INDIAN MEDICINAL PLANTS

INDIAN MEDICINAL PLANTS

BY

Lieutenant-Colonel K. R. KIRTIKAR, F.L.S., I.M.S., (Retired),

Major B. D. BASU, I.M.S., (Retired),

AND

I.C.S. (Retired).

PART III

PLATES

Published by

SUDHINDRA NATH BASU, M.B.

PANINI OFFICE, BHUWANESWARI ASRAMA, BAHADURGANJ,

Allahabad

PRINTED BY APURVA KRISHNA BOSE, AT THE INDIAN PRESS

1918

INDIAN MEDICINAL PLANTS

BY

Lieutenant-Colonel K. R. KIRTIKAR, F.L.S., I.M.S.,
(Retired),

Major B. D. BASU, I.M.S., (Retired),

AND

I. C. S. (Retired).

IN THREE PARTS

PART III

(PLATES)

GYAN

Published by

GYAN

Gyan Publishing House
5, Ansari Road
Daryaganj, New Delhi-110002
Phone: 011-47034999, 9811692060
E-mail: books@gyanbooks.com

Distribution Network
gyanbooks.com
India, USA, Canada, UK, Australia, France

ISBN: 978-81-212-5587-5 (Set)
978-81-212-5585-1 (PB)
First Published, 1918

2nd Impression 2023

Printed at: Gyan Press, Delhi.

INDIAN MEDICINAL PLANTS (PART III, PLATES)
Author: LIEUTENANT-COLONEL K. R. KIRTIKAR, Major B. D. BASU

PLATE No. 1.

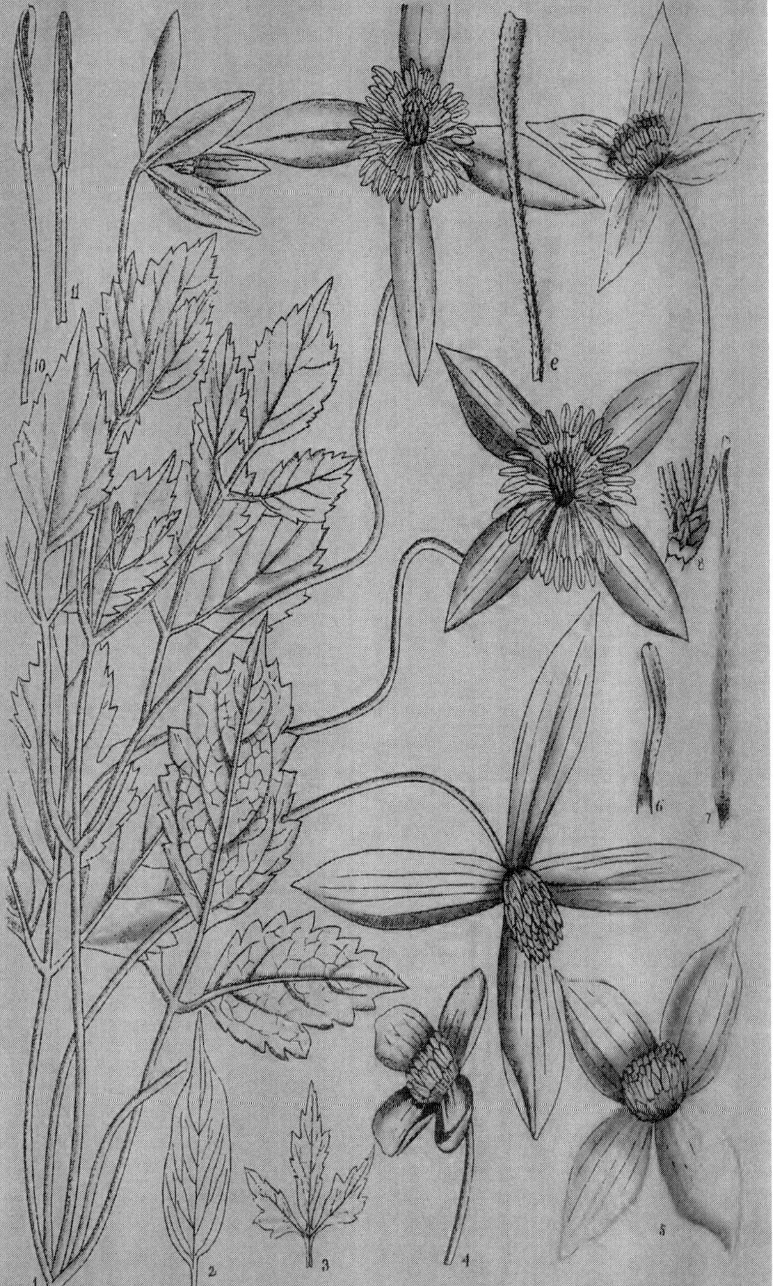

CLEMATIS NAPAULENSIS, DC.

PLATE No. 2.

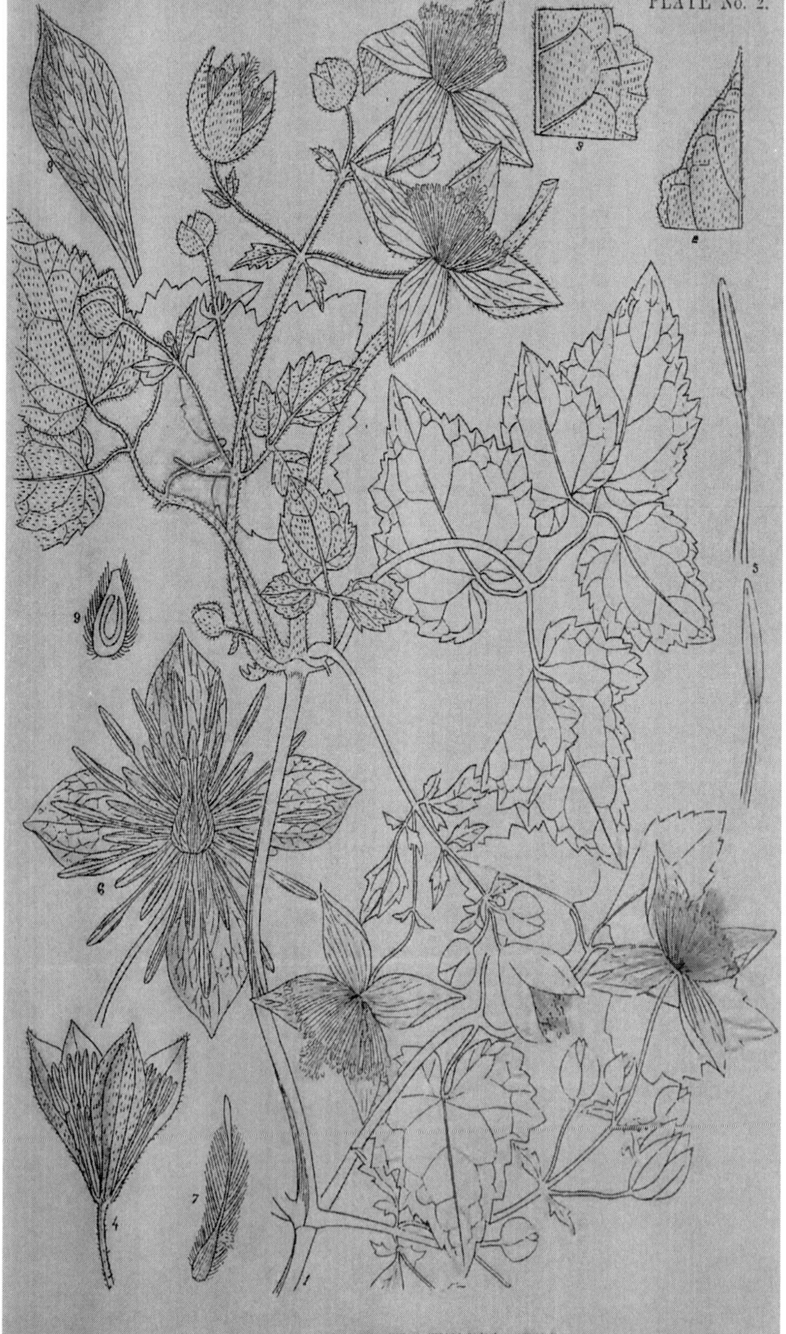

CLEMATIS TRILOBA, *Heyne*.

CLEMATIS GOURIANA, ROXB.

PLATE No. 3A.

CLEMATIS GOURIANA, ROXB.

PLATE No. 8.

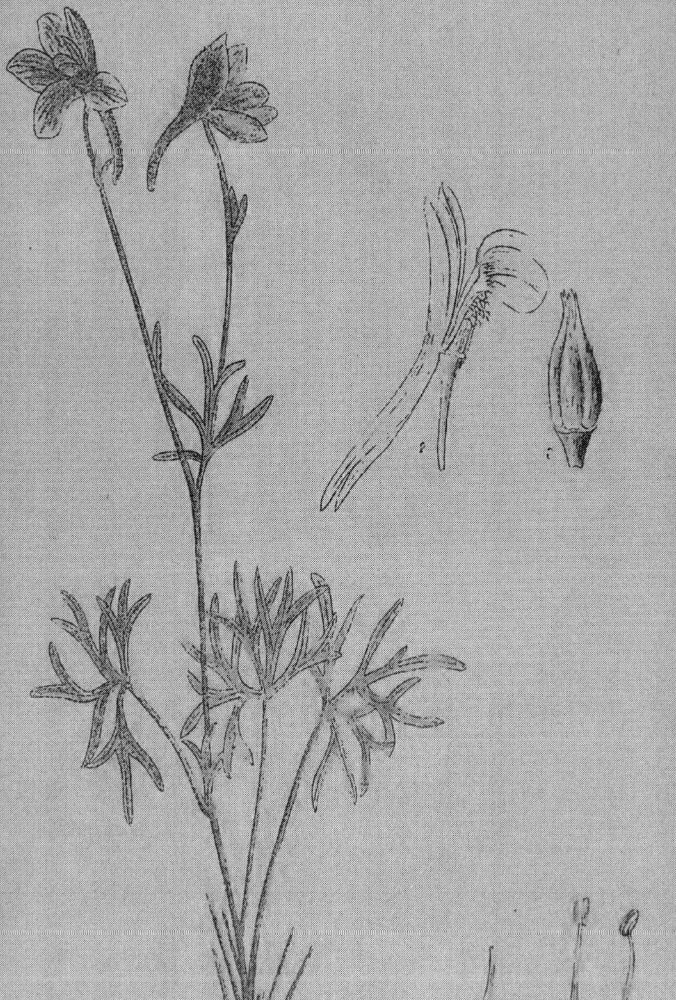

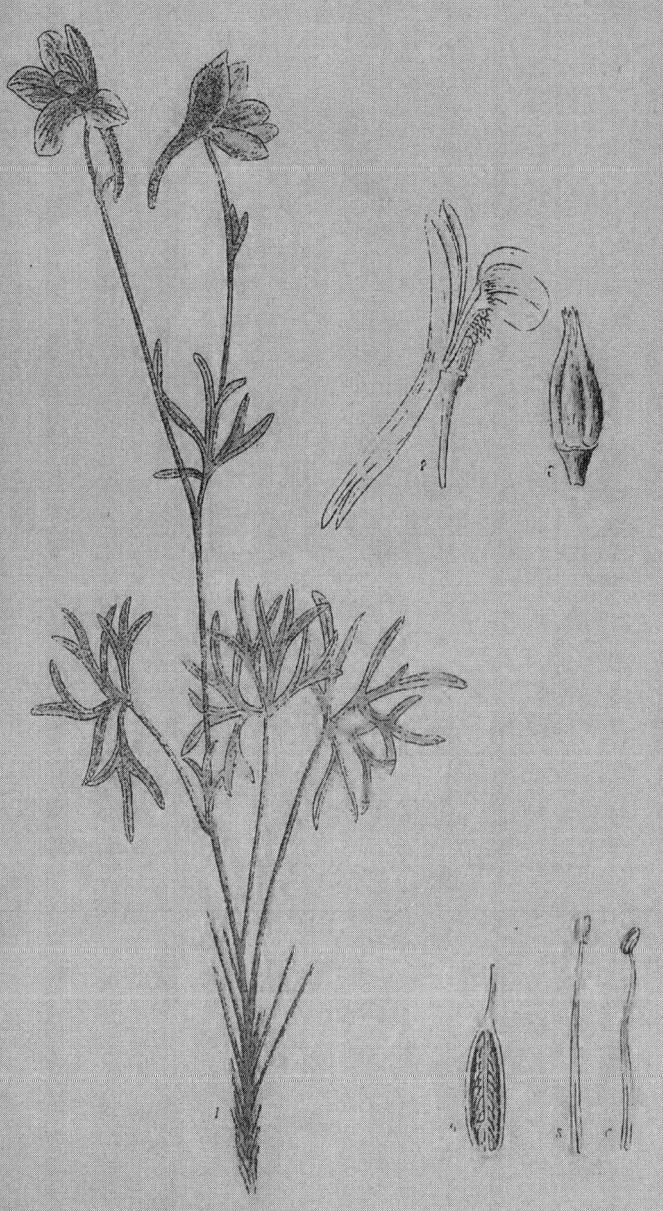

DELPHINIUM CÆRULEUM, JACQ.

PLATE No. 9.

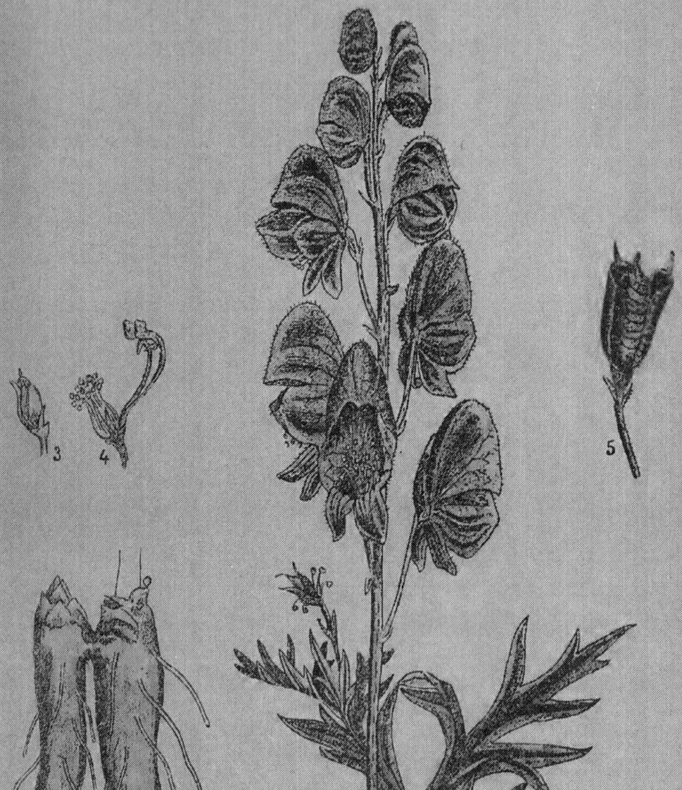

ACONITUM NAPELLUS, *LINN.*

PLATE No. 10.

ACONITUM SOONGARICUM, STAPF.

PLATE No. 11.

ACONITUM CHASMANTHUM, STAPF.

PLATE No. 12.

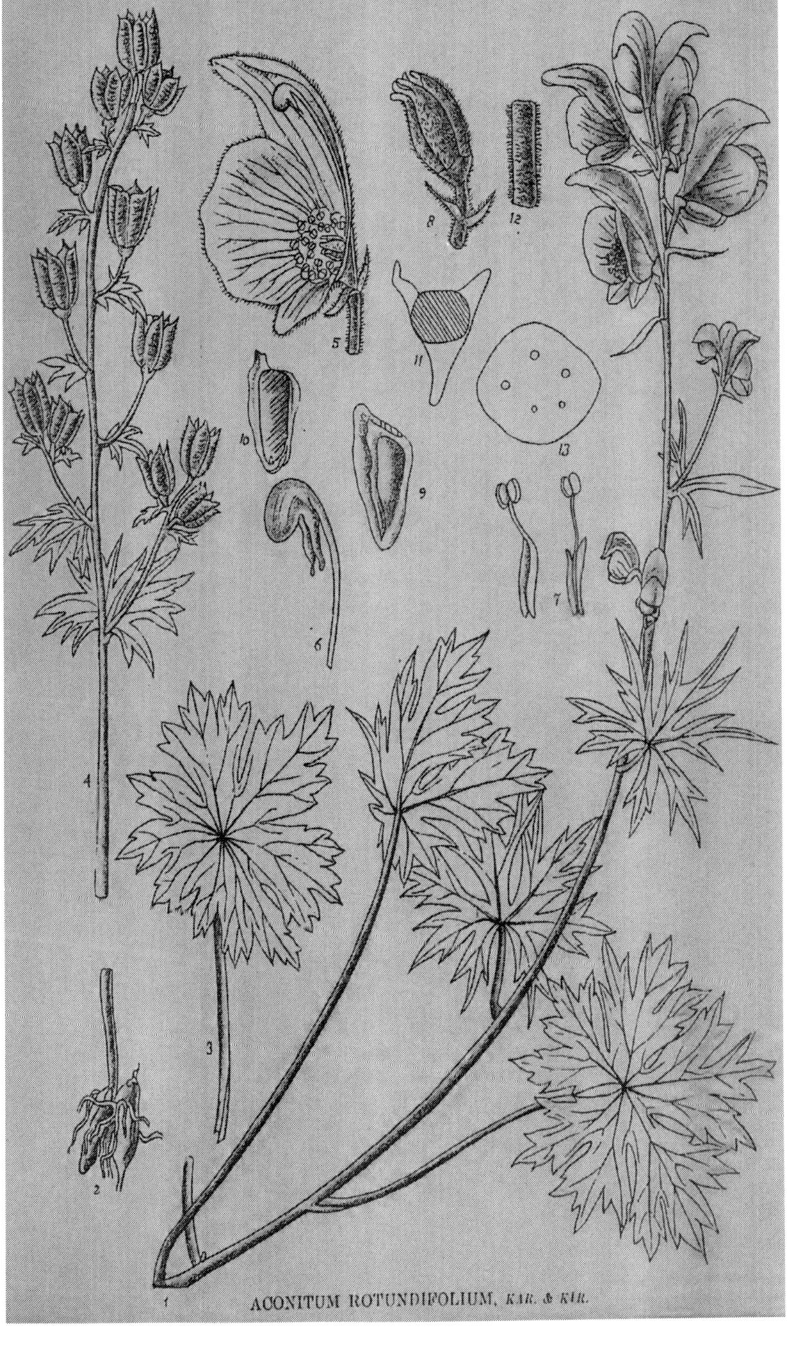

ACONITUM ROTUNDIFOLIUM, *Kar. & Kir.*

PLATE No. 13

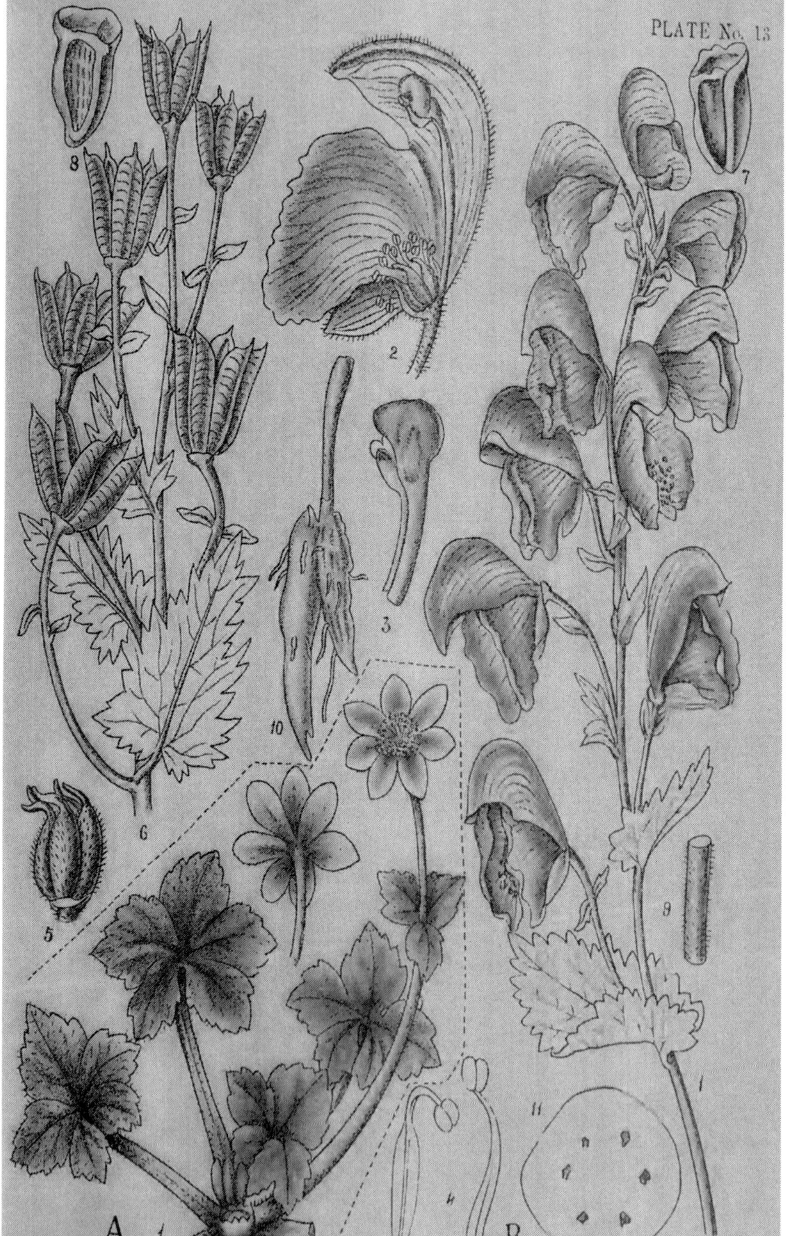

A—ANEMONE DISCOLOR, *ROYLE.*   B—ACONITUM HETEROPHYLLUM, *WALL.*

PLATE No. 14.

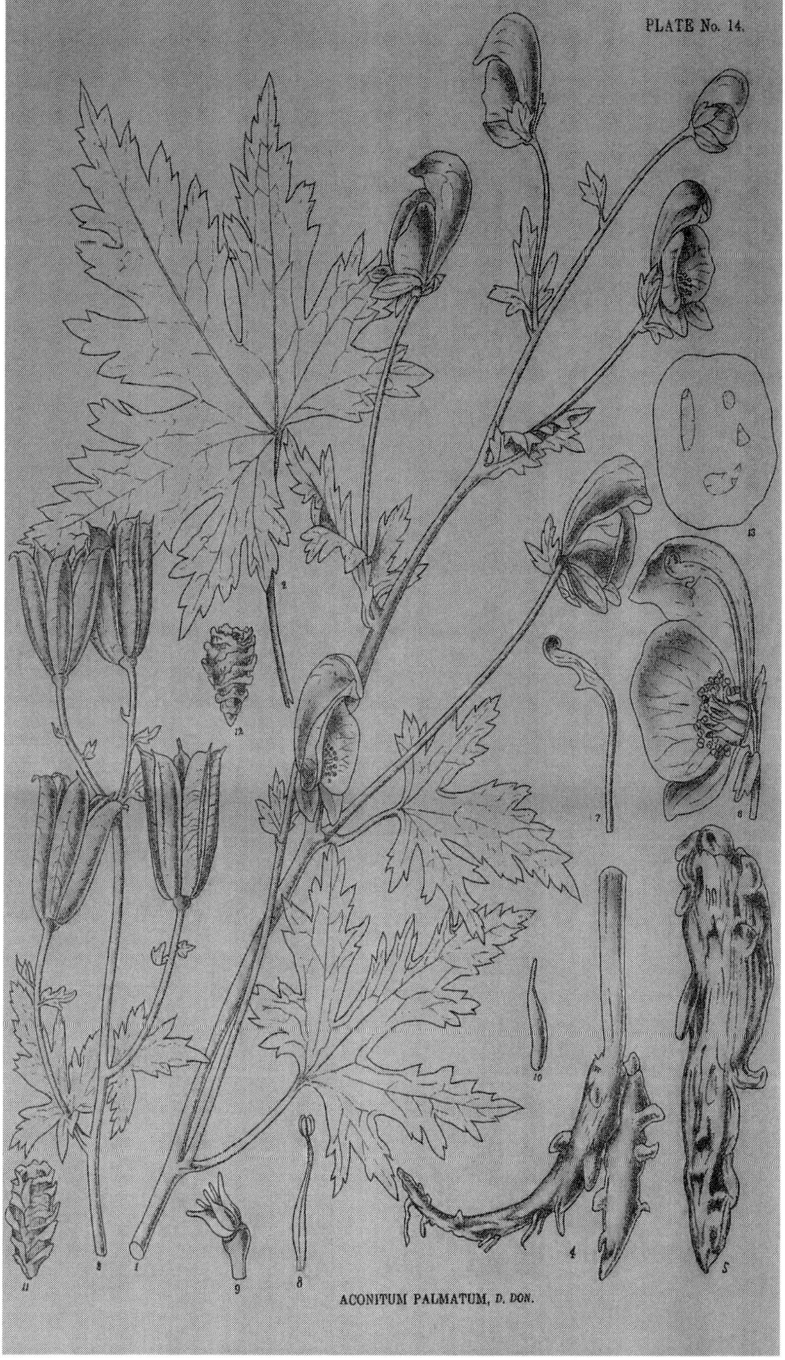

ACONITUM PALMATUM, *D. DON.*

PLATE No. 15.

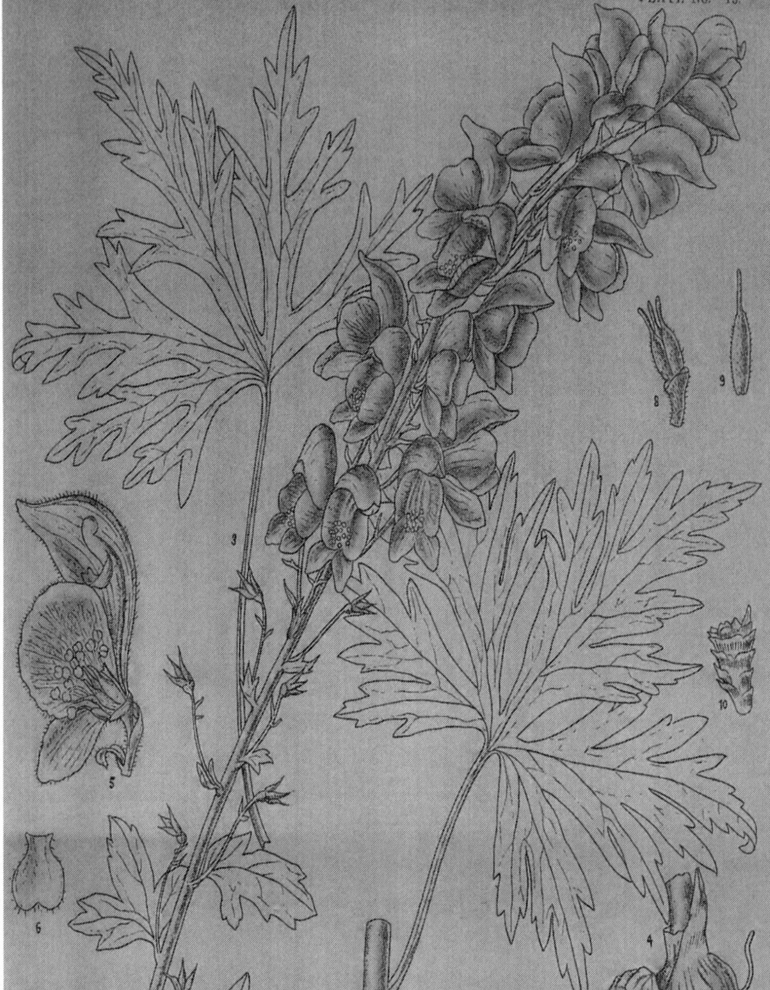

ACONITUM DEINORRHIZUM, STAPF.

PLATE No. 16.

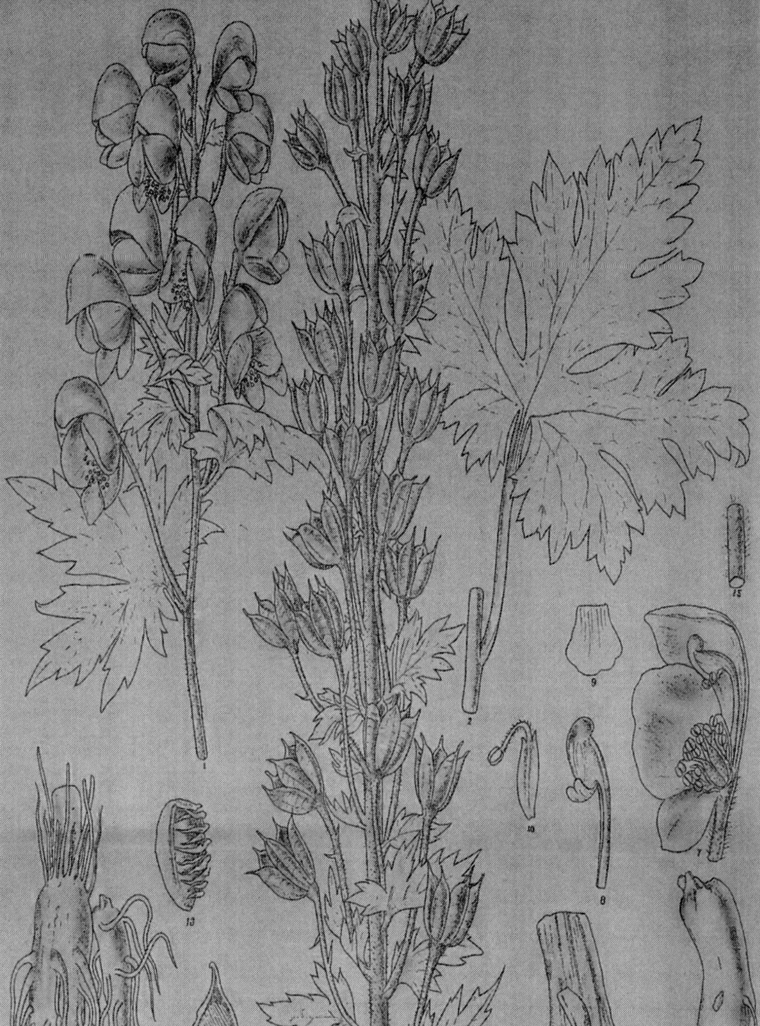

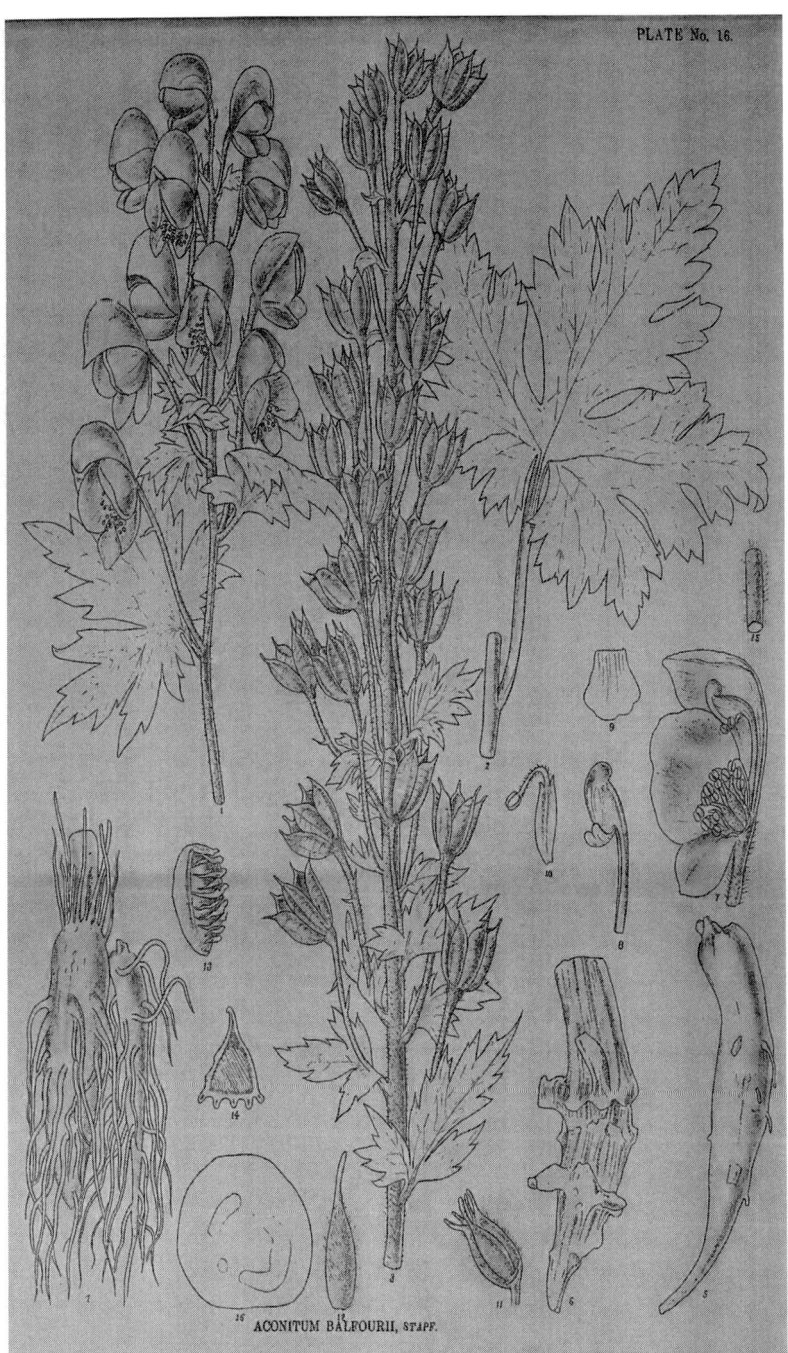

ACONITUM BALFOURII, STAPF.

PLATE No. 17.

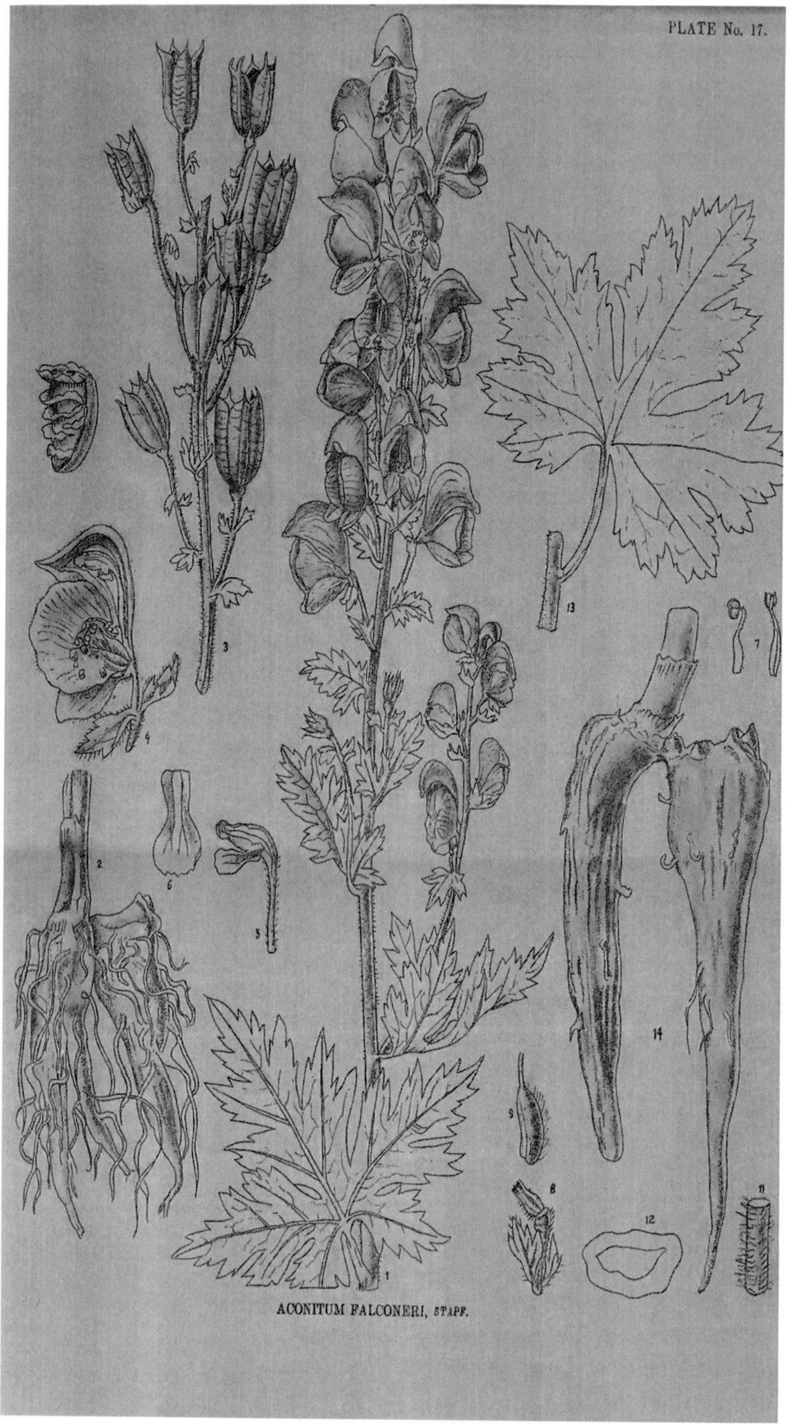

ACONITUM FALCONERI, STAPF.

PLATE No. 18.

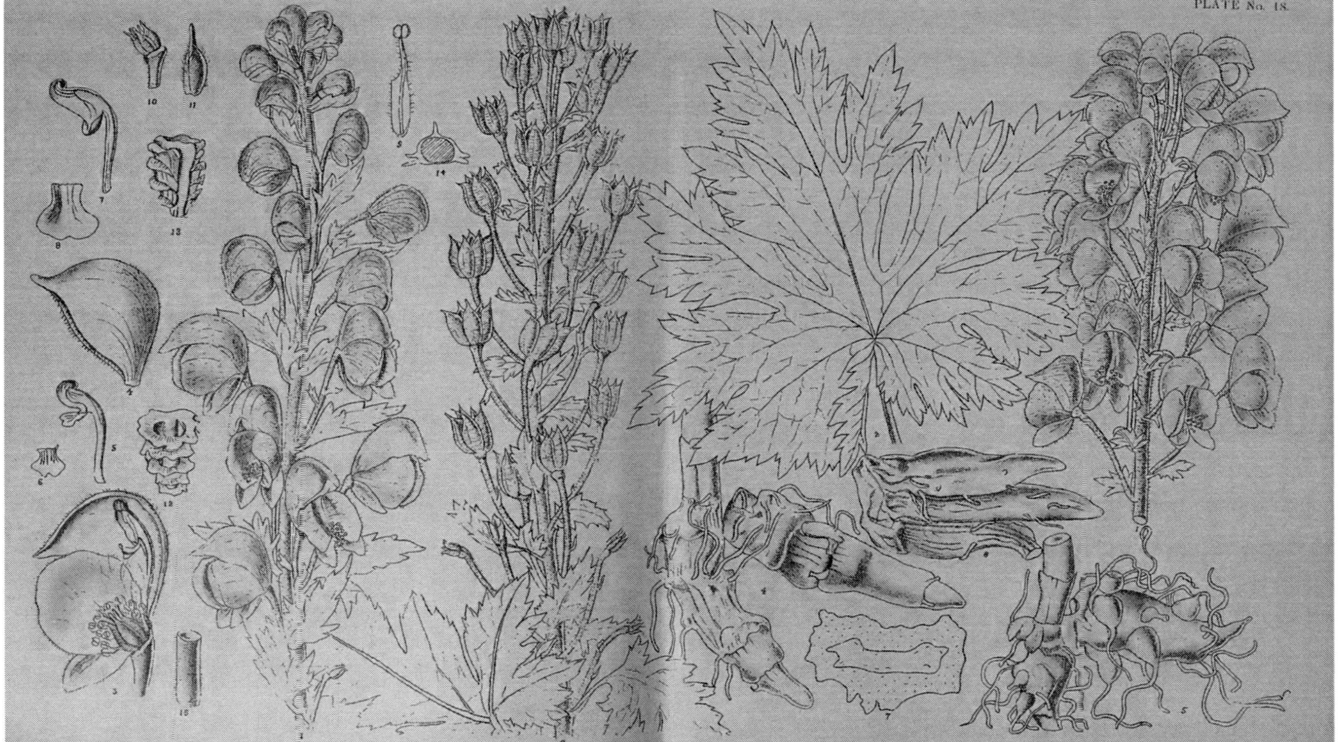

ACONITUM SPICATUM, Stapf.

PLATE No. 19.

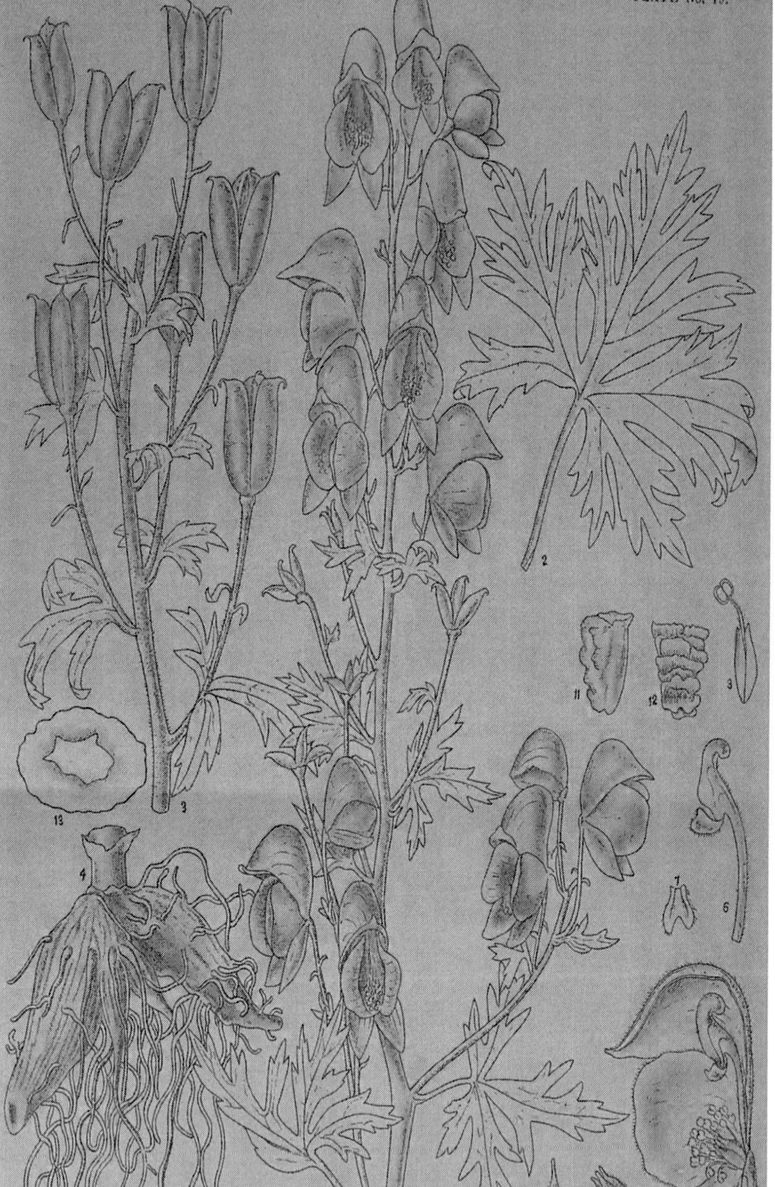

ACONITUM LACINIATUM, STAPF.

PLATE No. 20.

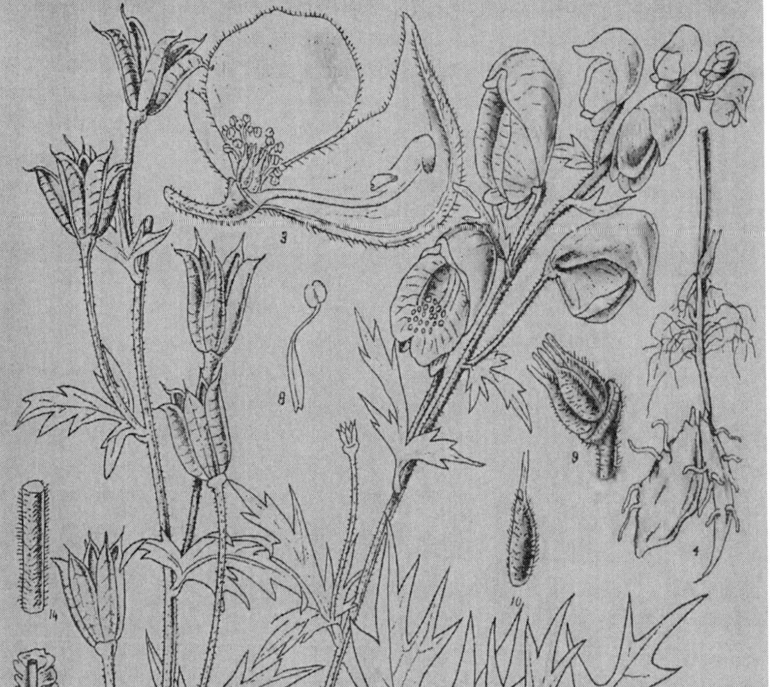

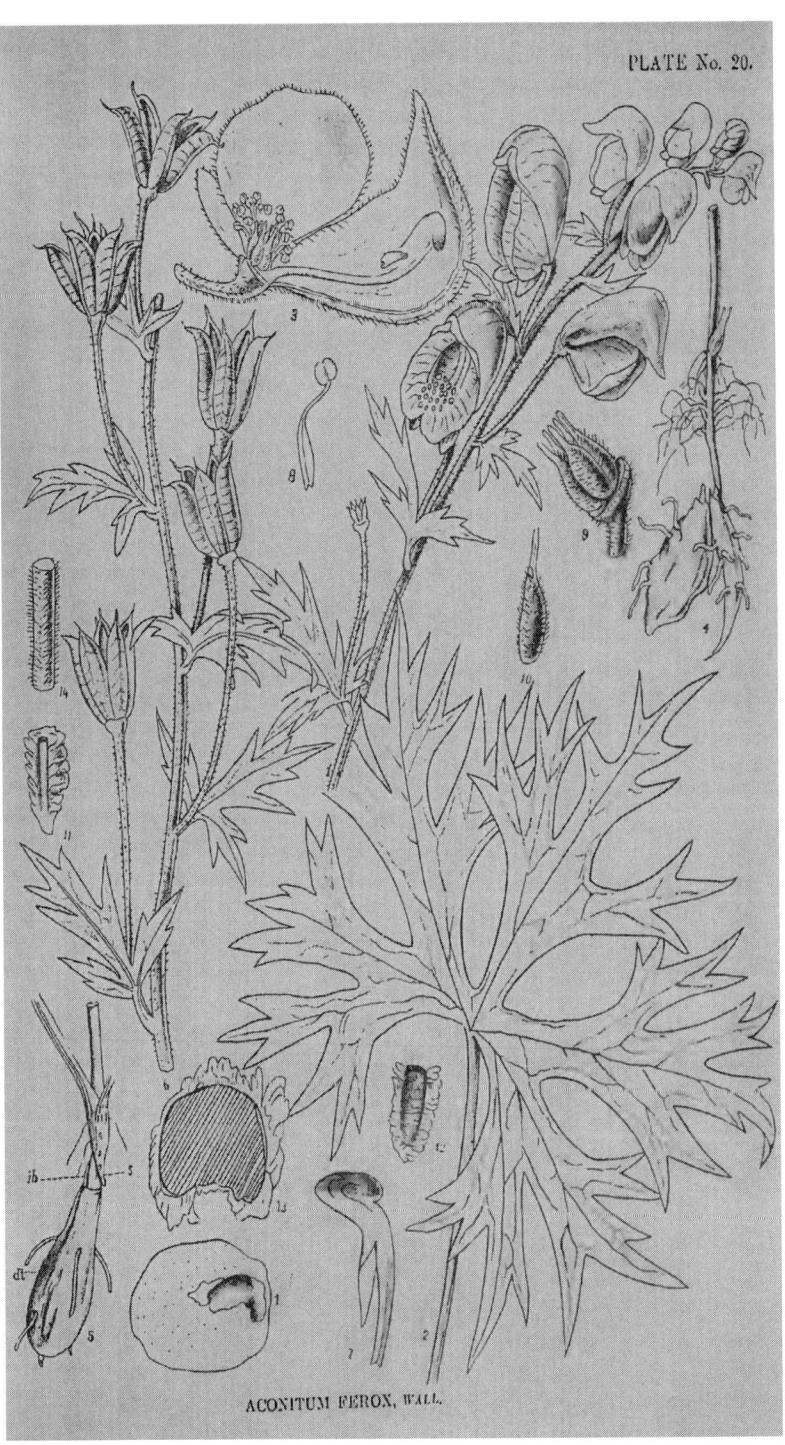

ACONITUM FEROX, WALL.

PLATE No. 21.

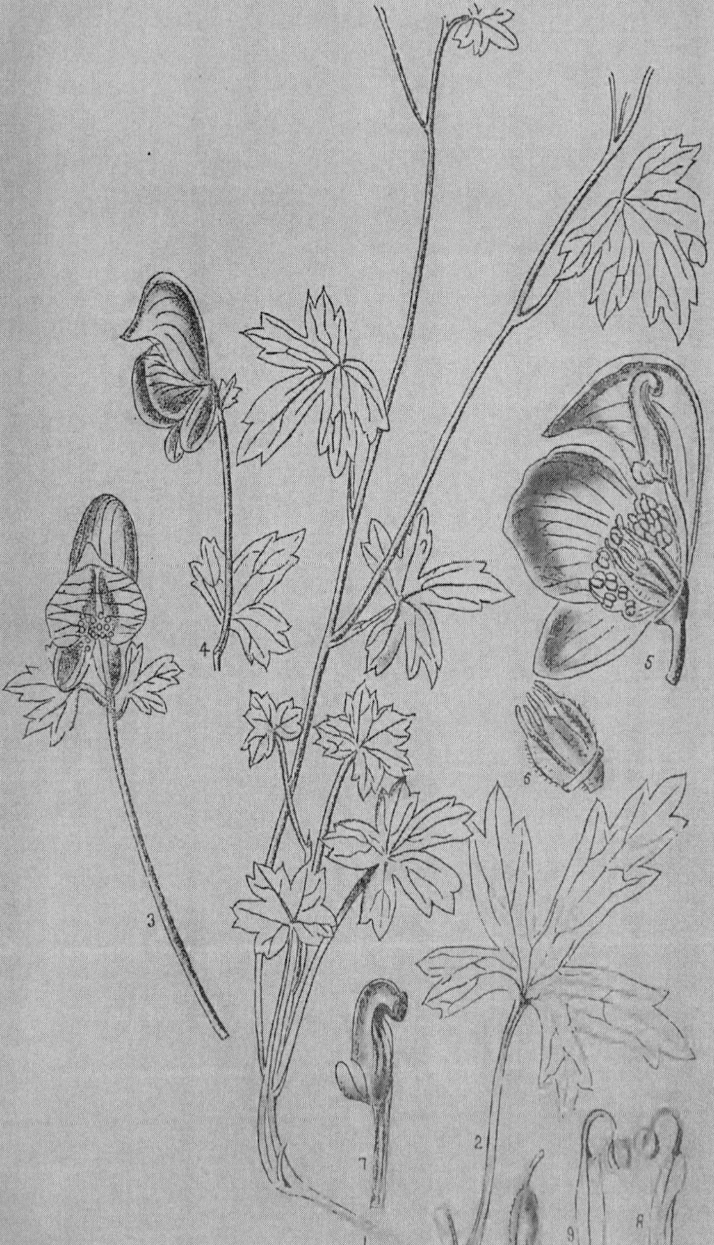

ACONITUM LETHALE, *GRIFF.*

PLATE No. 22.

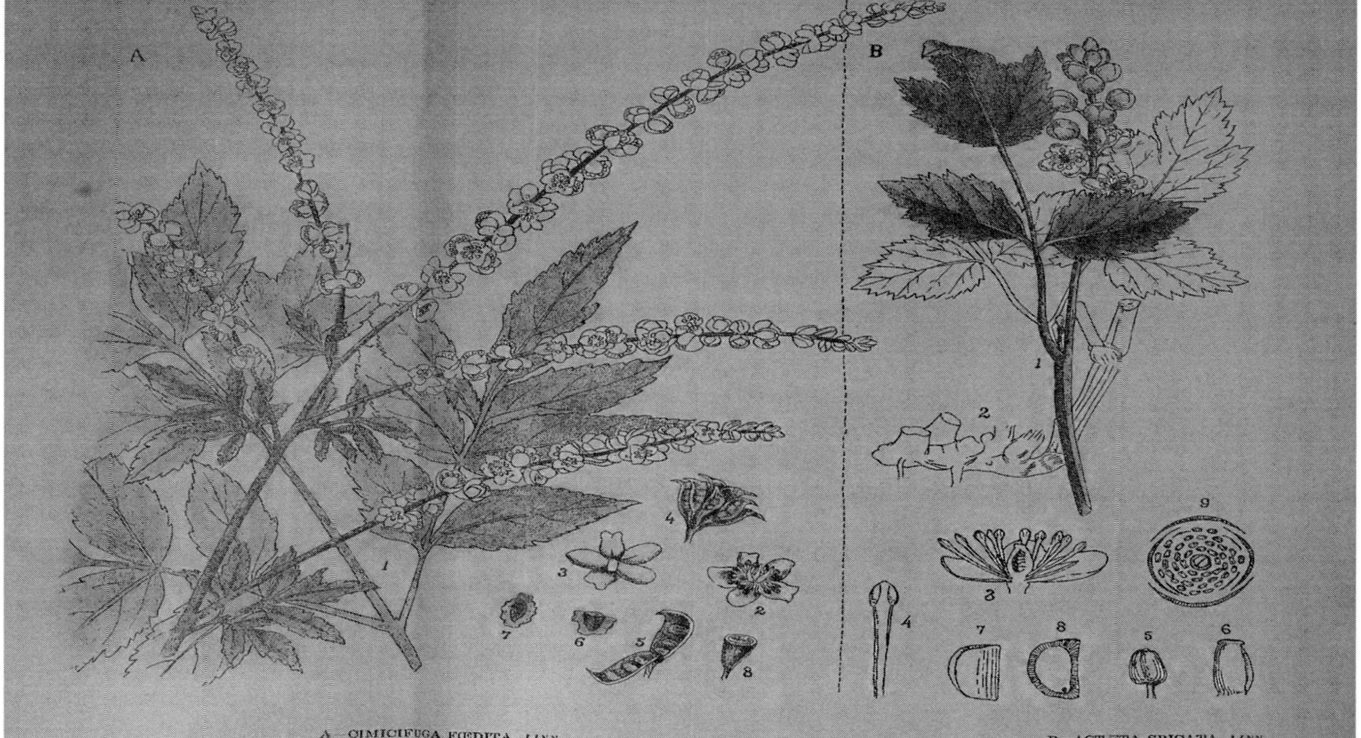

A—CIMICIFUGA FŒDITA, *LINN.*

B—ACTÆA SPICATA, *LINN.*

PLATE No. 23.

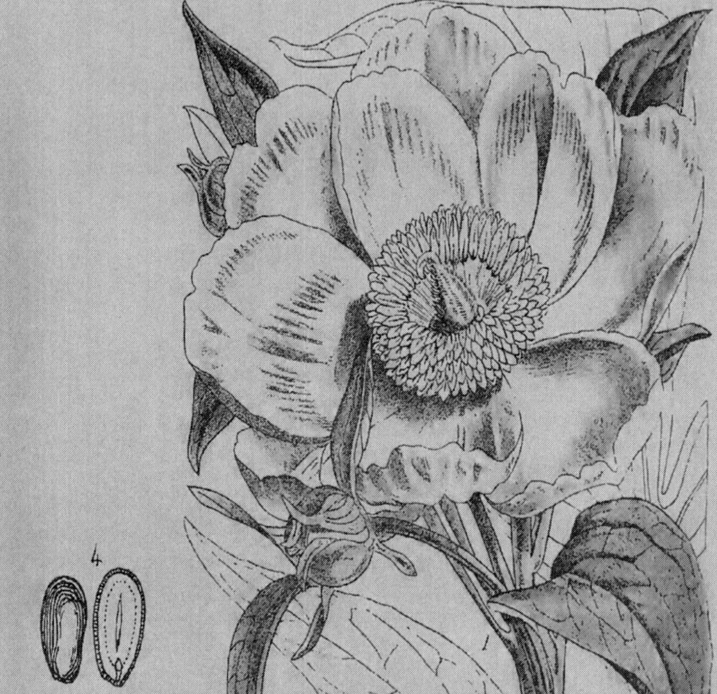

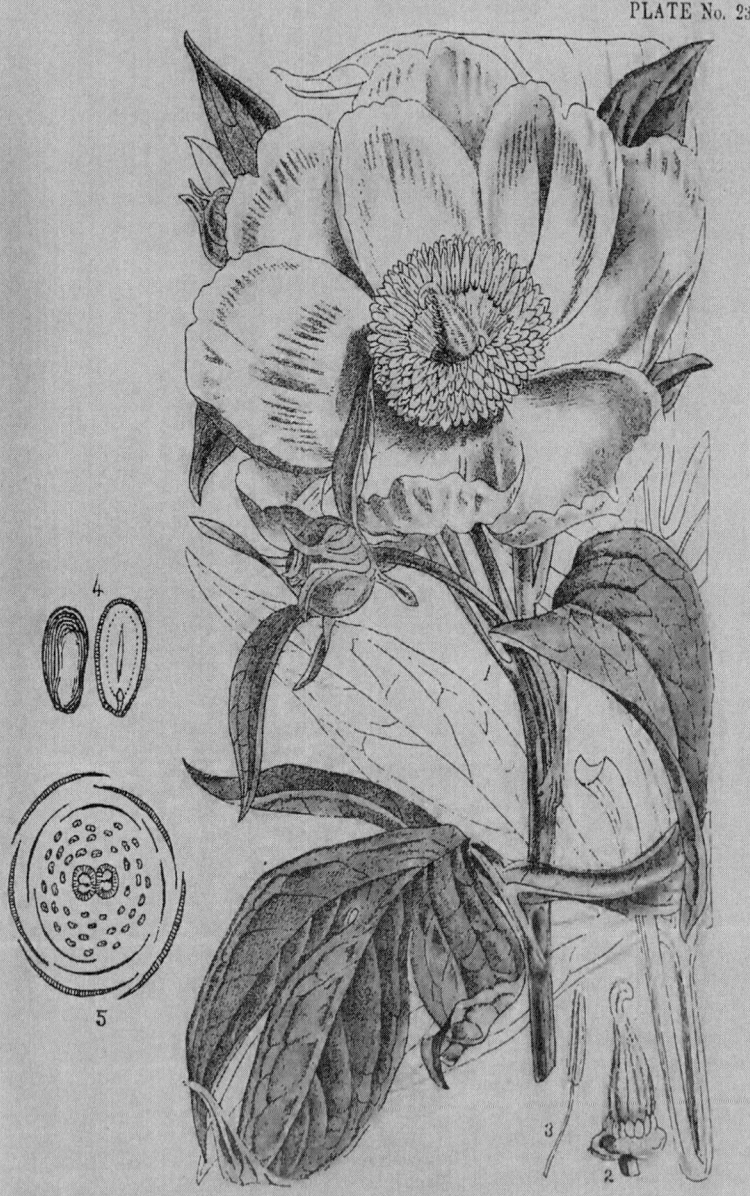

PÆONIA EMODI, WALL.

PLATE No. 24.

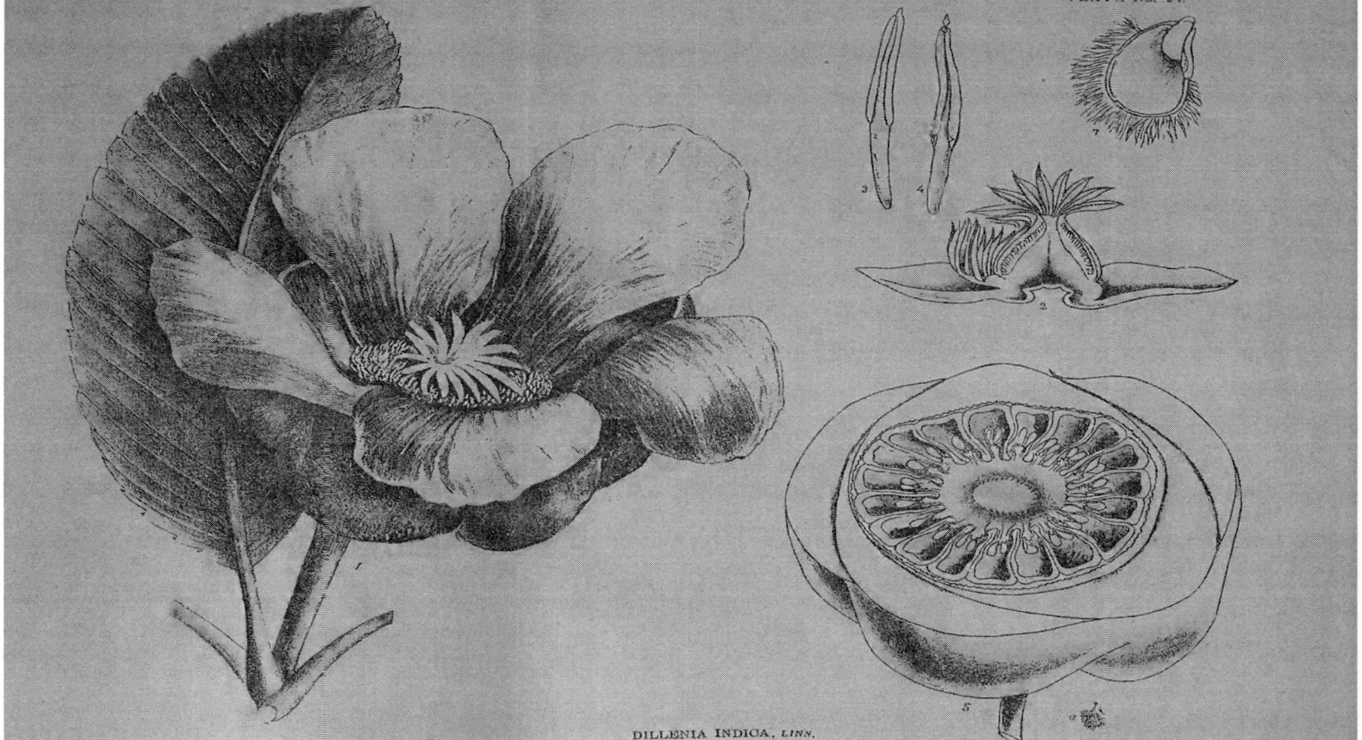

DILLENIA INDICA, *LINN.*

PLATE No. 25.

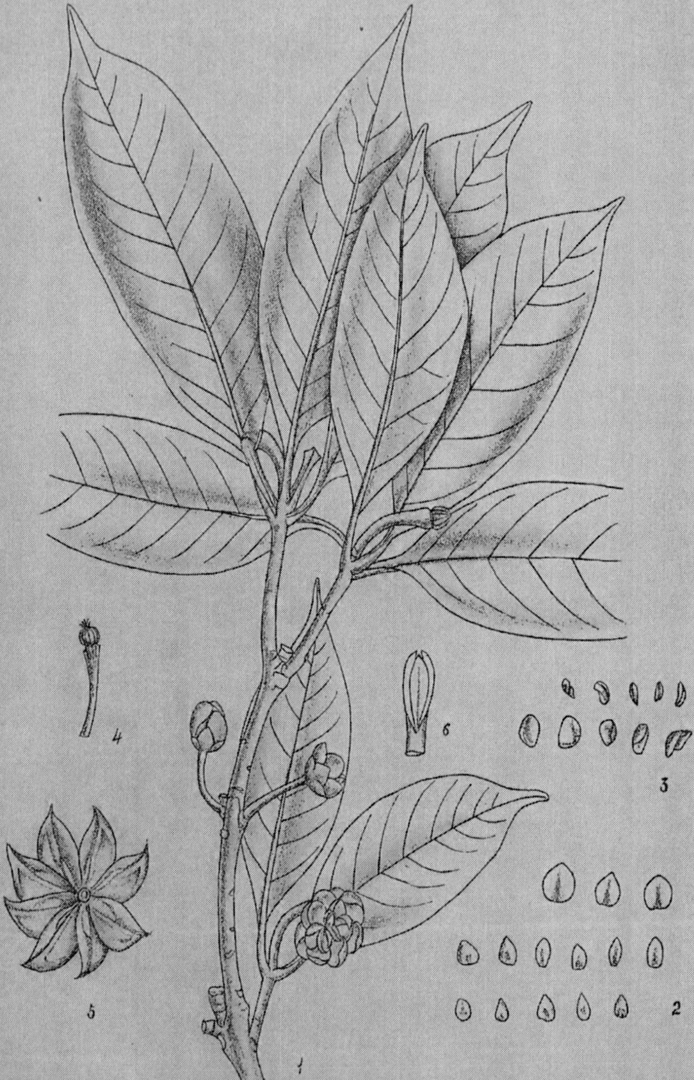

ILLICIUM GRIFFITHII, *H. F. & T.*

PLATE No. 26.

MICHELIA CHAMPACA, LINN.

PLATE No. 27.

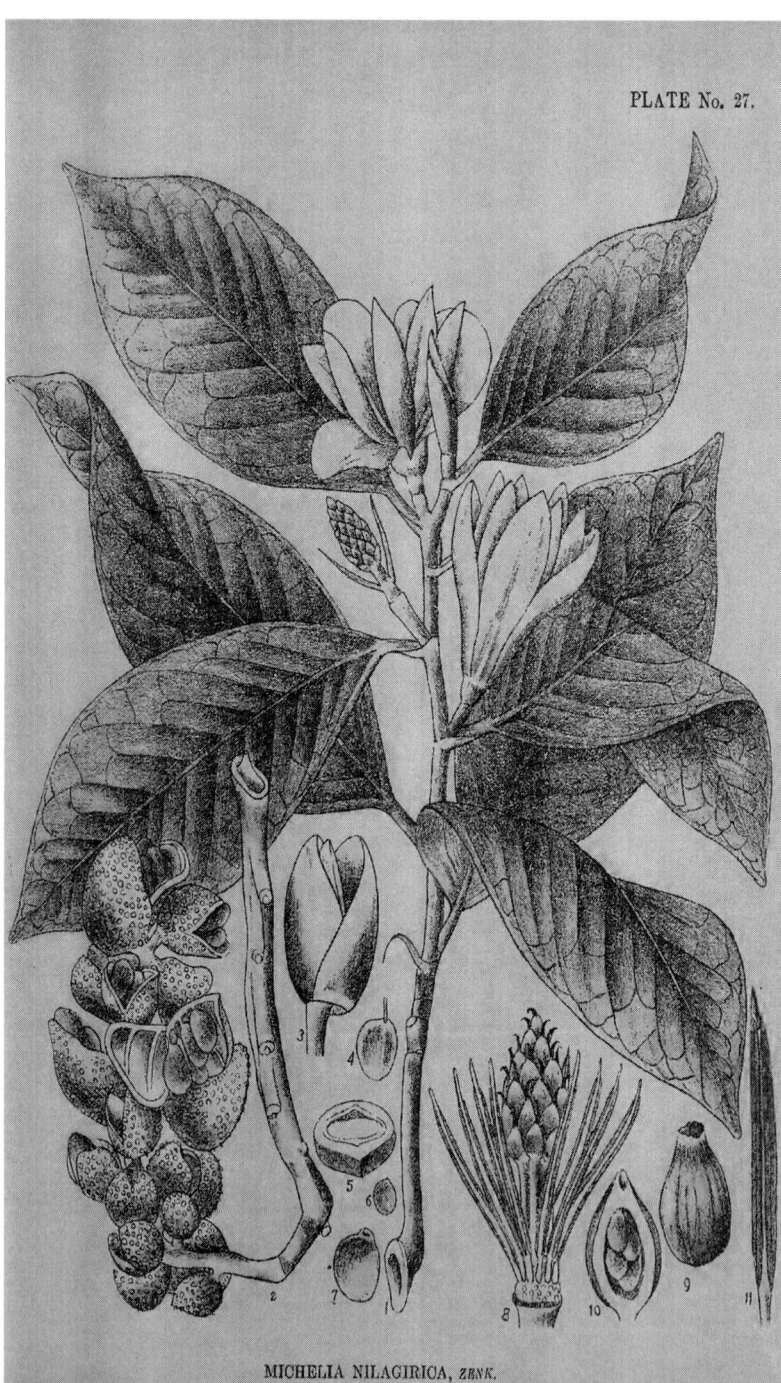

MICHELIA NILAGIRICA, *ZENK.*

PLATE No. 28.

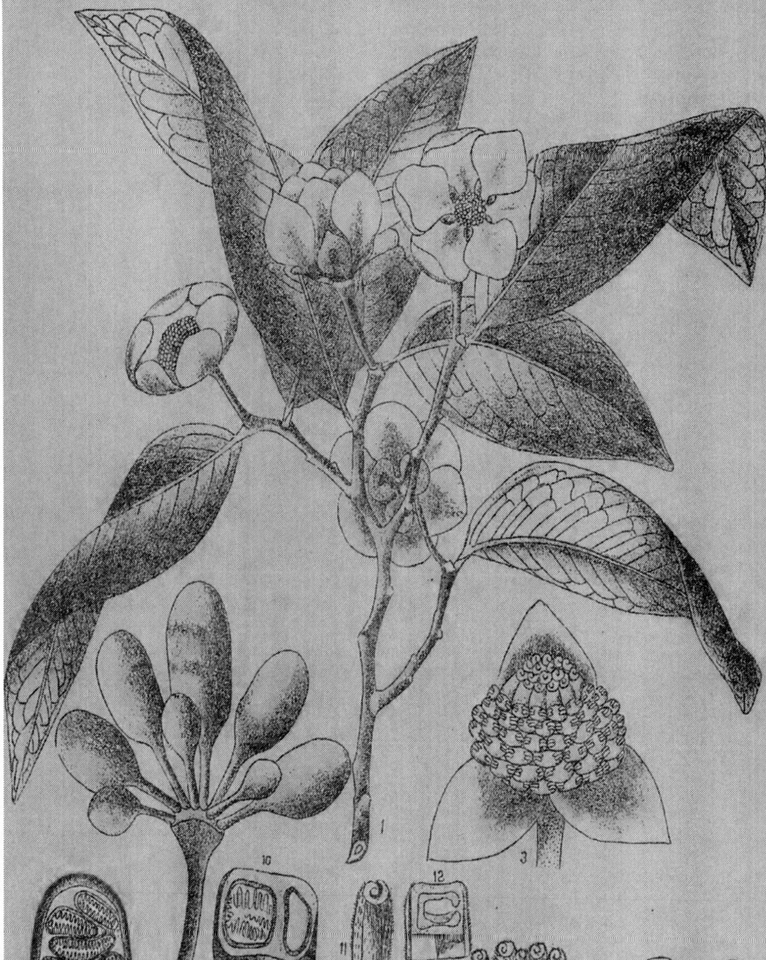

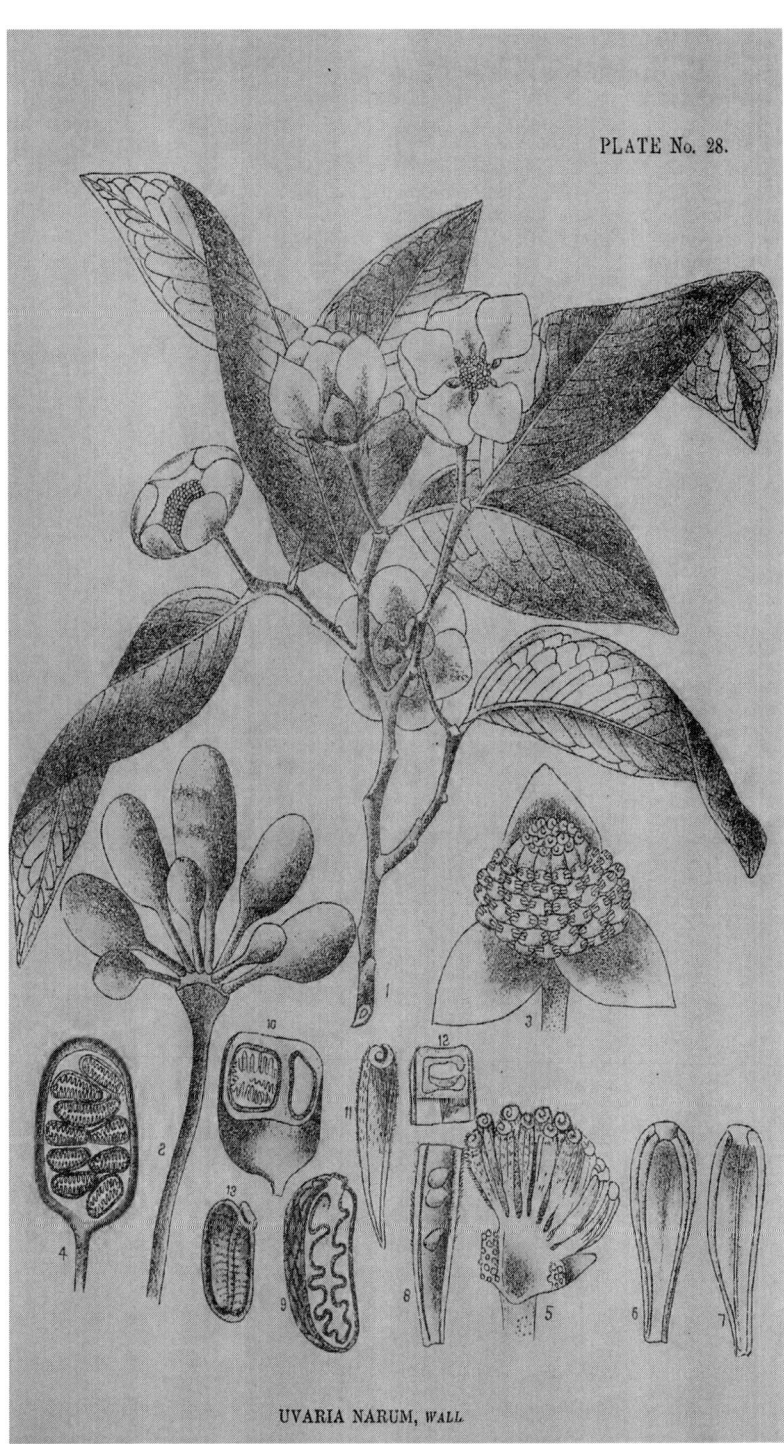

UVARIA NARUM, *WALL*

PLATE No. 29.

POLYALTHIA LONGIFOLIA, BENTH & HK. F.

PLATE No. 30

ANONA SQUAMOSA, *LINN.*

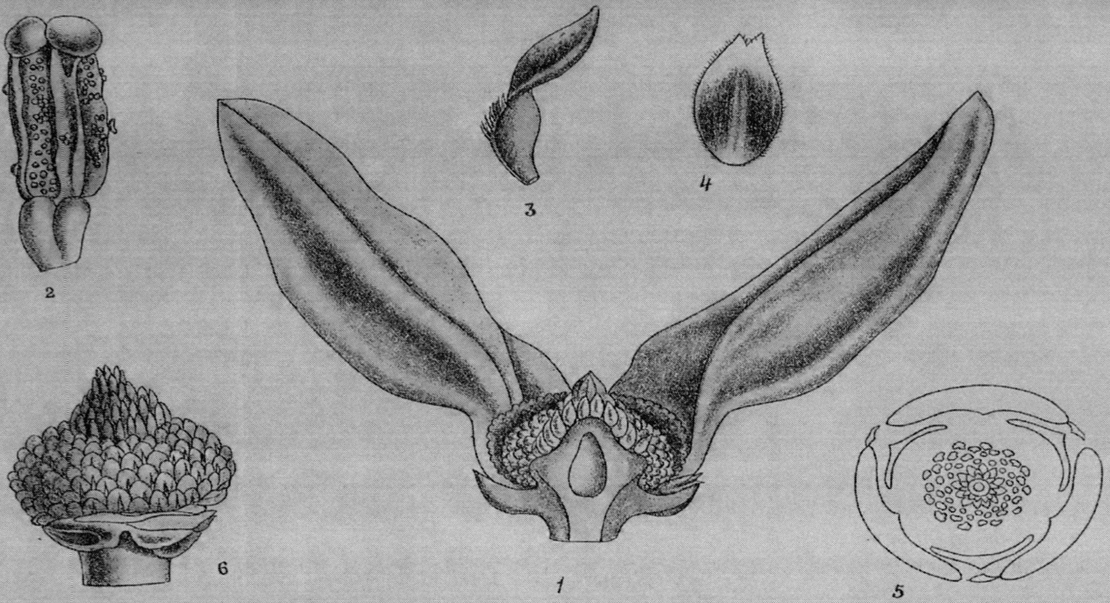

ANONA SQUAMOSA, *LINN.*

PLATE No. 31.

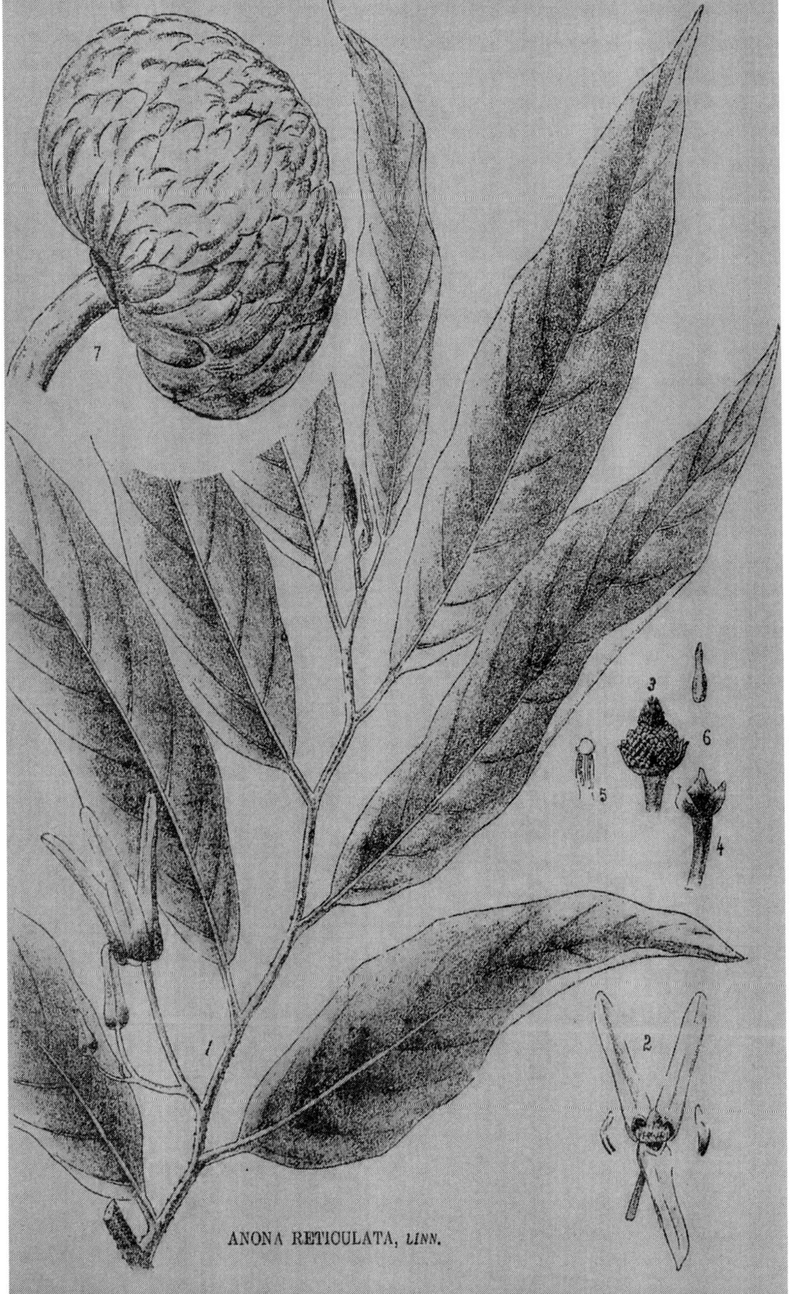

ANONA RETICULATA, *LINN.*

PLATE No. 32.

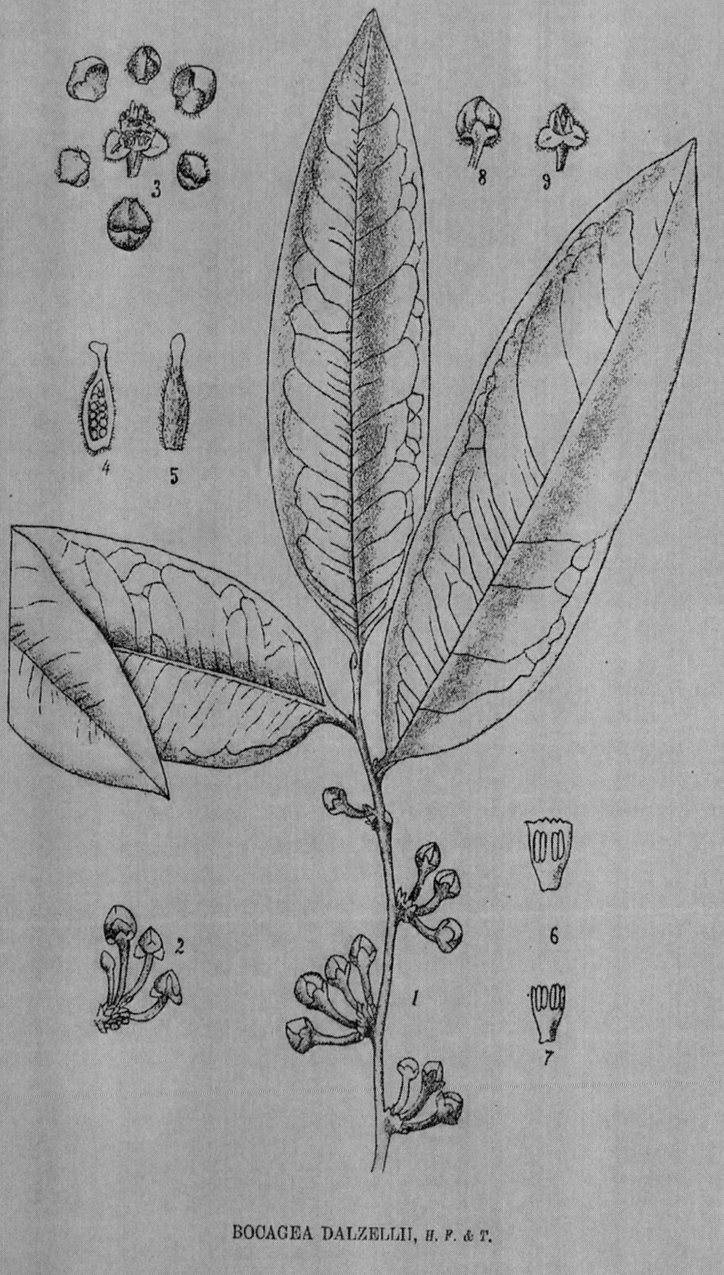

BOCAGEA DALZELLII, *H. F. & T.*

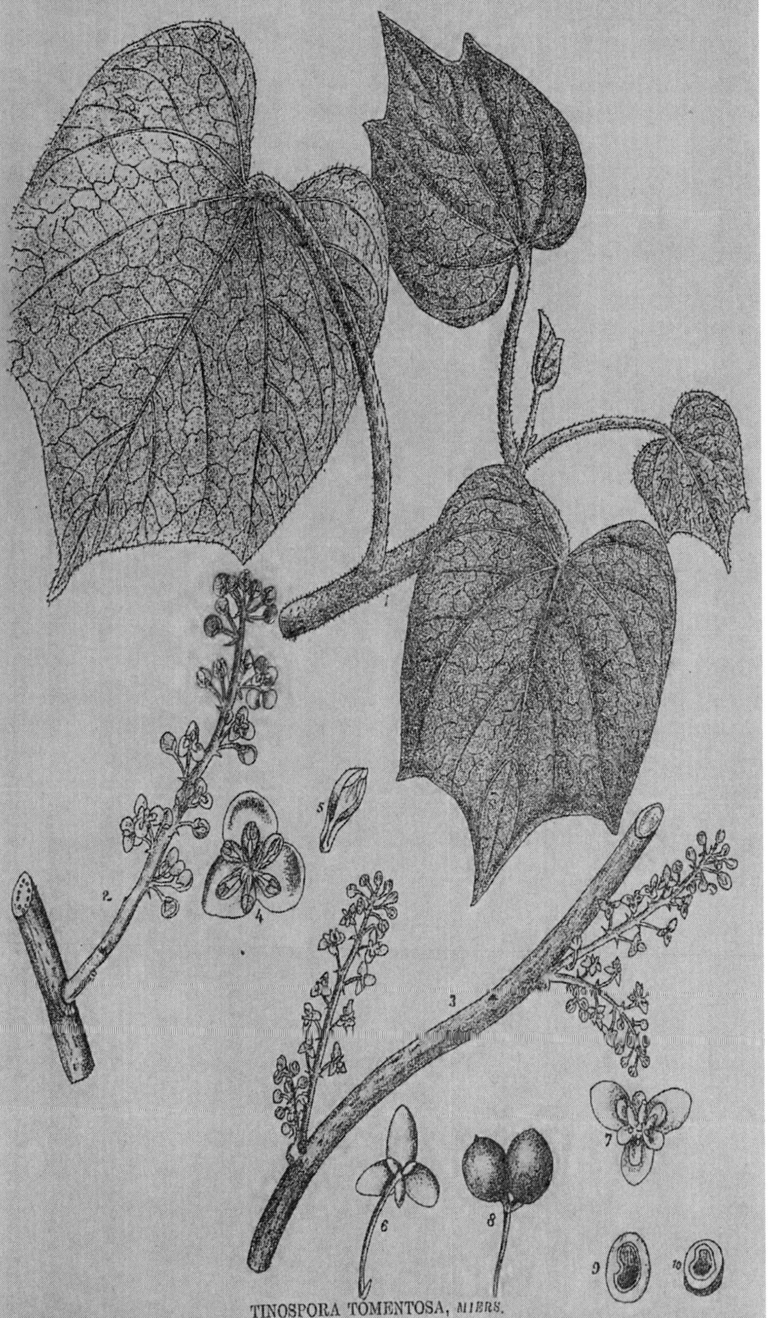

TINOSPORA TOMENTOSA, *MIERS.*

PLATE No. 34.

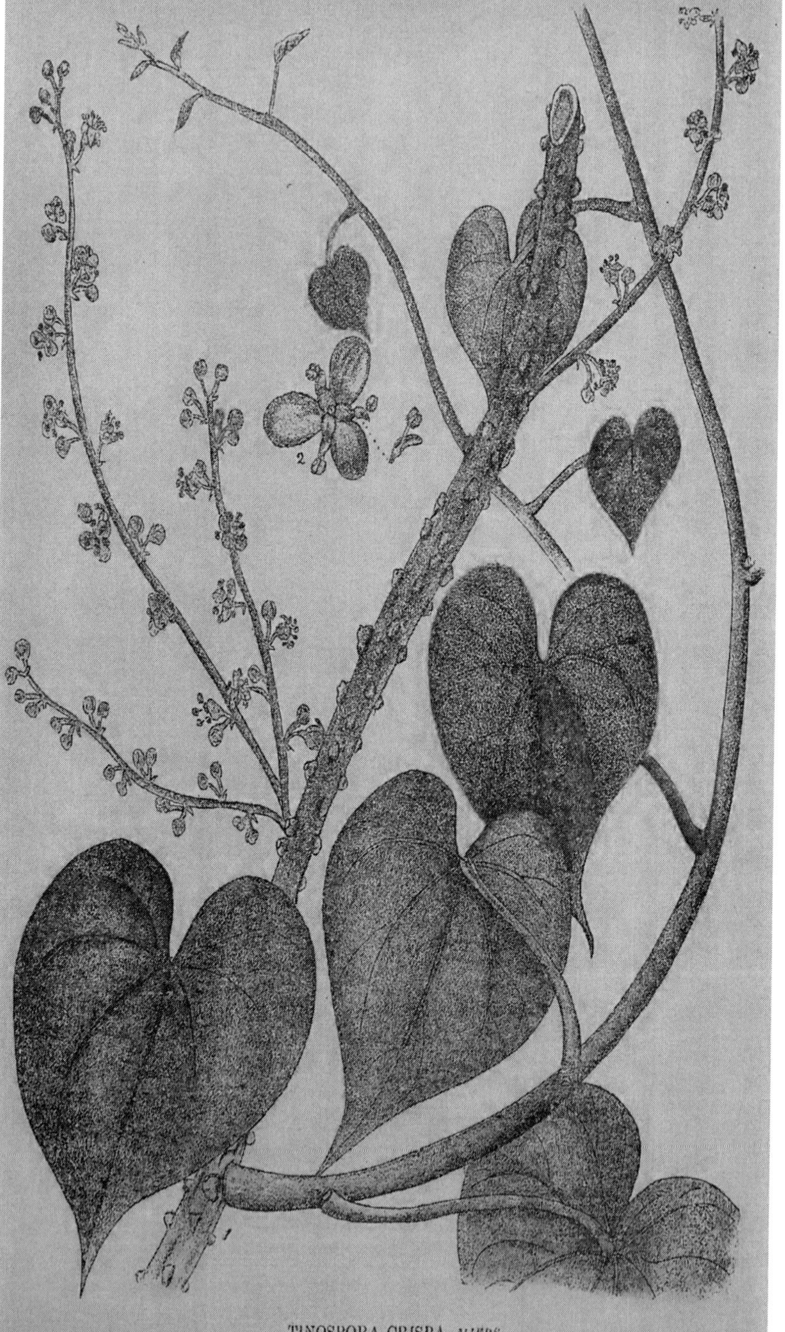

TINOSPORA CRISPA, MIERS.

PLATE No. 35.

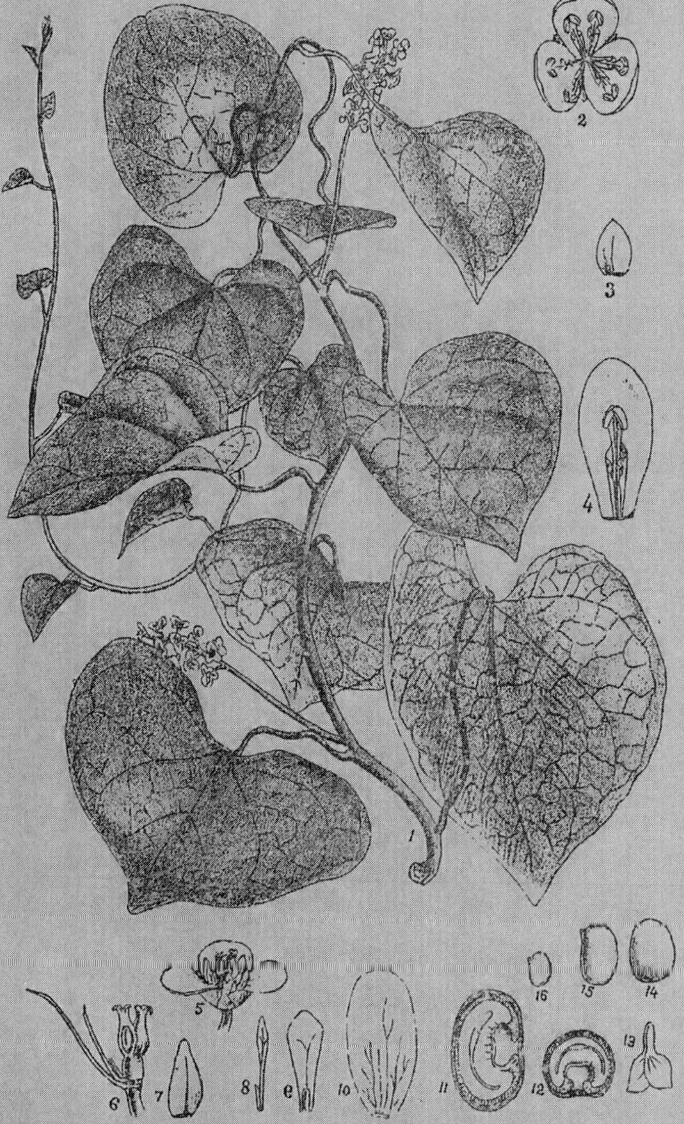

TINOSPORA CORDIFOLIA, *MIERS.*

PLATE No. 36.

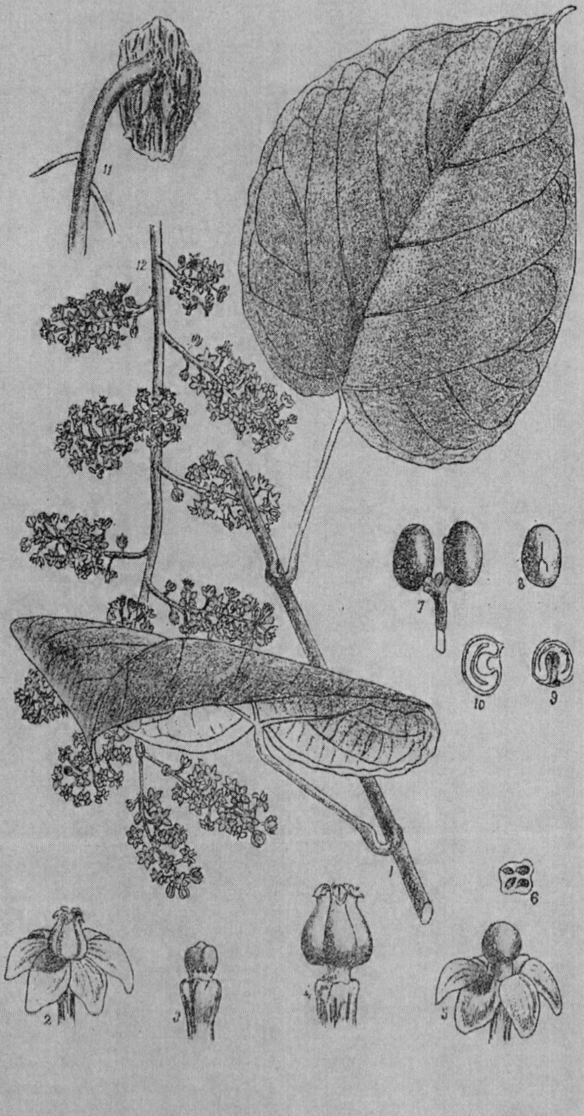

ANAMIRTA COCCULUS, *W. & A.*

PLATE No. 37.

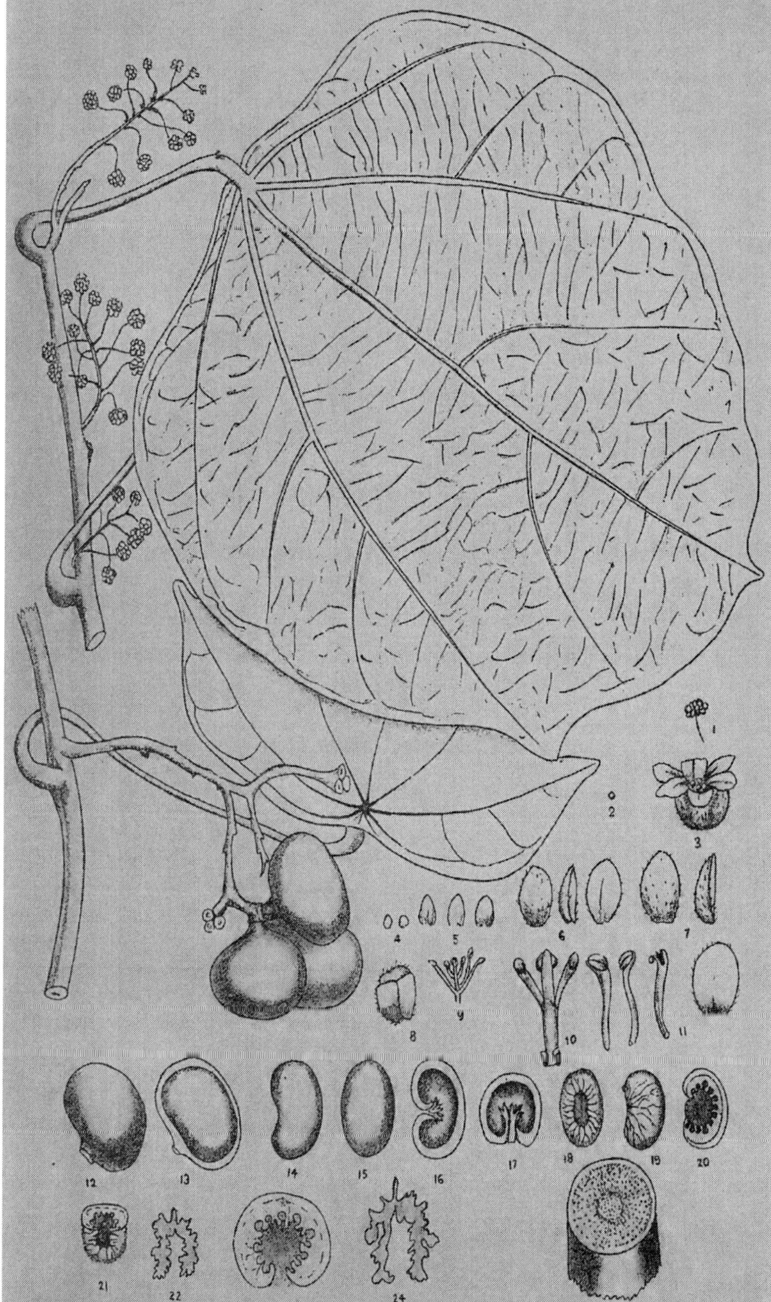

COSCINIUM FENESTRATUM, *COLEBROOKE.*

PLATE No. 38

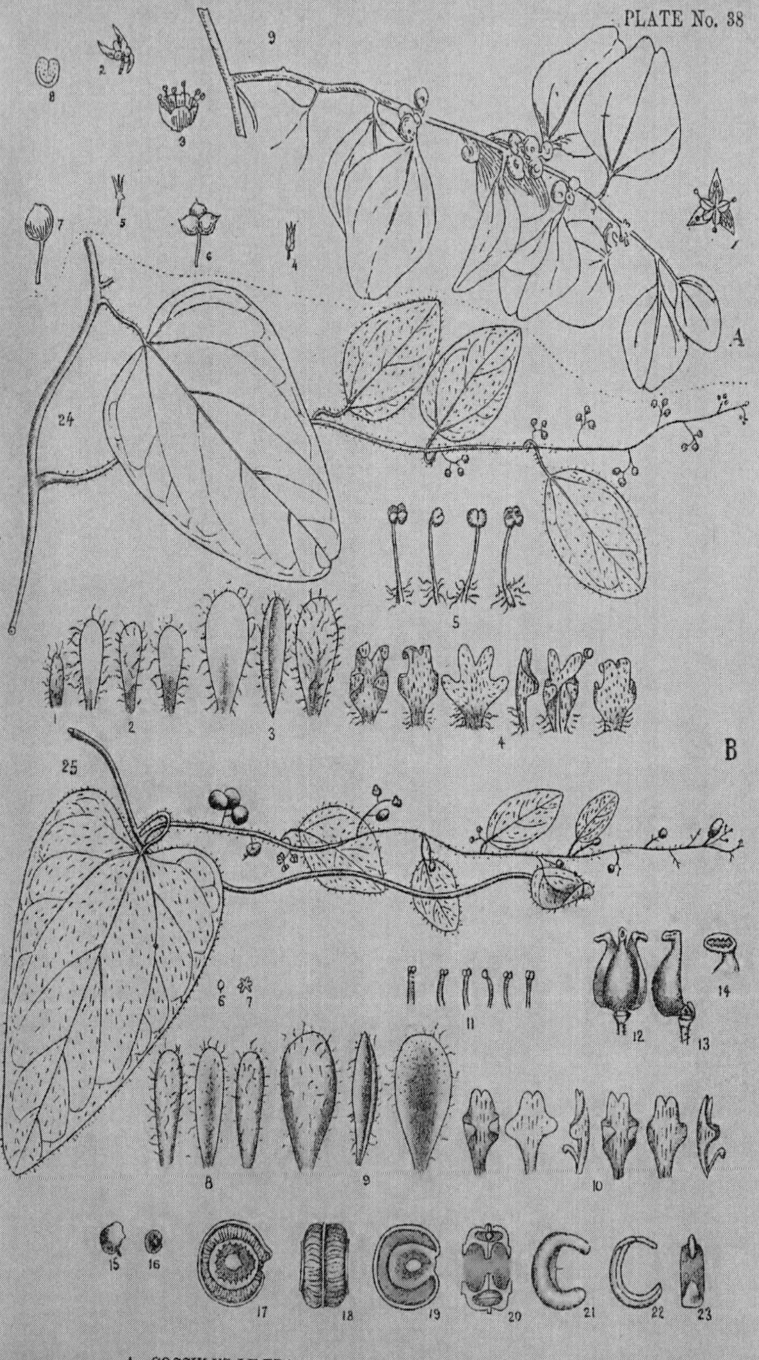

A—COOCULUS LEÆBA, *DC.* B—C. VILLOSUS, *DC.*

PLATE No. 39.

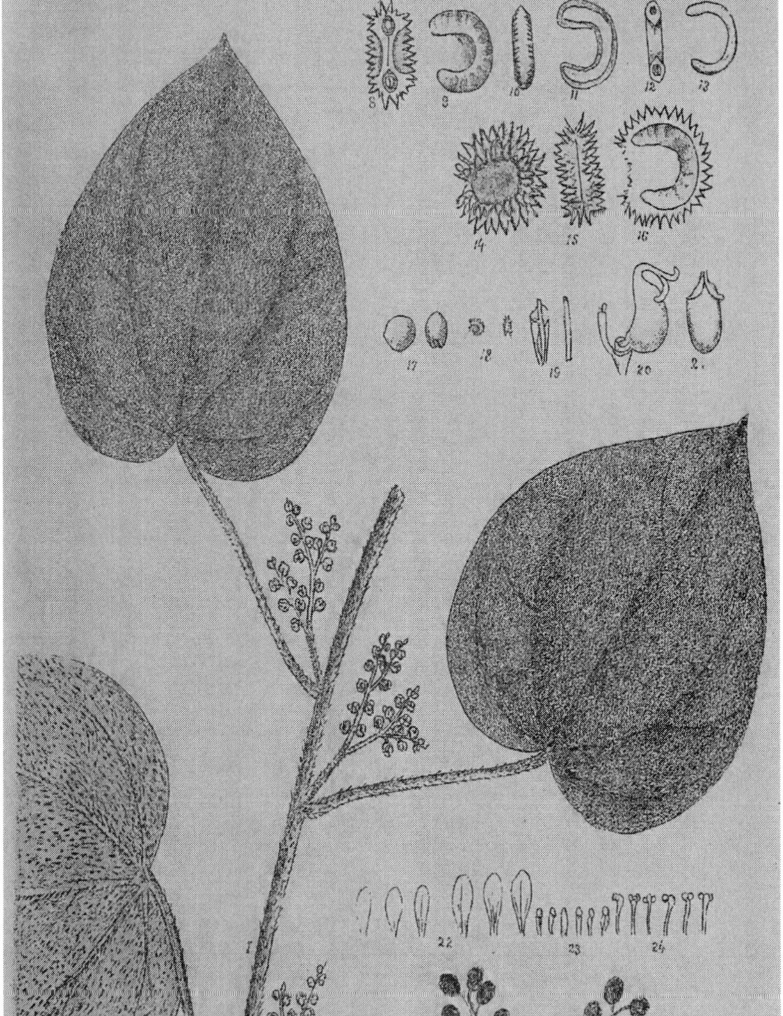

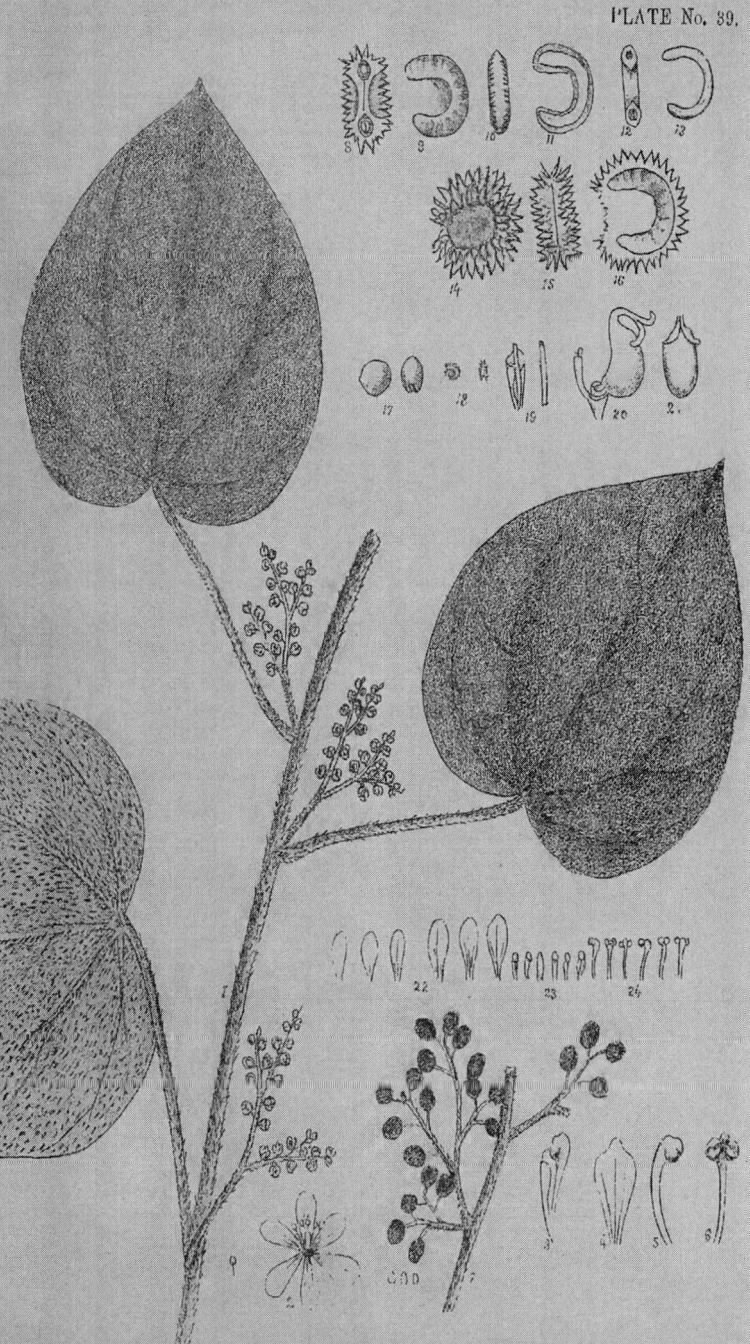

PERICAMPYLUS INCANUS, *MIERS.*

PLATE No. 40

STEPHANIA HERNANDIFOLIA, *WALP.*

PLATE No. 41.

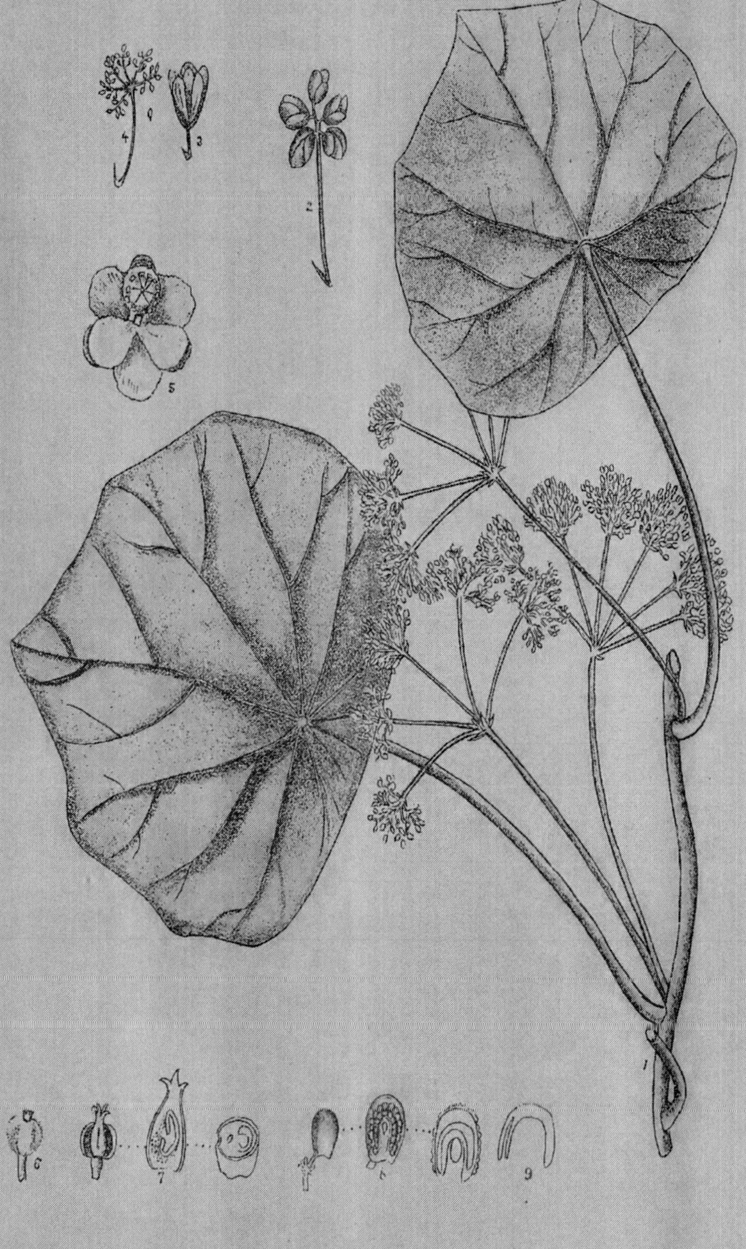

STEPHANIA ROTUNDA, *Lour.*

PLATE No. 42.

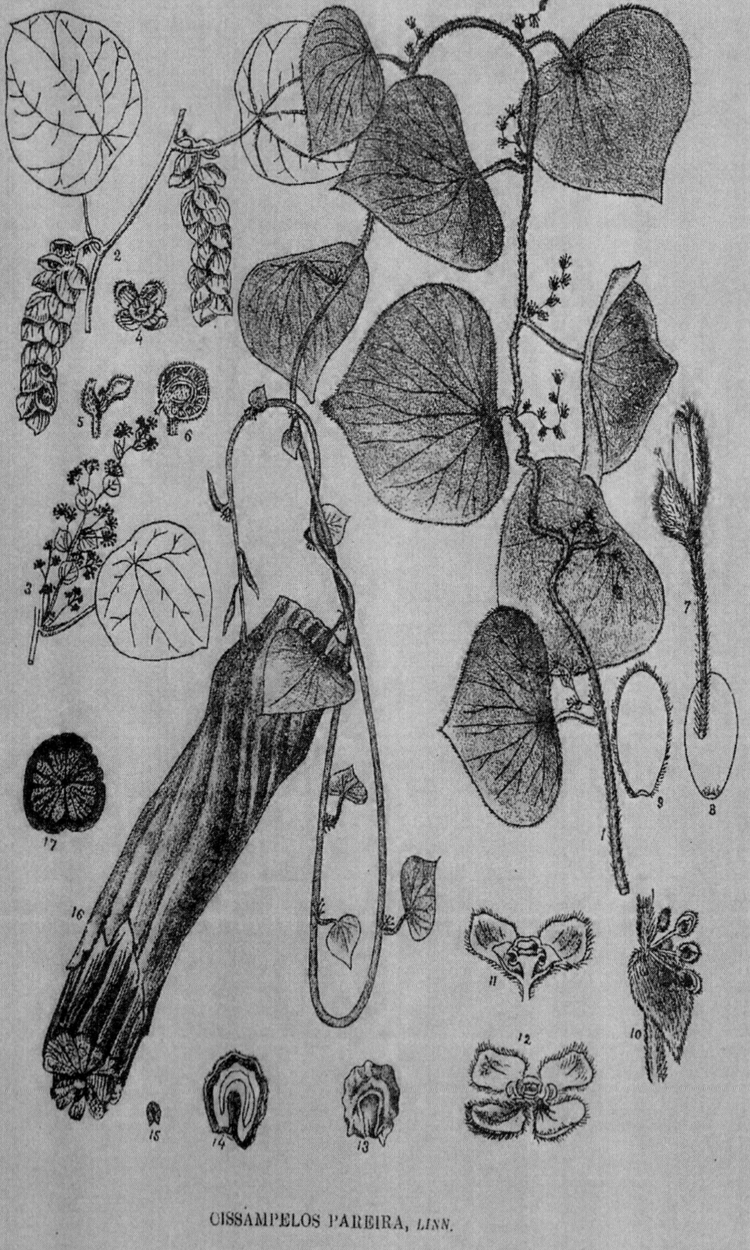

CISSAMPELOS PAREIRA, *LINN.*

PLATE No. 43.

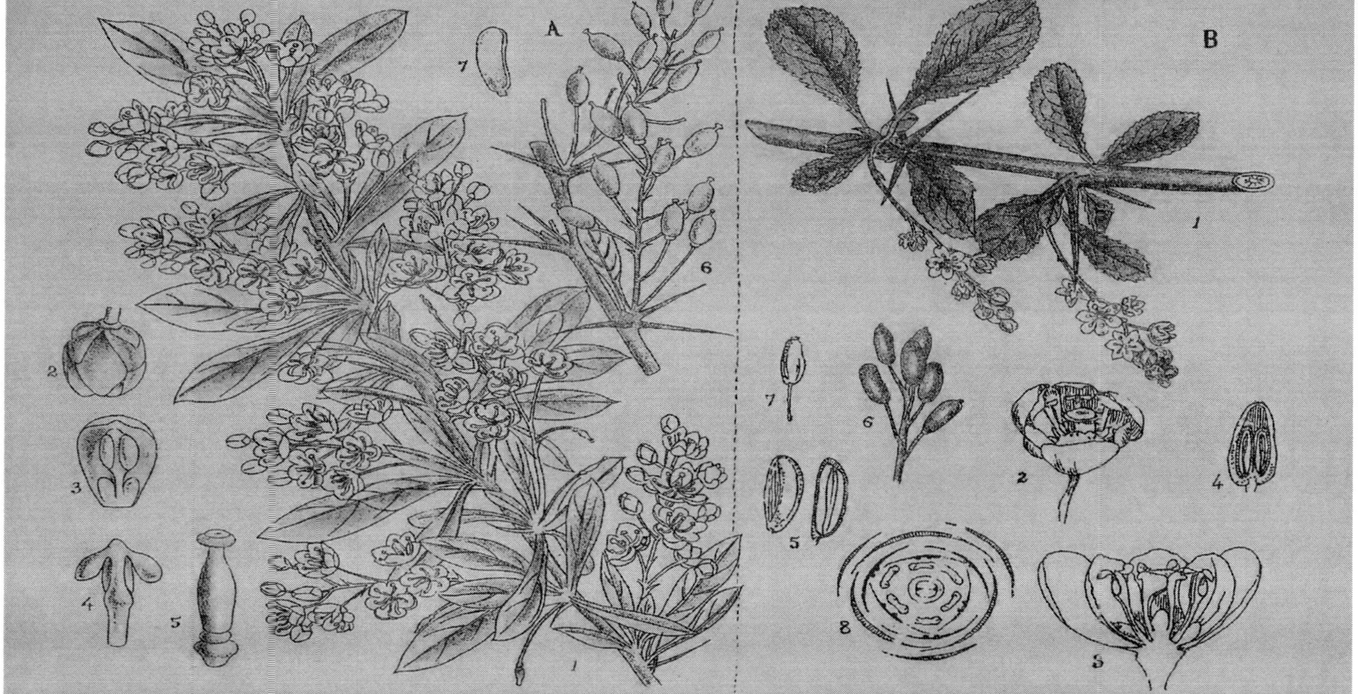

A—LERBERIS LYCIUM, *ROYLE.*

B—BERBERIS VULGARIS, *LINN.*

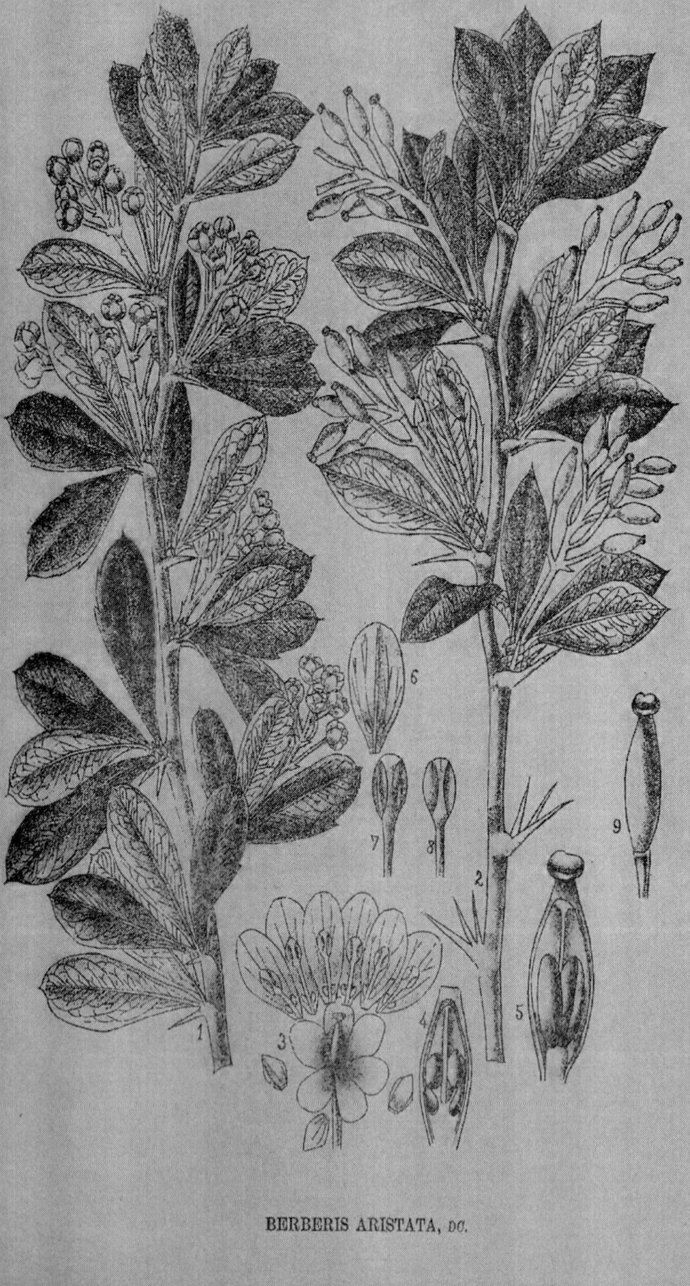

BERBERIS ARISTATA, *DC.*

BERBERIS ASIATICA, *ROXB.*

PLATE No. 46.

PODOPHYLLUM EMODI, *WALL.*

PLATE No. 47.

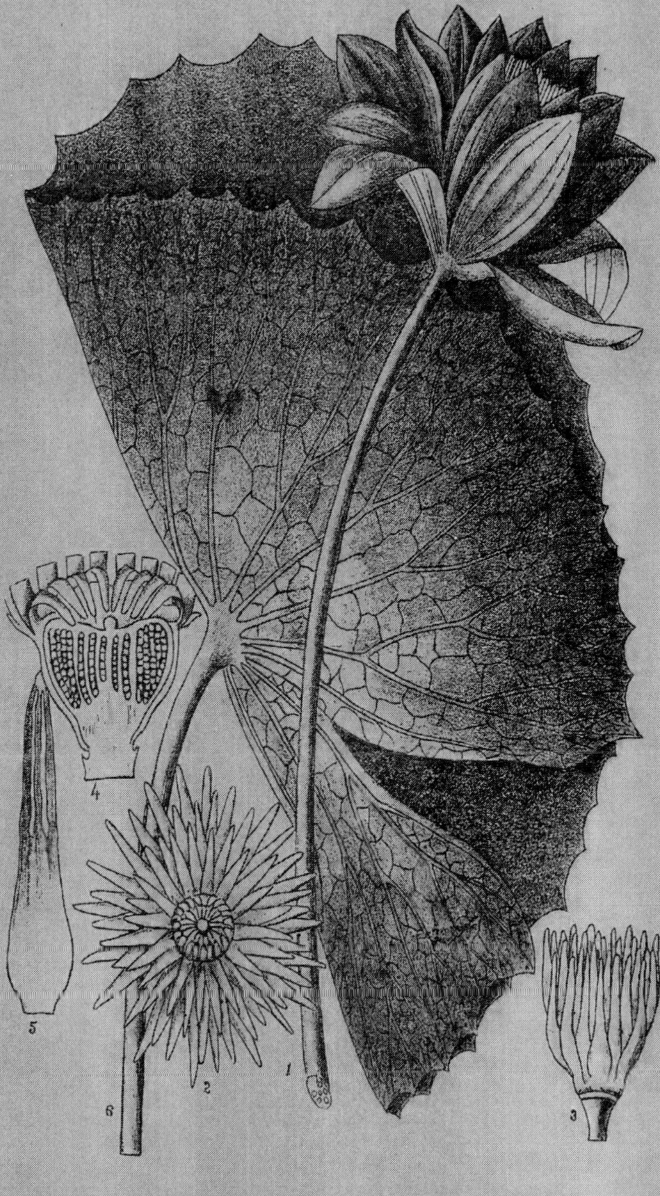

NYMPHÆA ALBA, *LINN.*

PLATE No. 48.

NYMPHÆA LOTUS, *Linn.*

PLATE No. 49.

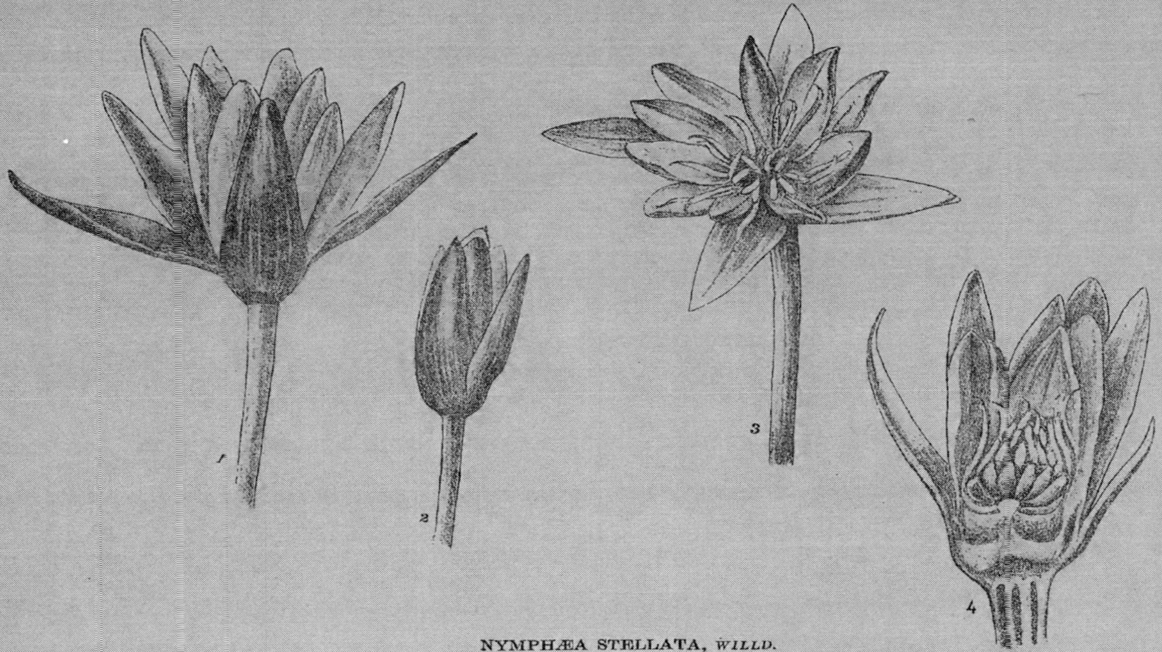

NYMPHÆA STELLATA, *WILLD.*

EURYALE FEROX, SALISB.

PLATE No. 51.

NELUMBIUM SPECIOSUM, *WILLD.*

PLTAE No. 52.

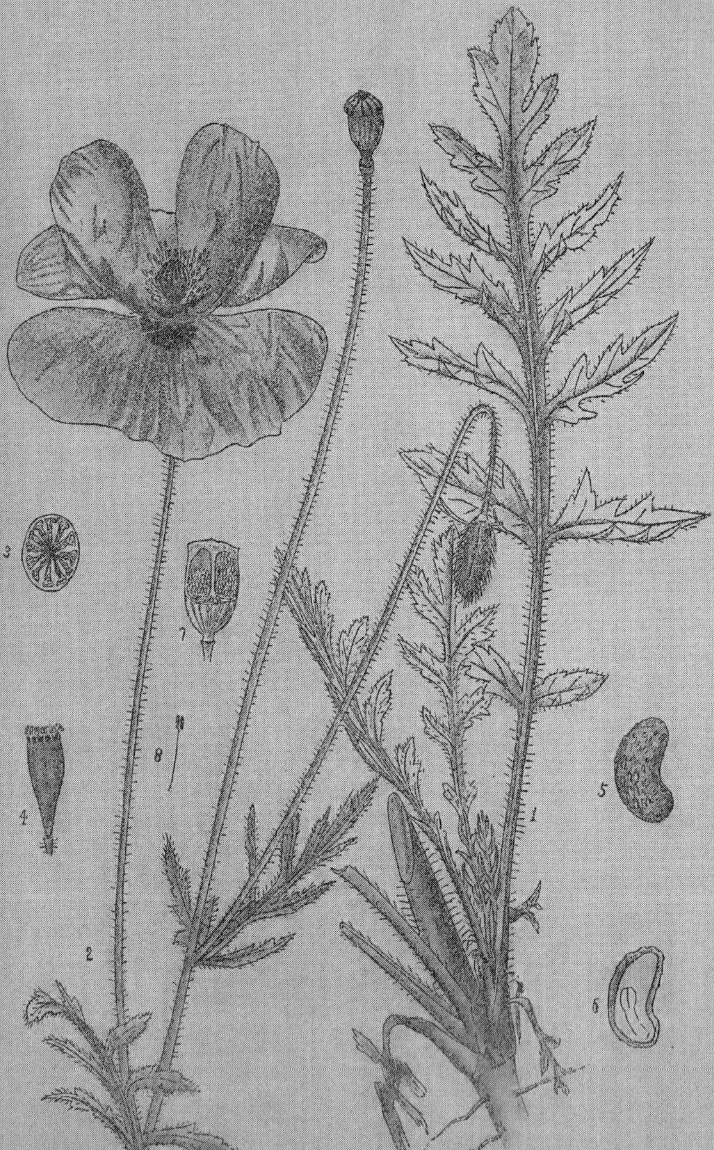

PAPAVER RHŒAS, *LINN.*

PLATE No. 53.

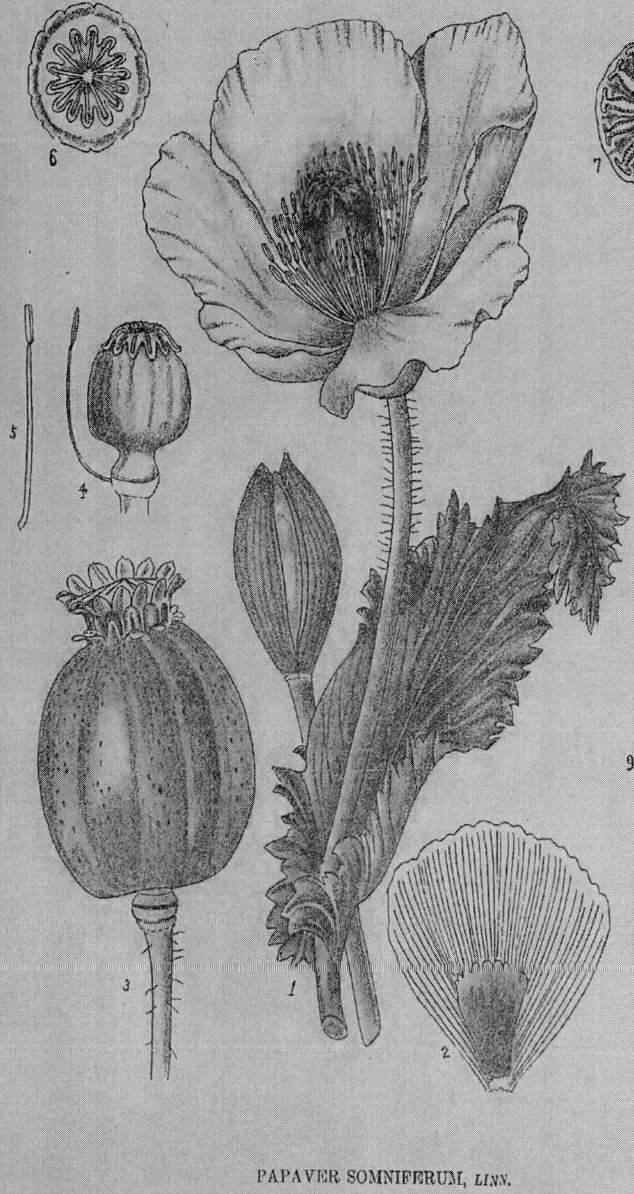

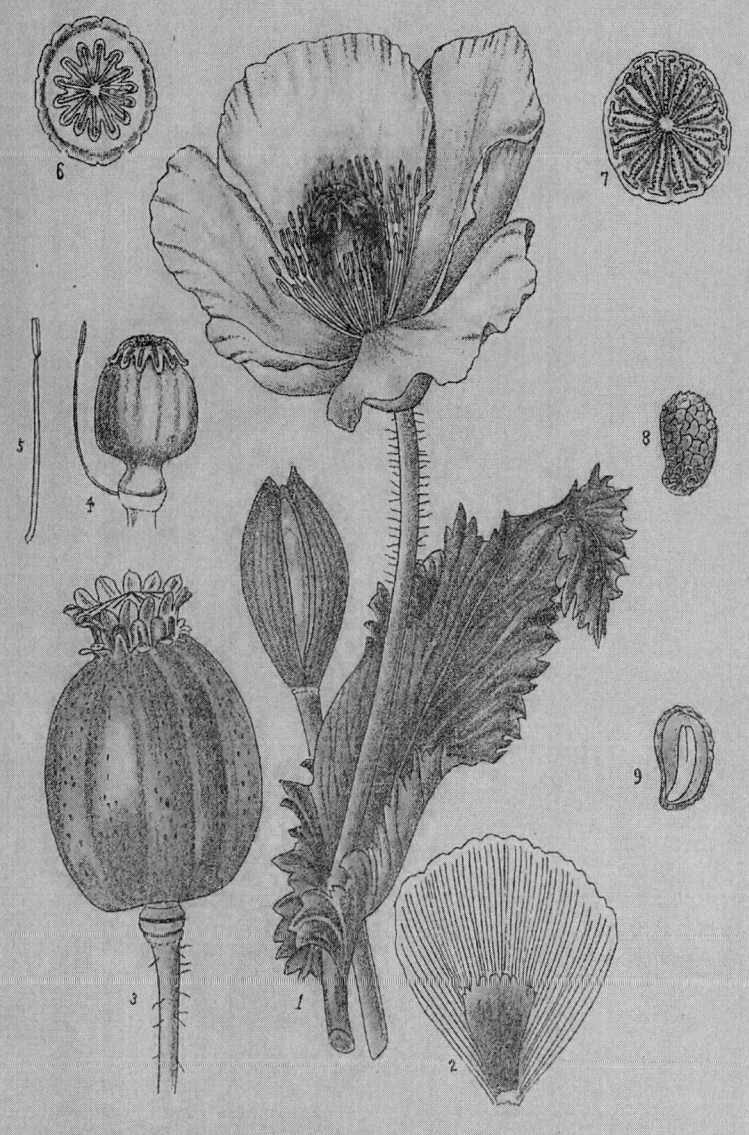

PAPAVER SOMNIFERUM, *LINN.*

PLATE No. 54

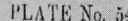

ARGEMOÆ MEXIČANA, *LINN*

PLATE No. 55.

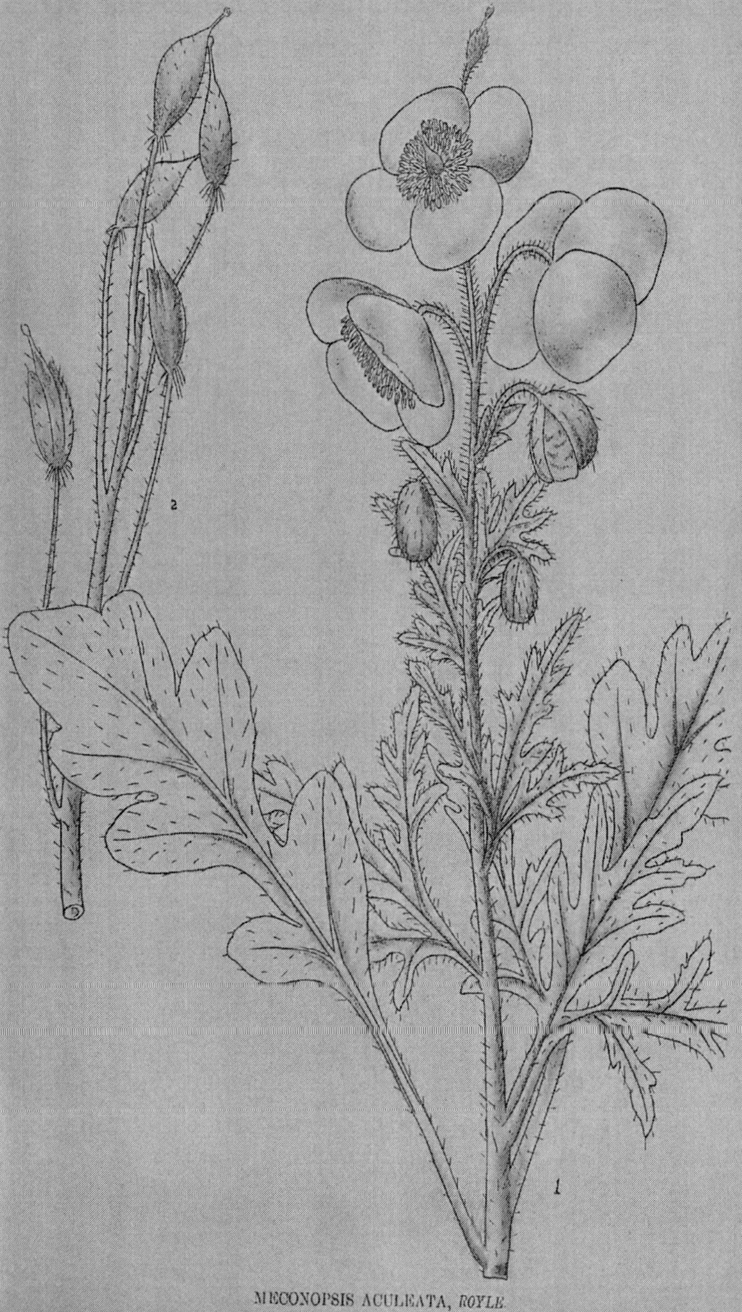

MECONOPSIS ACULEATA, *ROYLE.*

MECONOPSIS NIPALENSIS, *DC.*

PLATE No. 57.

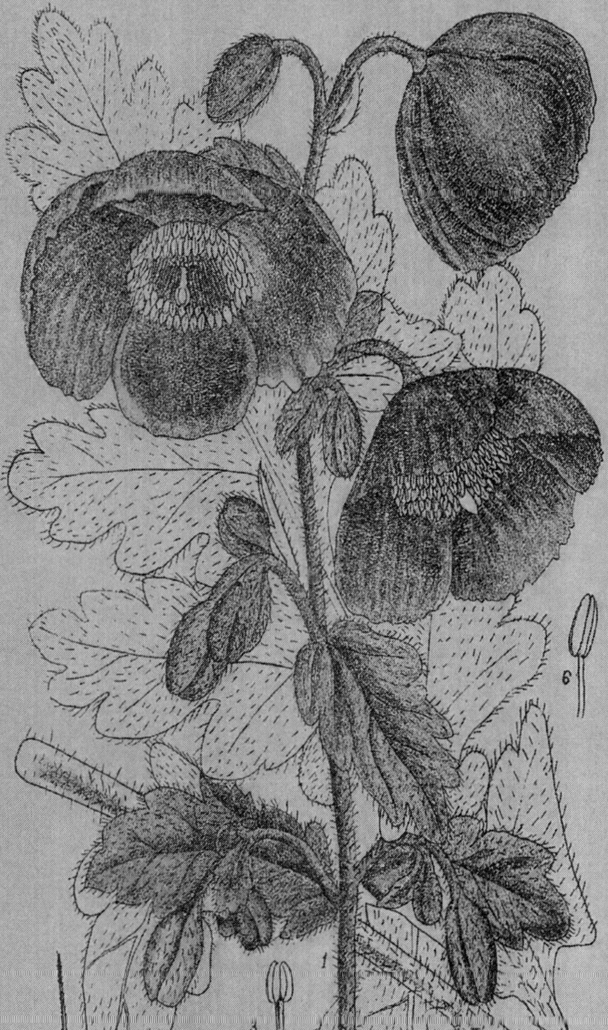

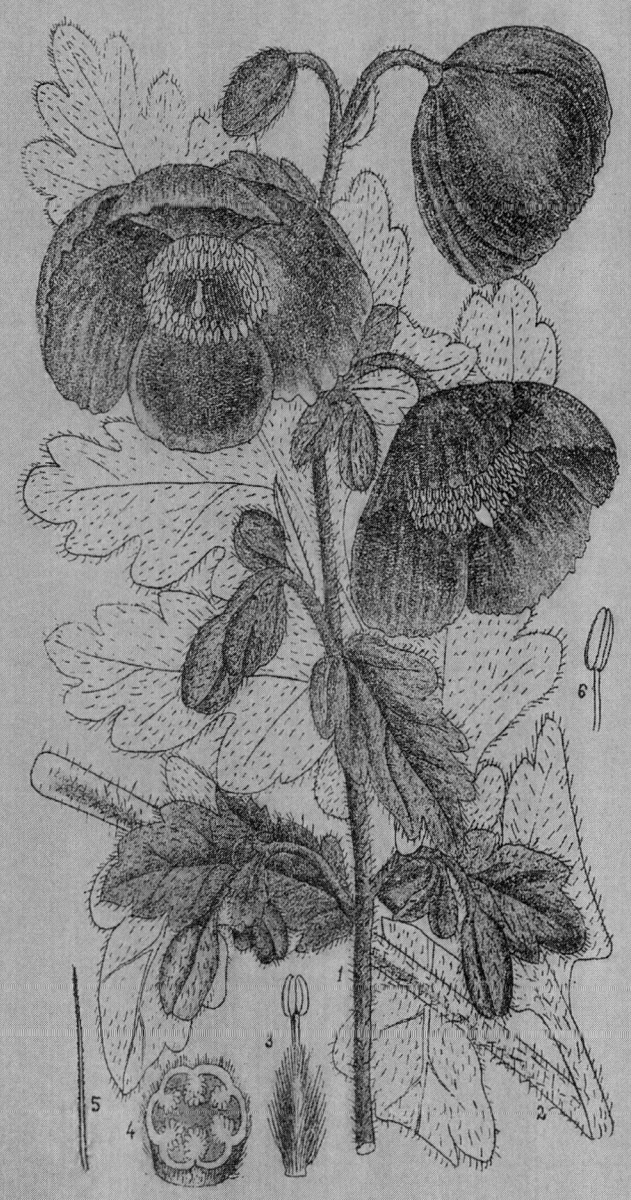

MECONOPSIS WALLICHII, HOOK.

PLATE No. 58.

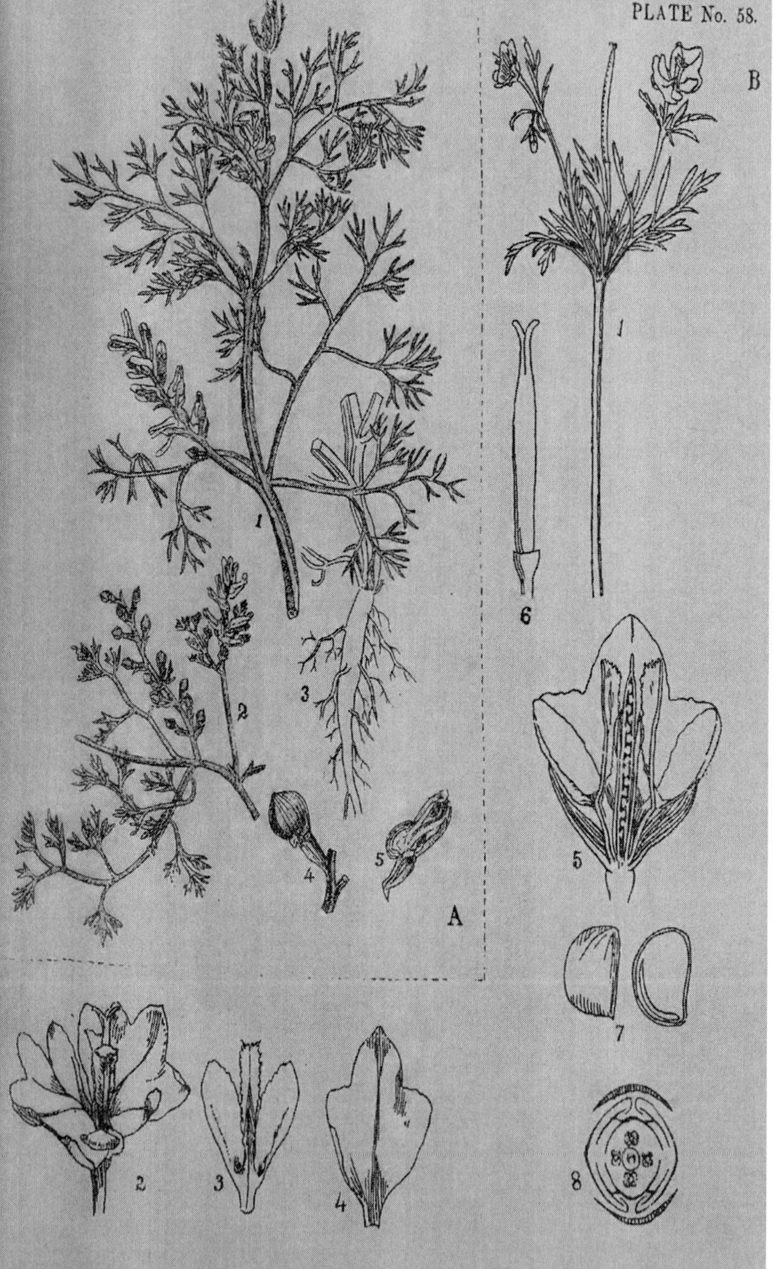

A—FUMARIA PAVIFLORA, *LAMK.*

B—HYPECOUM PROCUMBENS, *LINN.*

PLATE No. 59

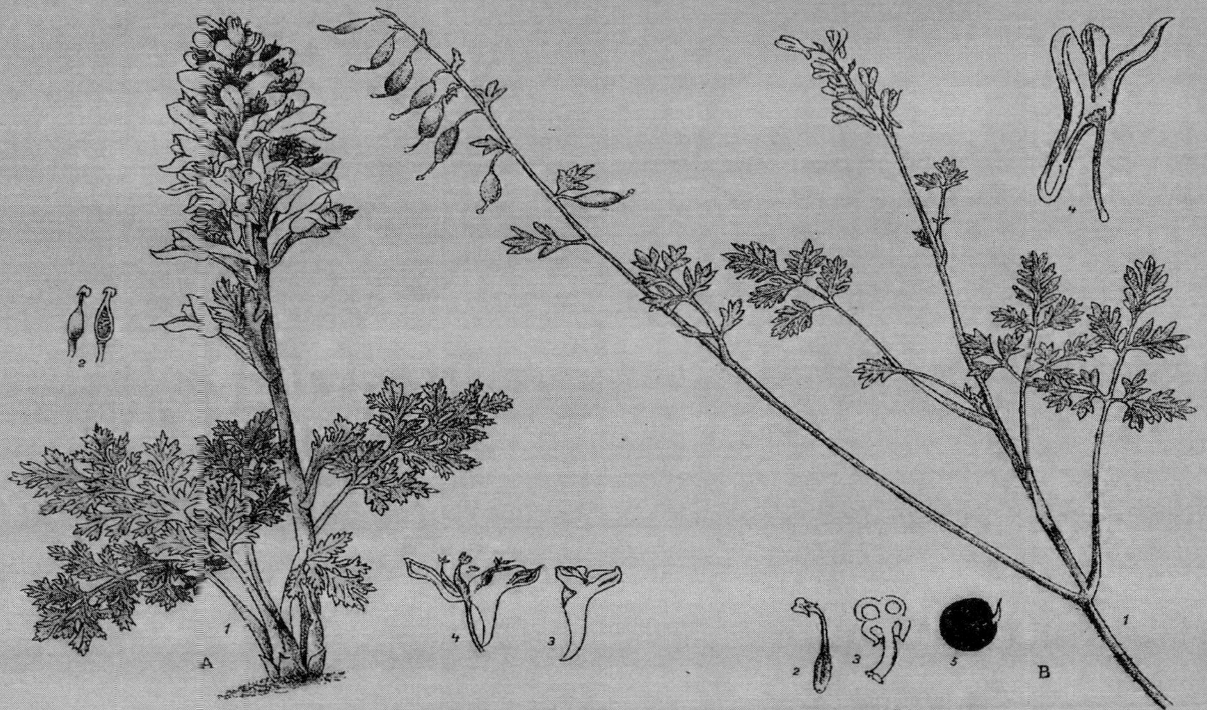

A—CORYDALIS GOVANIANA, *Wall.* B—C. RAMOSA, *Wall.*

PLATE No. 60.

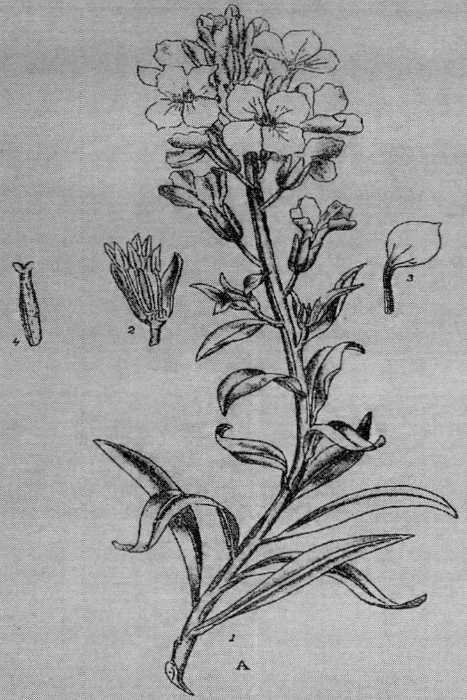

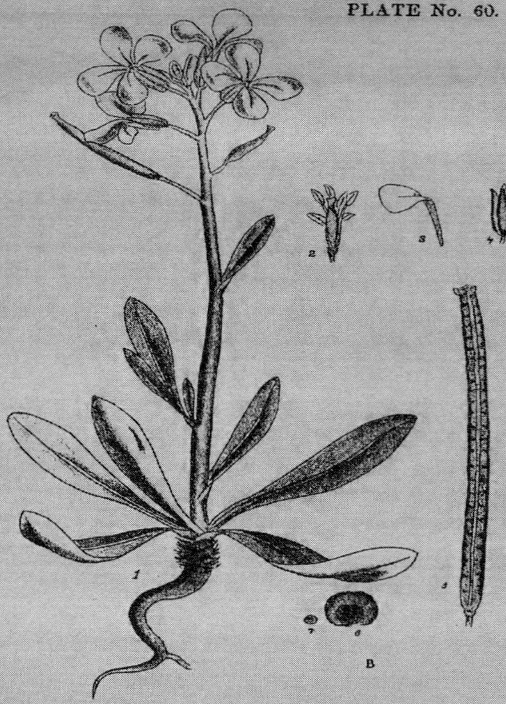

A—CHEIRANTHUS CHEIRI, *LINN.*

B—MATTHIOLA INCANA, *Br.*

PLATE No. 61.

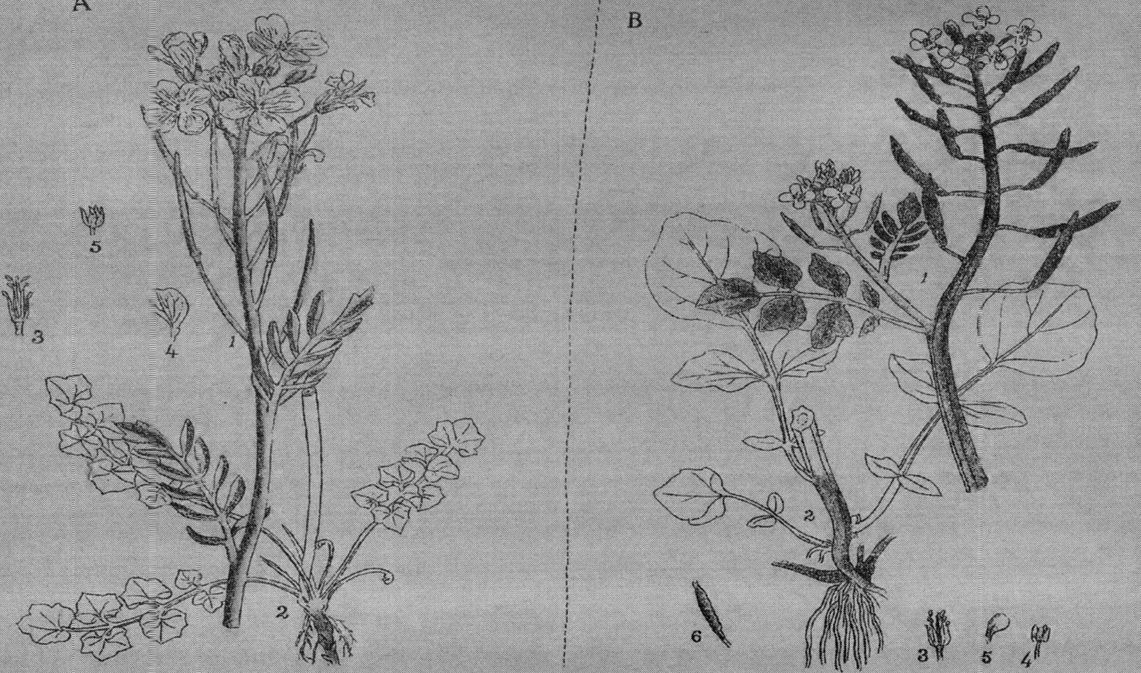

A—CARDAMINE PRATENSIS, *LINN.*

B—NASTURTIUM OFFICINALE, *BR.*

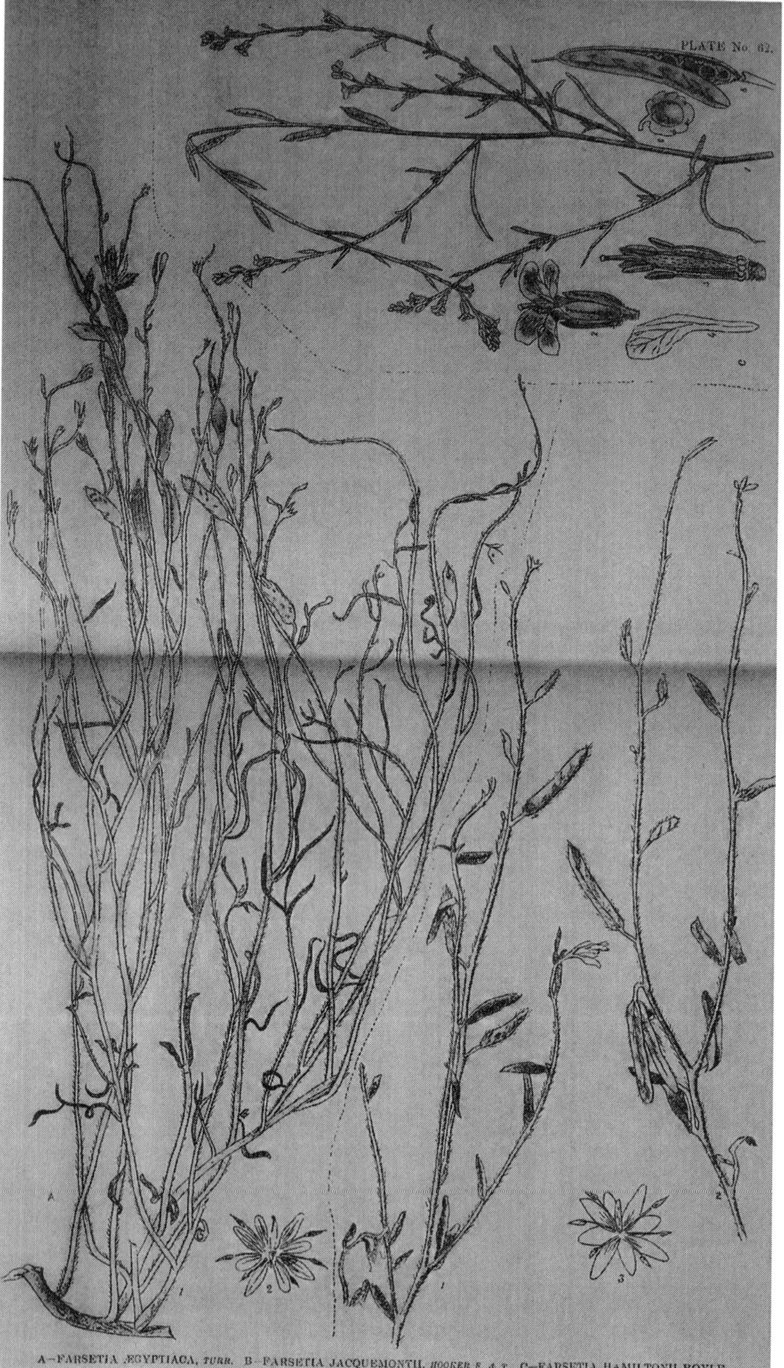

A—FARSETIA ÆGYPTIACA, *TURR.* B—FARSETIA JACQUEMONTII, *HOOKER F. & T.* C—FARSETIA HAMILTONII ROYLE.

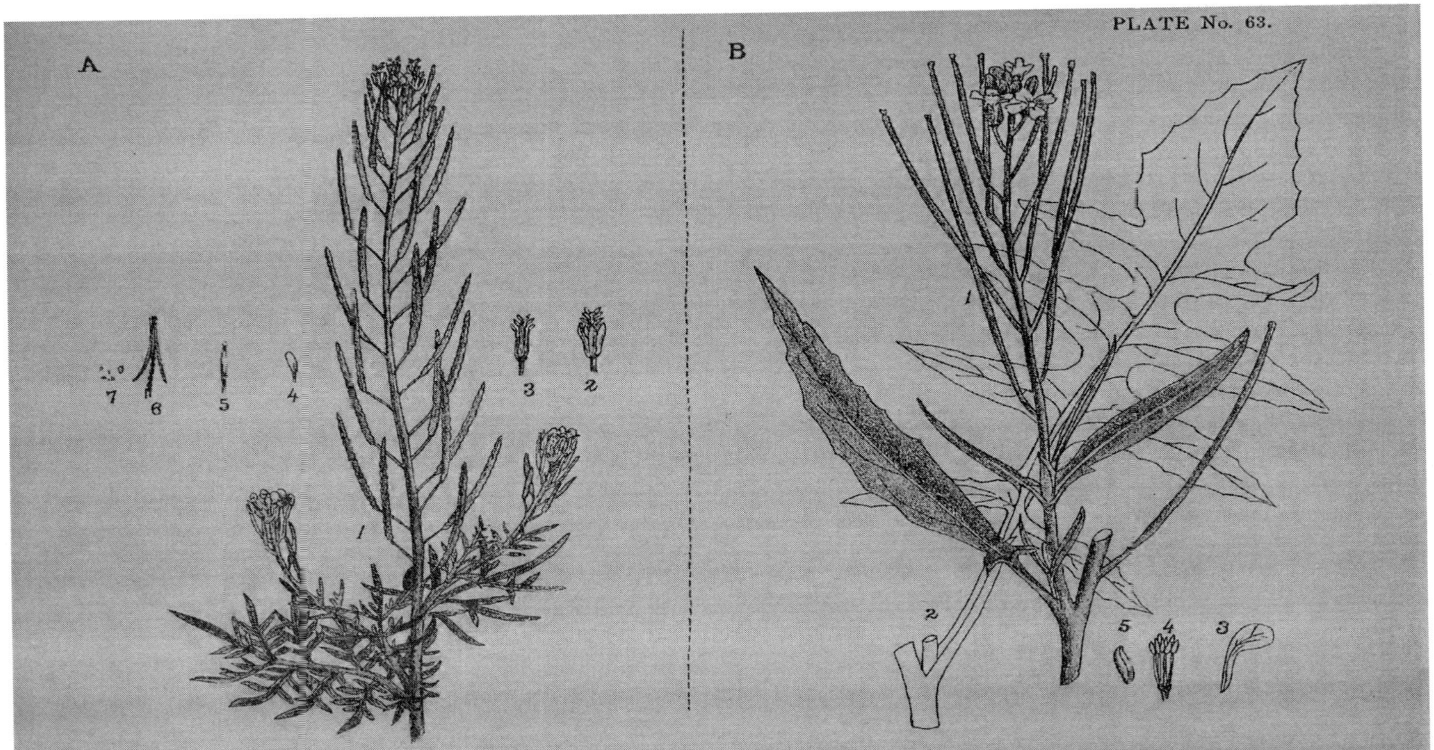

A—SISYMBRIUM SOPHIA, *LINN.*

B—SISYMBRIUM IRIO, *LINN.*

PLATE No. 64.

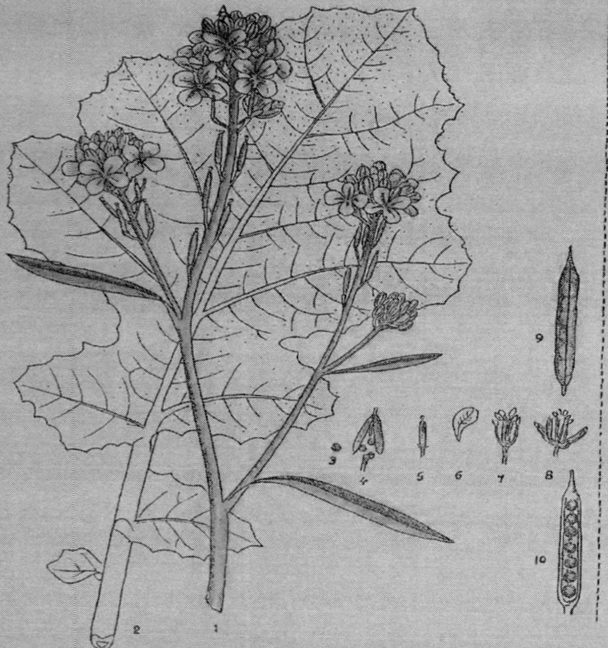

A—BRASSICA CAMPESTRIS, *LINN.*

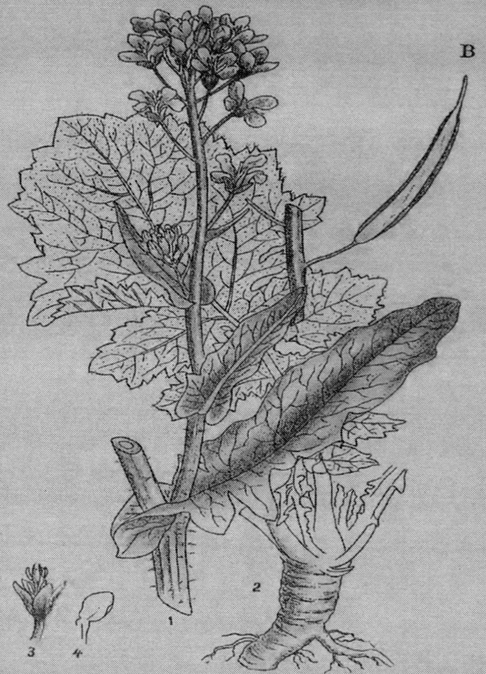

B—BRASSICA NIGRA, *KOCH.*

PLATE No. 65.

BRASSICA JUNCEA, *HK. F. & T.*

PLATE No. 66.

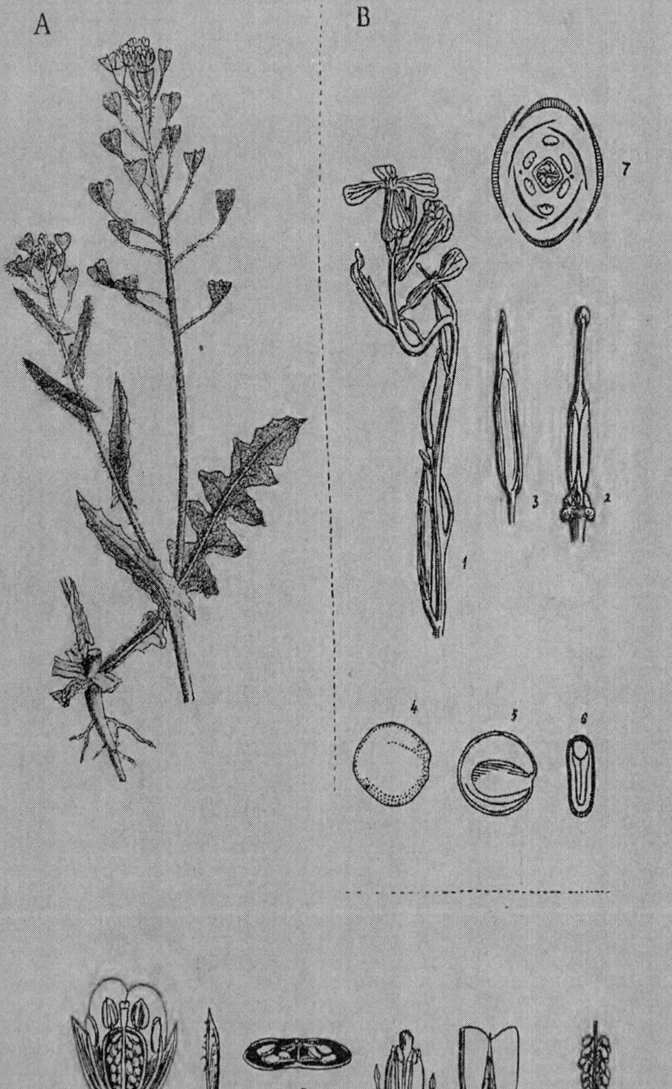

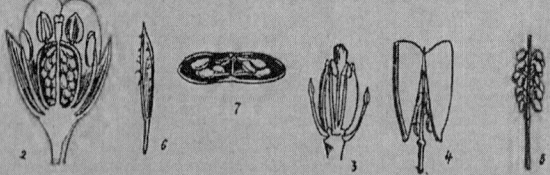

A—CAPSELLA BURSA-PASTORIS, *MŒNCH*

B—ERUCA SATIVA, *LAMK.*

PLATE No. 67.

LEPIDIUM SATIVUM, *LINN.*

PLATE No. 68.

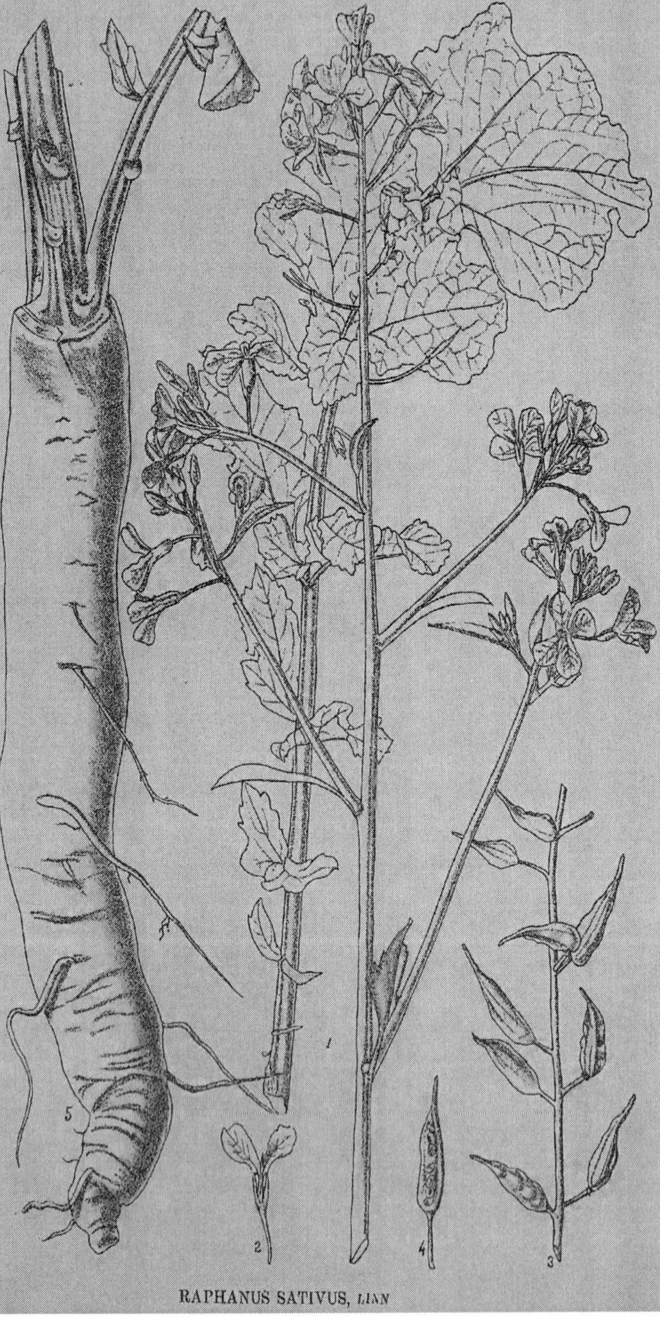

RAPHANUS SATIVUS, *LINN*

PLATE No. 69.

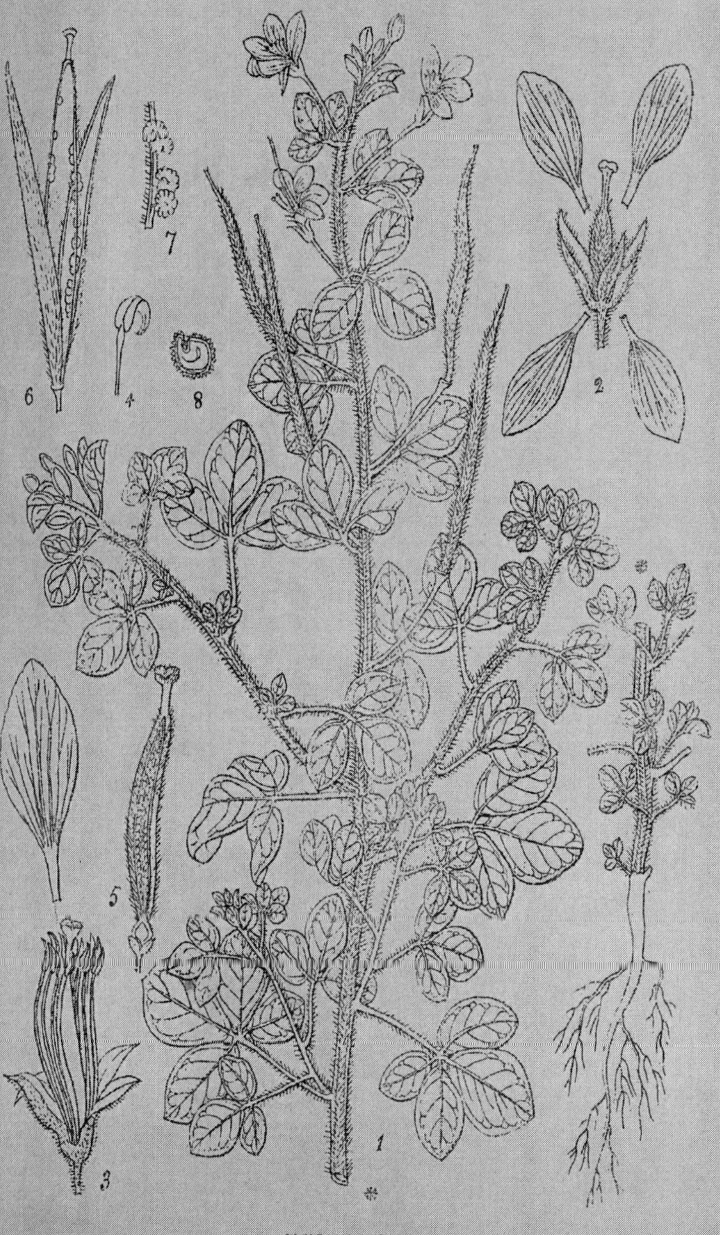

CLEOME VISCOSA, *LINN.*

PLATE No. 70.

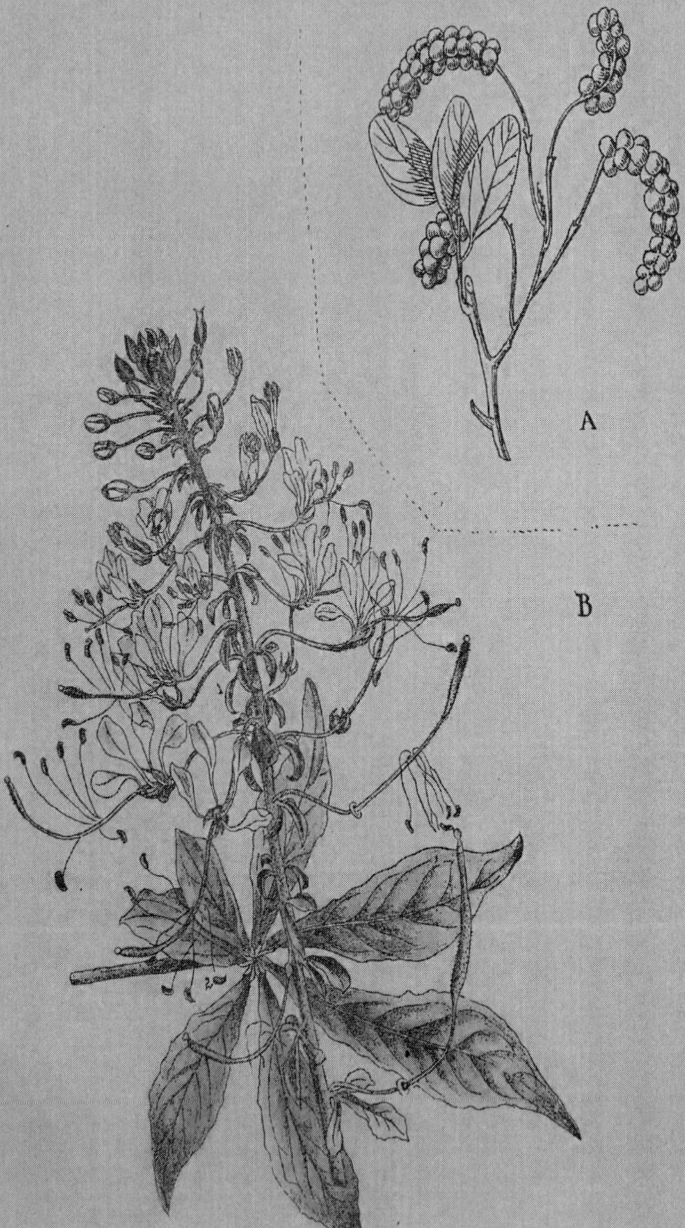

A—MÆRUA ARENARIA, *H. F. & T.*　　B—GYNANDROPSIS PENTAPHYLLA, *DC.*

PLATE No. 71.

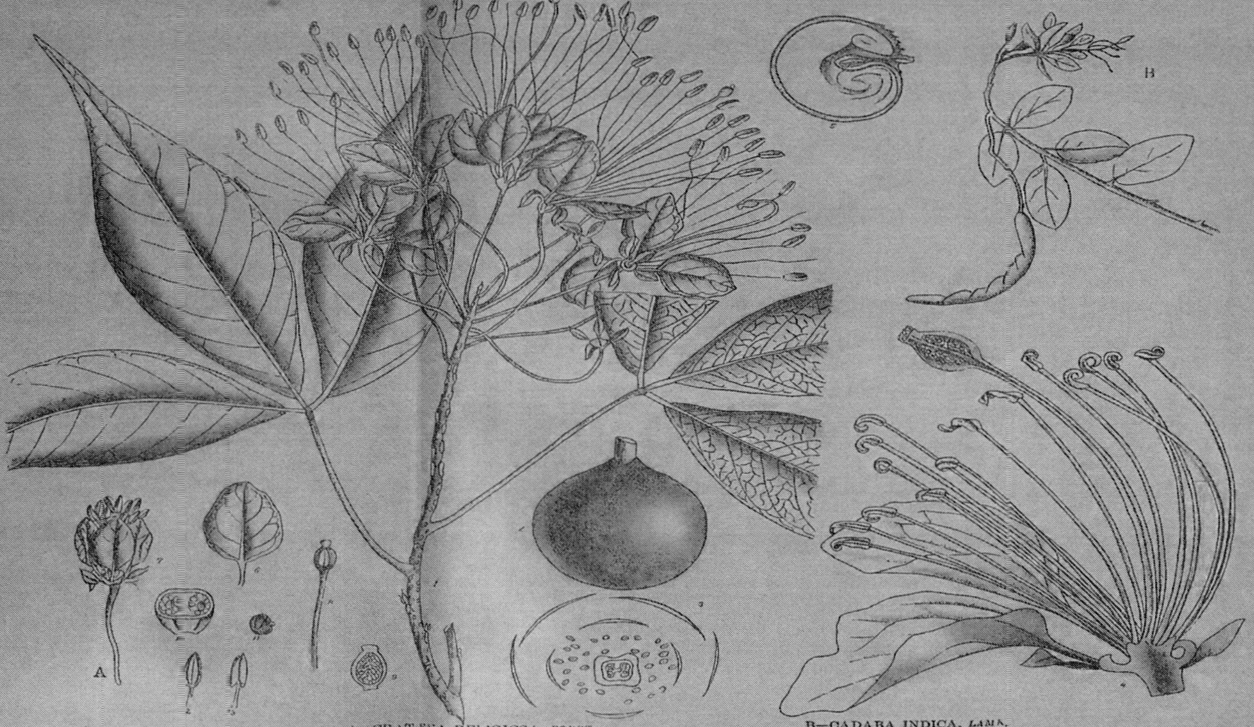

A—CRATÆVA RELIGIOSA, *Forst.* B—CADABA INDICA, *Lamk.*

PLATE No. 72.

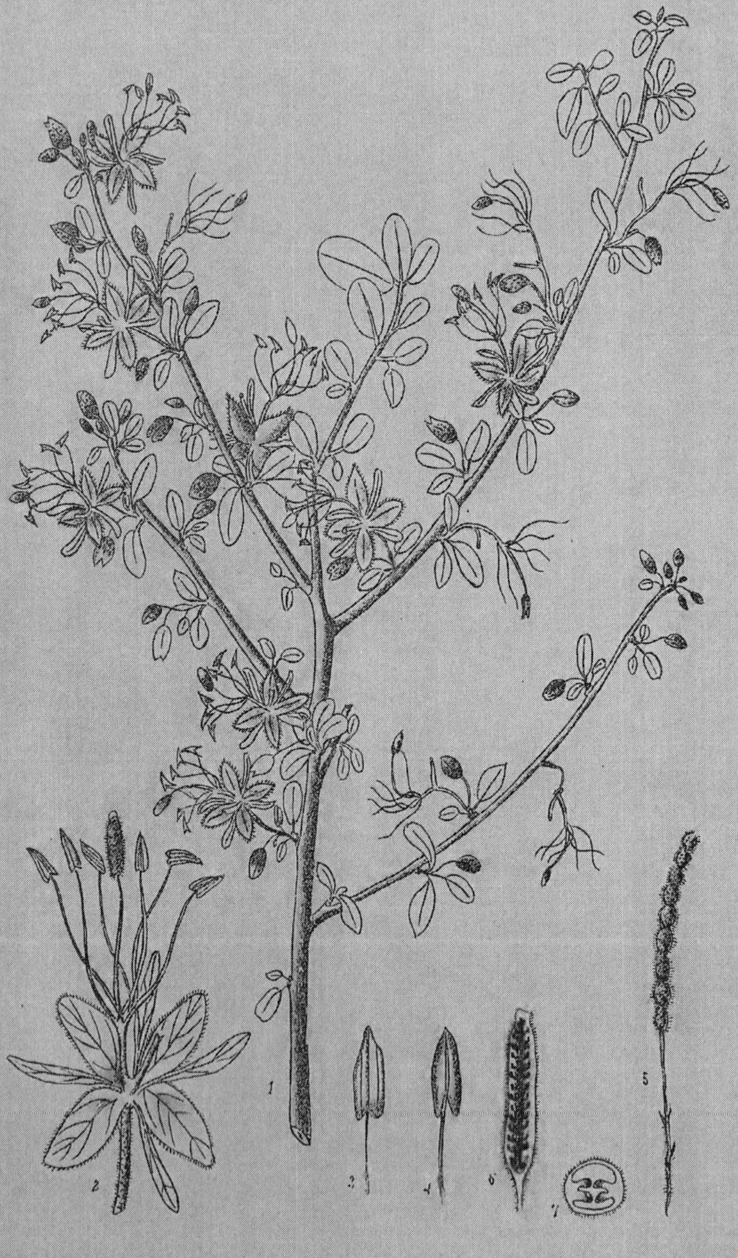

CADABA FARINOSA, *FORSK.*

PLATE No. 73.

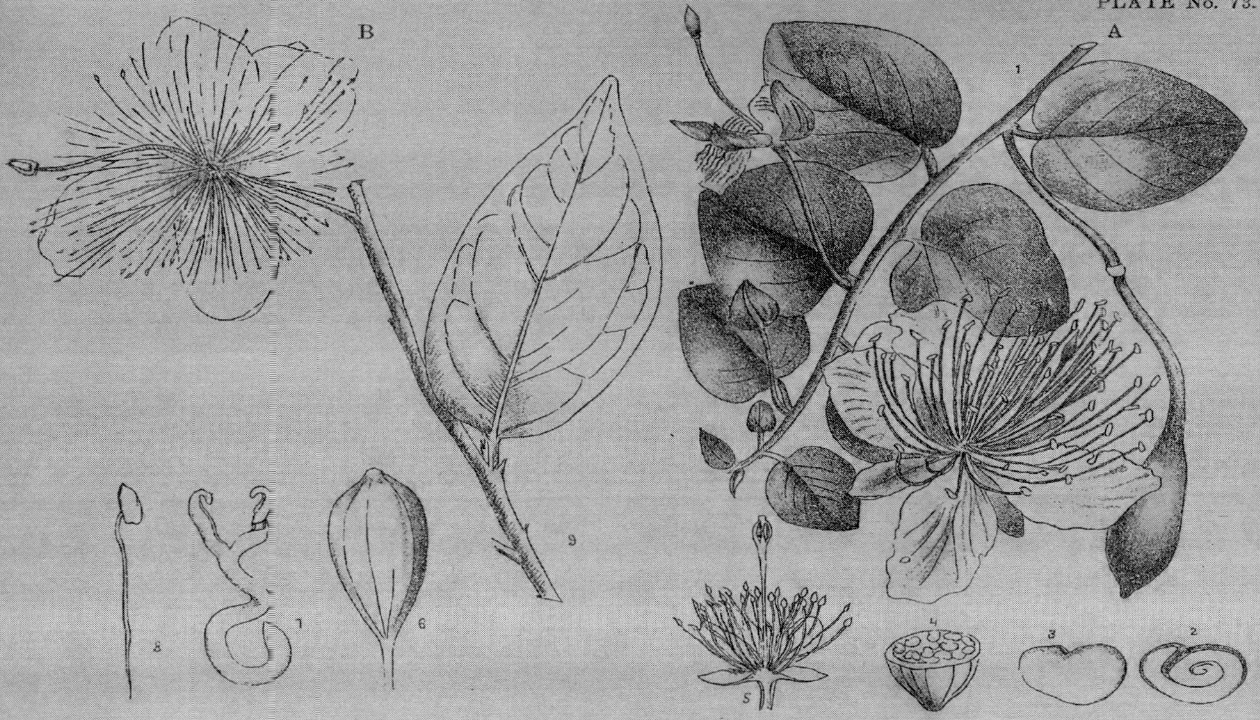

A—CAPPARIS SPINOSA, *LAMK.* (*FIG. 1—8.*) B—C. HEYNEANA, *WALL* (*FIG. 9.*)

PLATE No. 74.

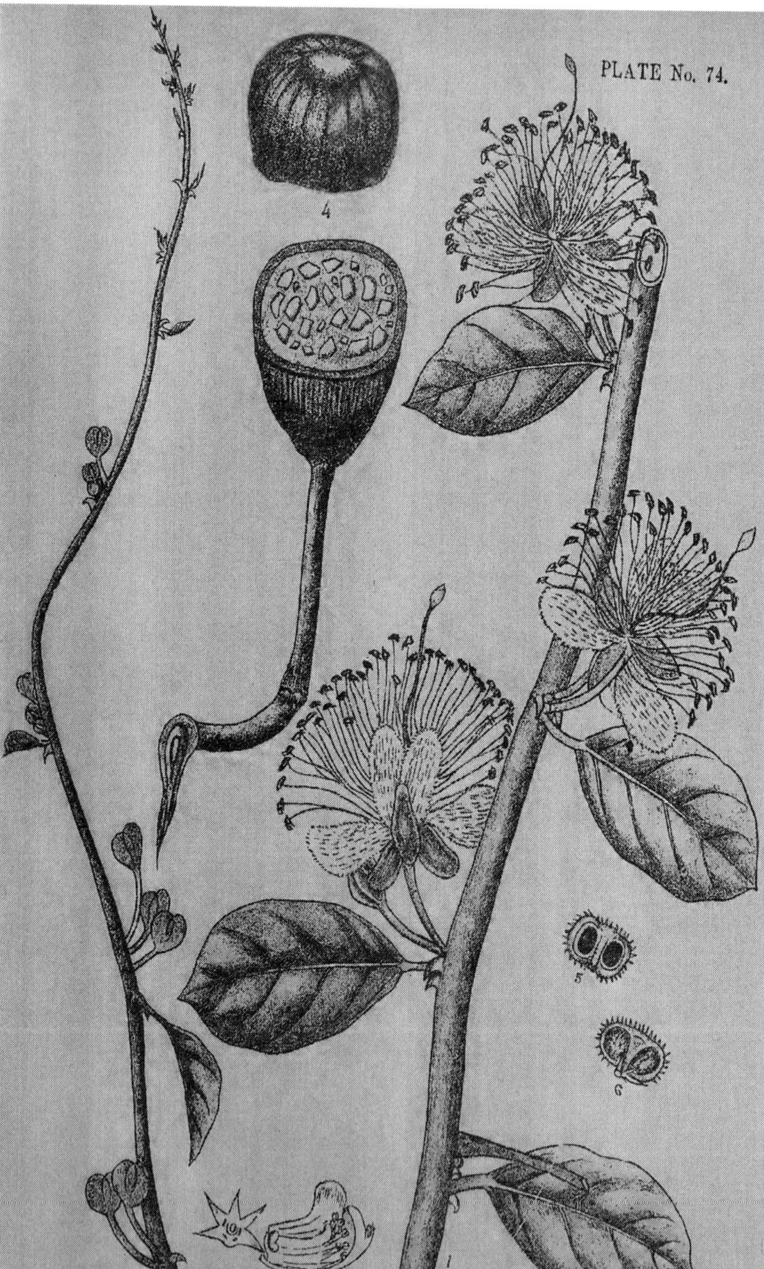

CAPPARIS ZEYLANICA, *LINN.*

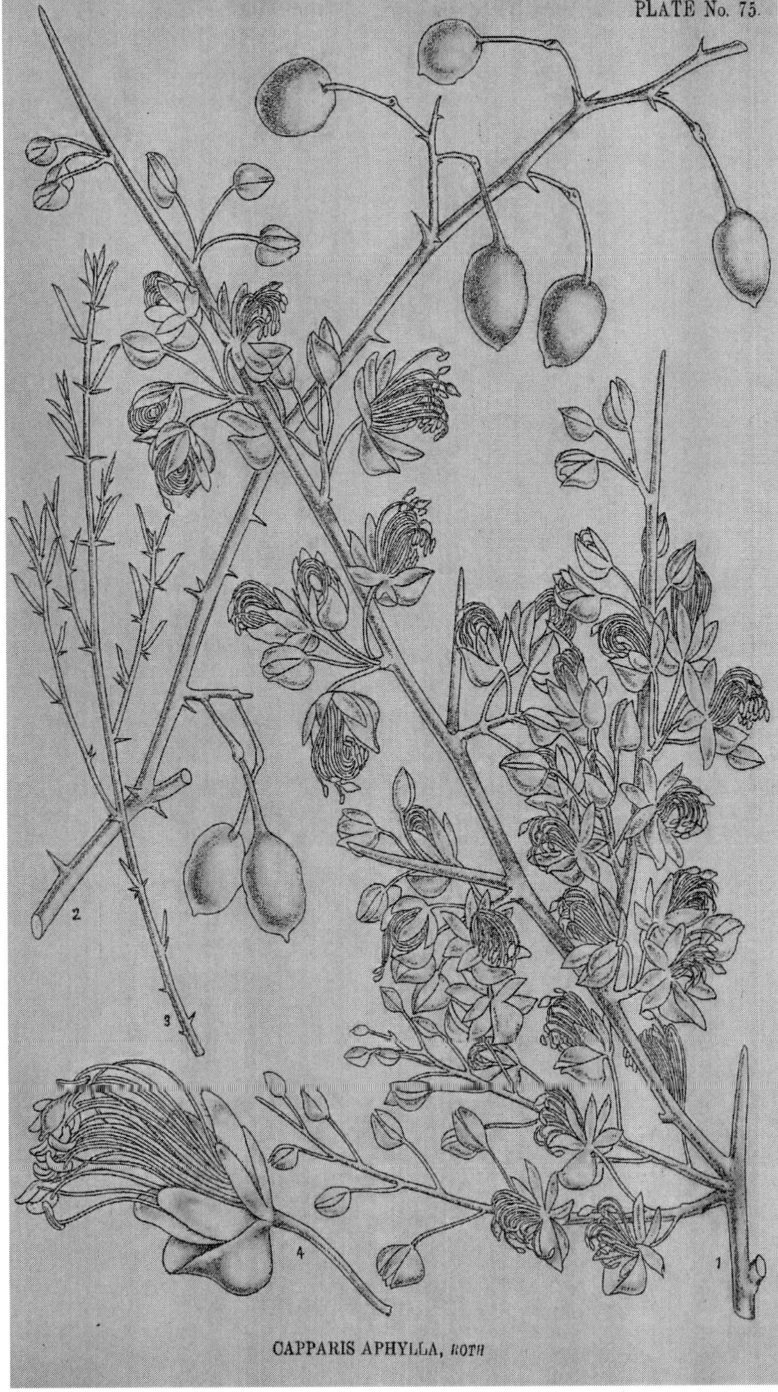

CAPPARIS APHYLLA, ROTH

PLATE No 76.

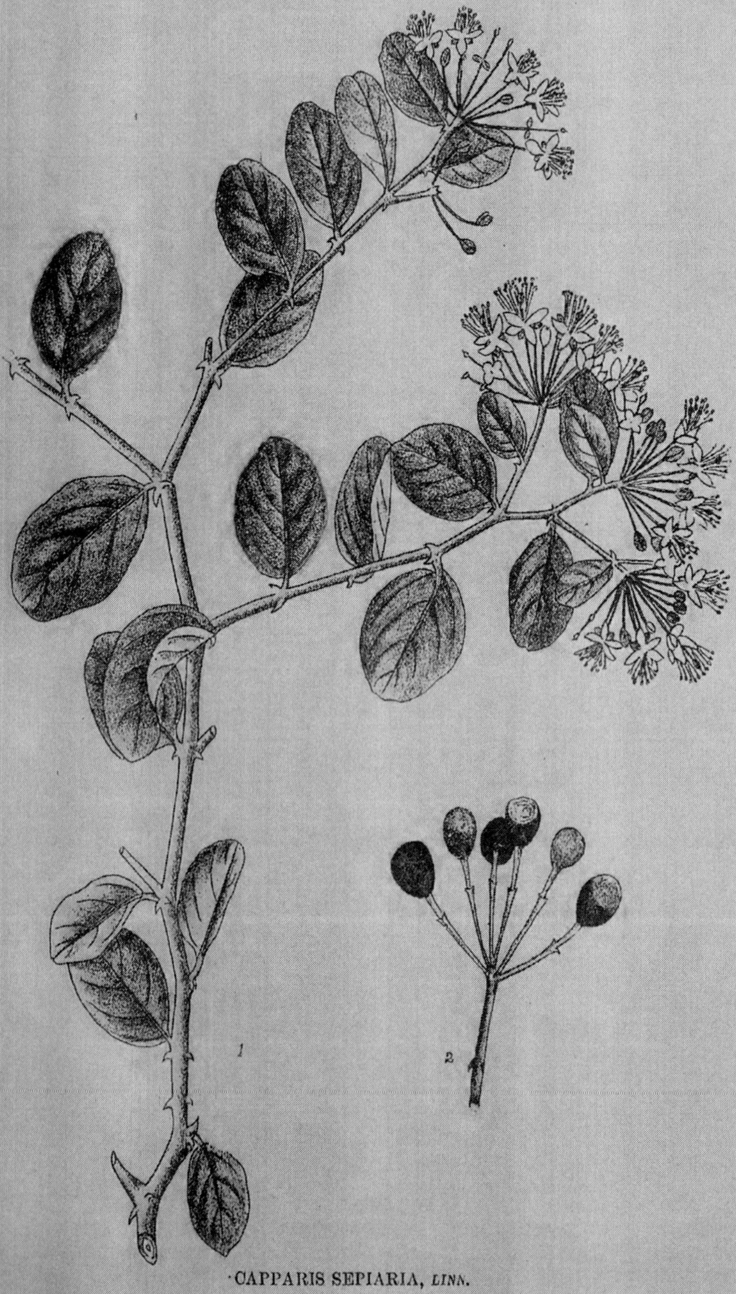

CAPPARIS SEPIARIA, LINN.

PLATE No. 77.

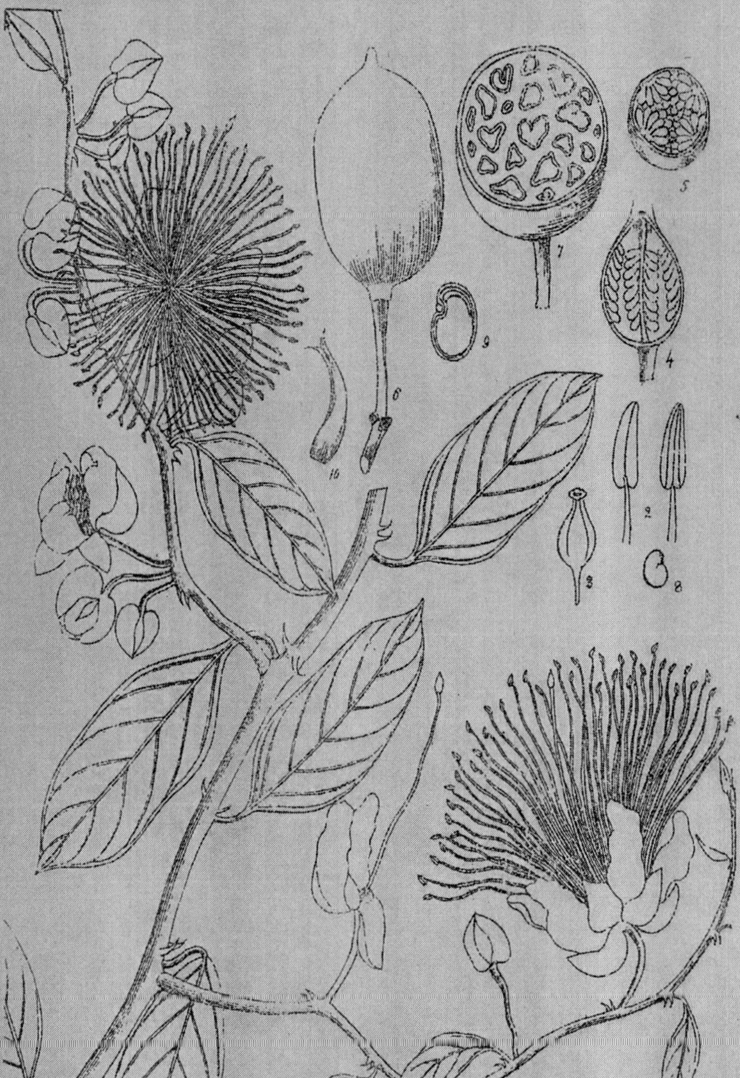

CAPPARIS HORRIDA, LINN. F.

PLATE No. 78.

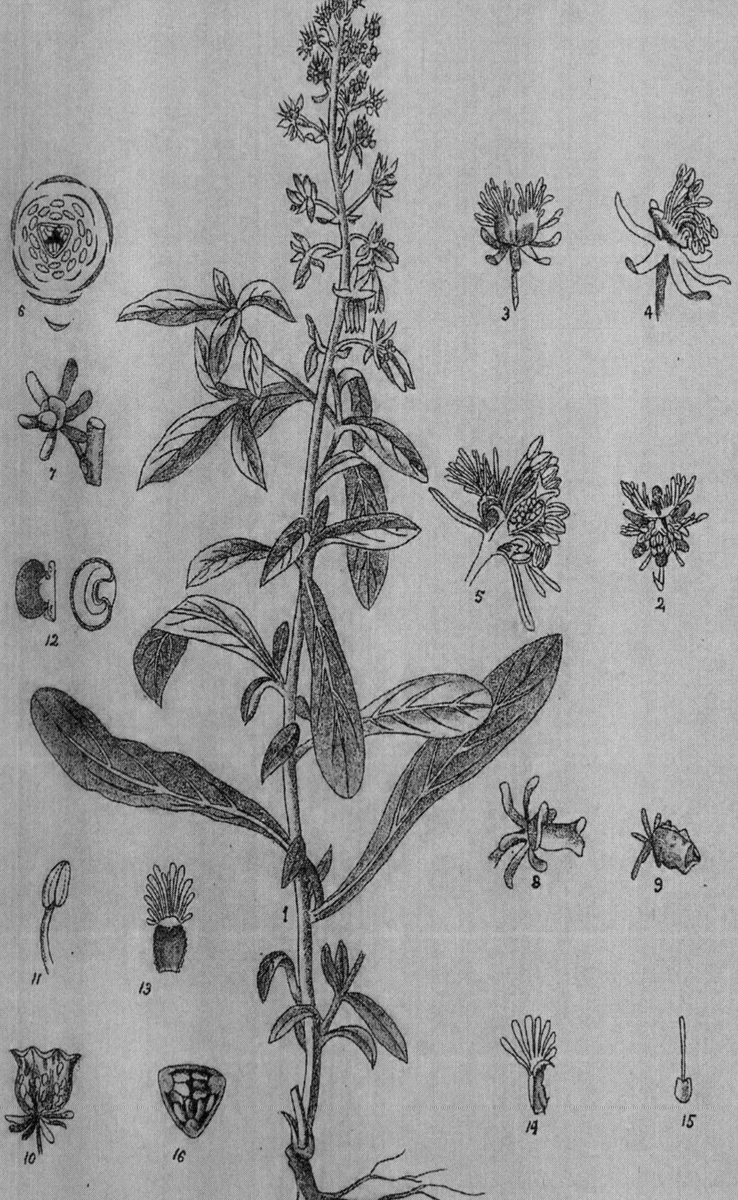

RESEDA ODORATA, *LINN.*

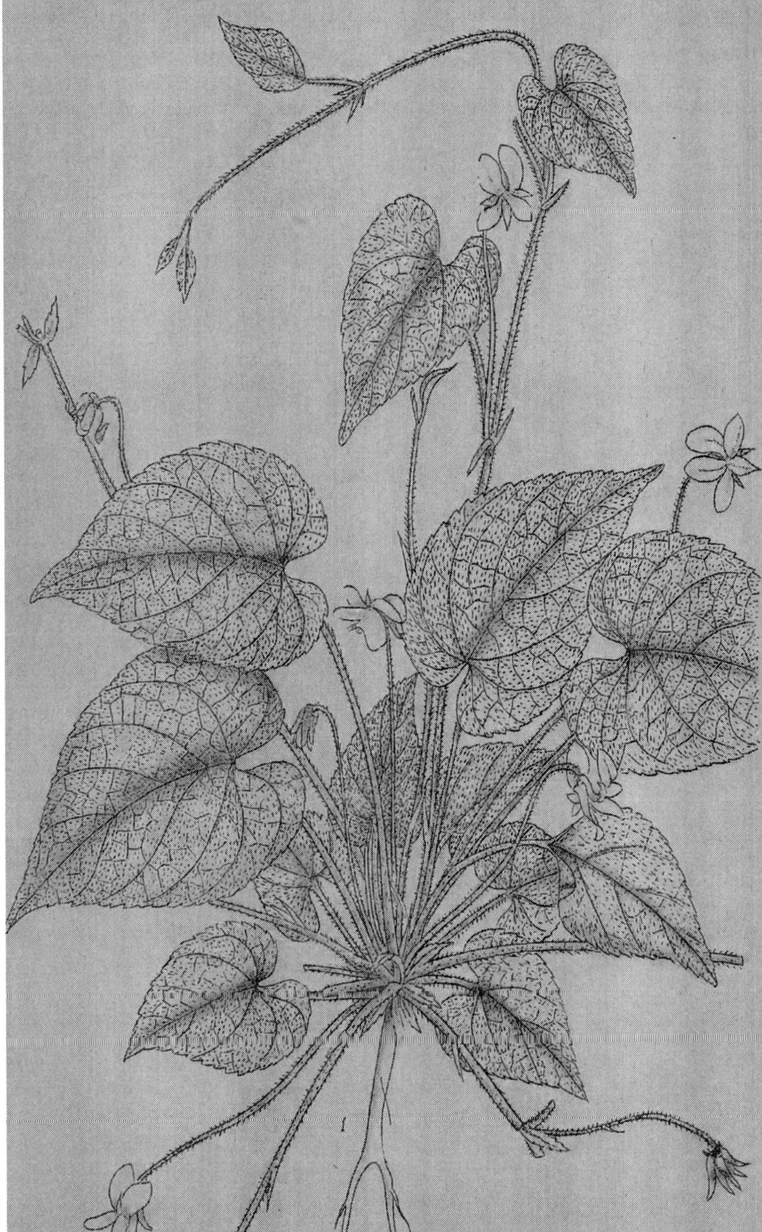

VIOLA SERPENS, *WALL*.

PLATE No. 80.

A—VIOLA CINEREA, *BOISS.*

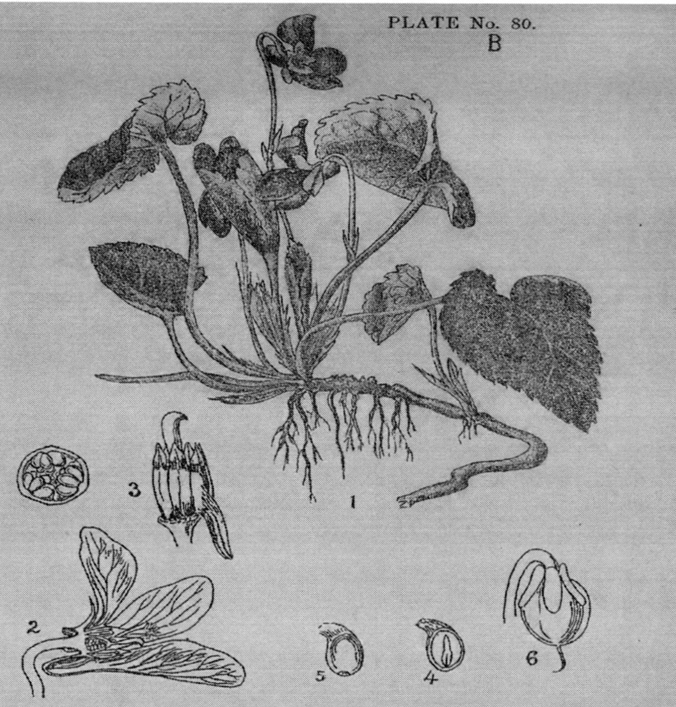

B—VIOLA ODORATA, *LINN.*

PLATE No. 81.

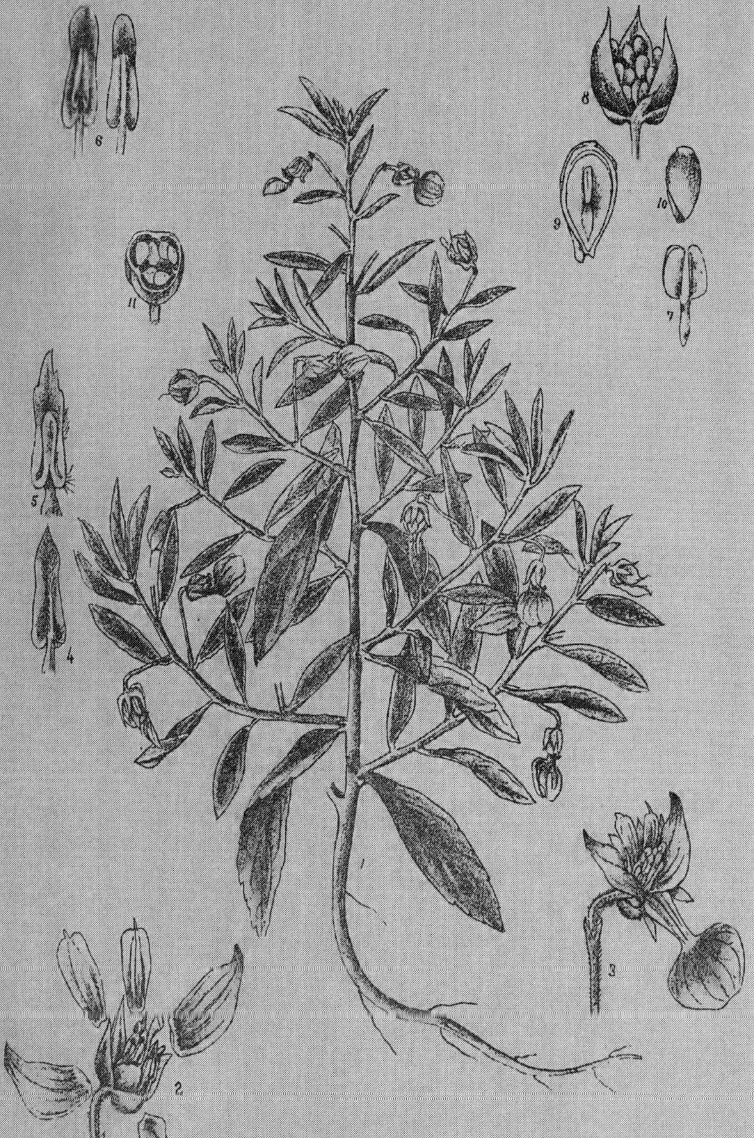

IONIDIUM SUFFRUTICOSUM, *GING.*

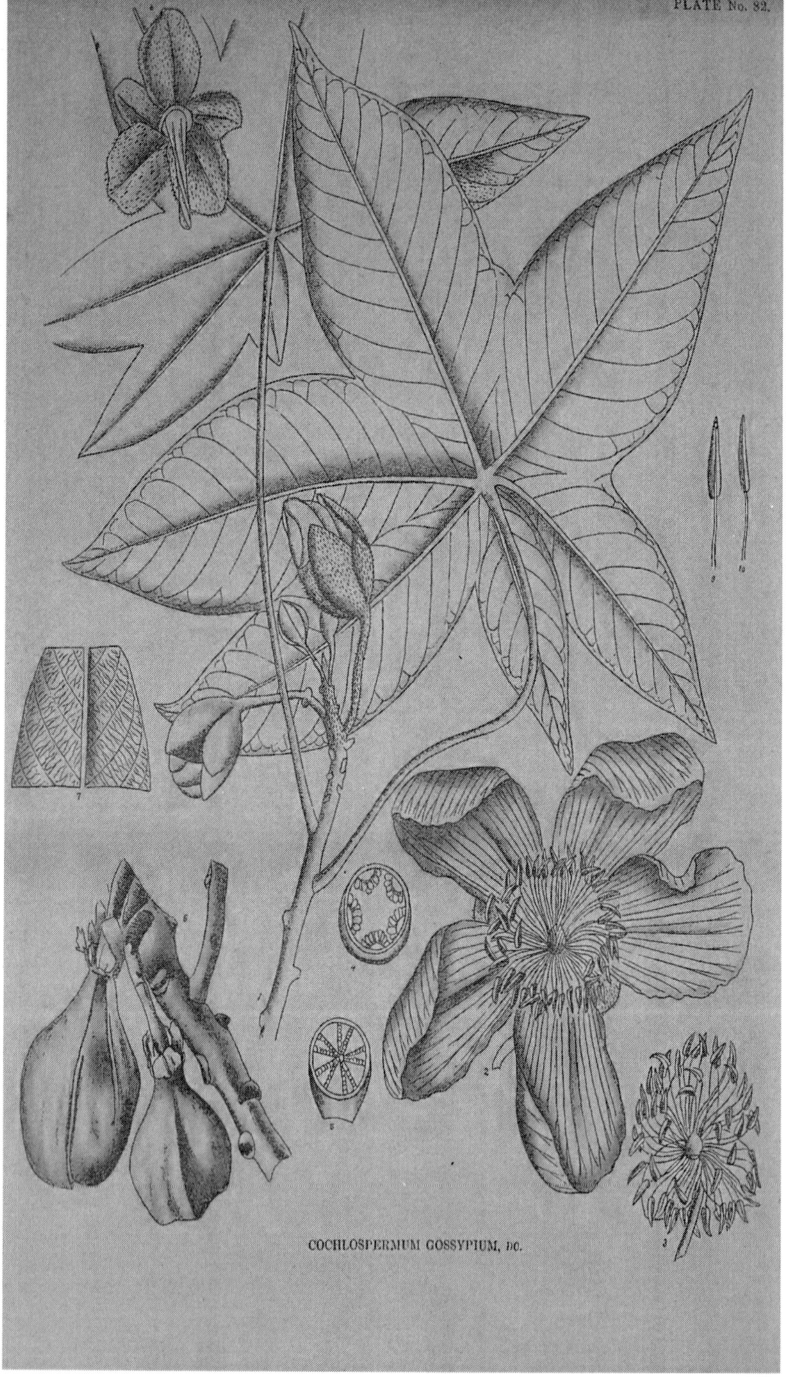

COCHLOSPERMUM GOSSYPIUM, DC.

PLATE No. 83.

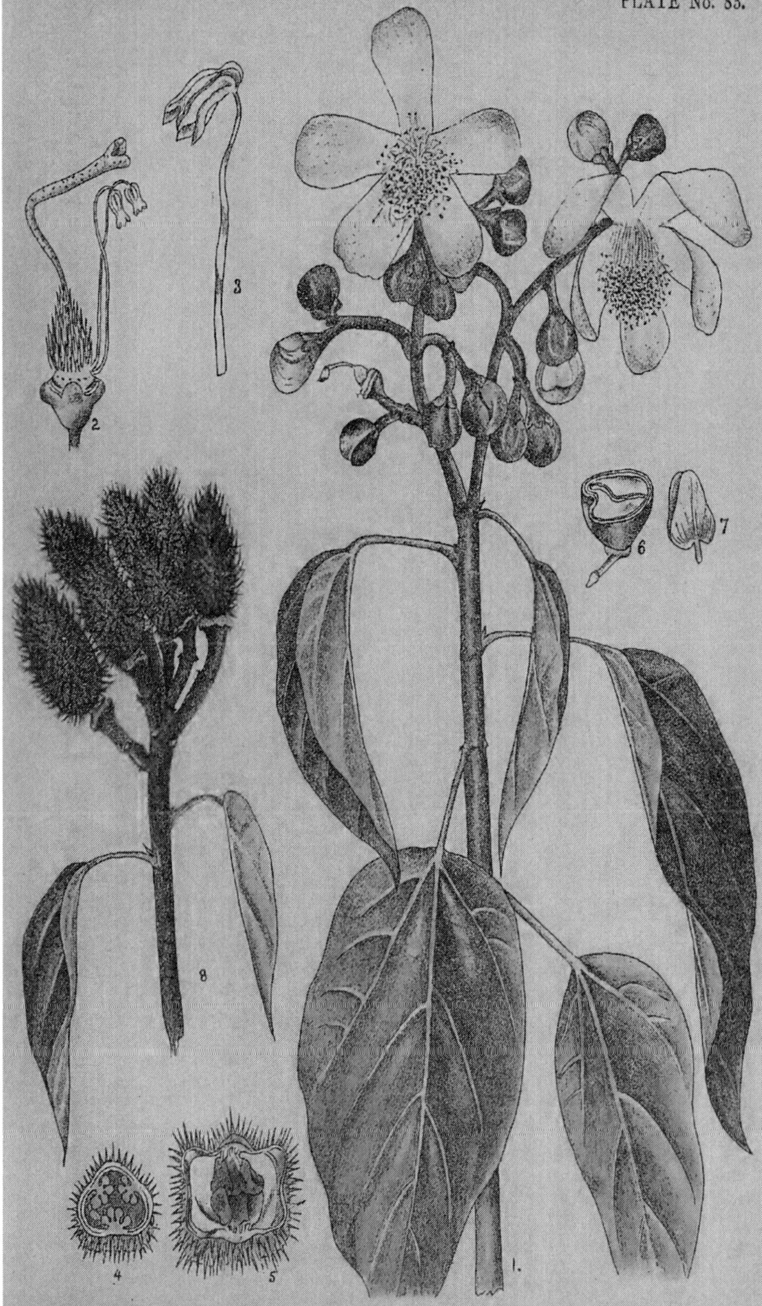

BIXA ORELLANA, *LINN.*

PLATE No 84.

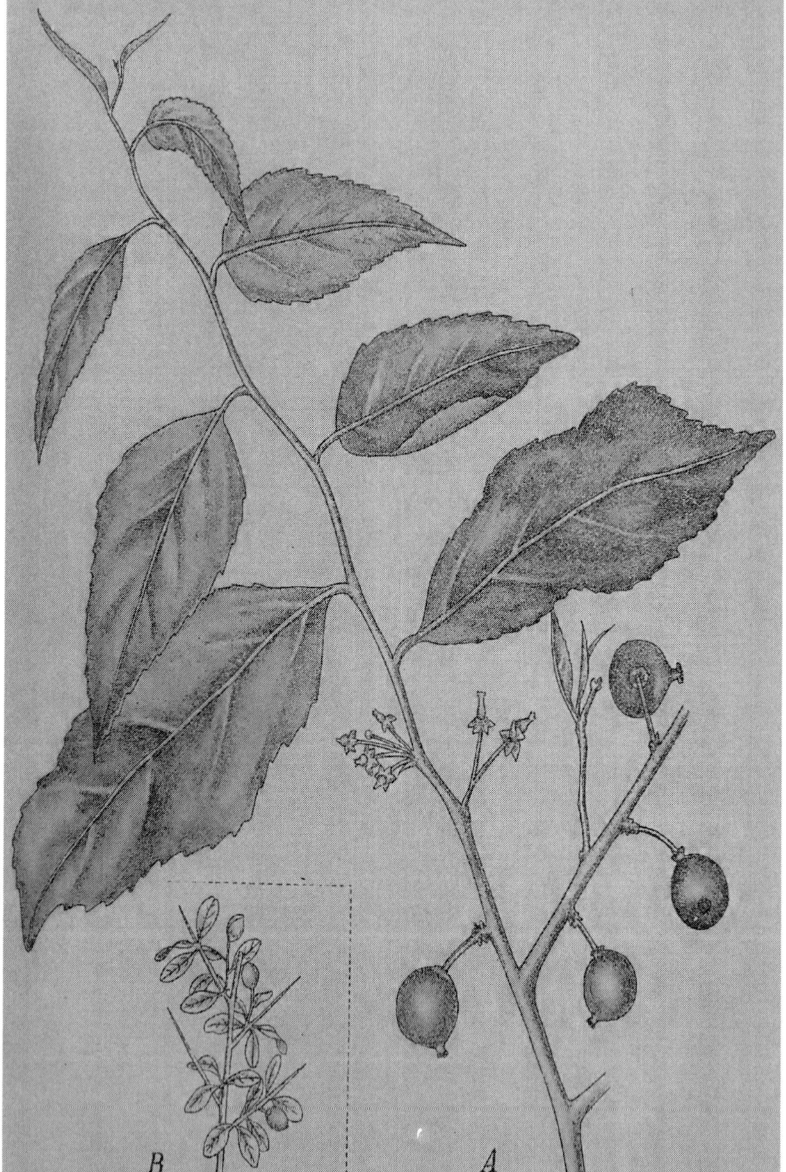

A—FLACOURTIA CATAPHRACTA, *ROXB.* B—FLACOURTIA RAMONTCHI, *L'HERIT.*

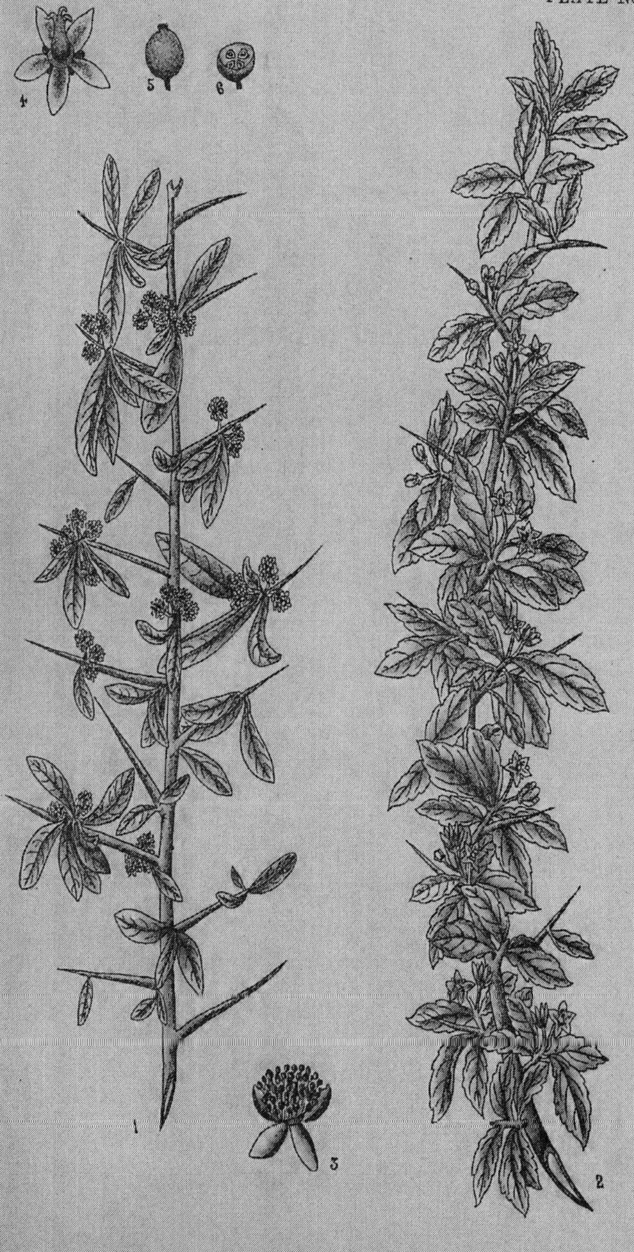

FLACOURTIA SEPIARIA, *ROXB.*

PLATE No. 86.

GYNOCARDIA ODORATA, *R Br.*

PLATE No. 87.

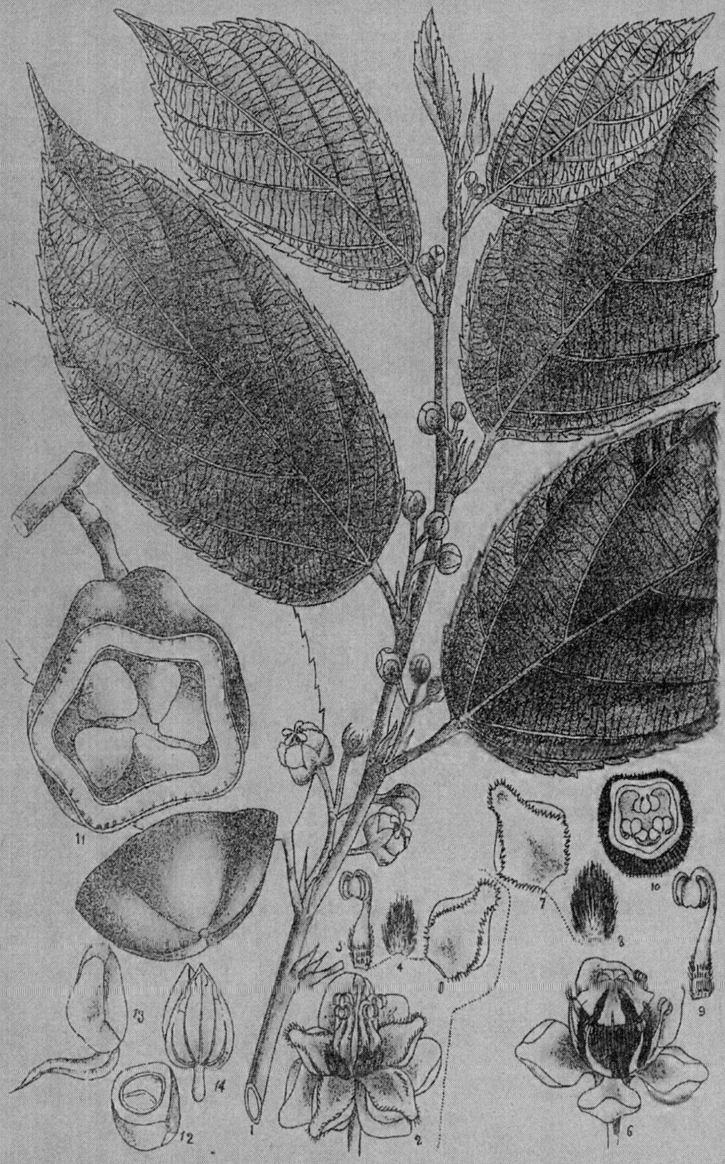

HYDNOCARPUS WIGHTIANA, *BLUME.*

TERAKTOGENOS KURZII, *KING.*

PLATE No. 89

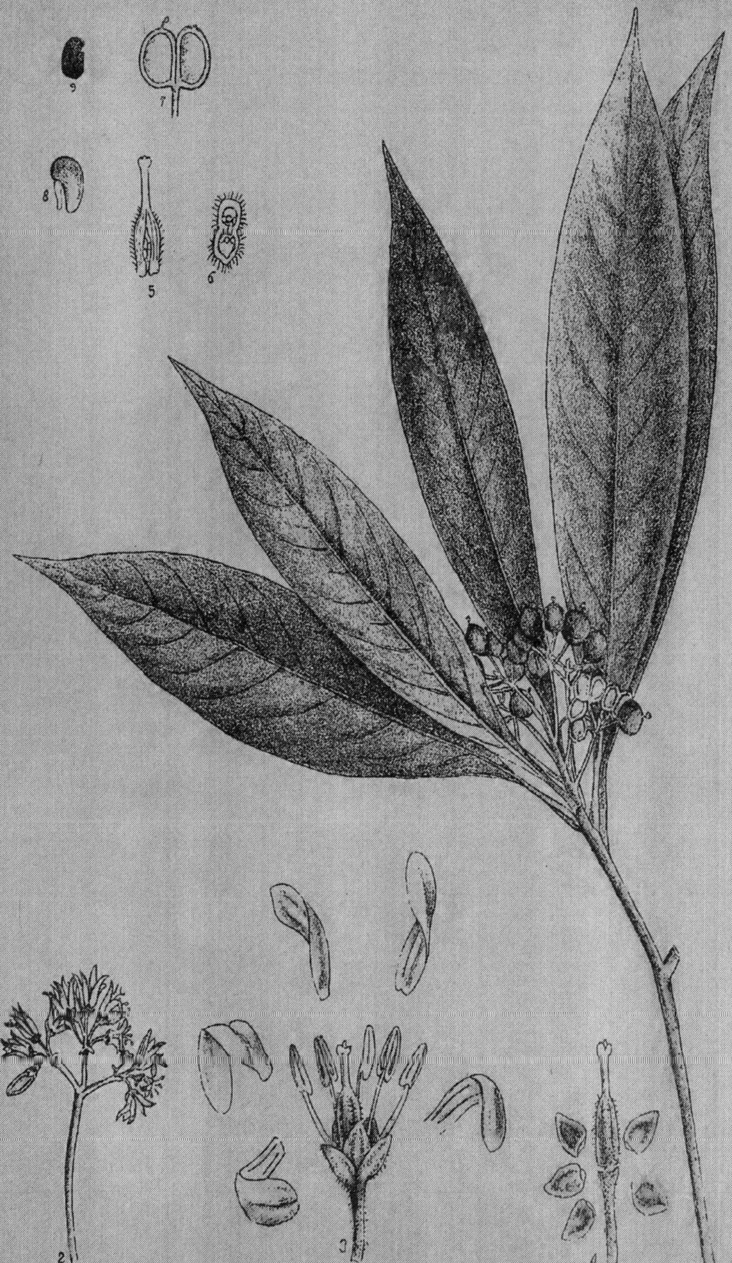

PITTOSPORUM FLORIBUNDUM, *W. & A.*

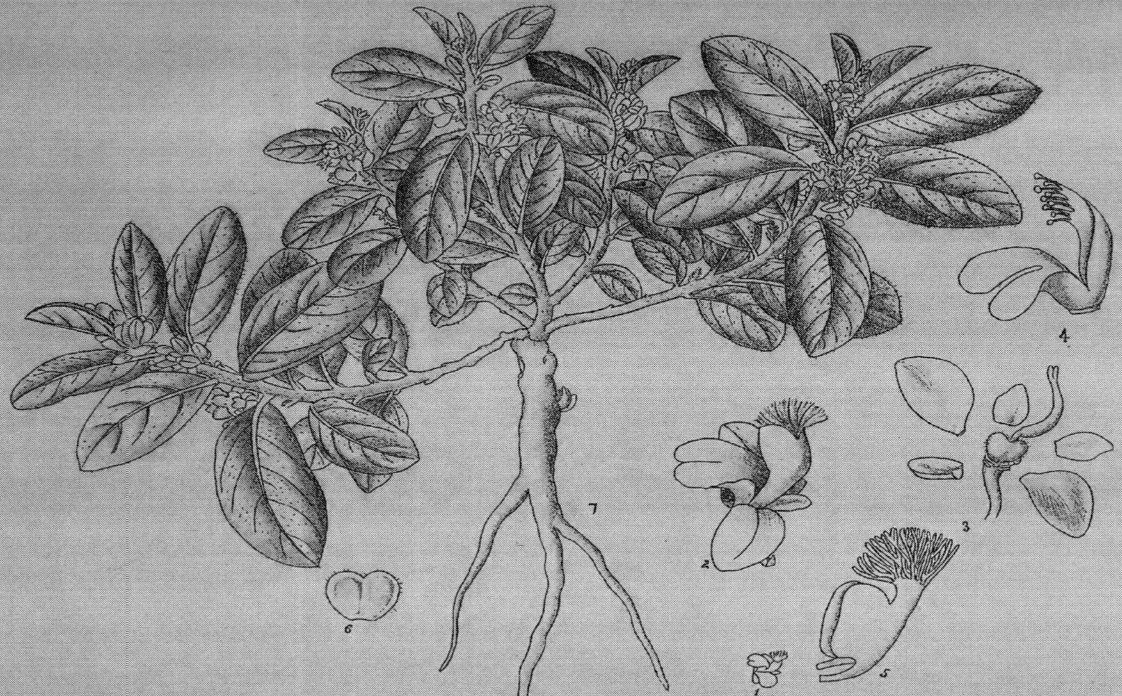

POLYGALA CROTALARIOIDES, *HAM.*

PLATE No. 91.

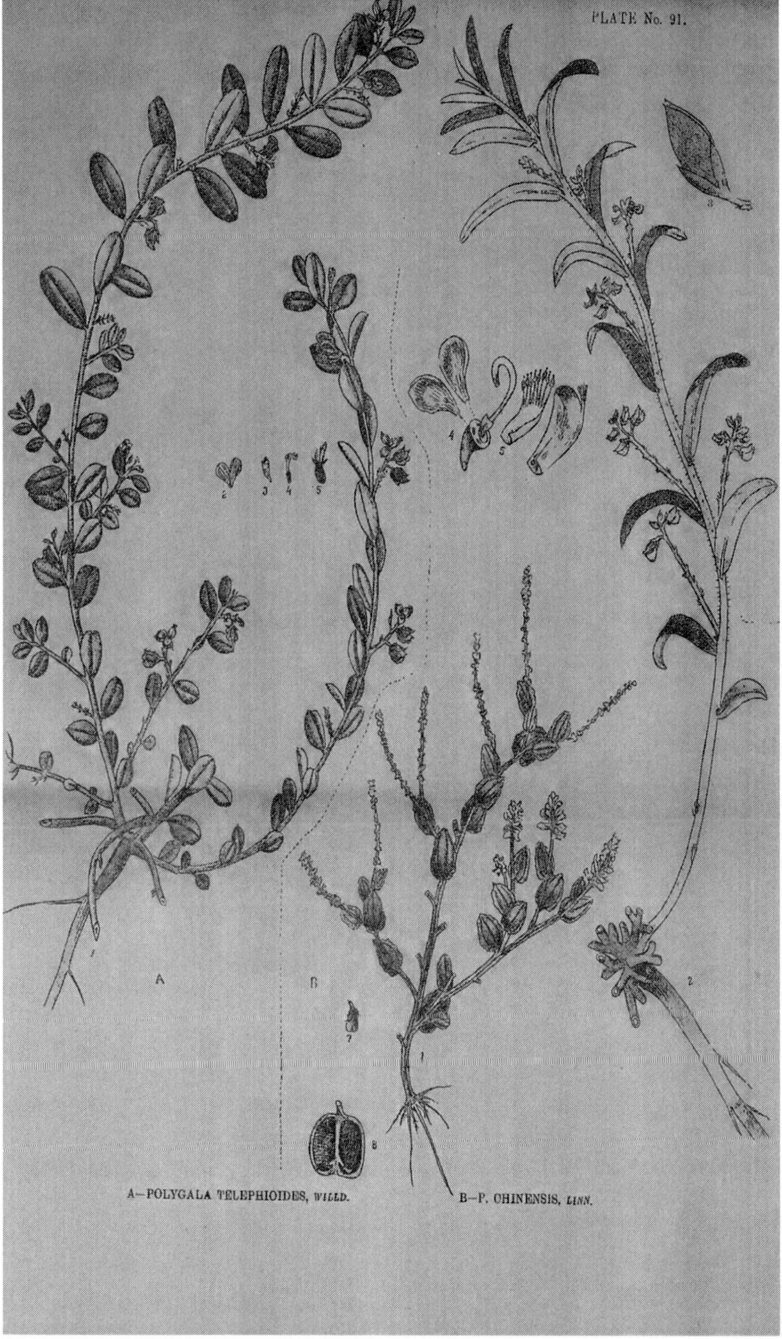

A—POLYGALA TELEPHIOIDES, *Willd.* B—P. CHINENSIS, *Linn.*

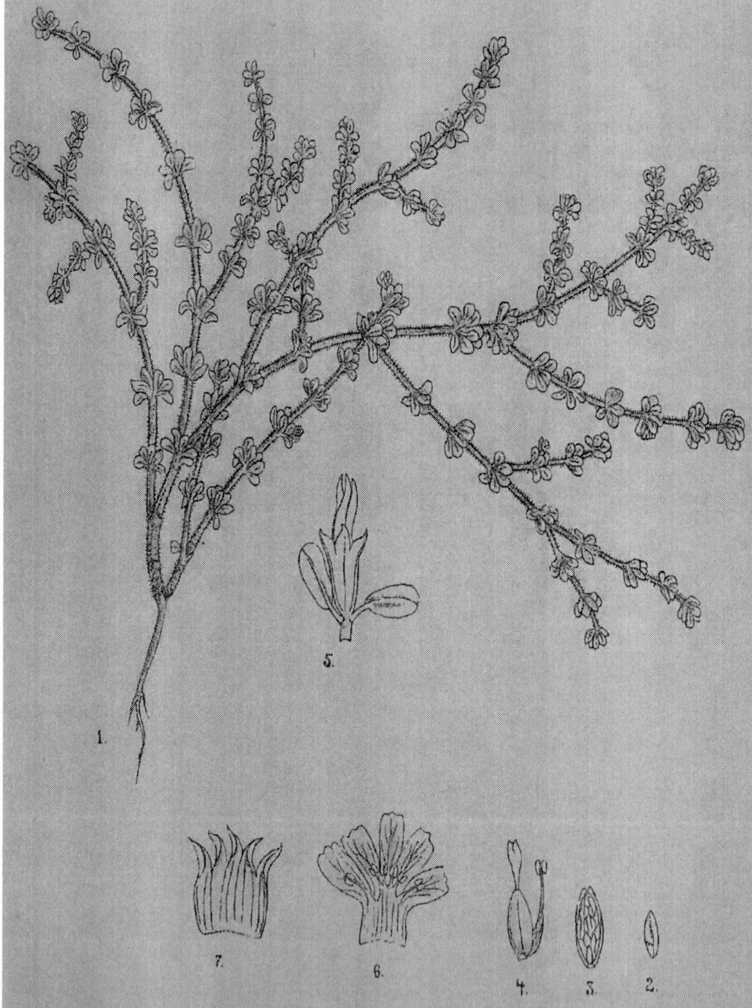

FRANKENIA PULVERULENTA, *LINN.*

PLATE No. 93.

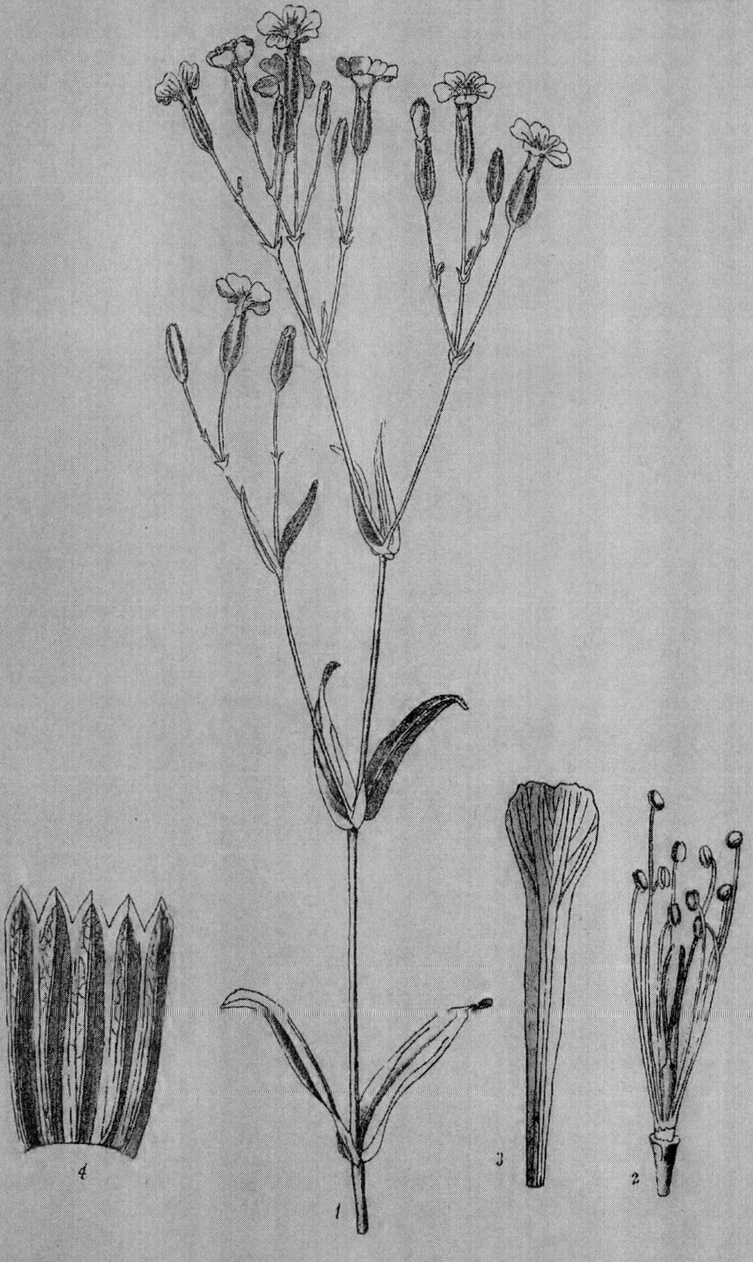

SAPONARIA VACCARIA, *LINN.*

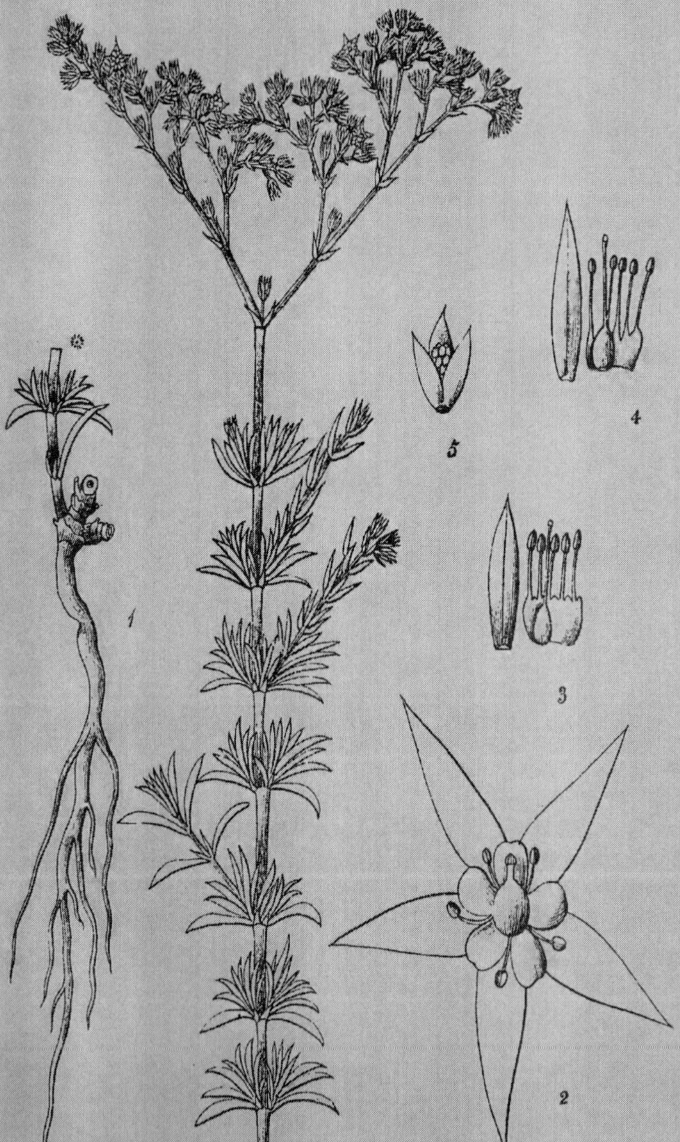

POLYARPÆA CORYMBOSA, LAMK.

PLATE No. 95.

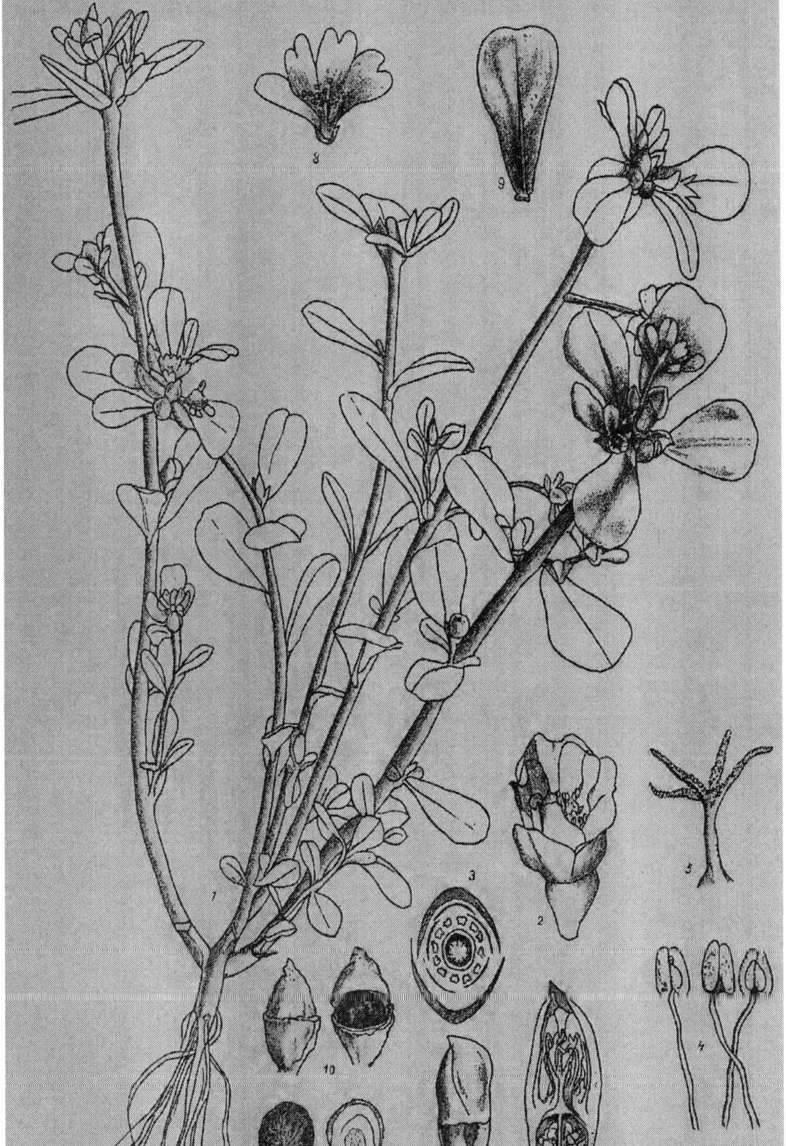

PORTULACA OLERACEA, *LINN*

PLATE No. 96

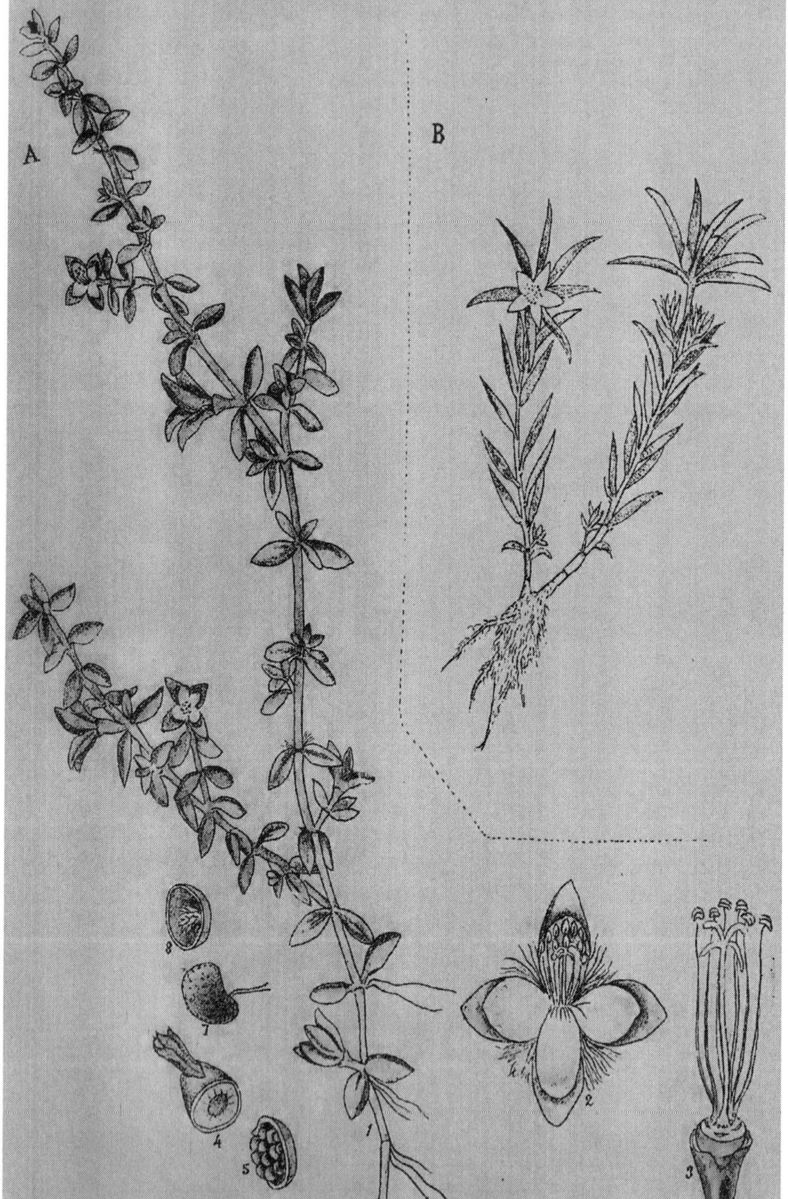

A–PORTULACA QUADRIFIDA, *LINN.*

B–P. TUBEROSA, *ROXB.*

PLATE No. 97

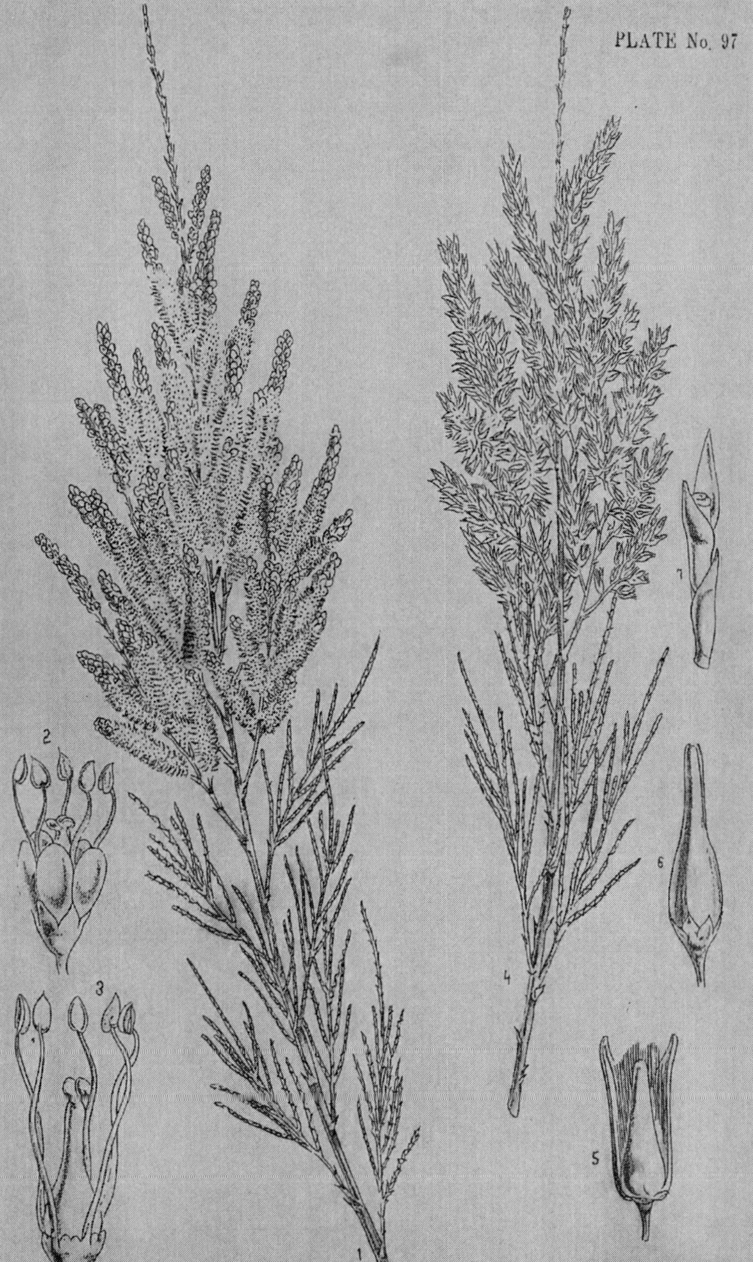

TAMARIX GALLICA, *Linn.*

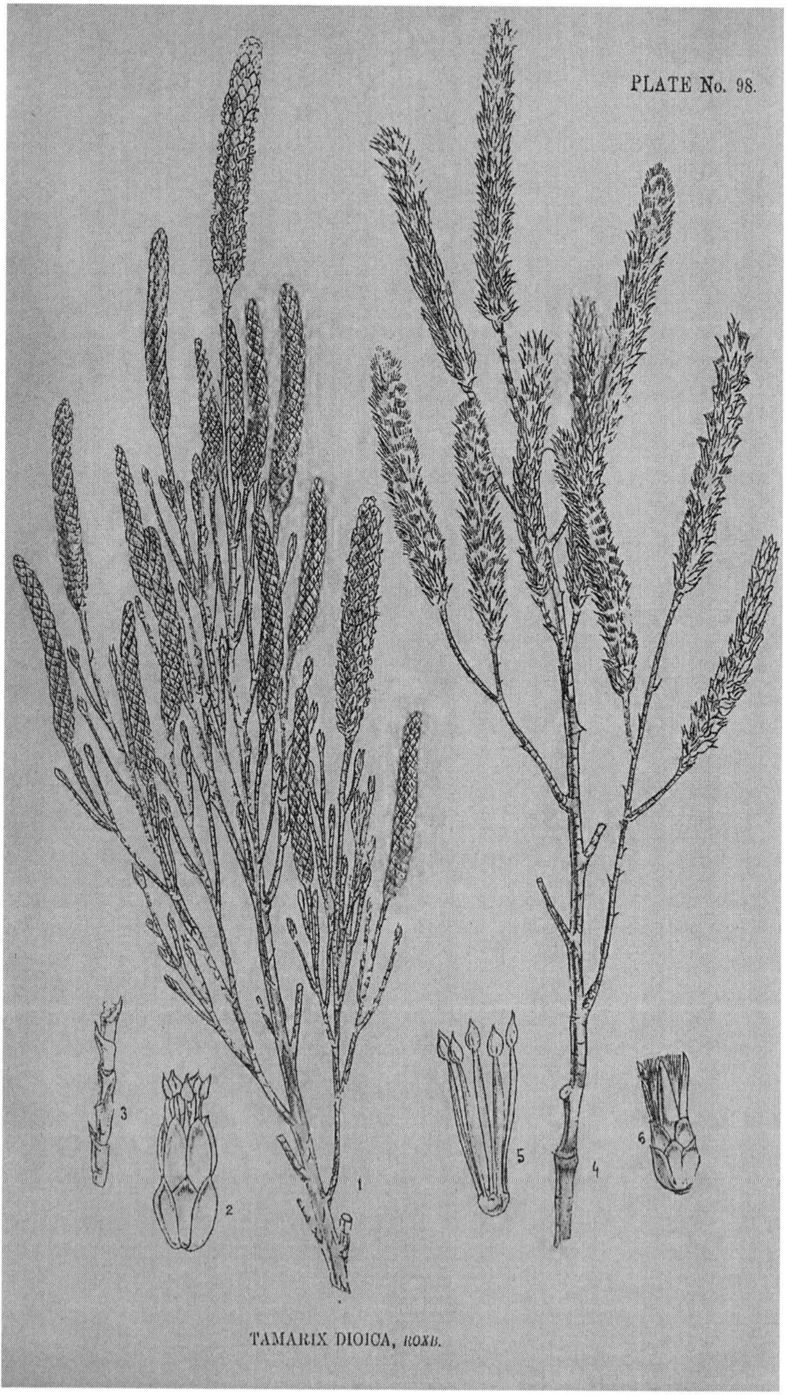

TAMARIX DIOICA, *ROXB.*

PLATE No 99

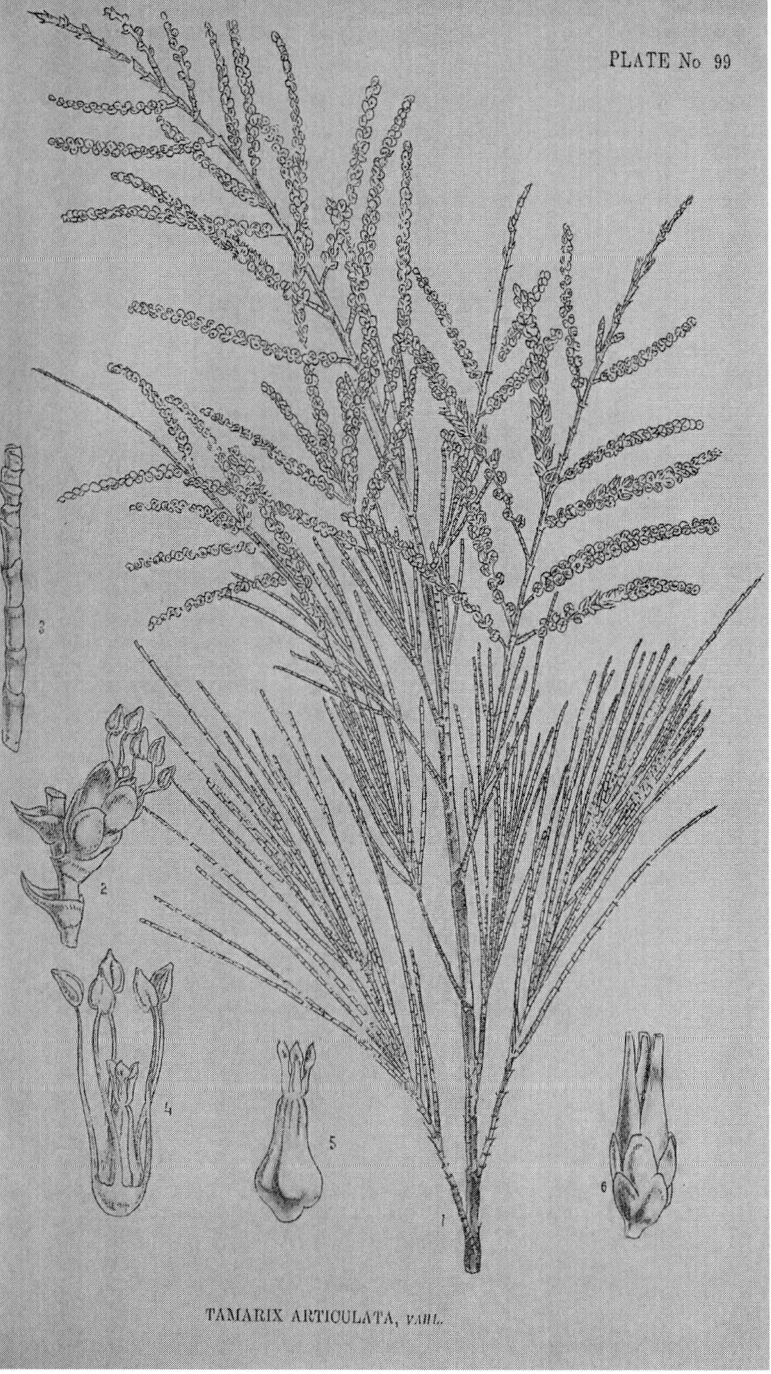

TAMARIX ARTICULATA, *VAHL.*

PLATE No. 100.

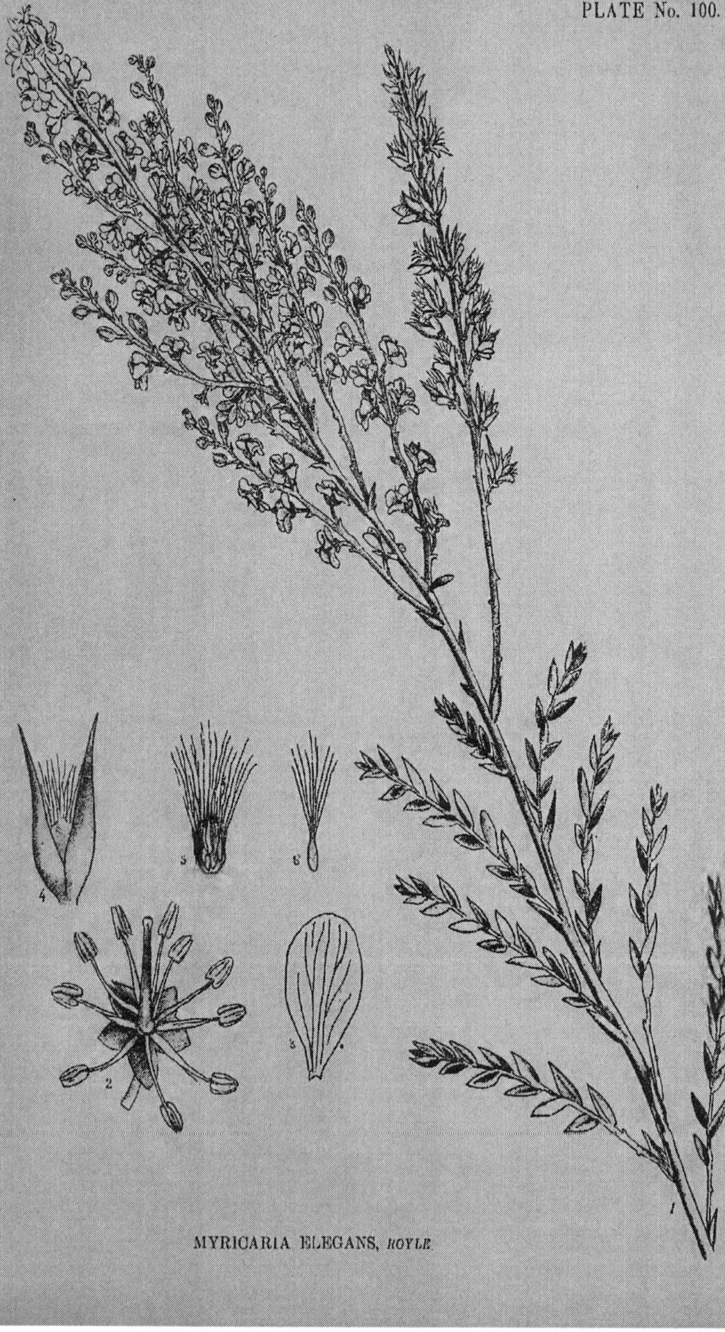

MYRICARIA ELEGANS, ROYLE.

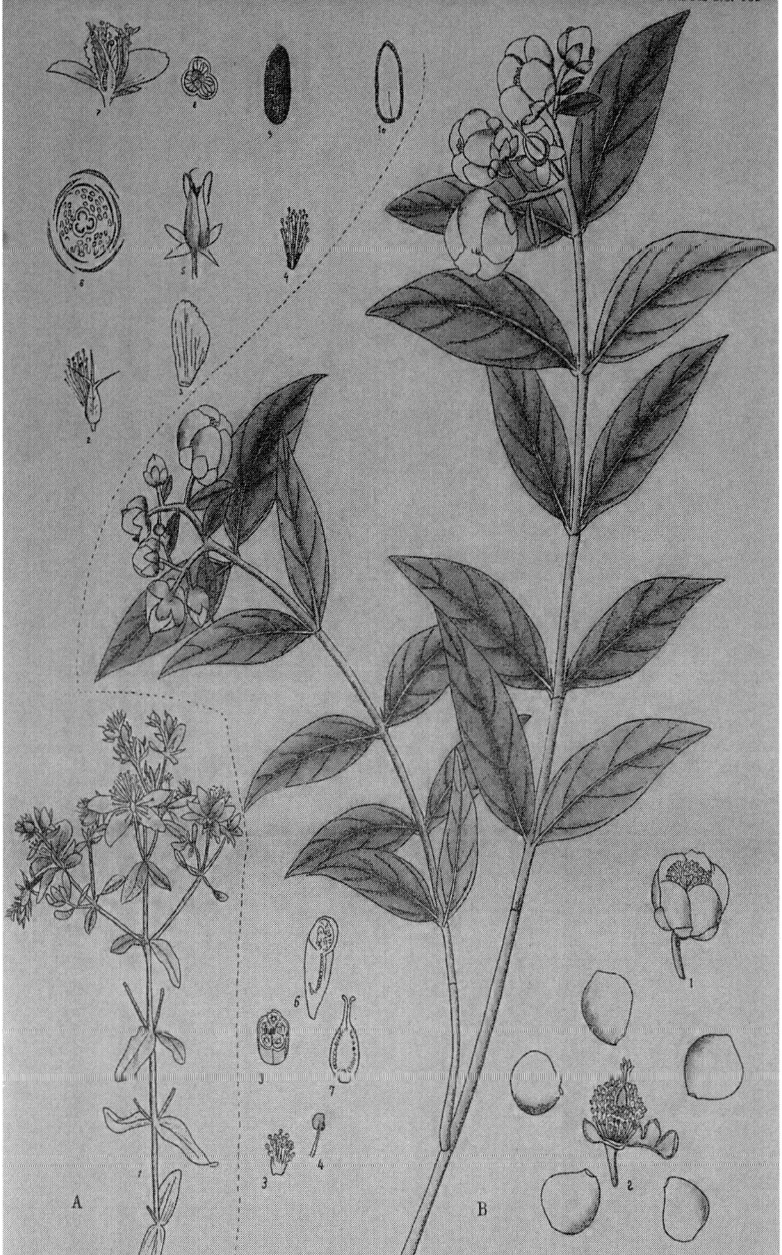

A— HYPERICUM PERFORATUM, LINN. B—H. PATULUM, THUNB.

PLATE No 102.

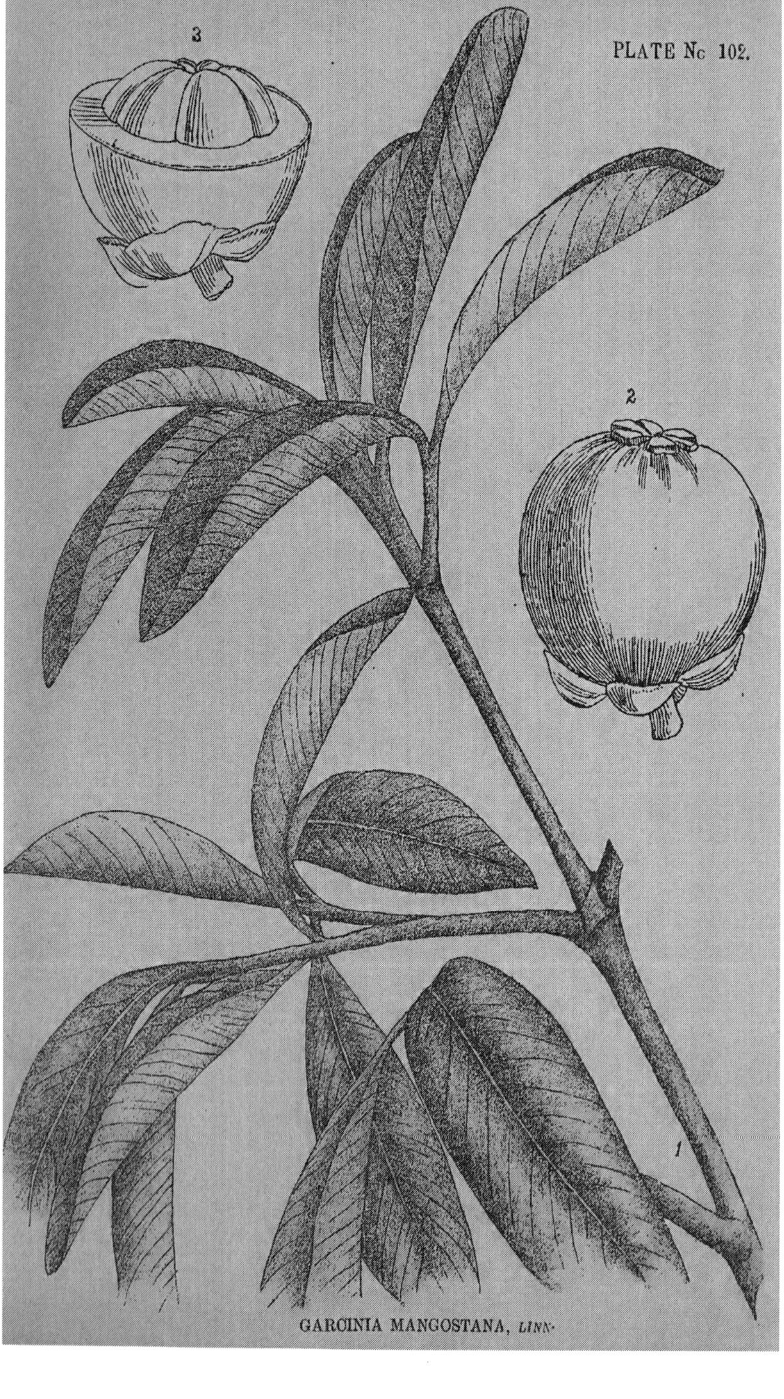

GARCINIA MANGOSTANA, *LINN.*

PLATE No. 103.

GARCINIA INDICA, Chois.

PLATE No. 104.

GARCINIA XANTHOCHYMUS, *HOOK. F.*

PLATE No. 105.

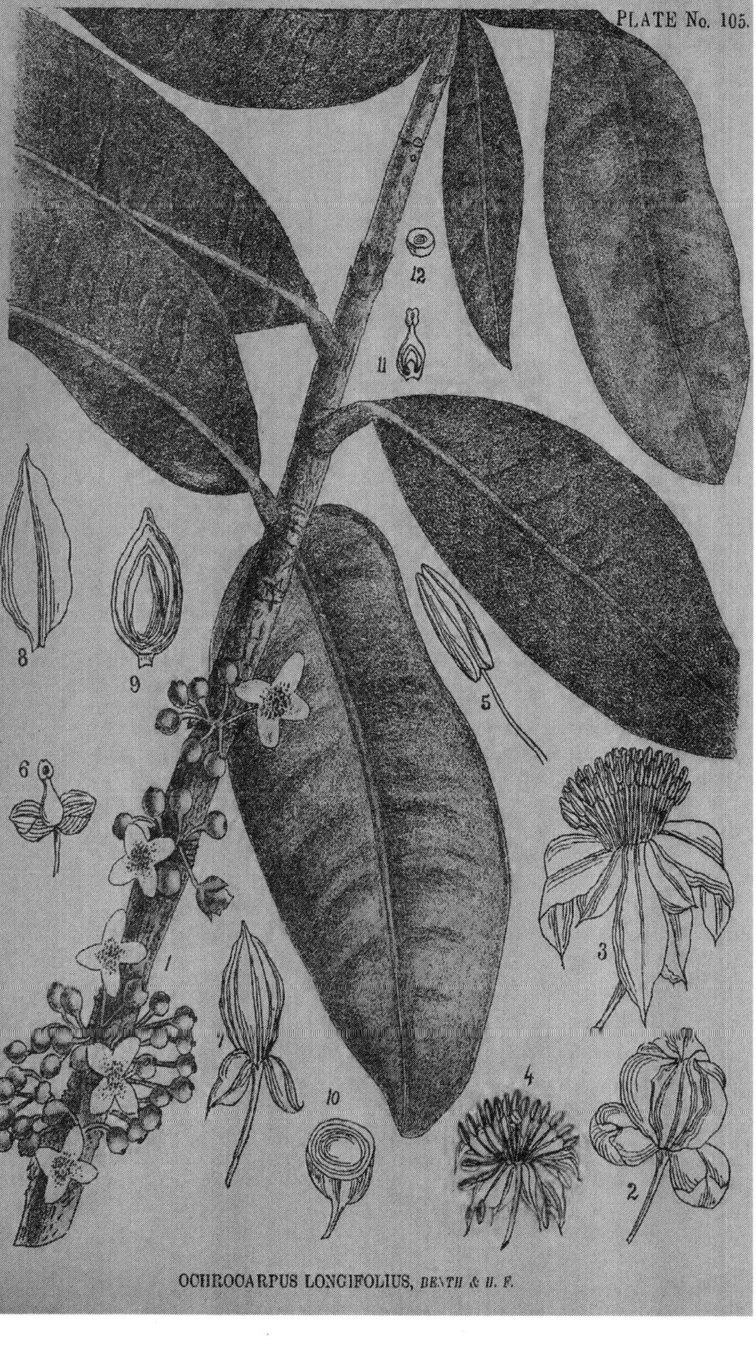

OCHROCARPUS LONGIFOLIUS, BENTH & H. F.

PLATE No. 106.

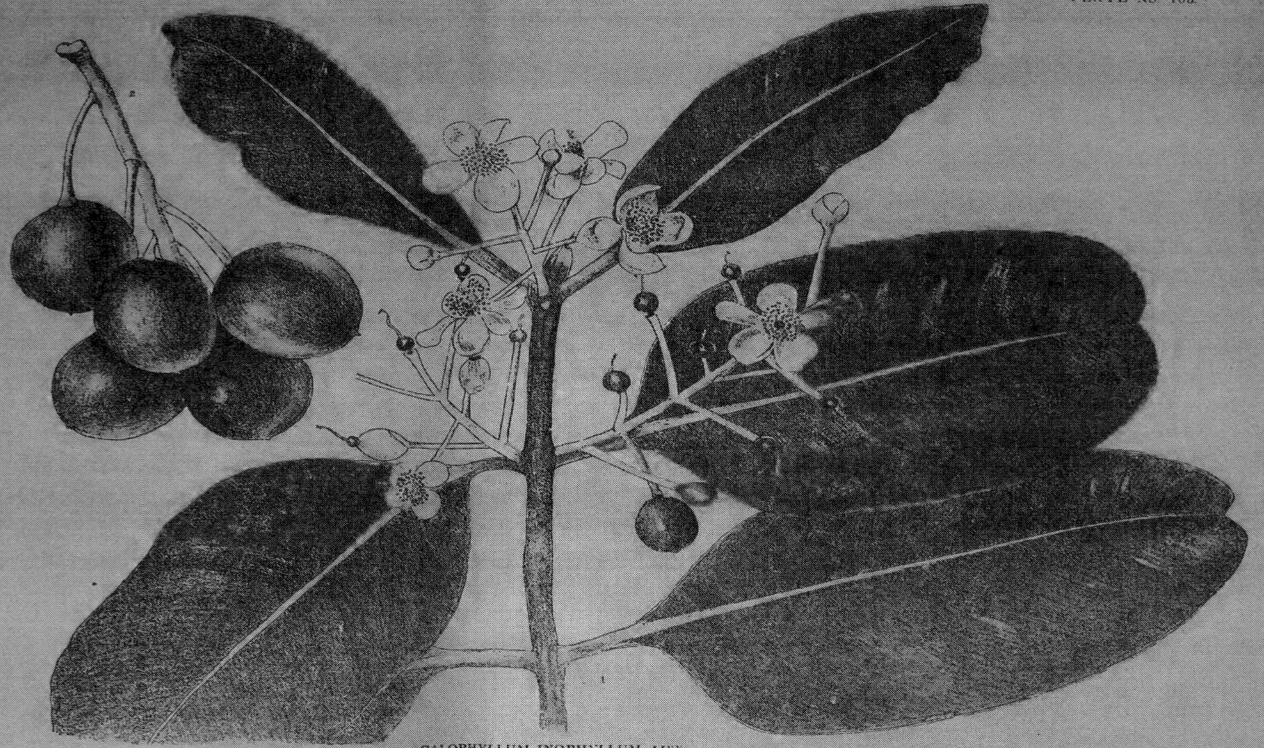

CALOPHYLLUM INOPHYLLUM, LINN.

PLATE No. 107.

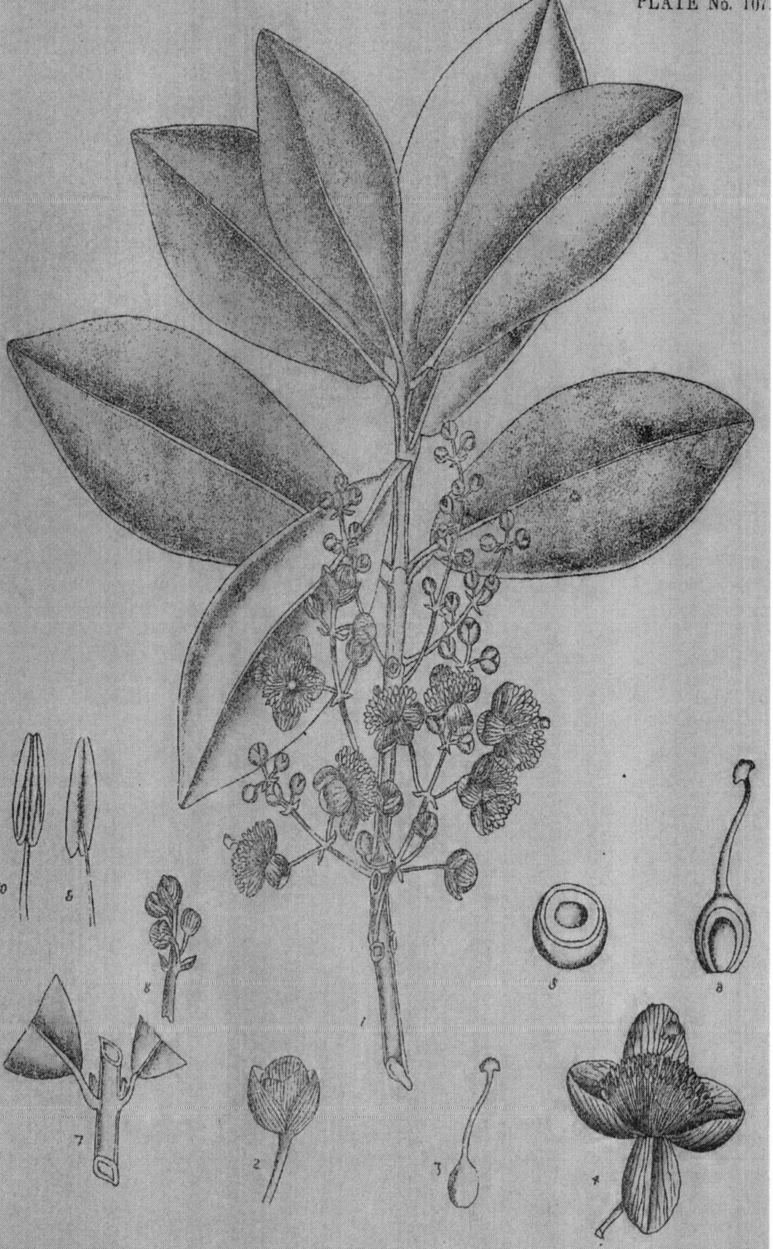

CALOPHYLLUM WIGHTIANUM, WALL.

PLATE No. 108.

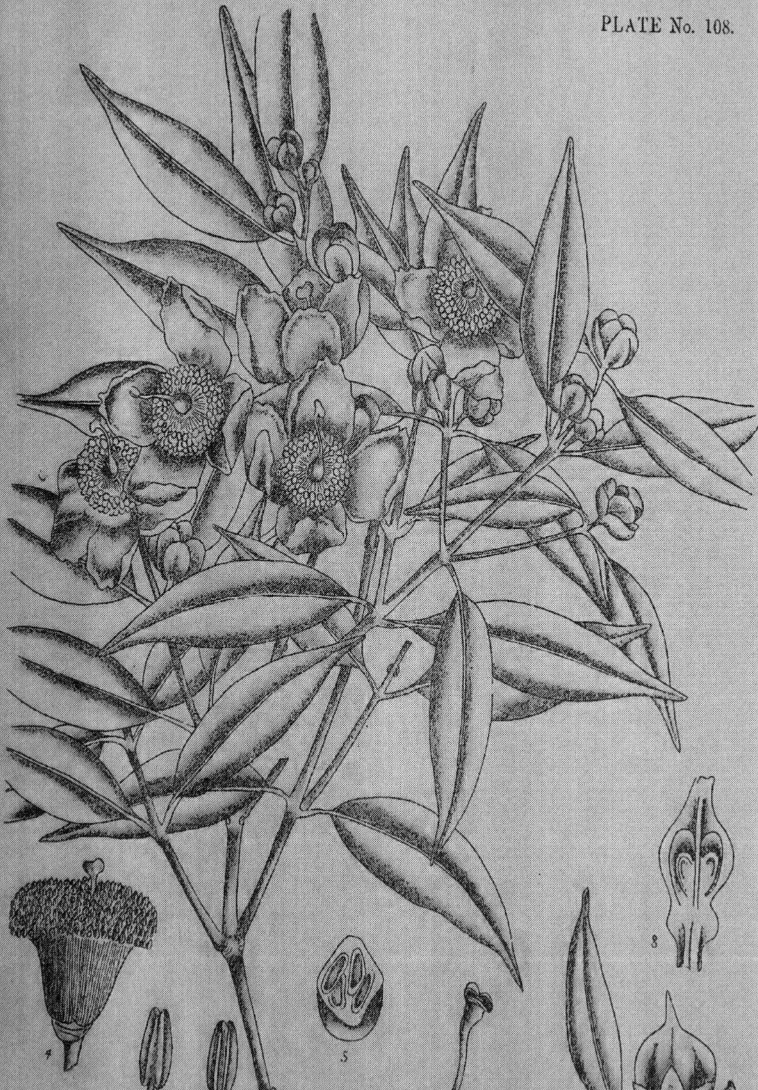

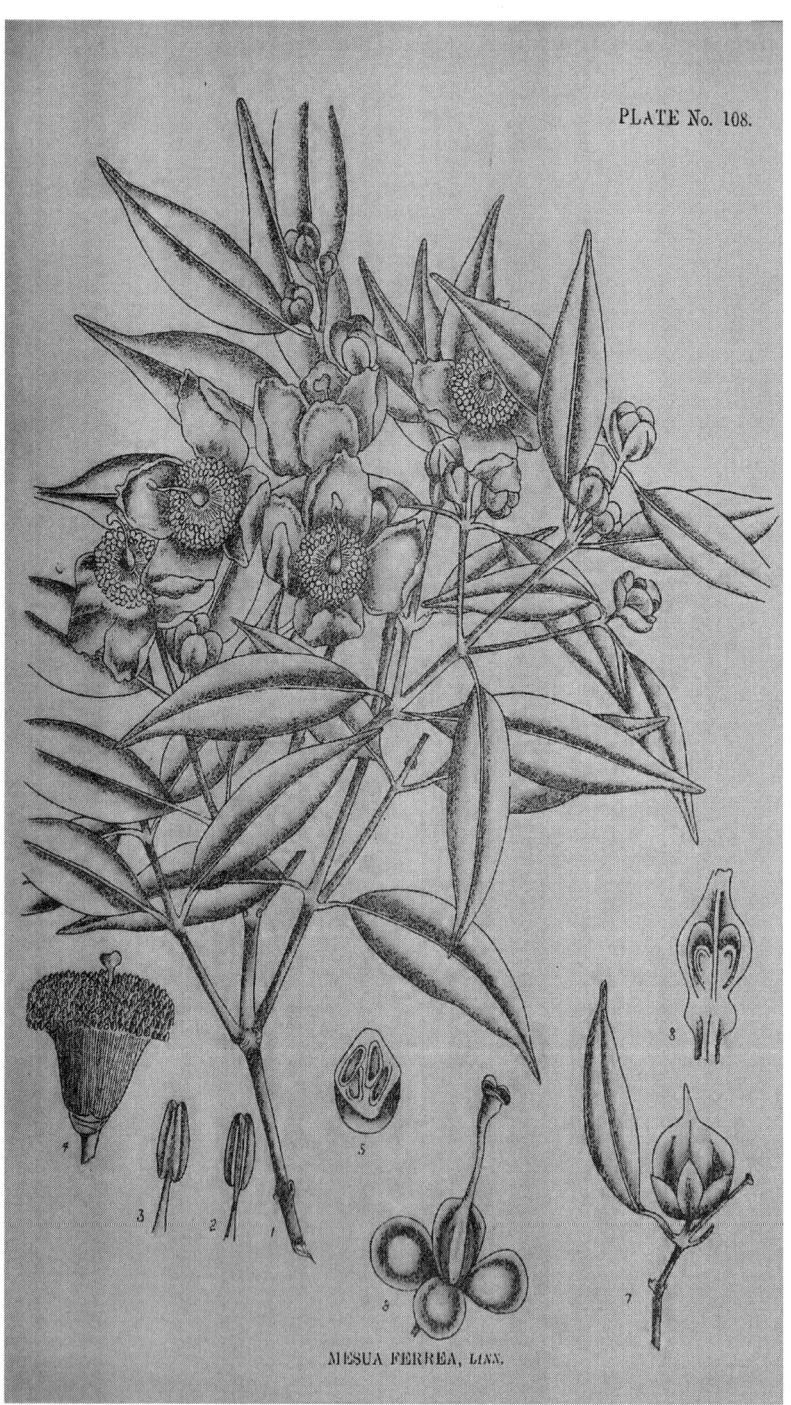

MESUA FERREA, LINN.

PLATE No. 109.

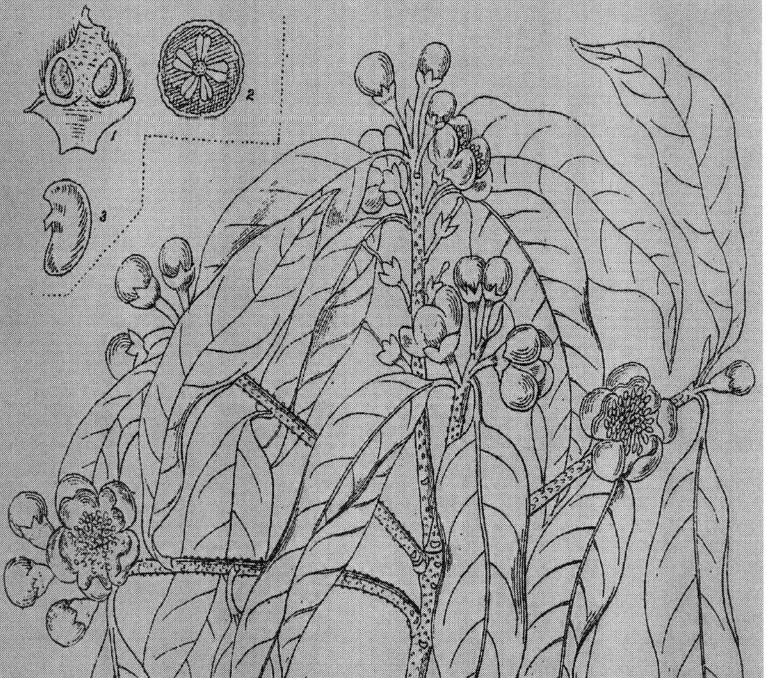

SCHIMA WALLICHII, *CHOIS.*

PLATE No. 110.

A—DIPTEROCARPUS TURBINATUS, GÆRTN. F. B—D. ALATUS, ROXB.

PLATE No. 111.

DIPTEROCRRPUS TUBERCULATUS, *ROXB*

PLATE No. 112.

DIPTEROCARPUS INCANUS, *ROXB.*

PLATE No. 113.

SHOREA ROBUSTA, *GÆRTN.*

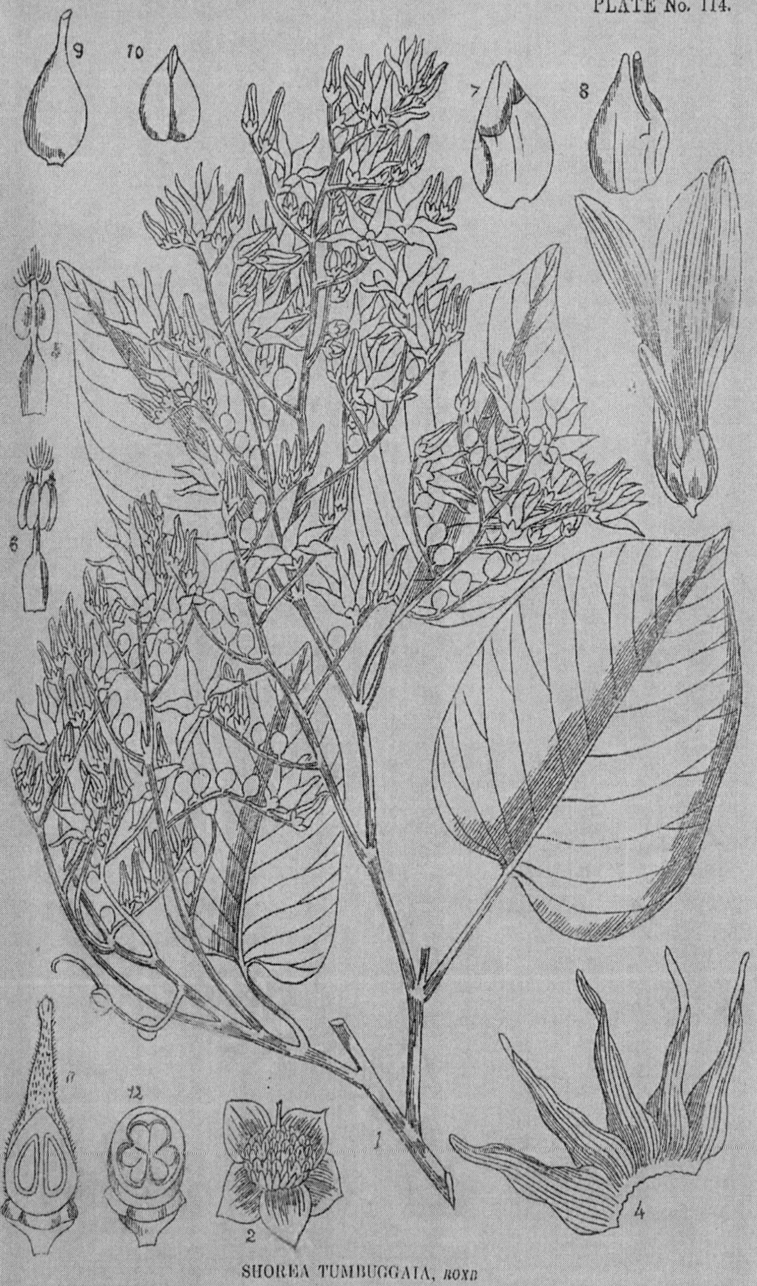

SHOREA TUMBUGGAIA, ROXB

PLATE No. 115.

VATERIA INDICA, *Linn*

PLATE No. 116

A—ALTHÆA OFFICINALIS, *LINN.*   B—A. ROSEA, *LINN.*

PLATE No. 117.

MALVA SILVESTRIS, *LINN.* M. ROTUNDIFOLIA, *LINN.*

PLATE No. 118

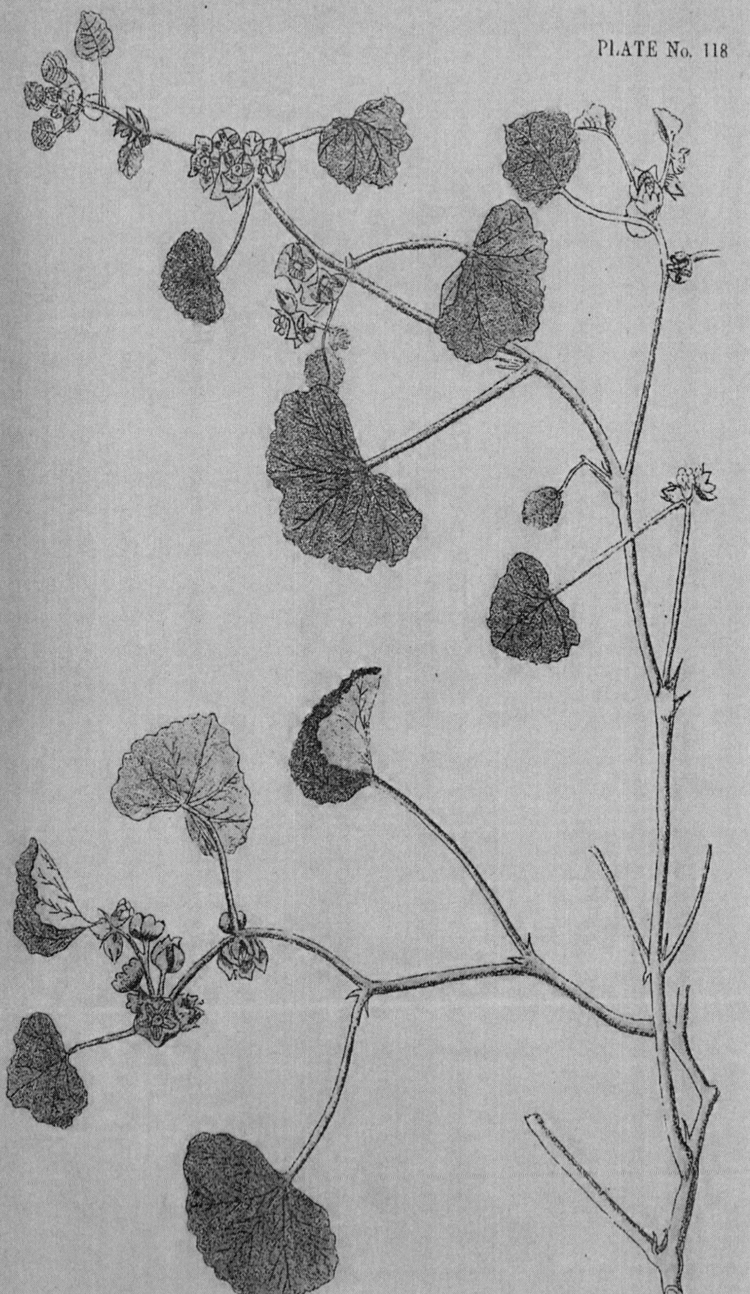

MALVA PARVIFLORA, LINN

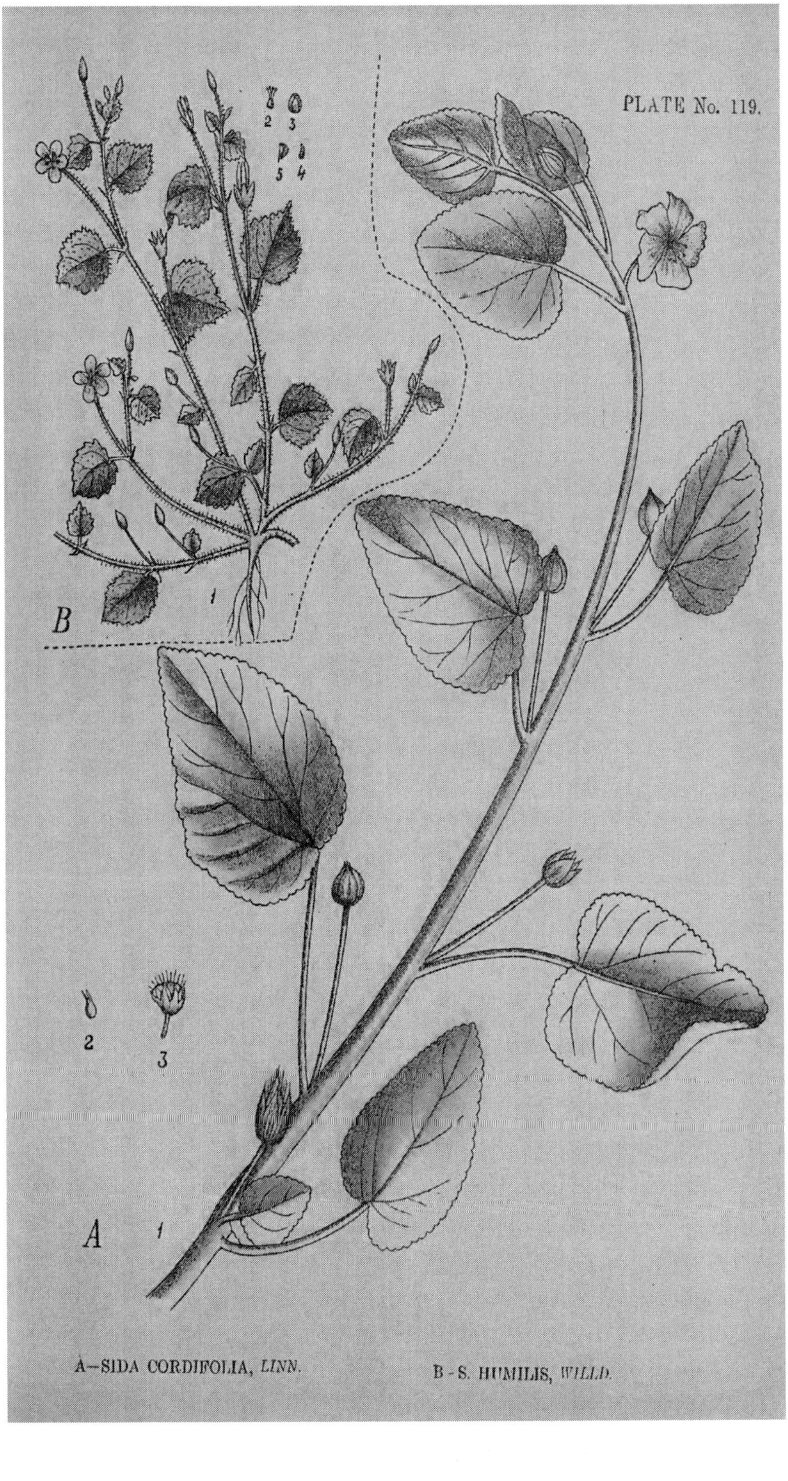
PLATE No. 119.
B
A
A—SIDA CORDIFOLIA, LINN.
B - S. HUMILIS, WILLD.

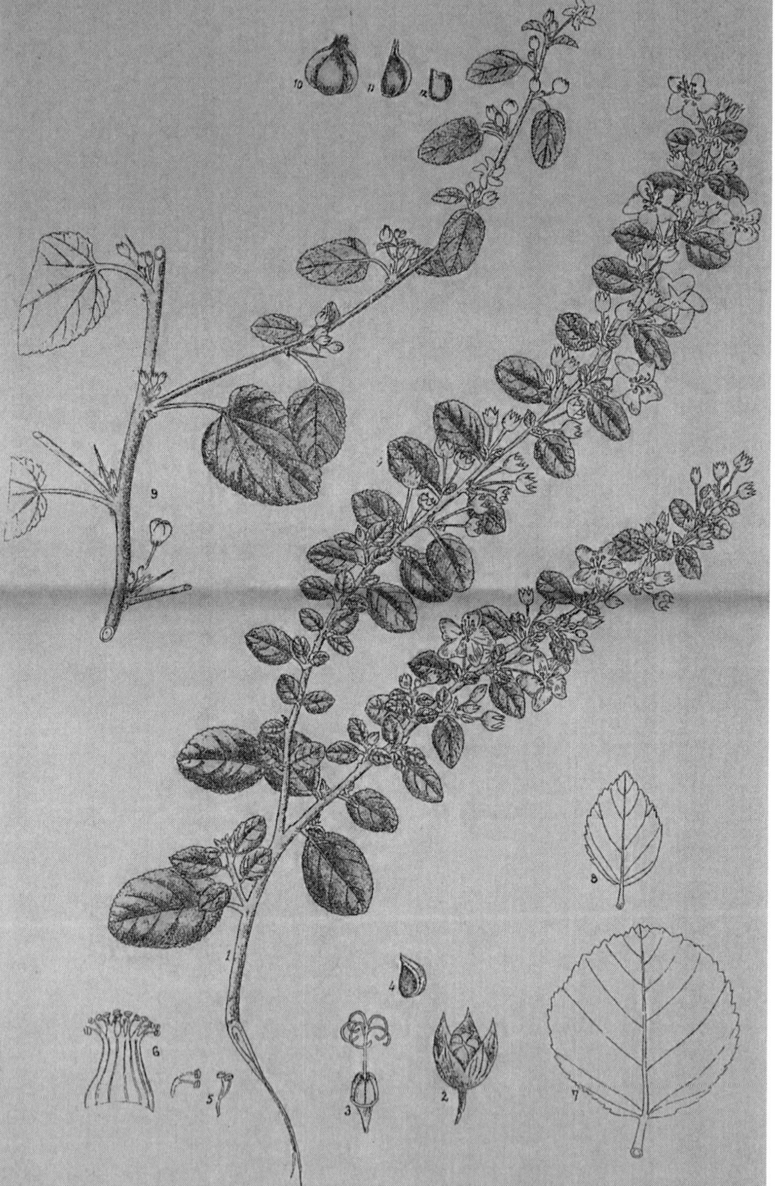

SIDA SPINOSA, *LINN.*

PLATE No. 121

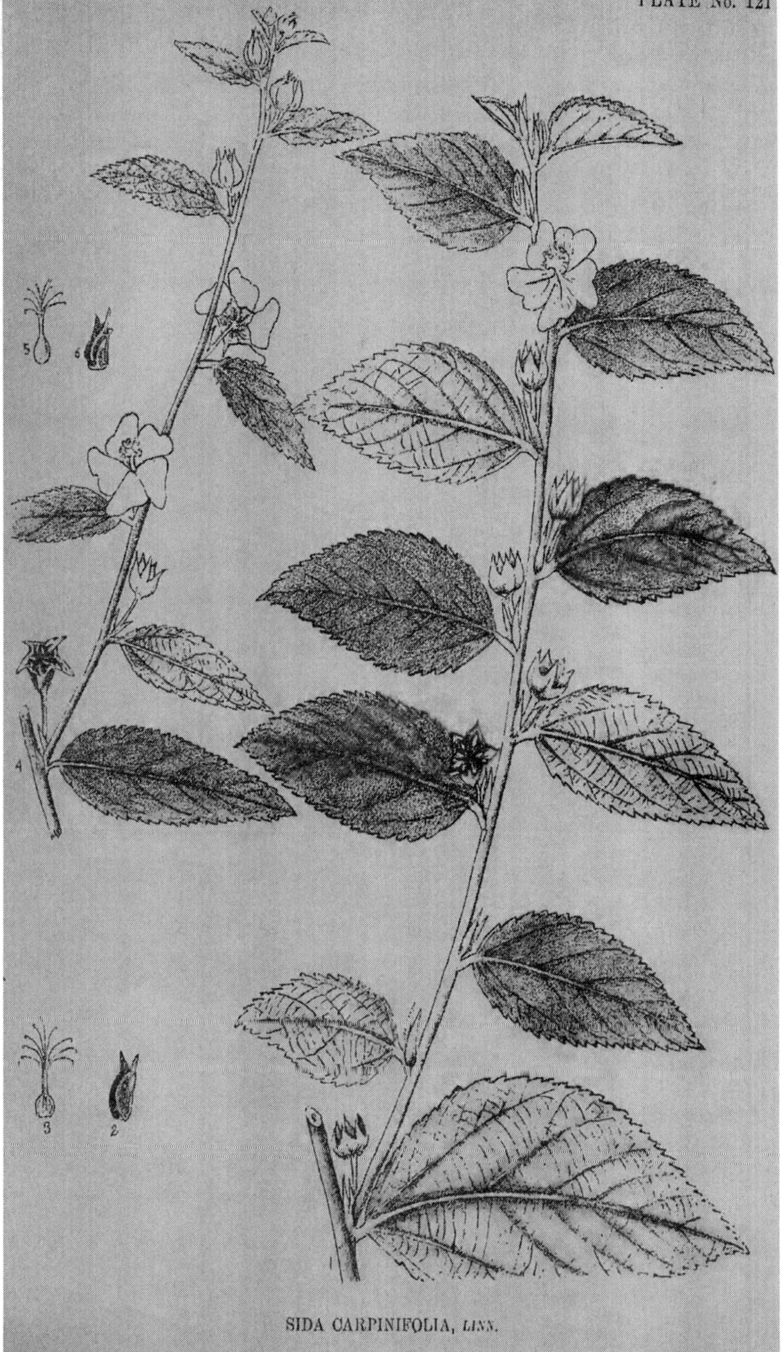

SIDA CARPINIFOLIA, *Linn.*

PLATE No. 122.

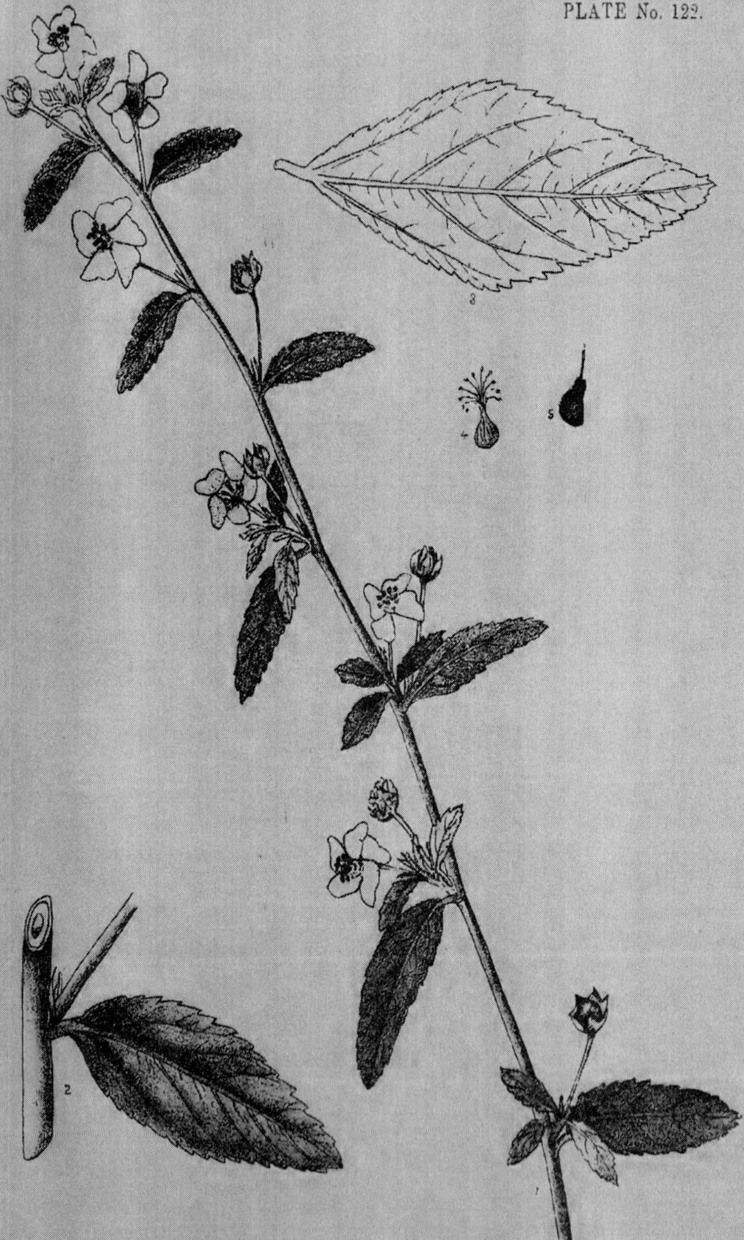

SIDA RHOMBIFOLIA, *LINN.*

PLATE No. 123.

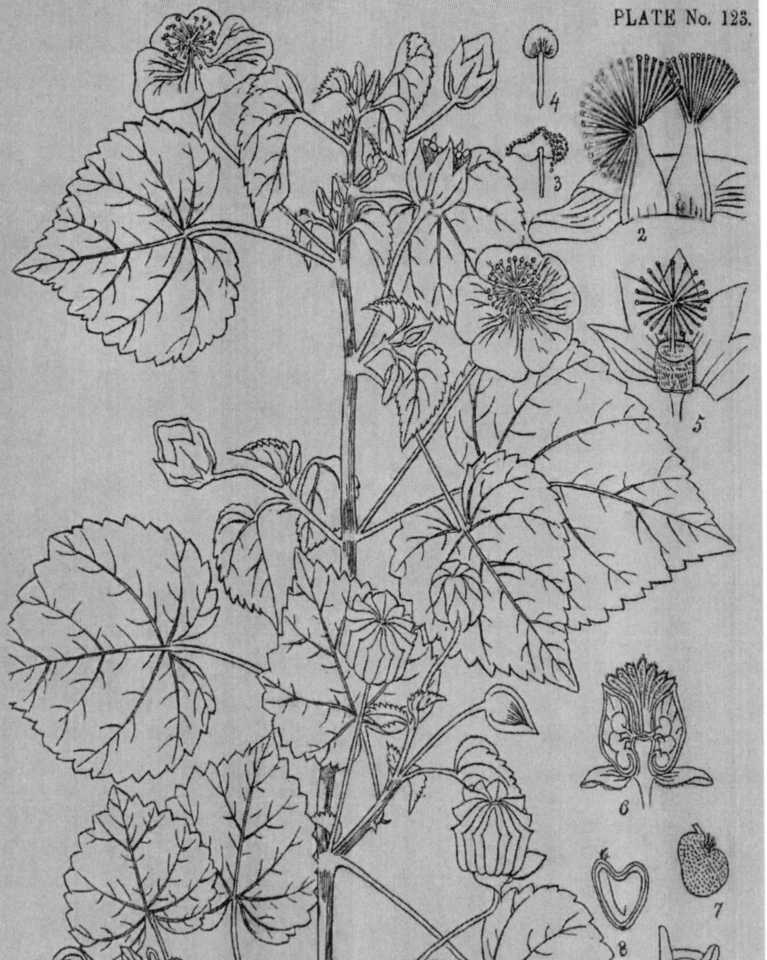

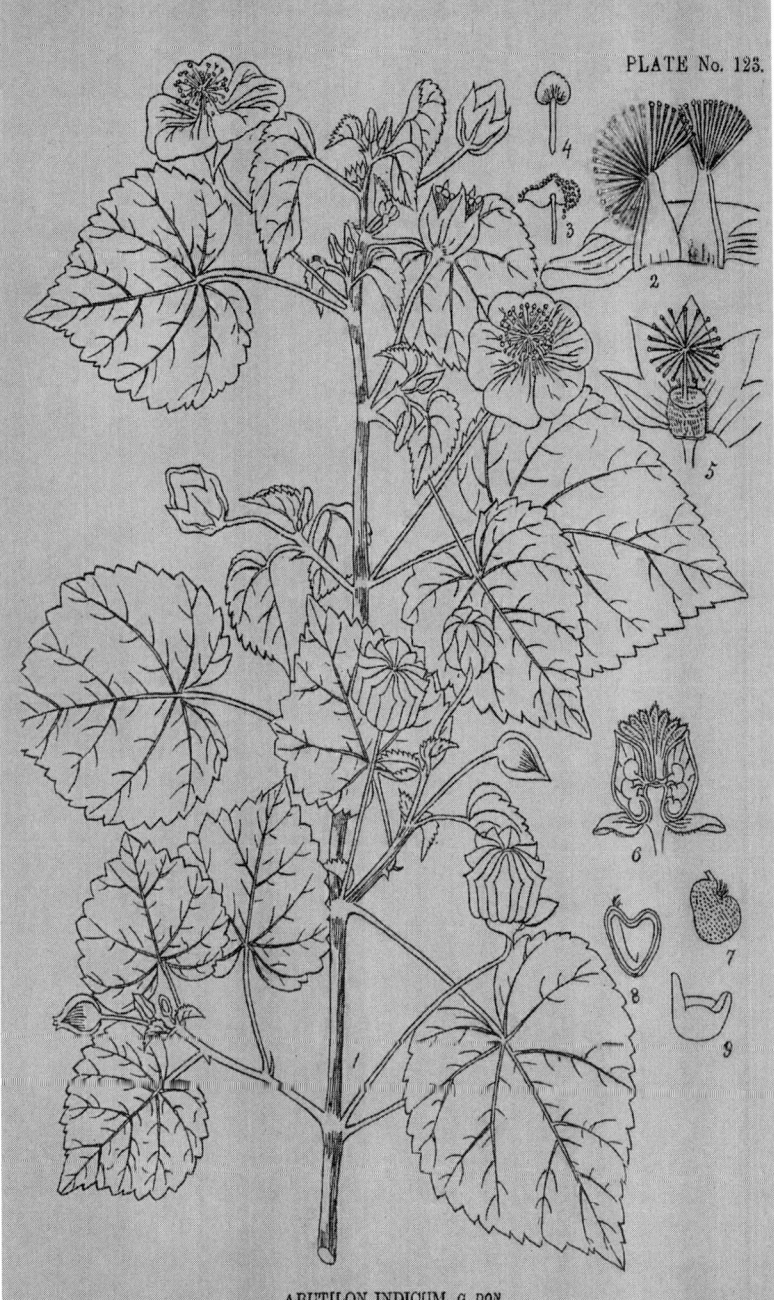

ABUTILON INDICUM, *G. DON.*

PLATE No. 124.

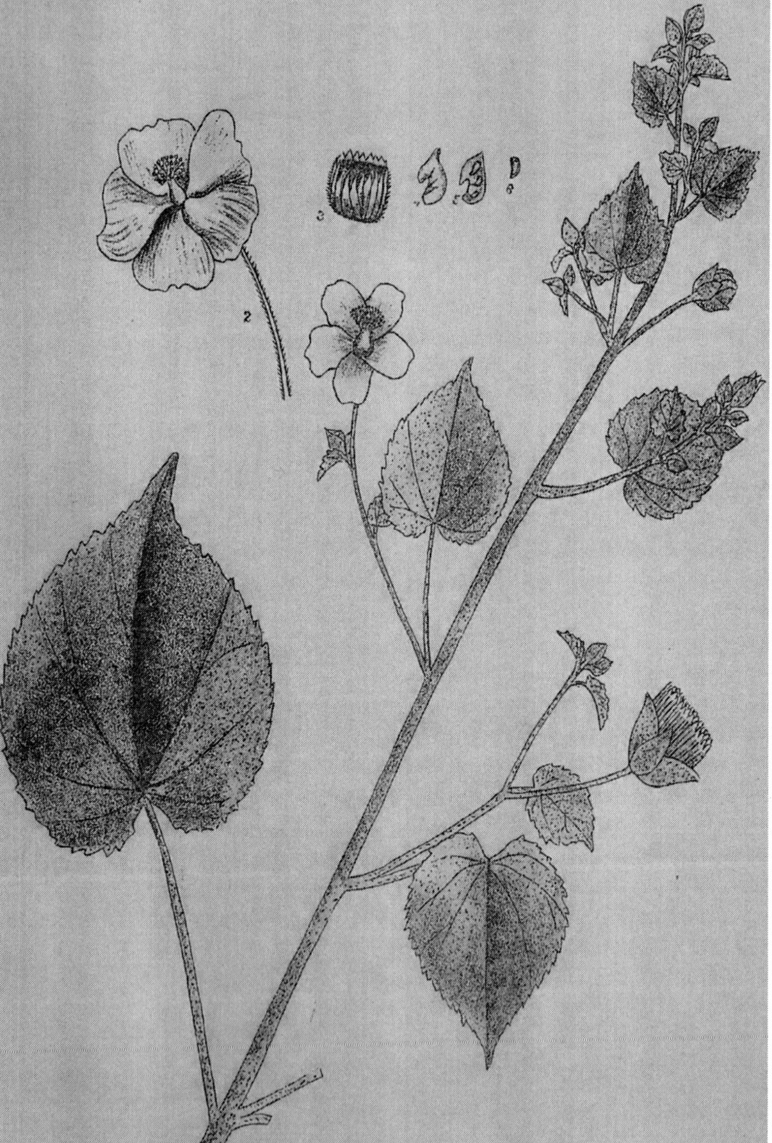

ABUTILON GRAVEOLENS, W. & A.

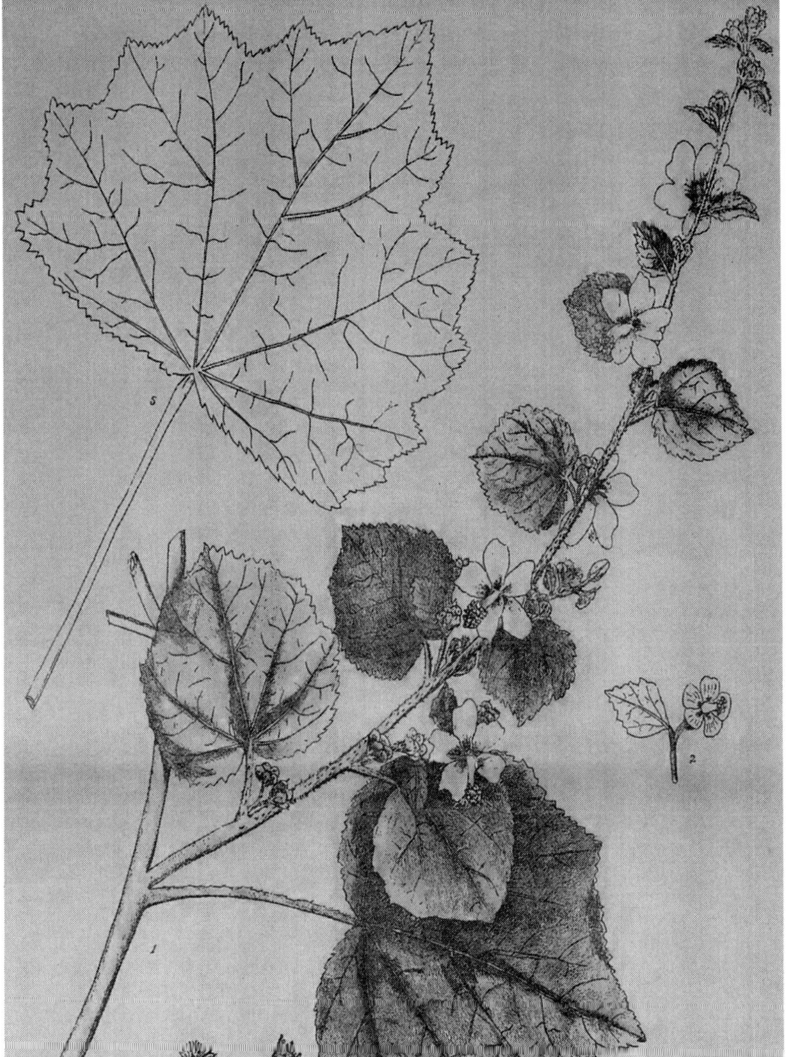

URENA LOBATA, LINN

URENA SINUATA, *LINN.*

PLATE No. 127.

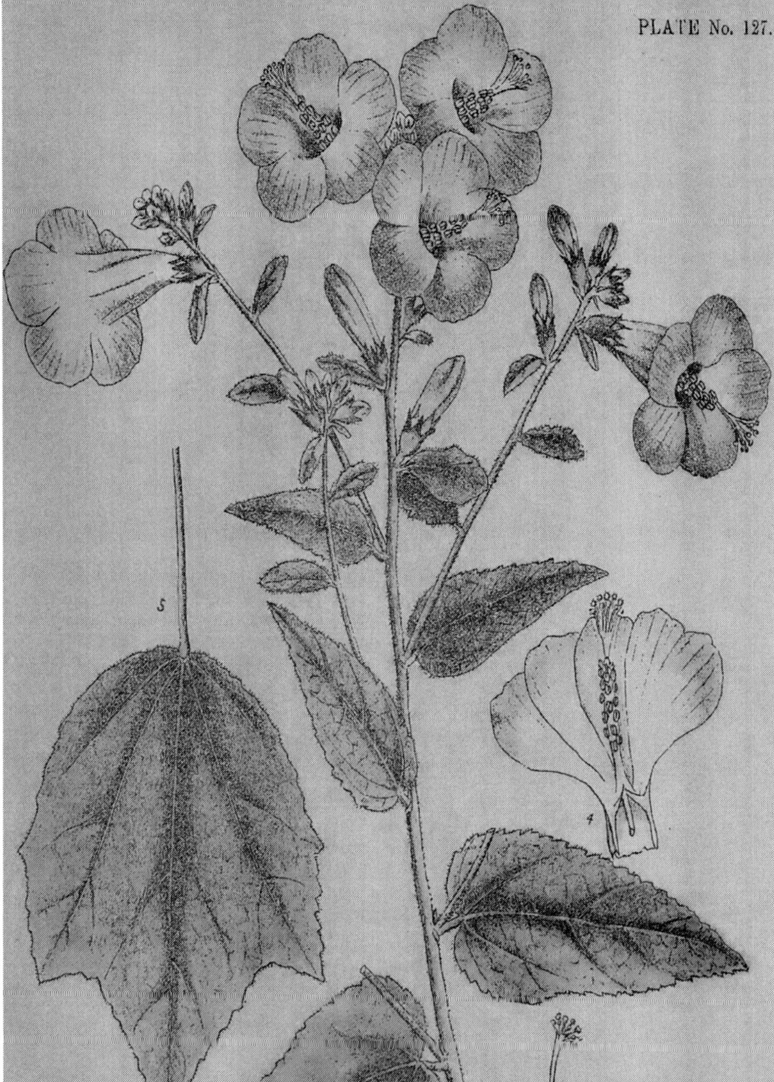

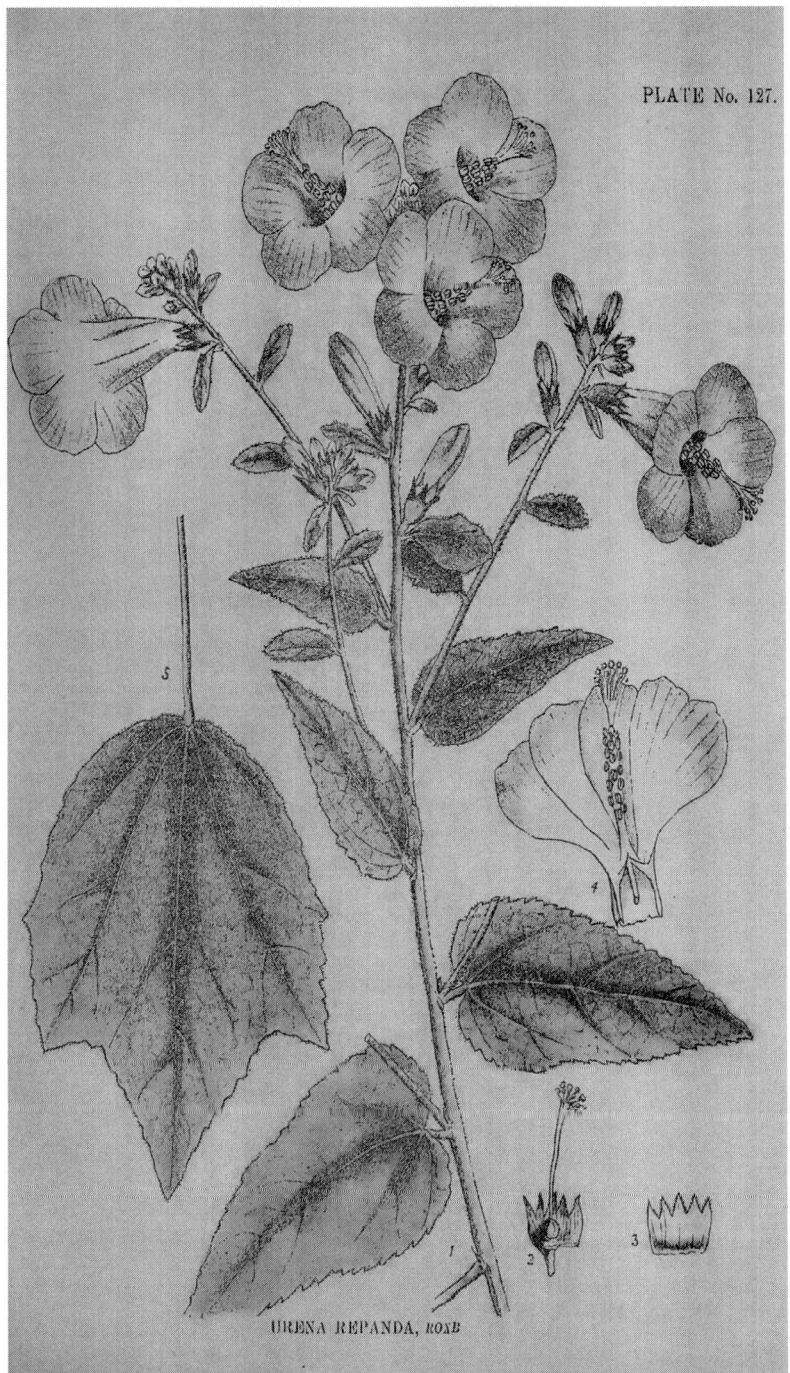

URENA REPANDA, ROXB

PLATE No. 128.

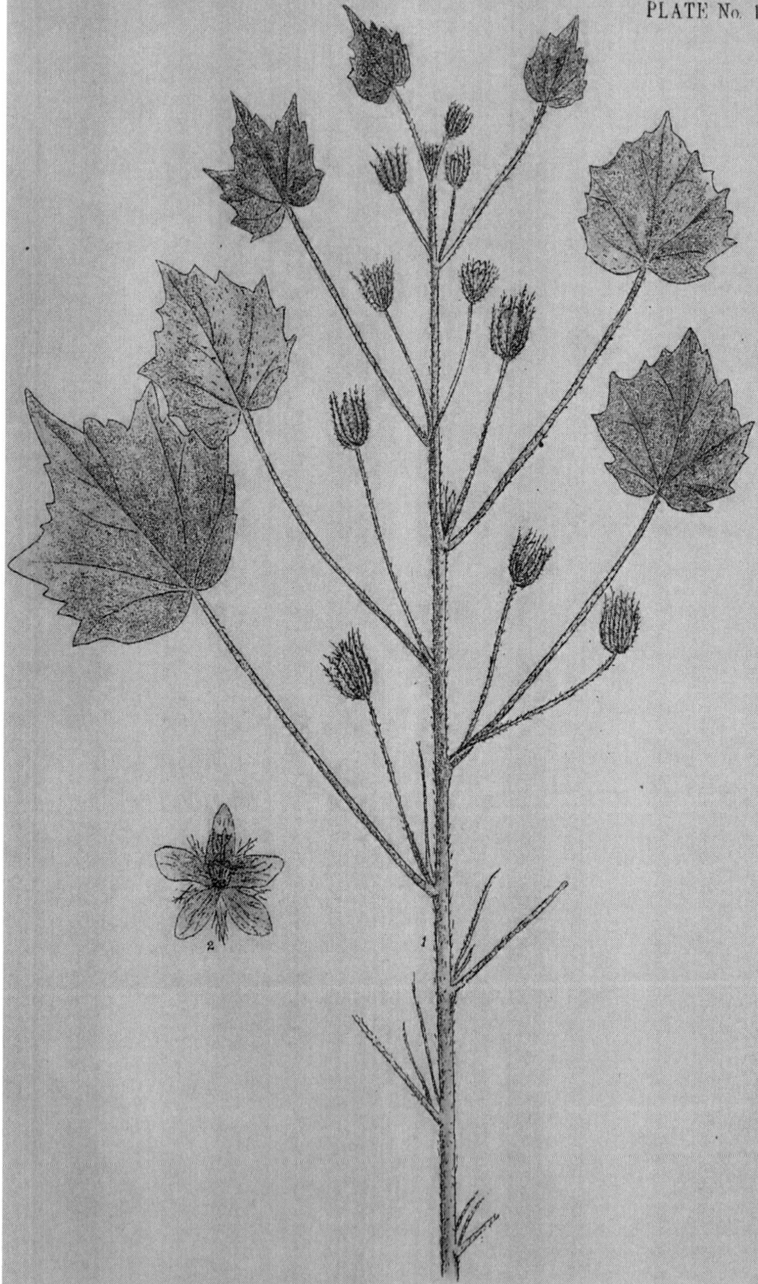

PAVONIA ODORATA, WILLD.

PLATE No. 129.

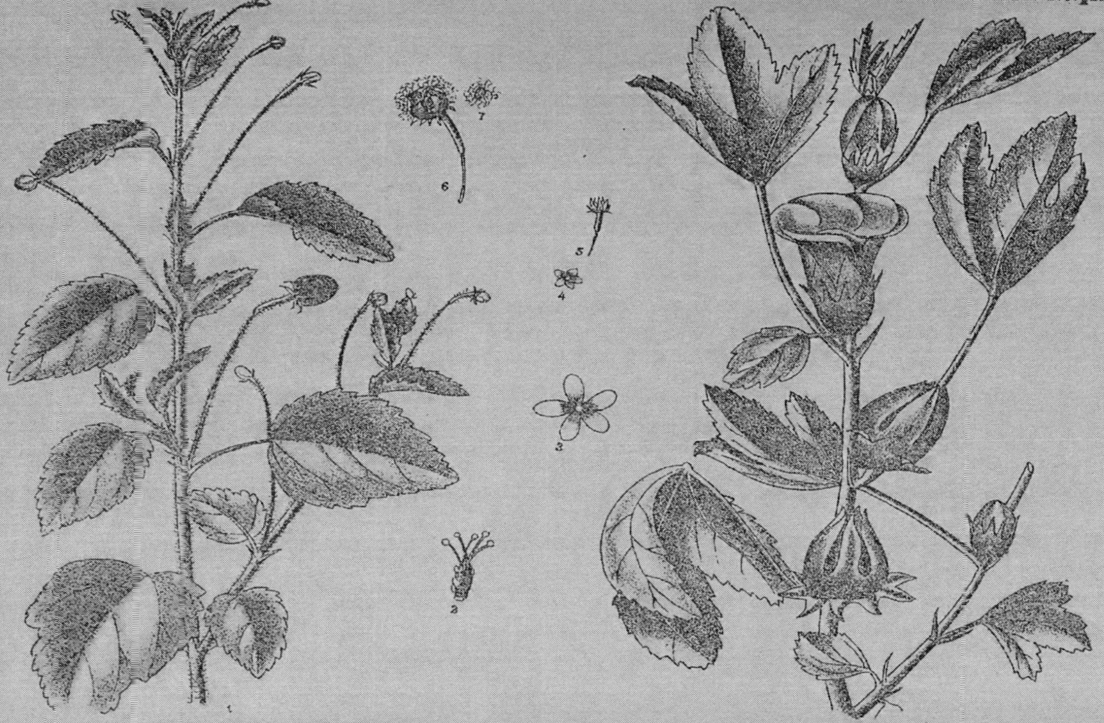

HIBISCOUS MICRANTHUS, *LINN.* H. SABDARIFFA, *LINN.*

PLATE No. 130.

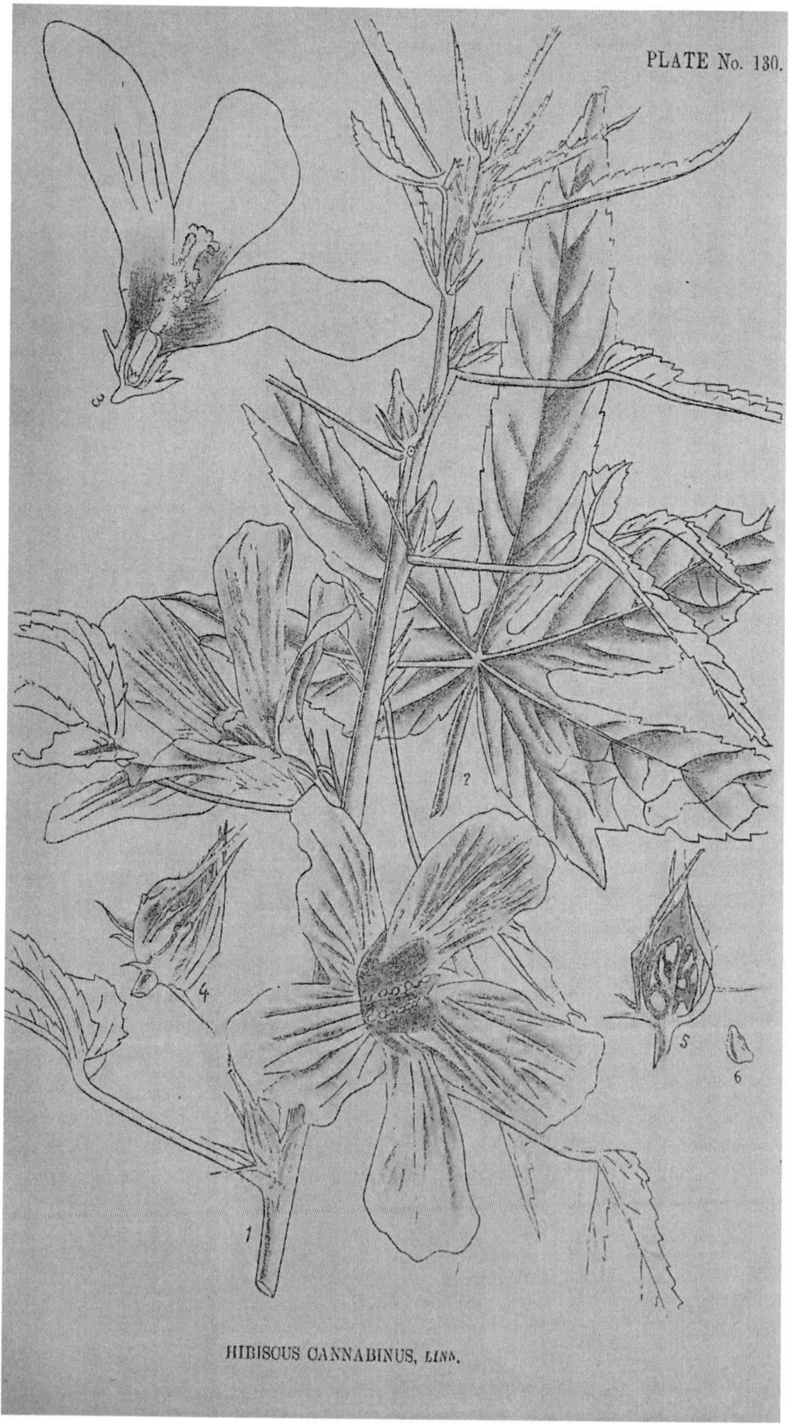

HIBISCUS CANNABINUS, *Linn.*

PLATE No. 131.

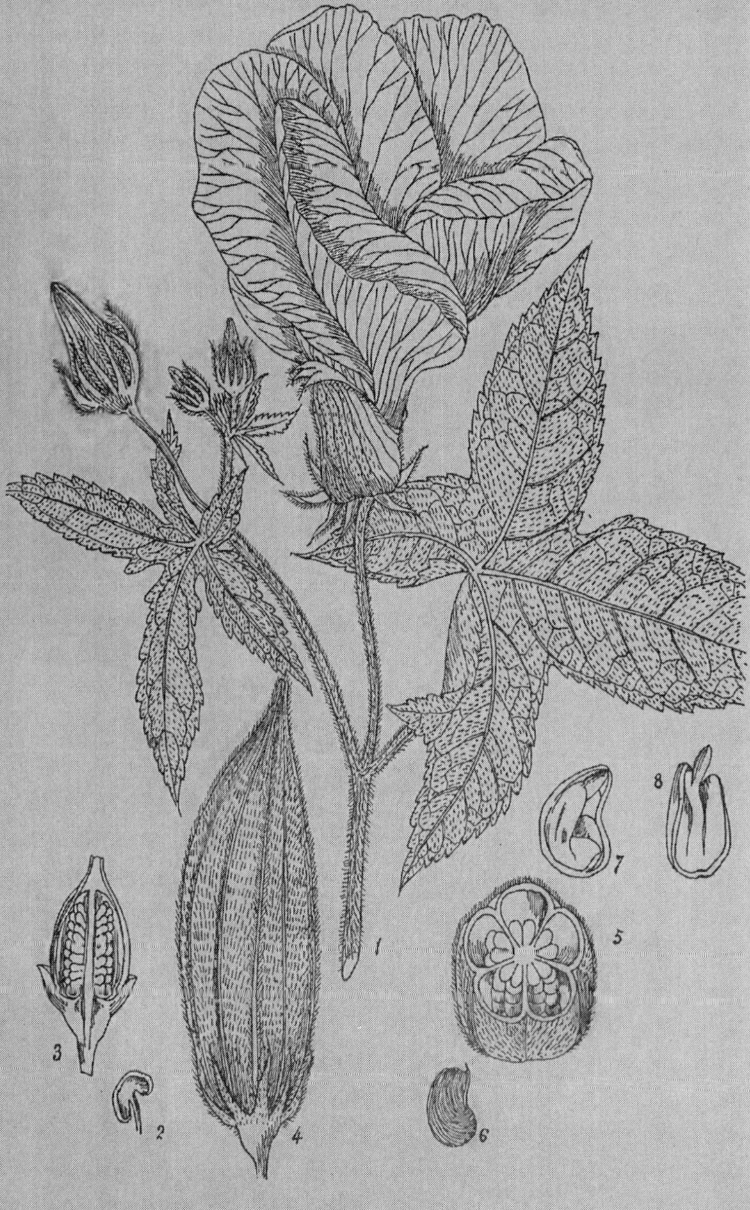

HIBISCUS ABELMOSCHUS, *LINN.*

PLATE No. 132.

HIBISCUS ESCULENTUS, *LINN.*

PLATE No. 133.

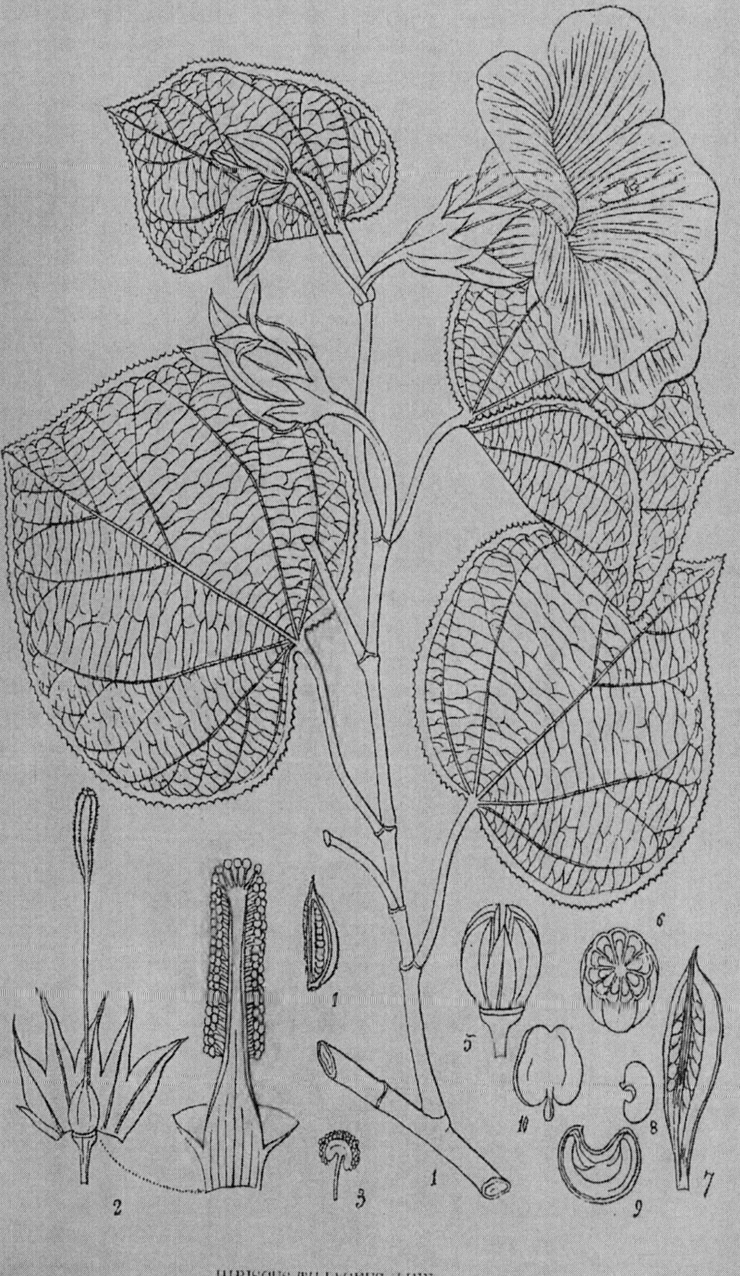

HIBISCUS TILIACEUS, *LINN.*

PLATE No. 134.

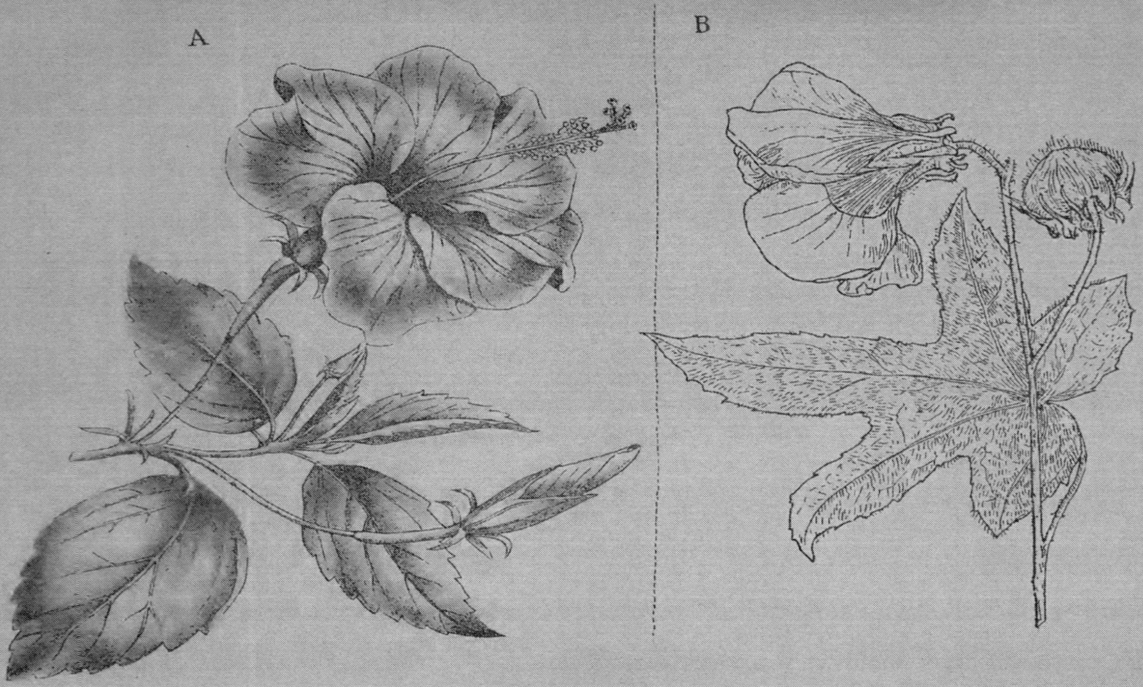

A—HIBISCUS ROSA-SINENSIS, *LINN.*

B—HIBISCUS FURCATUS, *ROXB.*

PLATE No. 135.

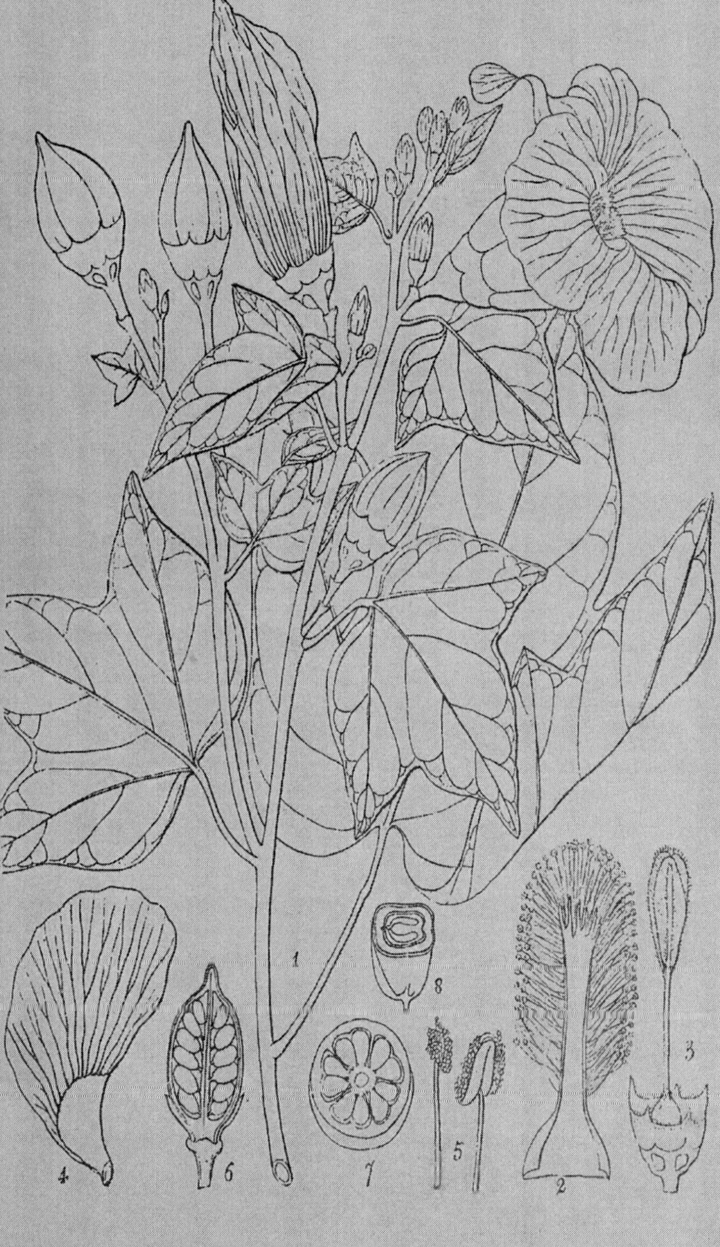

THESPASIA LAMPAS, DALZ & GIBS.

PLATE No. 136.

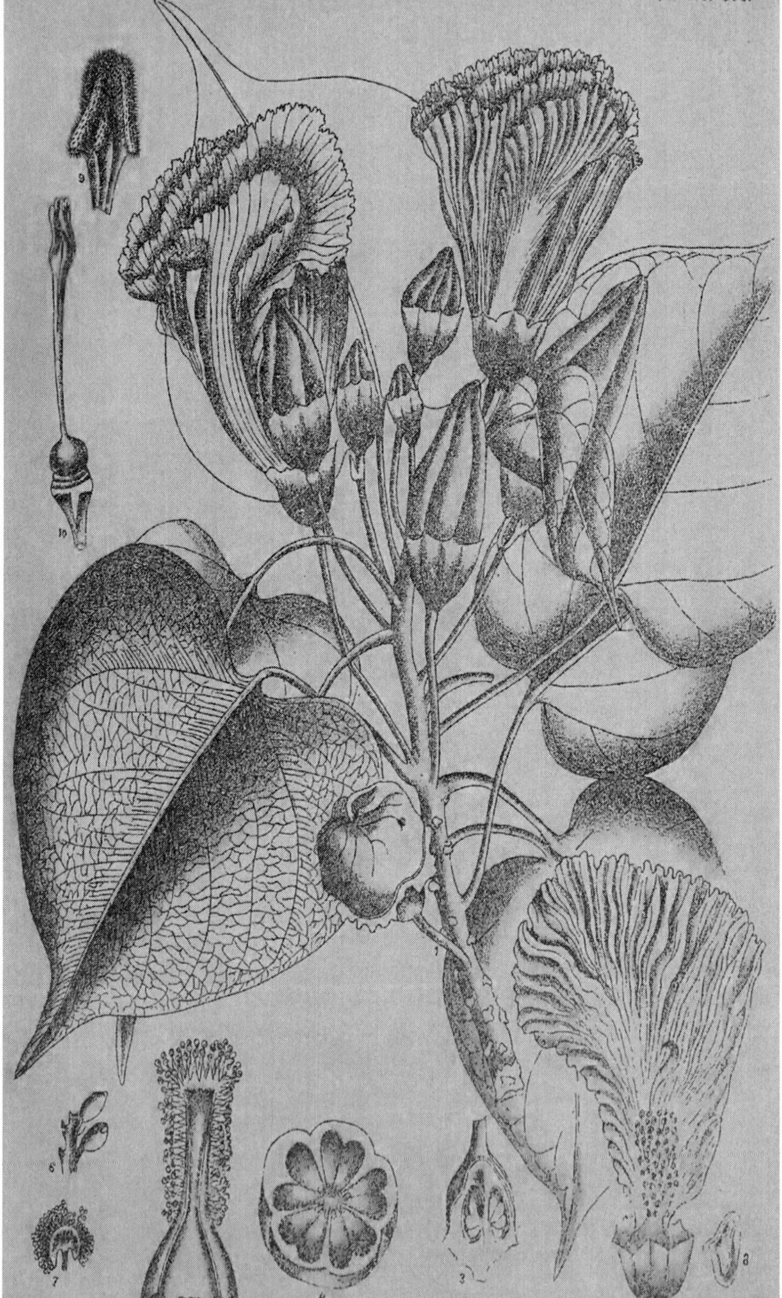

THESPESEA POPULNEA, CORR.

PLATE No. 137.

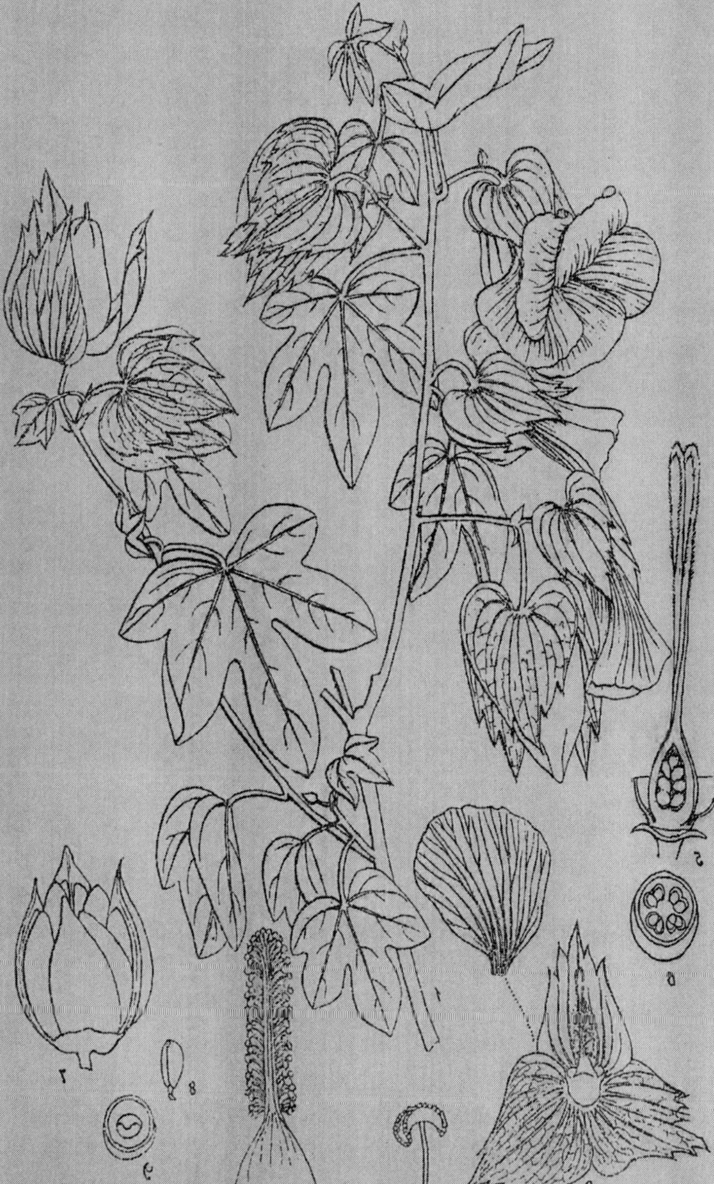

GOSSYPIUM HERBACEUM, *LINN.*

PLATE No. 138.

GOSSYPIUM HERBACEUM, *Linn.*

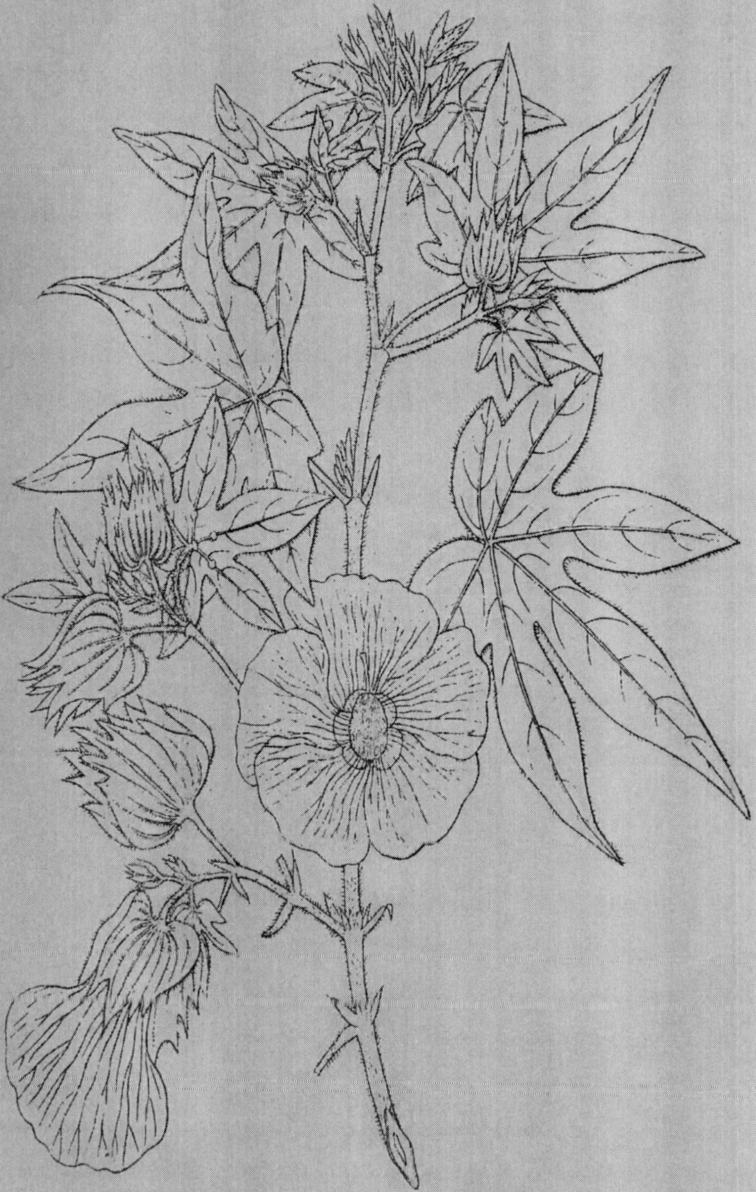

GOSSYPIUM ARBOREUM, *LINN.*

PLATE No. 140.

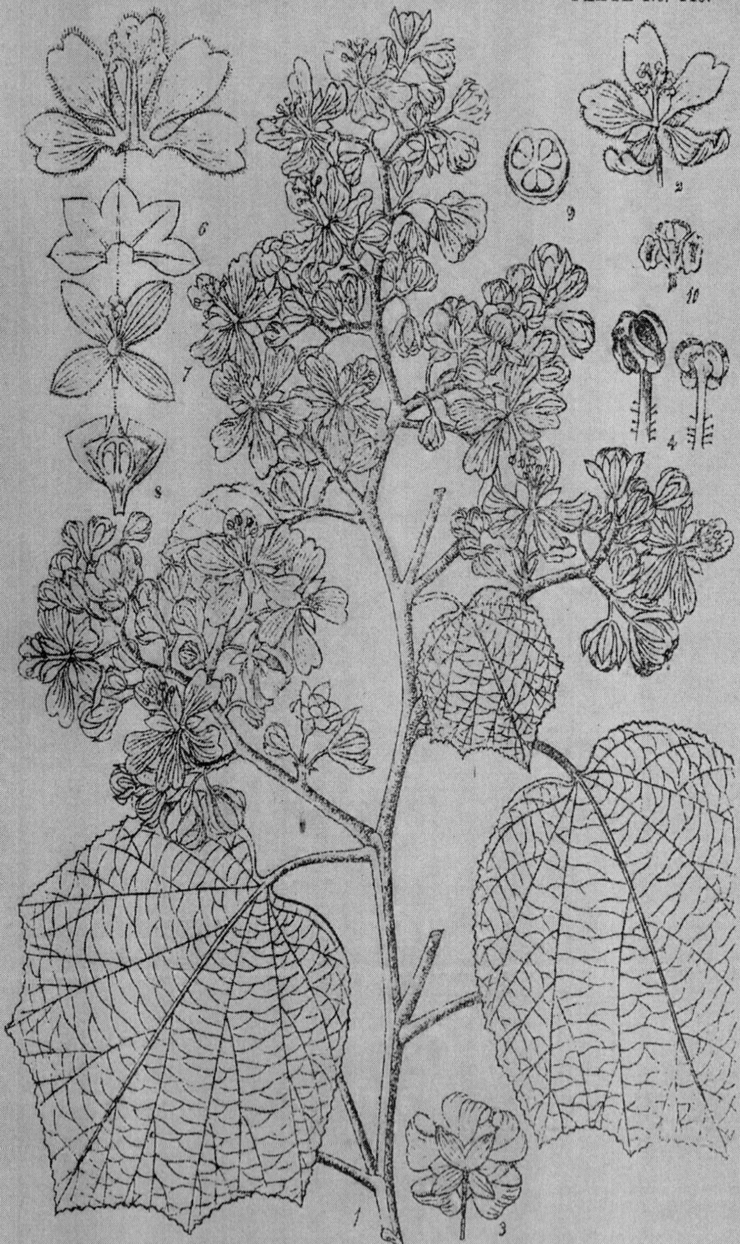

KYDIA CALYCINA, *ROXB.*

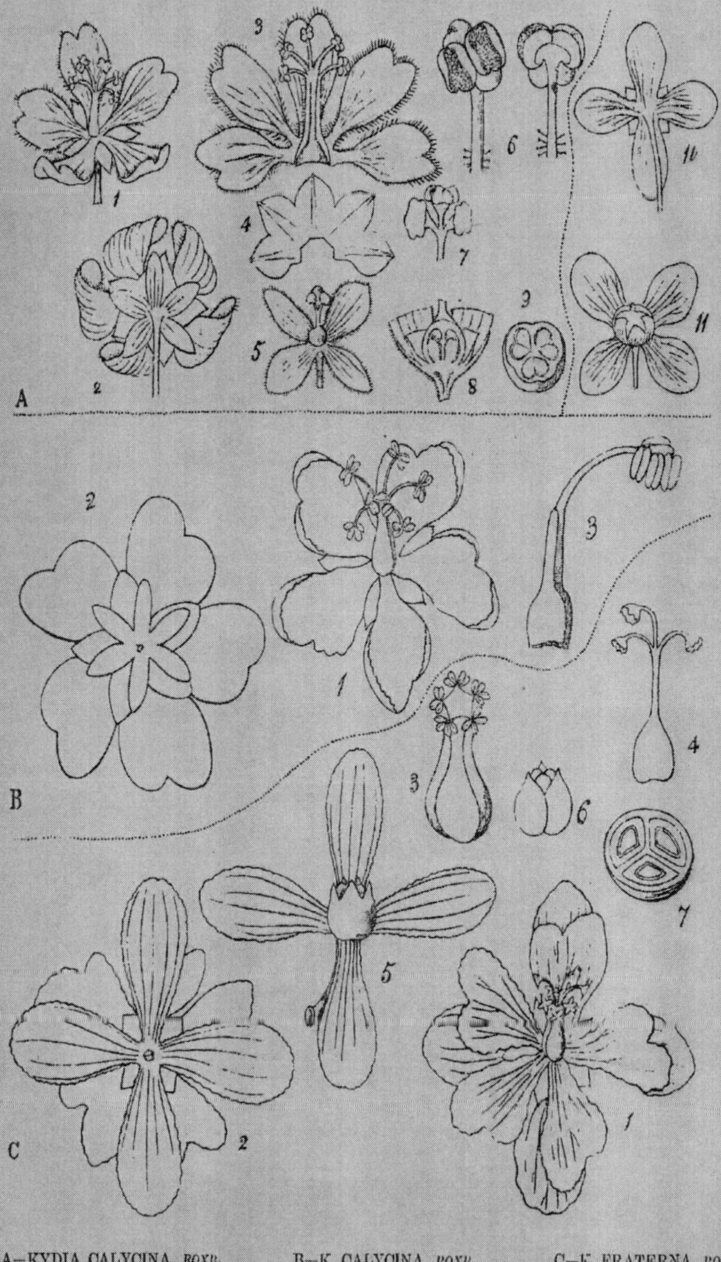

A—KYDIA CALYCINA, *ROXB.* B—K. CALYCINA, *ROXB.* C—K. FRATERNA, *ROXB.*

PLATE No. 142.

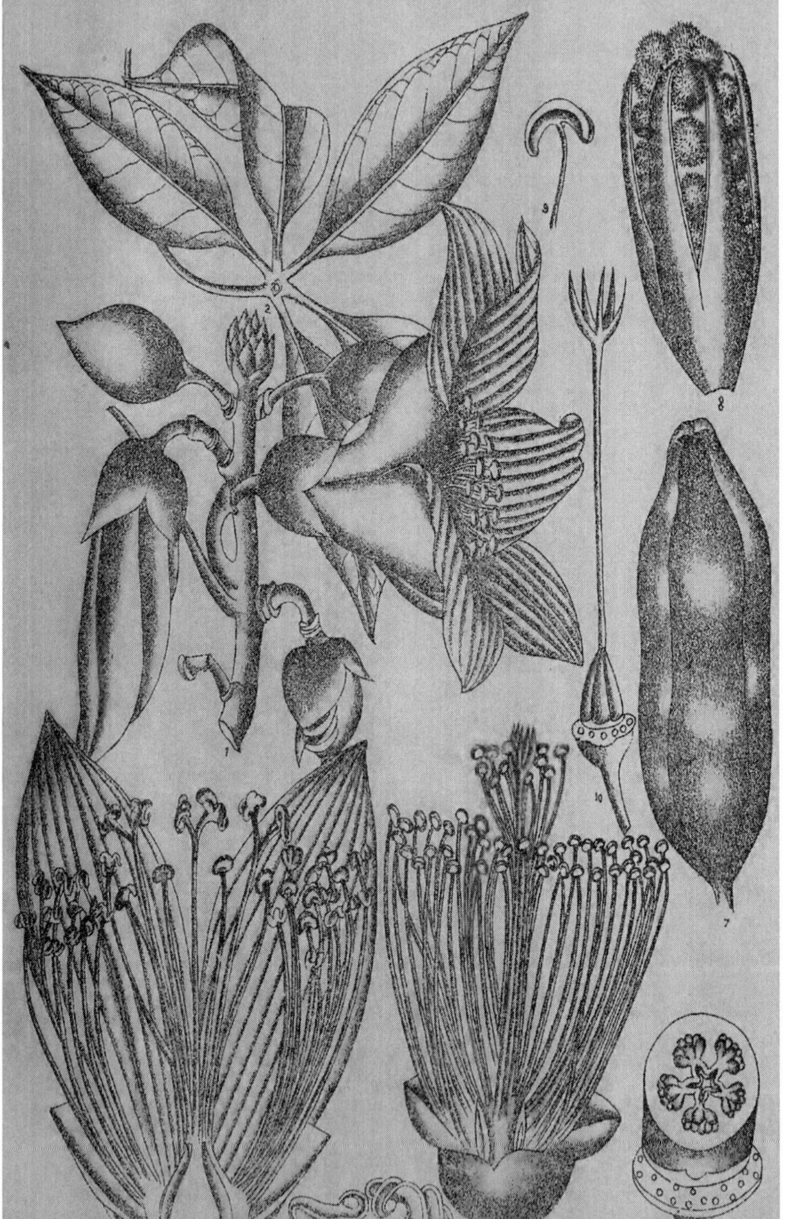

BOMBAX MALABARICUM, *DC.*

PLATE No 143.

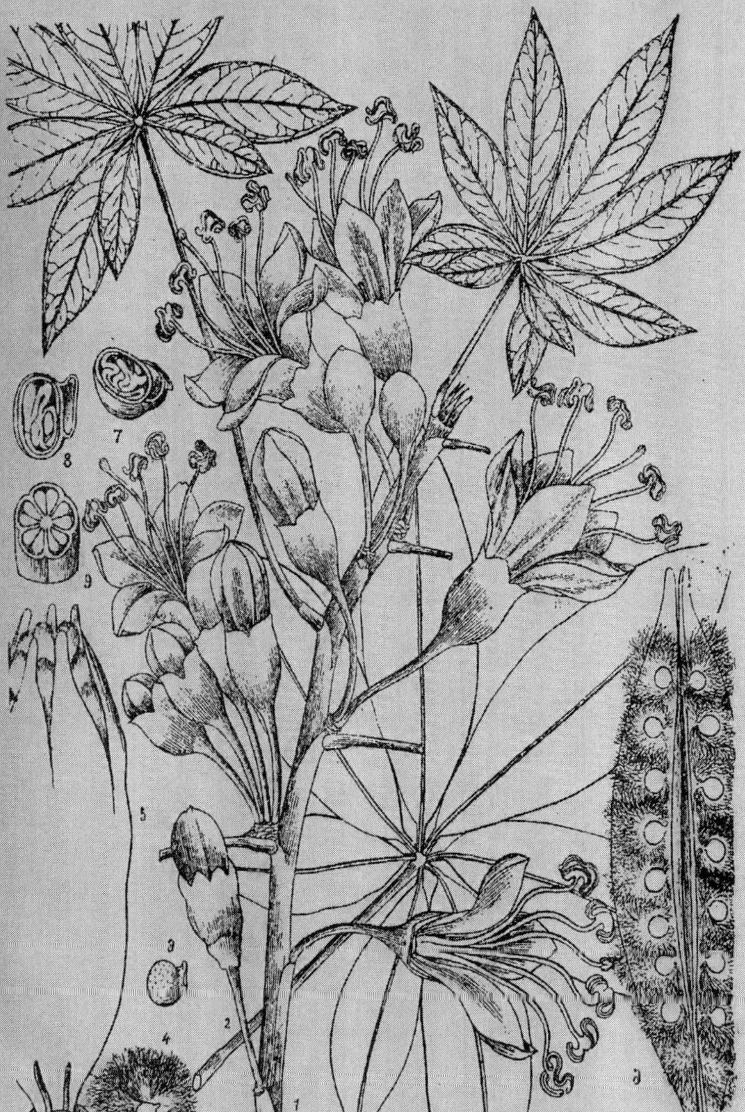

ERIODENDRON ANFRACTUOSUM, DC.

PLATE No 144.

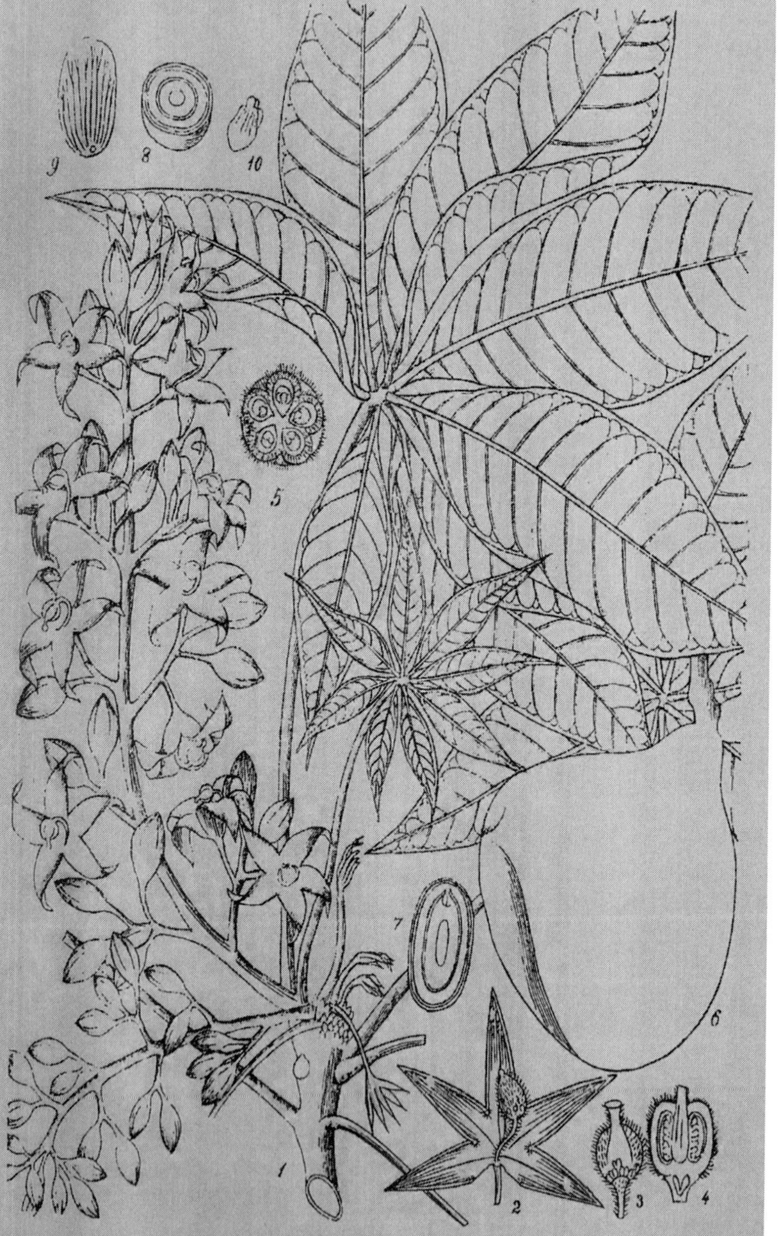

STERCULIA FŒTIDA, LINN.

PLATE No. 145.

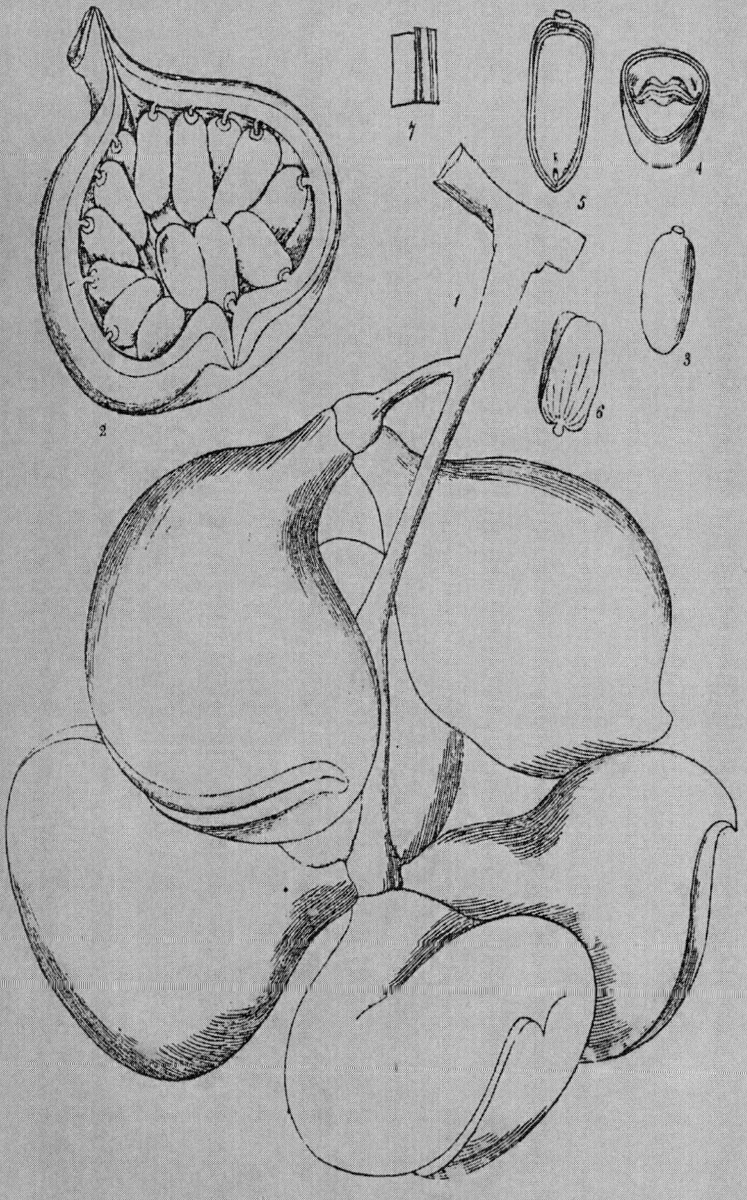

STERCULIA FOETIDA, LINN.

STERCULIA URENS, *ROXB.*

STERCULIA SCAPHIGERA, *WALL*

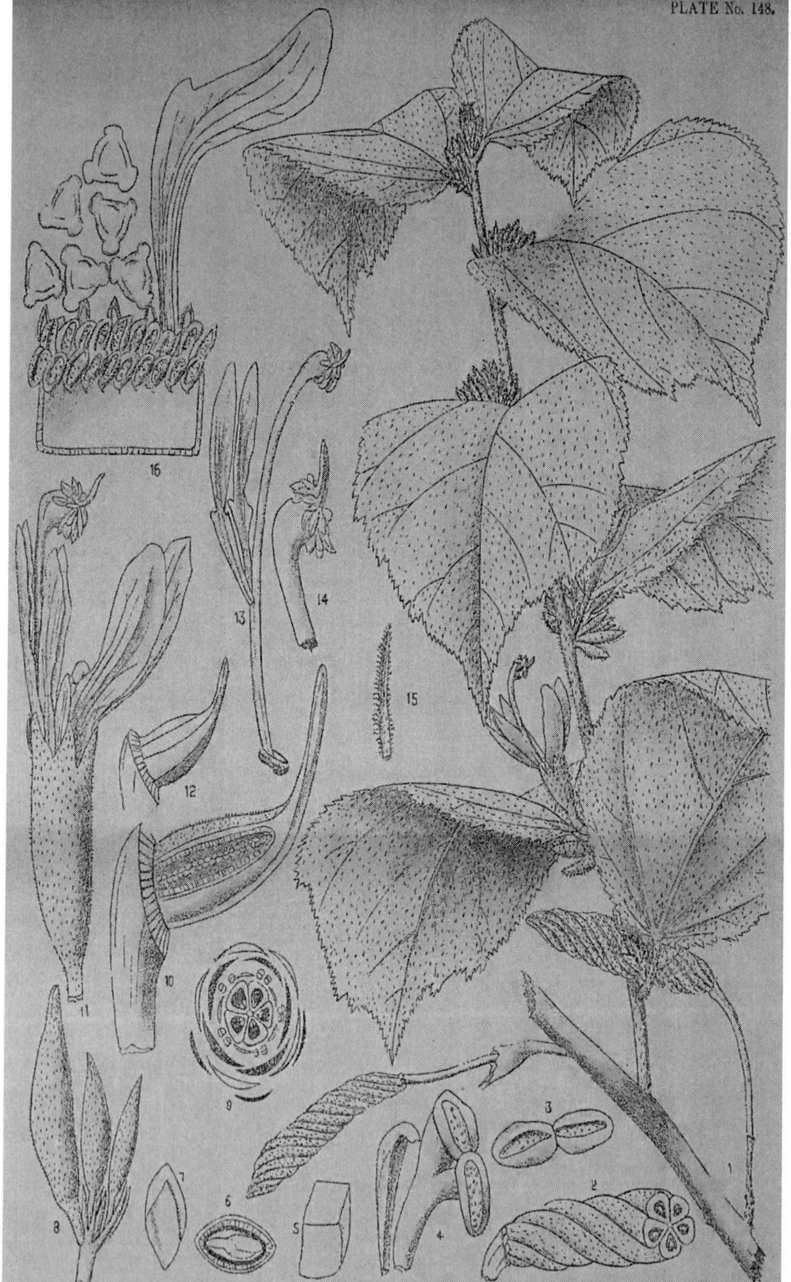

HELIOTERES ISORA, *LINN.*

PLATE No. 149.

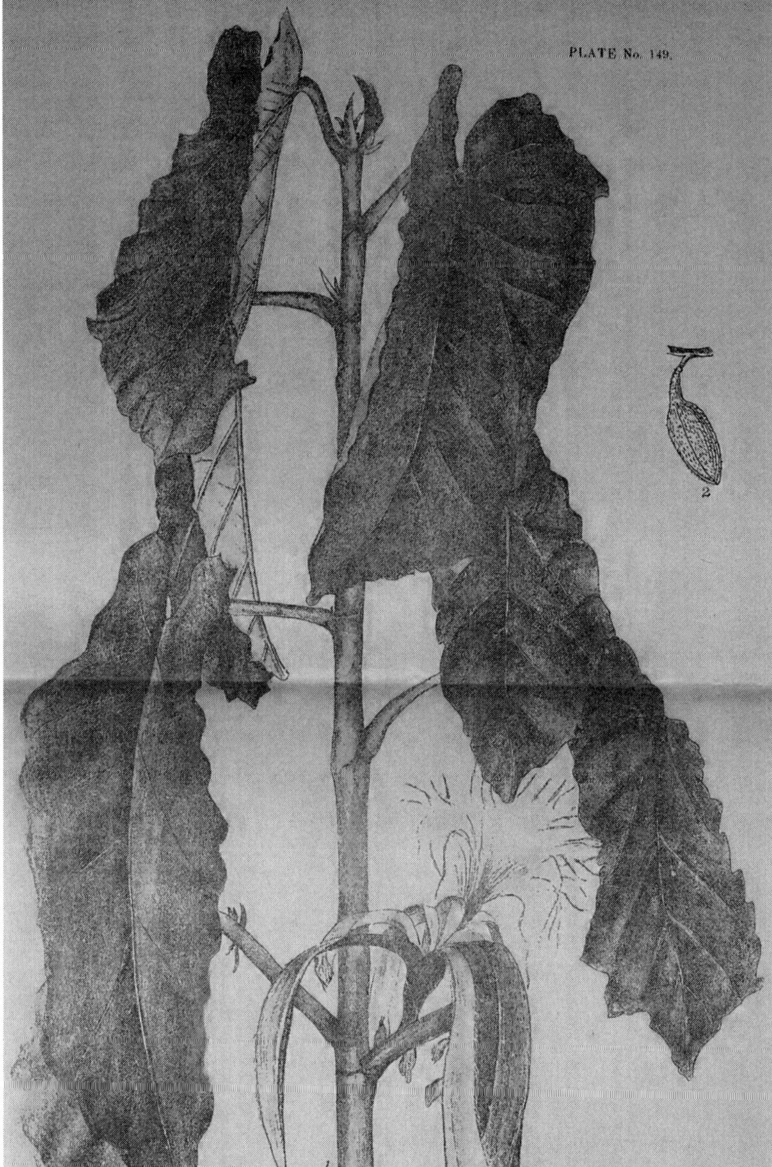

PTEROSPERMUM SUBERIFOLIUM, LAM.

PLATE No. 150.

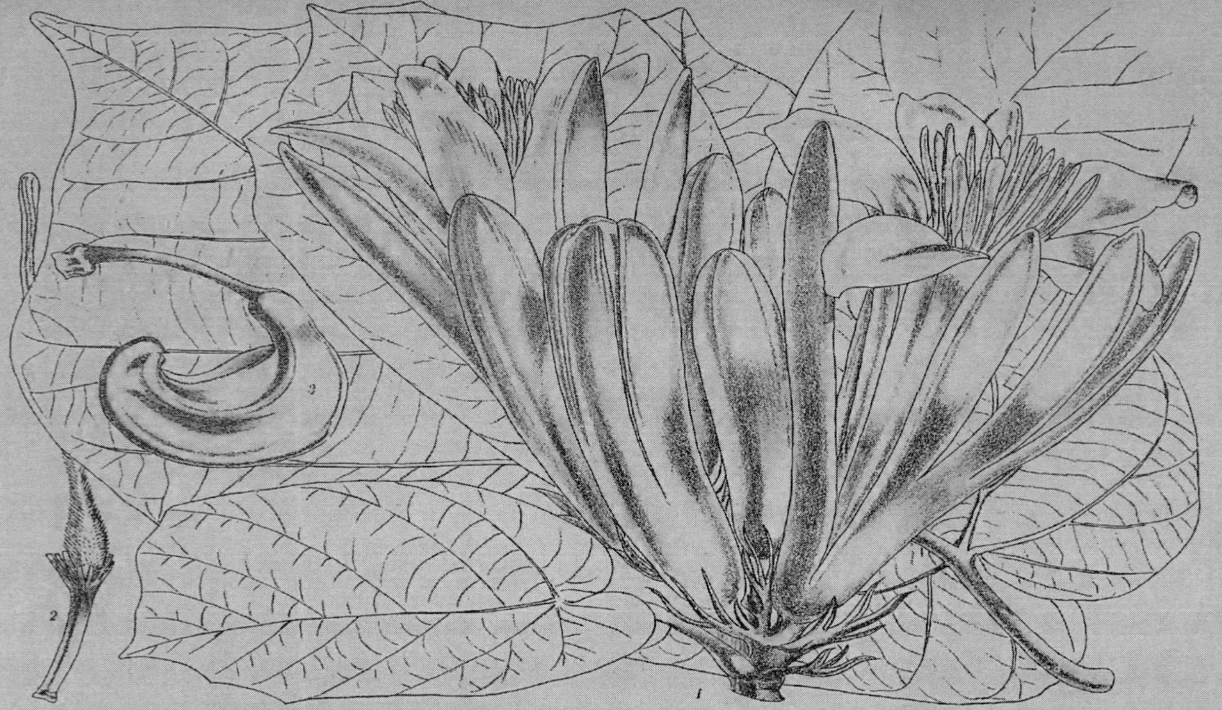

PTEROSPERMUM ACERIFOLIUM, *WILLD.*

PLTAE No. 151

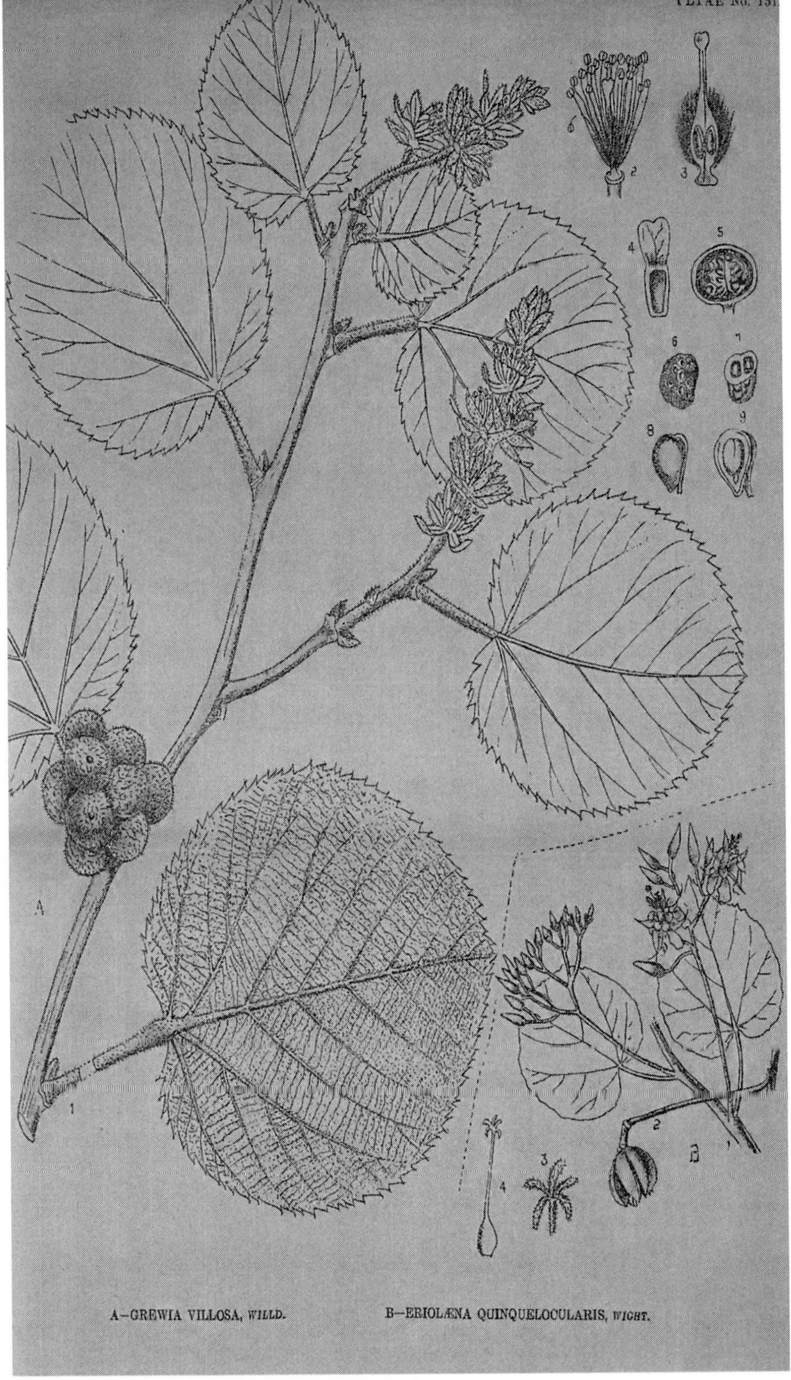

A—GREWIA VILLOSA, *WILLD.* B—ERIOLÆNA QUINQUELOCULARIS, *WIGHT.*

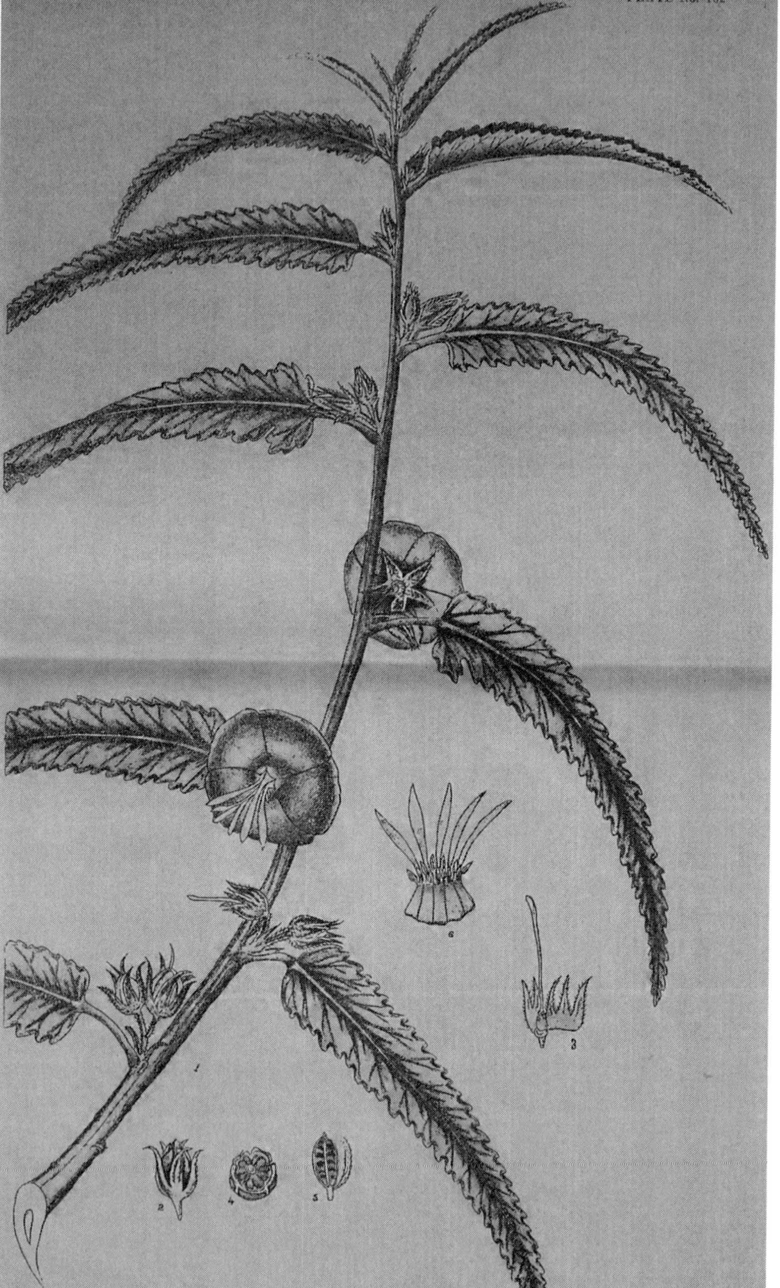

PENTAPETES PHŒNICEA, *Linn.*

PLATE No. 153

ABROMA AUGUSTA, *Linn.*

PLATE No. 154.

GUAZUMA TOMENTOSA, *KUNTH.*

PLATE No. 155.

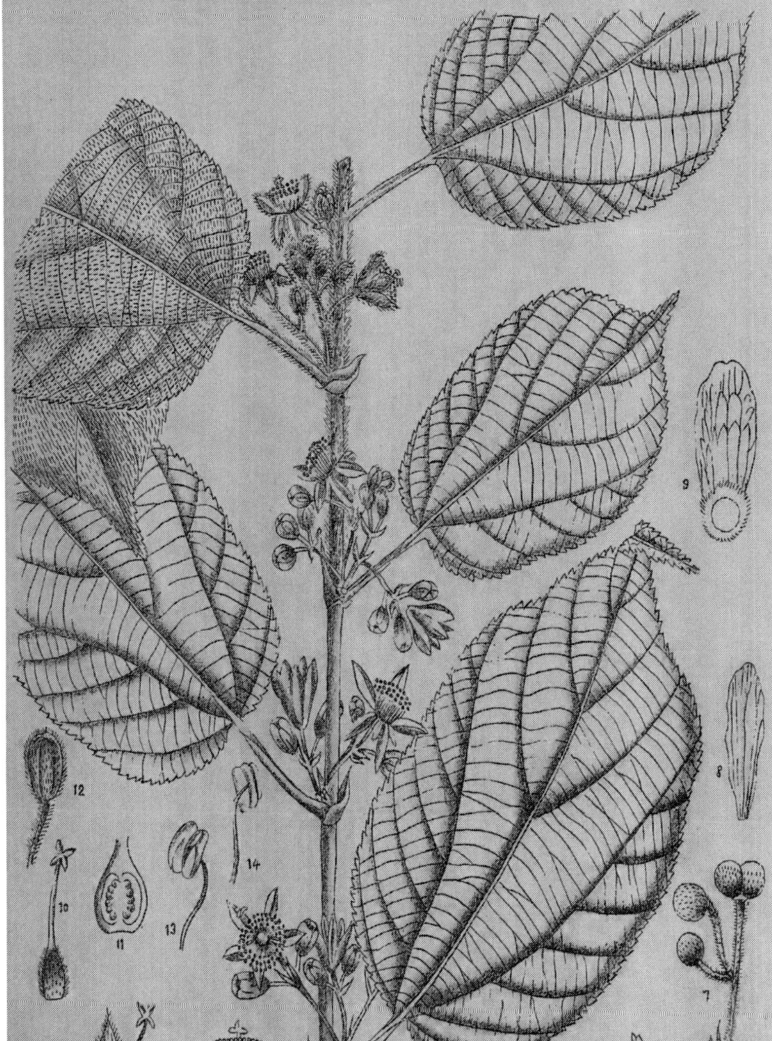

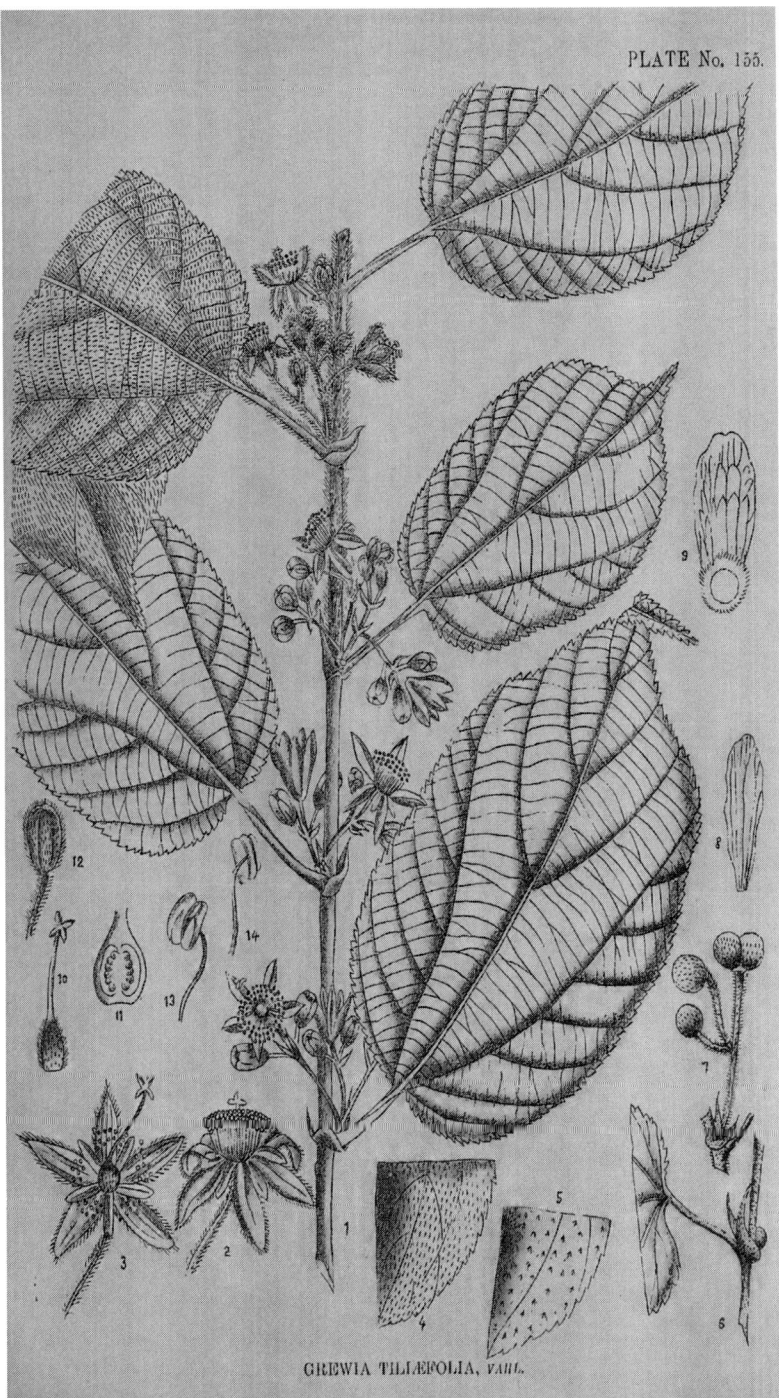

GREWIA TILIÆFOLIA, *VAHL.*

PLATE No. 156.

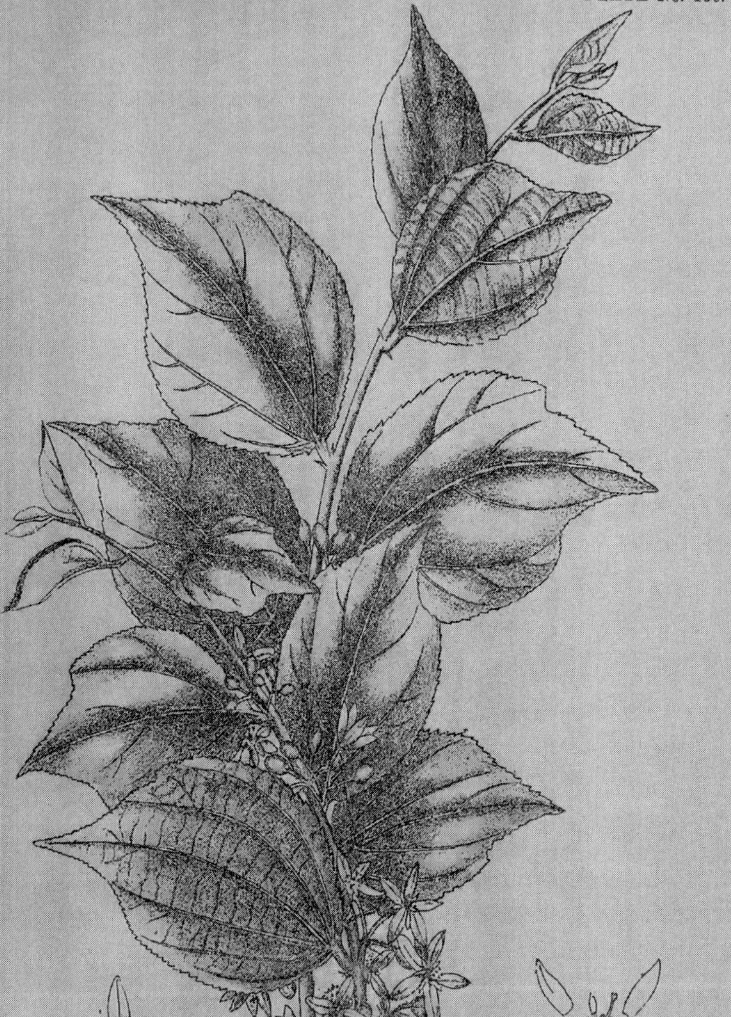

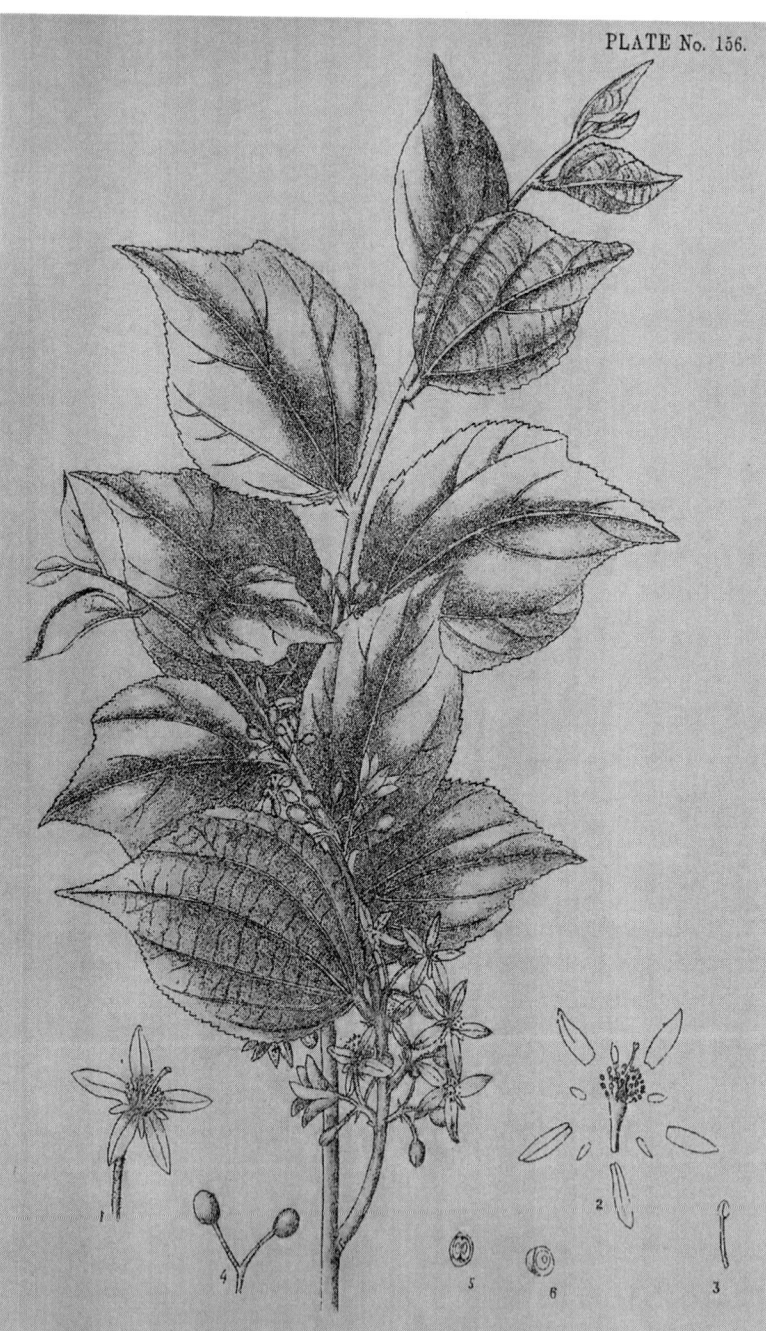

GREWIA ASIATIOA, *VAR. VESTITA, WALL.*

PLATE No. 157.

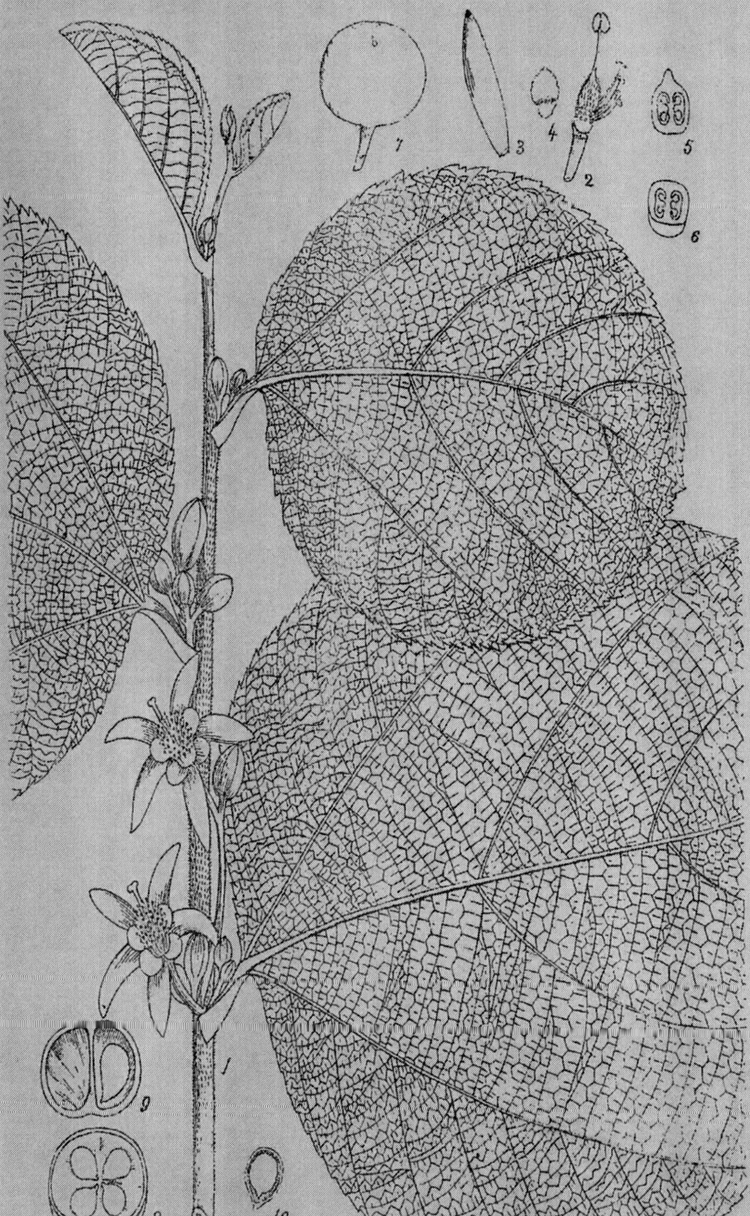

GREWIA SCABROPHYLLA, *ROXB.*

PLATE No. 158.

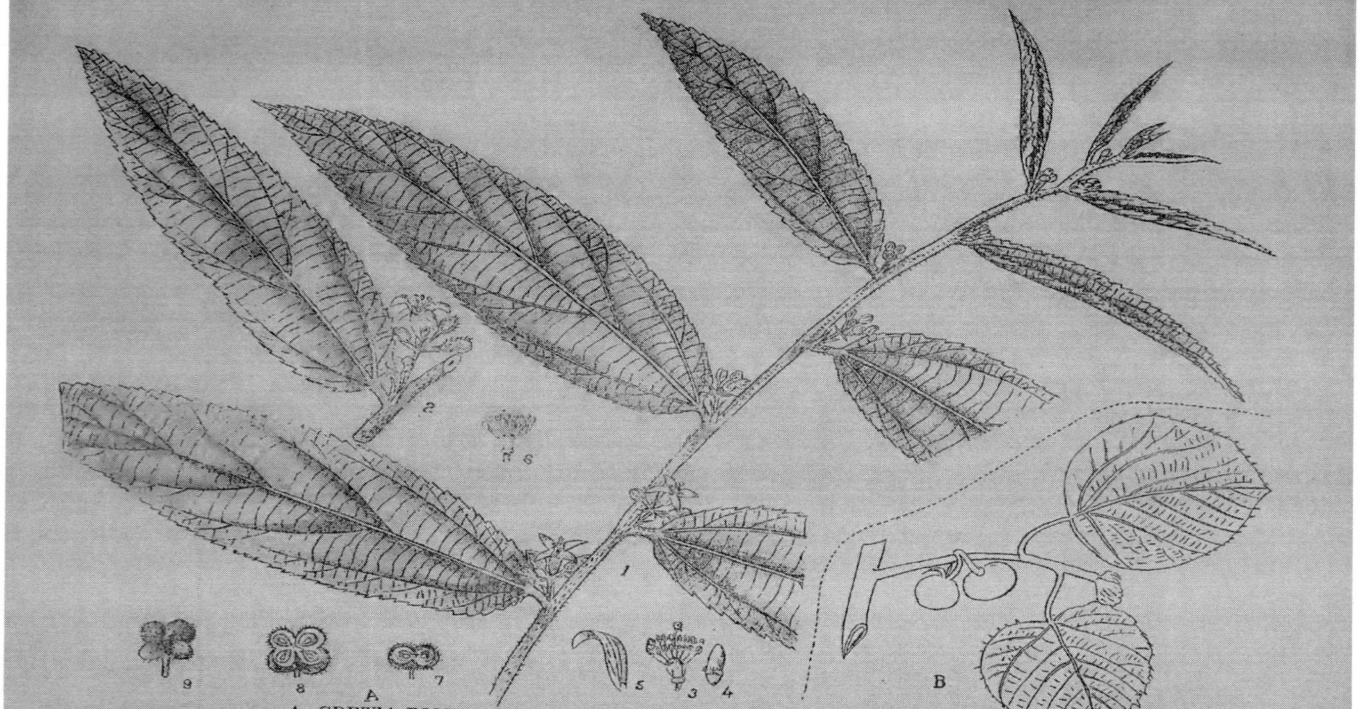

A—GREWIA POLYGAMA, *ROXB.*　　B—G. VILLOSA, *WILL.*

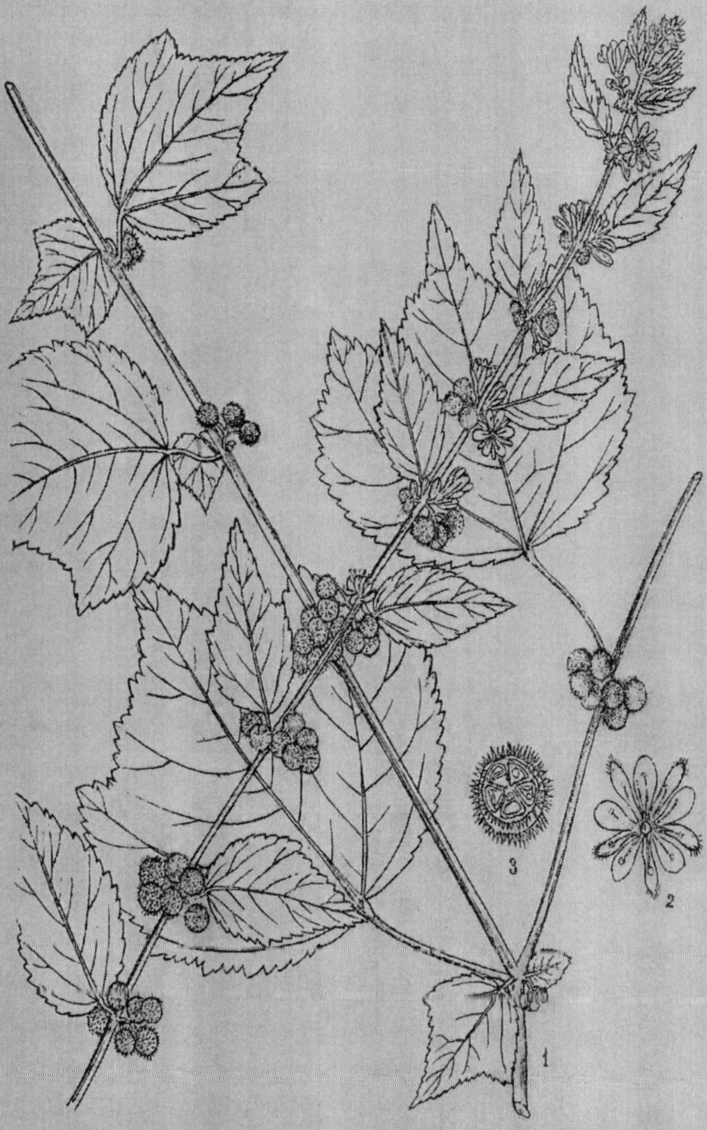

TRIUMFETTA RHOMBOIDEA, JACQ

PLATE No. 160.

CORCHORUS CAPSULARIS, LINN.

PLATE No. 161.

A—CORCHORUS OLITORIUS, *LINN.* B—C. FASCICULARIS, *LAMK*

PLATE No. 162.

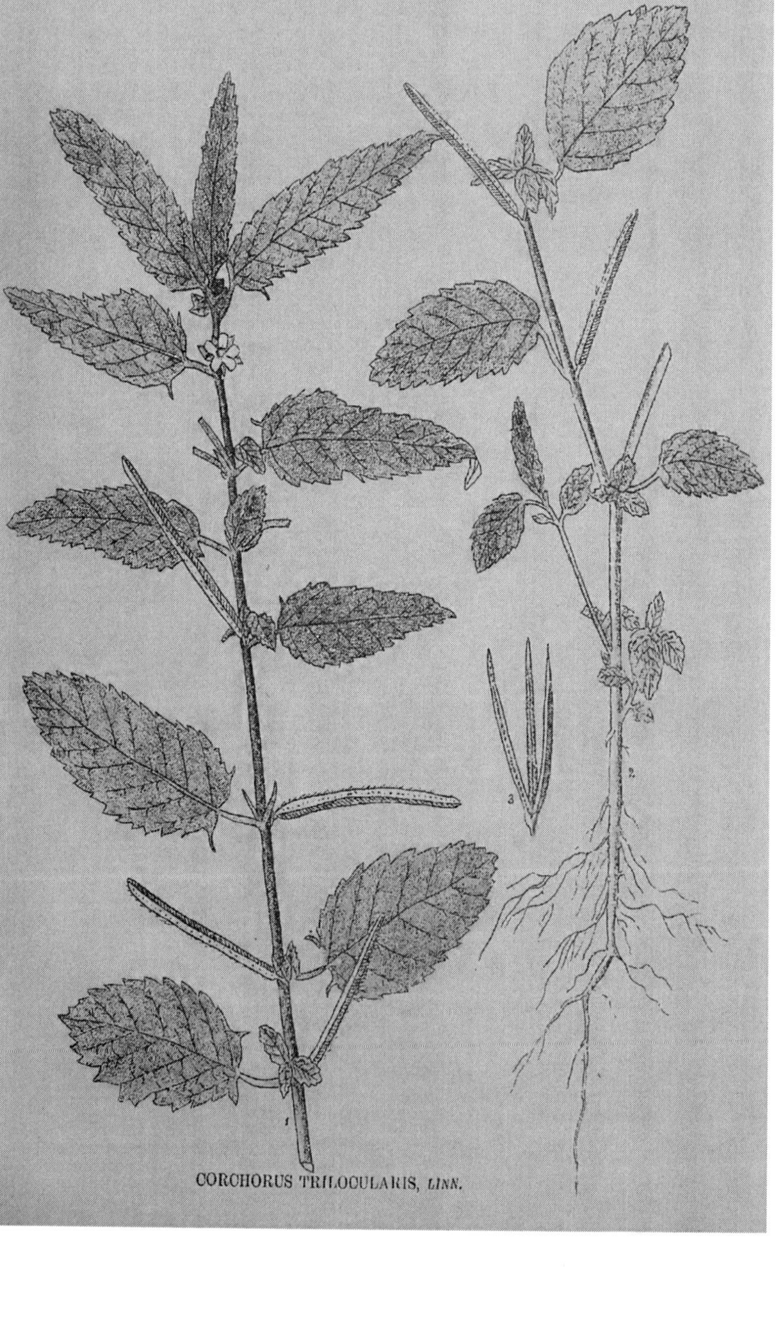

CORCHORUS TRILOCULARIS, *LINN.*

PLATE No. 163.

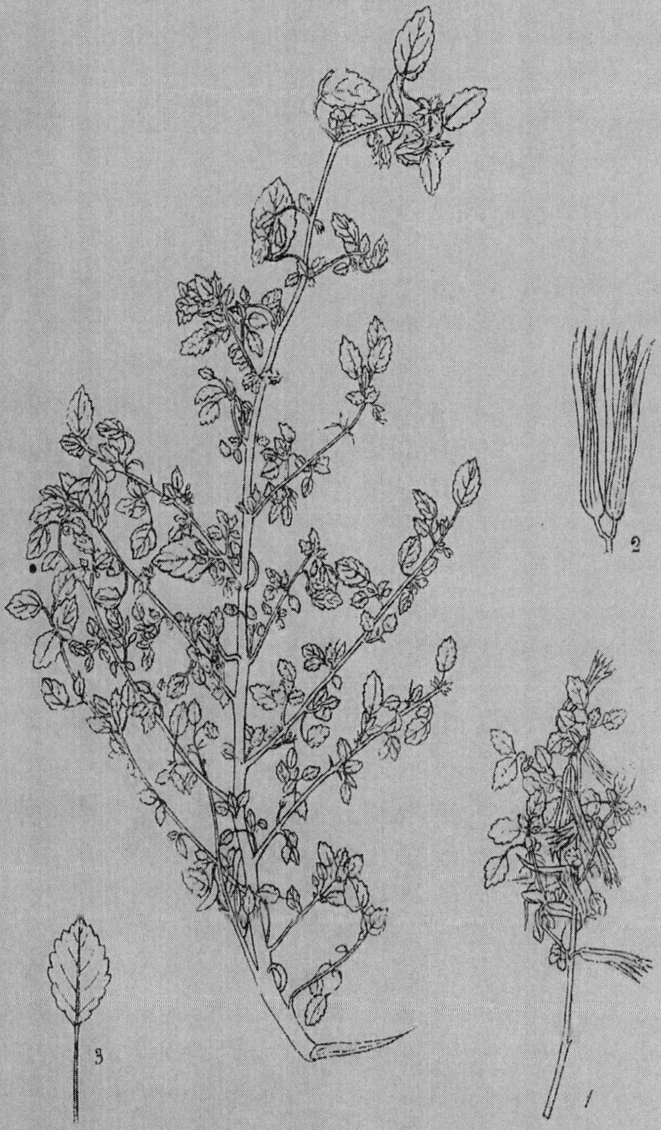

CORCHORUS ANTICHORUS, Rœusch

PLATE No. 164.

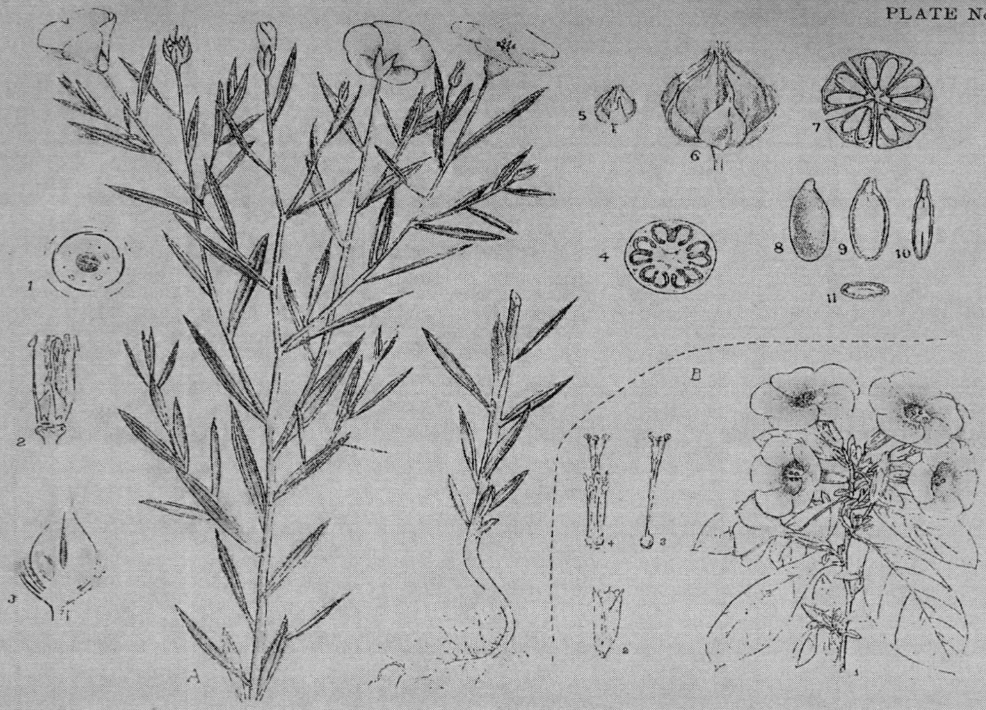

A—LINUM USITATISSIMUM, *LINN.* B—REINWARDTIA TRIGYANA, *PLANCH.*

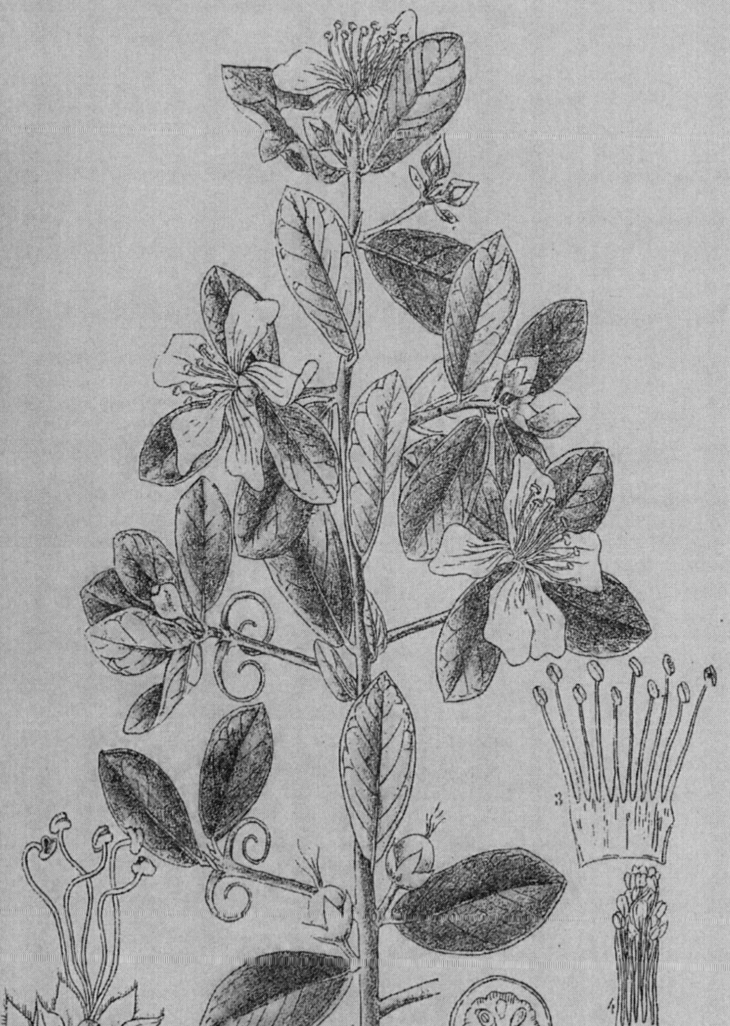

HUGONIA MYSTAX, *LINN.*

PLATE No. 166.

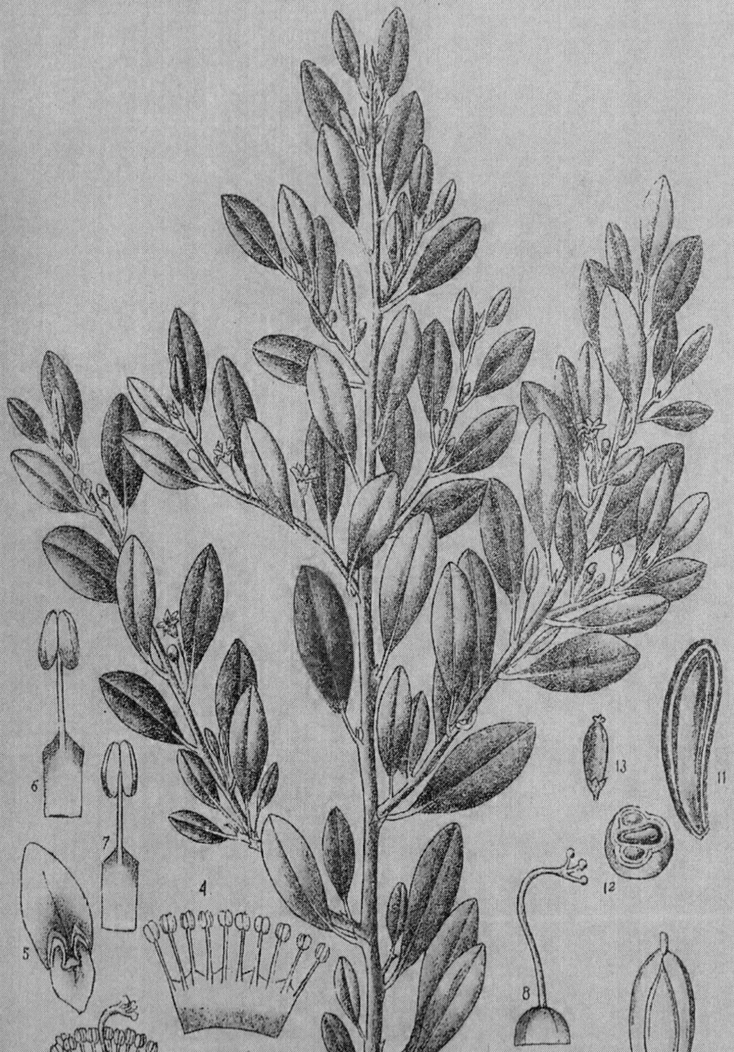

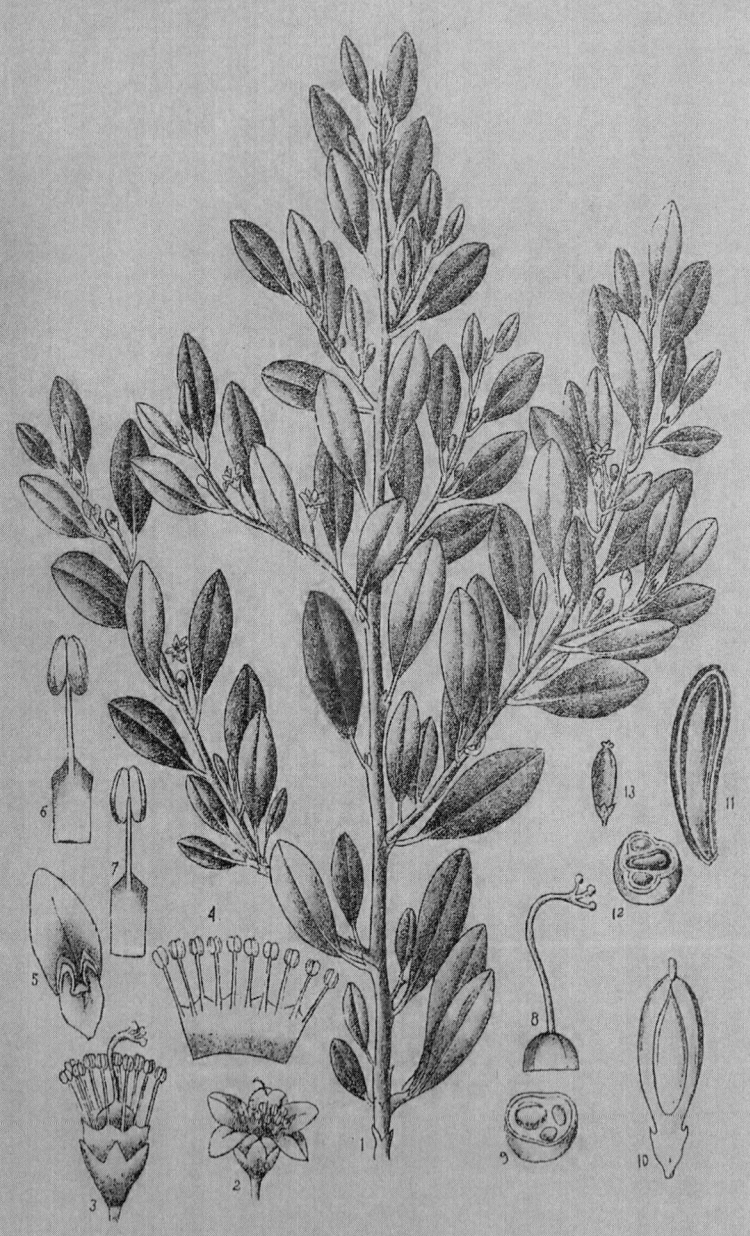

ERYTHROXYLON MONOGYNUM, ROXB.

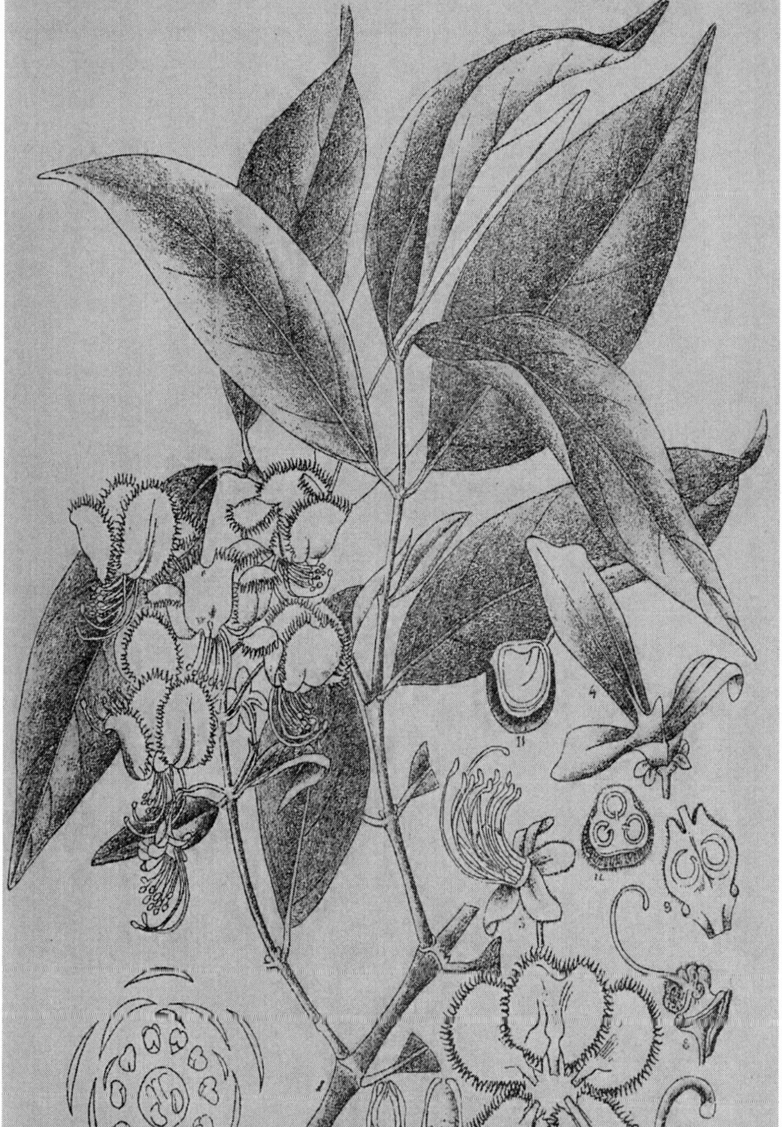

HIPTAGE MADABLOTA, Gærtn.

PLATE No. 168.

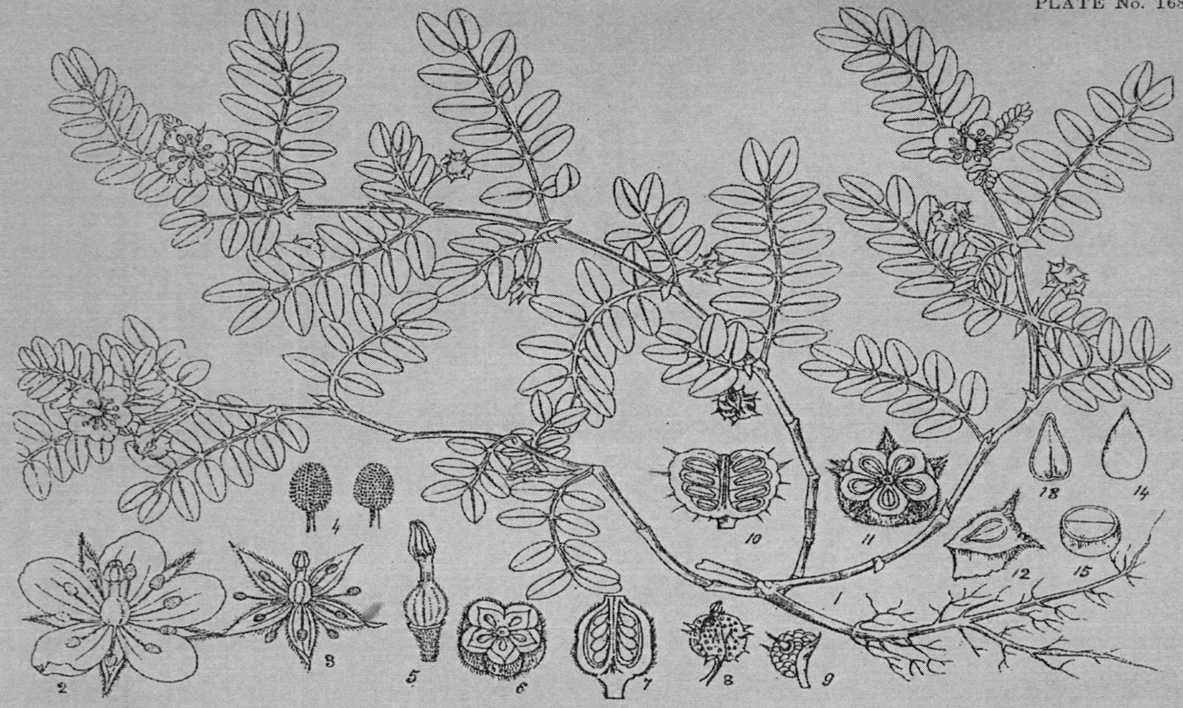

TRIBULUS TERRESTRIS, *LINN.*

PLATE No. 169

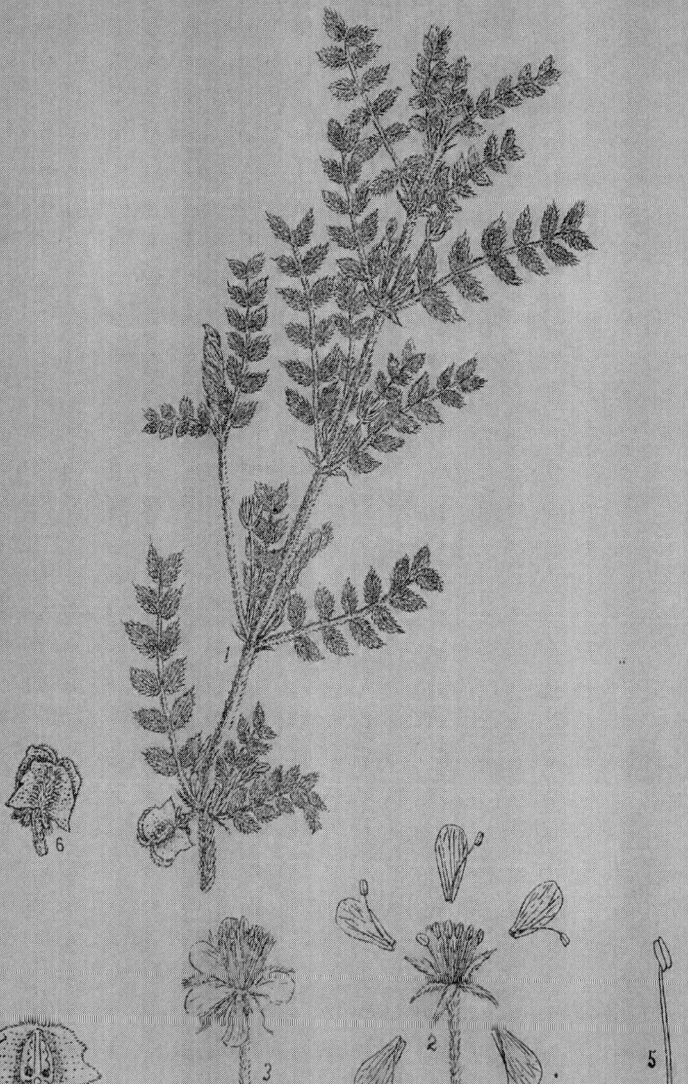

TRIBULUS ALATUS, *DELILE.*

PLATE No. 170.

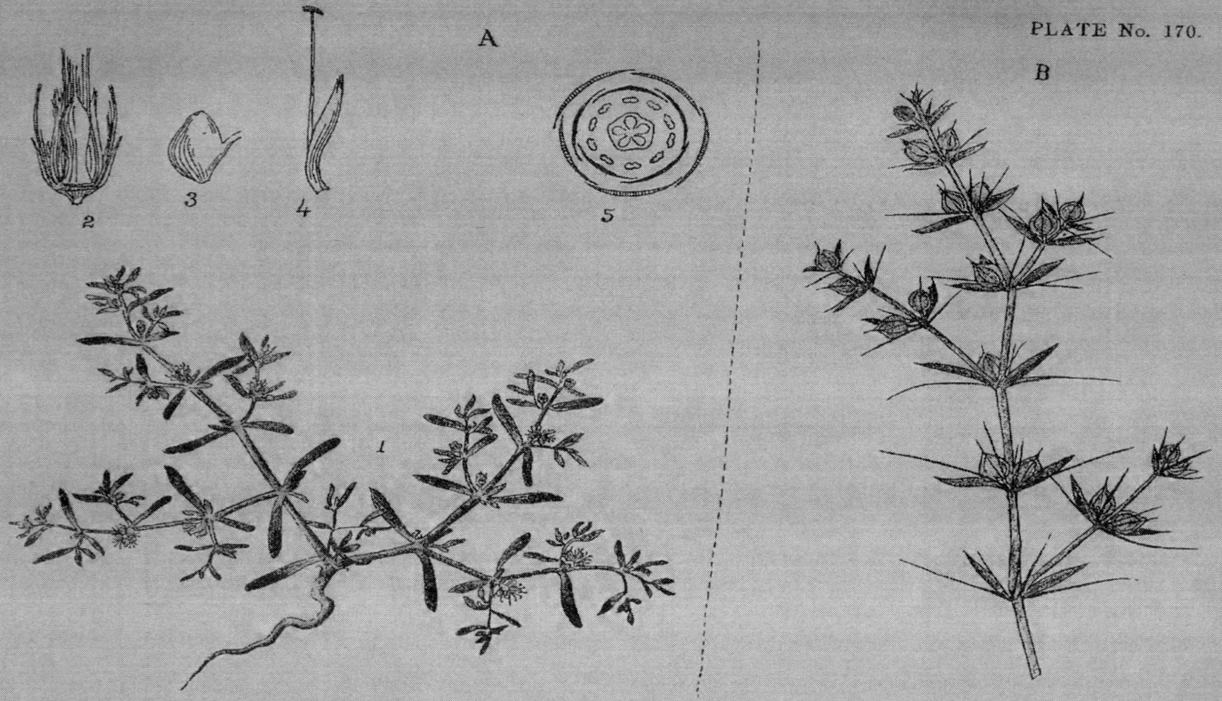

A—ZYGOPHYLLUM SIMPLEX, *LINN.*

B—FAGONIA BRUGUIERI, *DC.*

PLATE No. 171.

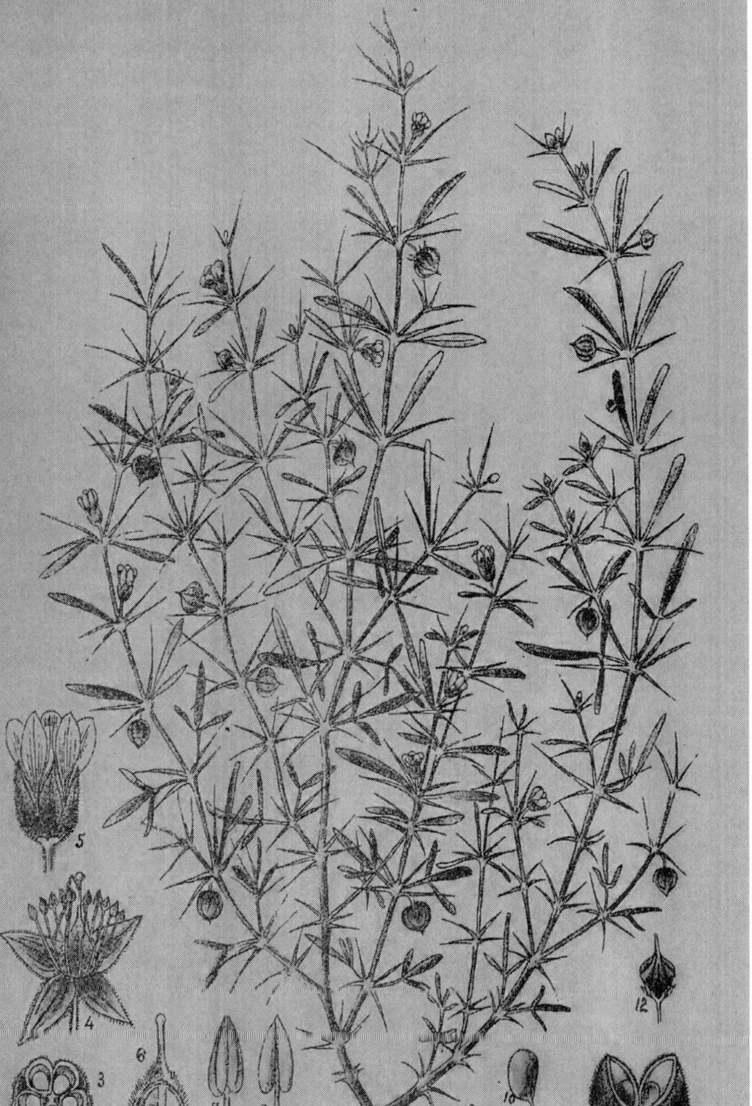

FAGONIA ARABICA, *LINN.*

PLATE No. 172.

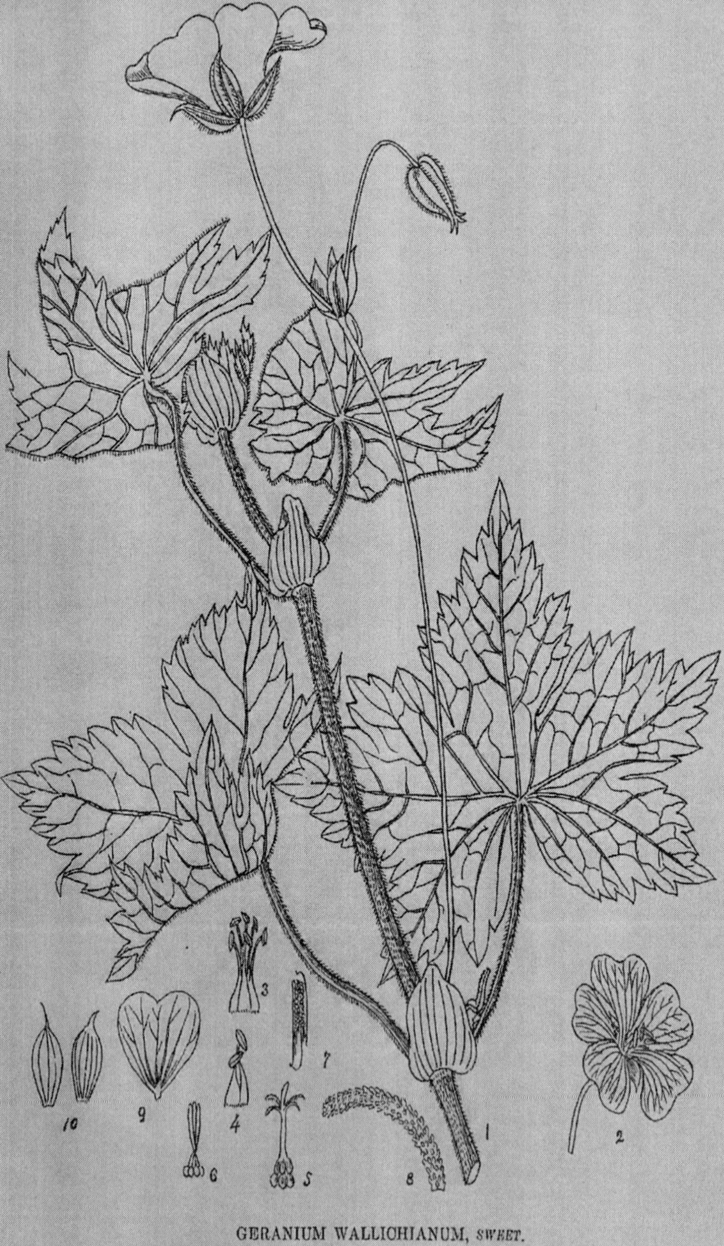

GERANIUM WALLICHIANUM, *SWEET.*

PLATE No. 173

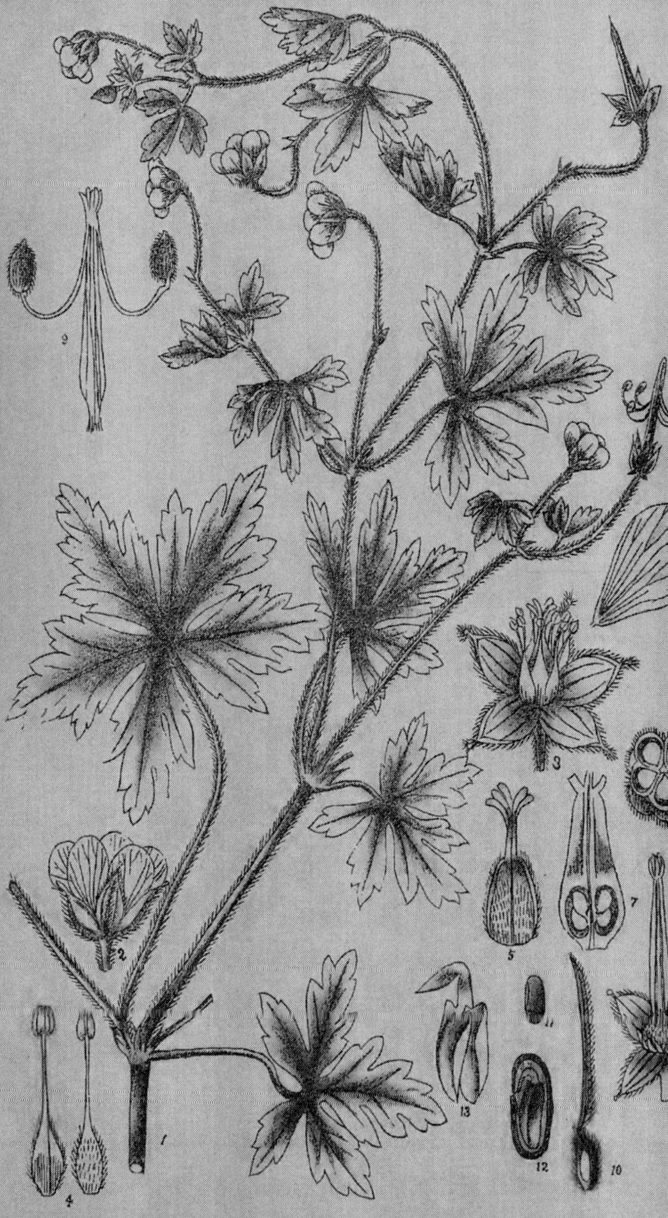

GERANIUM NEPALENSE, SWEET.

PLATE No 174.

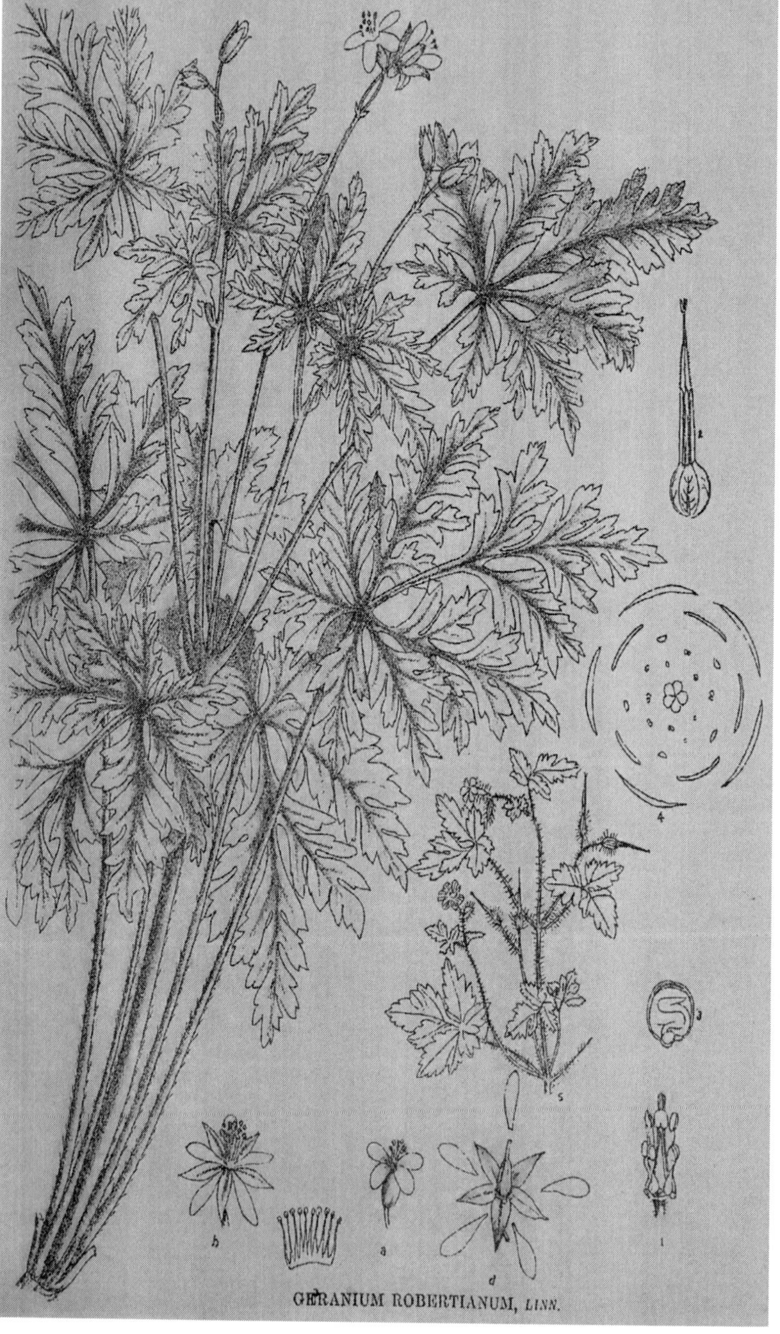

GERANIUM ROBERTIANUM, LINN.

PLATD No. 175.

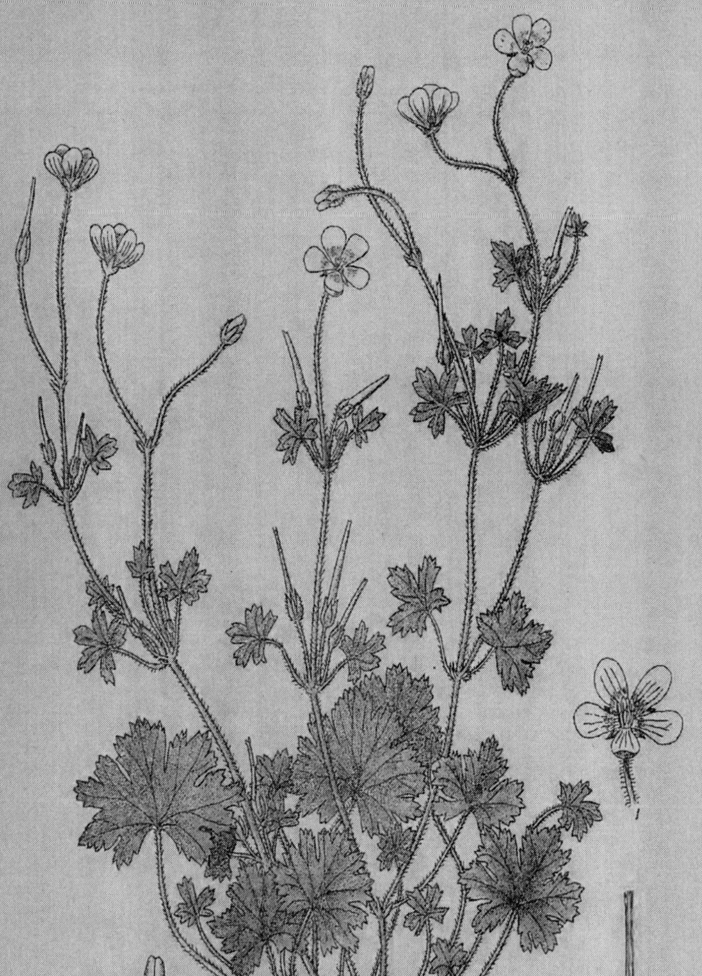

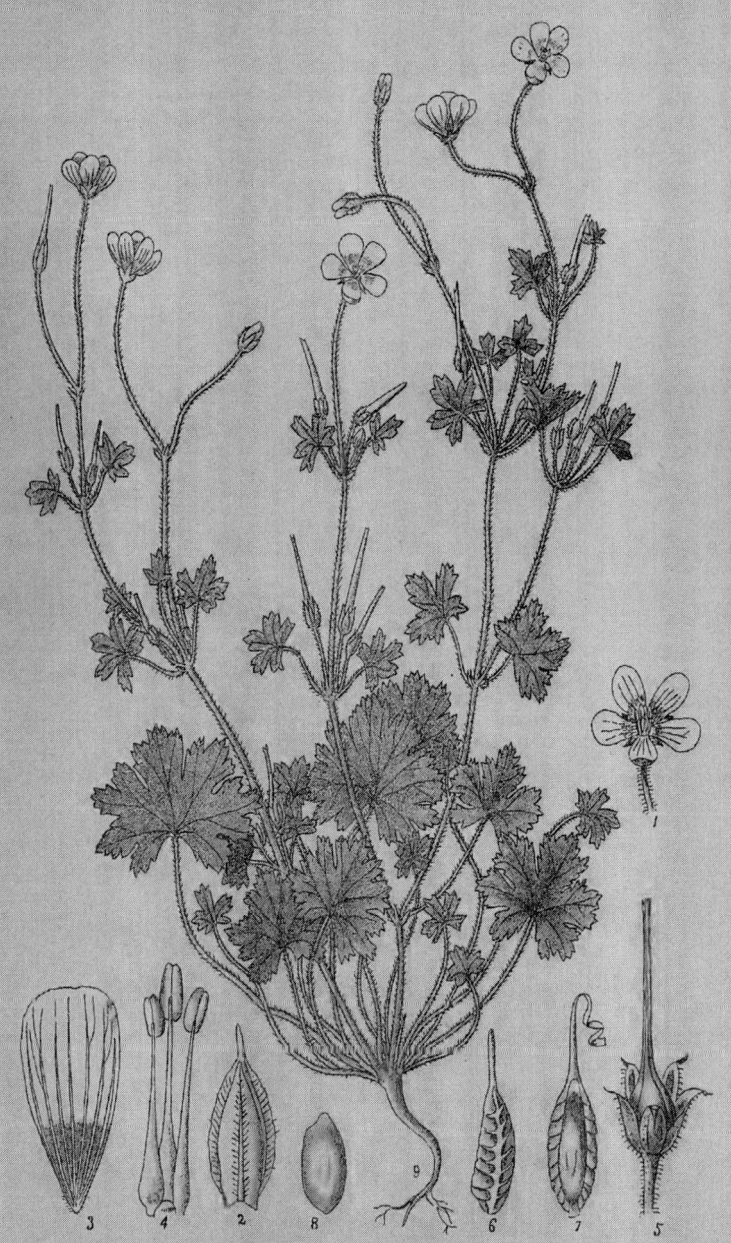

GERANIUM OCELLATUM, *CAMB.*

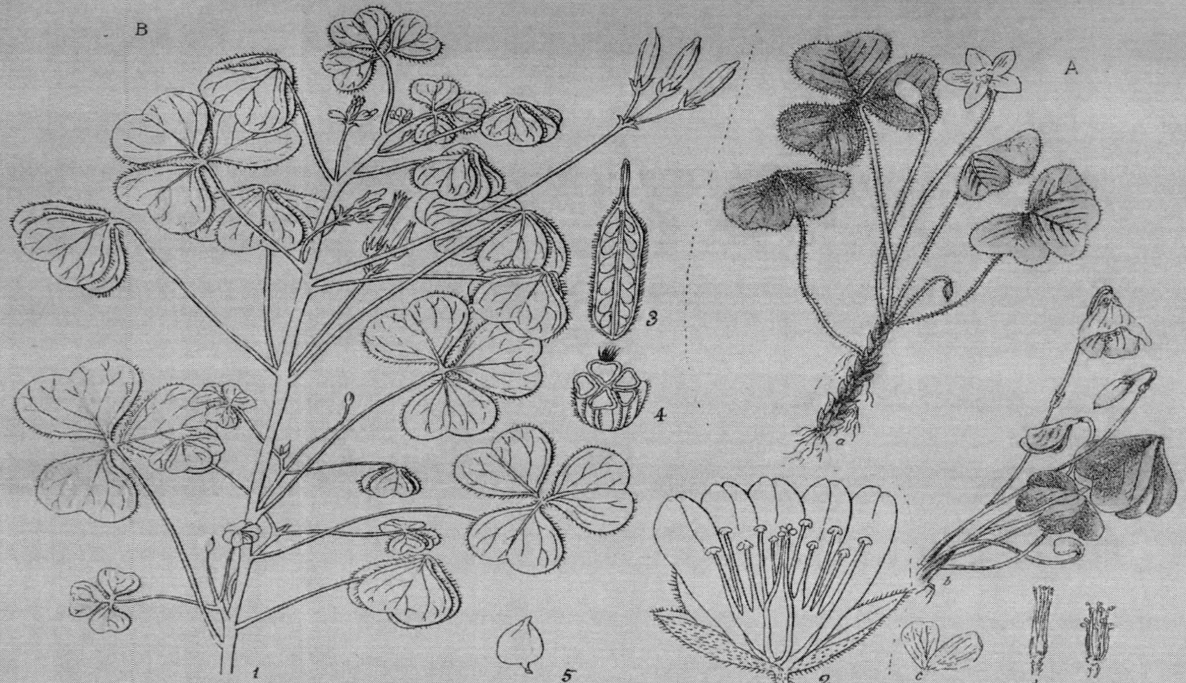

A—OXALIS ACETOSELLA, *LINN.* B—O. CORNICULATA, *LINN.*

PLATE No. 177

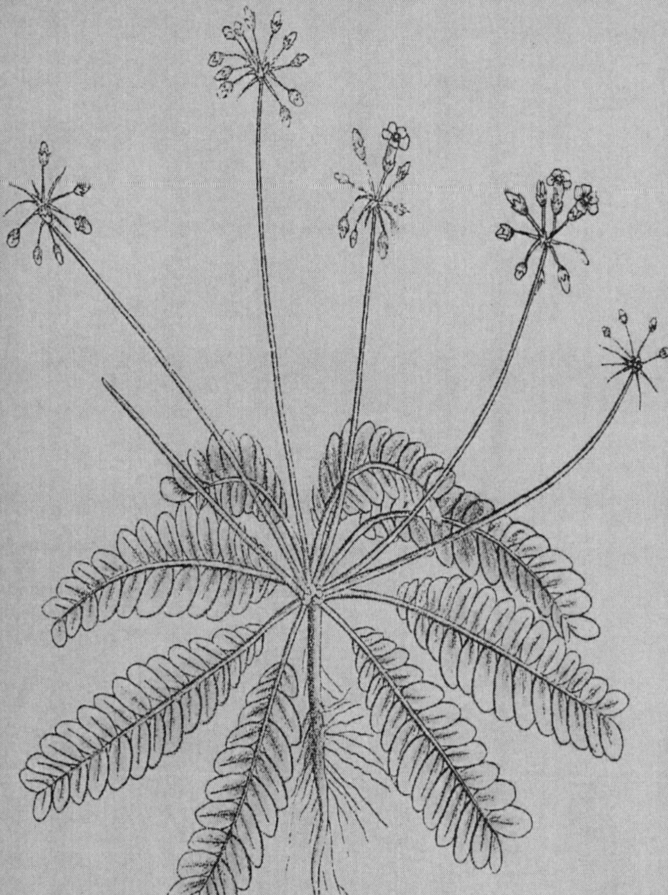

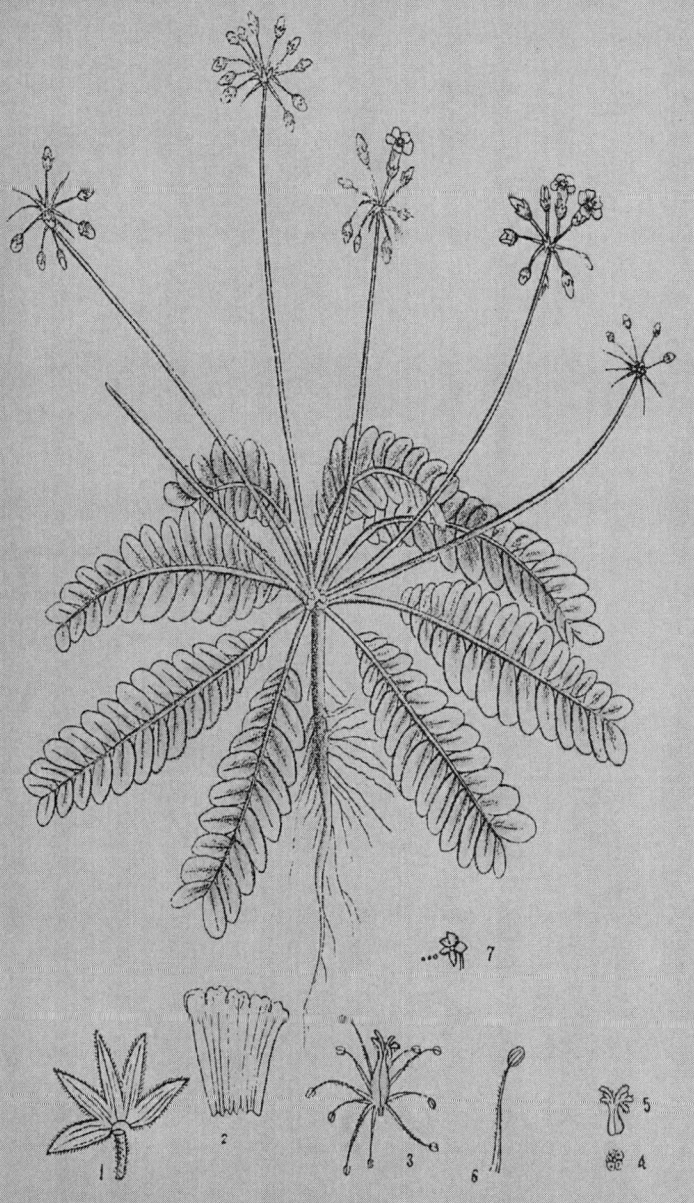

BIOPHYTUM SENSITIVUM. DC.

PLATE No. 178.

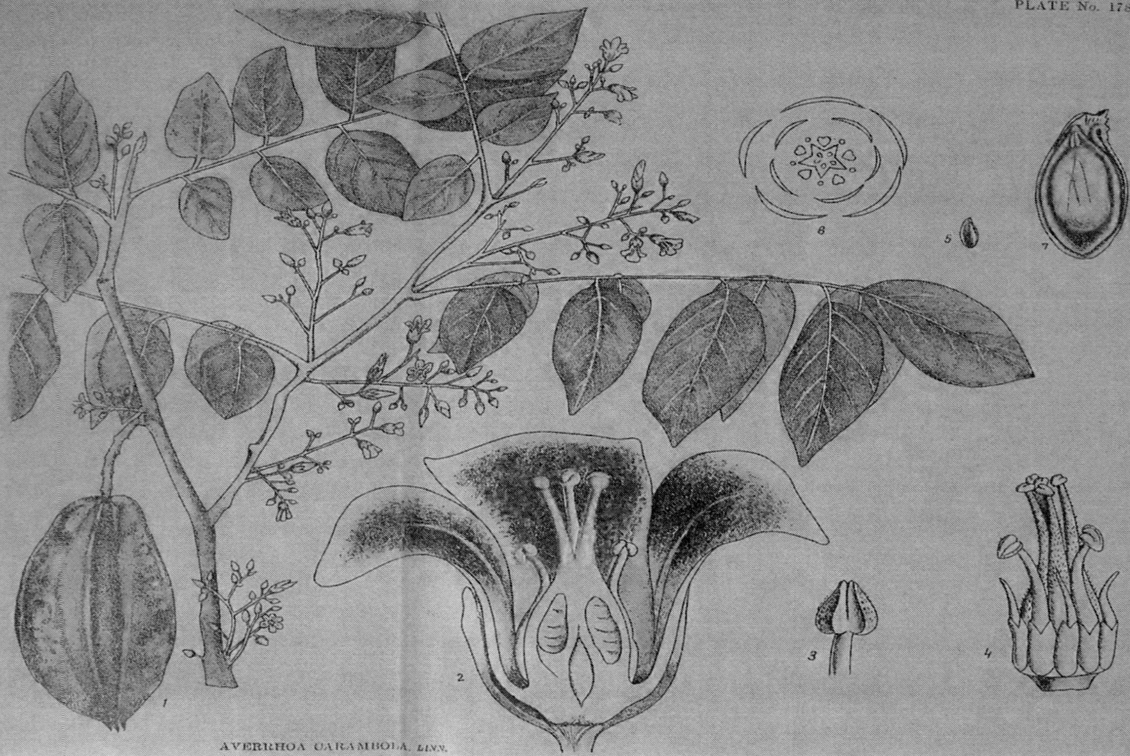

AVERRHOA CARAMBOLA, LINN.

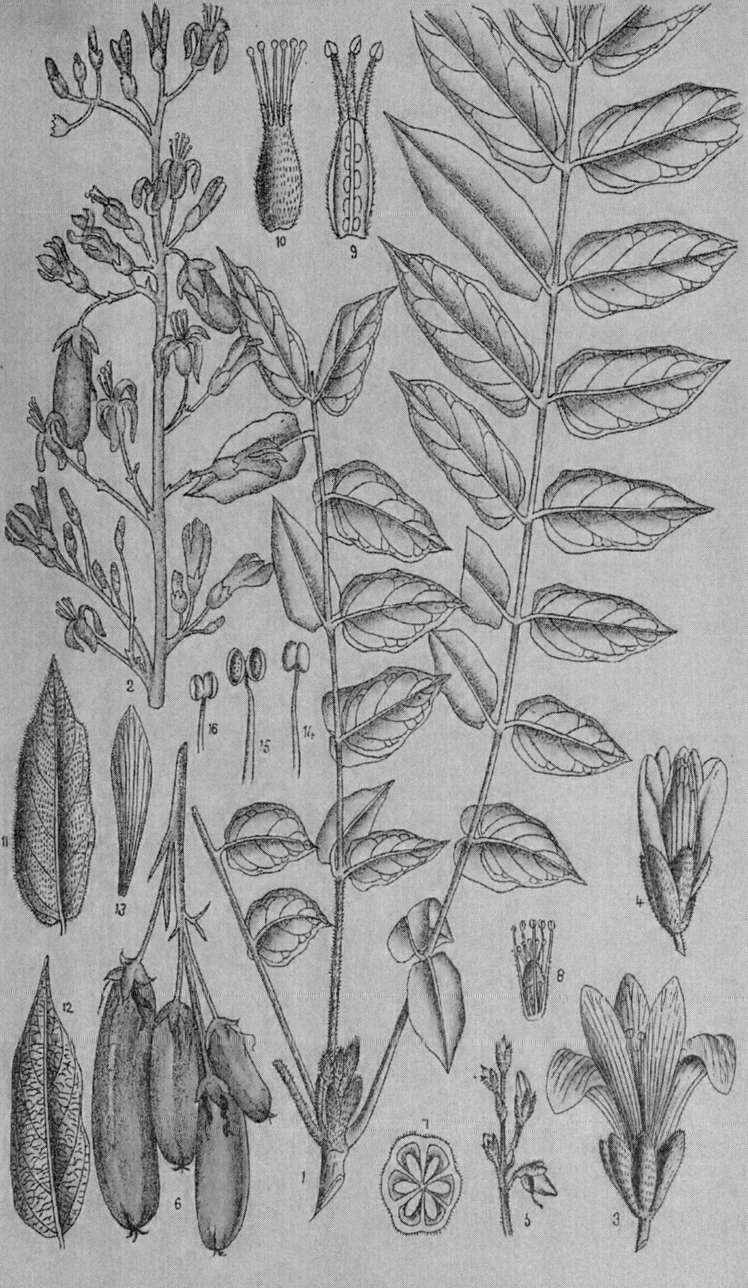

AVERRHOA BILIMBI, *LINN.*

PLATE No. 180.

IMPATIENS BALSAMINA, *LINN.*

PLATE No. 181.

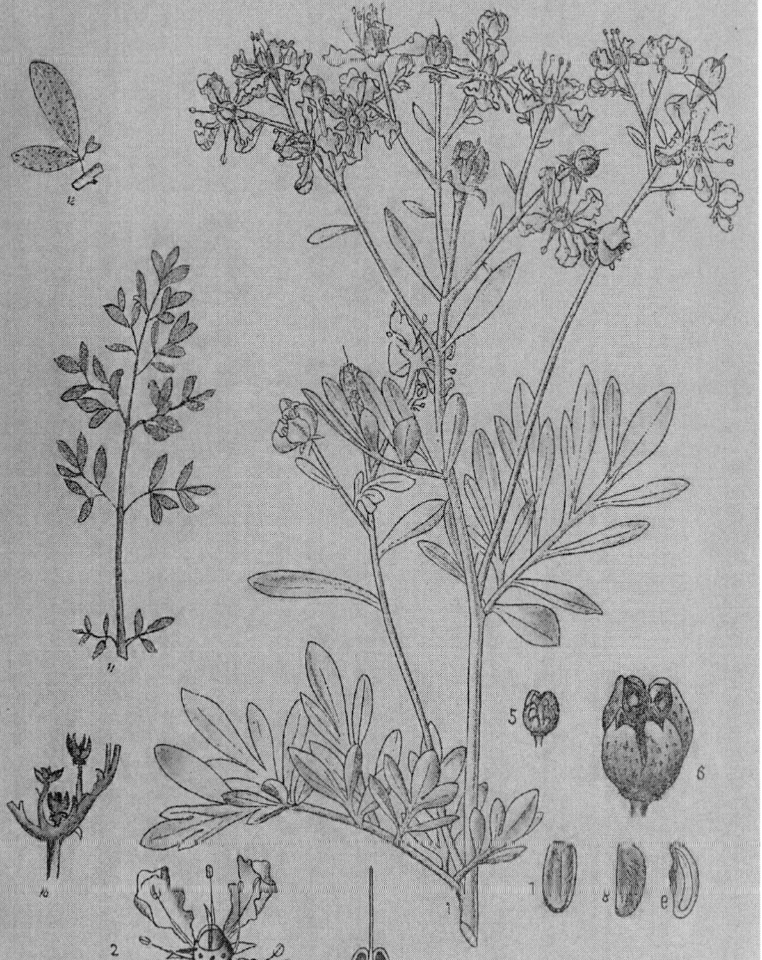

RUTA GRAVEOLENS, *LINN.*

PLATE No. 182.

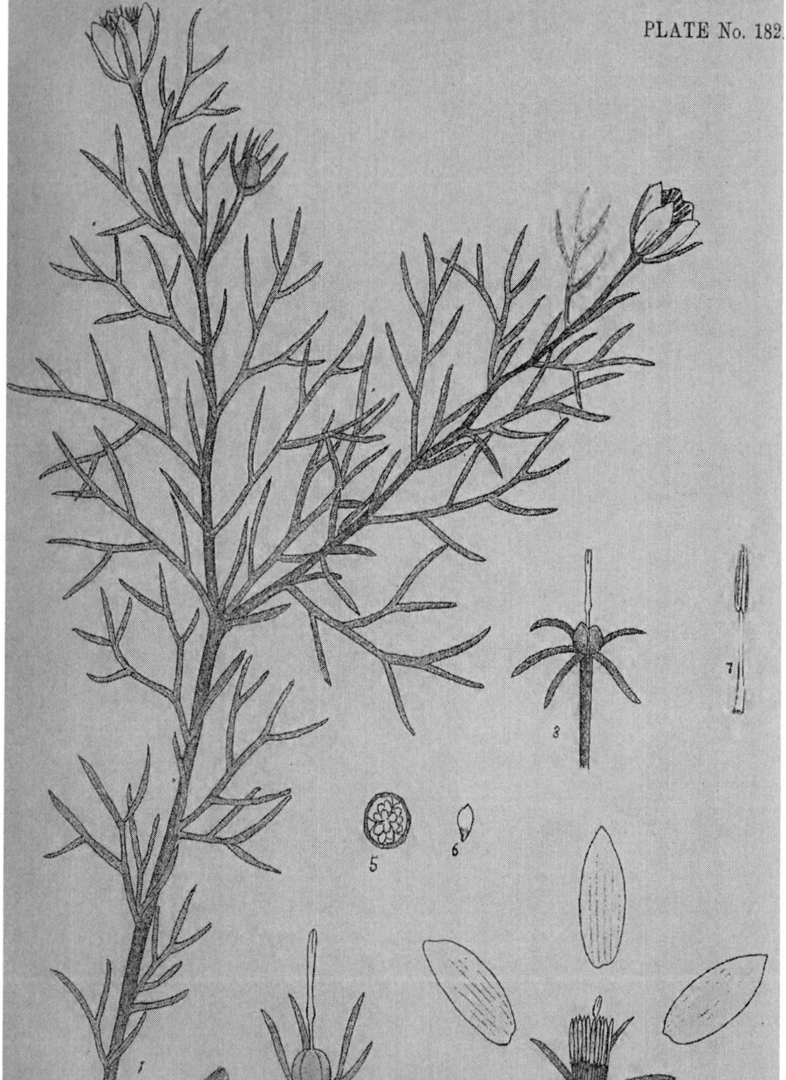

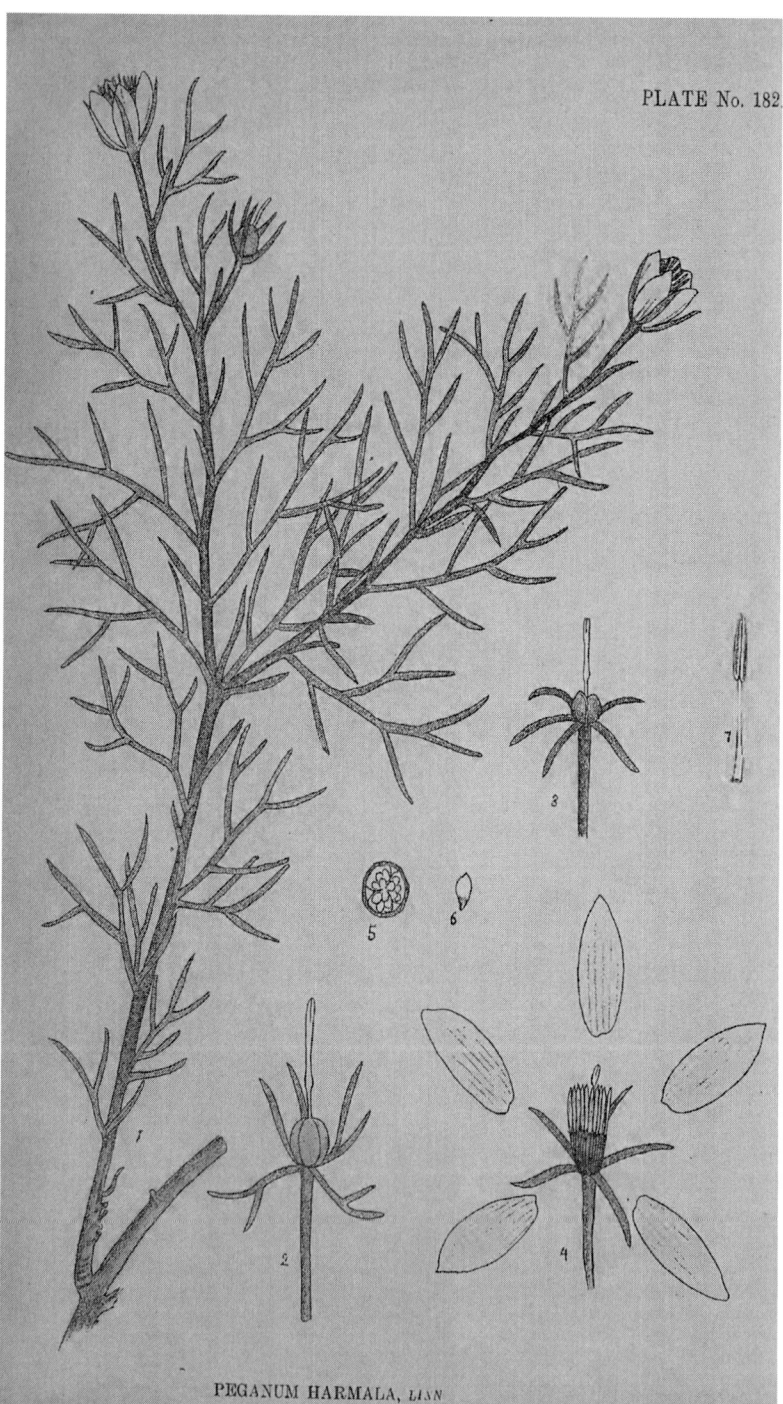

PEGANUM HARMALA, LINN

PLATE No. 183.

DIOTAMNUS ALBUS, *LINN.*

PLATE No. 184.

ZANTHOXYLUM ALATUM, ROXB.

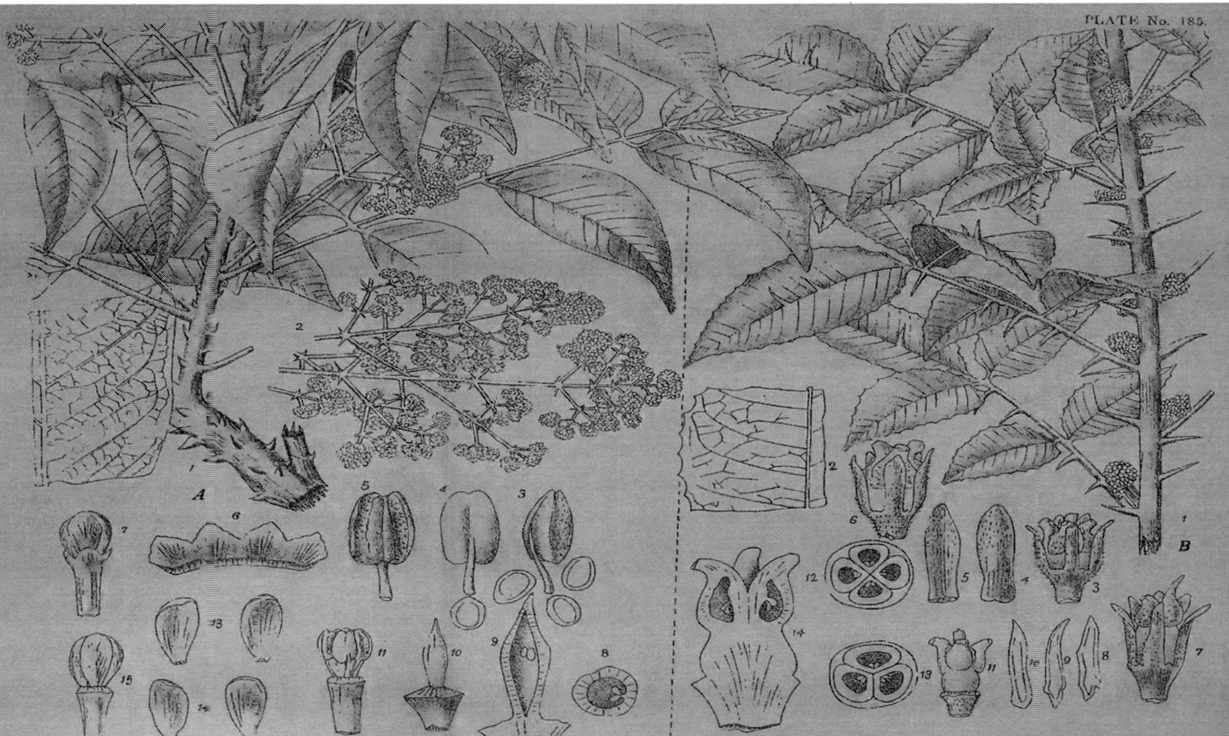

A—ZANTHOXYLUM RHETSA, *DC.* B—Z. ACANTHOPODIUM, *DC.*

PLATE No. 186

ZANTHOXYLUM OXYPHYLLUM, EDGEW.

PLATE No. 187.

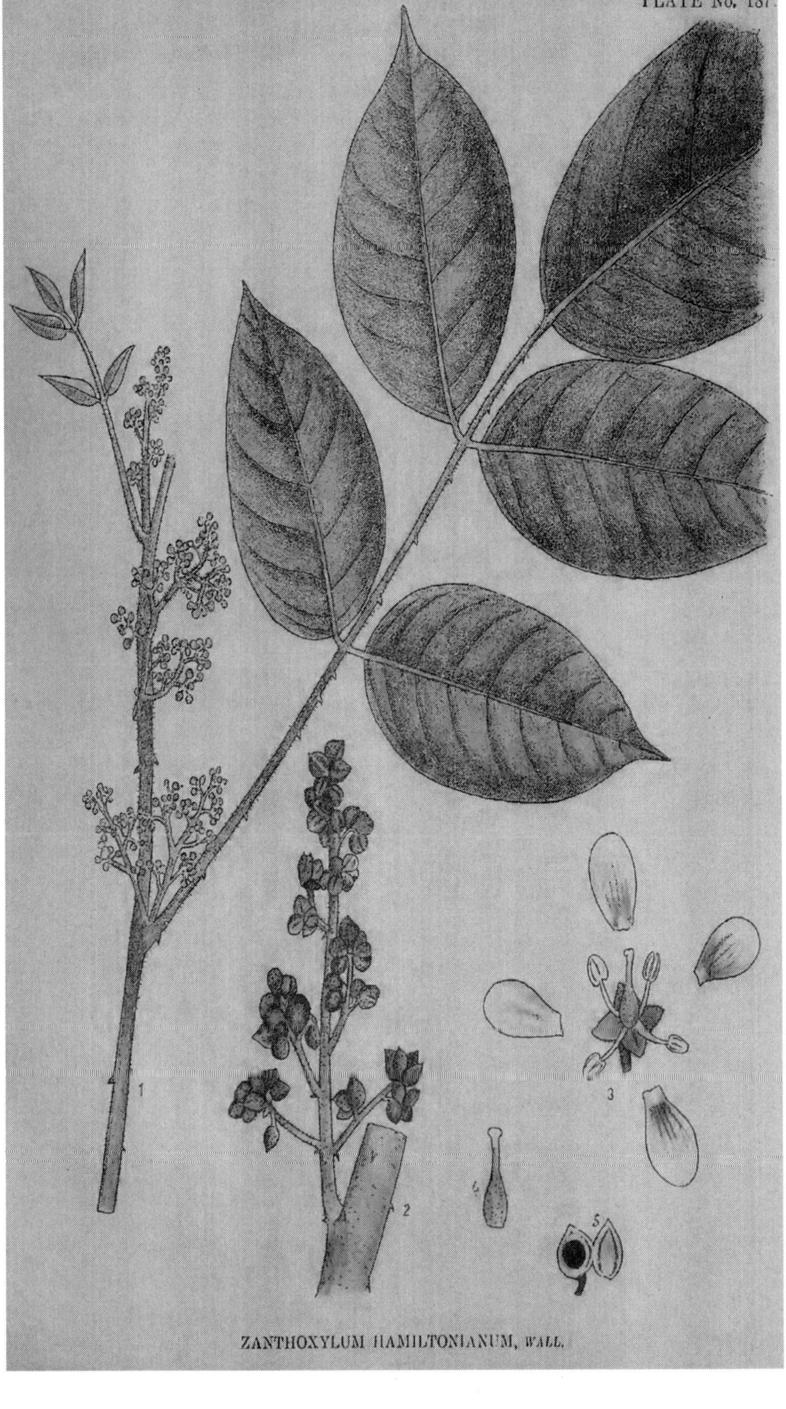

ZANTHOXYLUM HAMILTONIANUM, *WALL.*

PLATE No. 188.

ZANTHOXYLUM BUDRUNGA, WALL.

PLATE No. 189.

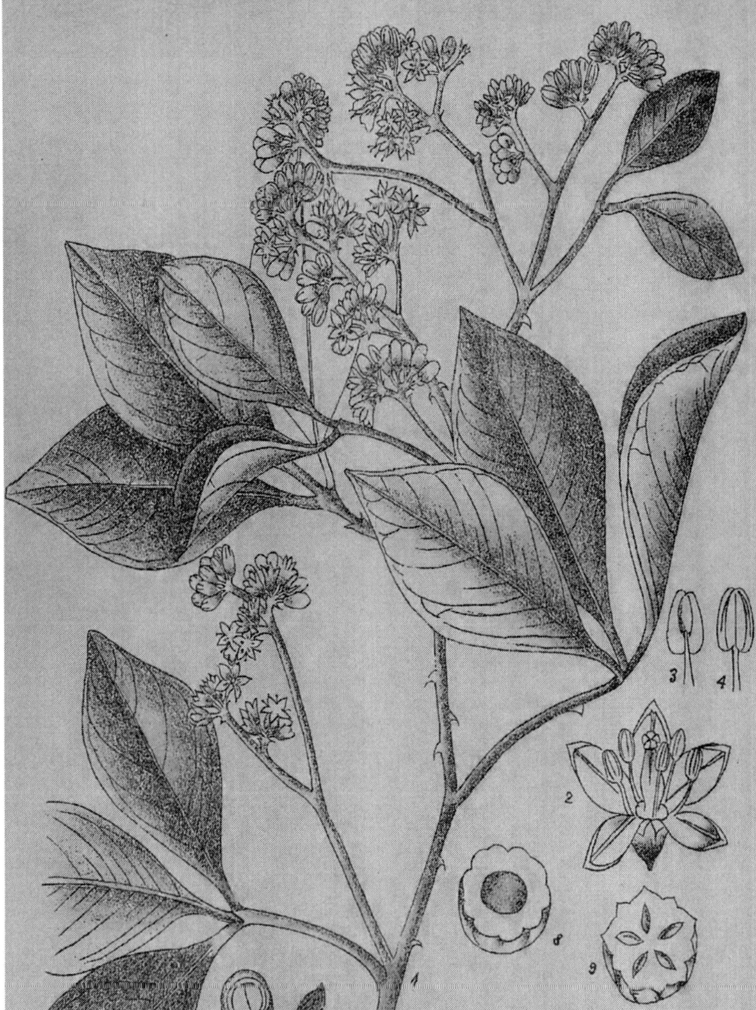

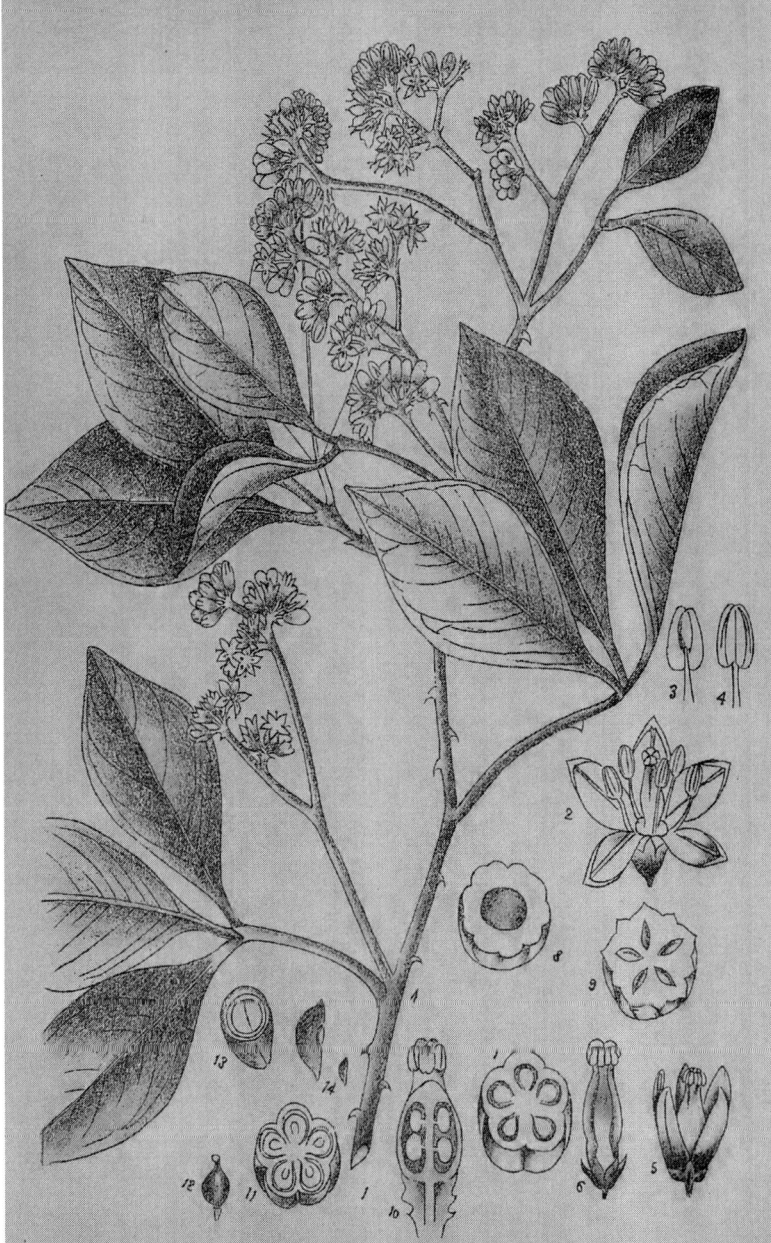

TODDALIA ACULEATA, *PERS.*

PLATE No. 190.

ACRONYCHIA LAURIFOLIA, *BLUME.*

PLATE No. 191.

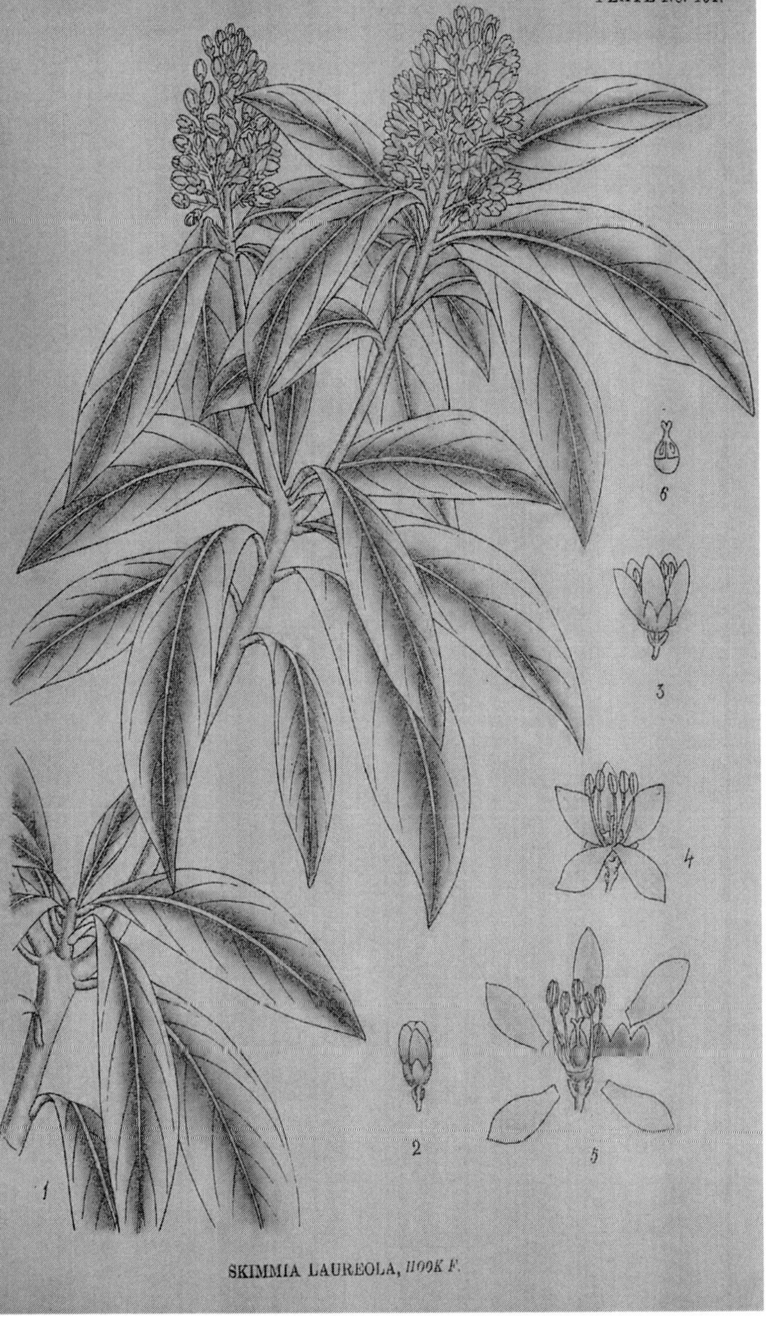

SKIMMIA LAUREOLA, *HOOK F.*

PLATE No. 192.

MURRAYA KŒNIGII, SPRENG.

PLATE No. 193

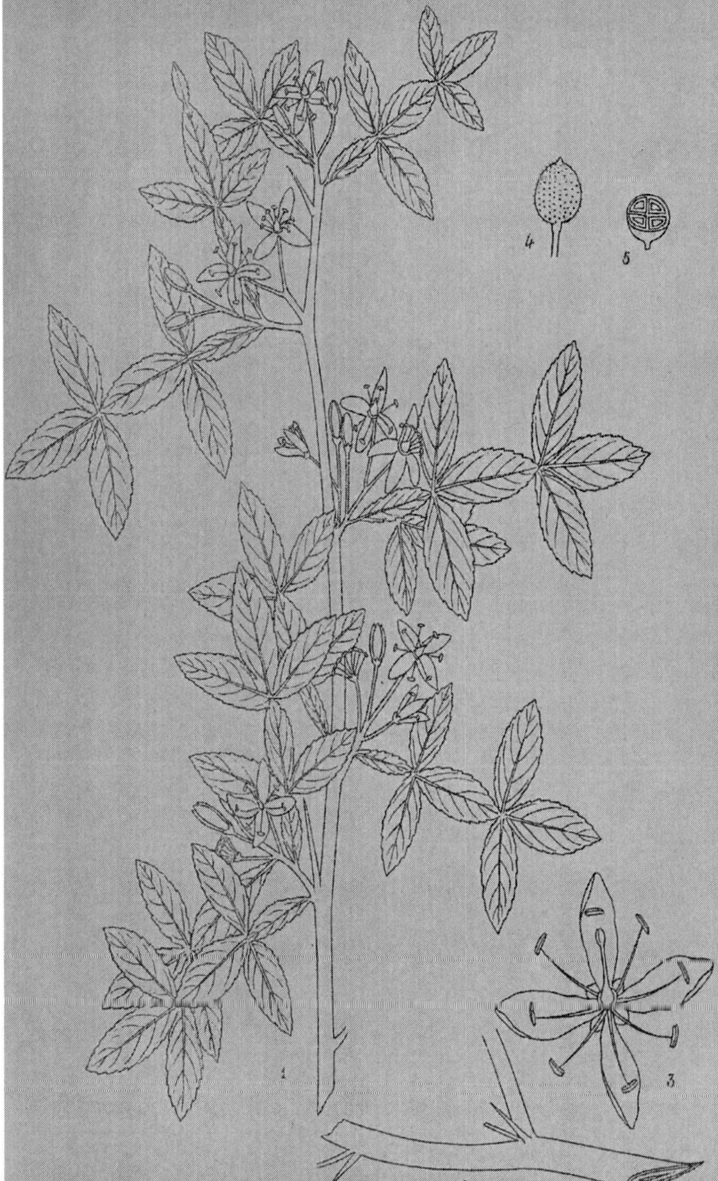

LIMONIA ACIDISSIMA, *LINN.*

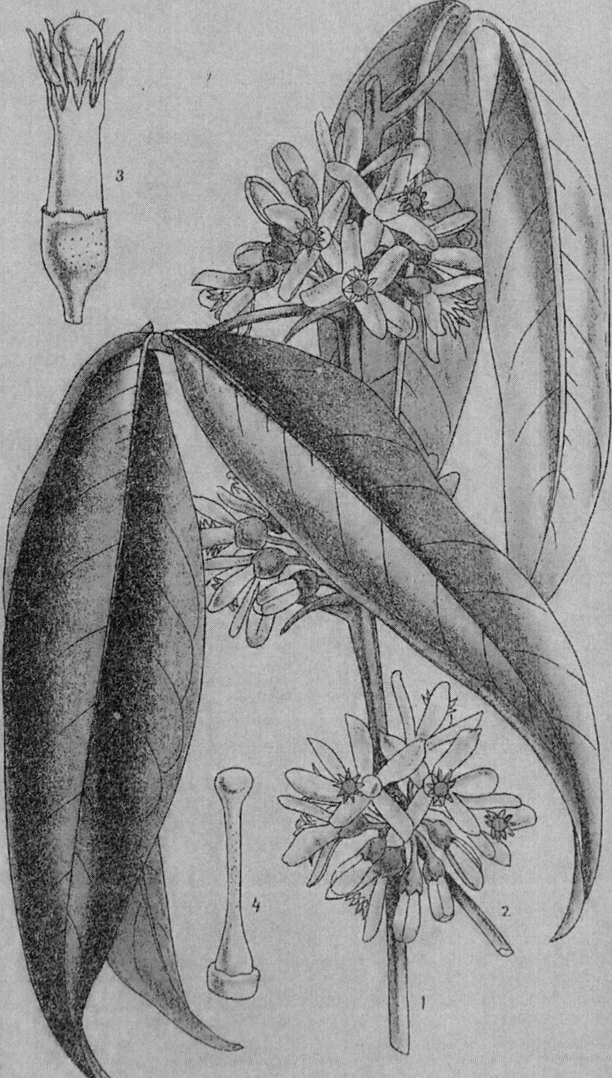

LUVUNGA SCANDENS, *HAM.*

PLATE No. 195.

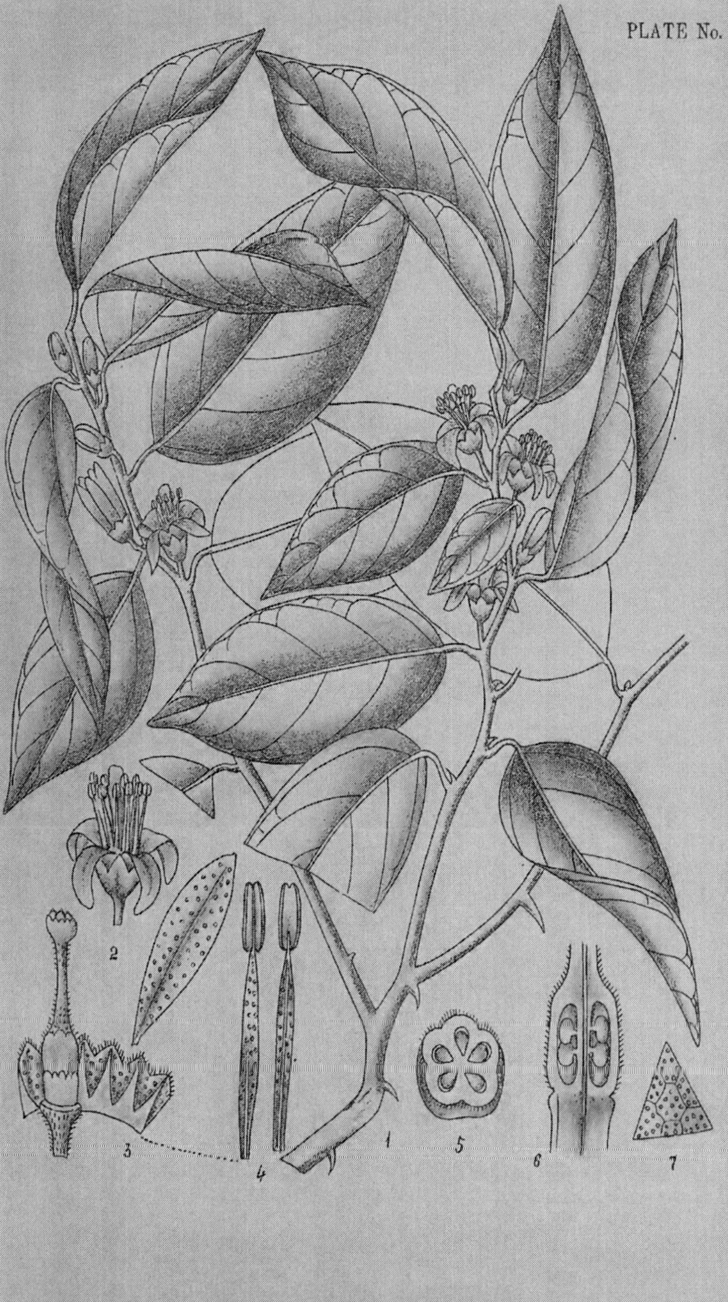

PARAMIGNYA MONOPHYLLA, WIGHT

PLATE No. 196.

PARAMIGNYA LONGISPINA, *HOOK. F.*

PLATE No. 197.

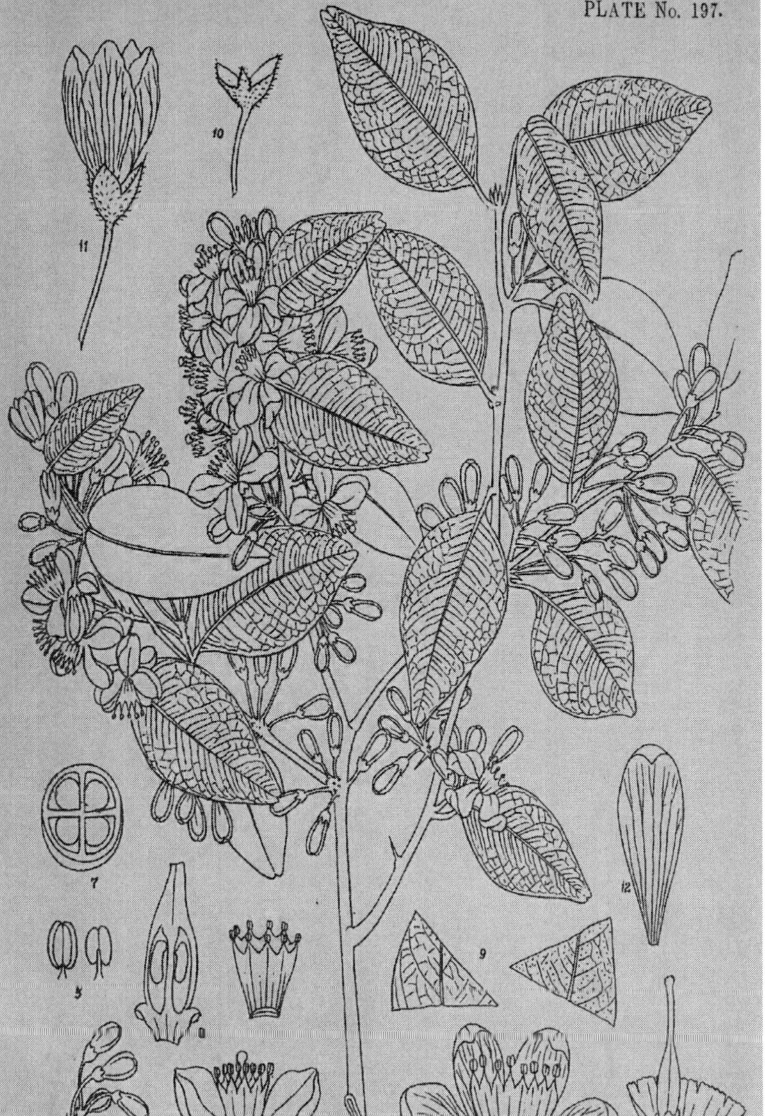

ATALANTIA MONOPHYLLA, CORR.

PLATE No. 198

CITRUS MEDICA, *LINN.*

PLATE No. 199

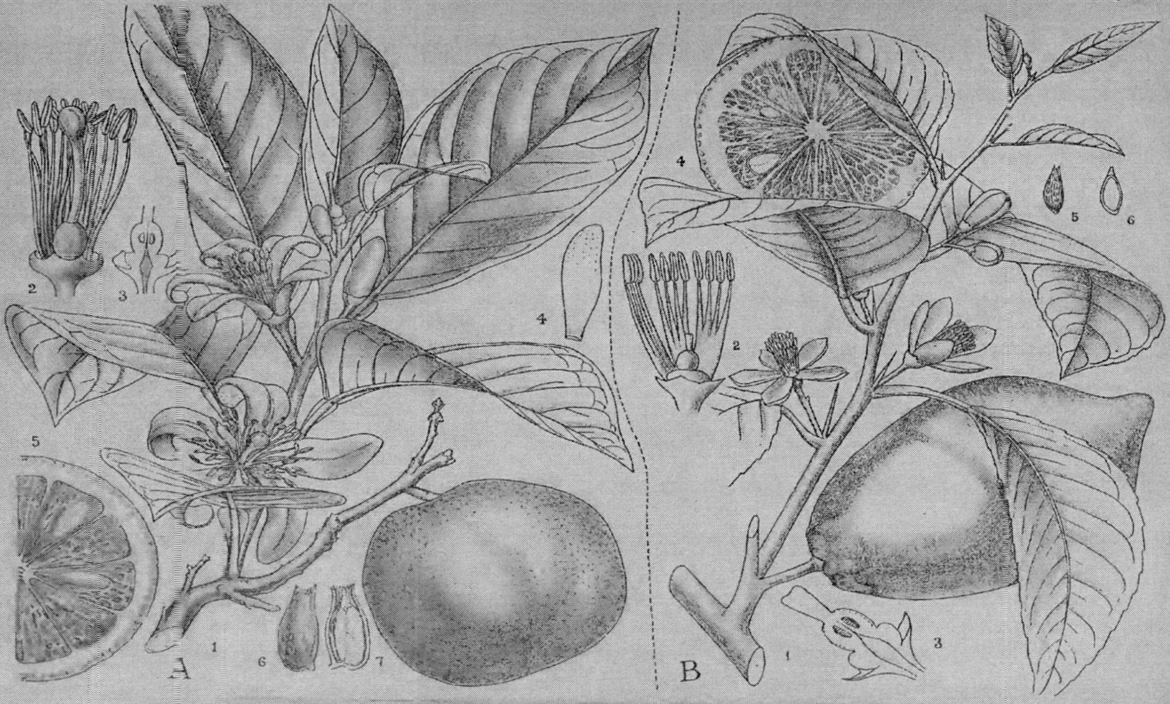

A—OITRUS AURANTIUM, *LINN.* B. CITRUS LIMONUM, *WALL*

PLATE No. 200.

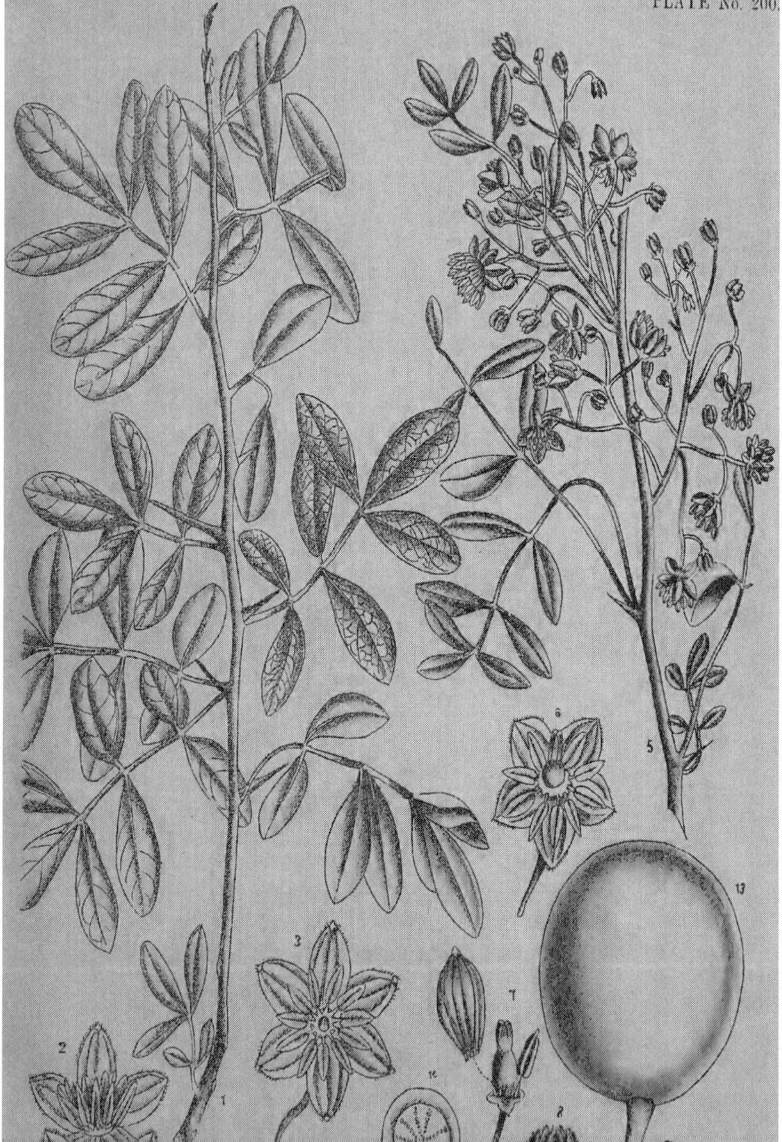

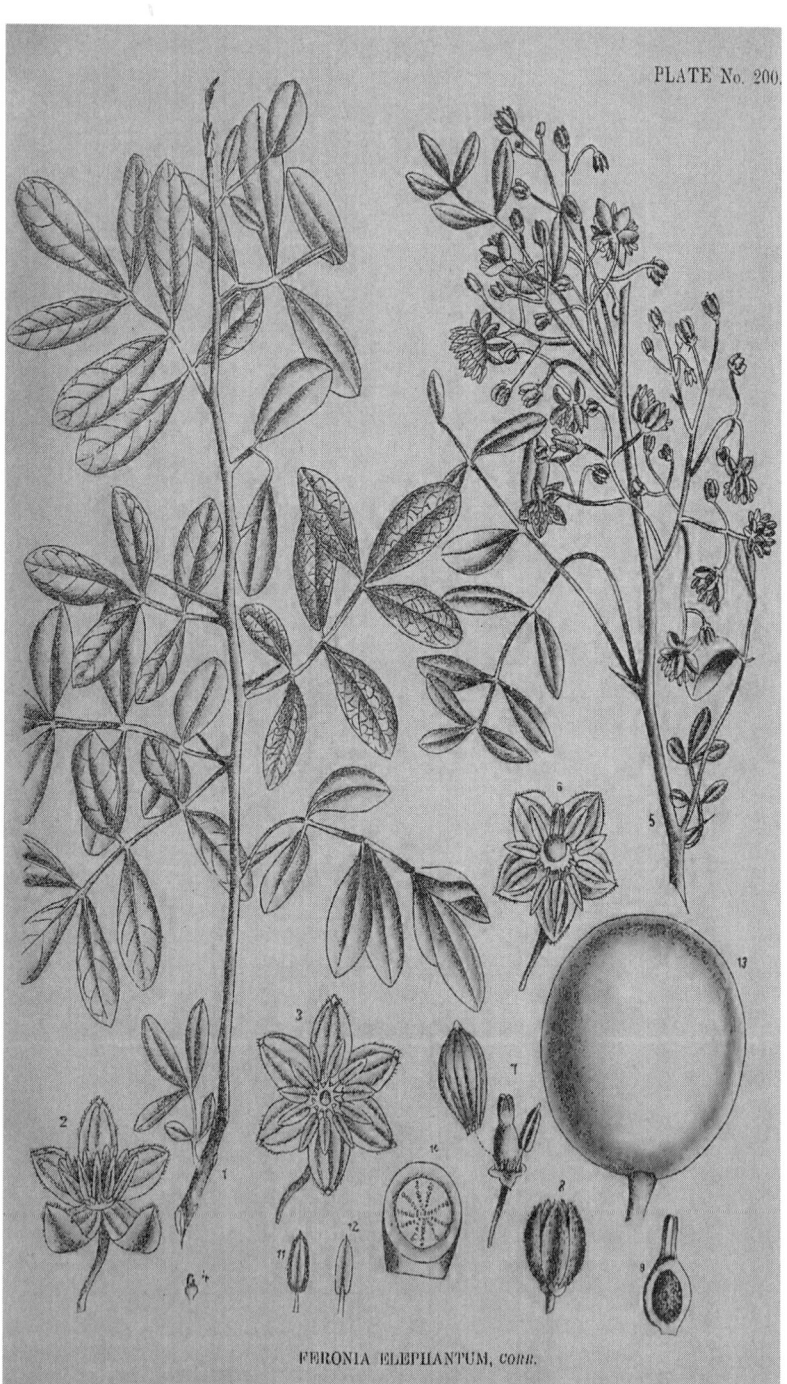

FERONIA ELEPHANTUM, CORR.

PLATE No. 201.

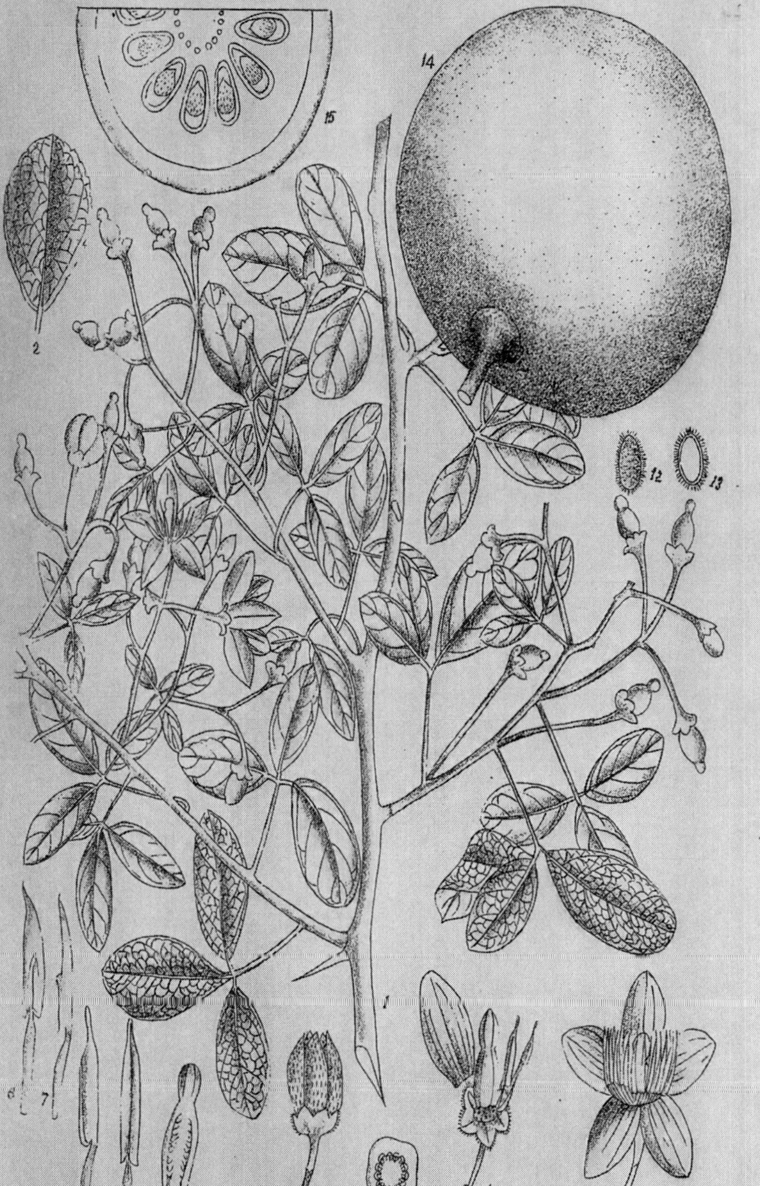

ÆGLE MARMELOS, *Correa.*

PLATE No. 202.

AILANTUS EXCELSA, *ROXB.*

PLATE No. 203.

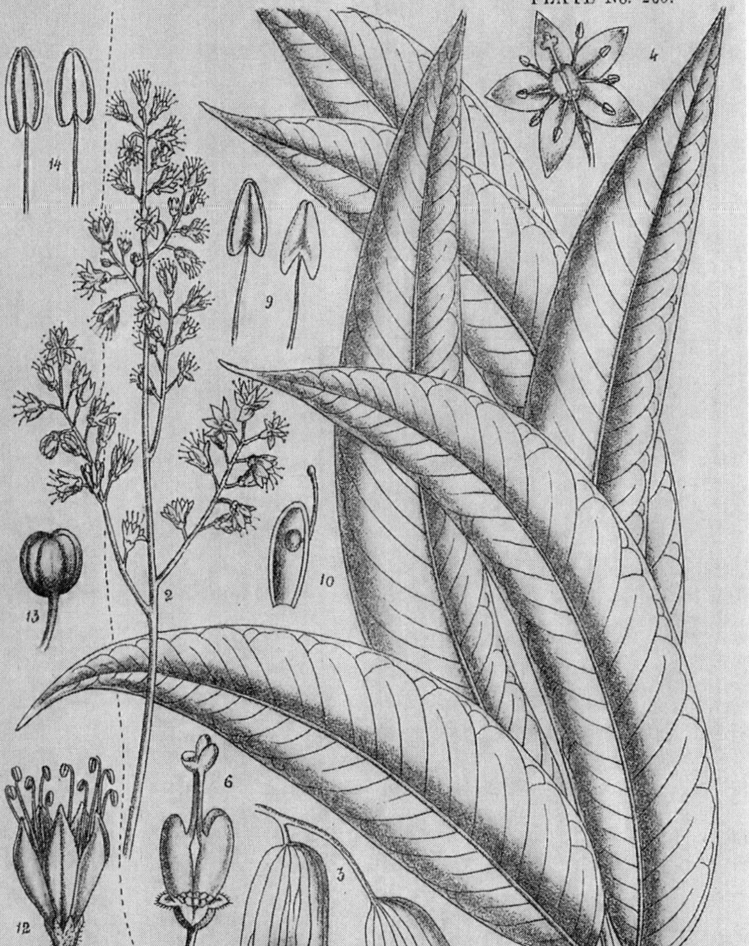

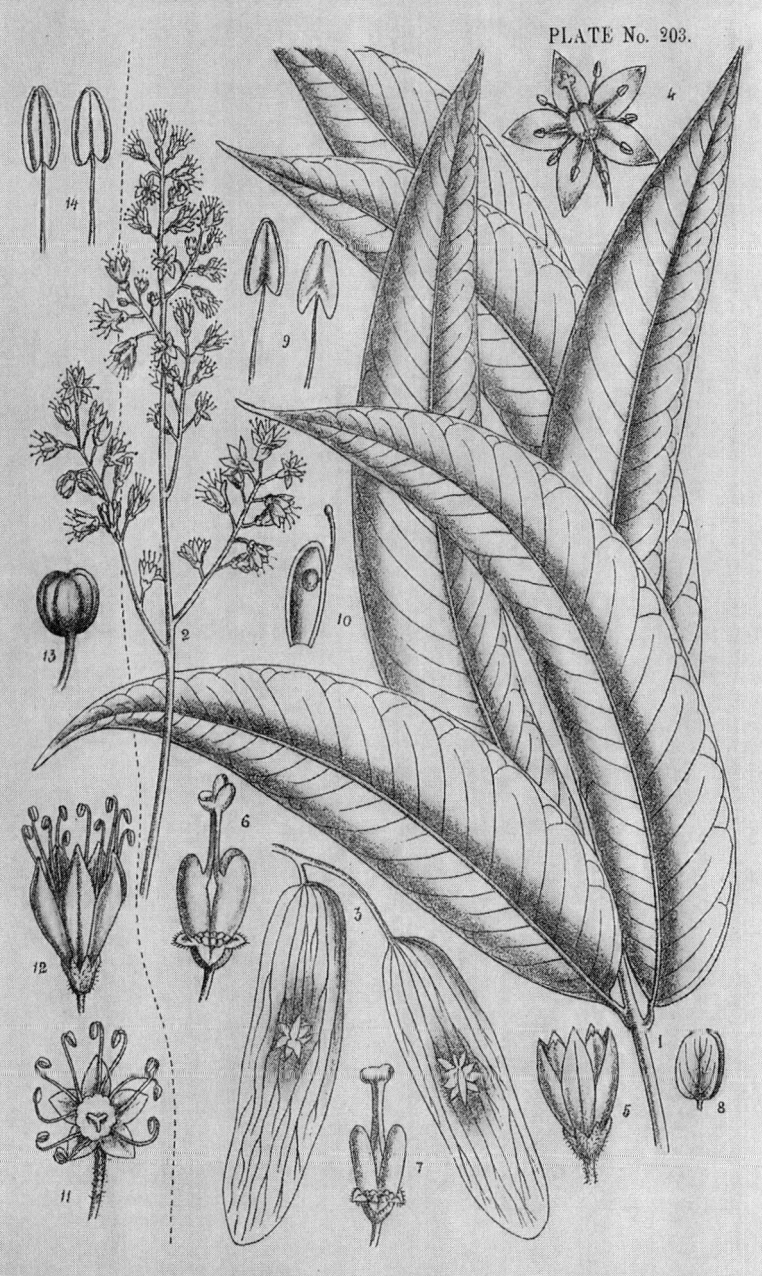

AILANTUS MALABARICA, *DC.*

PLATE No. 204.

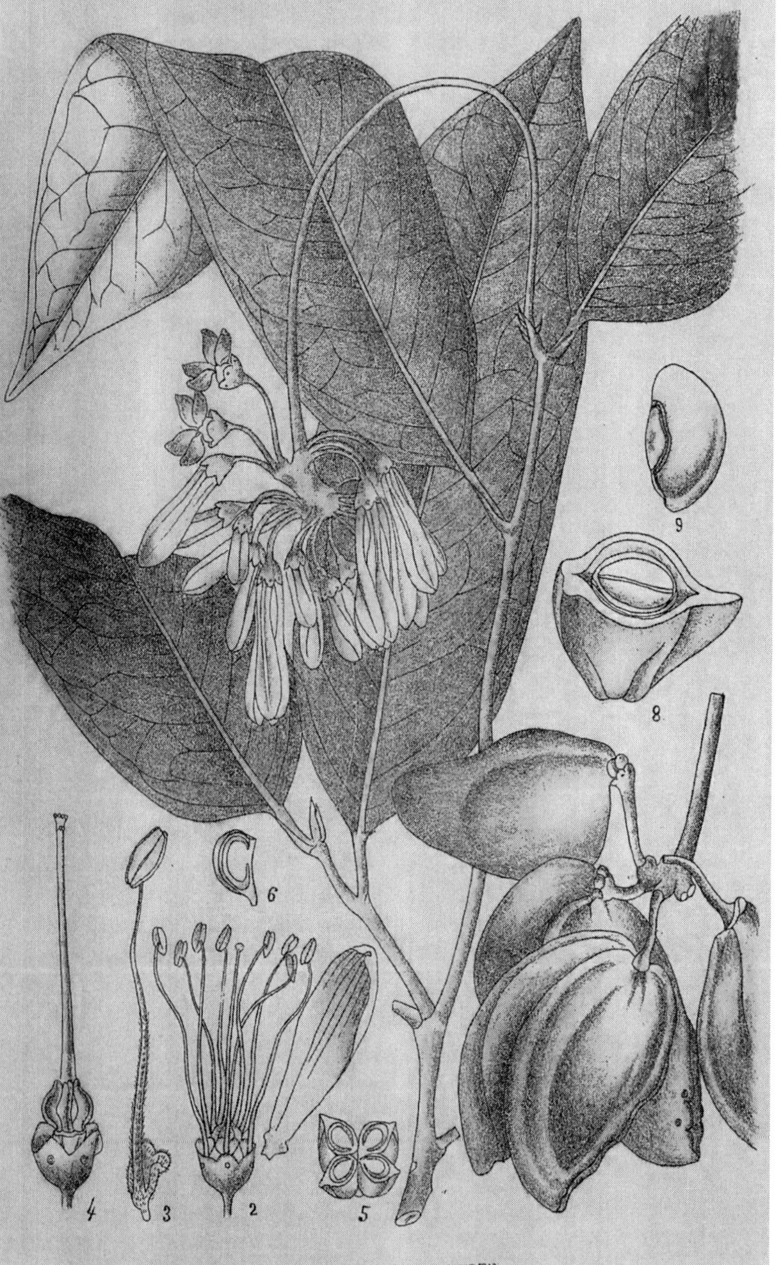

SAMADERA INDICA, *GÆRTN.*

PLATE No. 205.

PICRASMA QUASSIOIDES, *BENN.*

PLATE No 206.

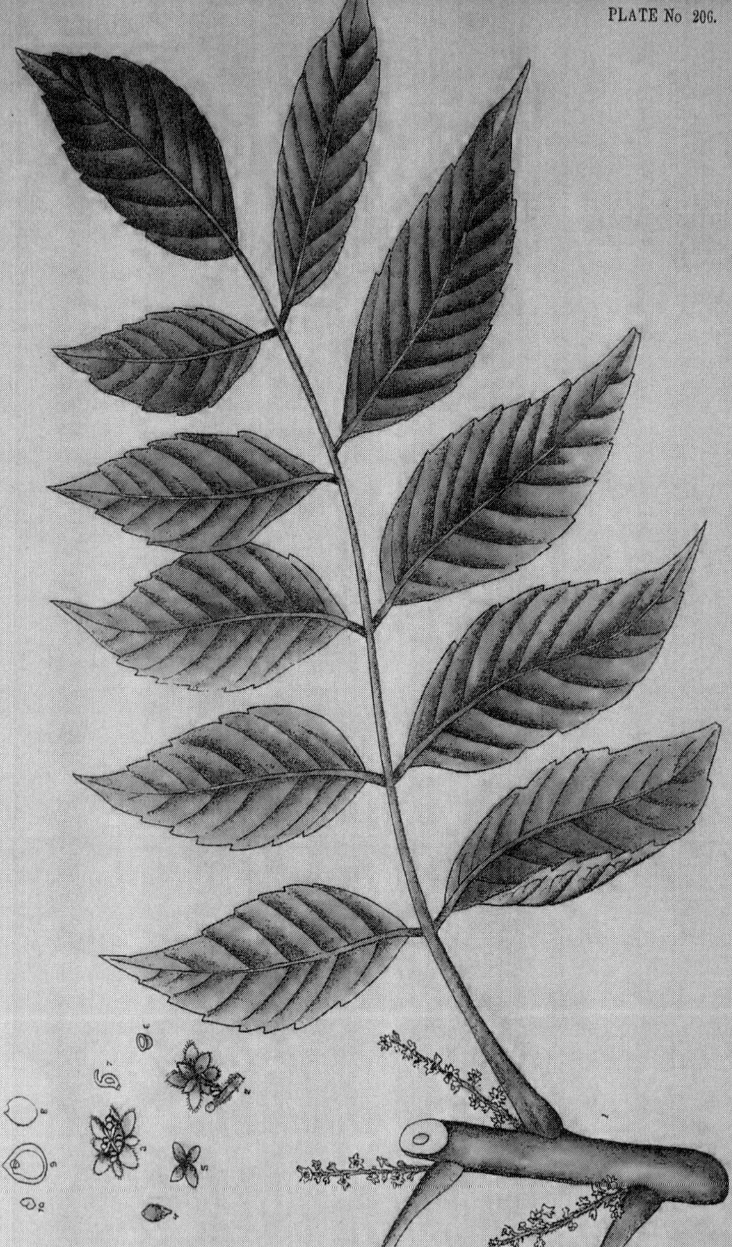

BRUCEA SUMATRANA, *ROXB.*

PLATE No. 207.

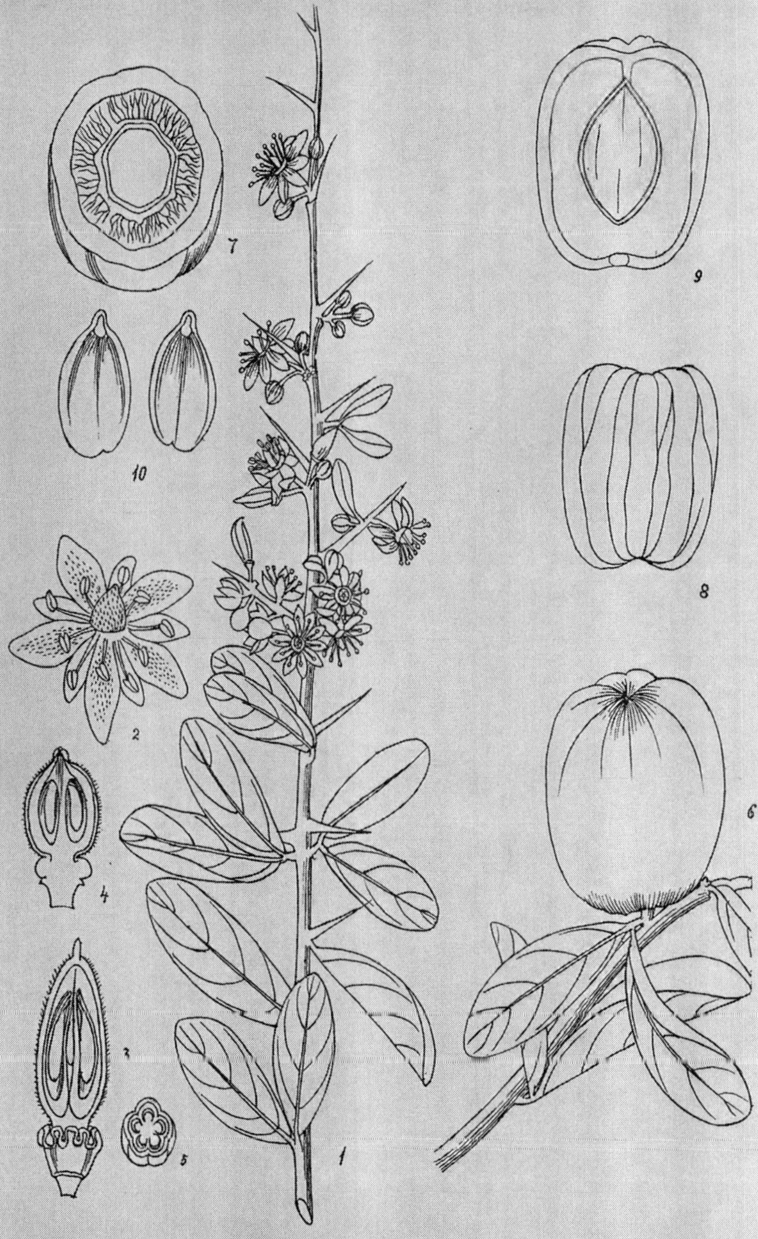

BALANITIS ROXBURGHII, *PLANCH.*

PLATE No. 208.

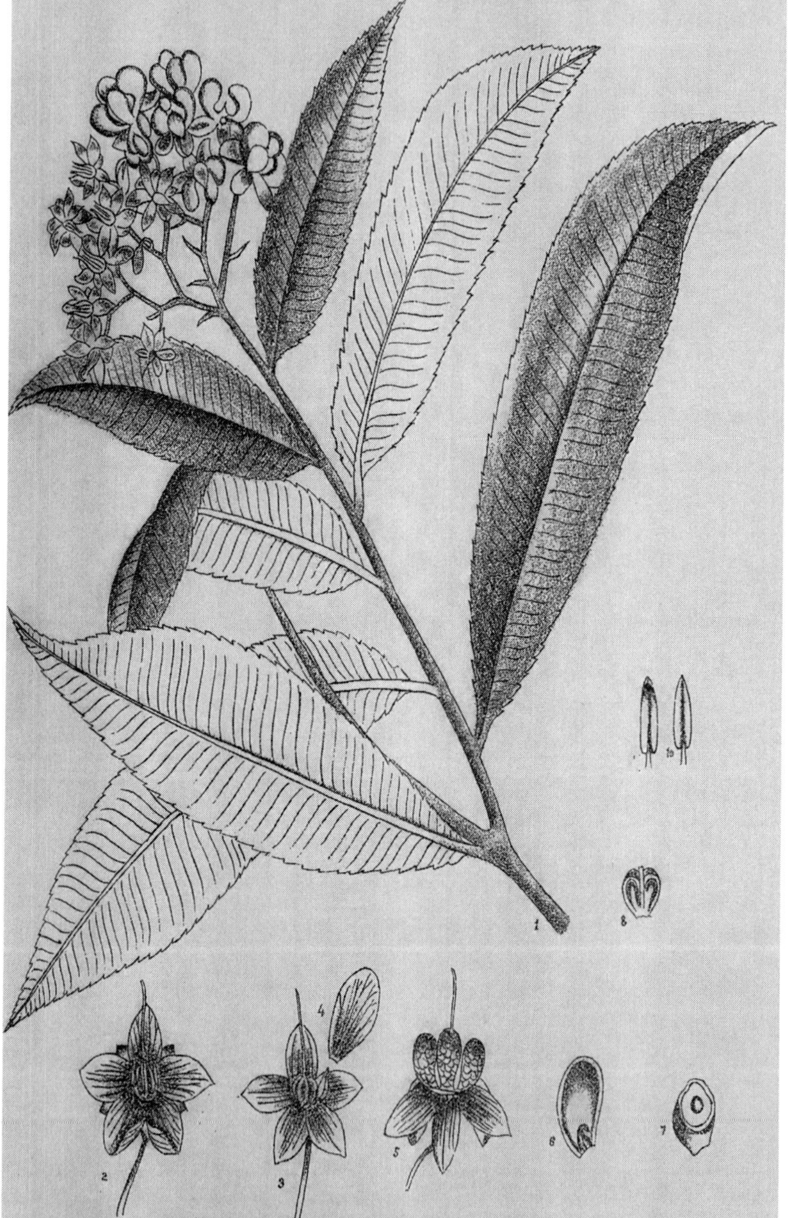

GOMPHIA ANGUSTIFOLIA, *VAHL.*

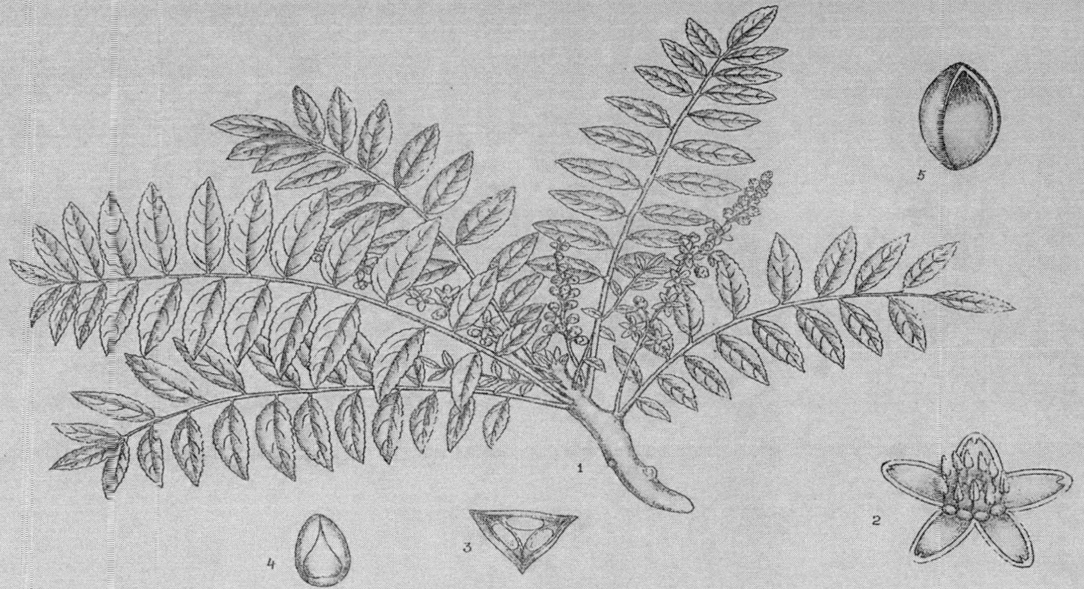

BOSWELLIA SERRATA, *ROXB.*

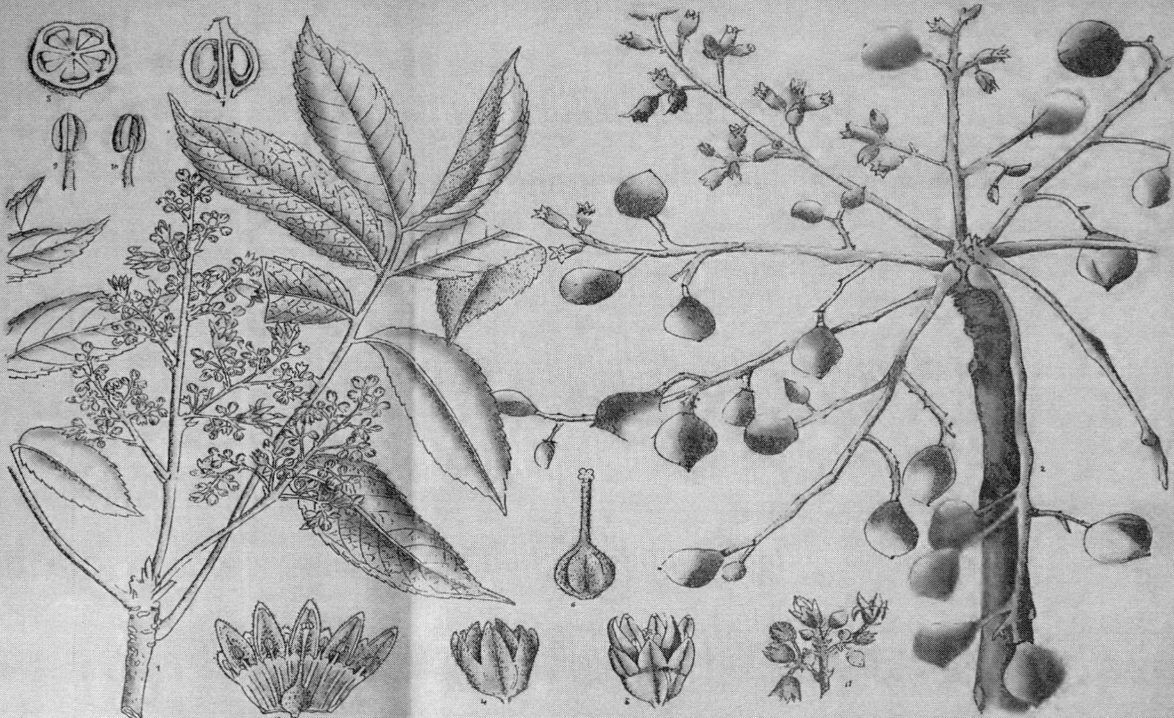

GARUGA PINNATA, *ROXB.*

PLATE No 211.

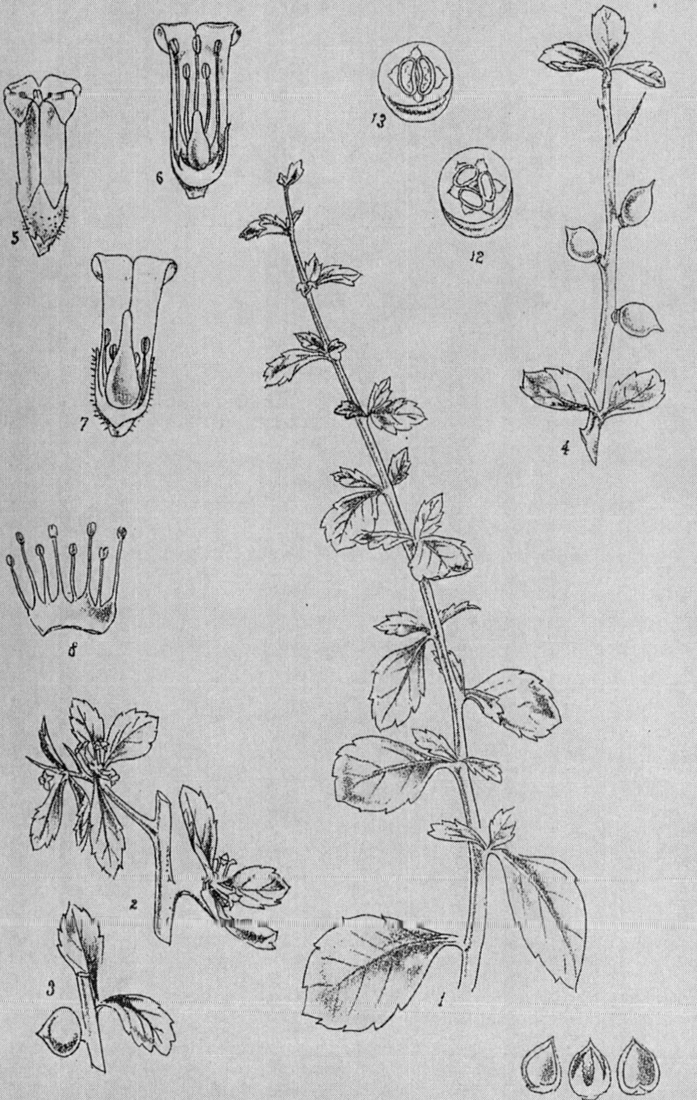

BALSAMODENDRON MUKUL, *STOCKS.*

PLATE No. 212.

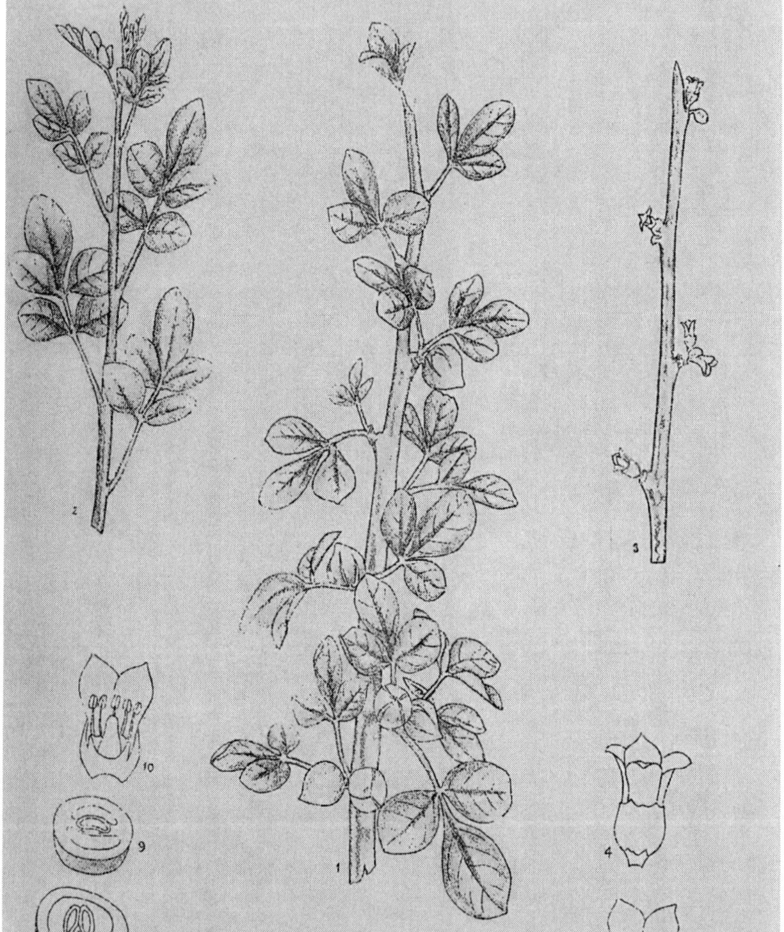

BALSAMODENDRON PUBESCENS, *STOCKS.*

PLATE No. 213.

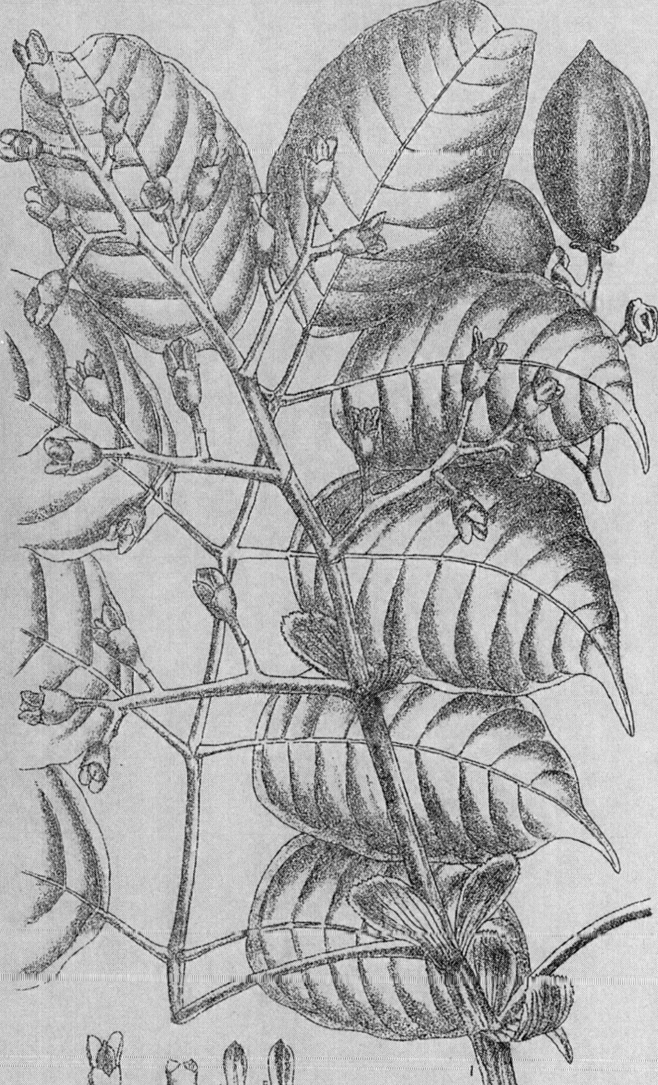

OANARIUM COMMUNE, *LINN.*

PLATE No. 214.

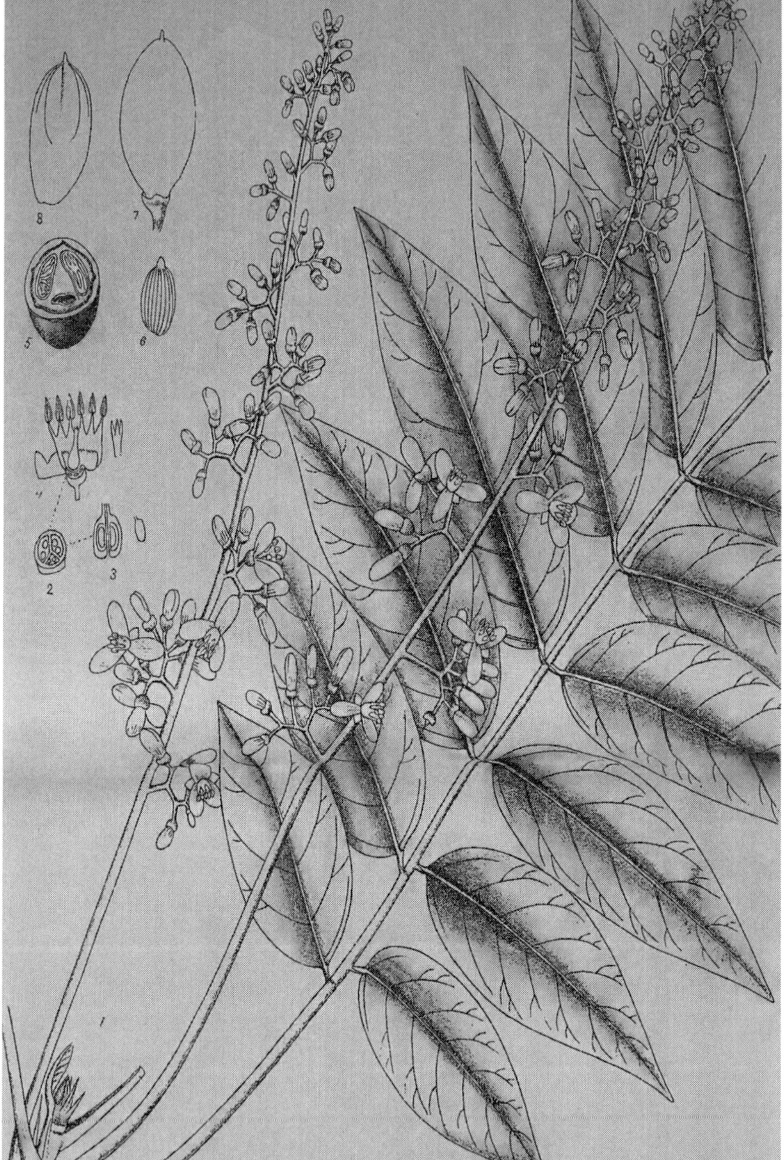

CANARIUM STRICTUM, *ROXB.*

PLATE No. 215.

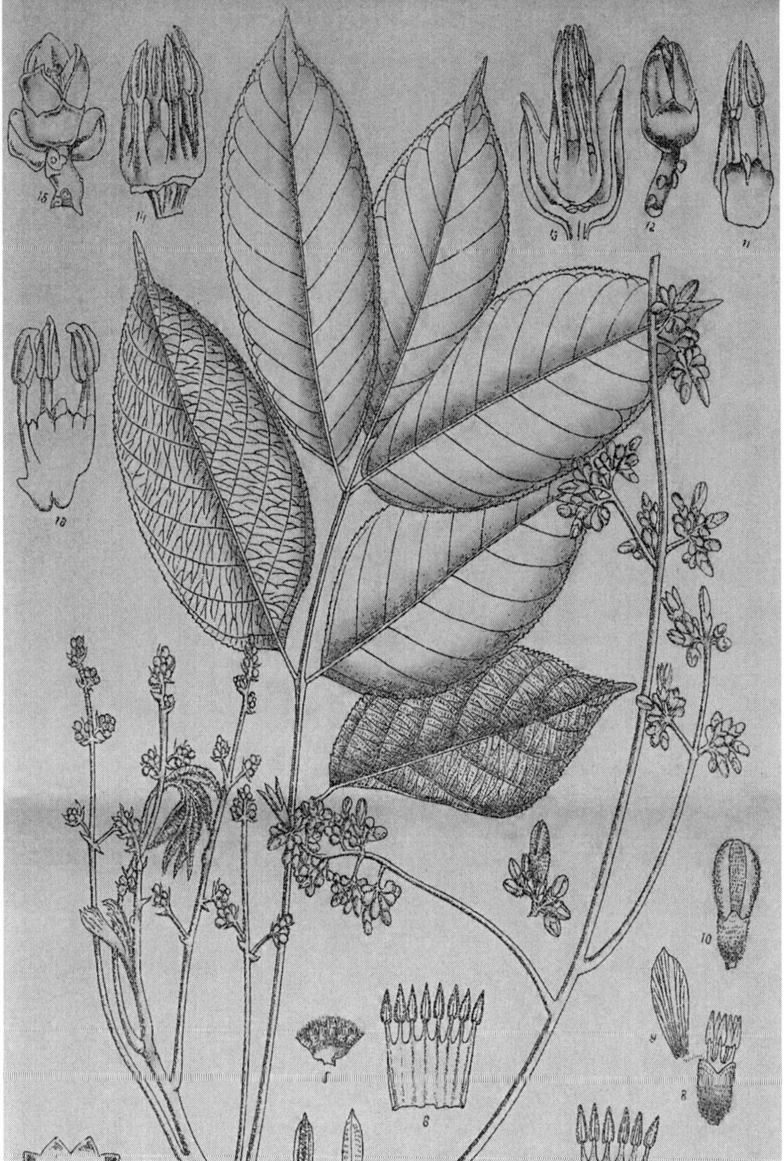

CANARIUM BENGALENSE, *ROXB.*

PLATE No. 216.

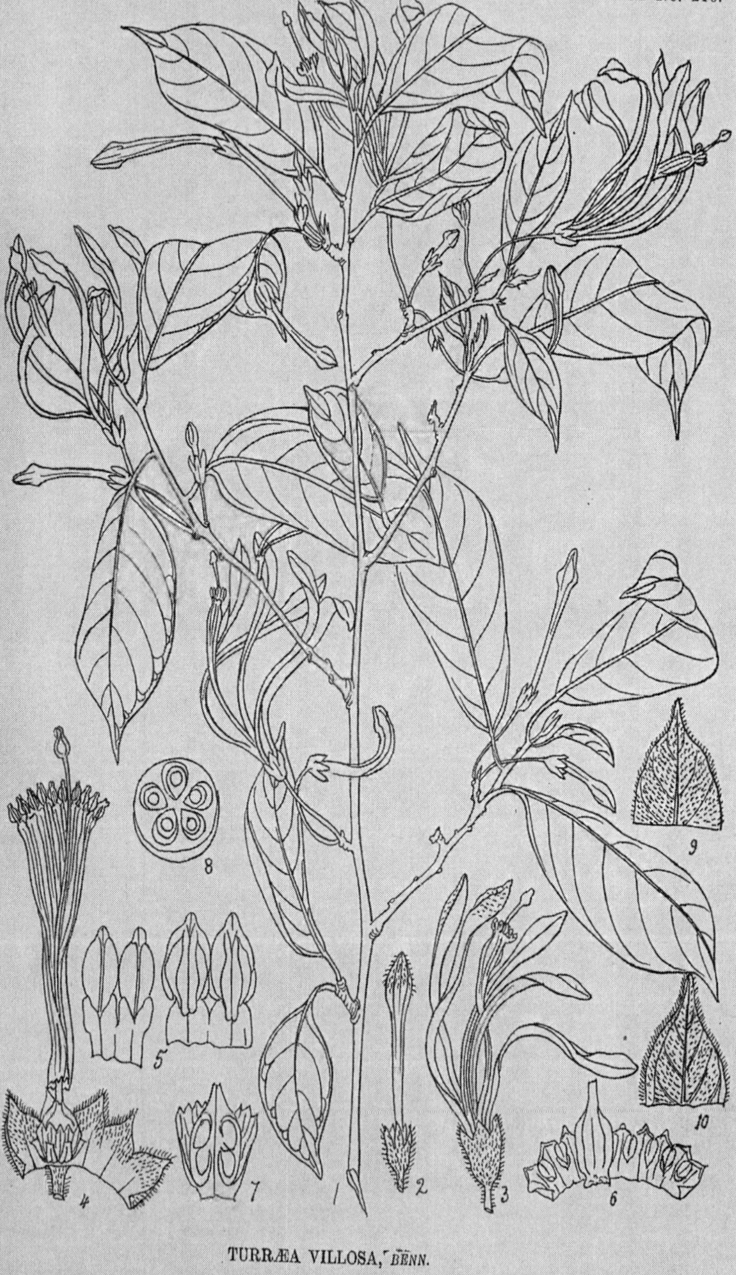

TURRÆA VILLOSA, BENN.

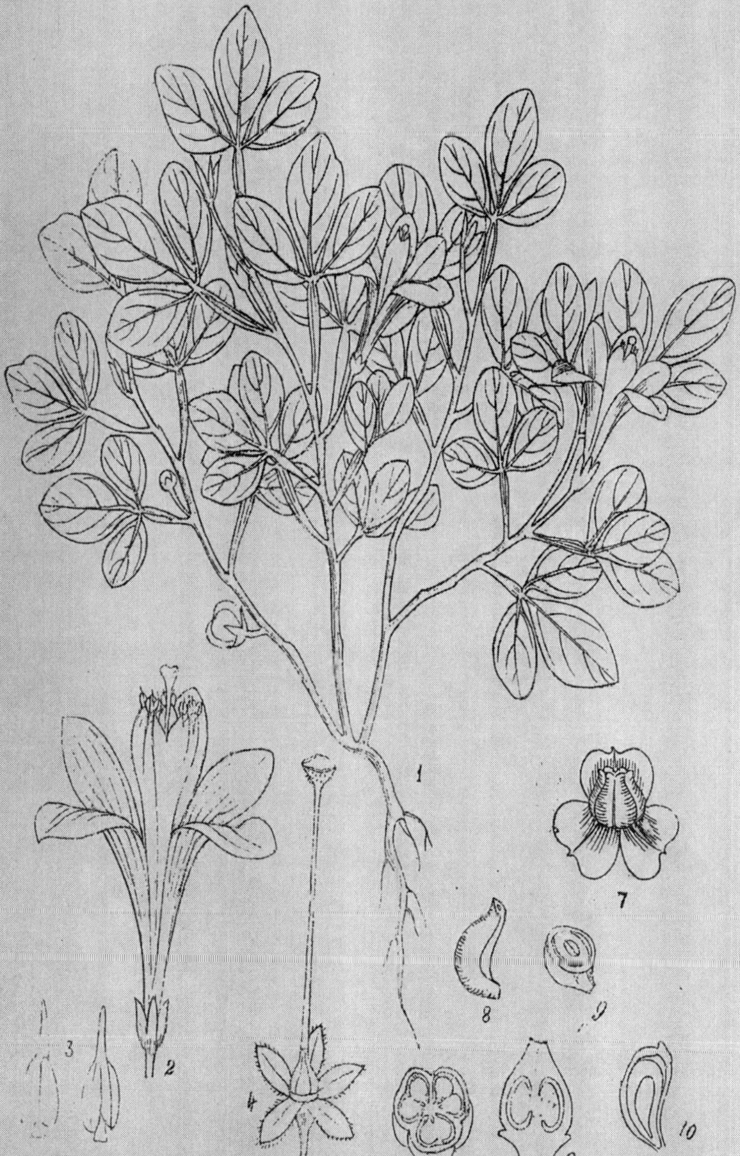

NAREGAMIA ALATA, W. & A.

PLATE No. 218.

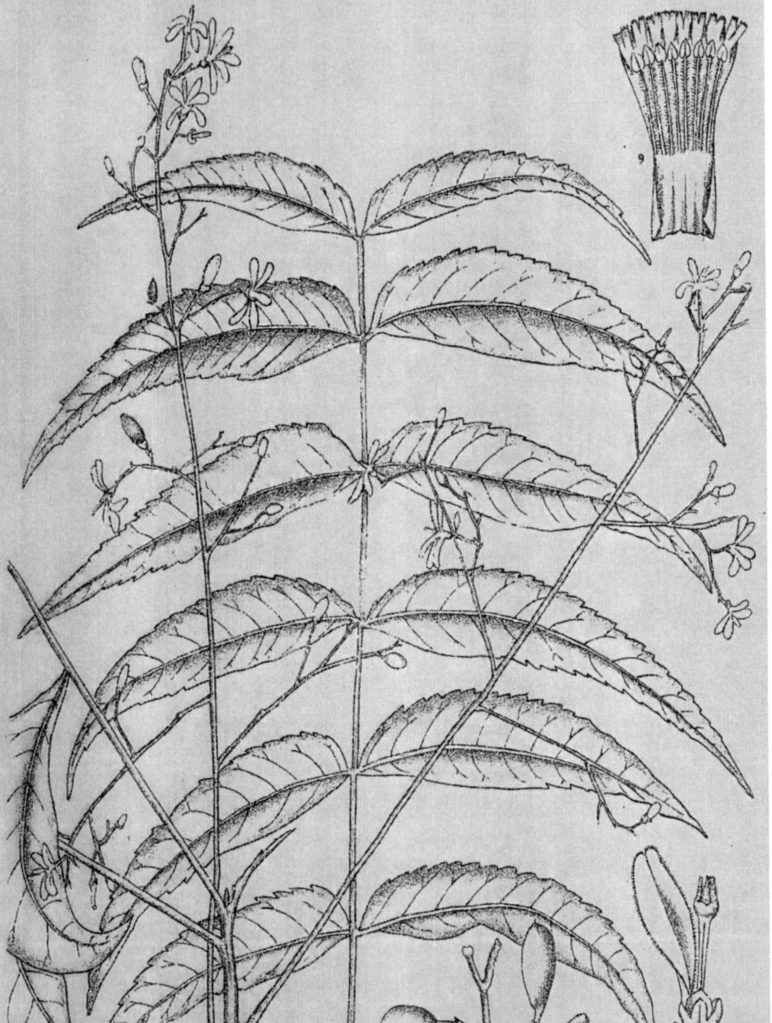

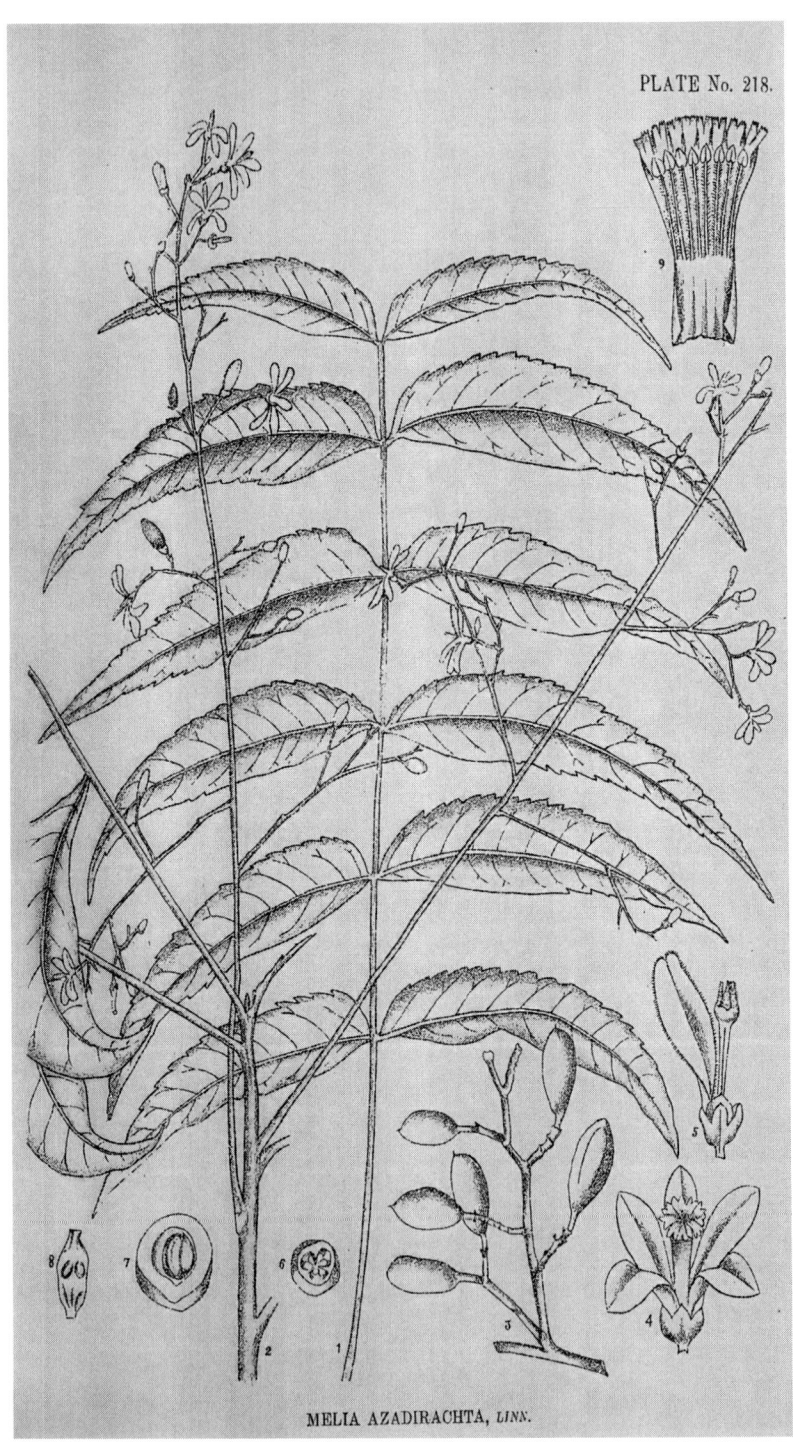

MELIA AZADIRACHTA, *LINN.*

PLATE No 219.

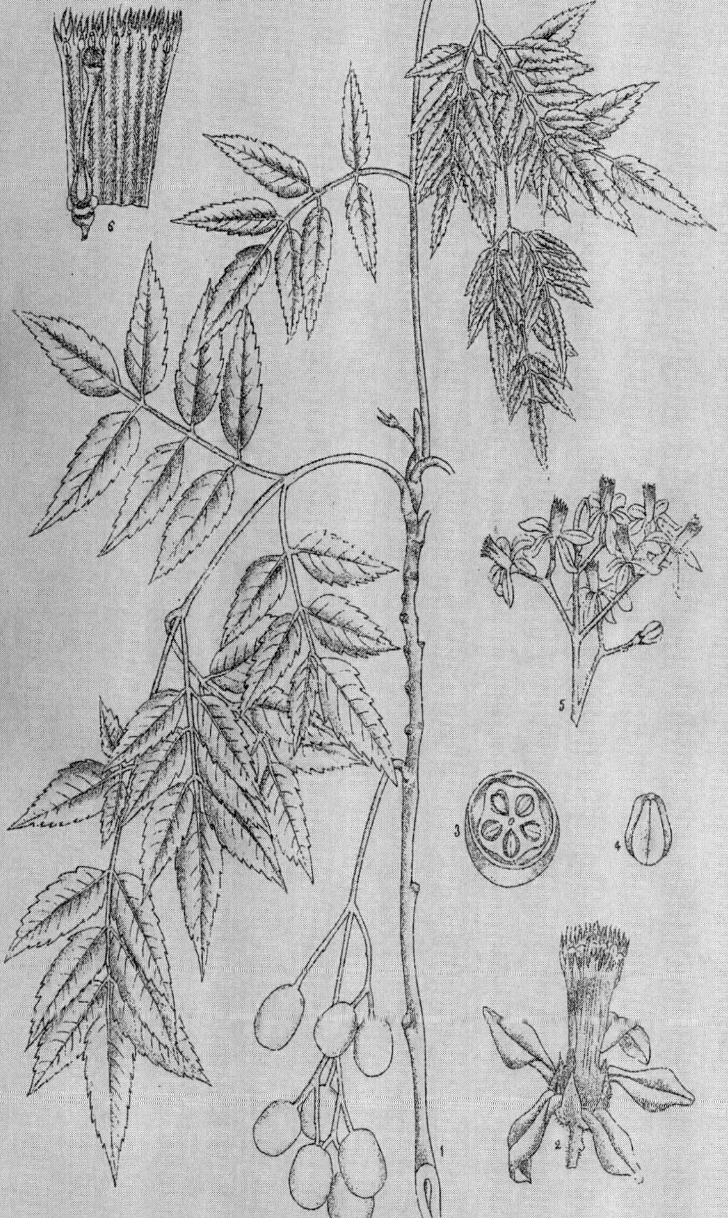

MELIA AZEDARACH, *LINN.*

PLATE No. 220.

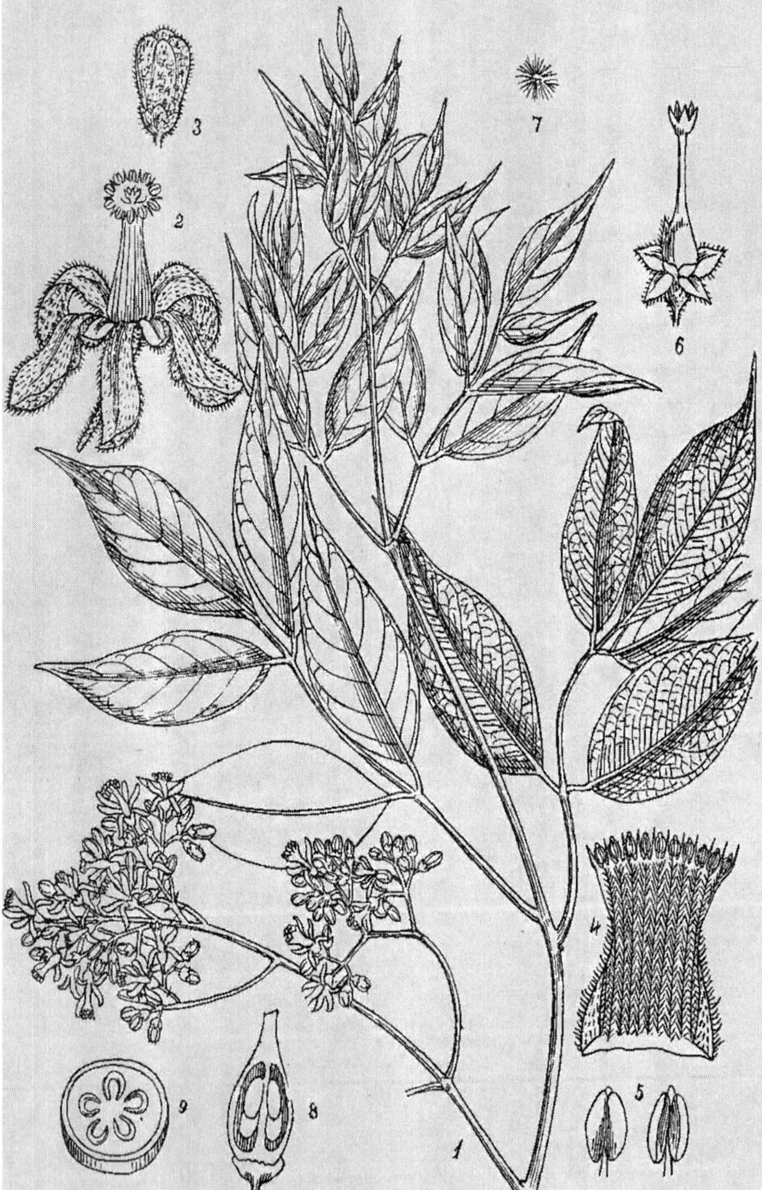

MELIA DUBIA, CAV.

PLATE No. 221.

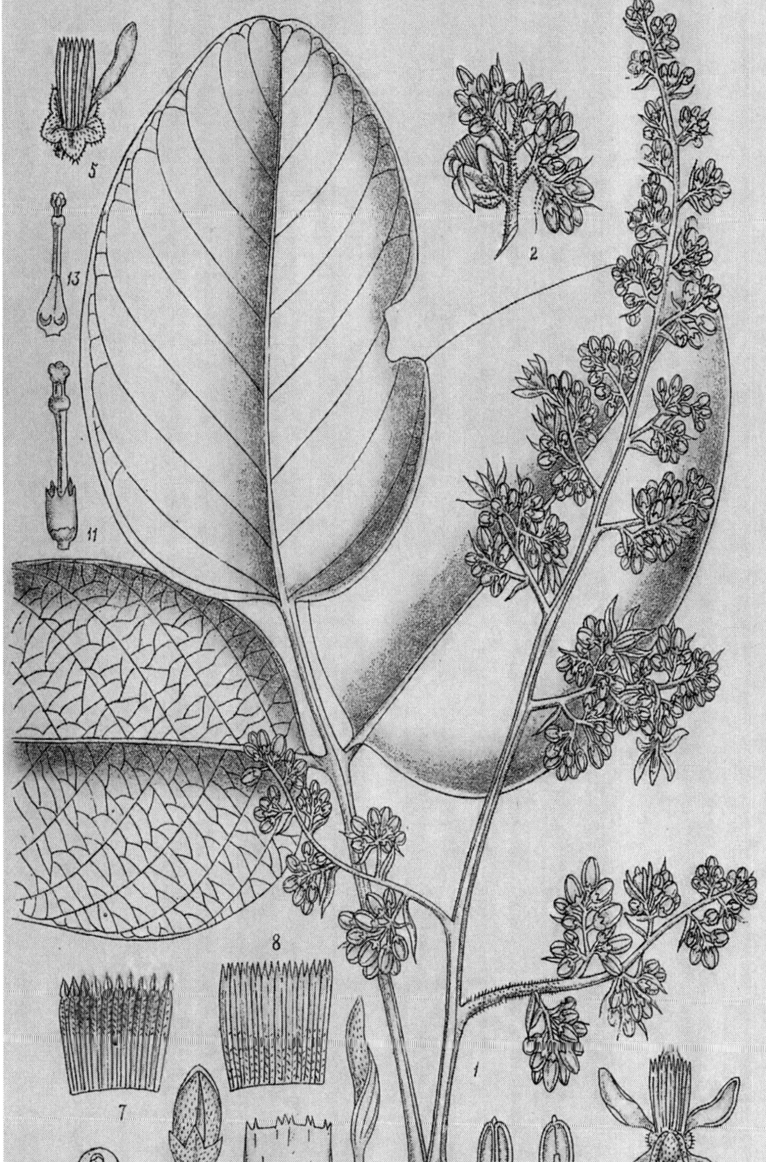

SANDORICUM INDICUM, CAV.

PLATE No. 222

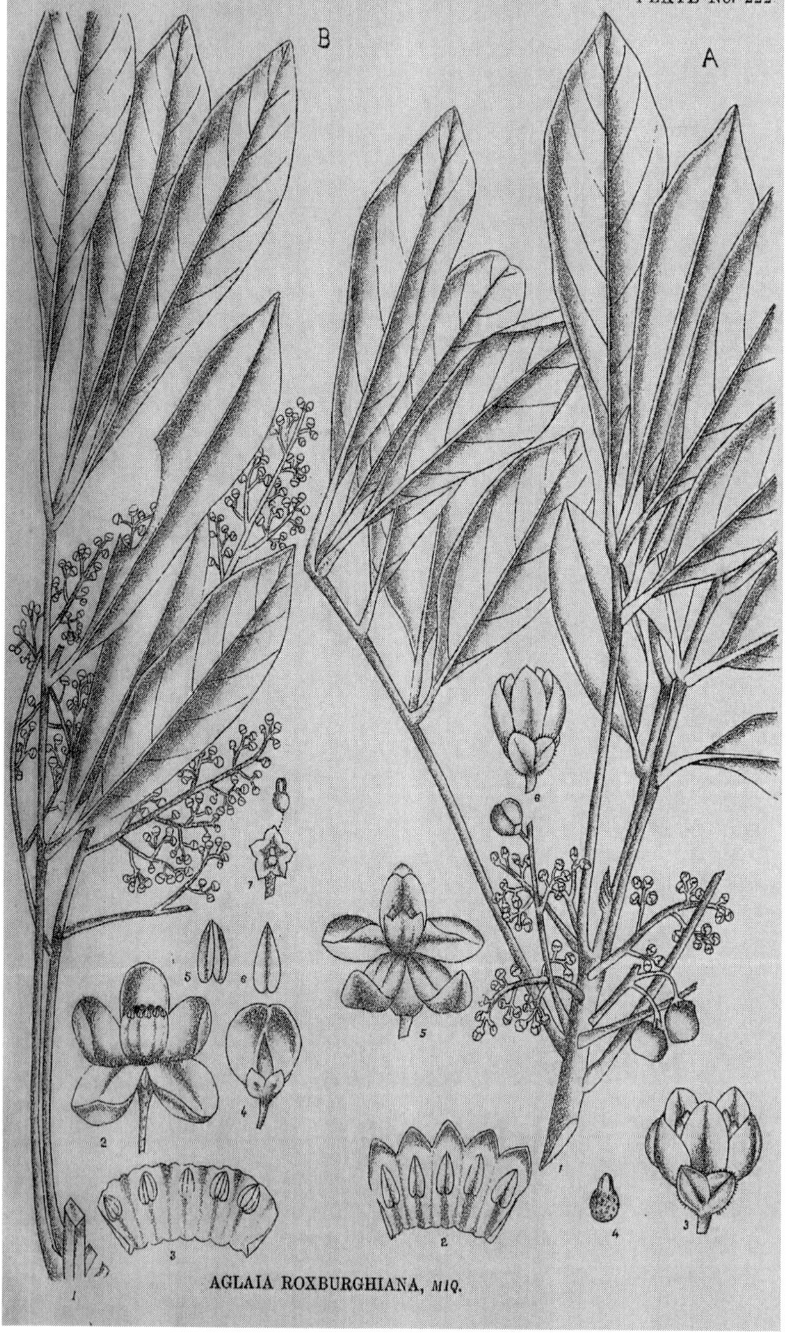

AGLAIA ROXBURGHIANA, *MIQ.*

PLTAE No. 223.

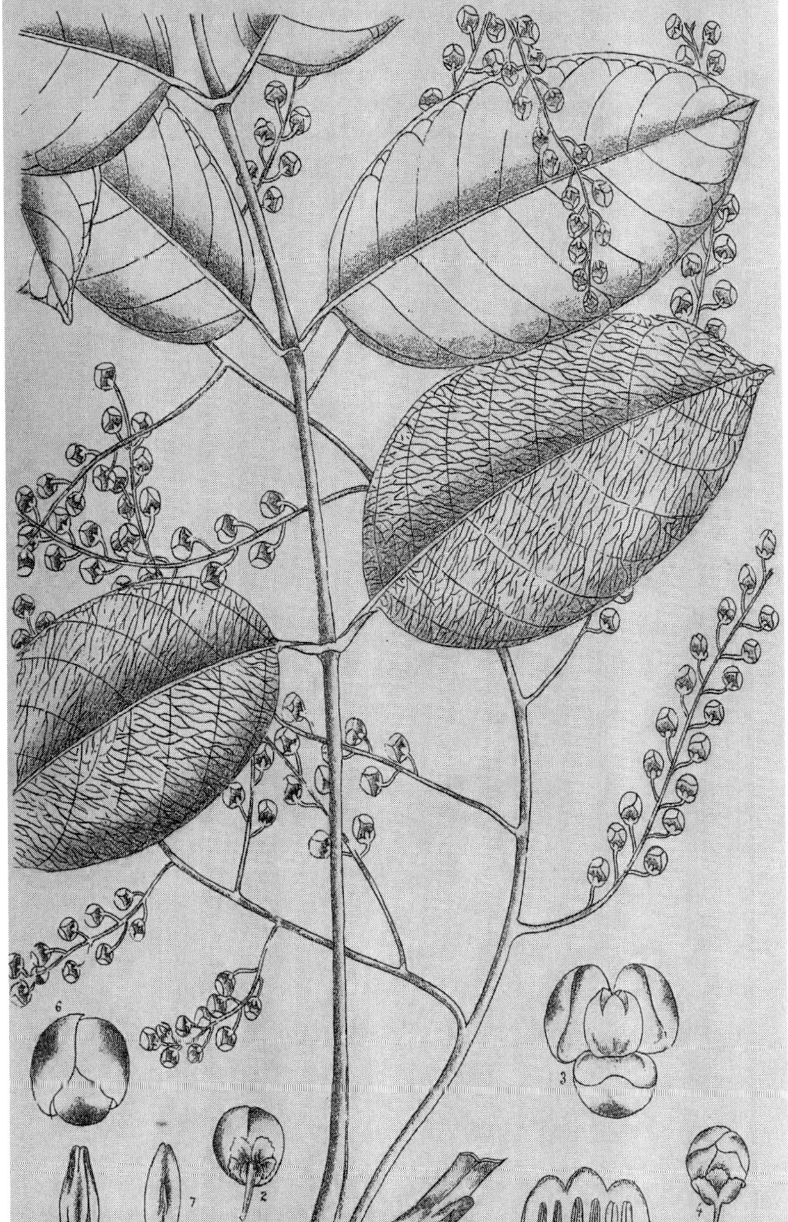

AMOORA ROHITUKA, *W. & A.*

PLATE No. 224.

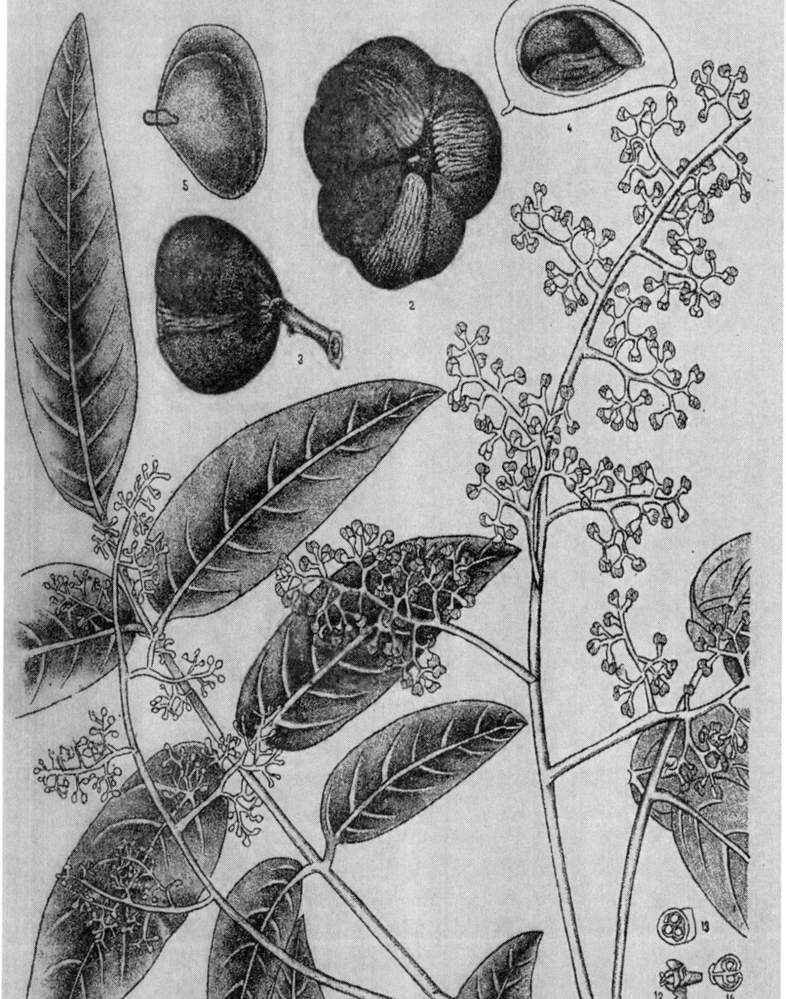

AMOORA CUCULLATA, ROXB.

PLATE No. 225.

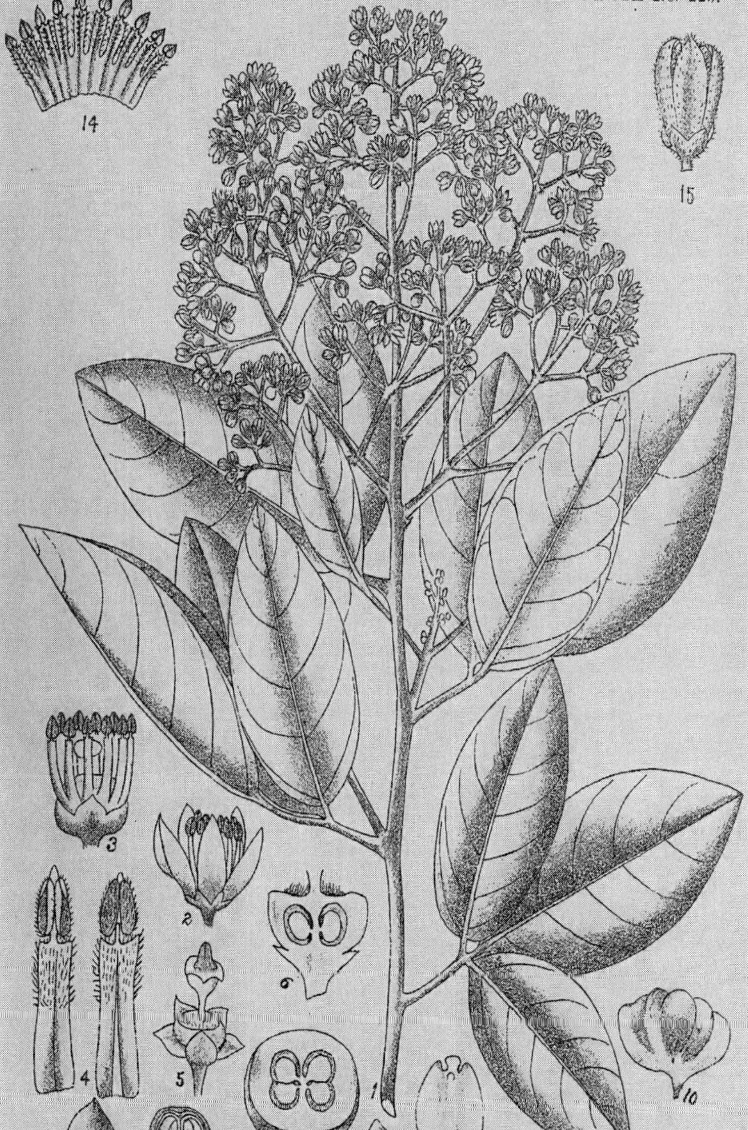

WALSURA PISCIDIA, *ROXB.*

PLATE No. 226.

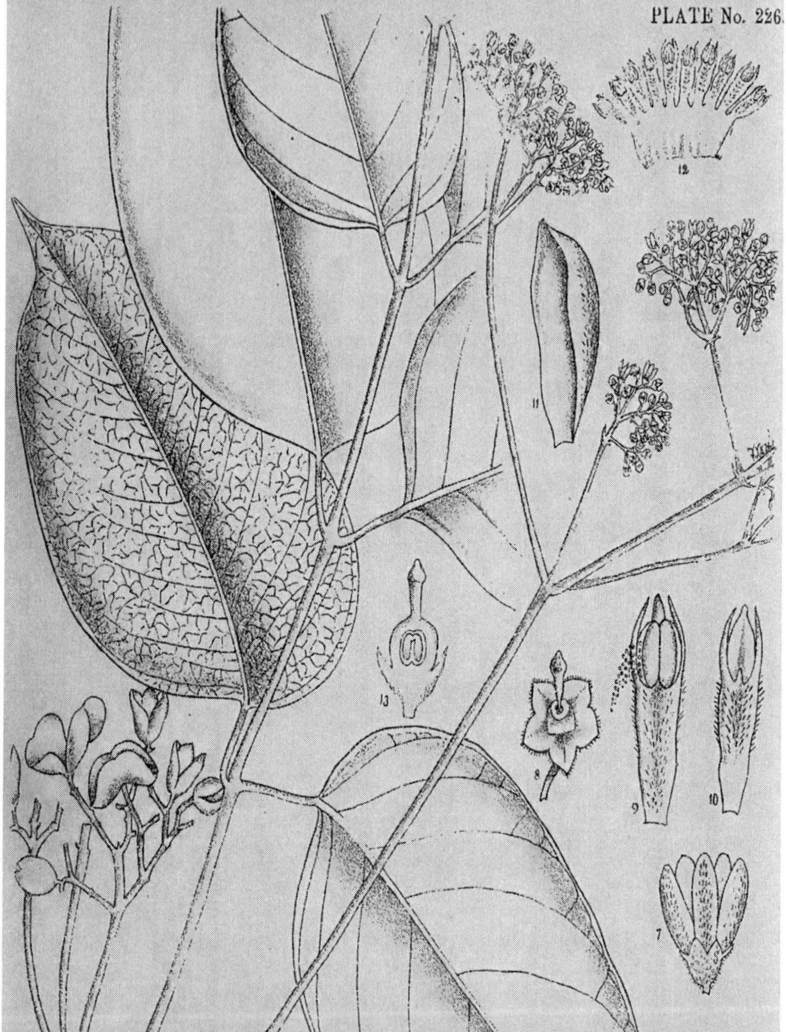

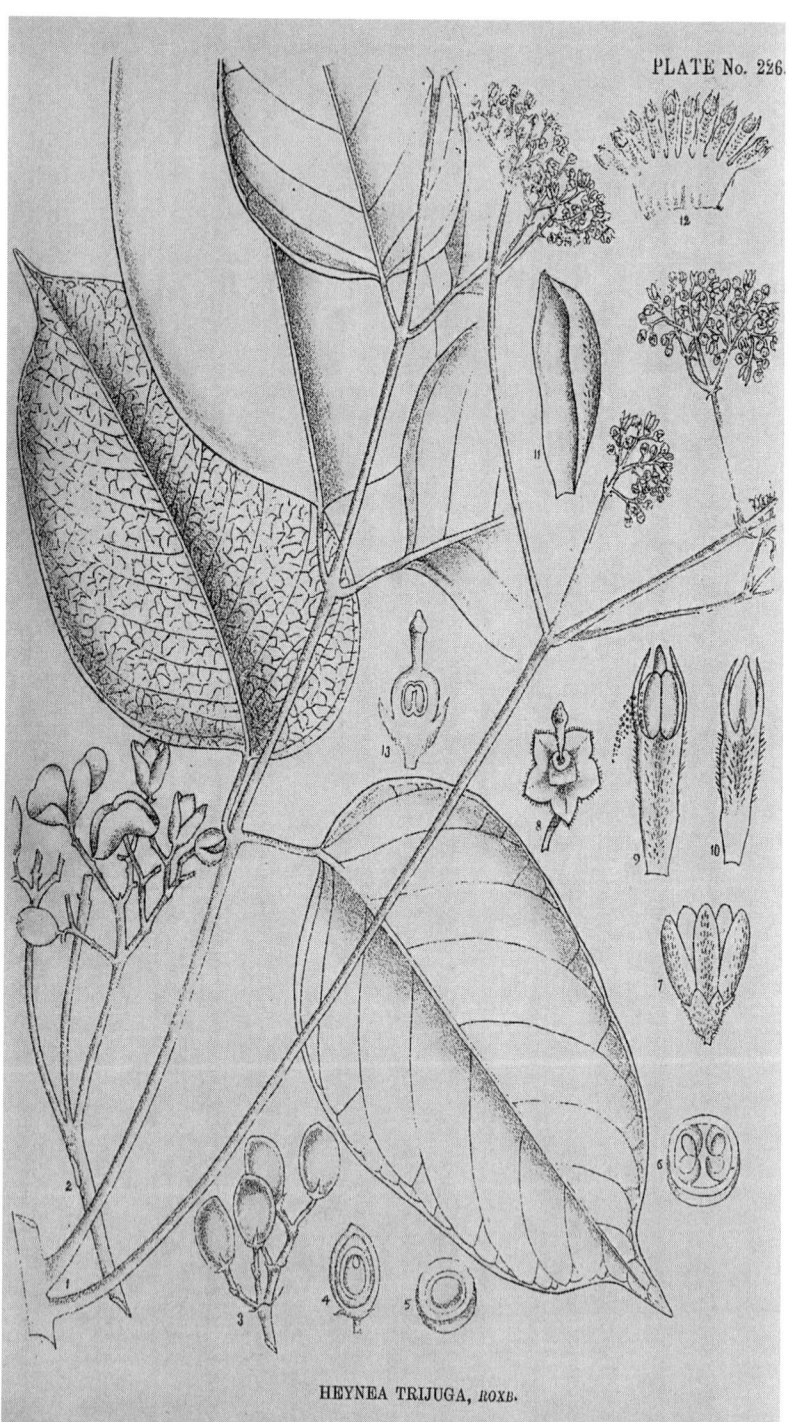

HEYNEA TRIJUGA, *ROXB.*

PLATE No. 227.

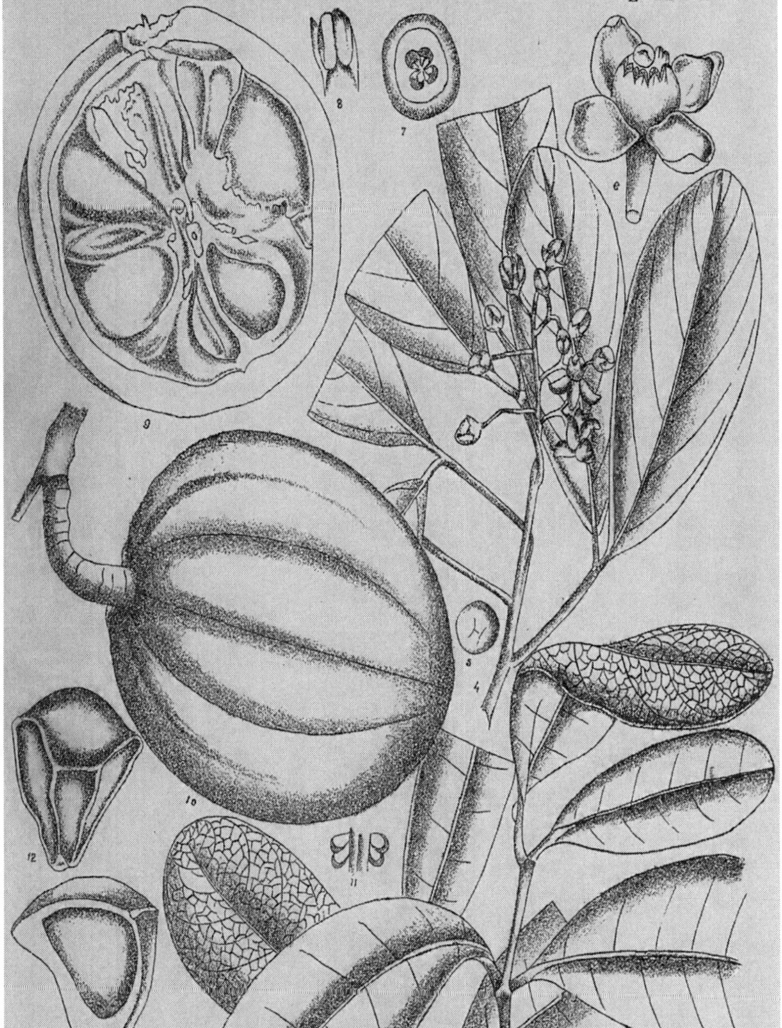

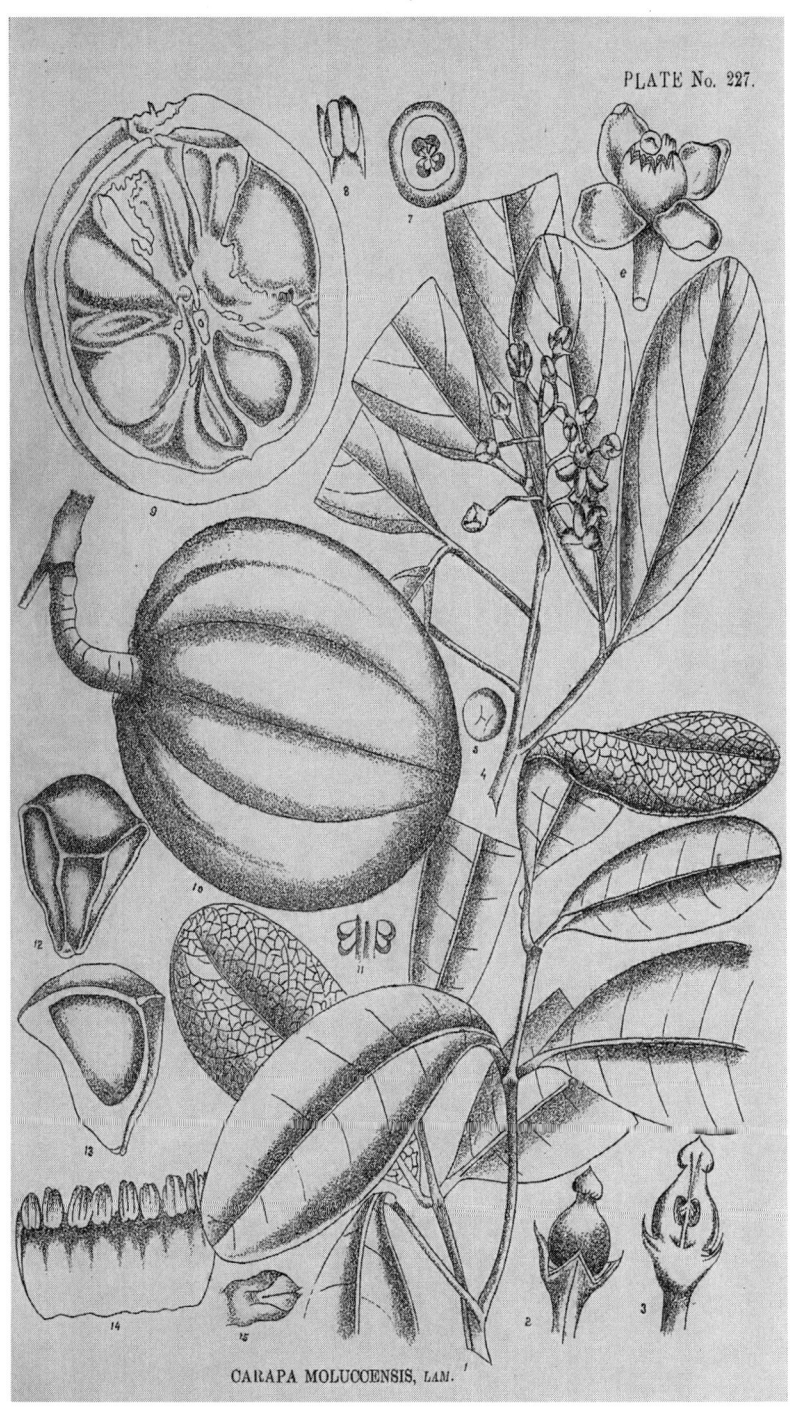

CARAPA MOLUCCENSIS, LAM.

PLATE No. 228.

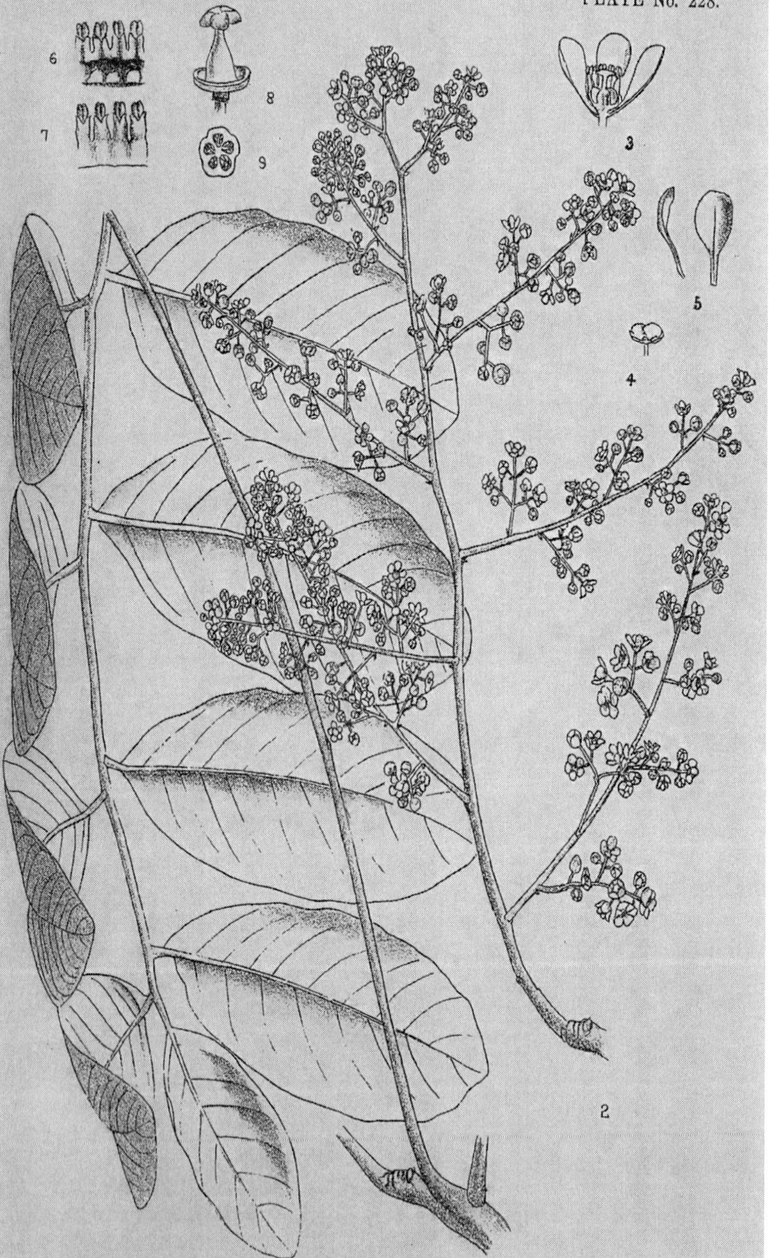

SOYMIDA FEBRIFUGA, ADR-JUSS.

PLATE No. 229.

CHICKRASSIA TABULARIS, *ADR. JUSS.*

PLATE No. 230.

CEDRELA TOONA, *ROXB.*

PLATE No. 231.

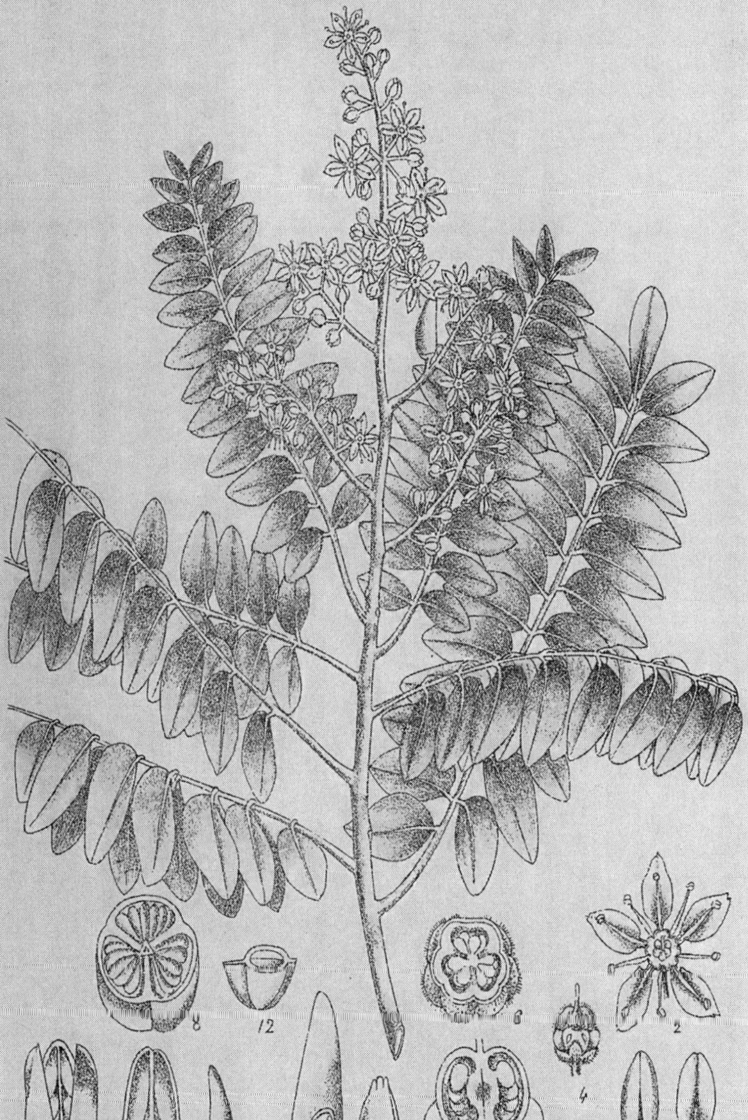

CHLOROXYLON SWIETENIA, *DC.*

PLATE No. 232.

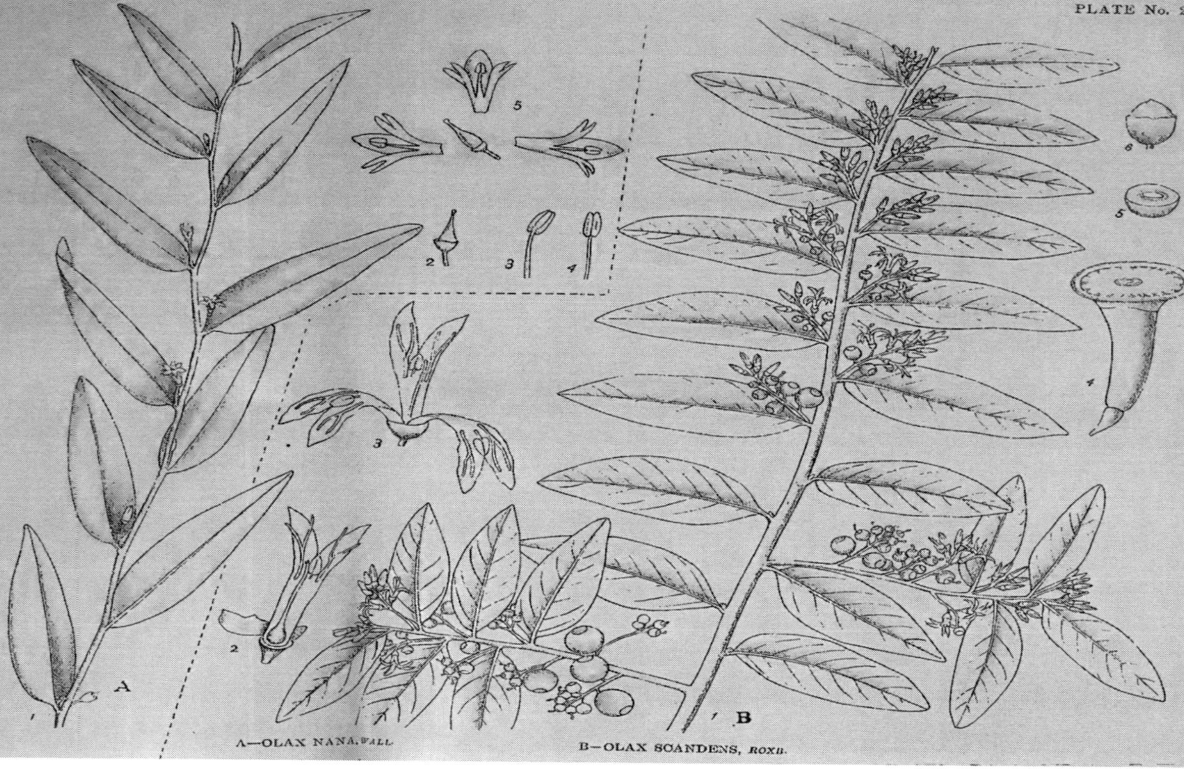

A—OLAX NANA, WALL.   B—OLAX SCANDENS, ROXB.

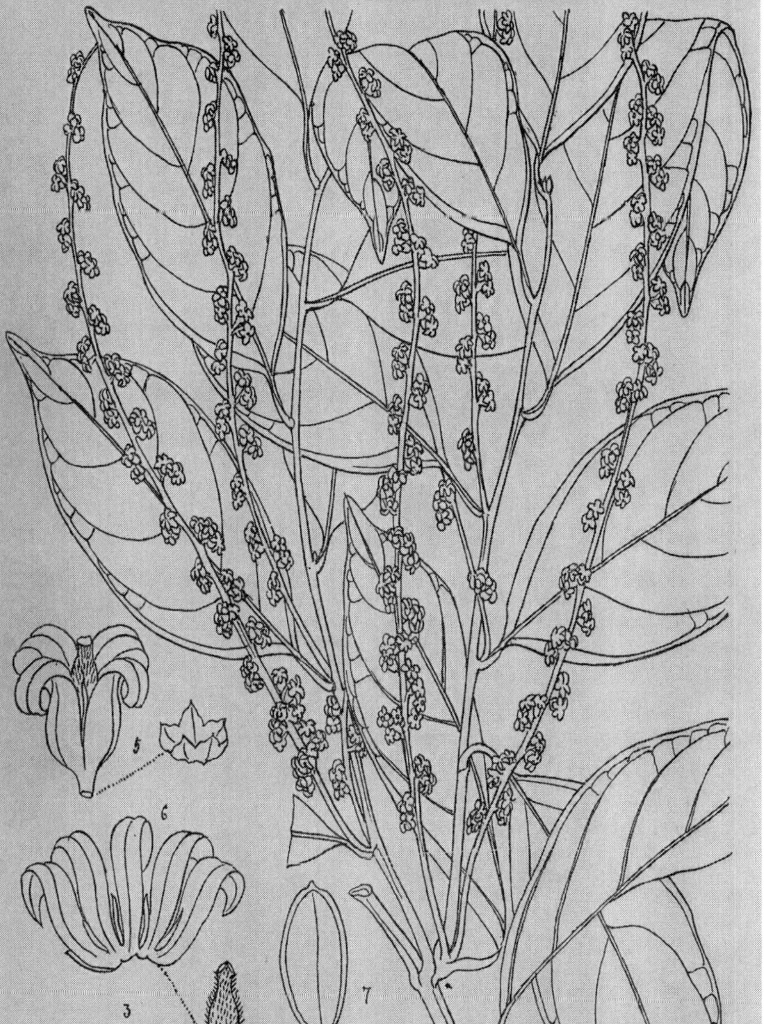

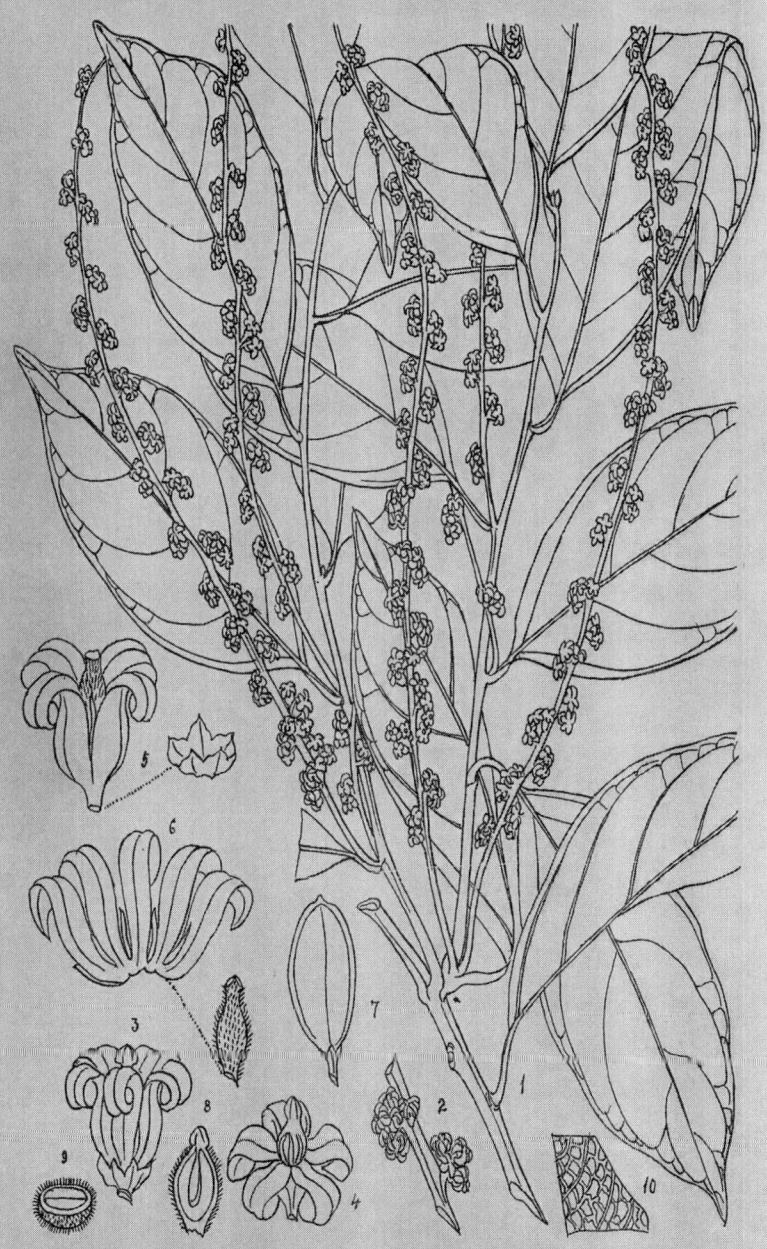

SARCOSTIGMA KLEINII, *W. & A.*

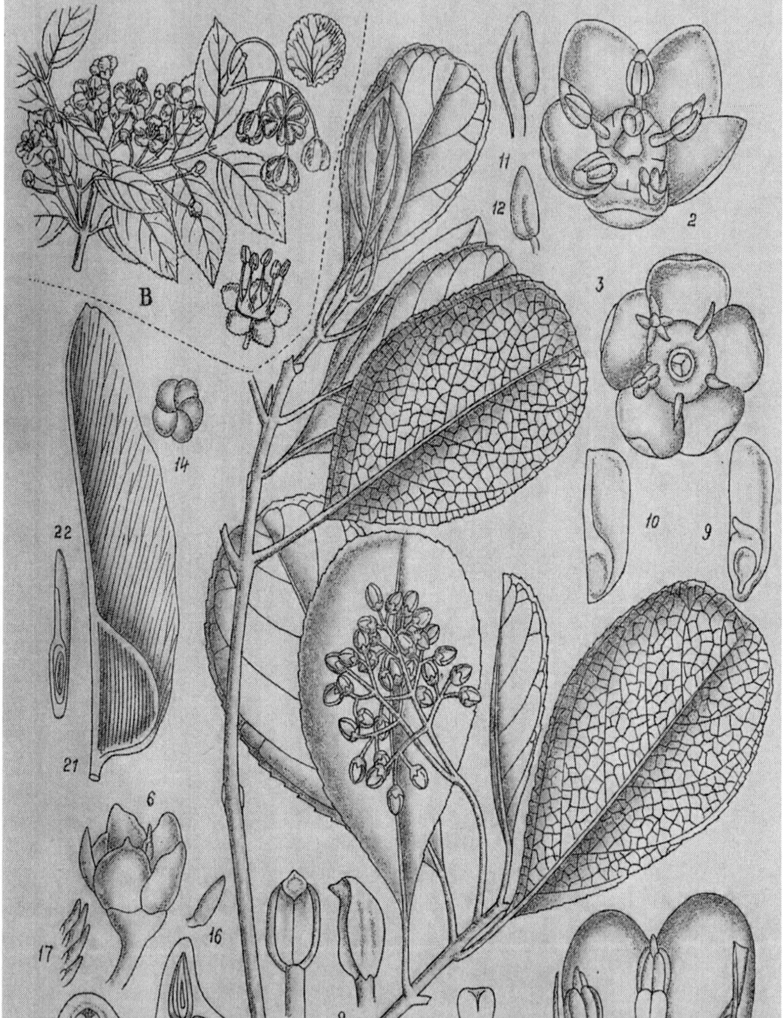

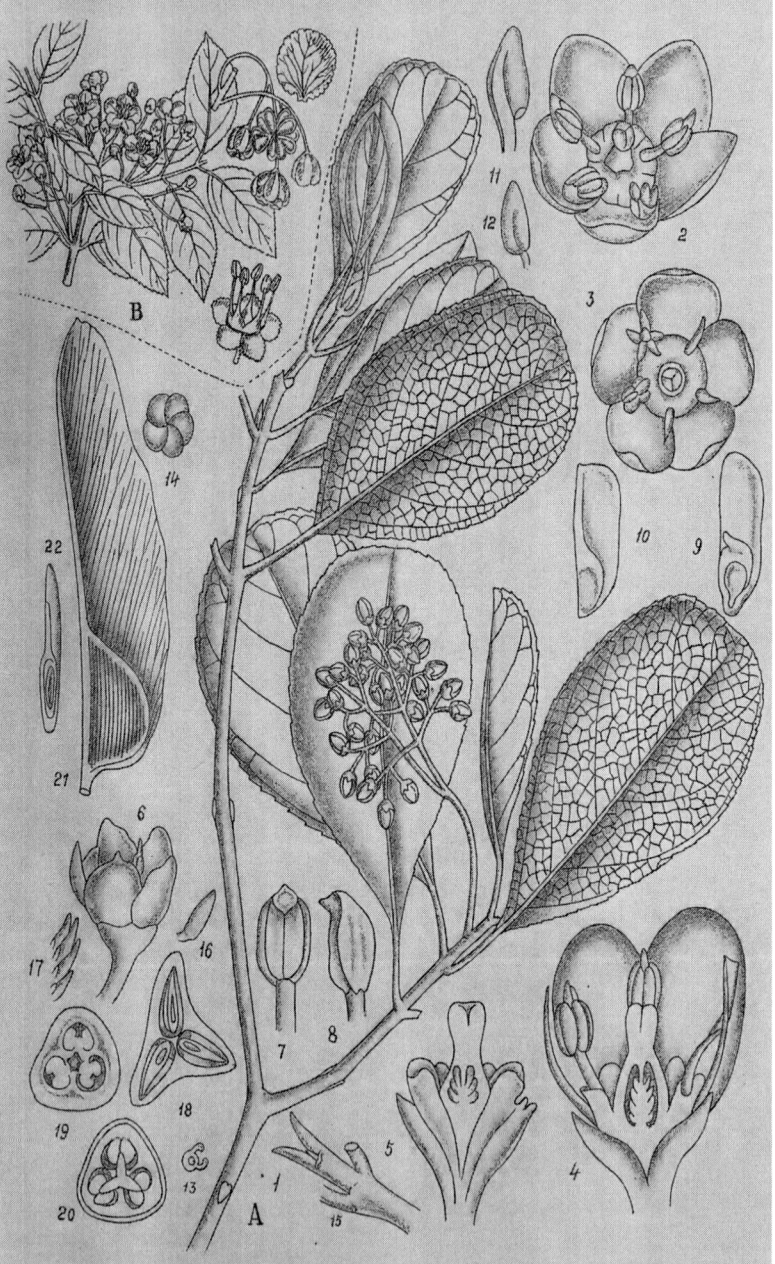

B—EUONYMUS TINGENS, *WALL.* A—KOKOONA ZEYLANICA, *THWAITES.*

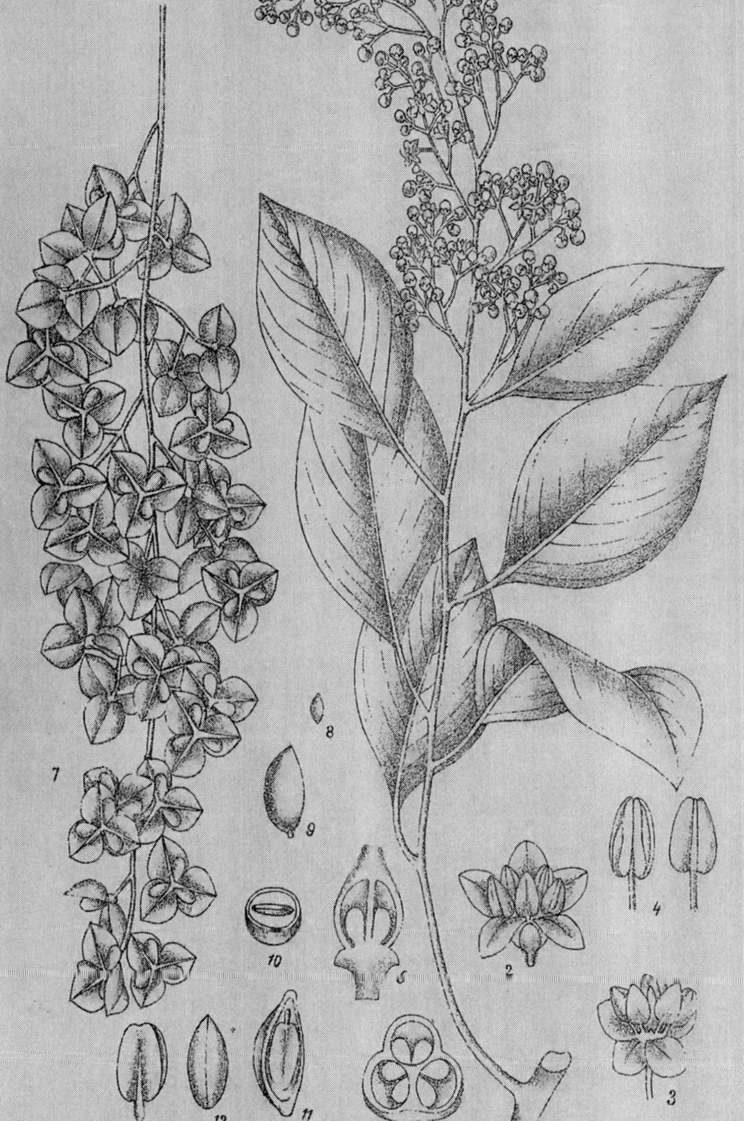

CELASTRUS PANICULATA, *WILLD.*

PLATE No. 236.

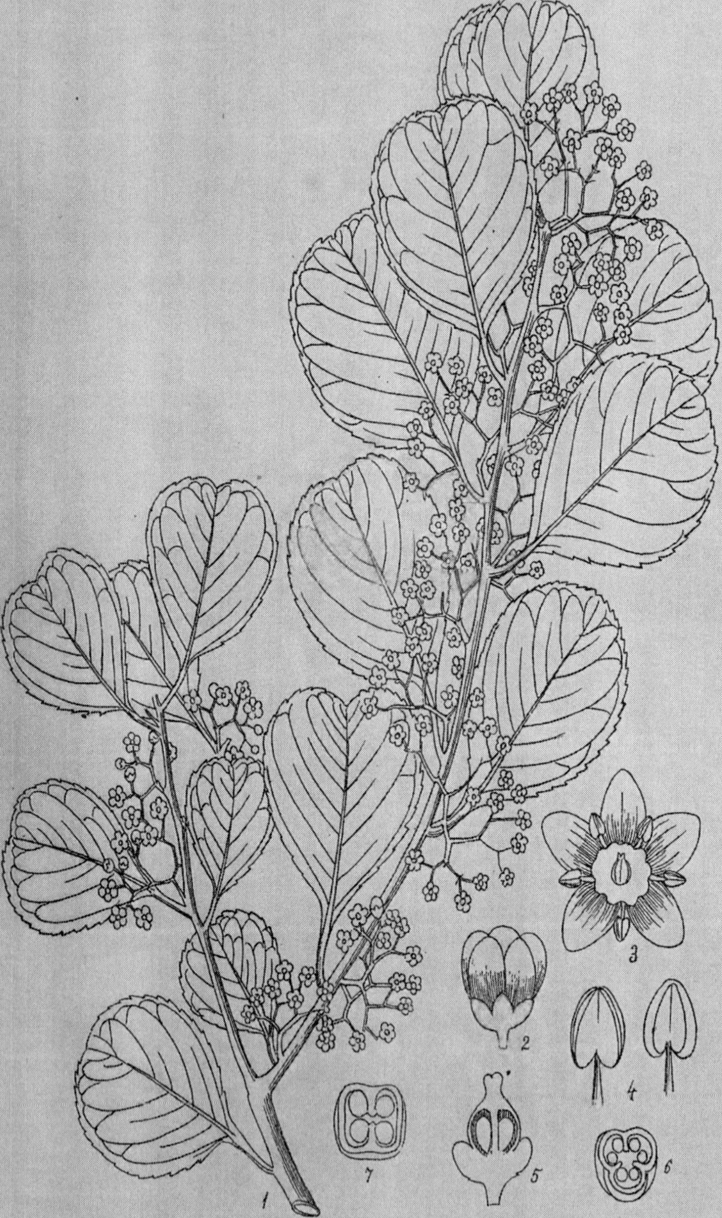

GYMNOSPORIA MONTANA, *BENTH.*

PLATE No. 237.

ELÆODENDRON GLAUCUM, PERS.

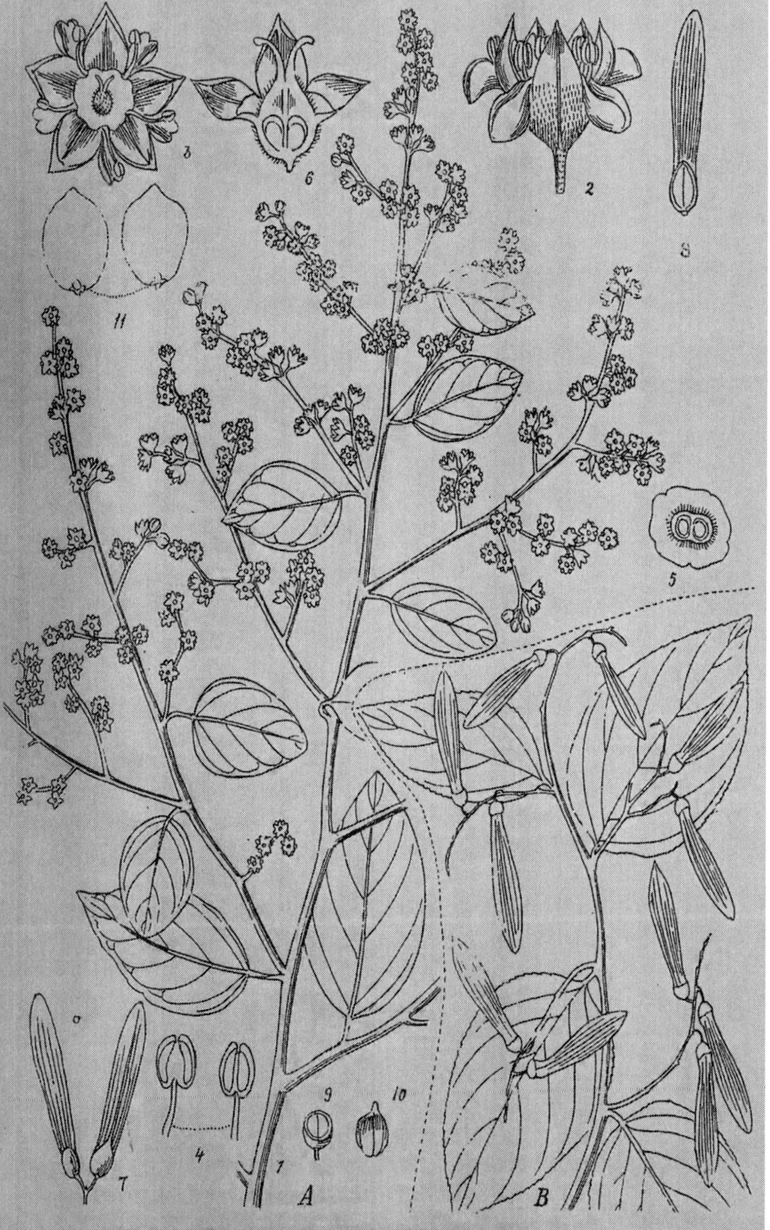

A—VENTILAGO MADRASPATANA, *GAERTN.* B—V. CALYCULATA, *TULSANE.*

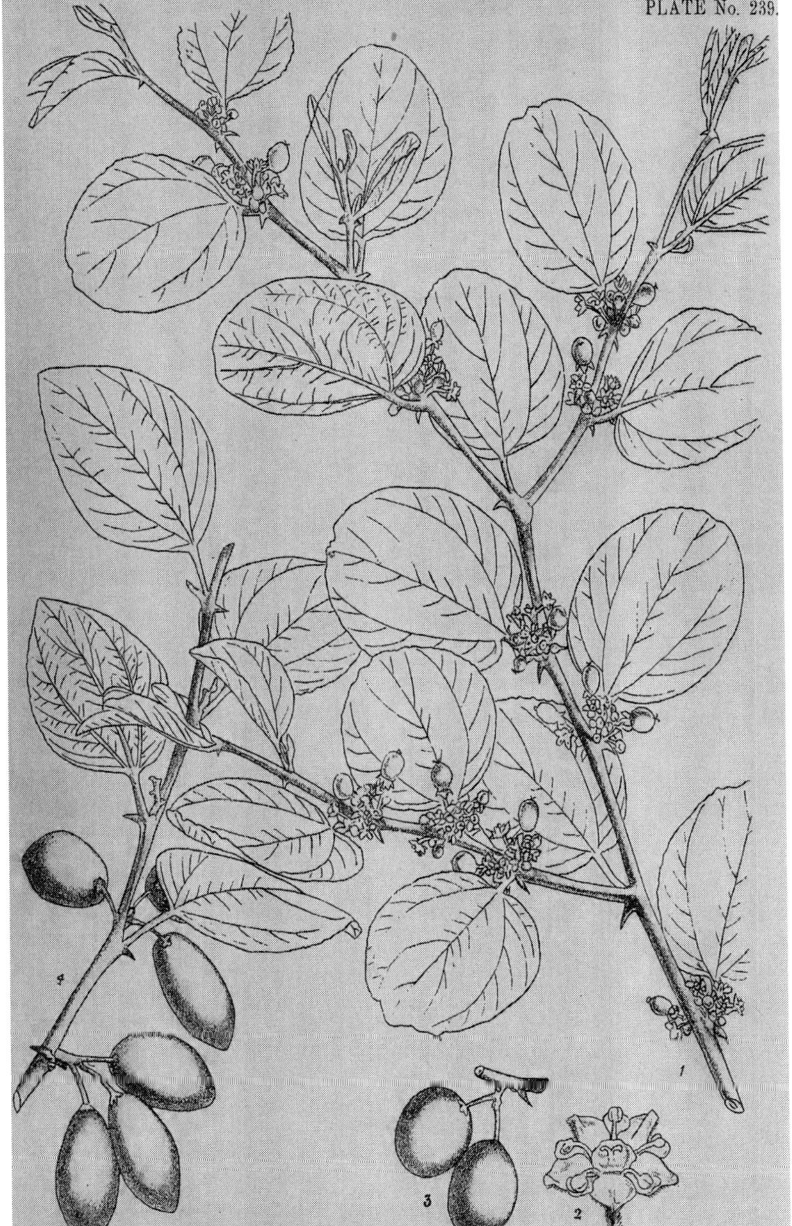

ZIZYPHUS JUJUBA, LAMK.

PLATE No. 240.

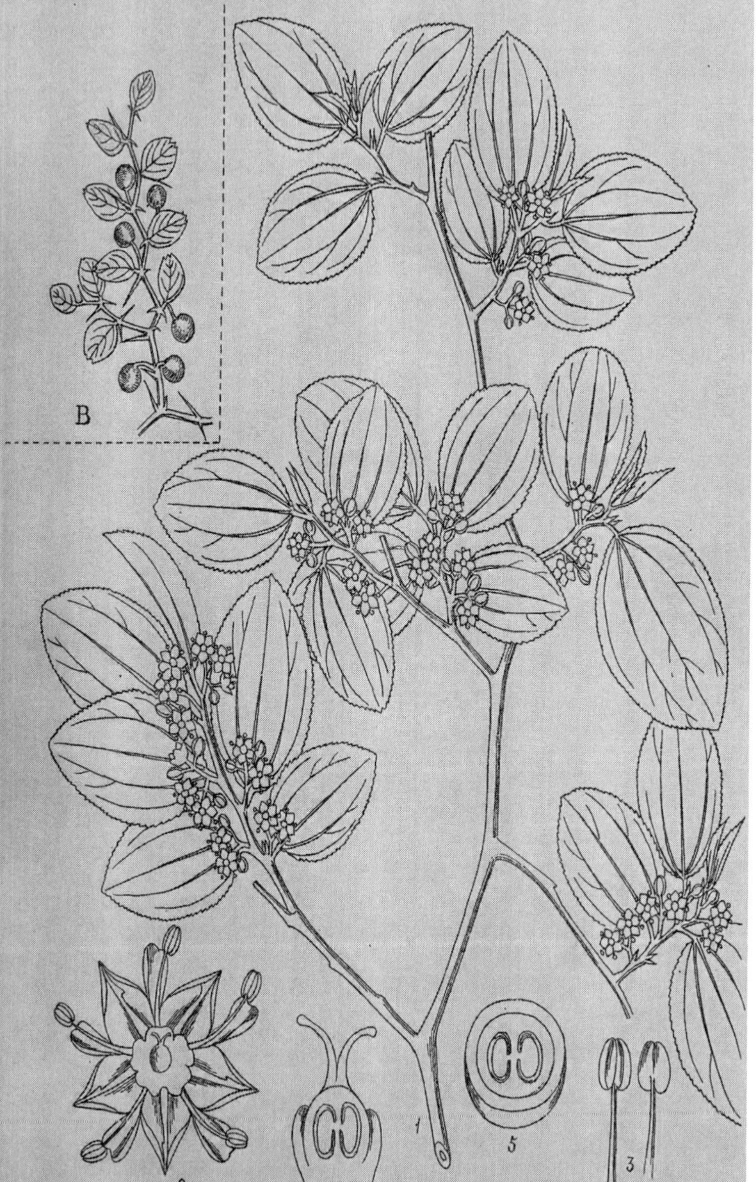

A—ZIZYPHUS GLABRATA, *HEYNE*. B—ZIZYPHUS NUMMULARIA, *W. & A.*

PLATE No. 241.

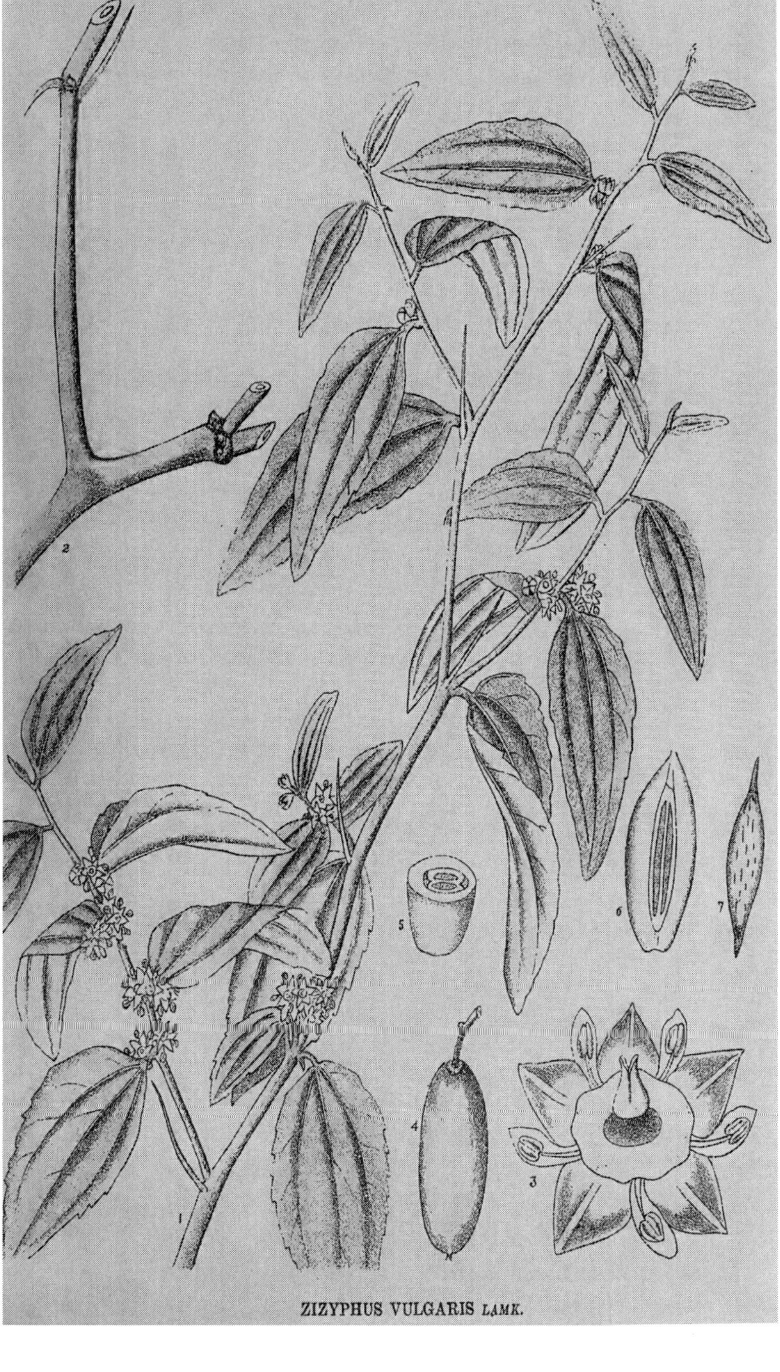

ZIZYPHUS VULGARIS LAMK.

PLATE No. 242

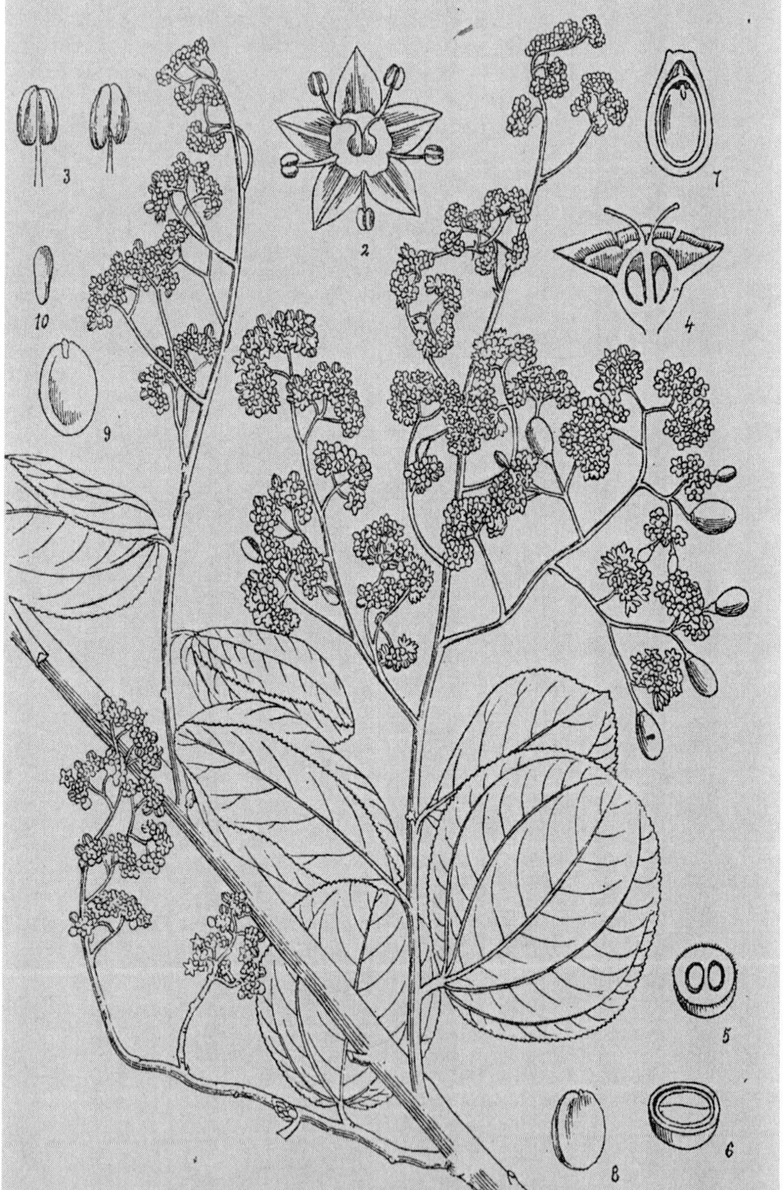

ZIZYPHUS RUGOSA, LAMK.

A - RHAMNUS PURPUREUS, *EDGEW.* B—R. DAHURIOUS, *PALL.*

PLATE No. 244.

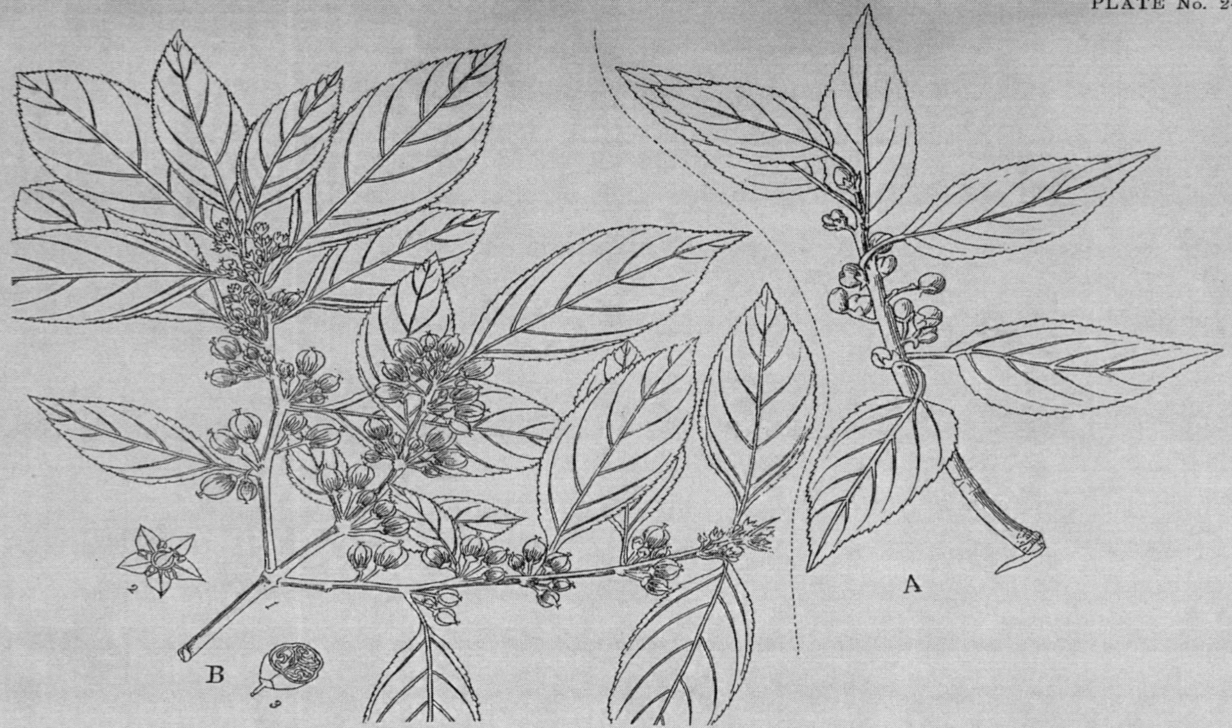

A—RHAMNUS TRIQETER, *LAWS.* B—RHAMNUS WIGHTII, *W. & A.*

PLATE No. 245.

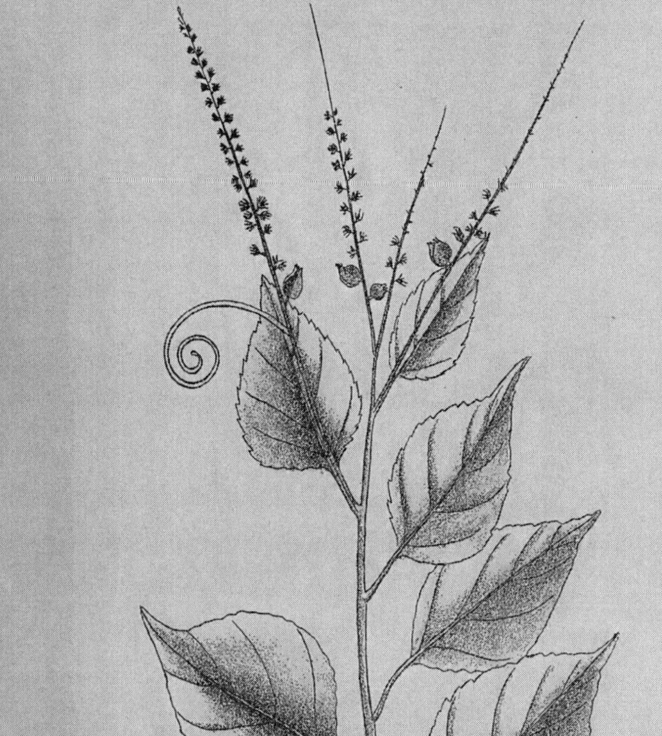

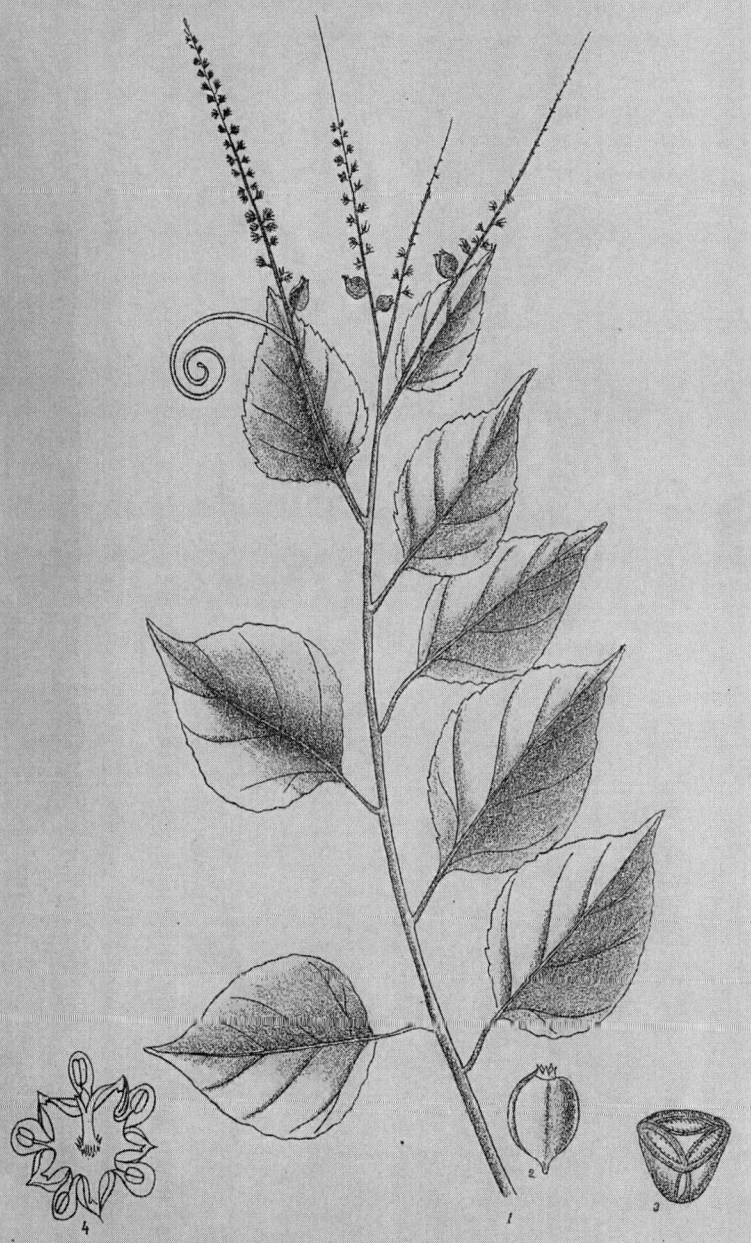

GOUANIA LEPTOSTACHYA, *DC.*

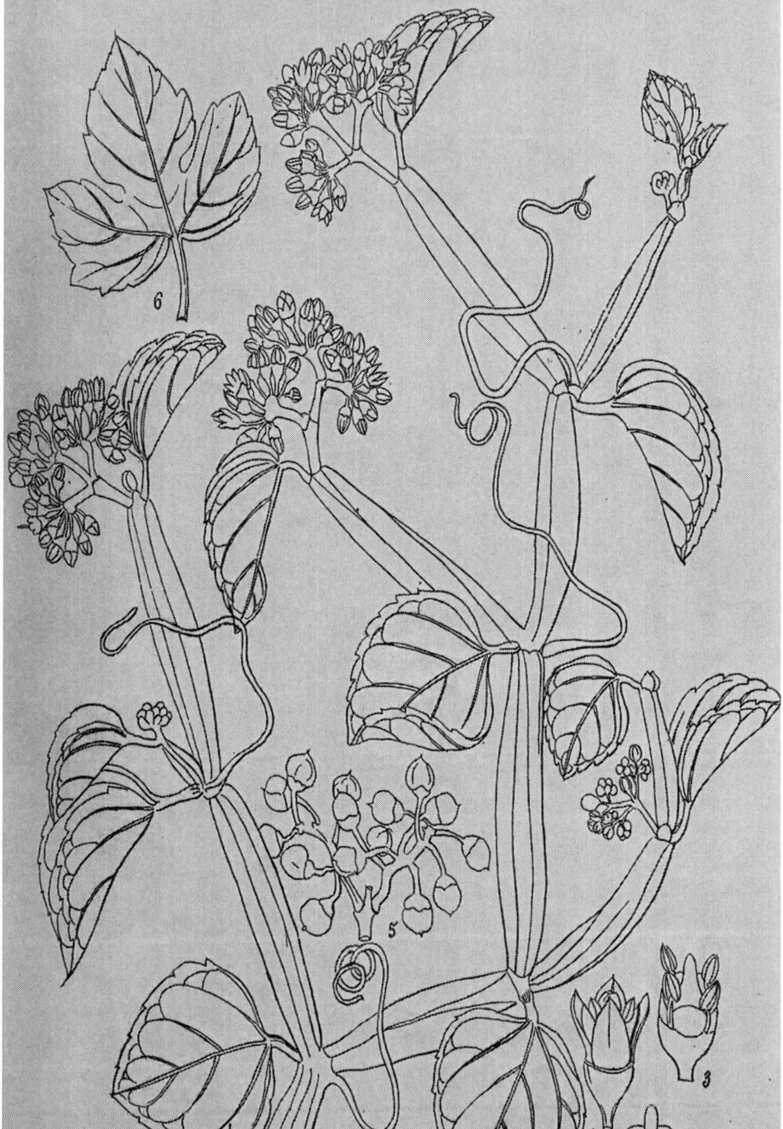

VITIS QUADRANGULARIS, *WALL.*

PLATE No. 247

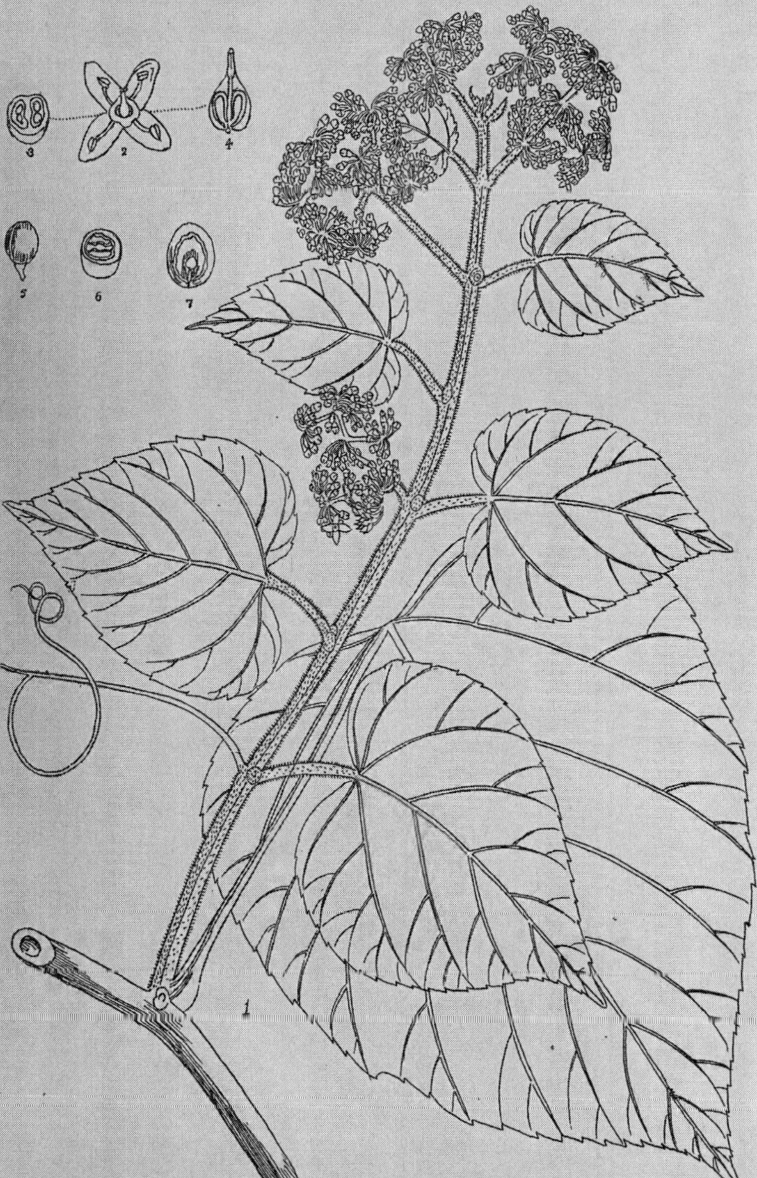

VITIS ADNATA, *WALL.*

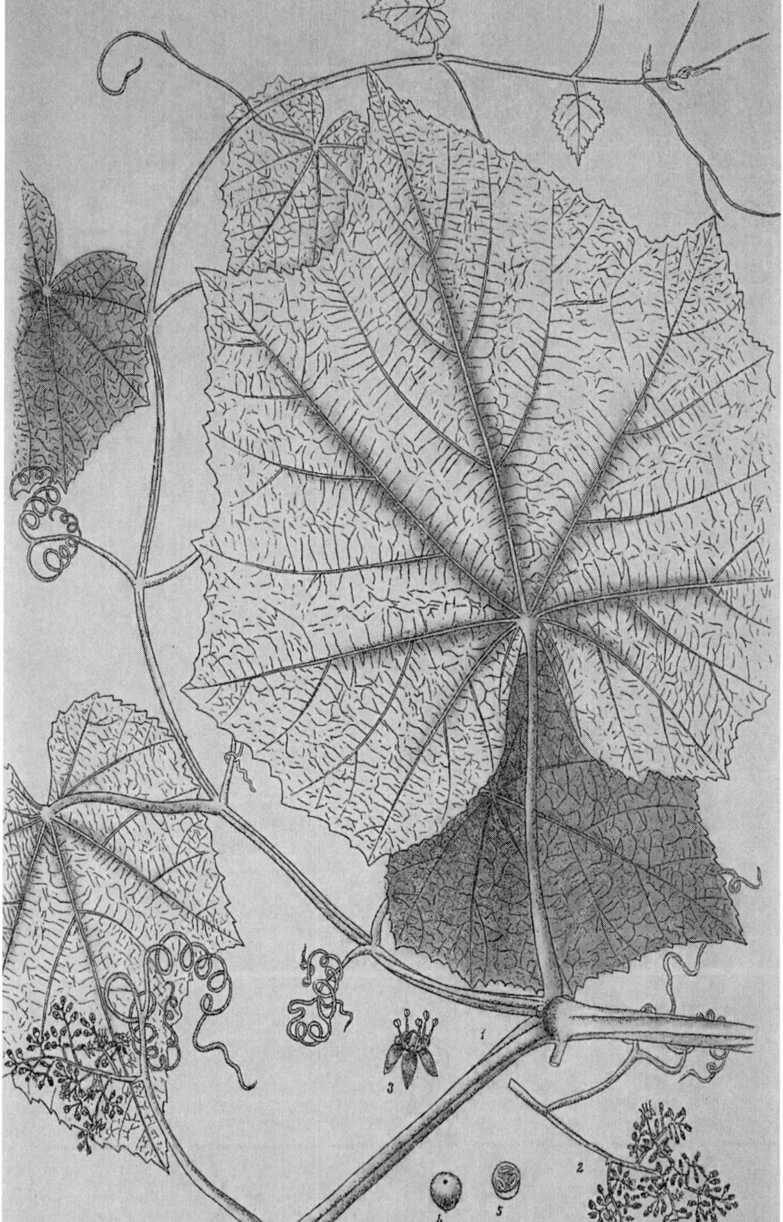

VITIS LATIFOLIA, *ROXB.*

PLATE No. 249.

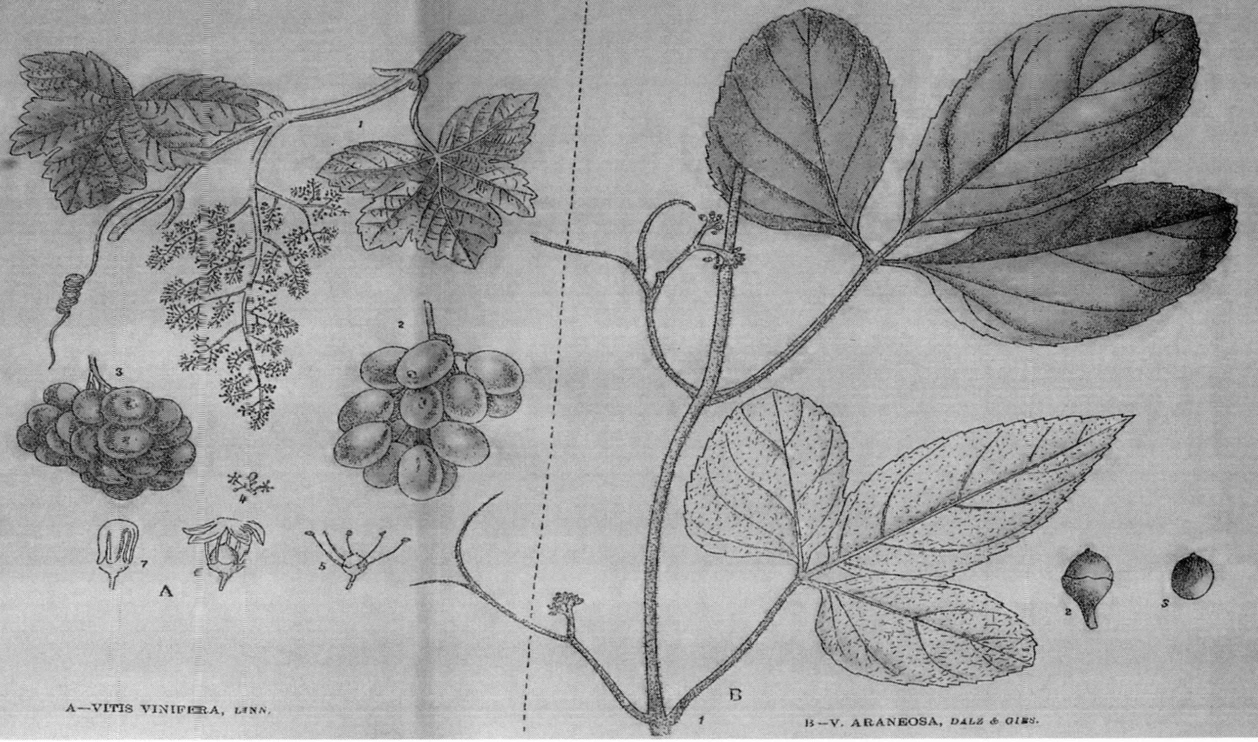

A—VITIS VINIFERA, LINN.

B—V. ARANEOSA, DALZ & GIBS.

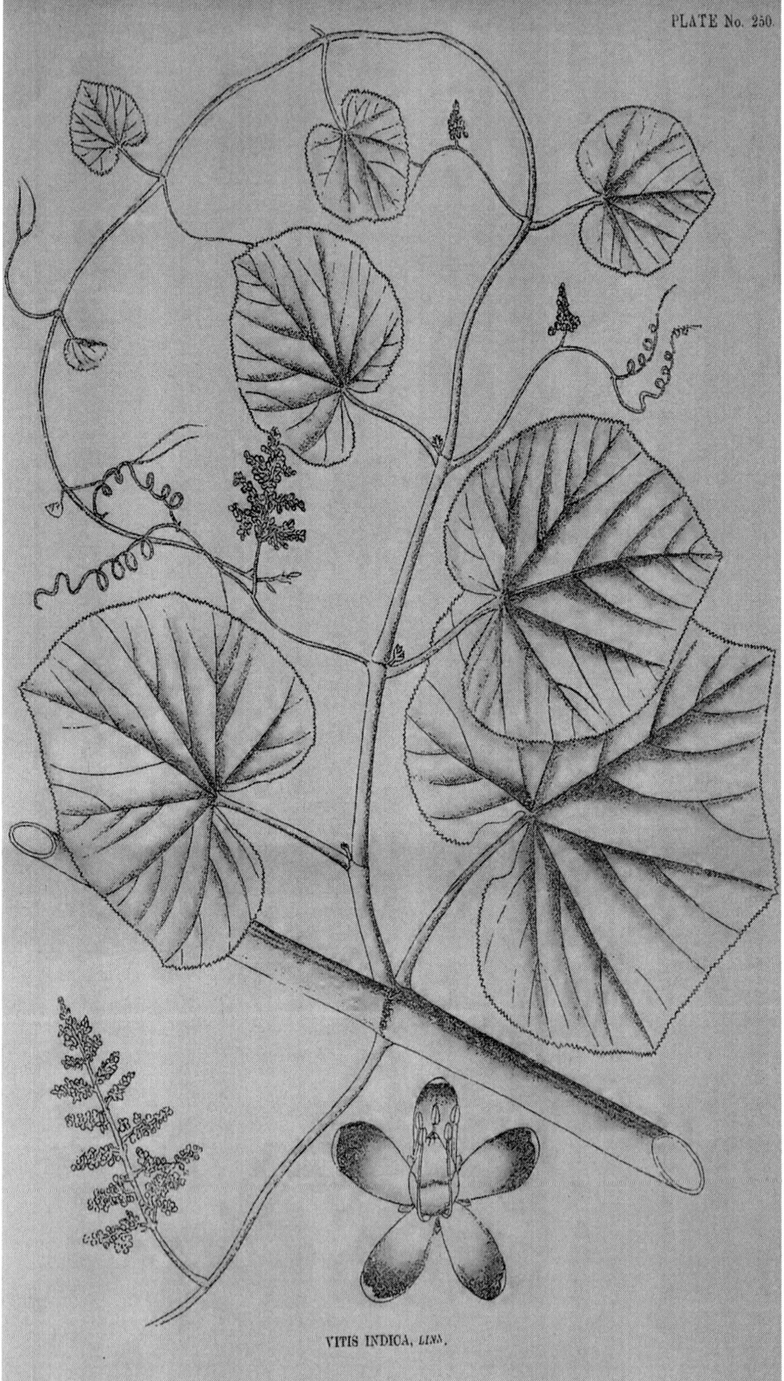

VITIS INDICA, *Linn.*

PLATE No. 251.

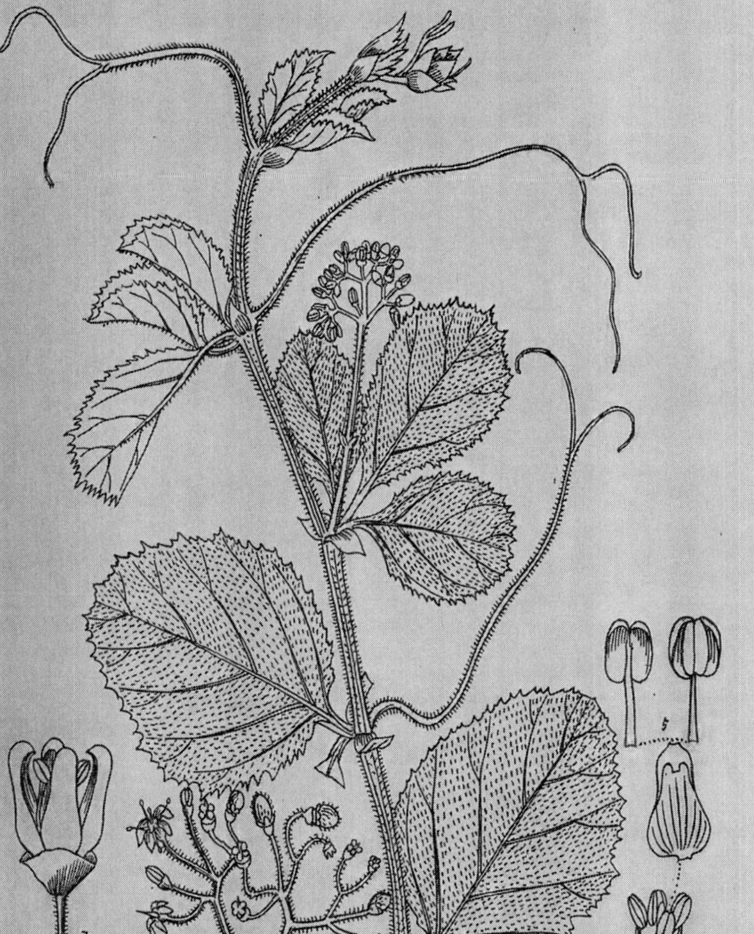

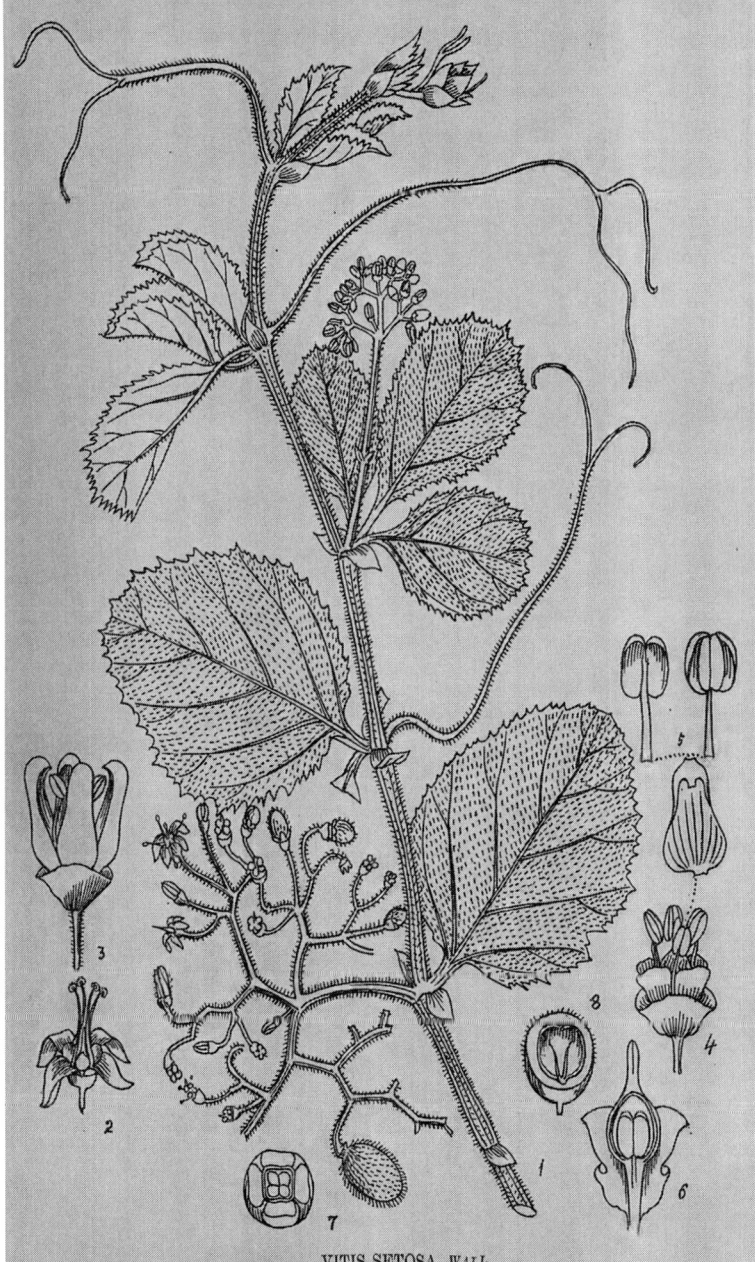

VITIS SETOSA, *Wall.*

PLATE No. 252.

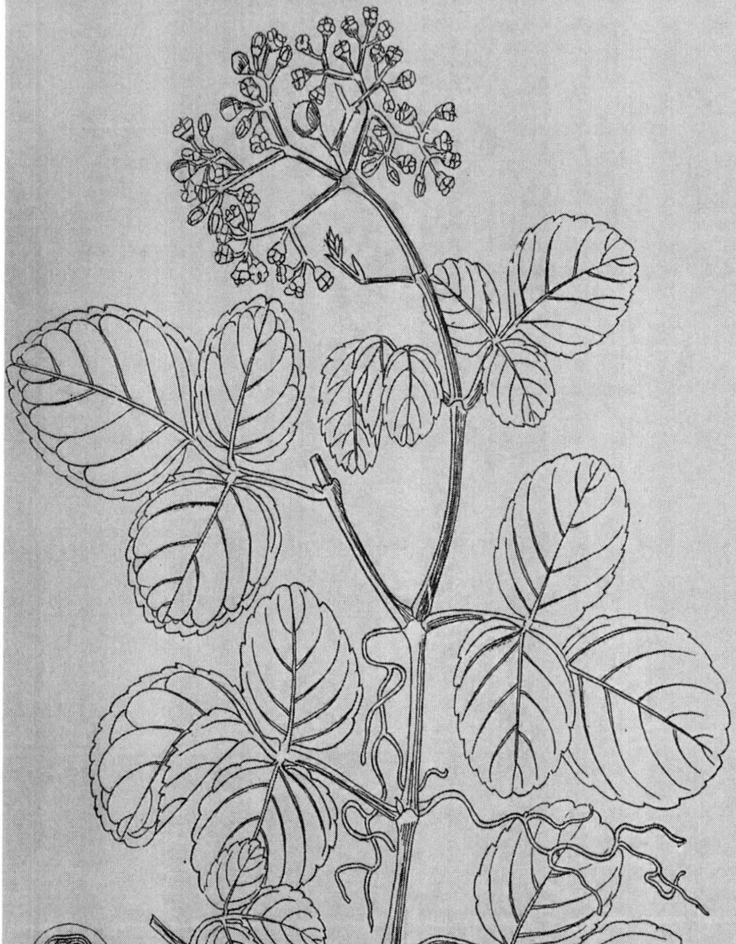

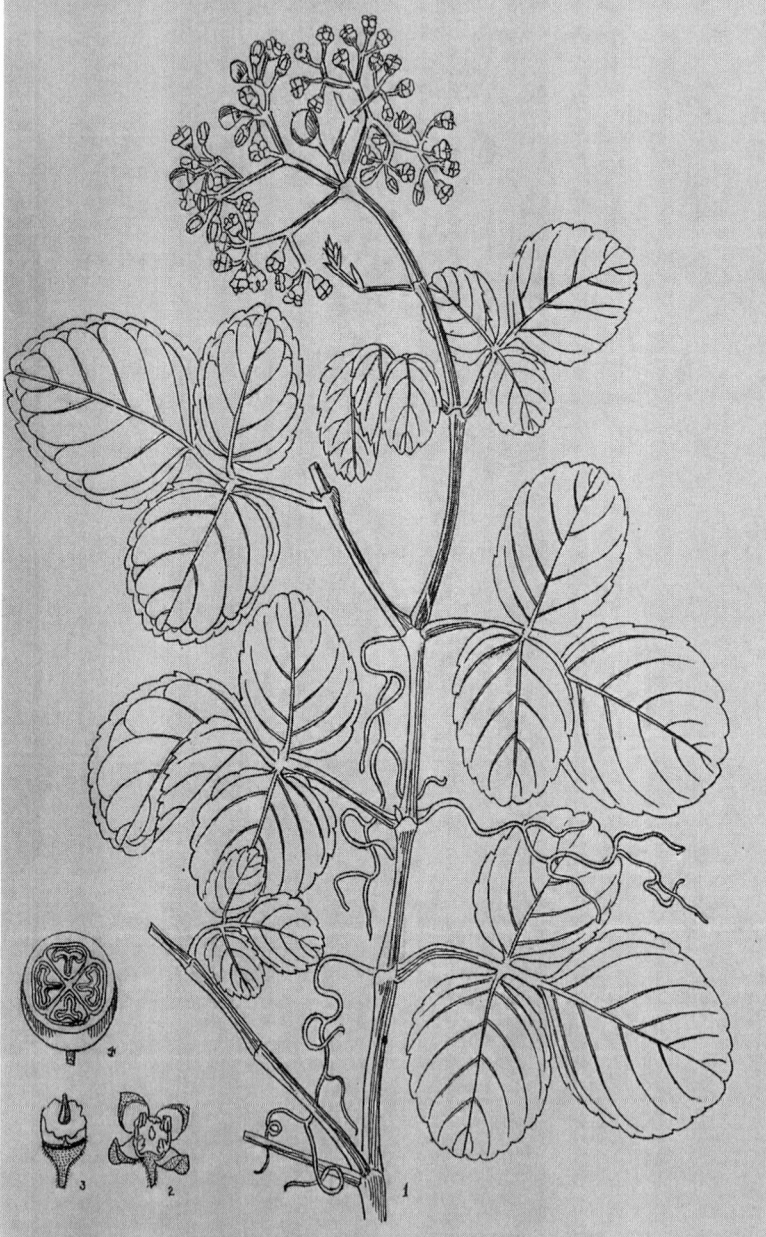

VITIS CARNOSA, *WALL*

VITIS PEDATA, Vahl.

LEEA MACROPHYLLA, *ROXB.*

PLATE No. 255.

LEEA CRISPA, *WILLD.*

PLATE No. 256.

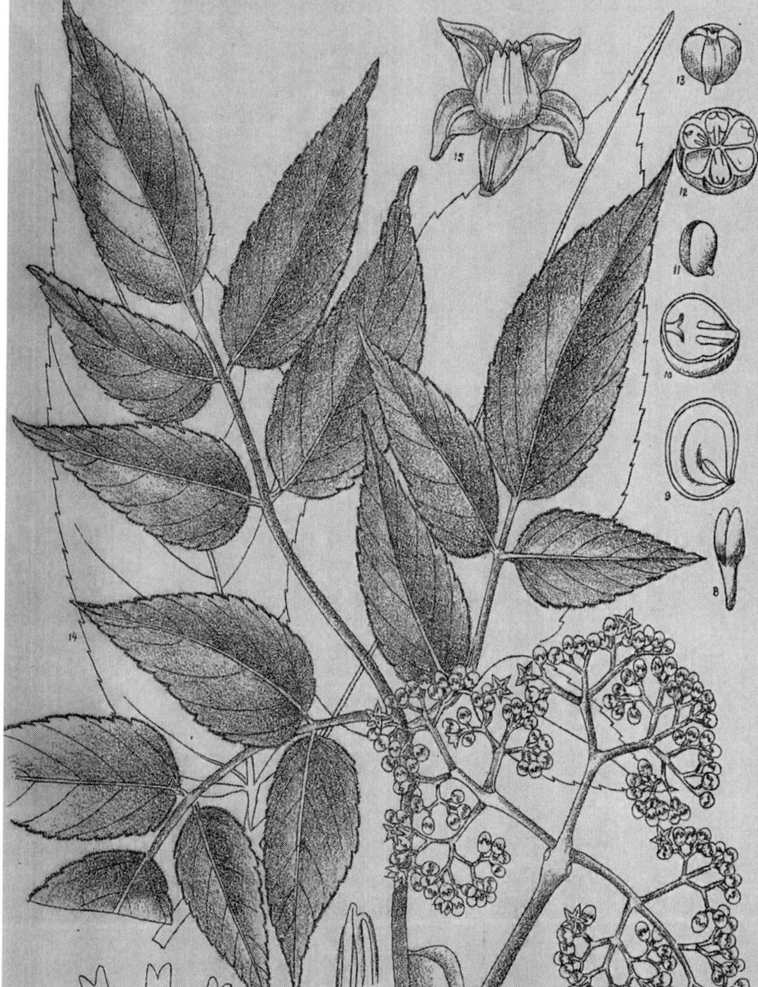

LEEA SAMBUCINA. *WILLD.*

PLATE No. 257.

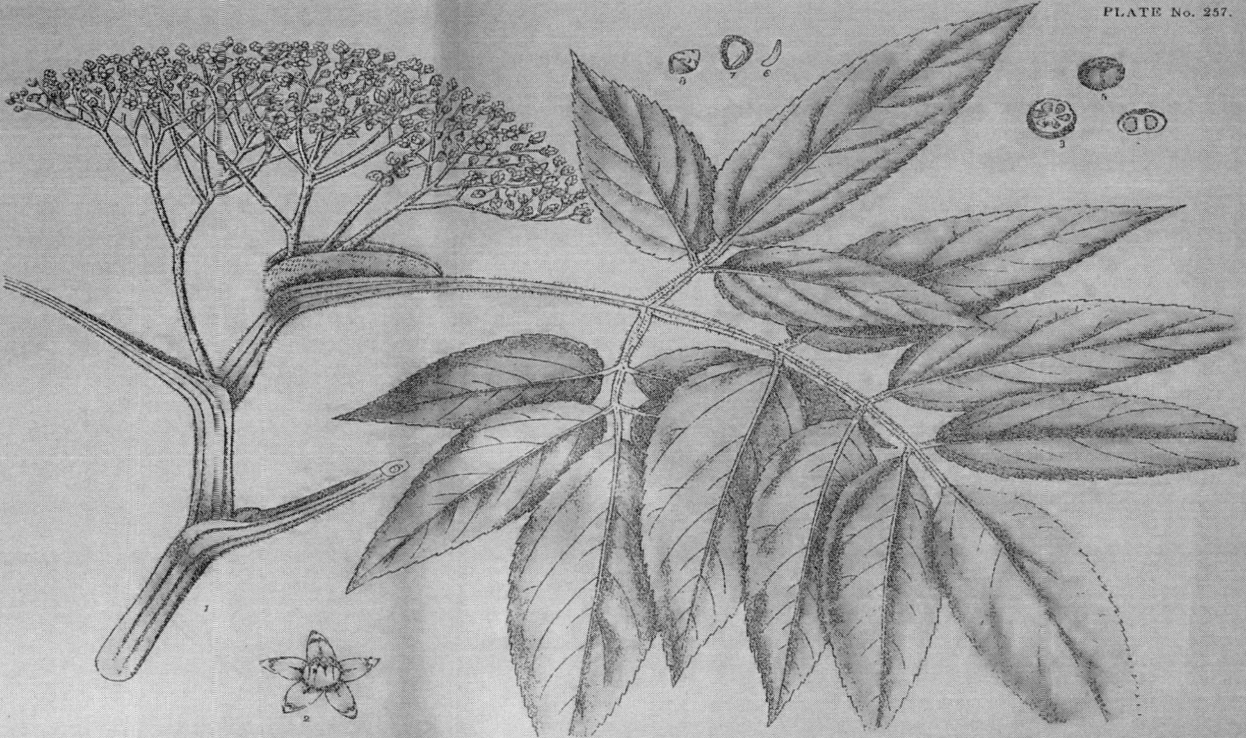

LEEA ROBUSTA, *Roxb.*

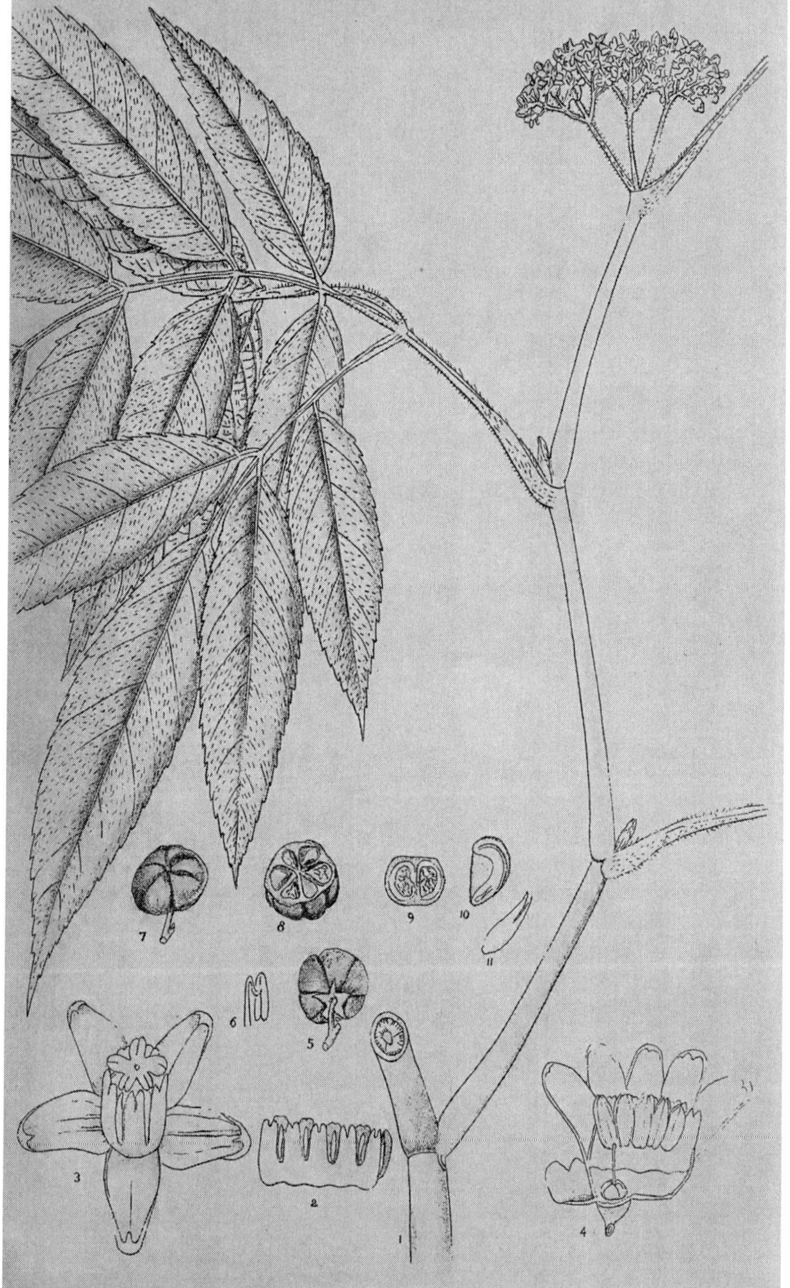

LEEA HIRTA, *ROXB.*

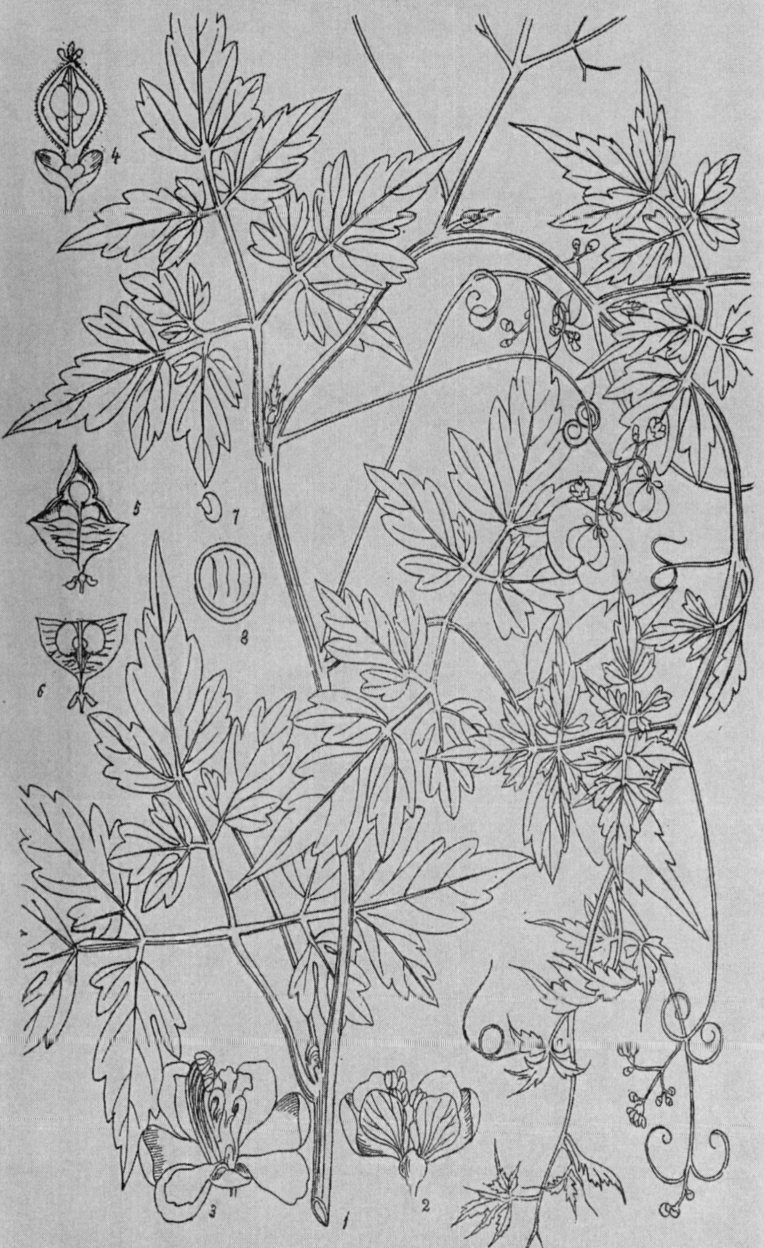

CARDIOSPERMUM HALICACABUM, *LINN.*

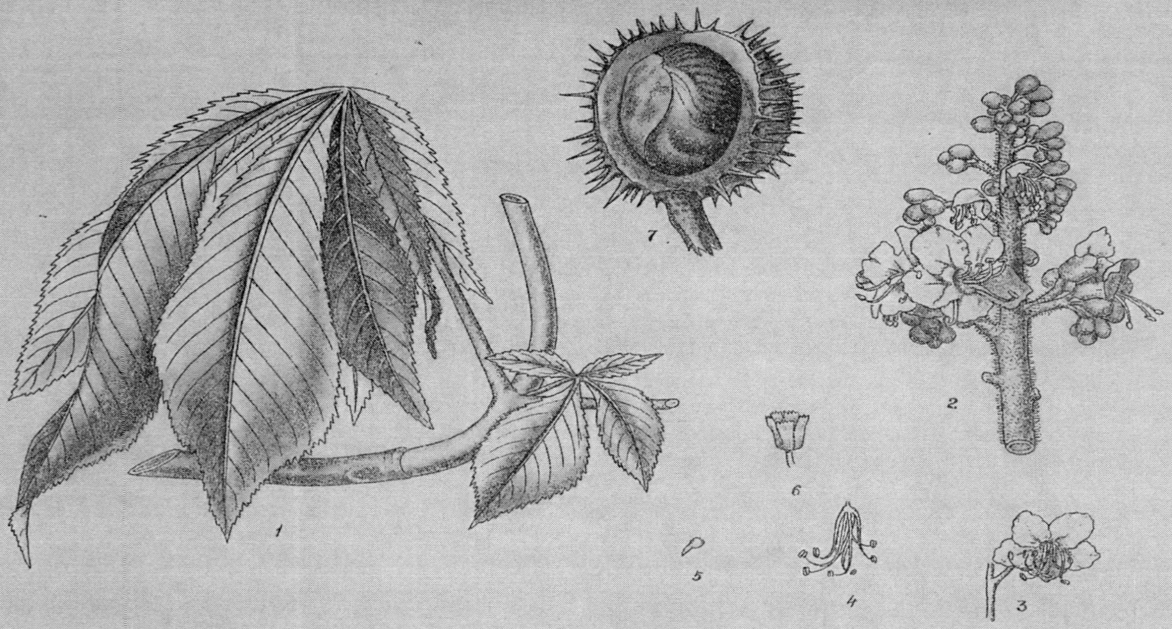

ÆSCULUS HIPPOCASTANUM, *LINN.*

PLATE No. 261.

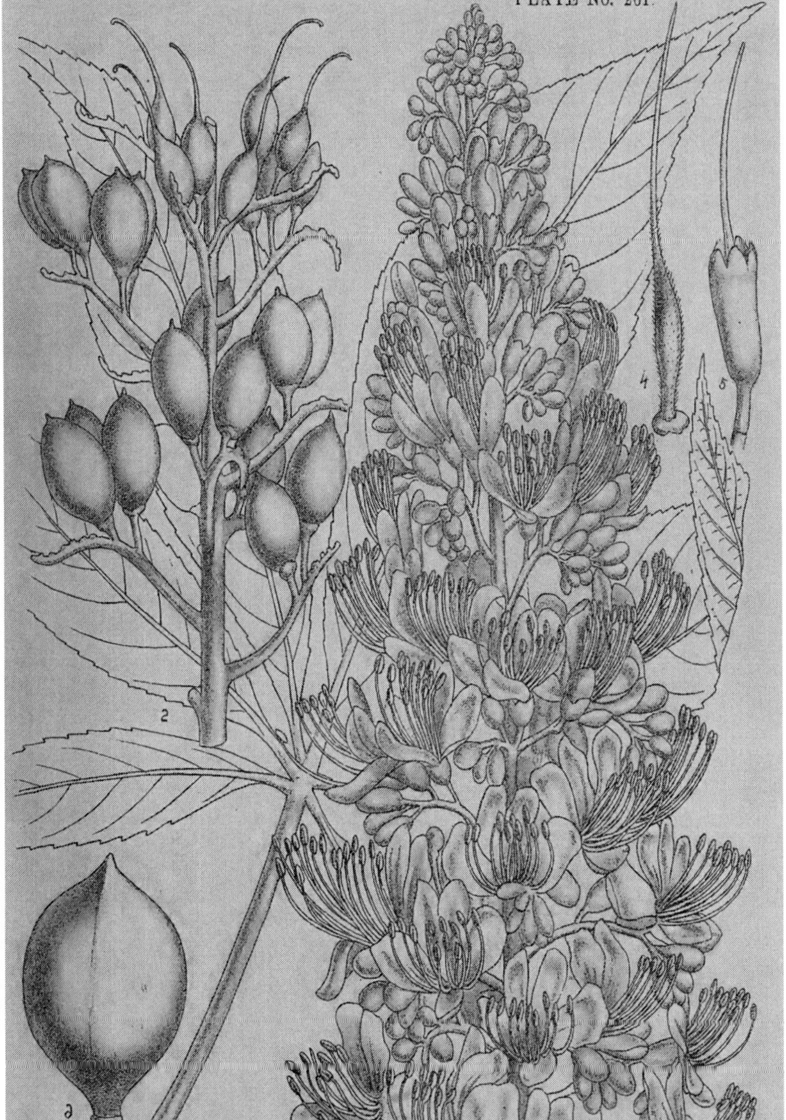

ÆSCULUS INDICA, *HIERN.*

PLATE No. 262

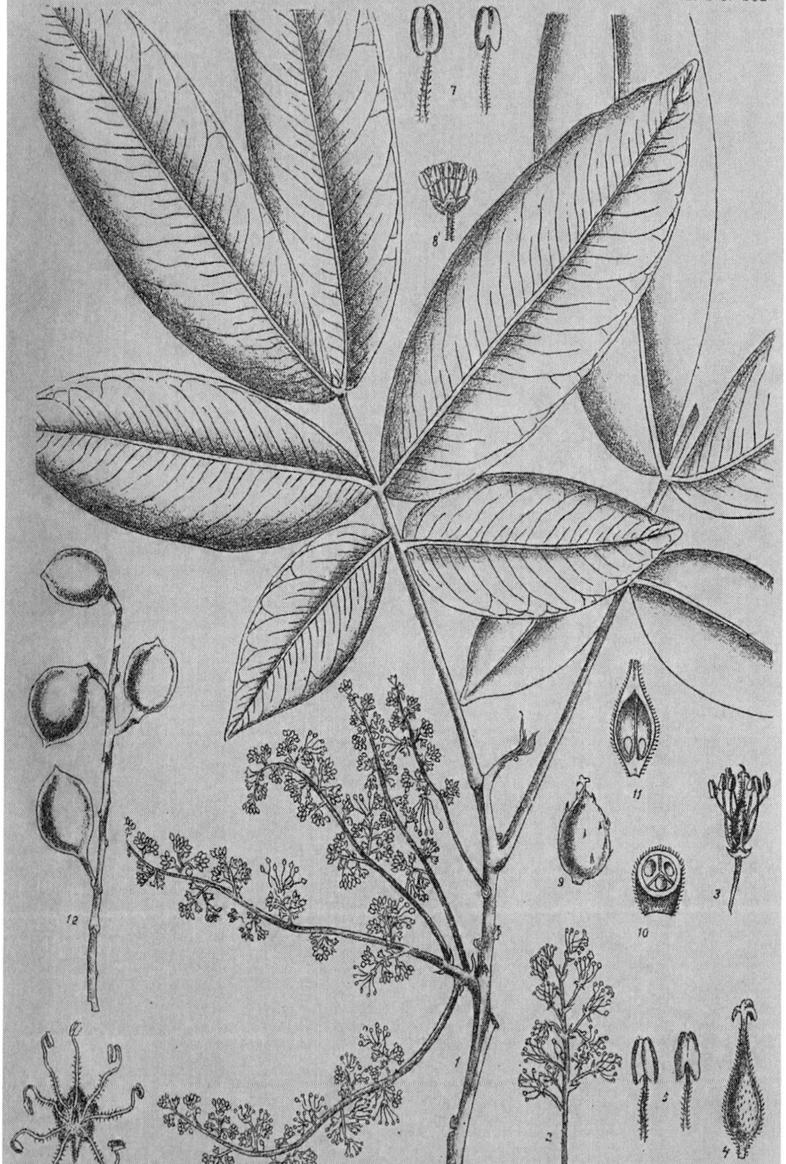

SCHLEICHERA TRIJUGA, *WILLD*

PLTAE No. 263.

SAPINDUS TRIFOLIATUS, *LINN.*

PLATE No. 264.

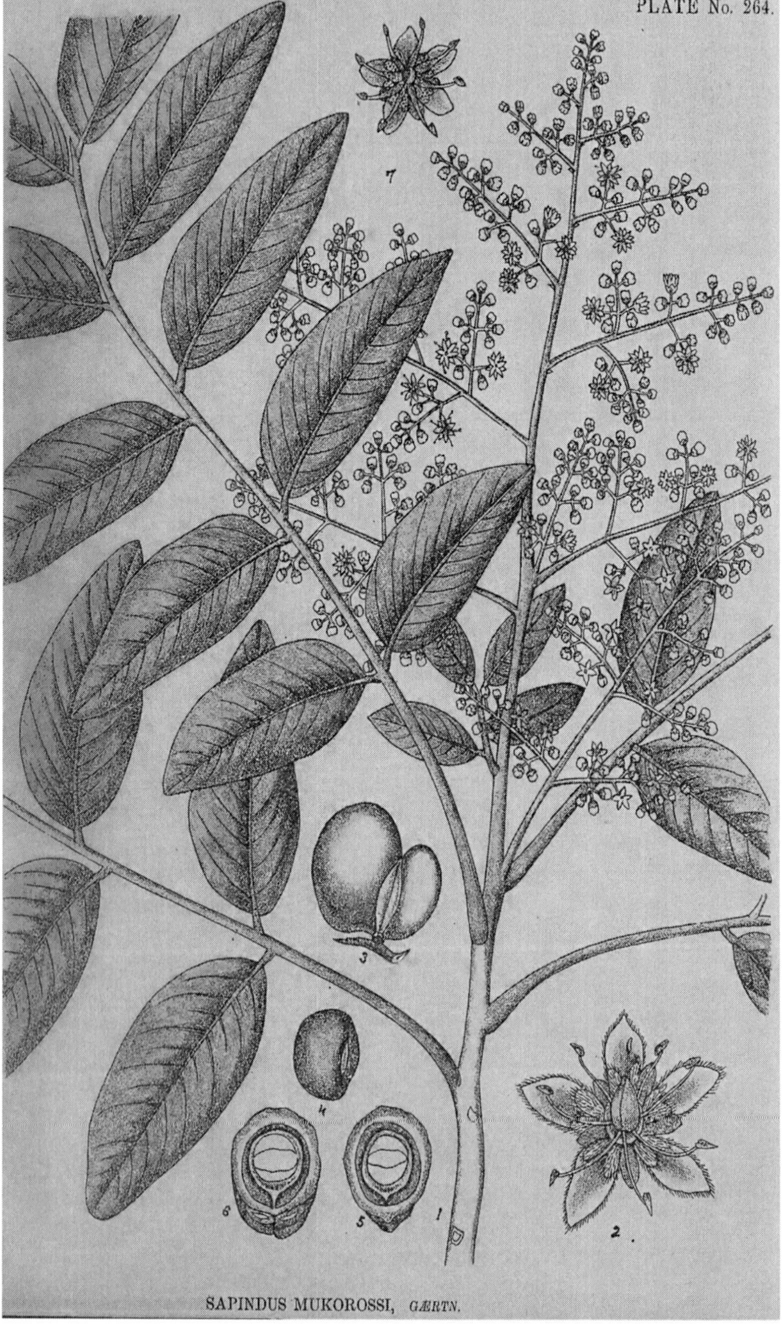

SAPINDUS MUKOROSSI, *GÆRTN.*

PLATE No. 265.

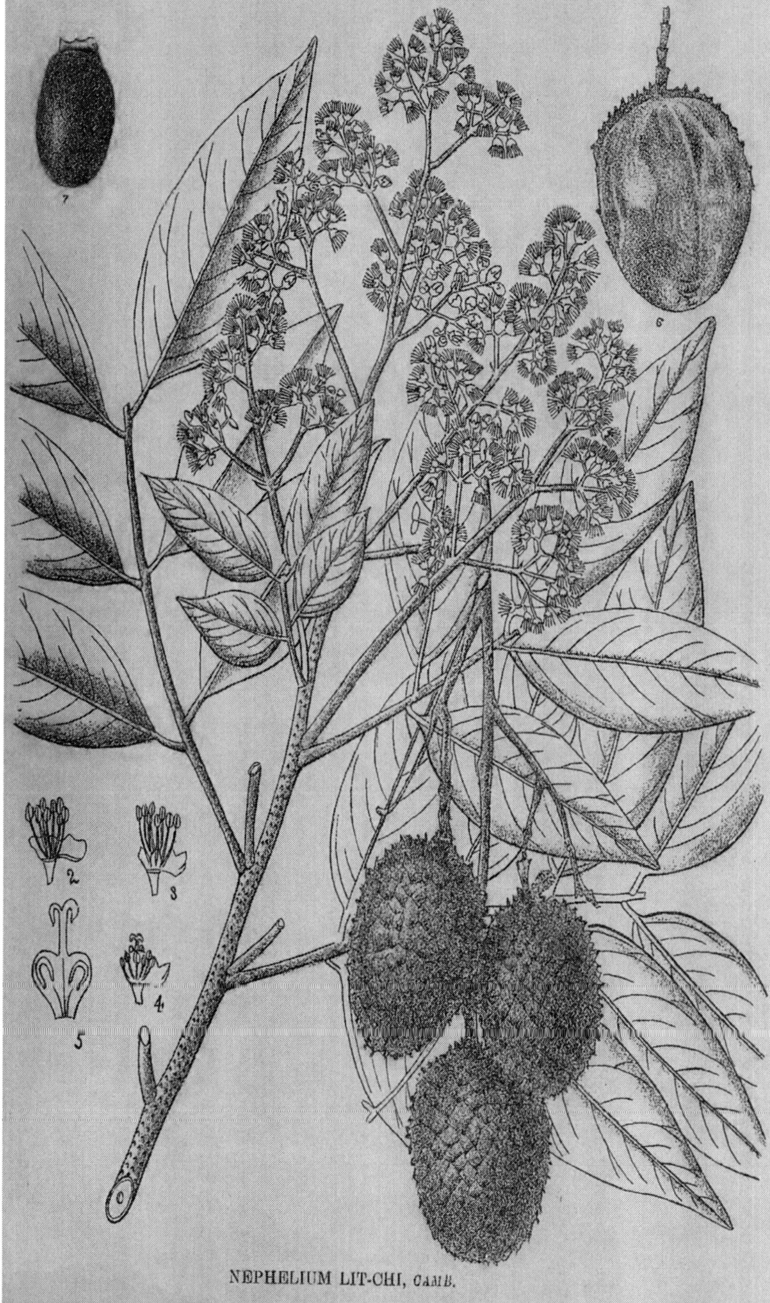

NEPHELIUM LIT-CHI, *Camb.*

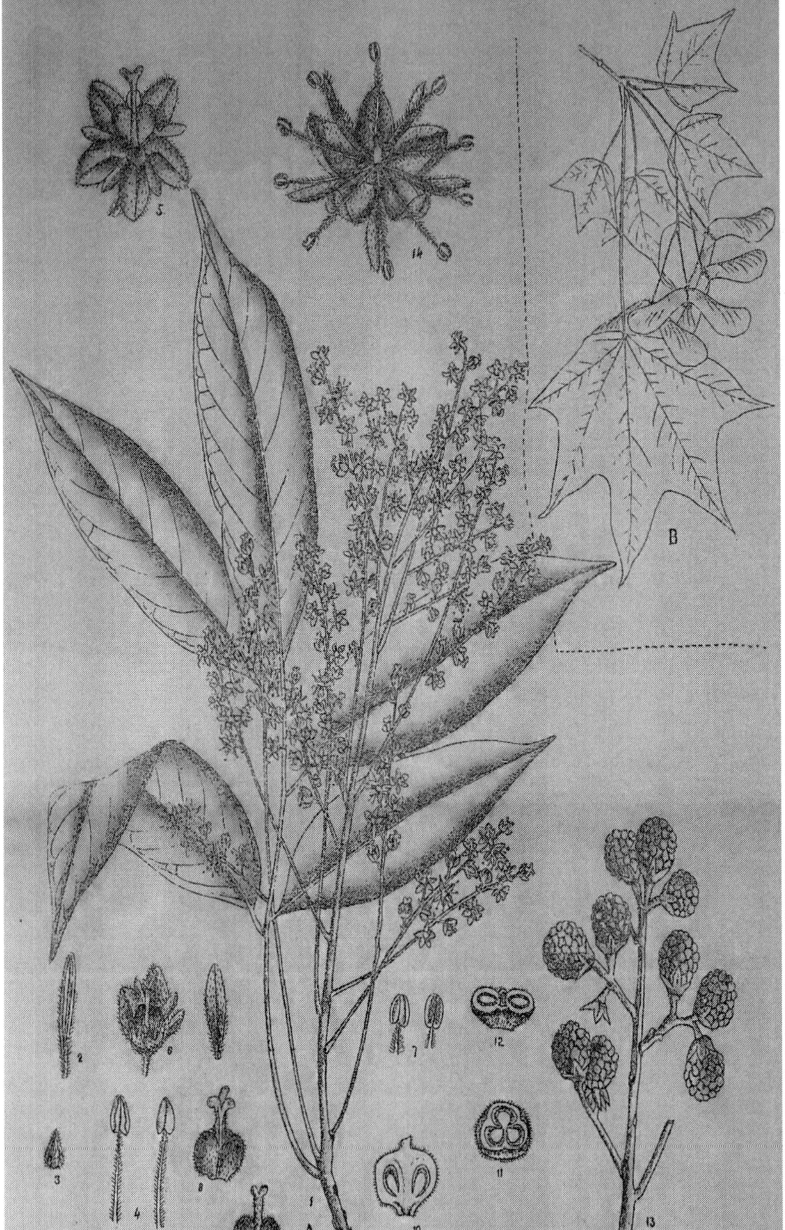

A--NEPHELIUM LONGANA, CAMB.   B--ACER PICTUM, THUMB.

PLATE No 267.

DODONÆA VISCOSA, LINN.

PLATE No. 268.

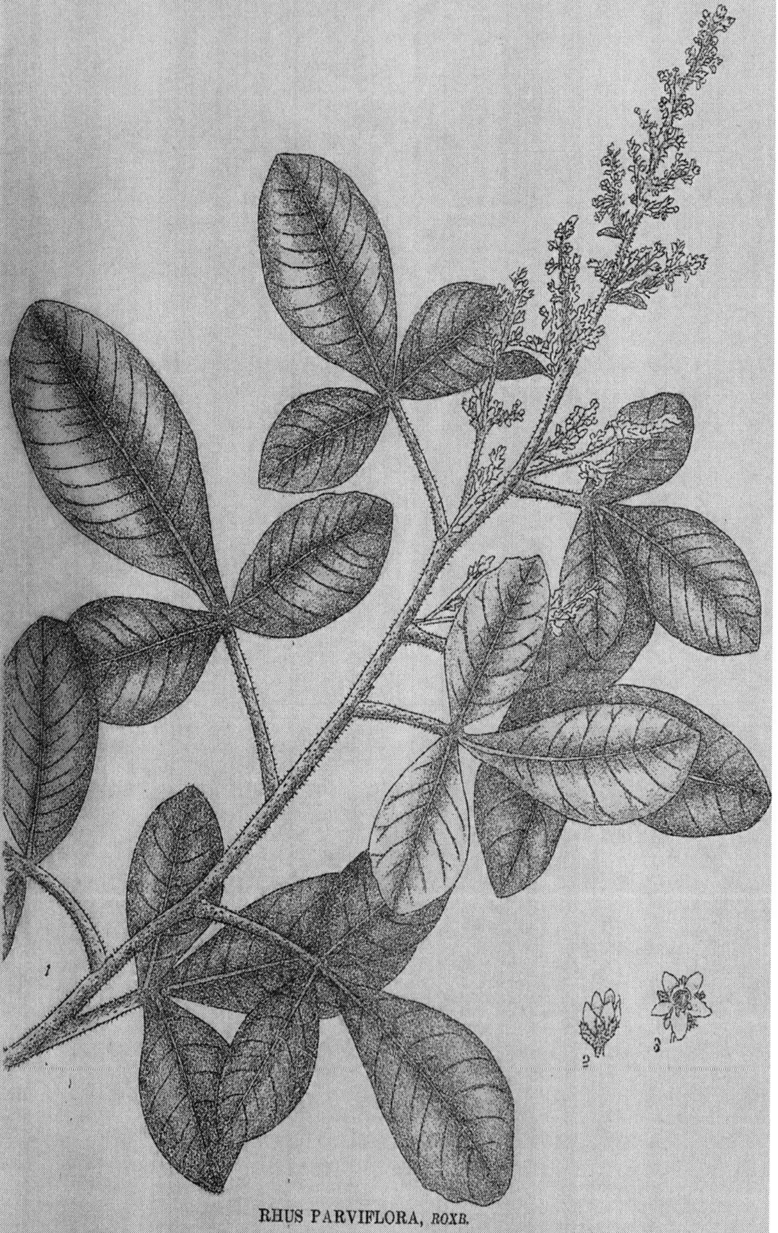

RHUS PARVIFLORA, *ROXB.*

PLATE No. 269.

RHUS SEMI-ALATA, *MURRAY*.

PLATE No 270.

RHUS WALLICHII, HOOK. F.

PLATE No. 271.

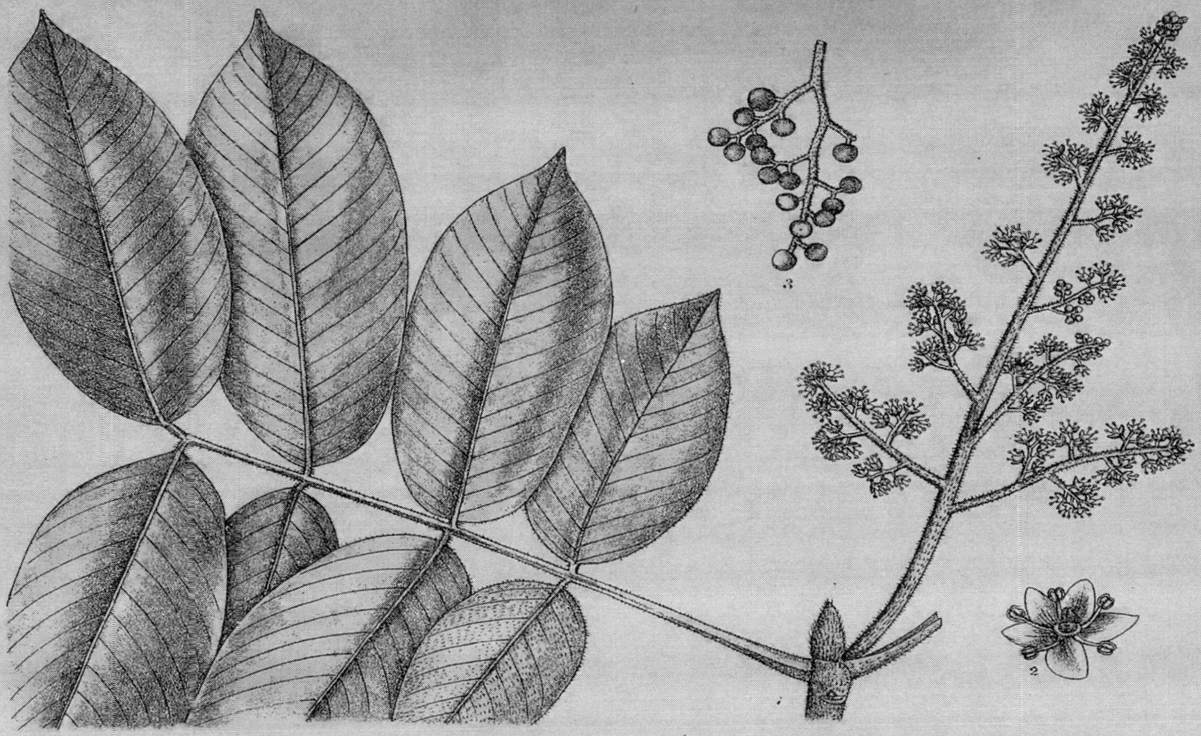

RHUS INSIGNIS, *HOOK. F.*

PLATE No. 272

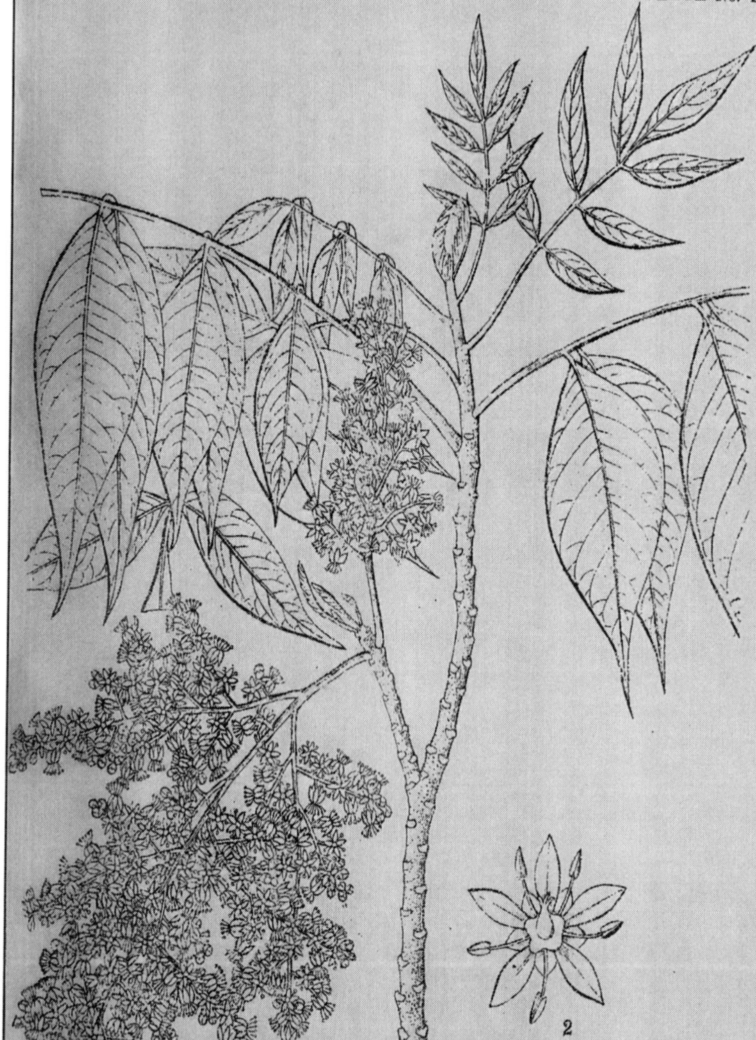

RHUS SUCCEDANEA, *LINN*

PISTACIA INTEGERRIMA, *STEWART.*

PLATE No 274.

MANGIFERA INDICA, *LINN.*

PLATE No. 275.

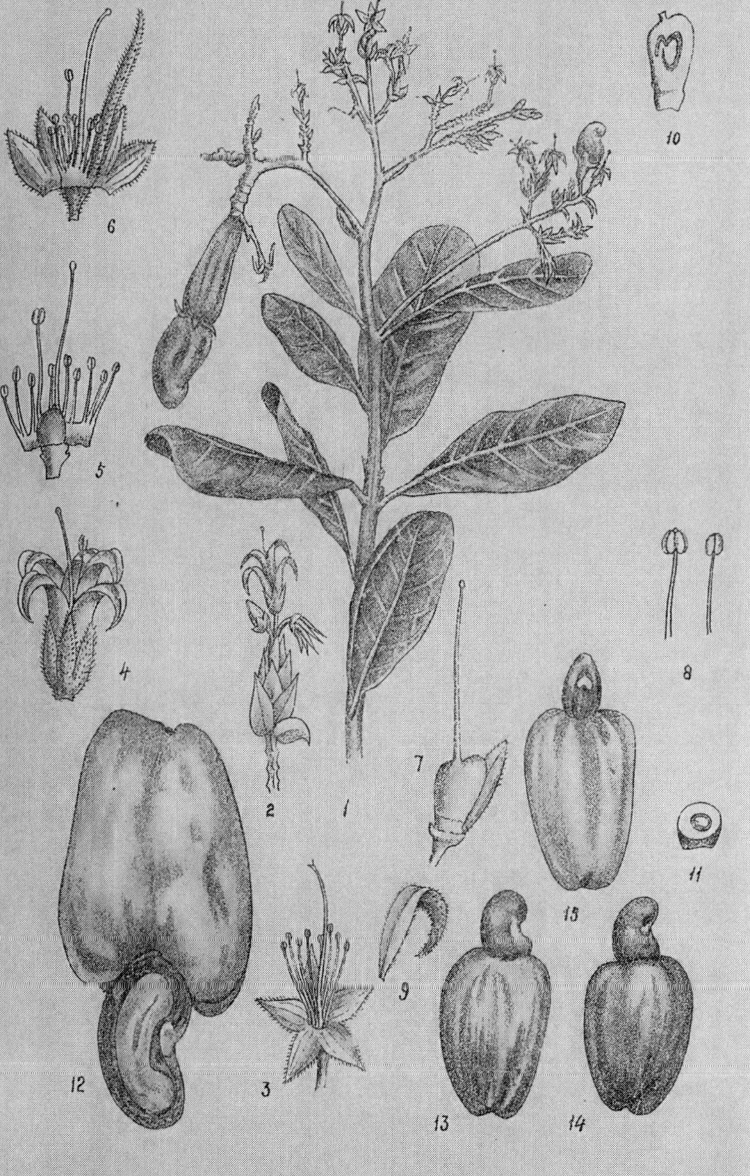

ANACARDIUM OCCIDENTALE, *LINN.*

PLATE No. 276.

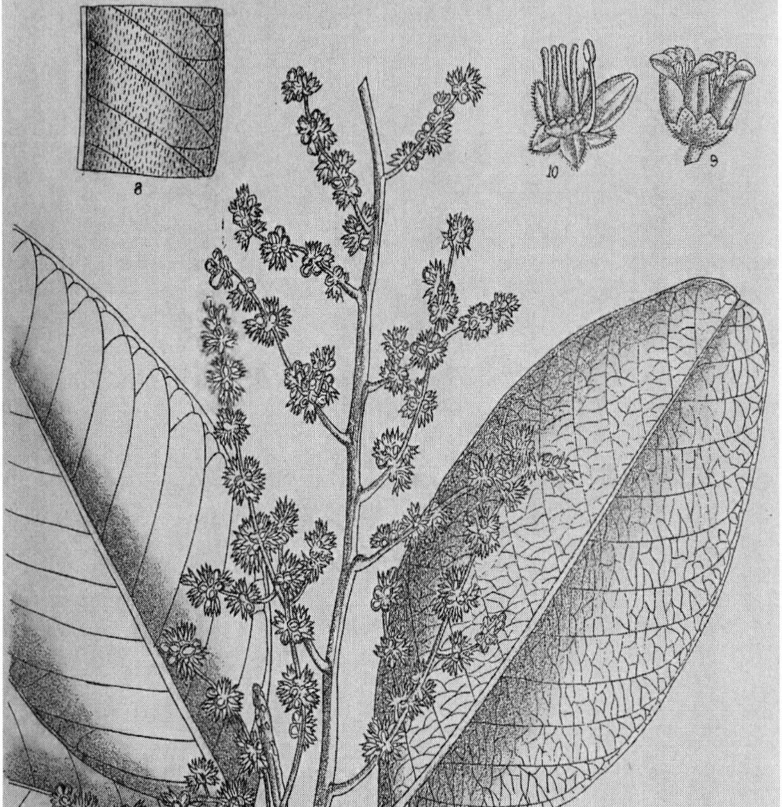

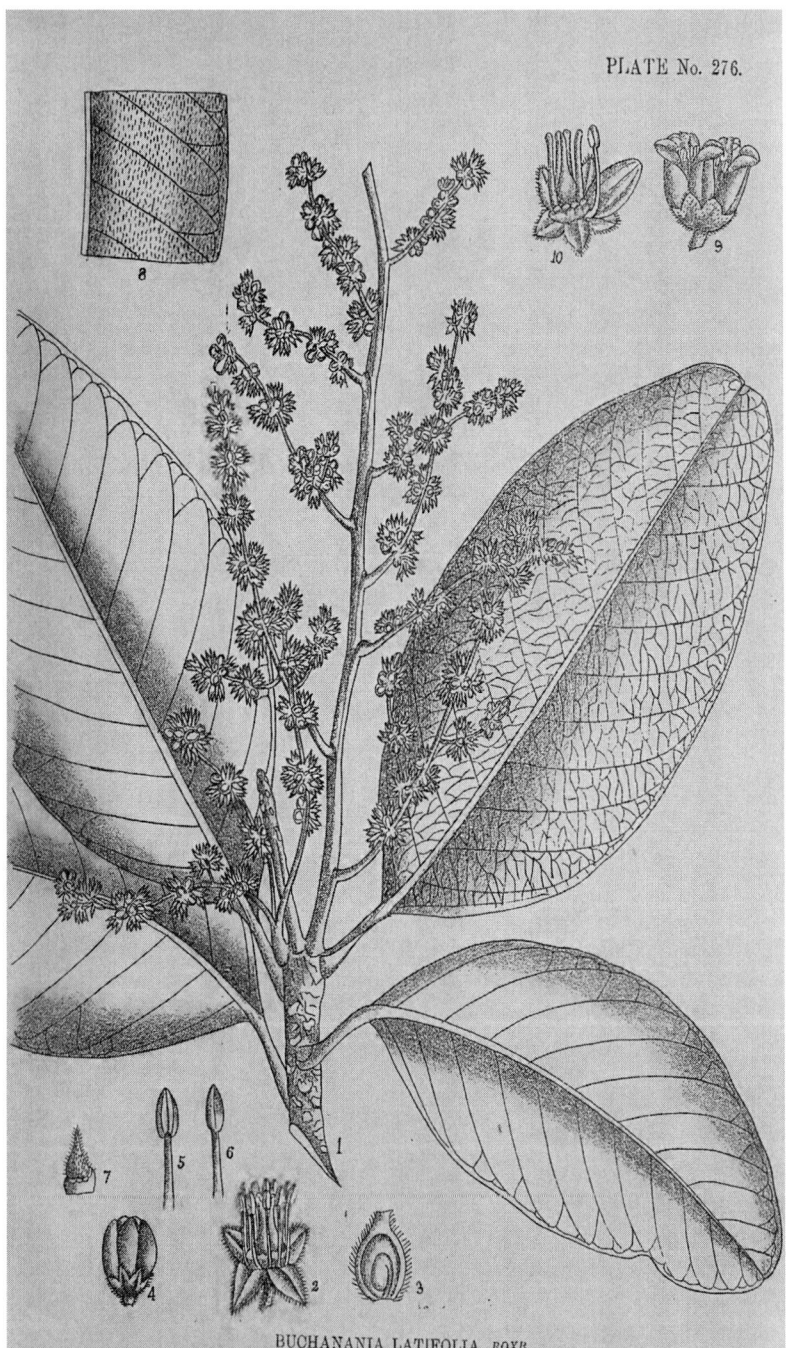

BUCHANANIA LATIFOLIA, *ROXB.*

PLATE No. 277.

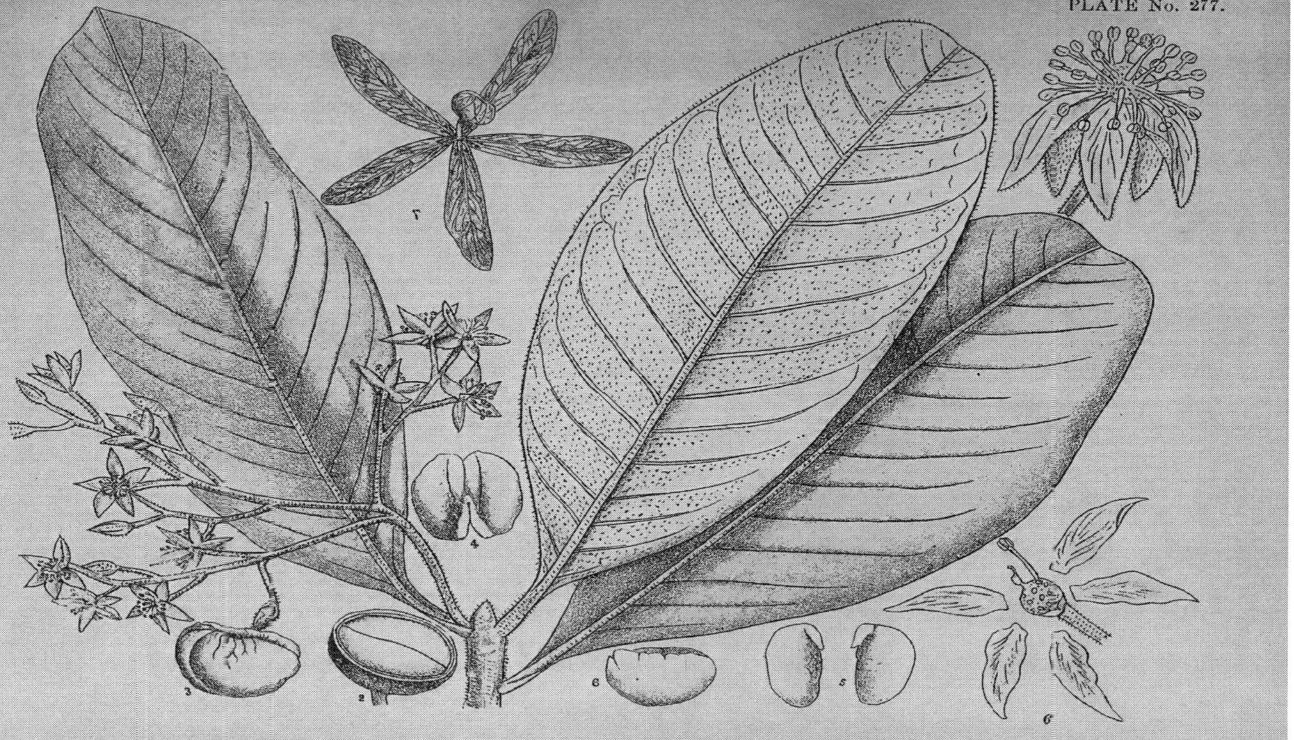

MELANORRHŒA USITATA, *Wall.*

ODINA WODIER, ROXB.

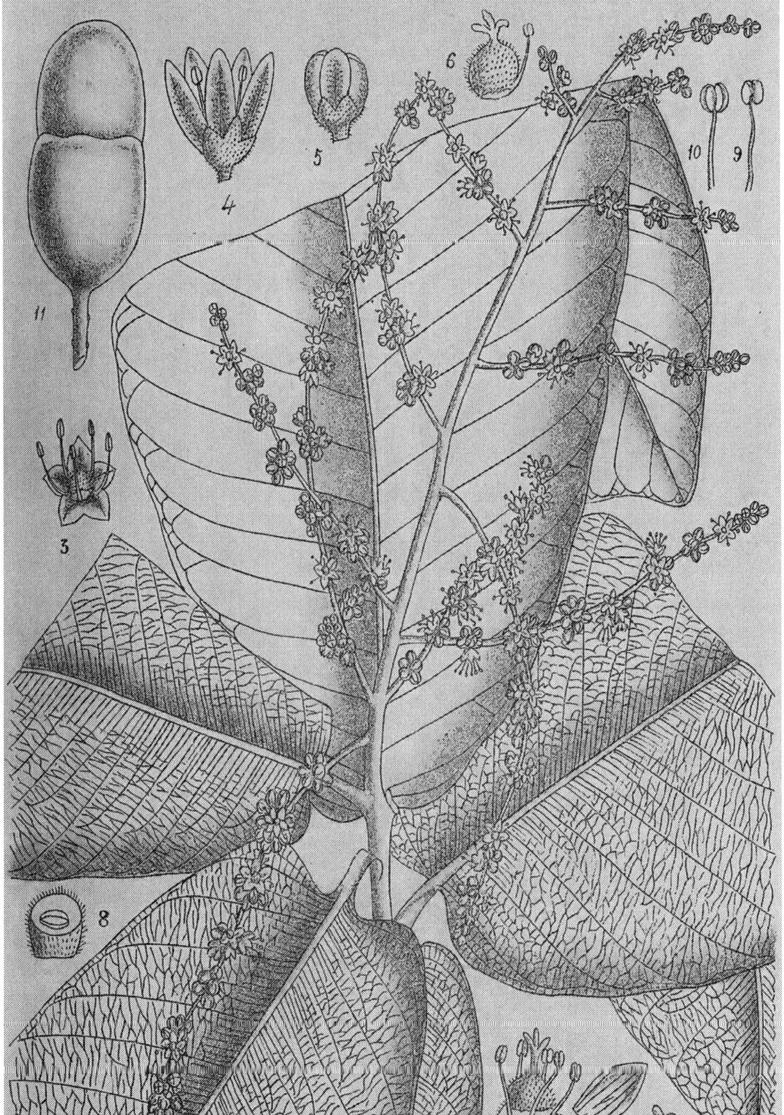

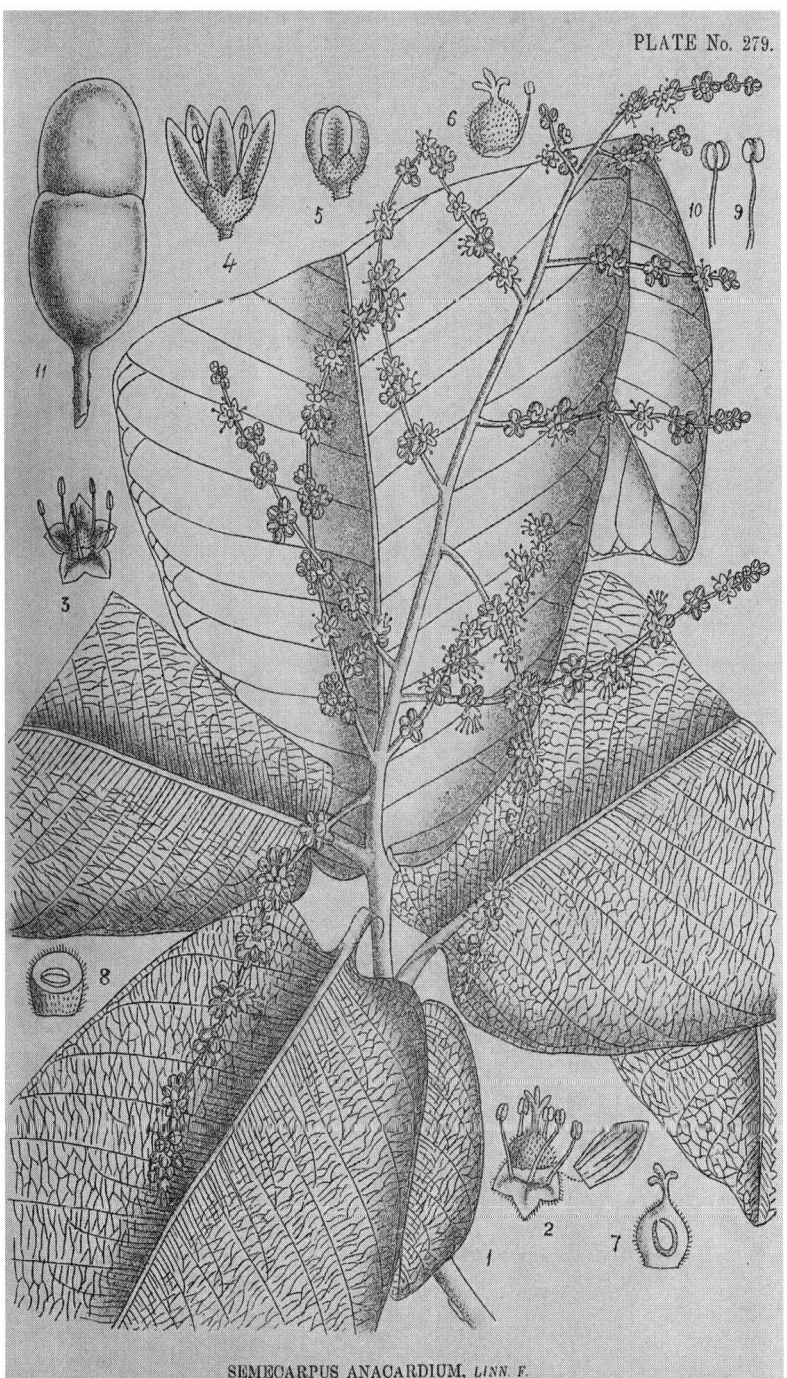

SEMECARPUS ANACARDIUM, LINN. F.

PLATE No 280.

HOLIGARNA ARNOTTIANA, HOOK F.

PLATE No. 281.

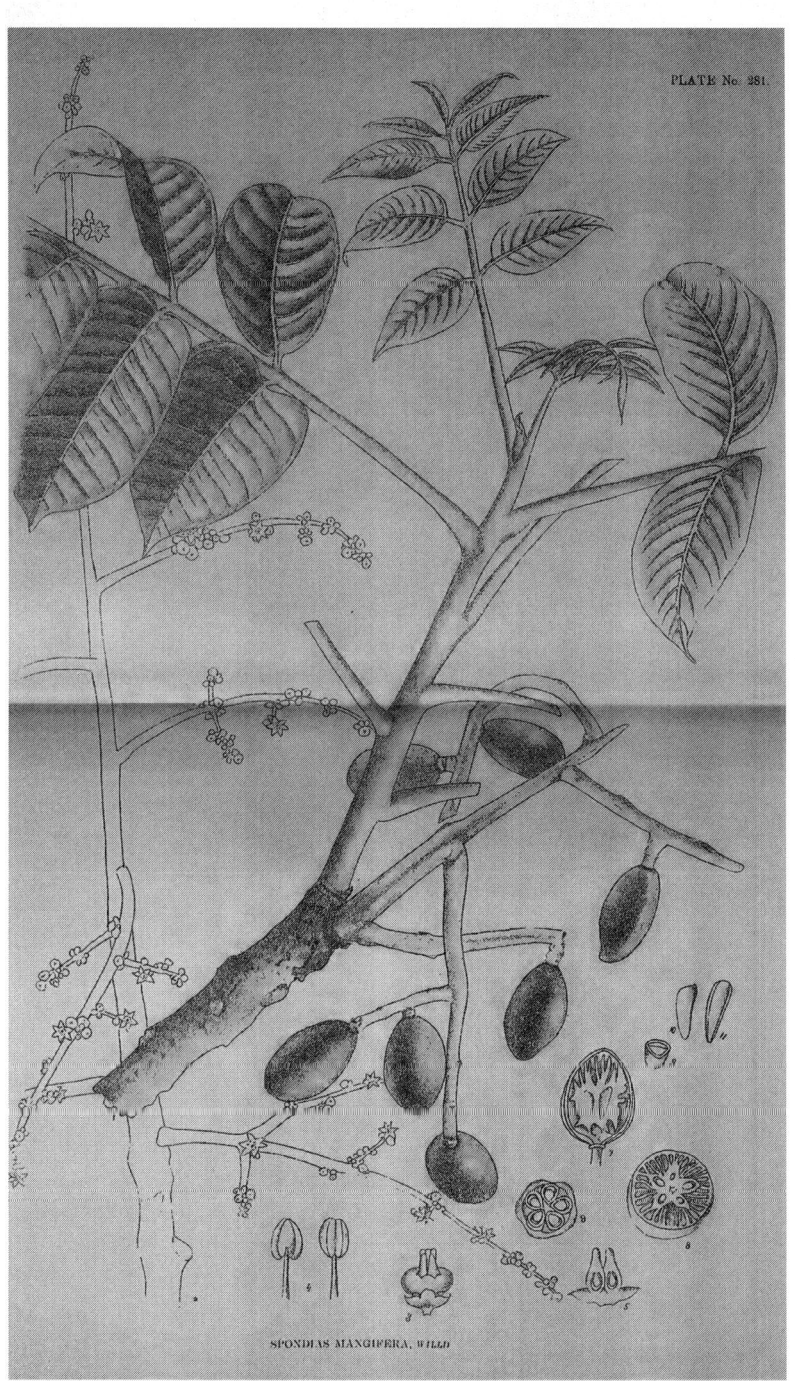

SPONDIAS MANGIFERA, *Willd*

PLATE No. 282.

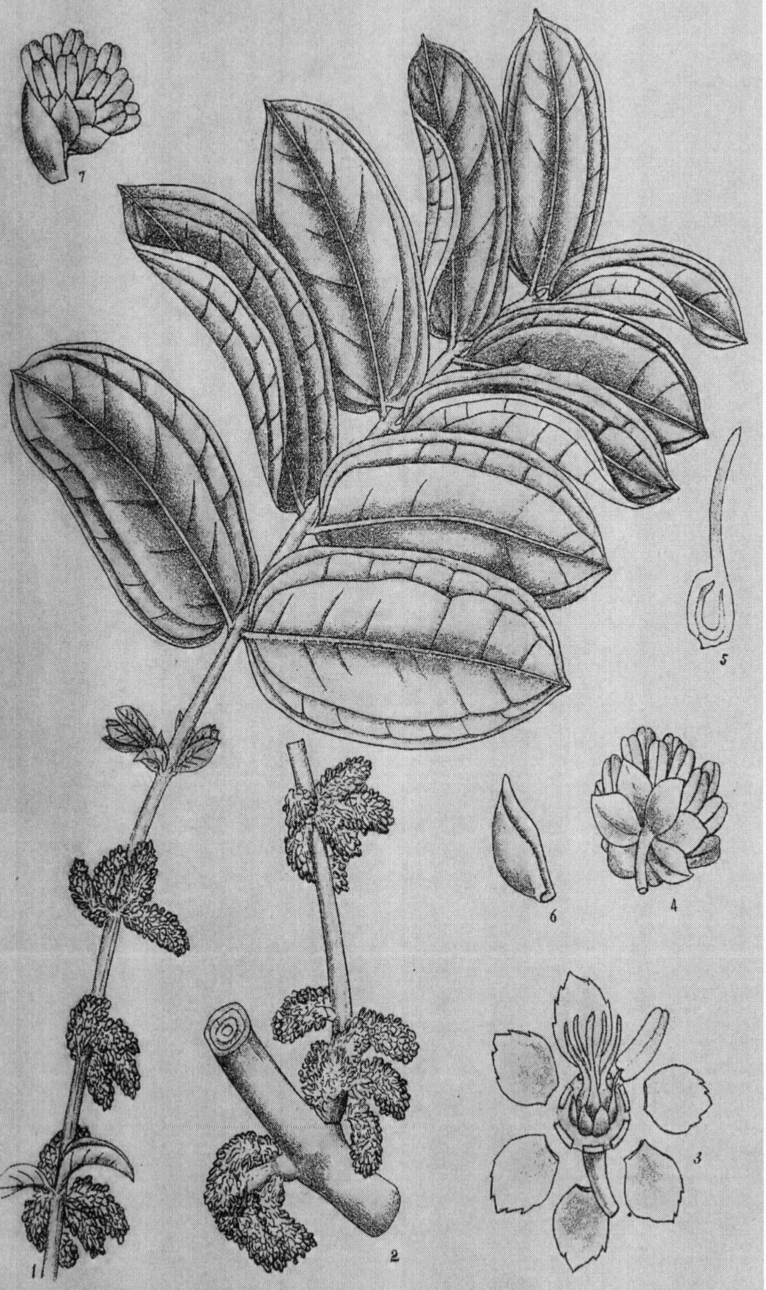

CORIARIA NEPALENSIS, WALL.

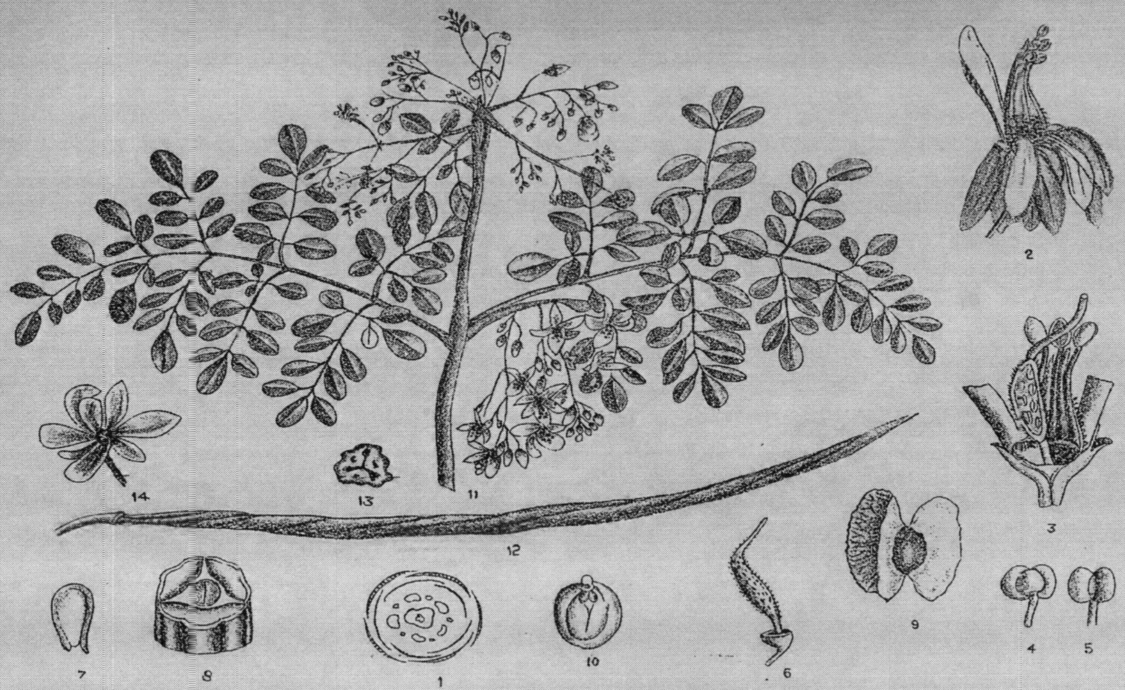

MORINGA PTERYGOSPERMA, *GAERTN.*

PLATE No. 284.

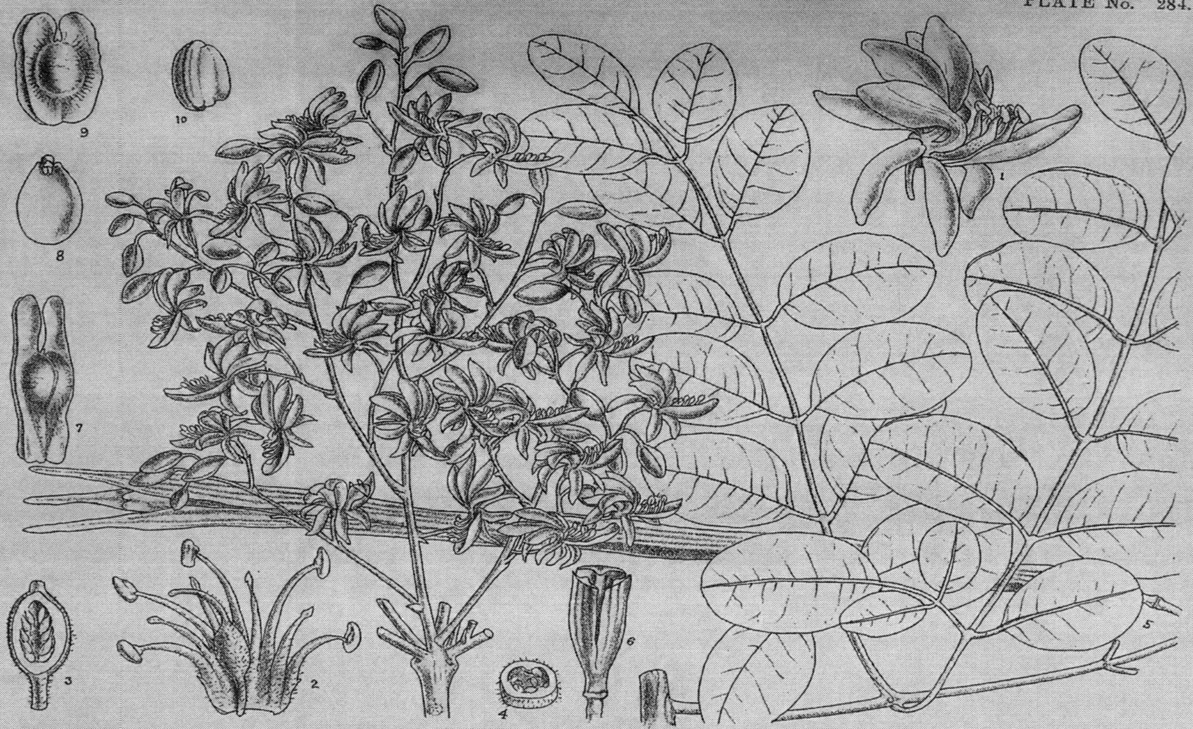

MORINGA CONCANENSIS, *NIMM.*

PLATE No. 285.

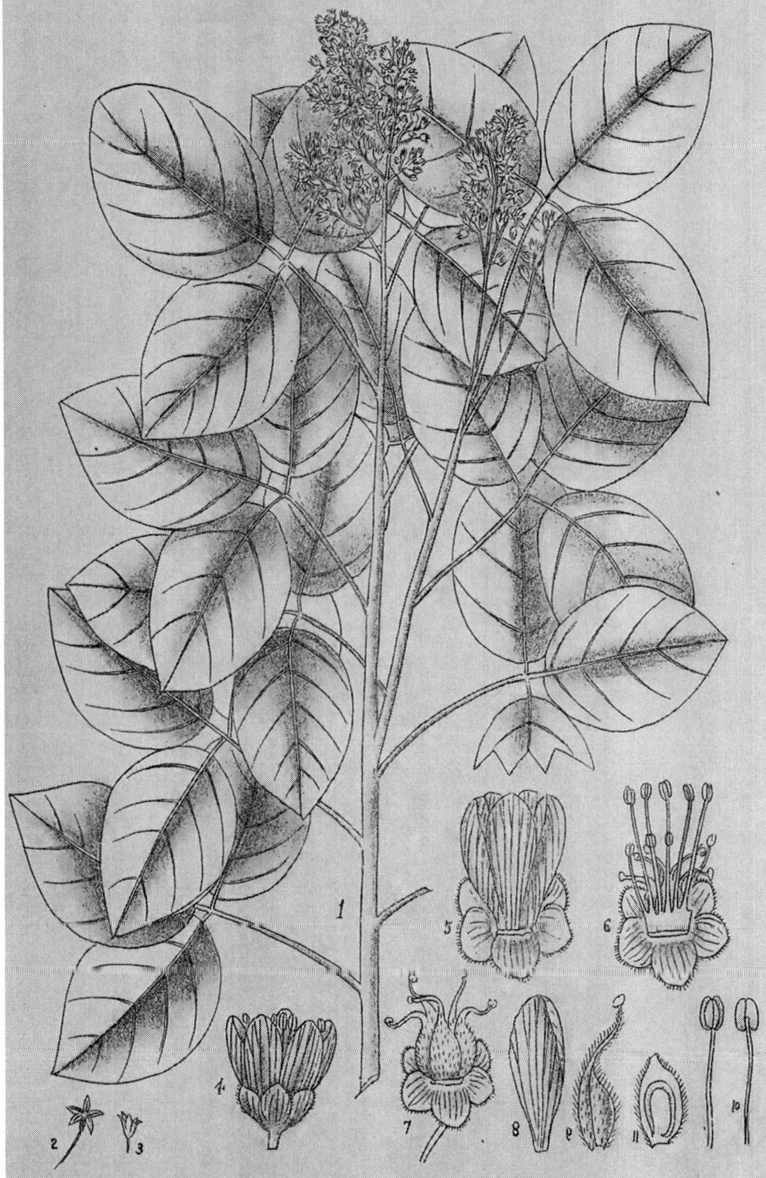

ROUREA SANTALOIDES, *W. & A.*

PLATE No 286.

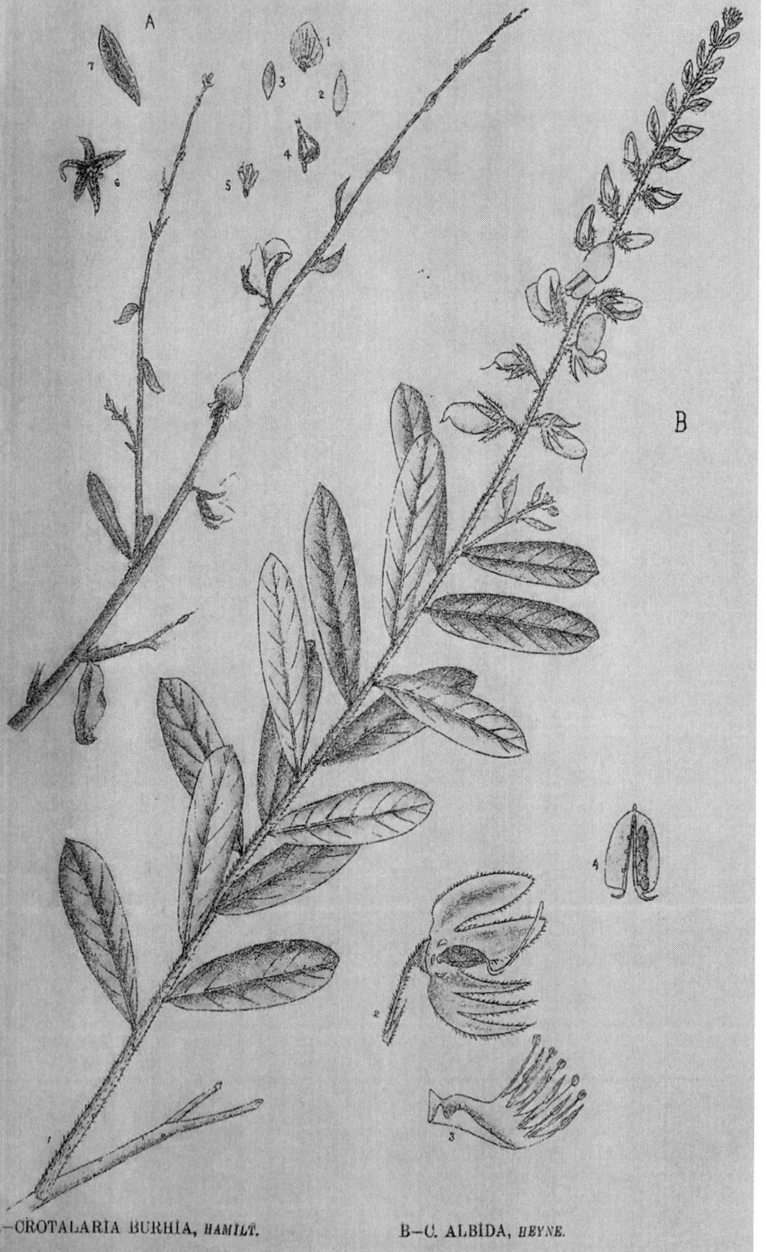

A—CROTALARIA BURHIA, *HAMILT.* B—C. ALBIDA, *HEYNE.*

PLATE No. 287

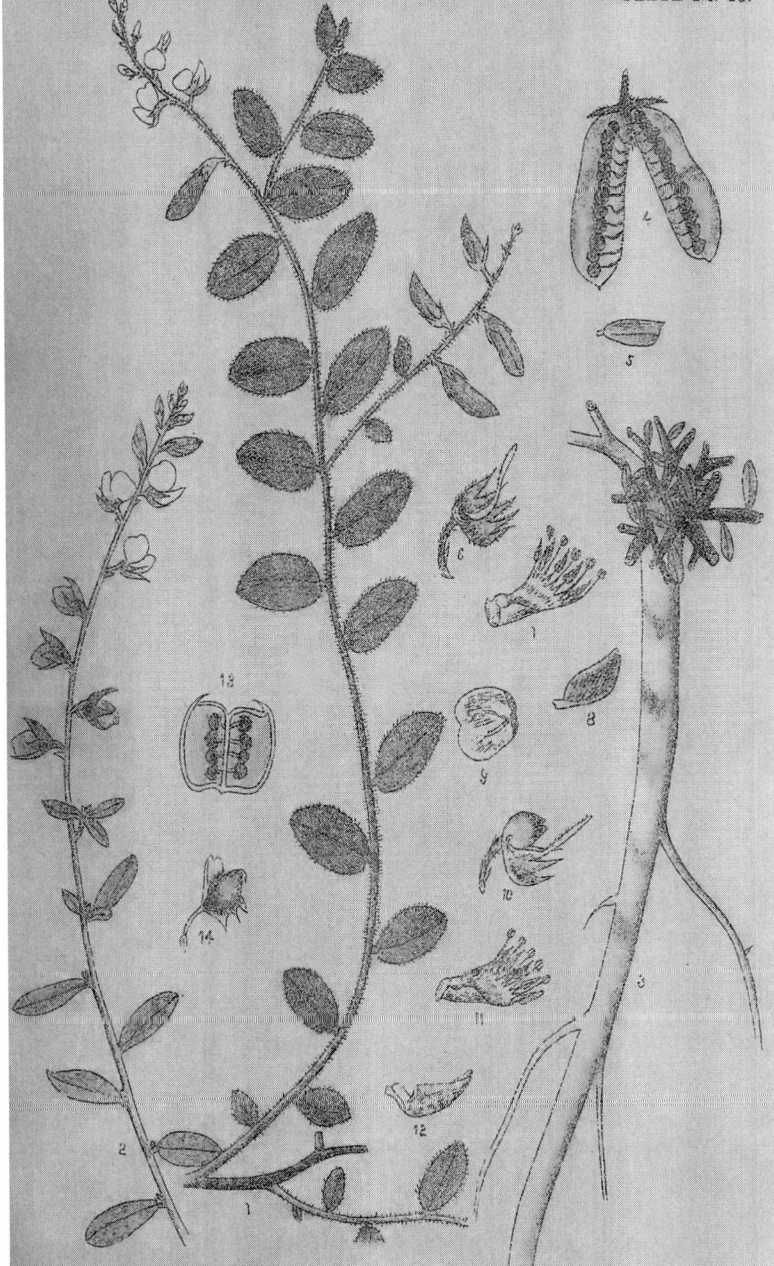

CROTALARIA PROSTRATA, *ROXB.*

PLATE No. 288

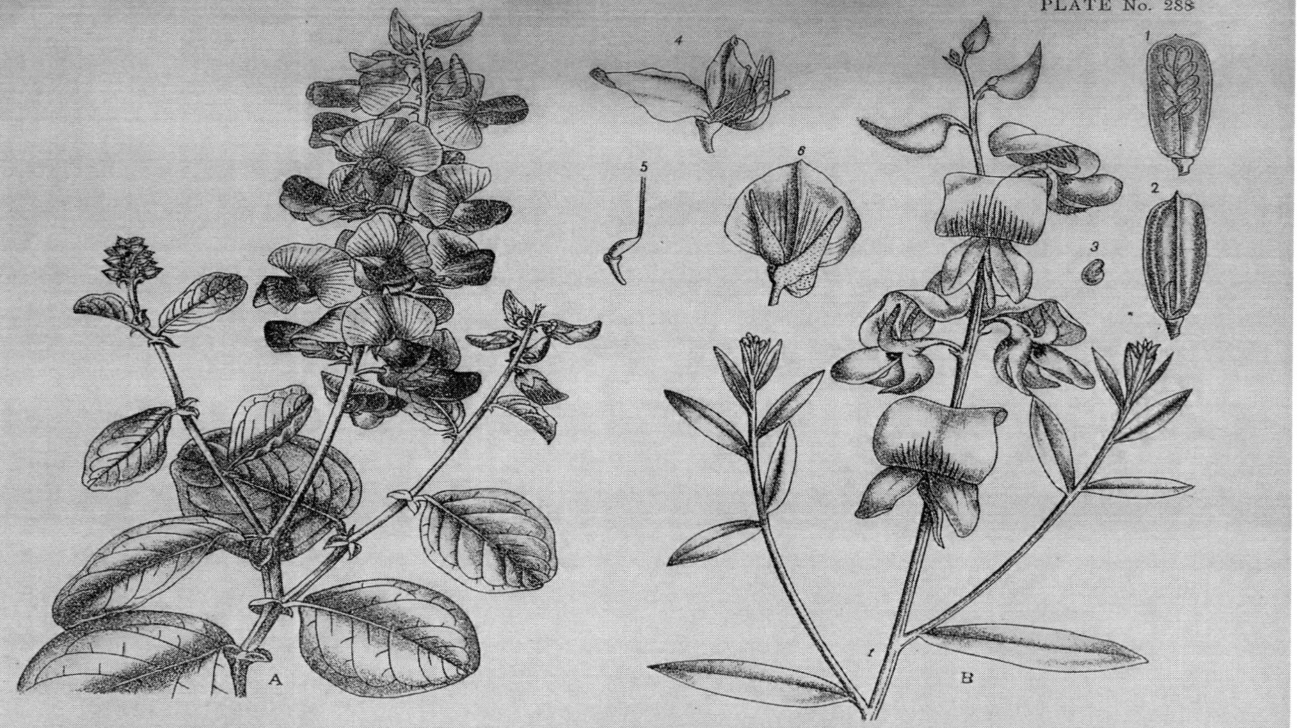

A—CROTALARIA VERRUCOSA, *LINN.* B—C. JUNCEA, *LINN.*

A--CROTALARIA TRIFOLIASTRUM, *WILLD.* B--C. MEDICAGINEA, *LAMK.*

PLATE No. 290.

A—TRIGONELLA OCCULTA, DELILE B—T. FŒNUM GRÆCUM. LINN.

PLATE No. 291.

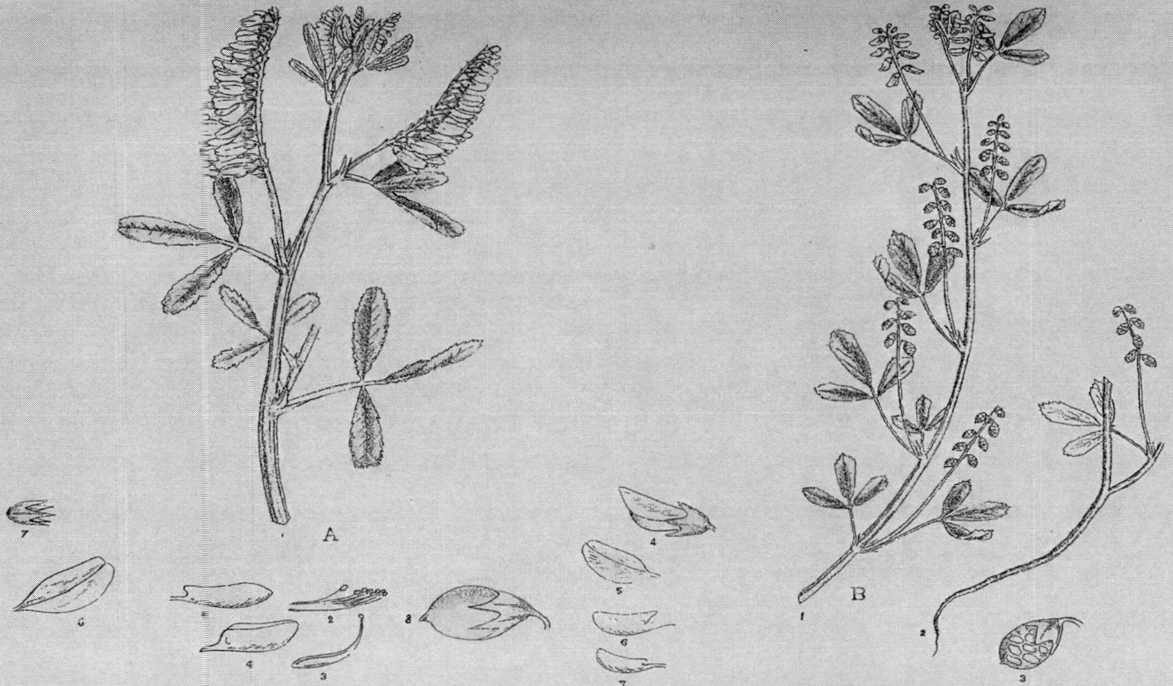

A—MELILOTUS OFFICINALIS, *WILLD.*

B—M. PARVIFLORA, *DESF.*

PLATE No. 292.

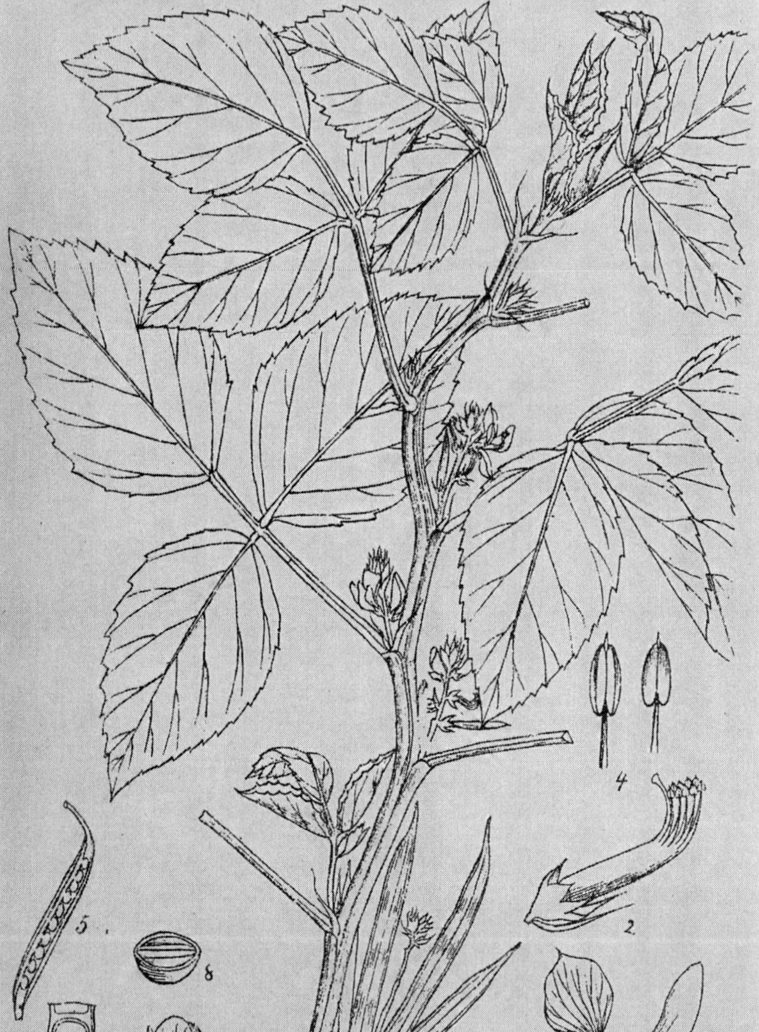

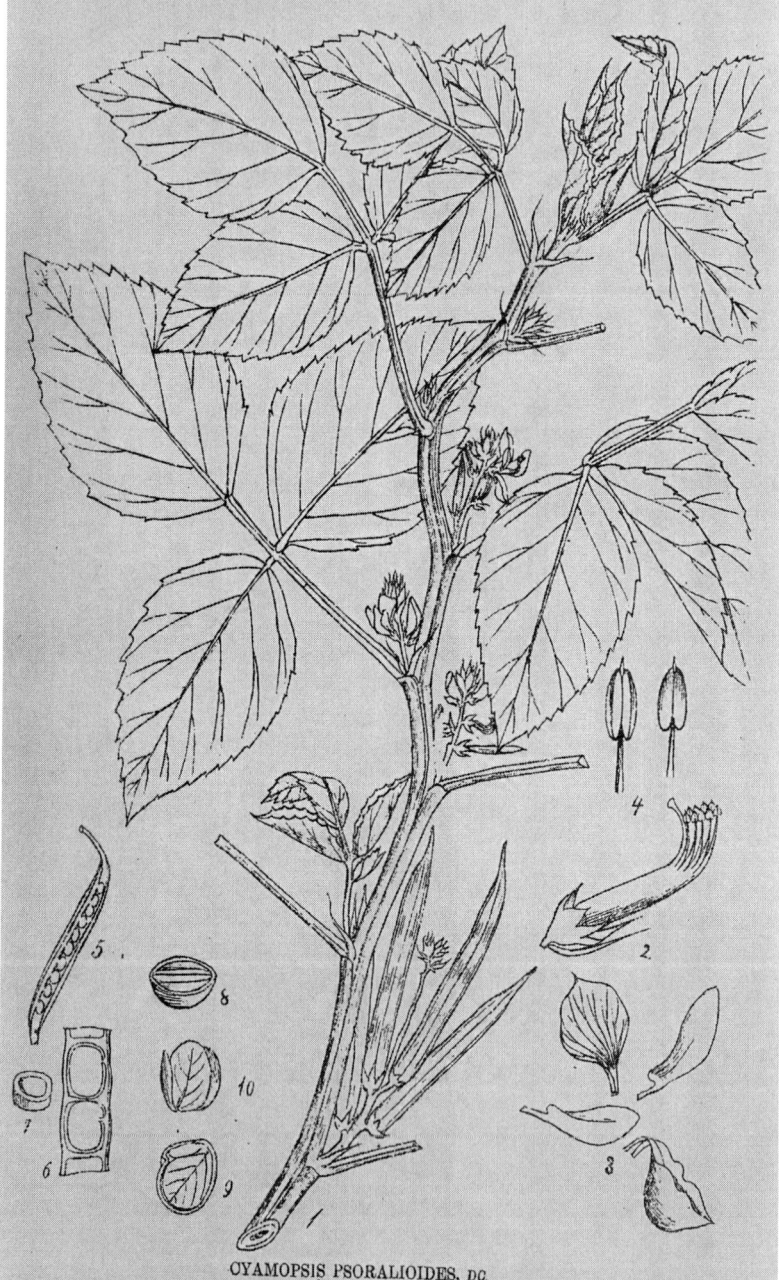

CYAMOPSIS PSORALIOIDES, DC.

PLATE No 293.

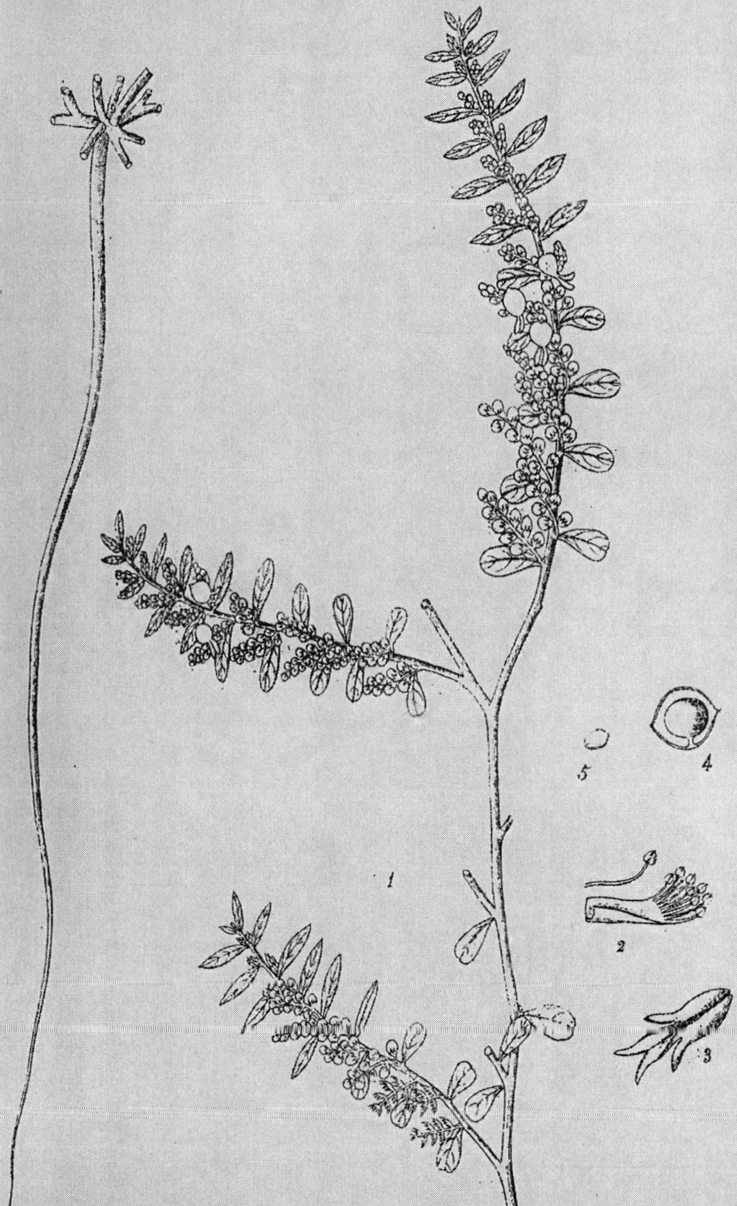

INDIGOFERA LINIFOLIA, *RETZ.*

PLATE No. 294.

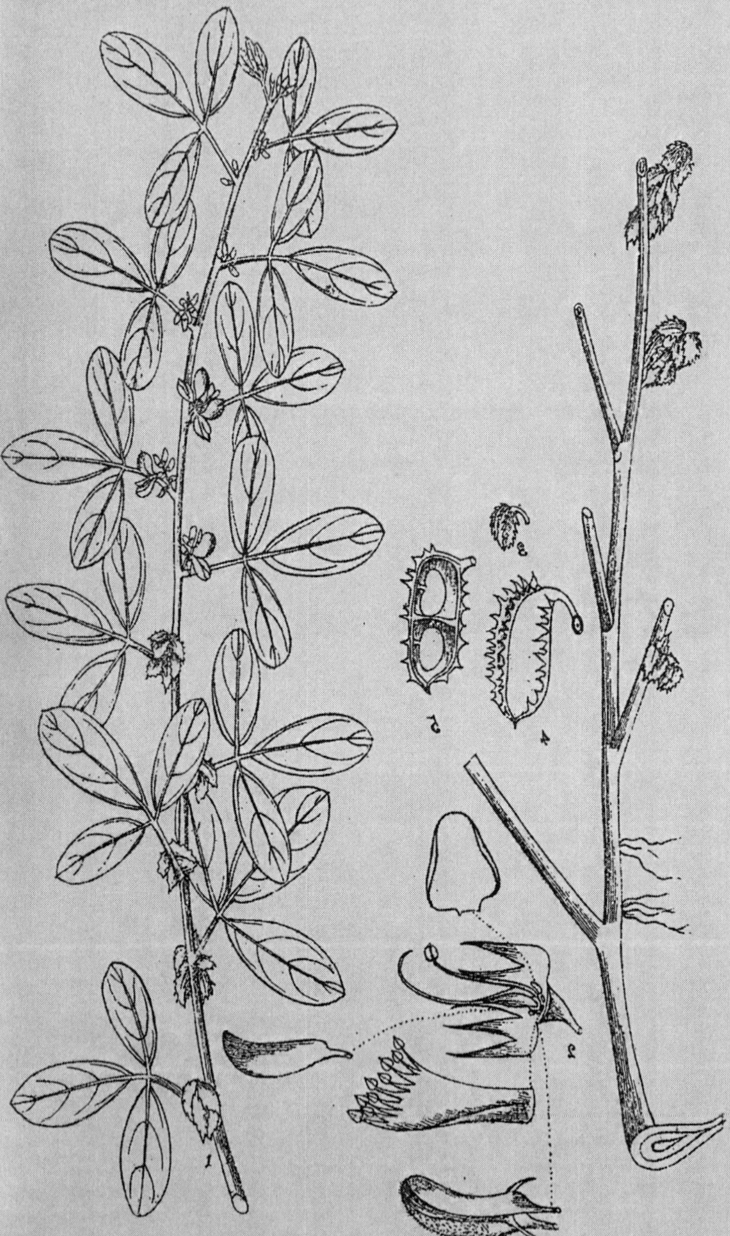

INDIGOFERA GLANDULOSA, *WILLD.*

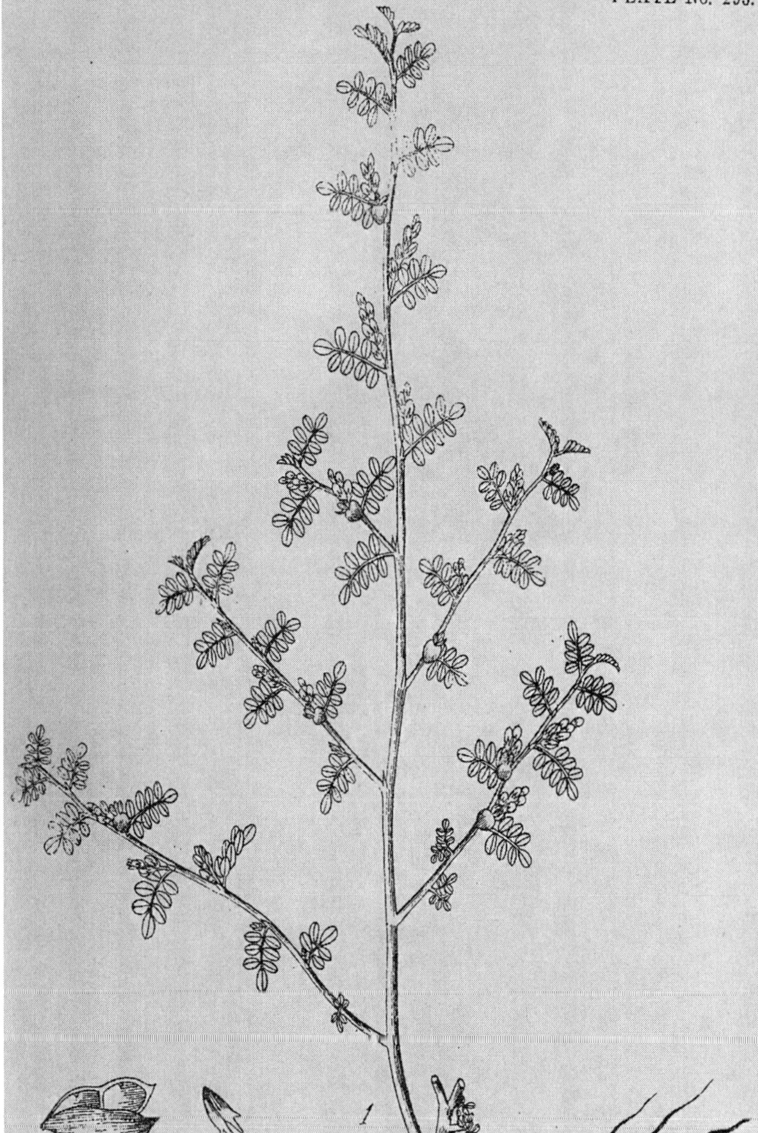

INDIGOFERA ENNEAPHYLLA, *LINN.*

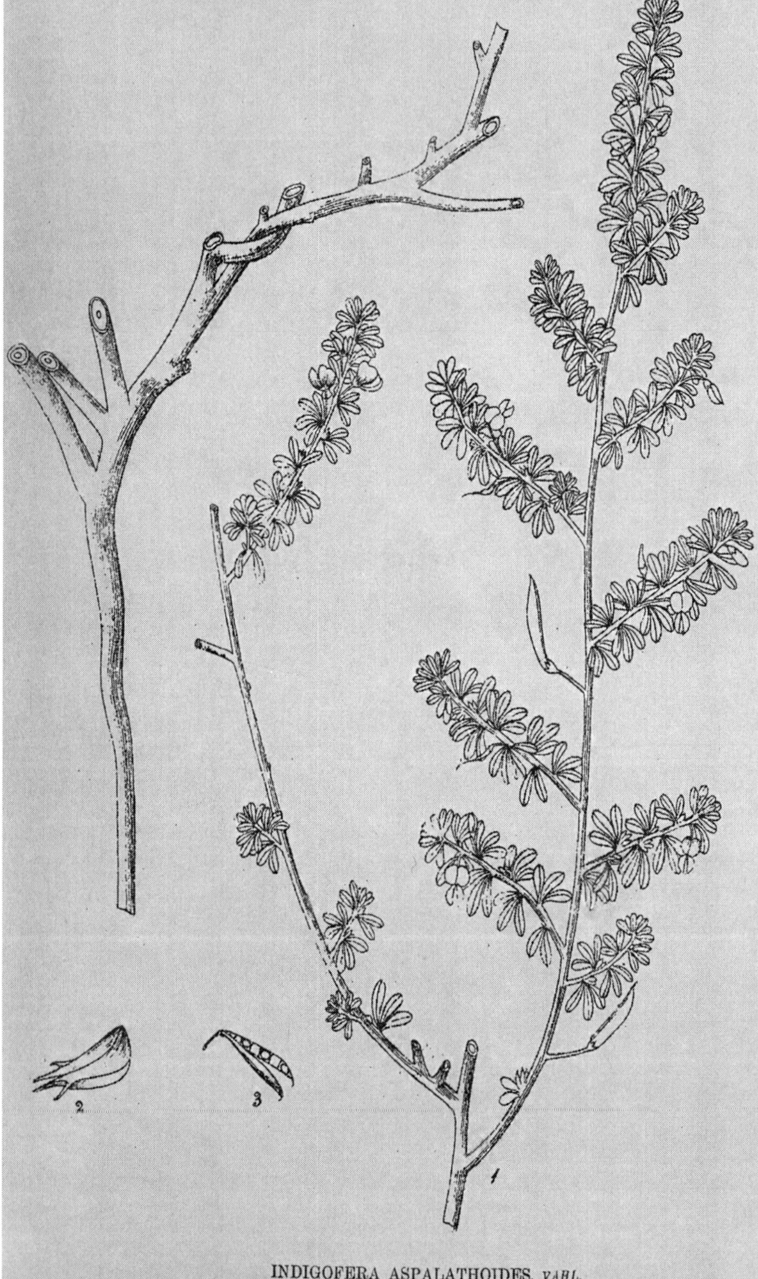

INDIGOFERA ASPALATHOIDES, VAHL.

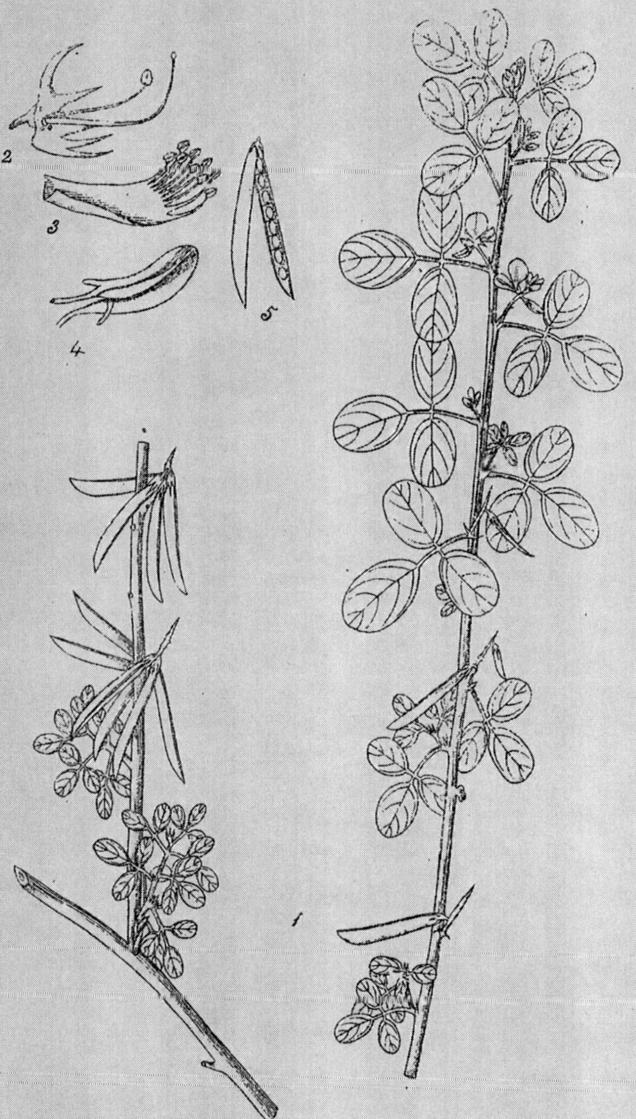

INDIGOFERA TRITA, *LINN. F.*

PLATE No. 298.

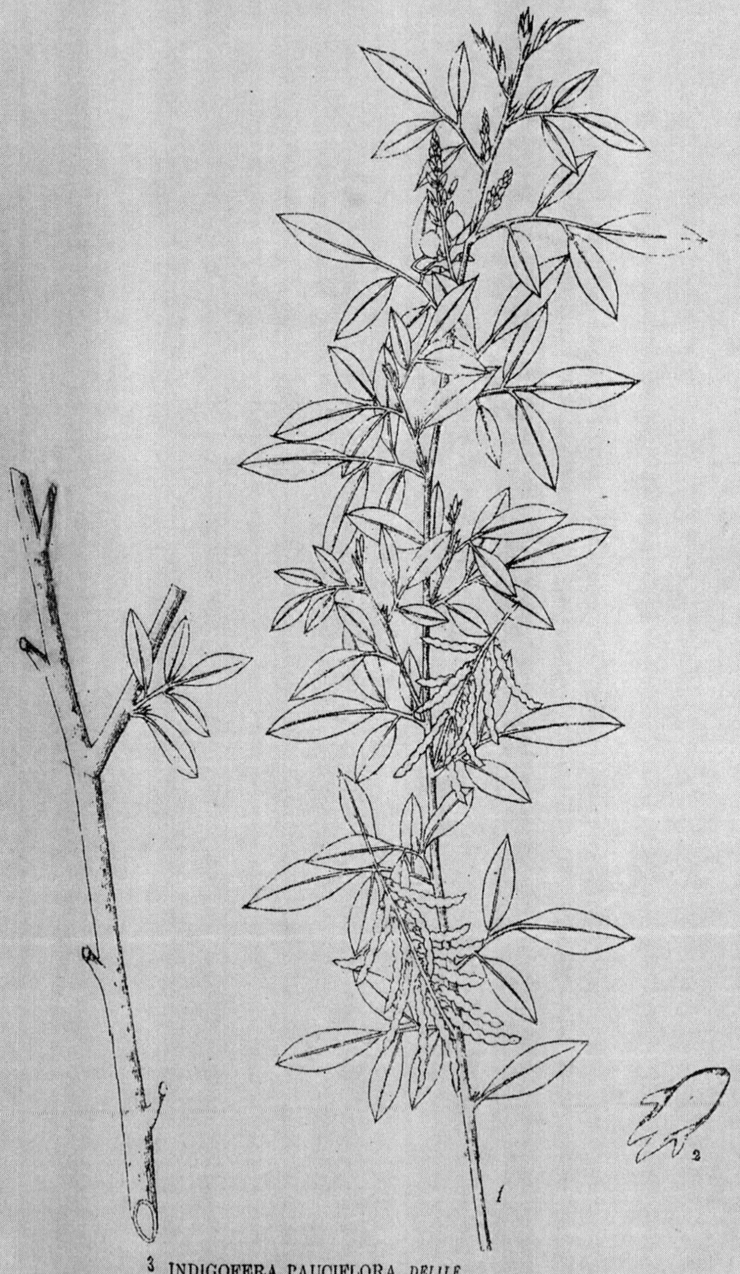

INDIGOFERA PAUCIFLORA, *DELILE.*

PLATE No. 299.

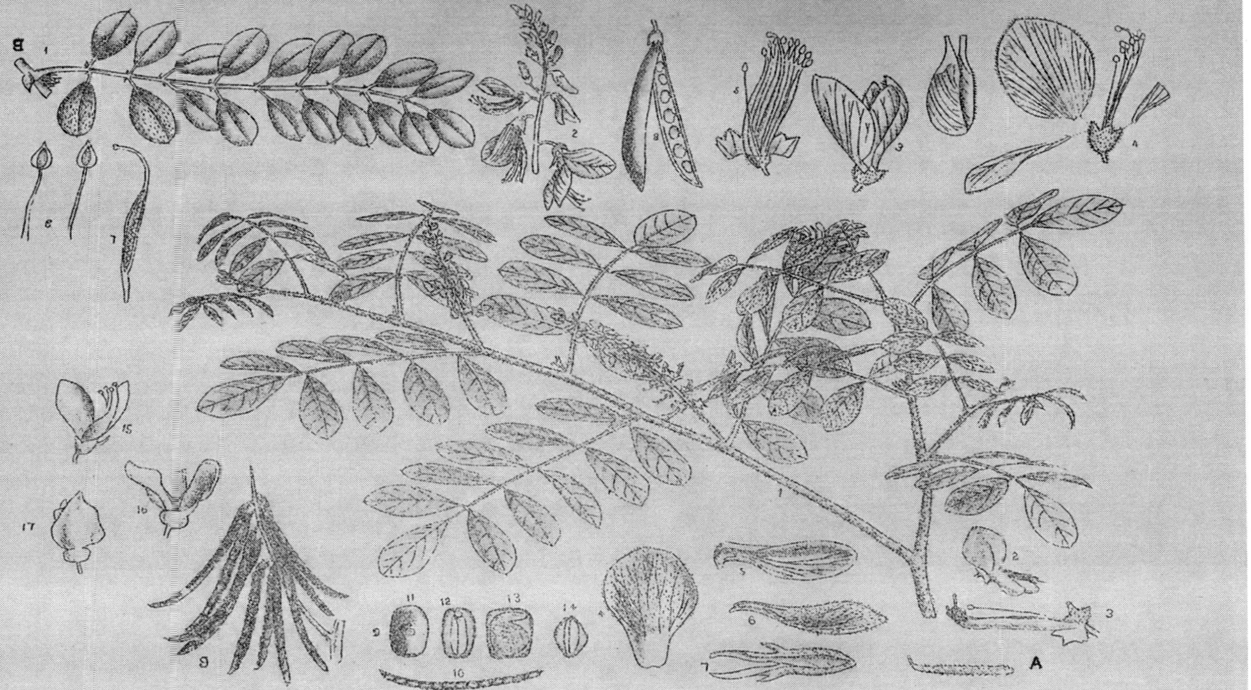

A—INDIGOFERA TINCTORIA, *LINN.* B—I. PULCHELLA, *ROXB.*

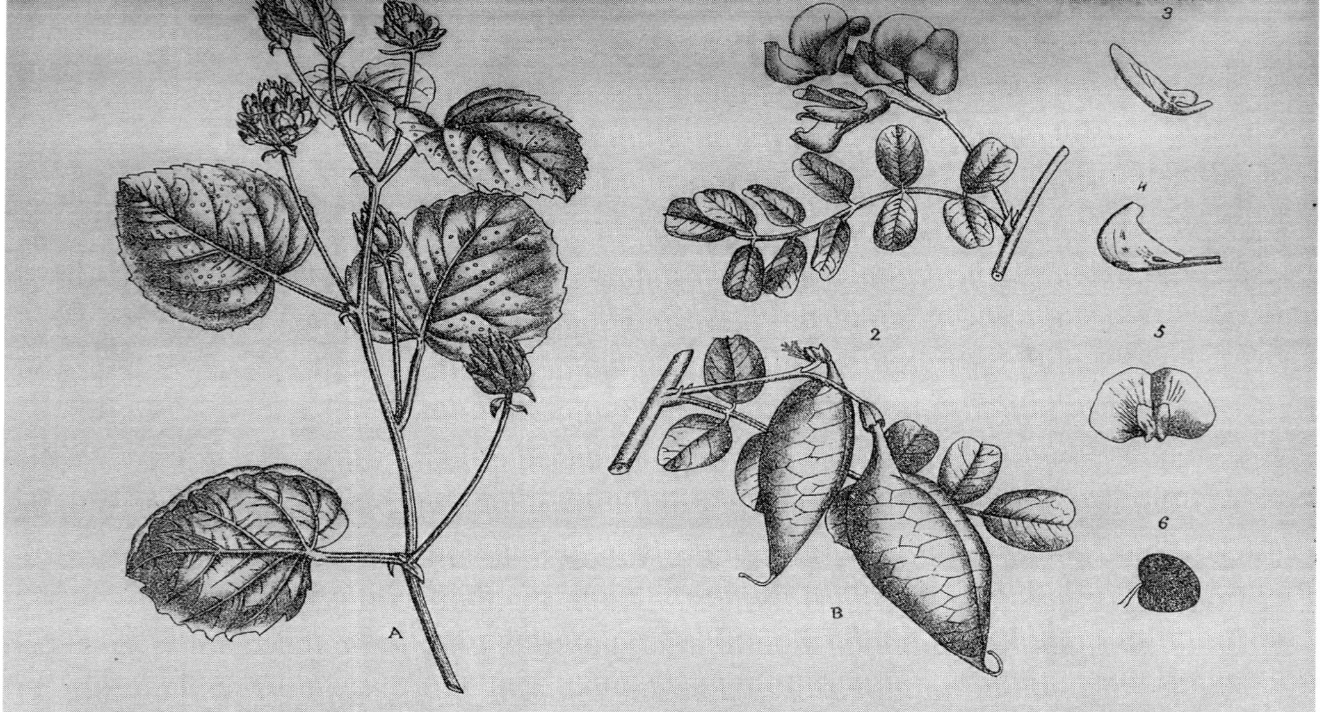

A—PSORALEA CORYLIFOLIA, LINN. B—COLUTEA ARBORESCENS, LINN.

PLATE No. 301

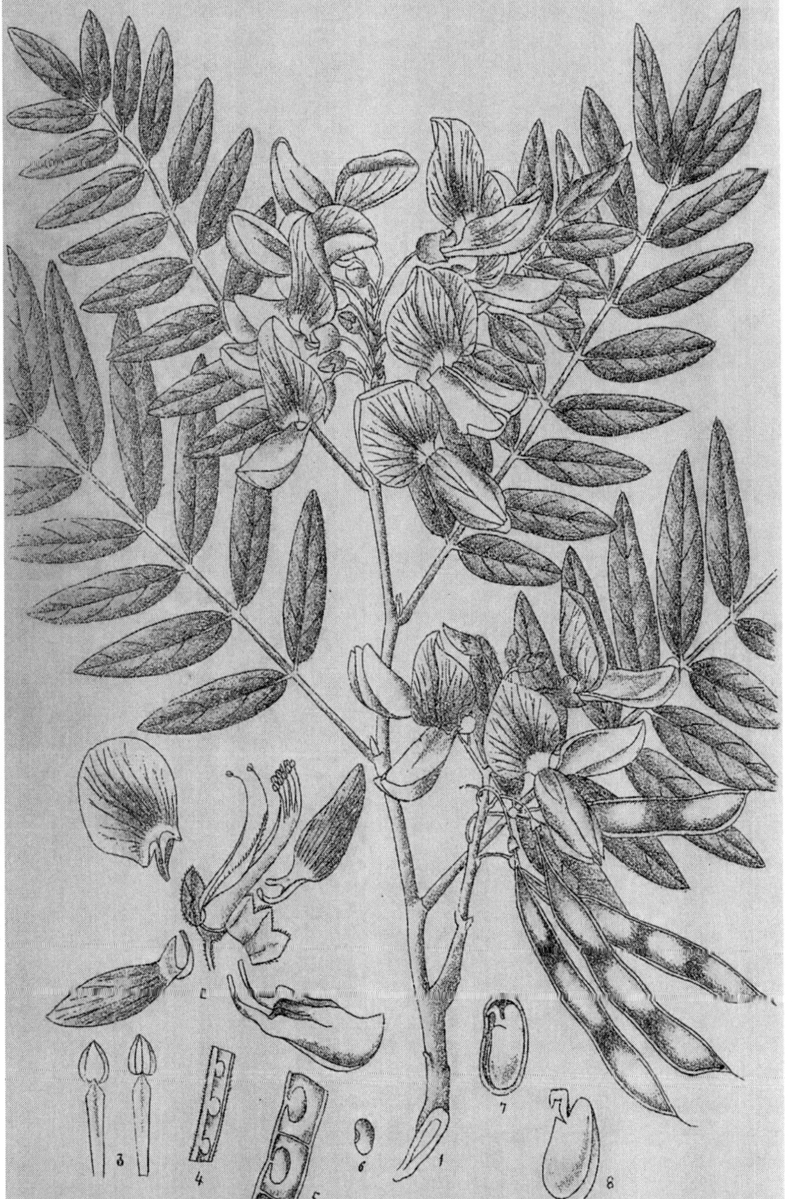

MUNDULEA SUBEROSA, *BENTH.*

PLATE No. 302.

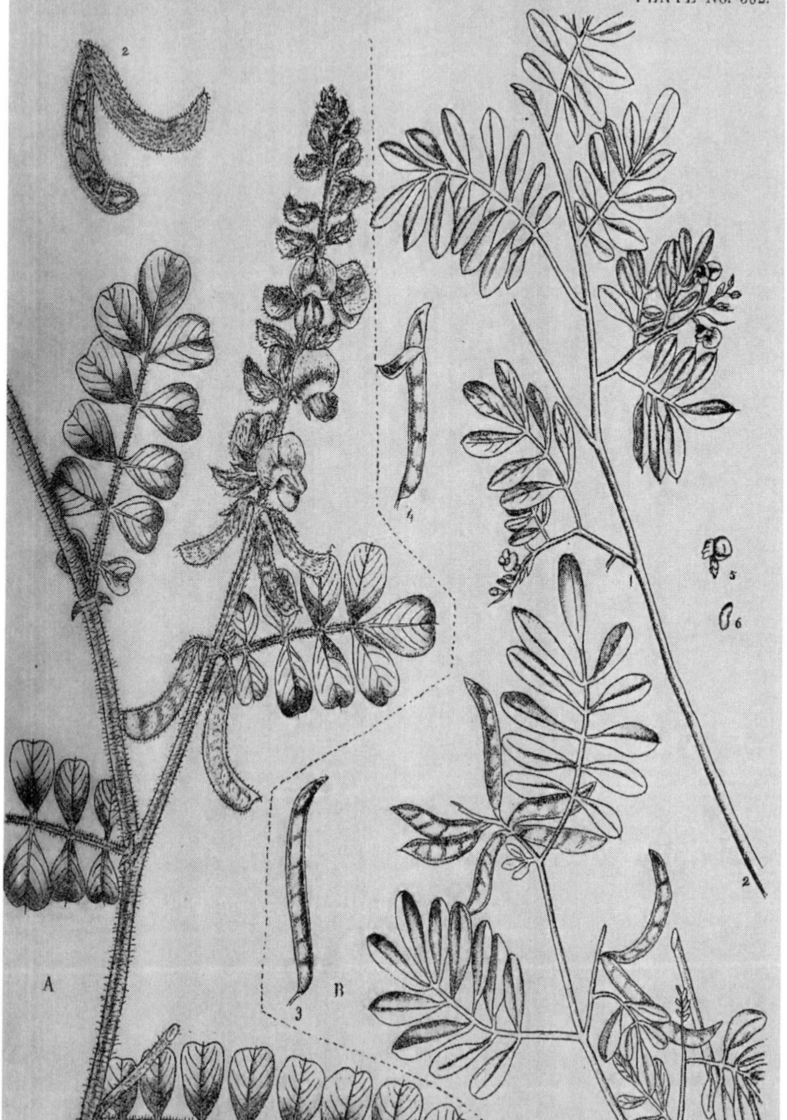

A—TEPHROSIA VILLOSA, *PERS.* B—TEPHROSIA PURPUREA, *PERS.*

PLATE No 303

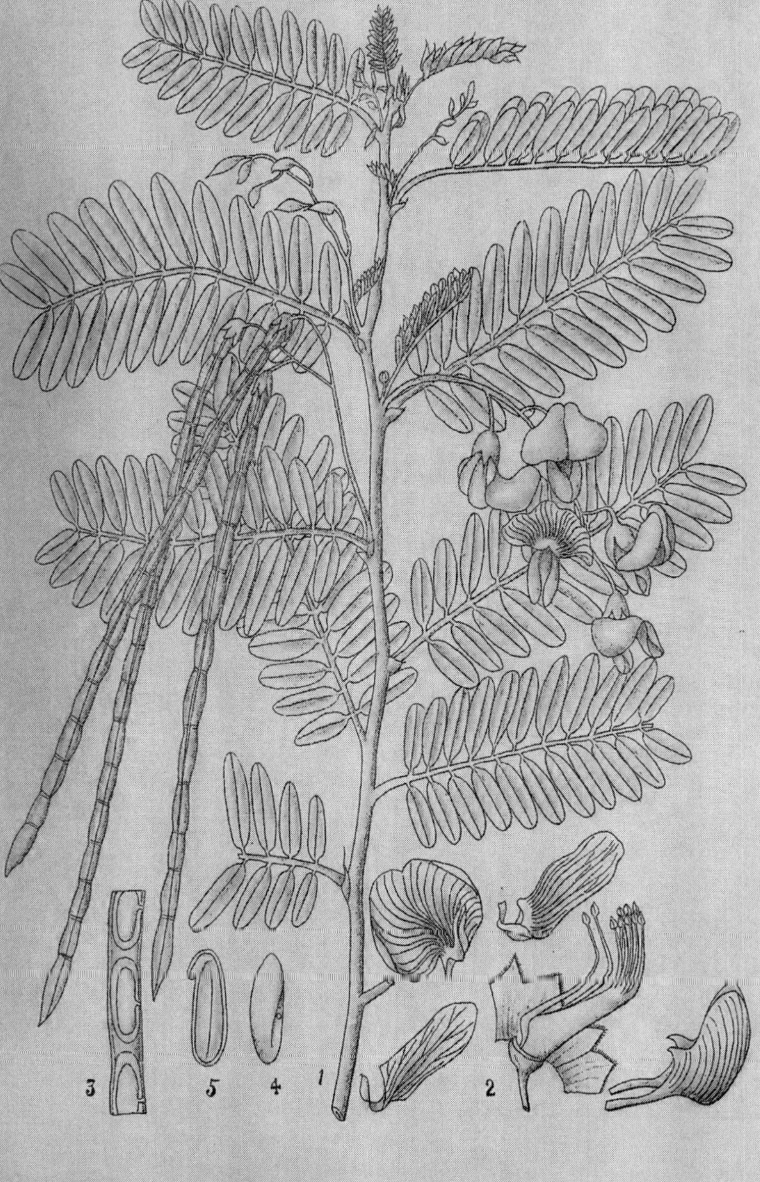

SESBANIA ÆGYPTIACA, PERS.

PLATE No. 304.

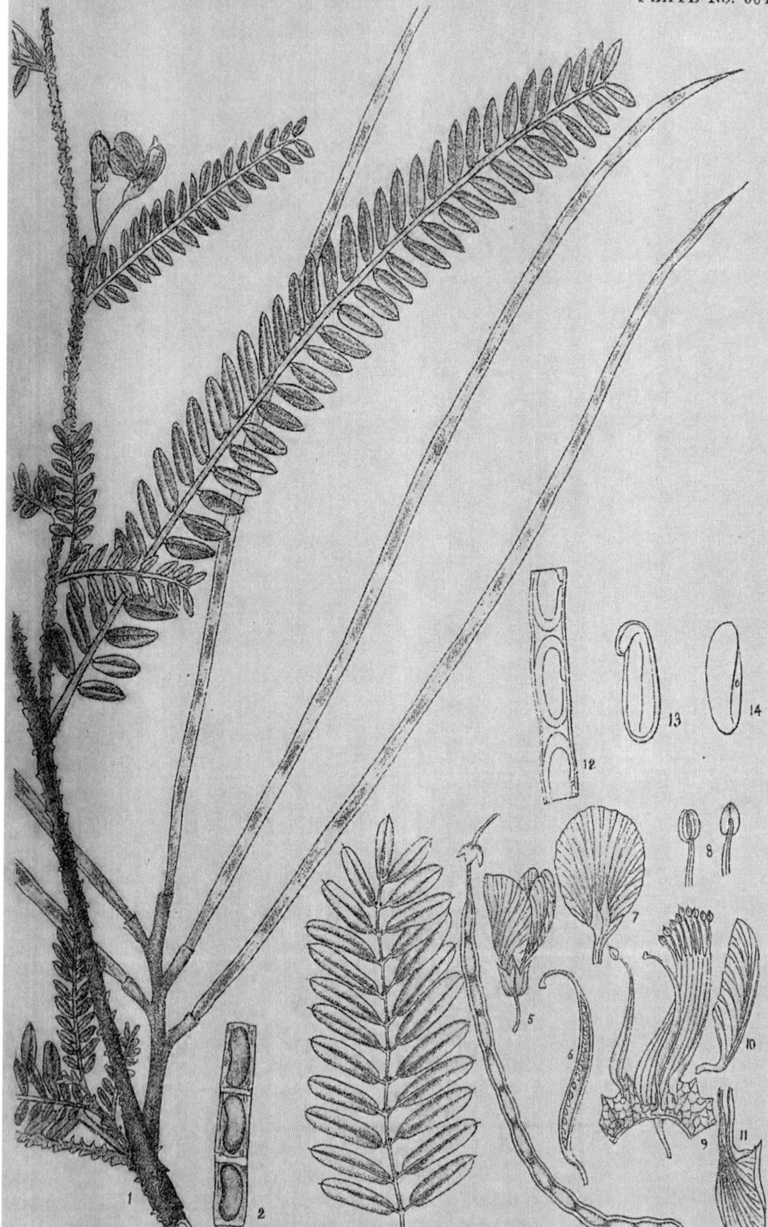

SESBANIA ACULEATA, *PERS.*

PLATE No. 305.

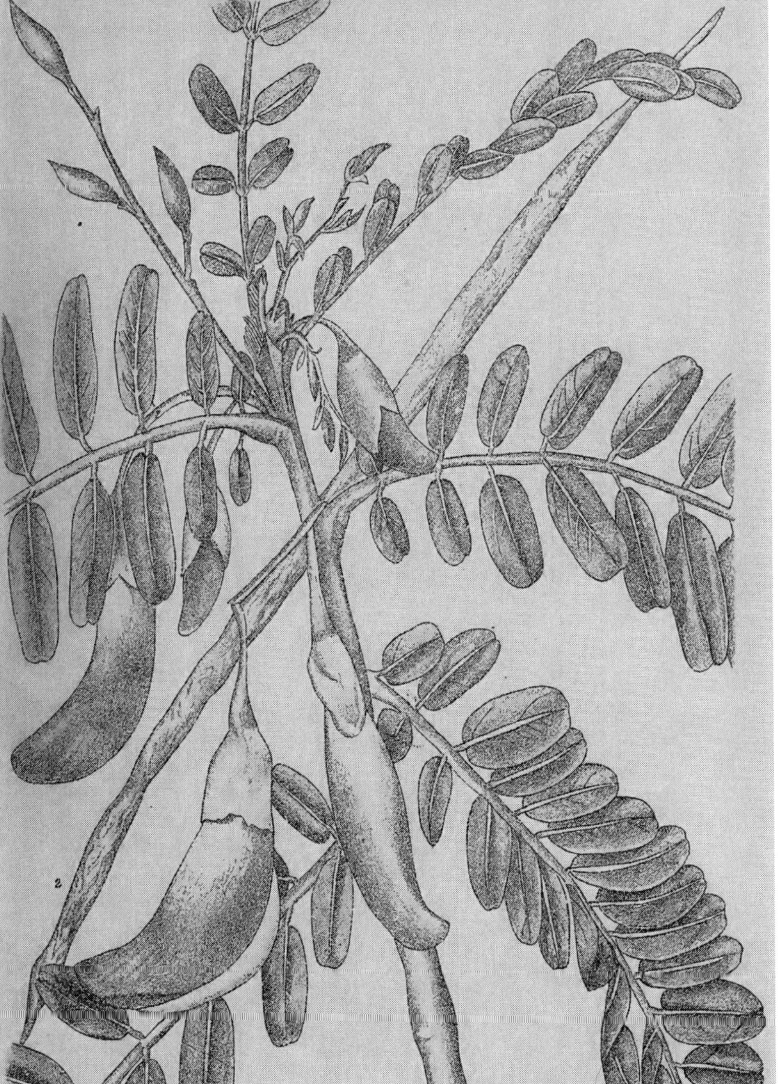

SESBANIA GRANDIFLORA, *PERS.*

PLATE No. 306.

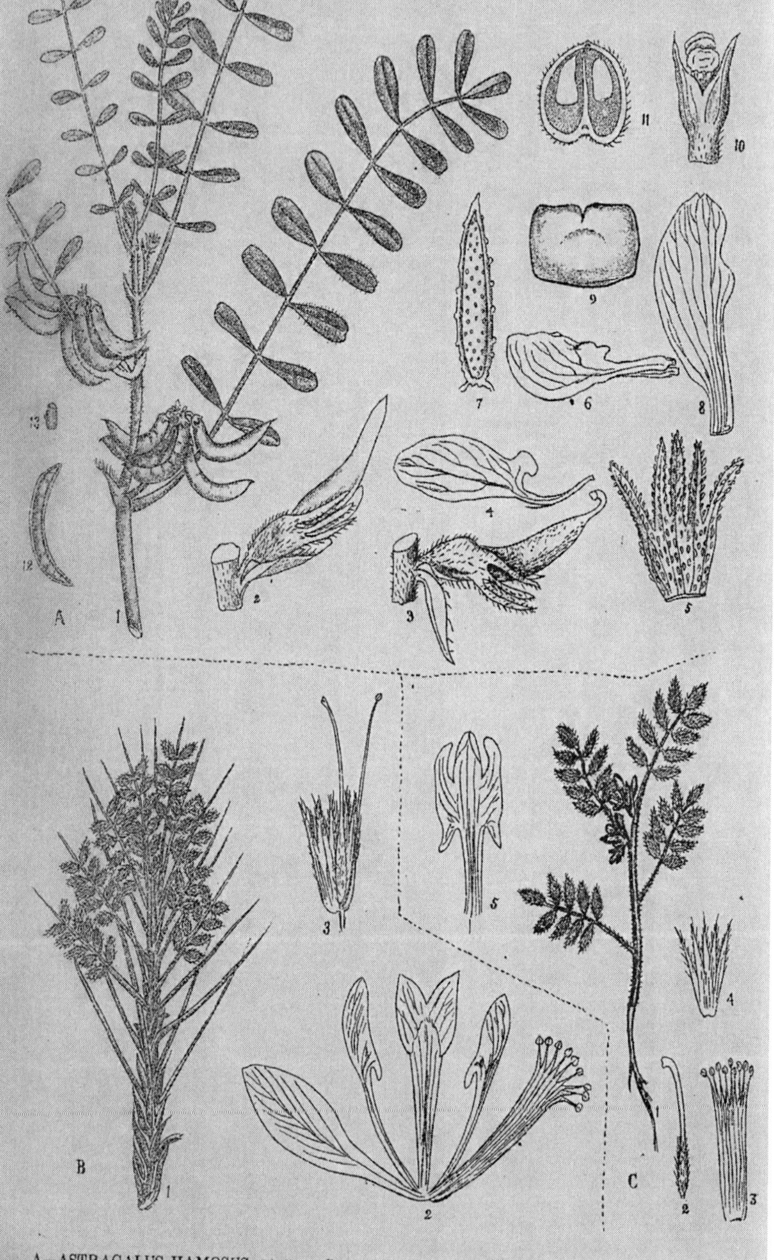

A—ASTRAGALUS HAMOSUS, LIN. B—A. MULTICEPS, WALL. C—A. TRIBULOIDES, DELILE.

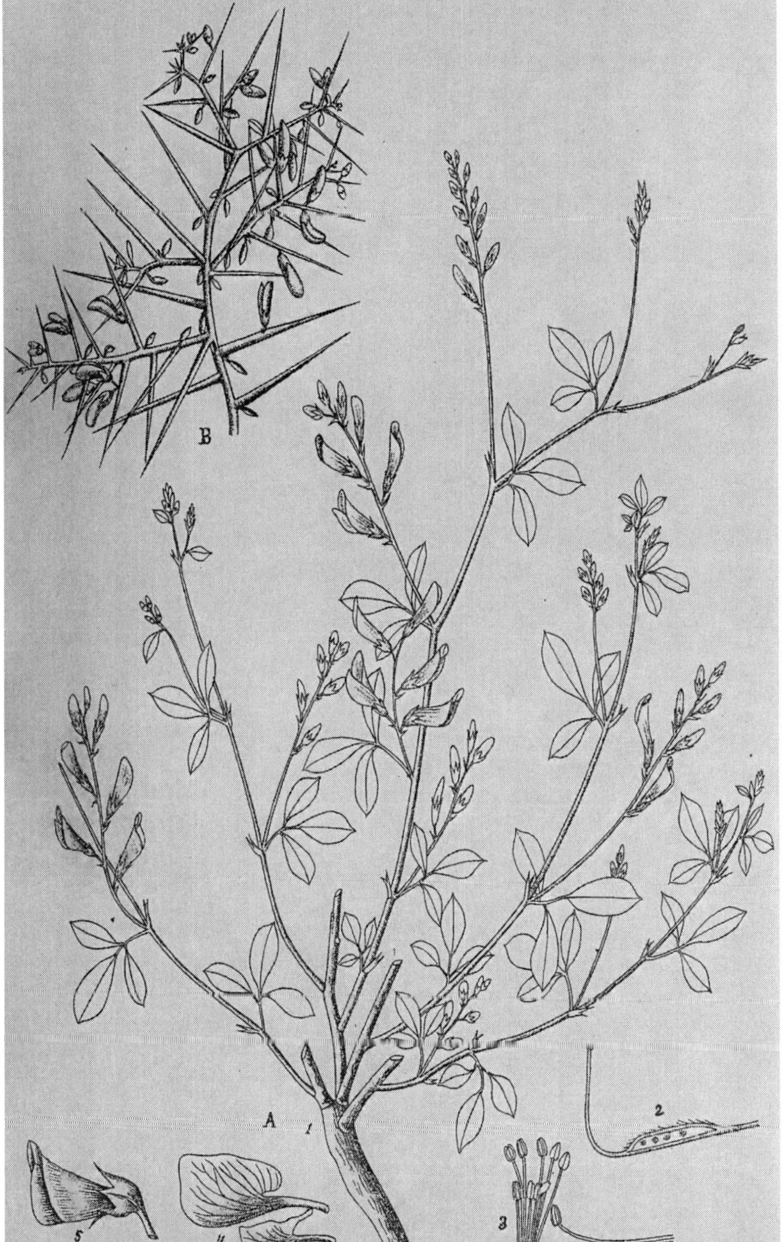

A—TAVERNIERA NUMMULARIA, DC   B—ALHAGI MAURORUM, DESV.

PLATE No. 308.

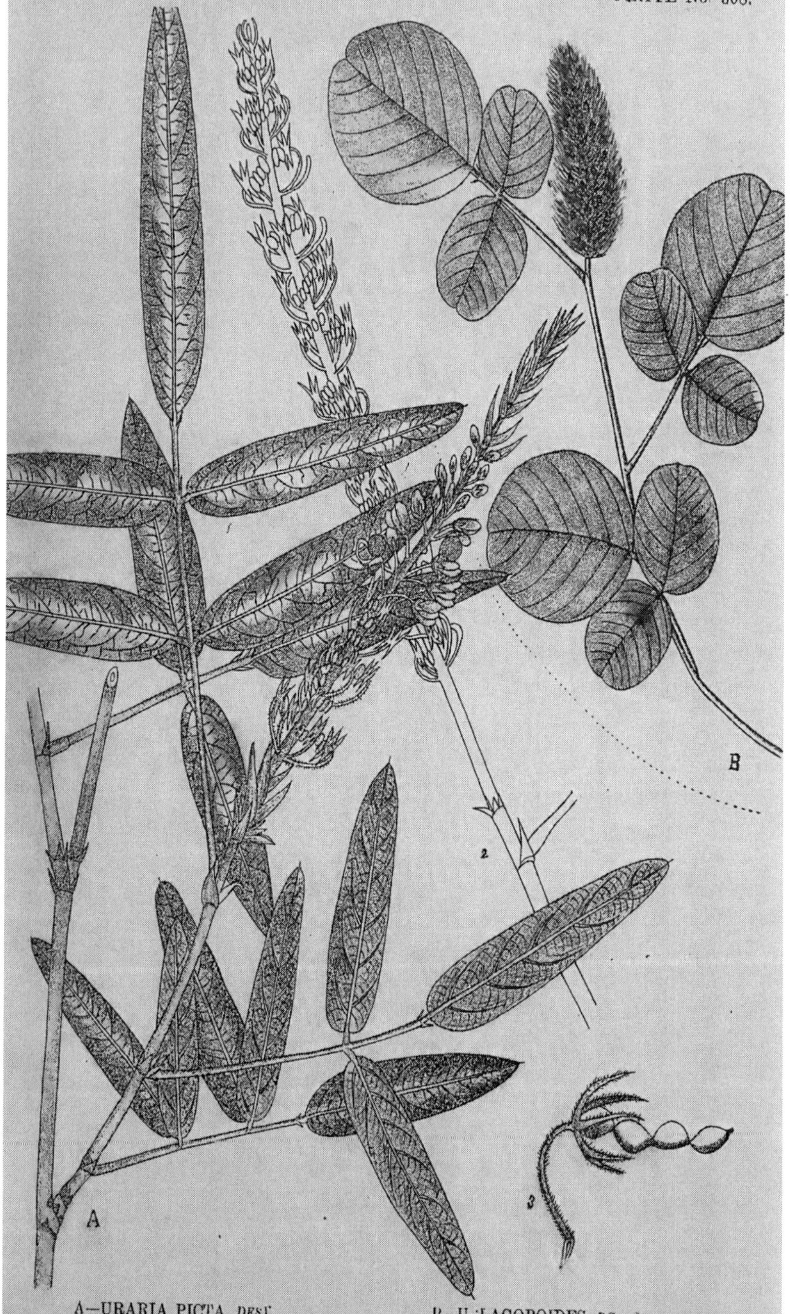

A—URARIA PICTA, DESV.   B—U. LAGOPOIDES, DC.

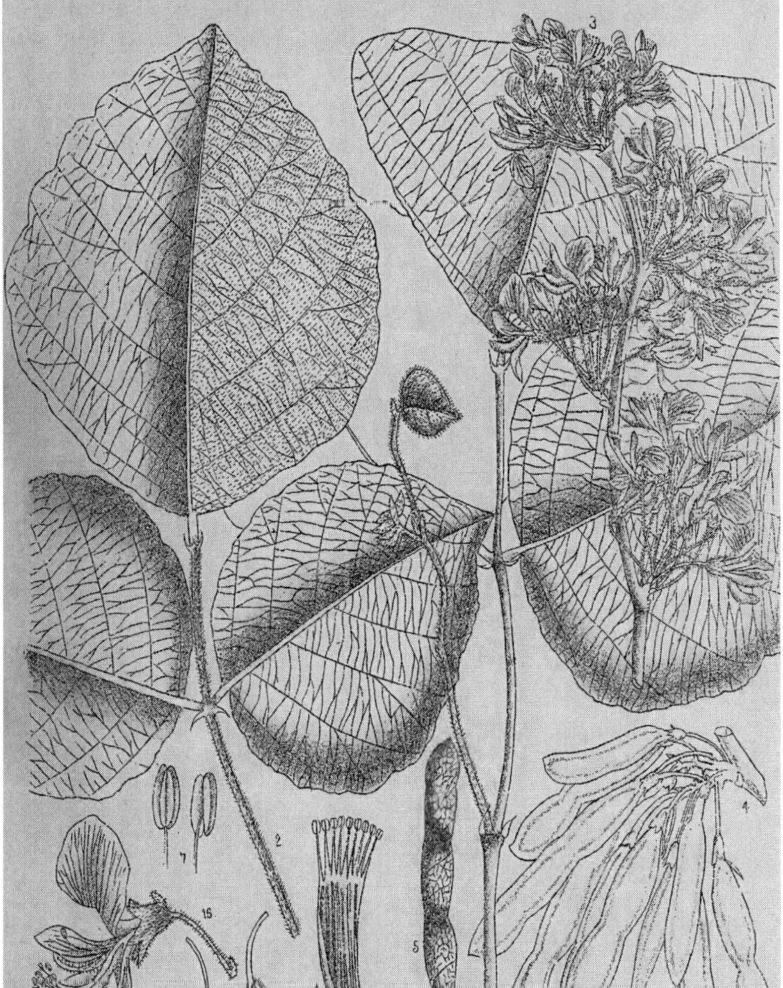

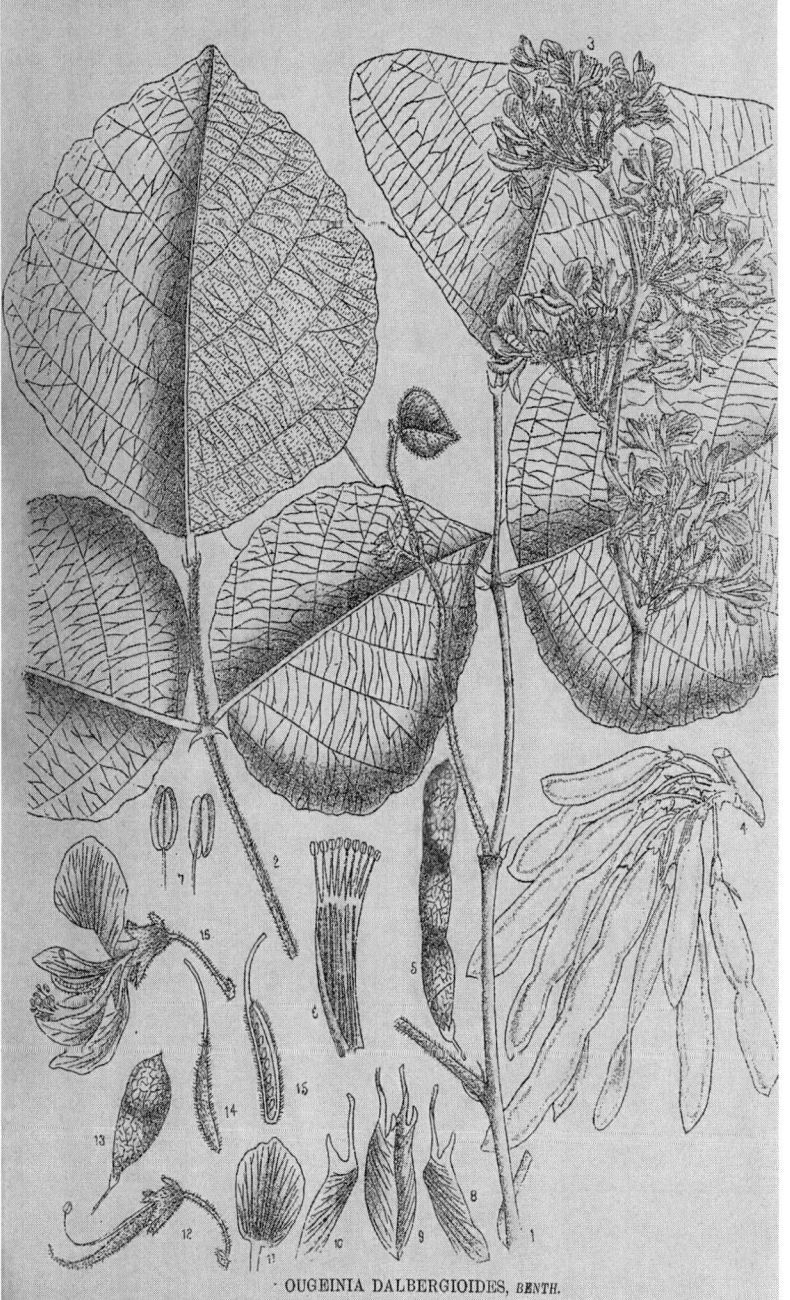

OUGEINIA DALBERGIOIDES, *Benth.*

PLATE No. 310.

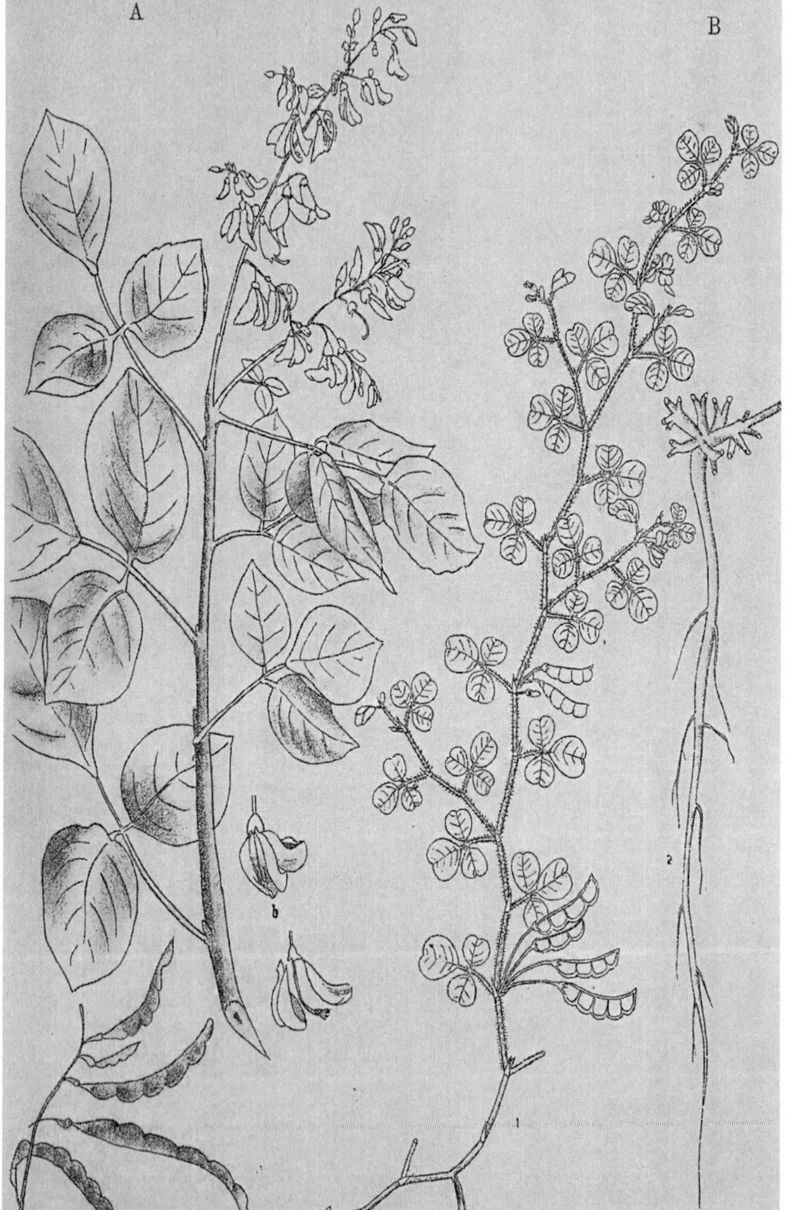

A--DESMODIUM TILIÆFOLIUM, *G. DON.* B—D. TRIFLORUM, *DC.*

PLATE No 311

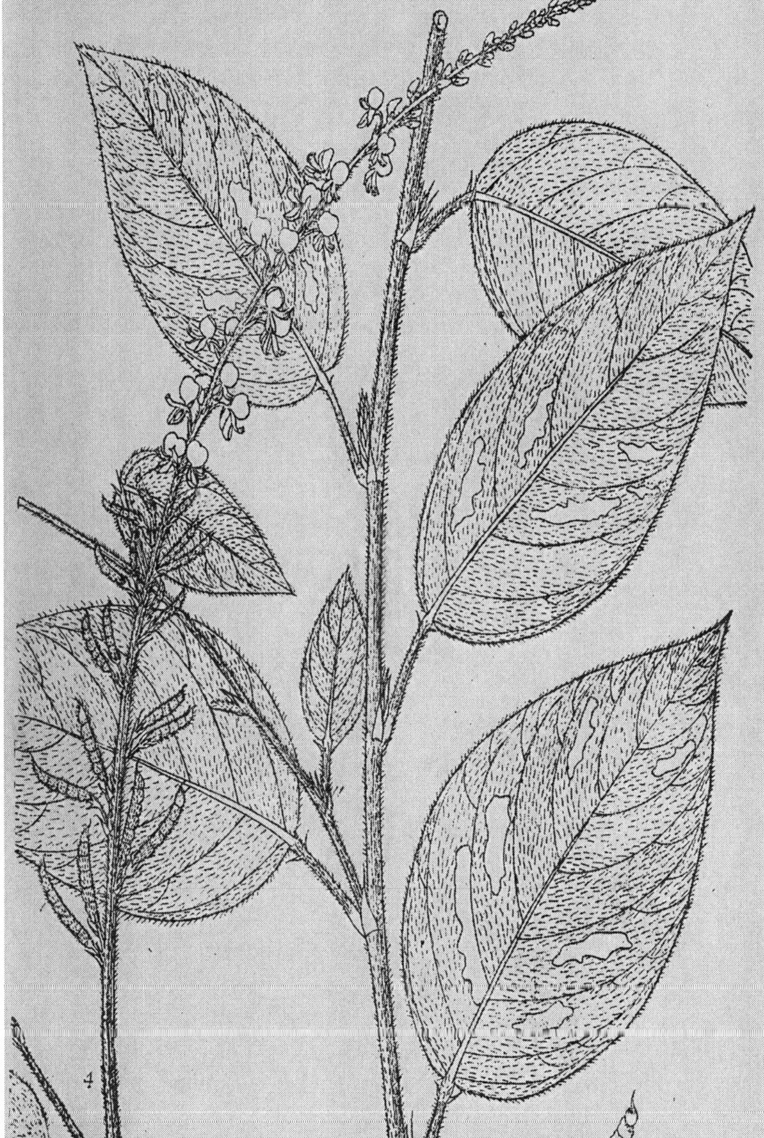

DESMODIUM GANGETICUM, DC.

PLATE No. 312.

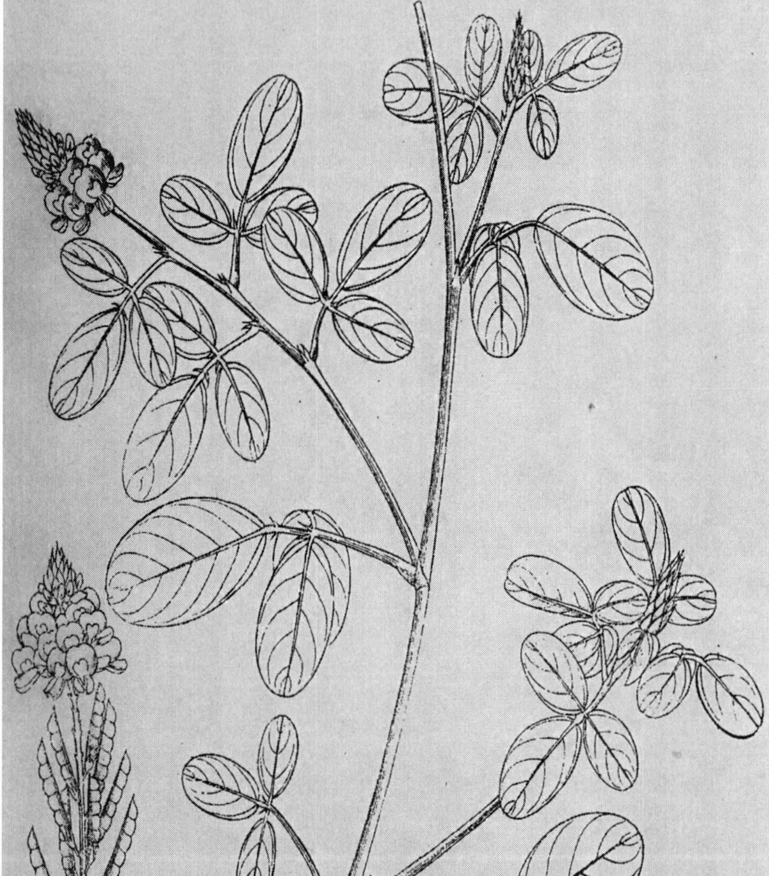

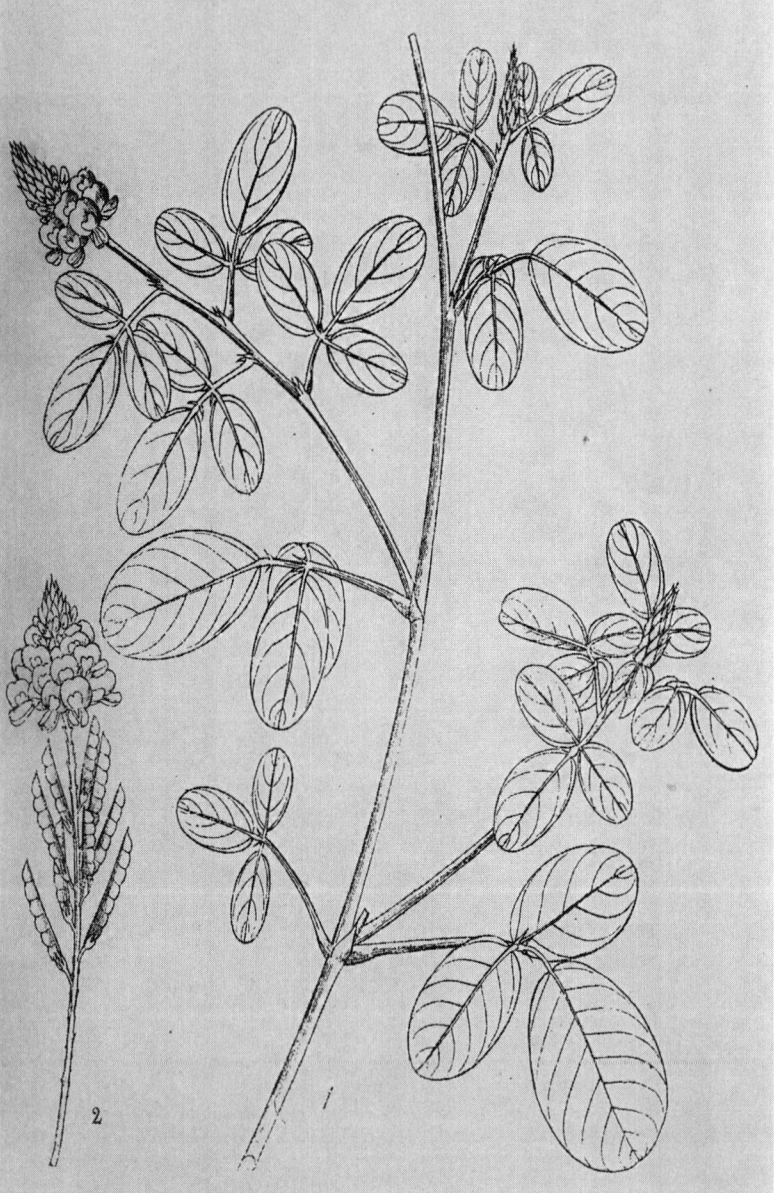

DESMODIUM POLYCARPUM, *DC.*

PLATE No. 329.

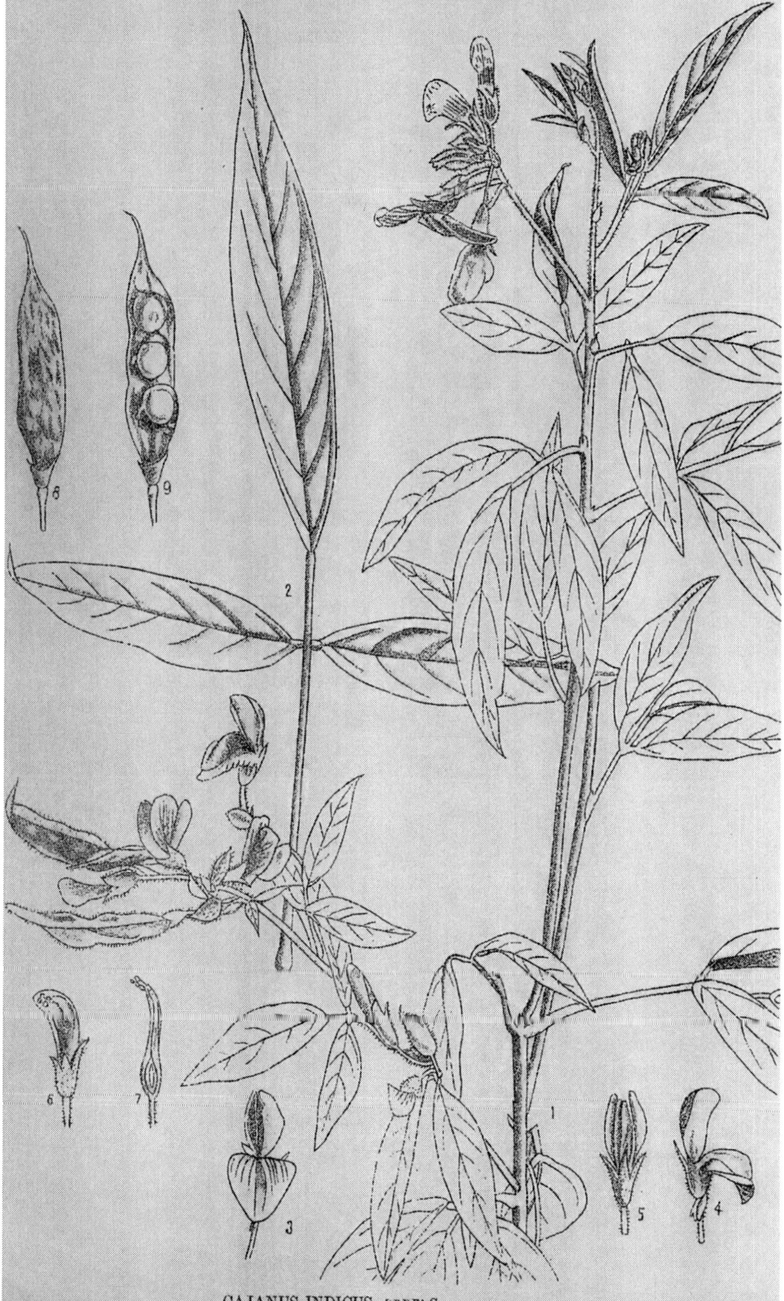

CAJANUS INDICUS, SPRENG.

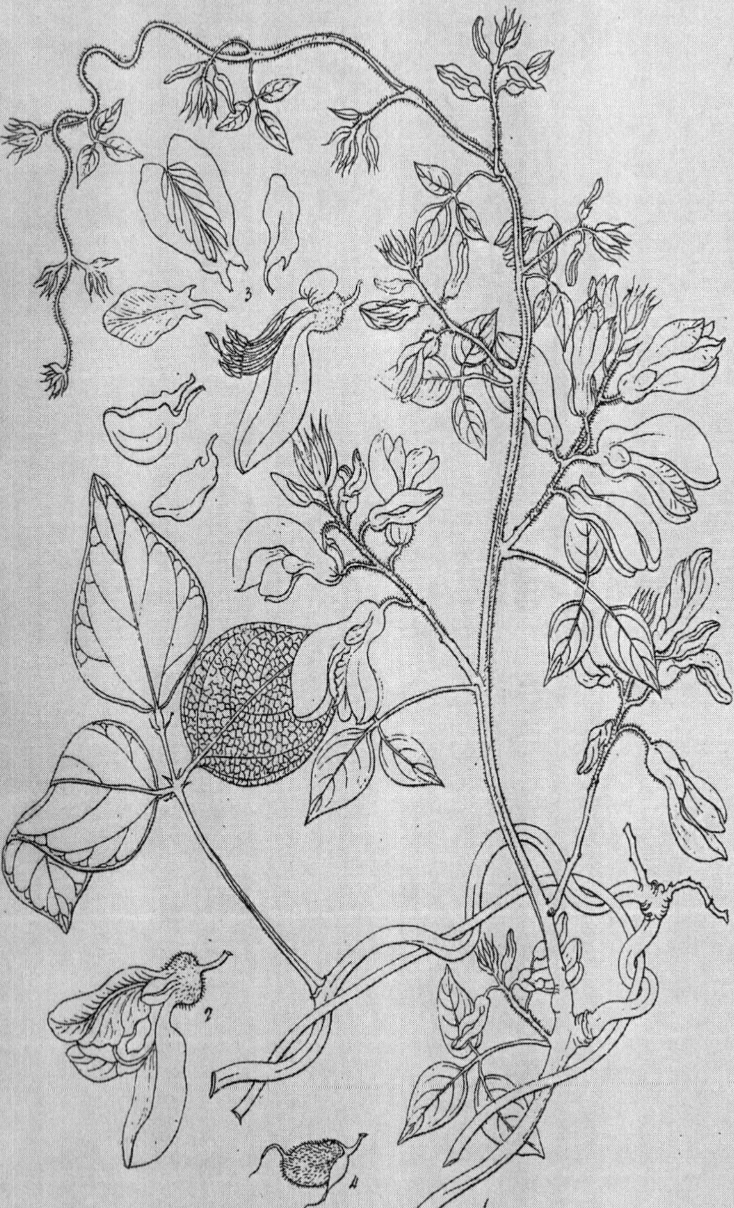

CYLISTA SCARIOSA, *AIT.*

PLATE No. 331.

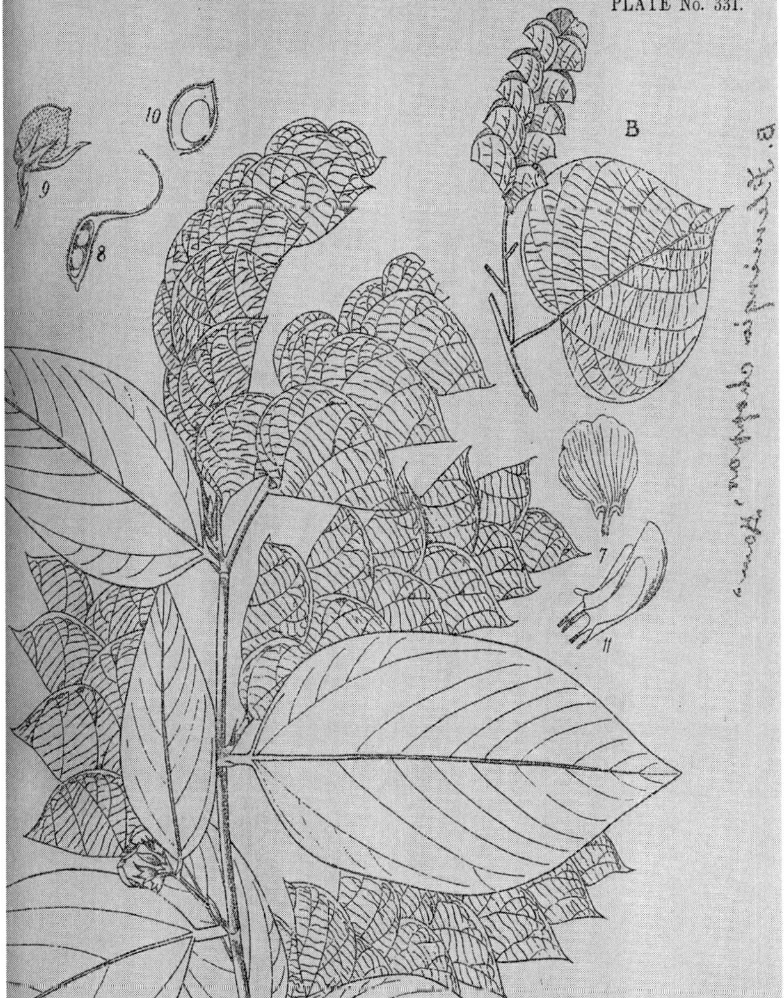

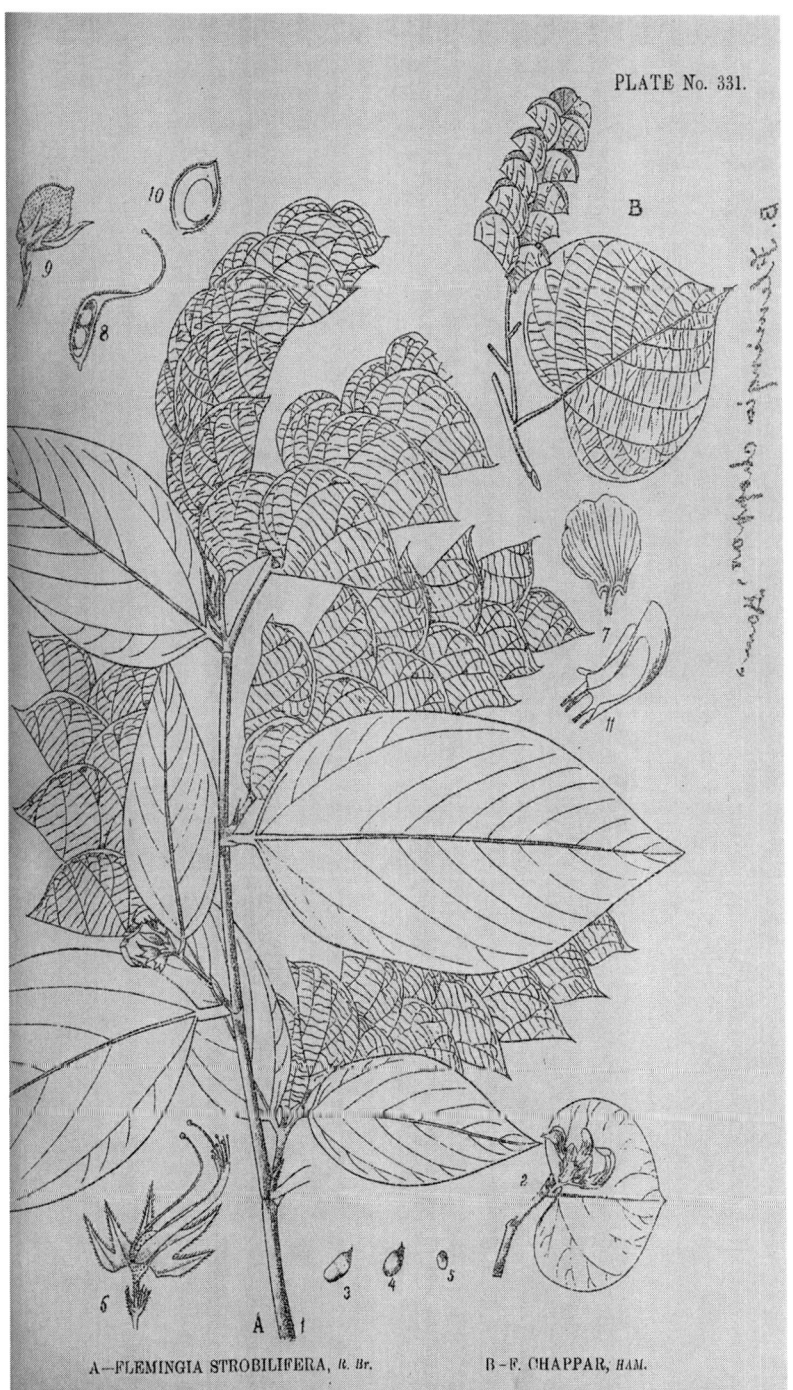

A—FLEMINGIA STROBILIFERA, *R. Br.* B—F. CHAPPAR, *HAM.*

PLATE No. 332.

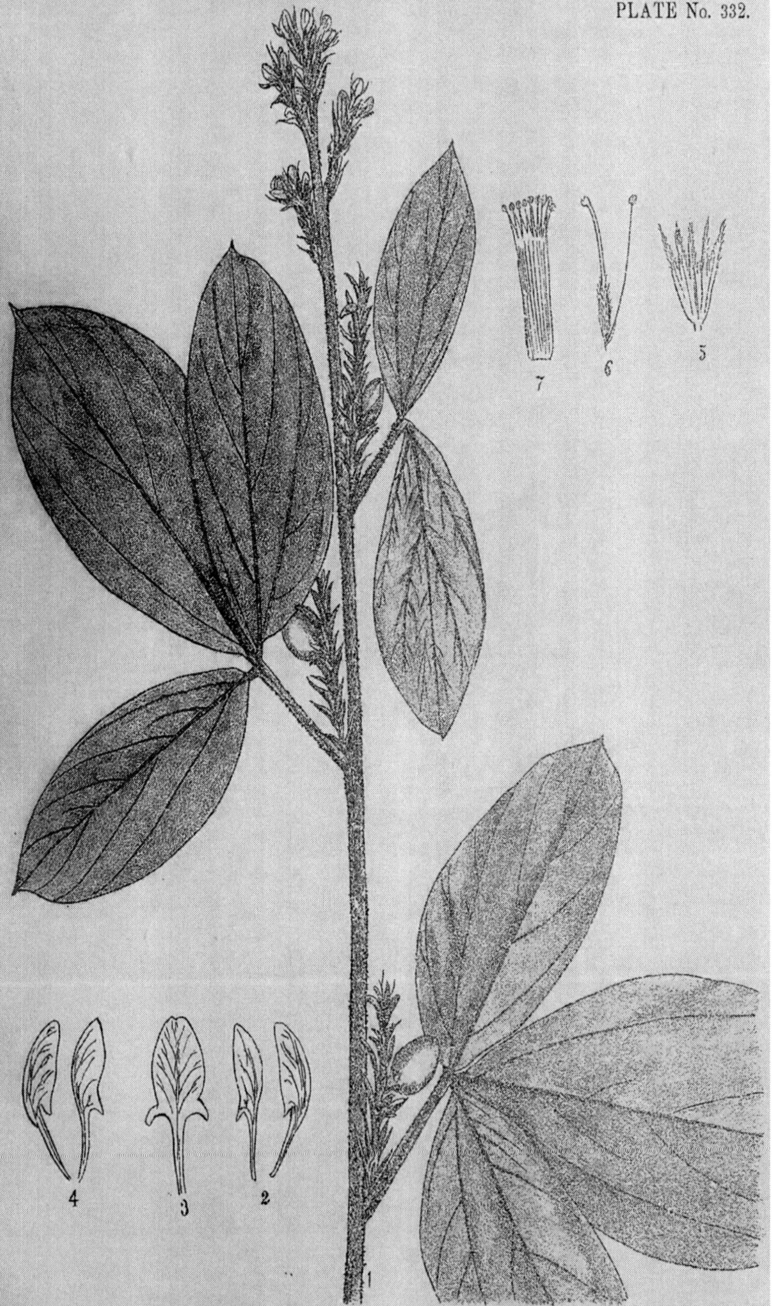

FLEMINGIA GRAHAMIANA, W. & A.

PLATE No. 333.

FLEMINGIA CONGESTA *ROXB.*

PLATE No. 334.

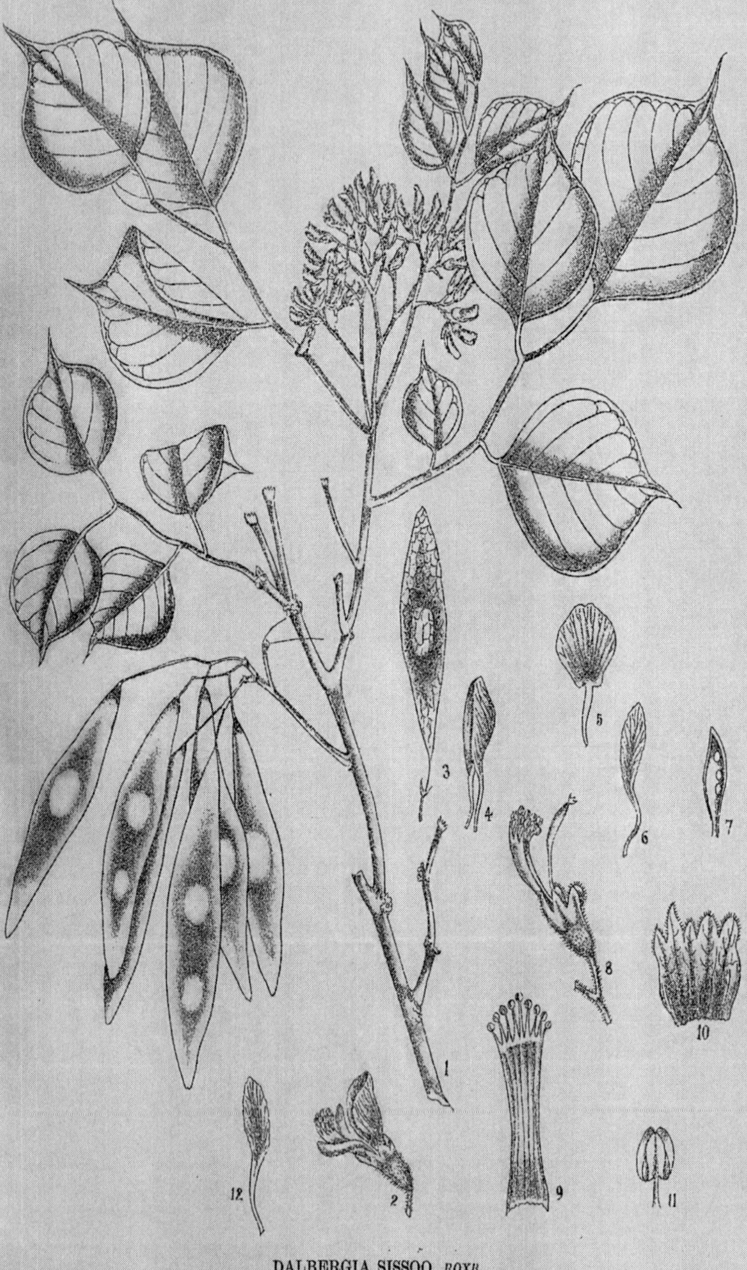

DALBERGIA SISSOO, *ROXB.*

PLATE No. 335.

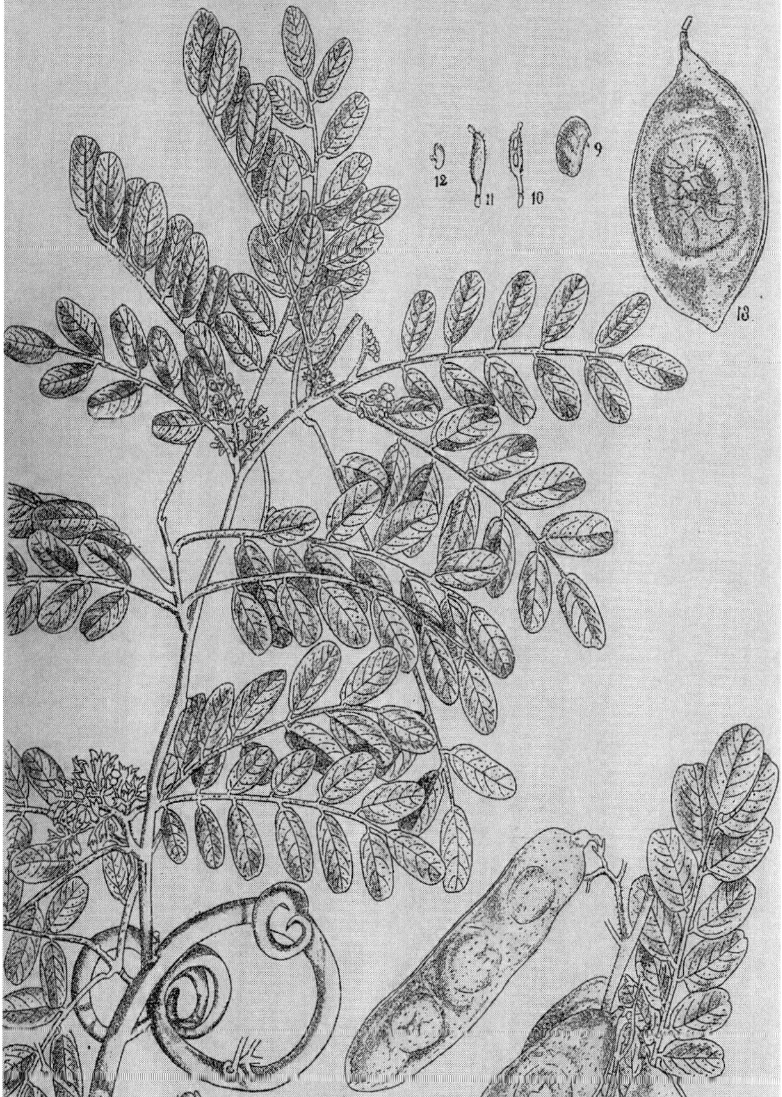

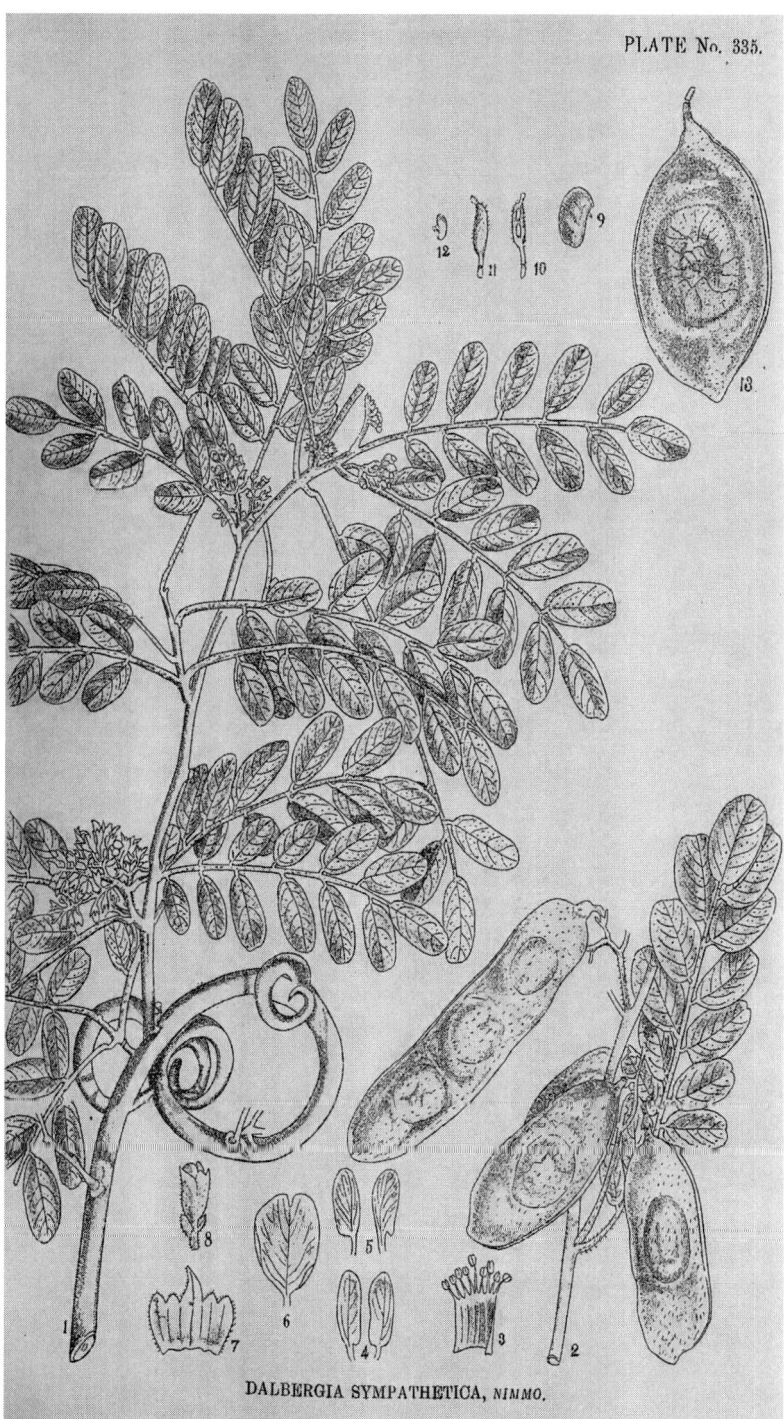

DALBERGIA SYMPATHETICA, *NIMMO.*

PLATE No. 336.

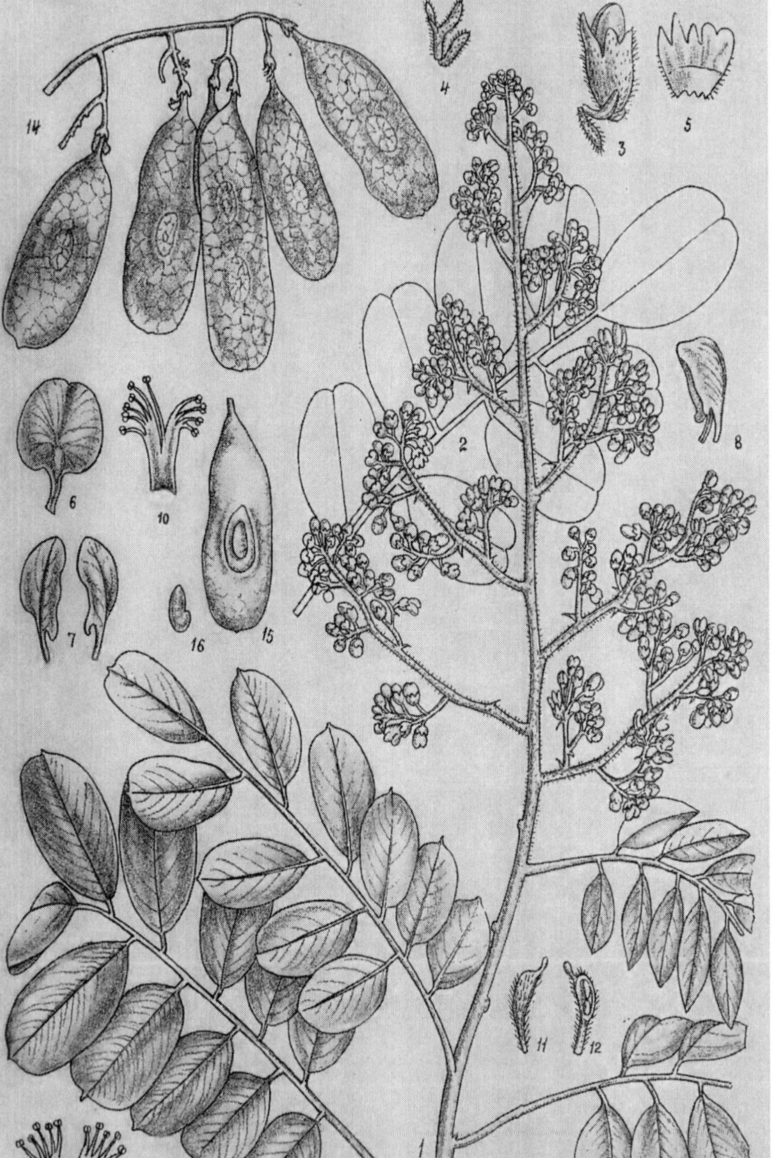

DALBERGIA VOLUBILIS, *ROXB.*

PLATE No. 337.

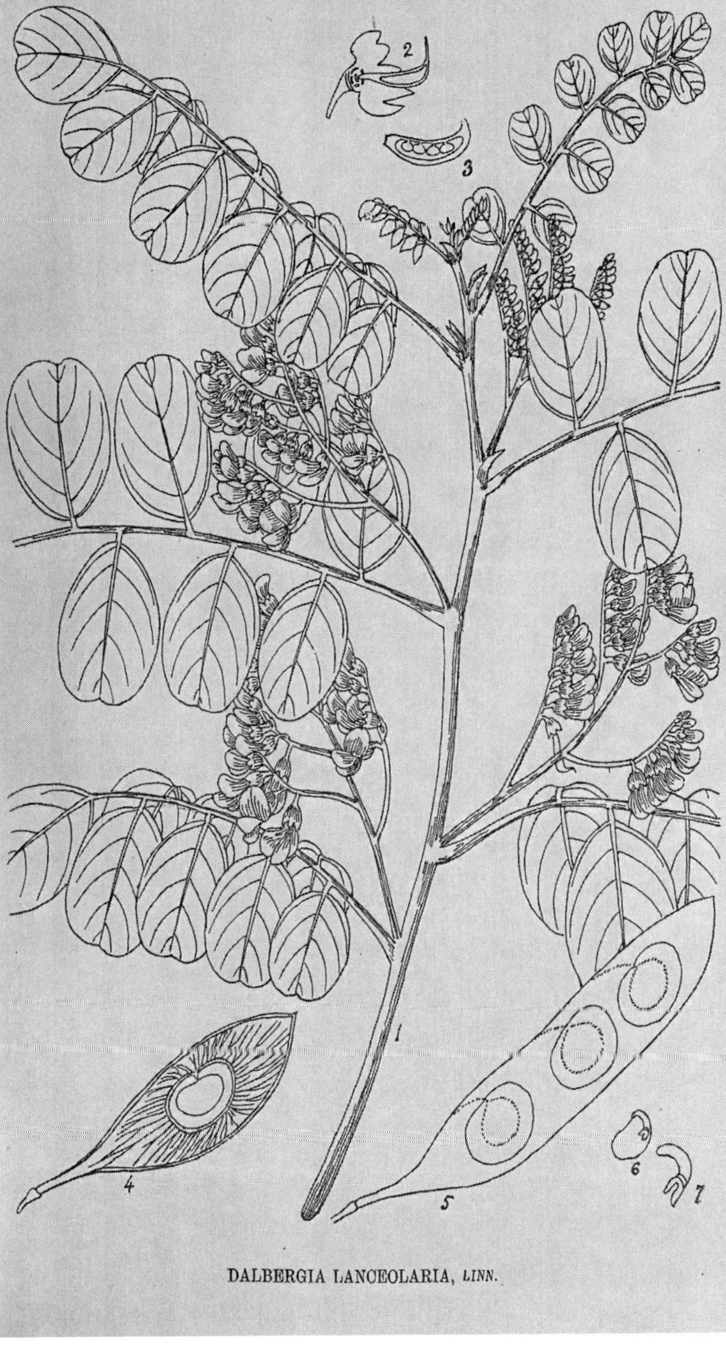

DALBERGIA LANCEOLARIA, *LINN.*

DALBERGIA SPINOSA, *ROXB.*

PLATE No. 339.

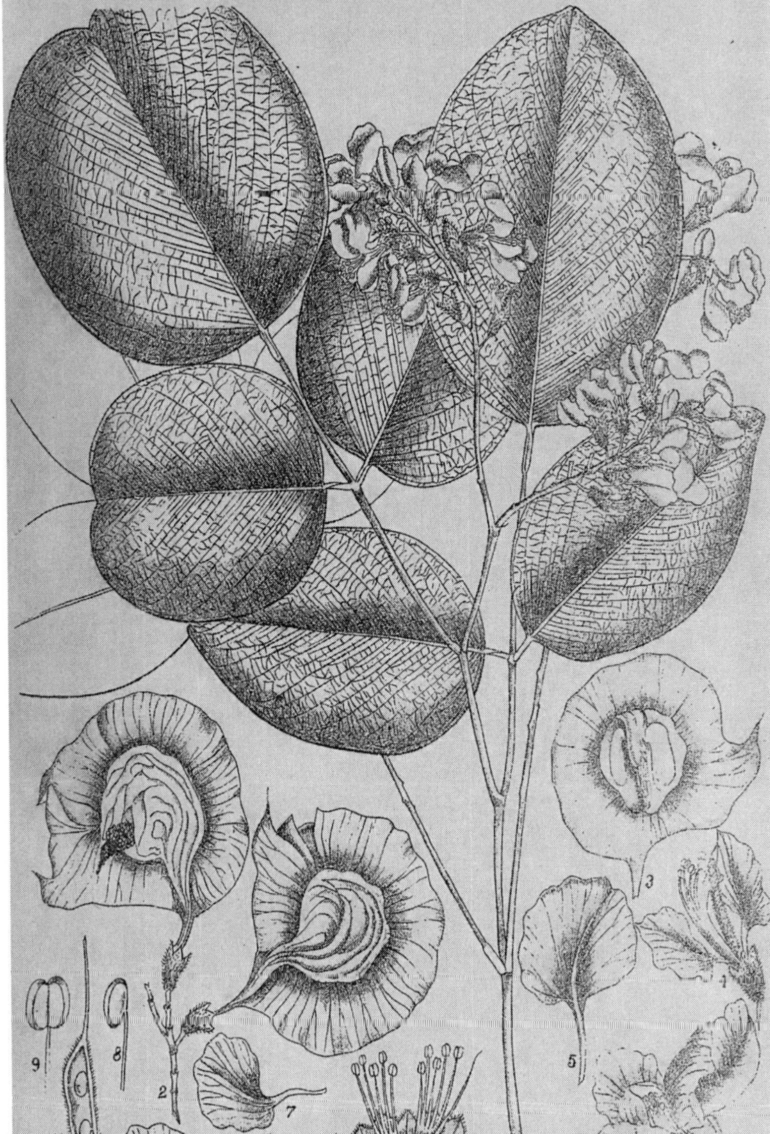

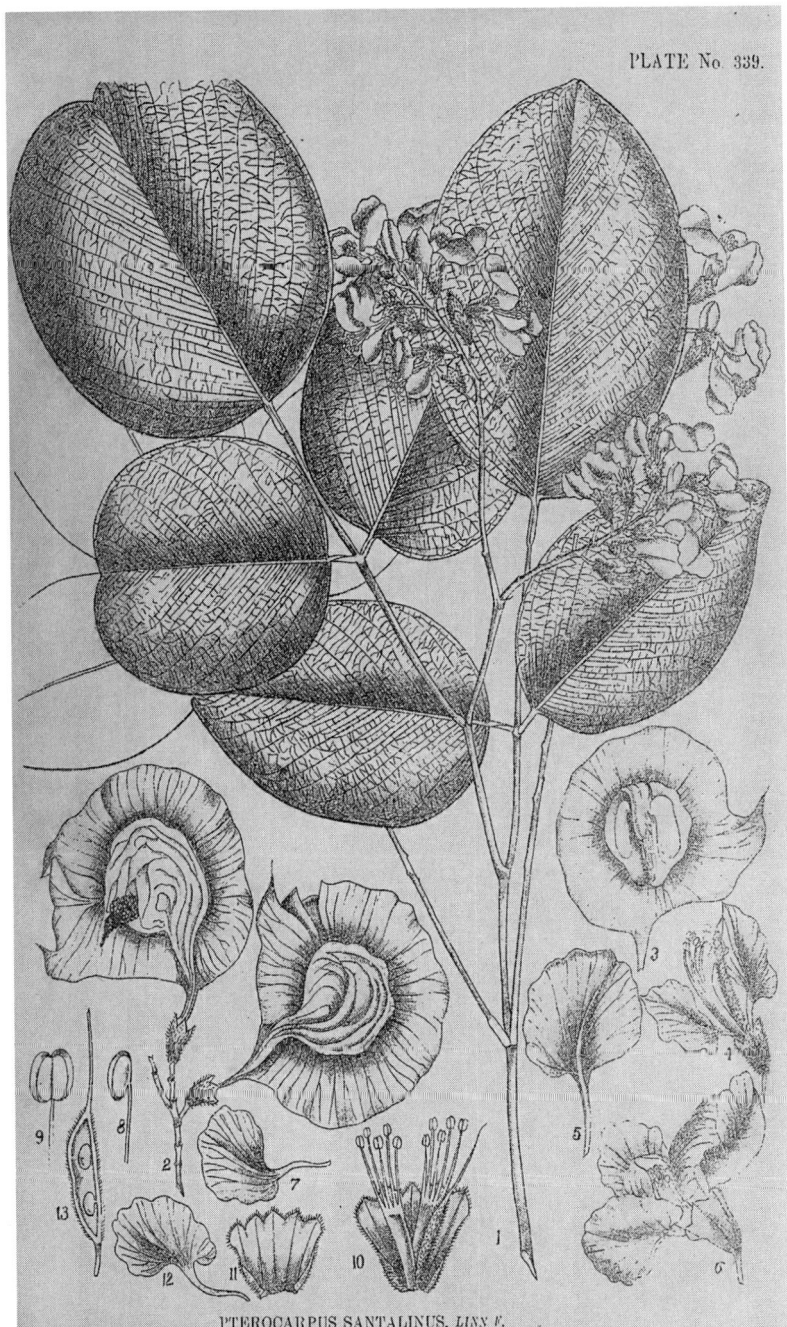

PTEROCARPUS SANTALINUS, *LINN F.*

PLATE No 340.

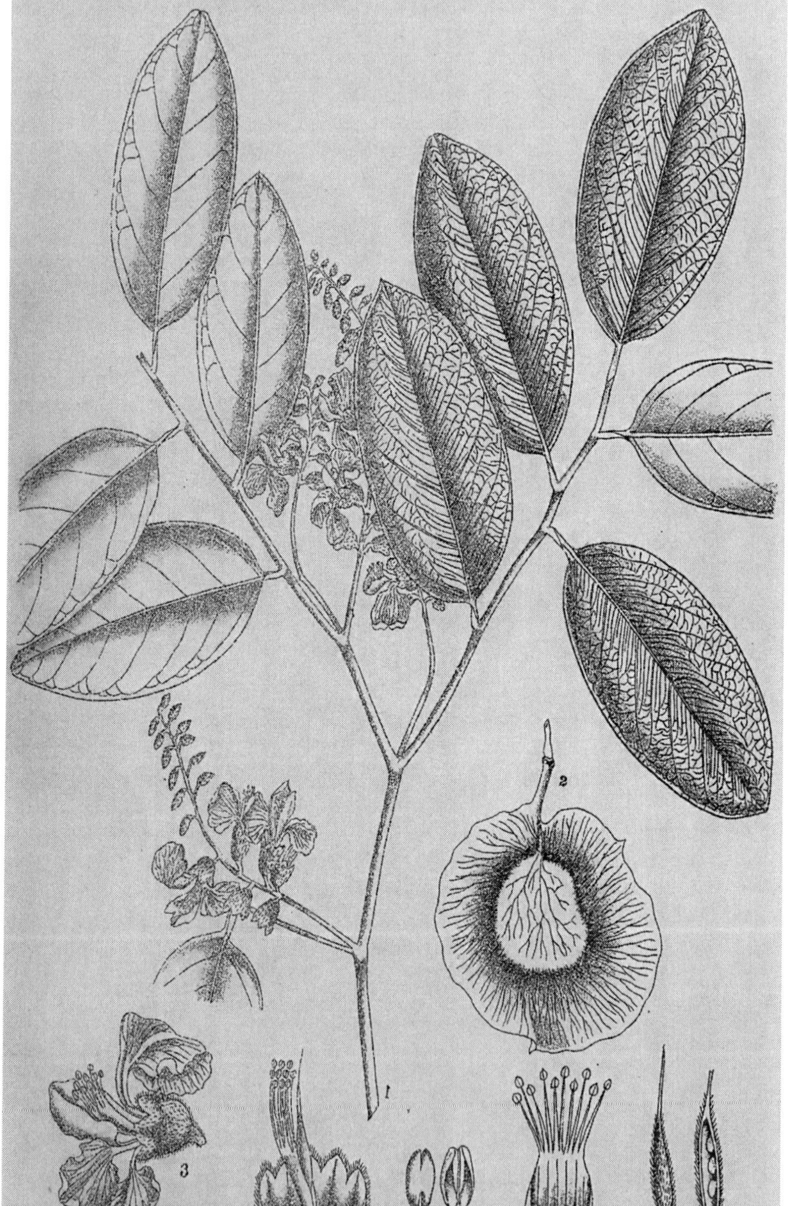

PTEROCARPUS MARSUPIUM, *ROXB.*

PLATE No. 341.

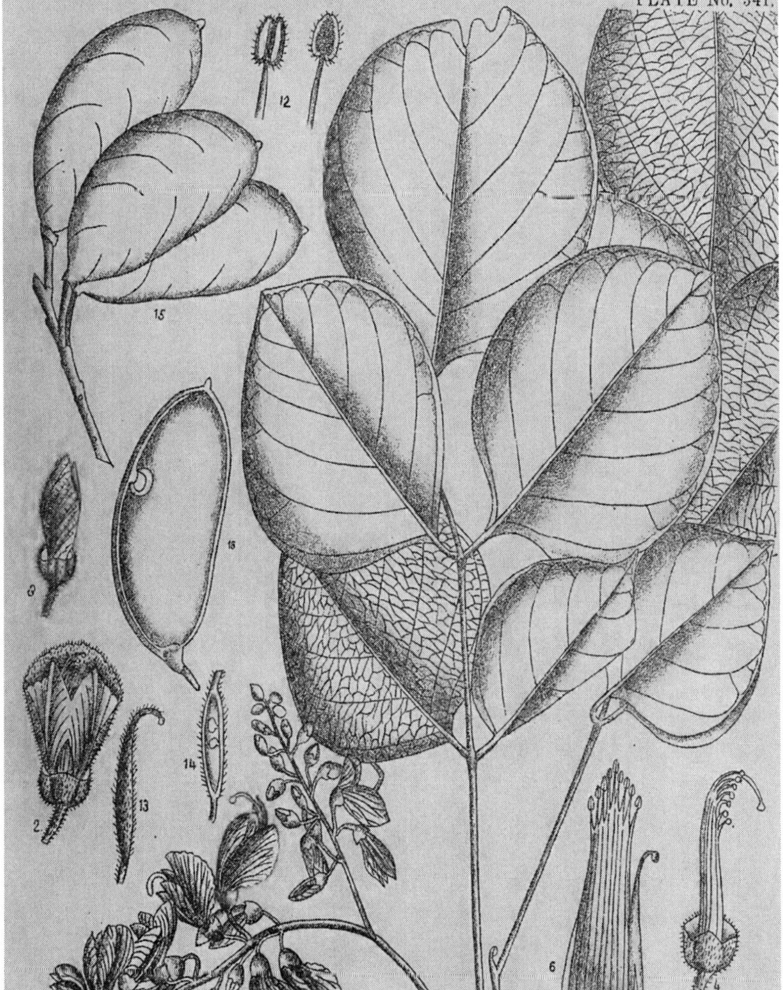

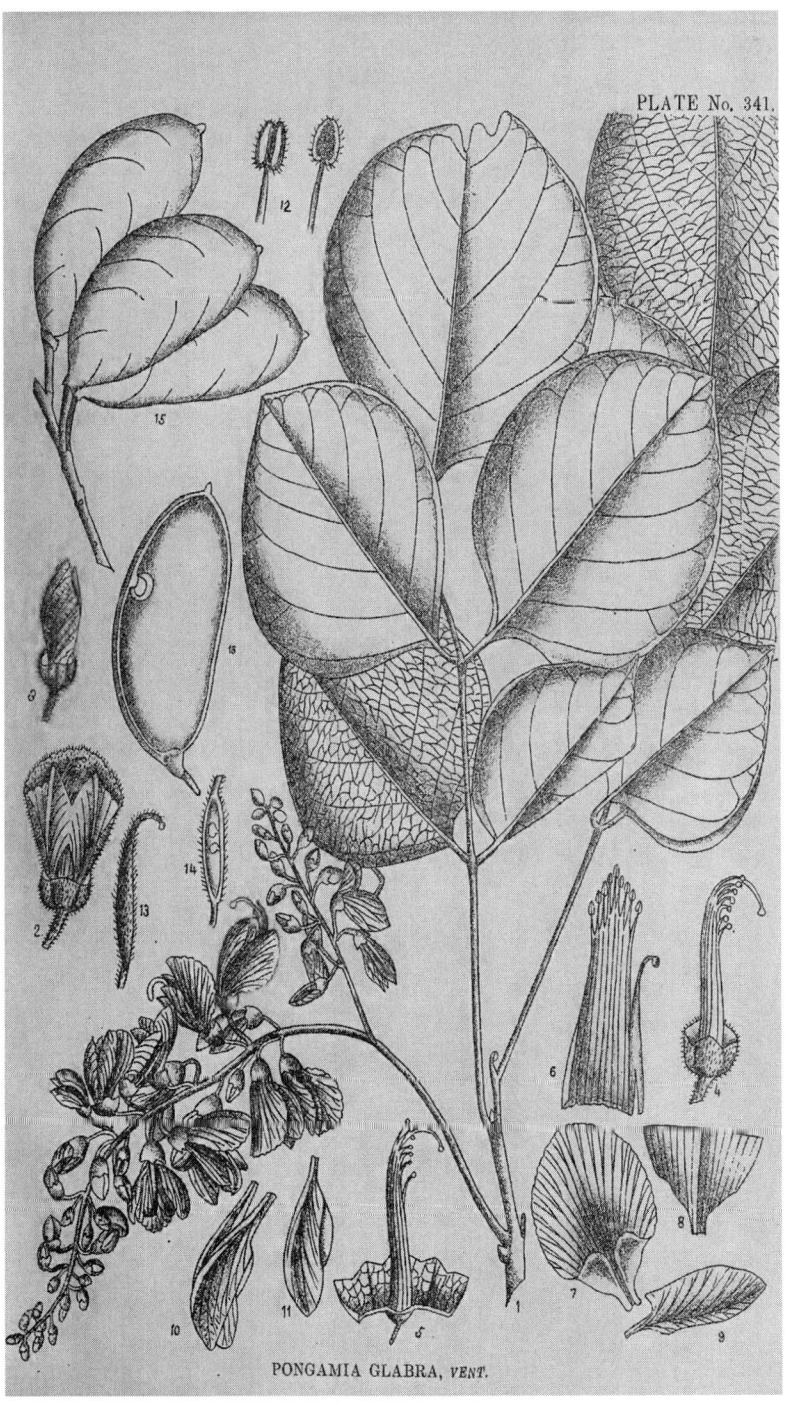

PONGAMIA GLABRA, *Vent.*

PLATE No. 342.

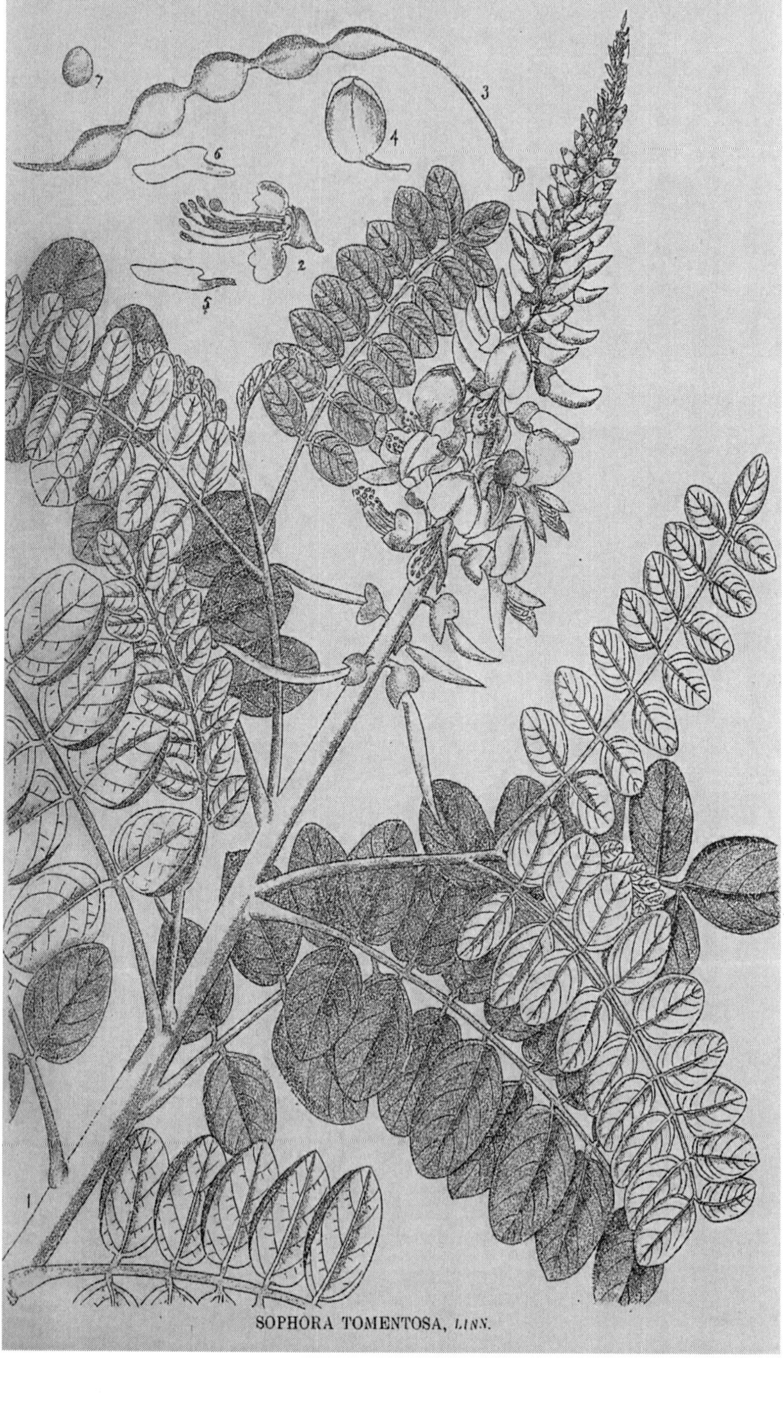

SOPHORA TOMENTOSA, *LINN.*

PLATE No. 343.

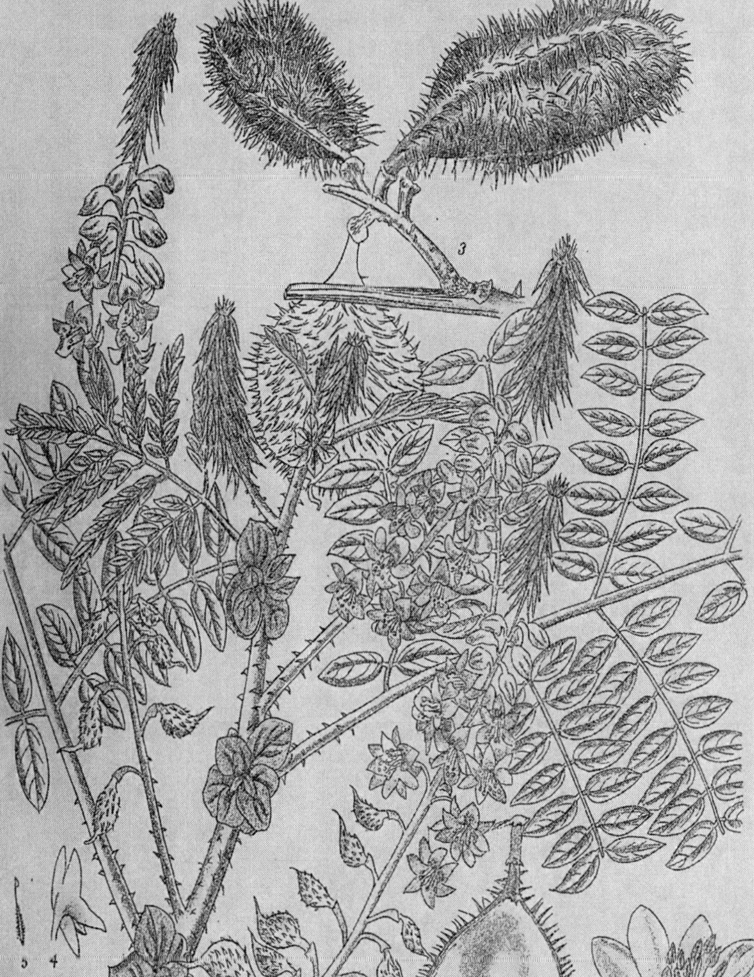

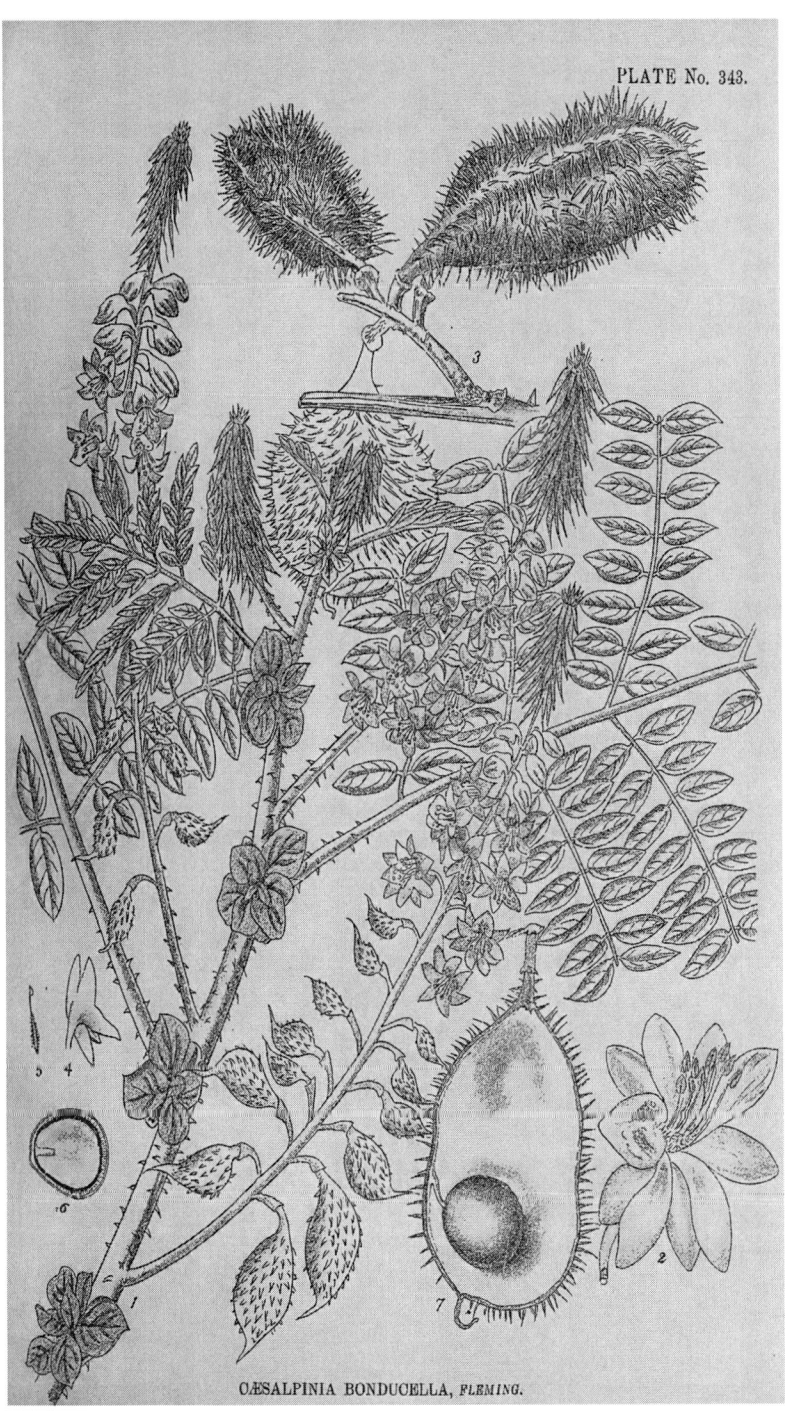

CÆSALPINIA BONDUCELLA, *FLEMING.*

PLATE No. 344

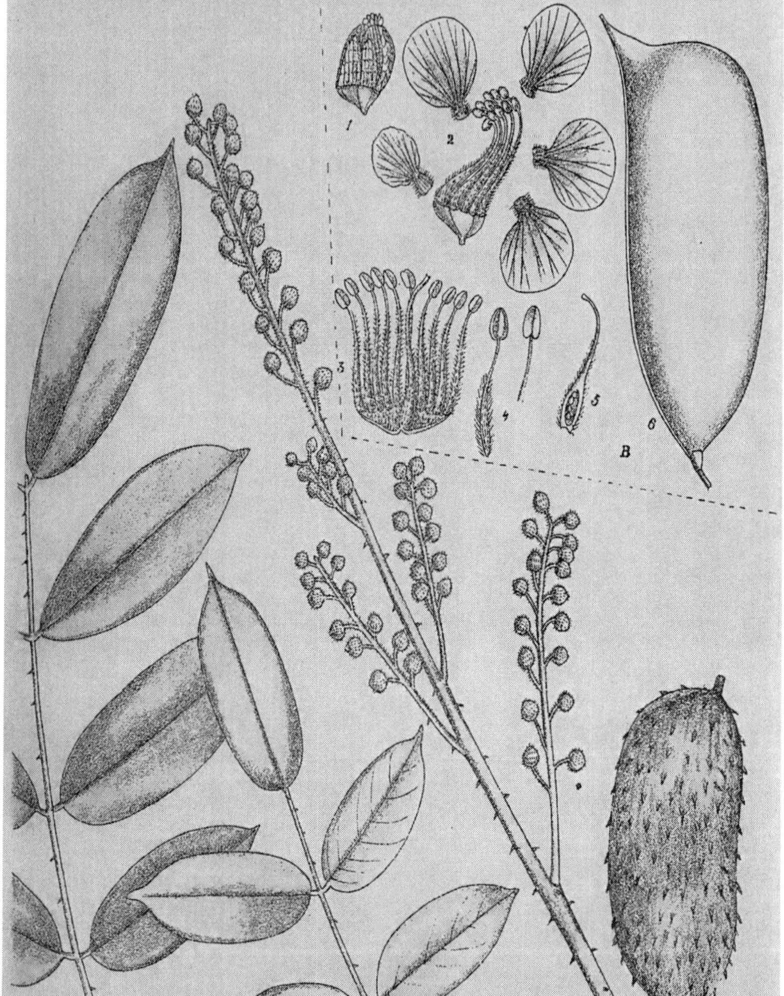

A—CÆSALPINIA BONDUC, *ROXB*　　　B—C. SAPPAN, *LINN.*

PLATE No. 313.

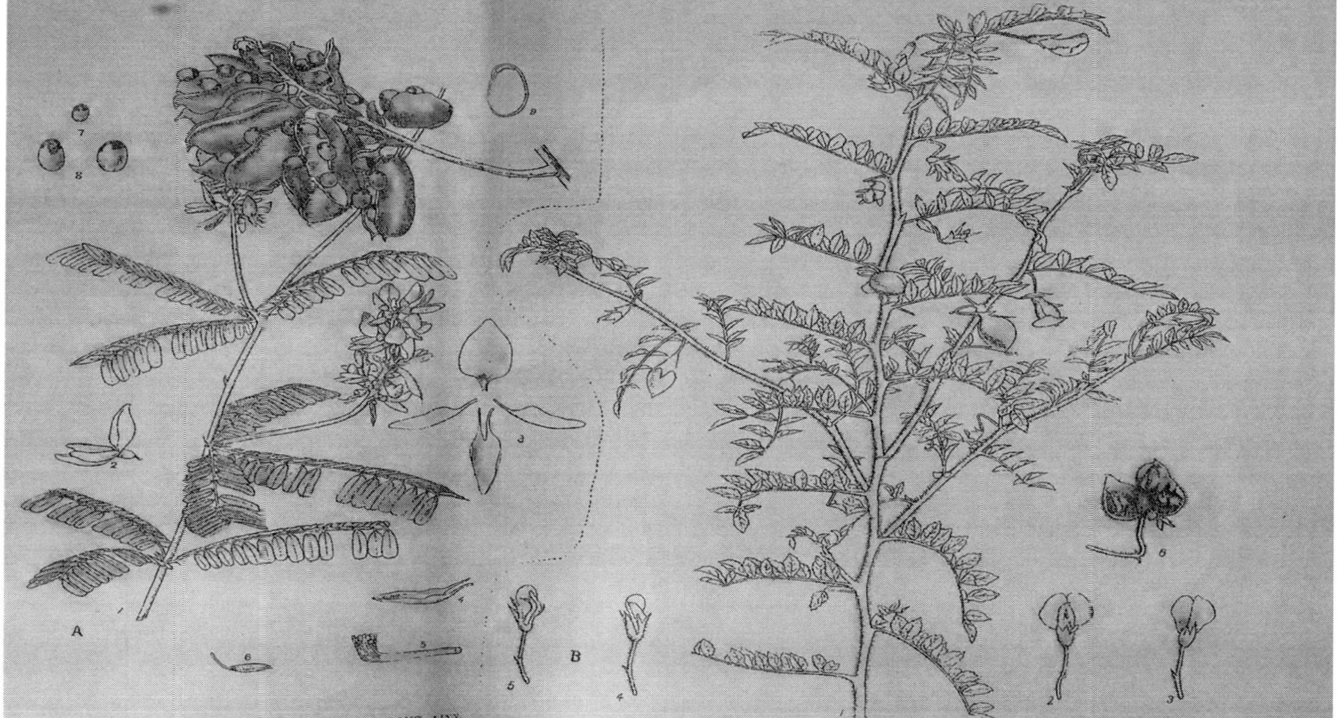

A—ABRUS PRECATORIUS, LINN.

B—CICER ARIETINUM, LINN.

PLATE No. 314.

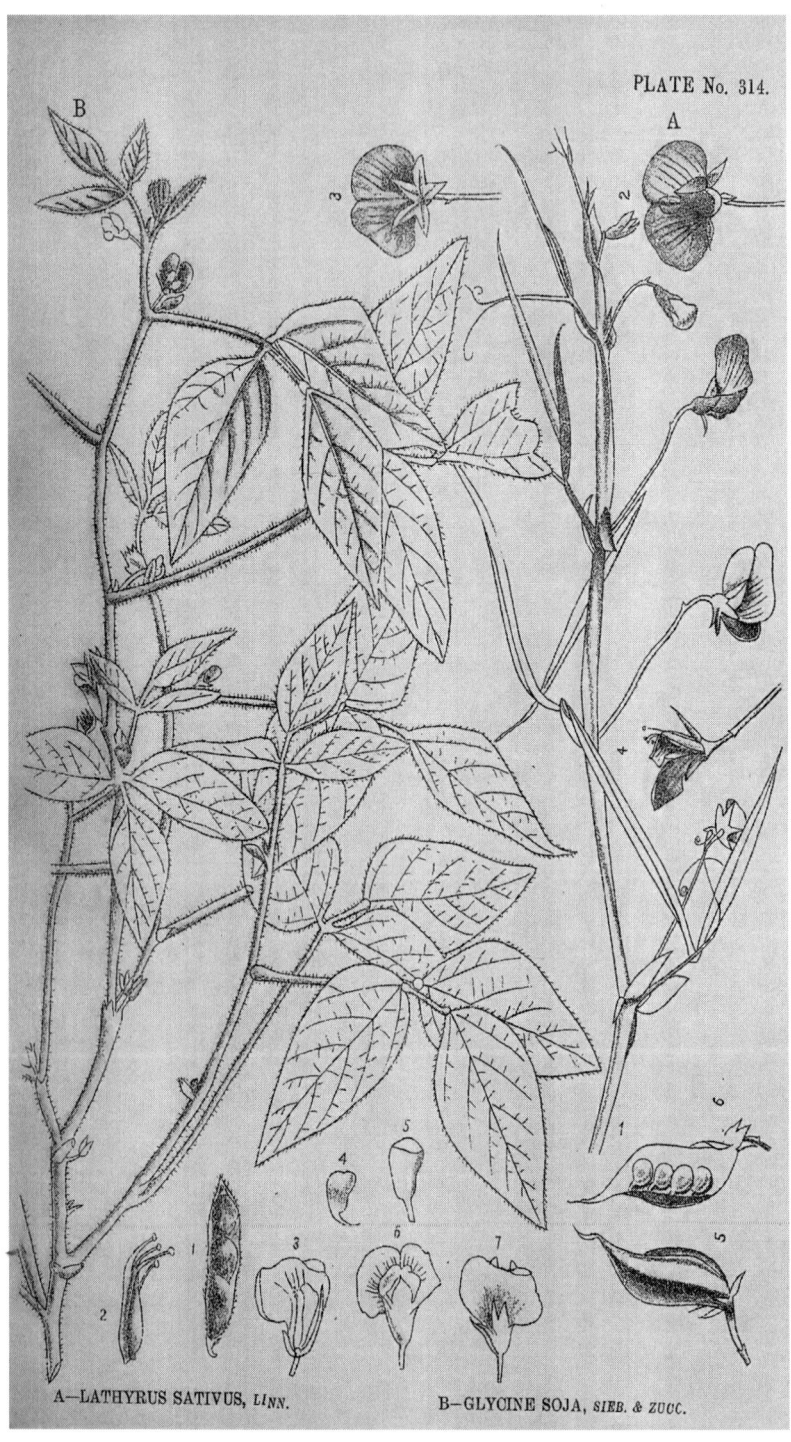

A—LATHYRUS SATIVUS, *Linn.* B—GLYCINE SOJA, *Sieb. & Zucc.*

TERAMNUS LABIALIS, SPRENG.

PLATE No. 316.

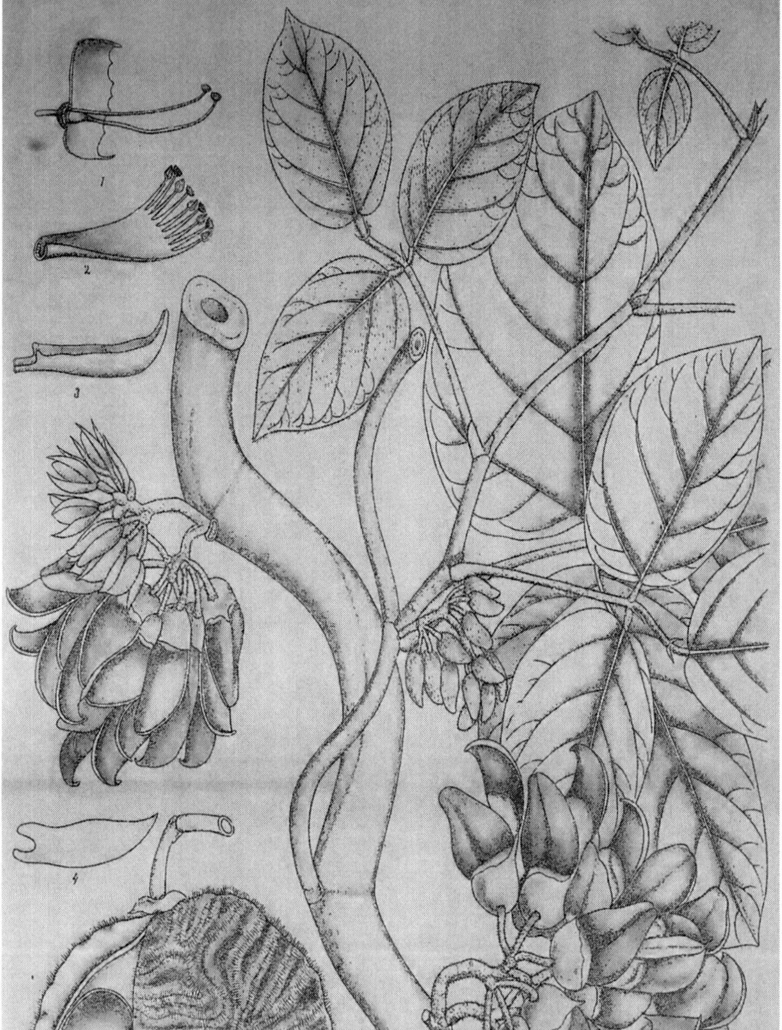

MUOUNA MONOSPERMA, *DC.*

PLATE No. 317

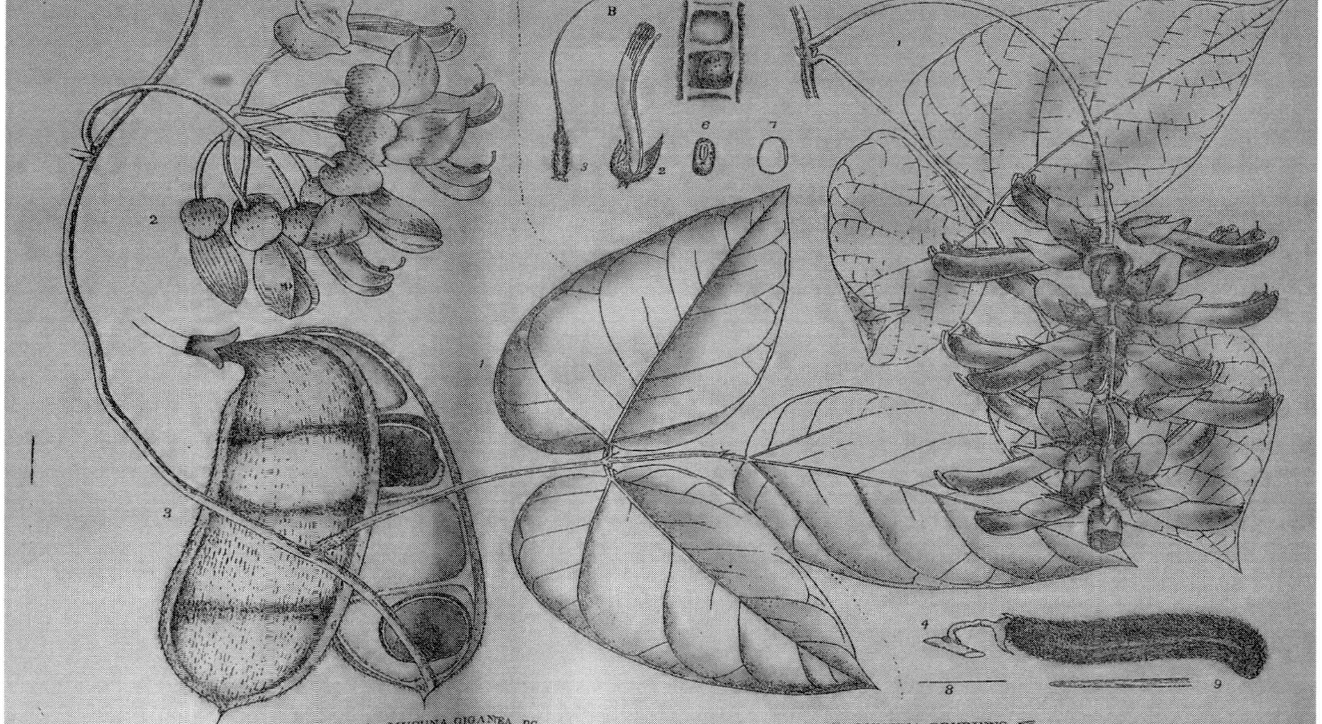

A—MUCUNA GIGANEA, DC. B—MUCUNA PRURIENS, DC.

PLATE No. 318

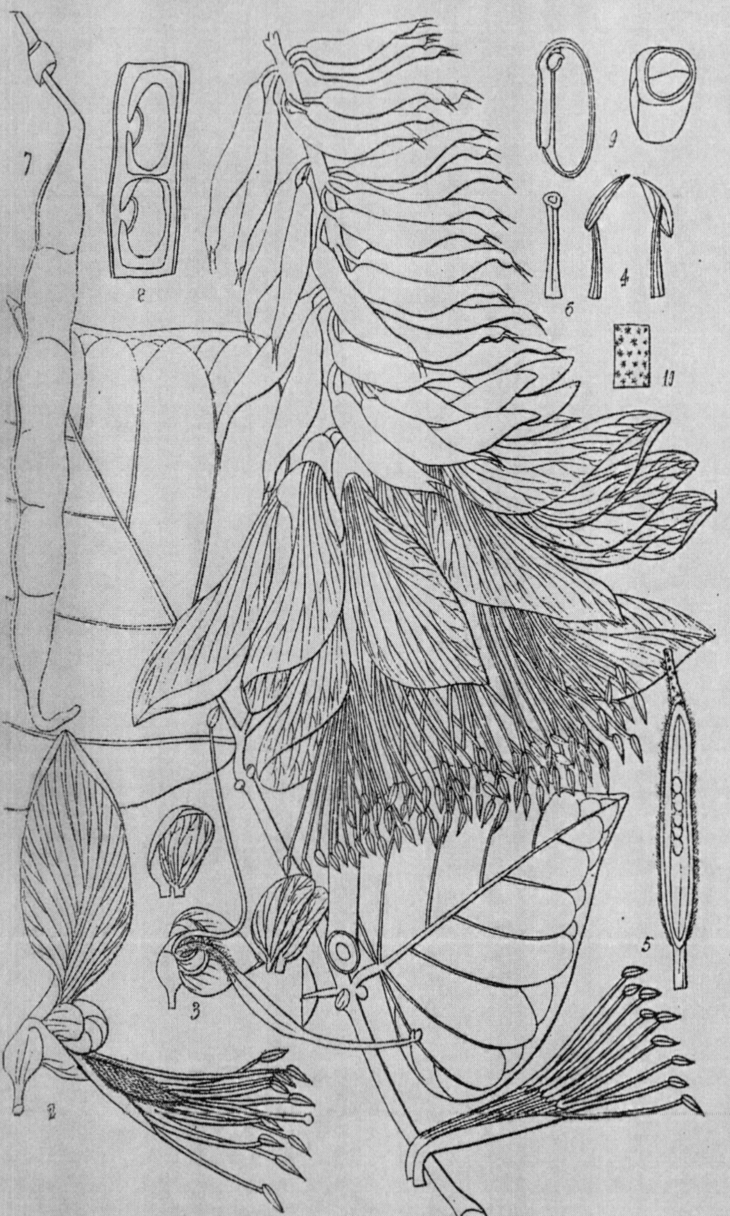

ERYTHRINA INDICA, *Lam.*

PLATE No. 319.

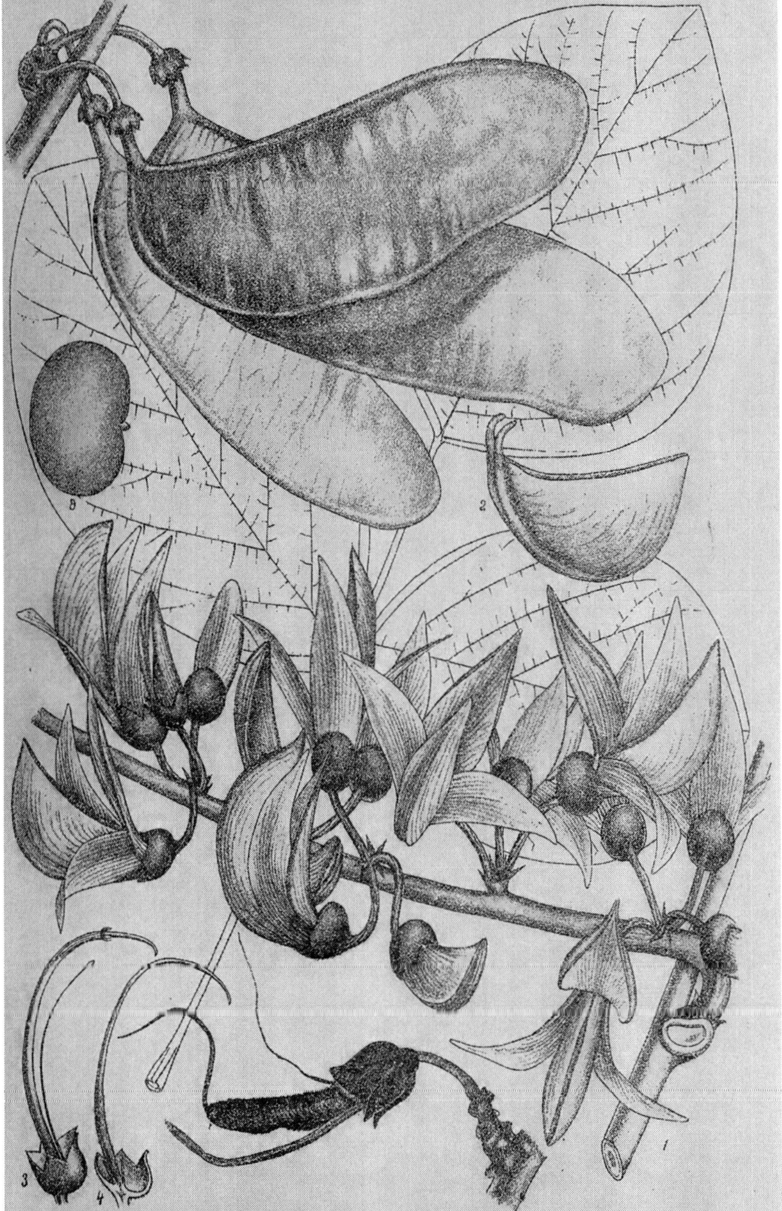

BUTEA FRONDOSA, *ROXB.*

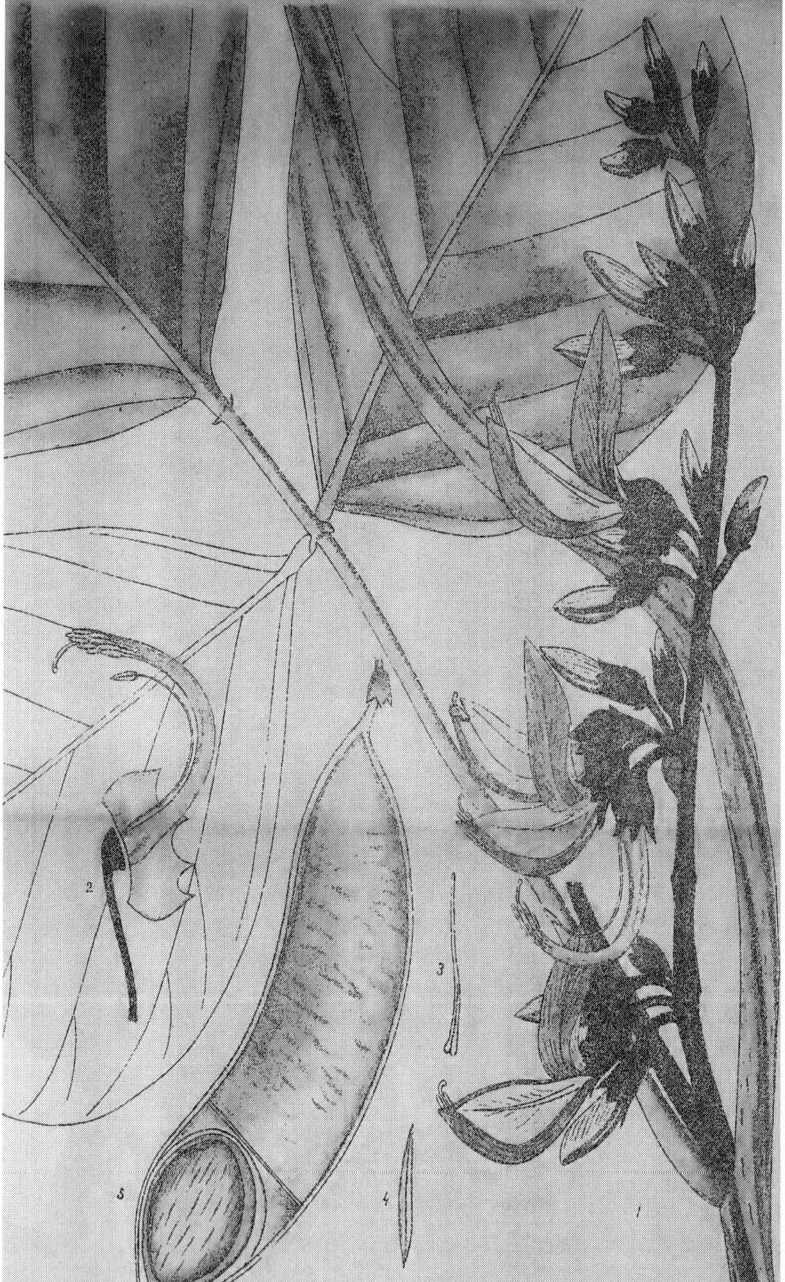

BUTEA SUPERBA, *Roxb.*

PLATE No. 321.

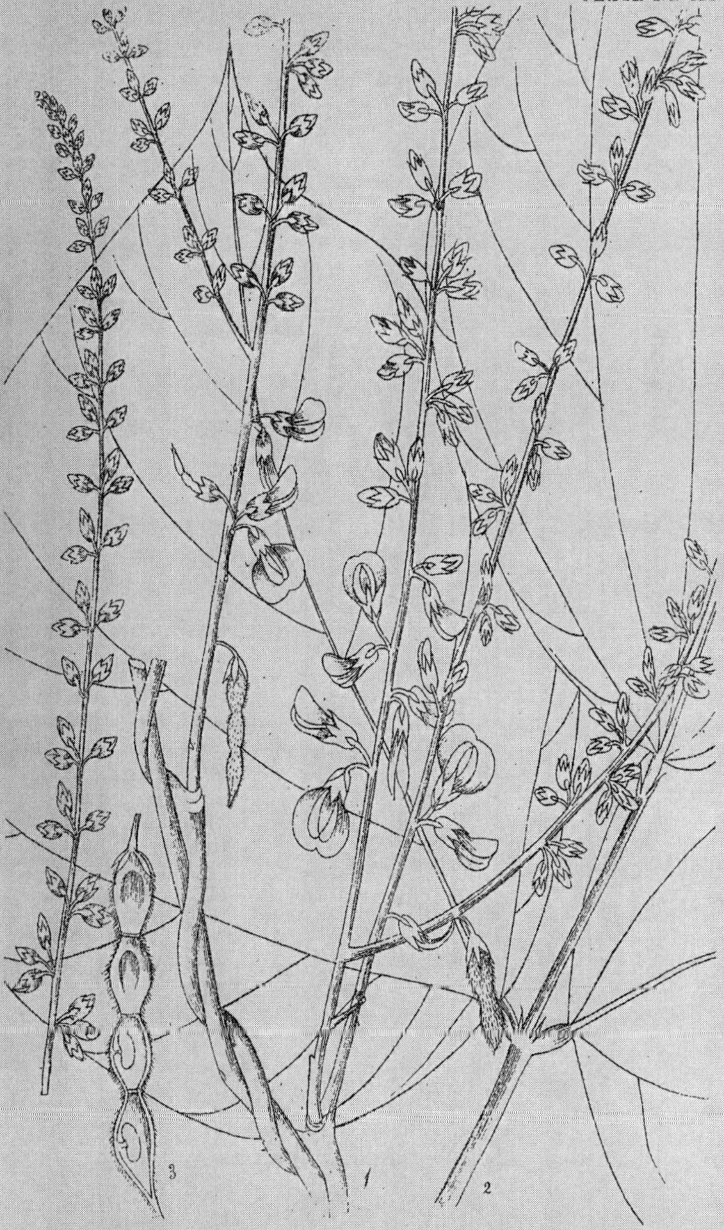

PUERARIA TUBEROSA, DC.

PLATE No. 322.

PHASEOLUS TRILOBUS, *AIT.*

PLATE No. 323.

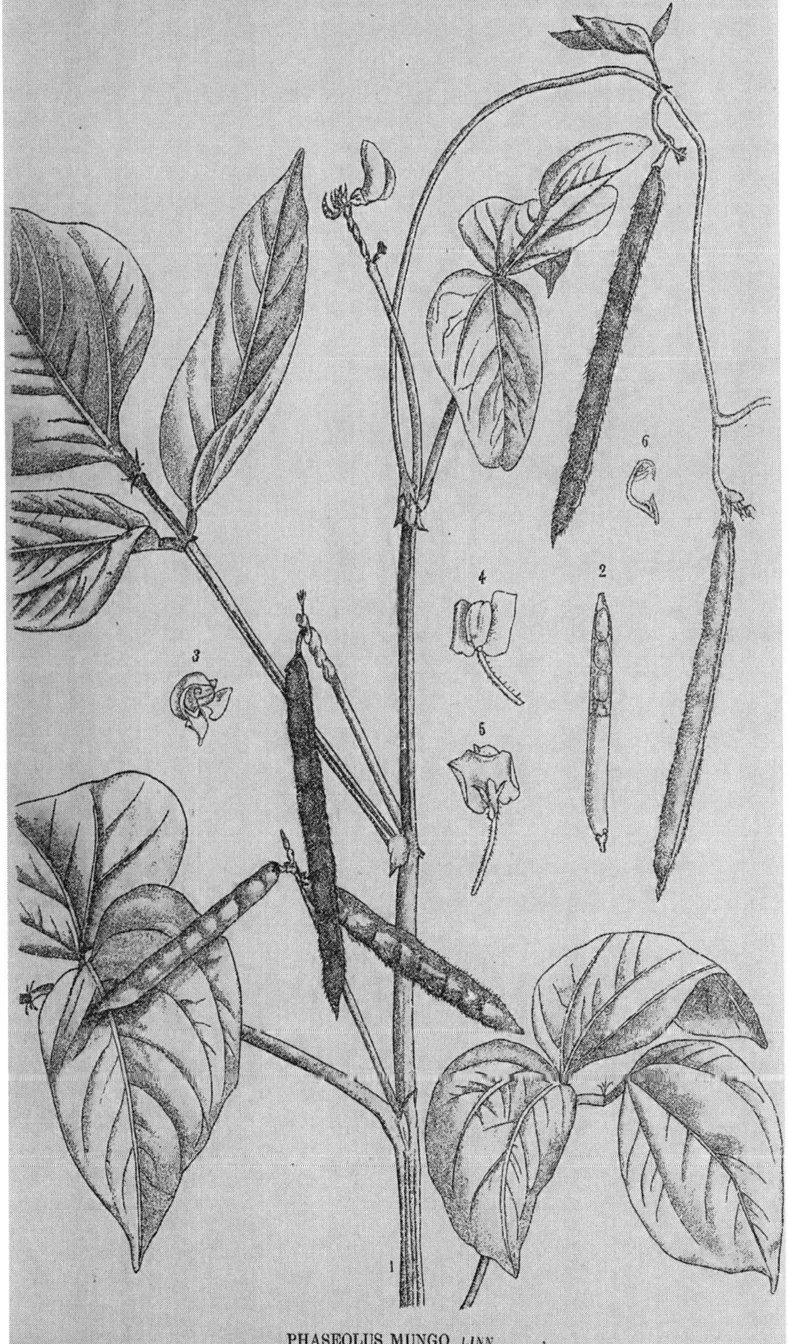

PHASEOLUS MUNGO, *LINN.*

PLATE No. 324.

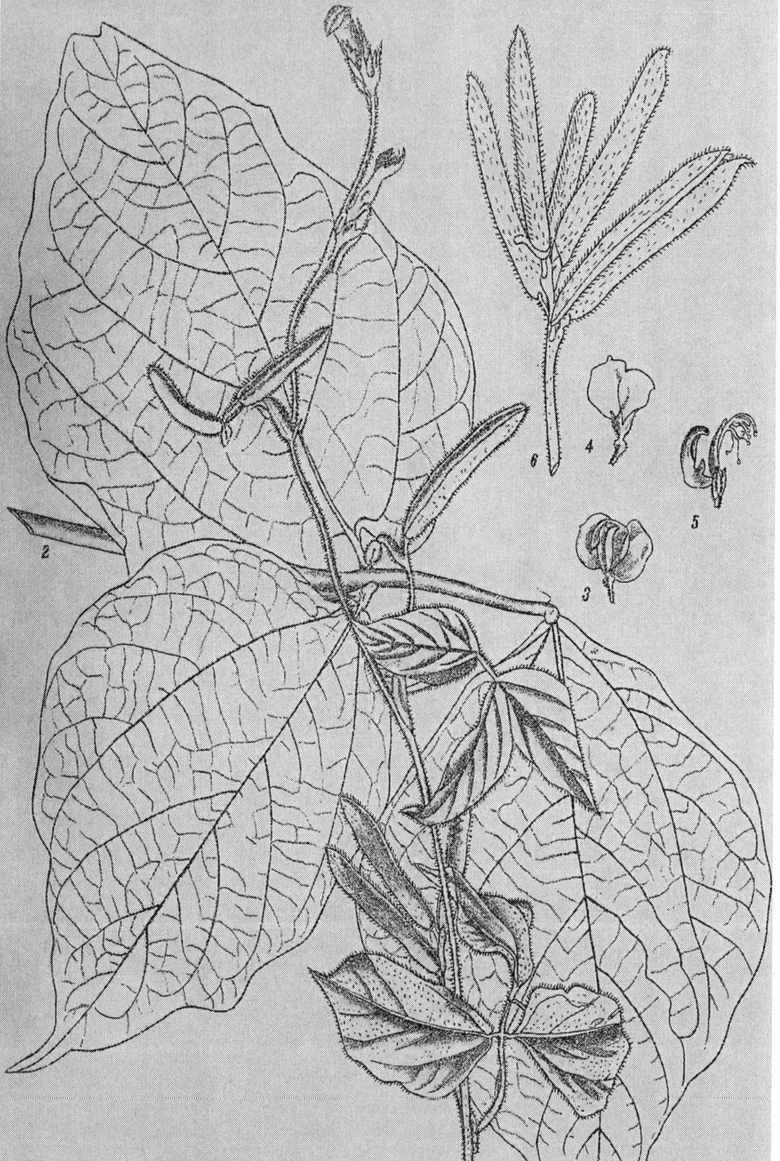

PHASEOLUS MUNGO, *L. VAR. RADIATUS.*

PLATE No. 325.

VIGNA CATIANG, *Endl.*

PLATE No. 326.

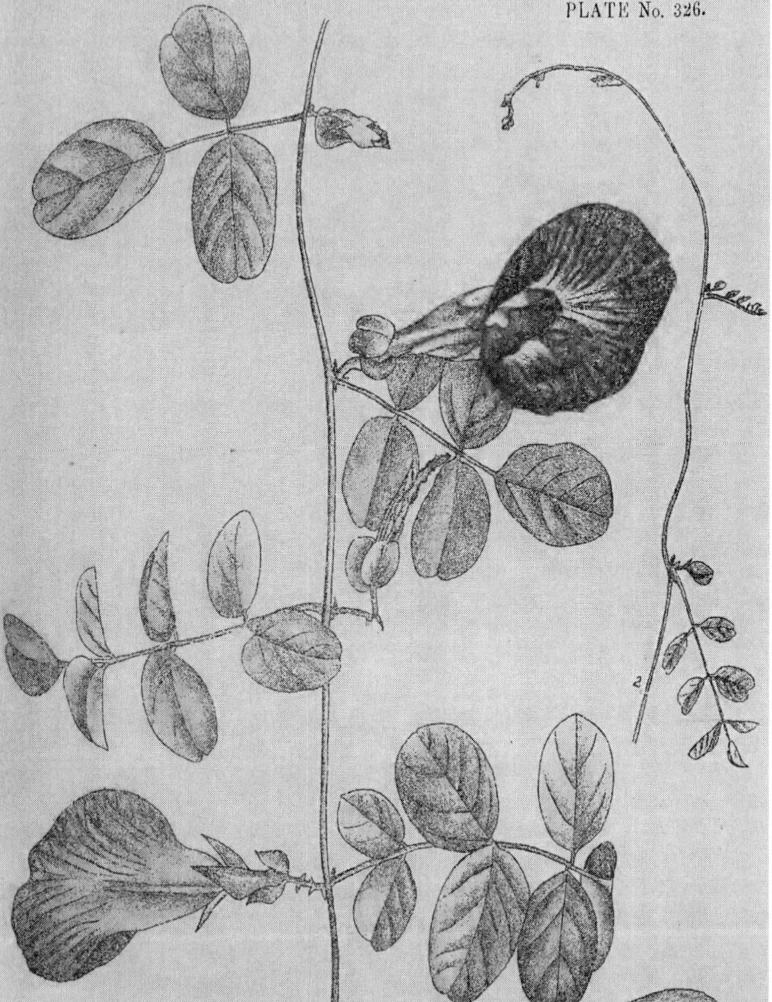

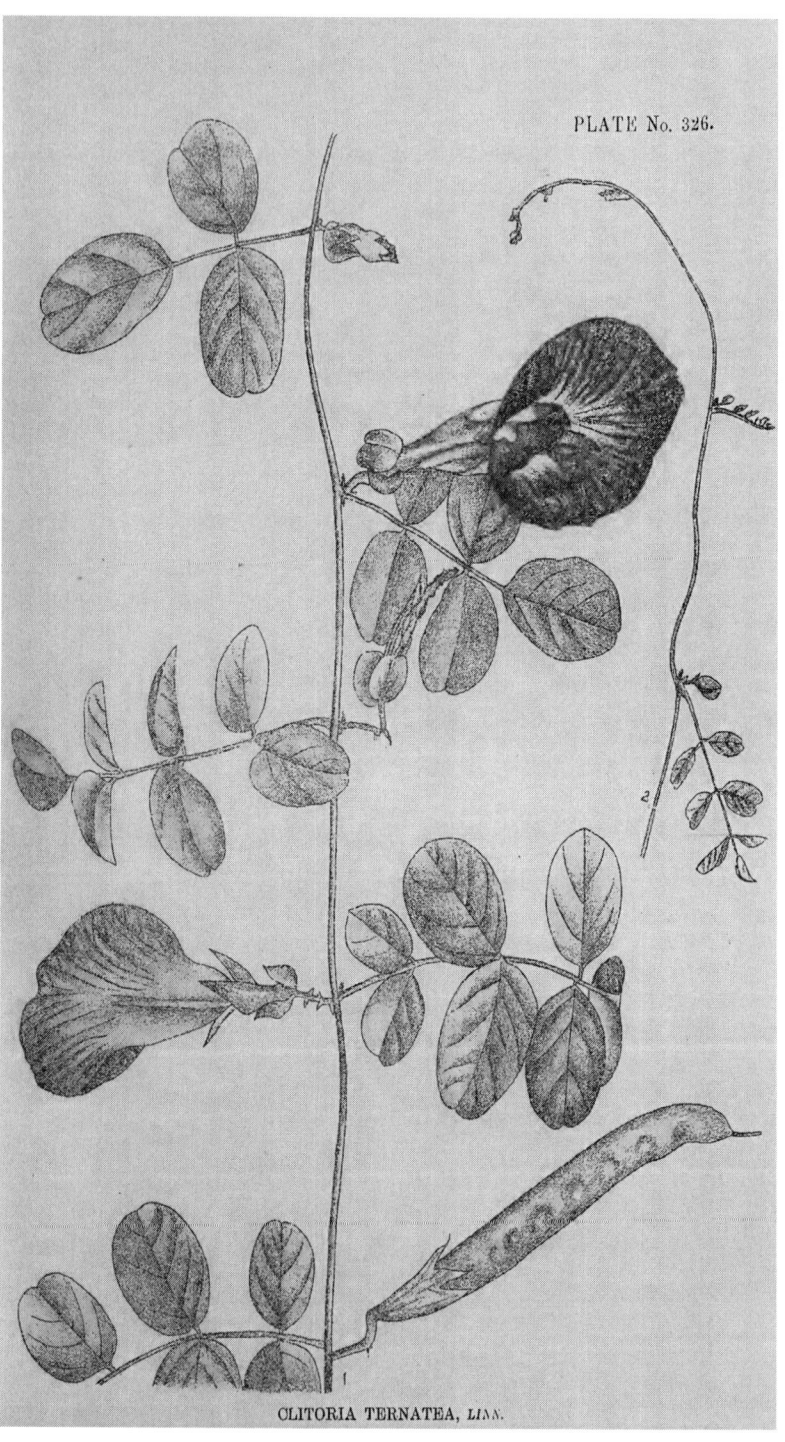

CLITORIA TERNATEA, *Linn.*

PLATE No. 327.

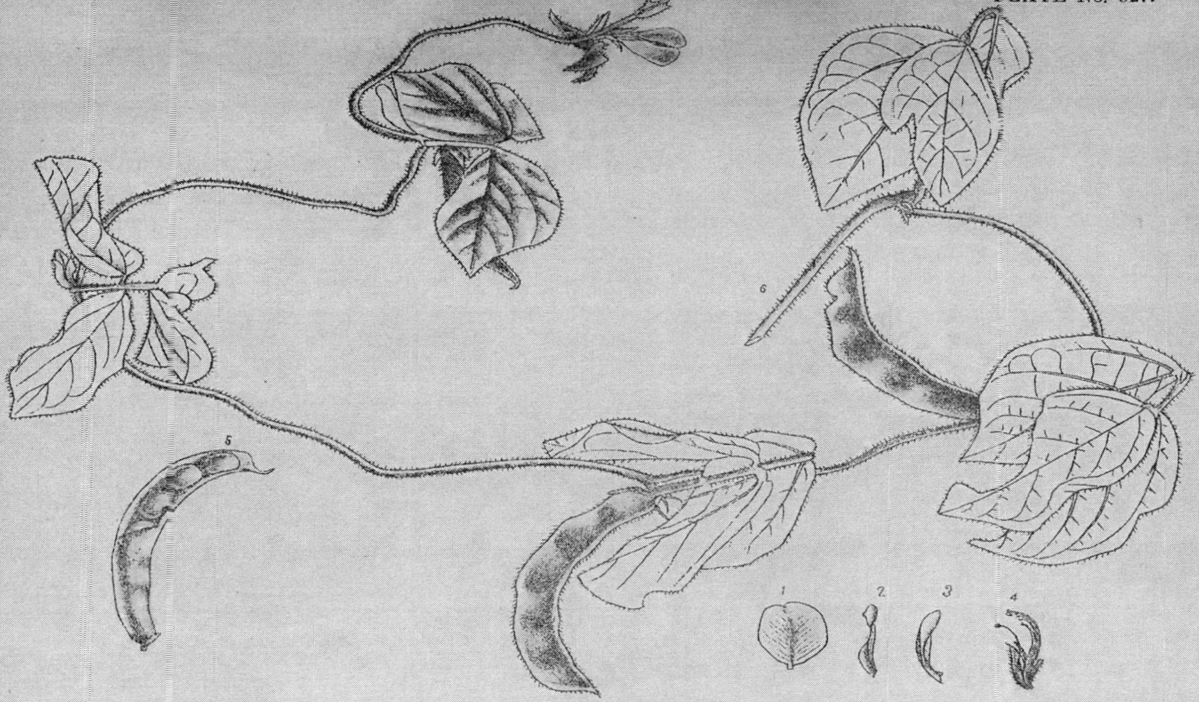

DOLICHOS BIFLORUS, *LINN.*

PLATE No. 328.

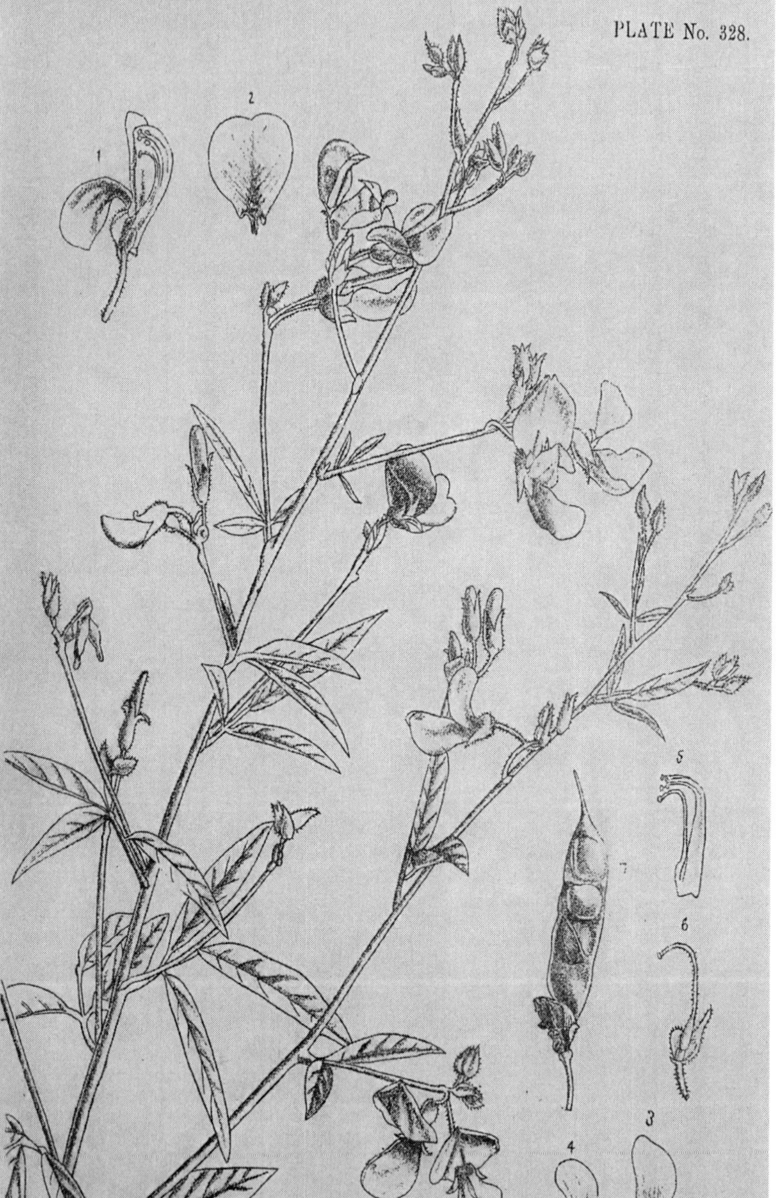

CAJANUS INDICUS, *SPRENG.*

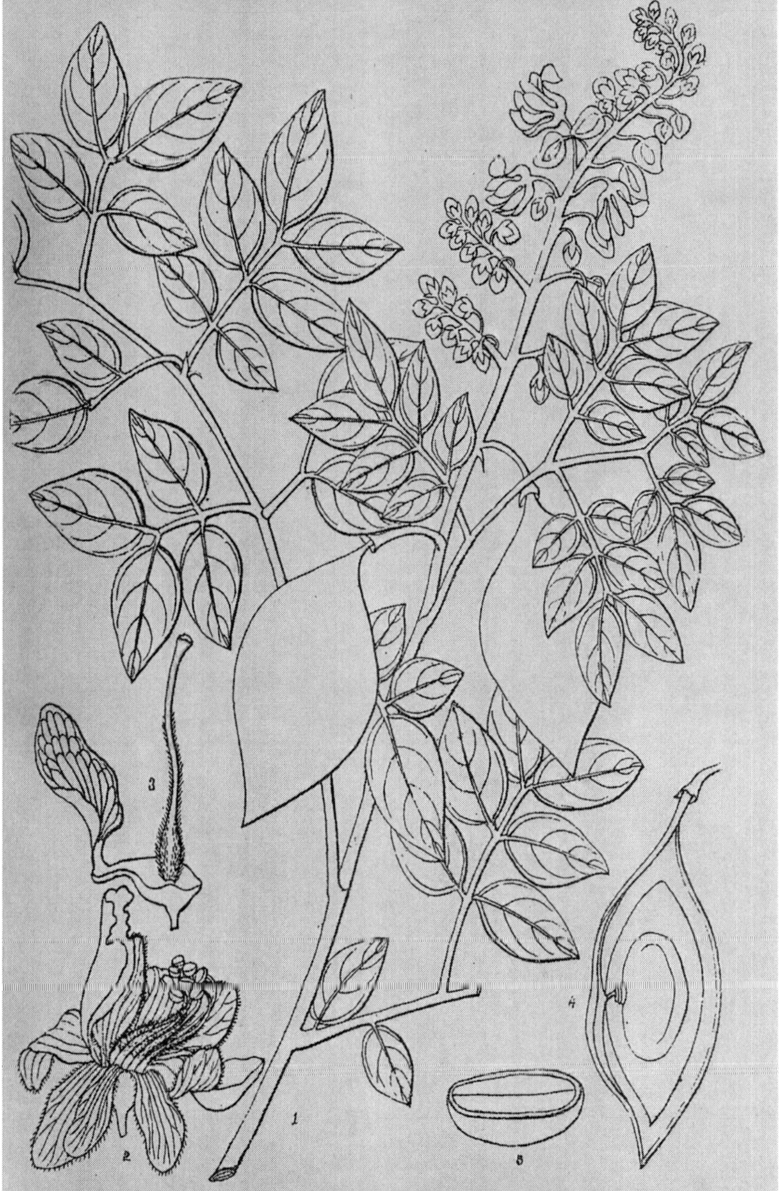

CÆSALPINIA NUGA, *AIT.*

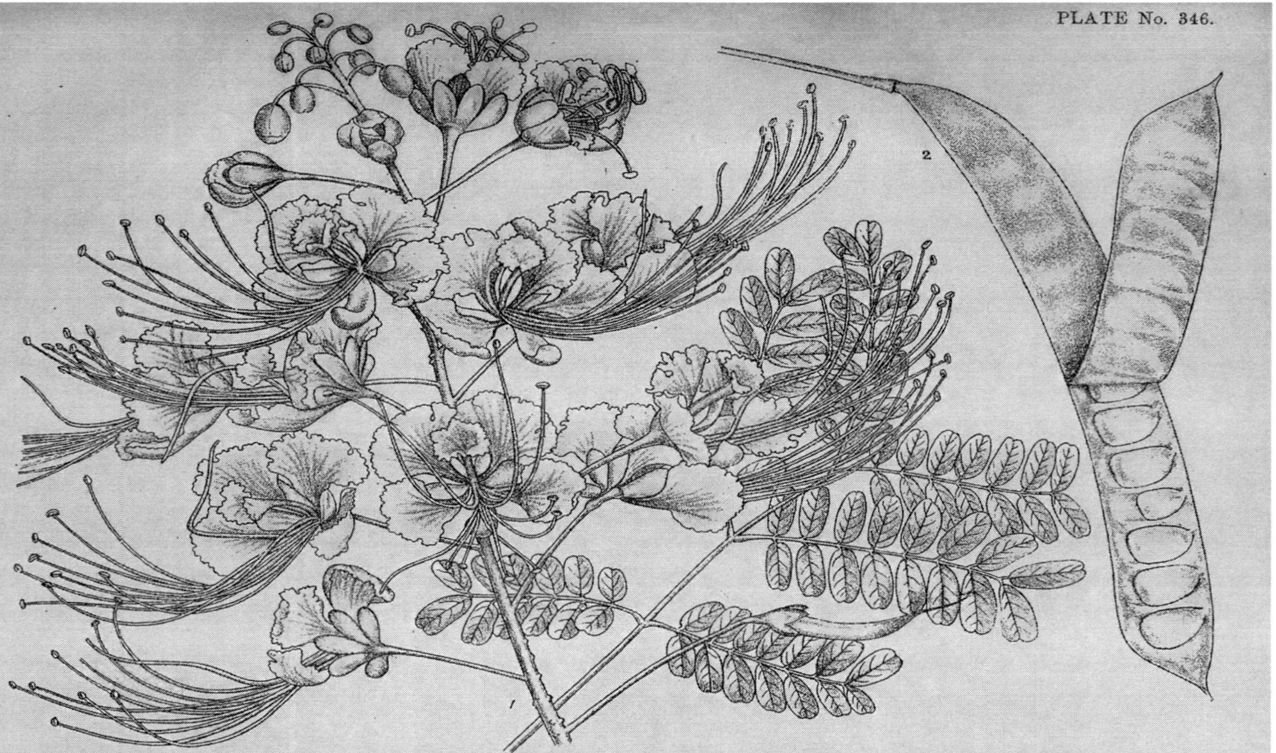

CÆSALPINIA PULCHERRIMA, *Swartz.*

PLATE No. 347.

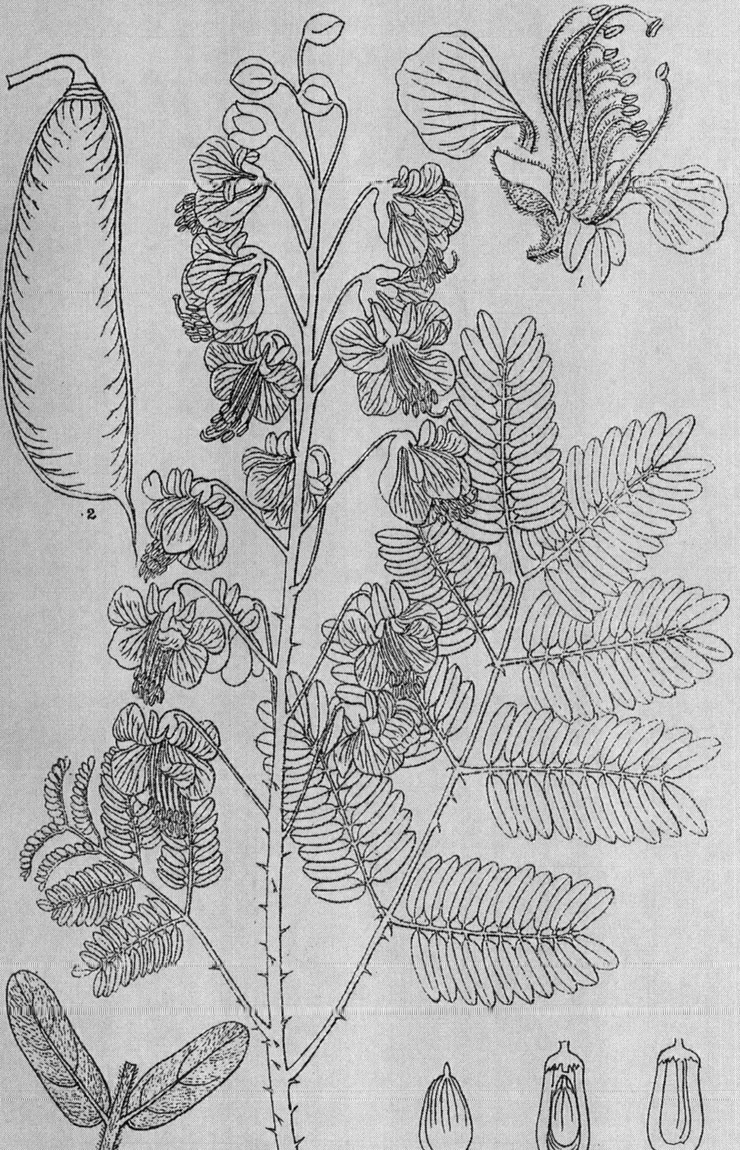

CÆSALPINIA SEPIARIA, *ROXB.*

PLATE No. 348

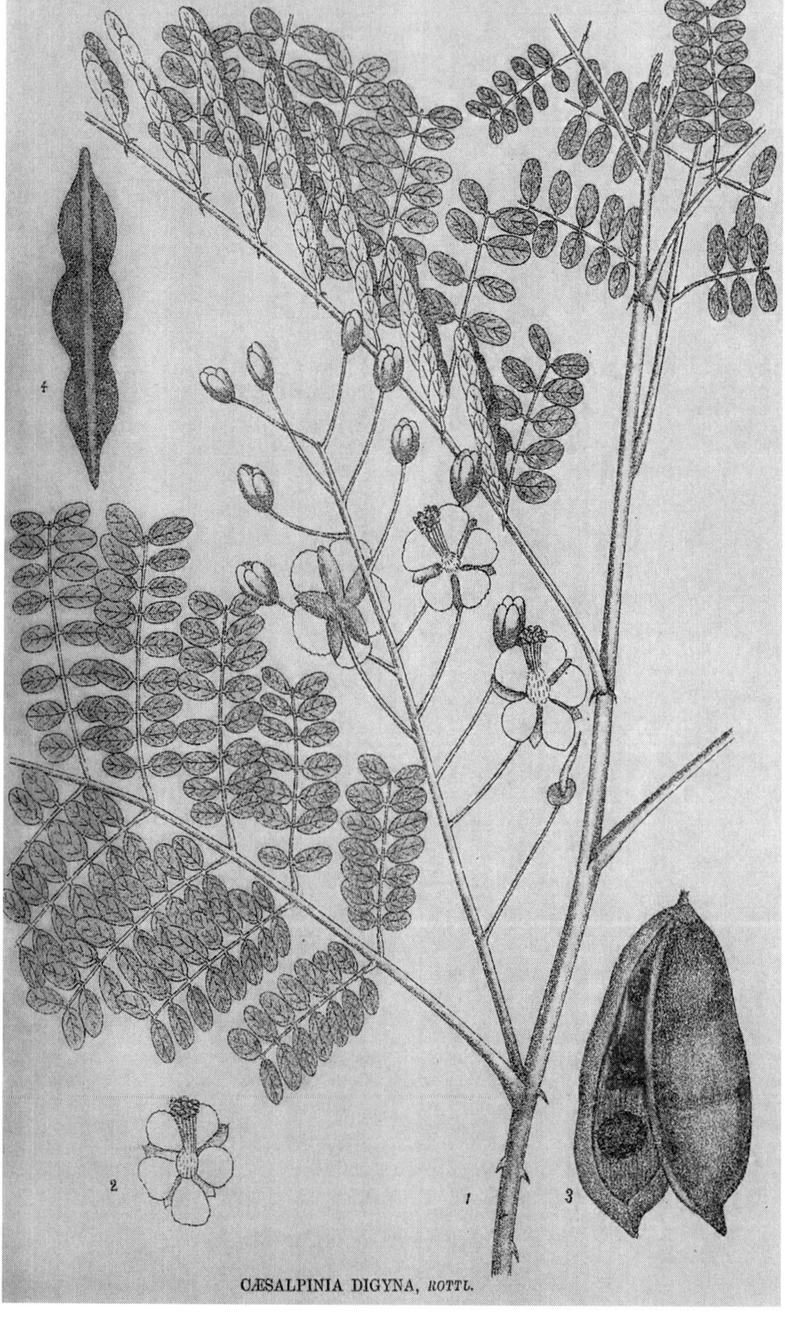

CÆSALPINIA DIGYNA, *ROTTL.*

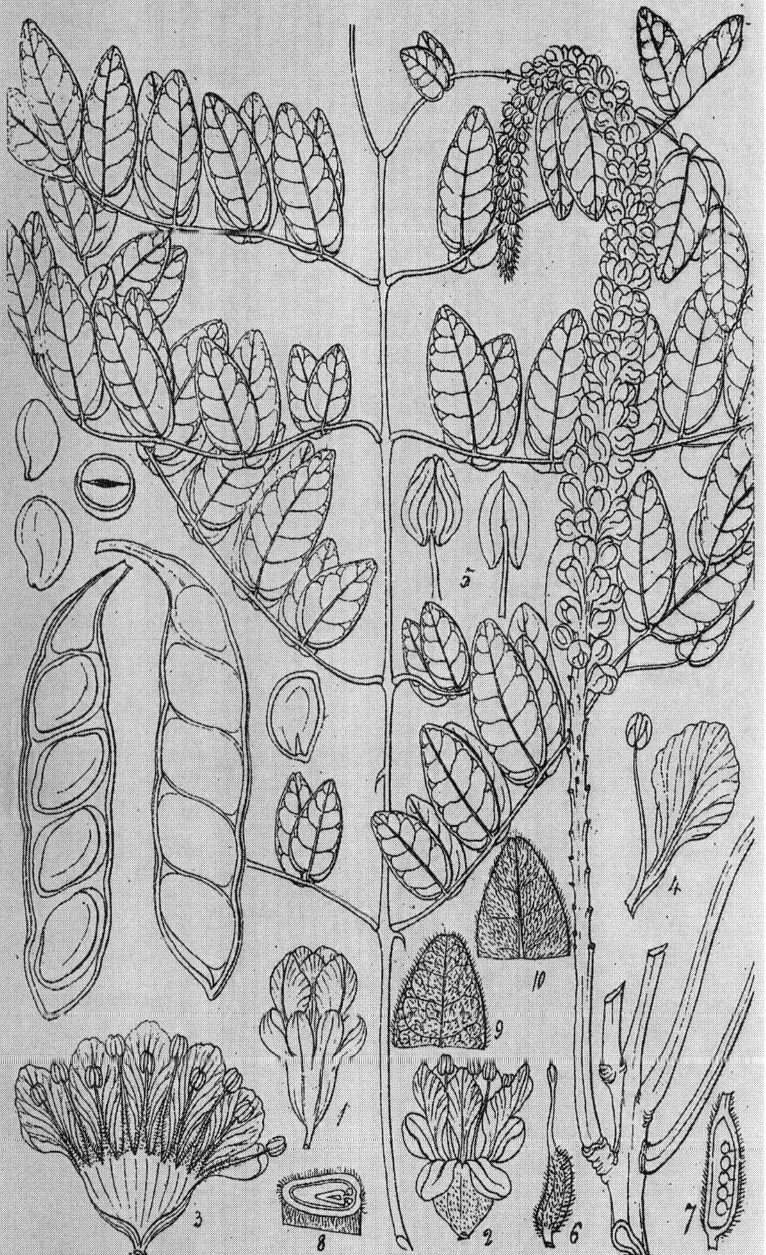

WAGATEA SPICATA, DALZELL.

PLATE No. 350.

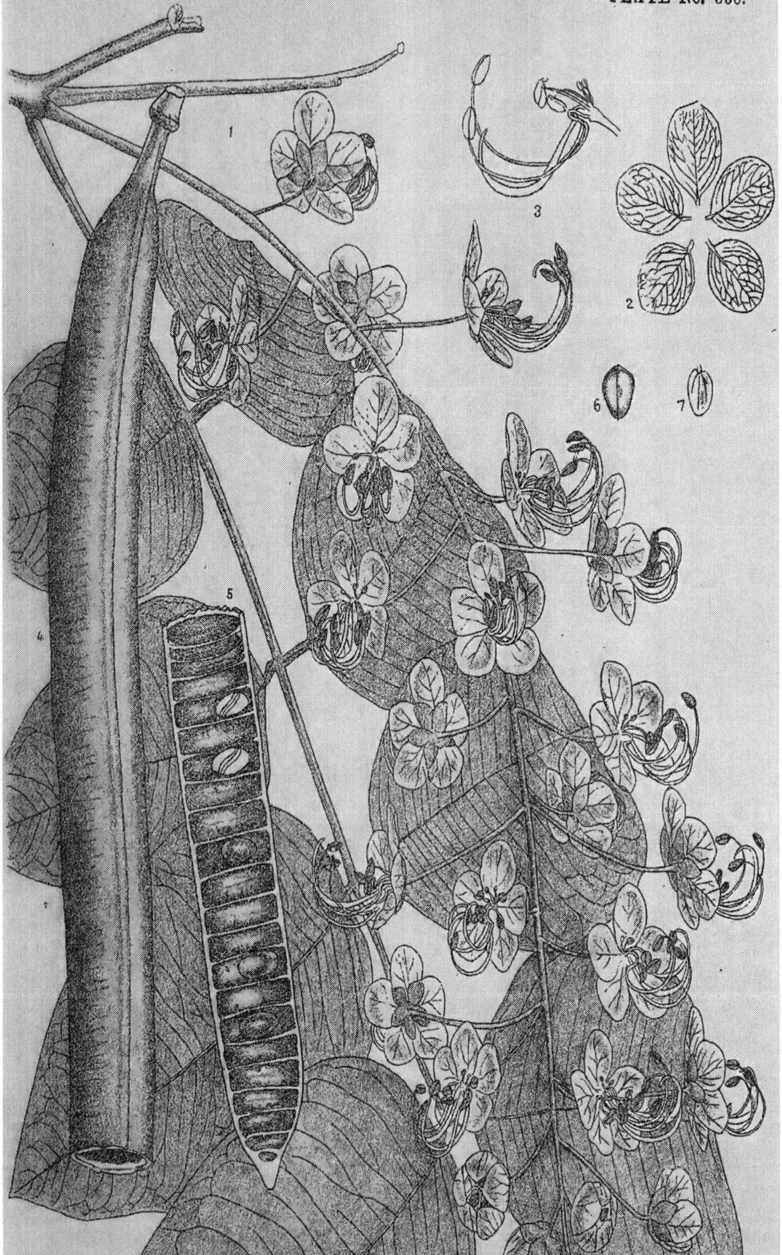

CASSIA FISTULA, *LINN.*

PLATE No. 351

CASSIA OCCIDENTALIS, *LINN.*

PLATE No. 352

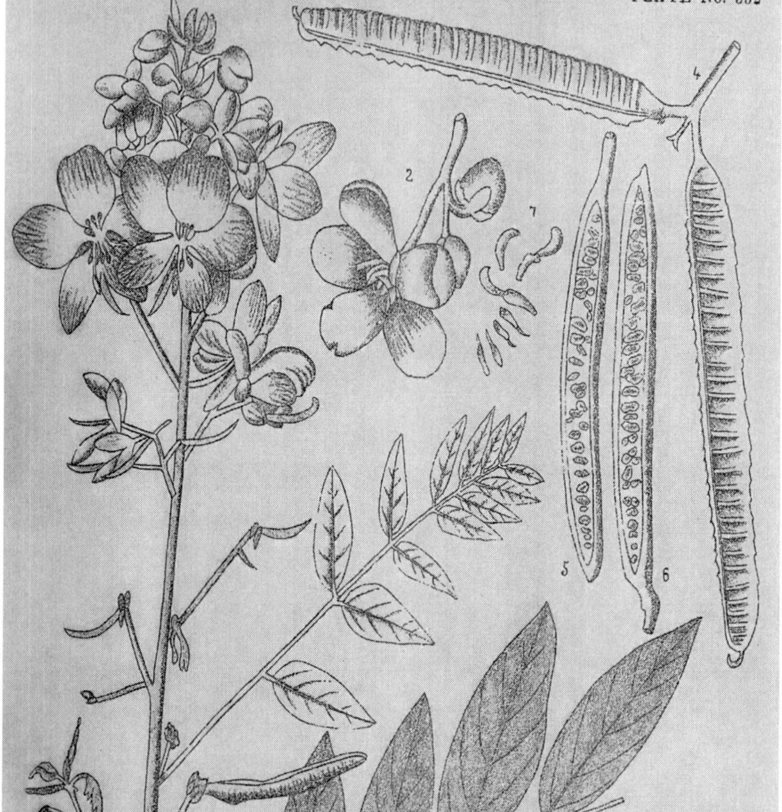

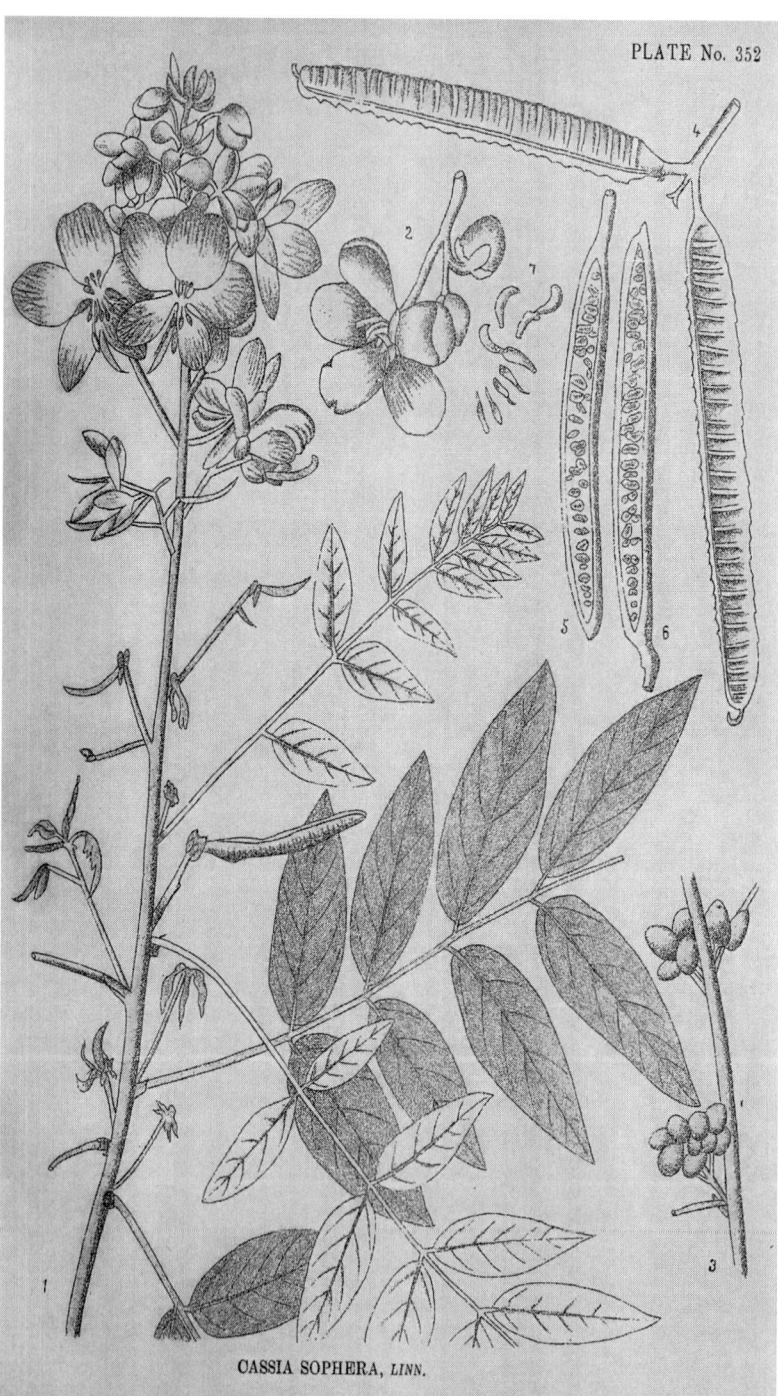

CASSIA SOPHERA, *LINN.*

PLATE No. 353.

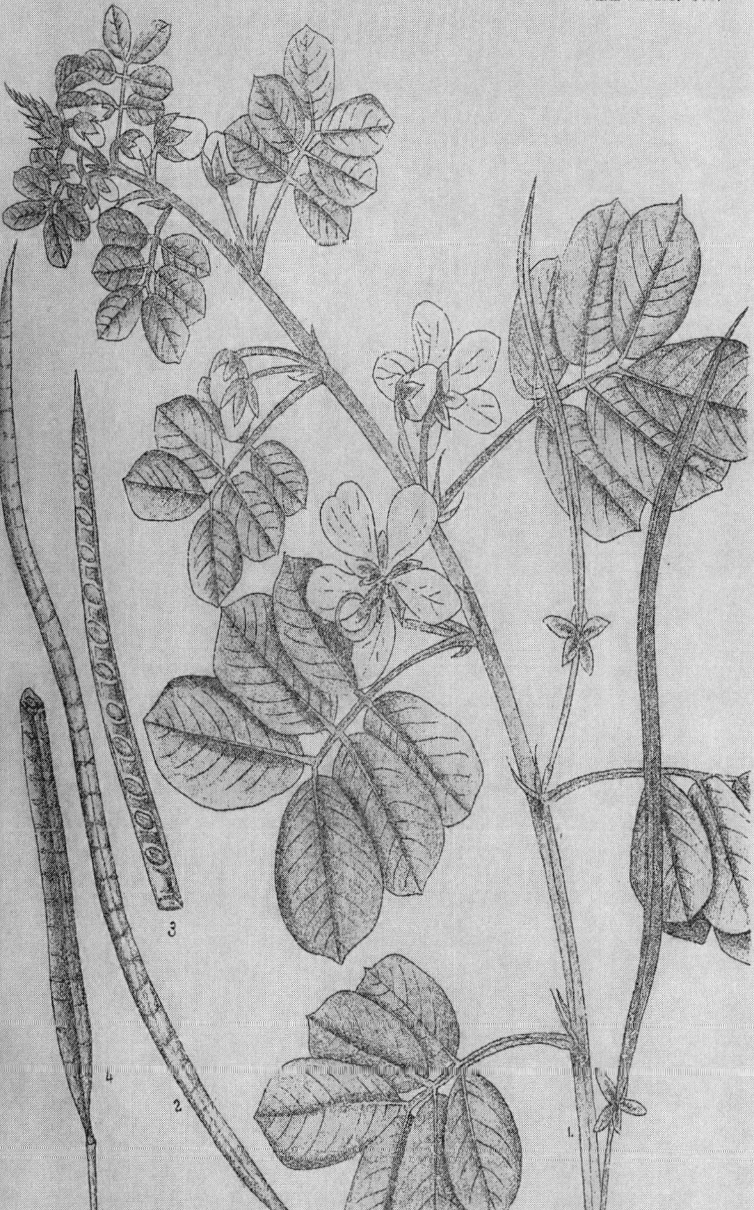

CASSIA TORA, *LINN.*

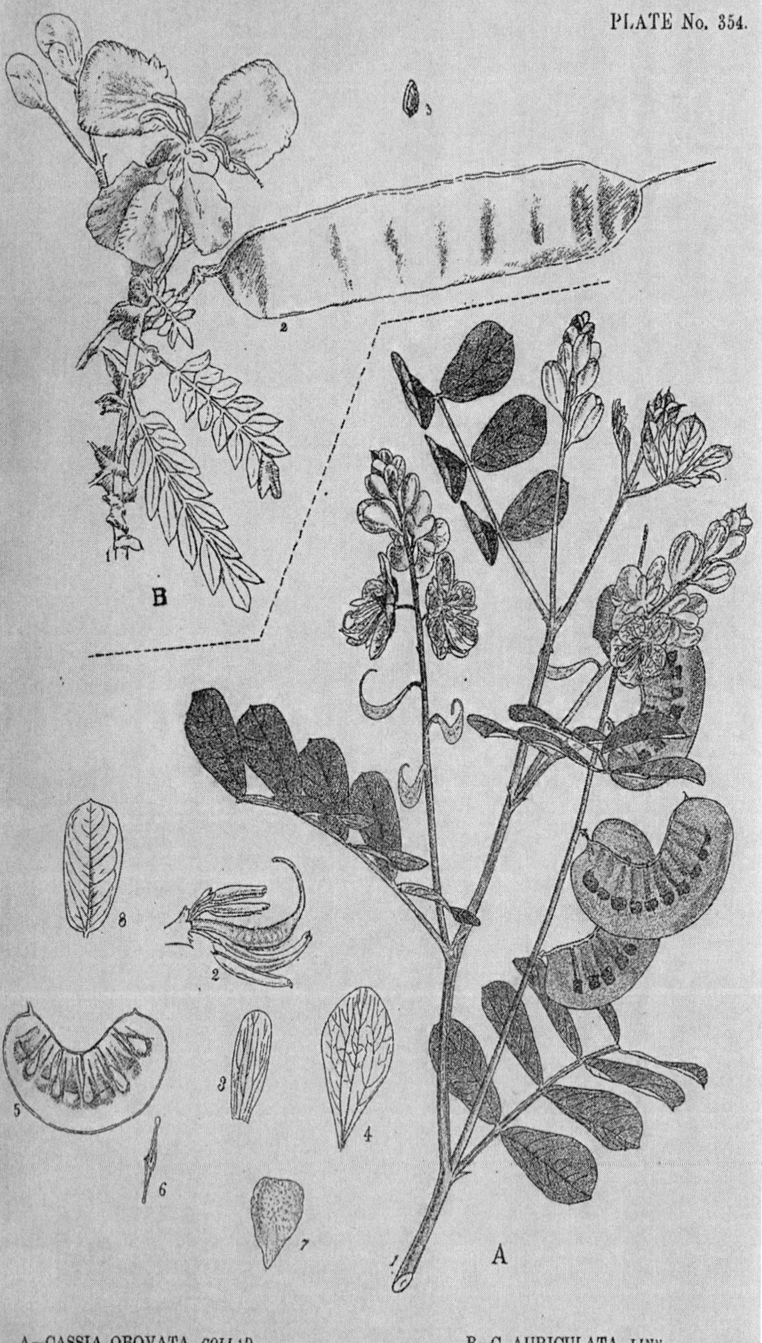

A—CASSIA OBOVATA, *COLLAD.*   B—C. AURICULATA, *LINN.*

PLATE No. 355.

CASSIA ALATA, *LINN.*

PLATE No. 356.

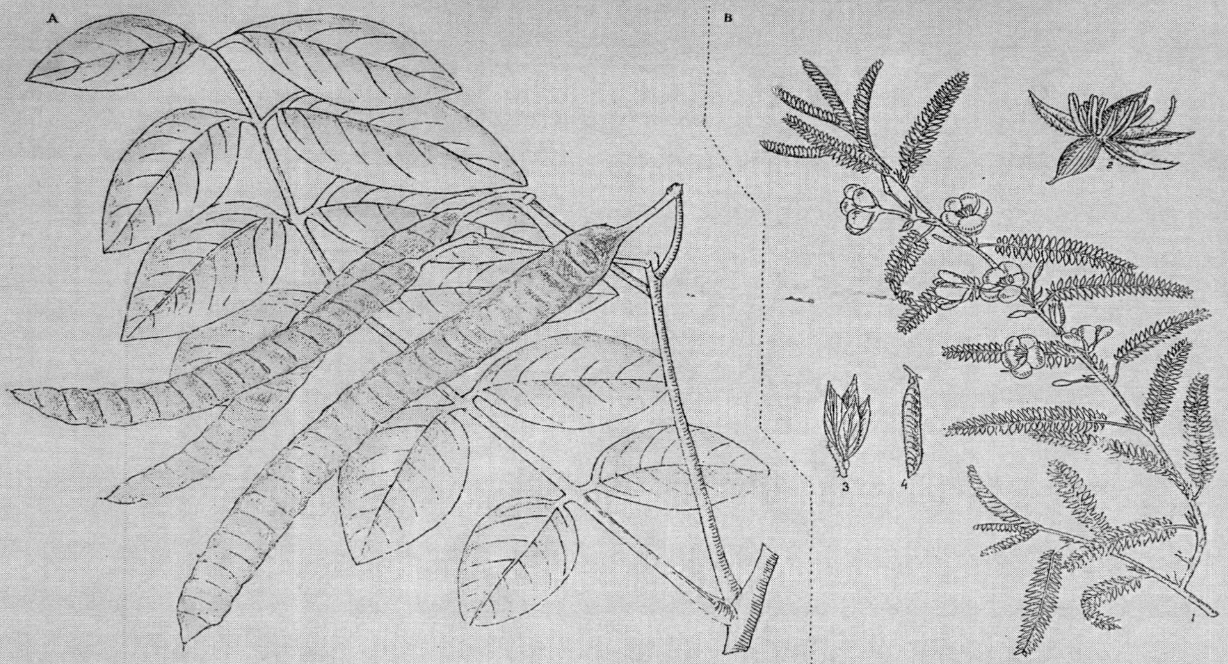

A—CASSIA GLAUCA, *LAM.*   B—C. MIMOSOIDES, *LINN.*

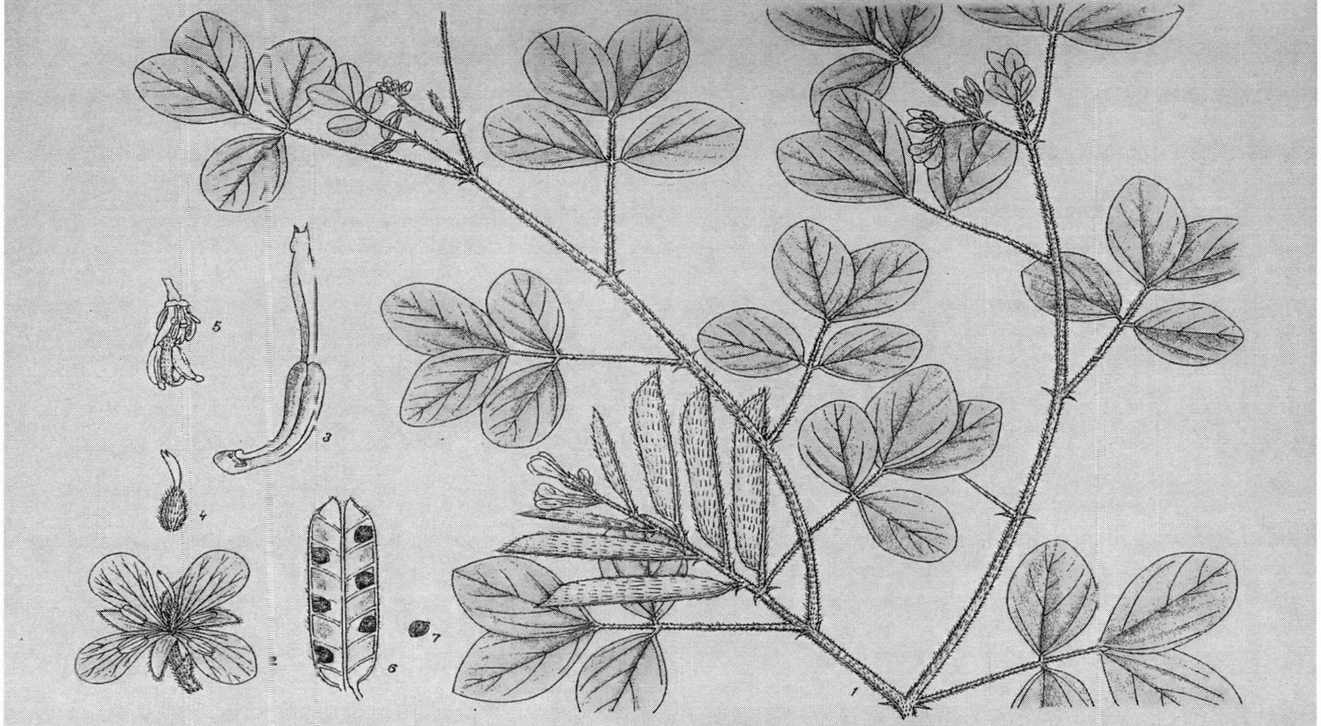

CASSIA ABSUS, *LINN.*

PLATE No. 358

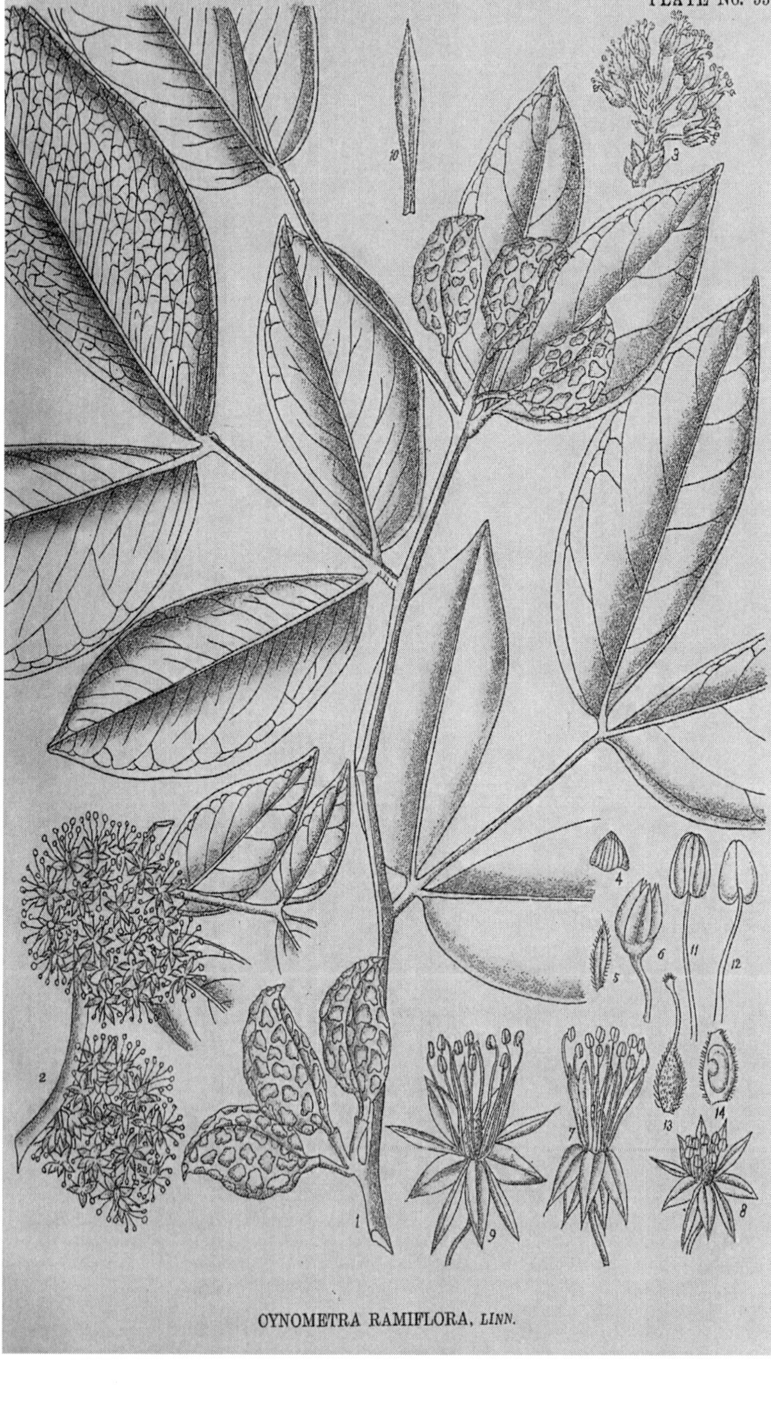

OYNOMETRA RAMIFLORA, LINN.

PLATE No. 359.

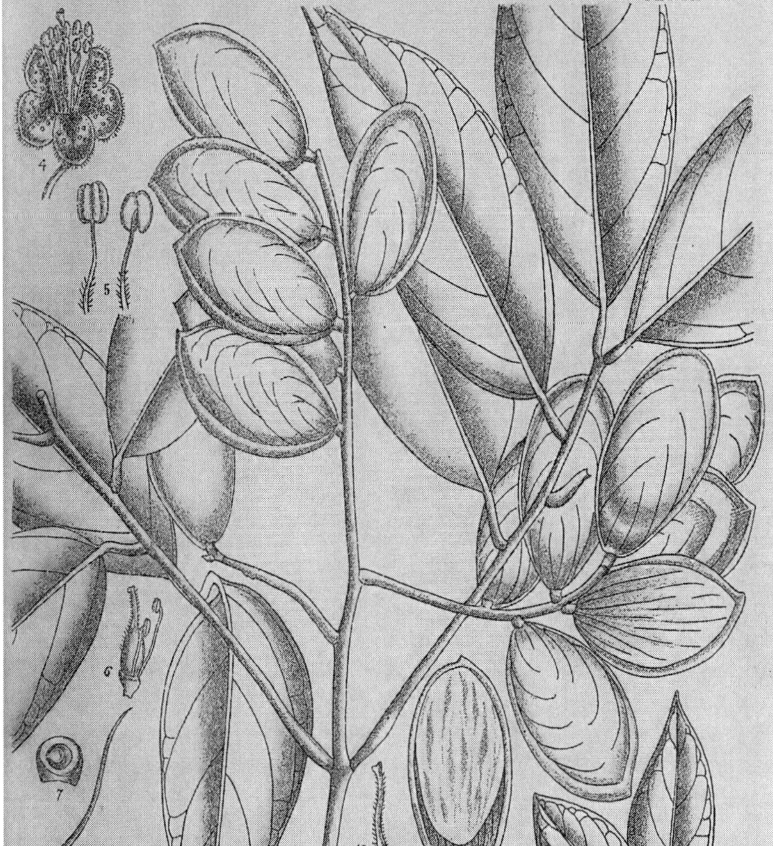

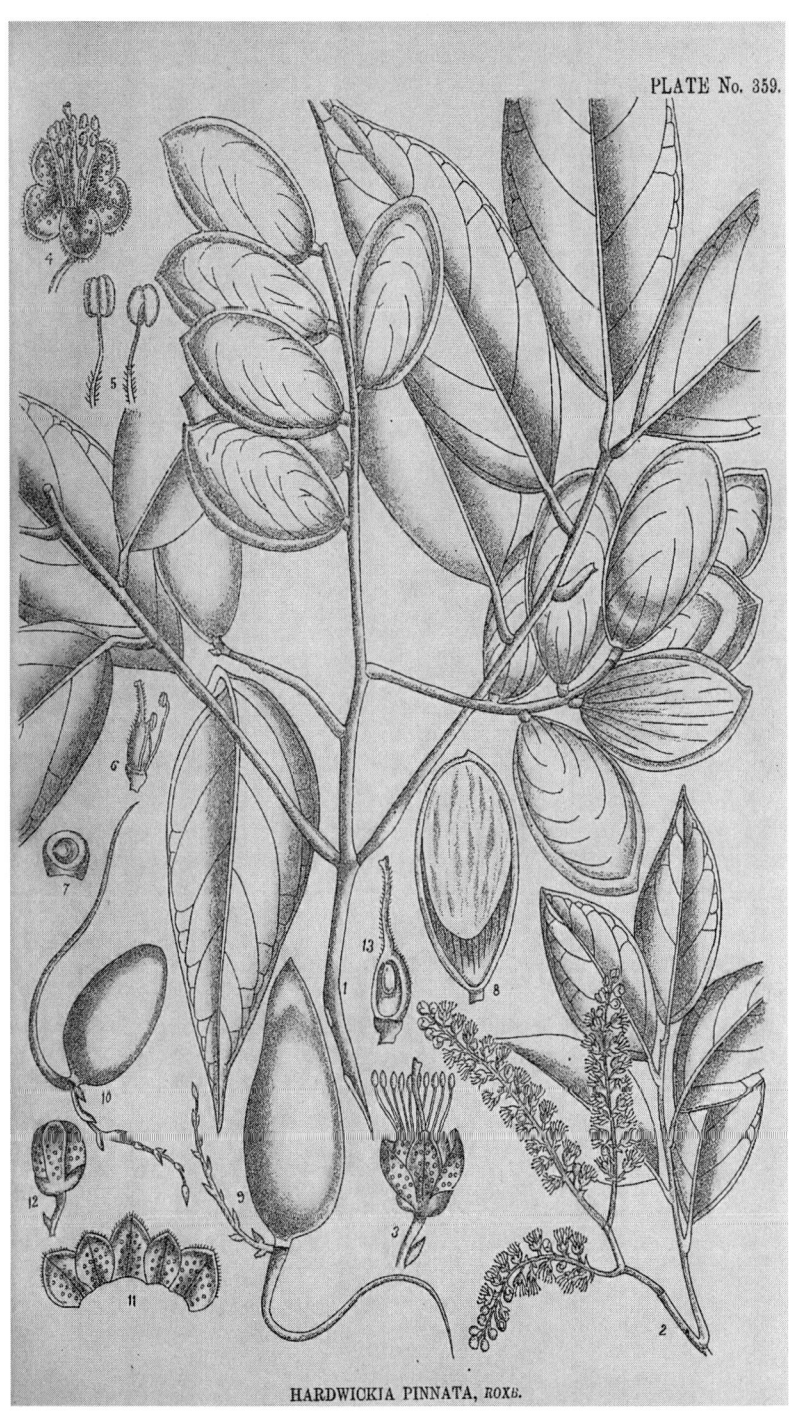

HARDWICKIA PINNATA, *ROXB.*

PLATE No. 360.

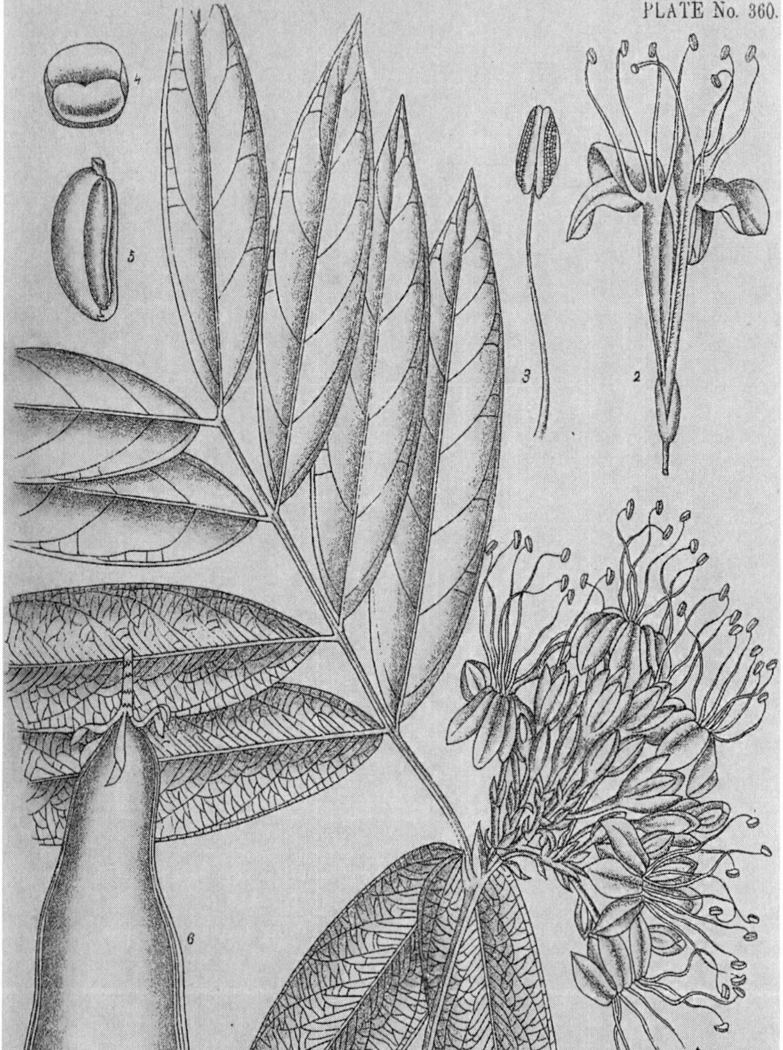

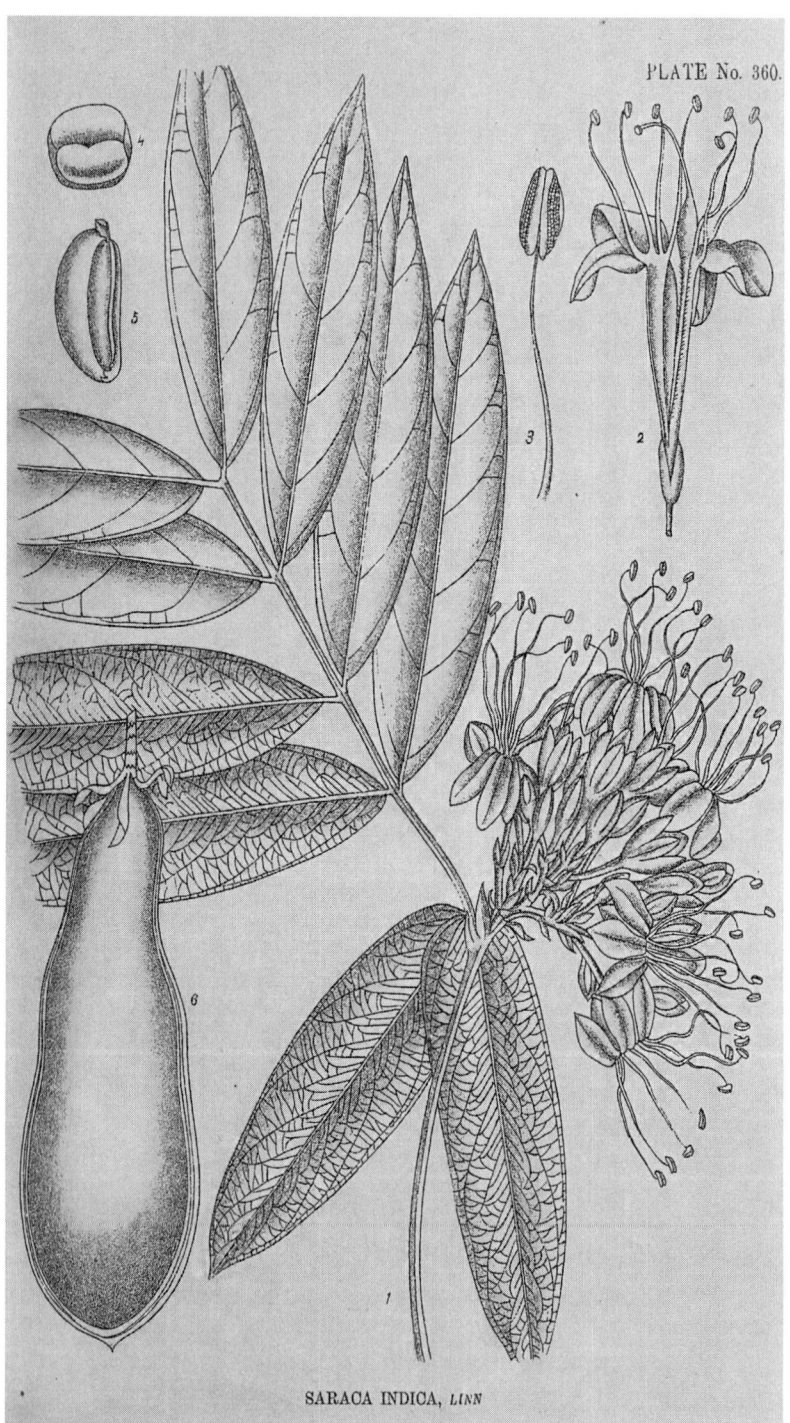

SARACA INDICA, *LINN*

PLATE No. 361.

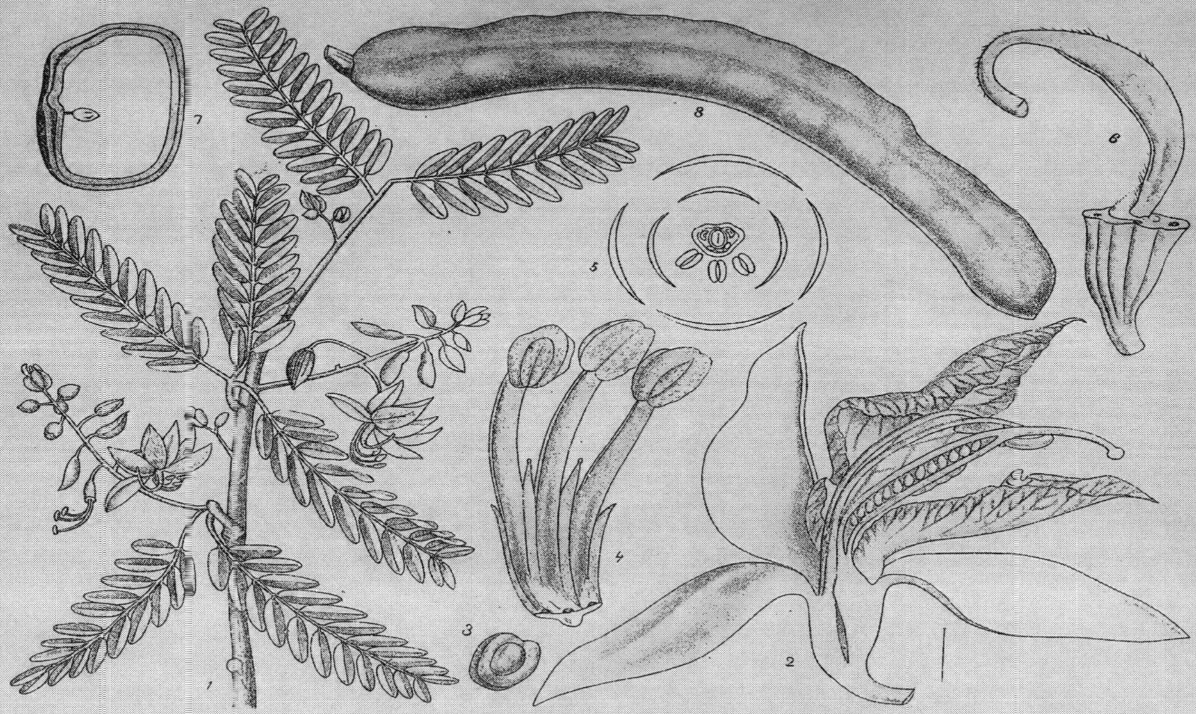

TAMARINDUS INDICA, *Linn.*

PLATE No. 362.

BAUHINIA TOMENTOSA, *LINN*

PLATE No. 363.

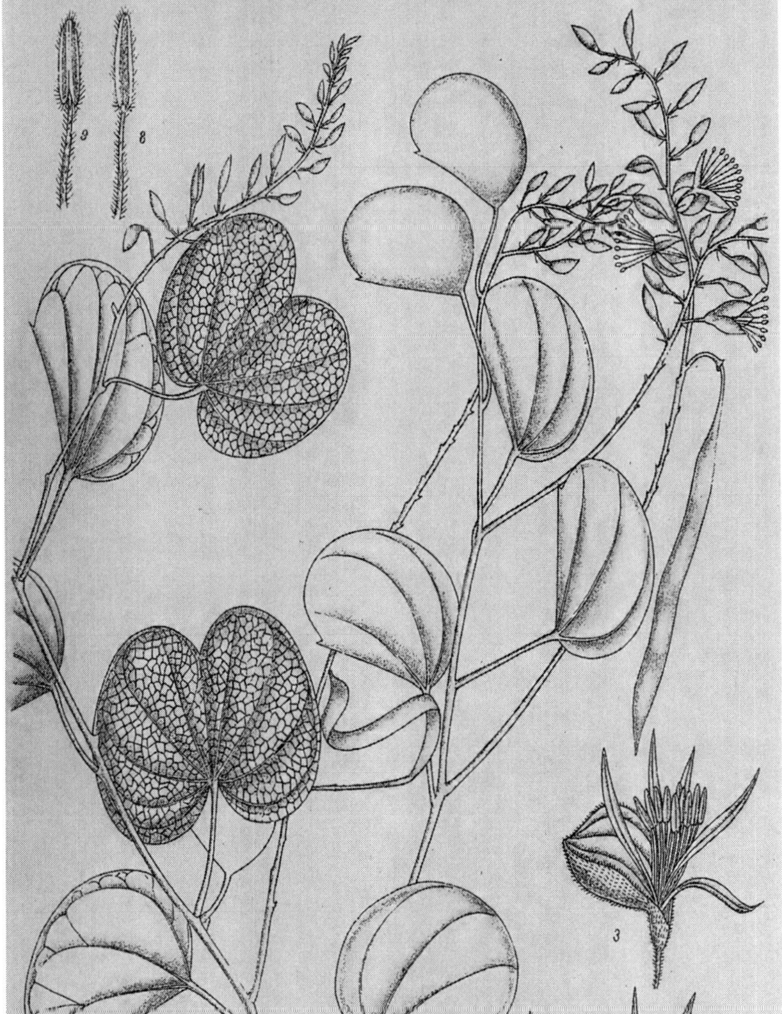

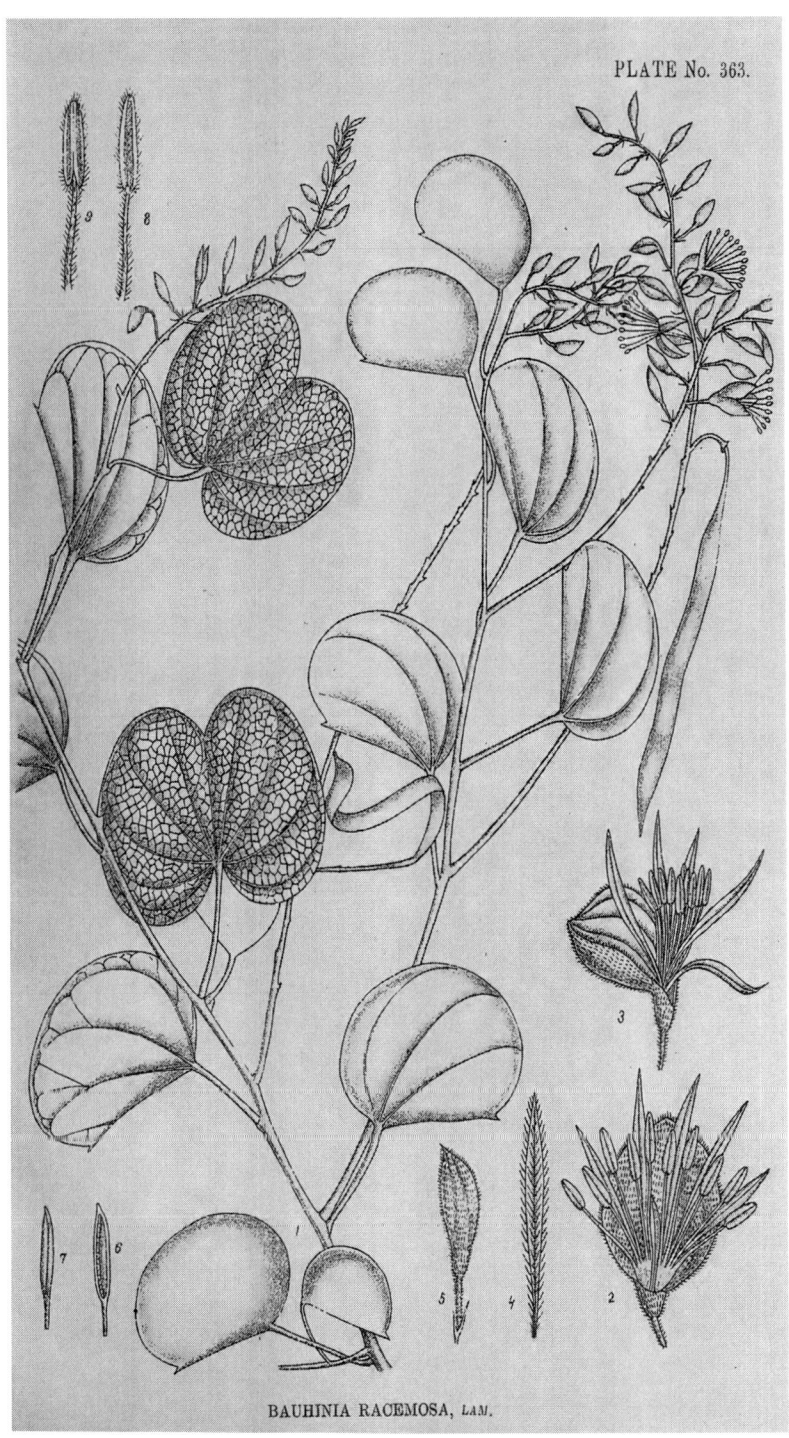

BAUHINIA RACEMOSA, LAM.

PLATE No. 364.

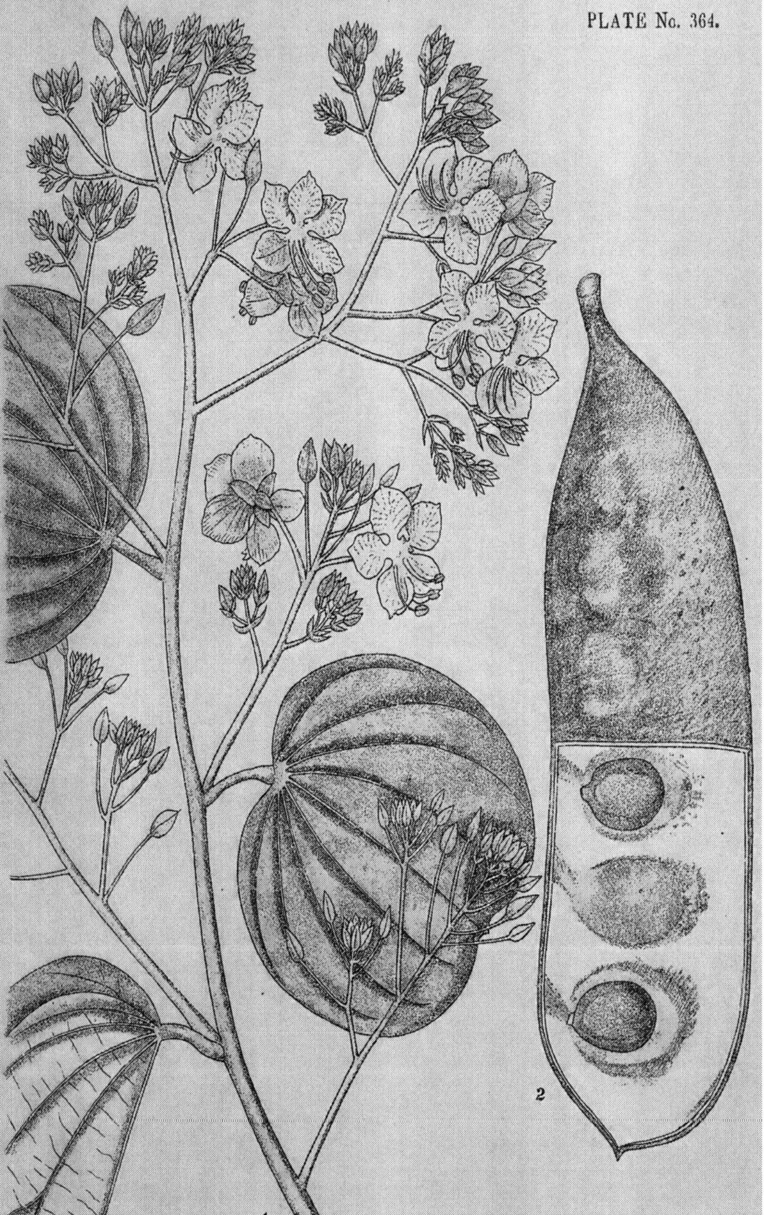

BAUHINIA RETUSA, *HAM.*

PLATE No 365

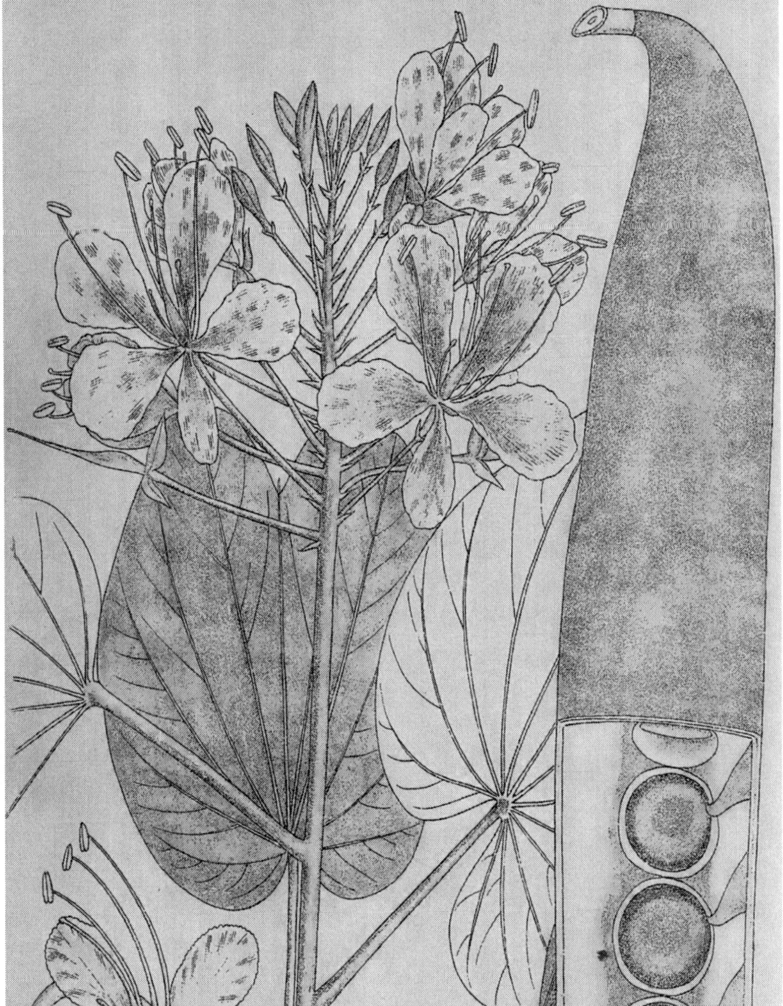

BAUHINIA VAHHLII, W. & A.

PLATE No. 366.

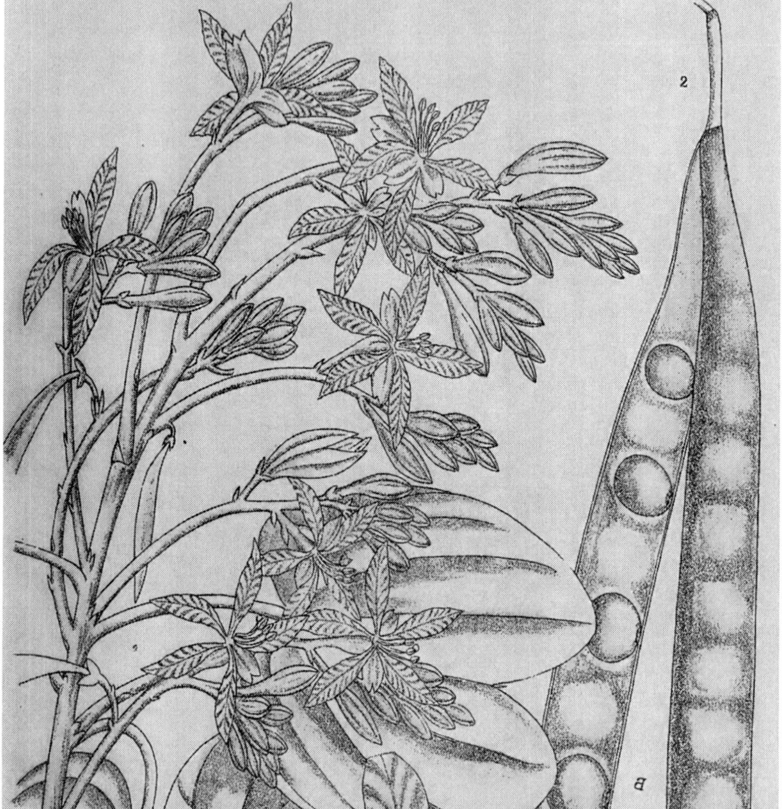

BAUHINIA PURPUREA, *LINN.*

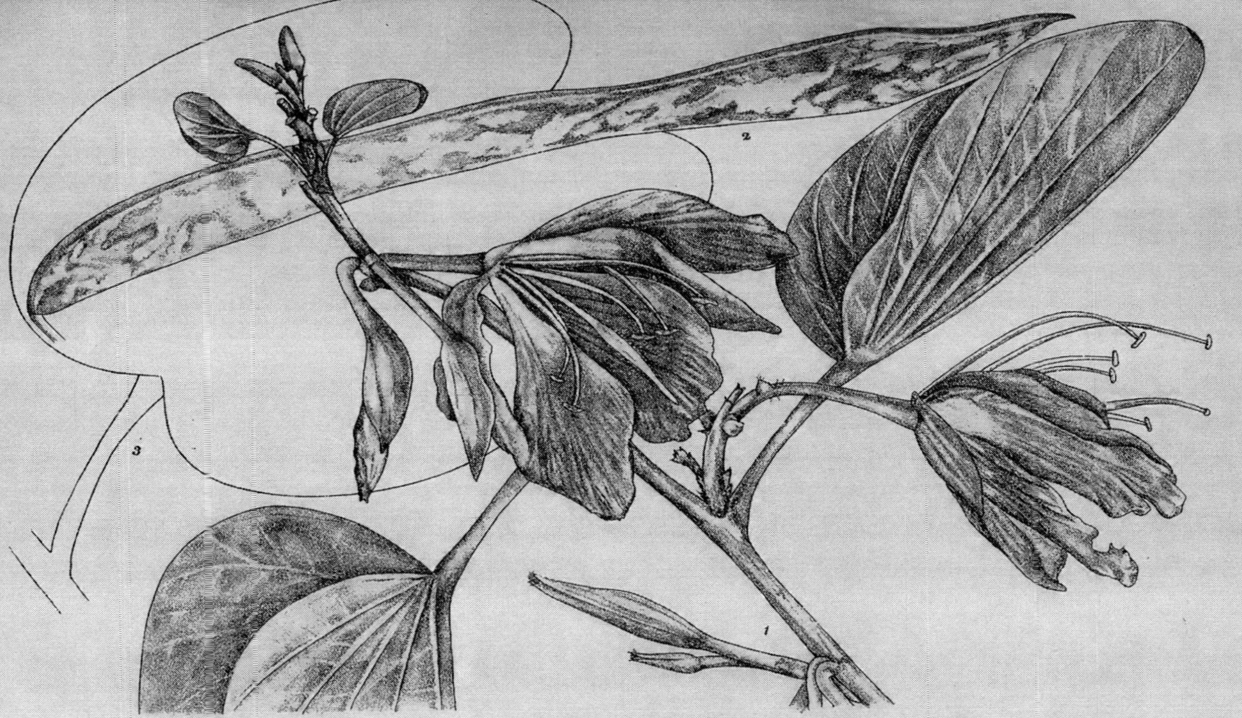

BAUHINIA VARIEGATA, *LINN.*

PLATE No. 368.

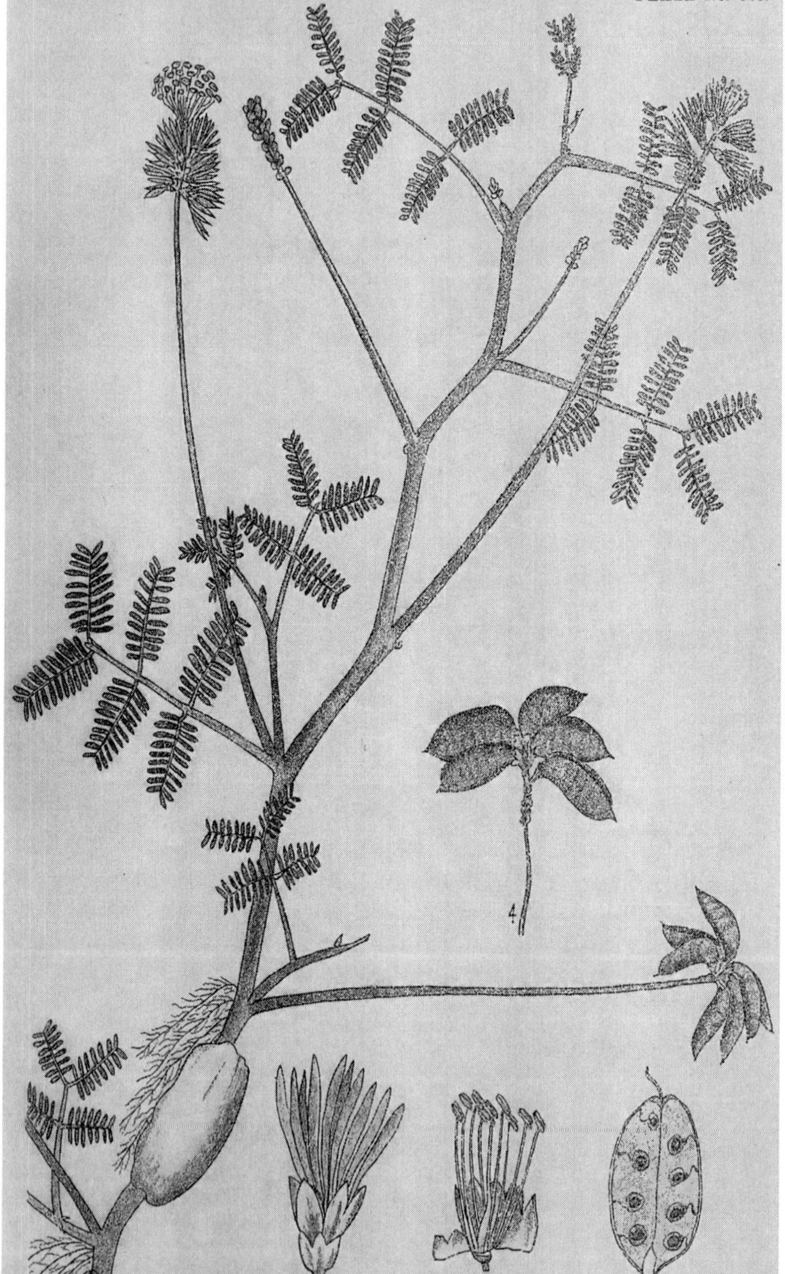

NEPTUNIA OLERACEA, *Lour.*

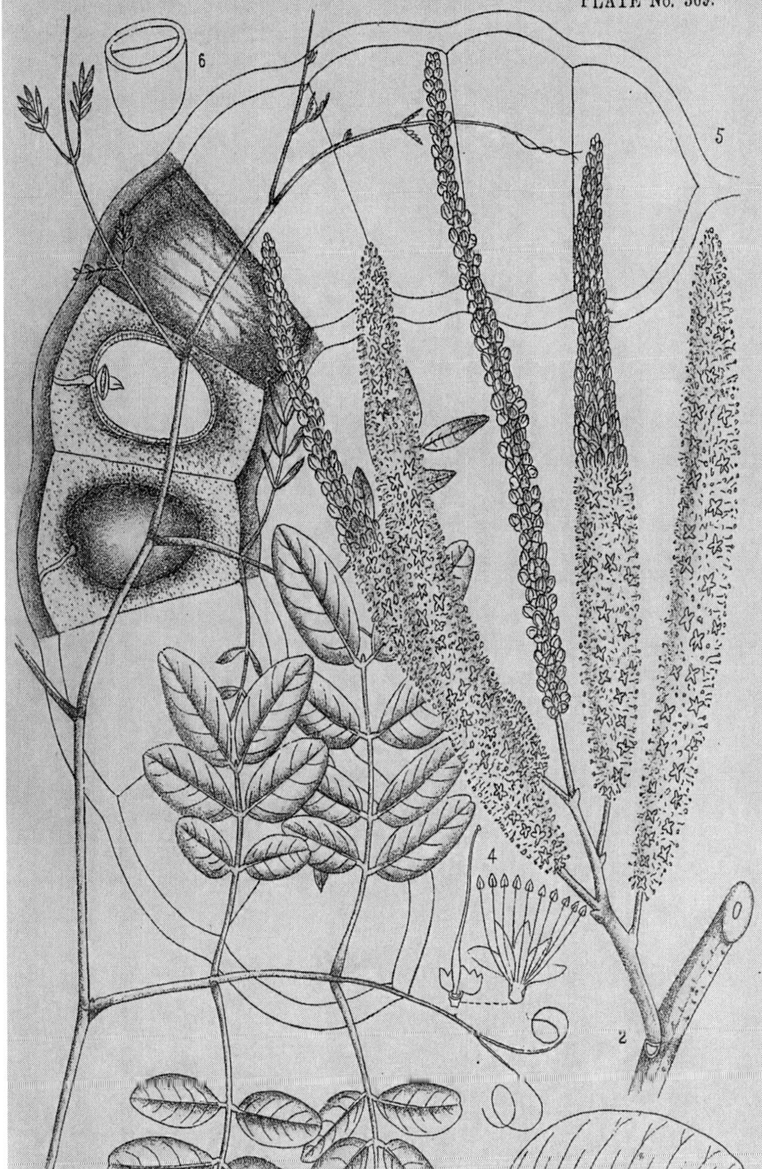

ENTADA SCANDENS, *BENTH.*

PLATE No 370.

ADENANTHERA PAVONINA, *LINN.*

PLATE No 371.

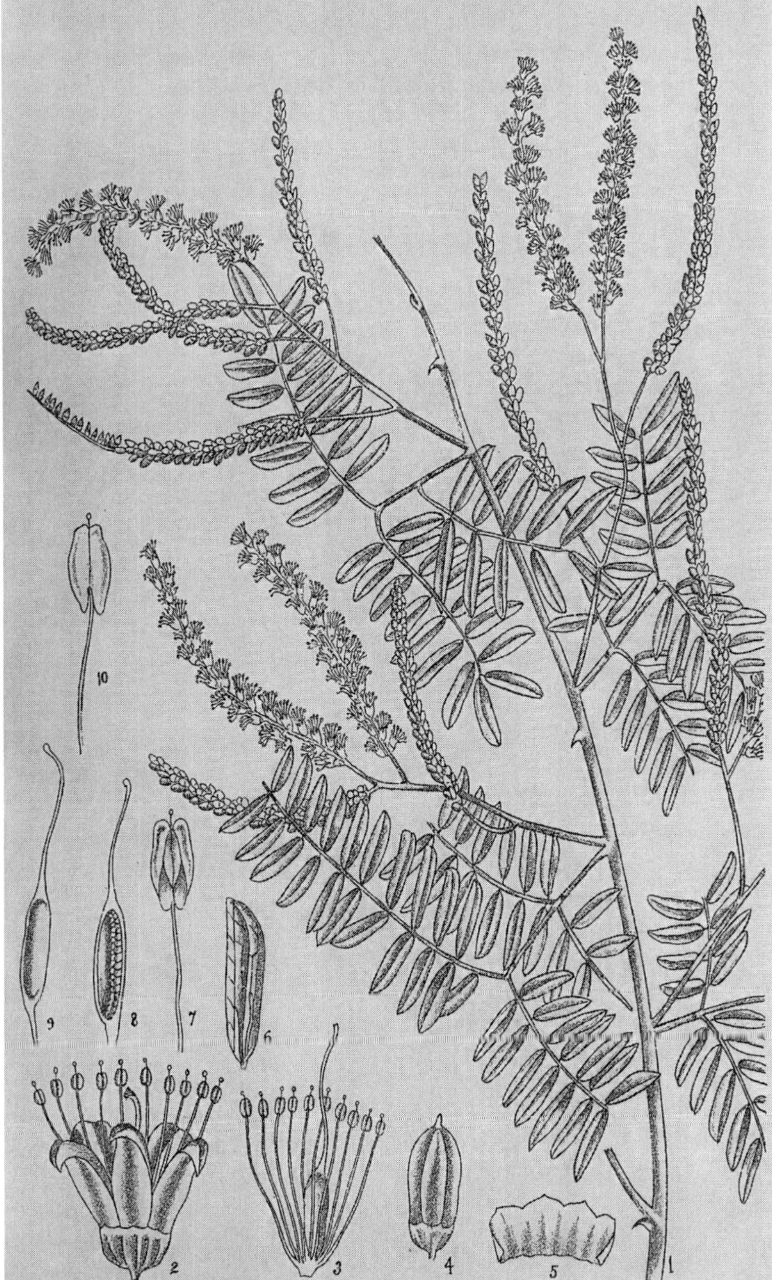

PROSOPIS SPICIGERA, *LINN.*

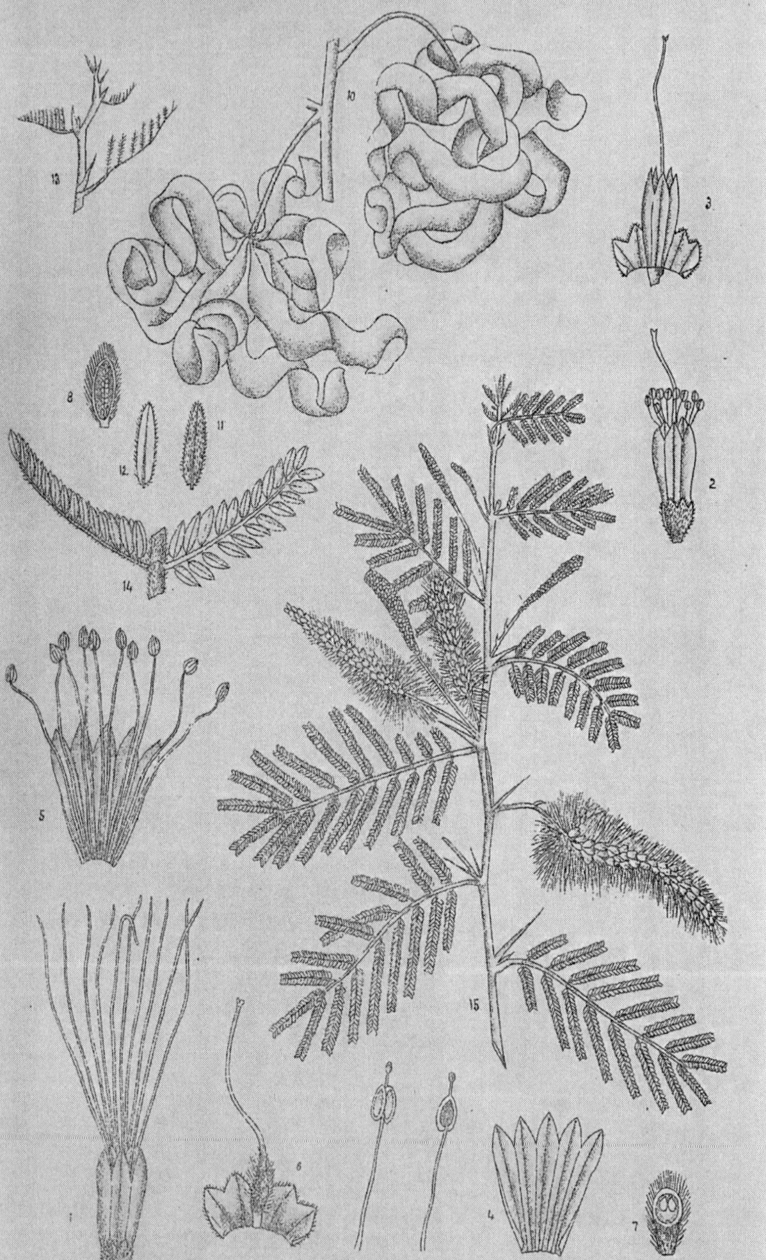

DICHROSTACHYS CINEREA, W. & A.

PLATE No. 373.

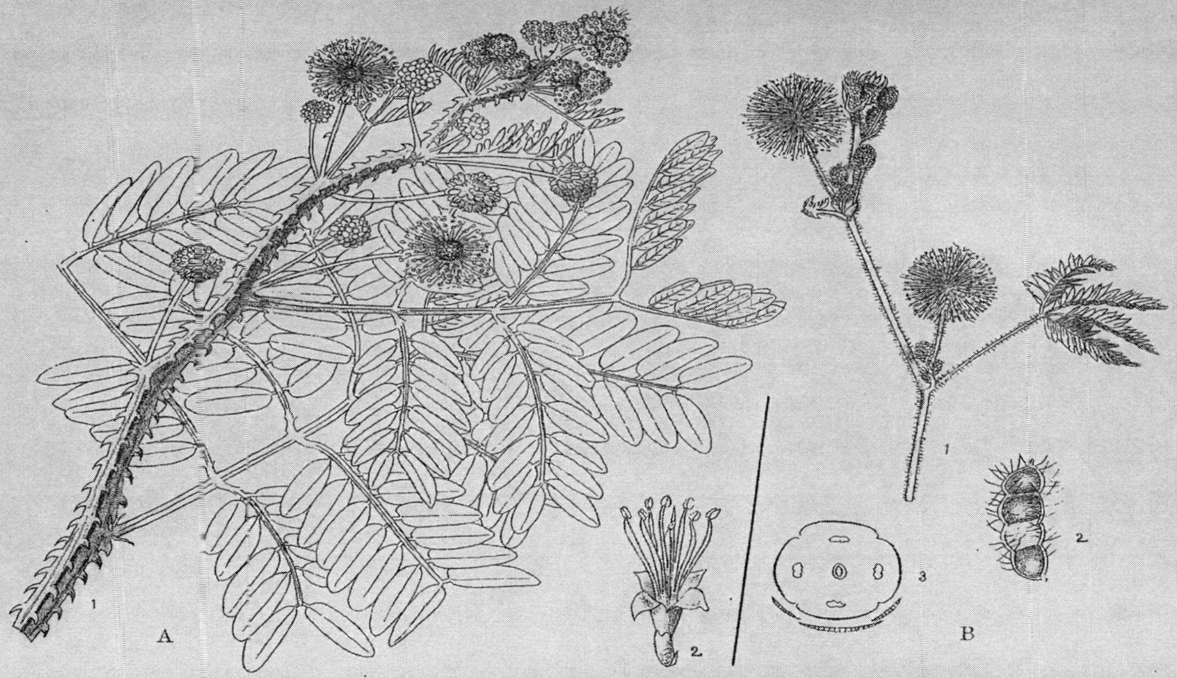

B—MIMOSA PUDICA *LINN.* A—M. RUBICAULIS, *LAM.*

PLATE No. 374.

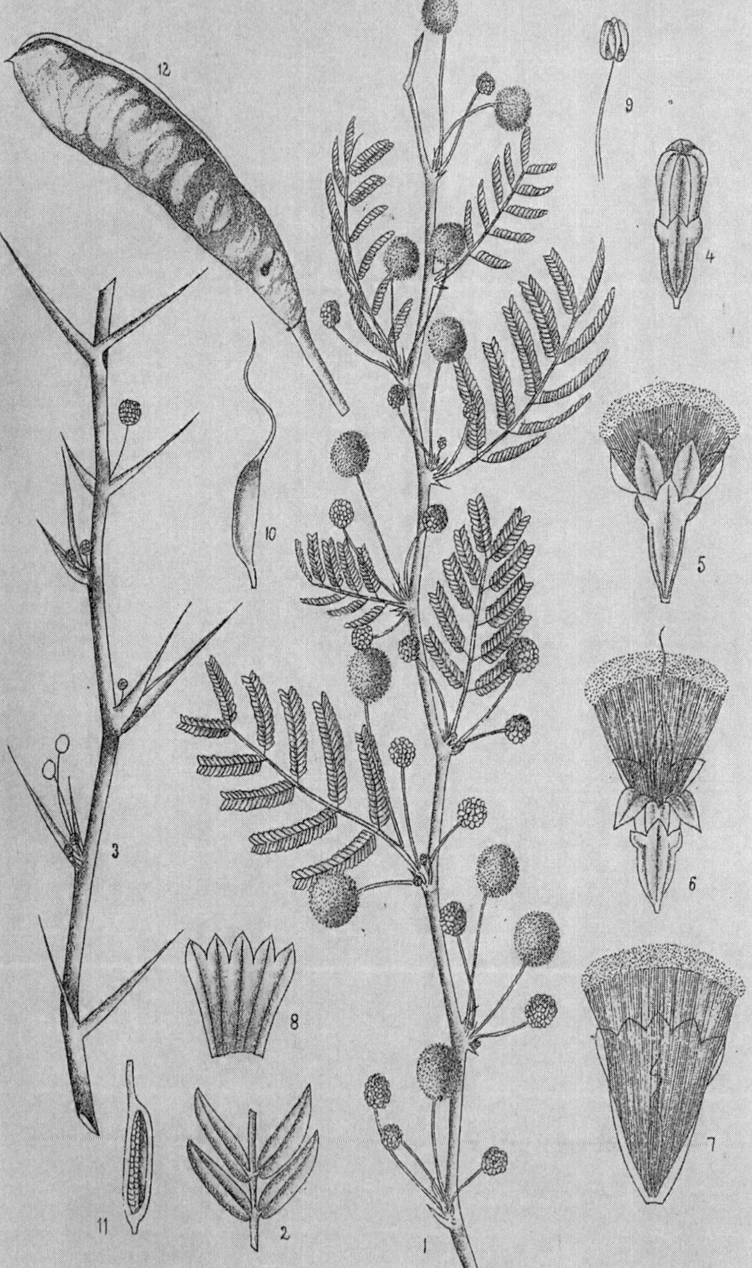

ACACIA FARNESIANA, *WILLD.*

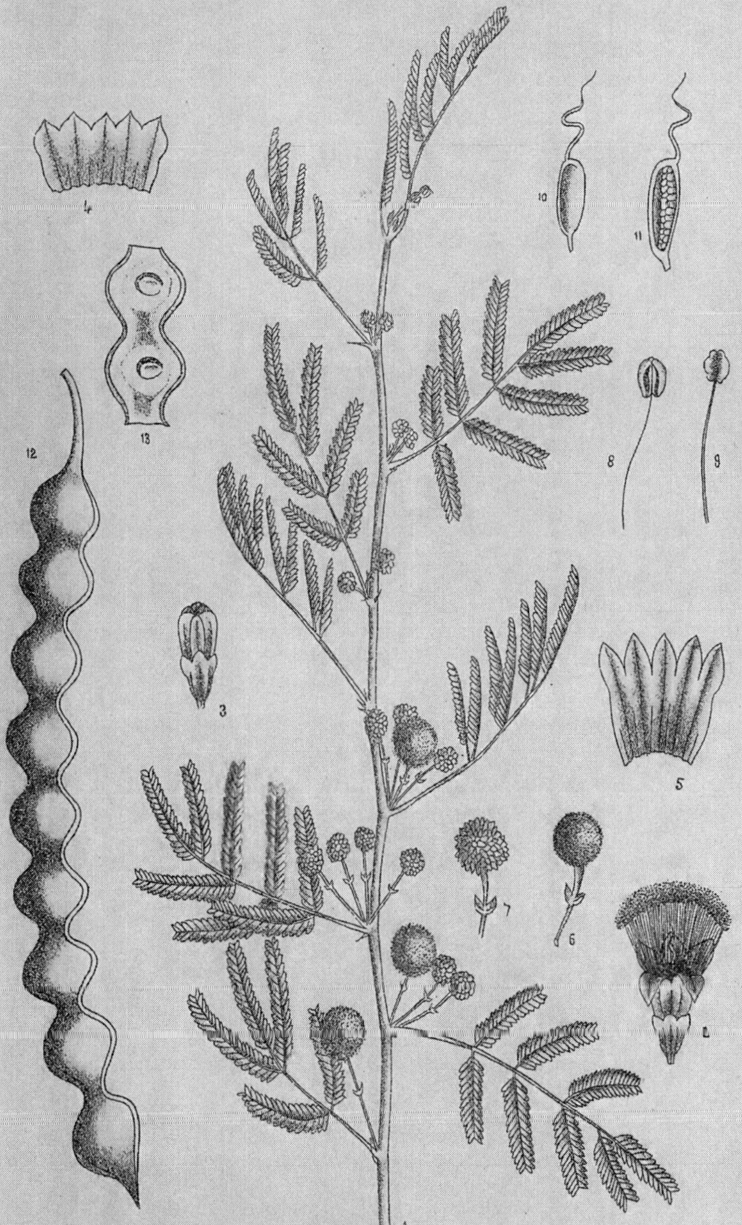

ACACIA ARABICA, *WILLD.*

PLATE No. 376.

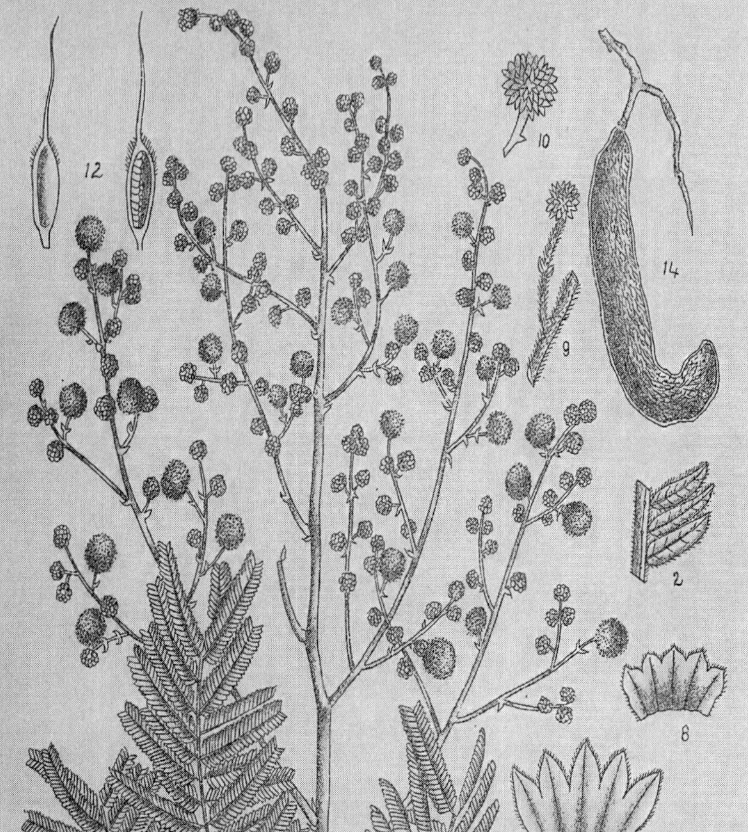

ACACIA LEUCOPHLÆA, *WILLD.*

PLATE No. 377.

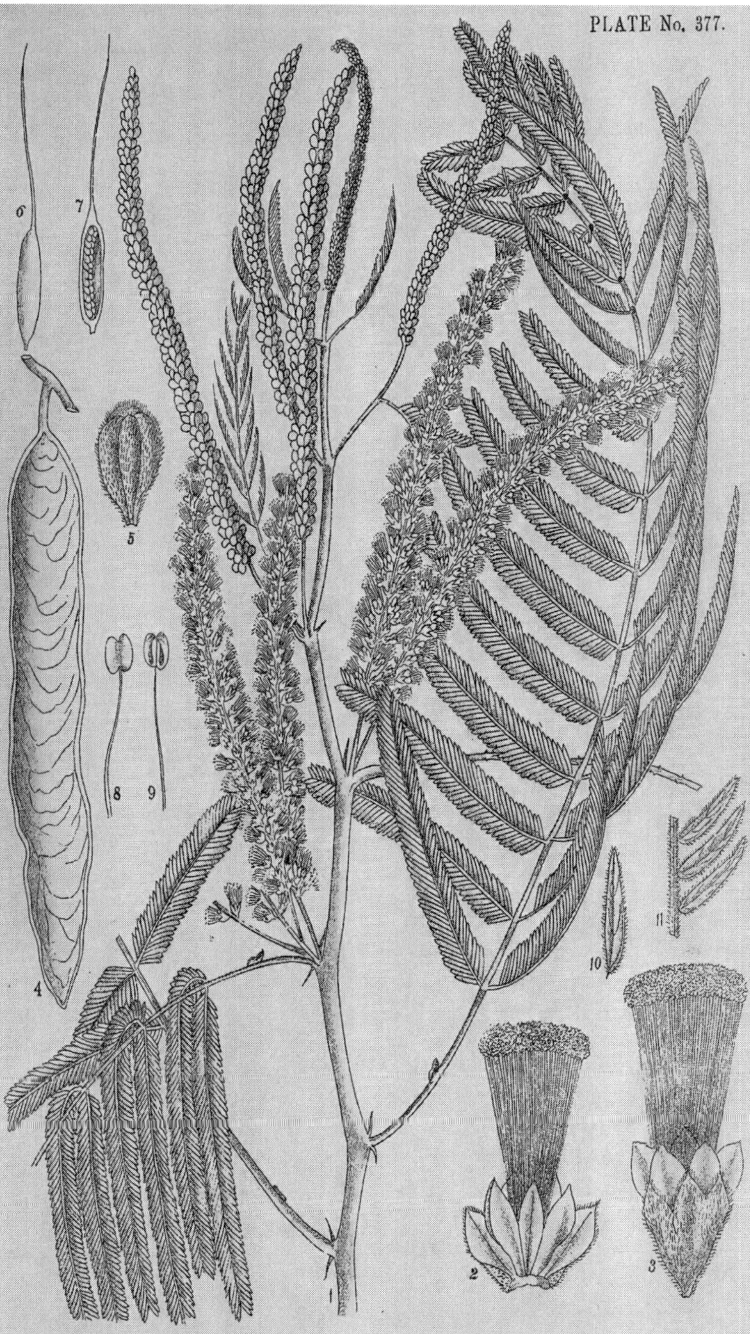

ACACIA CATECHU, *WILLD.*

PLATE No. 378.

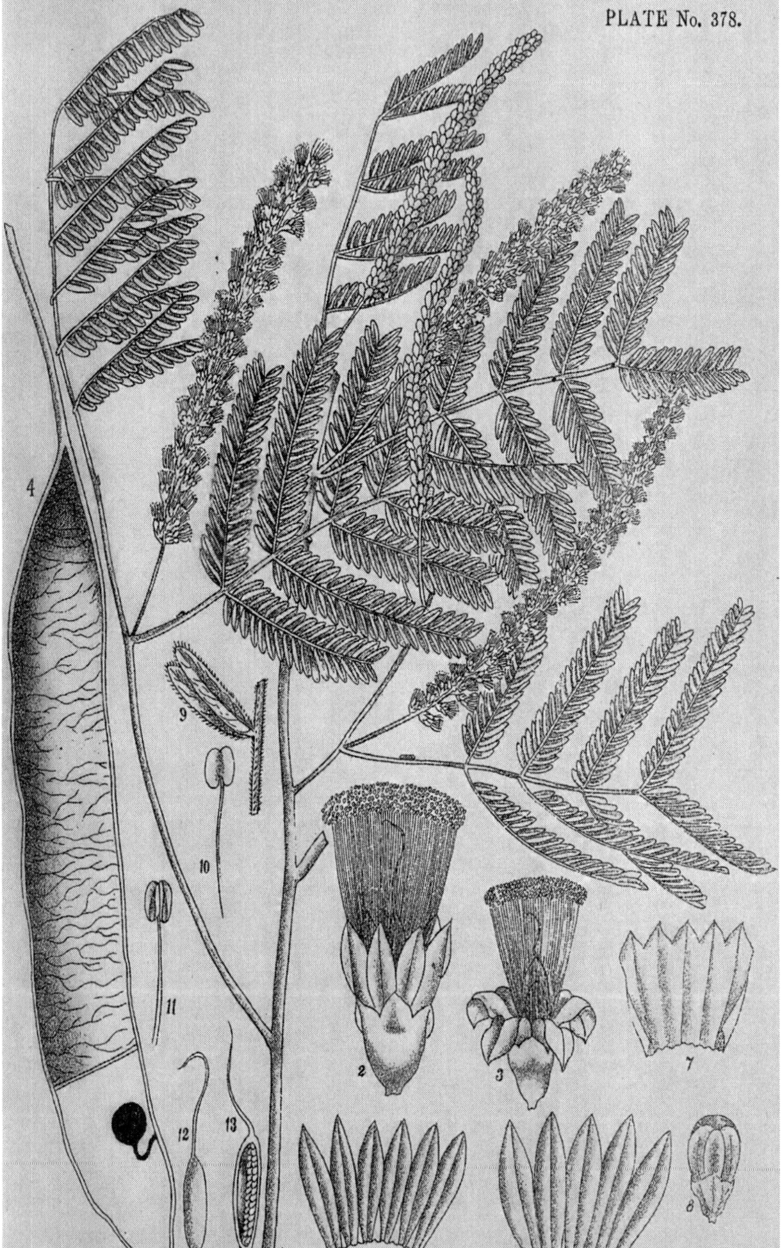

ACACIA FERRUGINEA, DC.

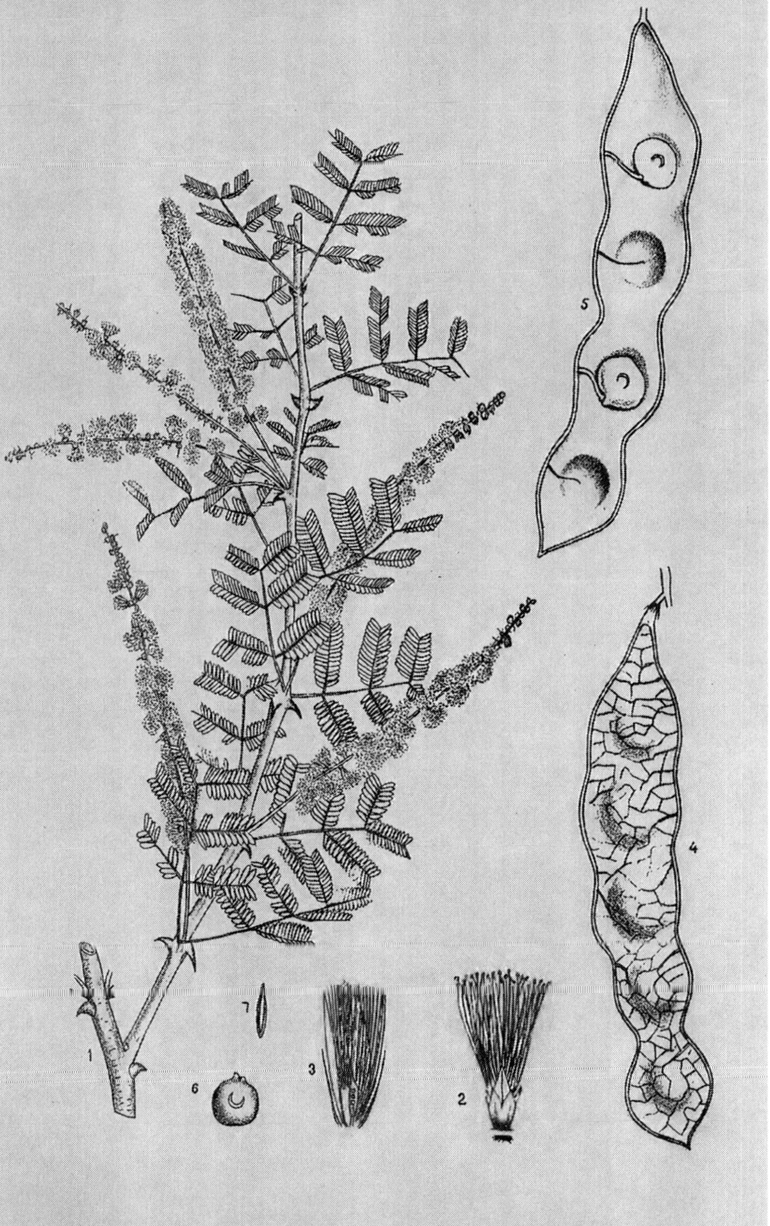

ACACIA SENEGAL, *WILLD.*

PLATE No. 380.

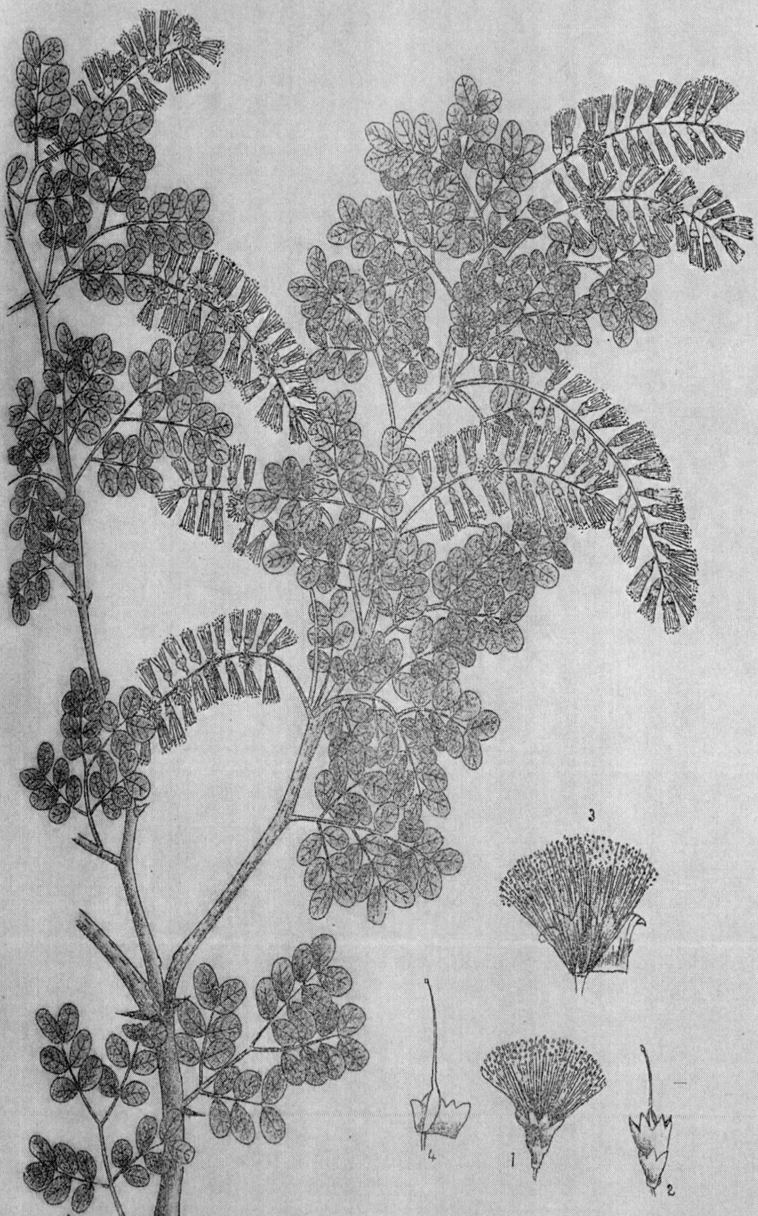

ACACIA MODESTA, *WALL.*

PLATE No. 381.

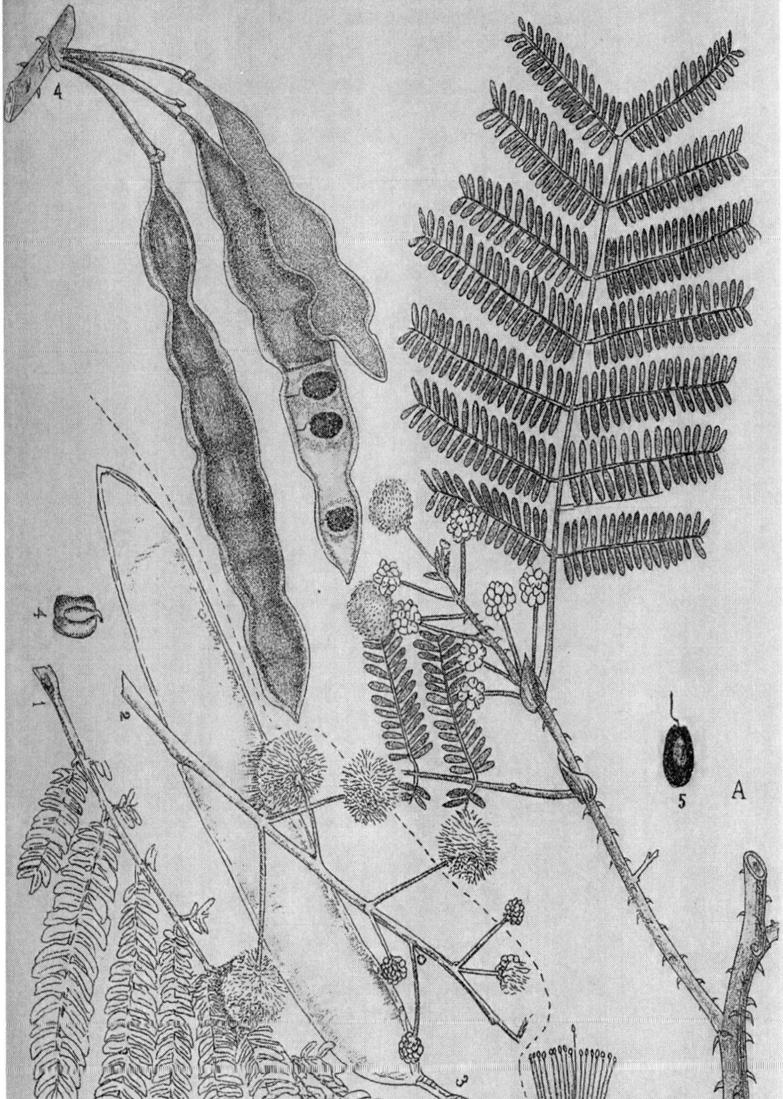

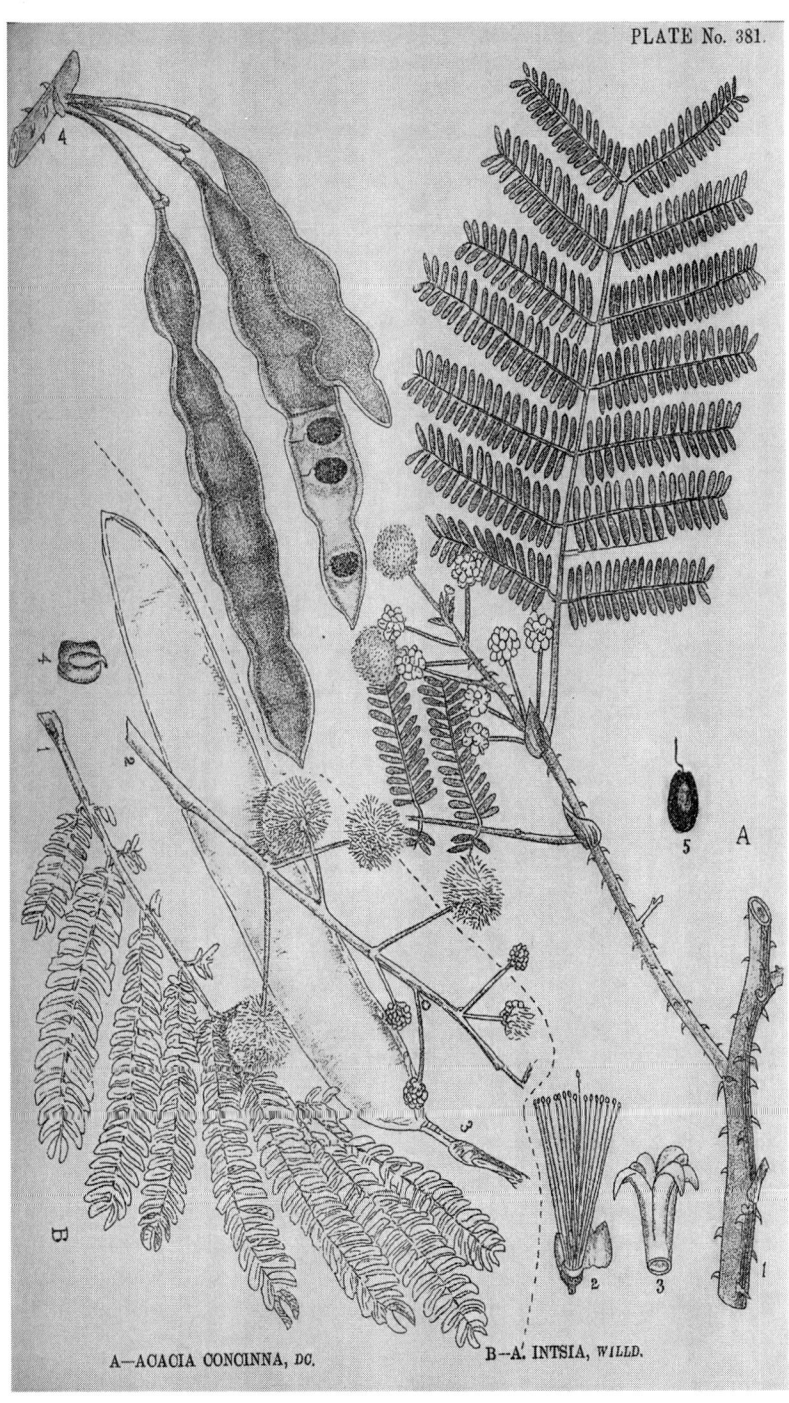

A—ACACIA CONCINNA, *DC.* B—A. INTSIA, *WILLD.*

PLATE No. 382.

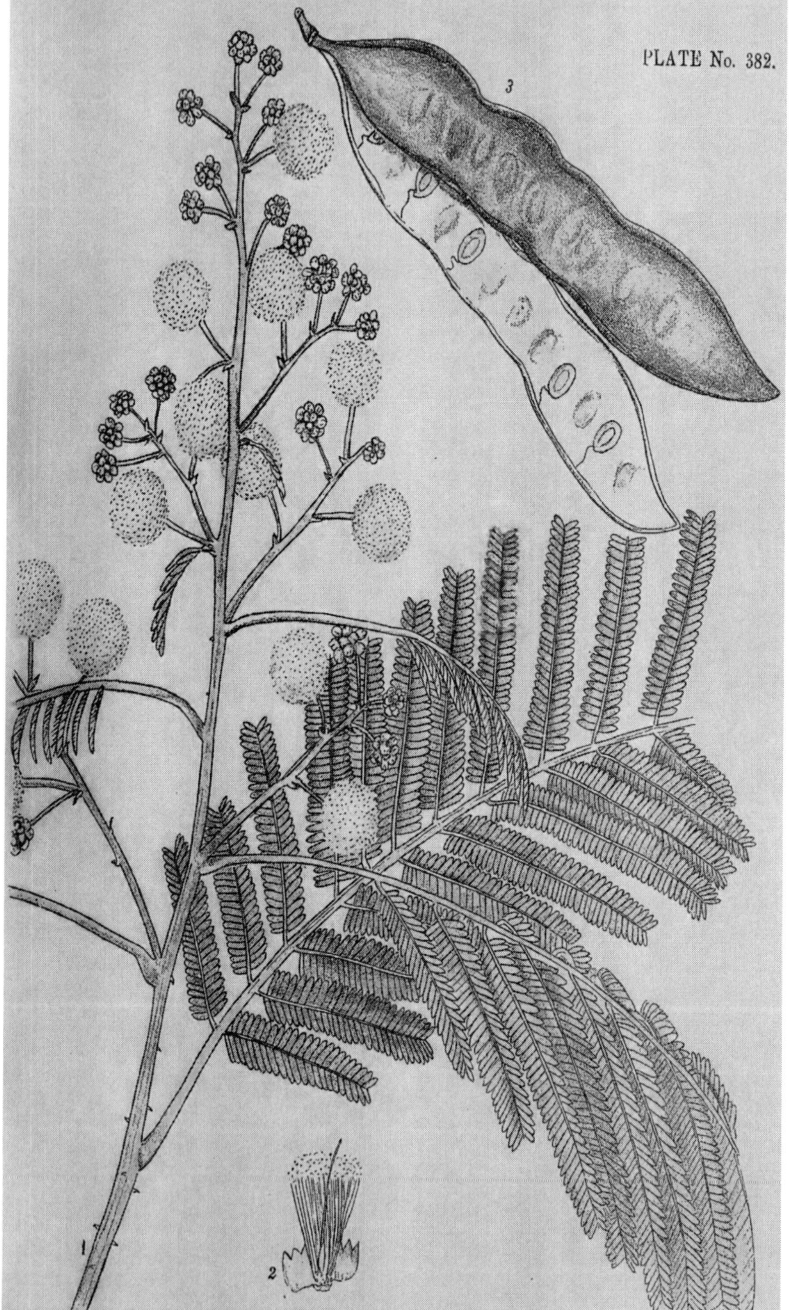

ACACIA PENNATA, *WILLD.*

ALBIZZIA LEBBEK, BENTH.

ALBIZZIA ODORATISSIMA, *BENTH.*

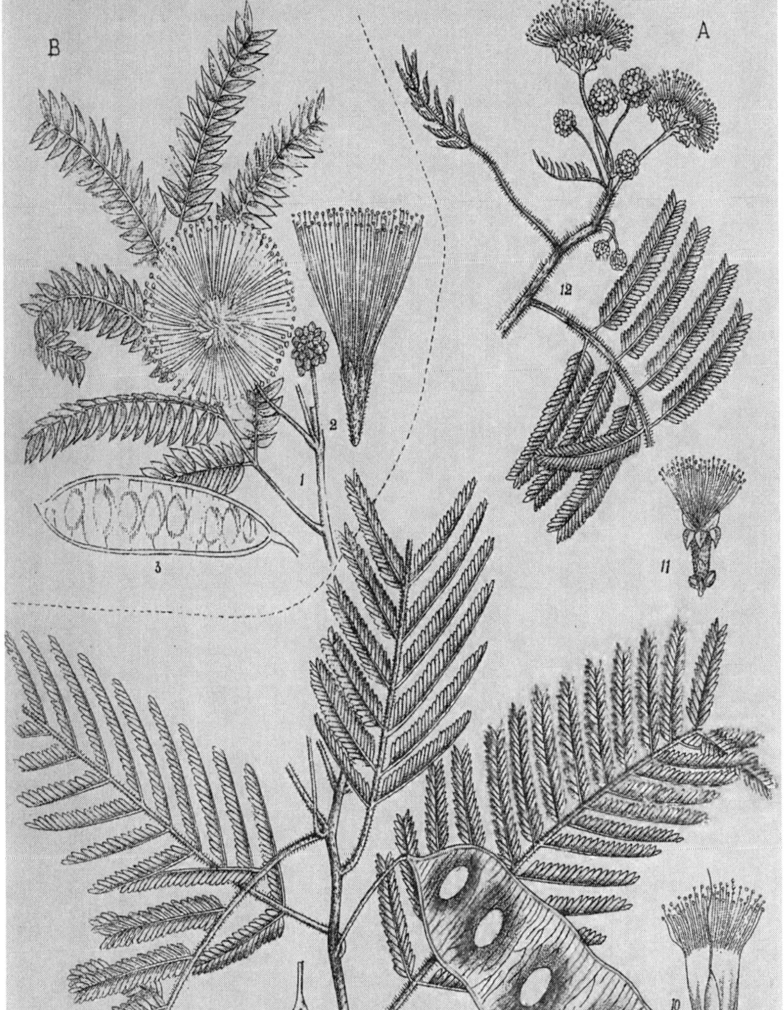

A--ALBIZZIA AMARA, *BOIV.*   B—A. JULIBRISSIN, *DURAZZ.*

PLATE No. 386.

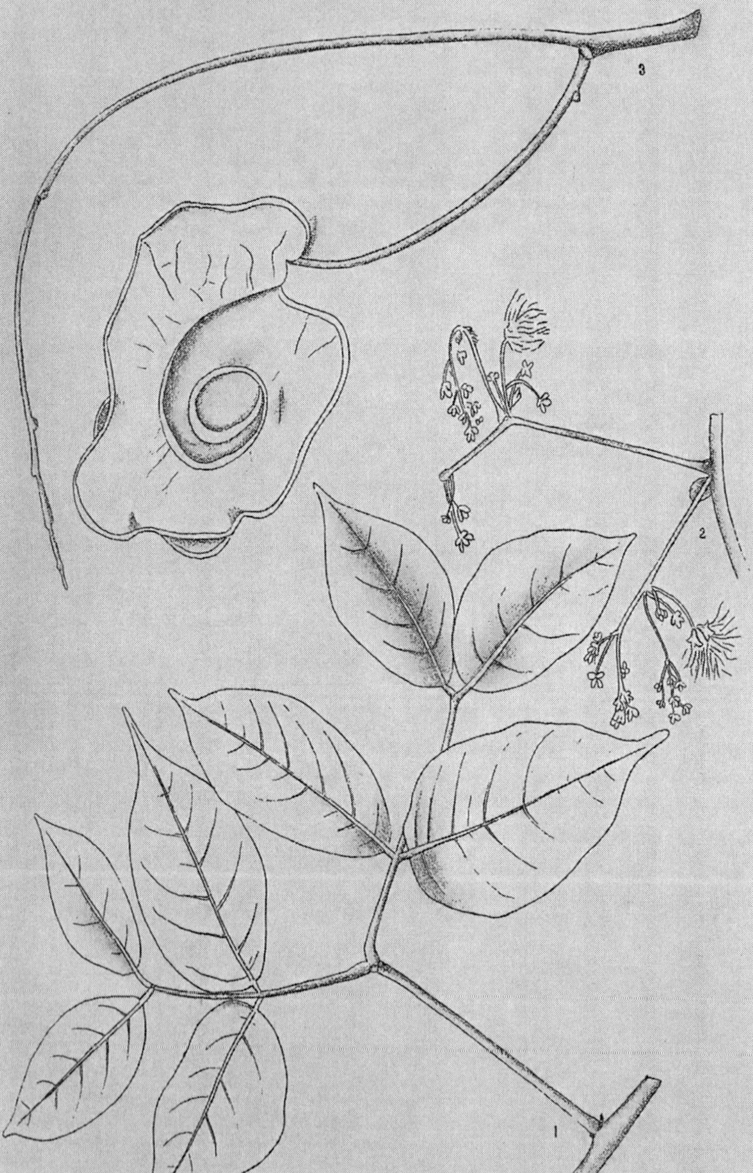

PITHECOLOBIUM BIGEMINUM, *BENTH.*

PLATE No. 387.

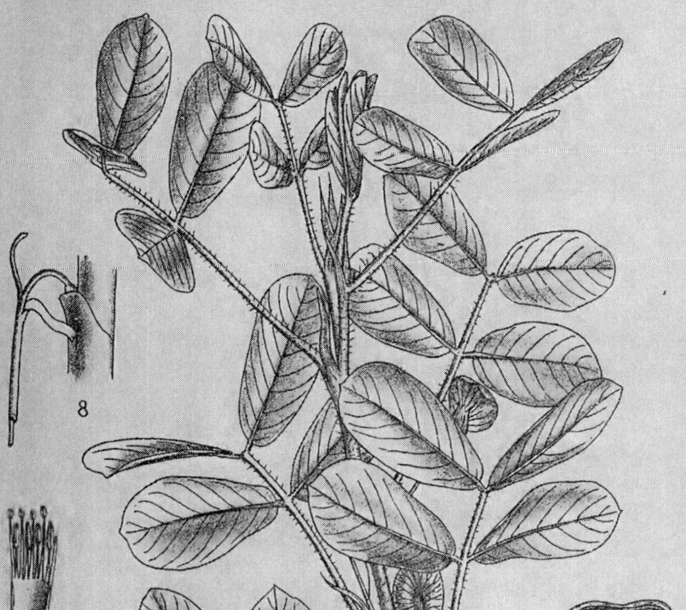

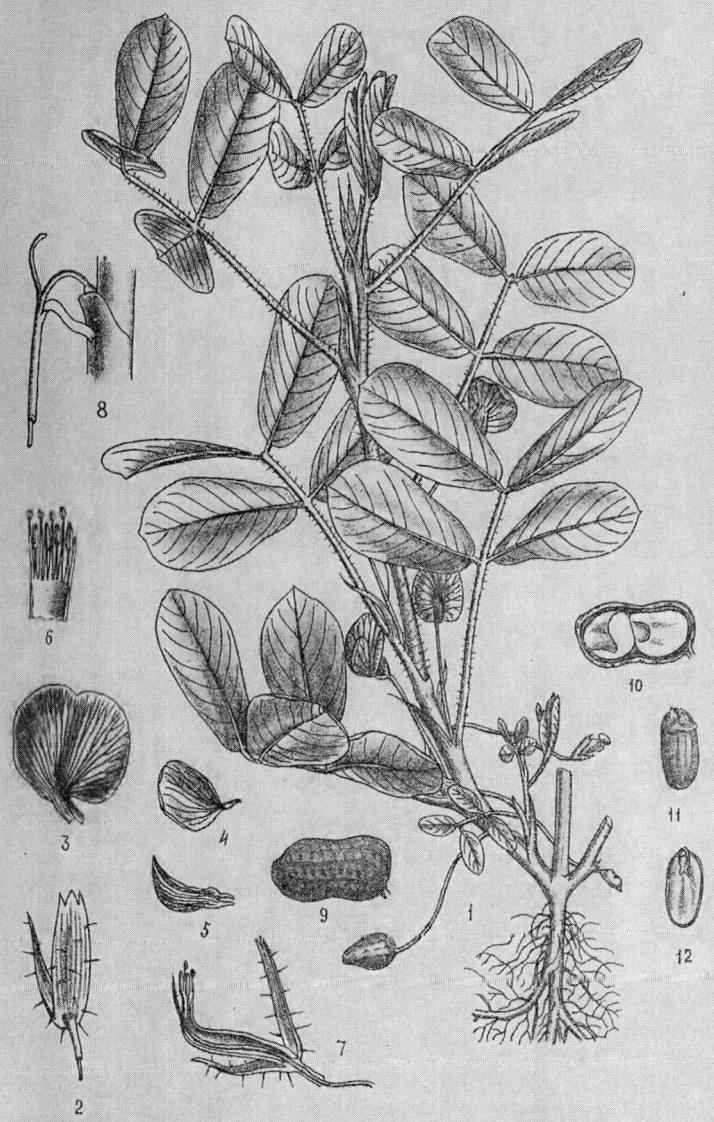

ARACHIS HYPOGÆA, *LINN.*

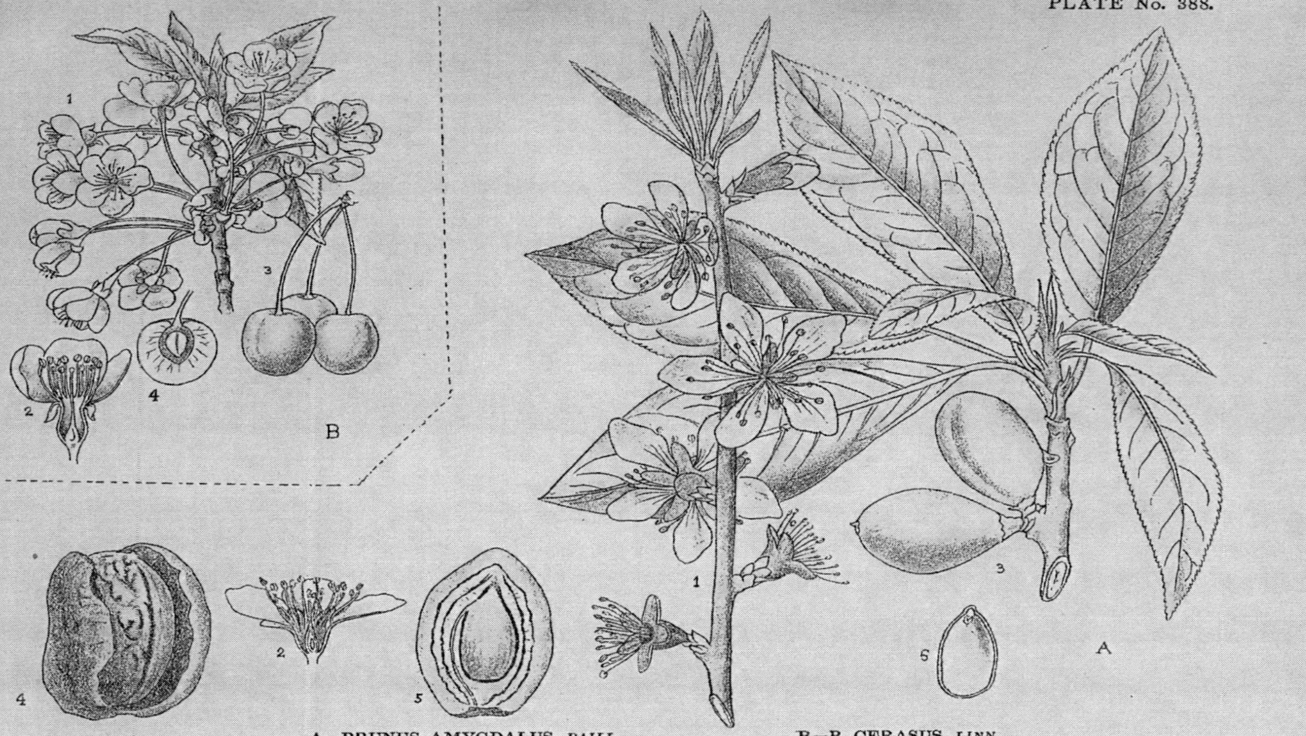

A—PRUNUS AMYGDALUS, *BAILL.* B—P. CERASUS, *LINN.*

A—PRUNUS PUDDUM, *ROXB.* B—PRUNUS ARMENIACA, *LINN.*

PLATE No. 390.

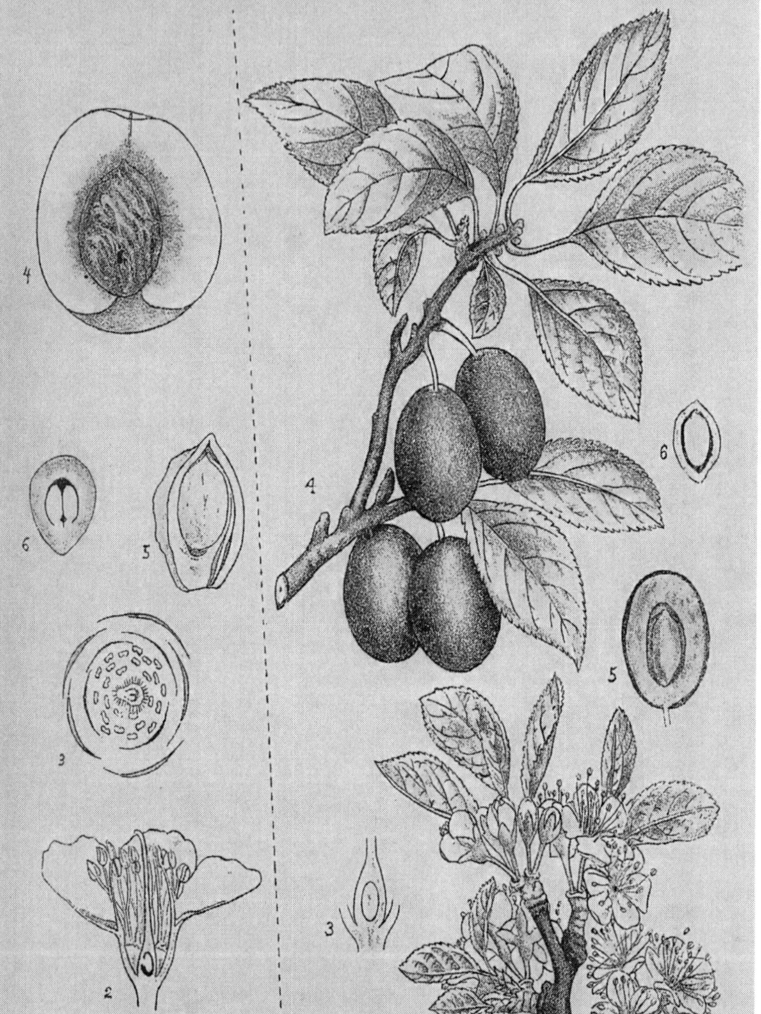

A—PRUNUS COMMUNIS, *var.* DOMESTICA. B—P. PERSICA, *Benth & Hook f.*

PLATE No. 391.

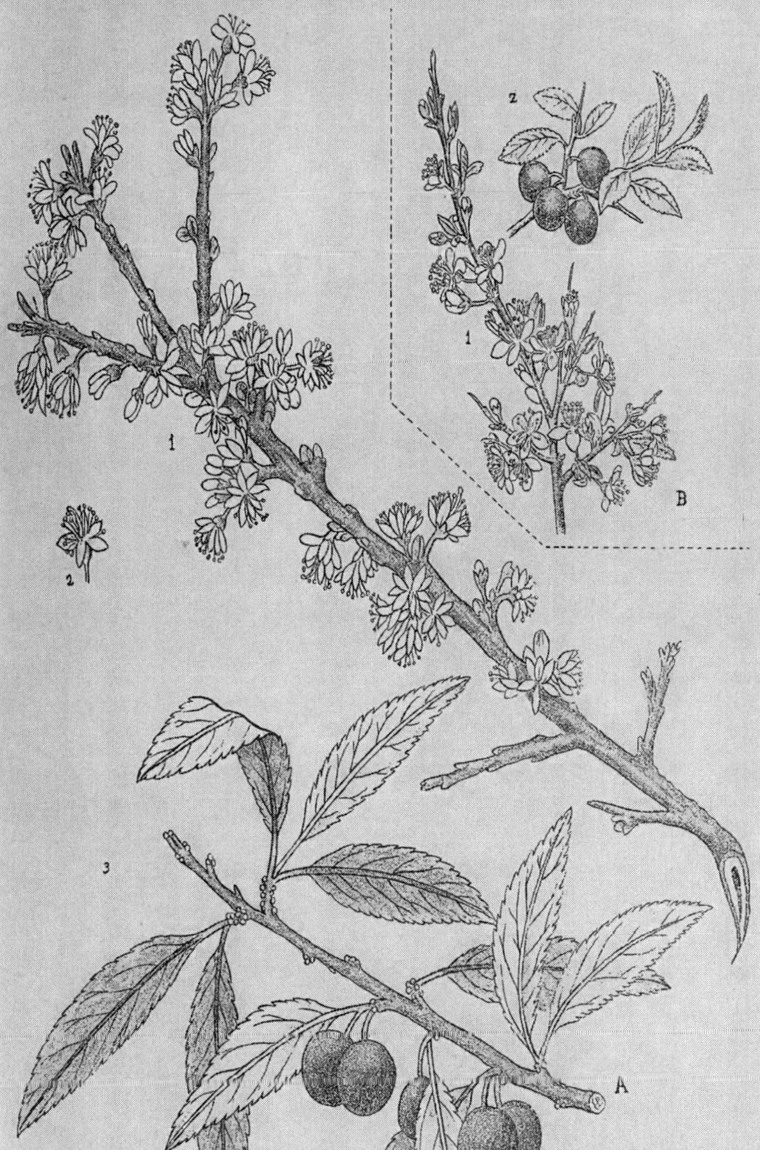

A—PRUNUS COMMUNIS, *HUDS.*   B—P. COMMUNIS, *VAR.* INSITITIA, *LINN.*

PLATE No. 392

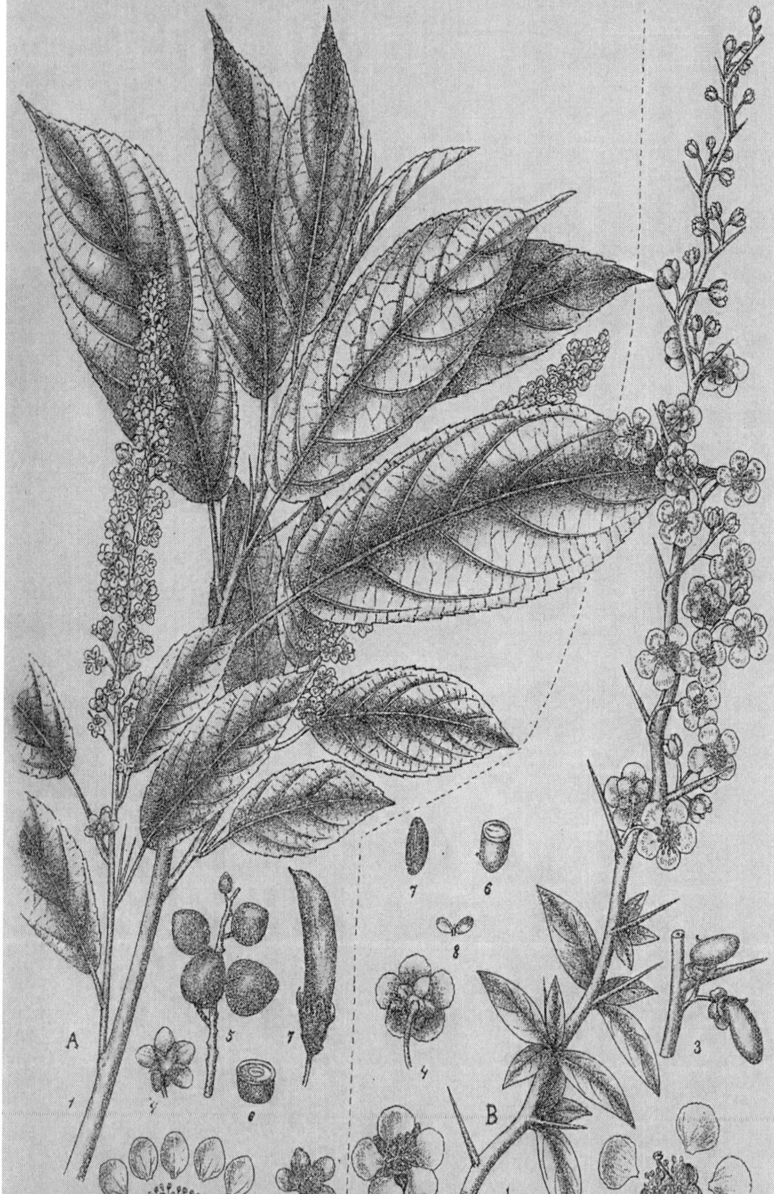

A—PRINSEPIA UTILIS, ROYLE. B—PRUNUS PADUS, LINN.

PLATE No. 393.

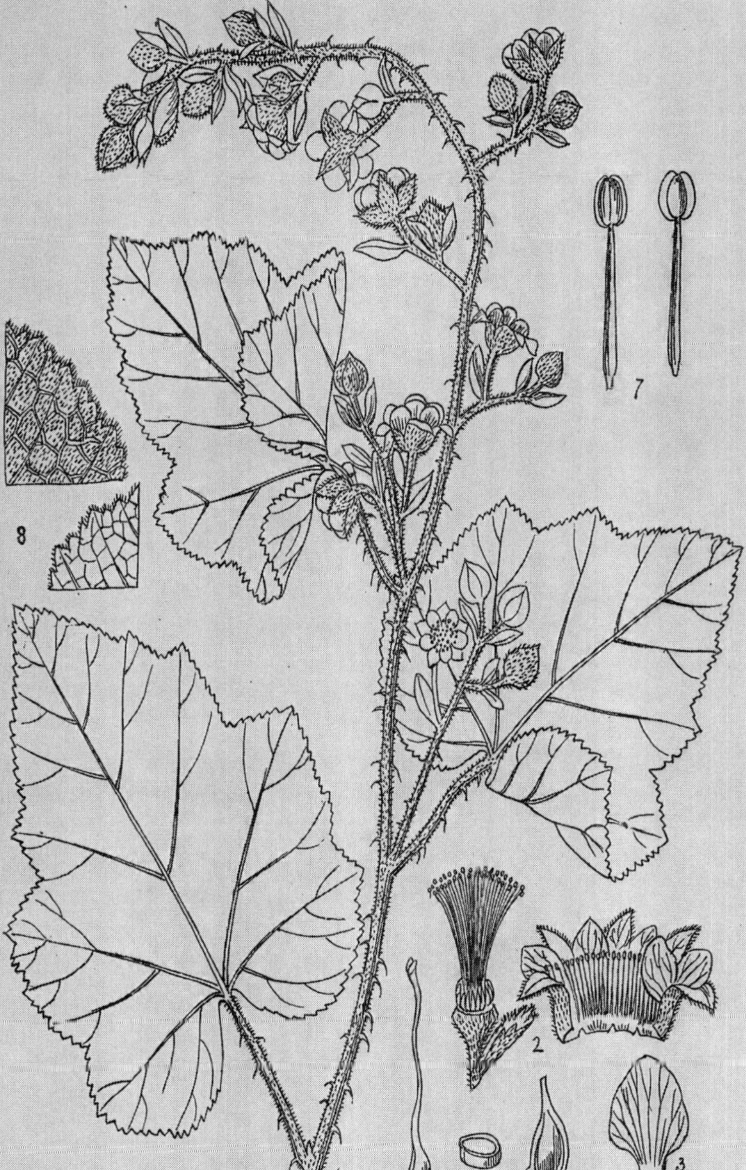

RUBUS MOLUCCANUS, *LINN.*

PLATE No. 394.

A—GEUM ELATUM, *WALL.*

B—G. URBANUM, *LINN.*

PLATE No. 395.

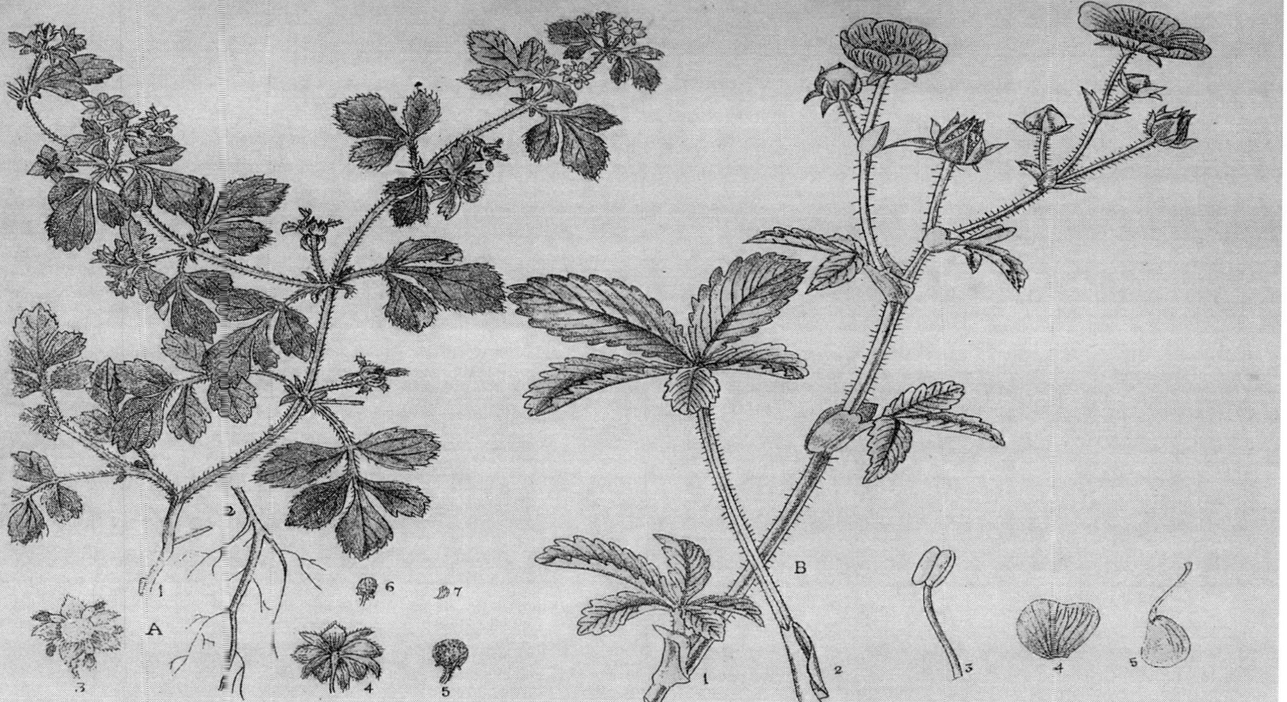

A—POTENTILLA SUPINA, *LINN.* B—P. NEPALENSIS, *HOOK.*

PLATE No. 396.

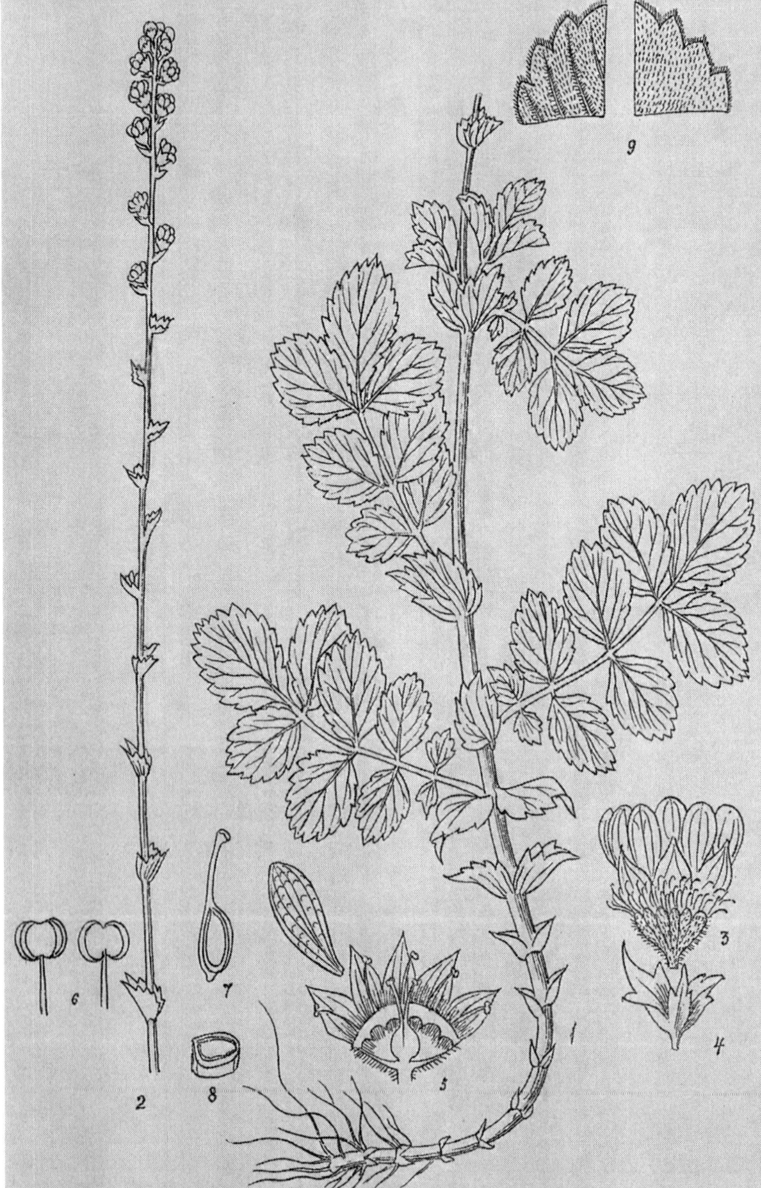

AGRIMONIA EUPATORIUM, *LINN.*

PLATE No. 397

ROSA DAMASCENA, *MILL.*

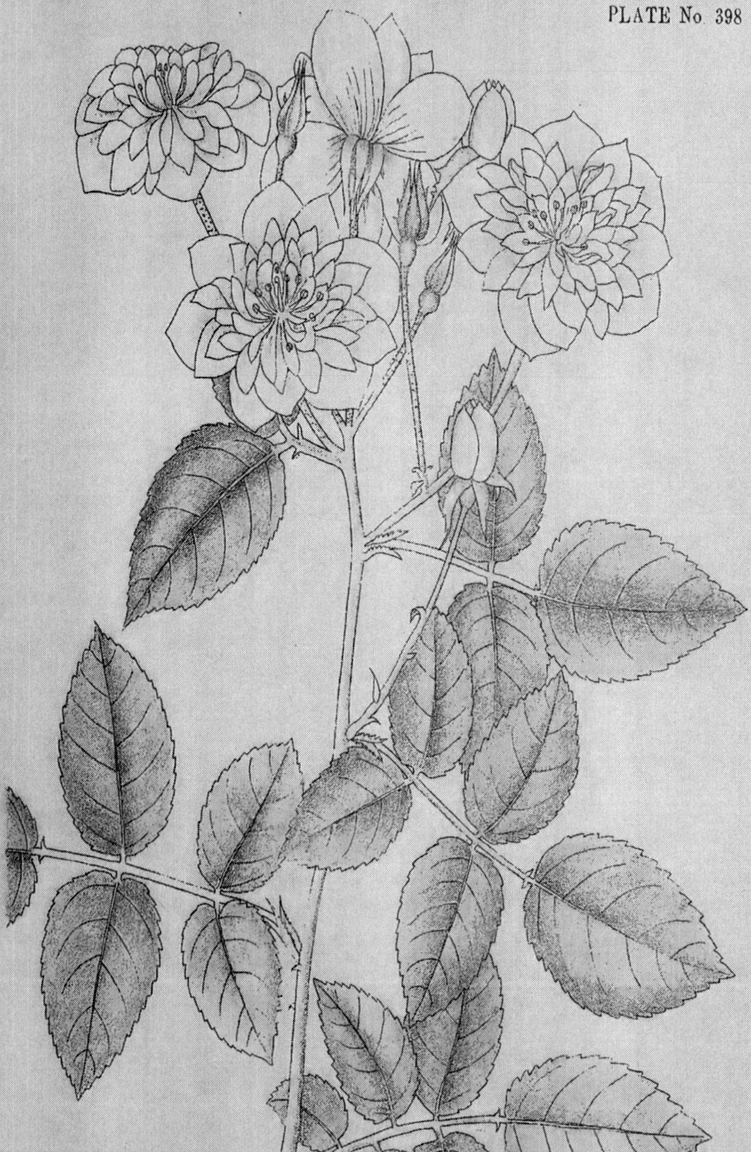

ROSA ALBA, *LINN.*

A CYDONIA VULGARIS, *PERS.*

B ROSA CENTIFOLIA, *LINN.*

C ROSA GALLICA, *LINN*

PLATE No. 400.

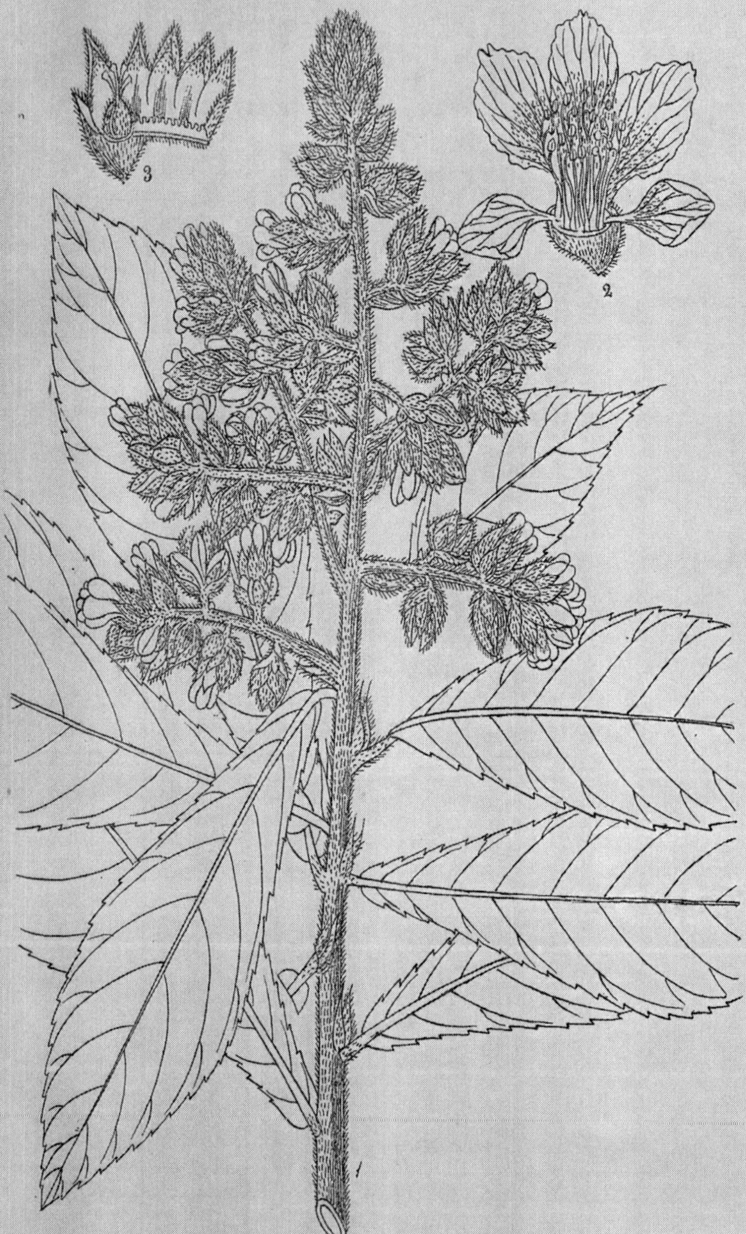

ERIOBOTRYA JAPONICA, *LINDL.*

PLATE No. 401.

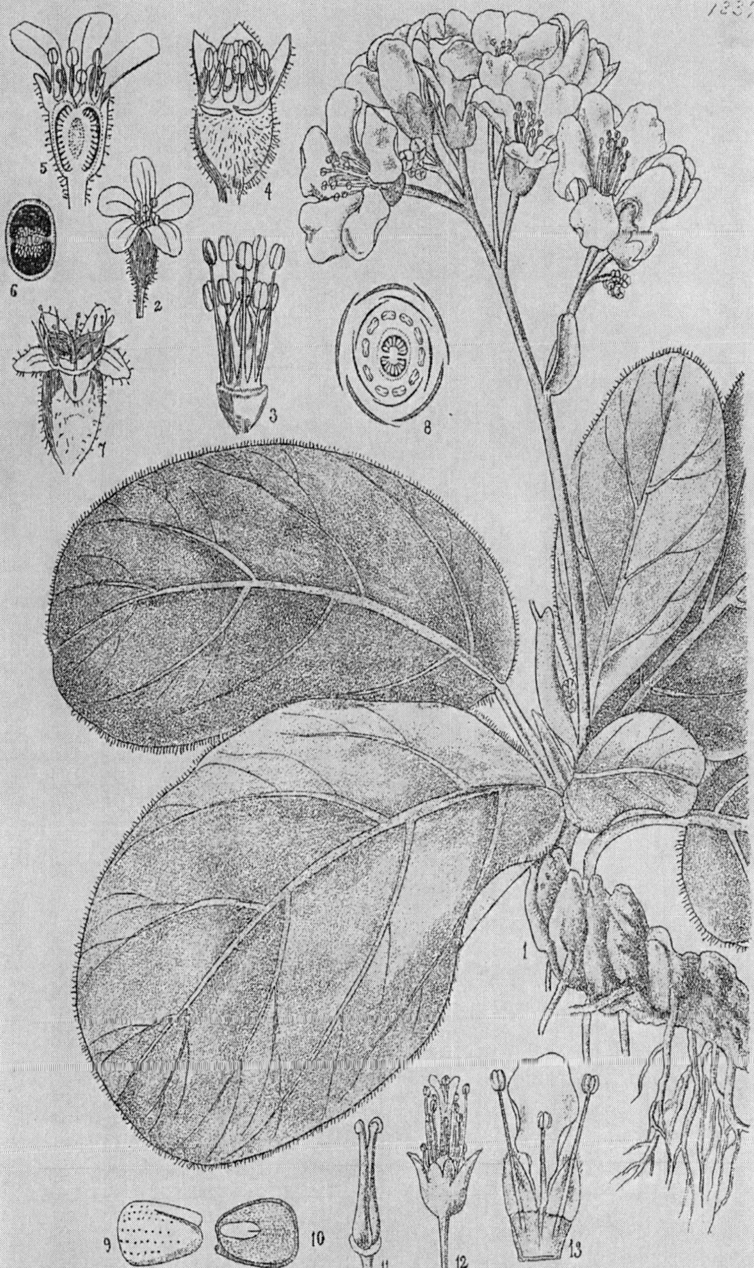

SAXIFRAGA LIGULATA, *WALL*.

PLATE No. 402.

DICHROA FEBRIFUGA, LOUR.

PLATE No. 403.

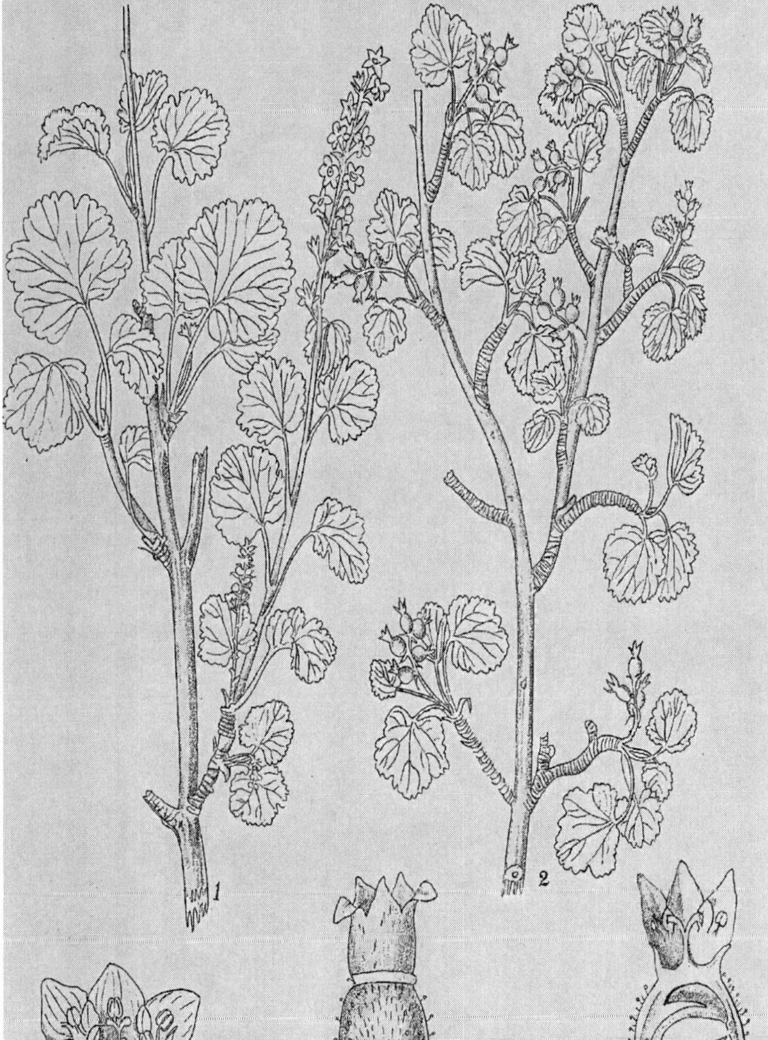

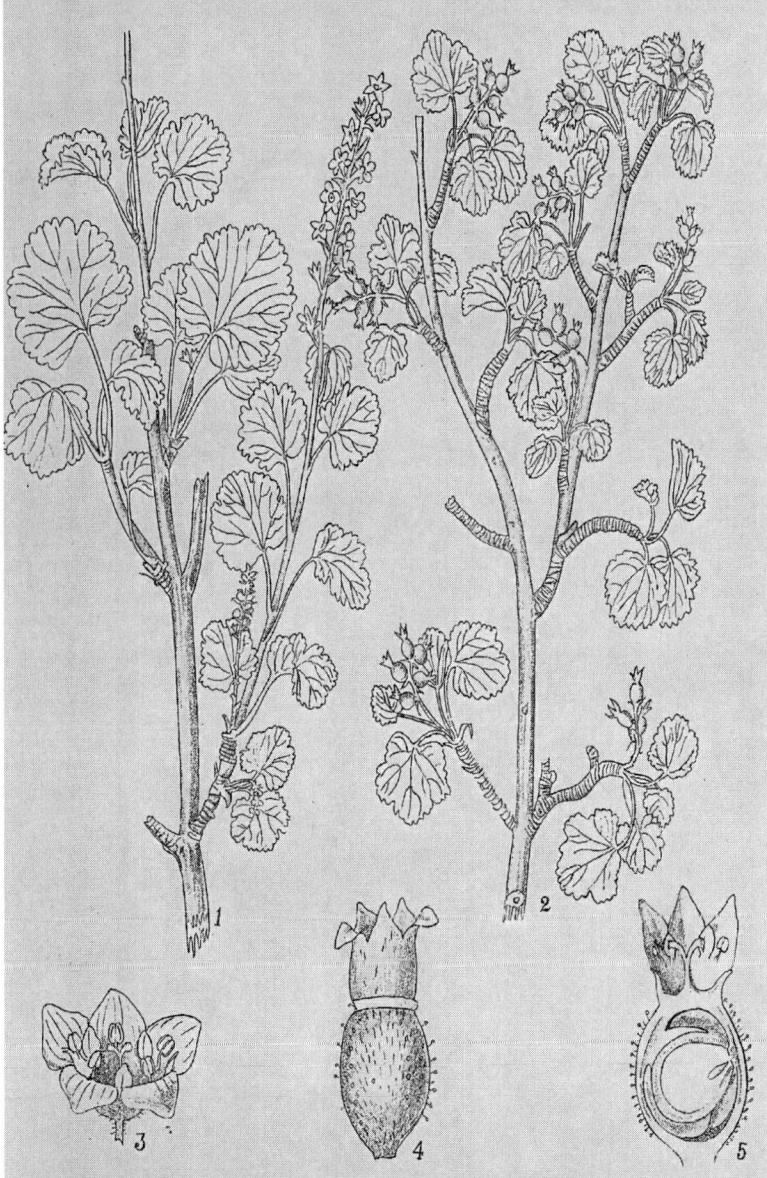

RIBES ORIENTALE, *POIR.*

PLATE No. 404.

BRYOPHYLLUM CALYCINUM, *SALISB.*

PLATE No. 405.

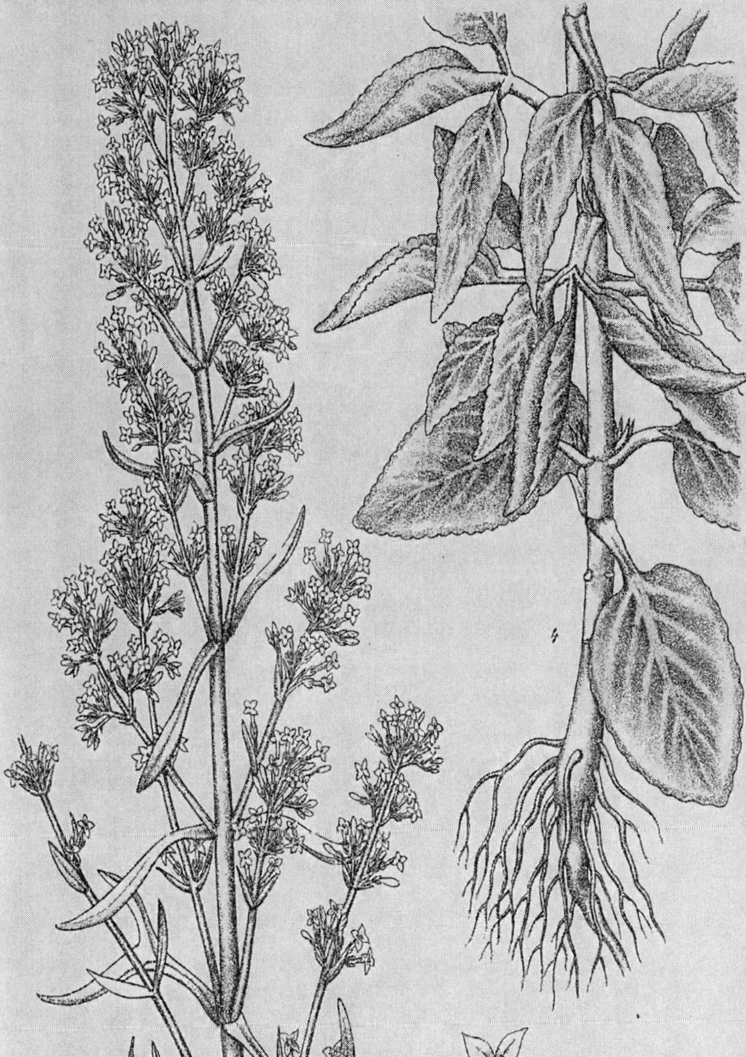

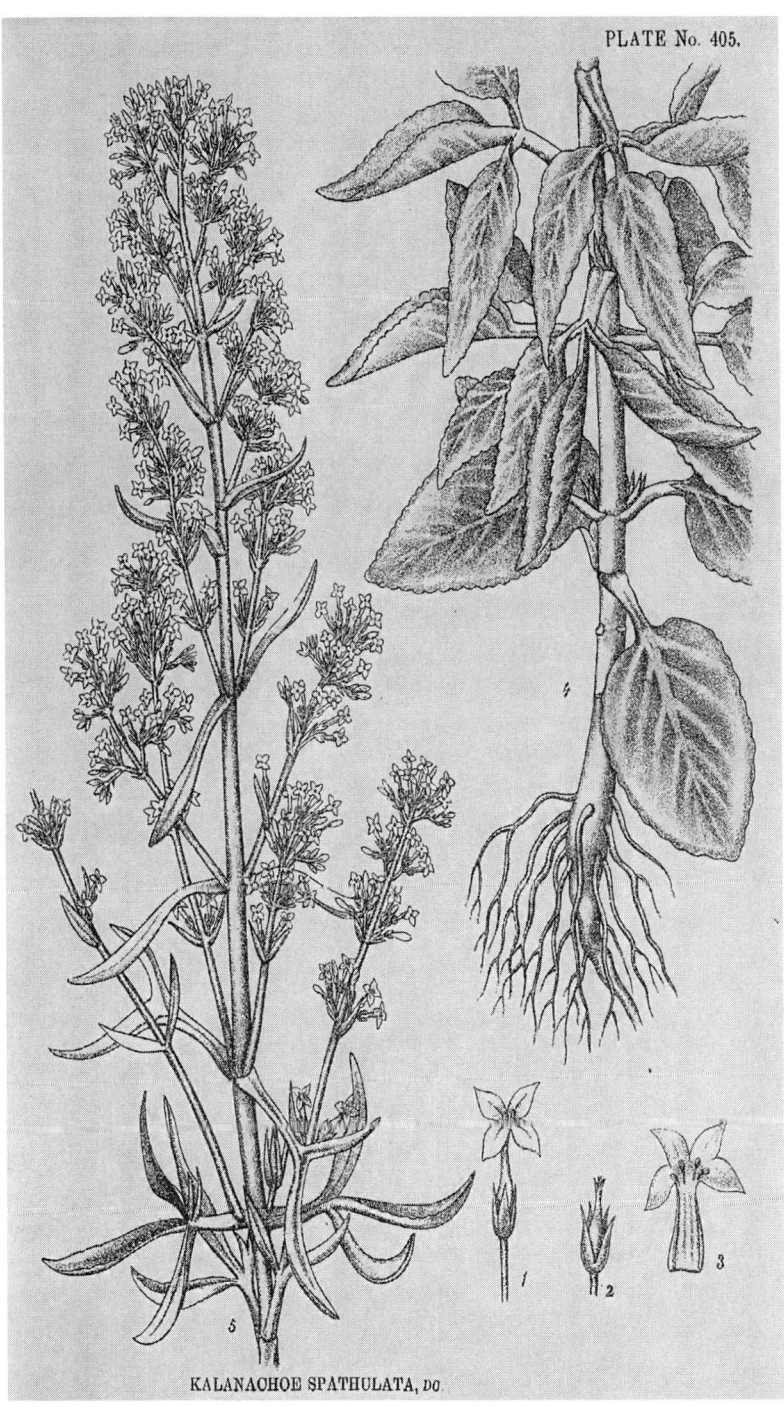

KALANACHOE SPATHULATA, *DC*

PLATE No. 406.

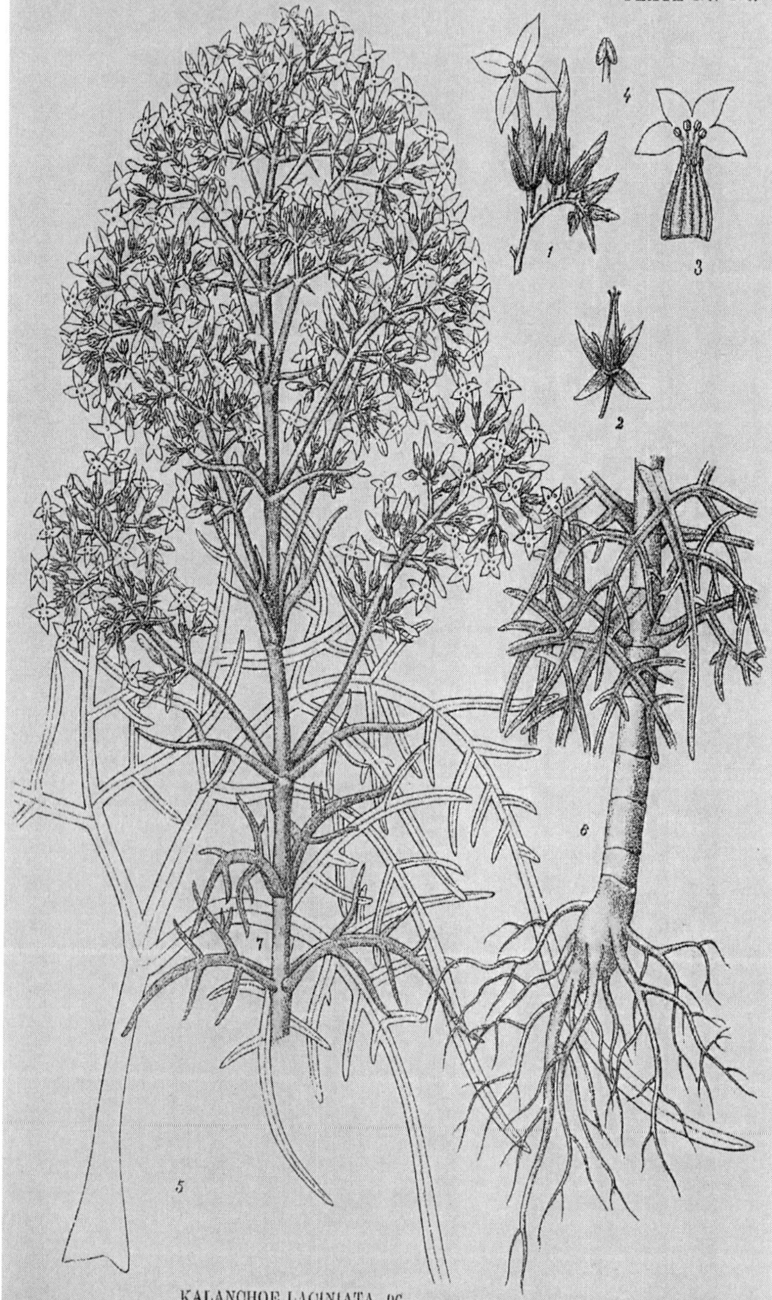

KALANCHOE LACINIATA, *DC.*

PLATE No. 407.

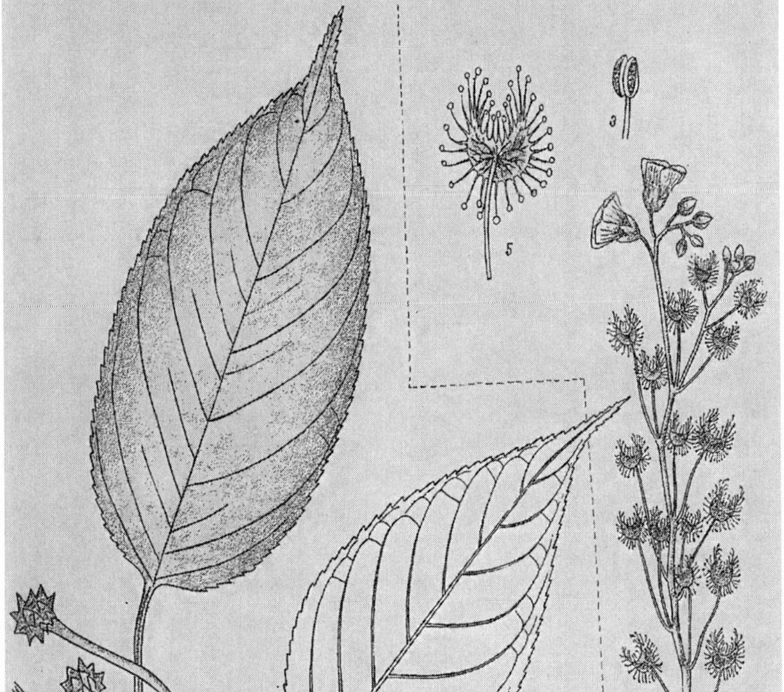

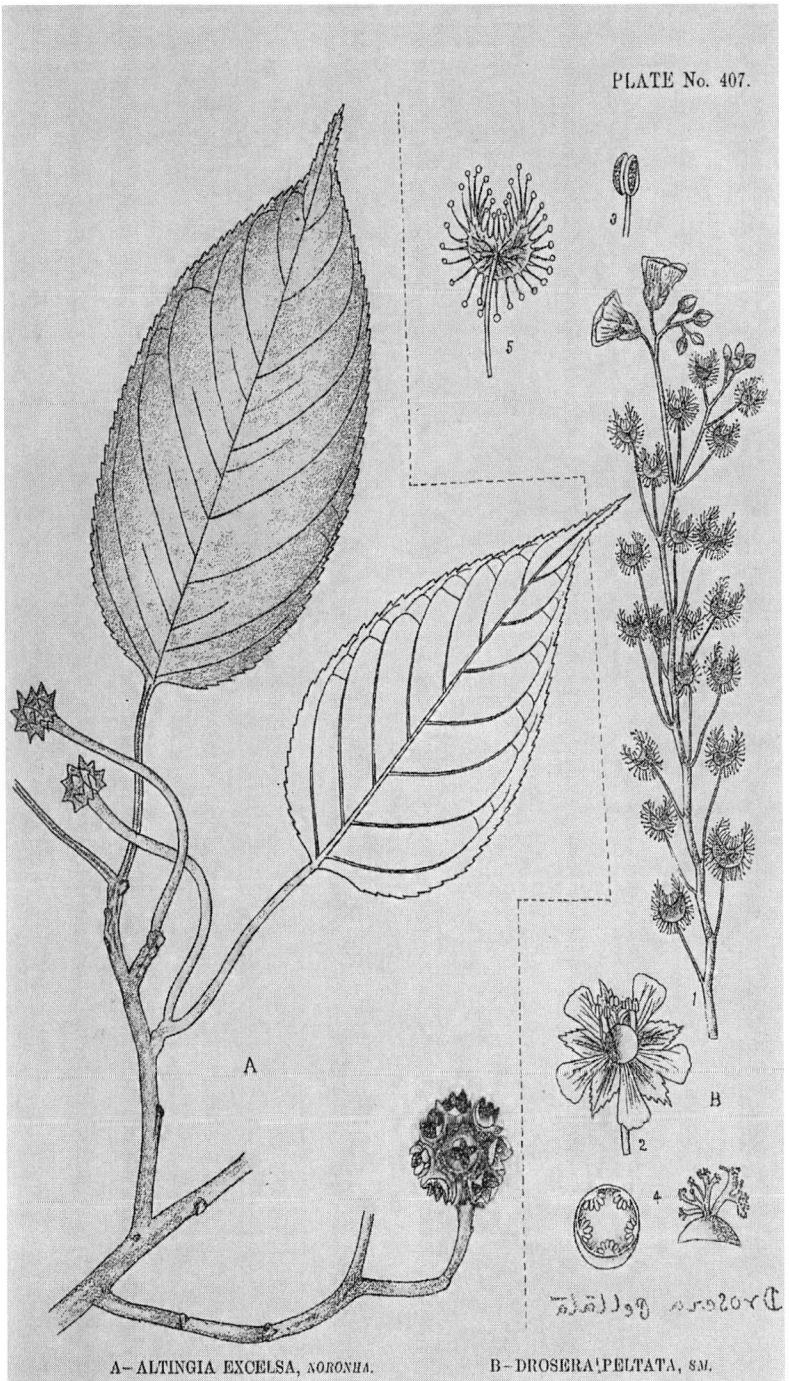

A– ALTINGIA EXCELSA, *NORONHA.* B– DROSERA PELTATA, *SM.*

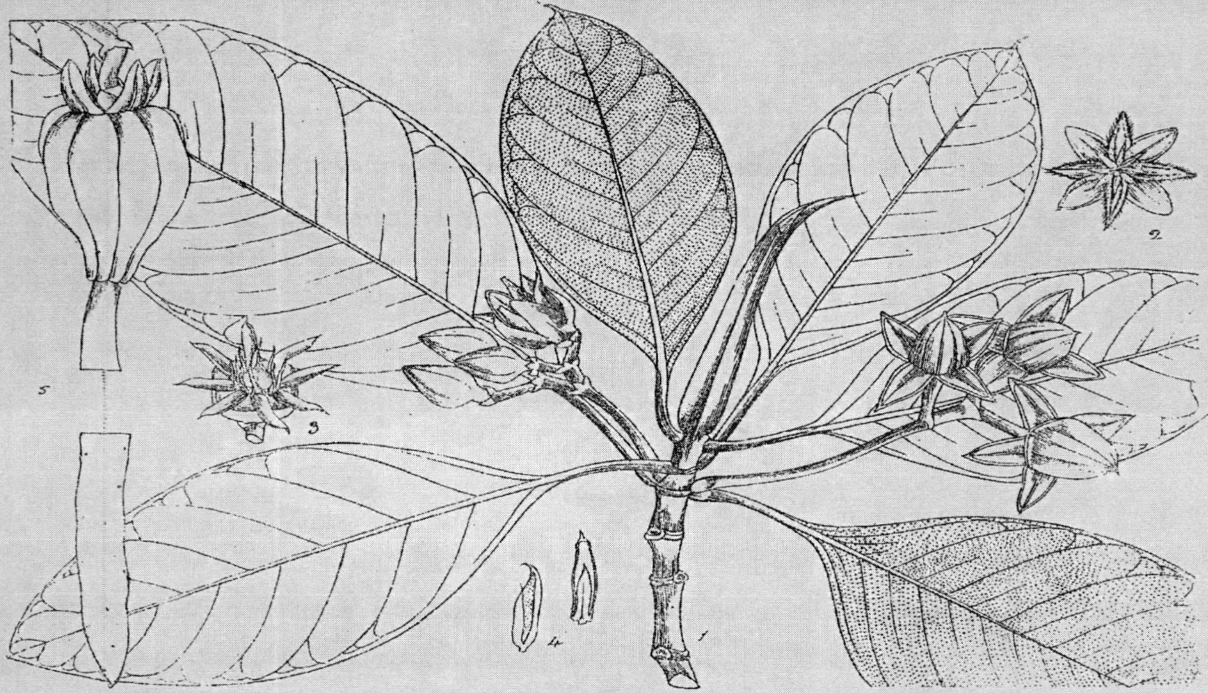

RHIZOPHORA MUCRONATA, *LAM.*

PLATE No. 409.

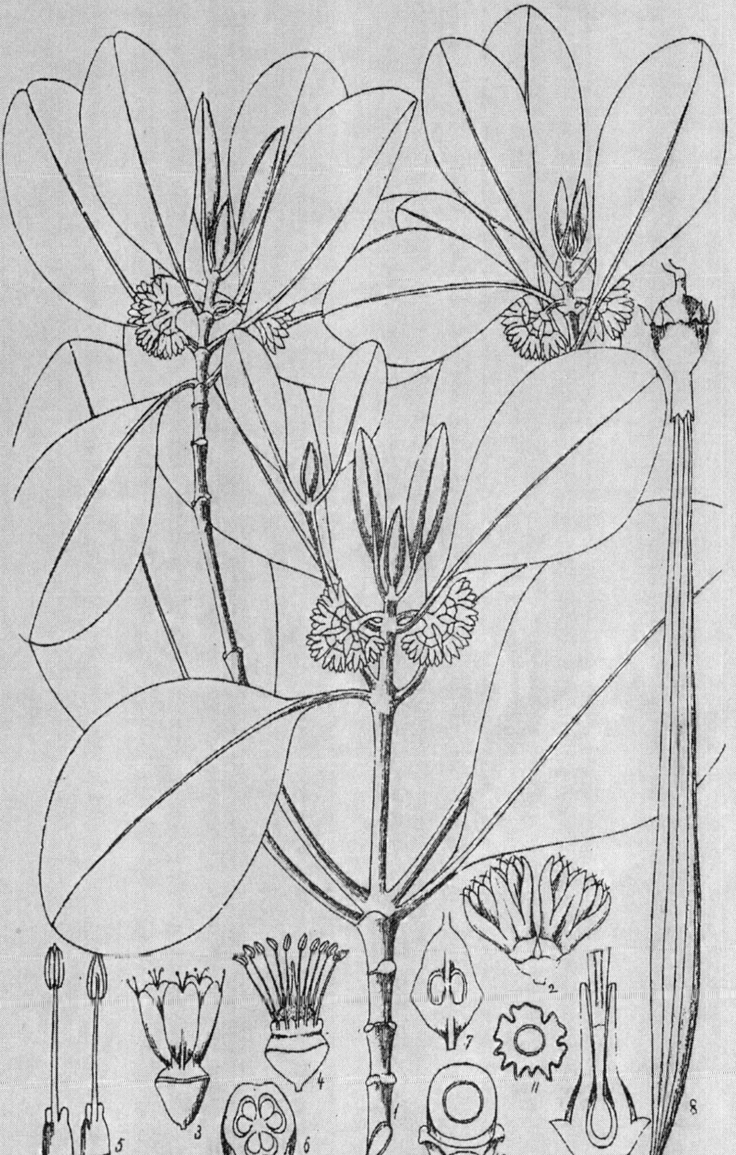

CERIOPS CANDOLLEANA, ARN.

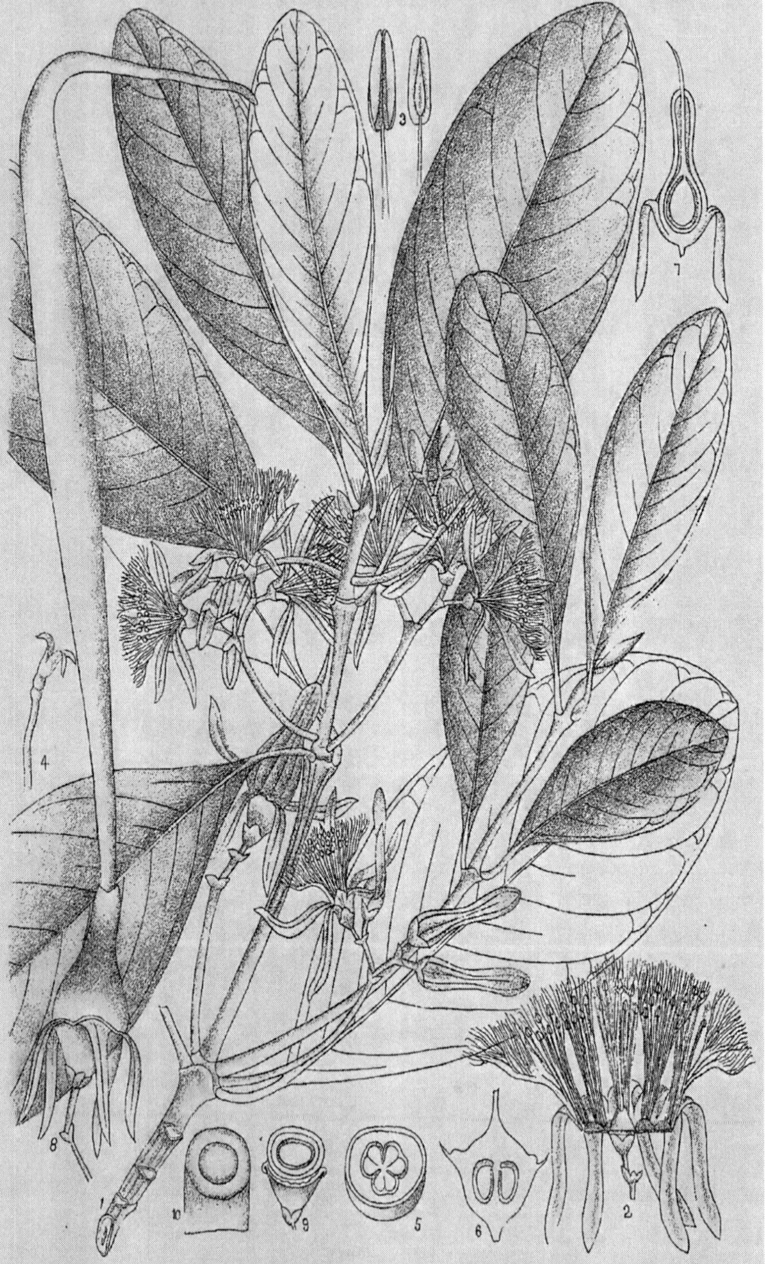

KANDELIA RHEEDII, *W.* & *A.*

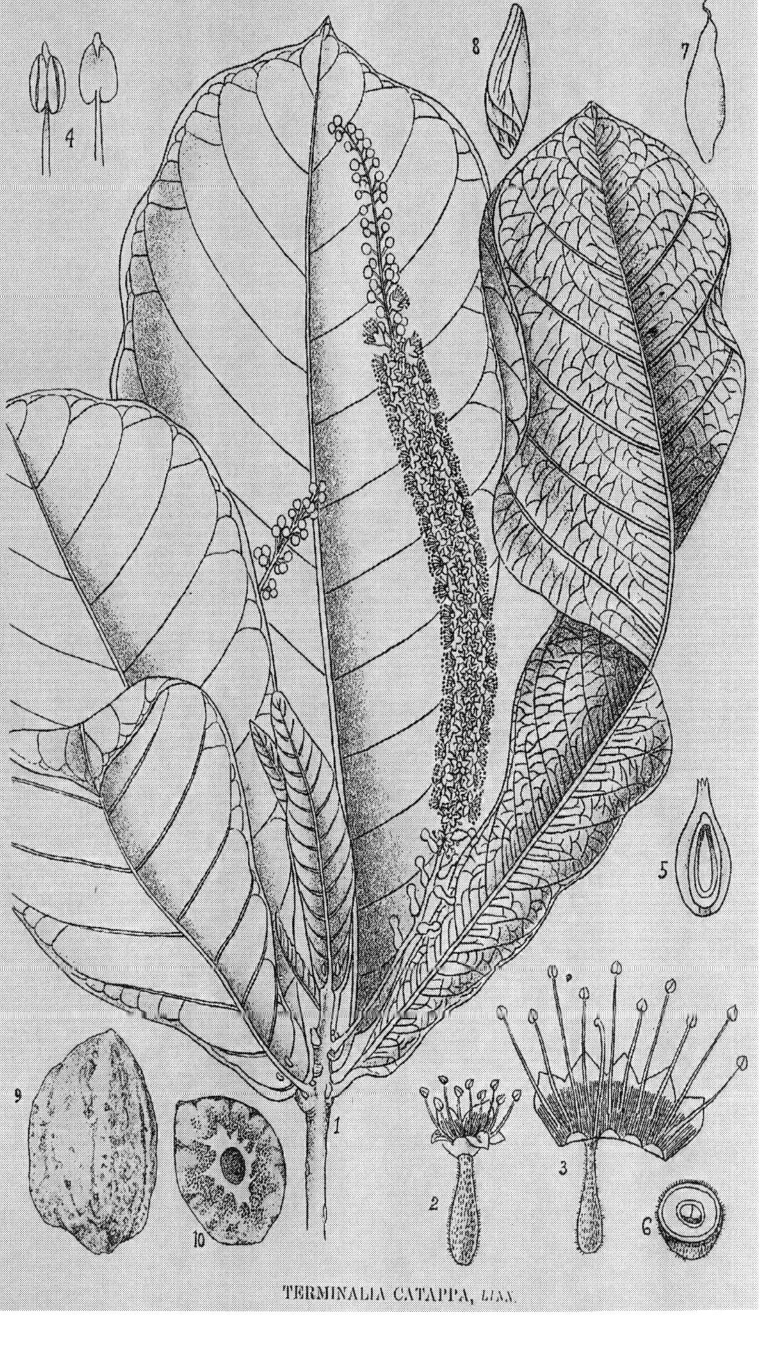

TERMINALIA CATAPPA, *Linn.*

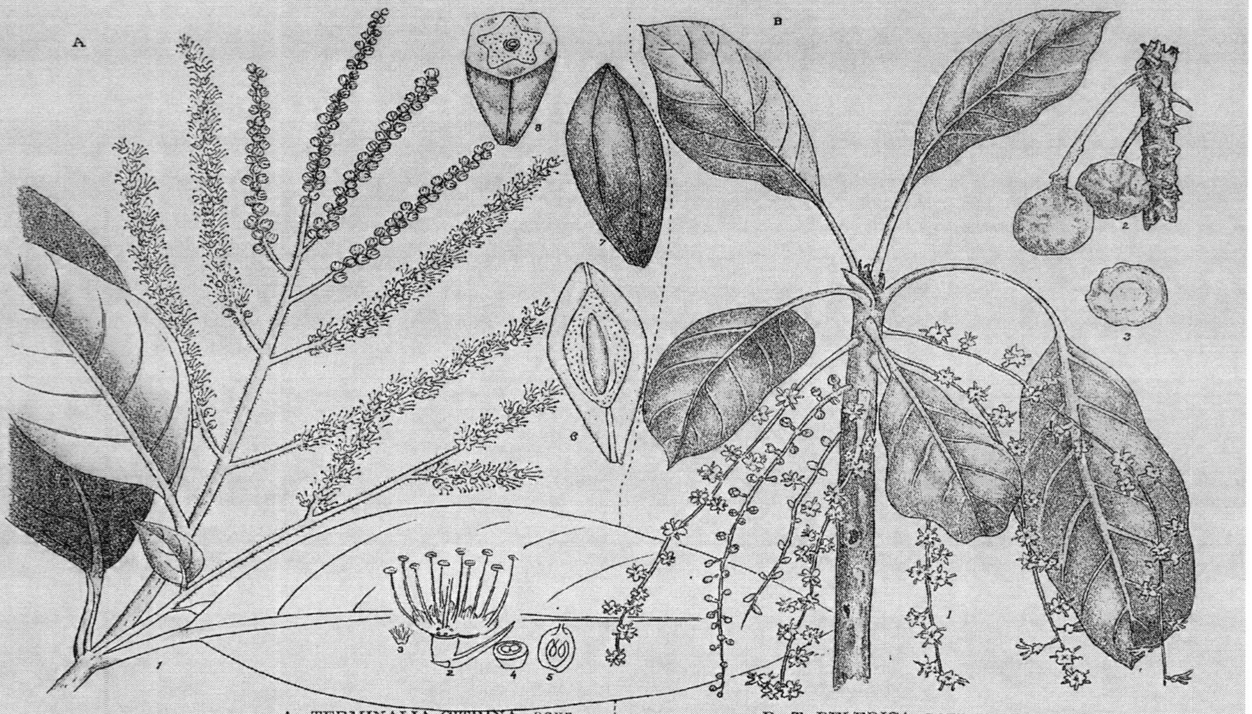

A—TERMINALIA CITRINA, *ROXB.*

B—T. BELERICA, *ROXB.*

PLATE No. 413

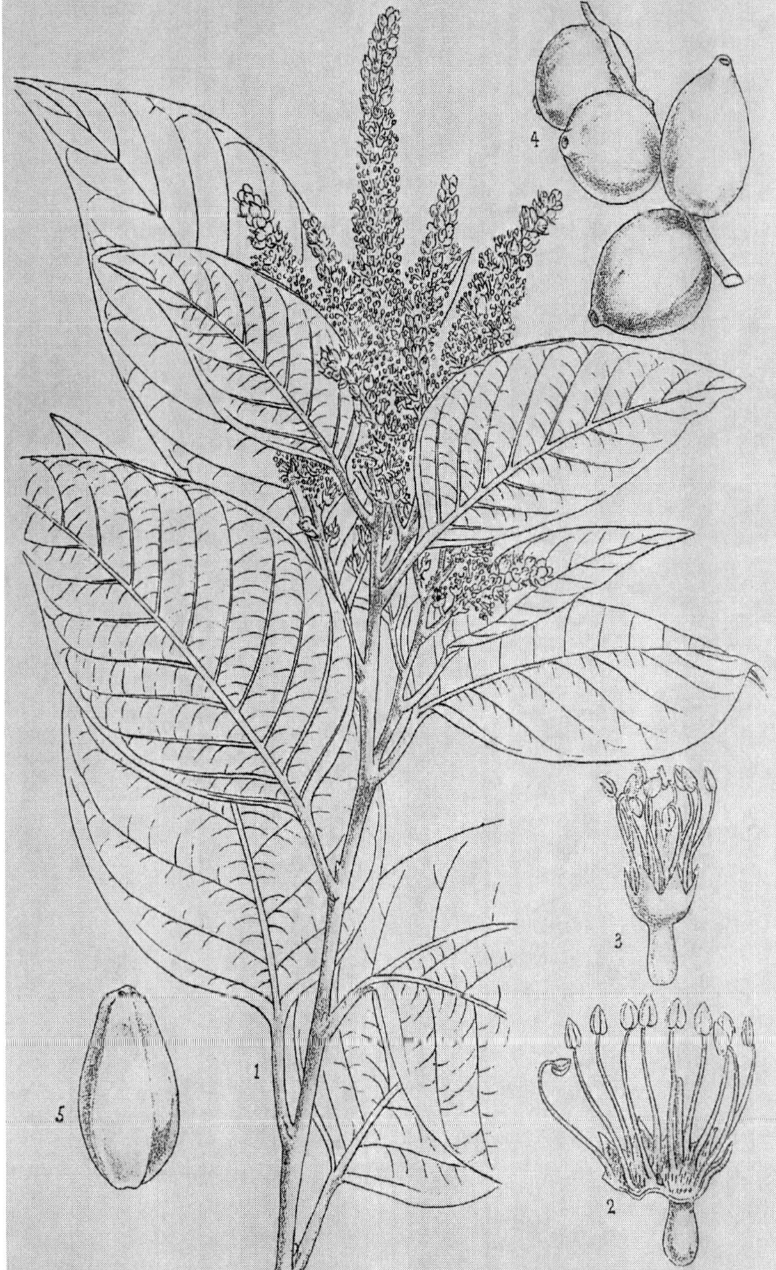

TERMINALIA CHEBULA, RETZ.

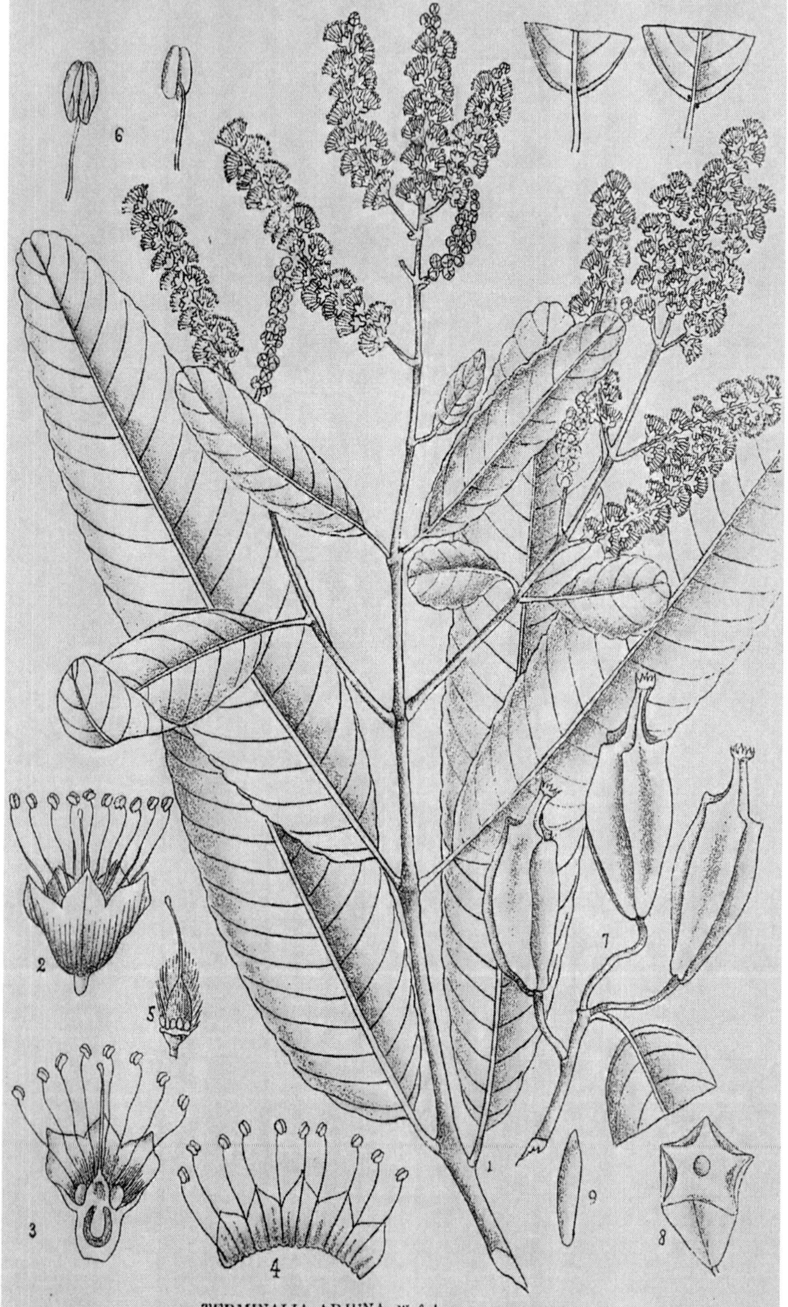

TERMINALIA ARJUNA, *W & A.*

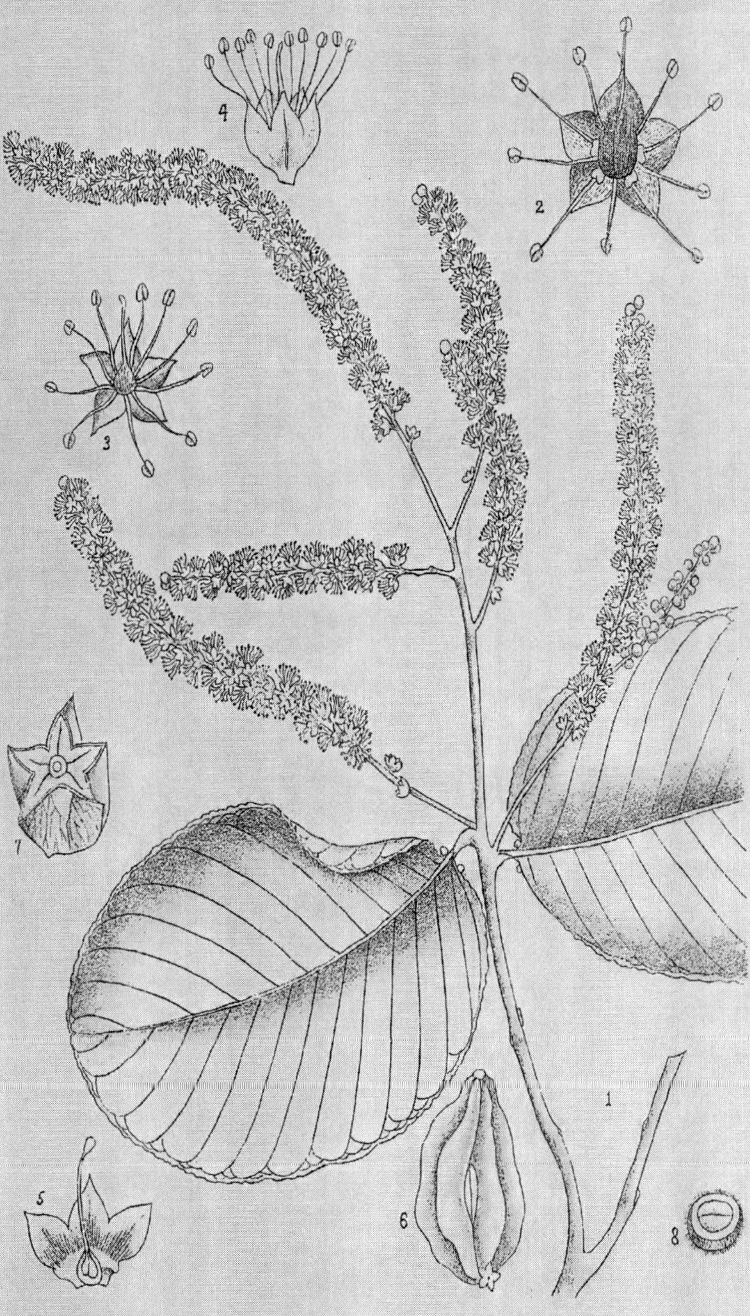

TERMINALIA TOMENTOSA, BEDD

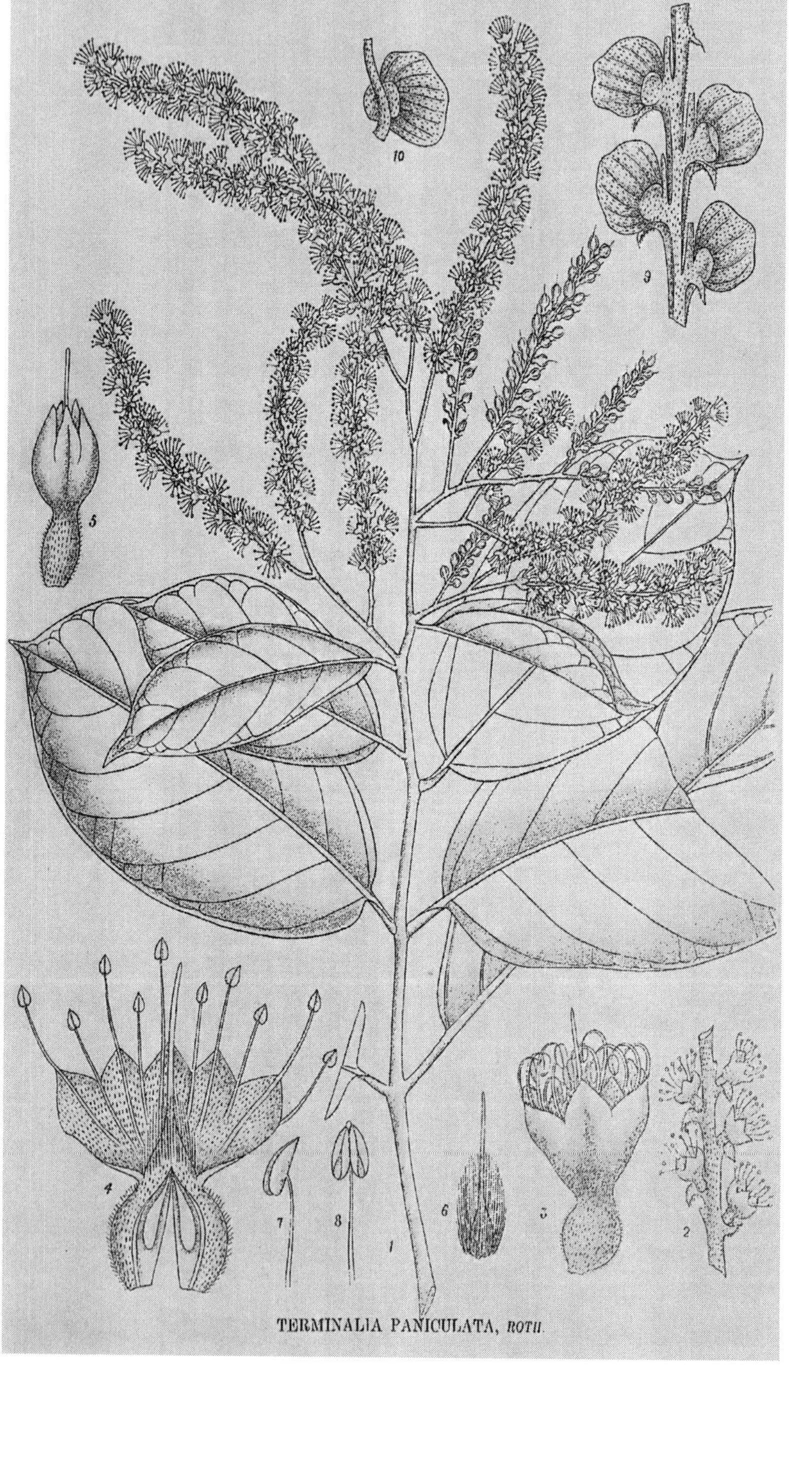

TERMINALIA PANICULATA, ROTH.

PLATE No. 417.

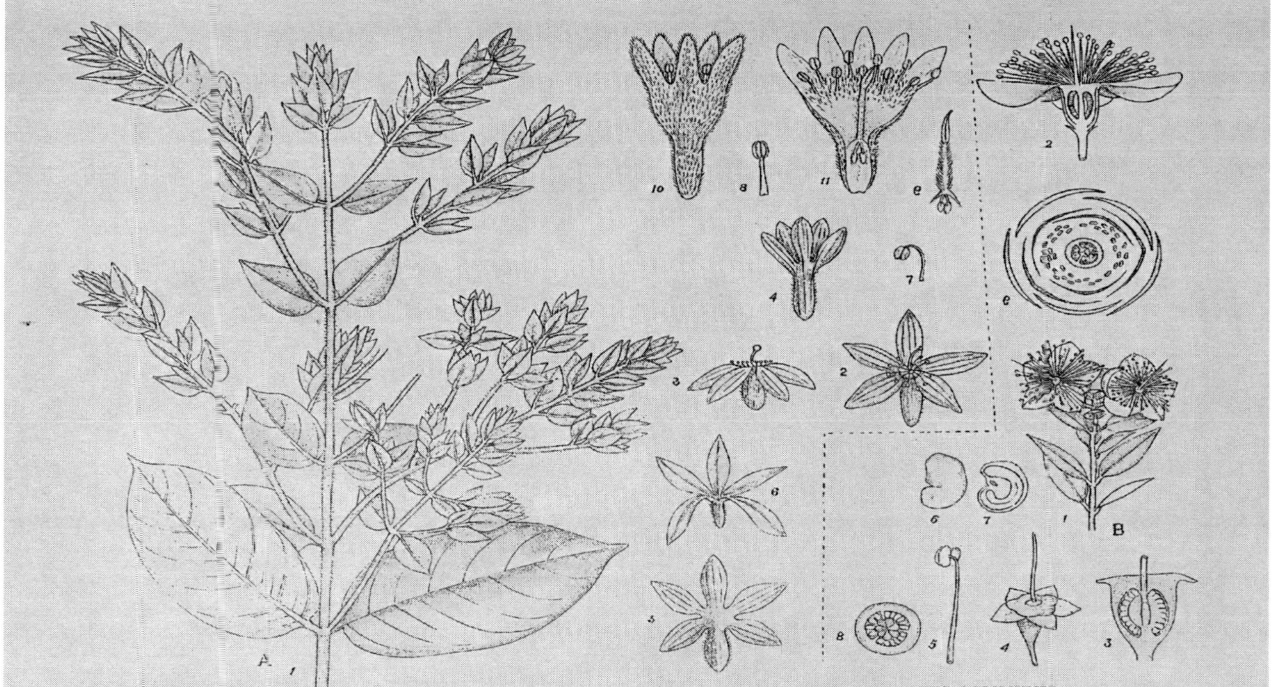

A—CALYCOPTERIS FLORIBUNDA, *LAMK.*

B—MYRTUS COMMUNIS, *LINN*

PLATE No. 418.

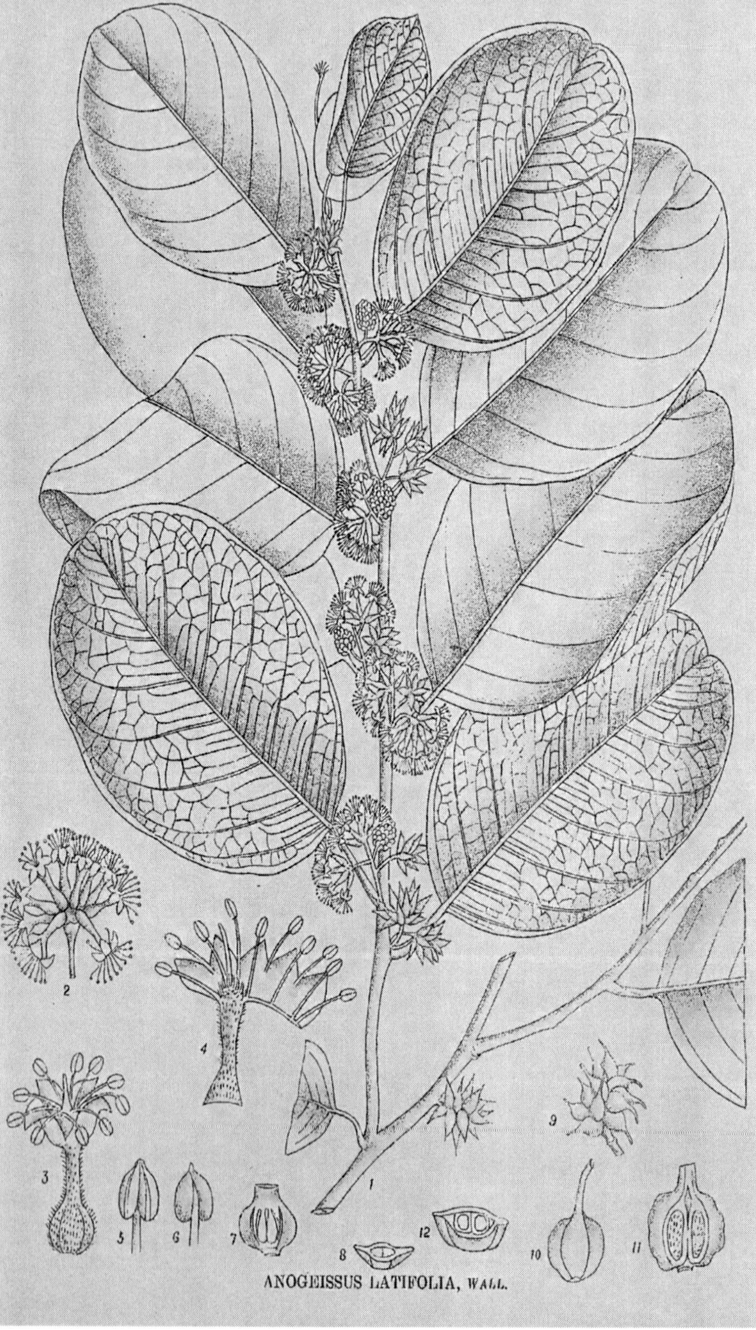

ANOGEISSUS LATIFOLIA, WALL.

PLATE No. 419.

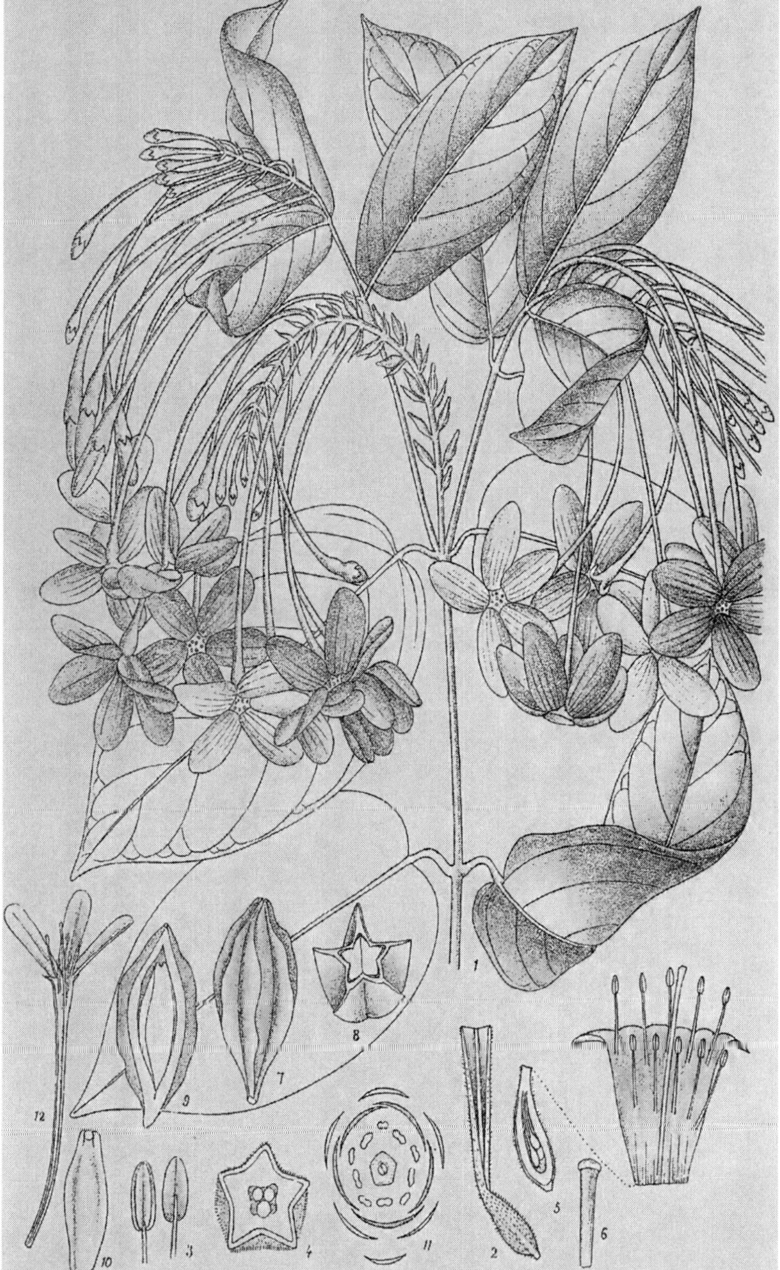

QUISQUALIS INDICA, *LINN.*

PLATE No. 420.

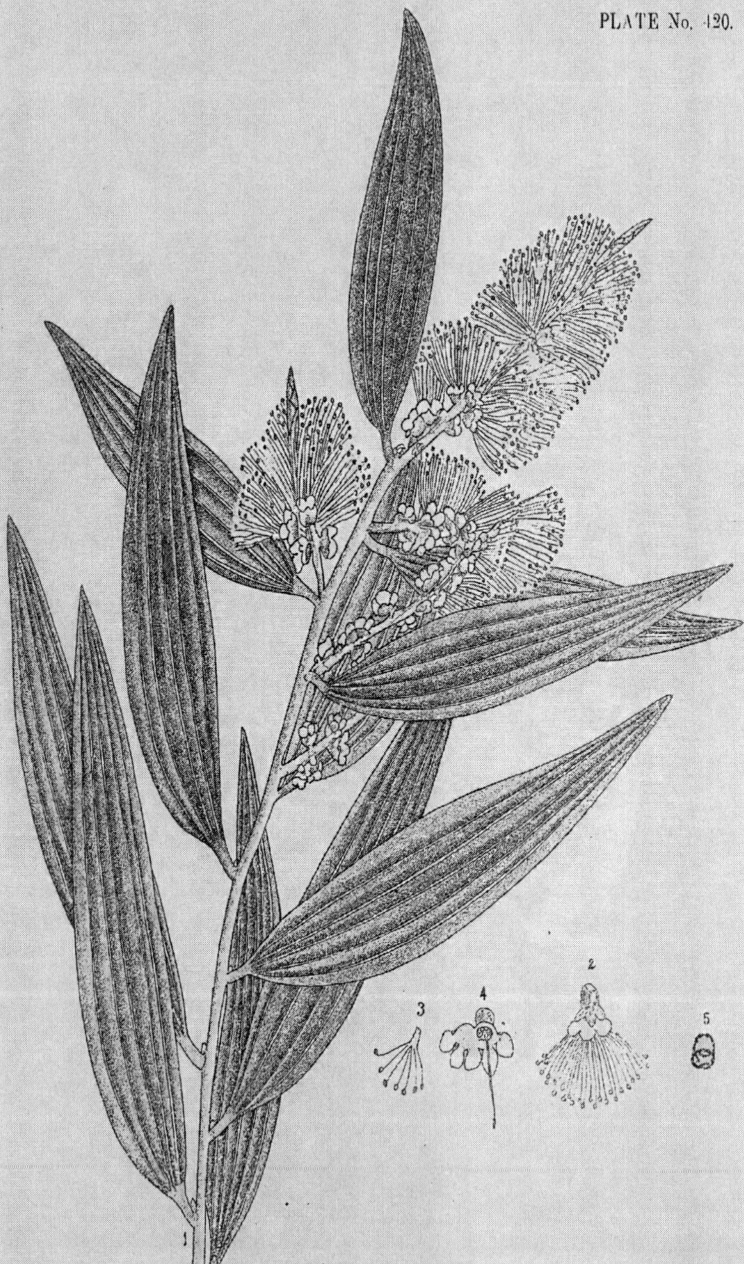

MELALEUCA LEUCADENDRON, *LINN.*

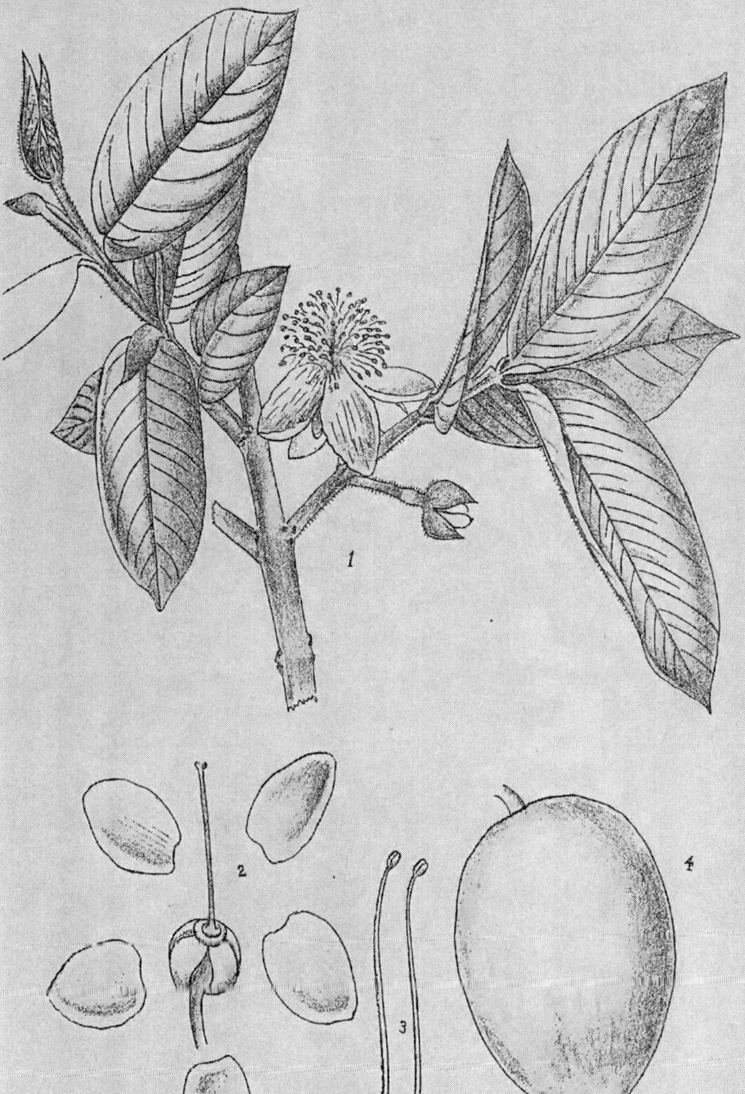

PSIDIUM GUYAVA, *LINN*

PLATE No. 422.

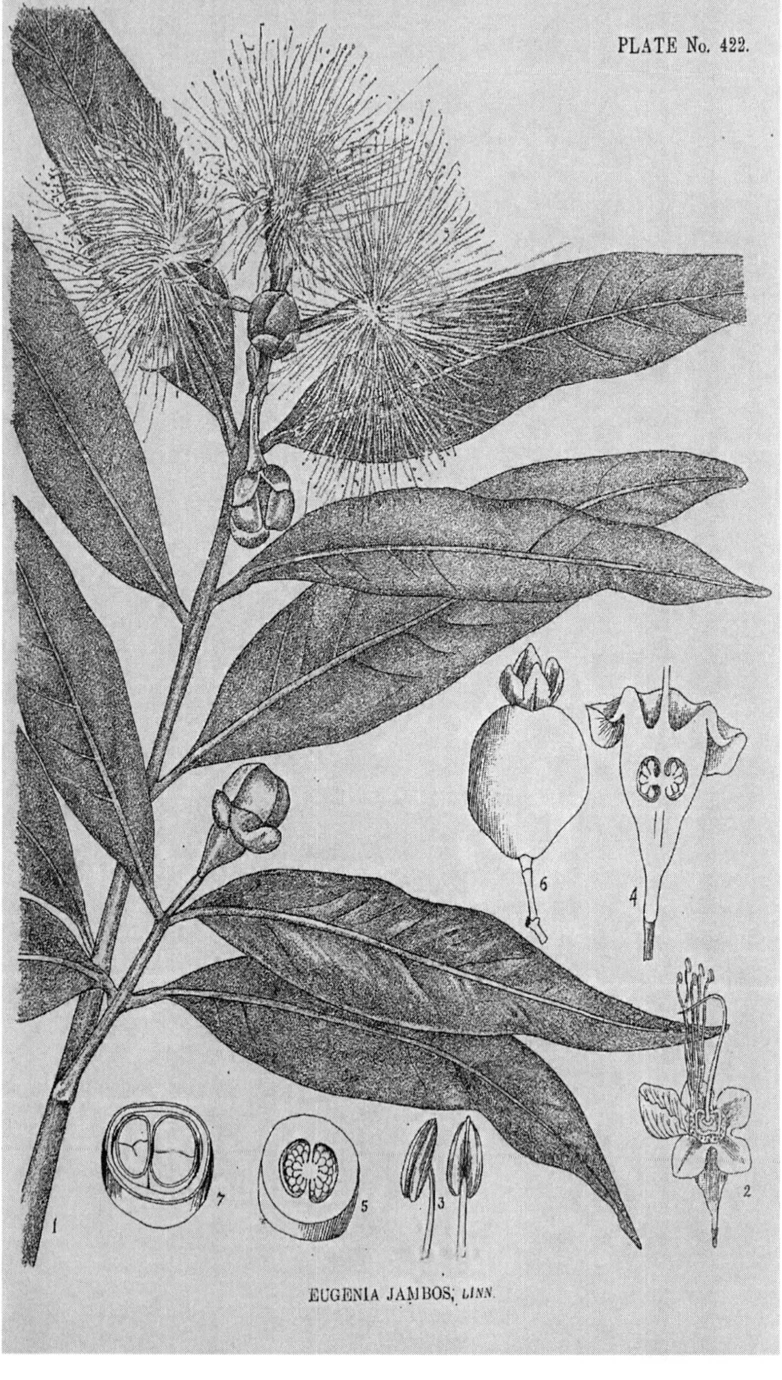

EUGENIA JAMBOS, LINN.

PLATE No. 423.

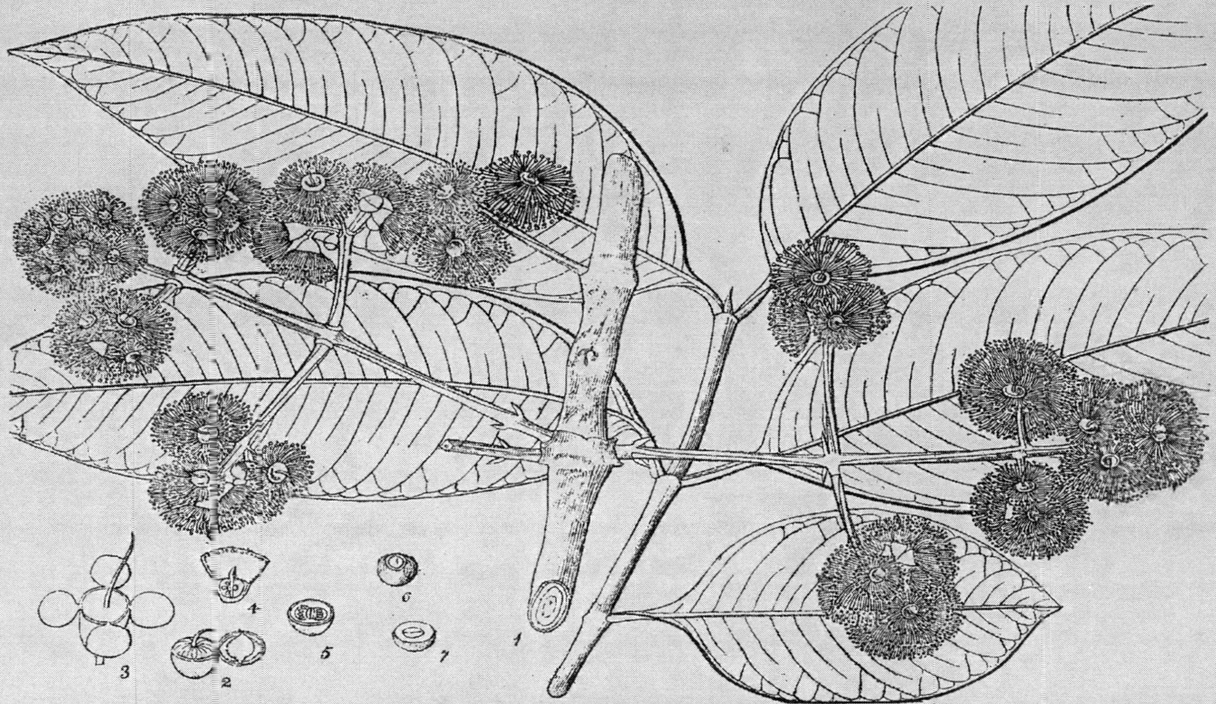

EUGENIA OPERCULATA, *ROXB.*

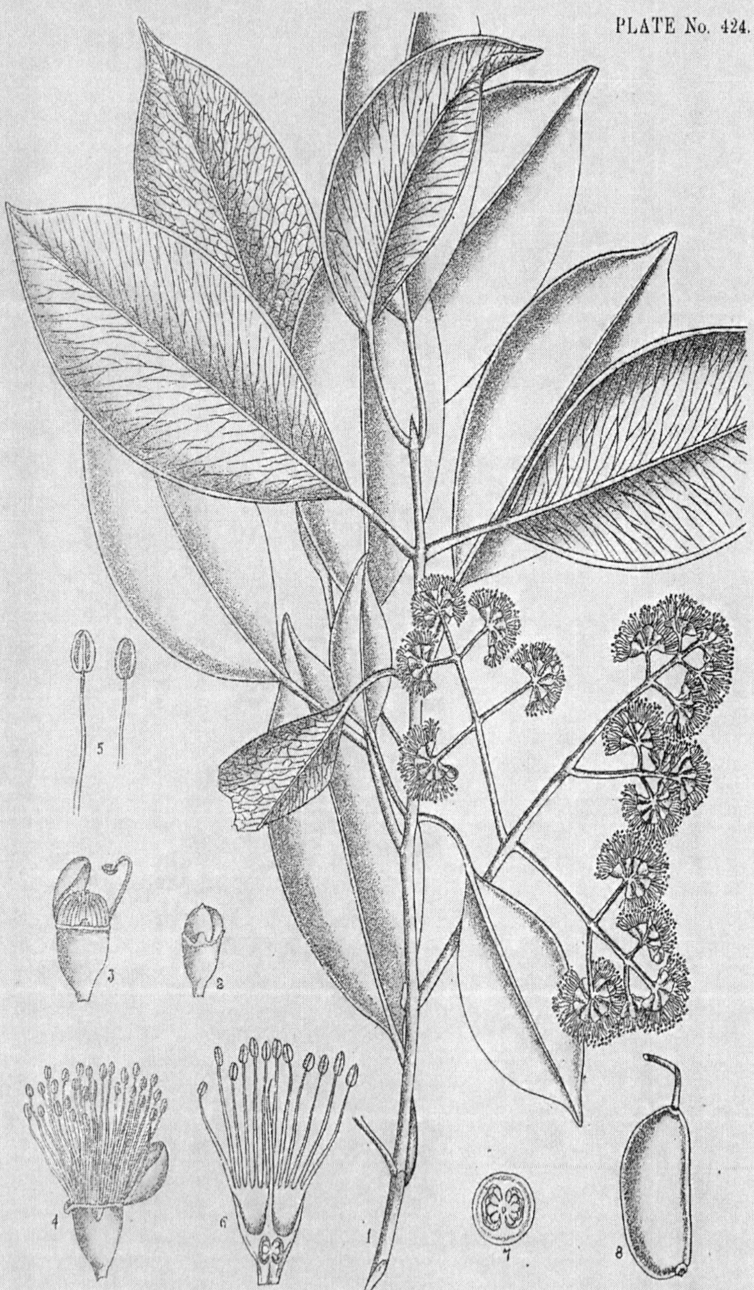

EUGENIA JOMBOLANA, LAM.

PLATE No. 425.

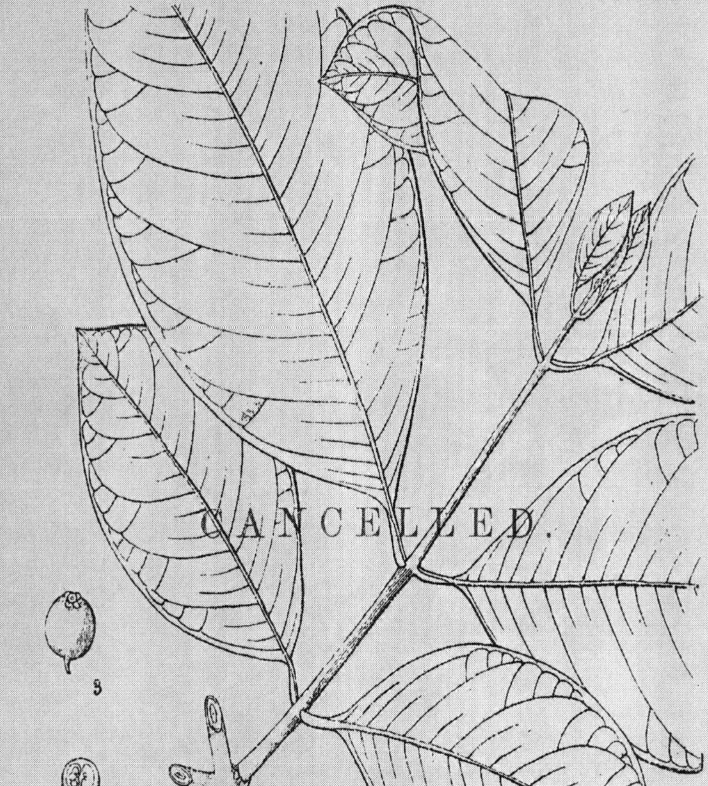

EUGENIA CERASOIDES, *ROXB.*

PLATE No 426.

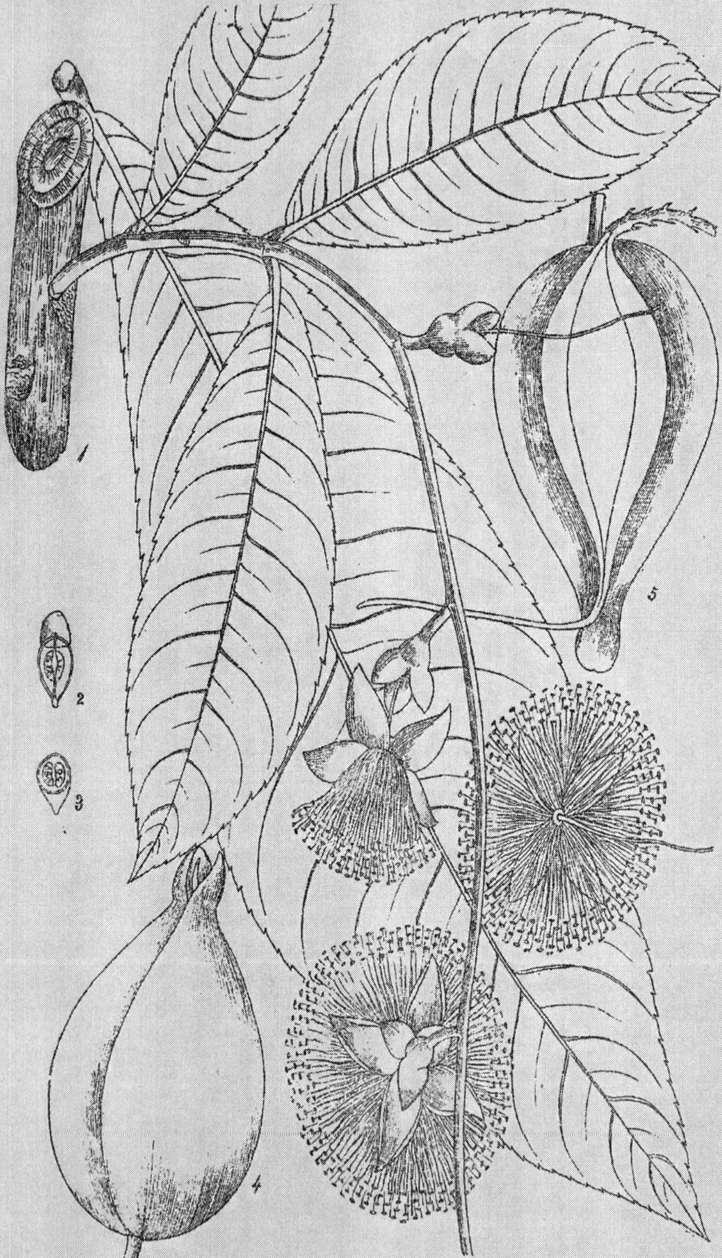

BARRINGTONIA RACEMOSA, BLUME.

PLATE No. 427.

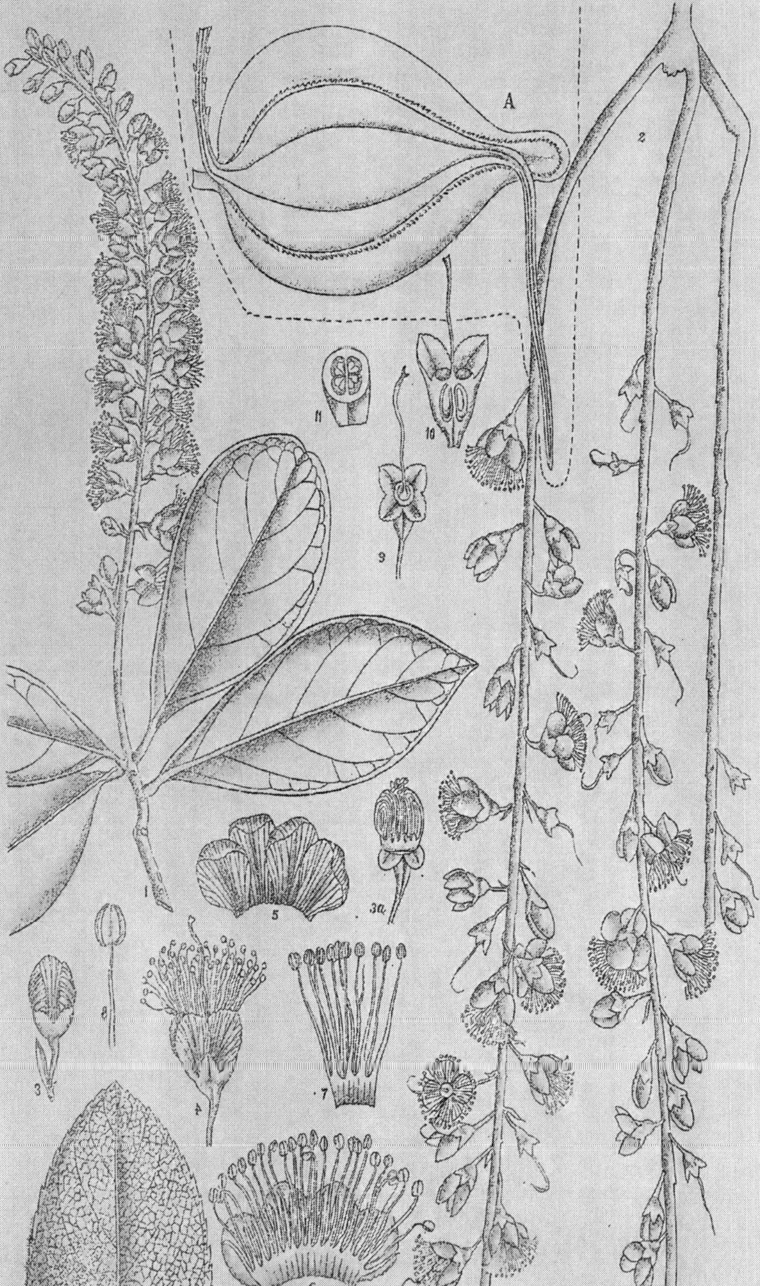

BARRINGTONIA ACUTANGULA, GÆRTN

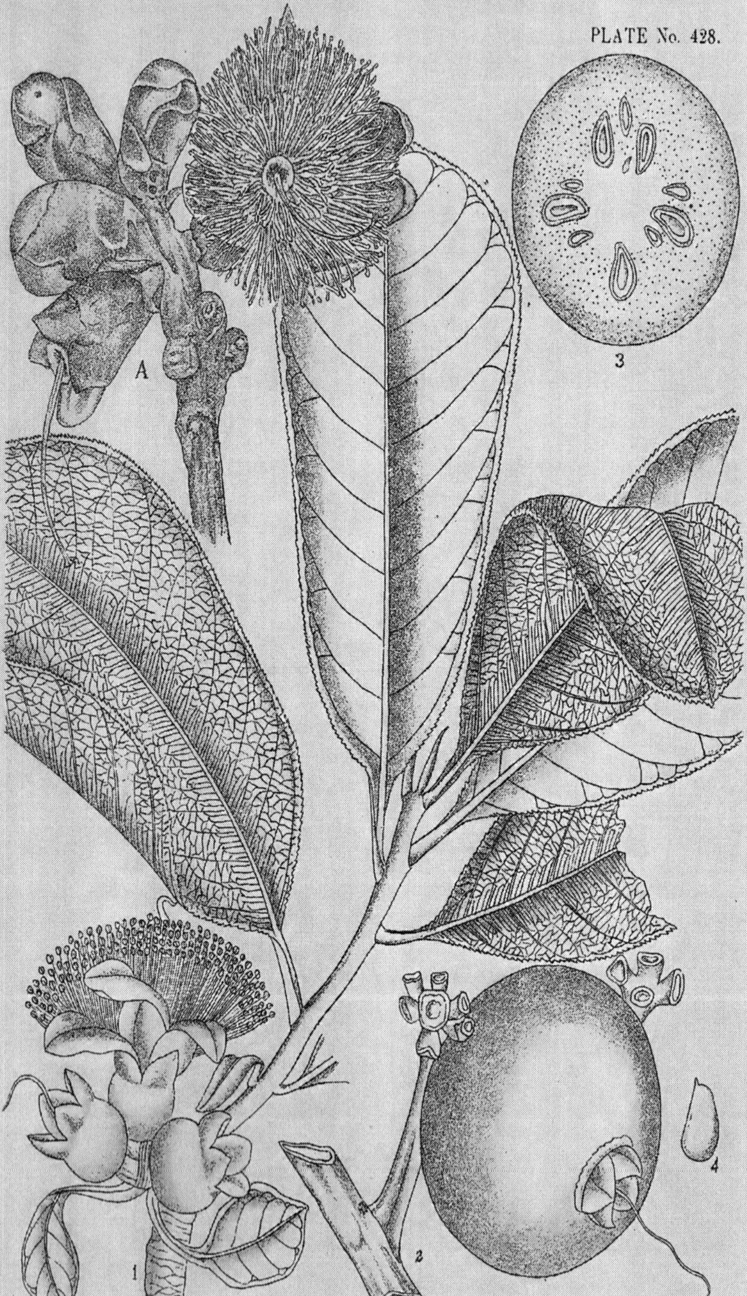

CAREYA ARBOREA, *ROXB.*

PLATE No. 129.

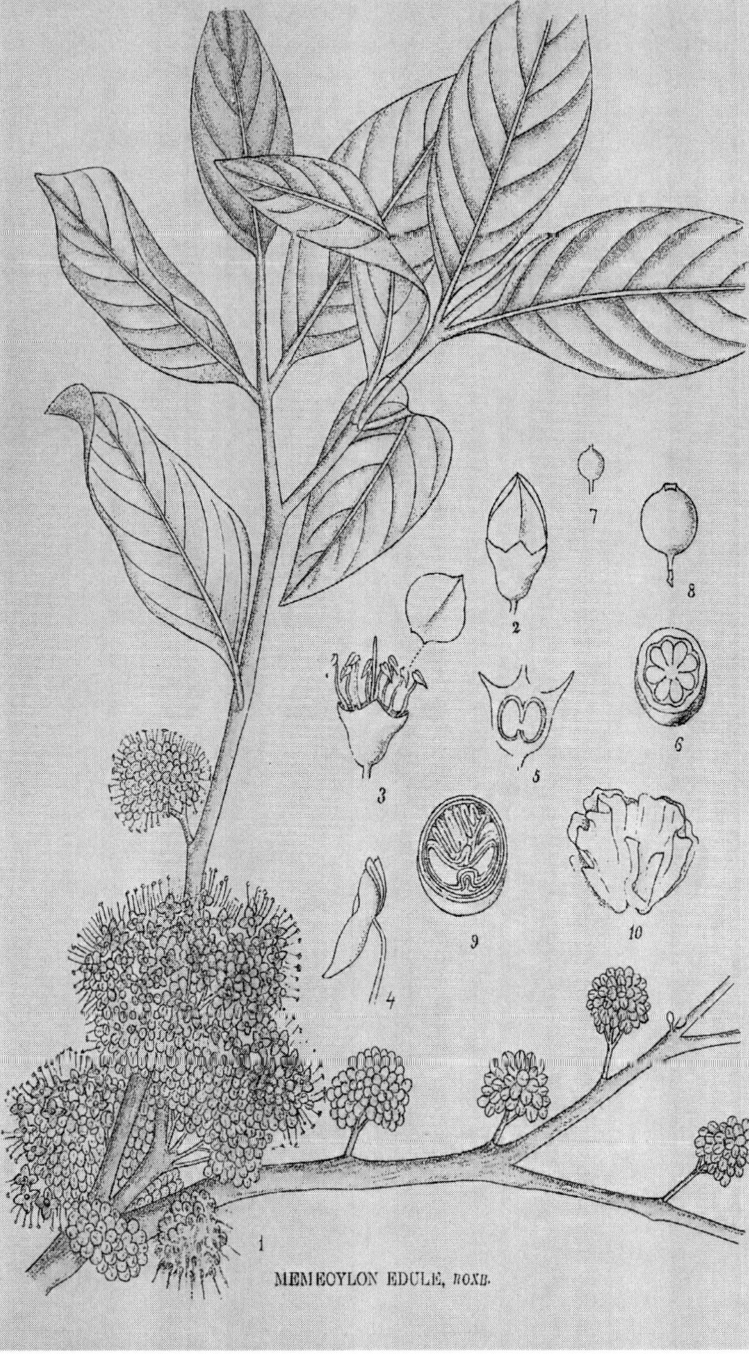

MEMECYLON EDULE, ROXB.

PLATE No. 430.

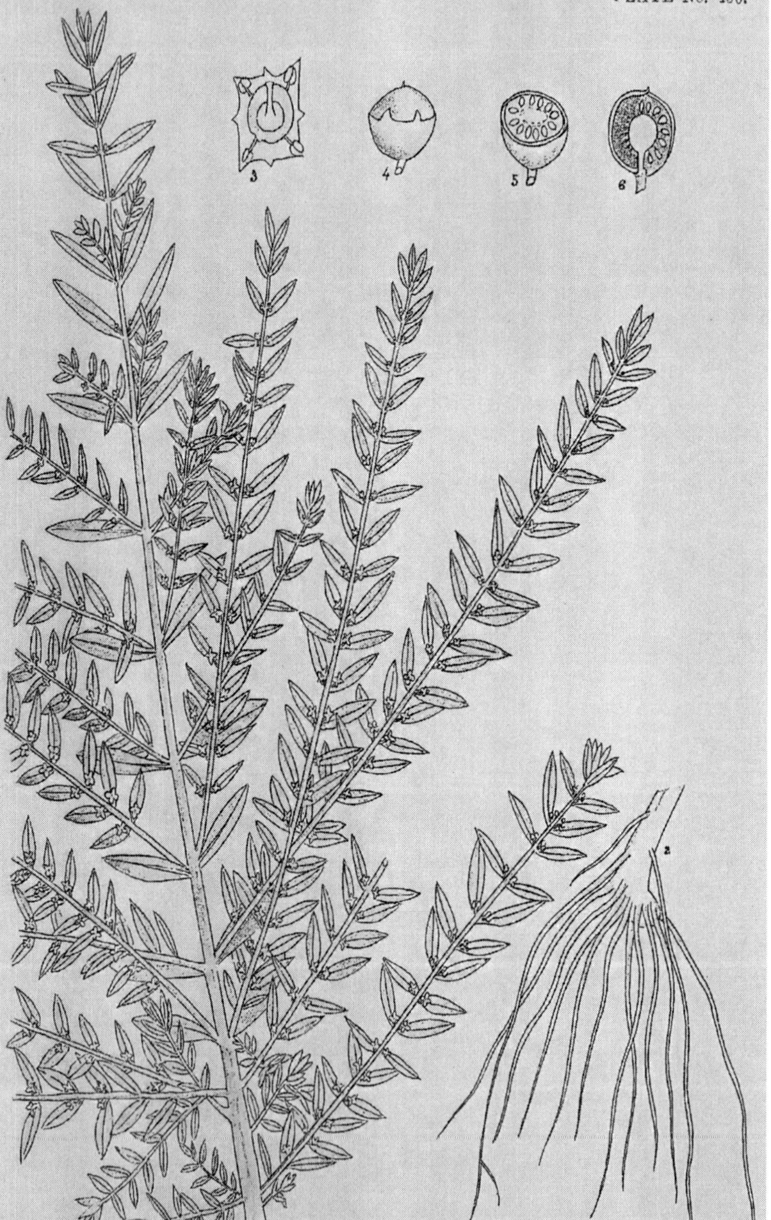

AMMANIA BACCIFERA, *LINN.*

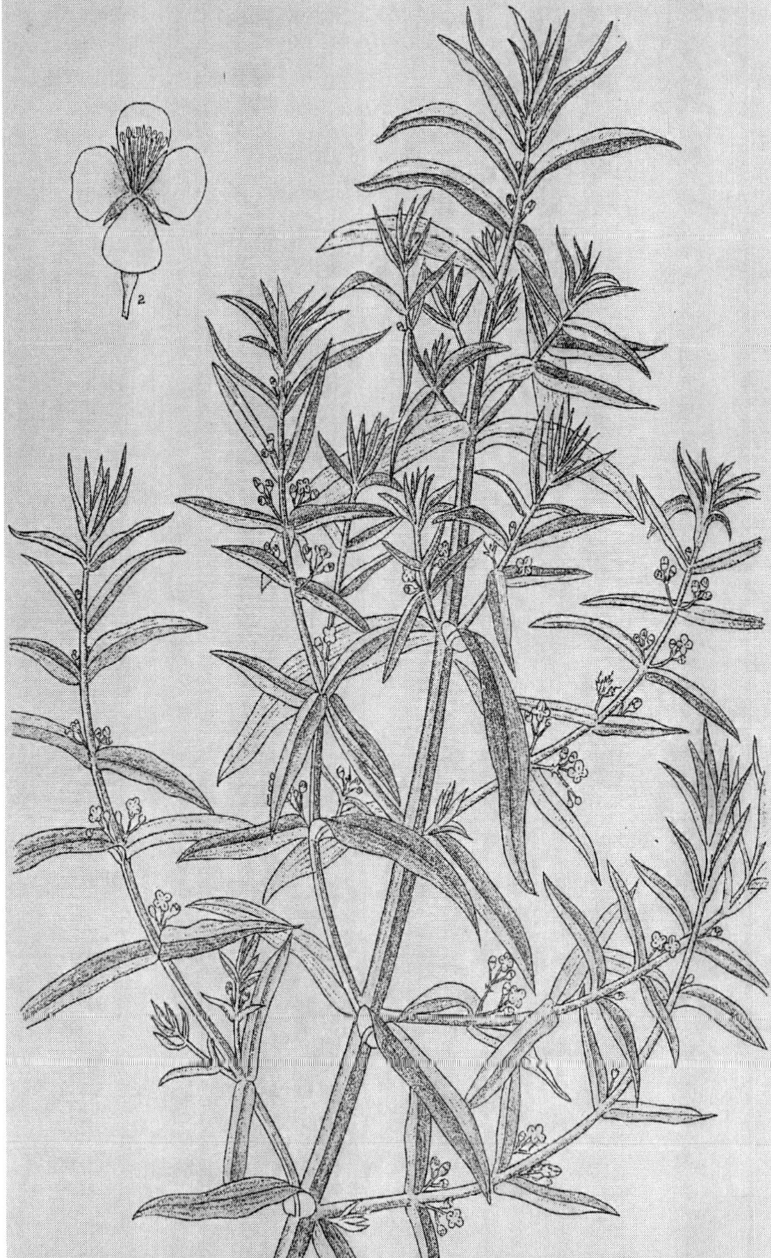

AMMANIA SENEGALENSIS, *LAMK.*

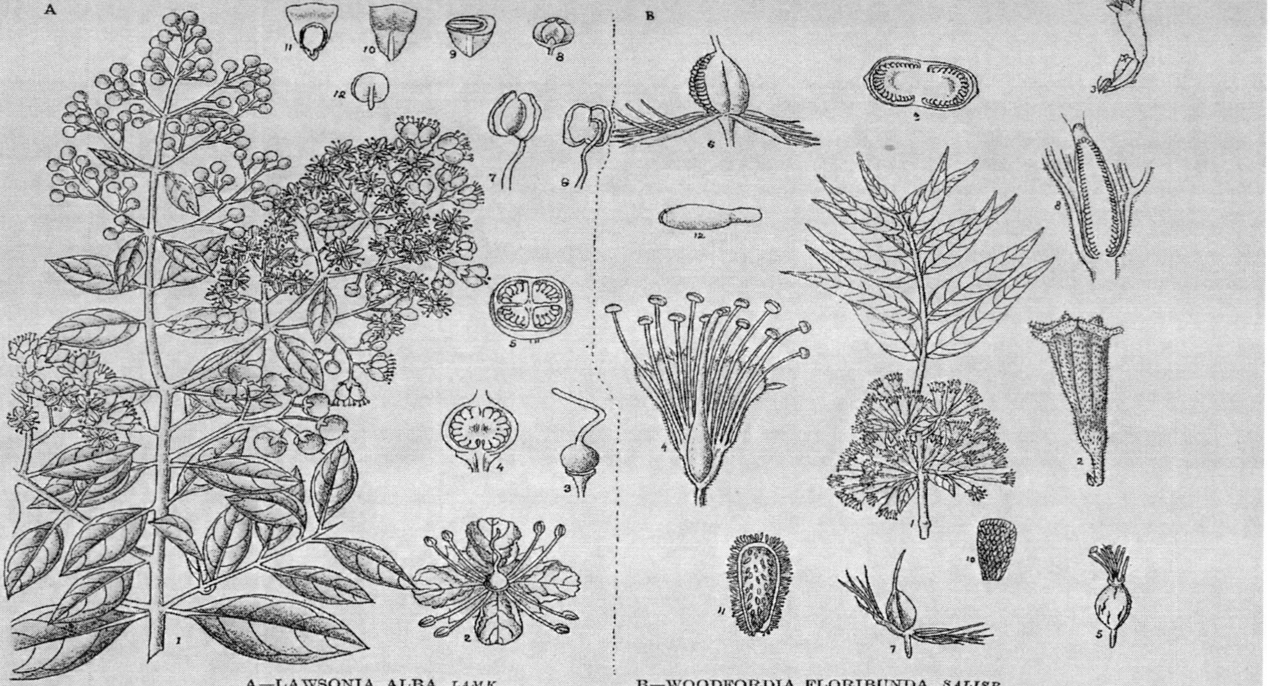

A—LAWSONIA ALBA, *LAMK.* B—WOODFORDIA FLORIBUNDA, *SALISB*

PLATE No. 433

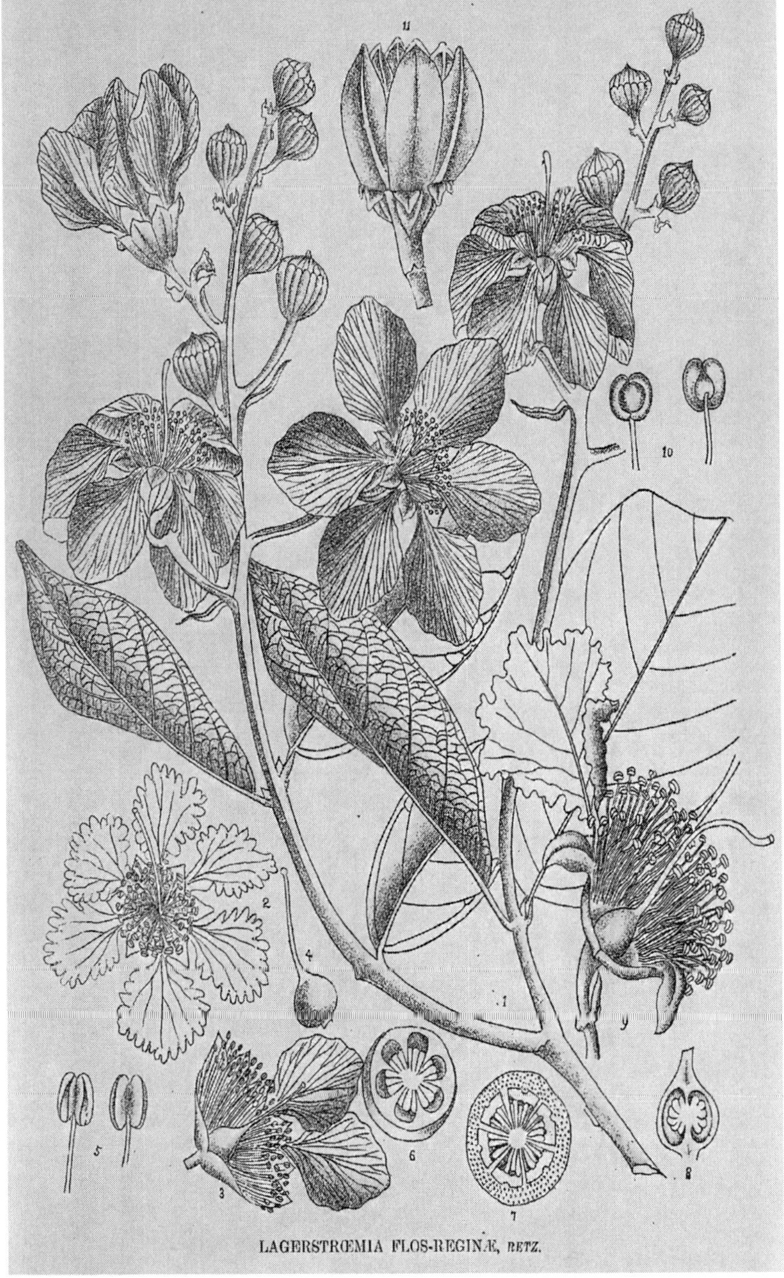

LAGERSTRŒMIA FLOS-REGINÆ, RETZ.

PLATE No. 434.

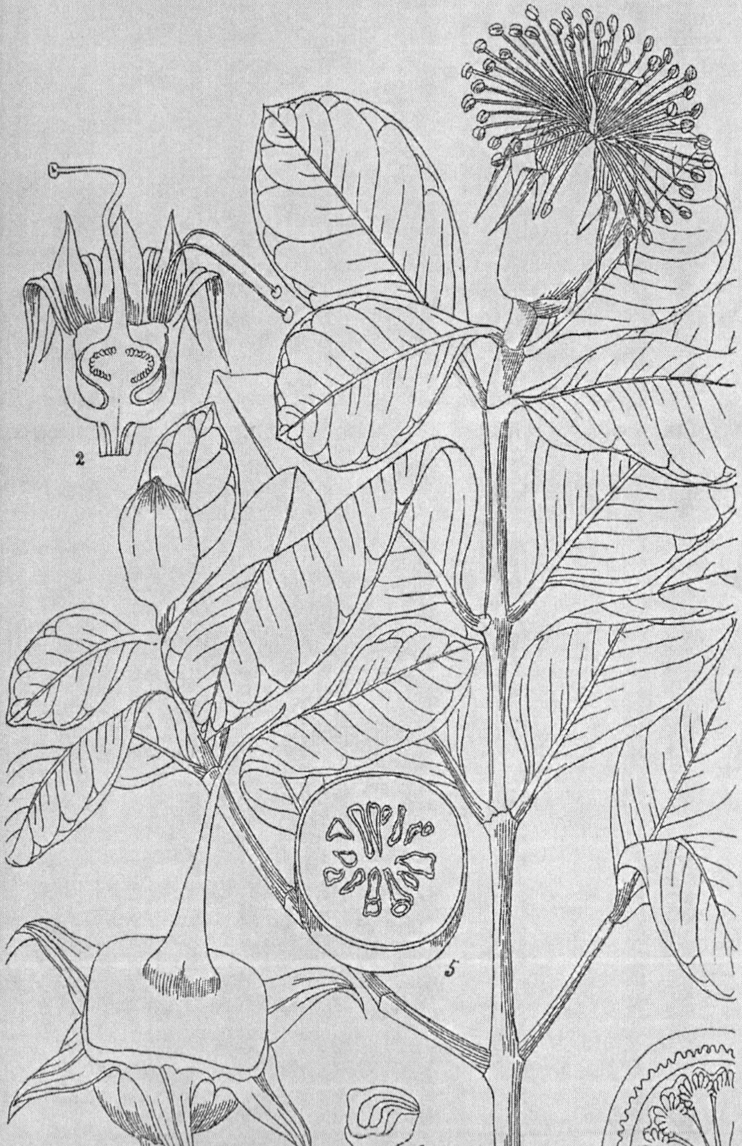

SONNERATIA ACIDA, *LINN. F.*

PLATE No 435.

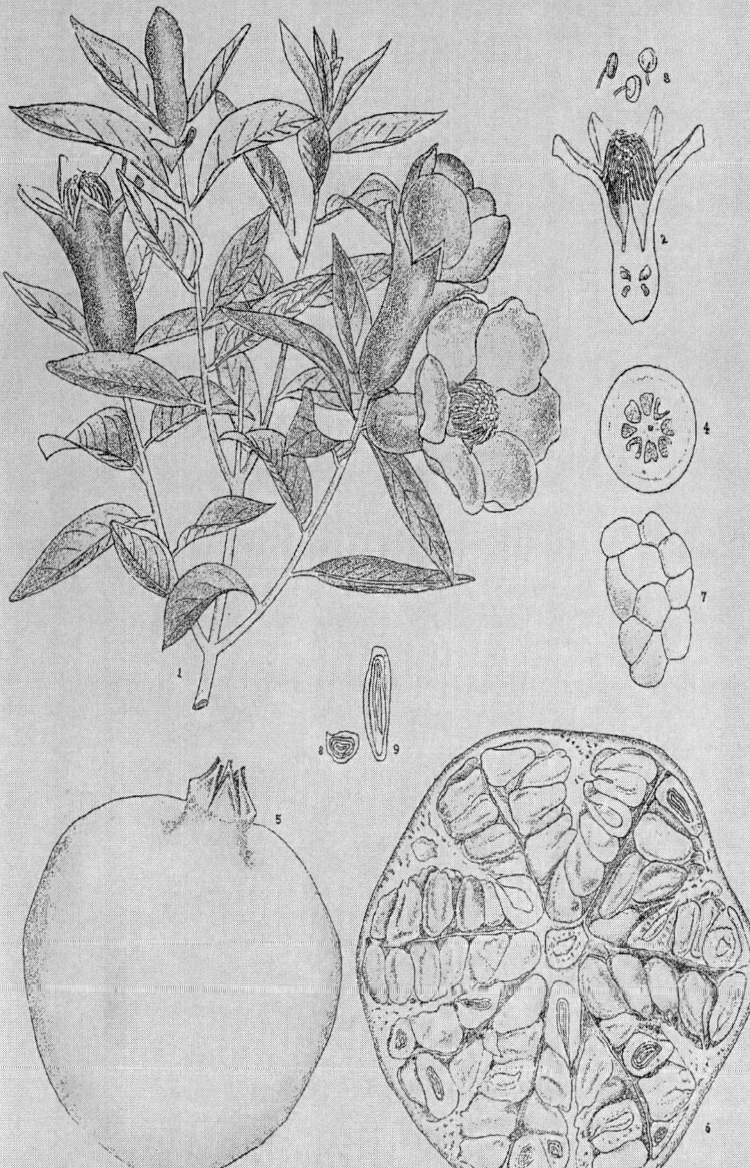

PUNICA GRANATUM, *Linn.*

PLATE No. 436.

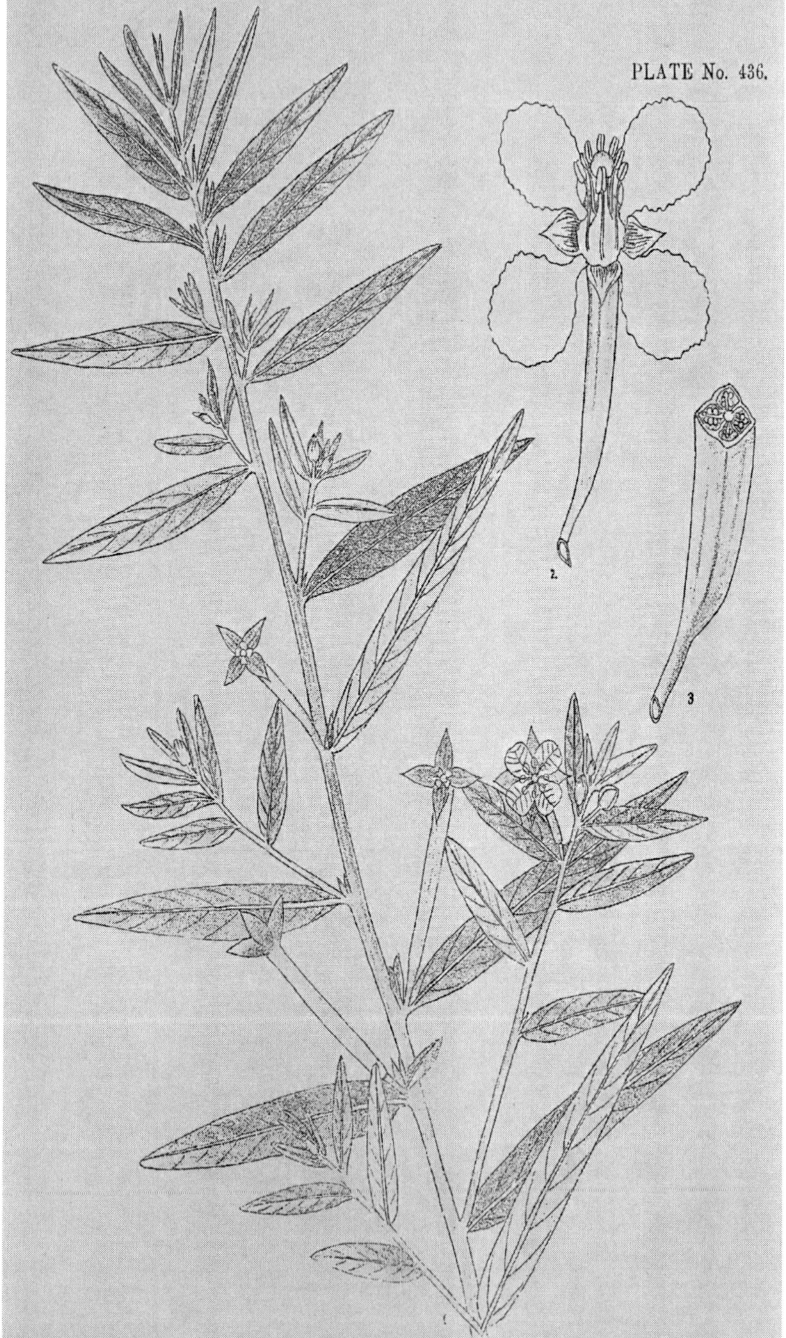

JUSSIÆA SUFFRUTICOSA, *LINN.*

PLATE No. 437.

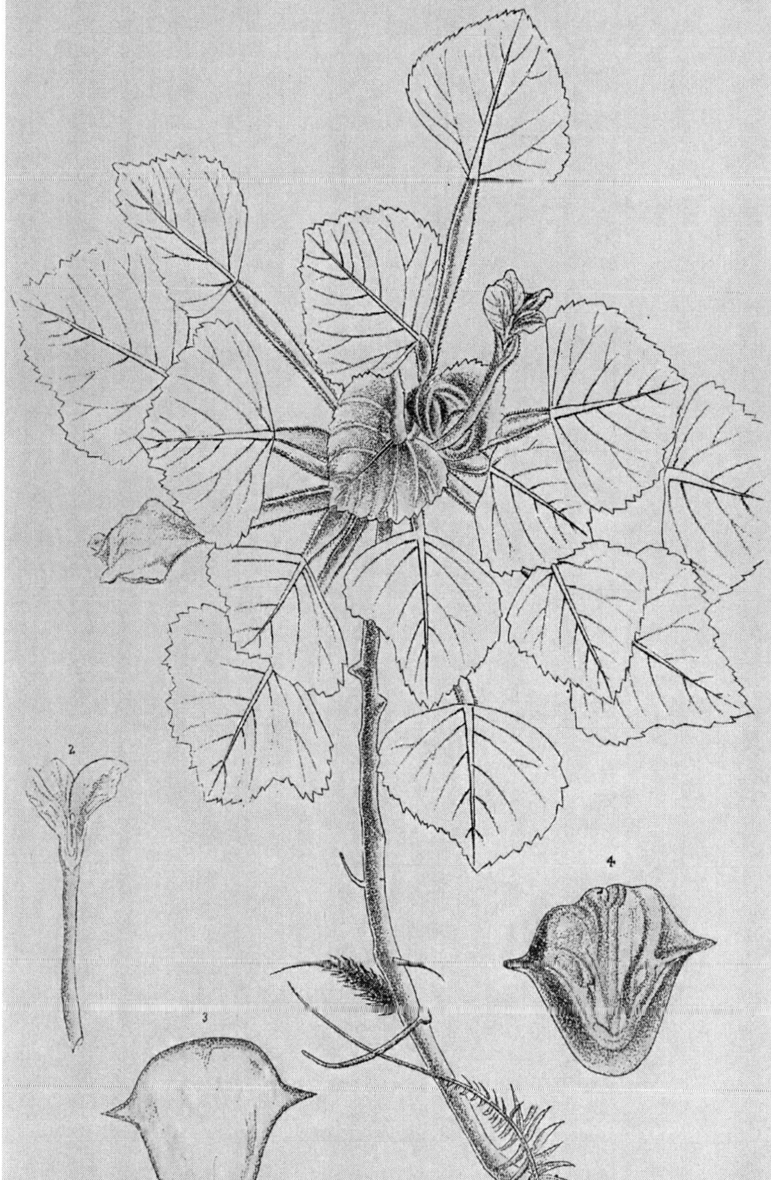

TRAPA BISPINOSA, ROXB.

PLATE No. 438.

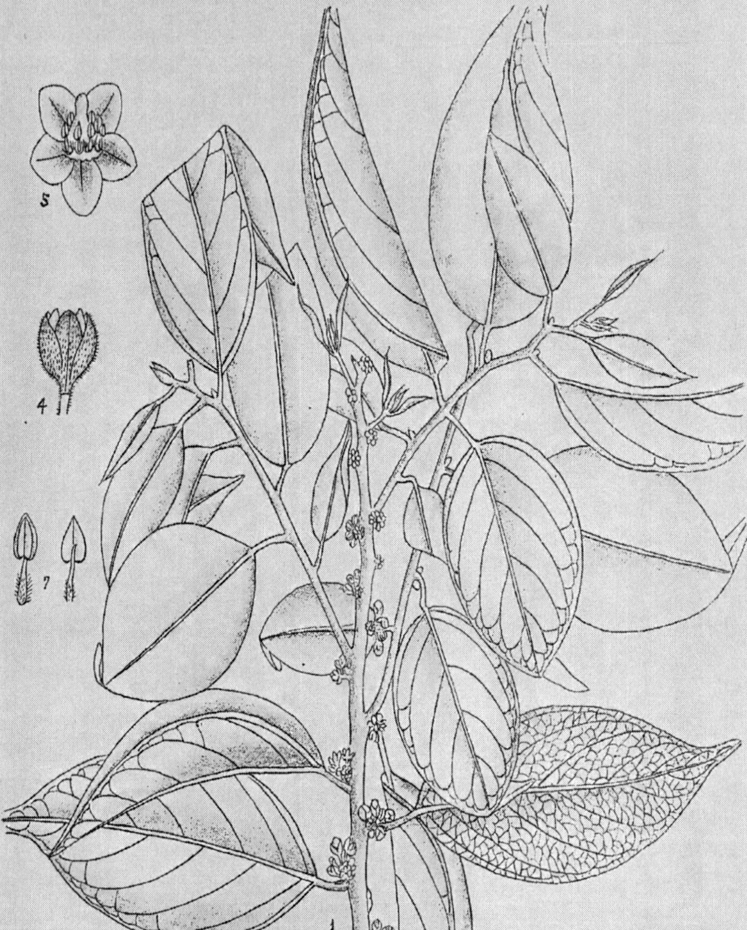

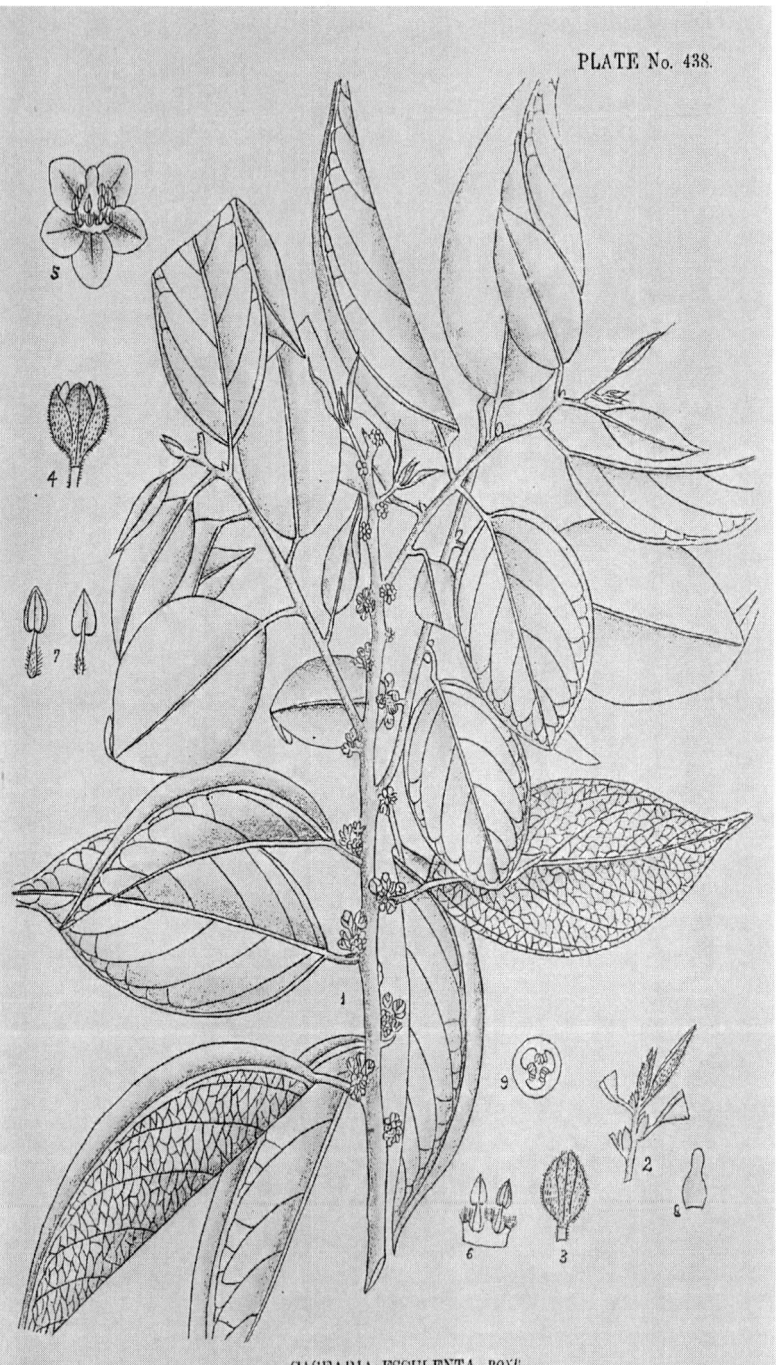

CASEARIA ESCULENTA, *ROXB.*

PLATE No. 439.

CASEARIA TOMENTOSA, *ROXB.*

PLATE No. 440.

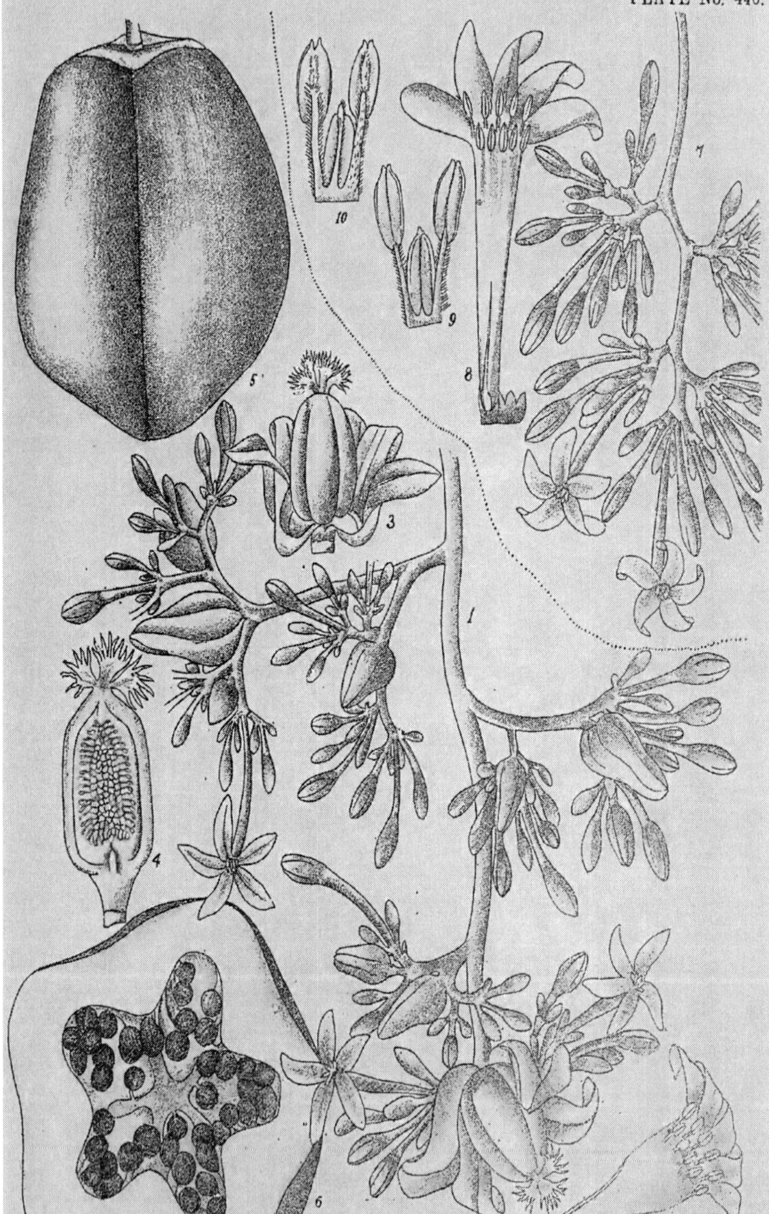

CARICA PAPAYA, *Linn.*

PLATE No. 441.

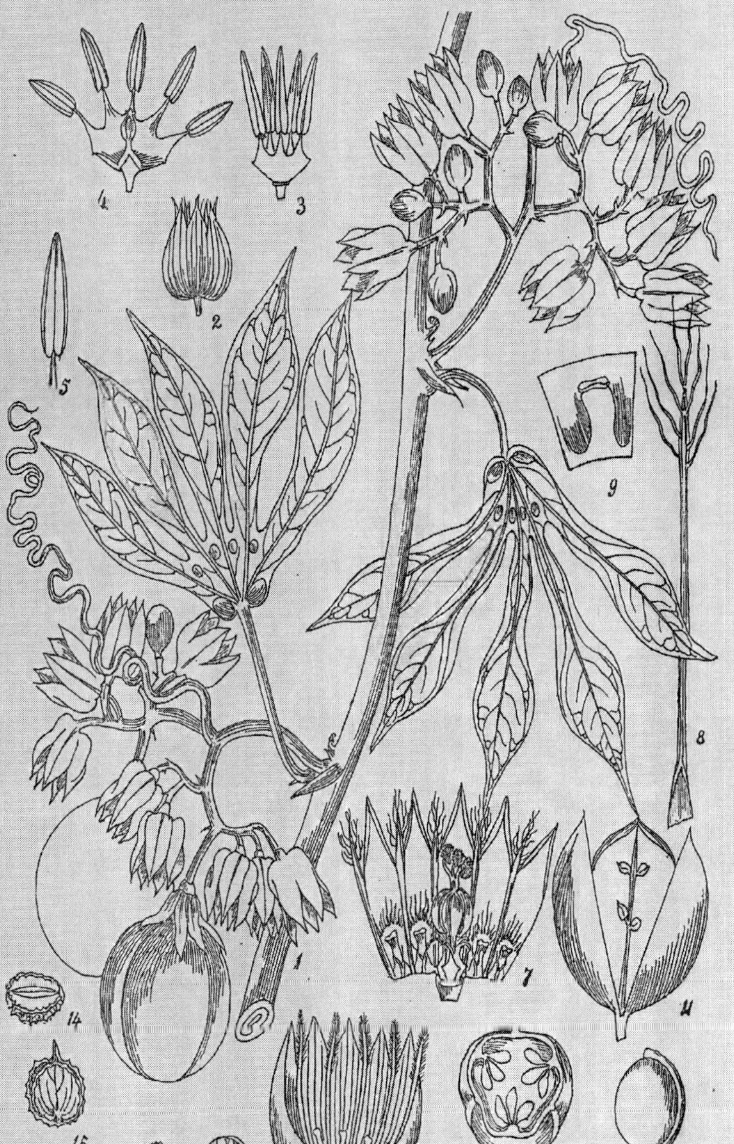

MODECCA PALMATA, LAM.

PLATE No 442.

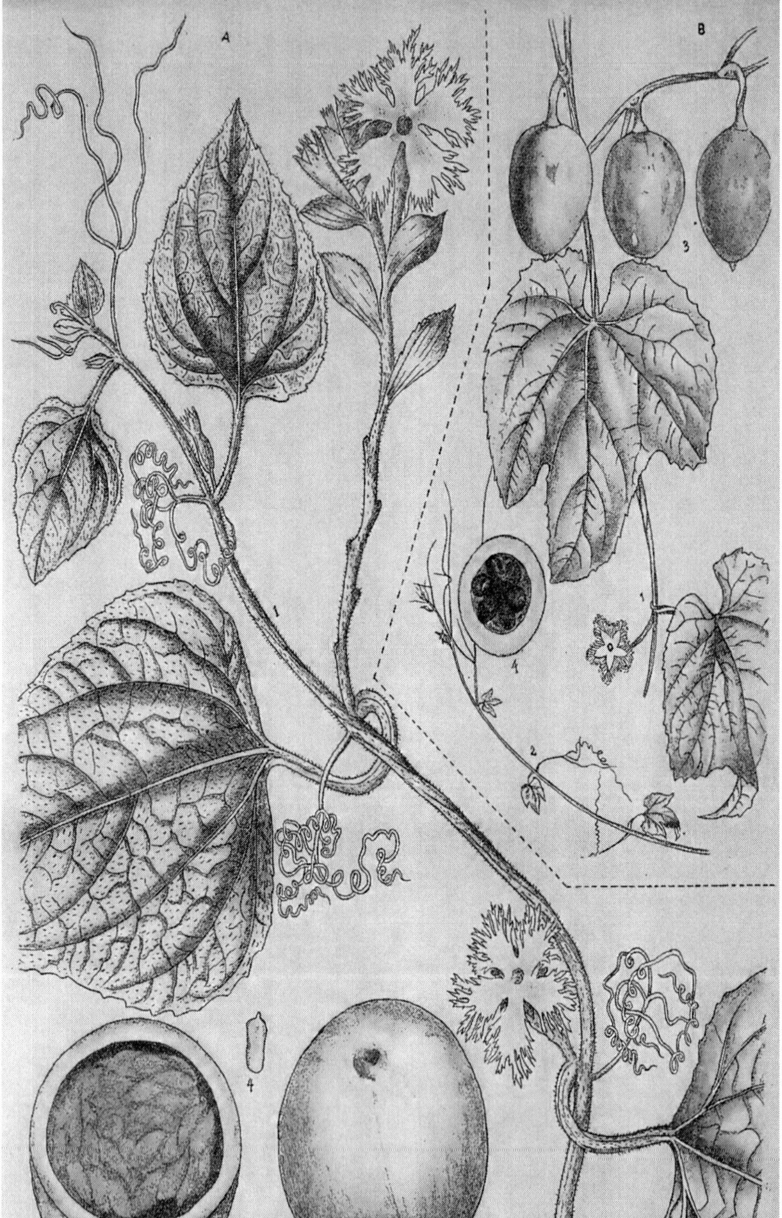

A—TRICHOSANTHES OORDATA, ROXB. B—T. PALMATA, ROXB.

PLATE No. 443.

TRICHOSANTHIS DIOICA, ROXB.

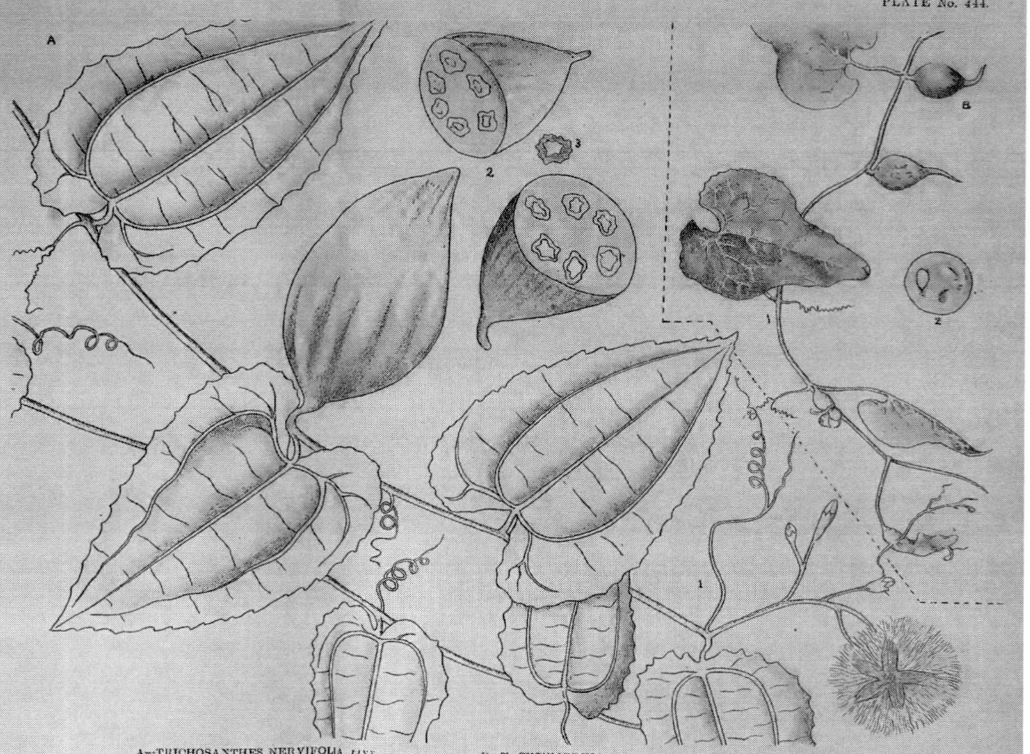

A—TRICHOSANTHES NERVIFOLIA, *Linn.* B—T. CUCUMERINA, *Linn.*

PLATE No. 445.

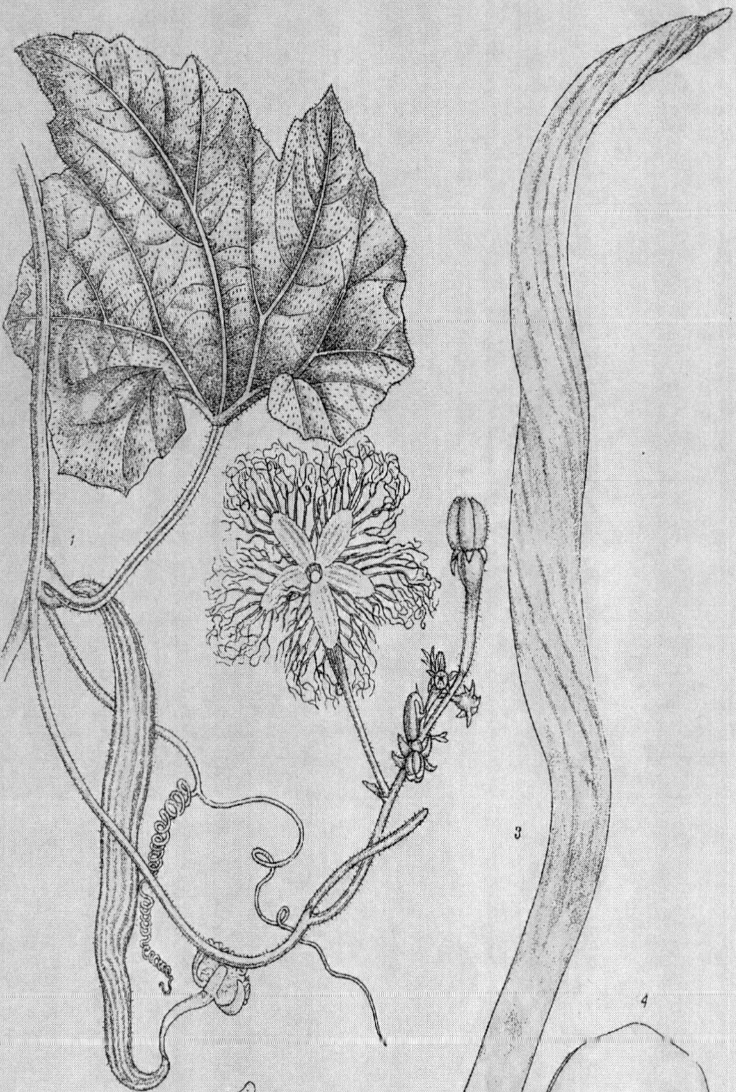

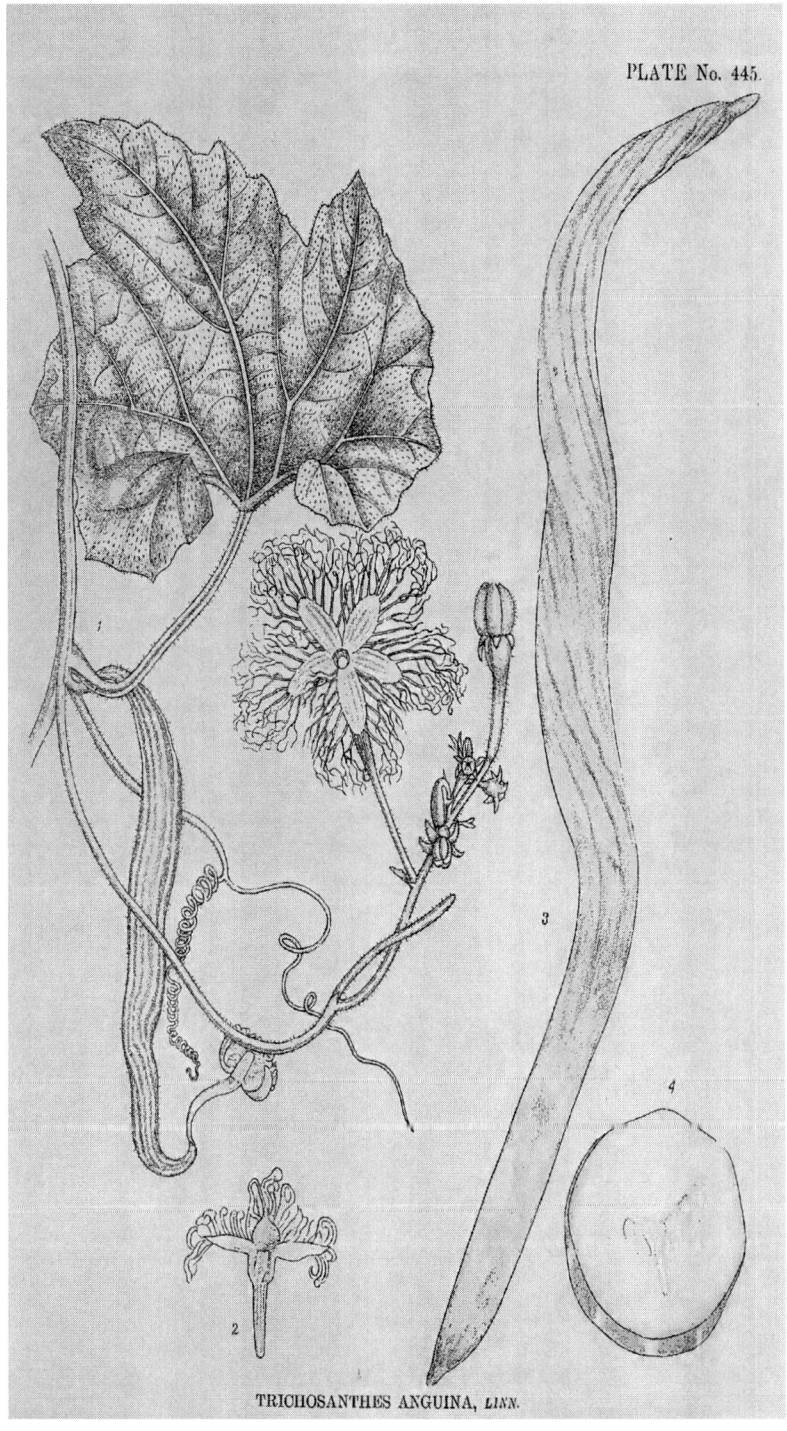

TRICHOSANTHES ANGUINA, *LINN.*

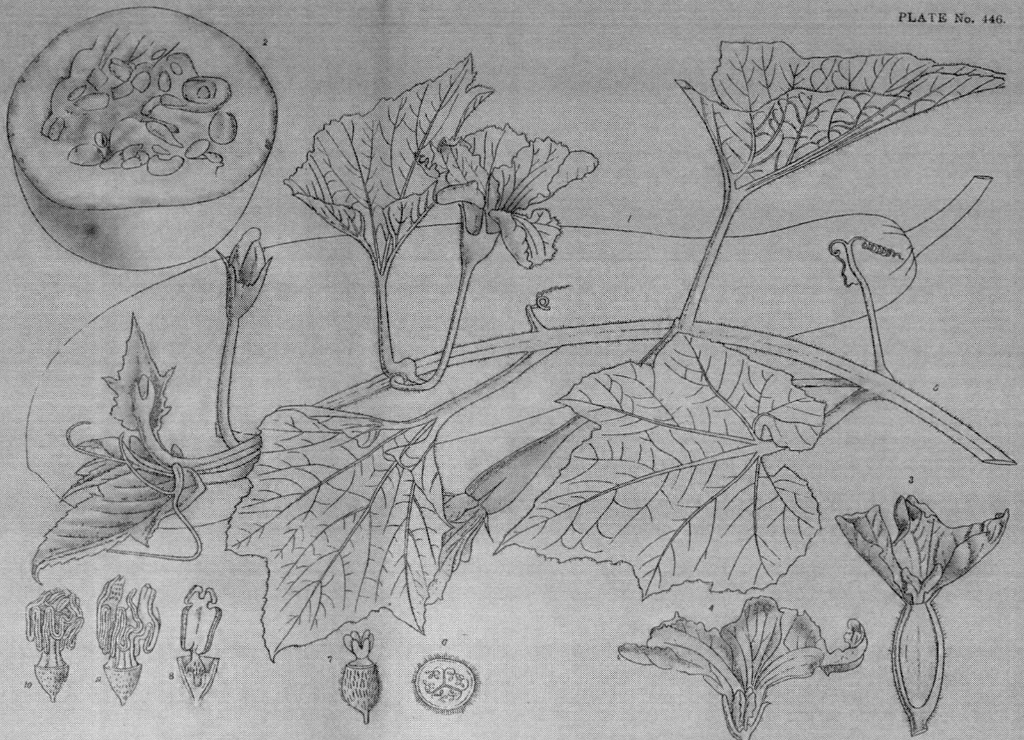

LAGENARIA VULGARIS, *Seringe.*

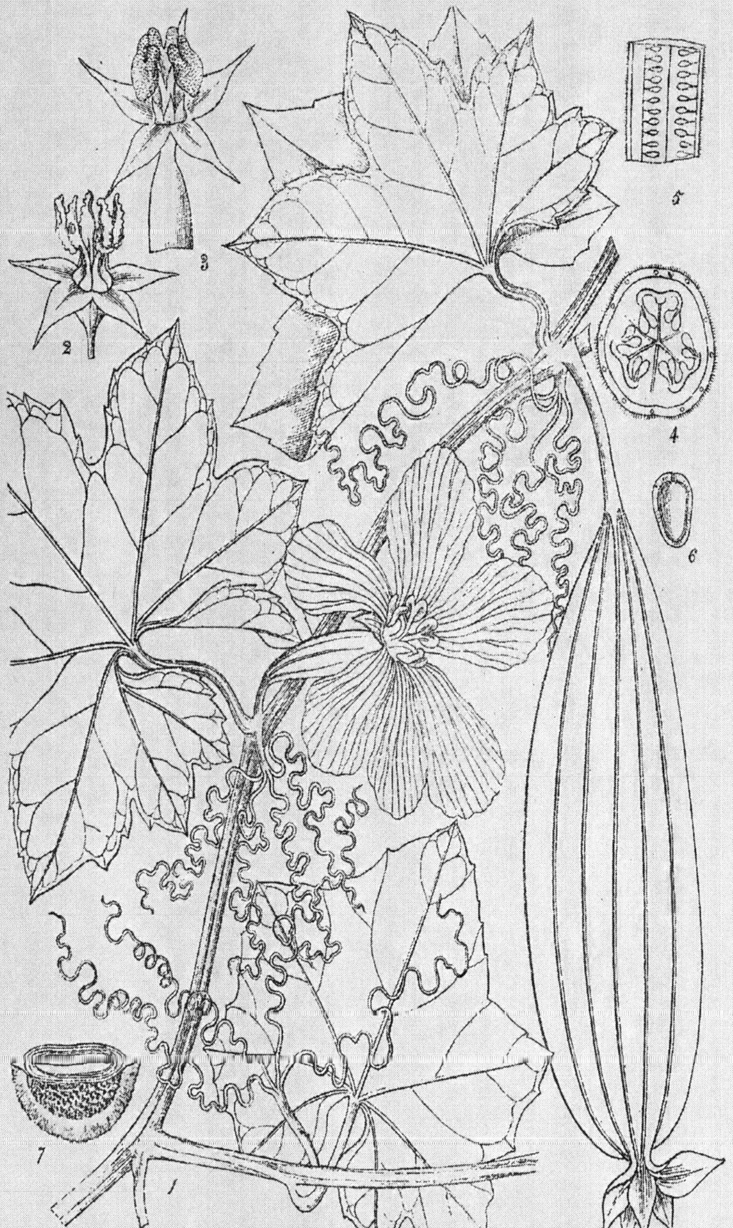

LUFFA ÆGYPTIACA, MILL.

PLATE No. 448.

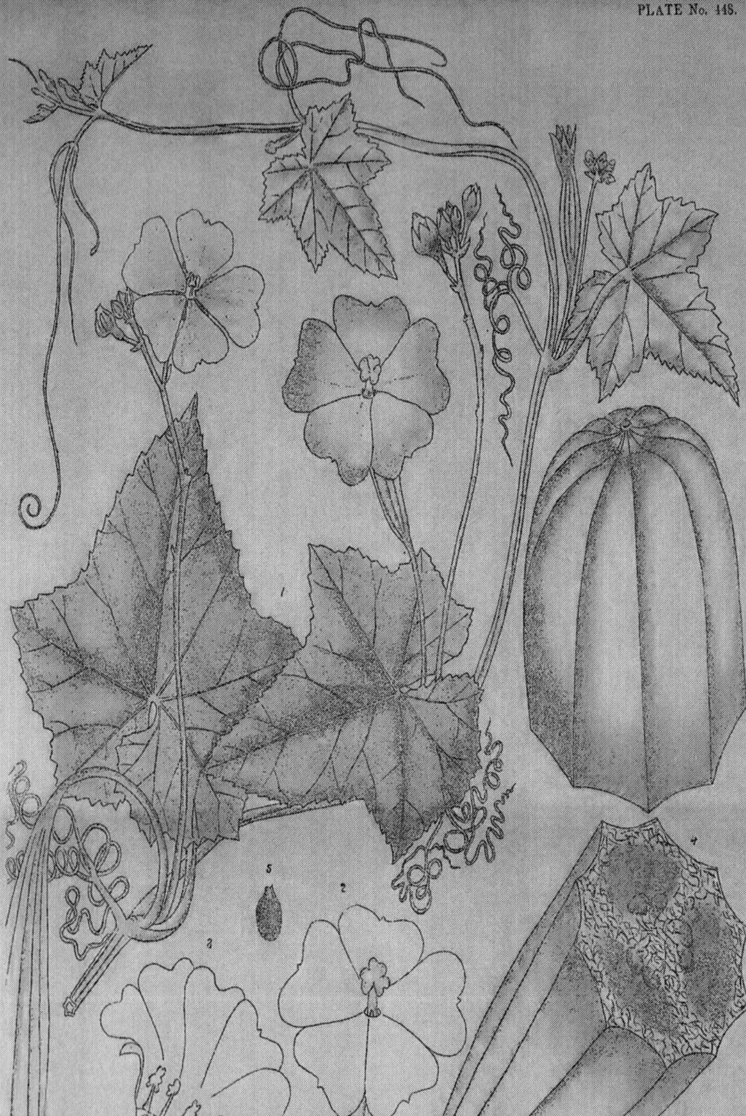

LUFFA ACUTANGULA, ROXB.

PLATE No. 449.

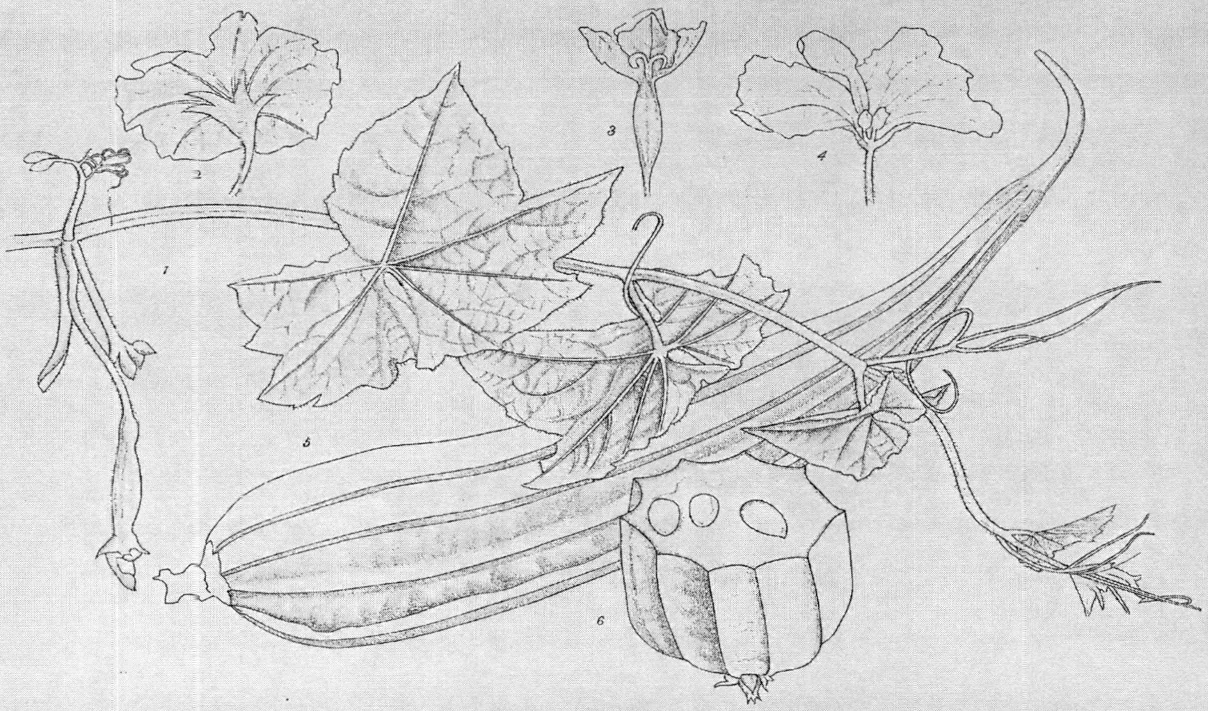

LUFFA ACUTANGULA, *ROXB.*

PLATE No. 450.

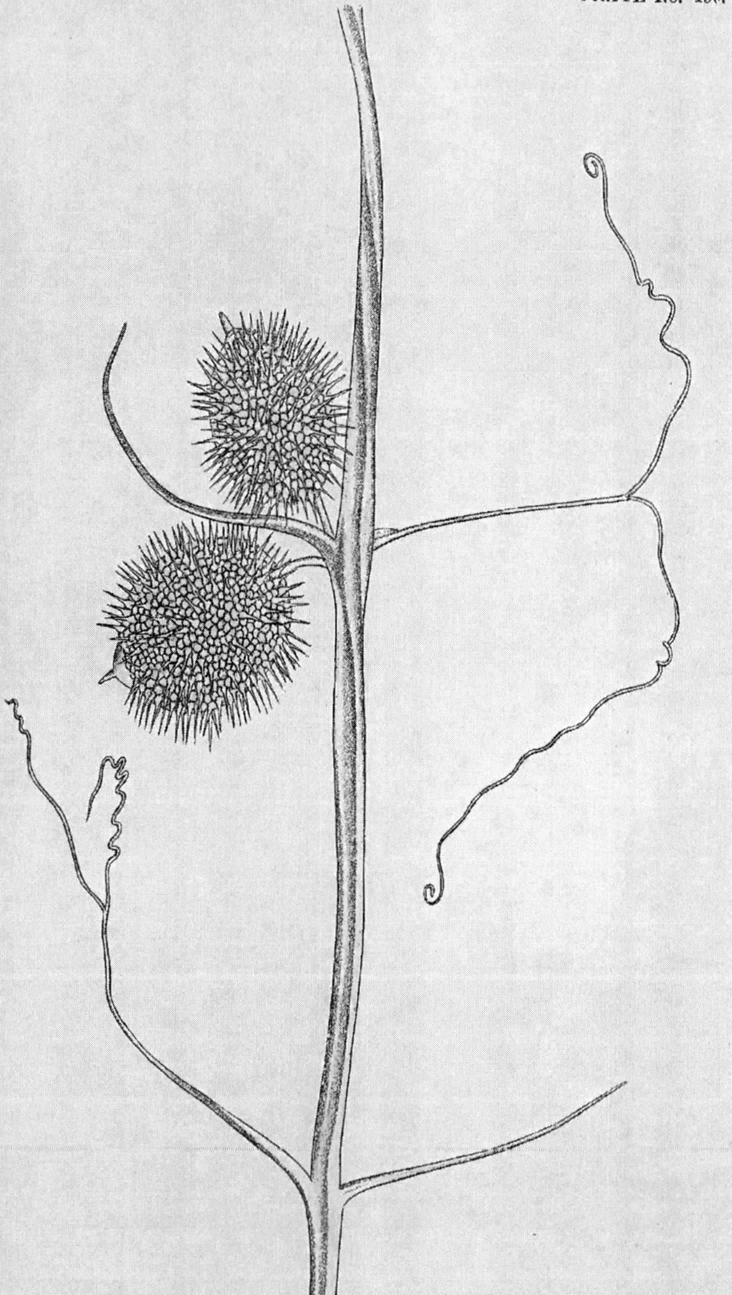

LUFFA ECHINATA, *ROXB.*

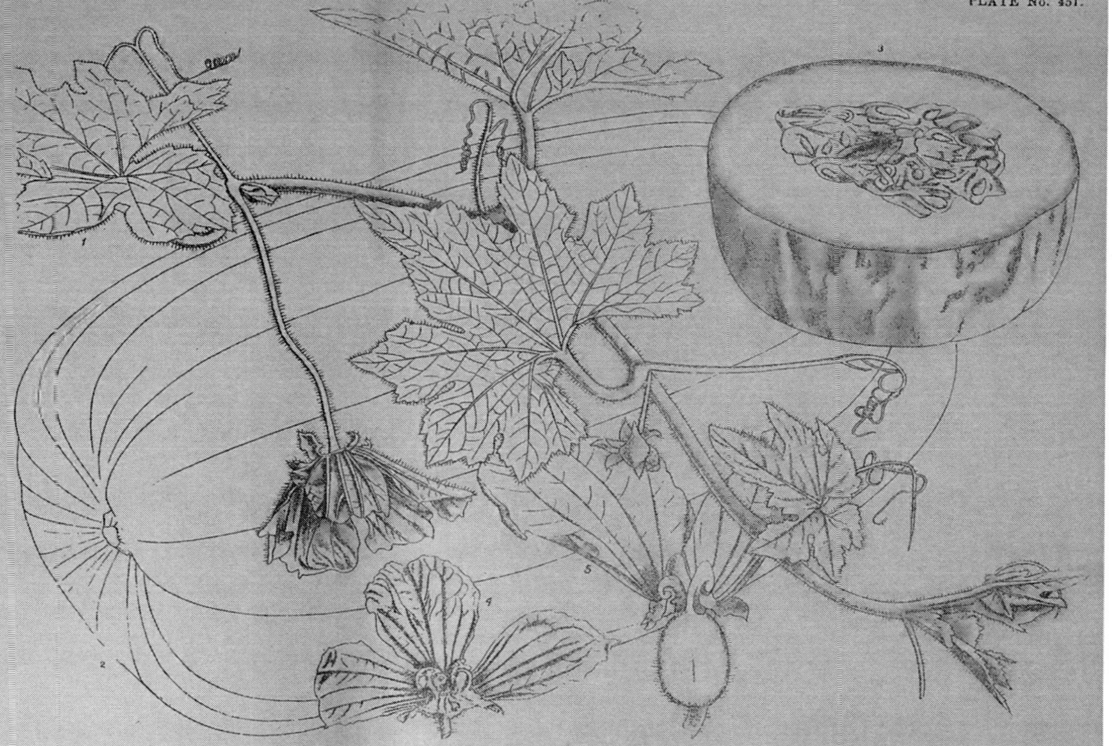

BENINCASA CERIFERA, *Savi.*

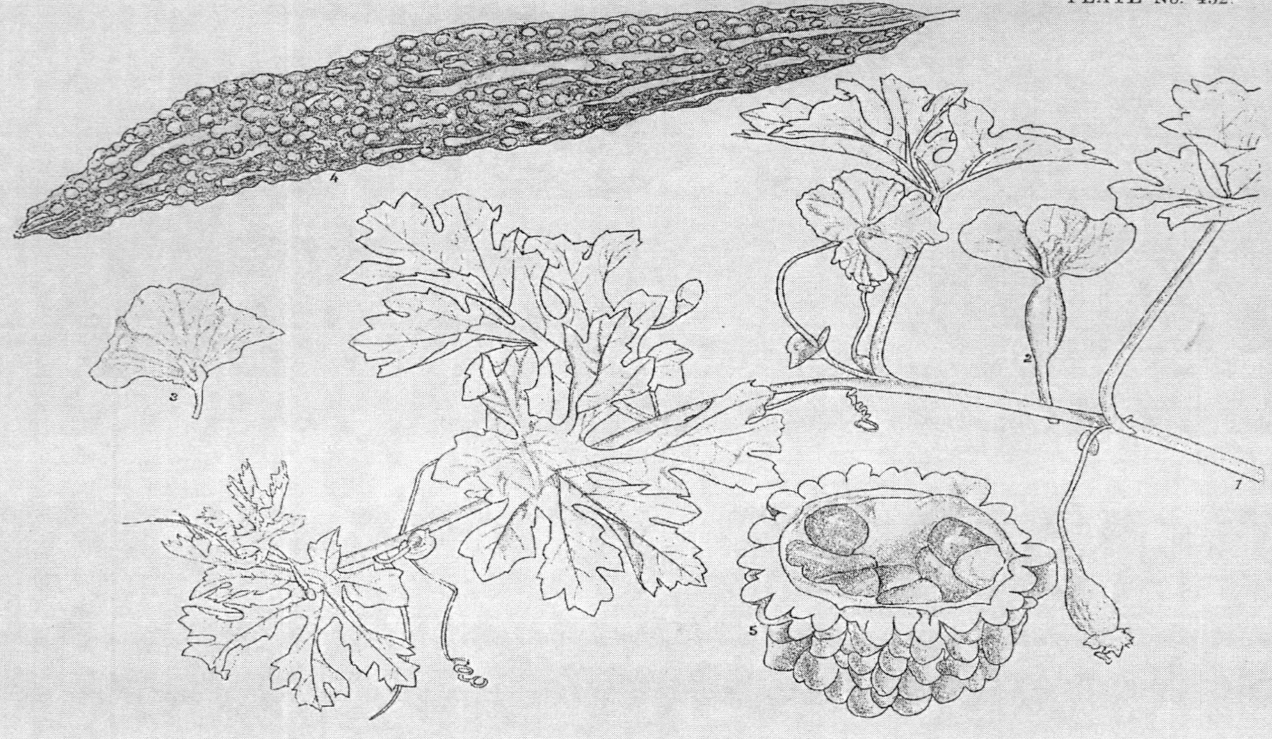

MOMORDICA CHARANTIA, *Linn.*

PLATE No. 453.

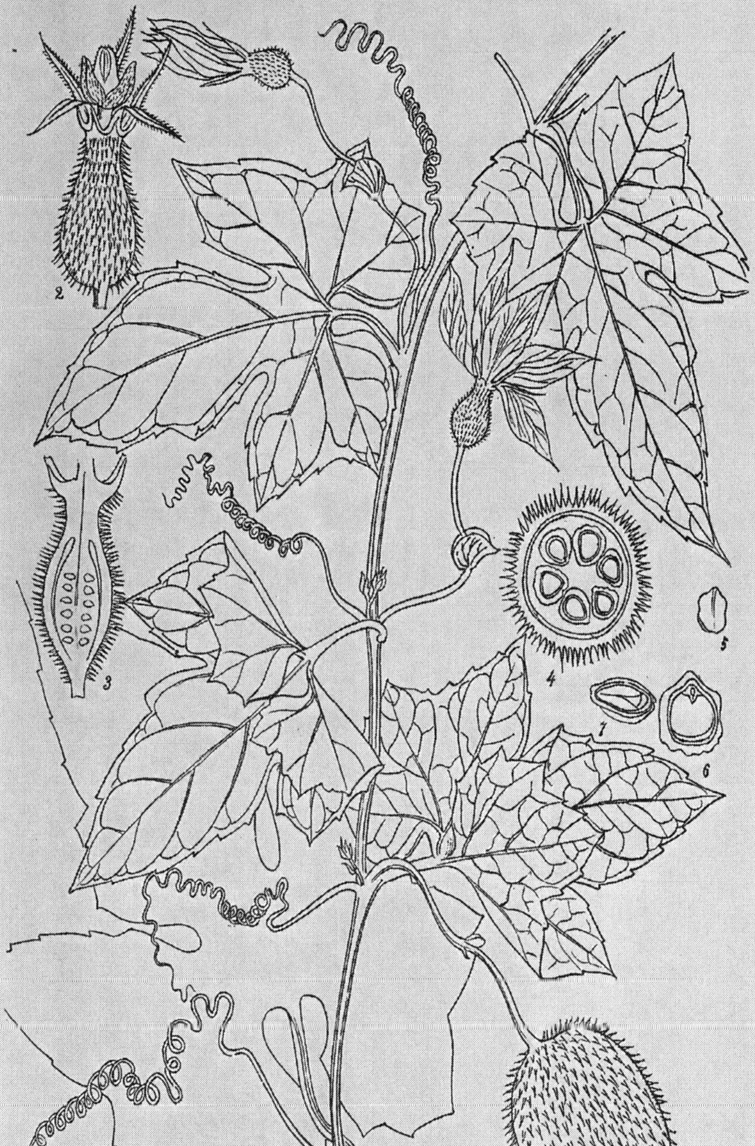

MOMORDICA DIOICA, ROXB.

PLATE No. 454.

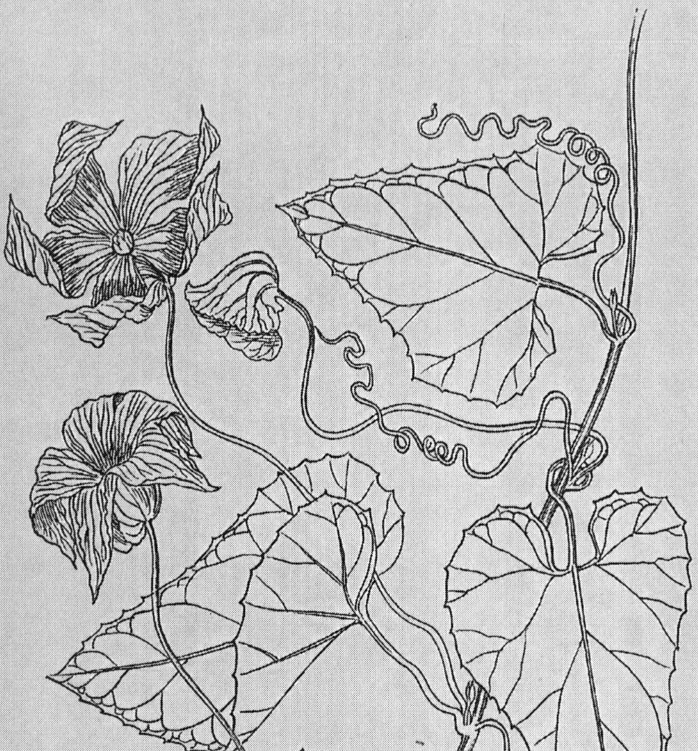

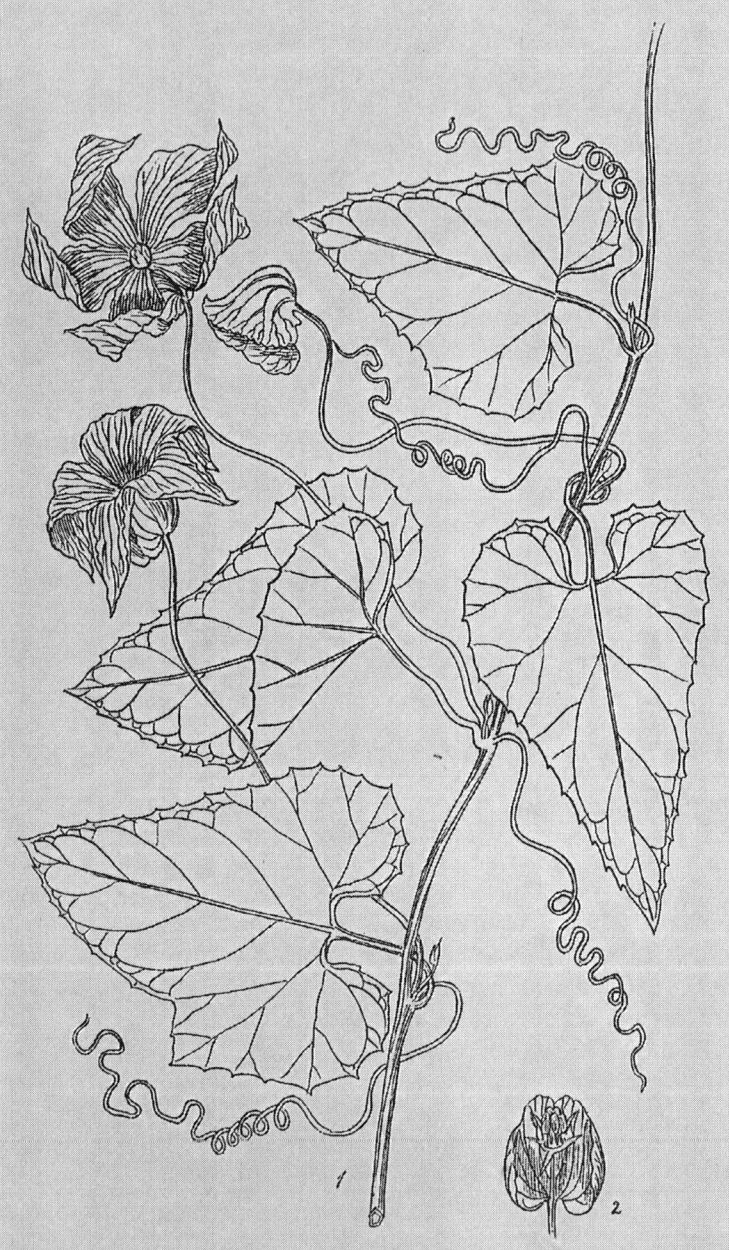

MOMORDICA DIOICA, ROXB.

PLATE No. 455

A—MOMORDICA COCHINCHINENSIS, *SPRENG.* B—M. CYMBALARIA, *FENZL.*

CUCUMIS TRIGONUS, *ROXB.*

PLATE No. 457.

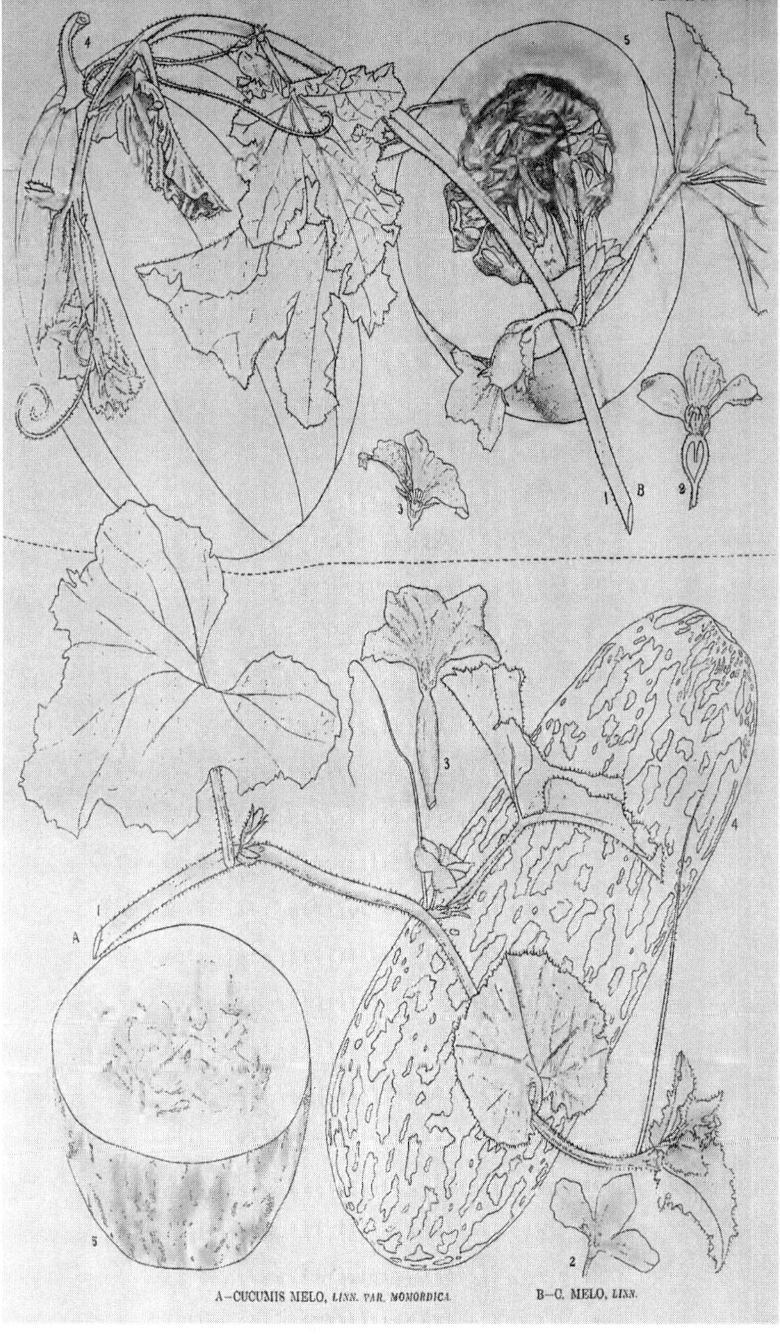

A—CUCUMIS MELO, *LINN. VAR. MOMORDICA.* B—C. MELO, *LINN.*

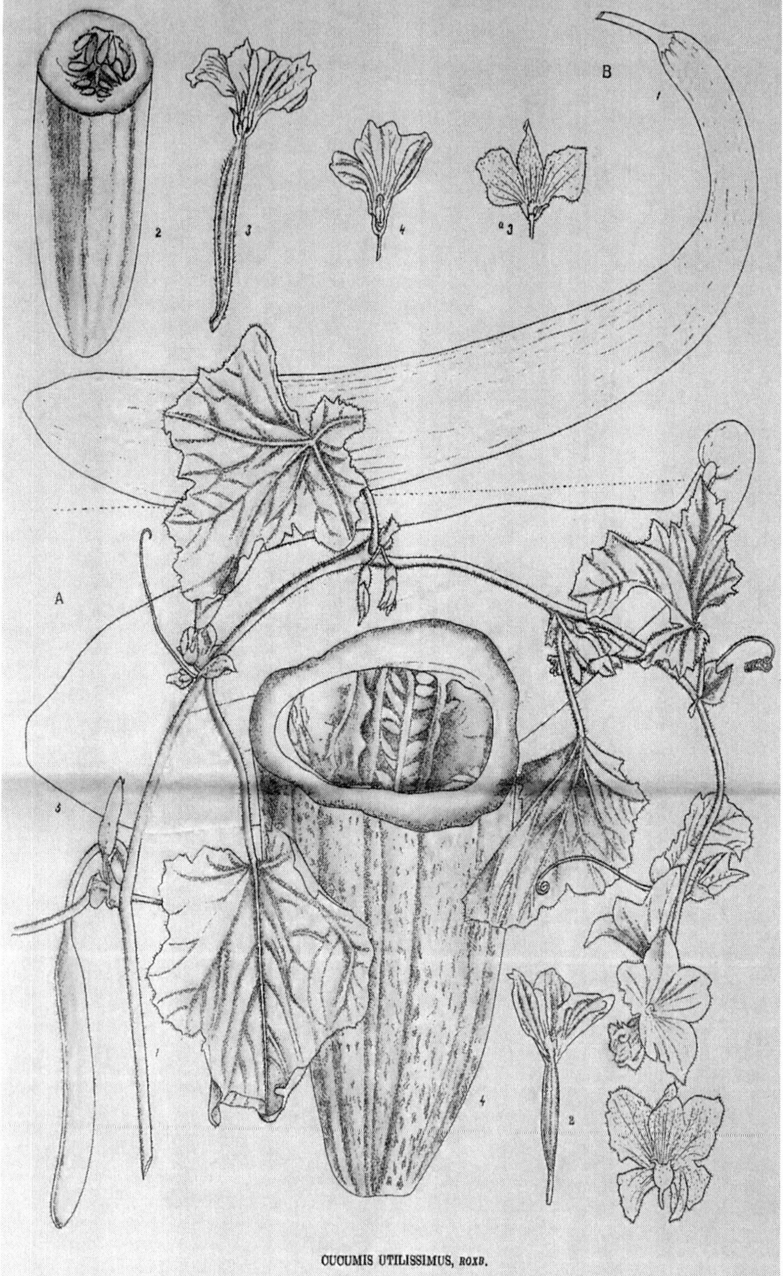

CUCUMIS UTILISSIMUS, ROXB.

PLATE No. 459.

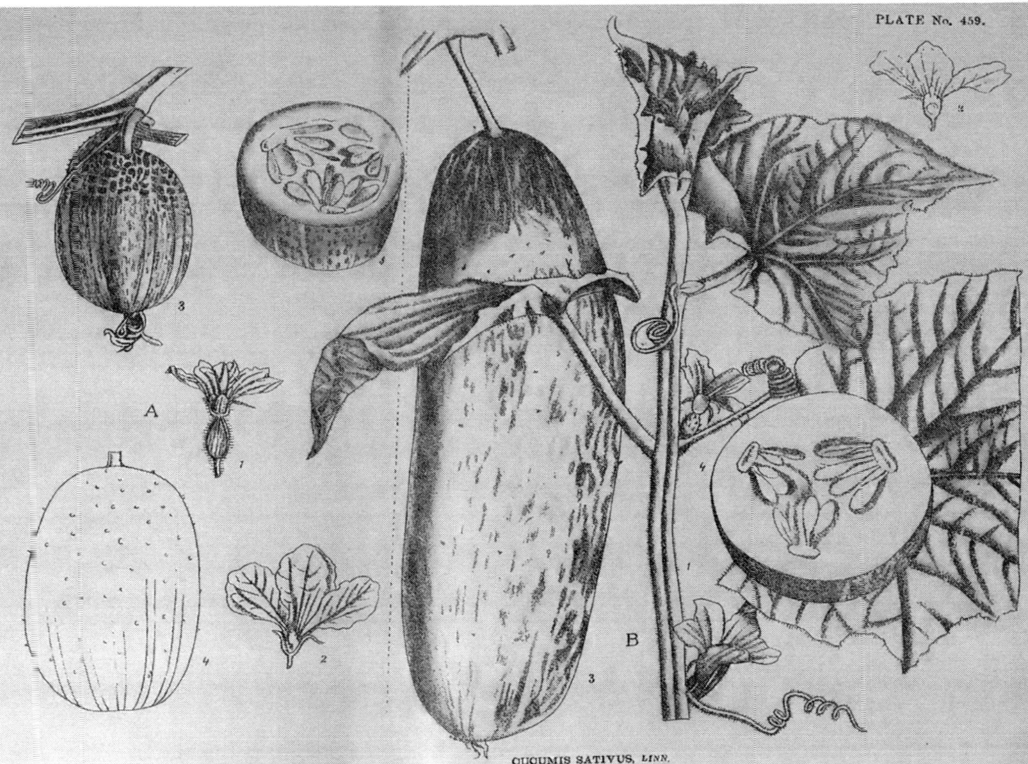

CUCUMIS SATIVUS, *Linn.*

PLATE No. 460.

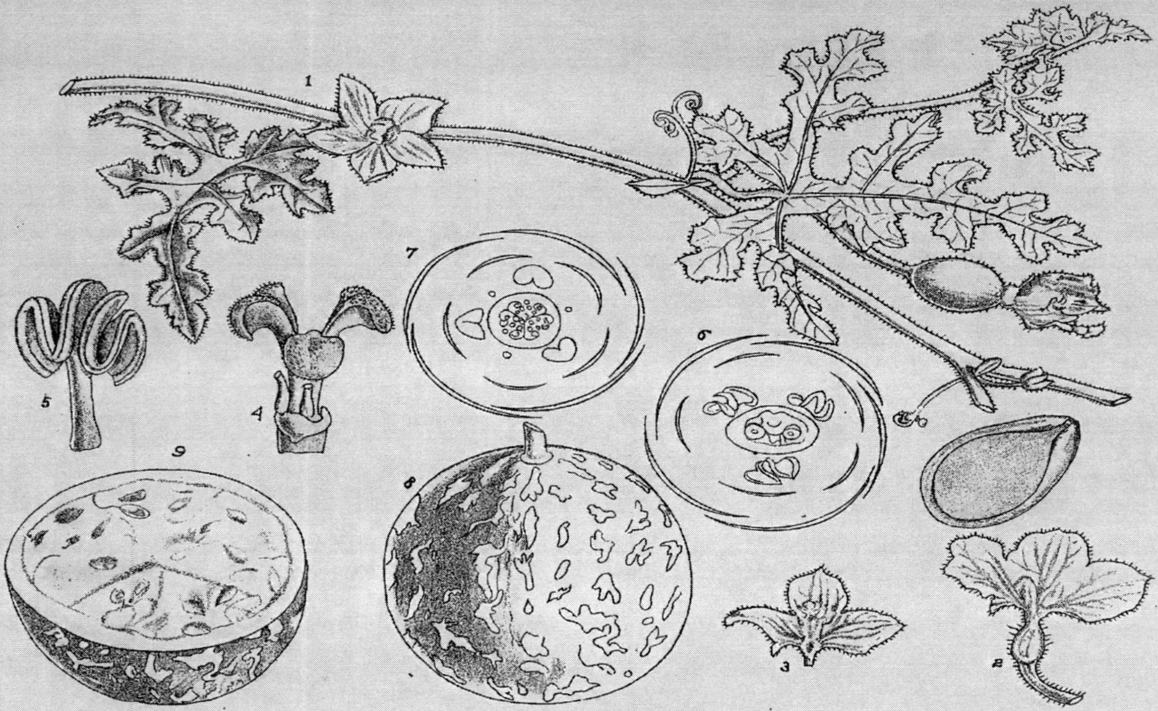

CITRULLUS COLOCYNTHIS, *SCHRAD.*

PLATE No. 461.

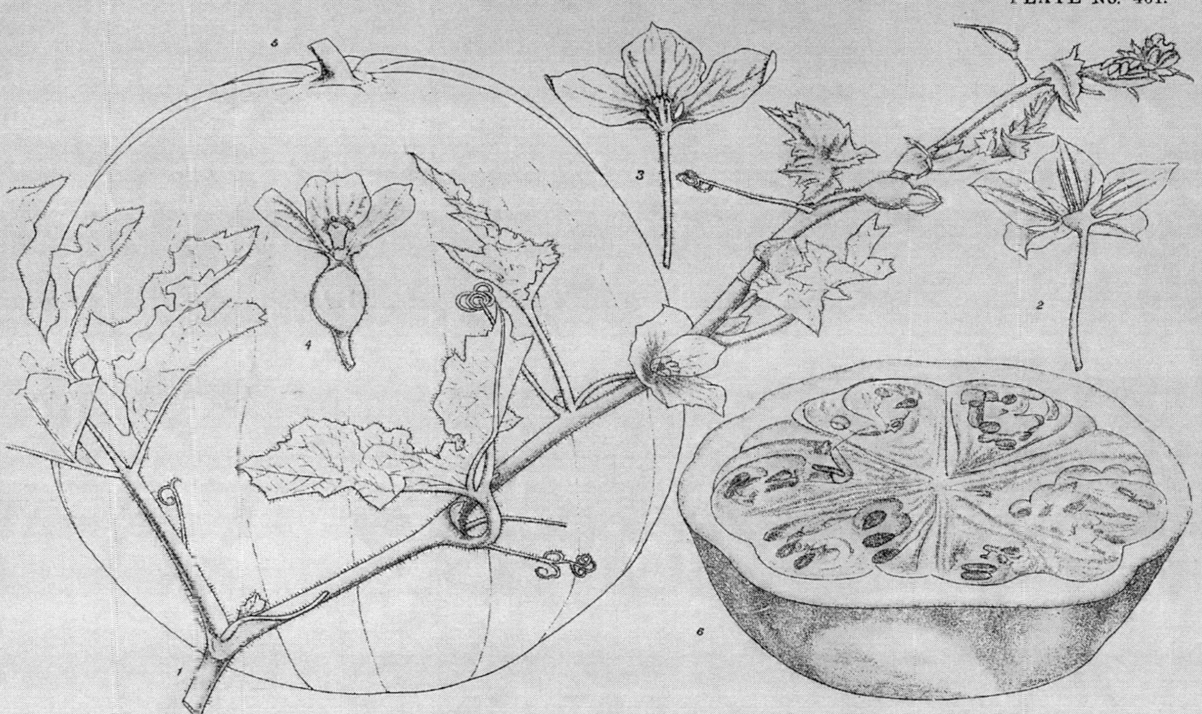

CITRULLUS VULGARIS, *SCHRAD.*

PLATE No. 461A.

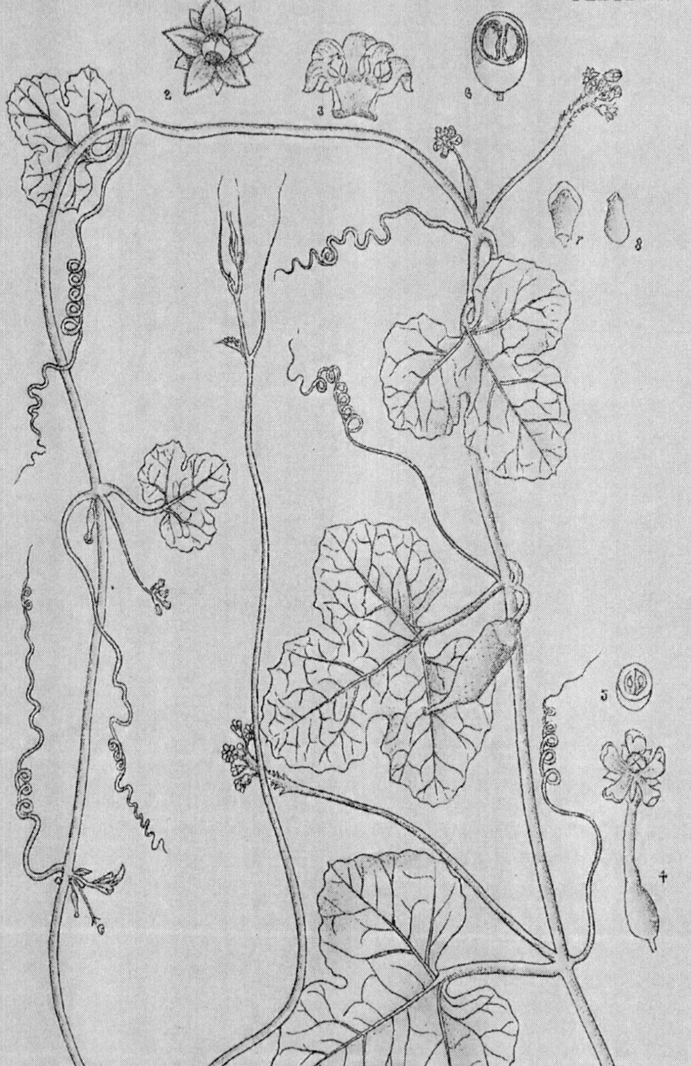

CORALLOCARPUS EPIGÆA, *HK. F.*

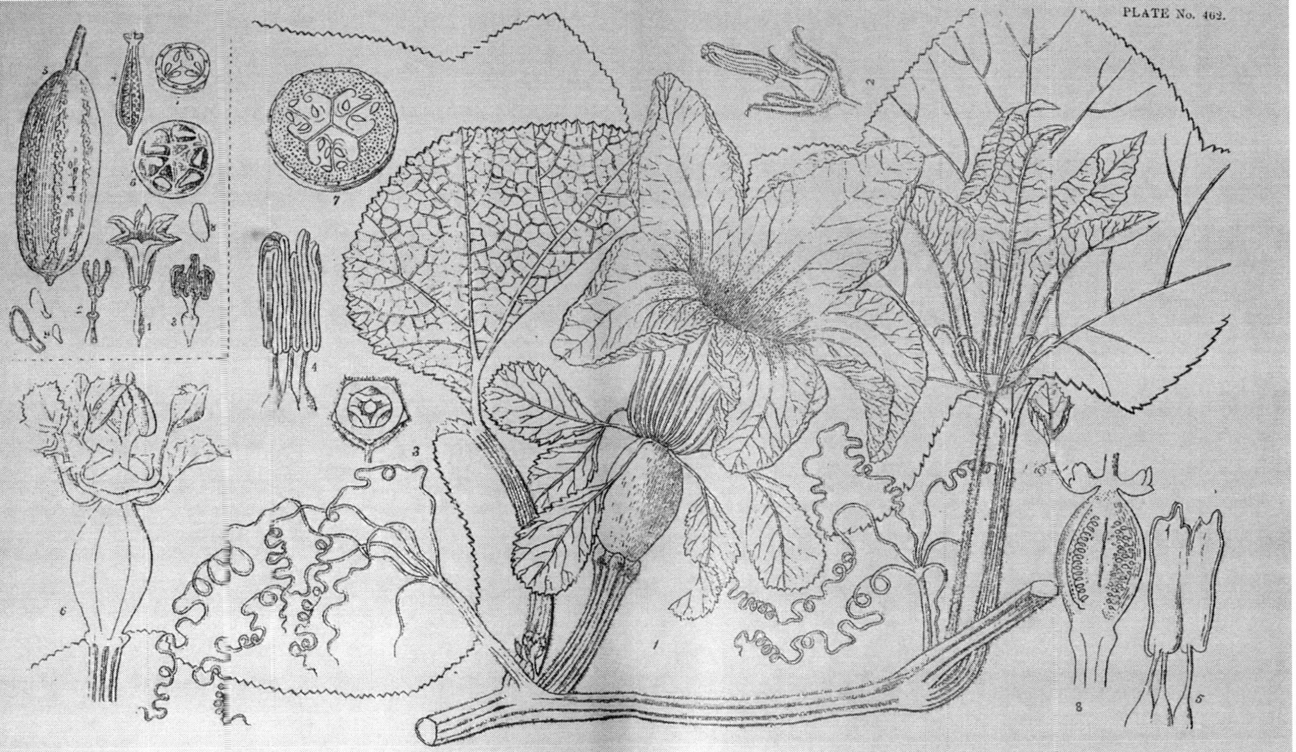

A.—CEPHALANDRA INDICA, *NAUD.* B—CUCURBITA MAXIMA, *DUCHESNE.*

PLATE No. 463.

CUCURBITA PEPO, *DC.*

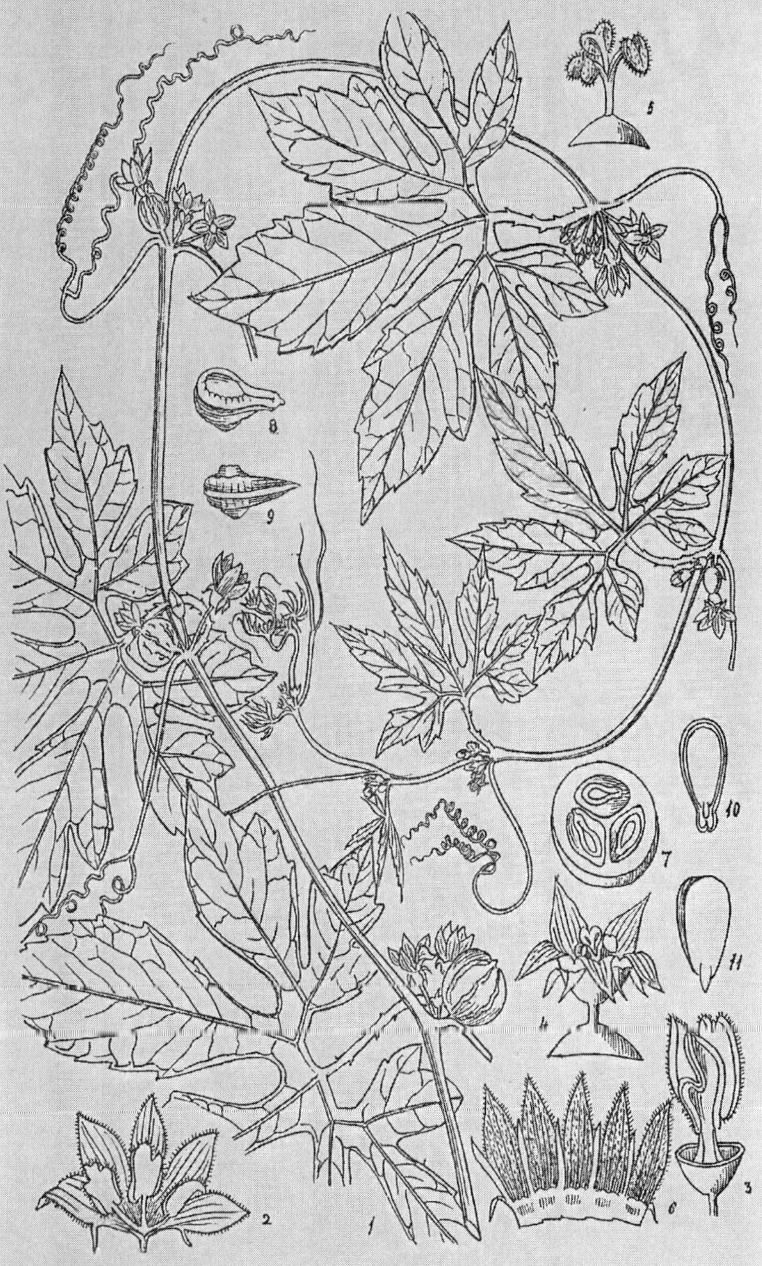

BRYONIA LACINIOSA, LINN.

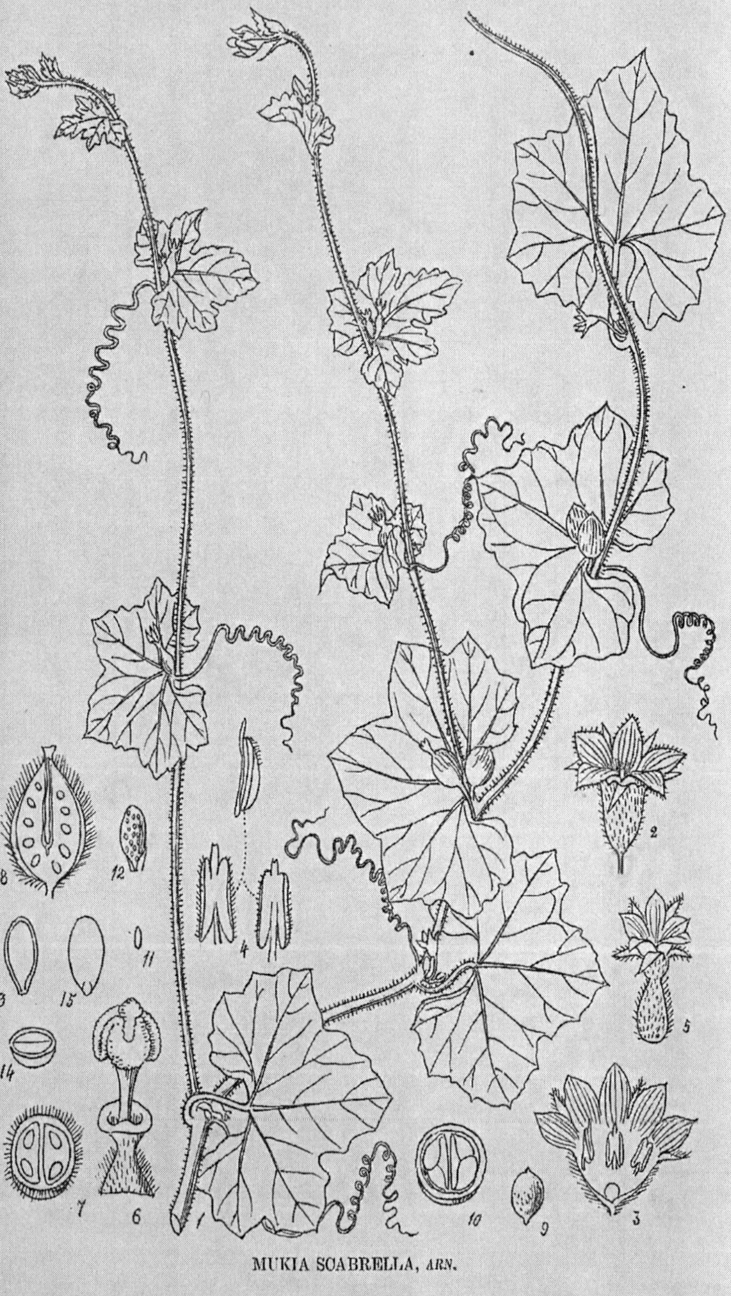

MUKIA SCABRELLA, ARN.

PLATE No. 466.

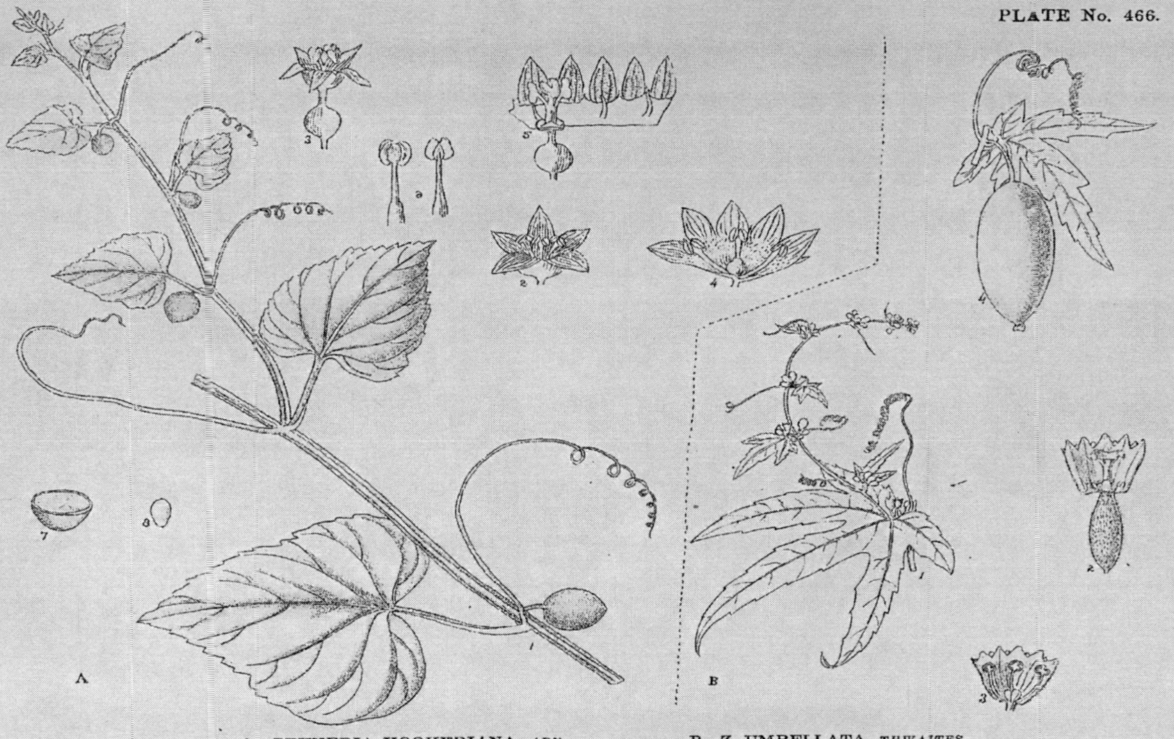

A—ZEHNERIA HOOKERIANA, *ARN.* B—Z. UMBELLATA, *THWAITES.*

PLATE No 467.

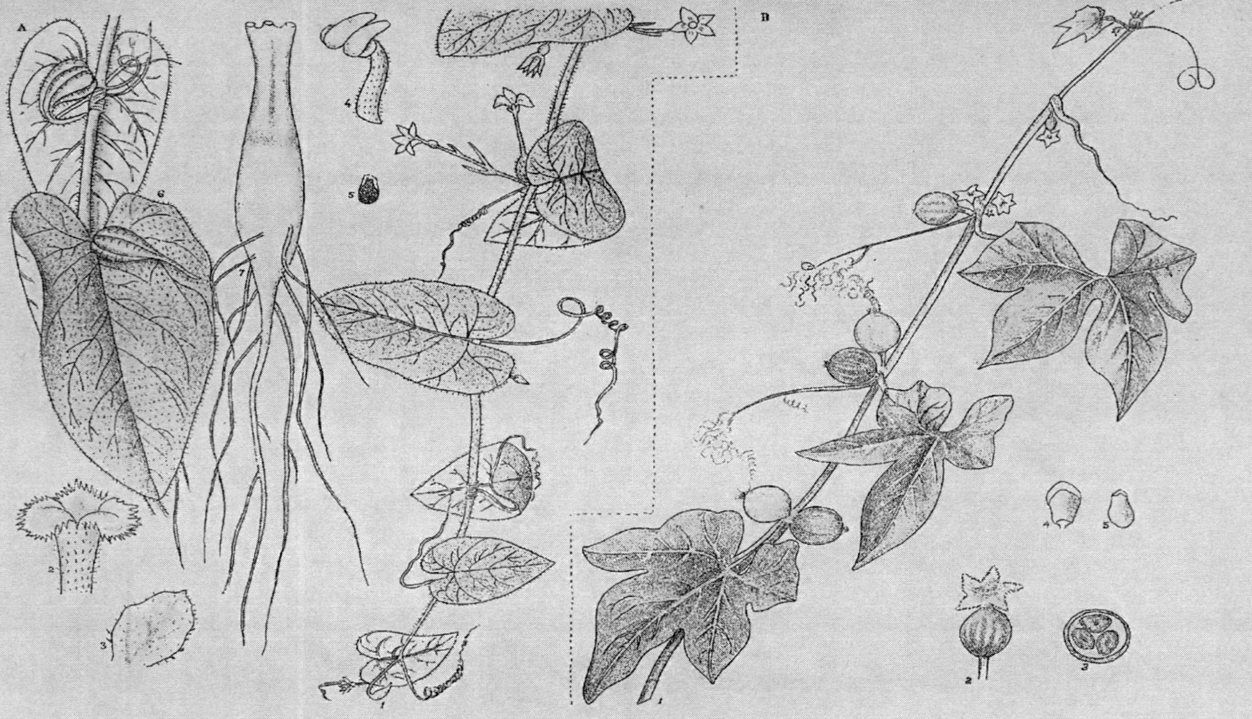

A—RHYNCHOCARPA FŒTIDA, *SCHRAD.* B—ƆTENOLEPIS CERASIFORMIS, *NAUD.*

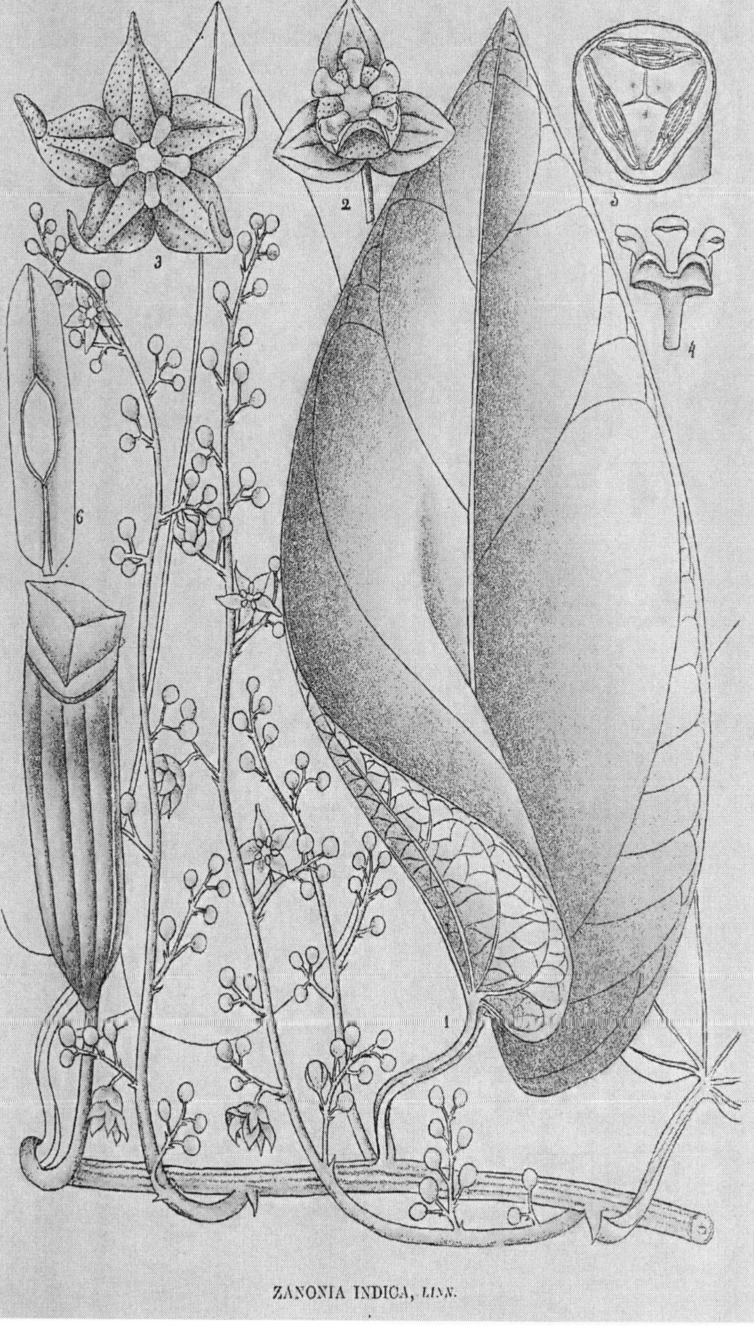

ZANONIA INDICA, LINN.

PLATE No. 469.

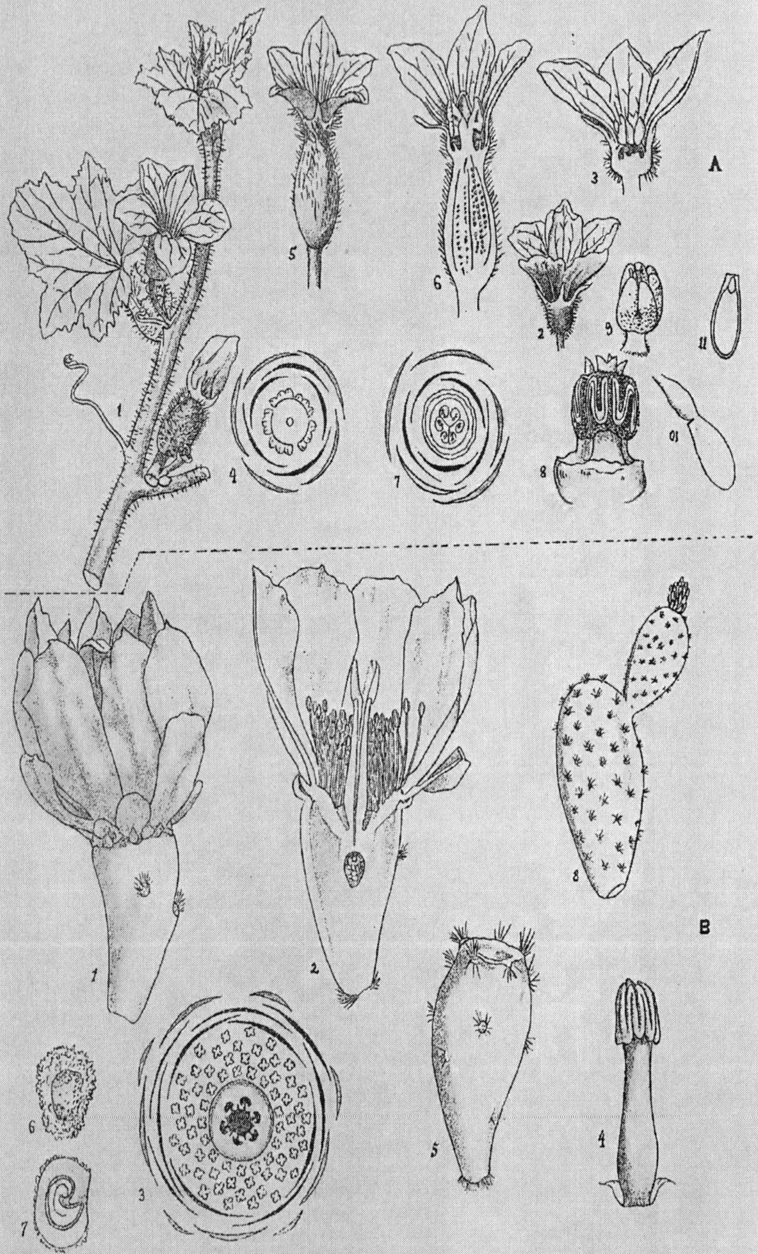

A—DATISCA CANNABINA, *LINN.* B—OPUNTIA DILLENII, *HAW.*

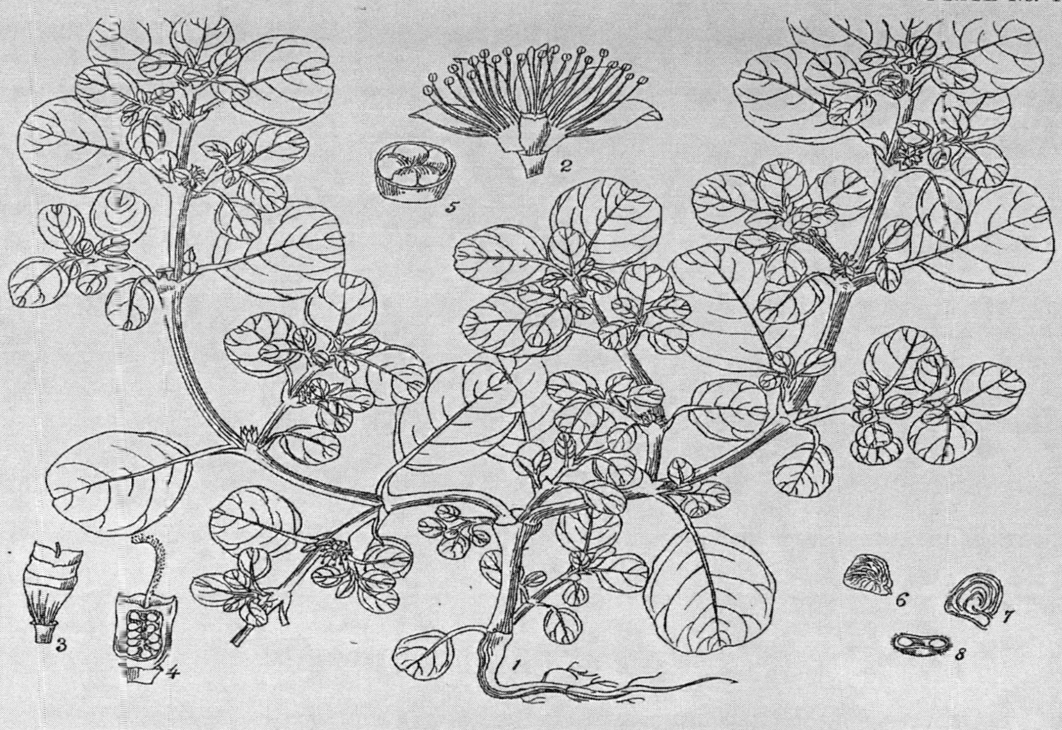

TRIANTHEMA MONOGYNA, *LINN.*

PLATE No. 471.

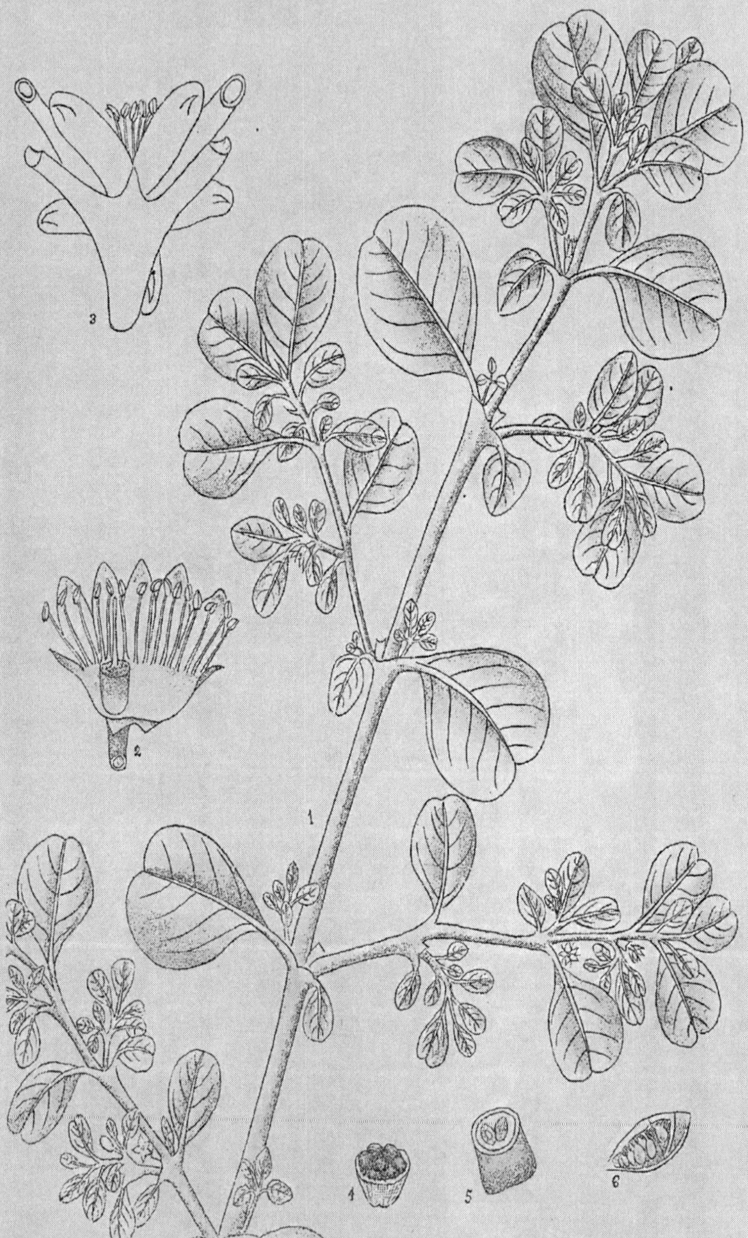

TRIANTHEMA PENTANDRA, *Linn*

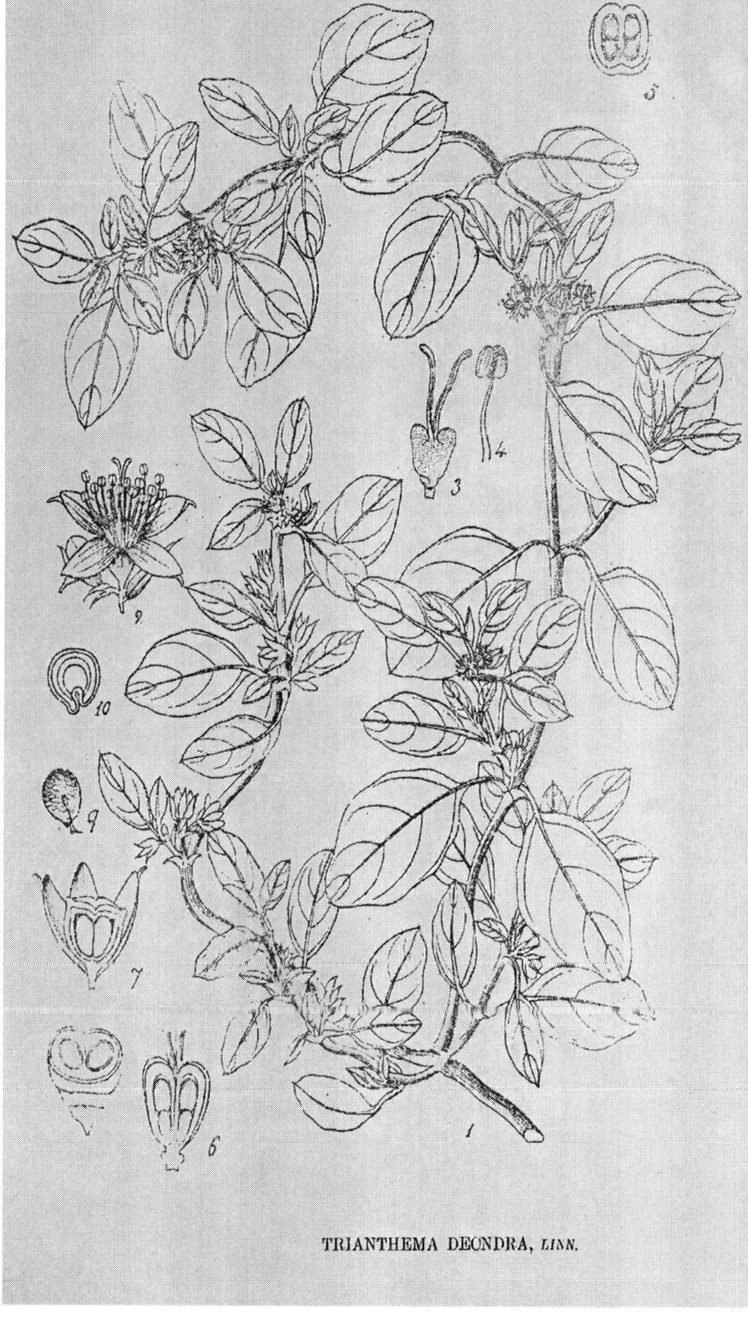

TRIANTHEMA DECANDRA, LINN.

PLATE No. 473.

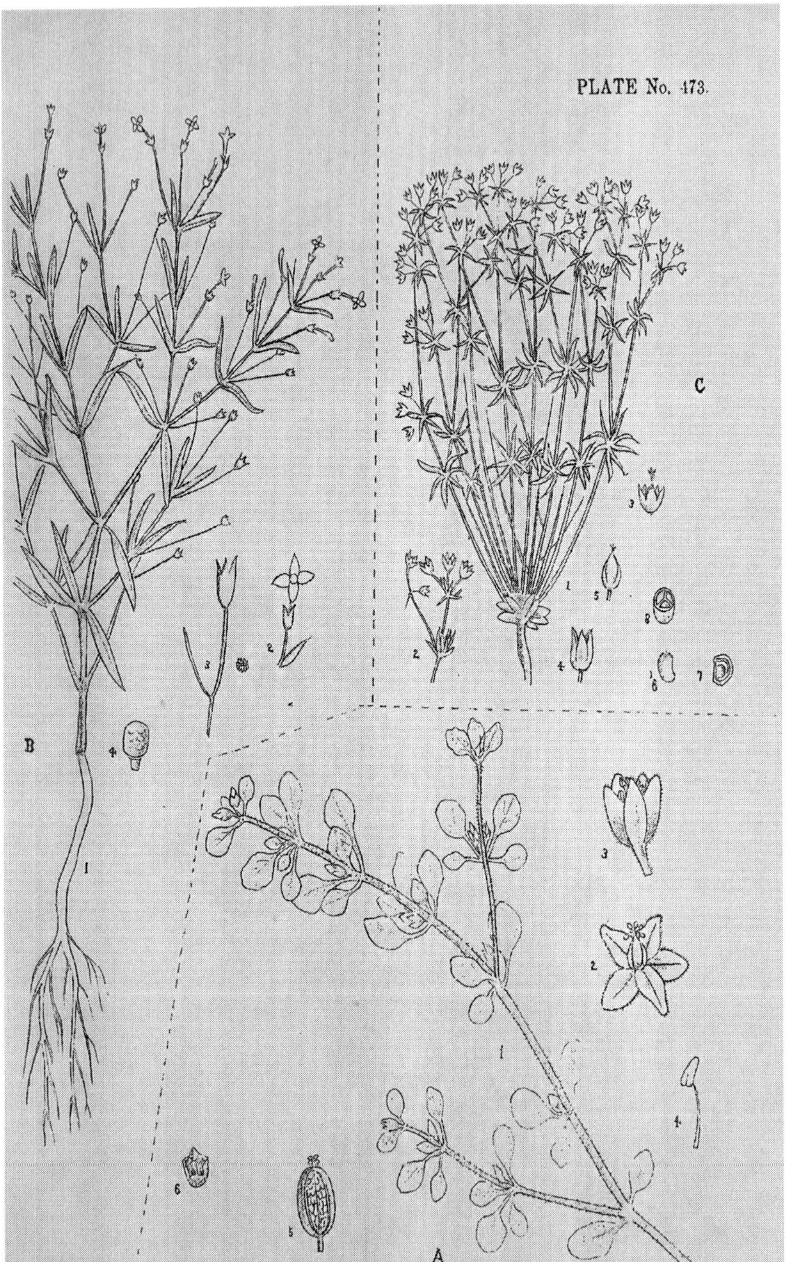

A—MOLLUGO HIRTA, *THUMB.* B—M. STRICTA, *LINN.* C—M. CERVIANA, *SERINGE.*

PLATE No. 474

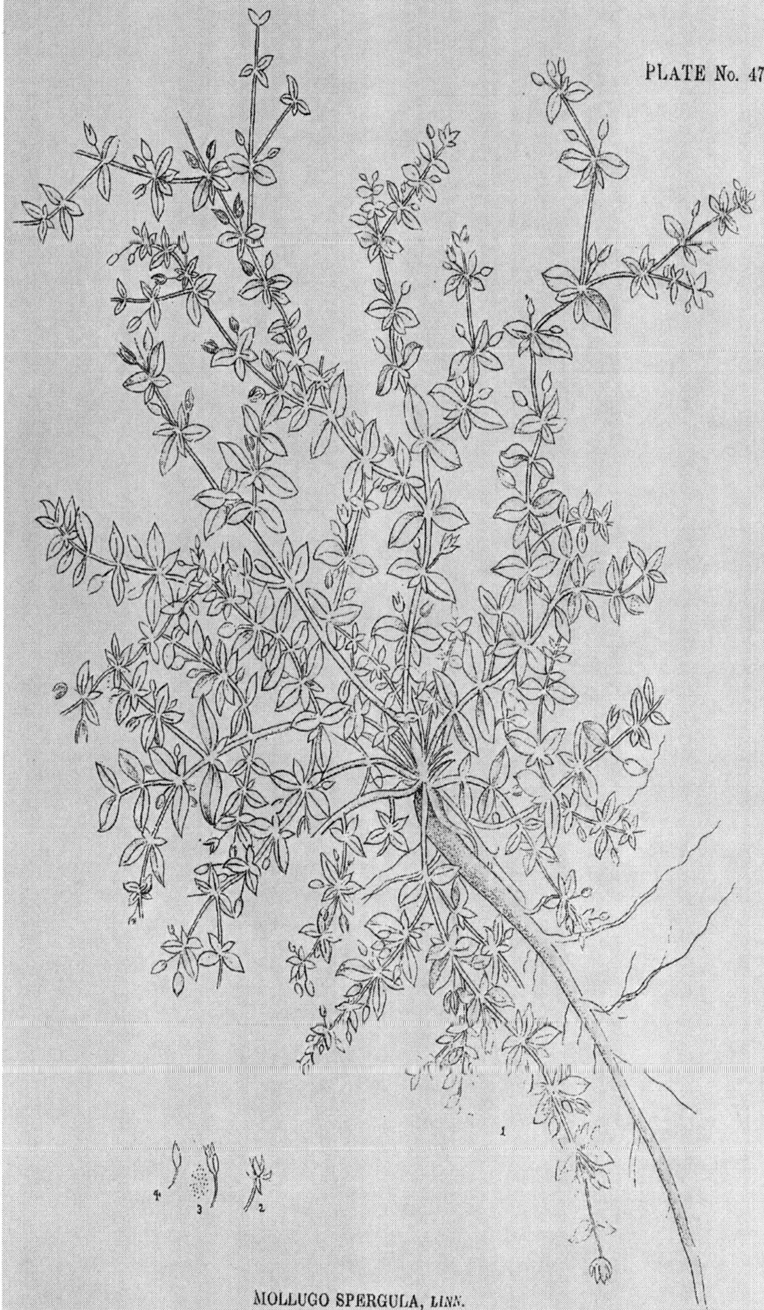

MOLLUGO SPERGULA, LINN.

PLATE No. 475

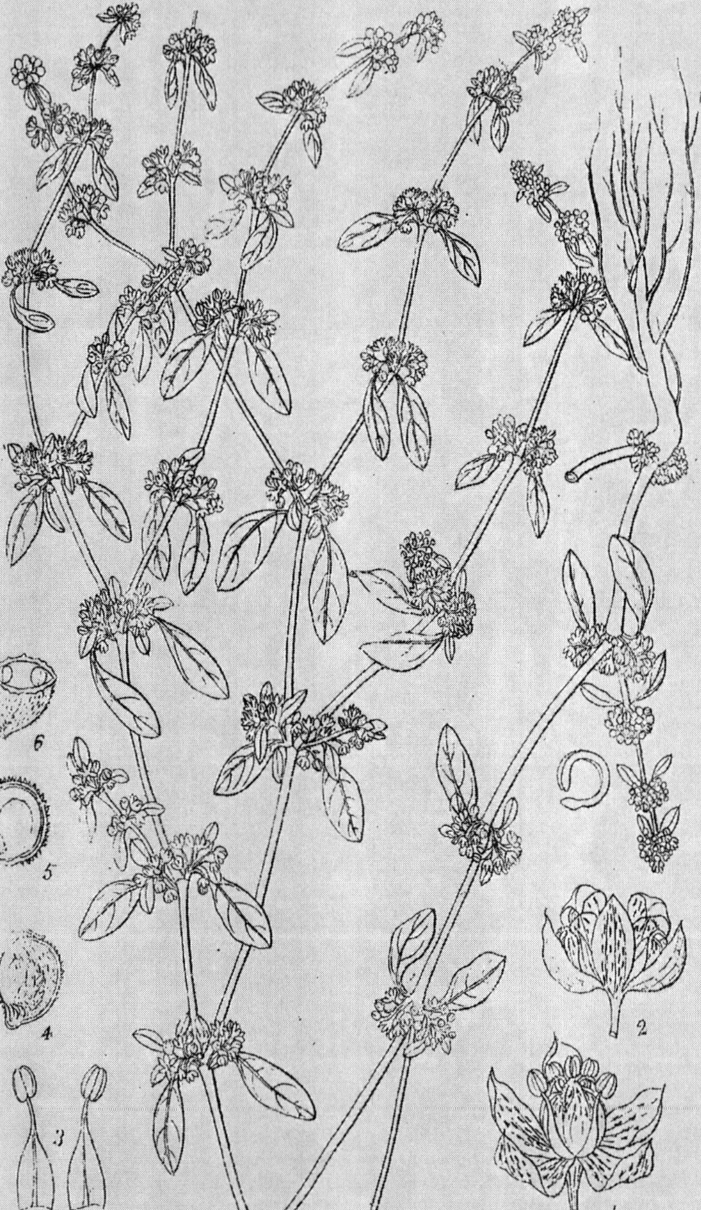

GISEKIA PHARNACEOIDES, *Linn.*

PLATE No. 476.

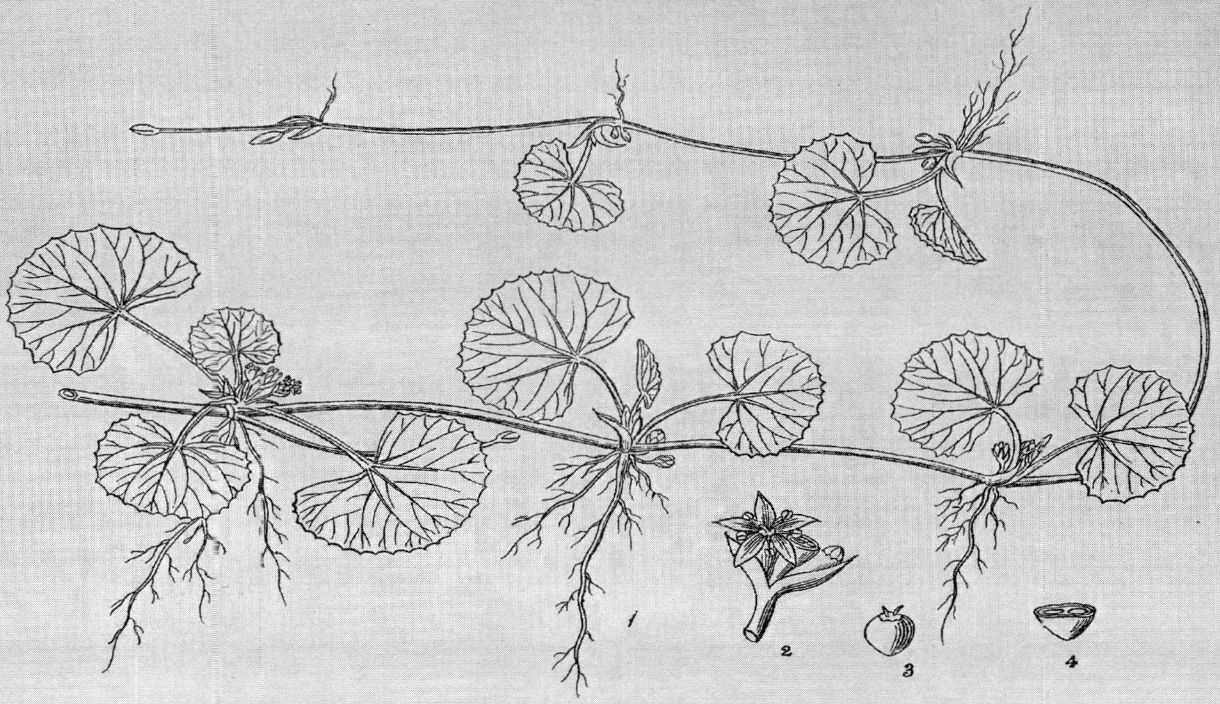

HYDROCOTYLE ASIATICA, *LINN.*

PLATE No. 477.

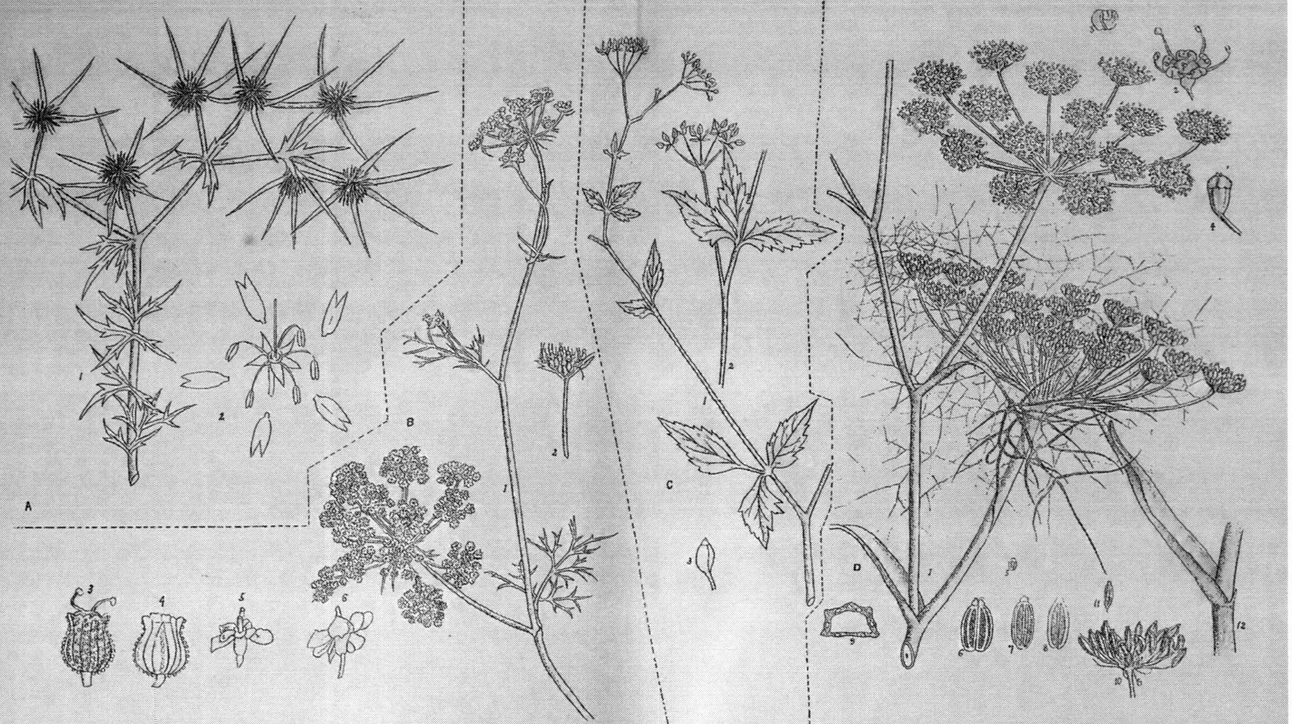

A—ERYNGIUM CÆRULEUM, BIEB. B—CARUM COPTICUM, BENTH. C—PIMPINELLA HEYNEANA, WALL. D—FŒNICULUM VULGARE, GÆRTN.

PLATE No 478.

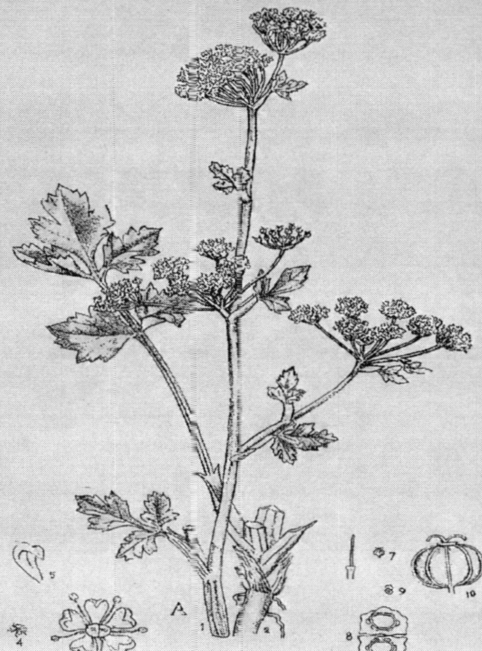

APIUM GRAVEOLENS, *LINN.*

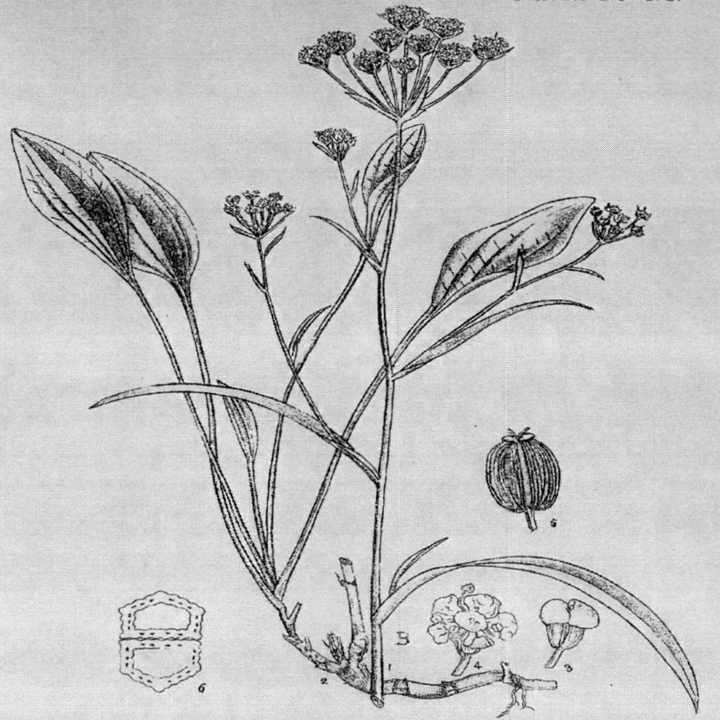

BUPLEURUM FALCATUM, *LINN.*

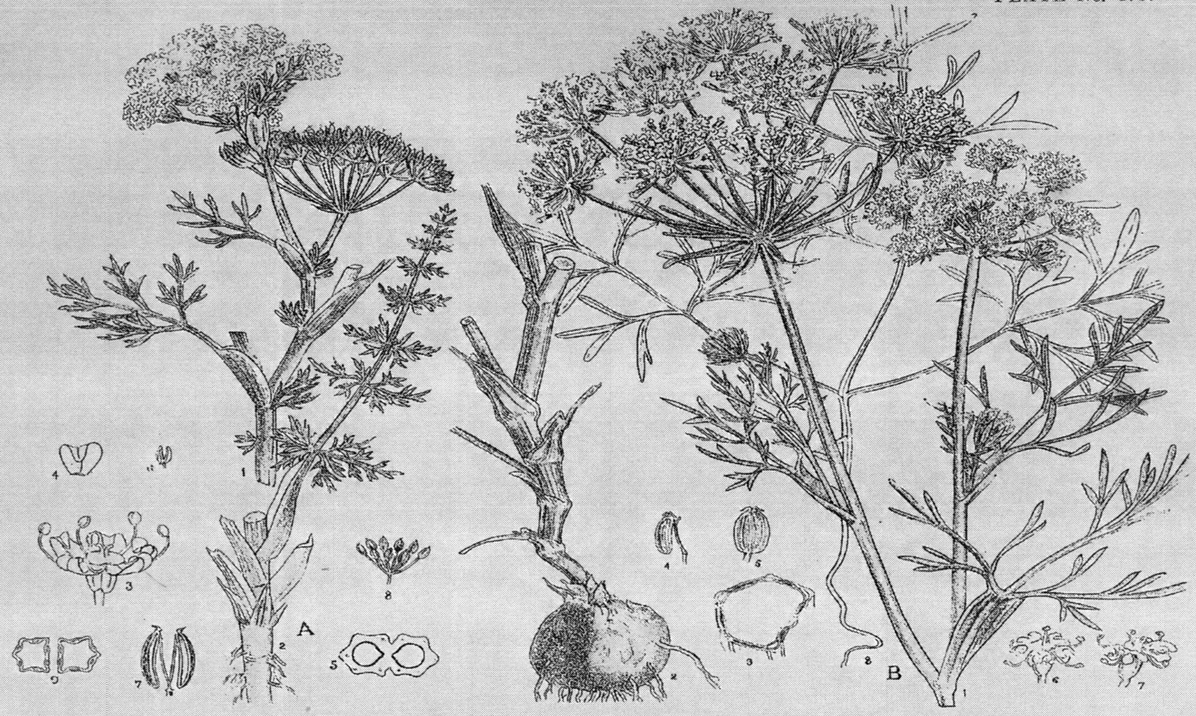

A—CARUM CARUI, *LINN.*

B—CARUM BULBOCASTANUM, *C. KOCH.*

PLATE No. 480.

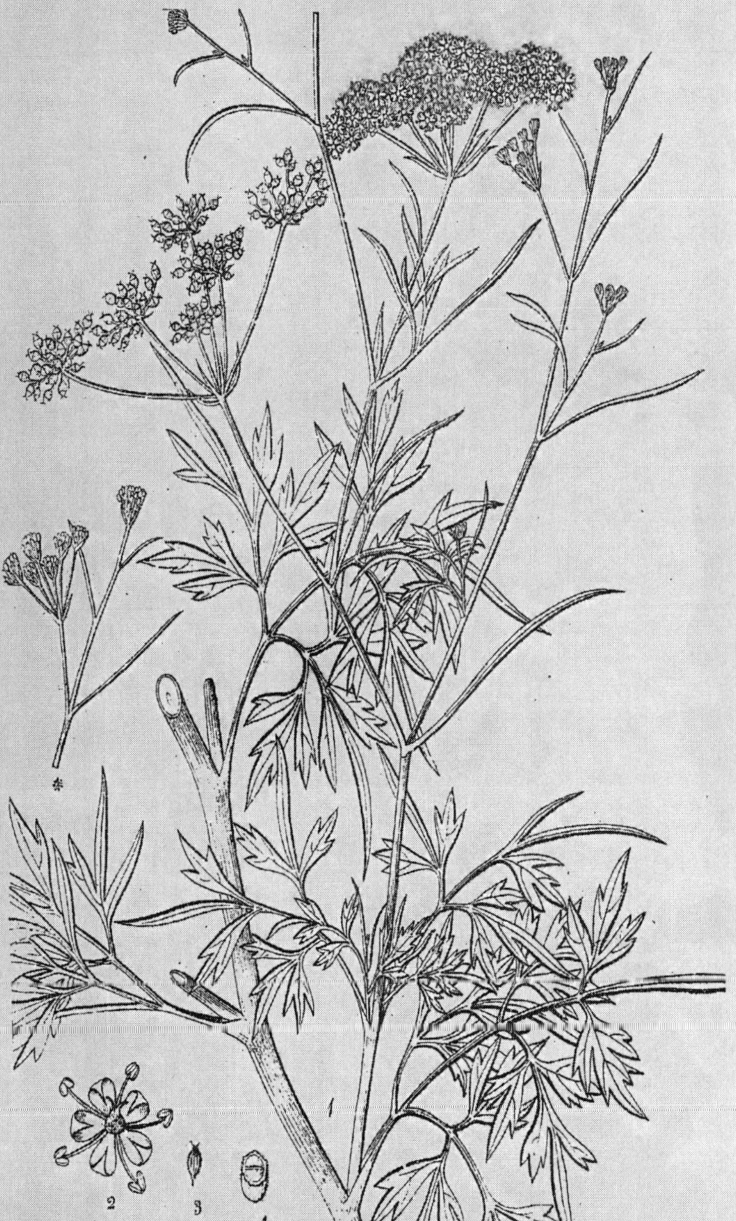

CARUM ROXBURGHIANUM, BENTH.

PLATE No. 481

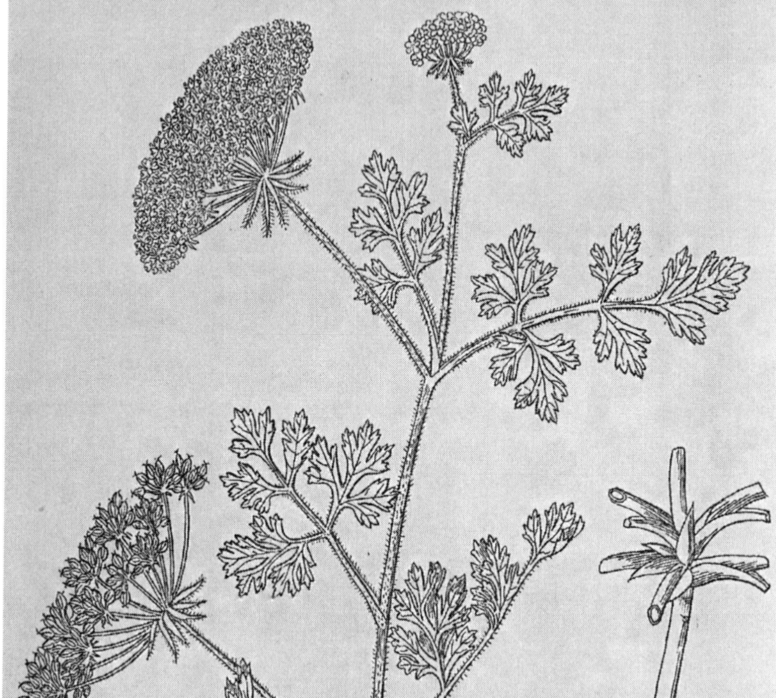

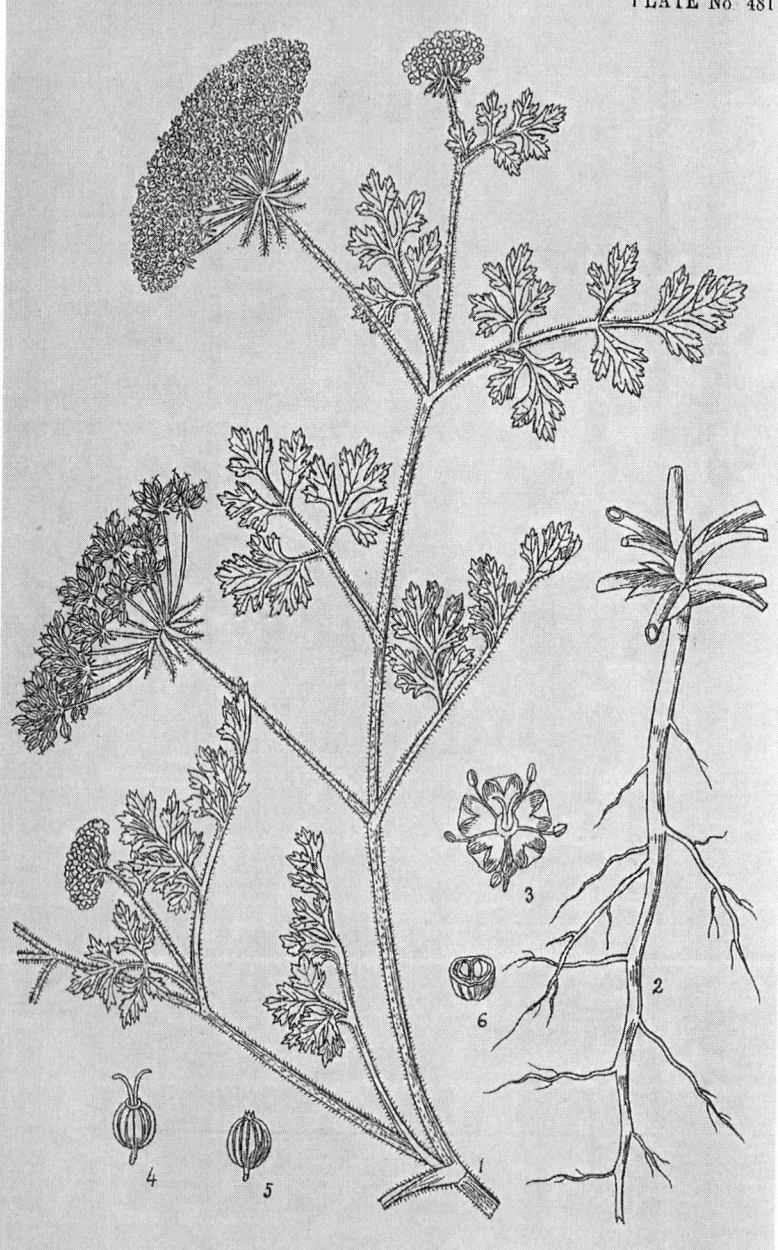

SESELI INDICUM, *W. & A.*

PLATE No. 482.

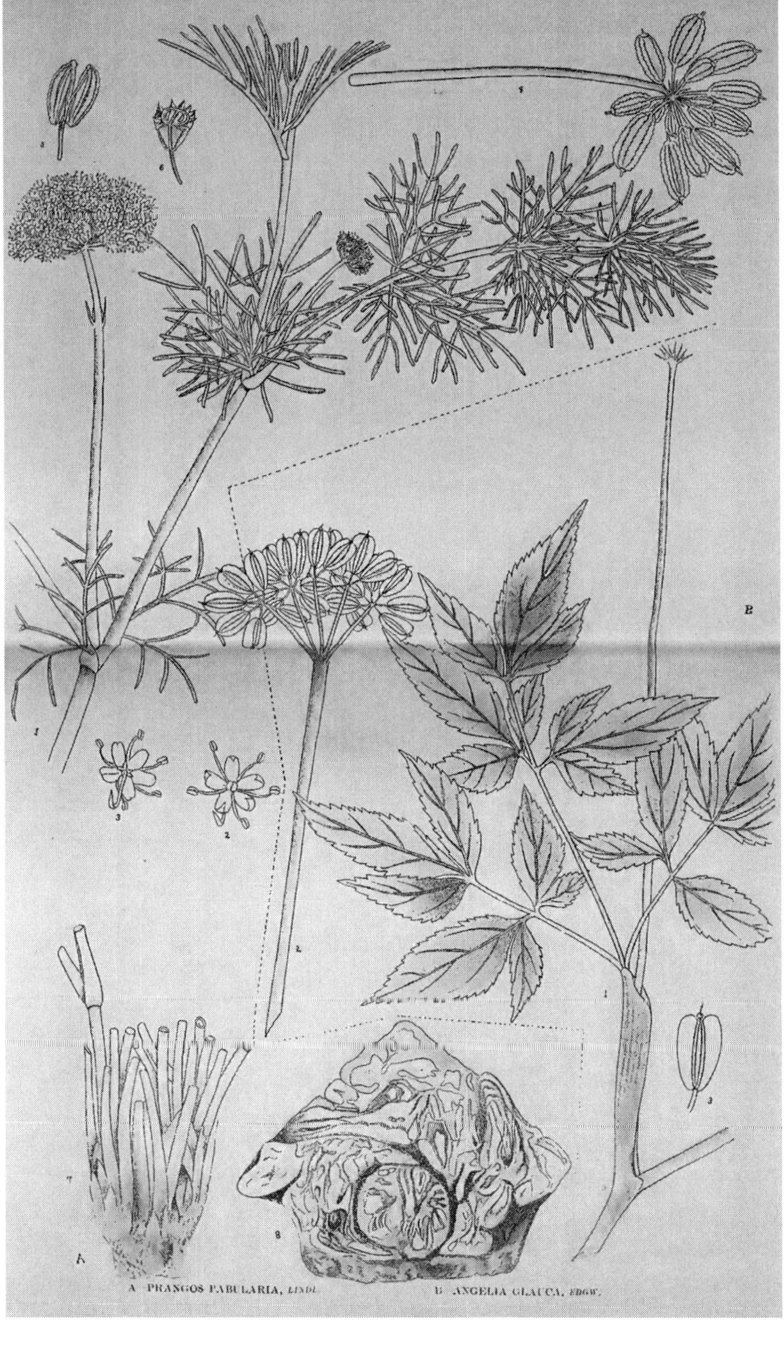

A PRANGOS PABULARIA, LINDL. B ANGELIA GLAUCA, EDGW.

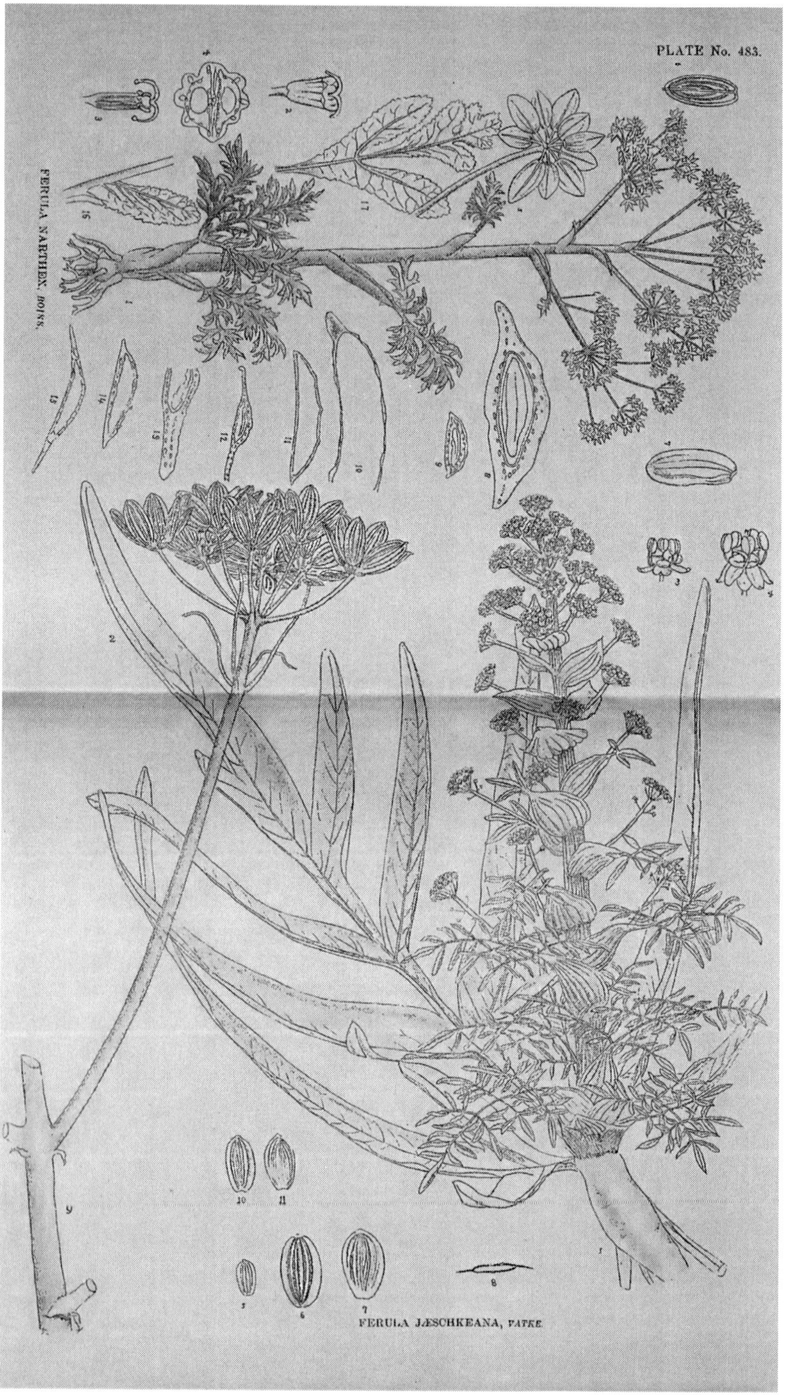
PLATE No. 483.
FERULA NARTHEX, BOISS.
FERULA JÆSCHKEANA, VATKE

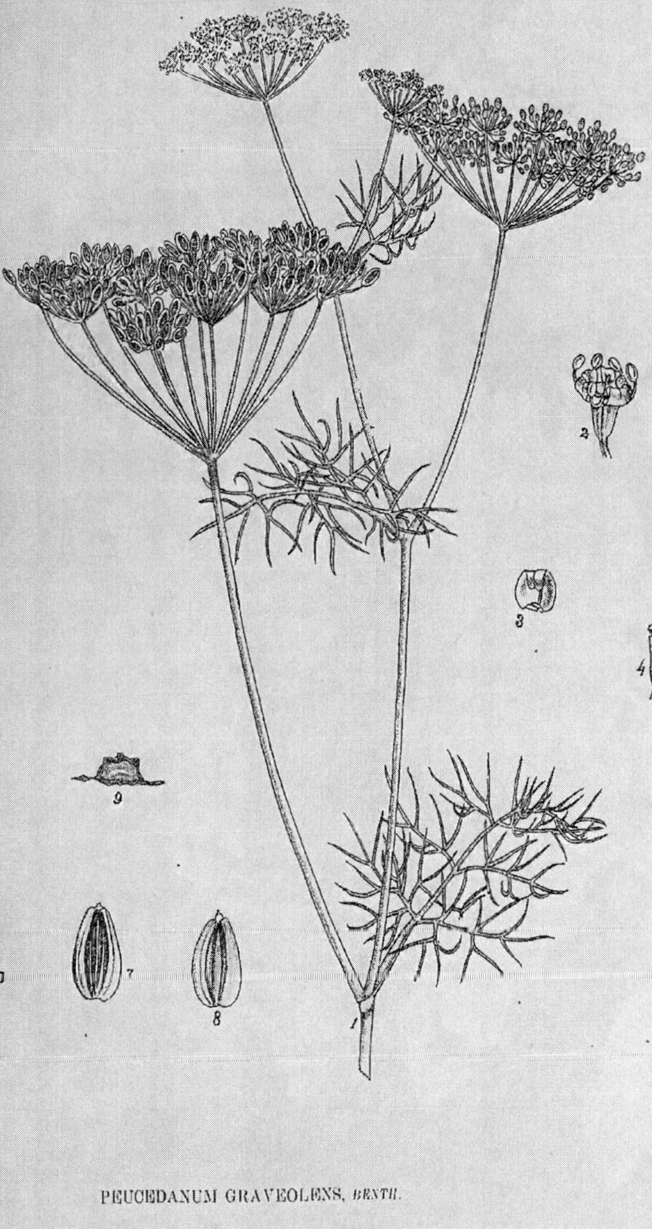

PEUCEDANUM GRAVEOLENS, BENTH.

PLATE No. 484 A

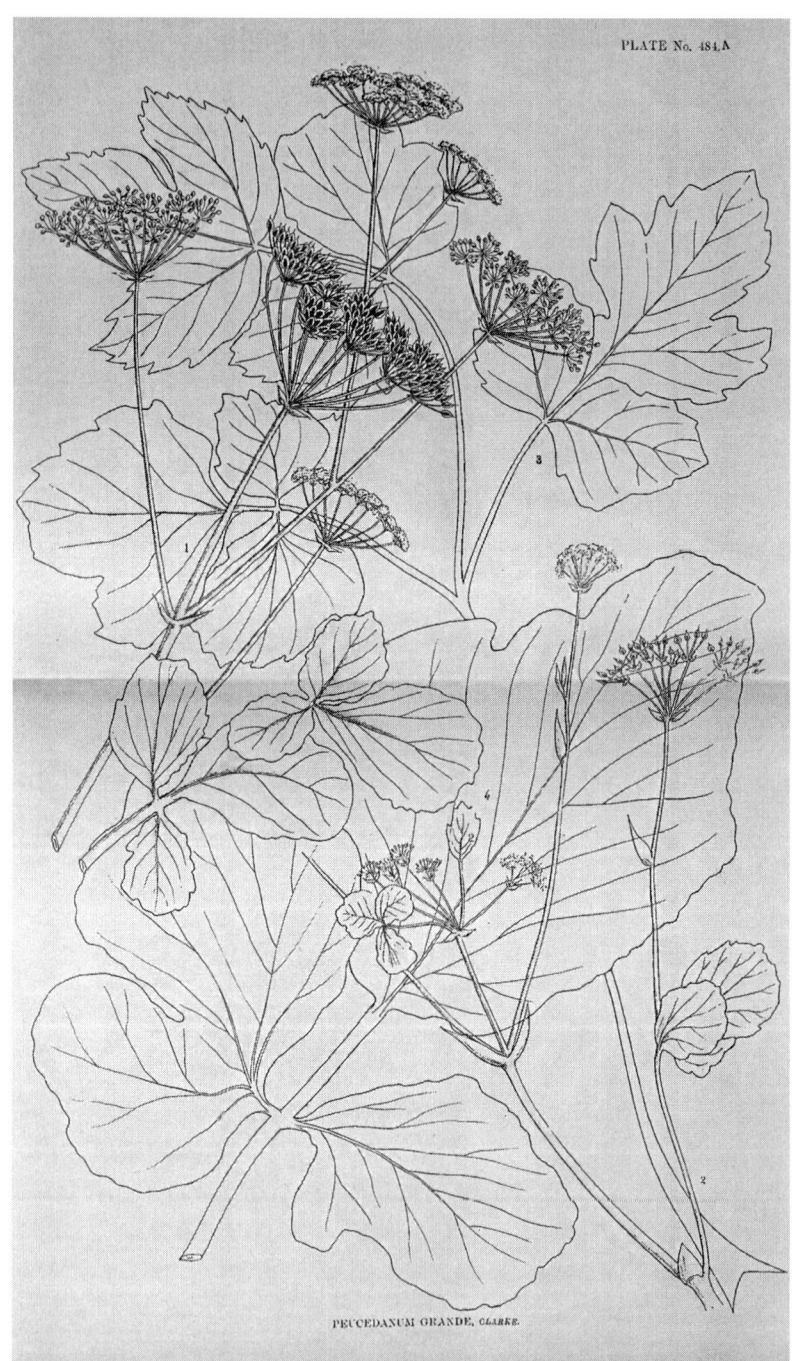

PEUCEDANUM GRANDE, *Clarke.*

A—CUMINUM CYMINUM, LINN.

B—DAUCUS CAROTA, LINN.

C—CORIANDRUM SATIVUM, LINN.

PLATE No. 486.

A—ARALIA PSEUDO-GINSENG, *BENTH.*   B—HEDERA HELIX, *LINN.*

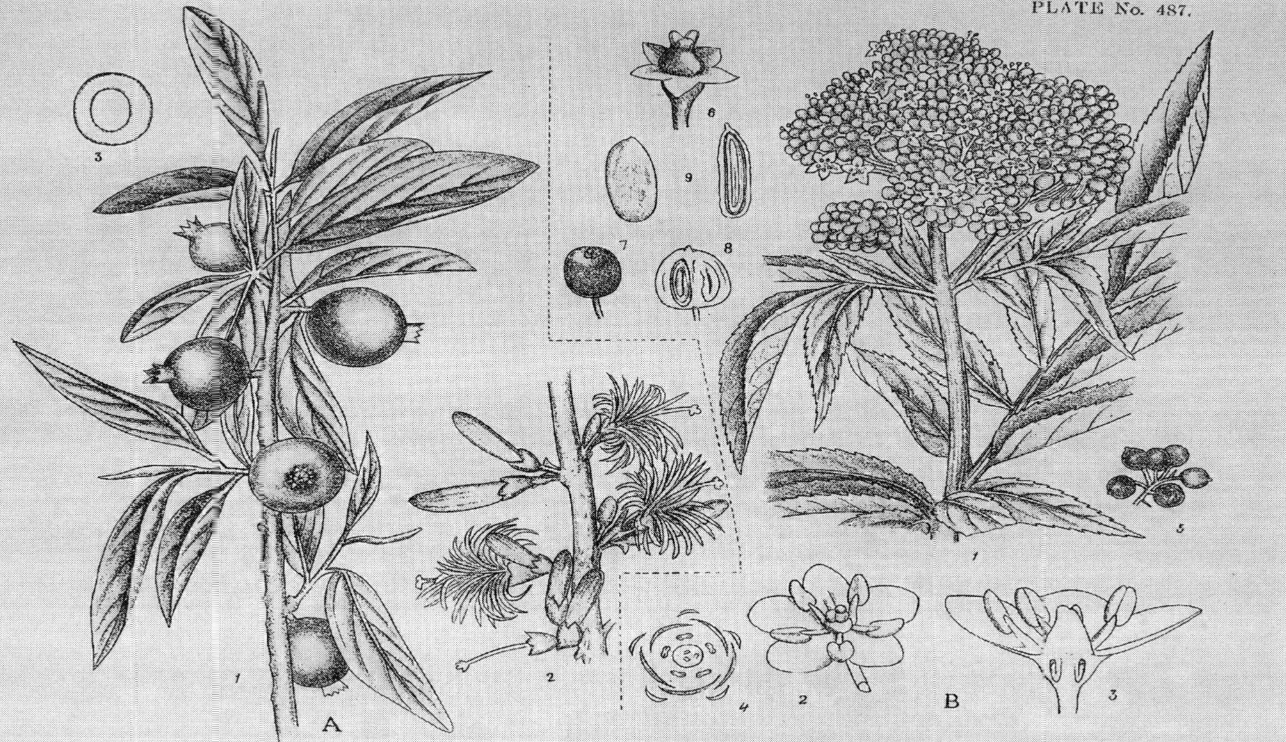

B—SAMBUCUS EBULUS, *LINN.*   A—ALANGIUM LAMARCKII, *THWAITES.*

PLATE No. 488.

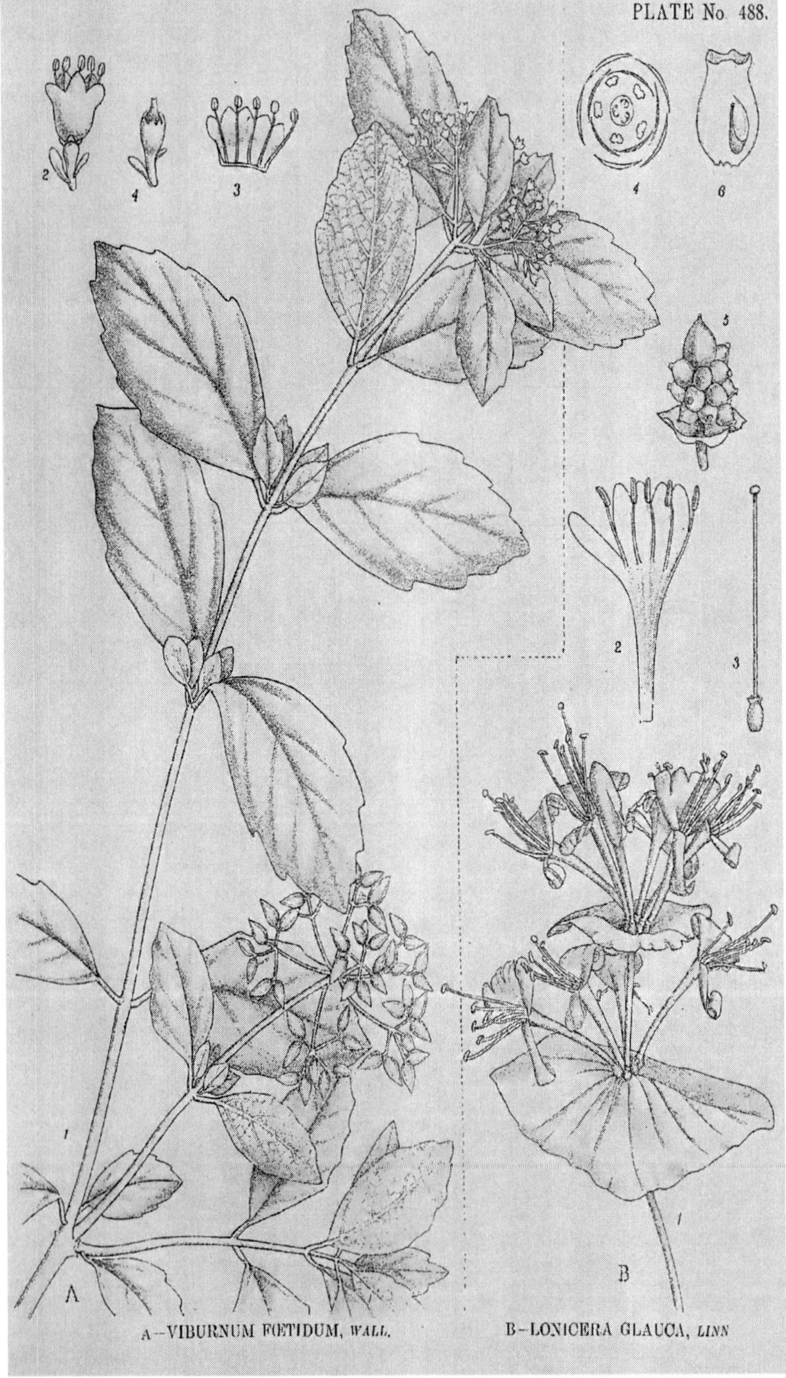

A—VIBURNUM FŒTIDUM, *WALL.*   B—LONICERA GLAUCA, *LINN*

PLATE No. 489.

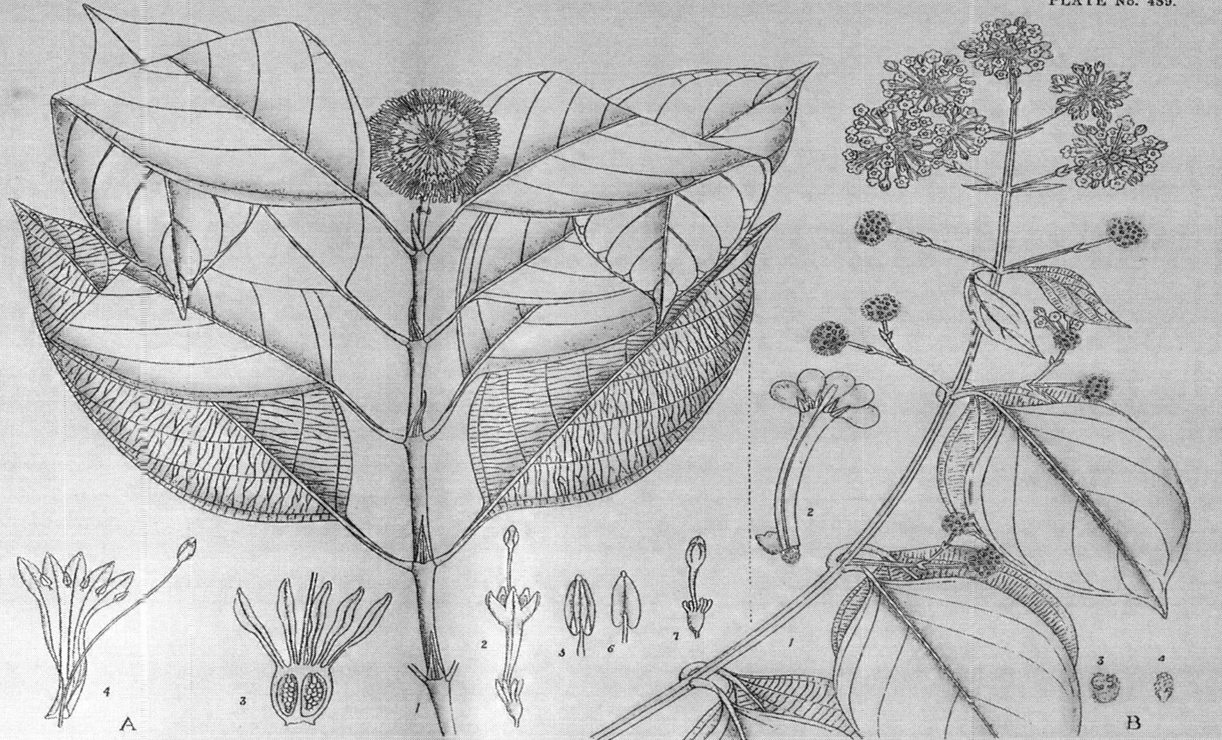

A—ANTHOCEPHALUS CADAMBA, *MIQ.* B—ADINA SESSILIFOLIA, *HOOK. F.*

PLATE No. 490.

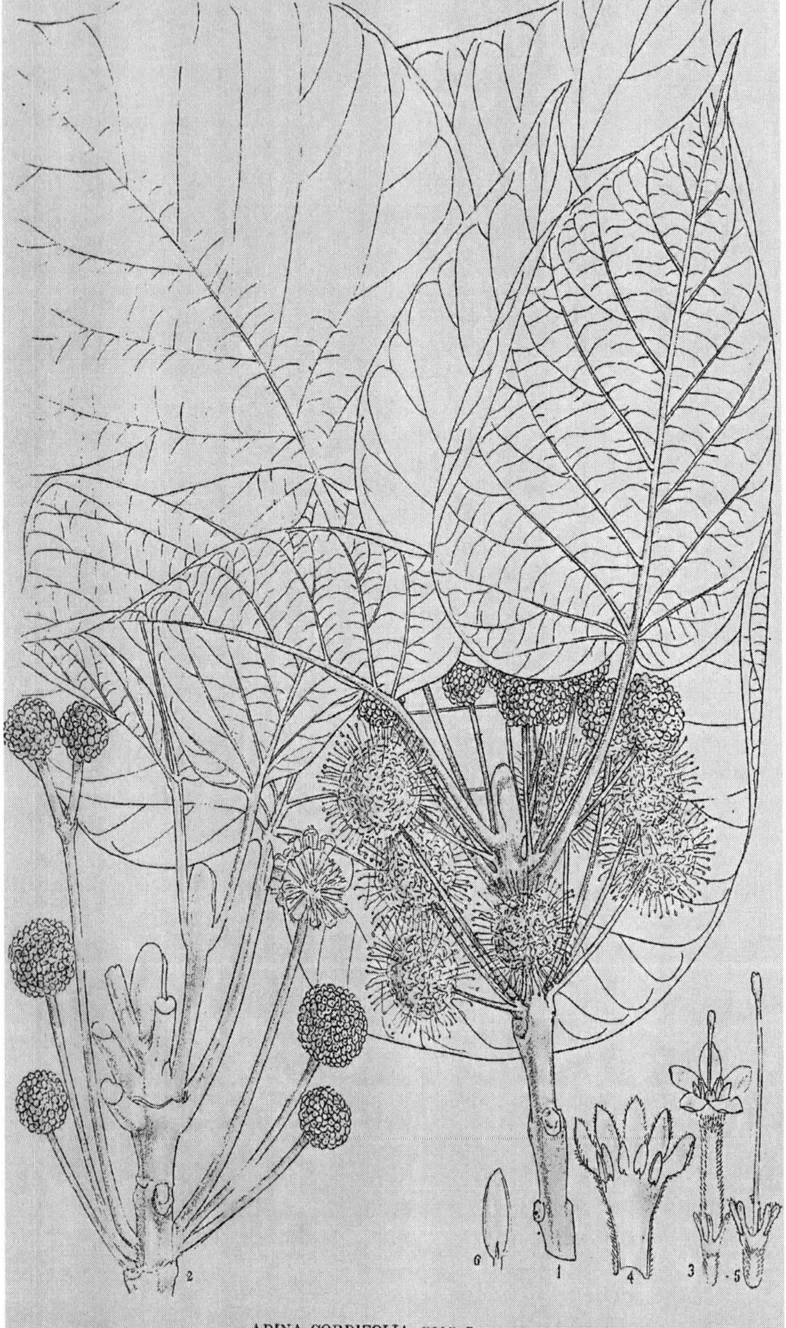

ADINA CORDIFOLIA, HOOK. F.

PLATE No. 491.

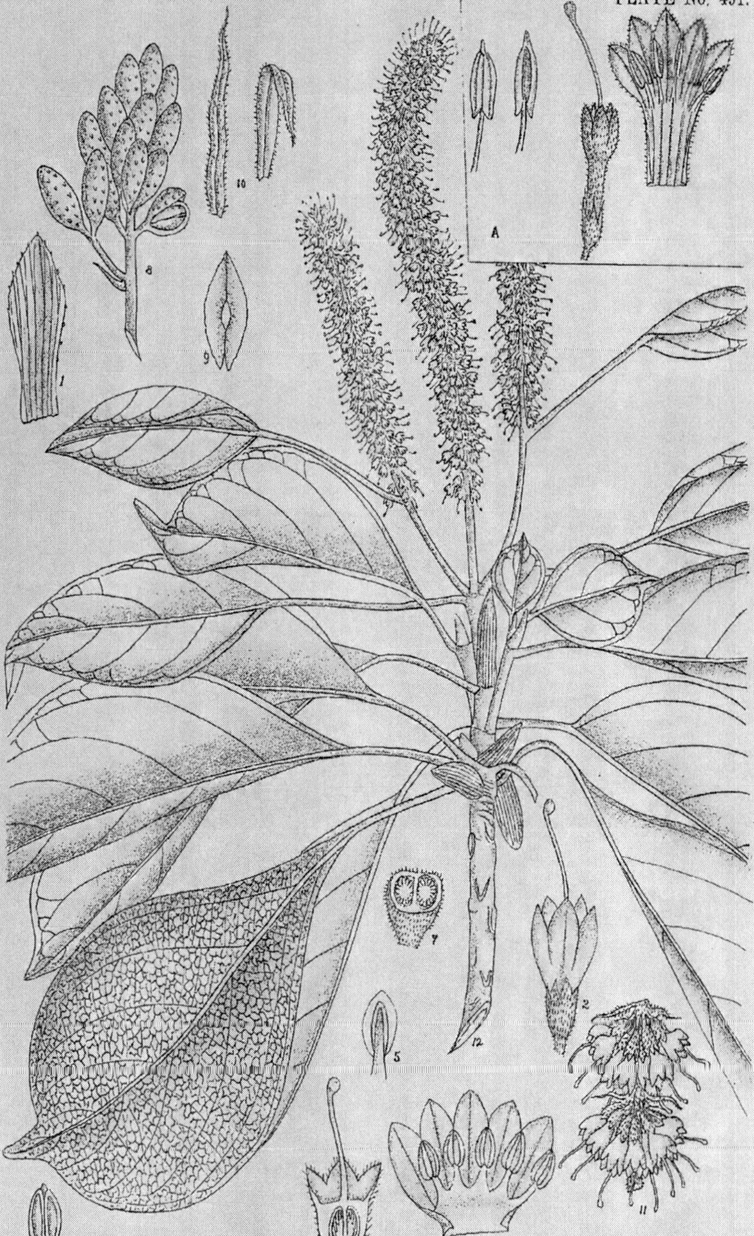

HYMENODICTYON EXCELSUM, *WALL.*

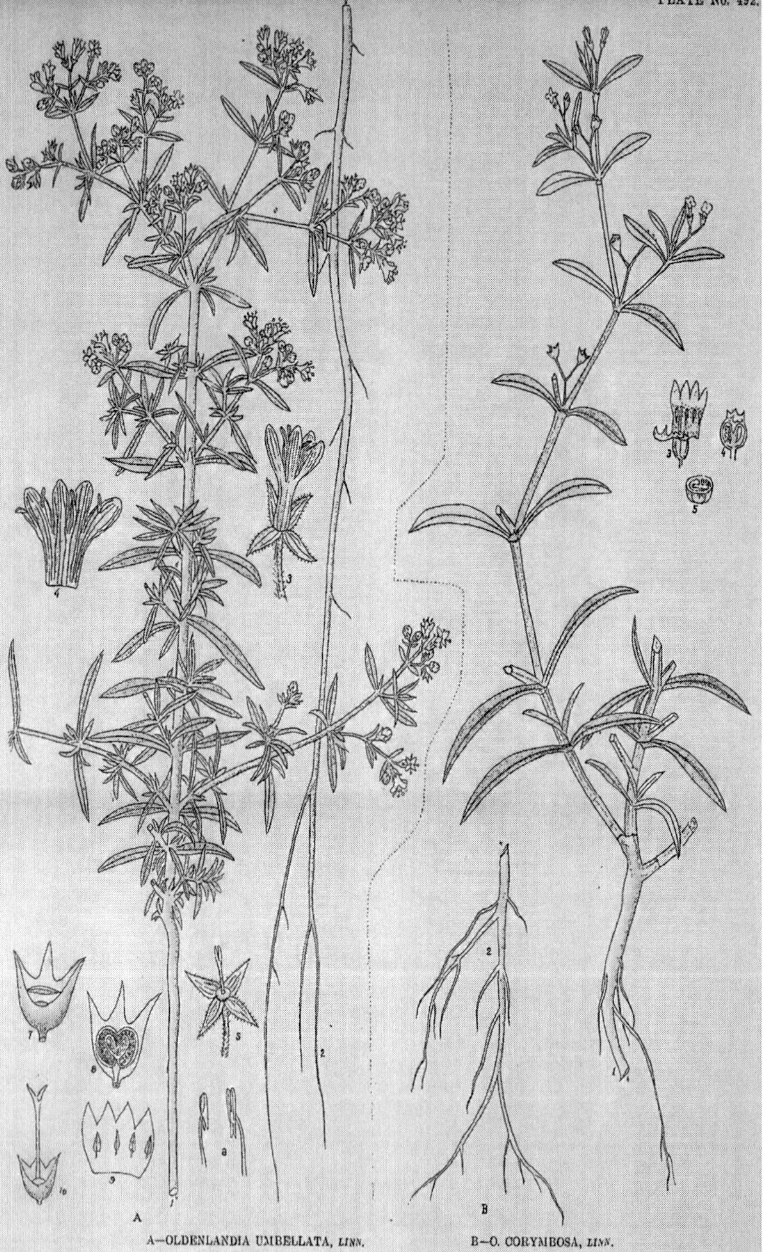

A—OLDENLANDIA UMBELLATA, *Linn.*

B—O. CORYMBOSA, *Linn.*

PLATE No. 493.

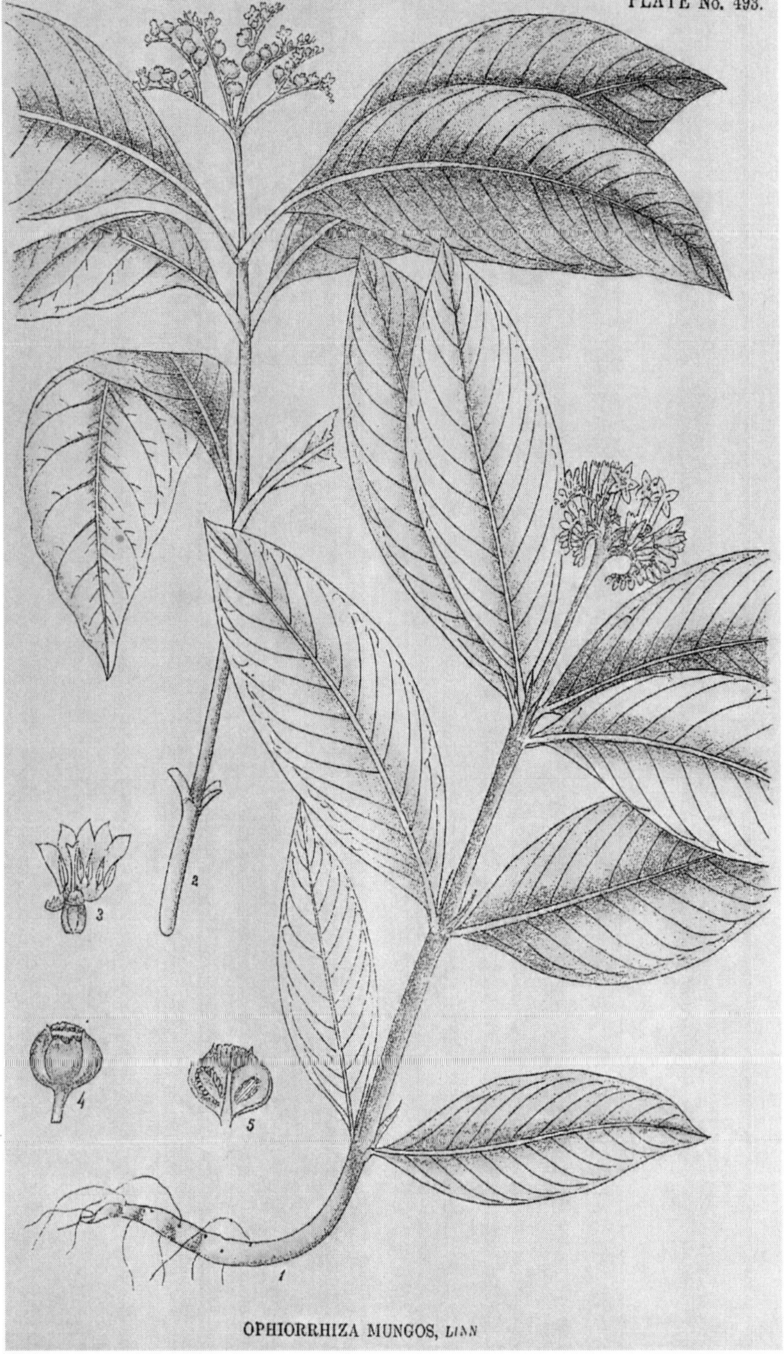

OPHIORRHIZA MUNGOS, *Linn*

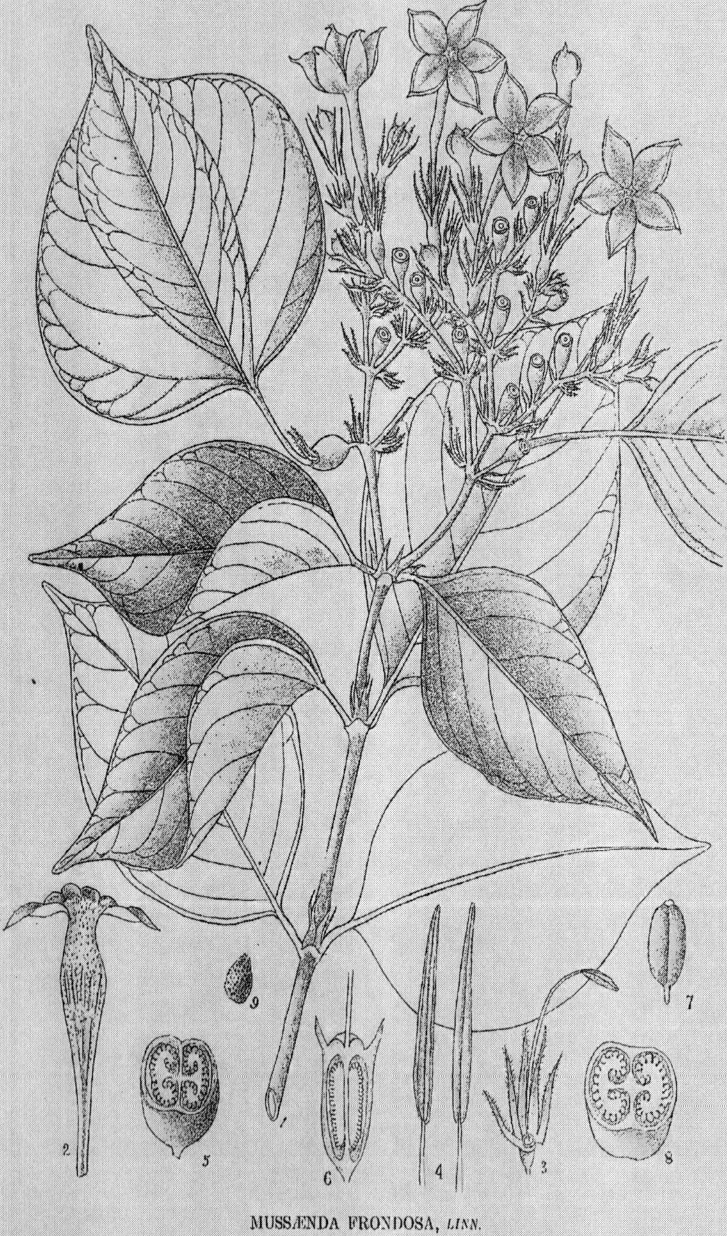

MUSSÆNDA FRONDOSA, *LINN.*

PLATE No. 495.

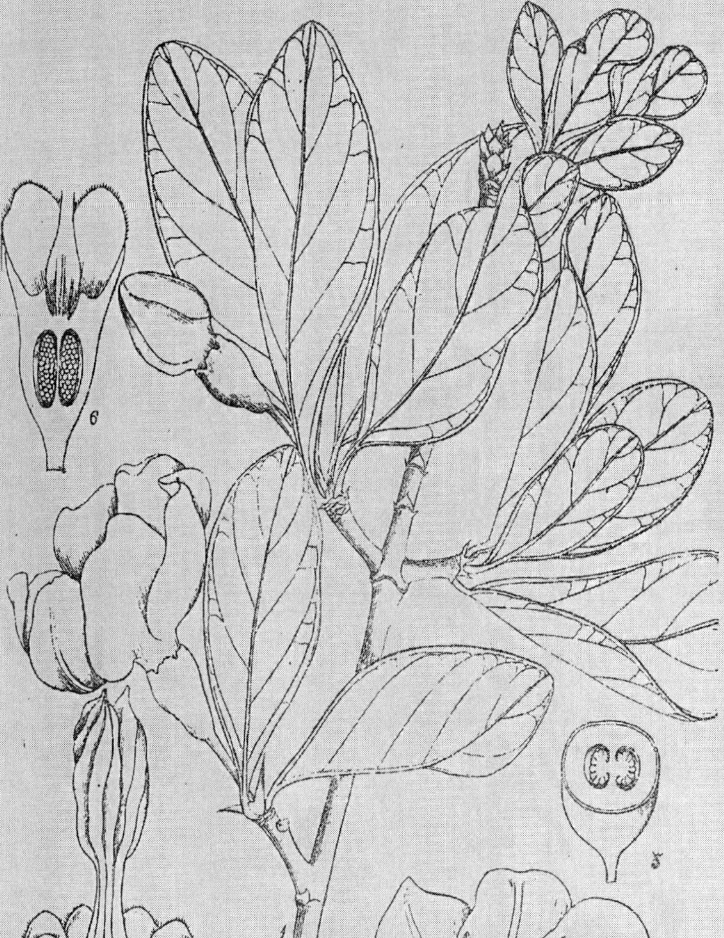

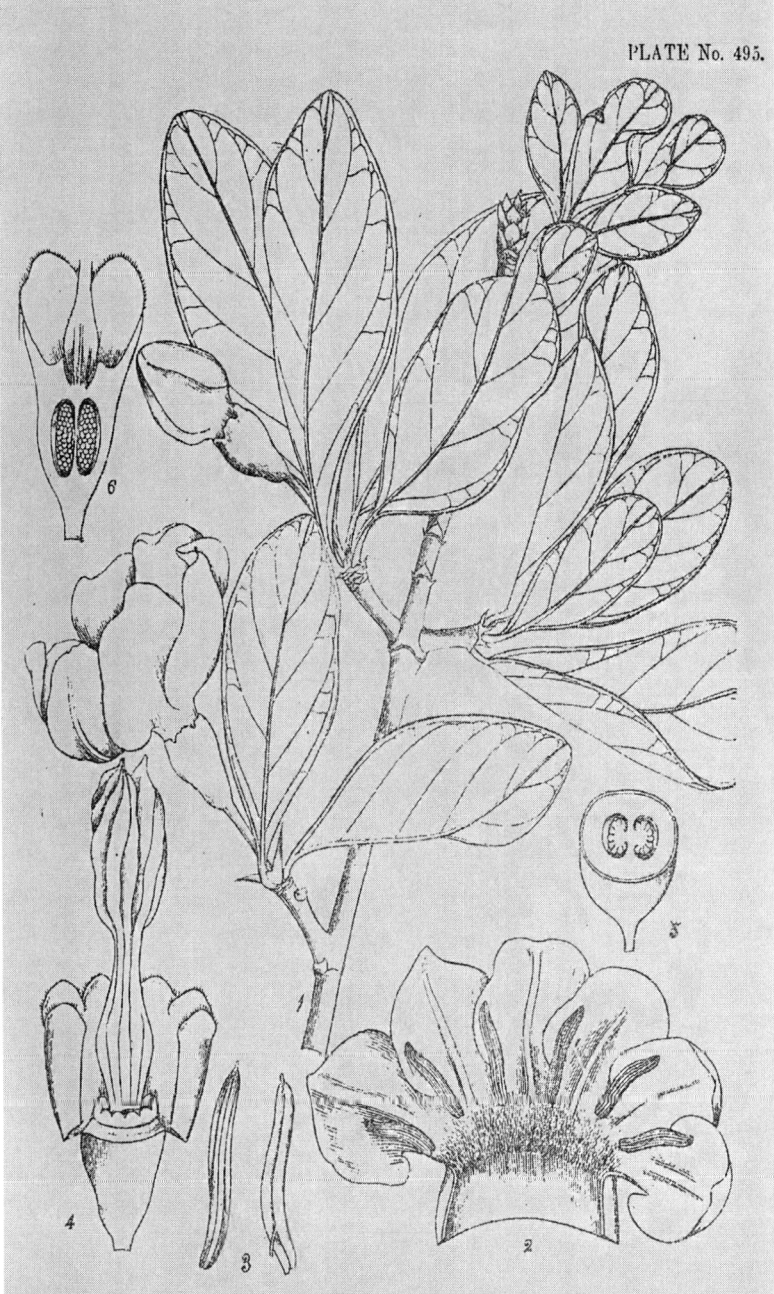

RANDIA ULIGINOSA, *DC.*

PLATE No. 496.

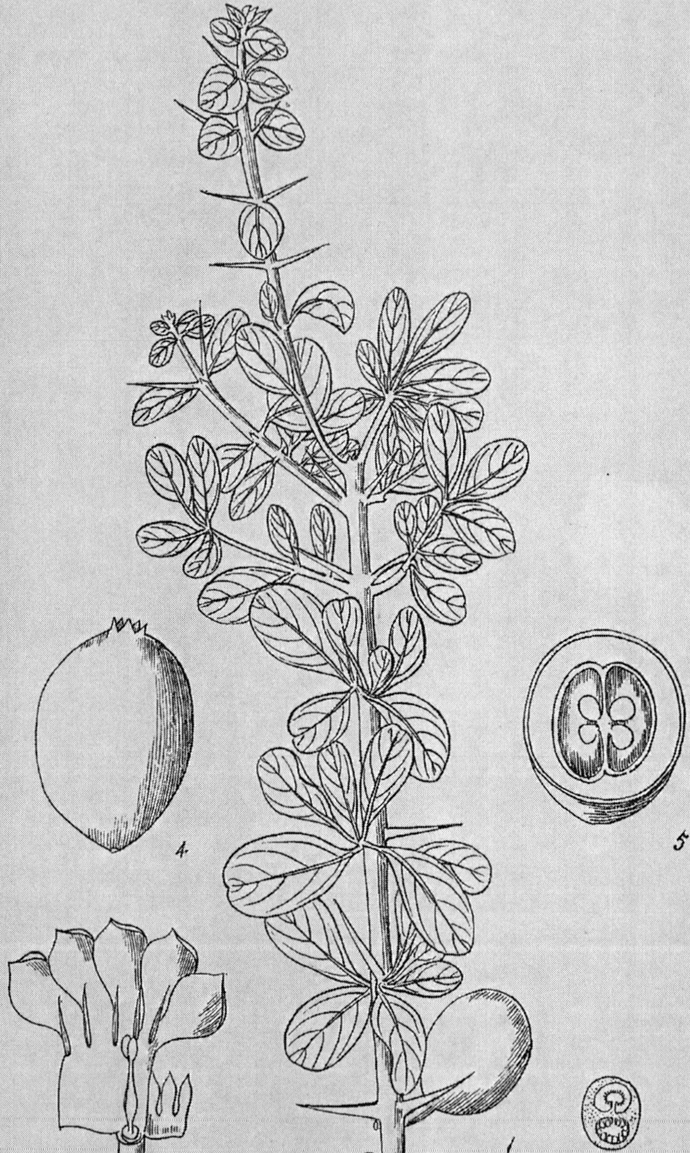

RANDIA DUMETORUM, *LAMK.*

PLATE No. 497.

GARDENIA LUCIDA, ROXB.

PLATE No. 498

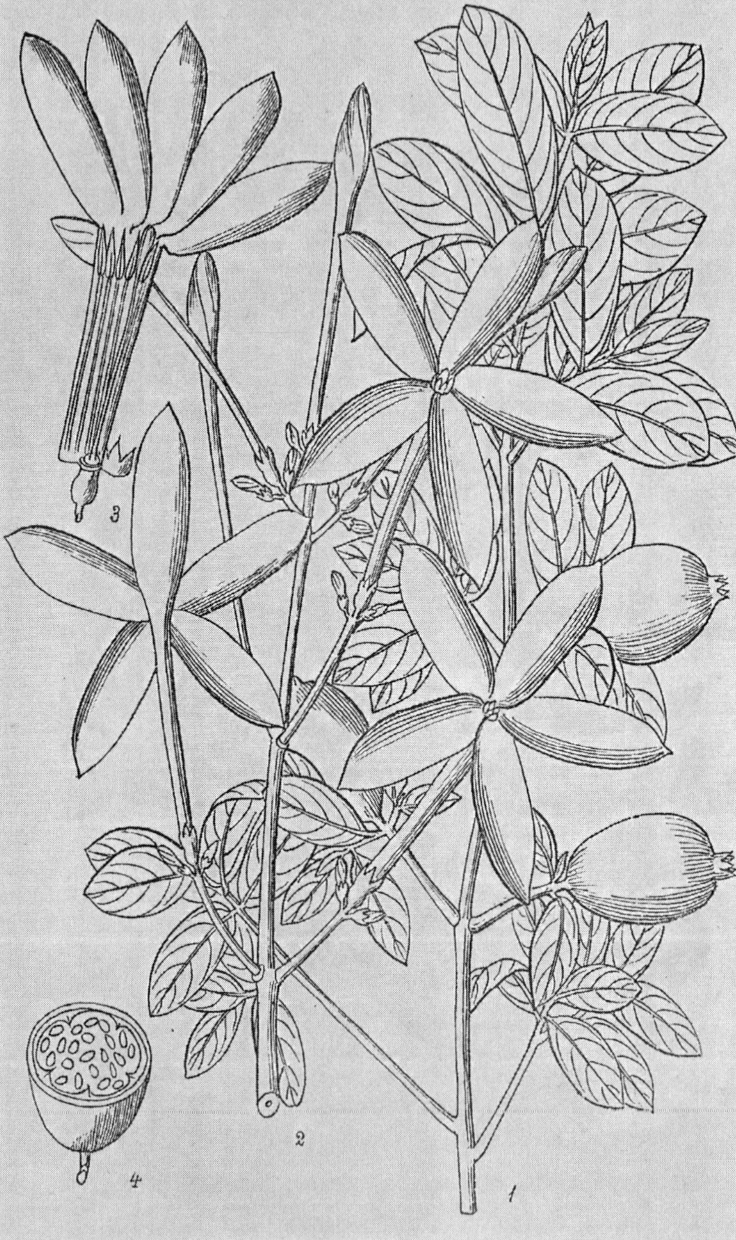

GARDENIA GUMMIFERA, *LINN F.*

PLATE No. 489.

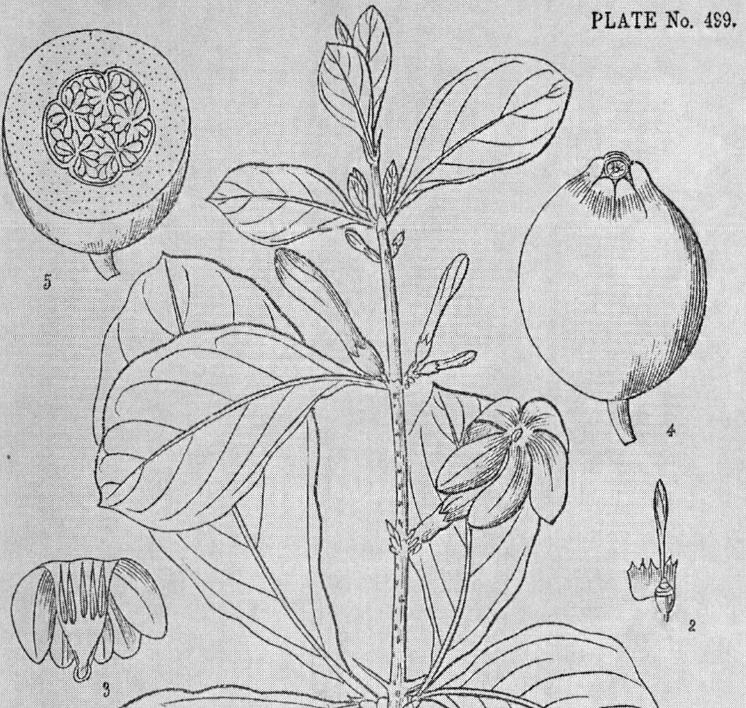

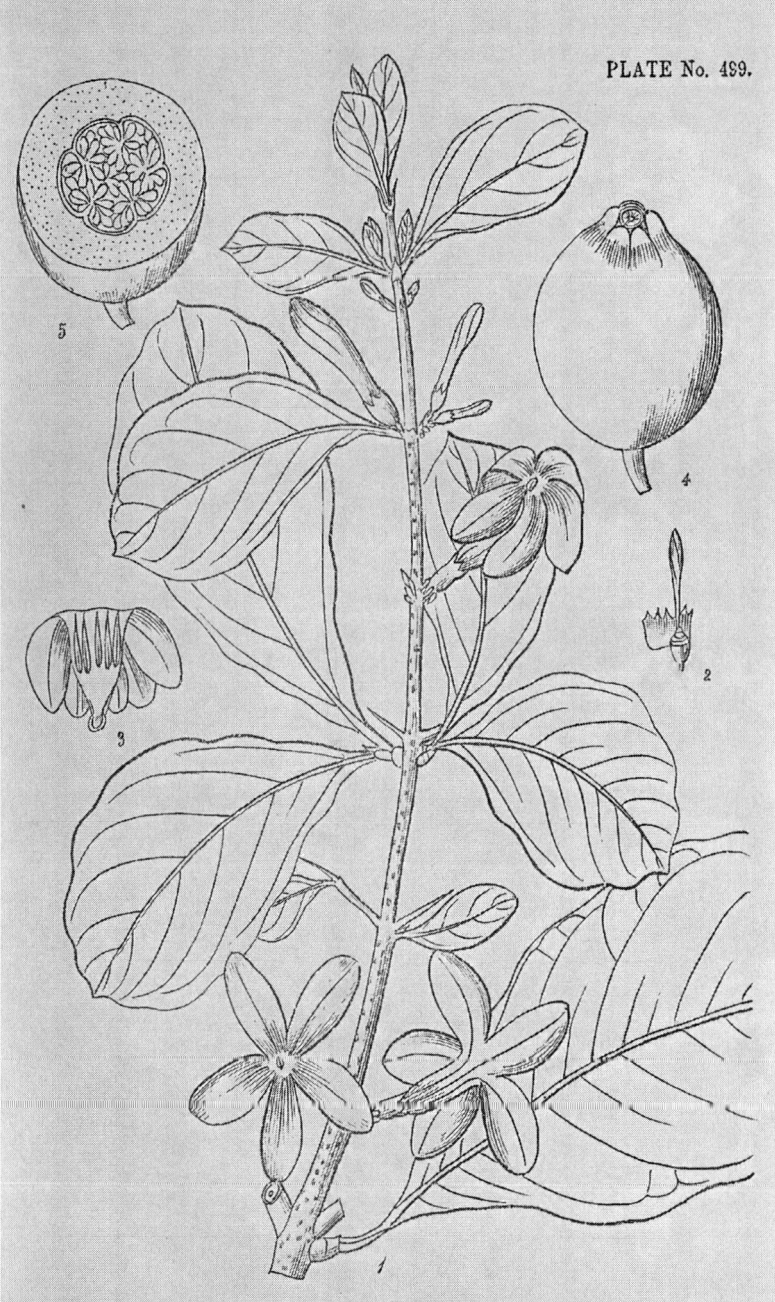

GARDENIA TURGIDA, ROXB.

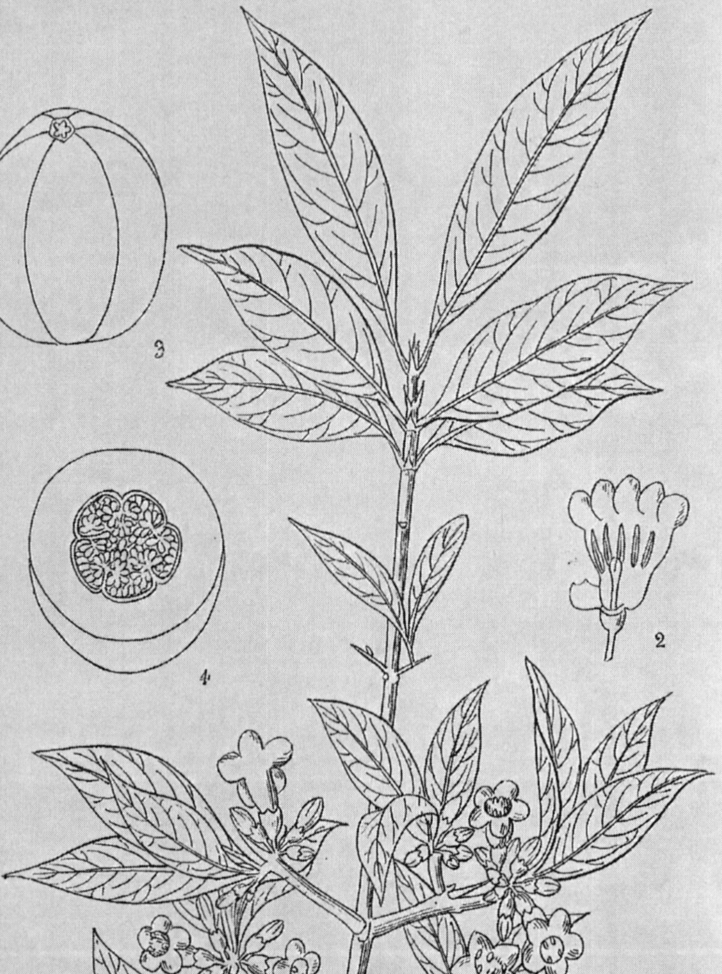

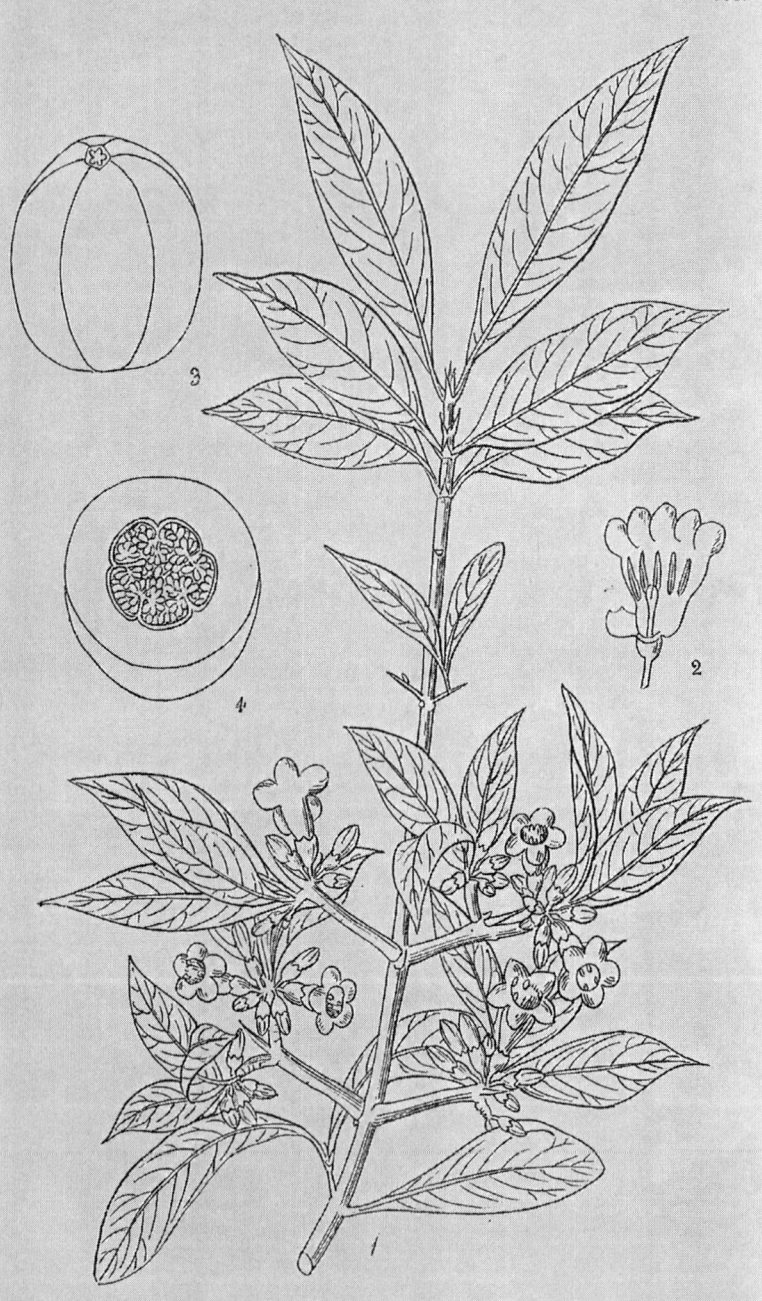

GARDENIA CAMPANULATA, ROXB.

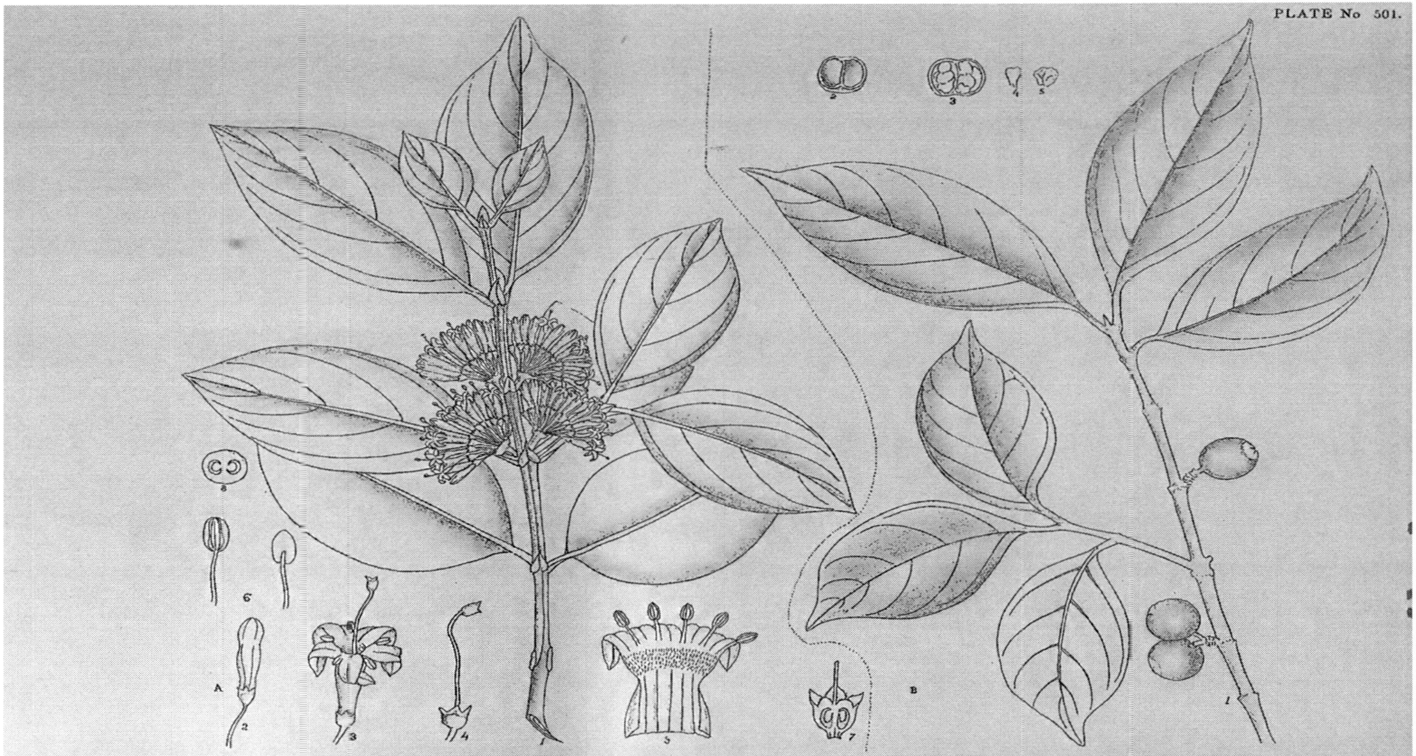

A—CANTHIUM DIDYMUM, *ROXB.* B - DIPLOSPORA SPHÆROCARPA, *HOOK. F.*

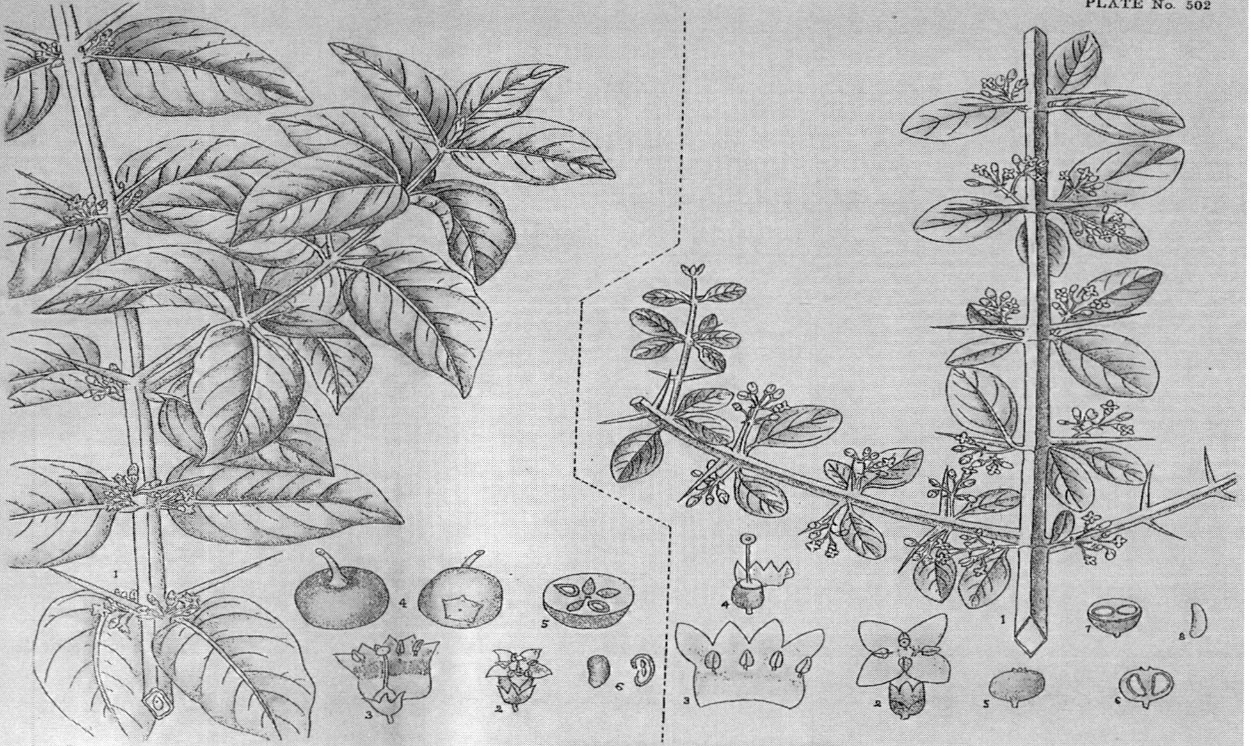

VANGUERIA SPINOSA, *Roxb.*　　CANTHIUM PARVIFLORUM, *Lamck.*

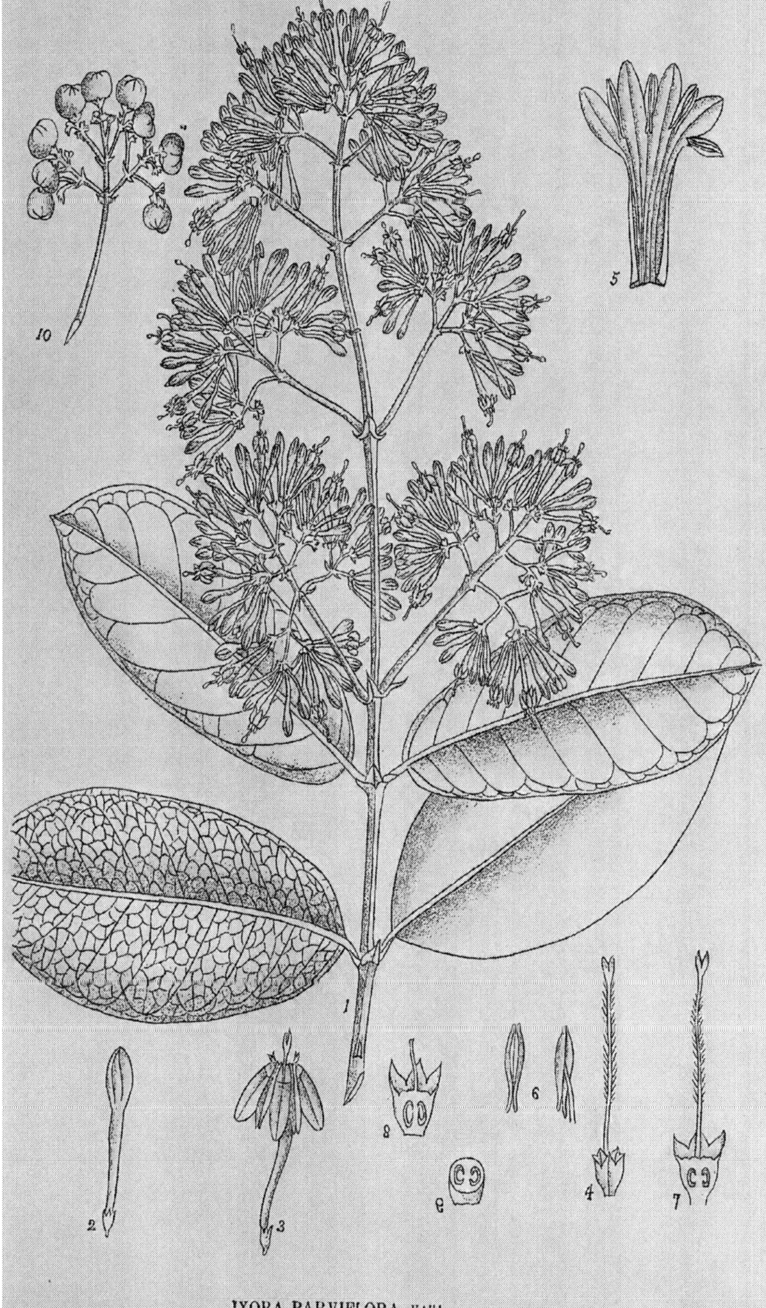

IXORA PARVIFLORA, VAHL.

PLATE No. 504.

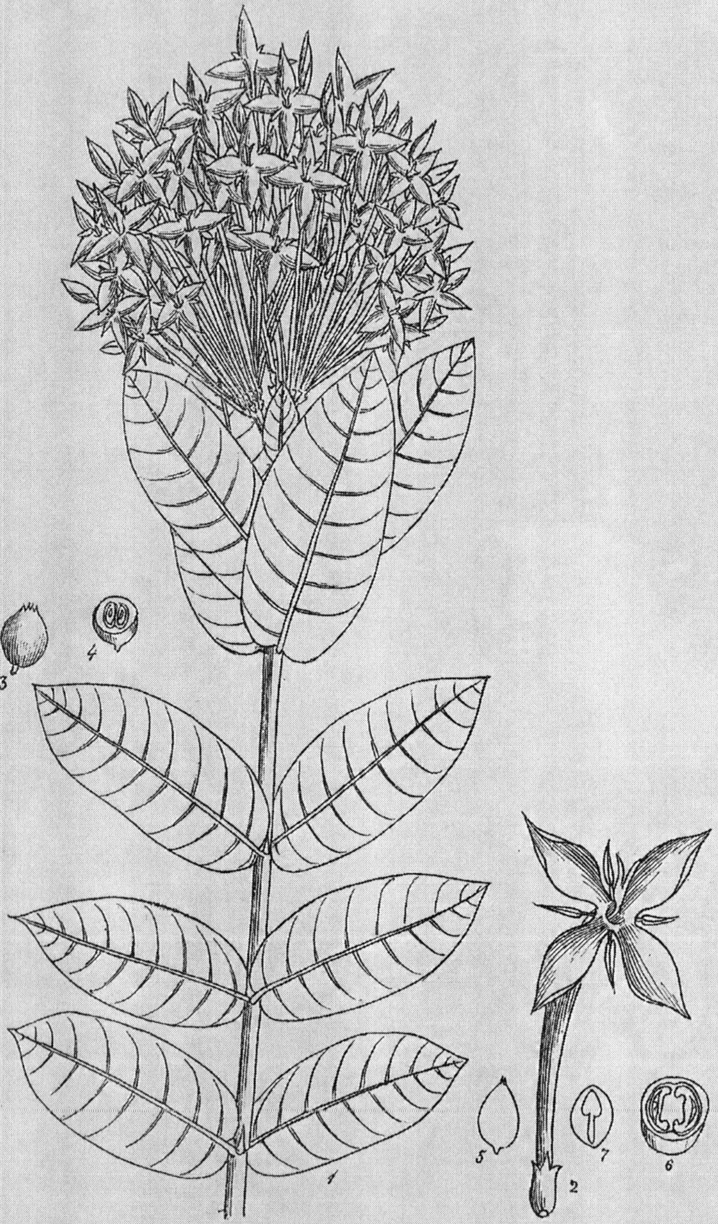

IXORA COCCINEA, *LINN.*

PLATE No. 505.

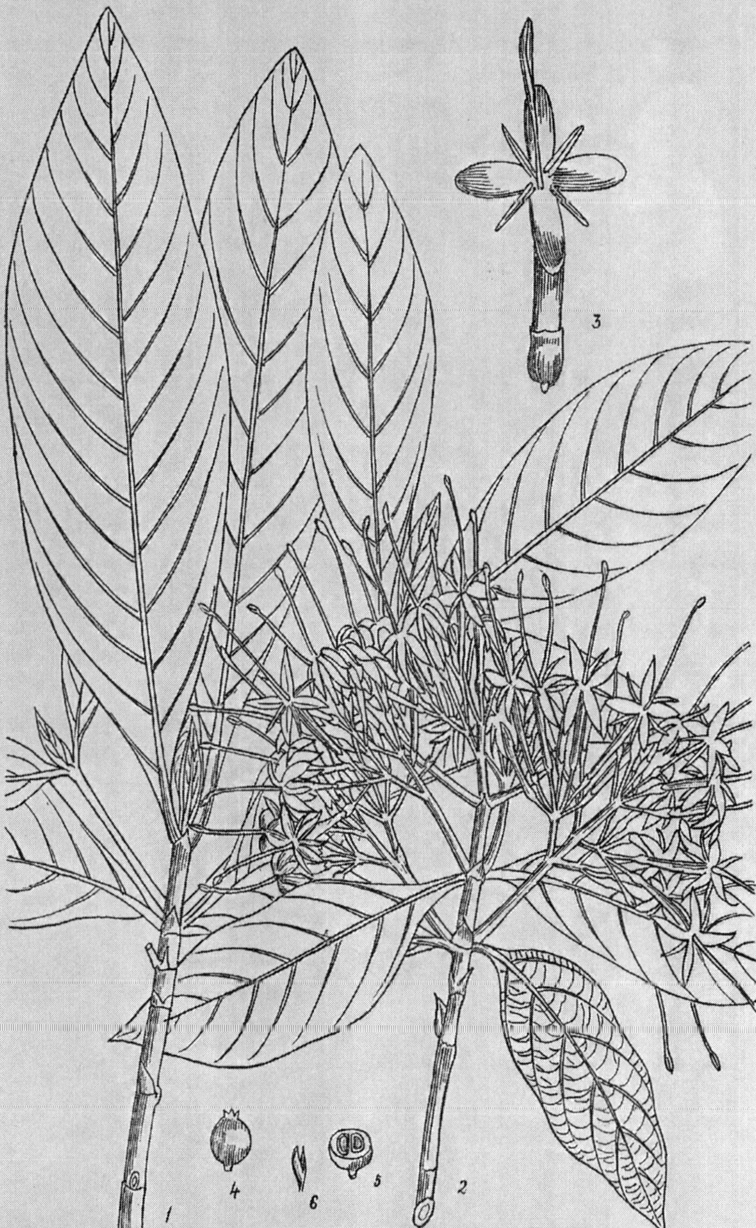

PAVETTA INDICA, LINN.

PLATE No. 506.

MORINDA CITRIFOLIA, *LINN.*

PLATE No. 507.

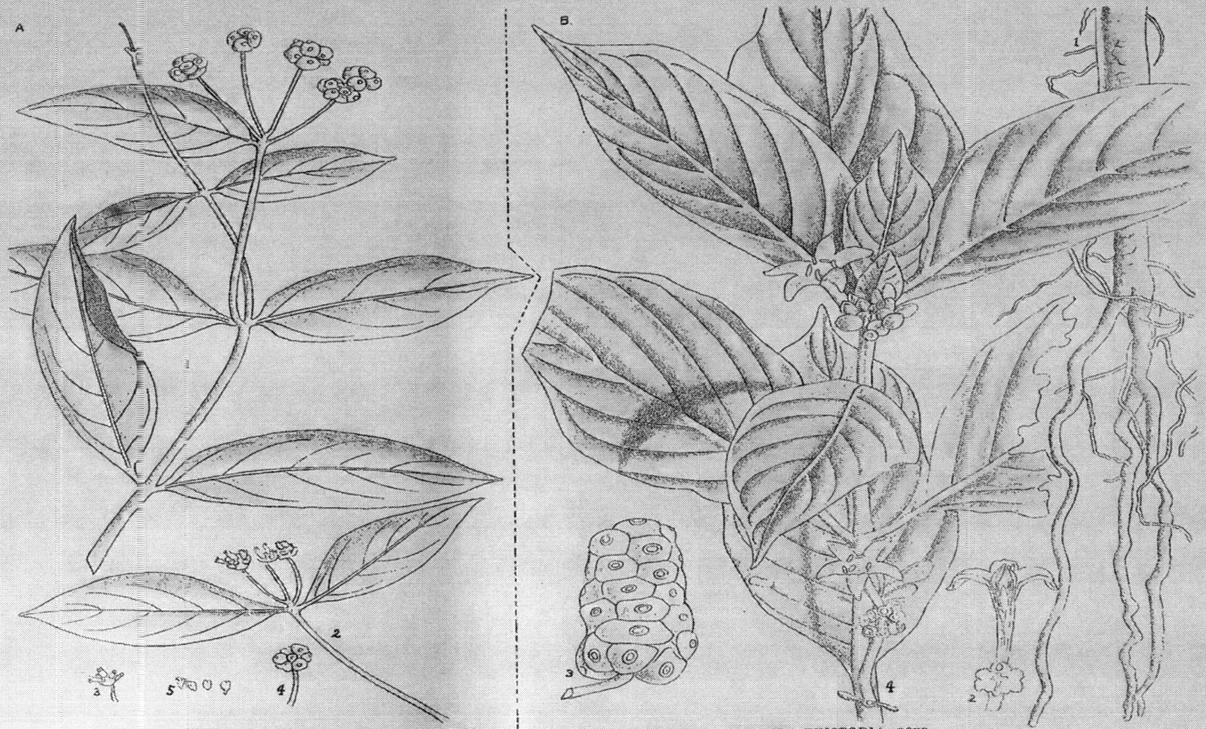

MORINDA UMBELLATA, LINN.

MORINDA TINCTORIA, ROXB

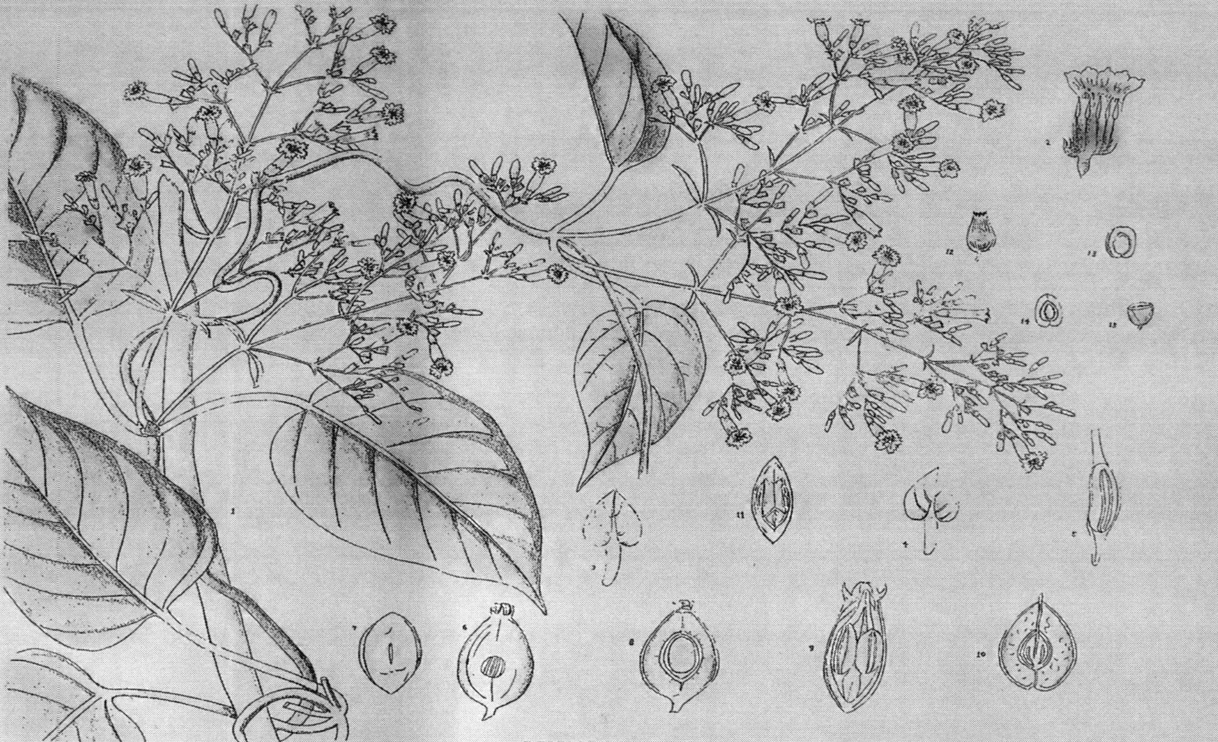

PÆDERIA FOETIDA, LINN.

PLATE No. 509.

B–NARDOSTACHYS JATAMANSI, *DC* A–SPERMACOCE HISPIDA, *LIN.*

PLATE No. 510.

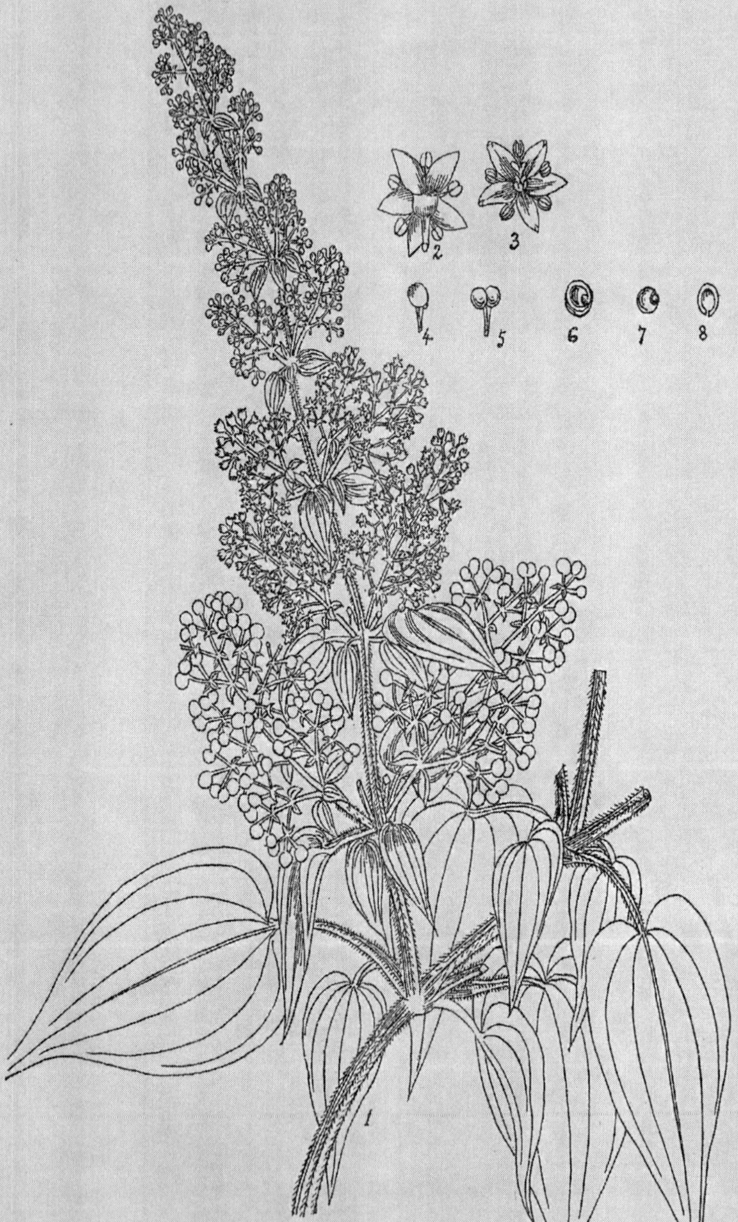

RUBIA CORDIFOLIA, *LINN.*

PLATE No. 511.

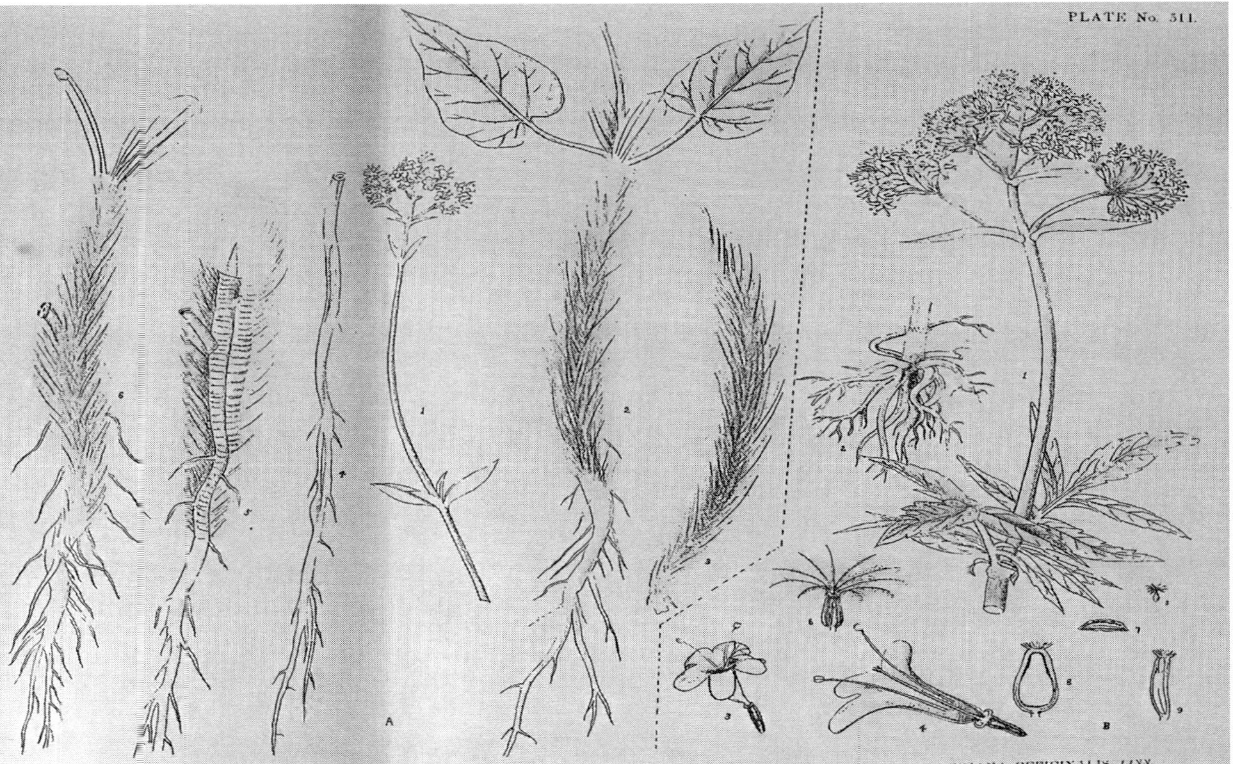

A—VALERIANA WALLICHII, *DC.*

B—VALERIANA OFFICINALIS, *LINN.*

PLATE No. 512

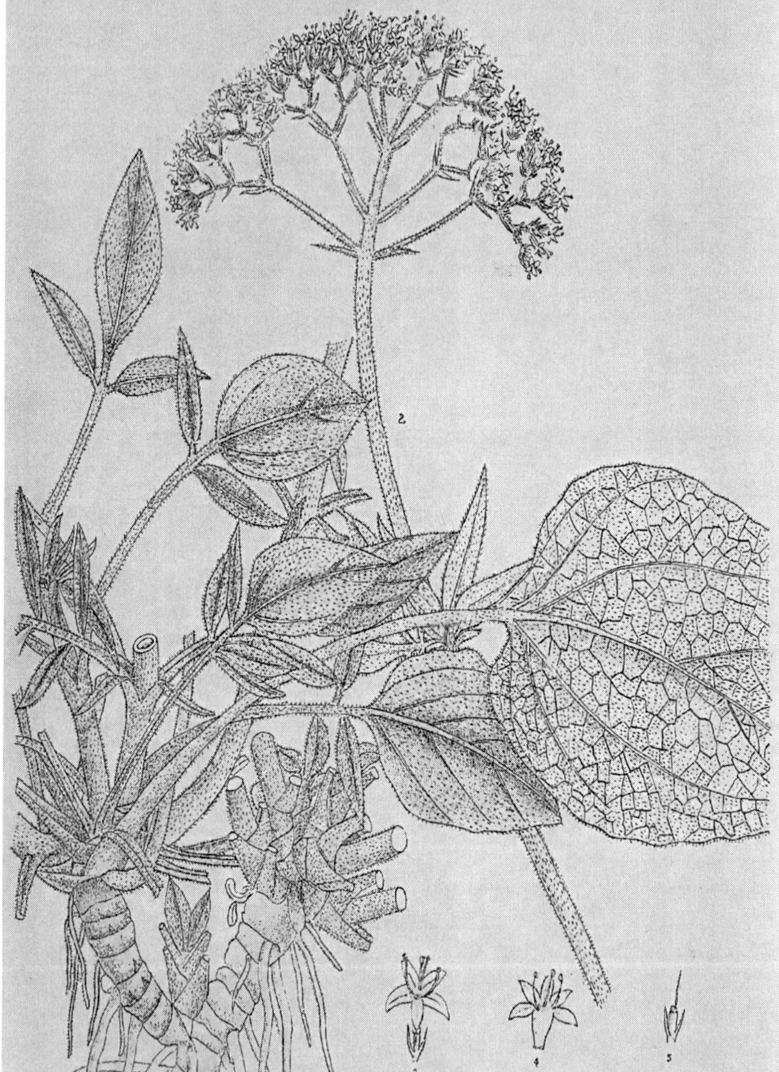

VALERIANA HARDWICKII, WALL.

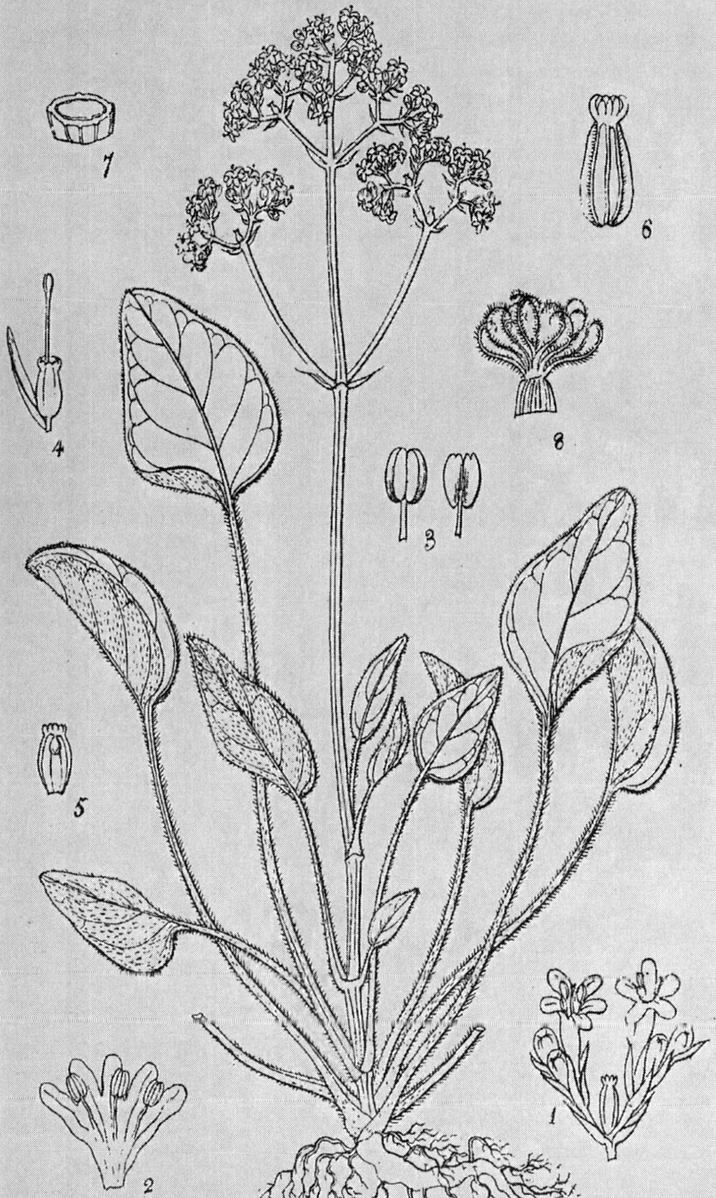

VALERIANA LESCHENAULTII, *DC. VAR. BRUNONIANA. W. & A.*

PLATE No. 514.

MORINA PERSICA, *LINN.*

PLATE No. 515.

A—VERNONIA ANTHELMINTICA, *WILLD.* B—LAMPRACHÆNIUM MICROCEPHALUM, *BENTH.*

PLATE No. 516.

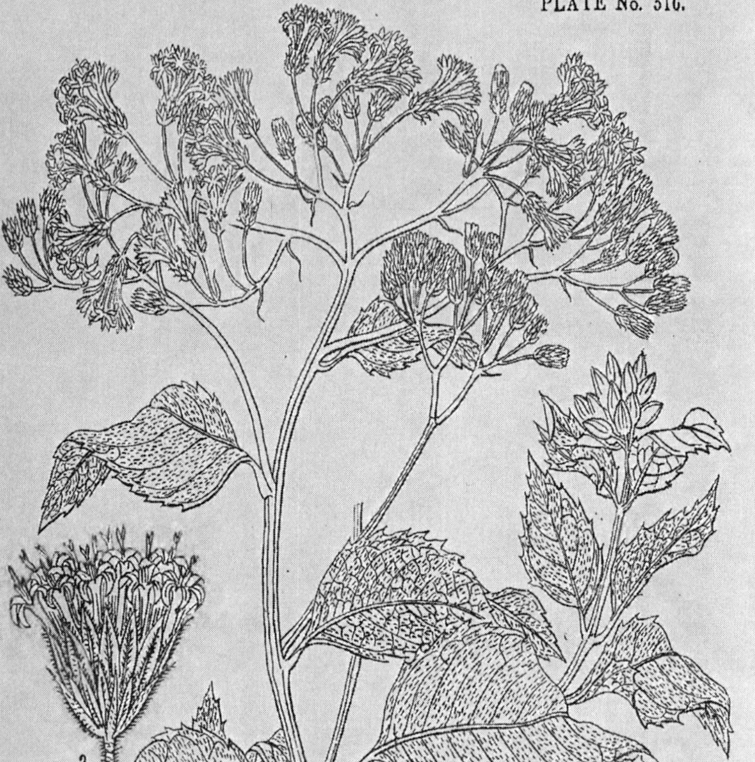

VERNONIA CINEREA, LESS.

PLATE No. 517.

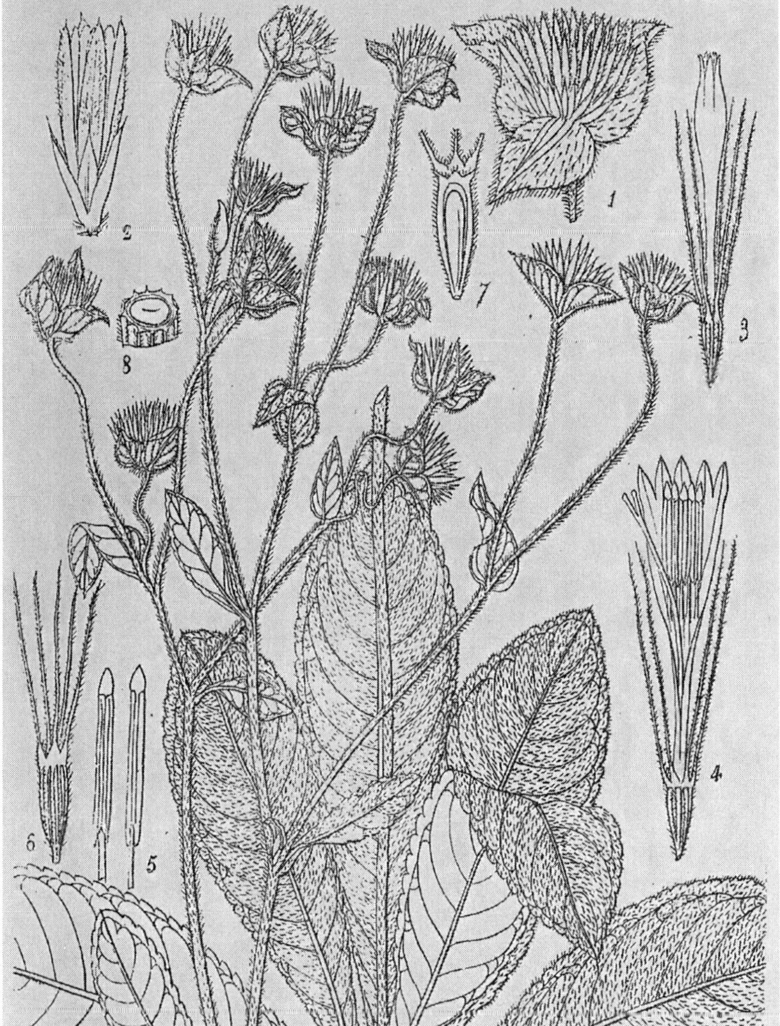

ELEPHANTOPUS SCABER, *LINN.*

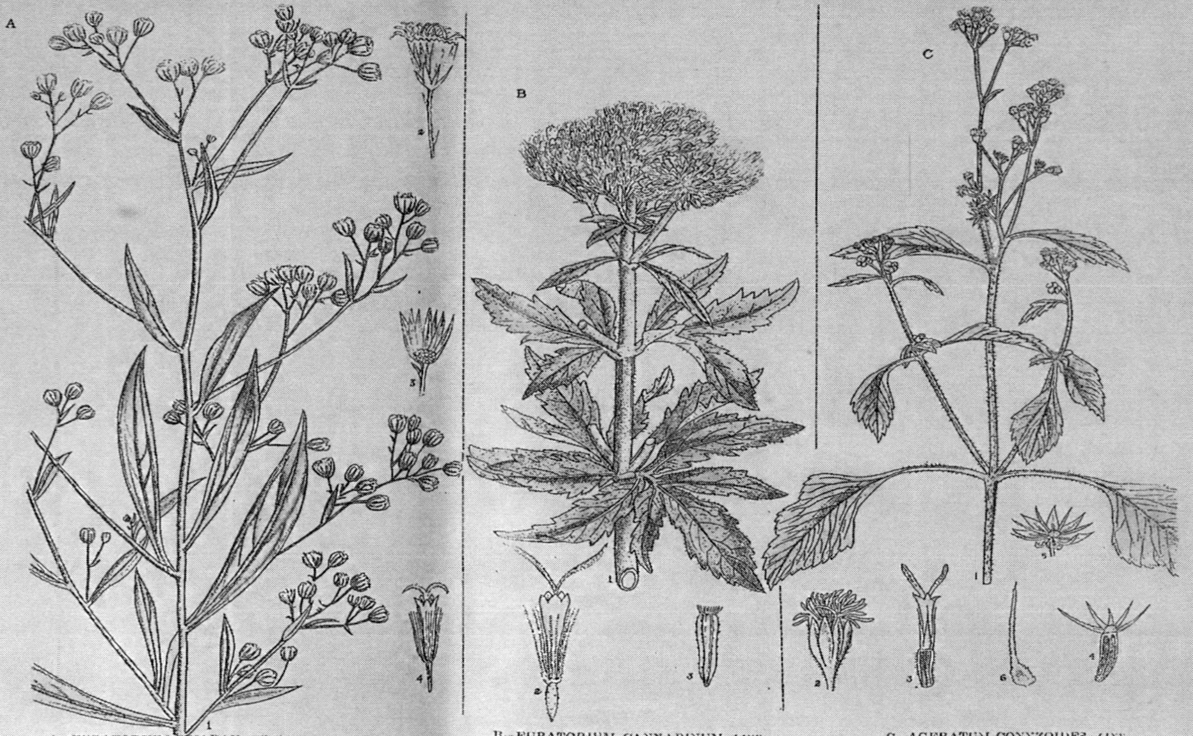

A.—EUPATORIUM AYAPAN, *Vent.* B.—EUPATORIUM CANNABINUM, *Linn.* C.—AGERATUM CONYZOIDES, *Linn.*

PLATE No. 519.

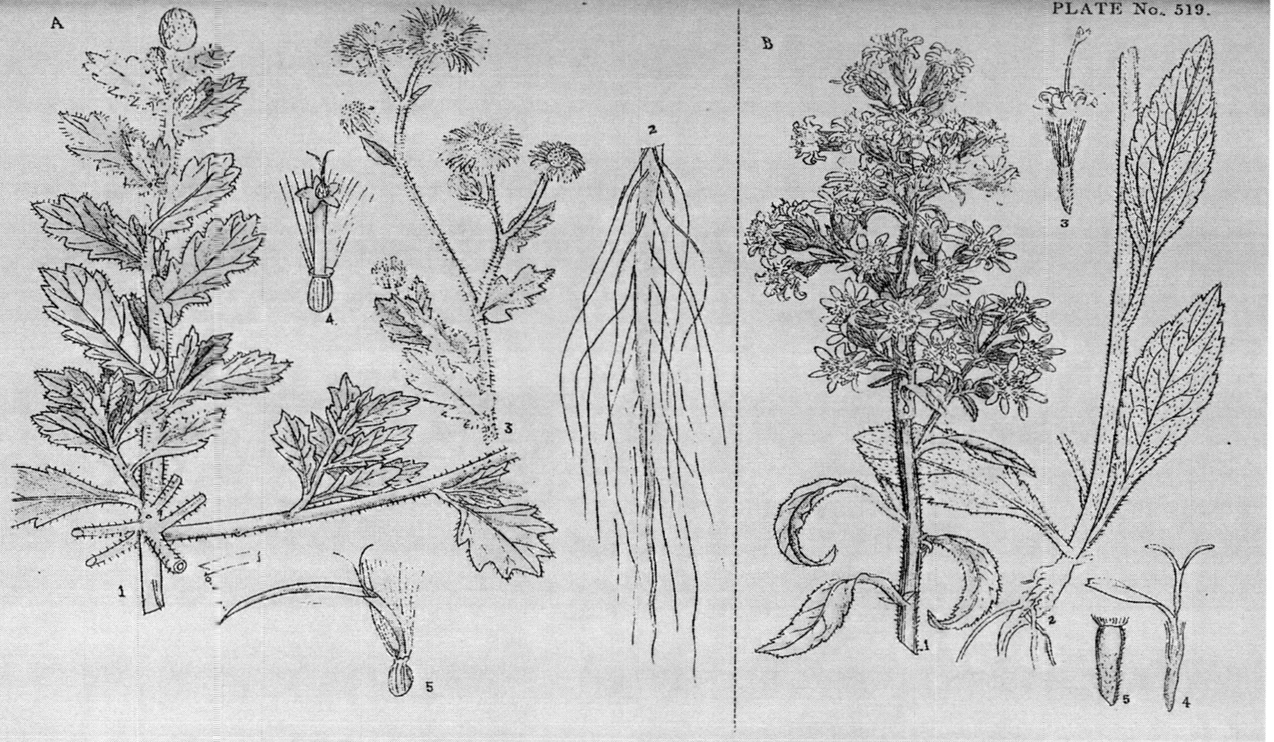

A—ERIGERON ASTEROIDES, *ROXB.*　　B—SOLIDAGO VIRGA-AUREA, *LINN.*

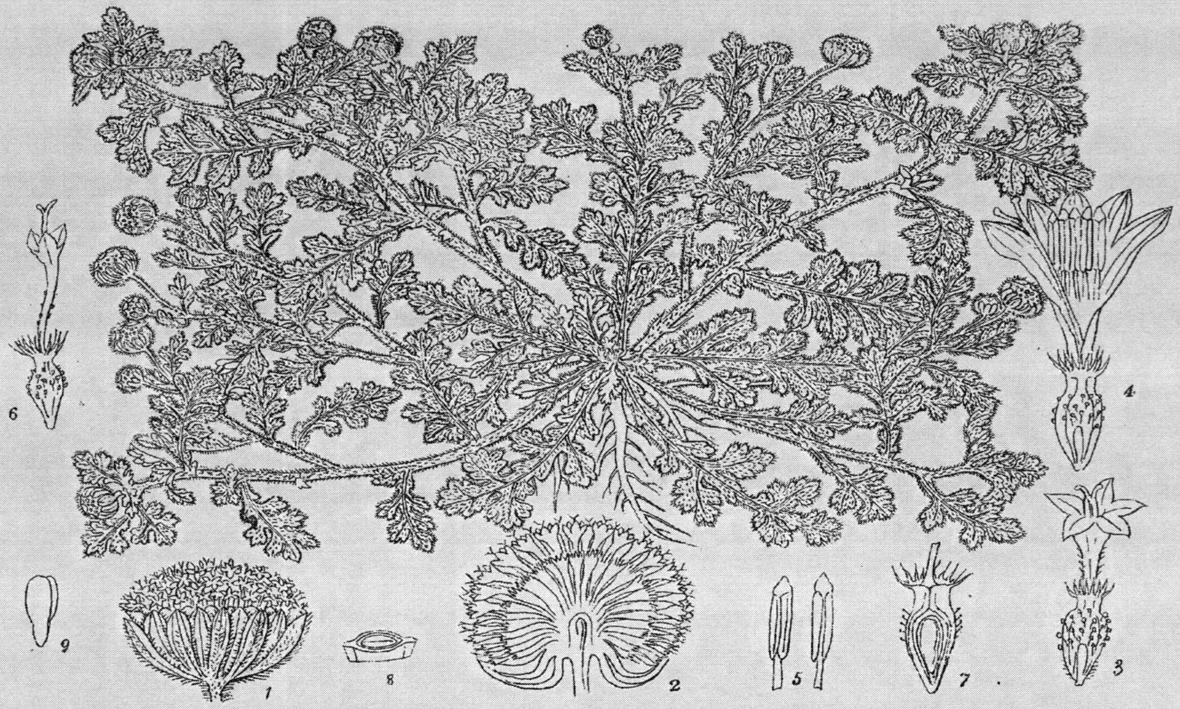

GRANGEA MADERASPATANA, POIR.

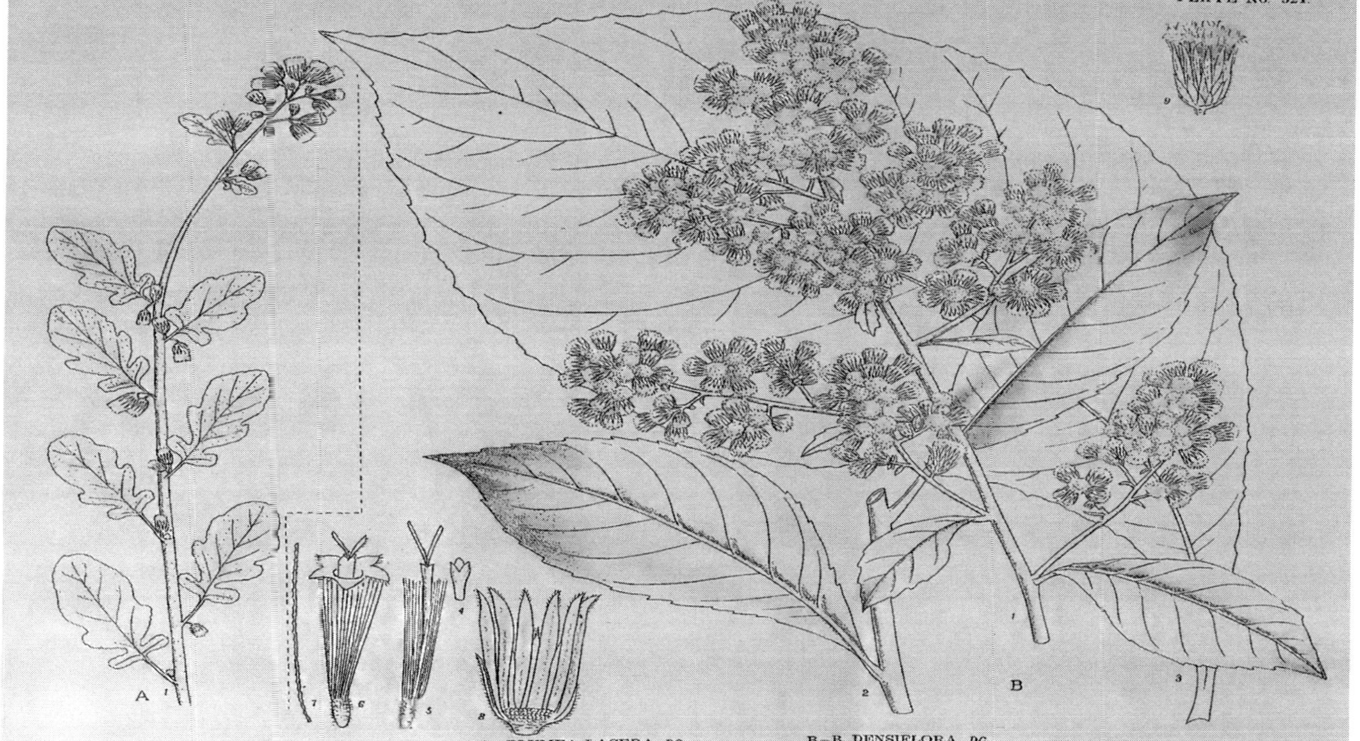

A—BLUMEA LACERA, *DC.*   B—B. DENSIFLORA, *DC.*

PLATE No. 522.

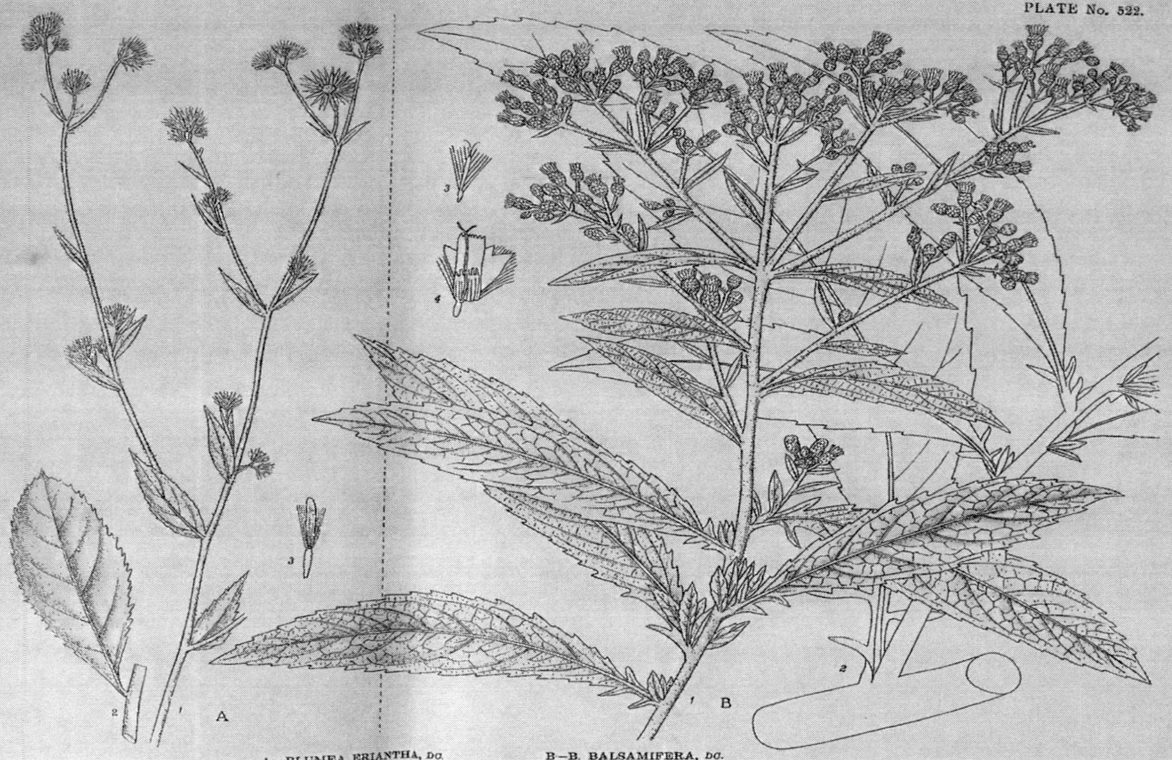

A -BLUMEA ERIANTHA, *DC.* B-B. BALSAMIFERA, *DC.*

PLATE No. 523.

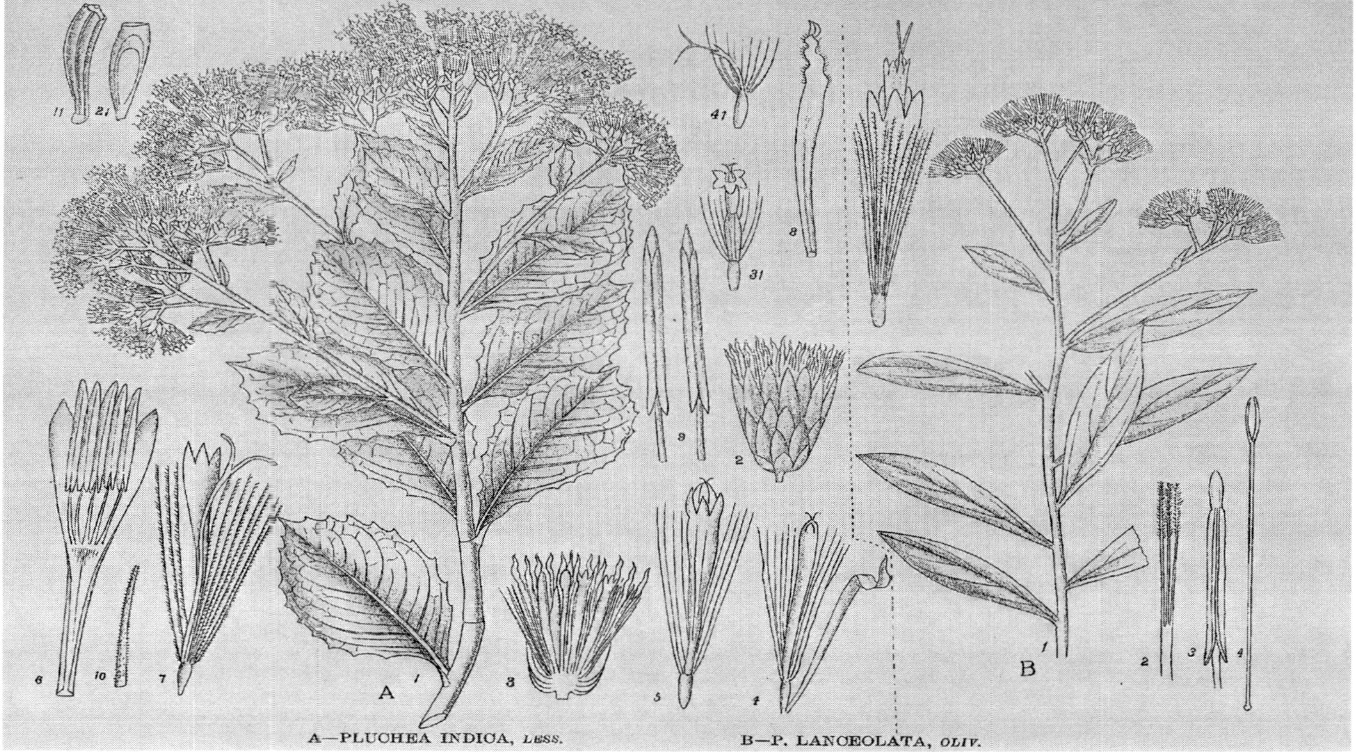

A—PLUCHEA INDICA, *LESS.*

B—P. LANCEOLATA, *OLIV.*

PLATE No 524.

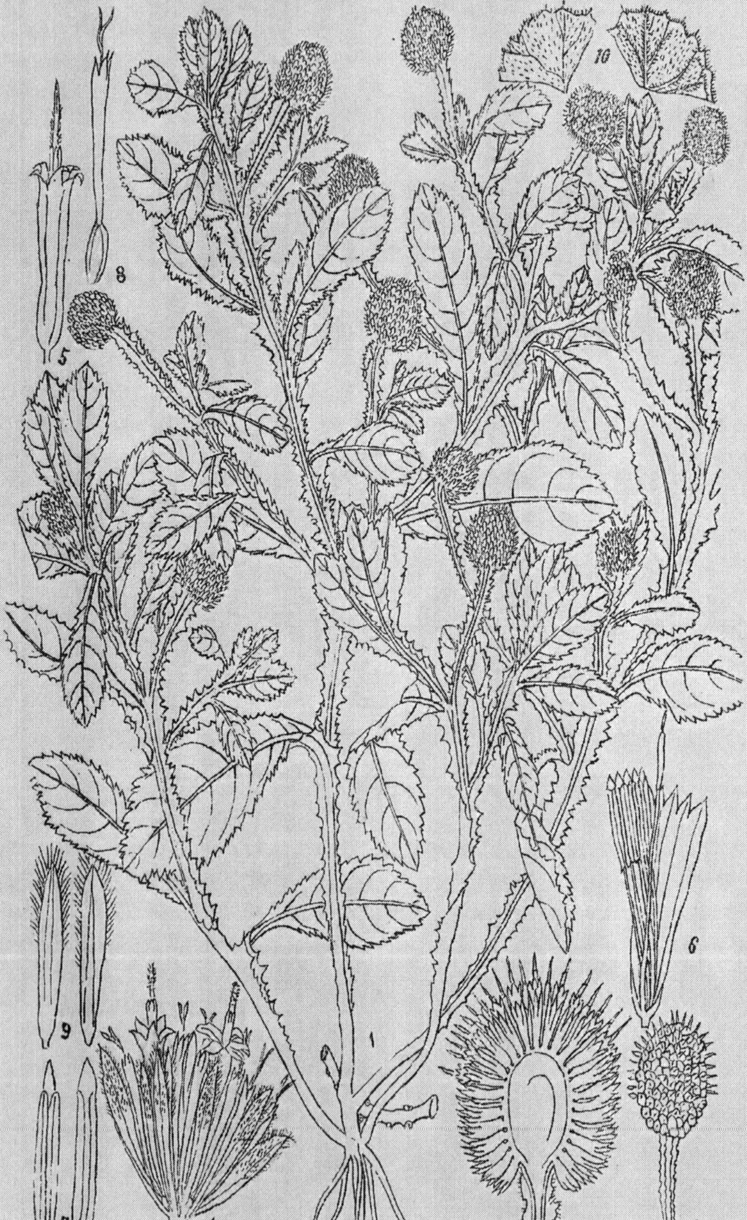

SPHÆRANTHUS INDICUS, *LINN.*

PLATE No. 525.

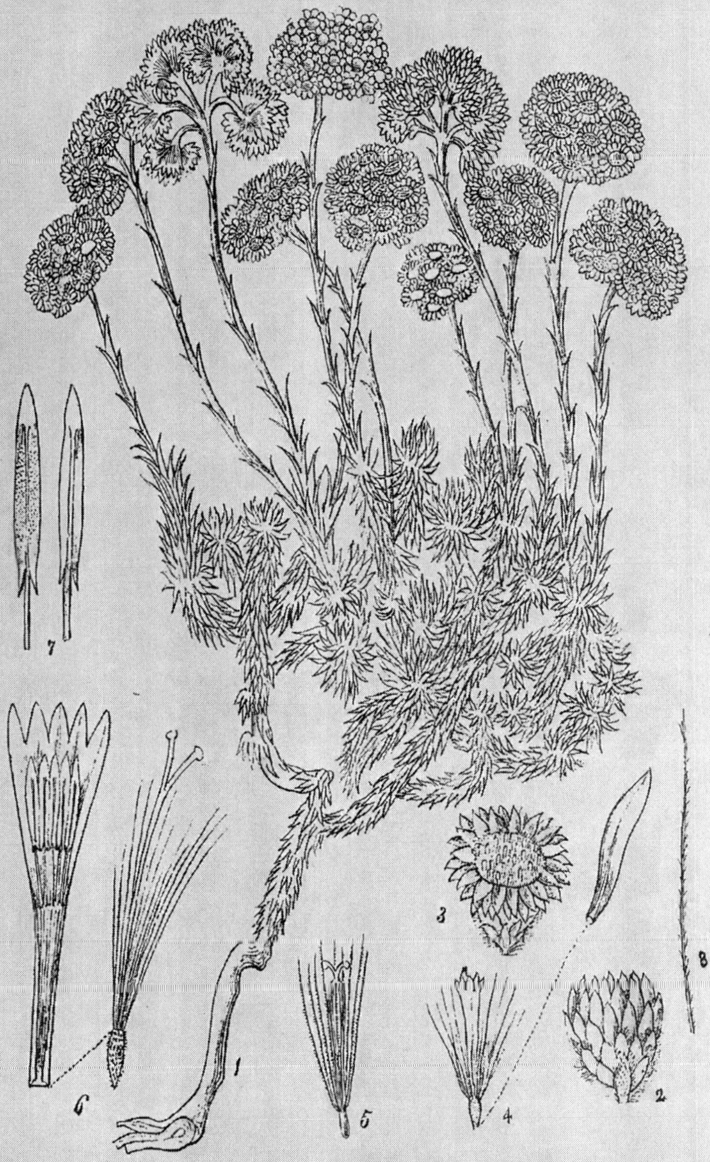

ANAPHALIS NEELGERRIANA, *DC.*

PLATE No. 526.

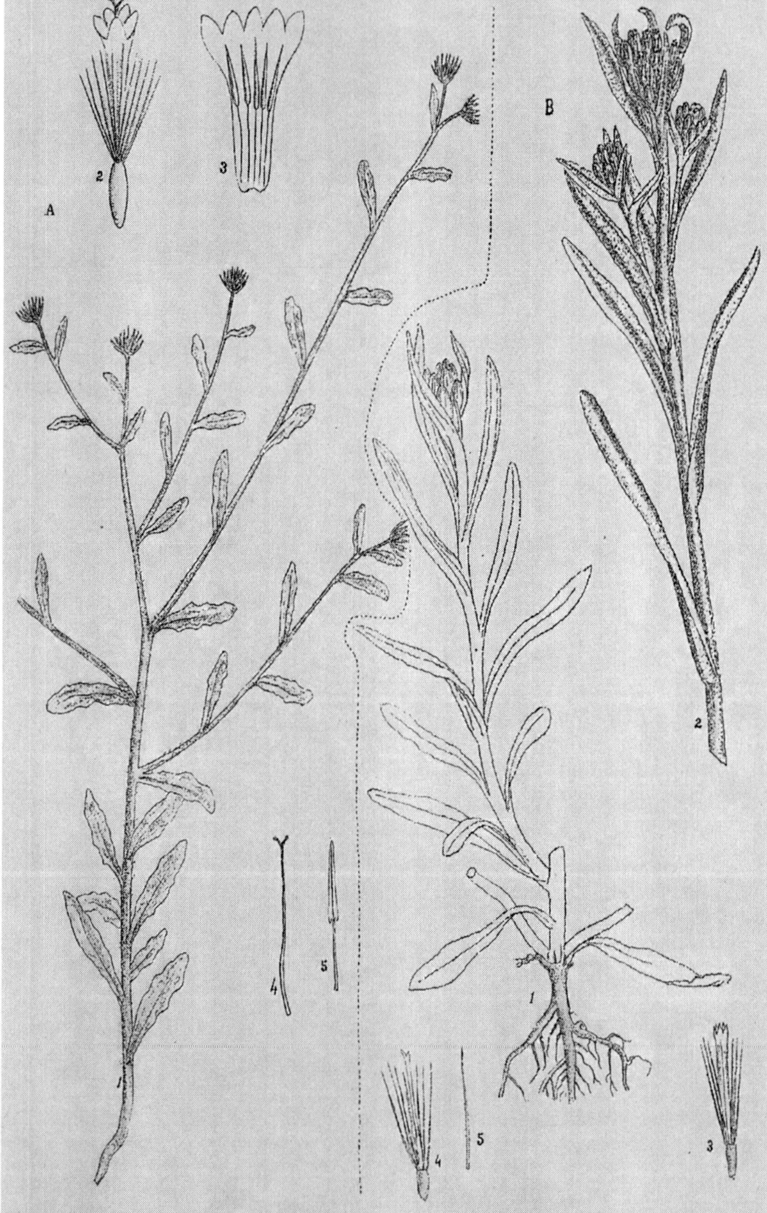

A – PULICARIA CRISPA, BENTH.

B – GNAPHALIUM LUTEO-ALBUM, LINN.

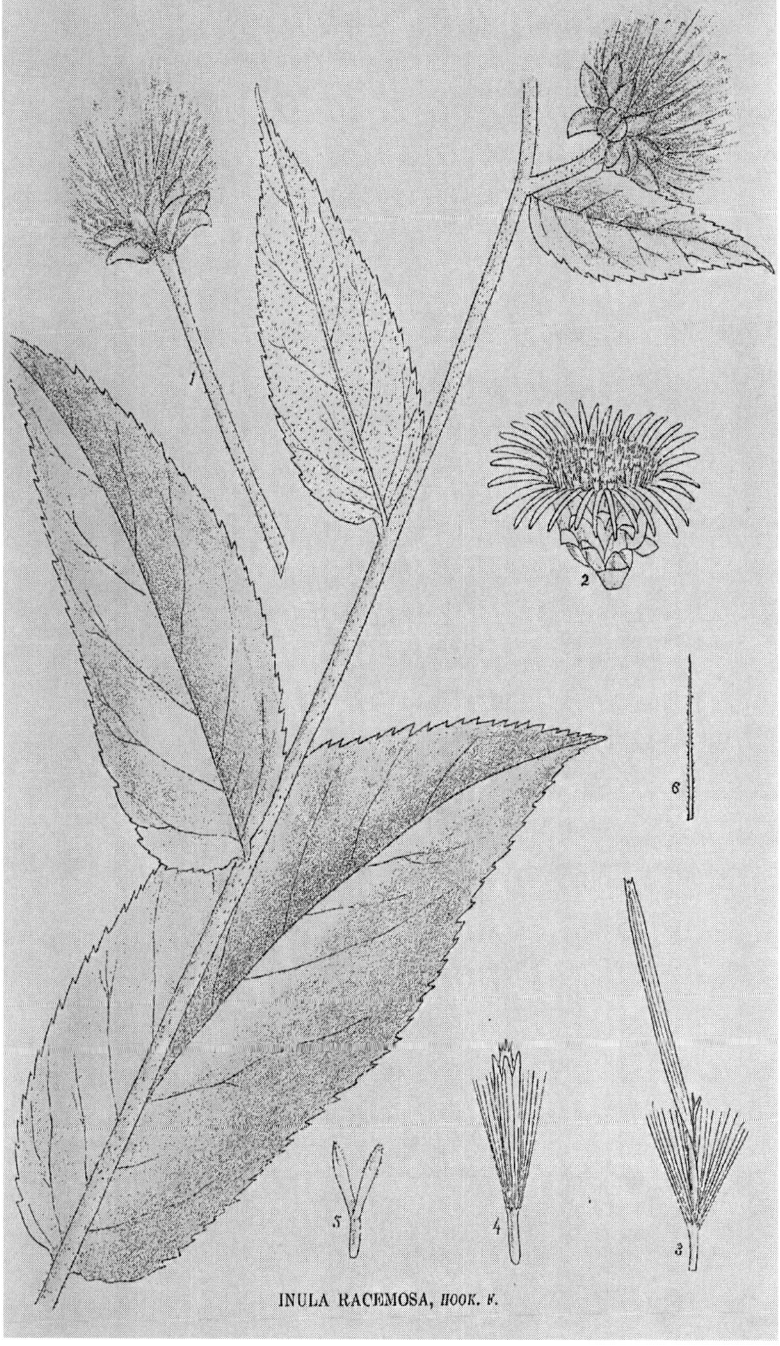

INULA RACEMOSA, HOOK. F.

PLATE No 528.

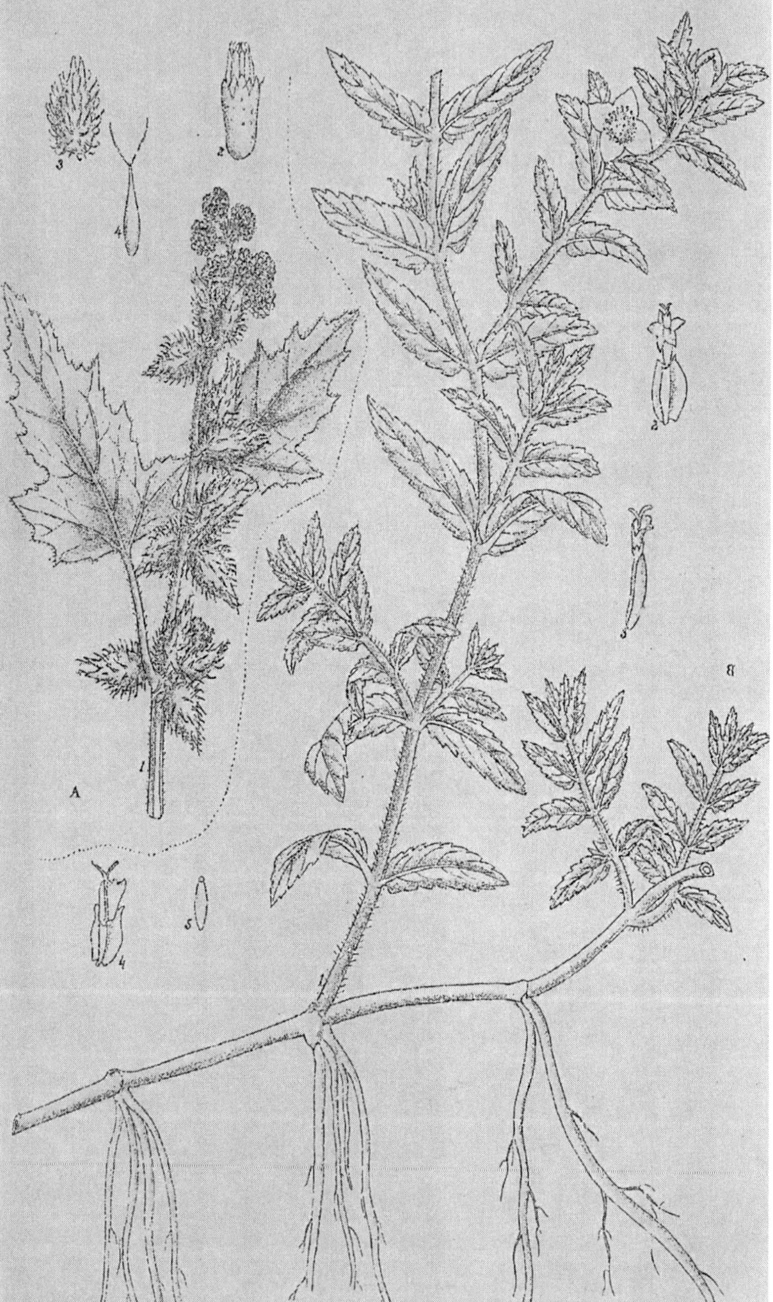

A—XANTHIUM STRUMARIUM, *LINN.* B—ENHYDRA FLUCTUANS, *LOUR*

PLATE No. 529.

SIEGESBECKIA ORIENTALIS, *Linn.*

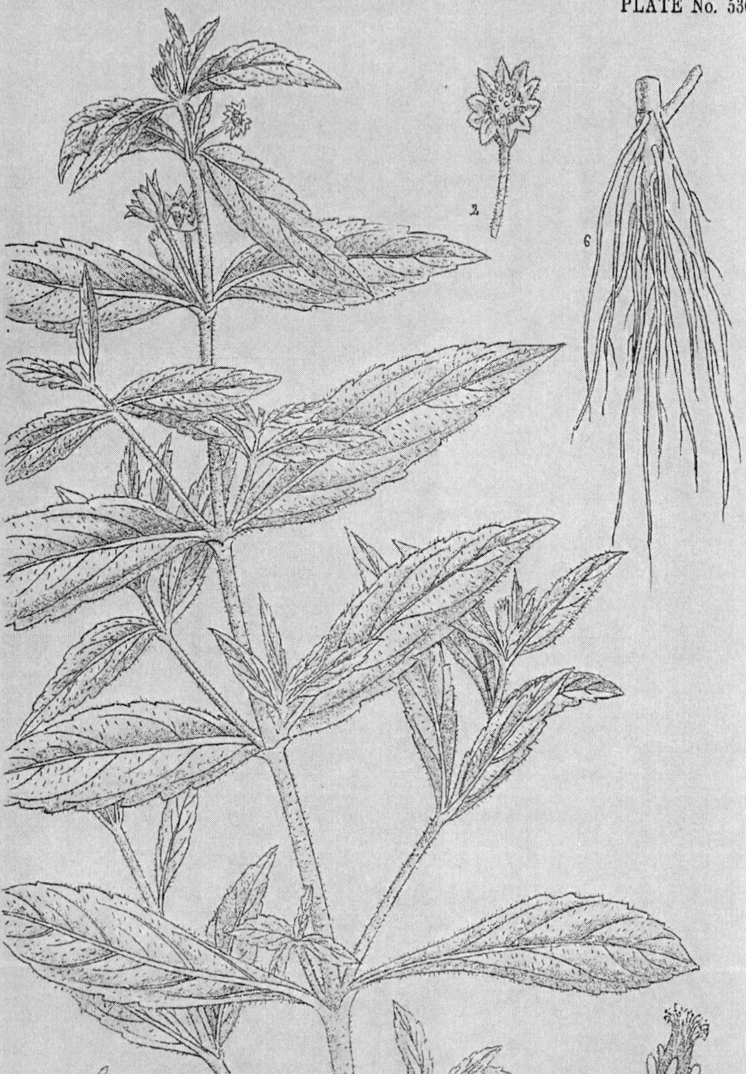

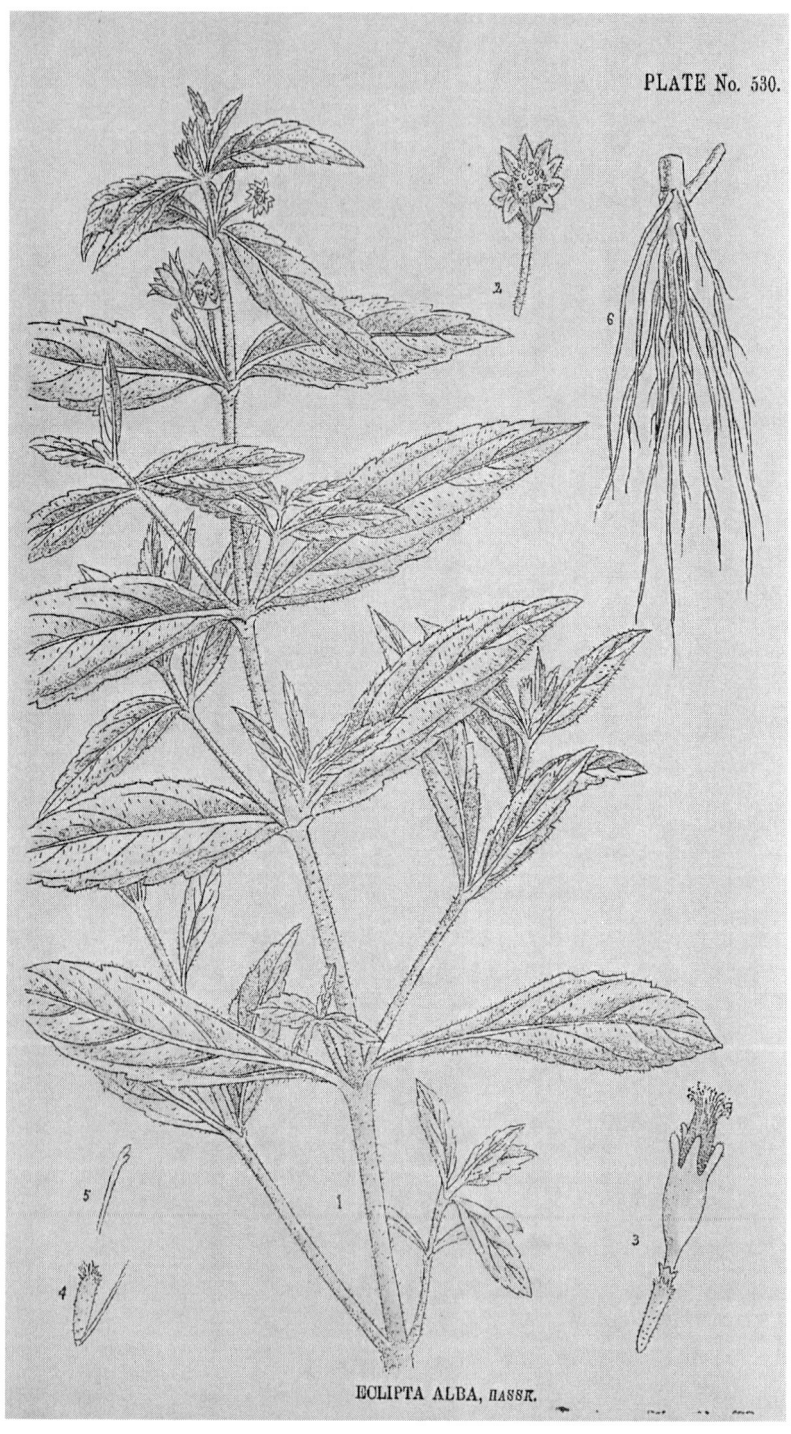

ECLIPTA ALBA, HASSK.

PLATE No. 531.

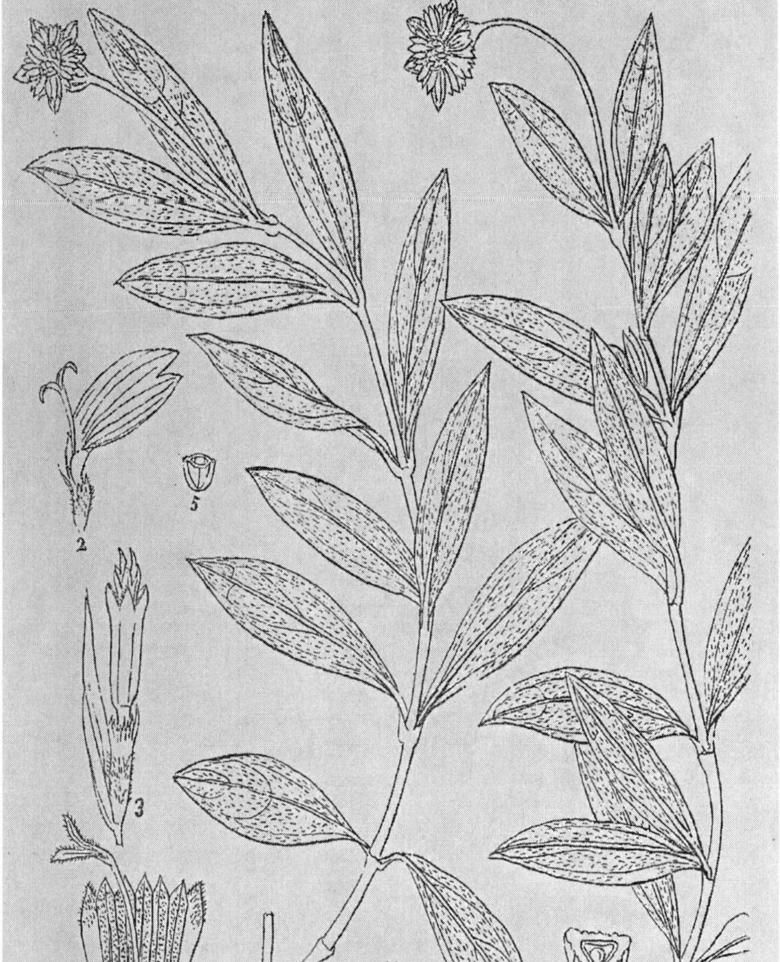

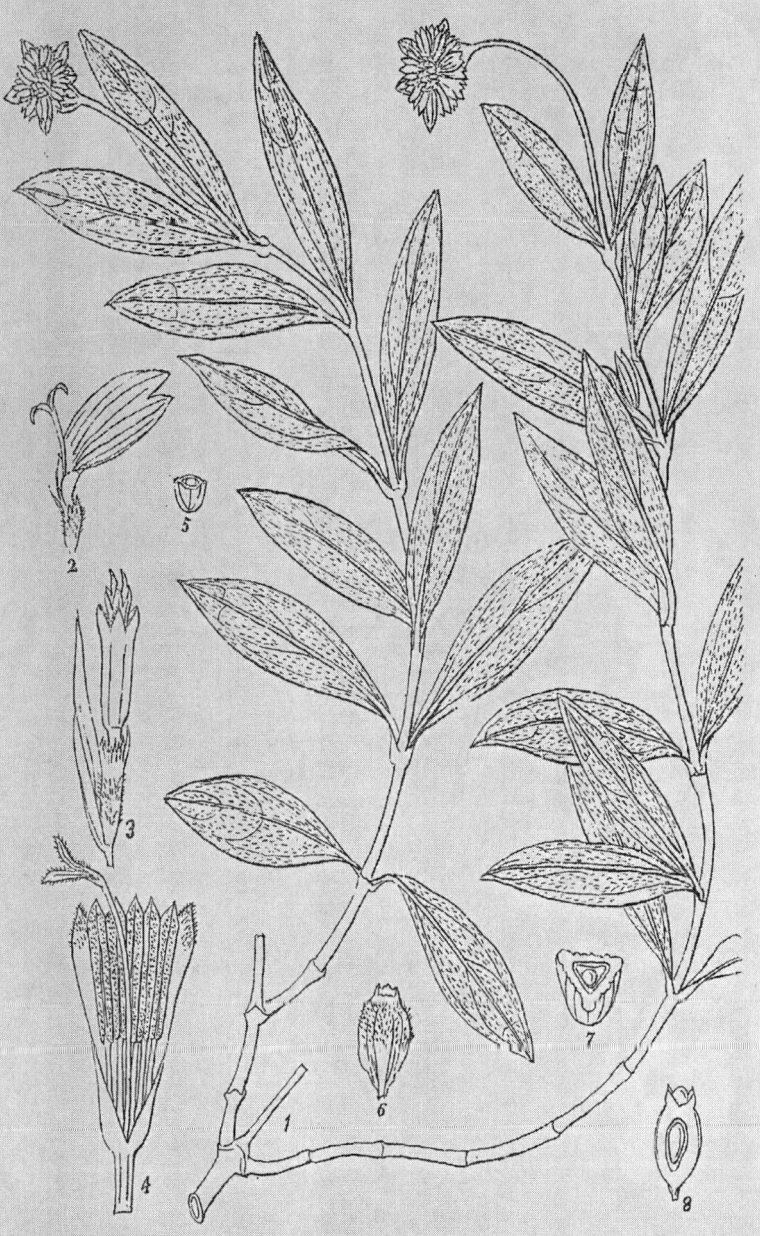

WEDELIA CALENDULACEA, LESS.

PLATE No. 532.

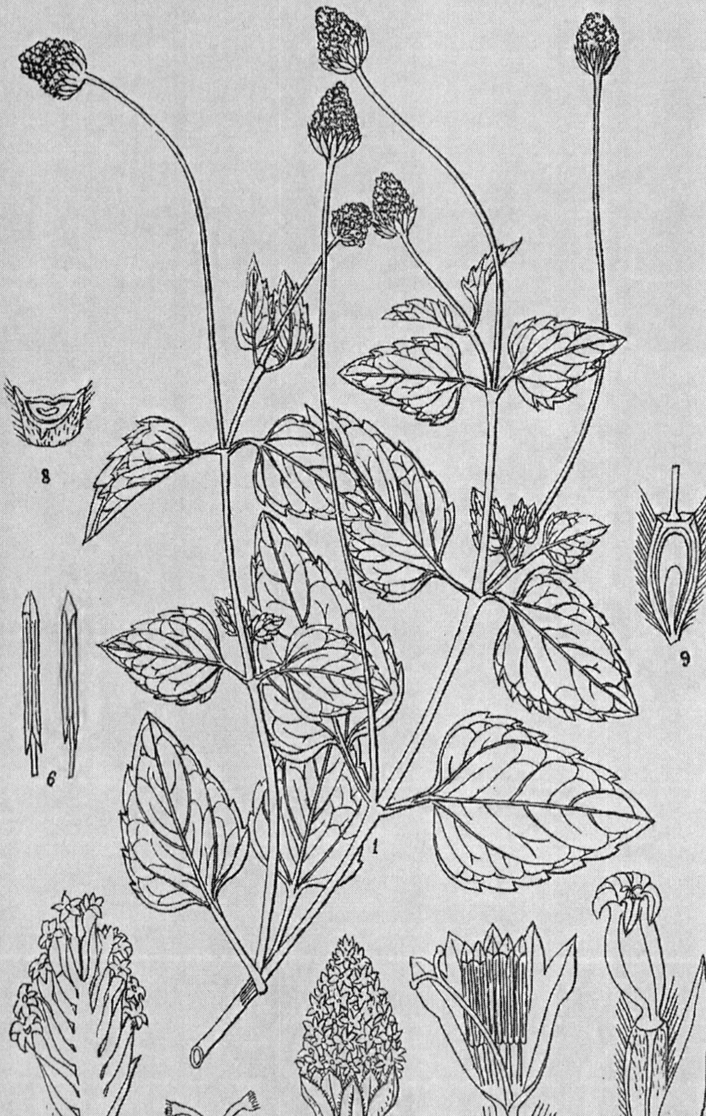

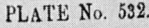

SPILANTHES ACMELLA, *LINN.*

PLATE No. 533

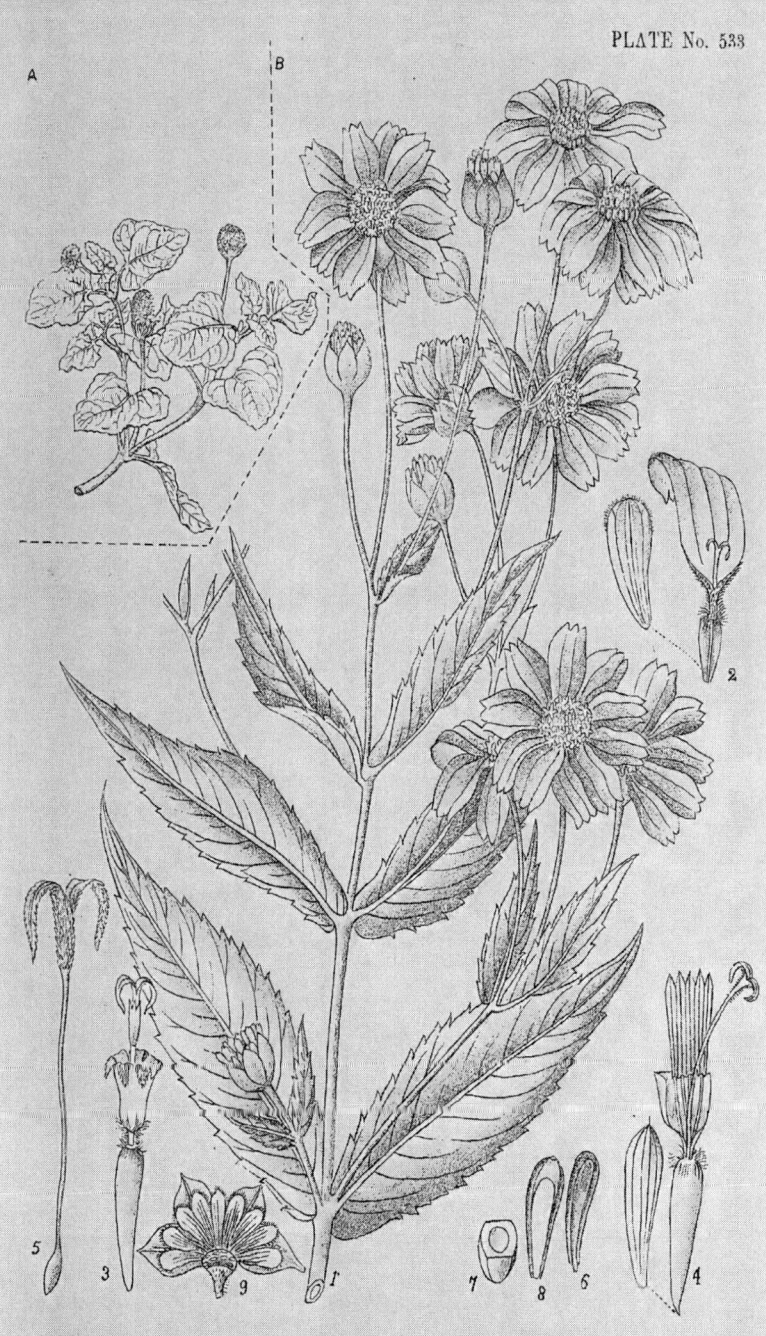

A—SPILANTHES OLERACEA, JACQ. B. GUIZOTIA ABYSSINICA, CASS.

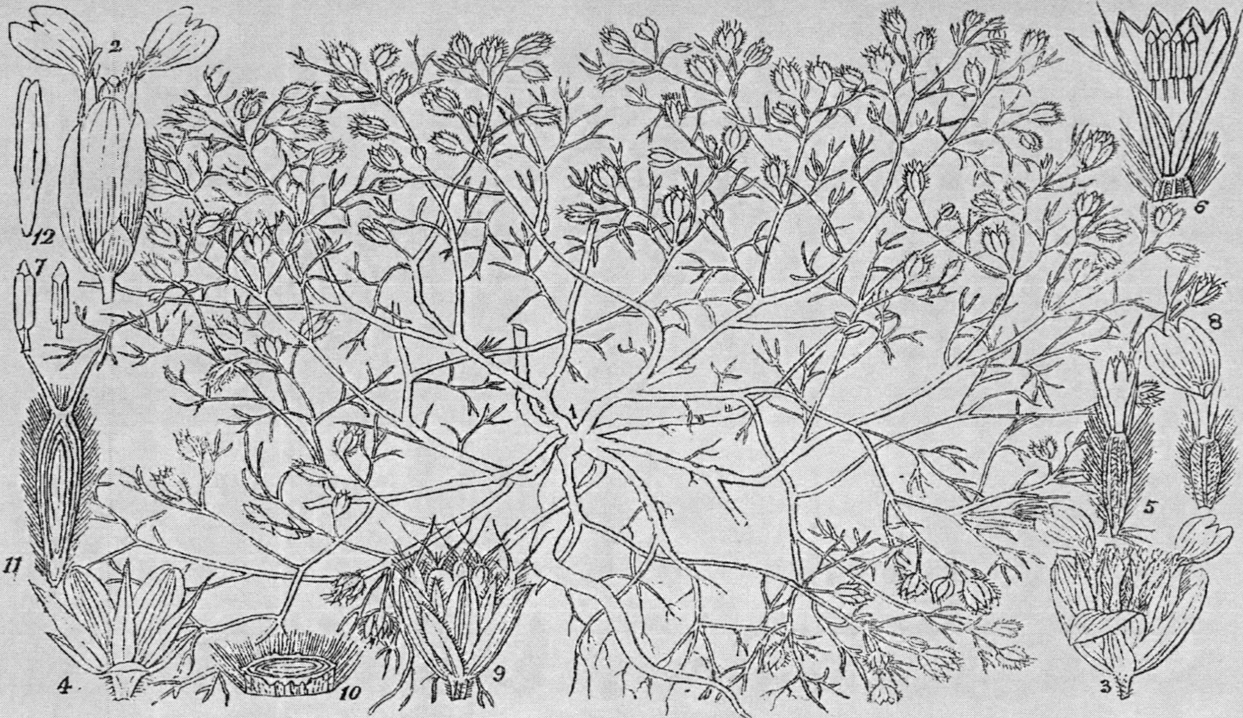

GLOSSOCARDIA LINEARIFOLIA, CASS.

PLATE No. 535.

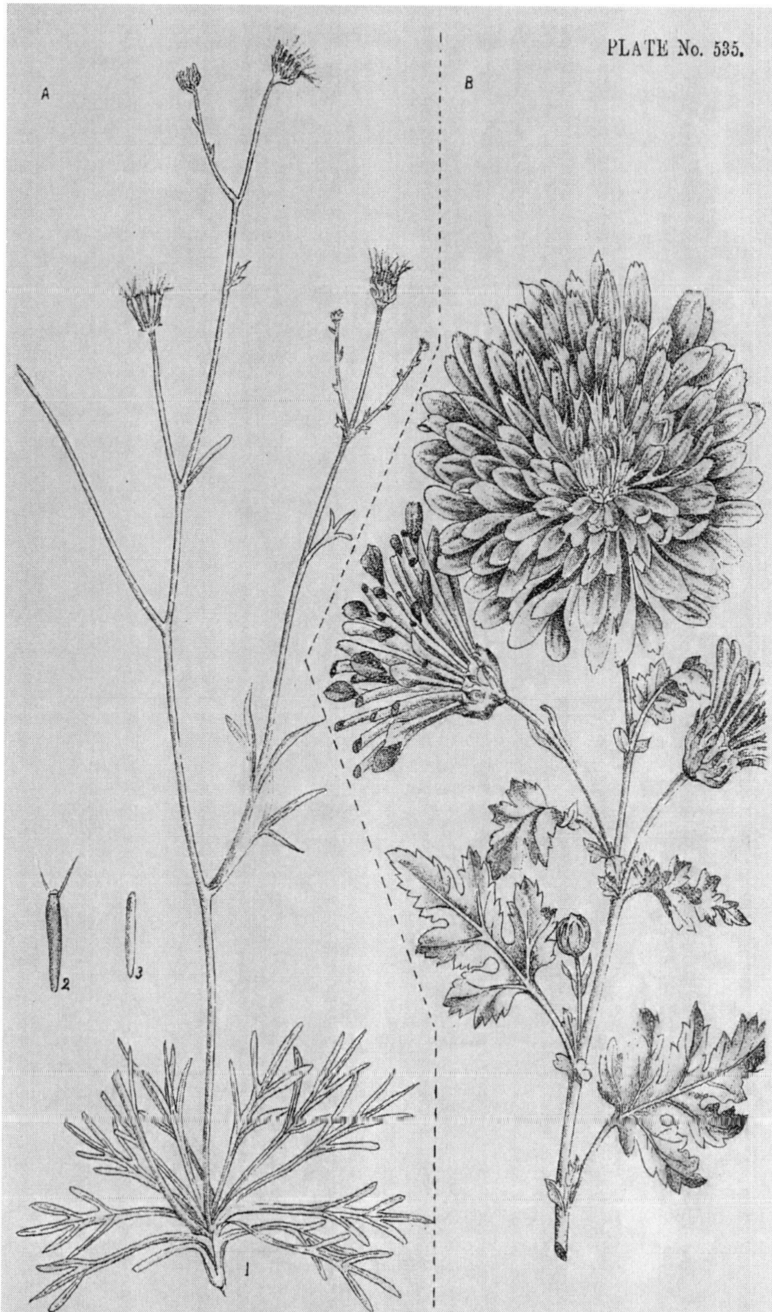

A–GLOSSOGYNE PINNATIFIDA, *DC.* B–CHRYSANTHEMUM INDICUM, *LINN.*

PLATE No. 536.

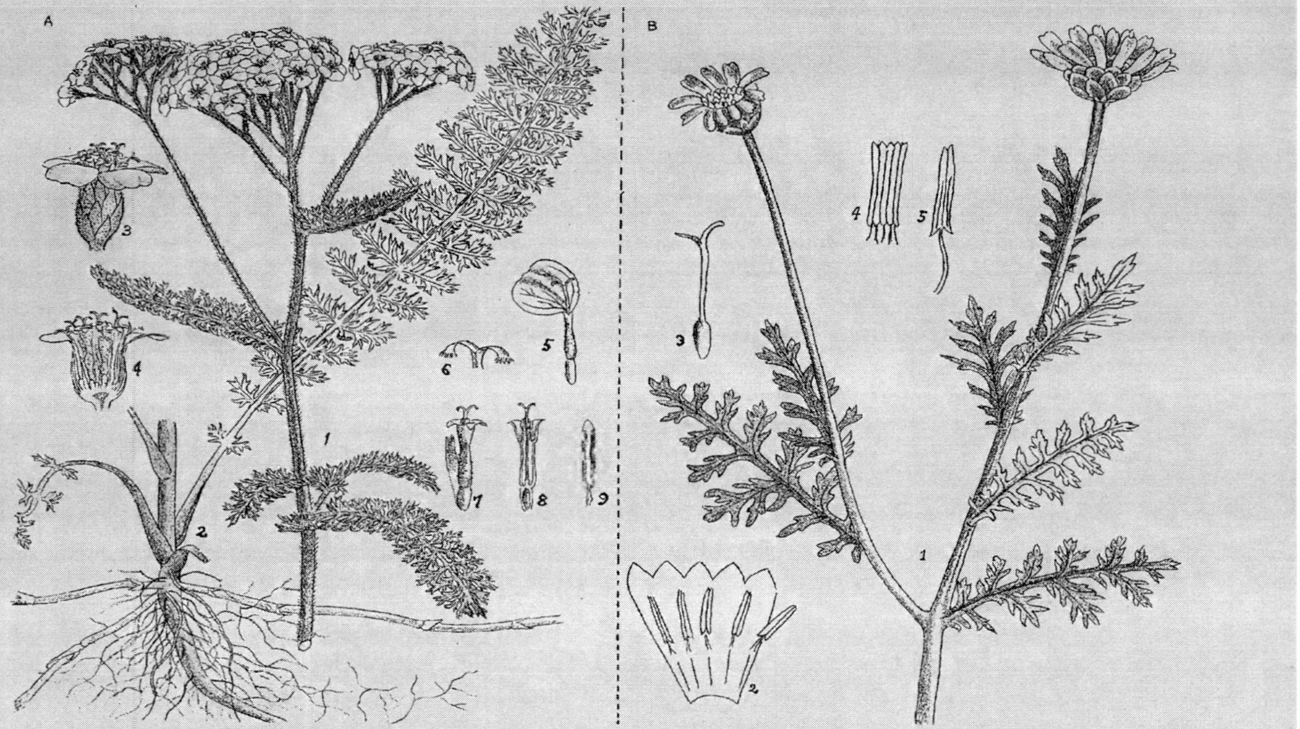

A – ACHILLEA MILLEFOLIUM, *LINN.*

B – CHRYSANTHEMUM CORONARIUM, *LINN.*

PLATE No 537.

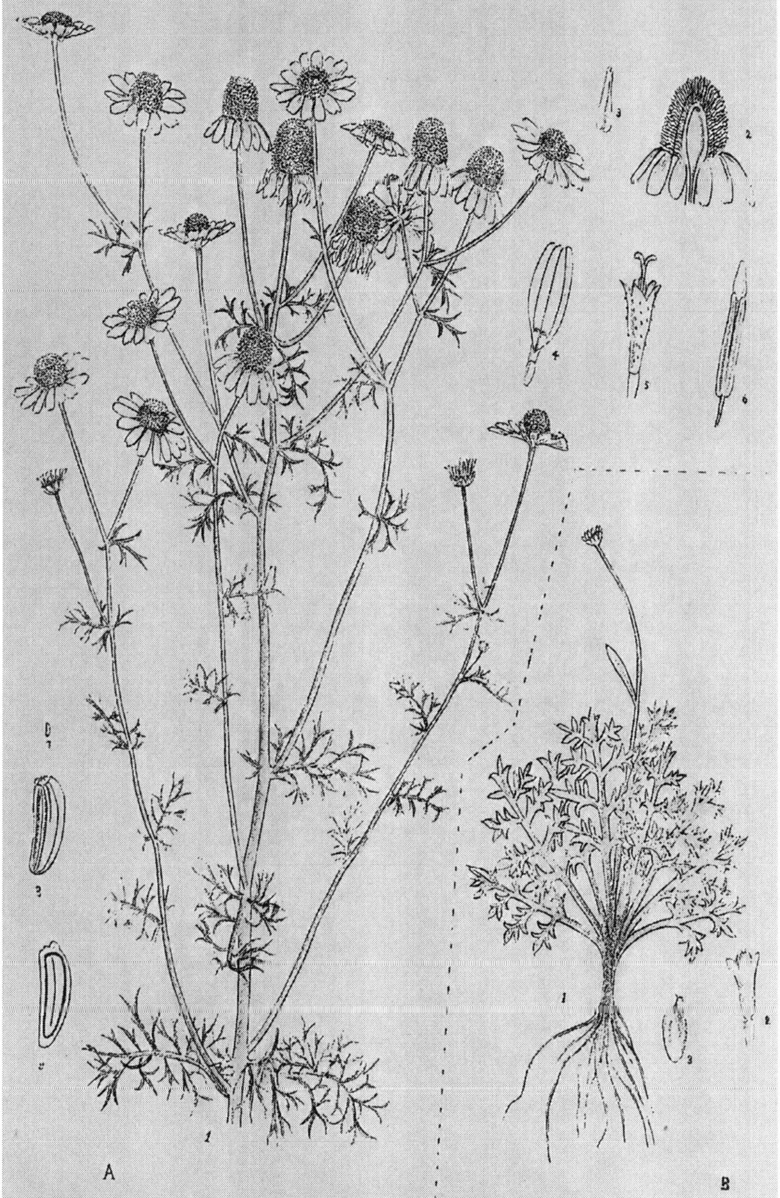

A—MATRICARIA CHAMOMILLA, *Linn.*

B—COTULA ANTHEMOIDES, *Linn.*

PLATE No. 538.

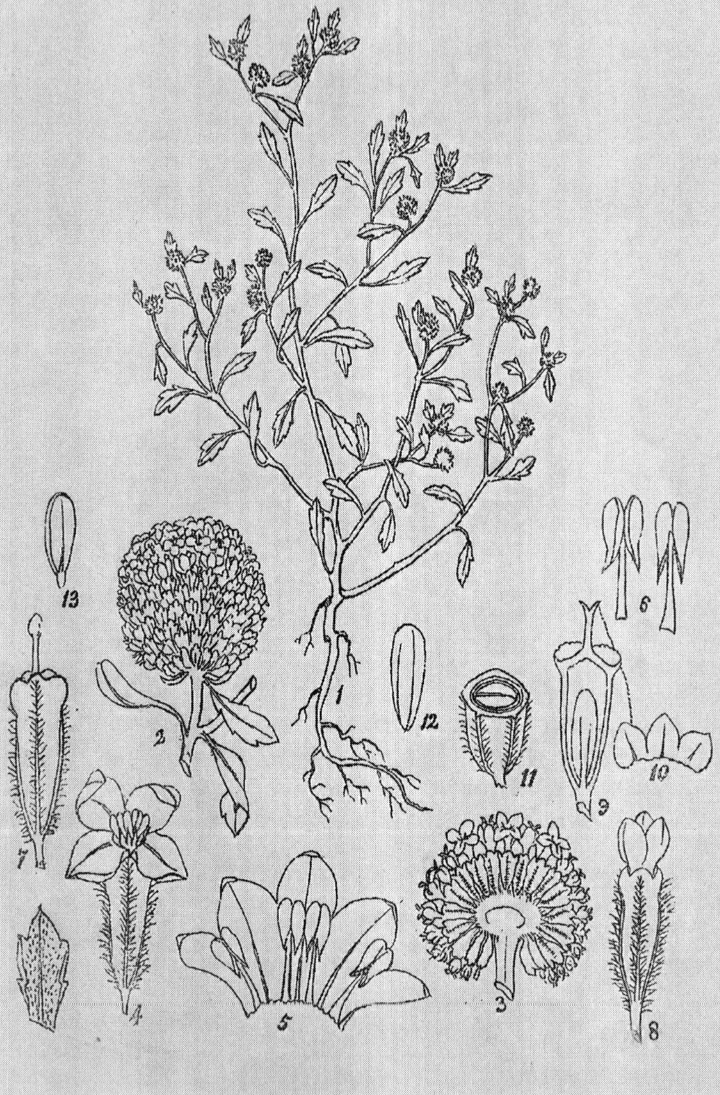

CENTIPEDA ORBICULARIS, LOUR.

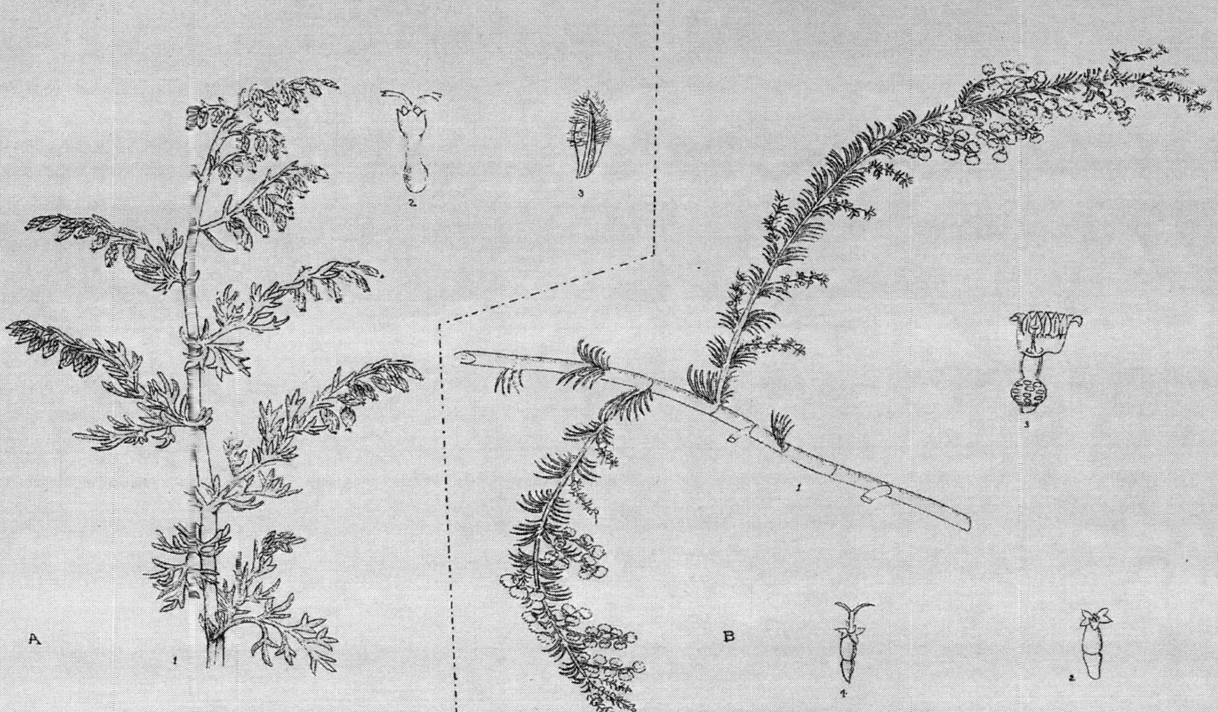

A—ARTEMISIA MARITIMA, *Linn.* B—A. SCOPARIA, *Waldst. & Kit.*

PLATE No. 540.

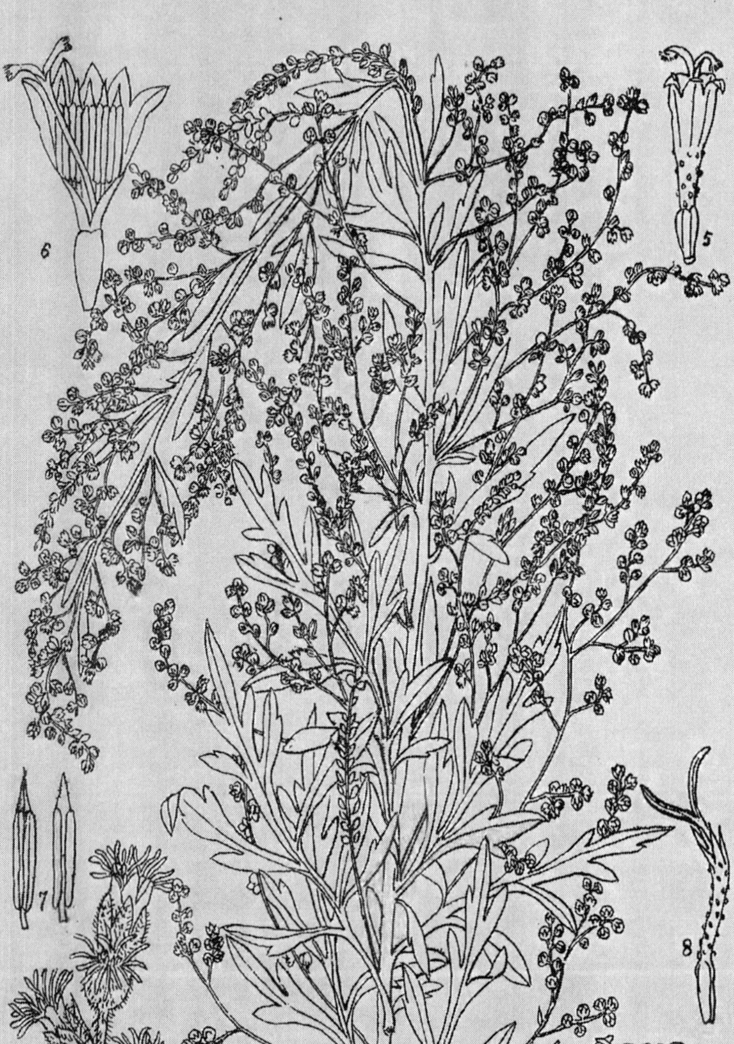

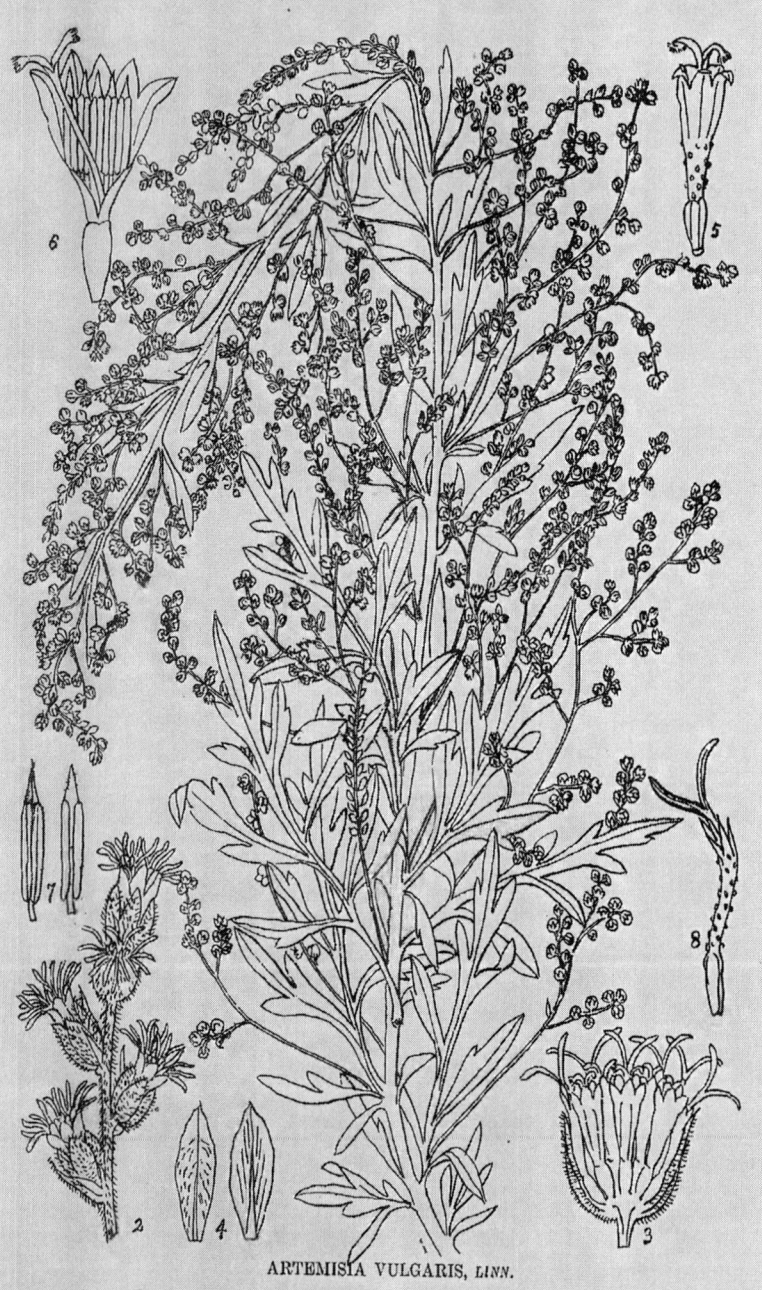

ARTEMISIA VULGARIS, *LINN.*

PLATE No. 541.

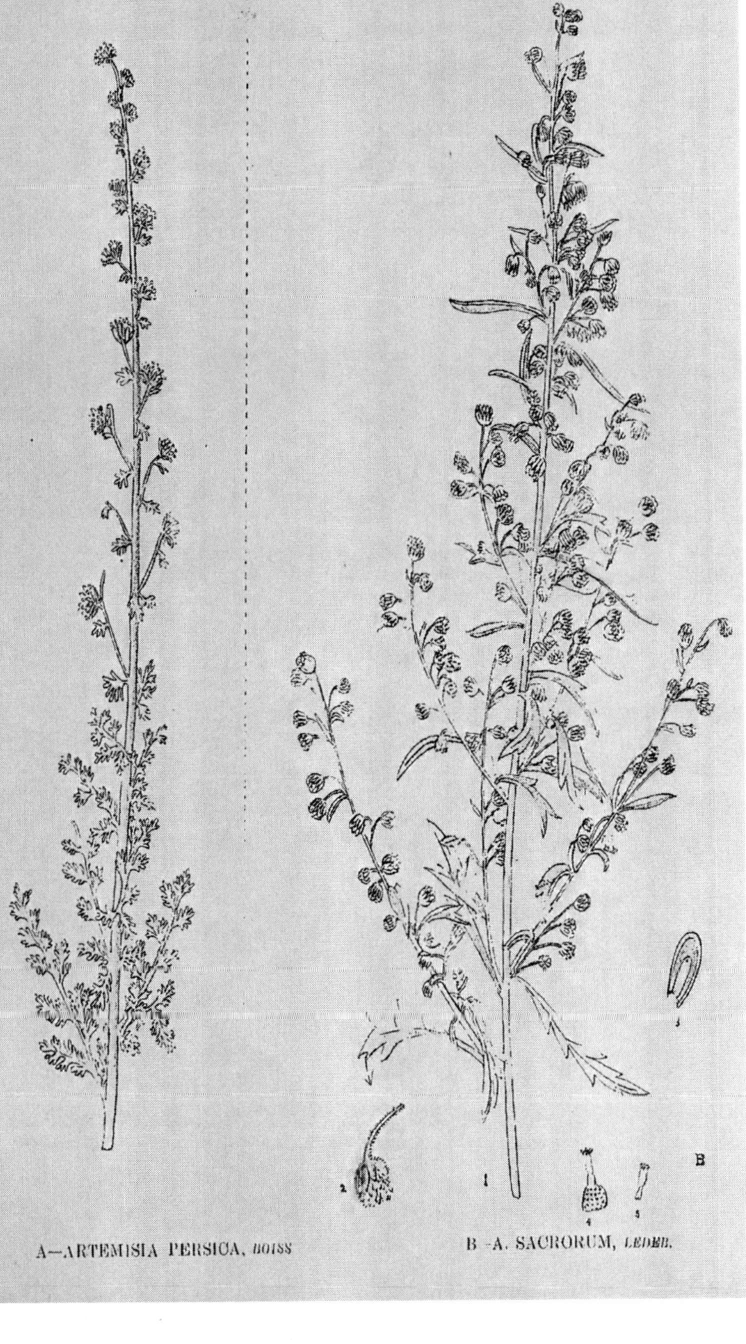

A—ARTEMISIA PERSICA, *BOISS* B—A. SACRORUM, *LEDEB.*

PLATE No. 542.

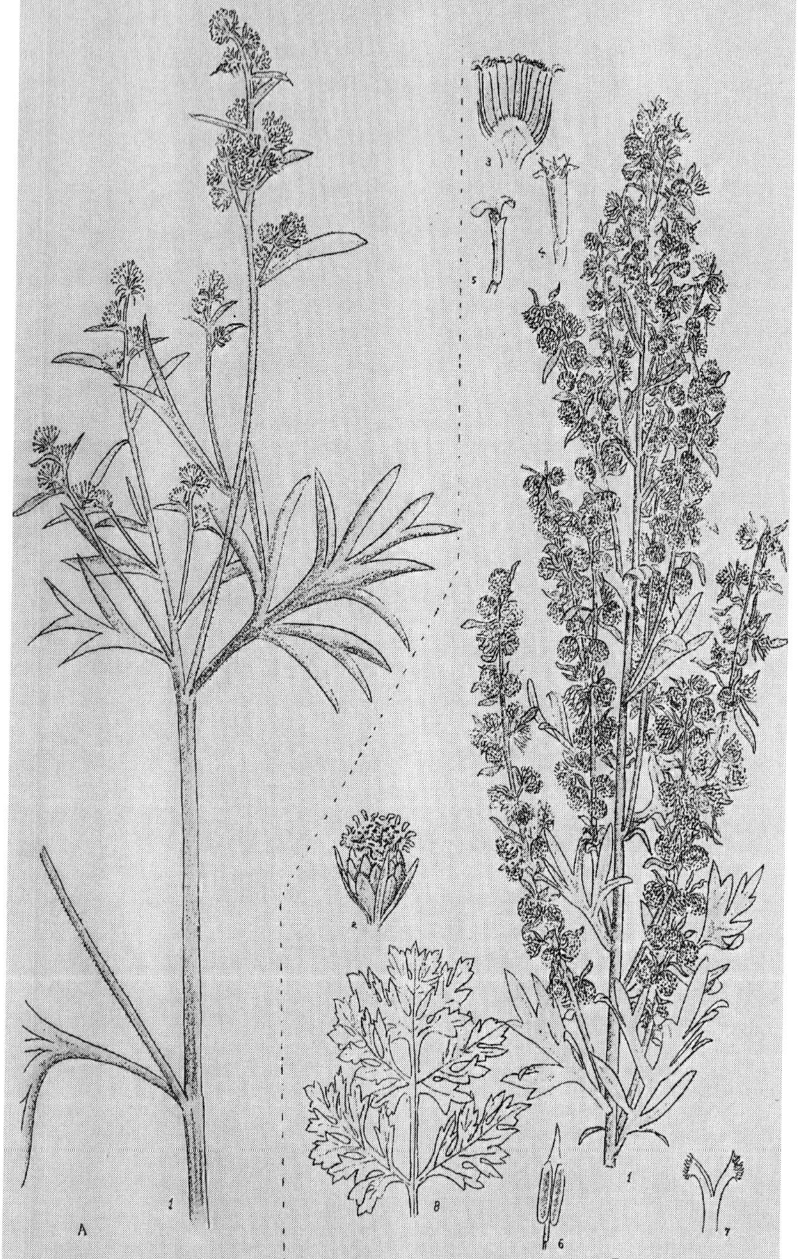

A—ARTEMISIA SIVERSIANA, *Willd.* B—A. ABSINTHIUM, *Linn.*

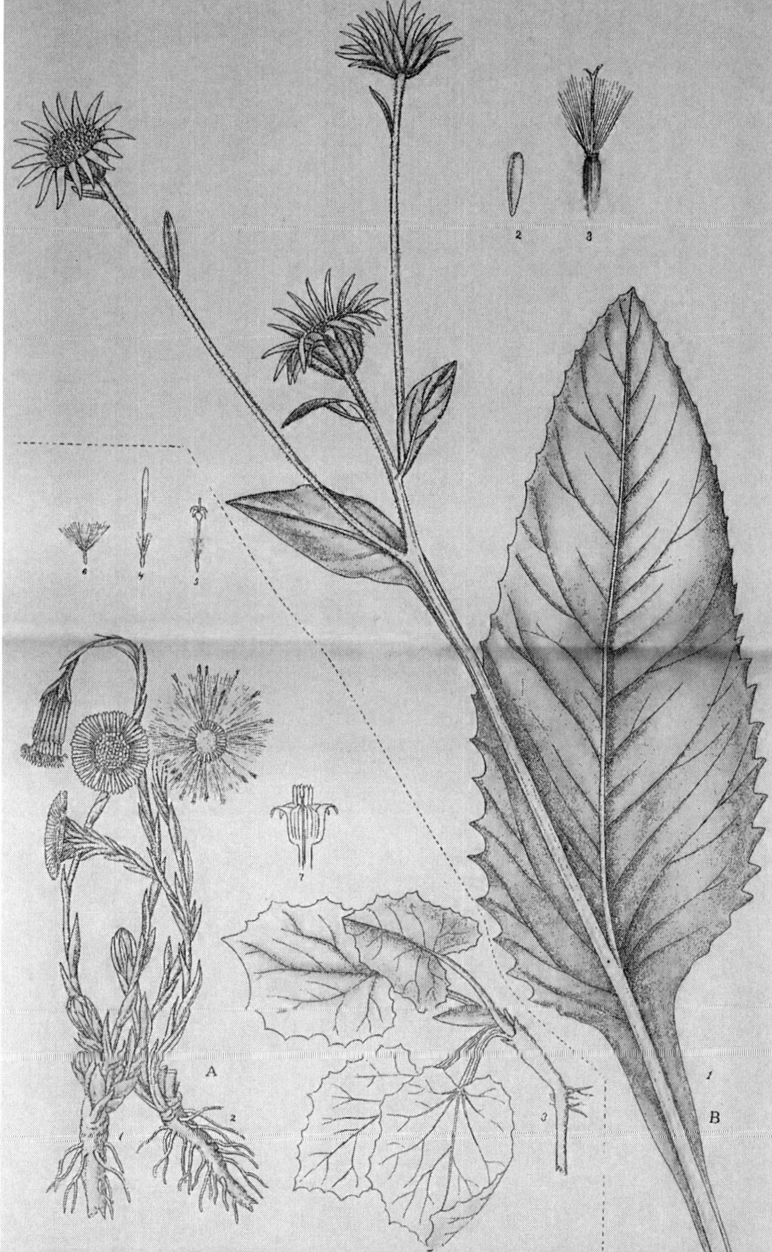

A—TUSSILAGO FARFARA, *LINN.* B—DORONICUM HOOKERI, *CLARKE.*

PLATE No. 544.

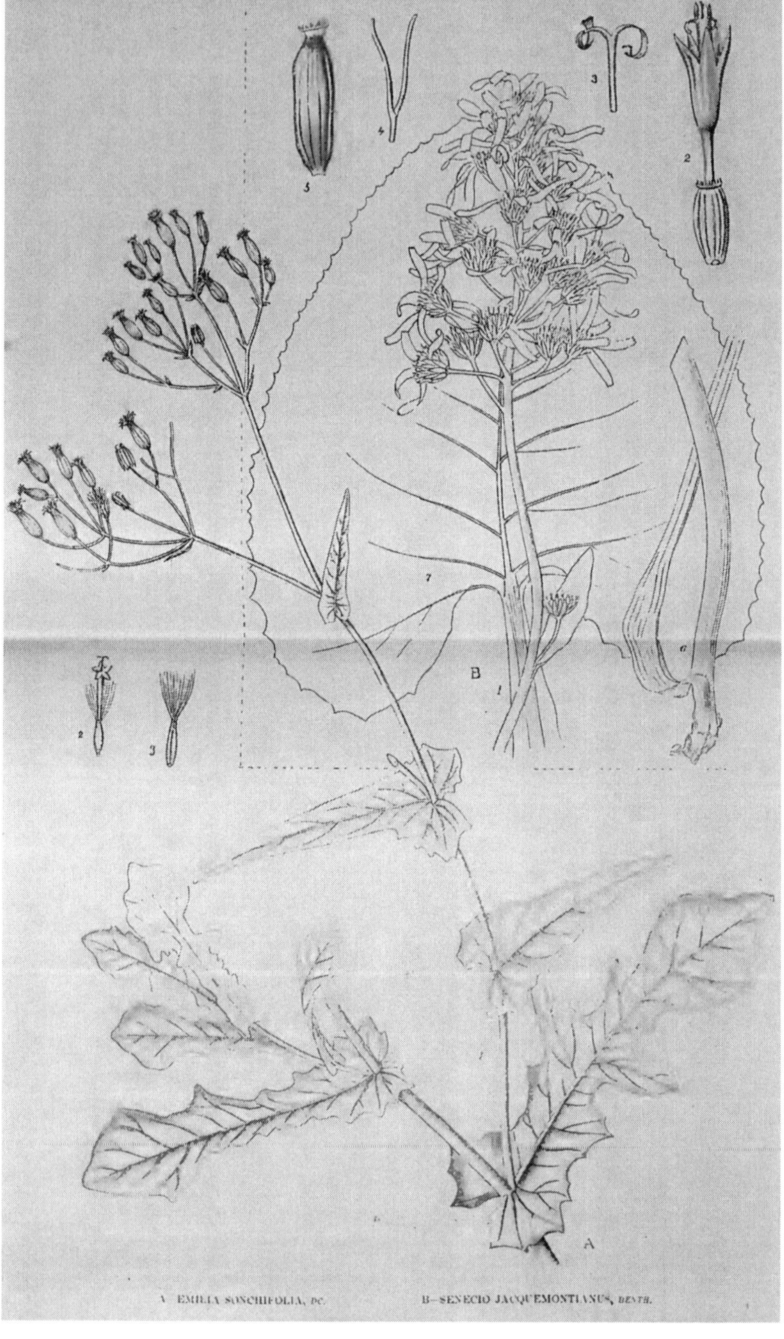

A—EMILIA SONCHIFOLIA, DC.　　B—SENECIO JACQUEMONTIANUS, BENTH.

PLATE No. 545.

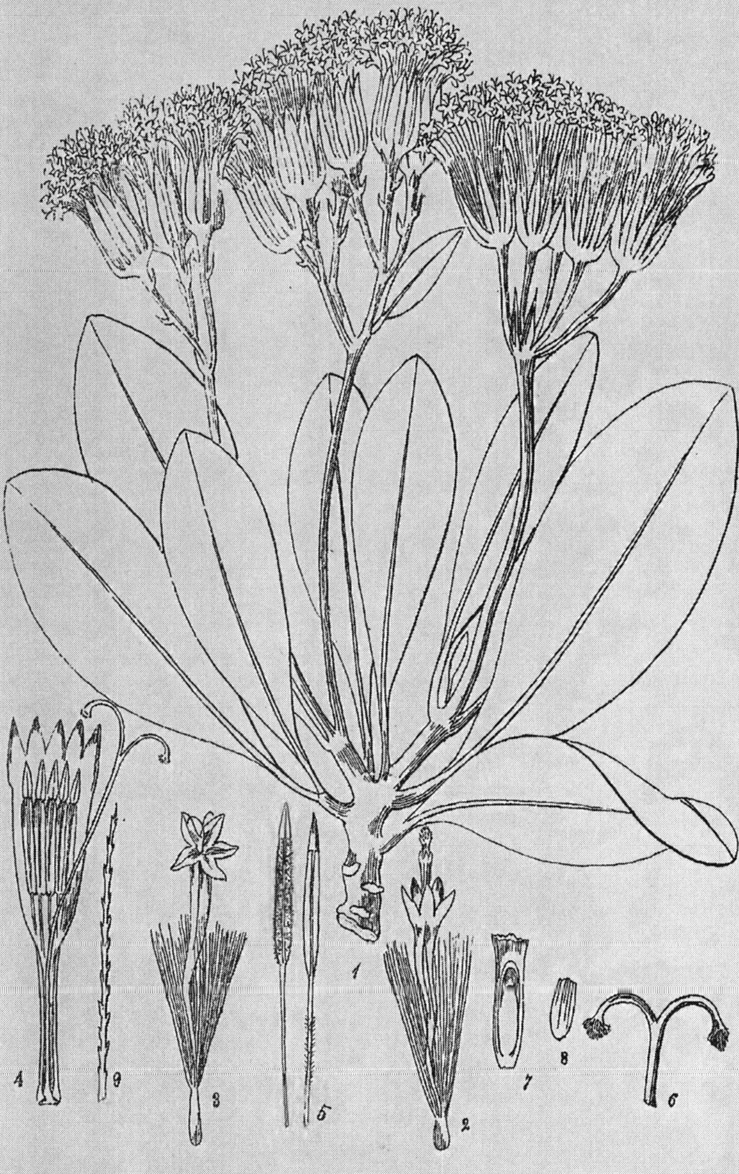

NOTONIA GRANDIFLORA, DC.

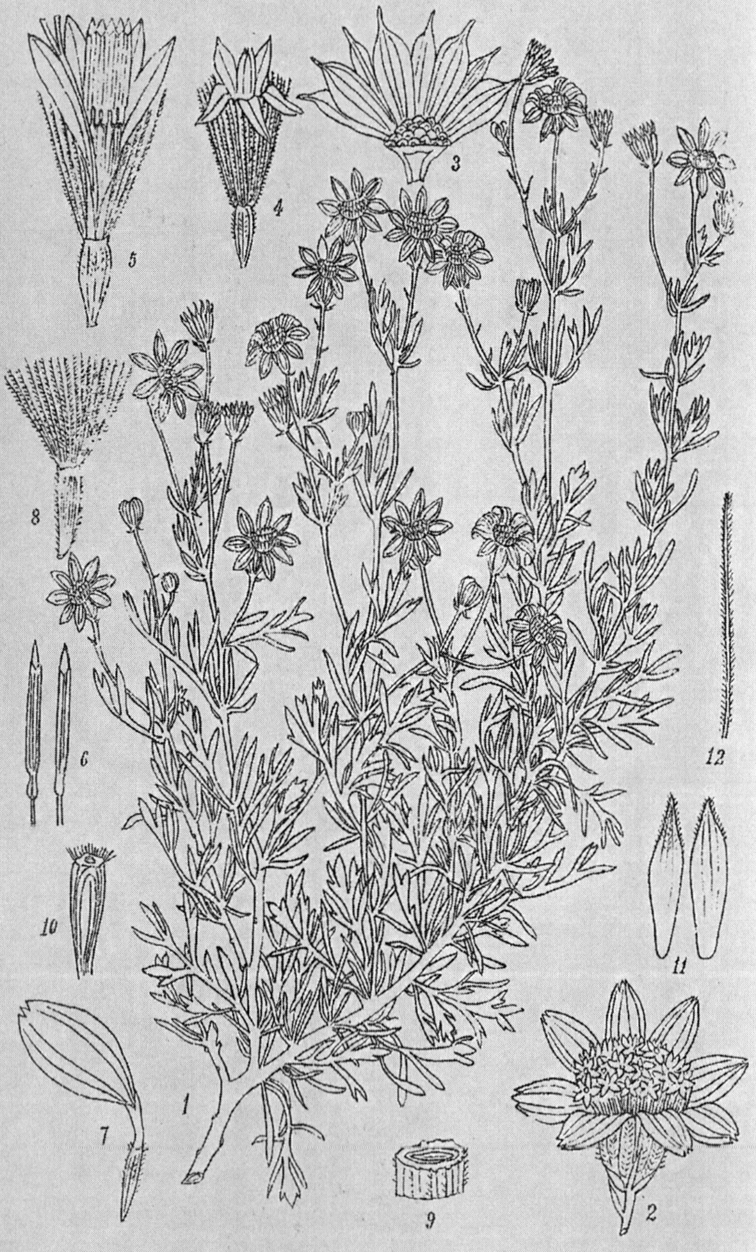

SENECIO TENUIFOLIUS, *BURM.*

PLATE No. 547.

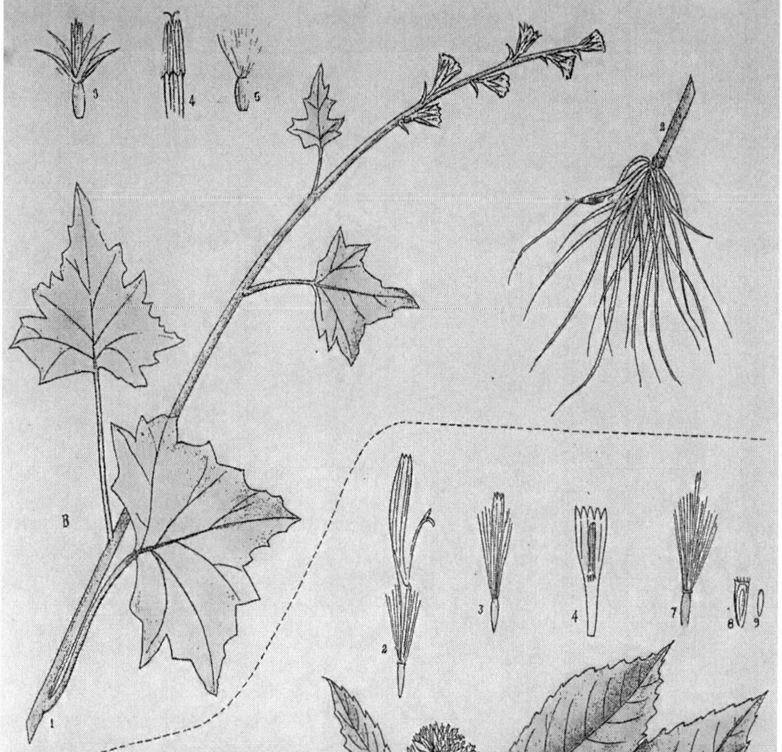

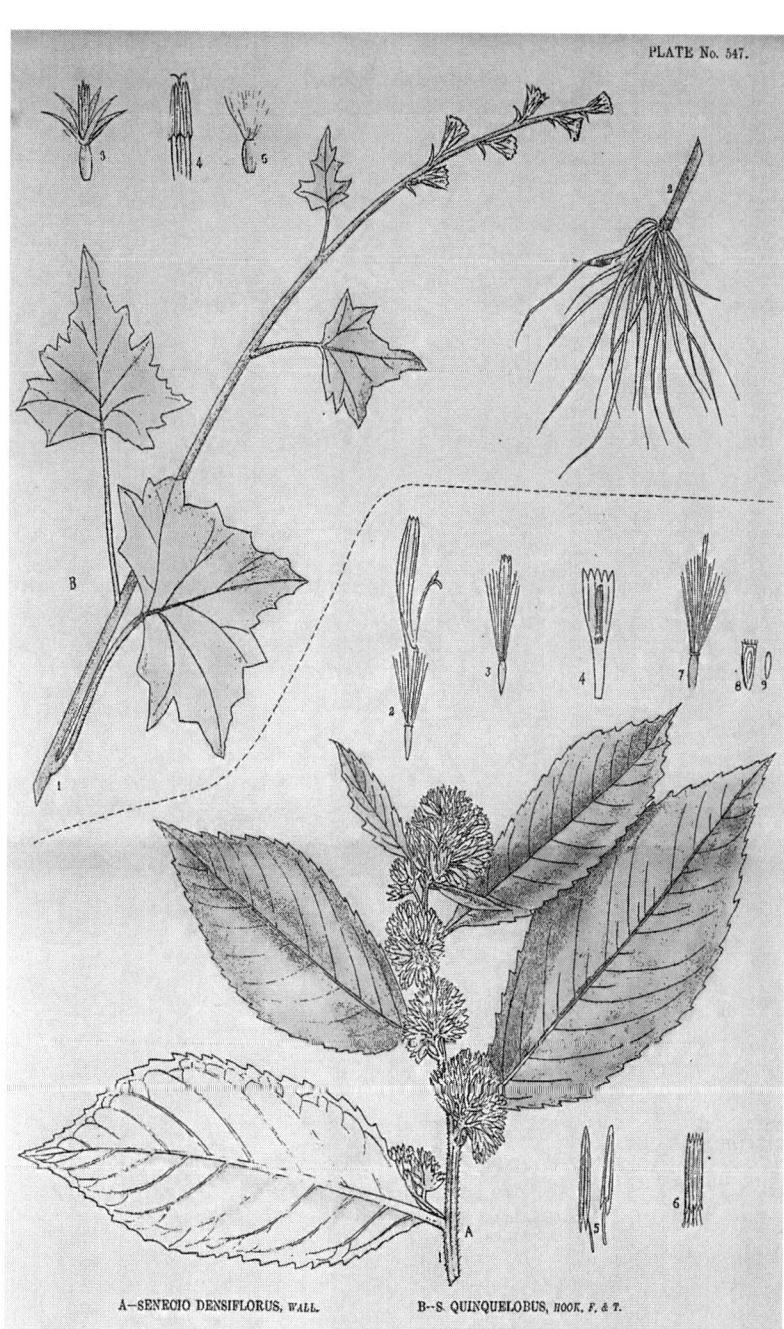

A—SENECIO DENSIFLORUS, *Wall.* B—S. QUINQUELOBUS, *Hook. f. & T.*

PLATE No. 548.

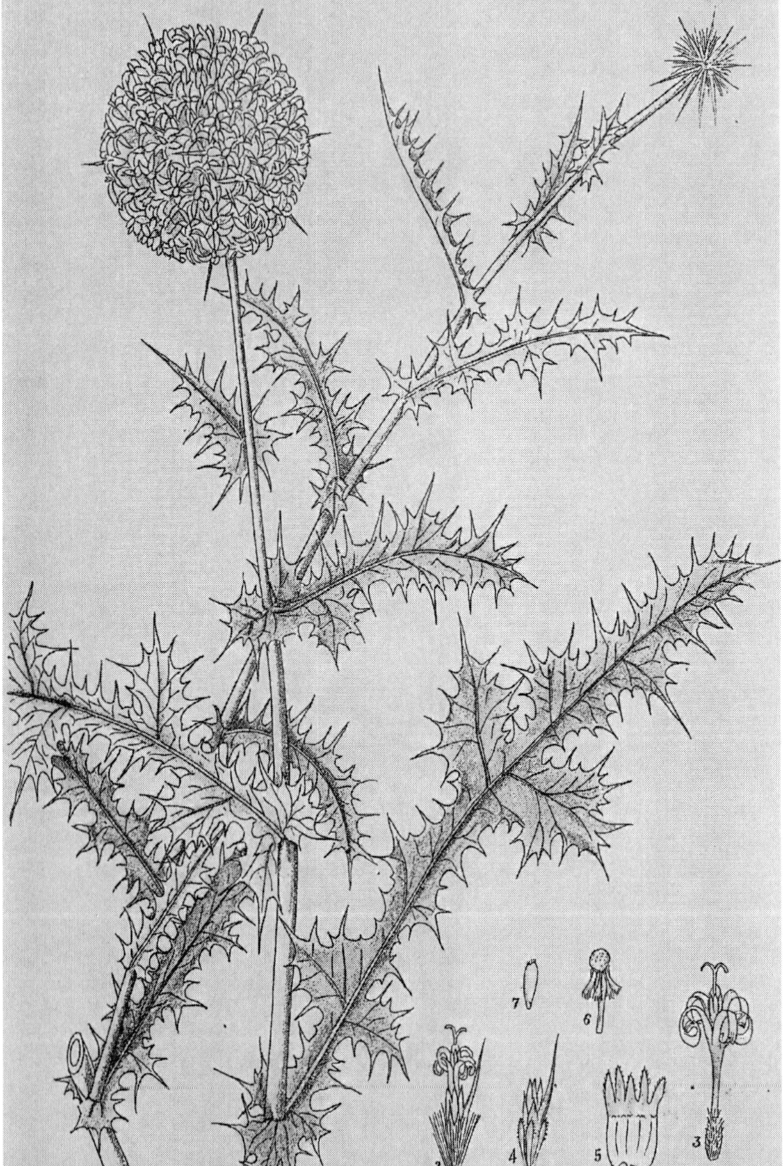

ECHINOPS ECHINATUS, *DC.*

PLATE No. 549.

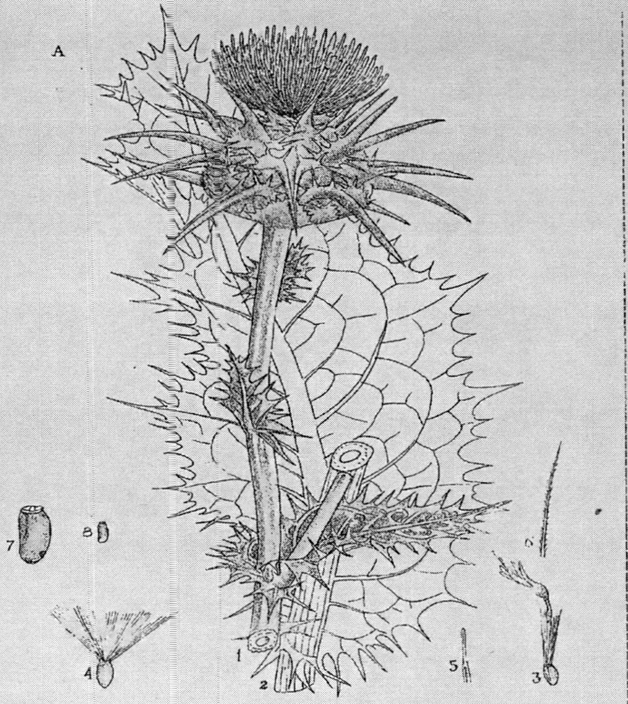

A—SILYBUM MARIANUM, *GAERTN.*

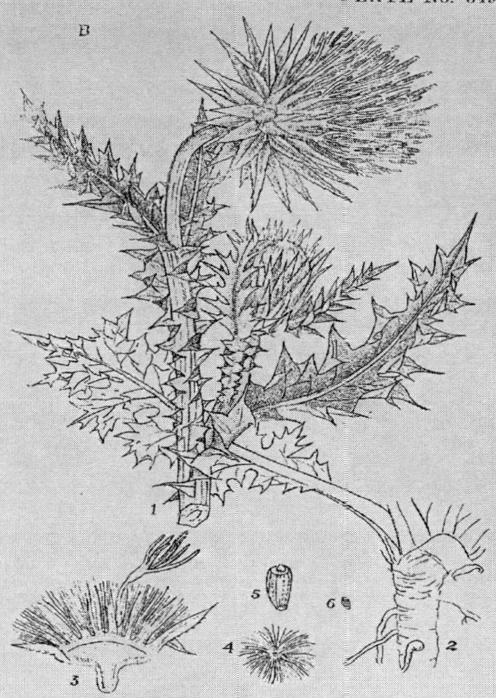

B—CARDUUS NUTANS, *LINN.*

PLATE No. 550.

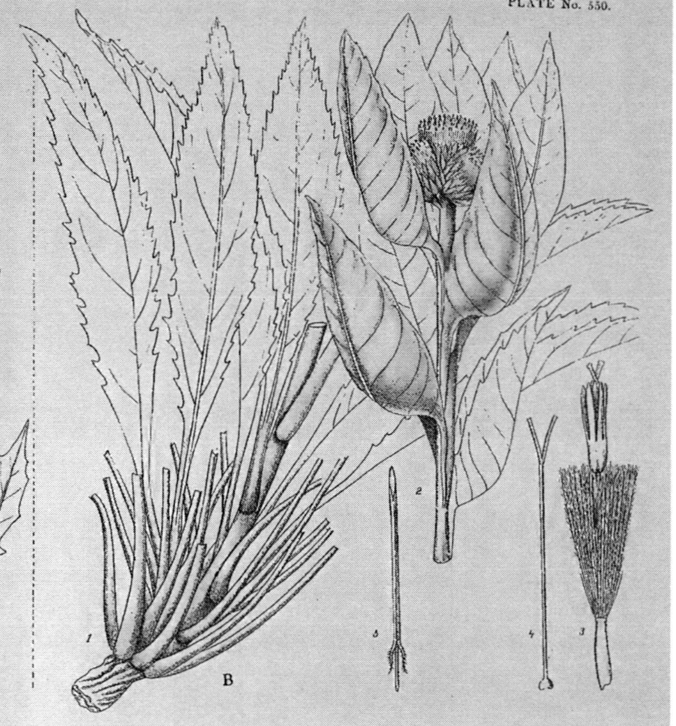

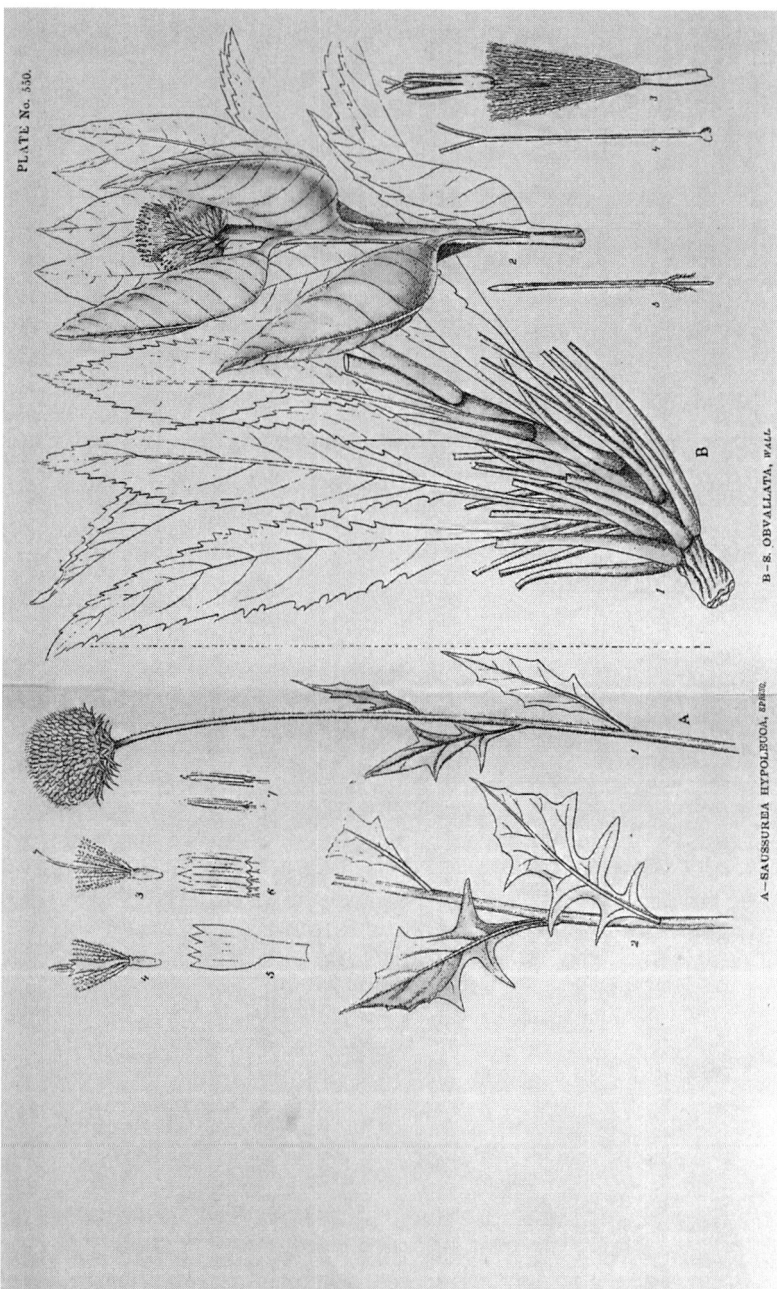

A—SAUSSUREA HYPOLEUCA, *Spreng.* B—S. OBVALLATA, *Wall.*

PLATE No. 551.

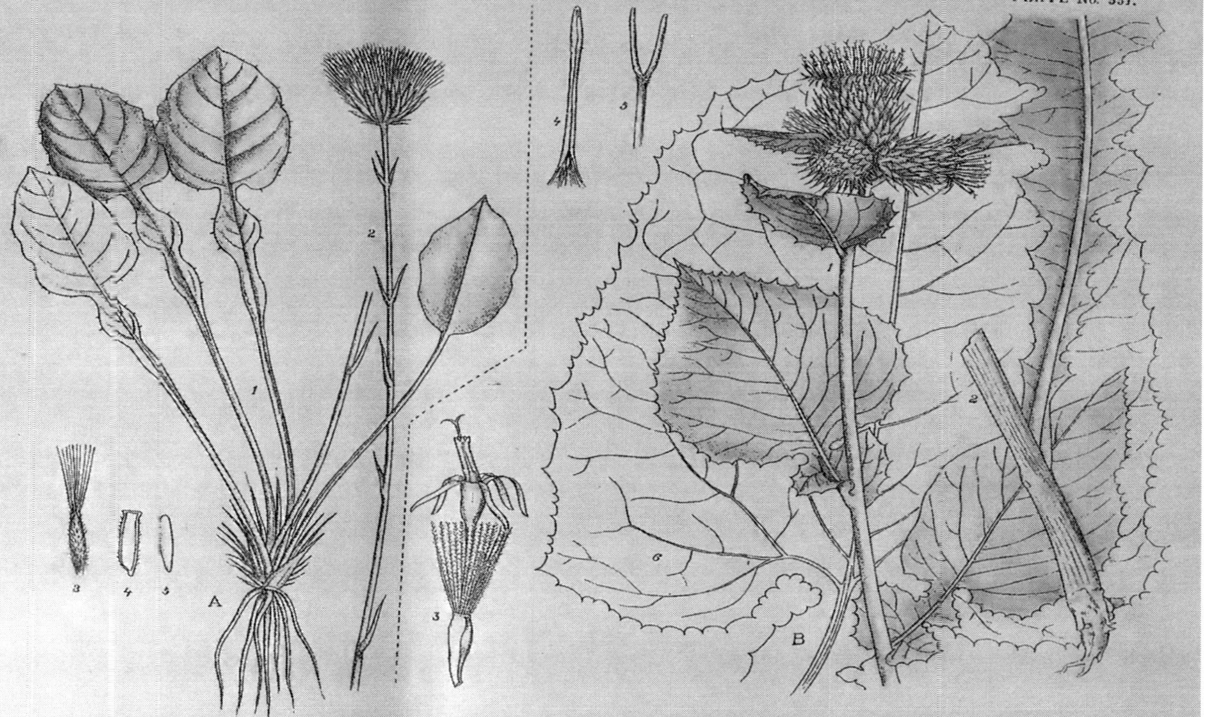

A—SAUSSUREA CANDICANS, *CLARKE*. B—S. LAPPA, *CLARKE*.

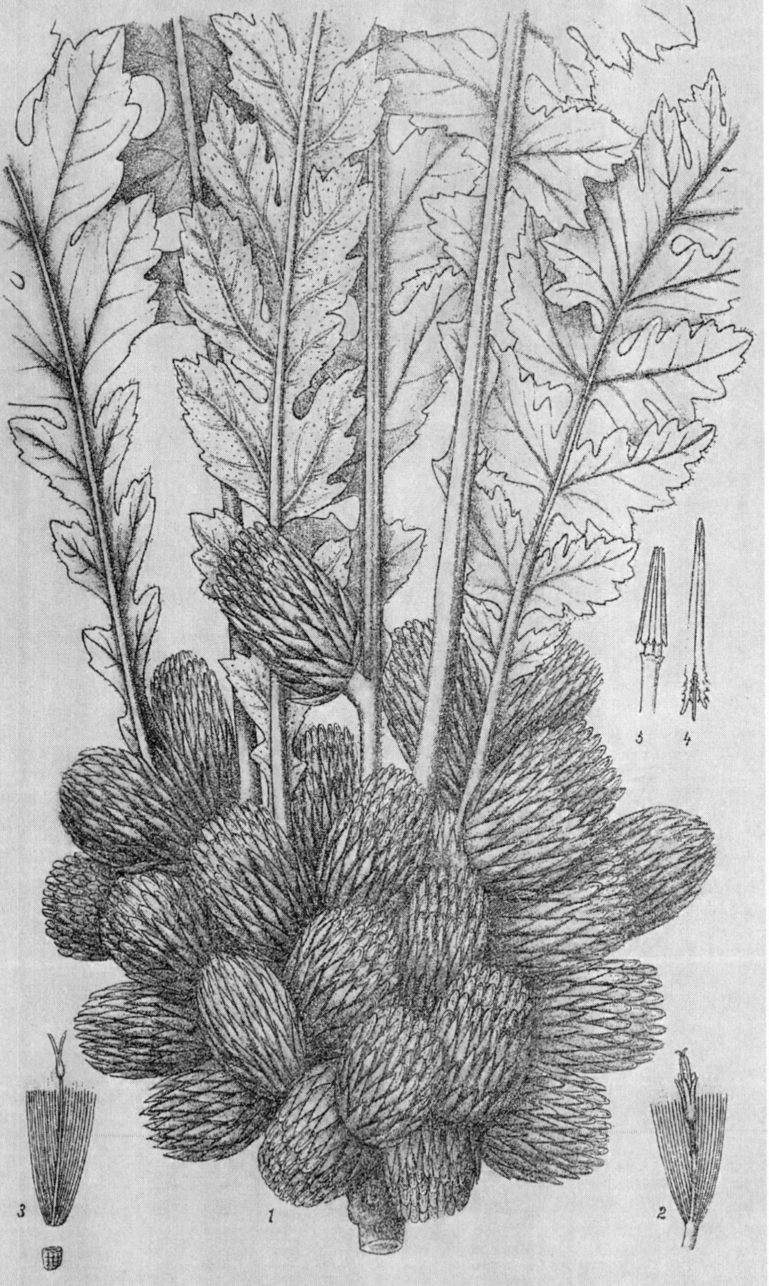

JURIÑEA MACROCEPHALA, BENTH.

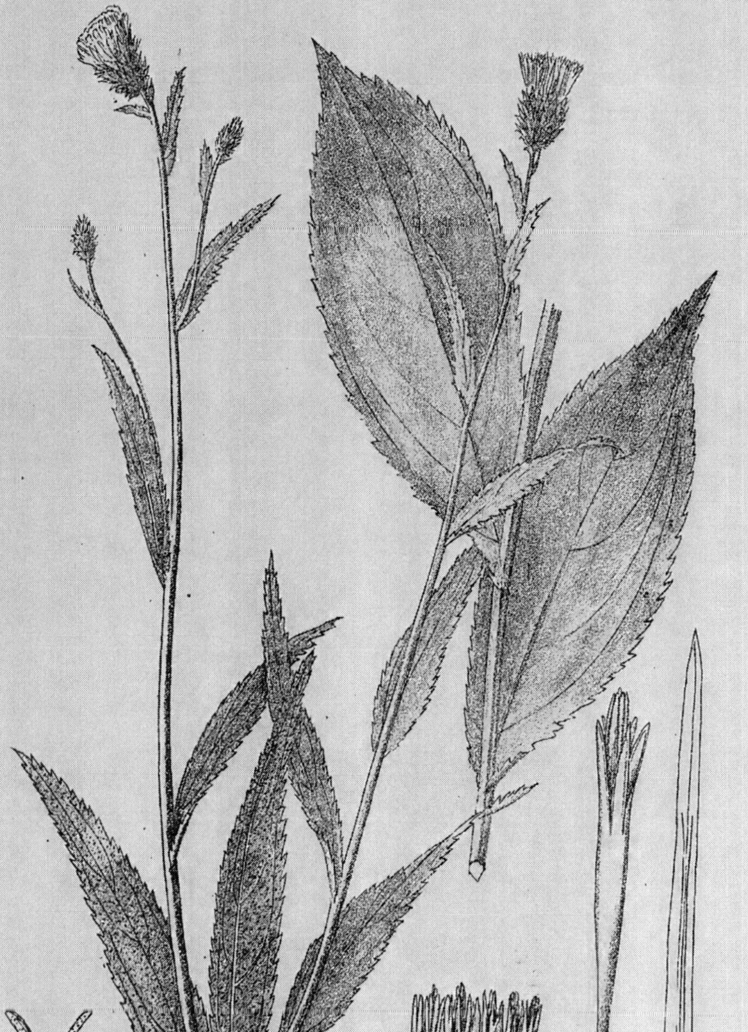

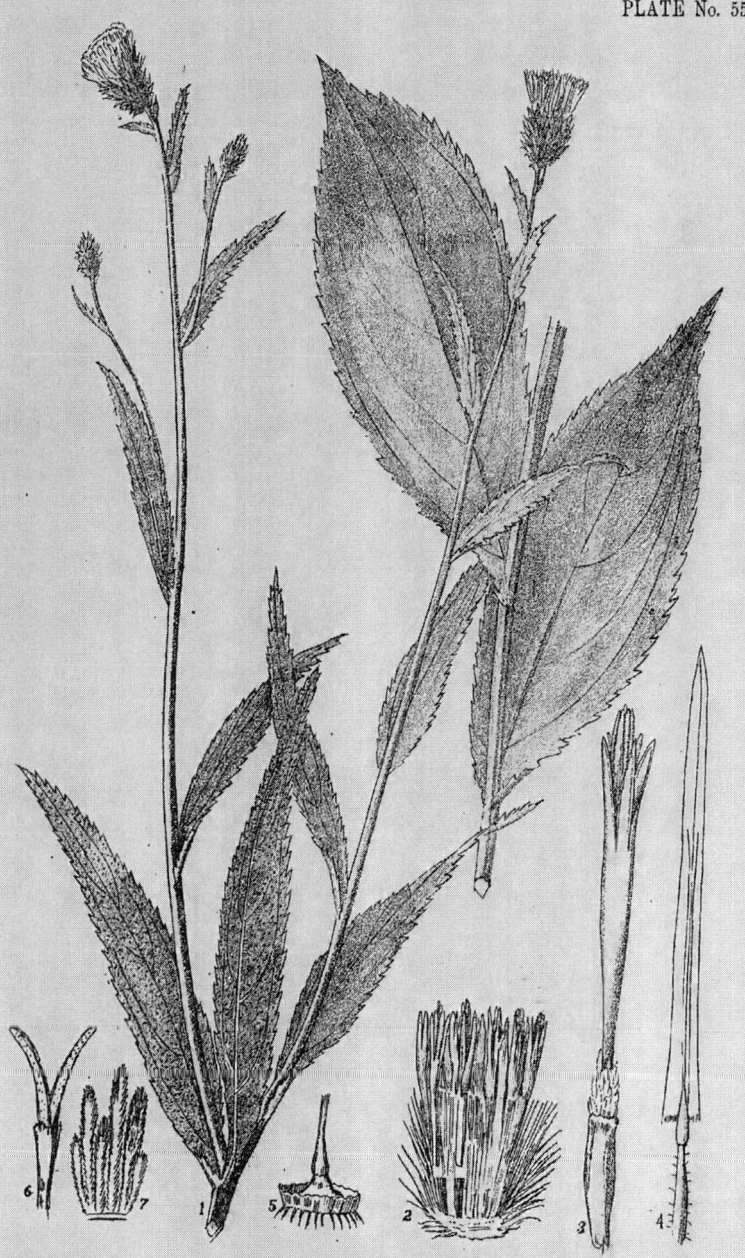

TRICHOLEPIS GLABERRIMA, DC.

PLATE No. 554.

VOLUTARELLA DIVARICATA, *BENTH.*

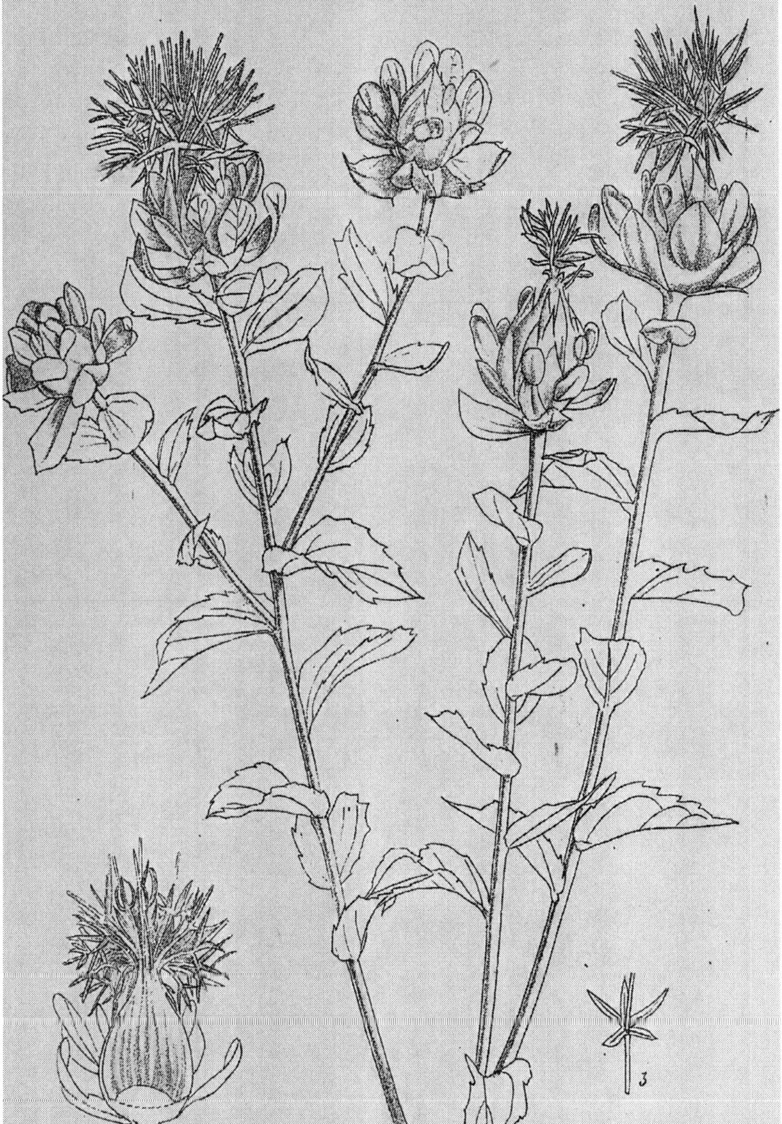

CARTHAMUS TINCTORIUS, *LINN.*

PLATE No. 556.

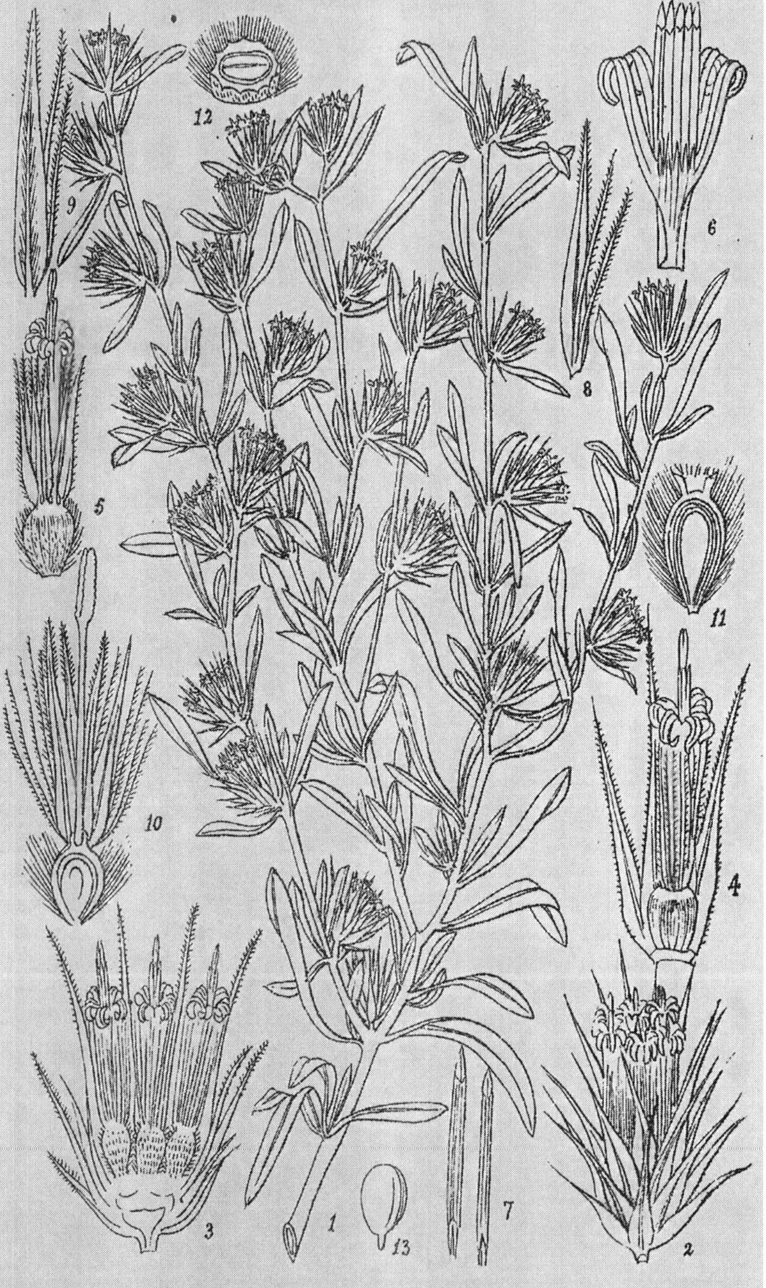

DICOMA TOMENTOSA, CASS.

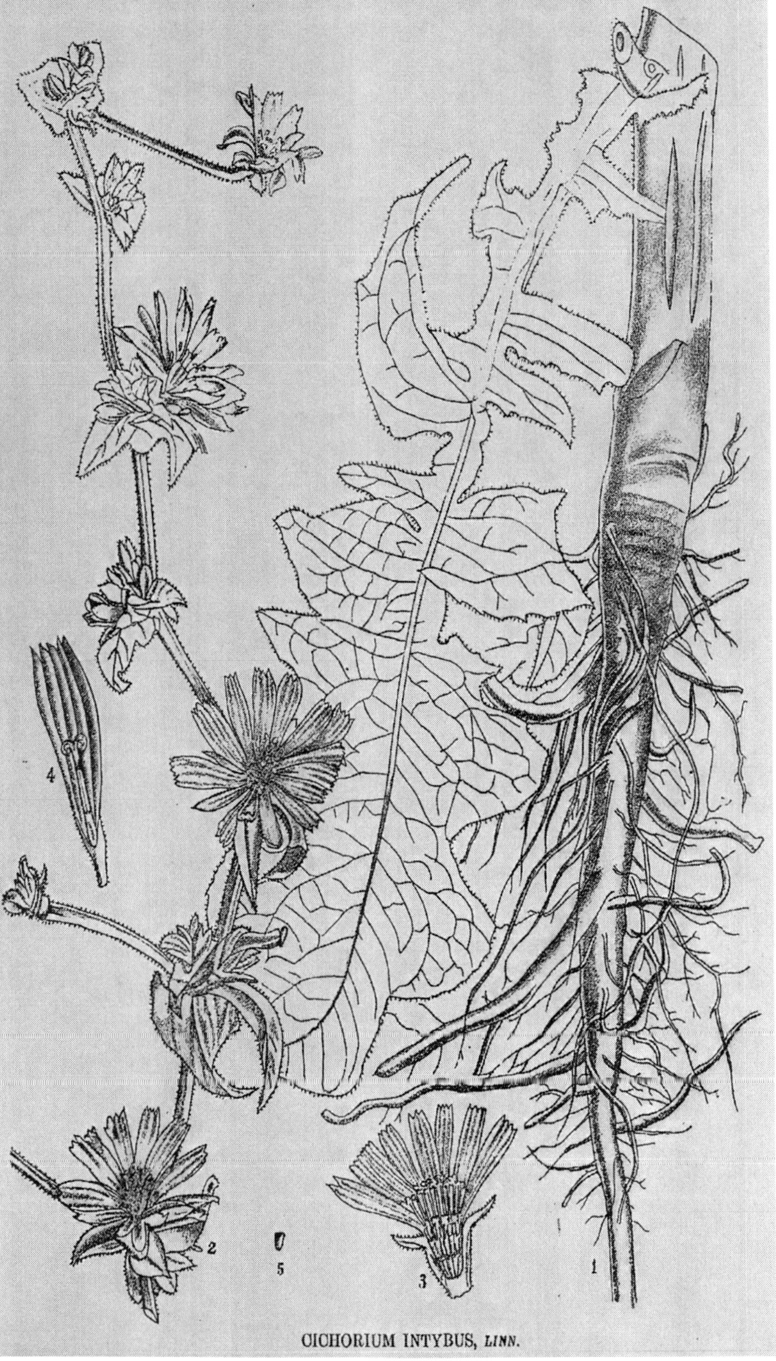

CICHORIUM INTYBUS, *LINN.*

PLATE No. 558.

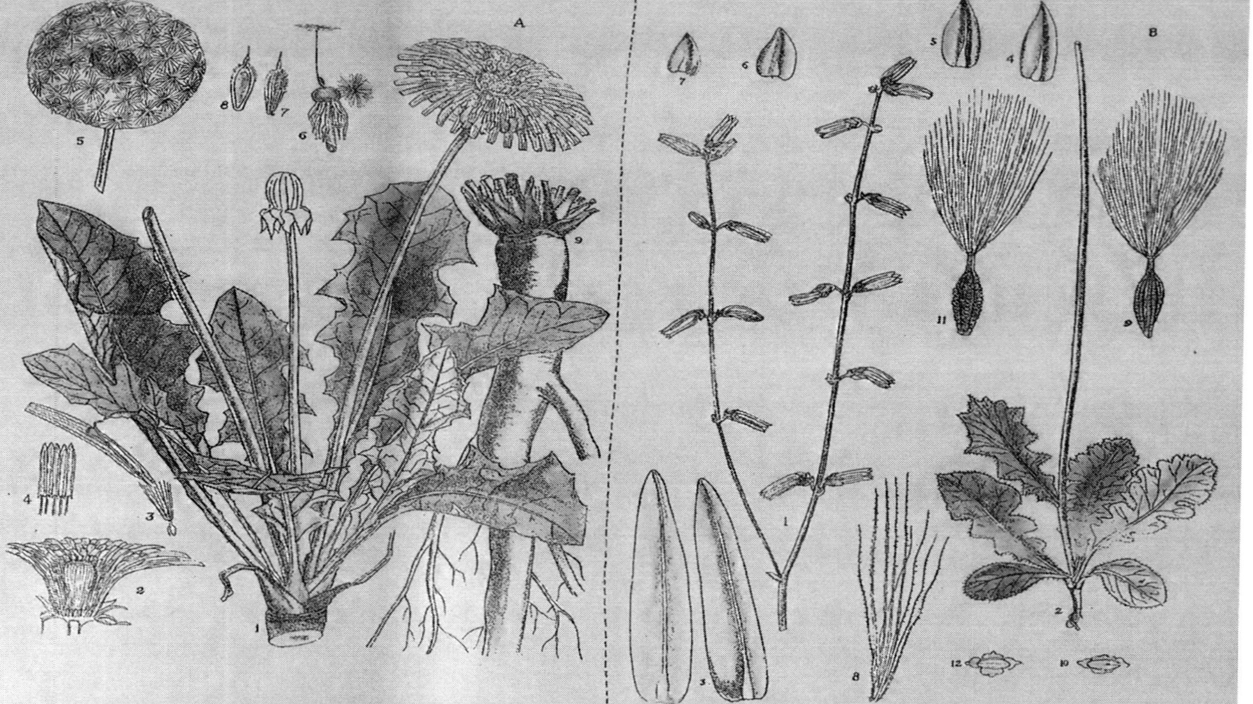

A—TARAXACUM OFFICINALE, *Wigg.*   B—LACTUCA REMOTIFLORA, *DC.*

LACTUCA HEYNEANA, *DC.*

PLATE No. 560.

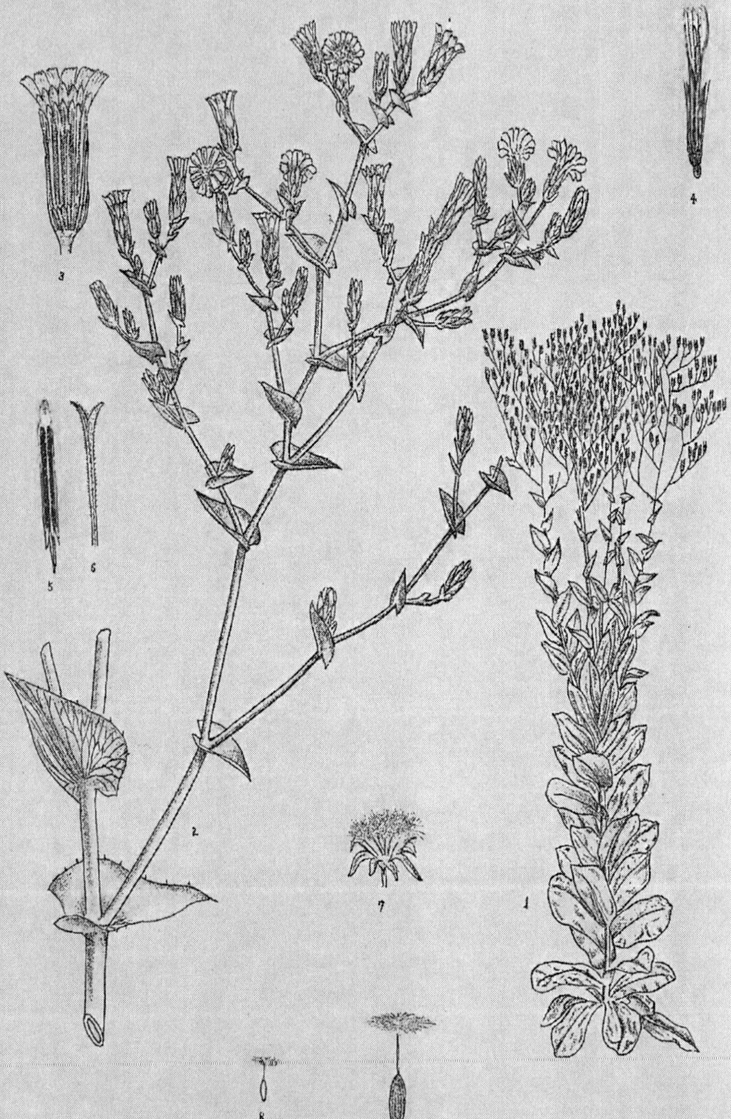

LACTUCA SCARIOLA, *LINN VAR. SATIVA.*

PLATE No. 561.

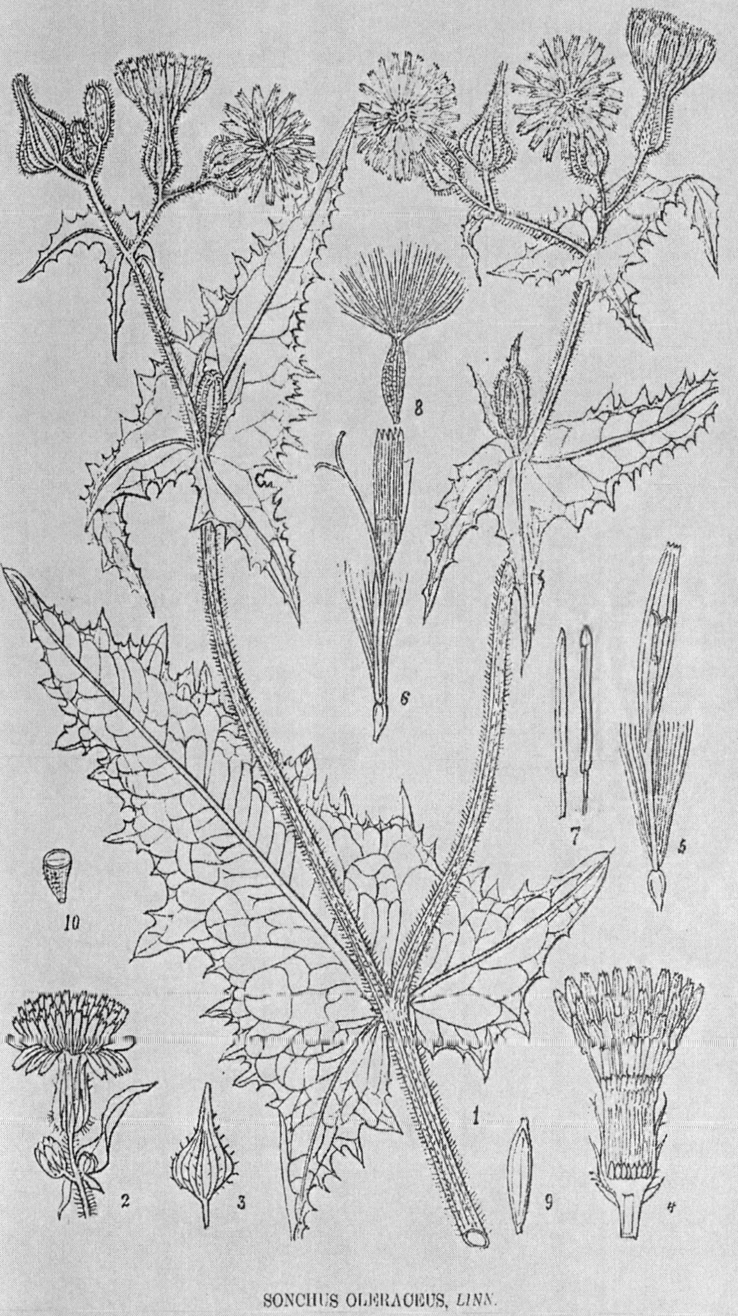

SONCHUS OLERACEUS, *LINN.*

PLATE No. 56

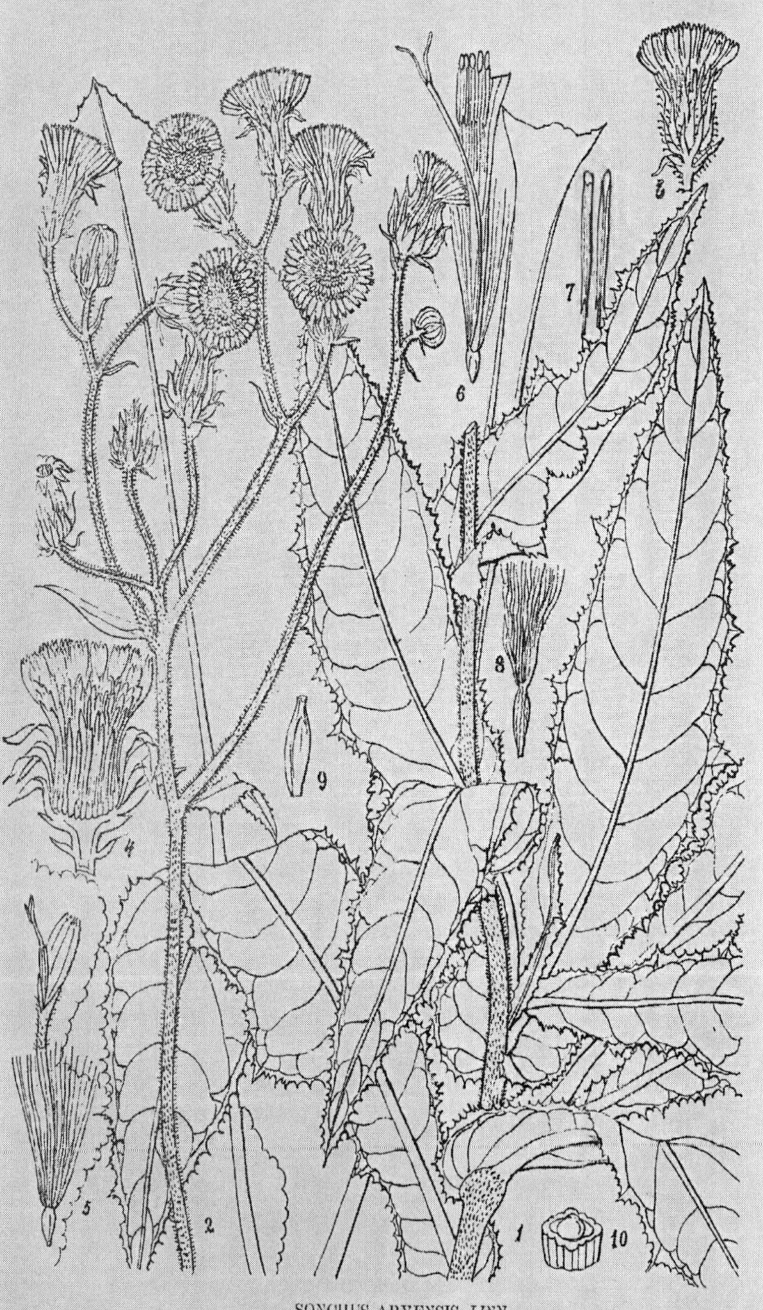

SONCHUS ARVENSIS, *LINN.*

PLATE No. 563.

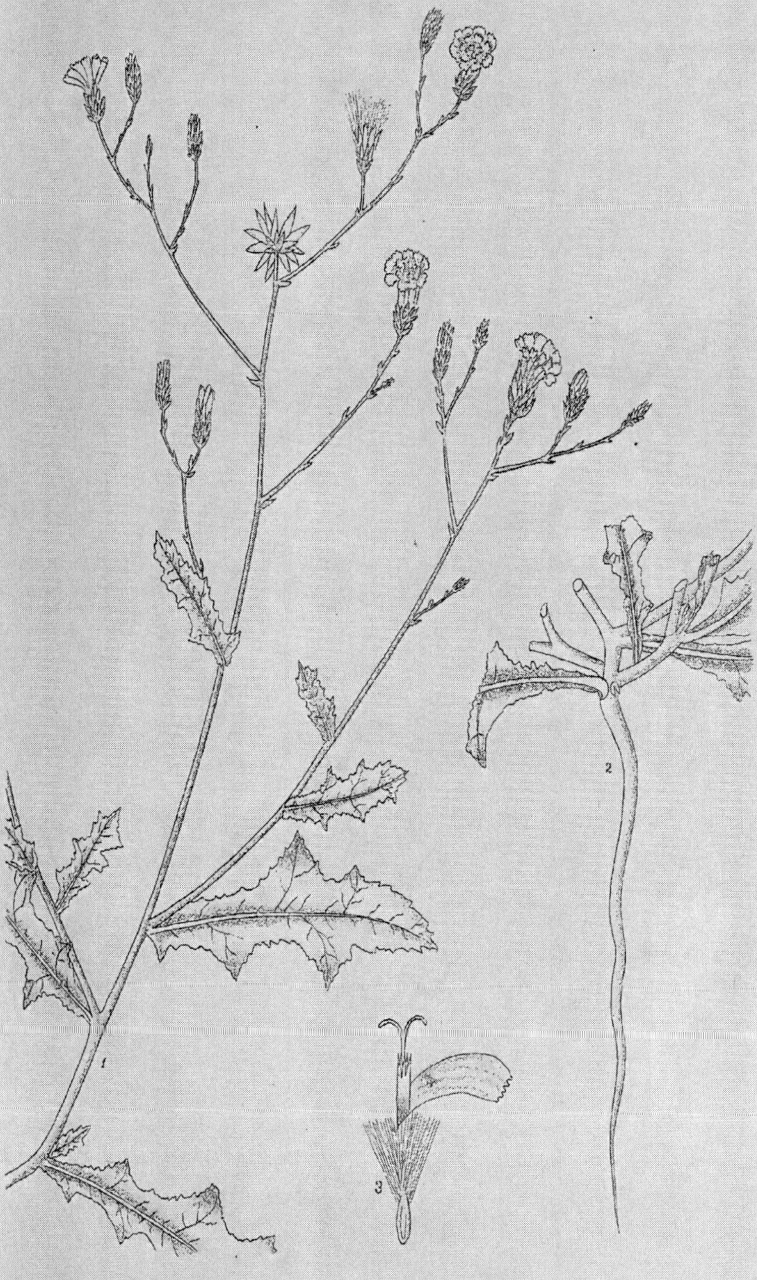

LAUNÆA ASPLENIFOLIA, HOOK. FIL.

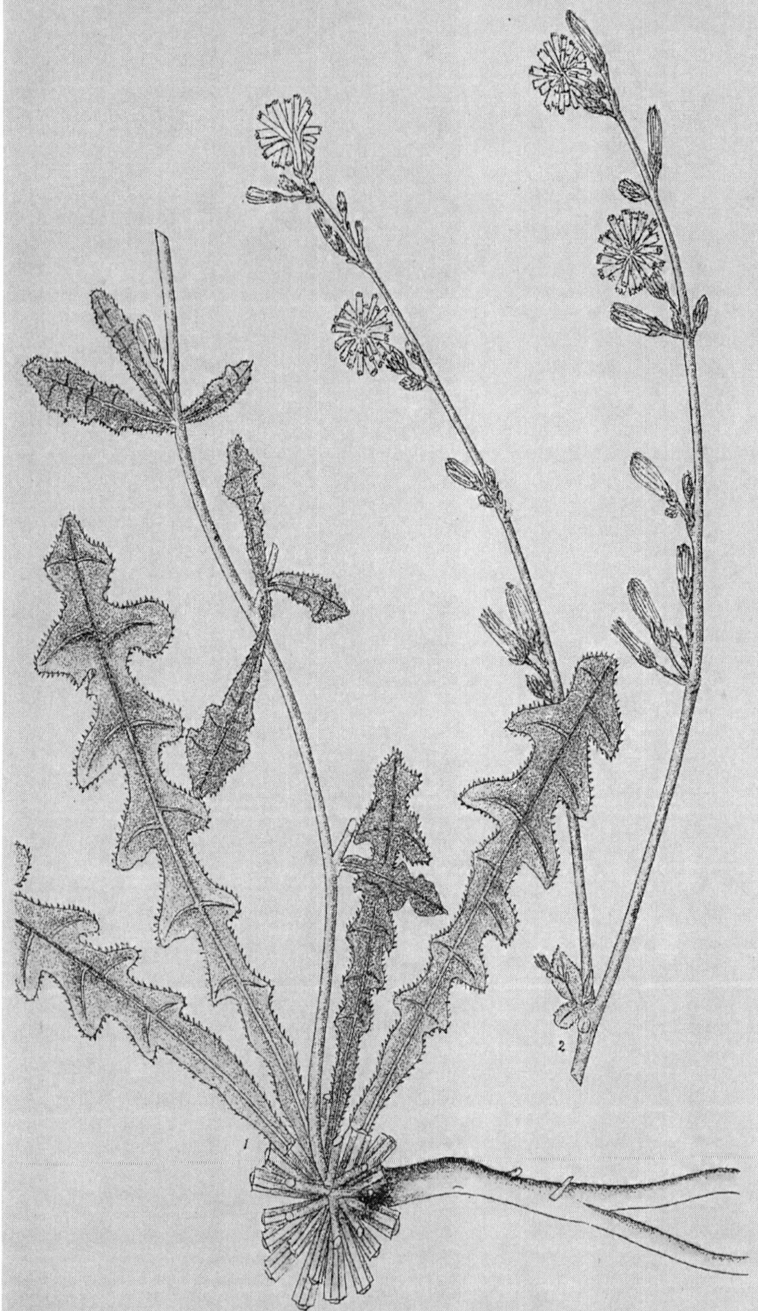

LAUNÆA NUDICAULIS, *HOOK. FIL.*

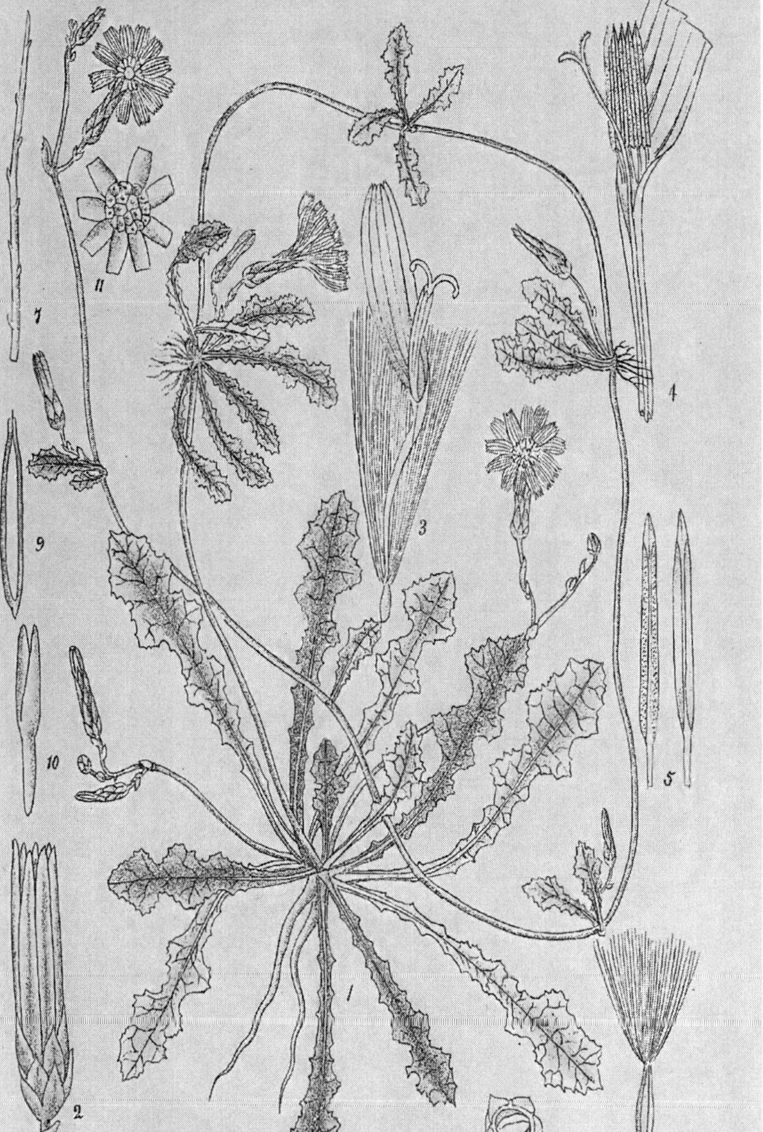

LAUNÆA PINNATIFIDA, CASS.

PLATE No. 566.

SCÆVOLA KŒNIGII, VAHL.

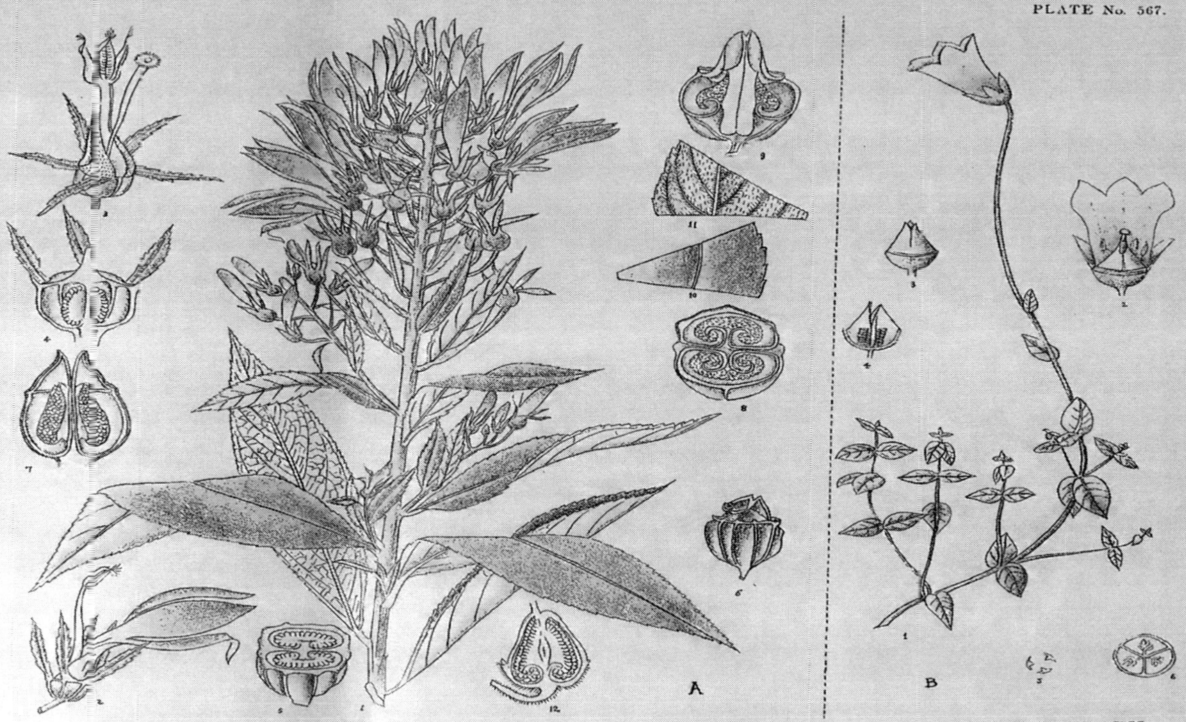

A—LOBELIA NICOTIANÆFOLIA, *HEYNE.*

B—CODONOPSIS OVATA, *BENTH.*

PLATE No. 568.

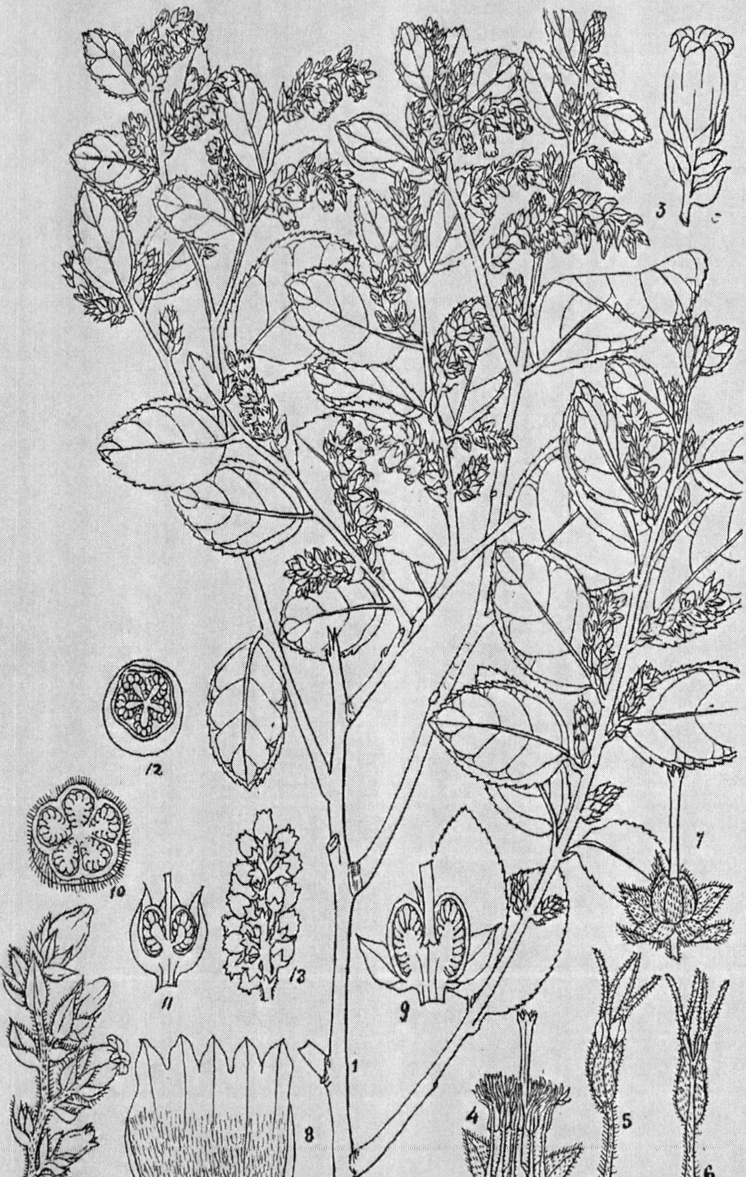

GAULTHERIA FRAGRANTISSIMA, WALL.

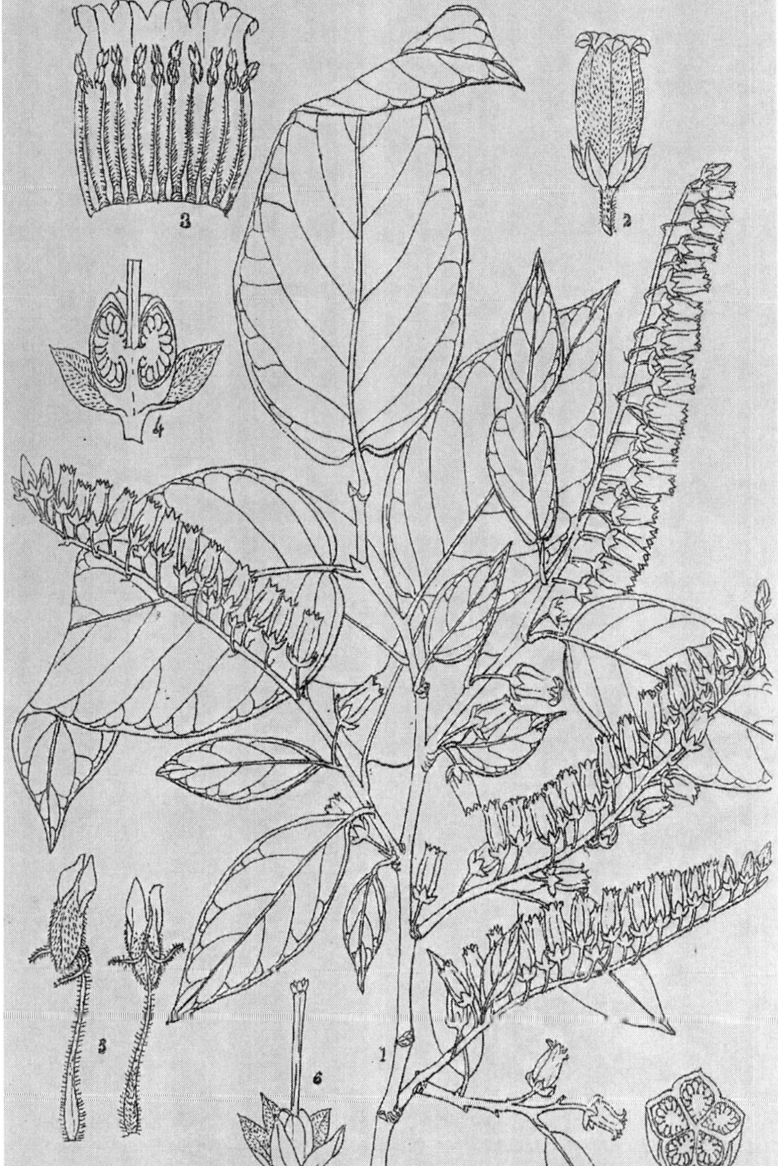

PIERIS OVALIFOLIA, *D. DON.*

PLATE No. 570.

RHODODENDRON ARBOREUM, SM.

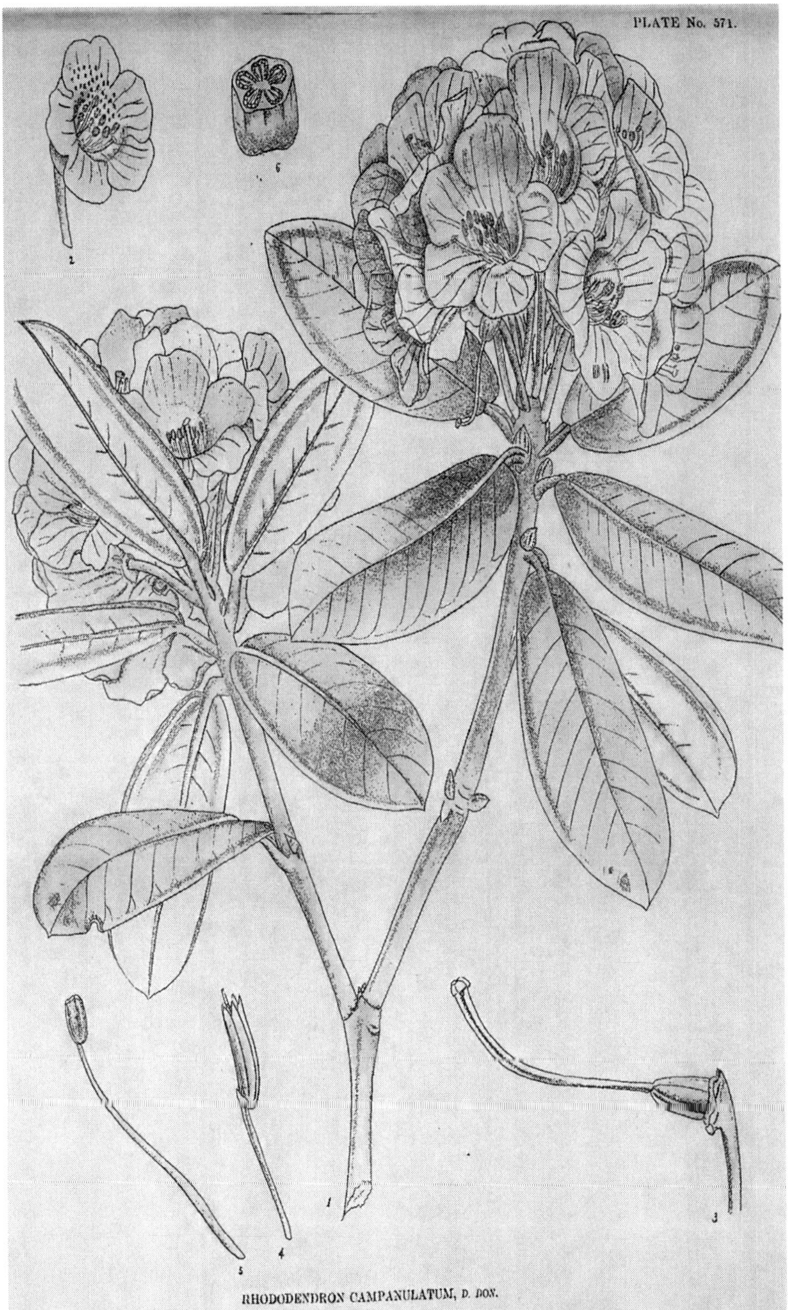

RHODODENDRON CAMPANULATUM, D. DON.

PLATE No. 572.

B—RHODODENDRON SETOSUM, *D. DON.*

A—RHODODENDRON LEPIDOTUM, *WALL.*

PLATE No. 573.

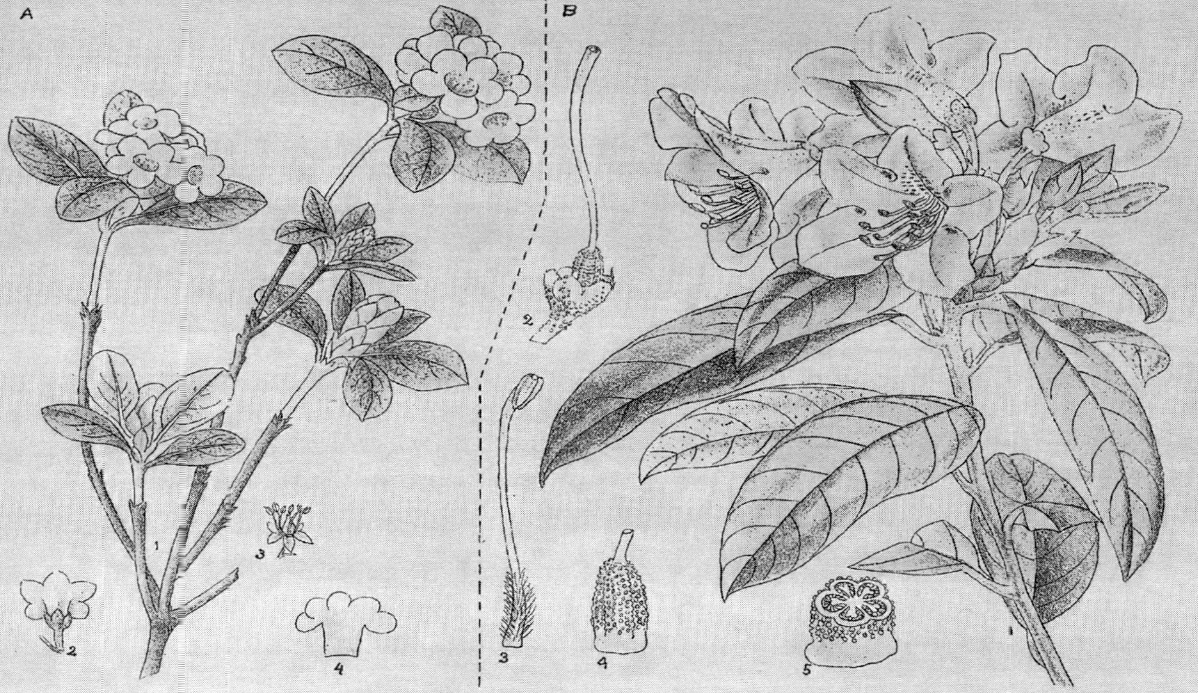

A—RHODODENDRON ANTHOPOGON, *D. DON.*   B—R. CINNABARINUM, *HOOK F.*

PLATE No. 574.

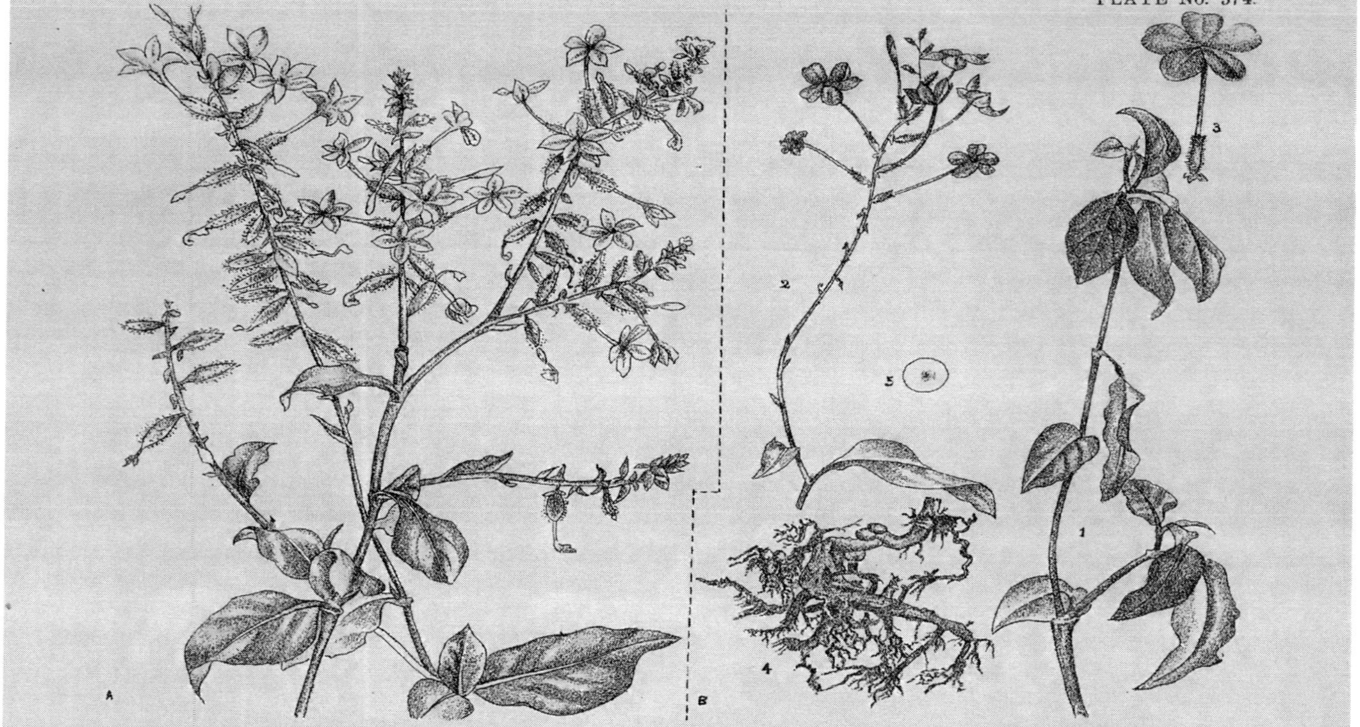

A—PLUMBAGO ZEYLANICA, *LINN.* B—PLUMBAGO ROSEA, *LINN.*

PLATE No. 575.

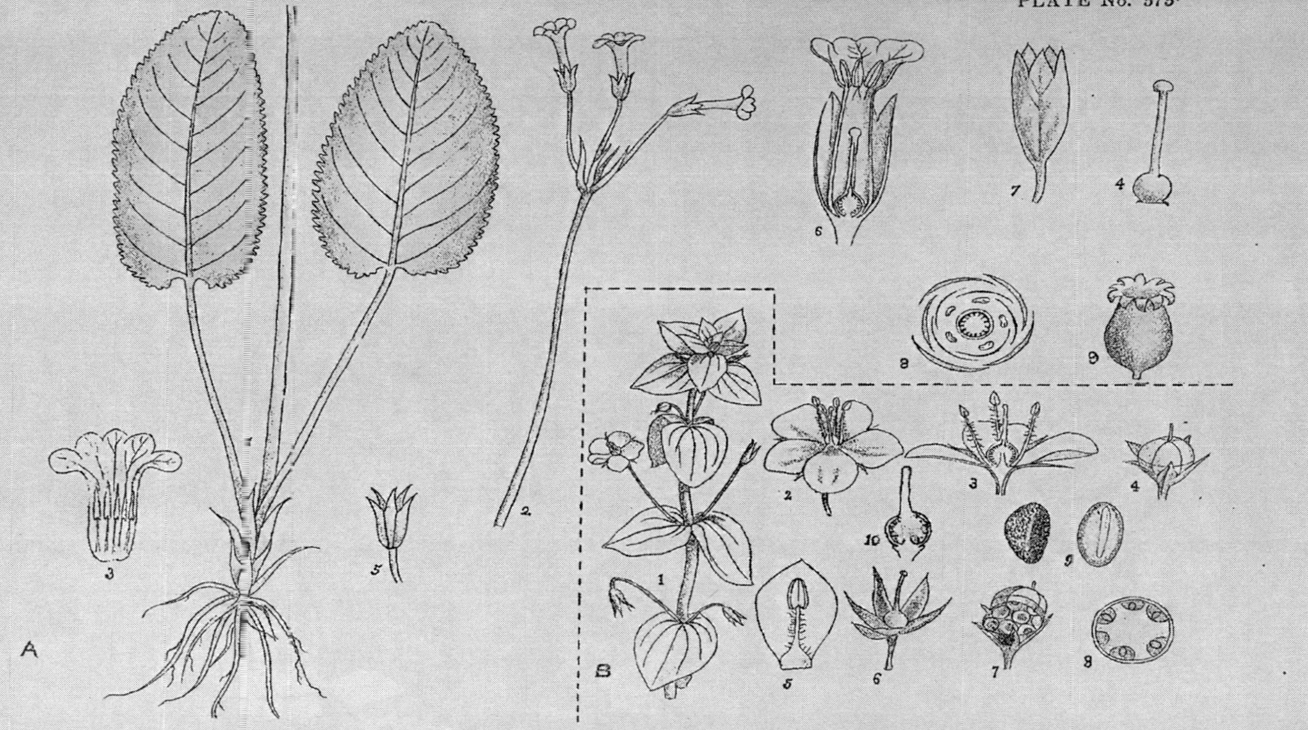

A—PRIMULA RETICULATA, *Wall.*   B—ANAGALLIS ARVENSIS, *Linn.*

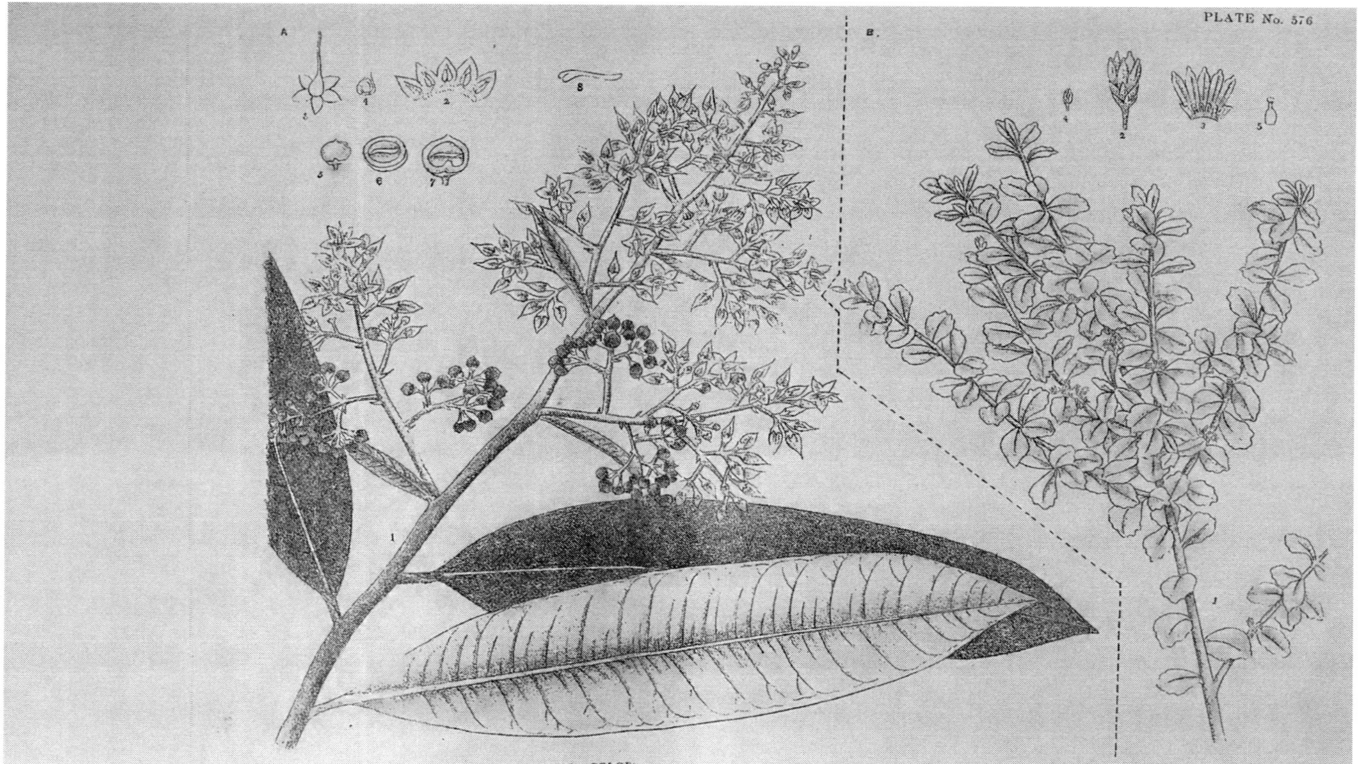

A. ARDISIA COLORATA, *Roxb.*

B. MYRSINE AFRICANA, *Linn.*

PLATE No. 577.

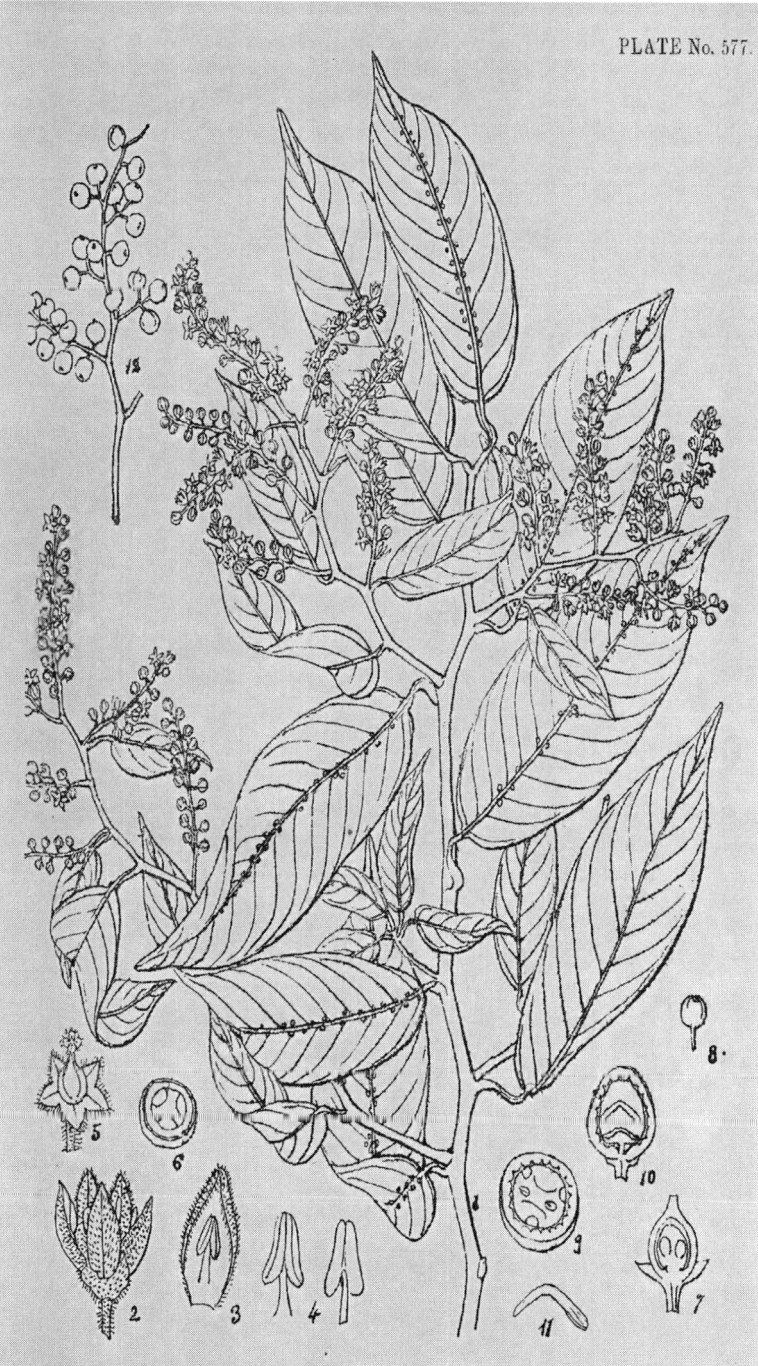

EMBELIA RIBES, *BURM.*

PLATE No. 578.

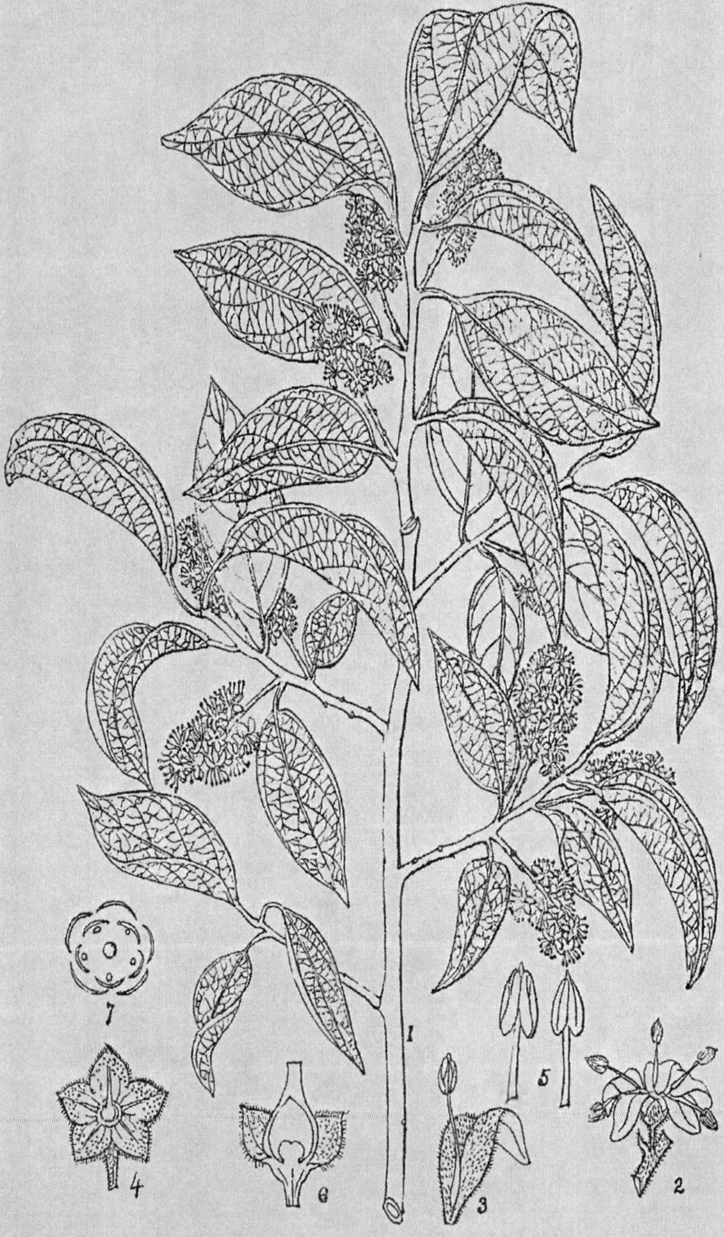

EMBELIA ROBUSTA, *ROXB.*

PLATE No. 579

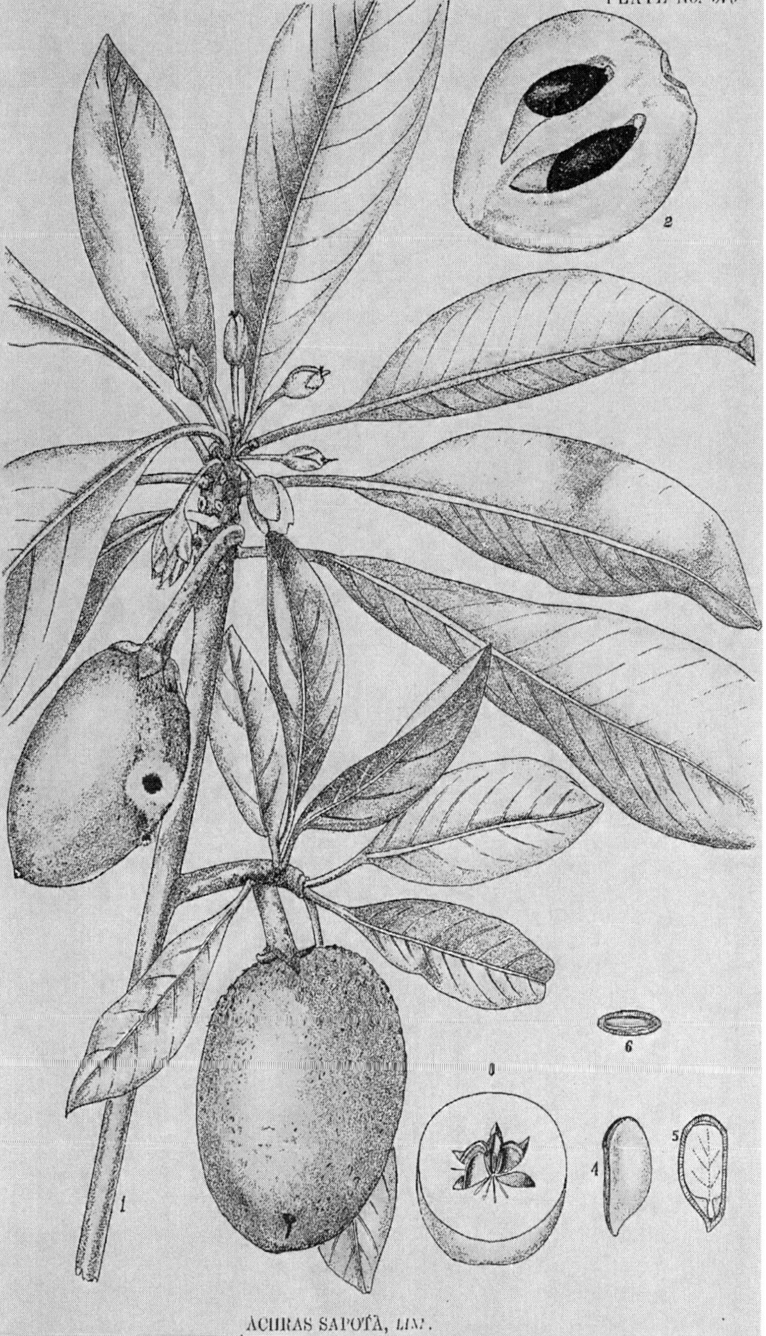

ACHRAS SAPOTA, Linn.

PLATE No. 580.

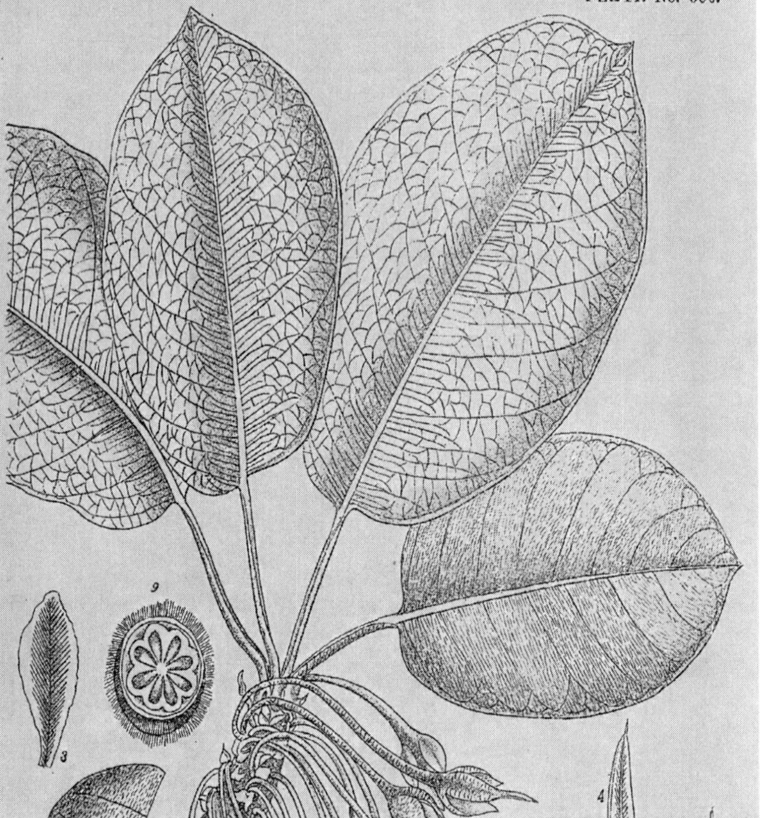

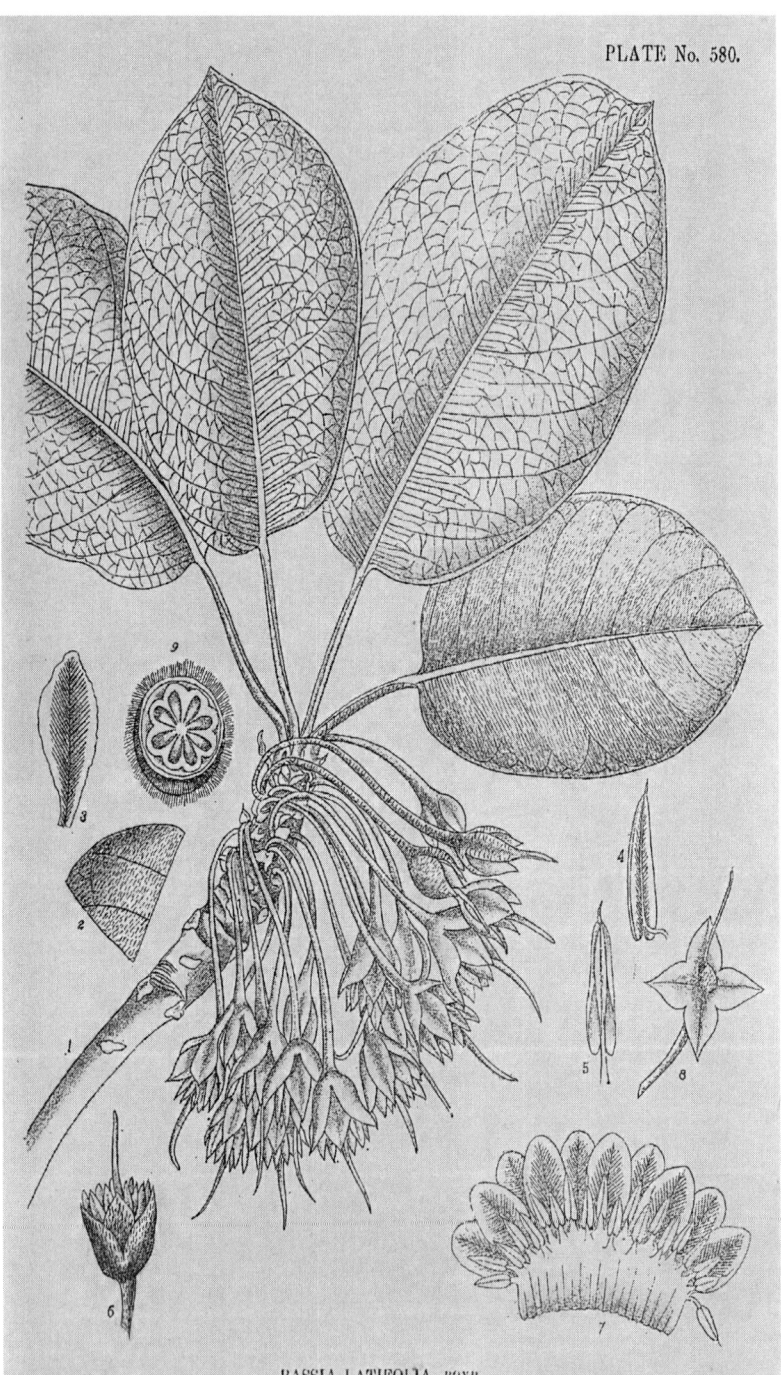

BASSIA LATIFOLIA, ROXB.

PLATE No. 581.

BASSIA LONGIFOLIA, *LINN.*

PLATE No. 582.

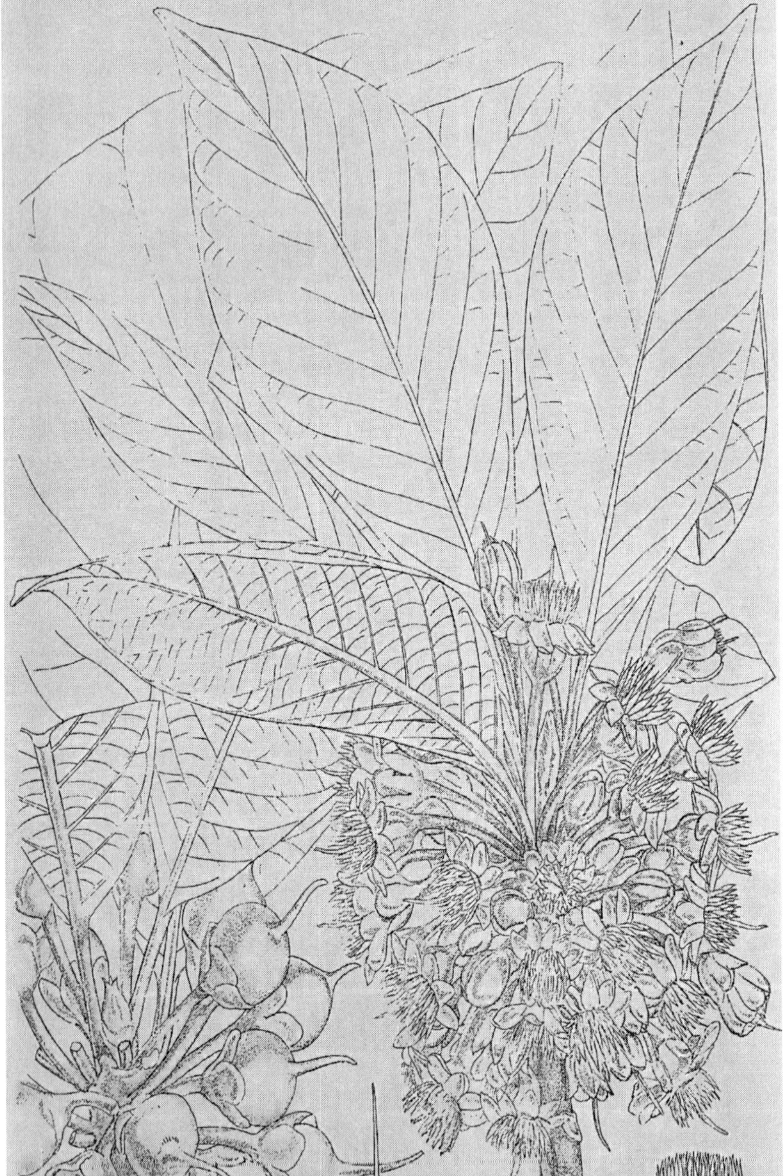

BASSIA BUTYRACEA, *ROXB.*

PLATE No. 583.

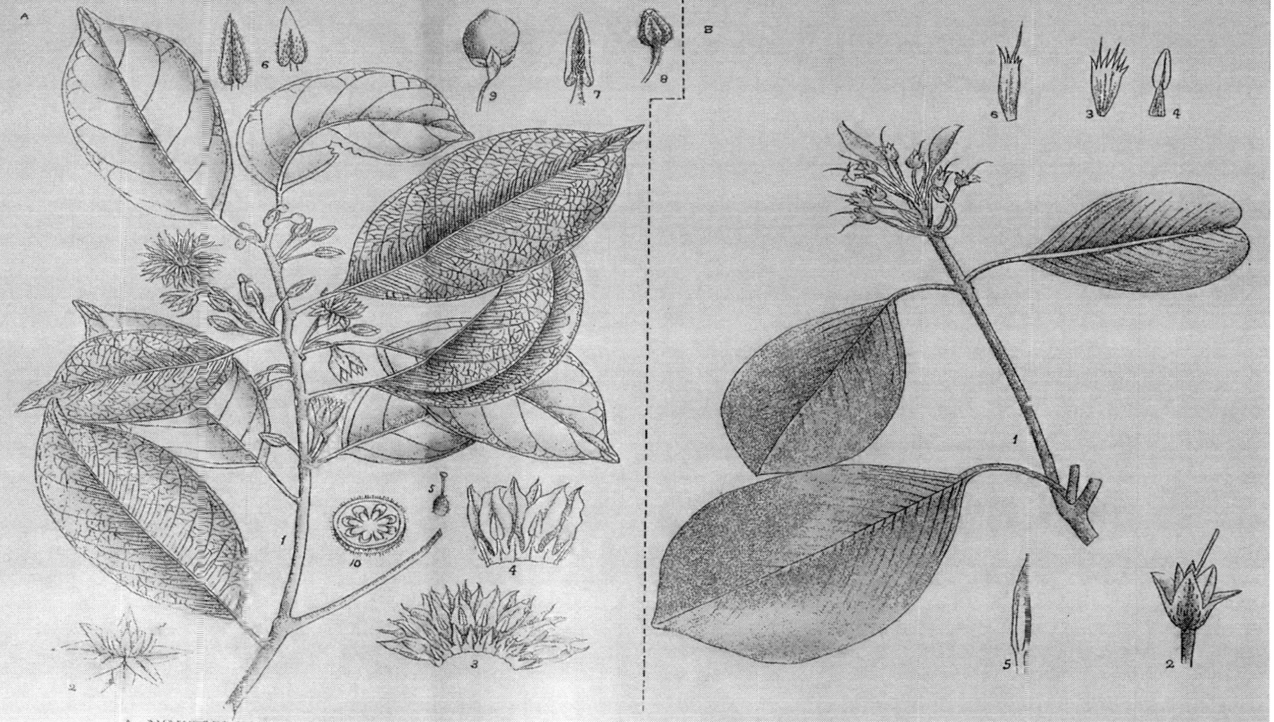

A -MIMUSOPS ELENGI, *LINN.*

MIMUSOPS KAUKI *LINN.*

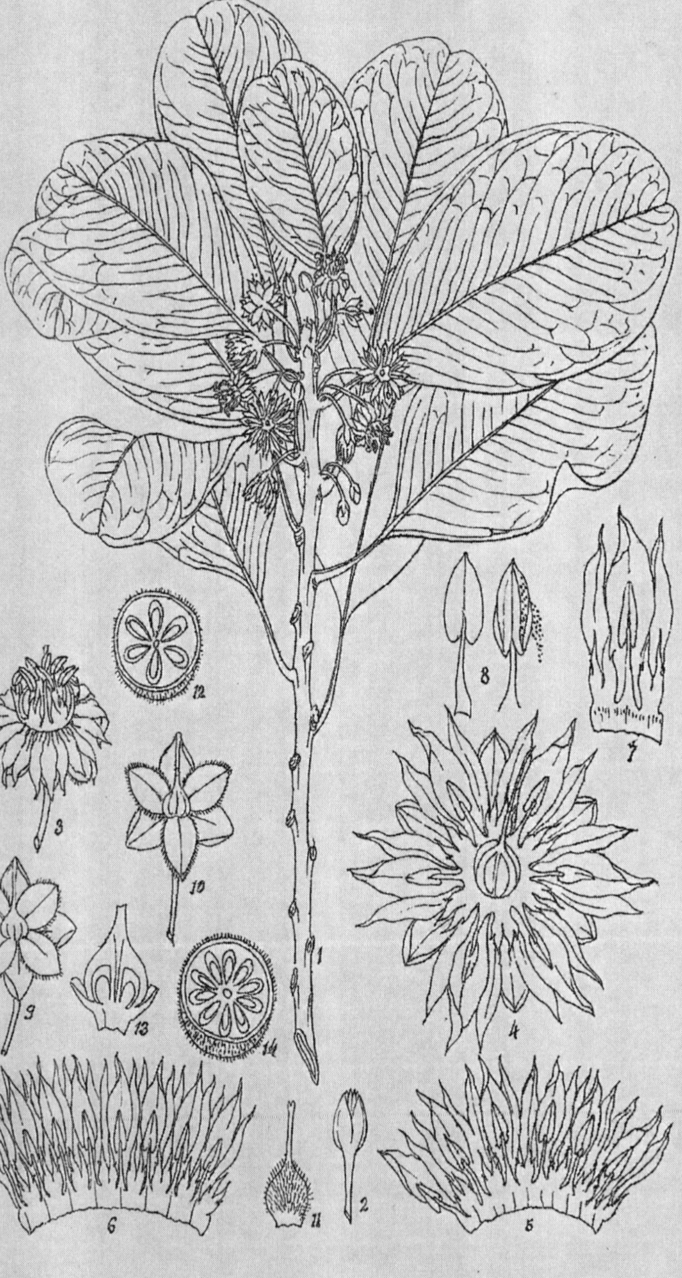

MIMUSOPS HEXANDRA, *ROXB.*

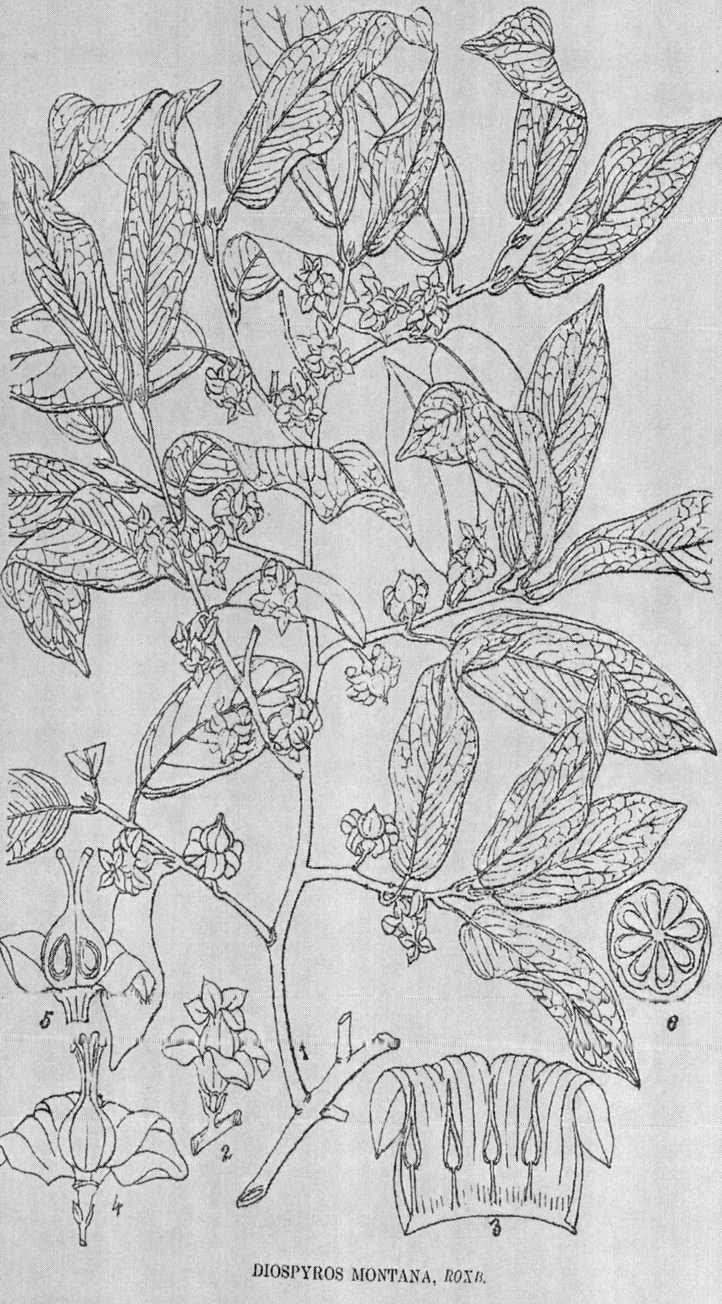

DIOSPYROS MONTANA, *ROXB.*

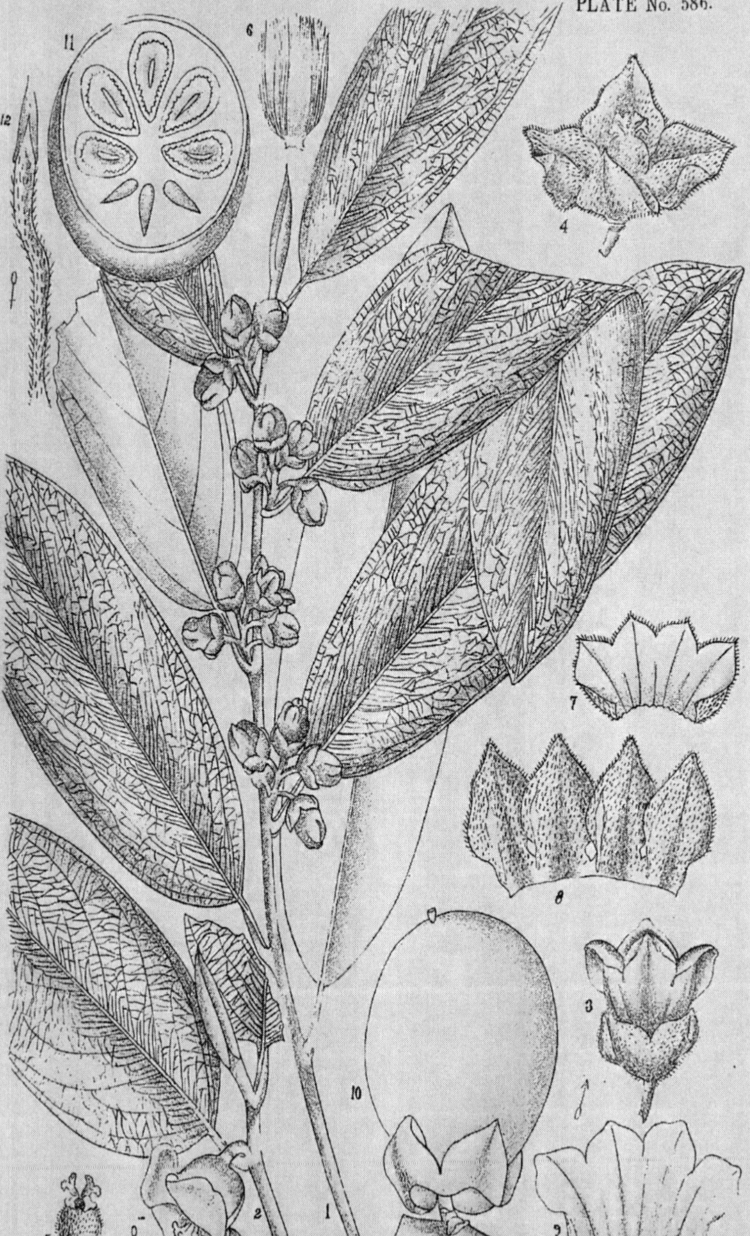

DIOSPYROS EMBRYOPTERIS, *PERS.*

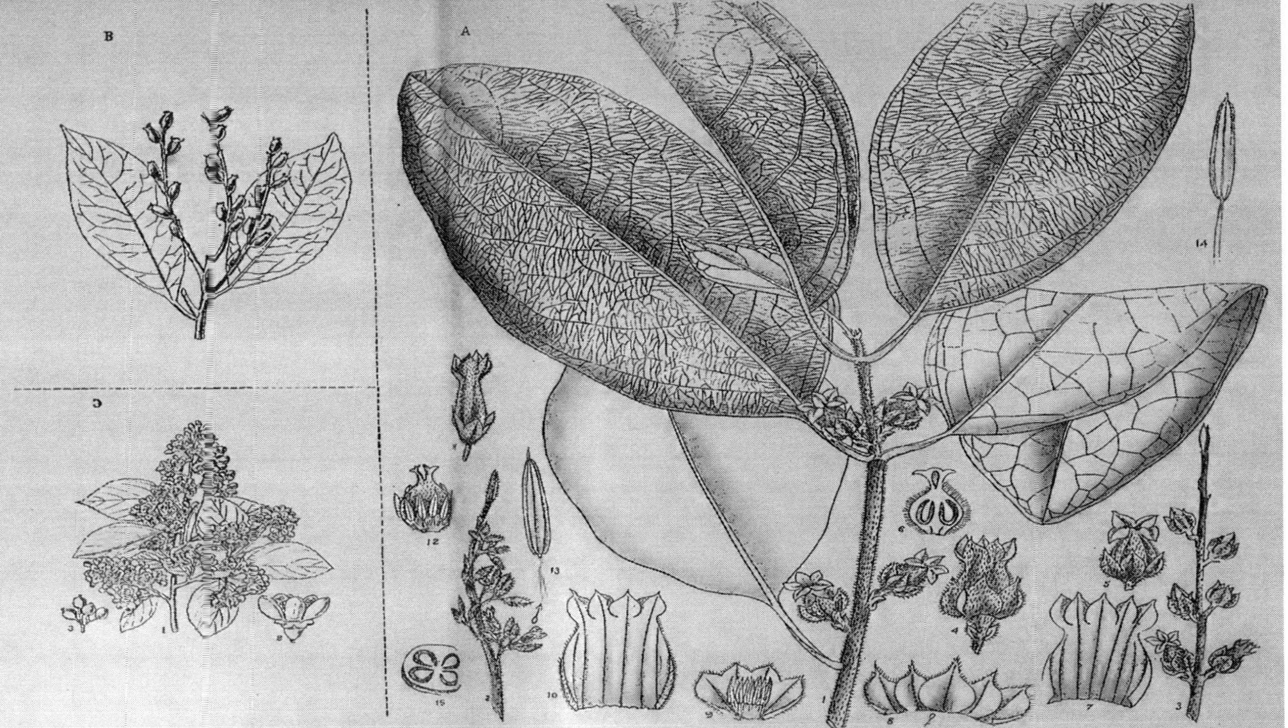

B—SYMPLOCOS RACEMOSA, ROXB.   C—S. CRATÆGOIDES, HAM.   A—DIOSPYROS MELANOXYLON, ROXB.

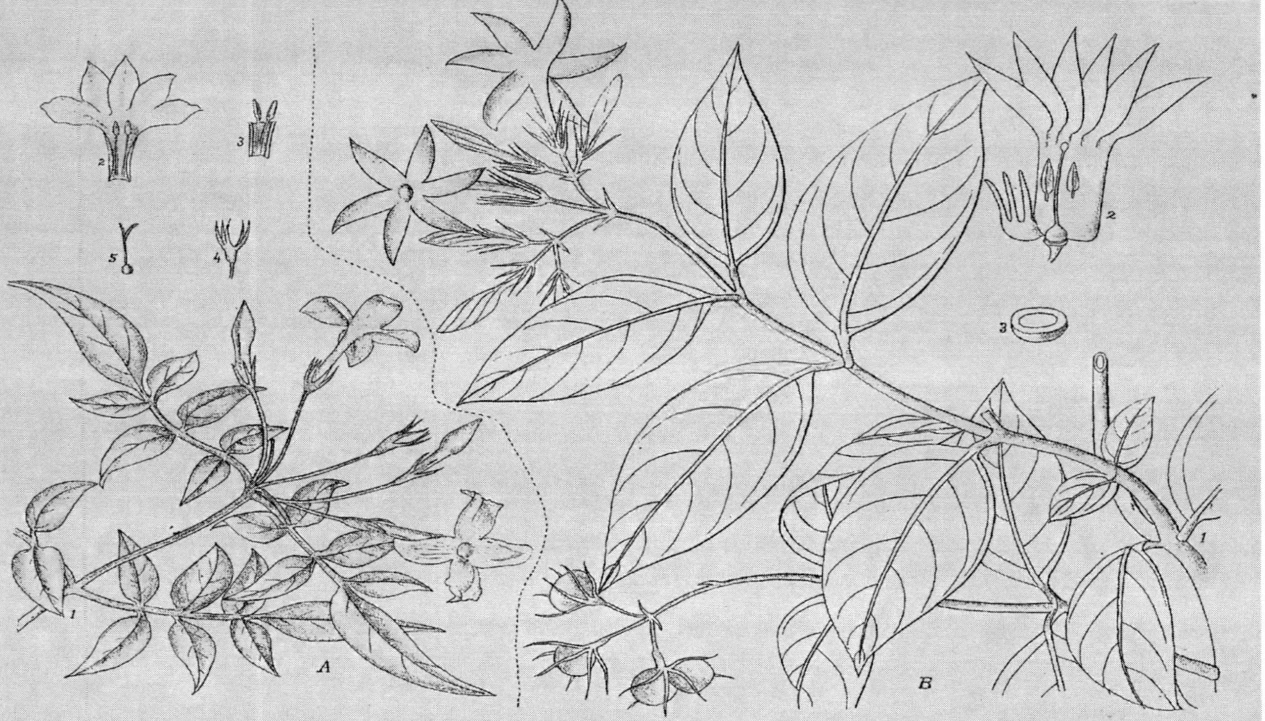

A—JASMINUM OFFICINALE, *LINN.* B—JASMINUM SAMBAC, *AIT.*

PLATE No. 589.

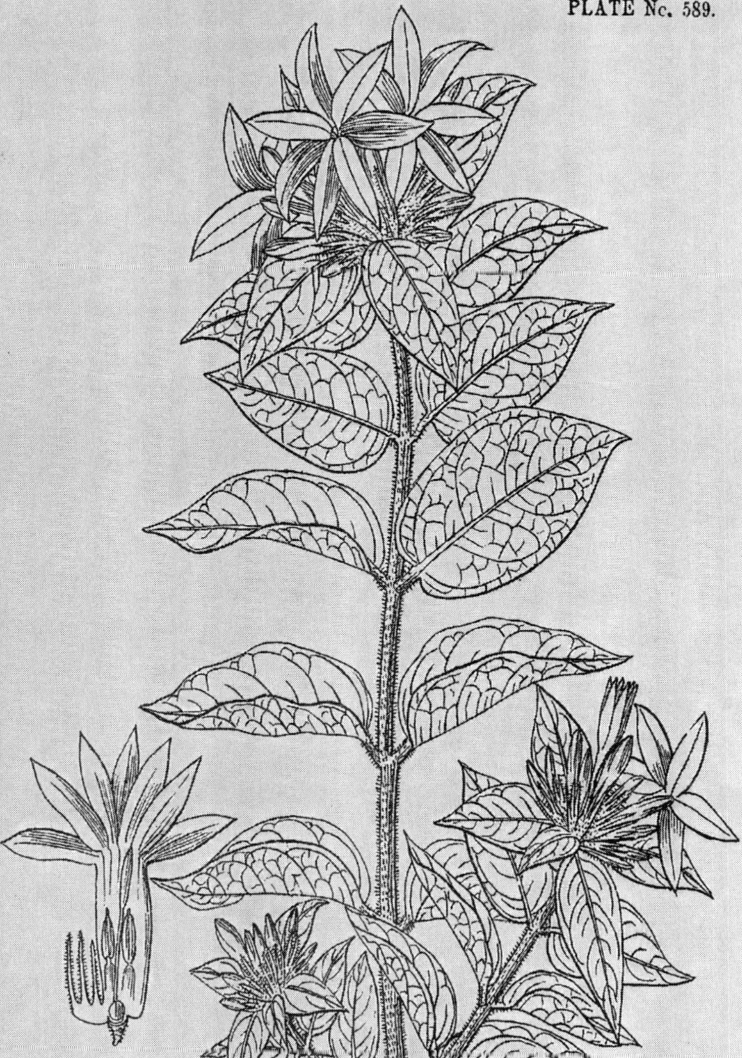

JASMINUM PUBESCENS, *WILLD.*

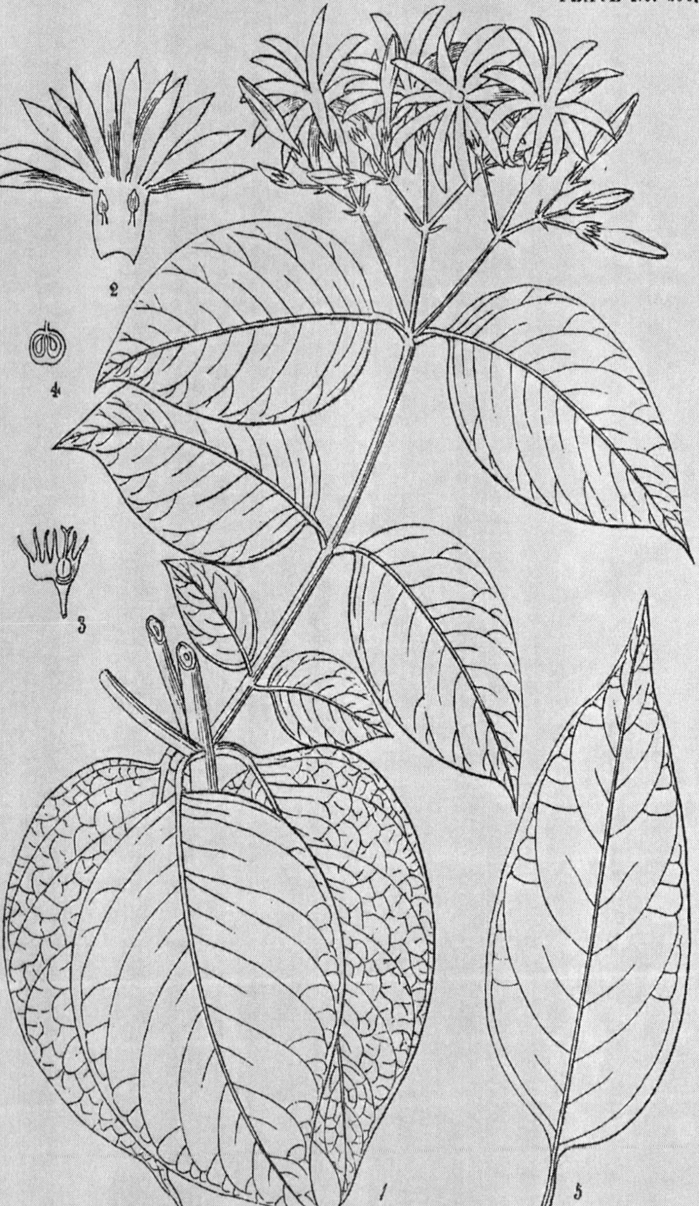

JASMINUM ARBORESCENS, *ROXB.*

PLATE No. 591.

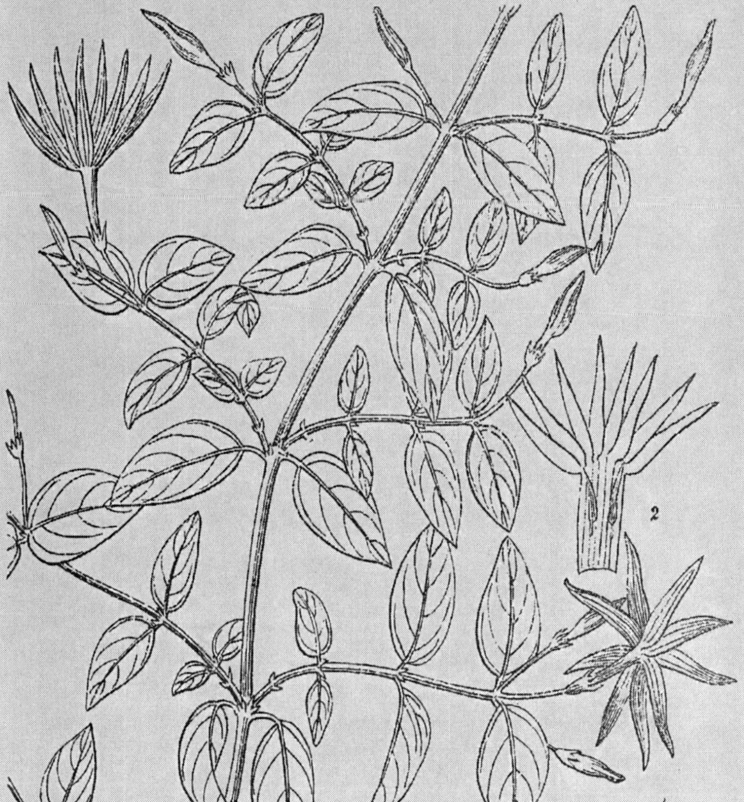

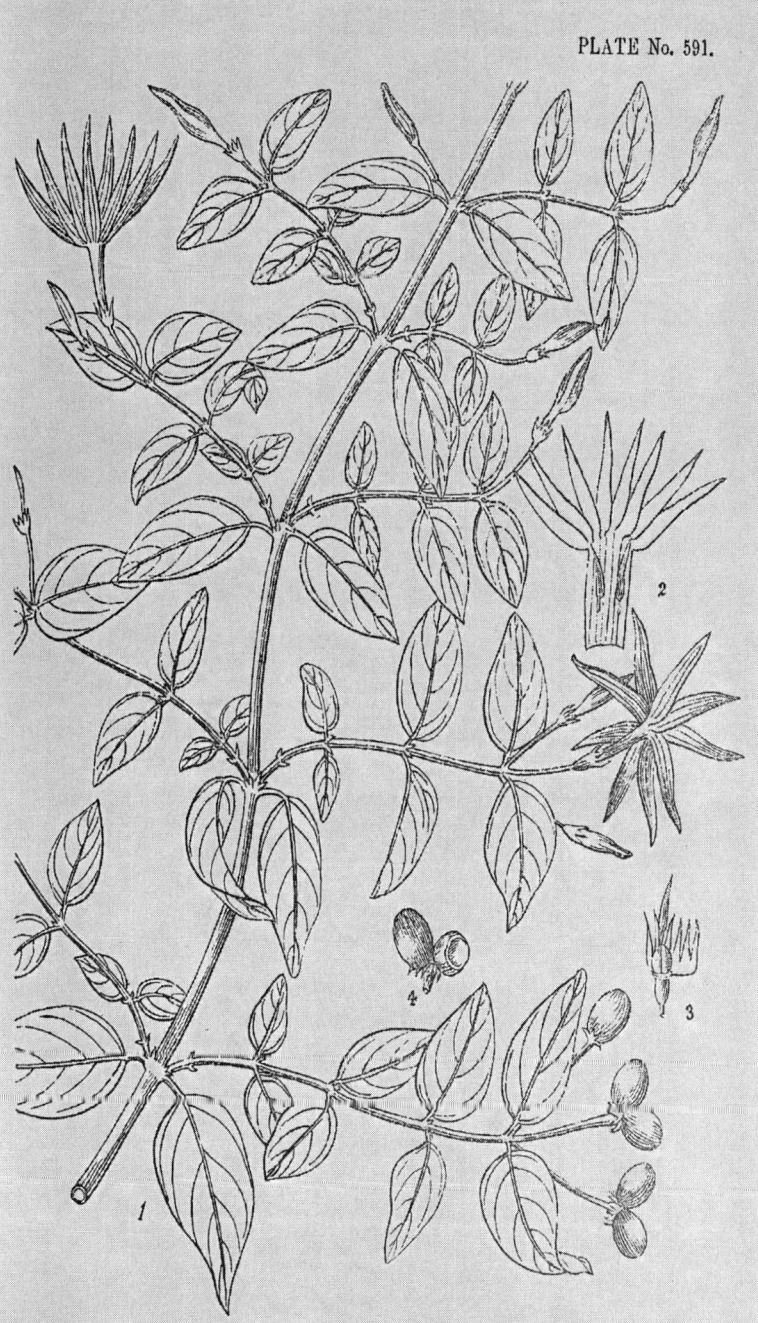

JASMINUM ANGUSTIFOLIUM, VAHL.

PLATE No 592.

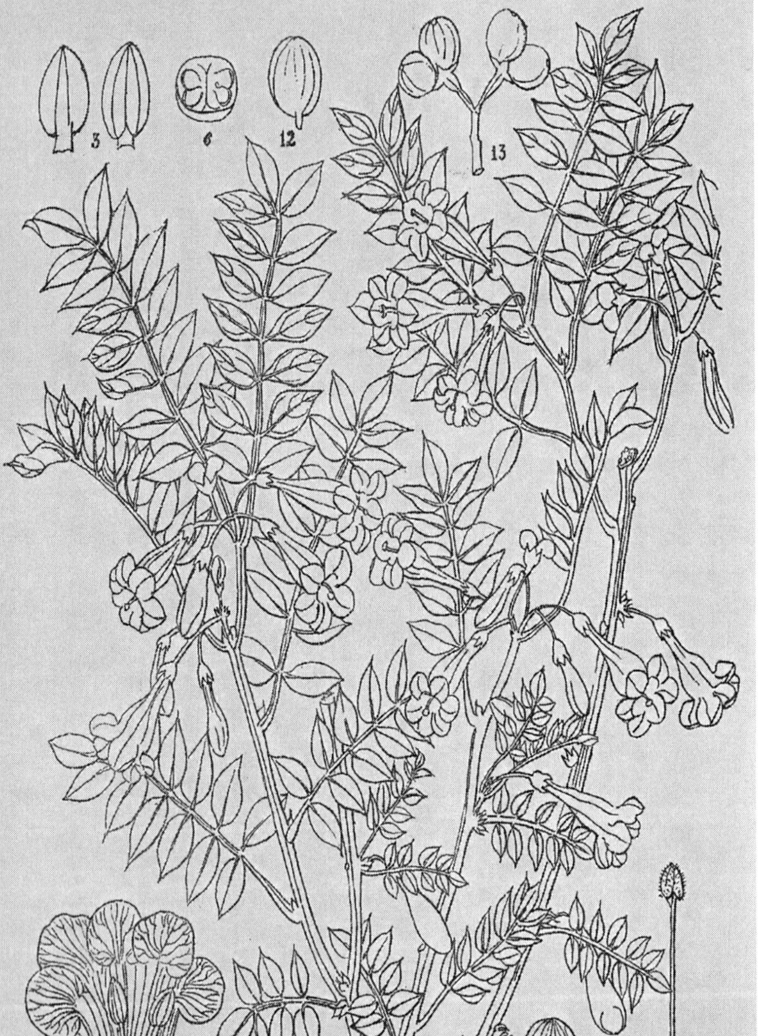

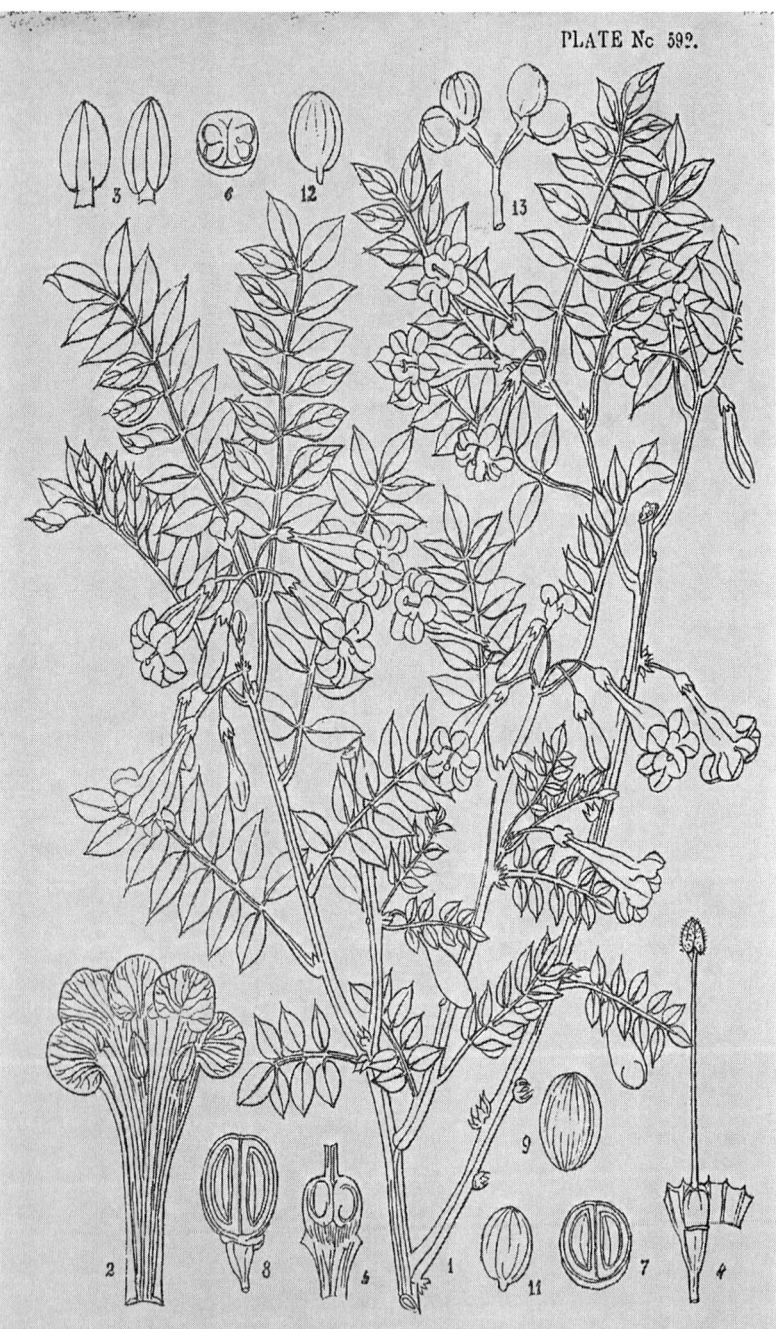

JASMINUM HUMILE, *Linn.*

PLATE No. 593

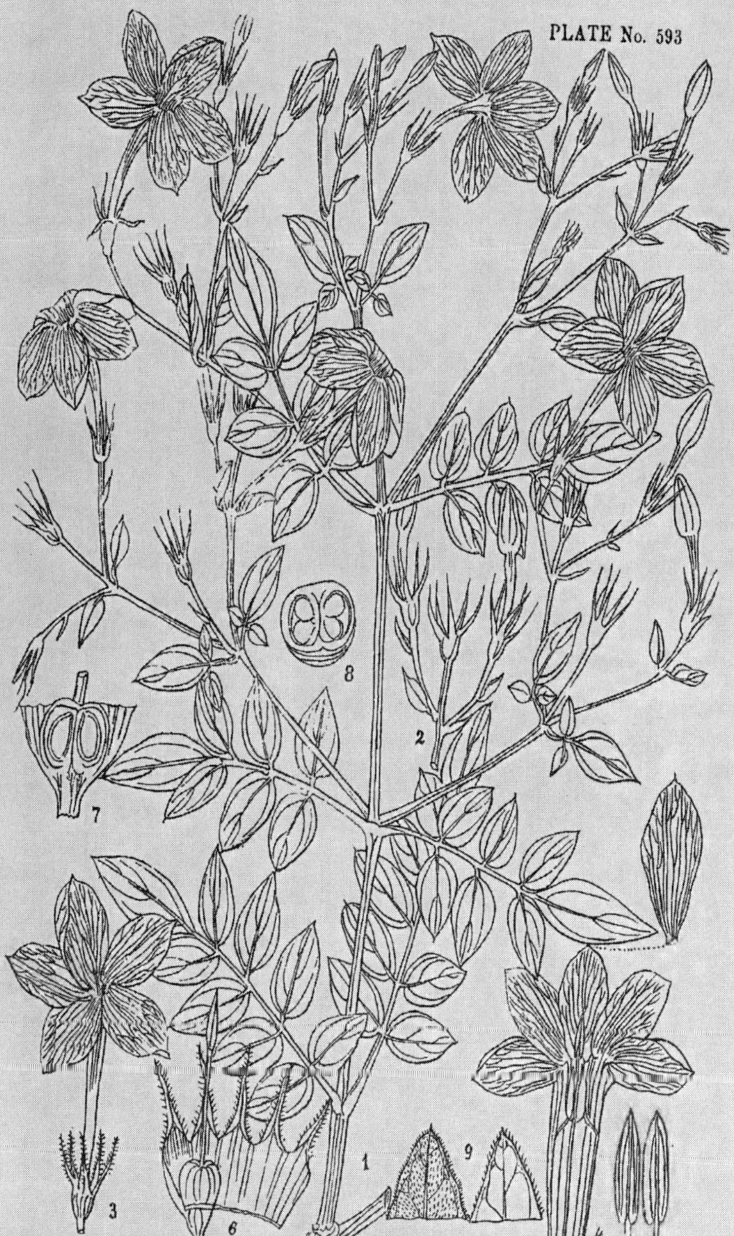

JASMINUM GRANDIFLORUM, LINN.

PLATE No. 594.

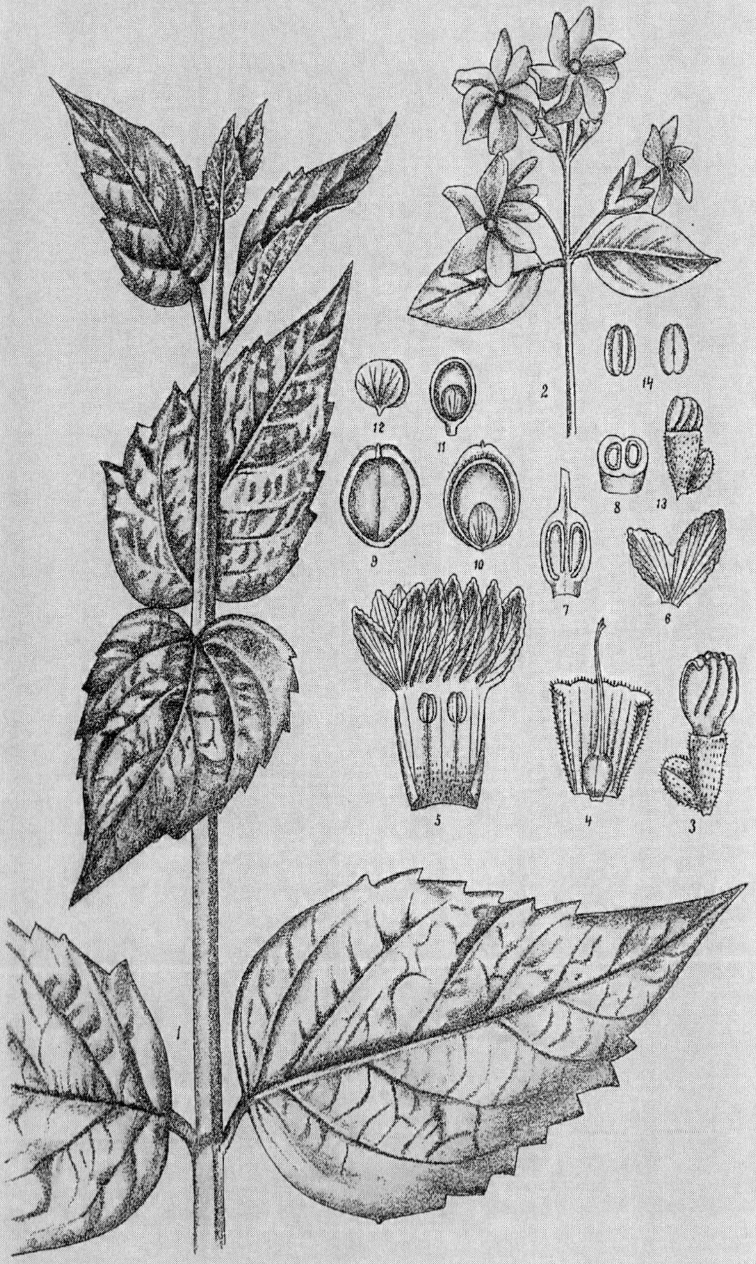

NYCTANTHES ARBOR-TRISTIS, *LINN.*

A—FRAXINUS FLORIBUNDA, *WALL.* B—FRAXINUS EXCELSIOR, *LINN.*

PLATE No 596.

OLEA CUSPIDATA, WALL.

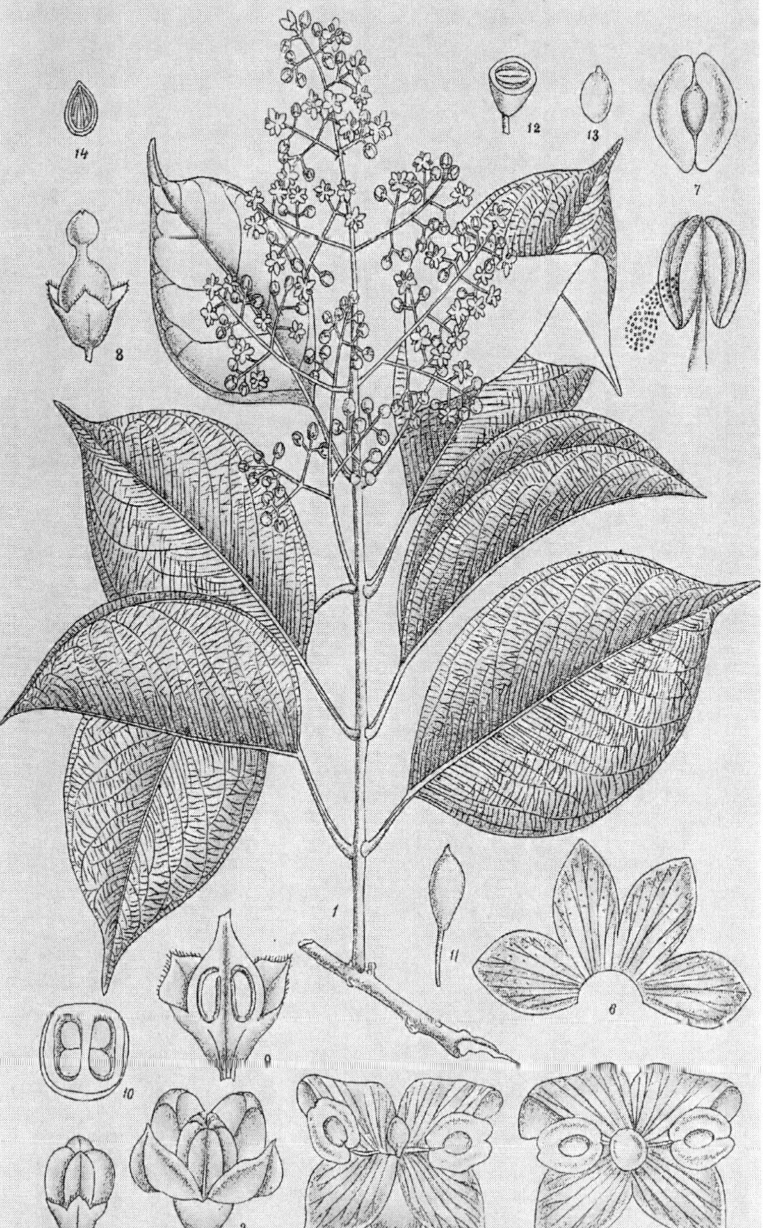

OLEA GLANDULIFERA, *WALL.*

PLATE No. 598.

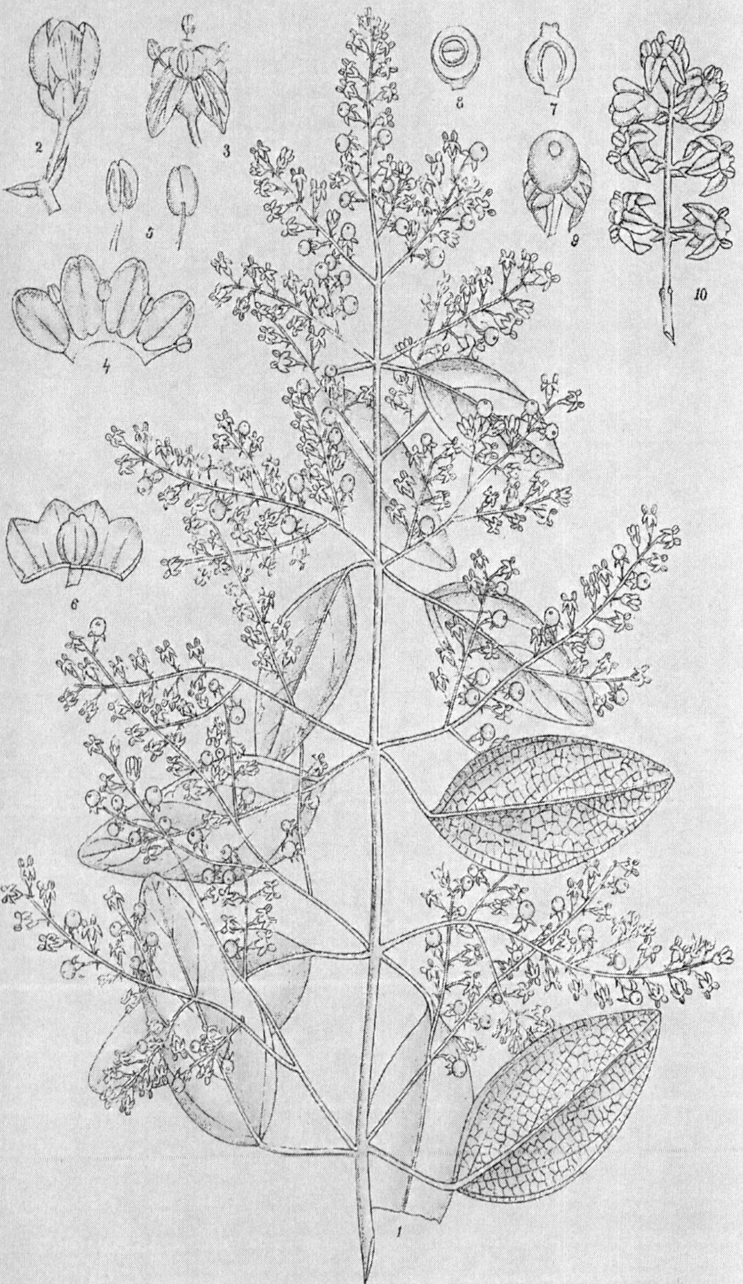

SALVADORA PERSICA, *LINN.*

PLATE No 599.

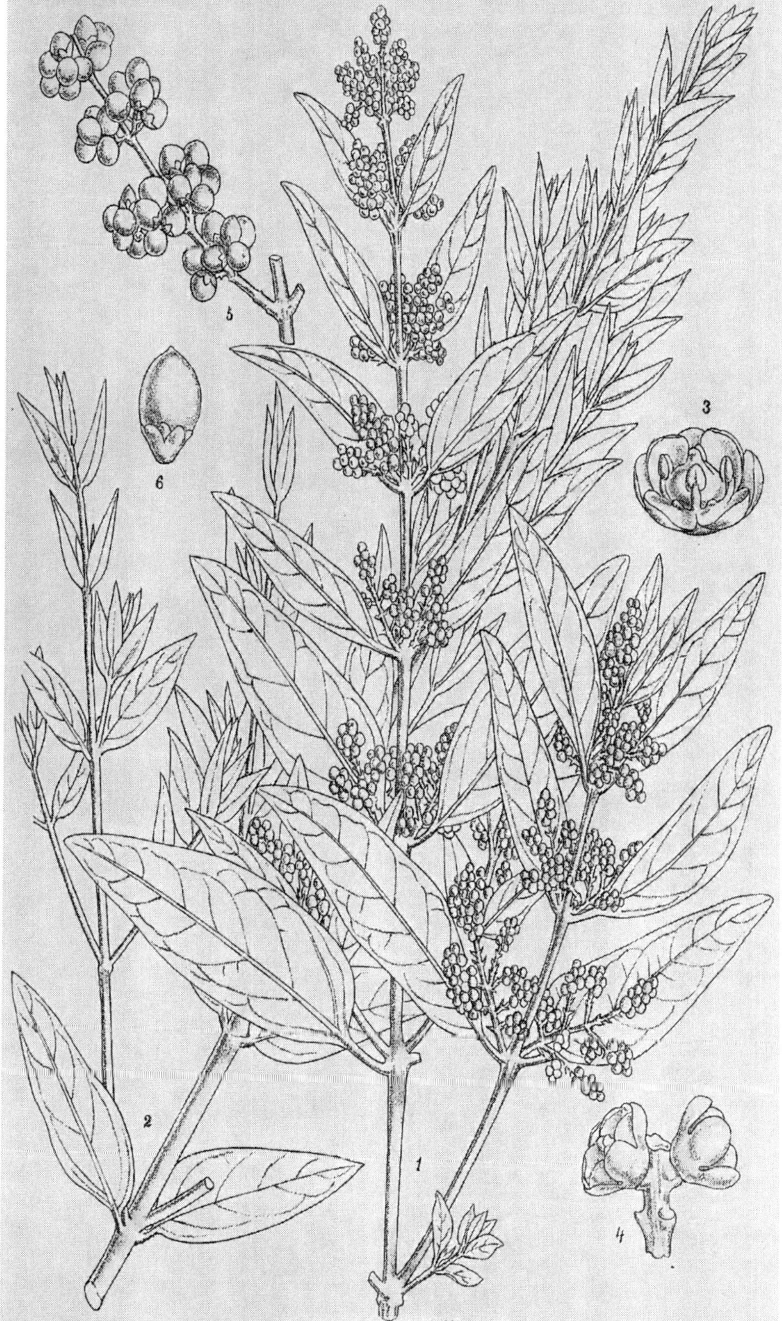

SALVADORA OLEOIDES, DCNE.

PLATE No. 600.

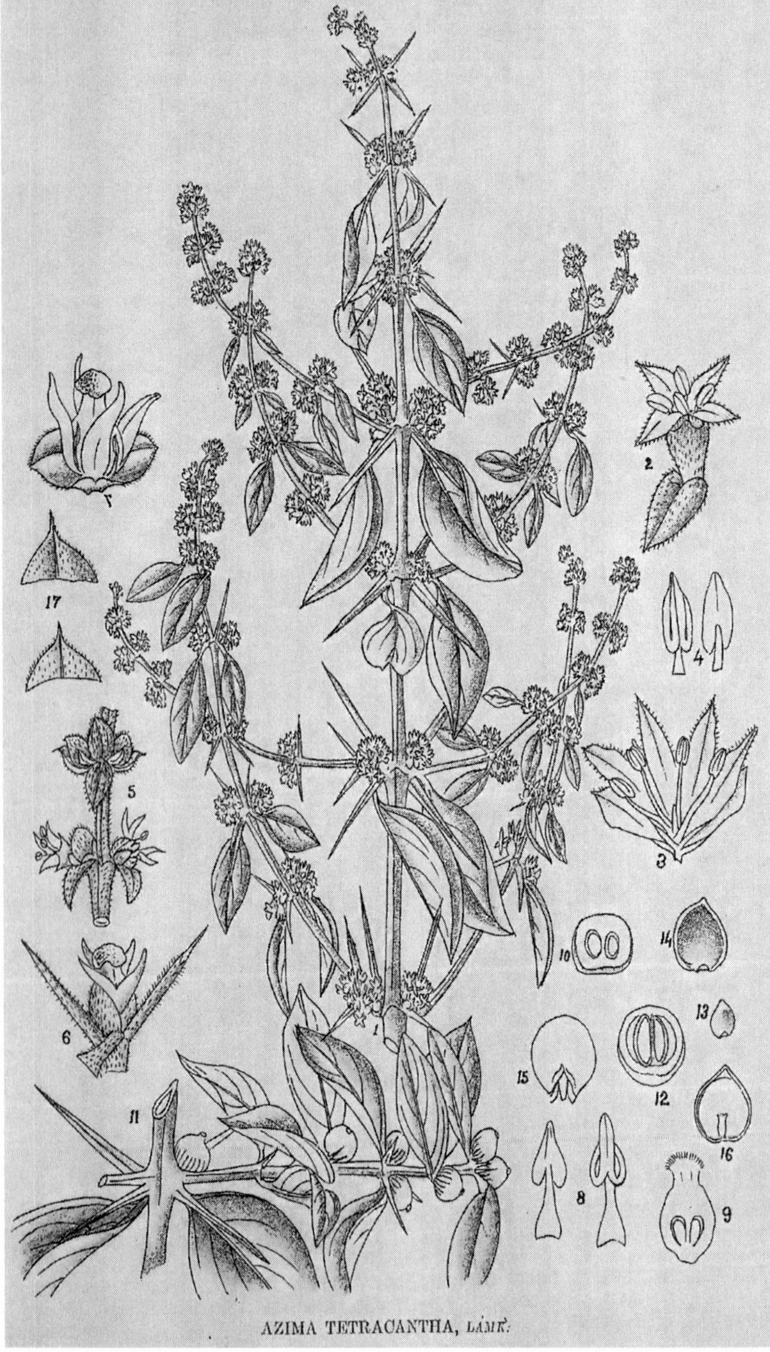

AZIMA TETRACANTHA, LAMK.

PLATE No. 601.

CARISSA CARANDAS, LINN.

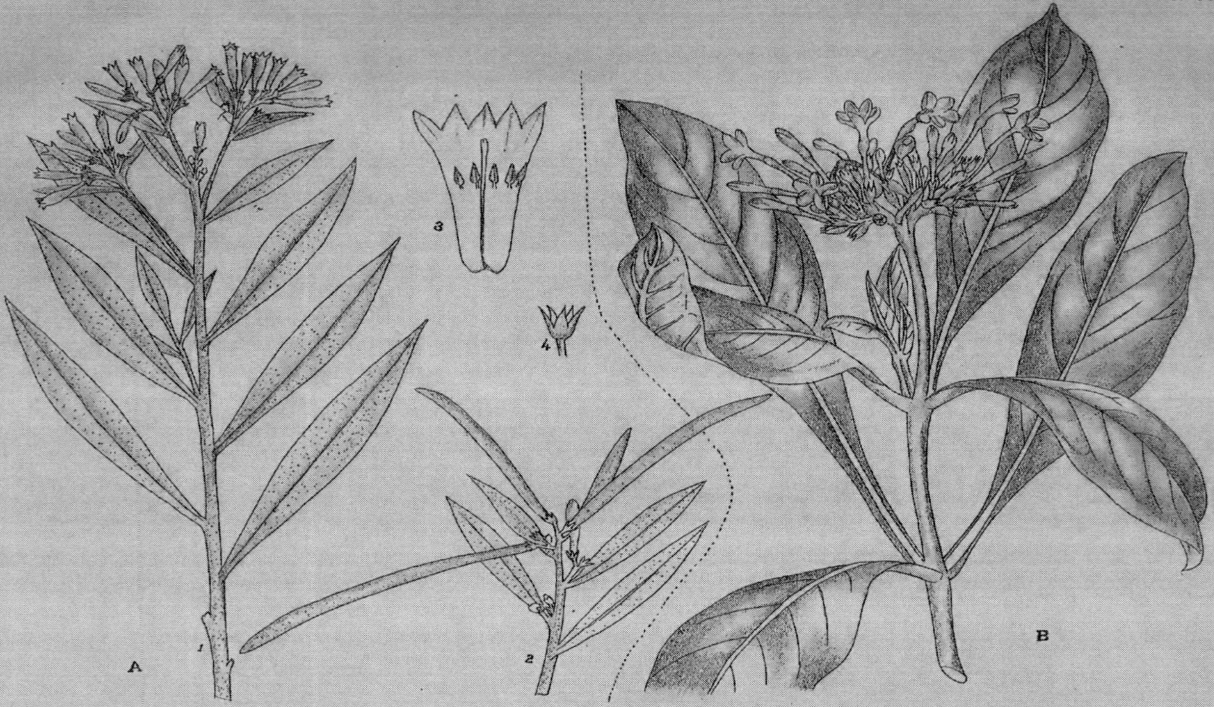

A—RHAZYA STRIOTA, *DECAISNE.*

B—RAUWOLFIA SERPENTINA, *BENTH.*

PLATE No. 603.

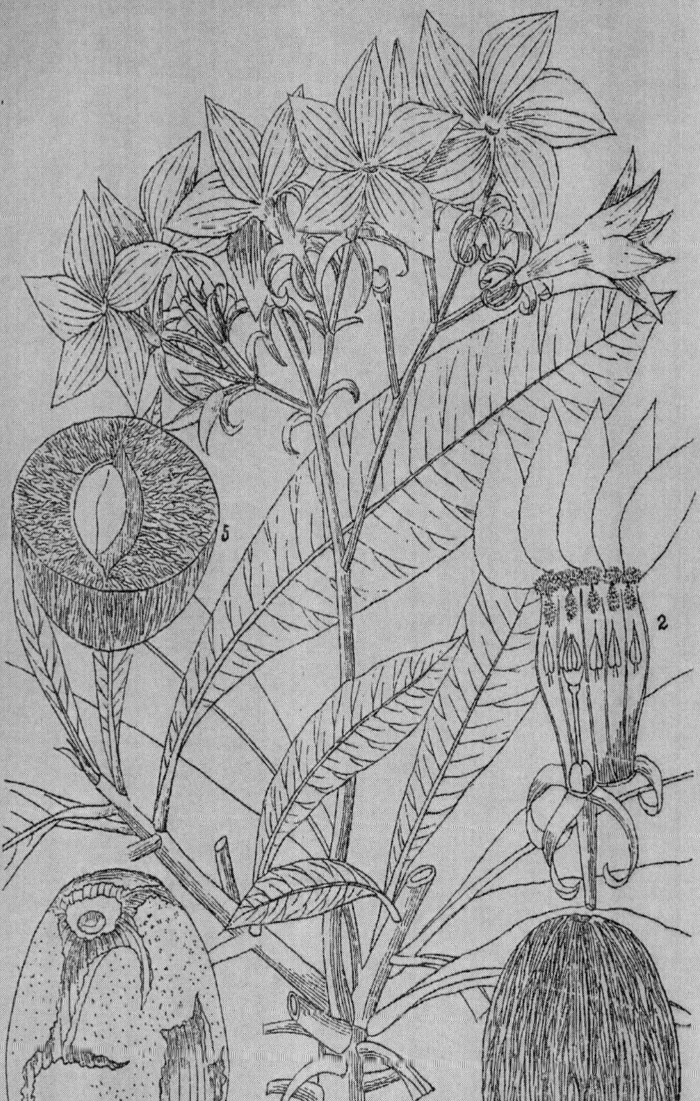

CERBERA ODOLLAM, A. GÆRTN.

PLATE No. 604.

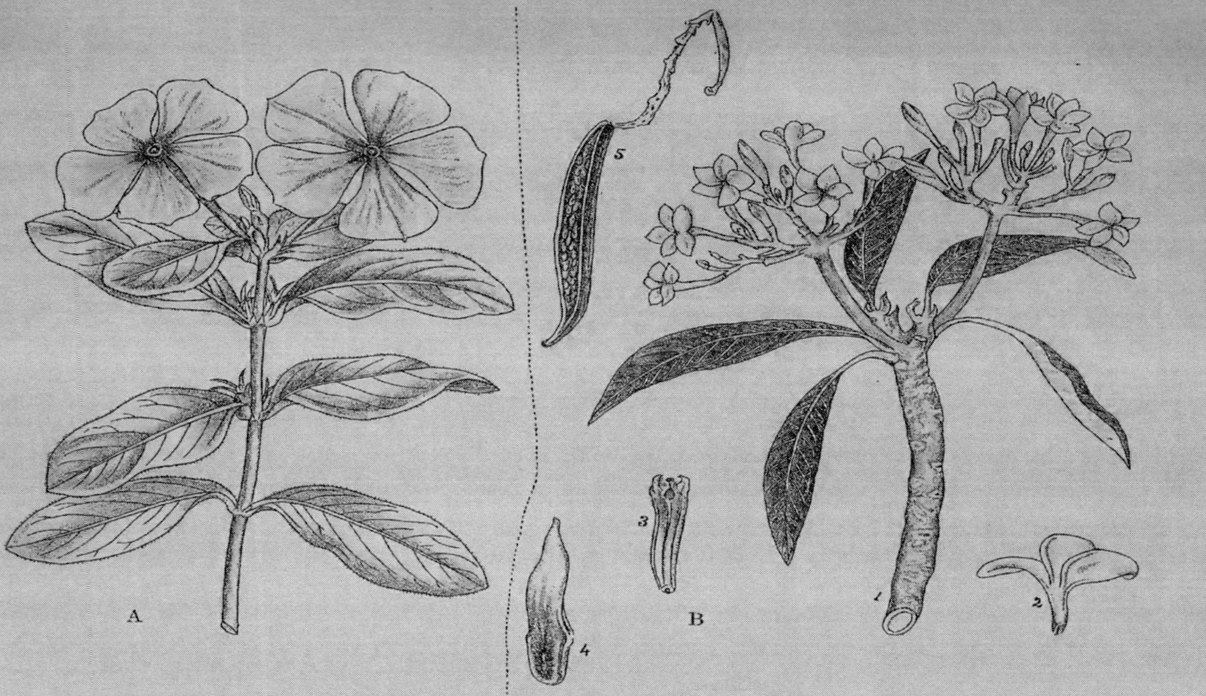

A—VINCA ROSEA, *Linn.*　　B—PLUMERIA ACUTIFOLIA, *Poiret.*

PLATE No. 605

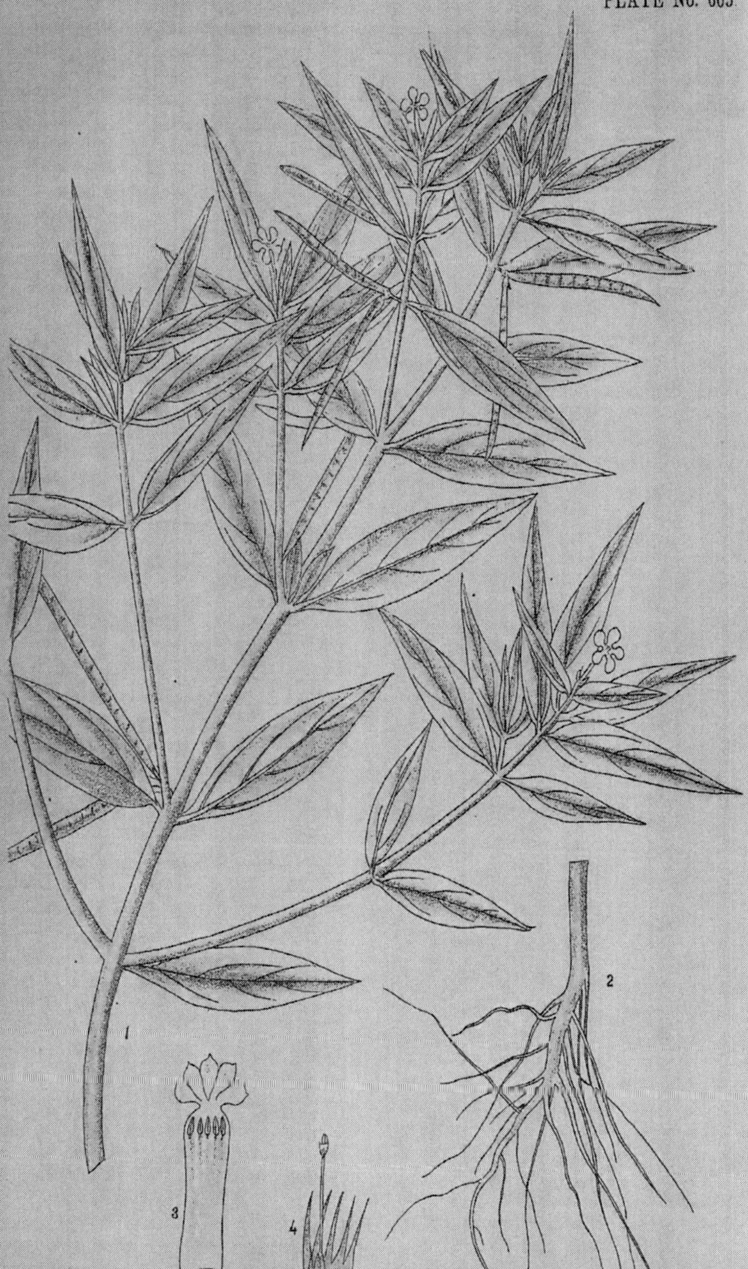

VINCA PUSILLA, *MURR*

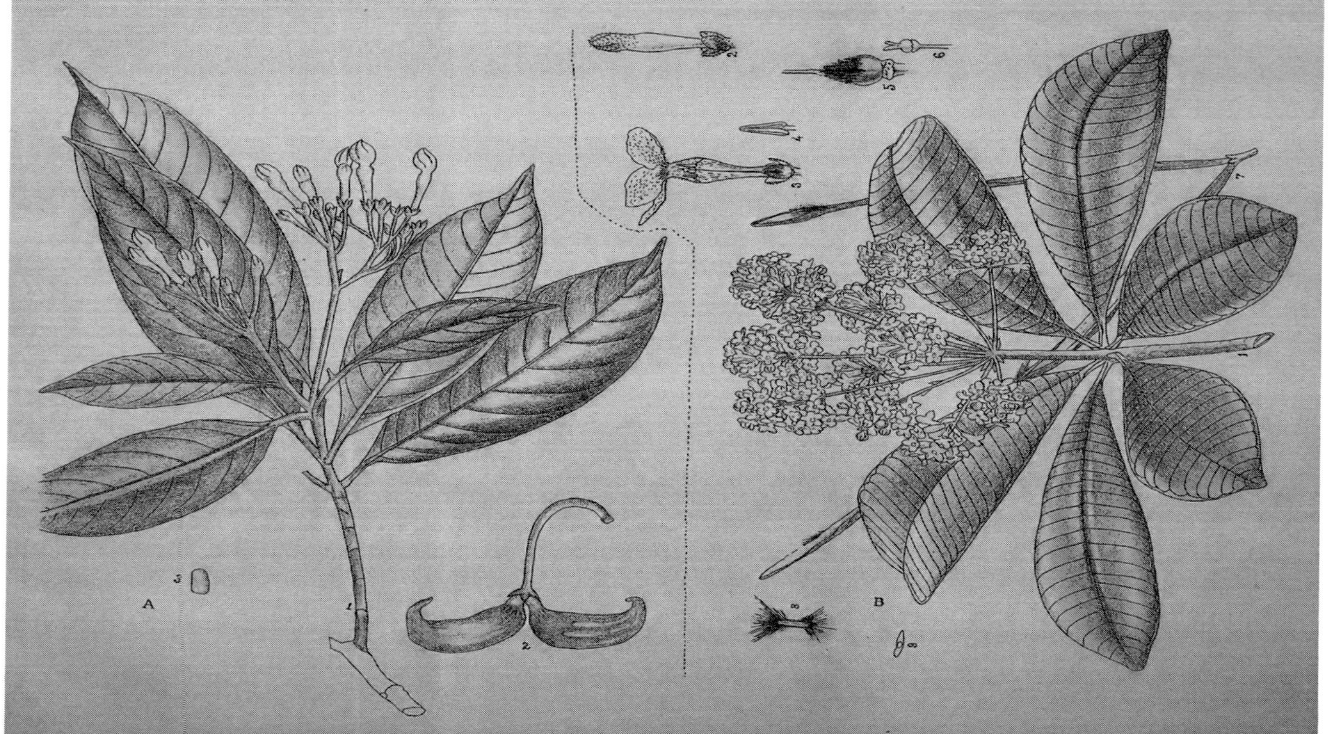

A—TABERNÆMONTANA HEYNEANA, *WALL.*

B—ALSTONIA SCHOLARIS, *R. BROWN.*

PLATE No. 607.

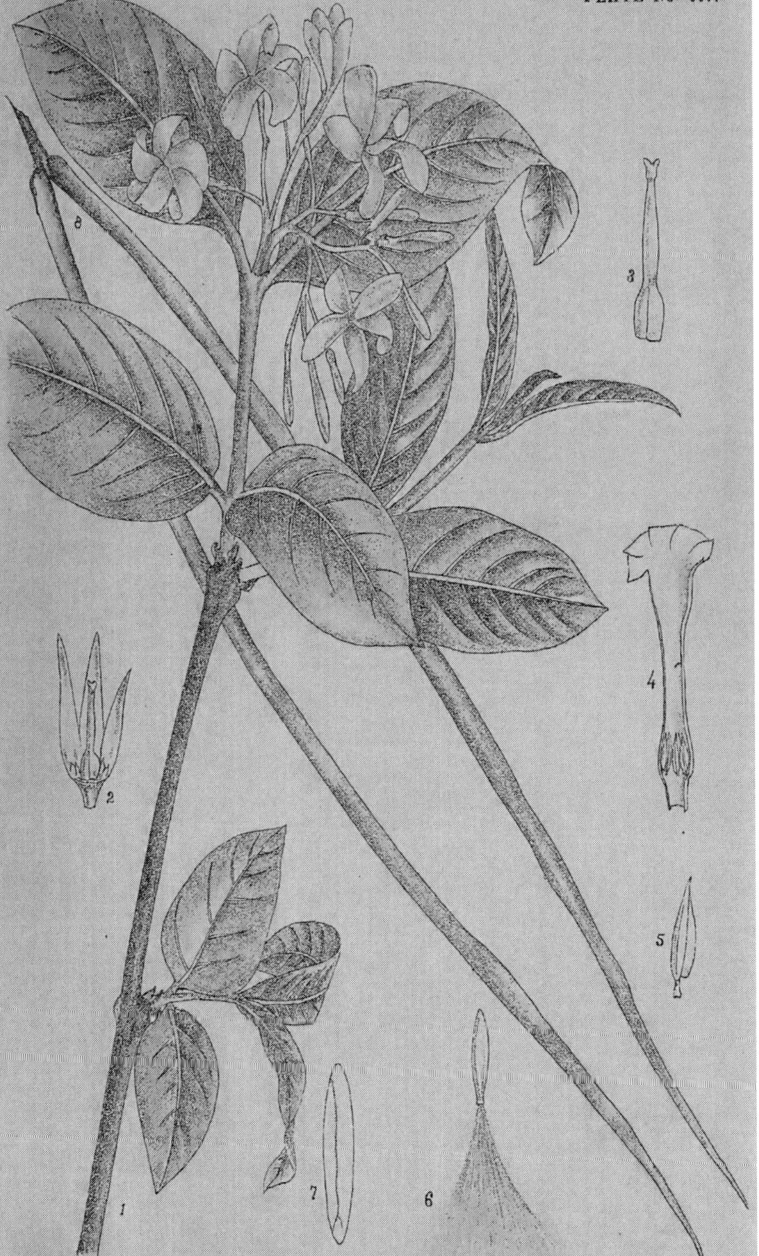

HOLARRHENA ANTIDYSENTERICA, *WALL.*

PLATE No. 608.

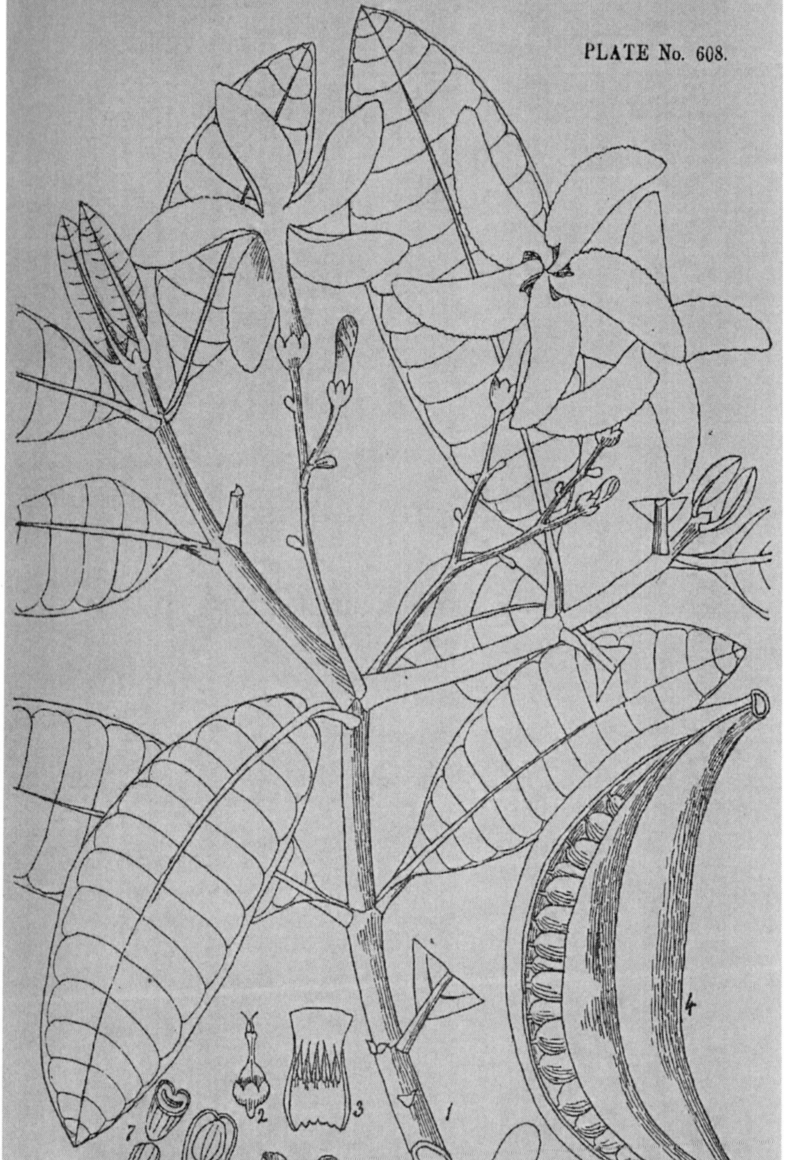

TABERNÆMONTANA DICHOTOMA *ROXB.*

PLATE No. 609.

TABERNÆMONTANA CORONARIA, *Br.*

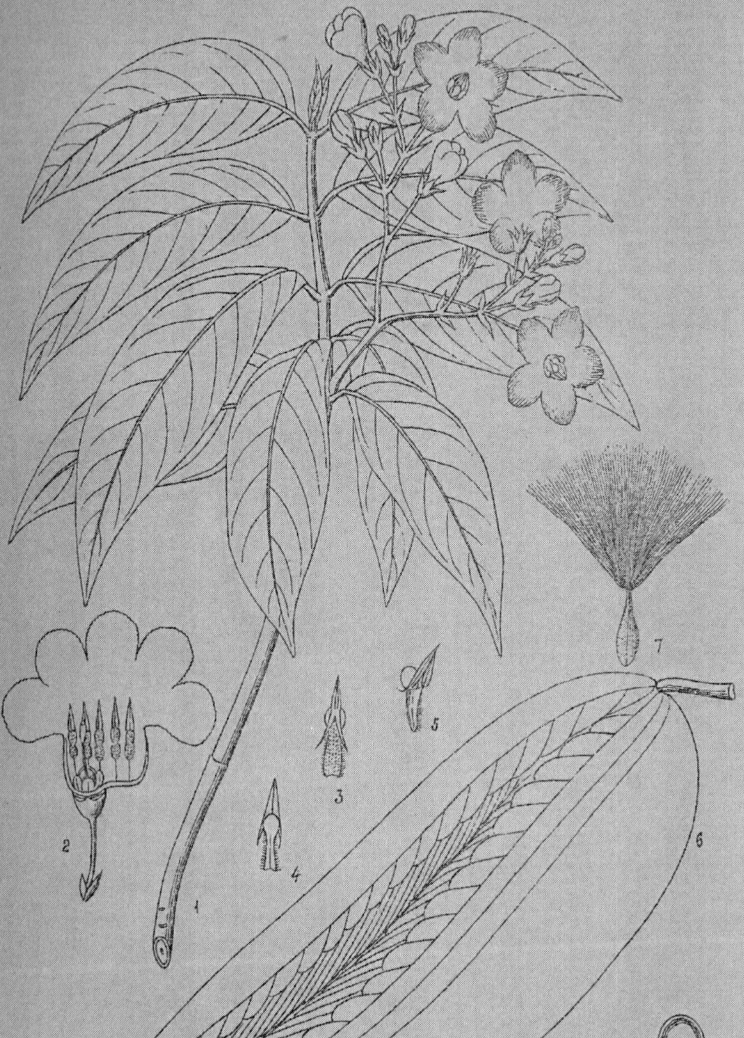

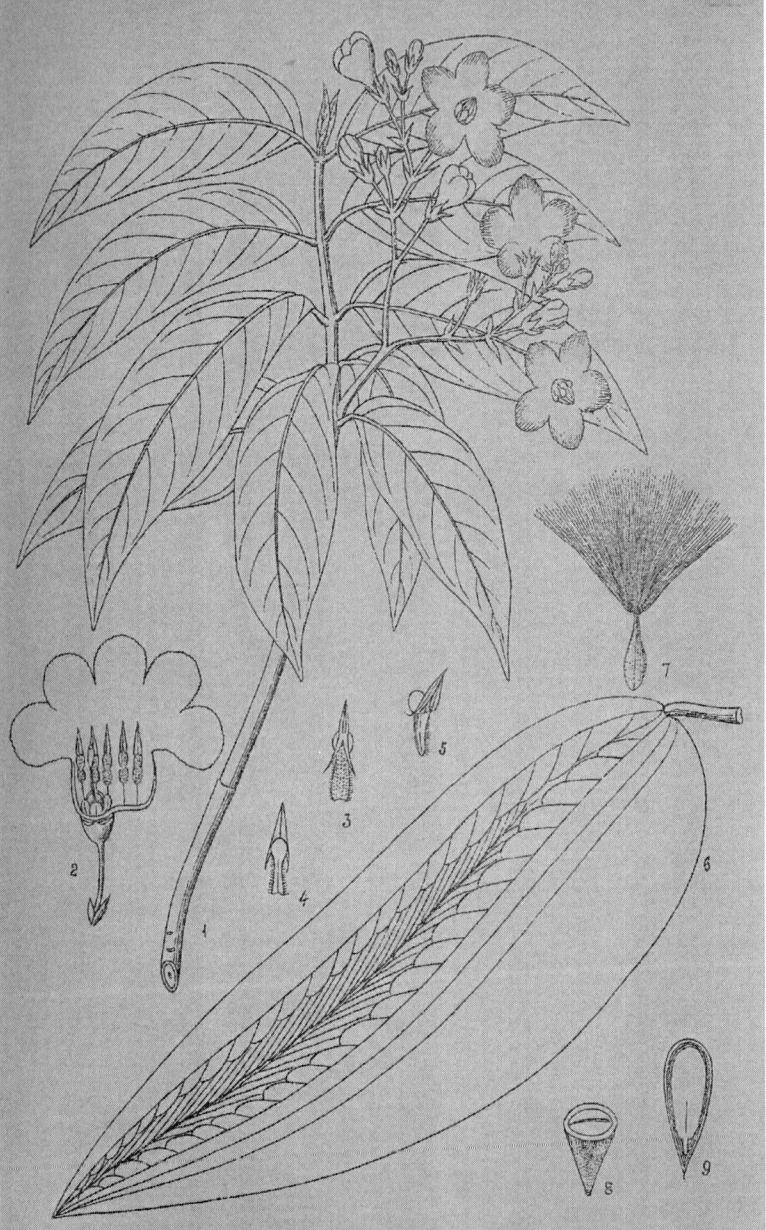

VALLARIS HEYNEI, *SPRENG.*

PLATE No. 611.

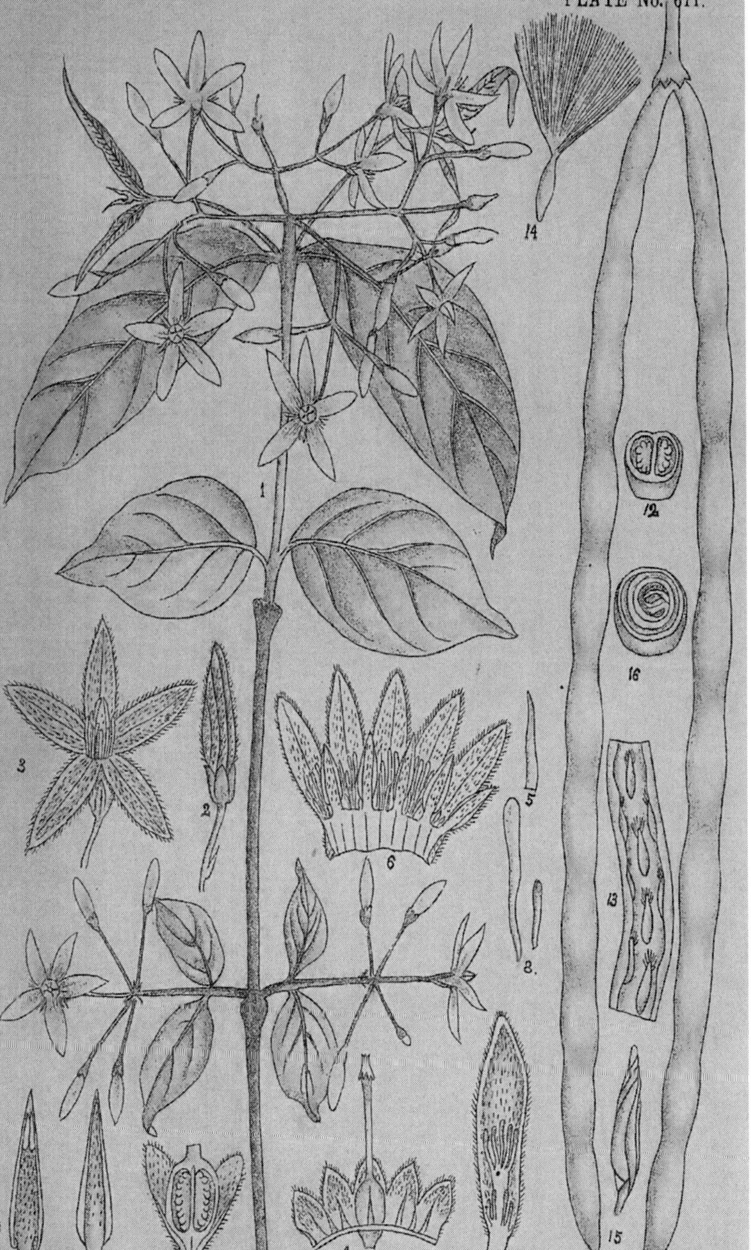

WRIGHTIA TINCTORIA, *BR.*

PLATE No. 612.

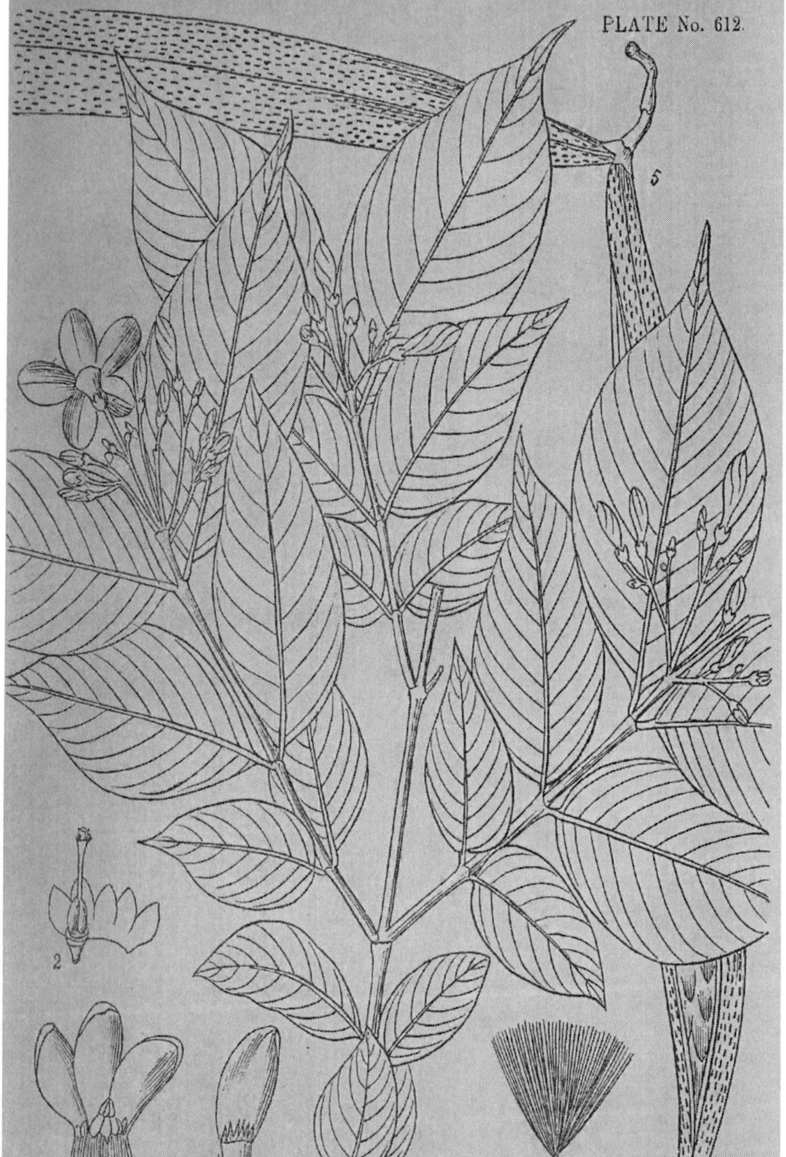

WRIGHTIA TOMENTOSA, R. & S.

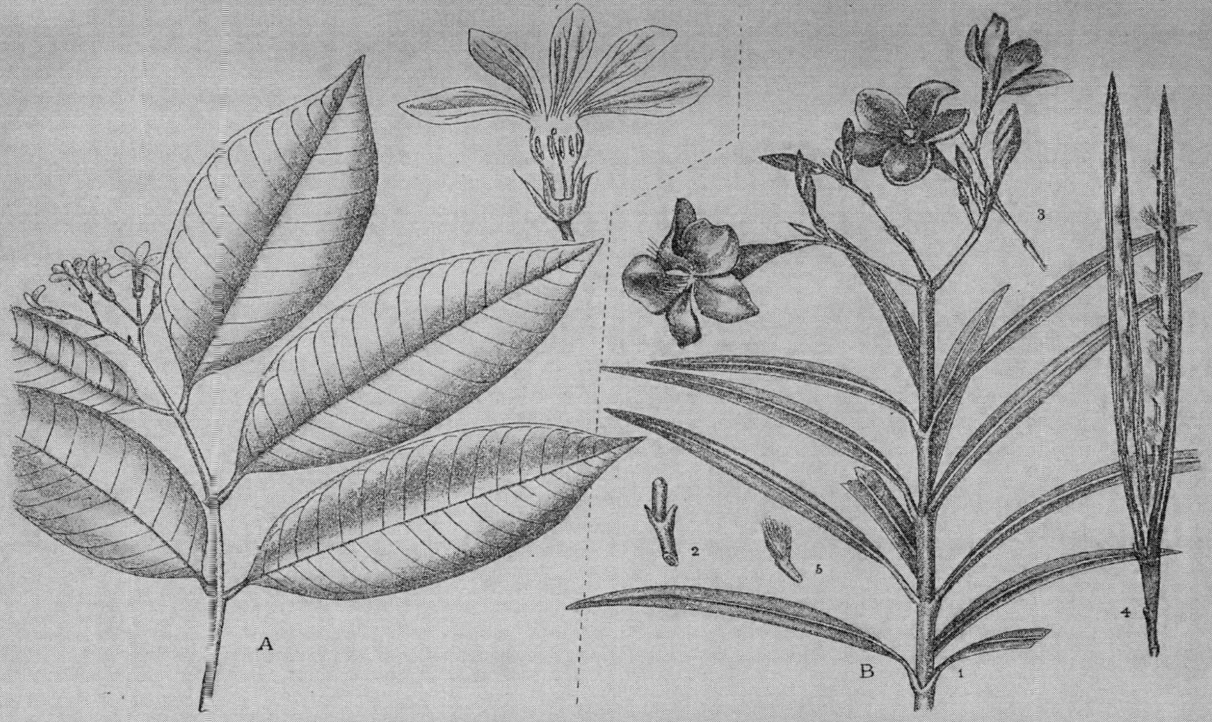

A—TRACHELOSPERMUM FRAGRANS, *Hook. f.* B—NERIUM ODORUM, *Soland*

PLATE No. 614.

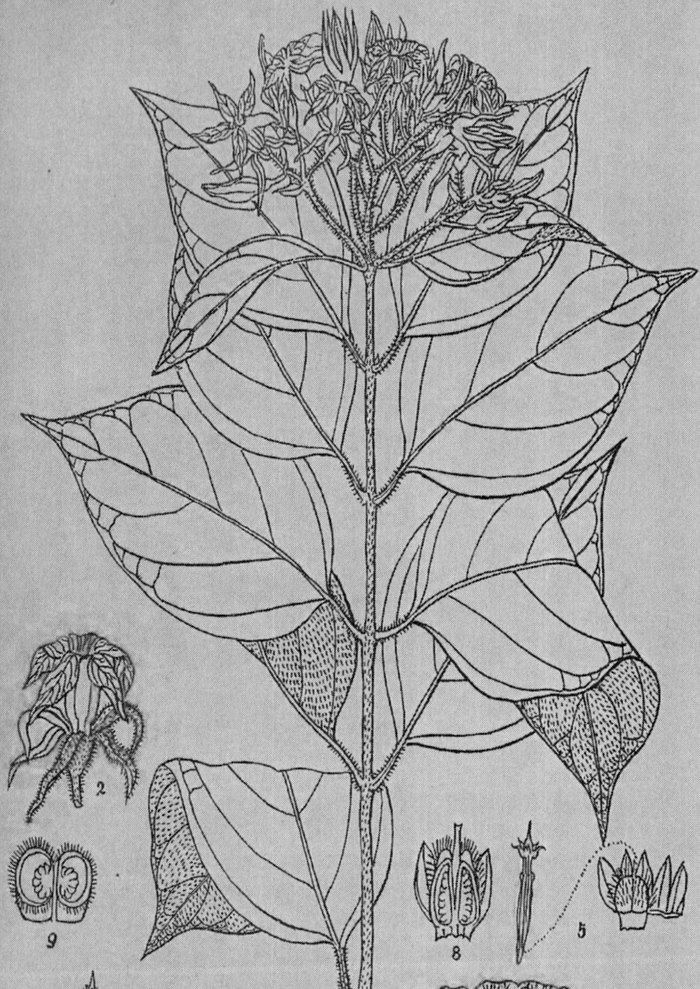

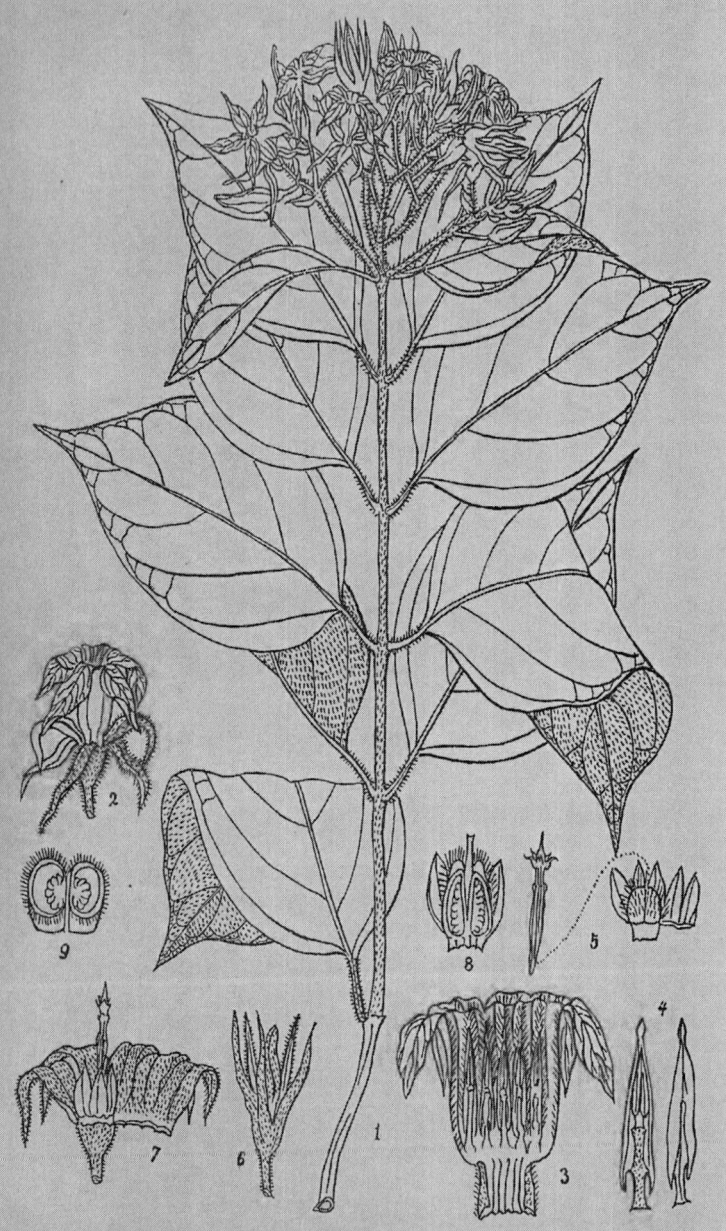

AGANOSMA CARYOPHYLLATA, *G. DON.*

PLATE No. 615.

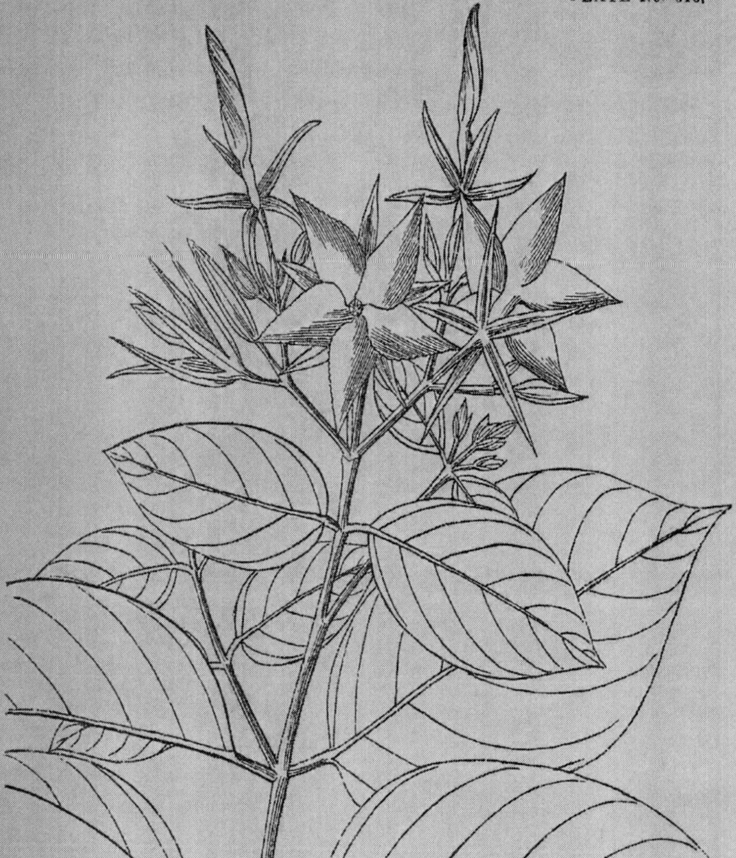

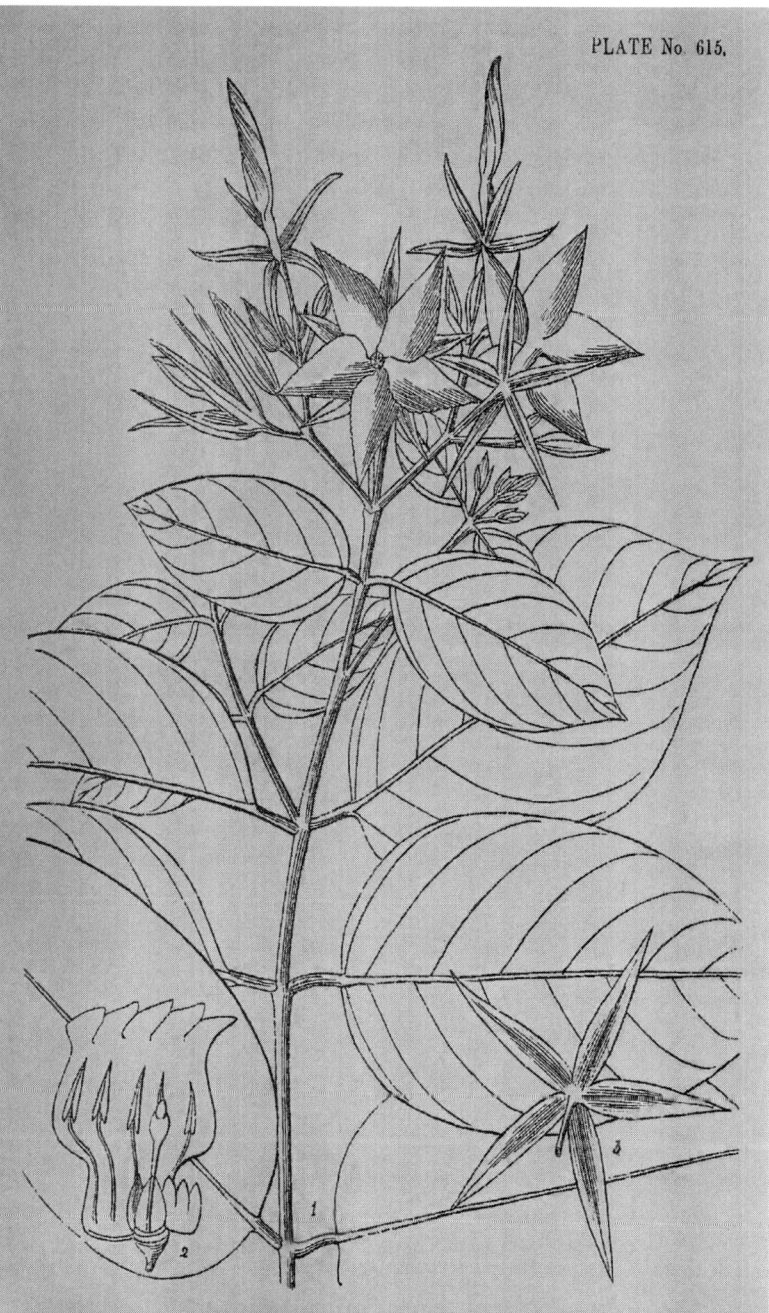

AGANOSMA CALYCINA, *A. DC.*

PLATE No. 616.

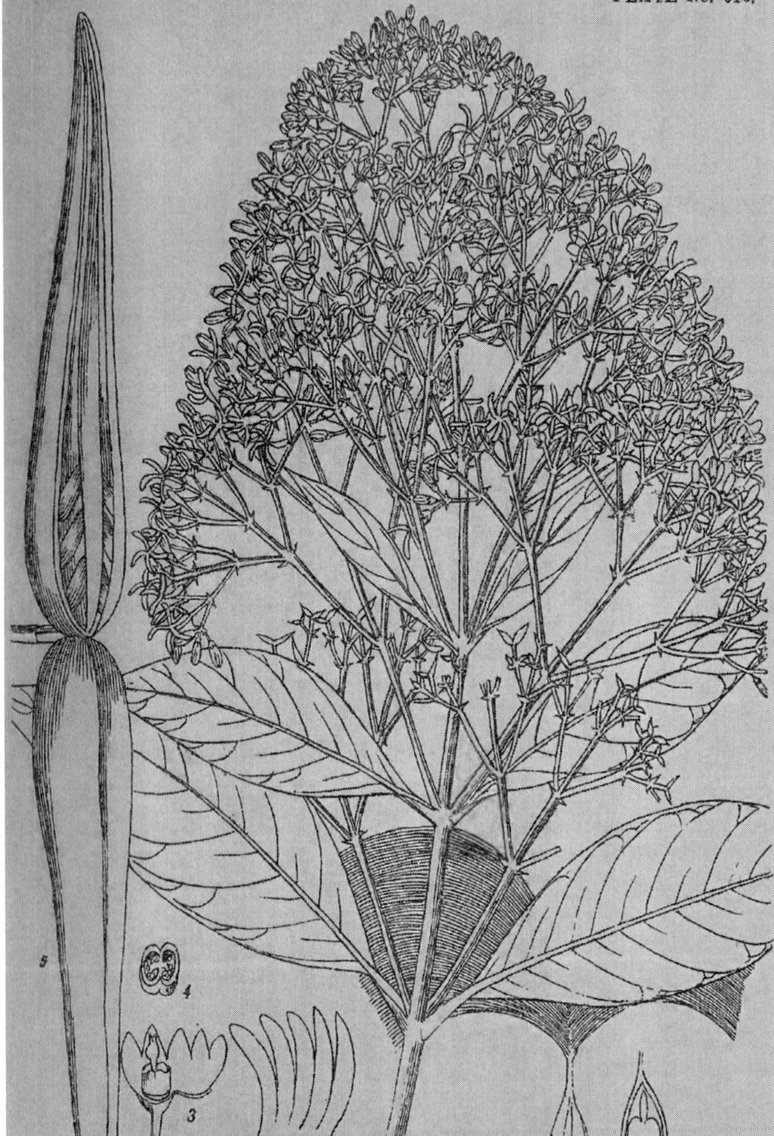

ANODENDRON PANICULATUM, A. DC.

PLATE No. 617.

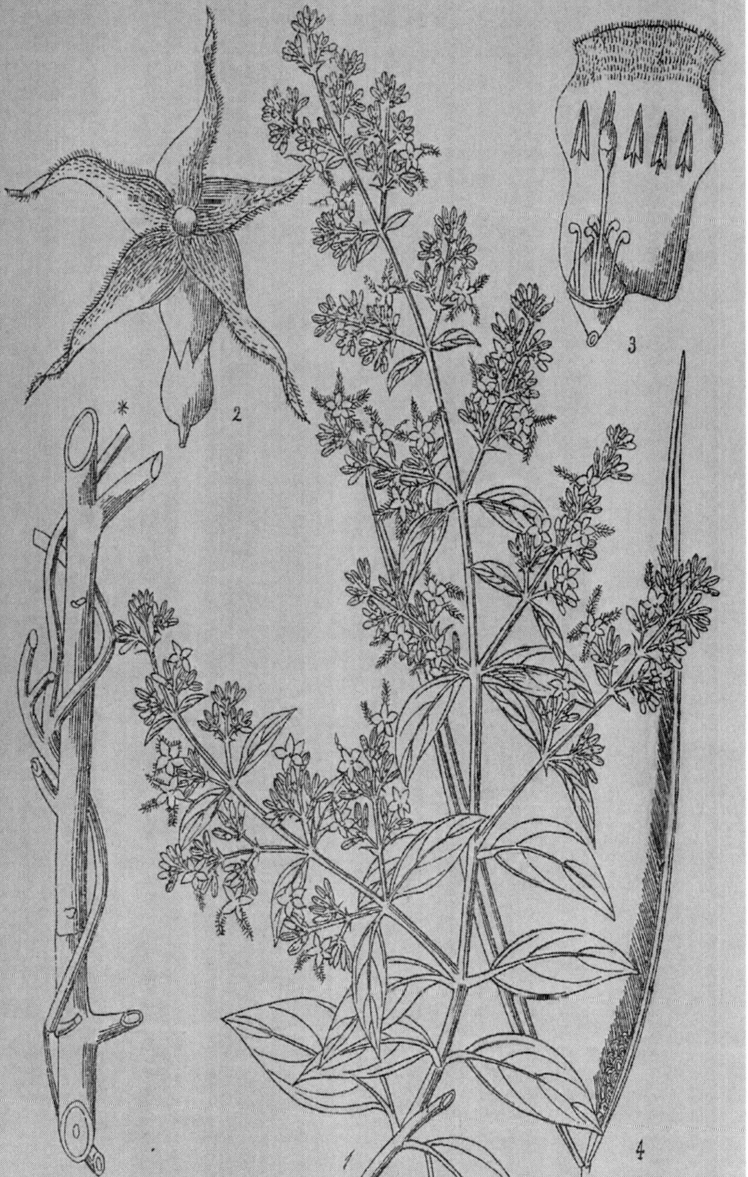

ICHNOCARPUS FRUTESCENS, *Br.*

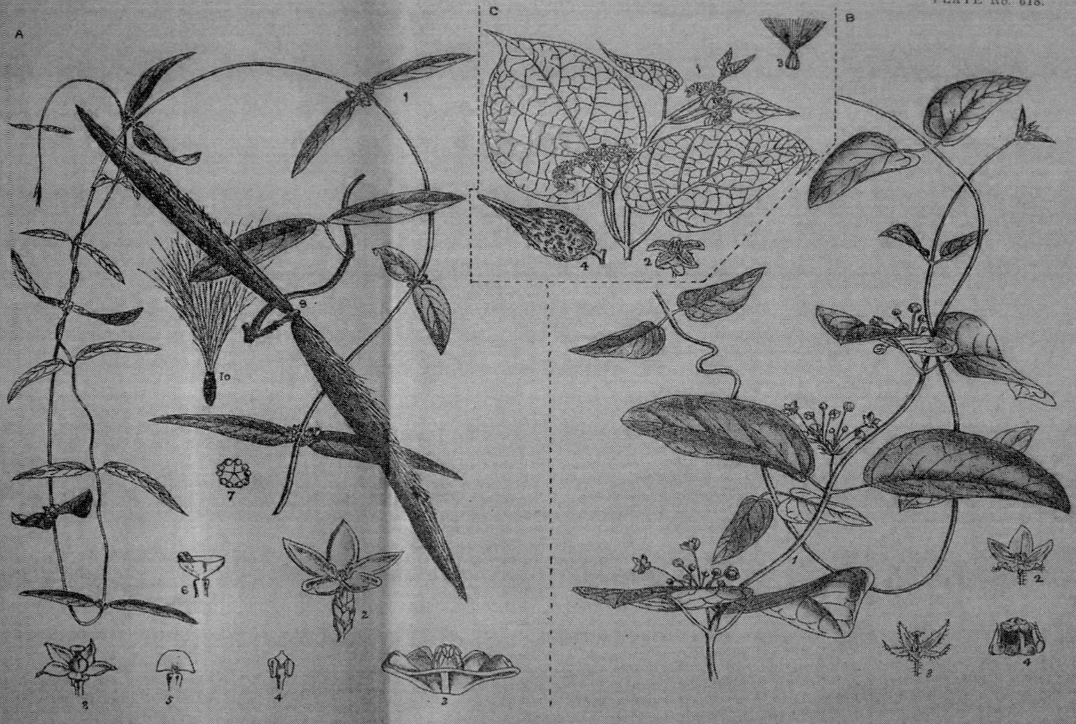

A—HEMISDESMUS INDICUS, Br.   C—MARSDENIA ROYLEI, Wight.   B—TYLOPHORA ASTHMATICA, Wight & Arn.

PLATE No. 619

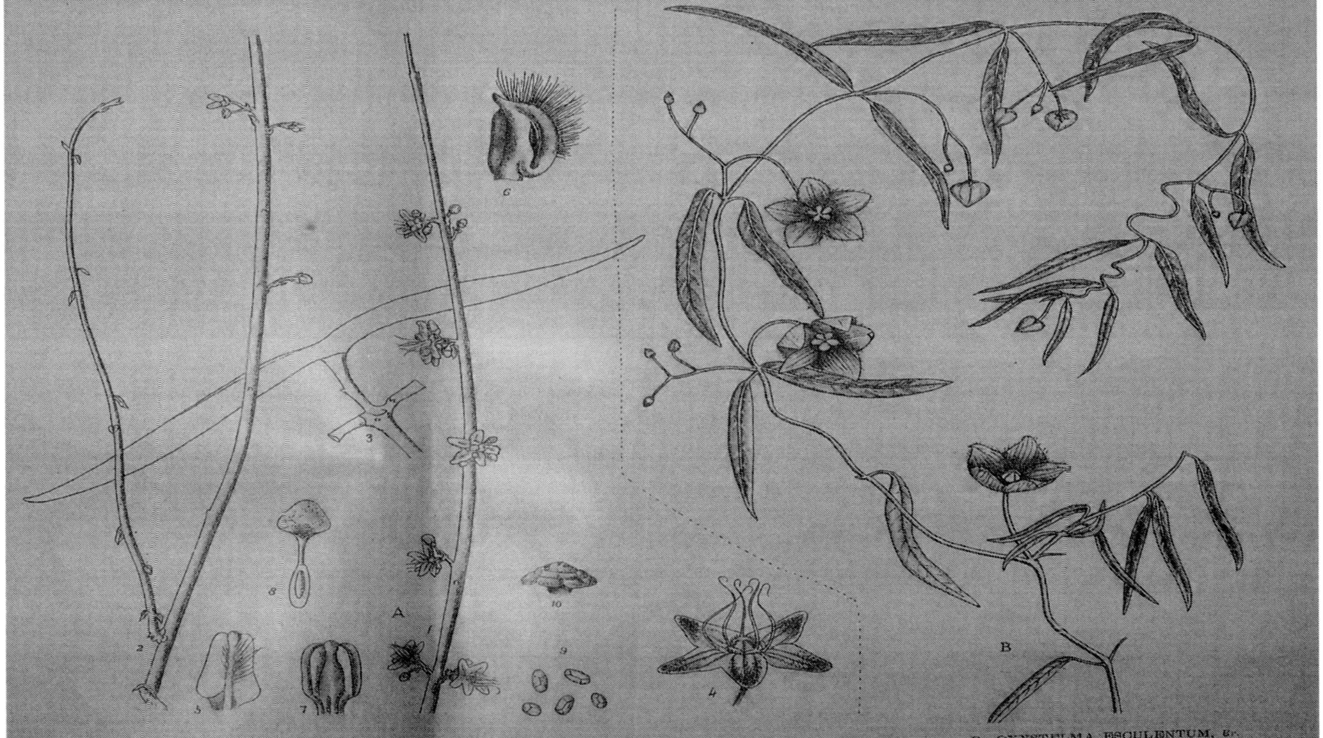

A—PERIPLOCA APHYLLA, *Dcne.*   B—OXYSTELMA ESCULENTUM, *Br.*

PLATE No. 620.

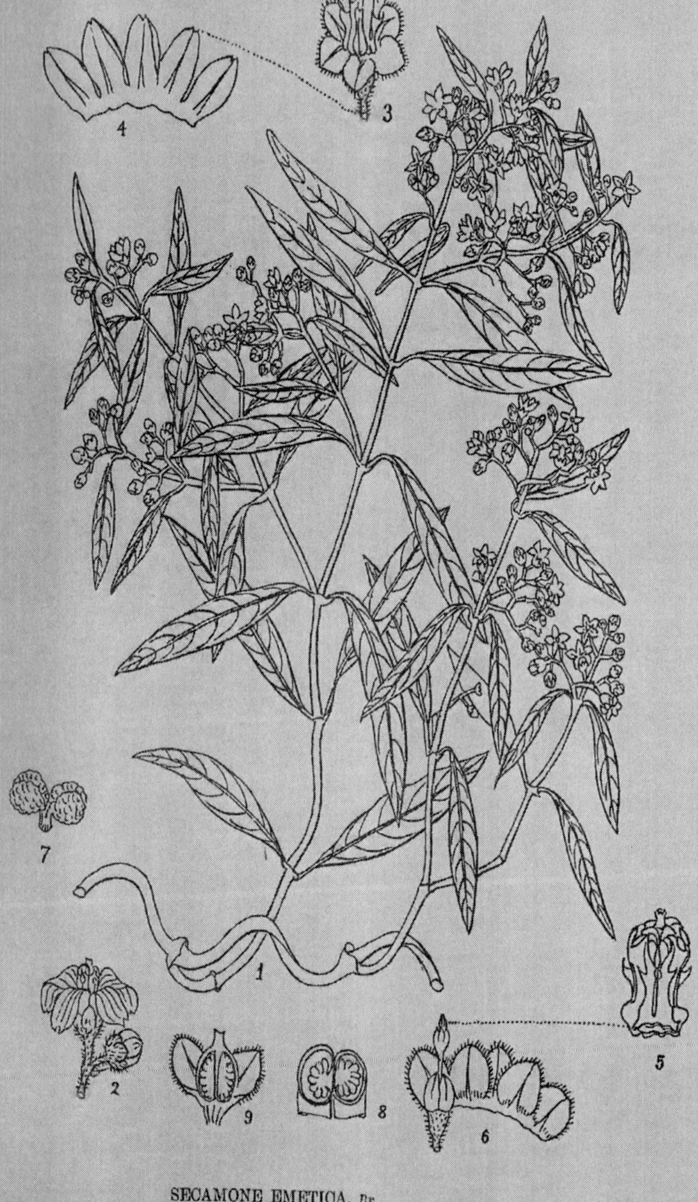

SECAMONE EMETICA, *Br.*

PLATE No. 621.

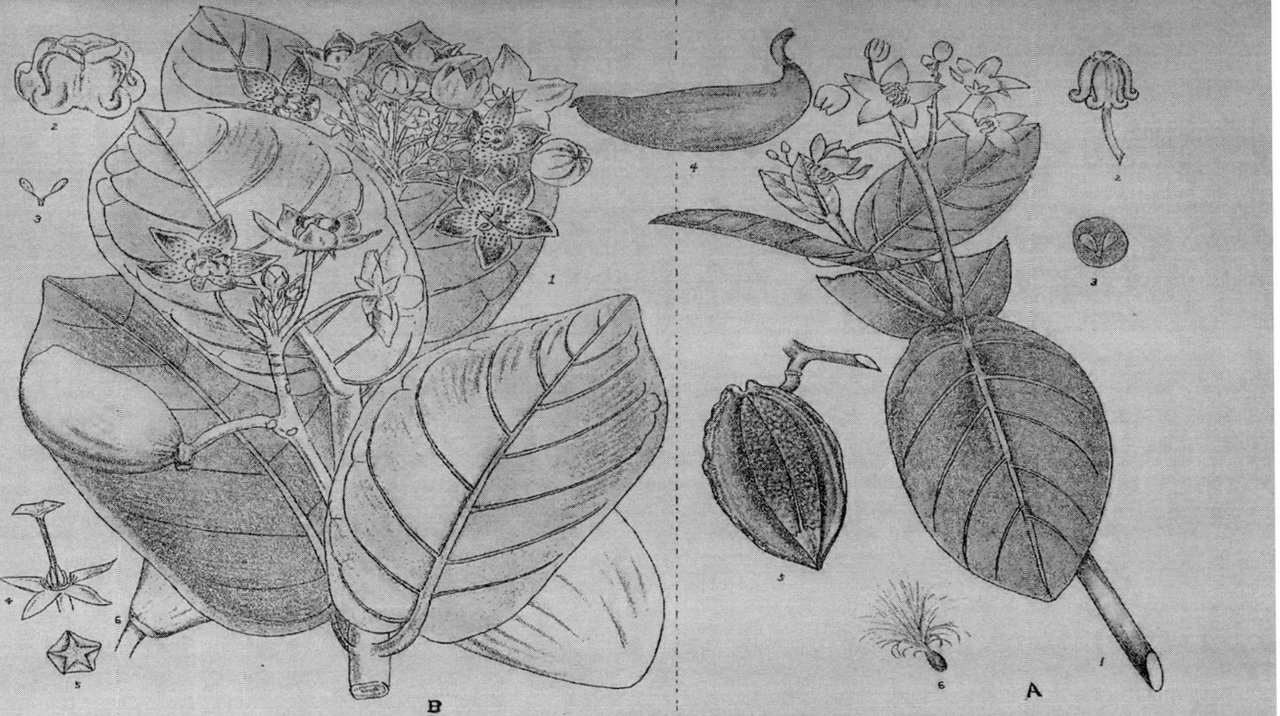

B—CALOTROPIS PROCERA, *Br.*

A—CALOTROPIS GIGANTEA, *Br.*

PLATE No. 622.

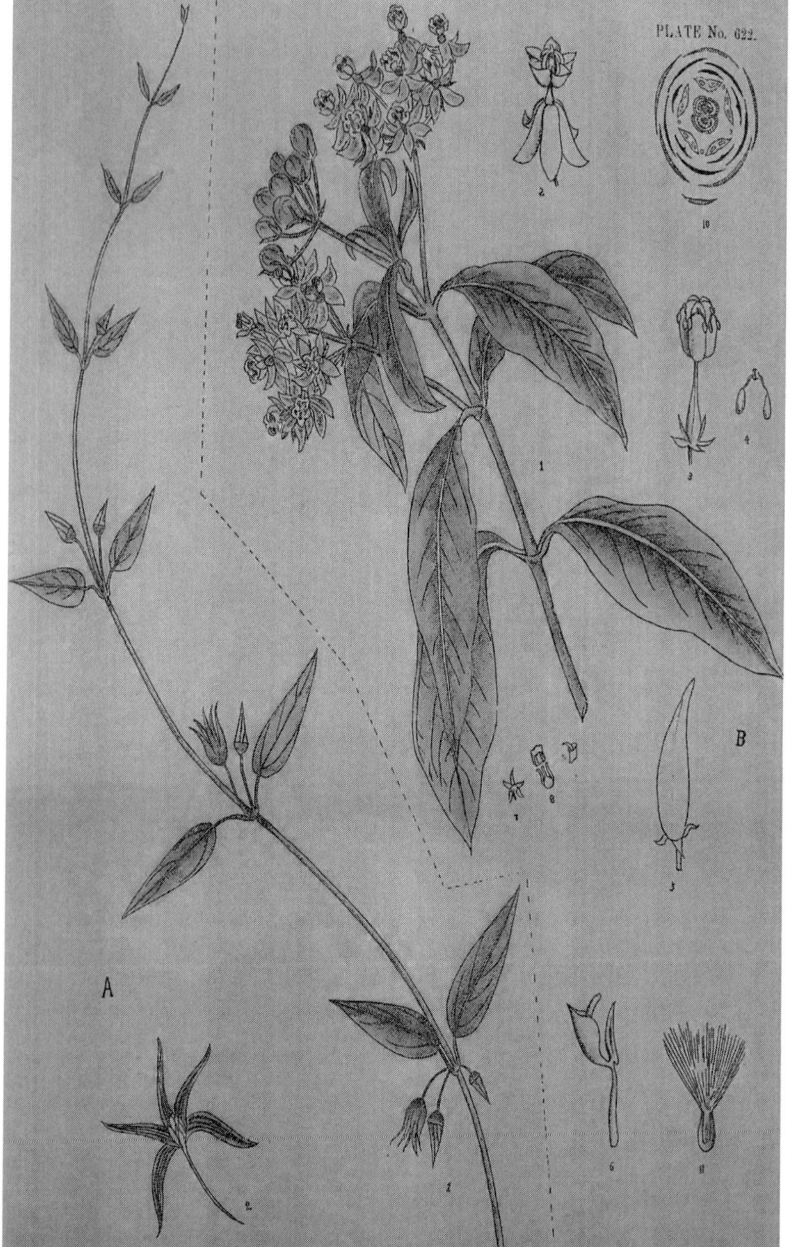

A—PENTATROPIS SPIRALIS, *DCNS.*

B—ASCLEPIAS CURASSAVICA, *LINN.*

PLATE No. 623.

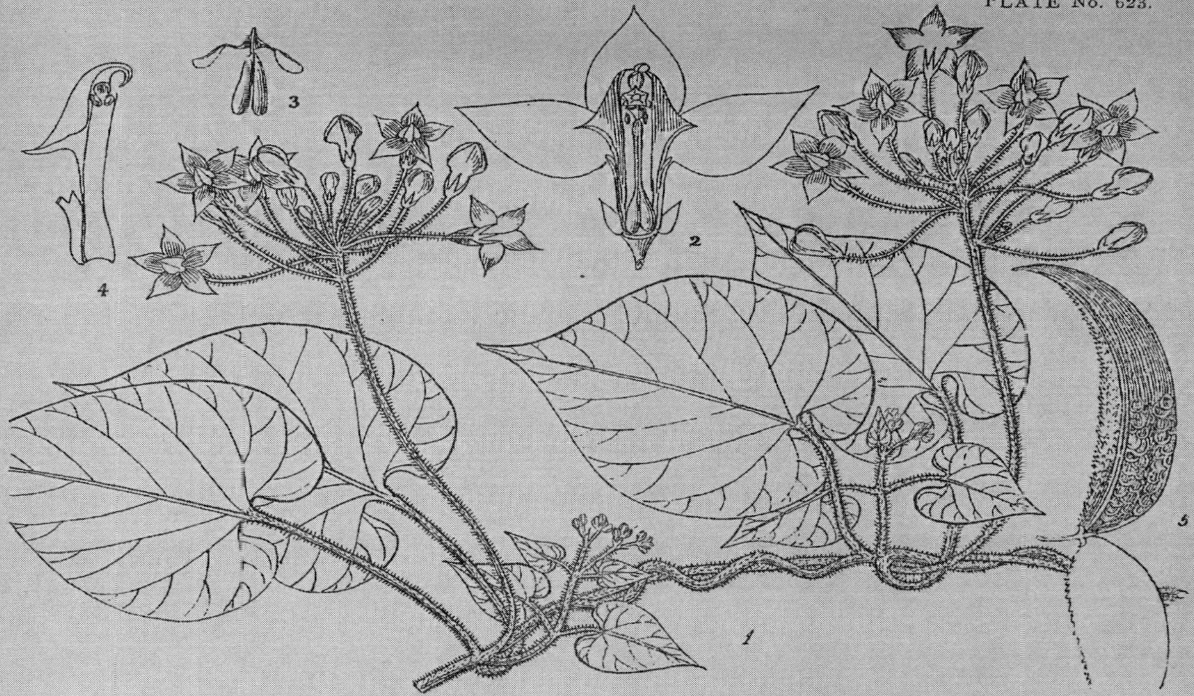

DÆMIA EXTENSA, *Br.*

PLATE No. 624.

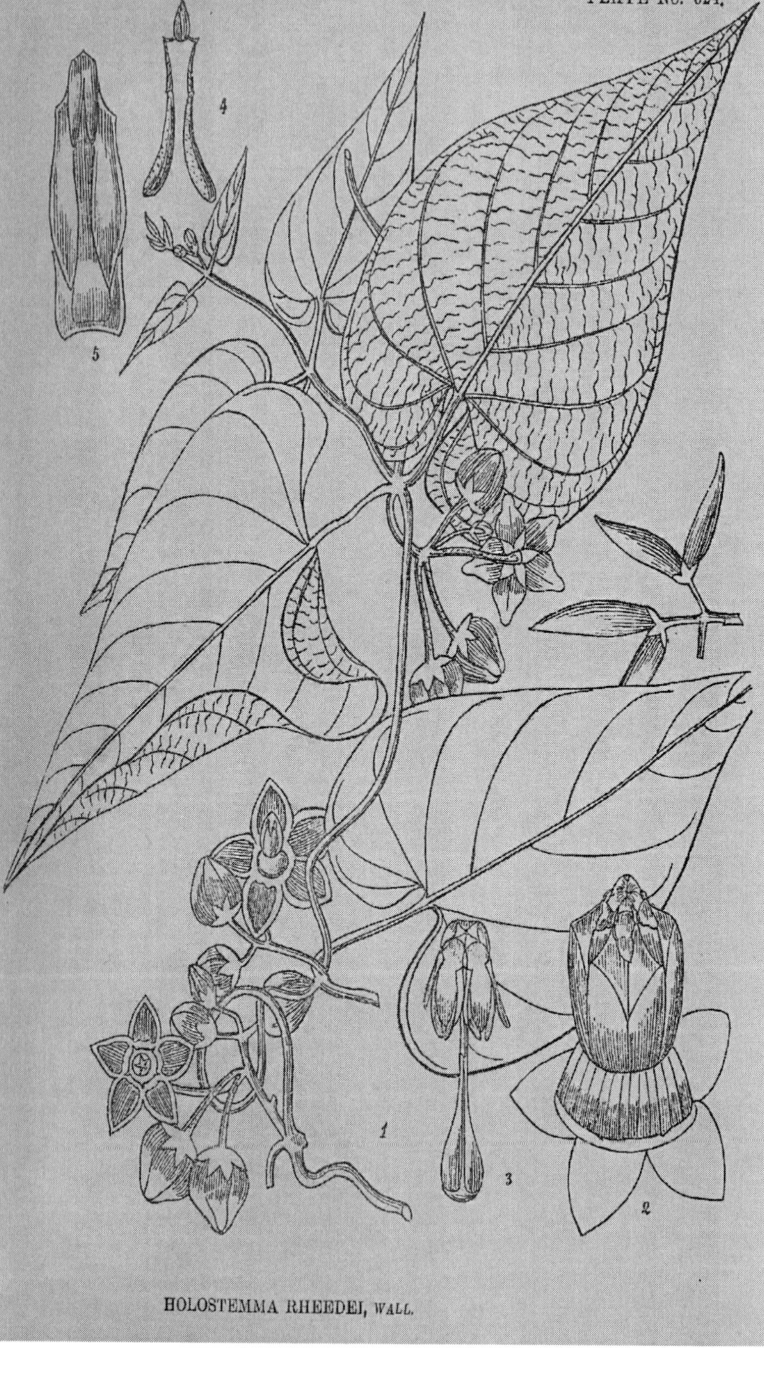

HOLOSTEMMA RHEEDEI, *WALL.*

PLATE No. 625.

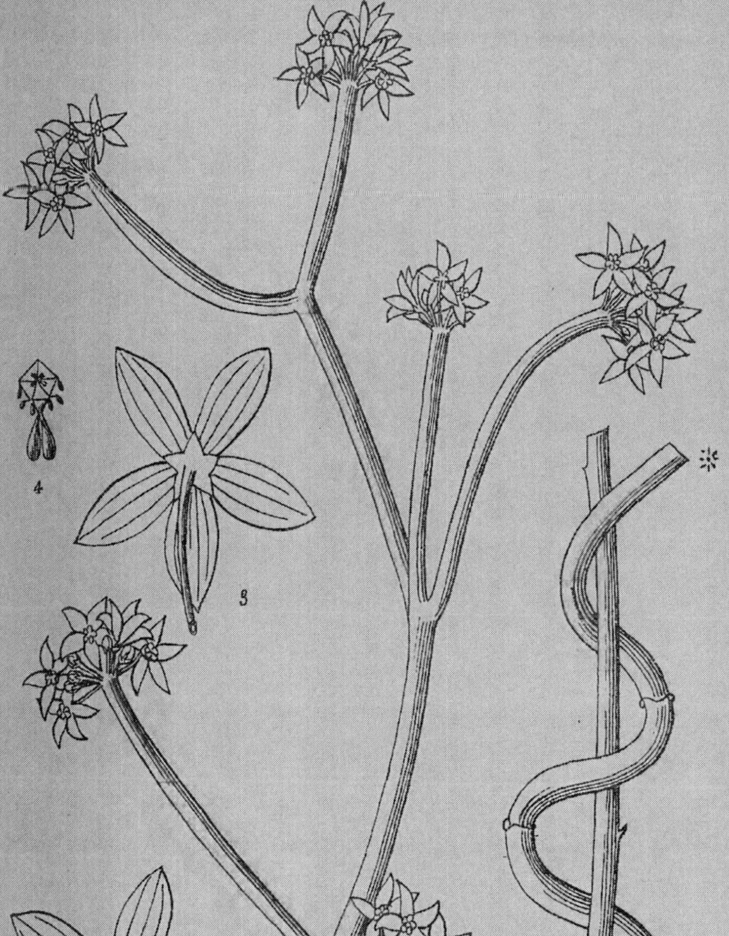

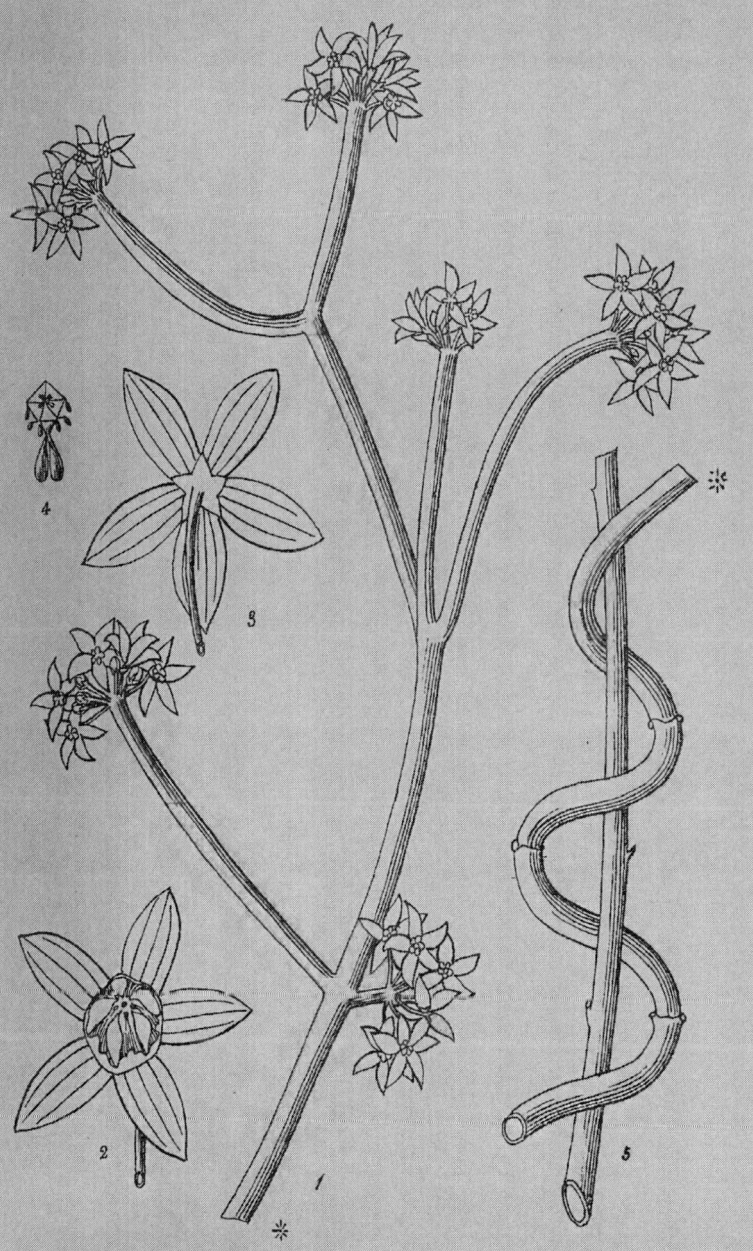

SARCOSTEMMA BREVISTIGMA, *W. & A.*

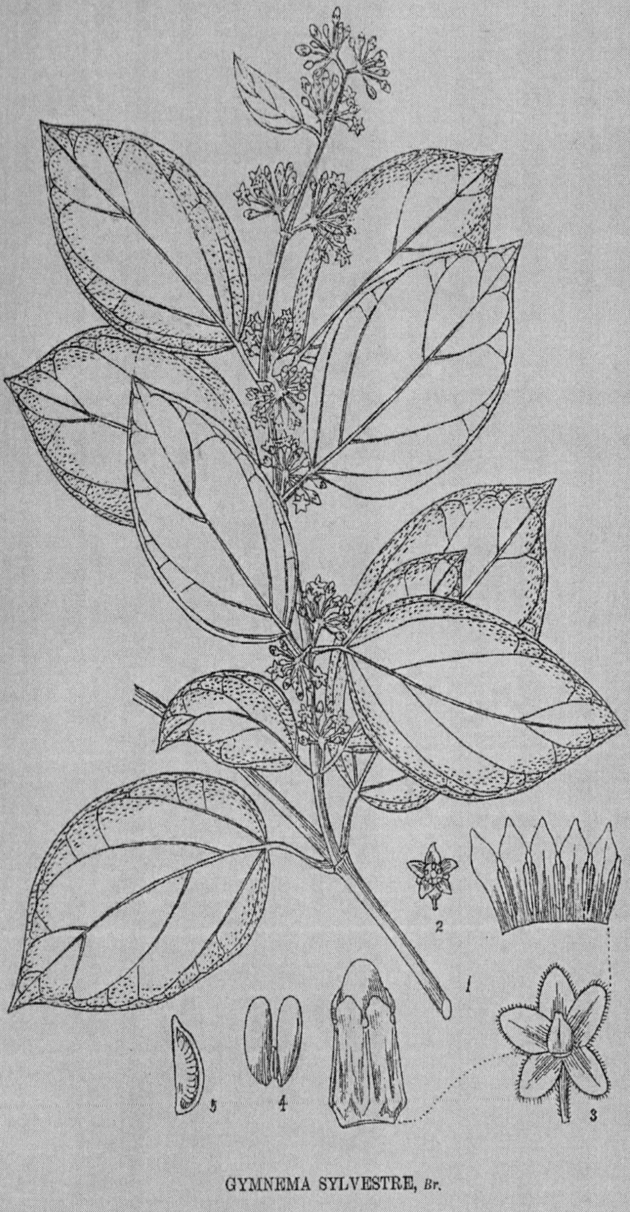

GYMNEMA SYLVESTRE, *Br.*

PLATE No 627

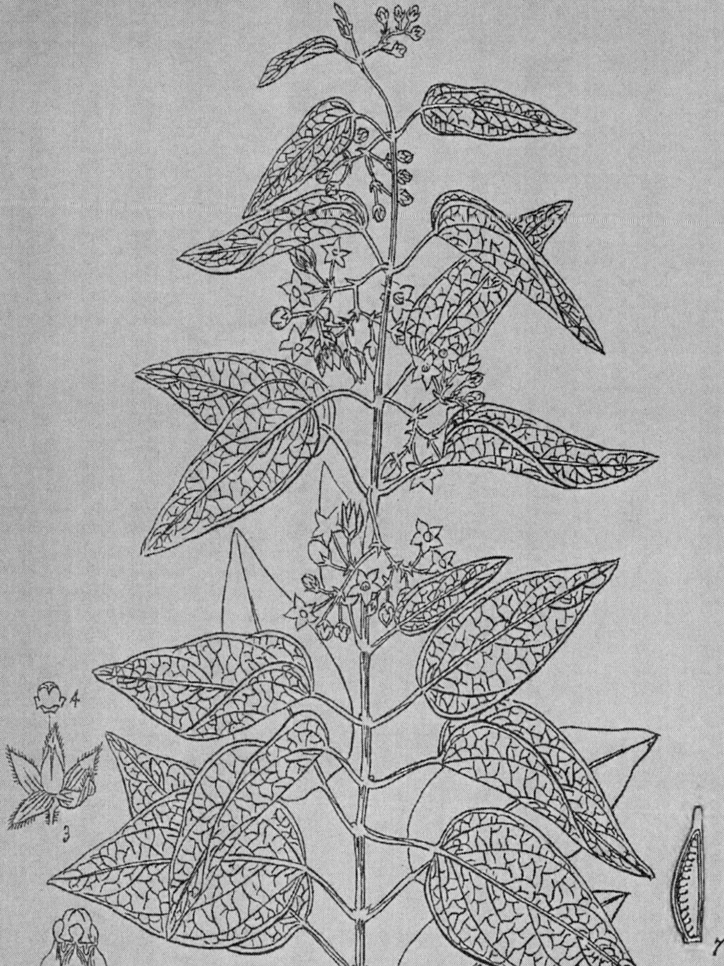

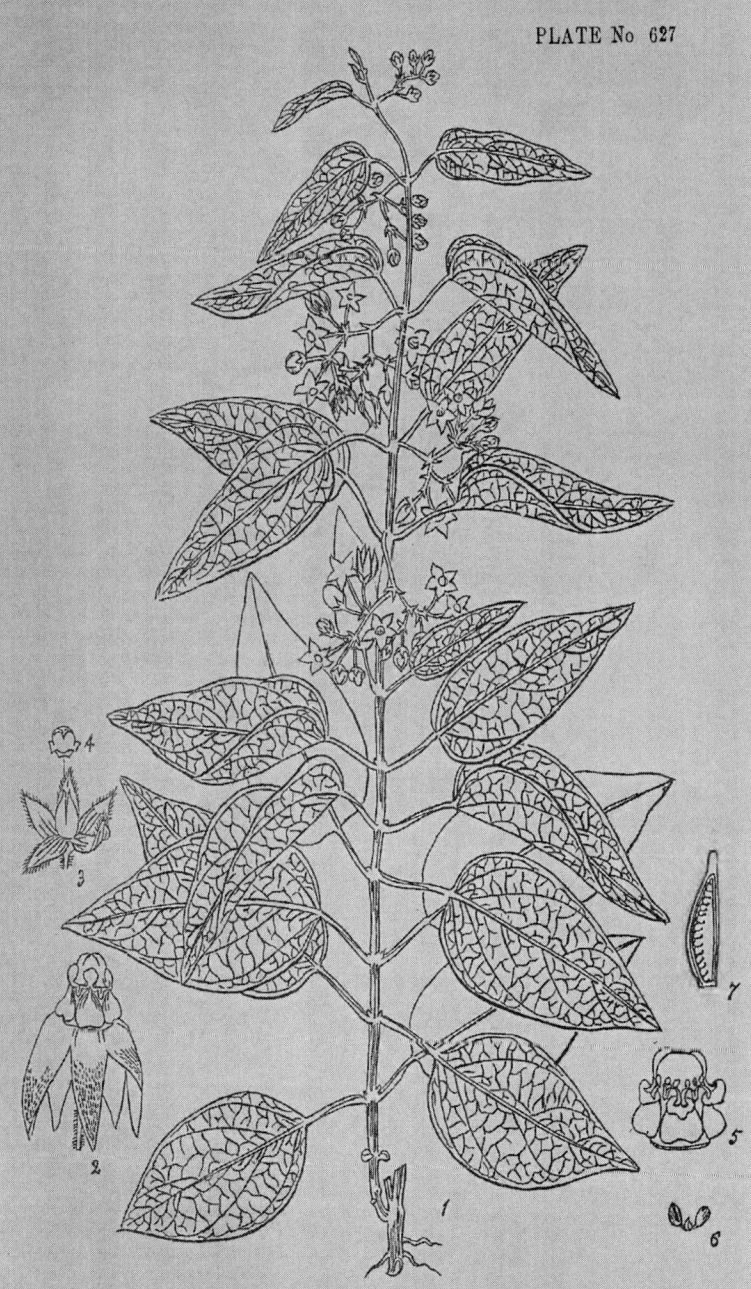

TYLOPHORA FASCICULATA, *HAM.*

PLATE No. 628.

COSMOSTIGMA RACEMOSUM, *WIGHT*.

PLATE No. 629.

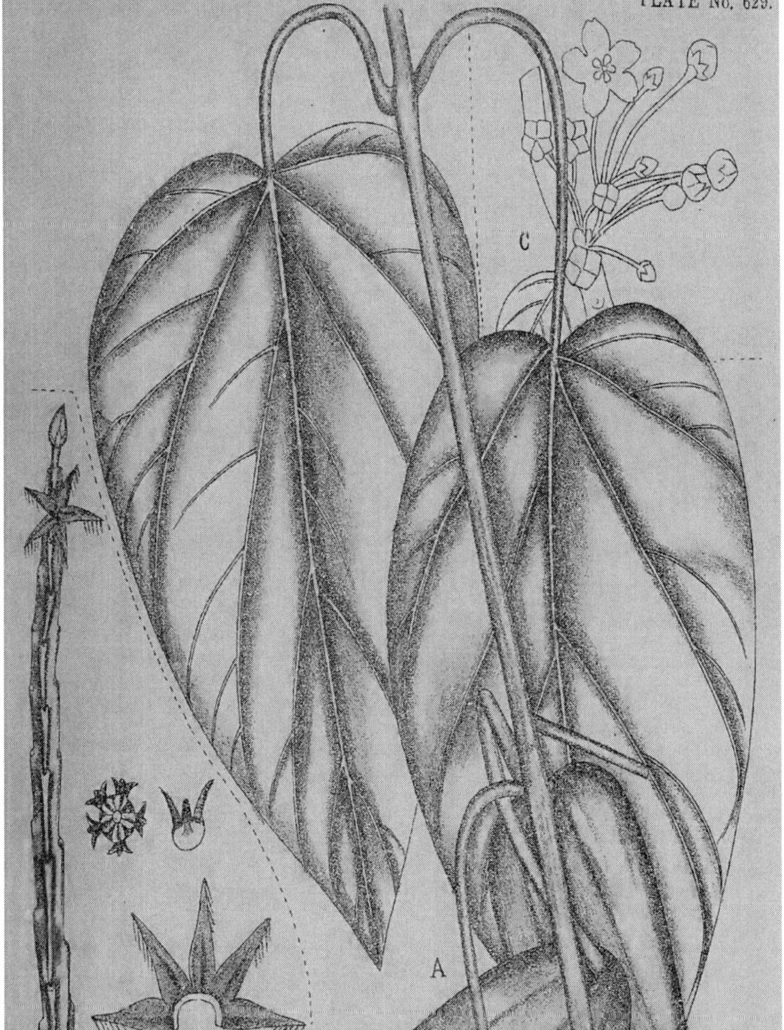

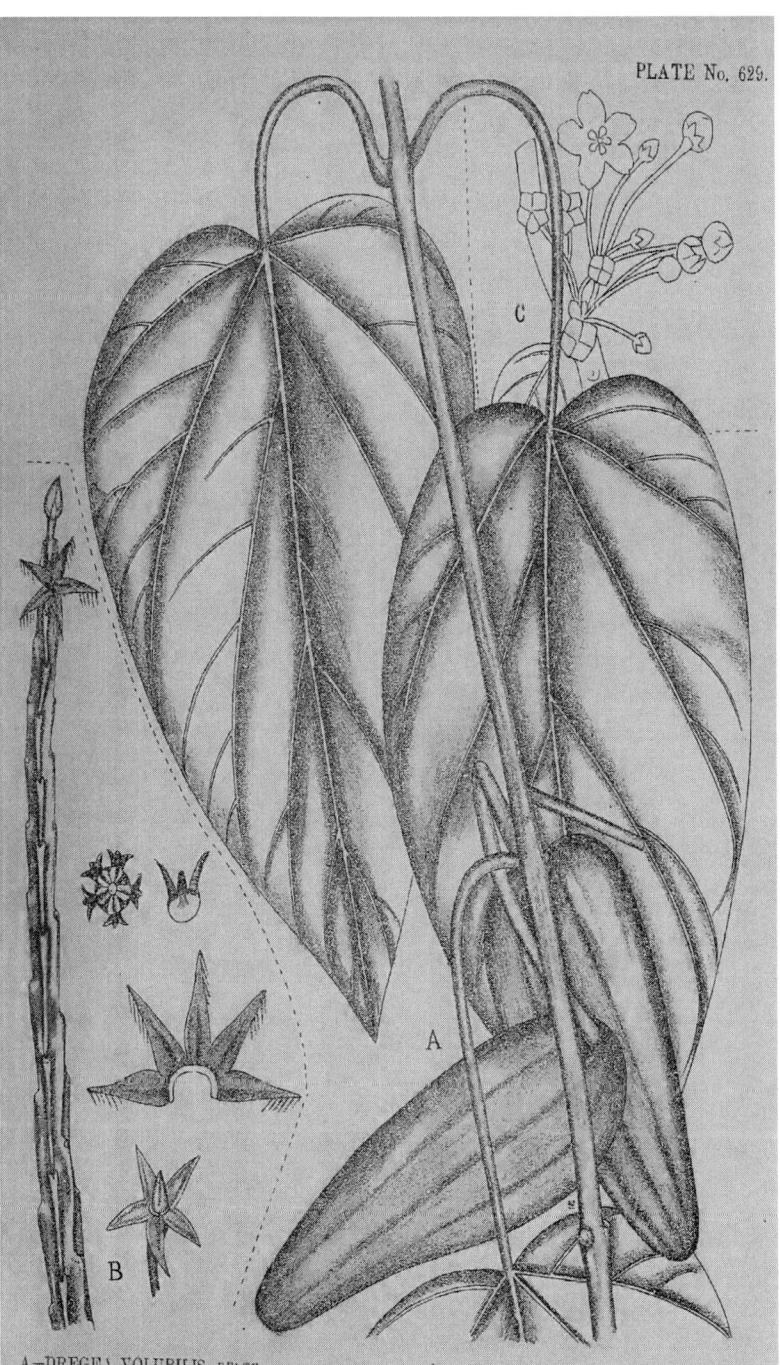

A—DREGEA VOLUBILIS, BENTH.   B—BOUCEROSIA AUCHERIANA, DCNE.

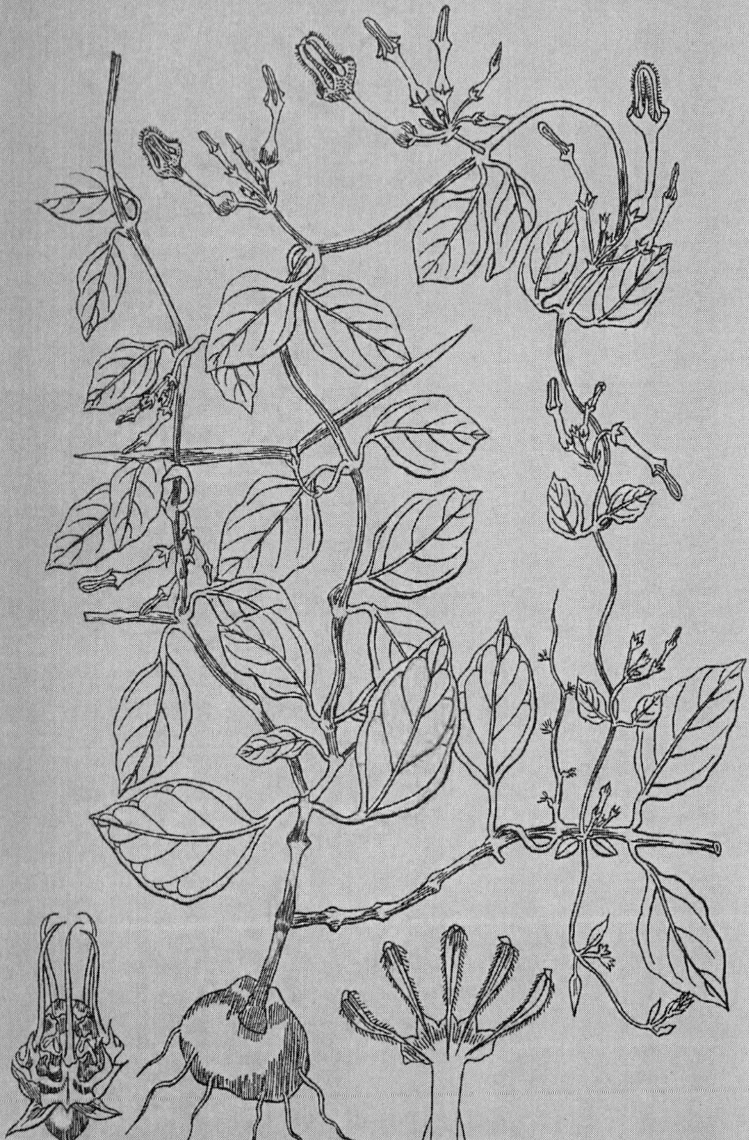

CEROPEGIA BULBOSA, *ROXB.*

PLATE No. 631.

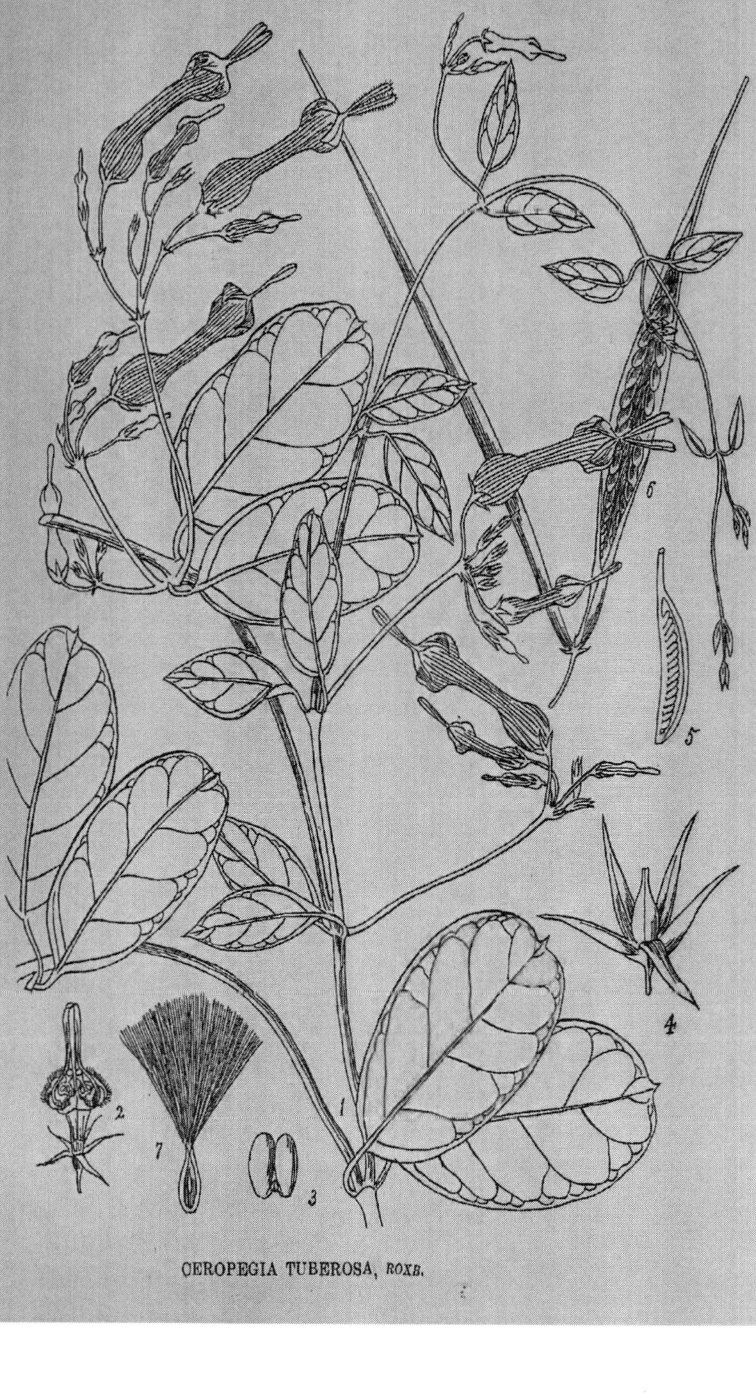

CEROPEGIA TUBEROSA, ROXB.

PLATE No. 632.

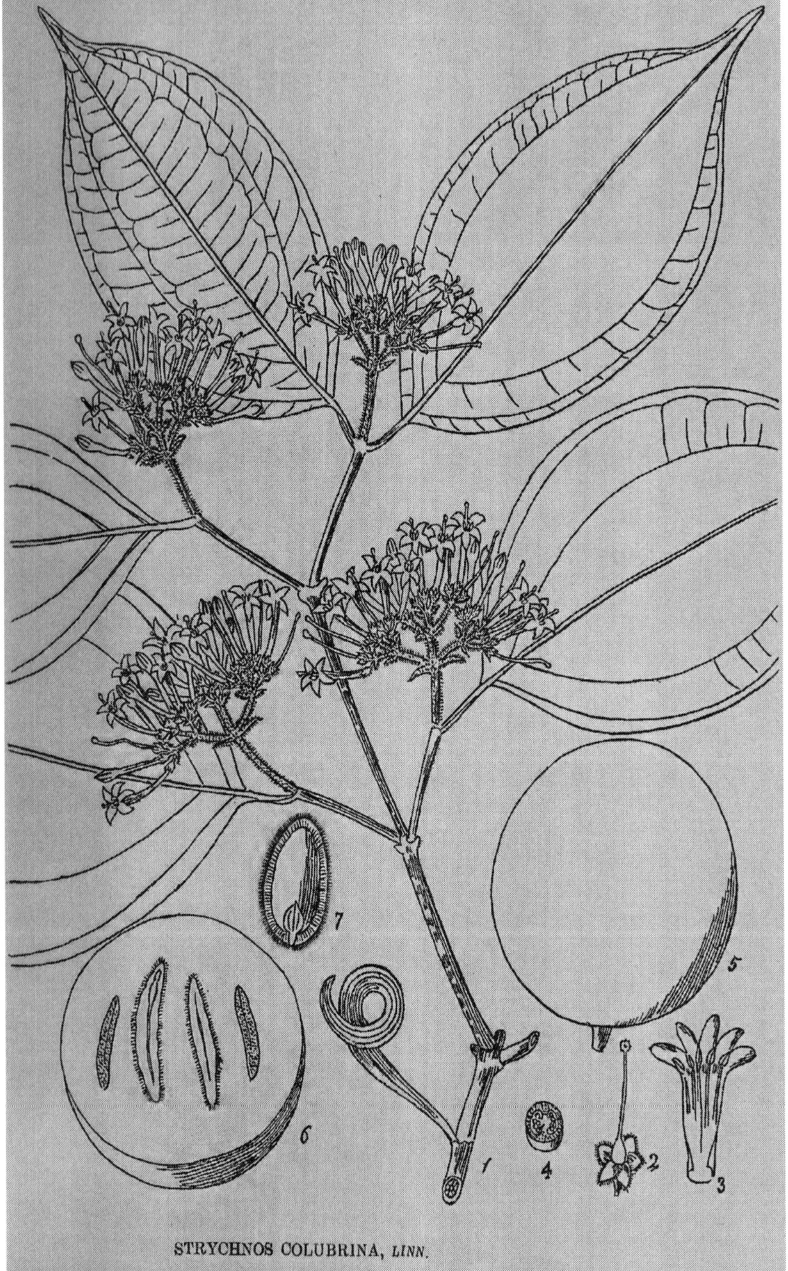

STRYCHNOS COLUBRINA, *LINN.*

A STRYCHNOS NUX-VOMICA, *Linn.* B—STRYCHNOS POTATORUM, *Linn f.*

PLATE No. 634.

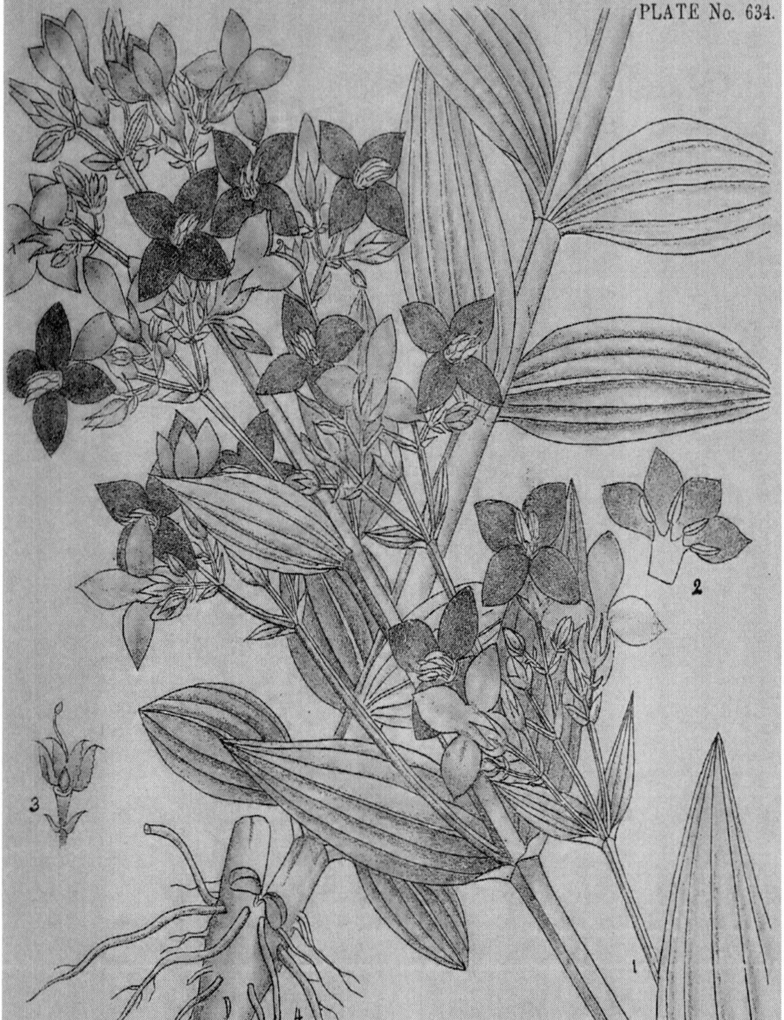

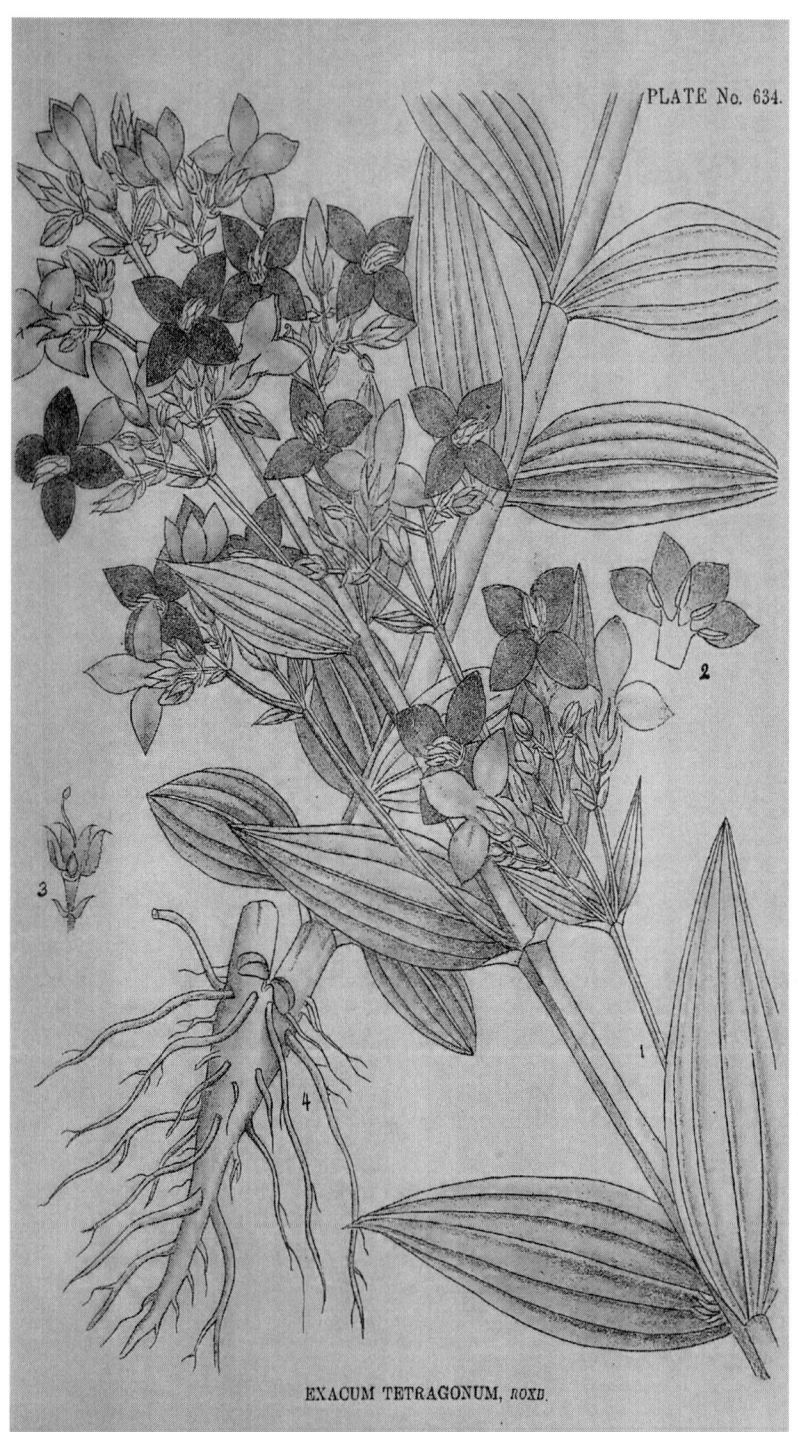

EXACUM TETRAGONUM, *ROXB.*

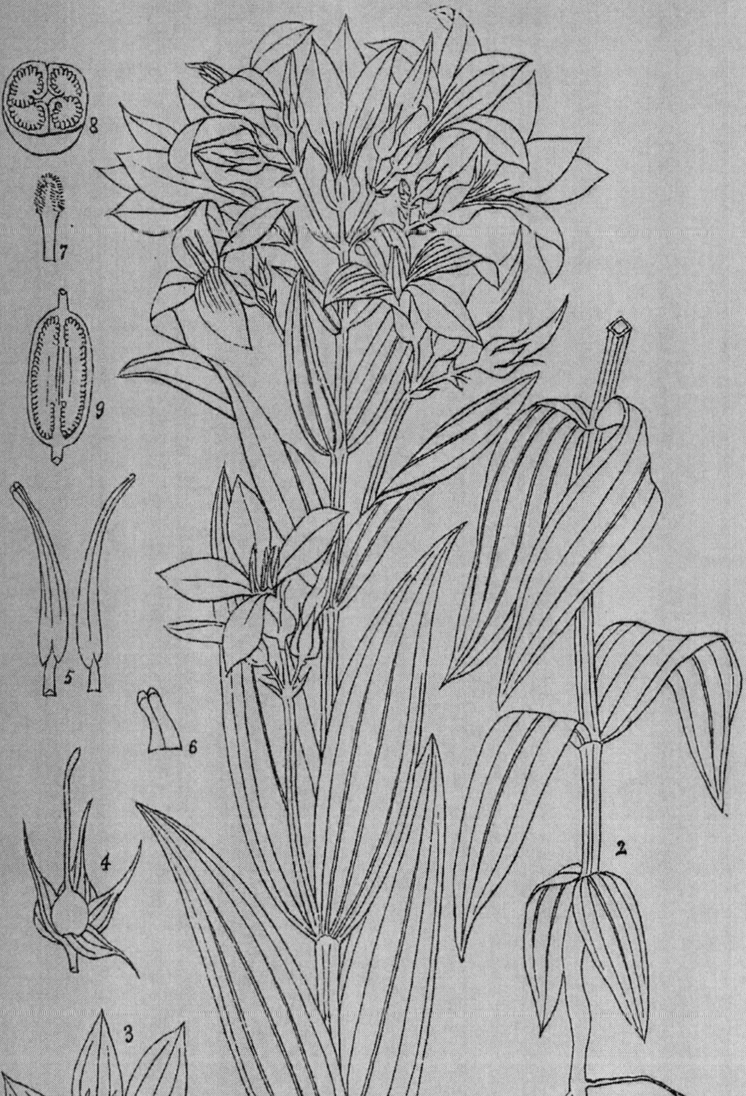

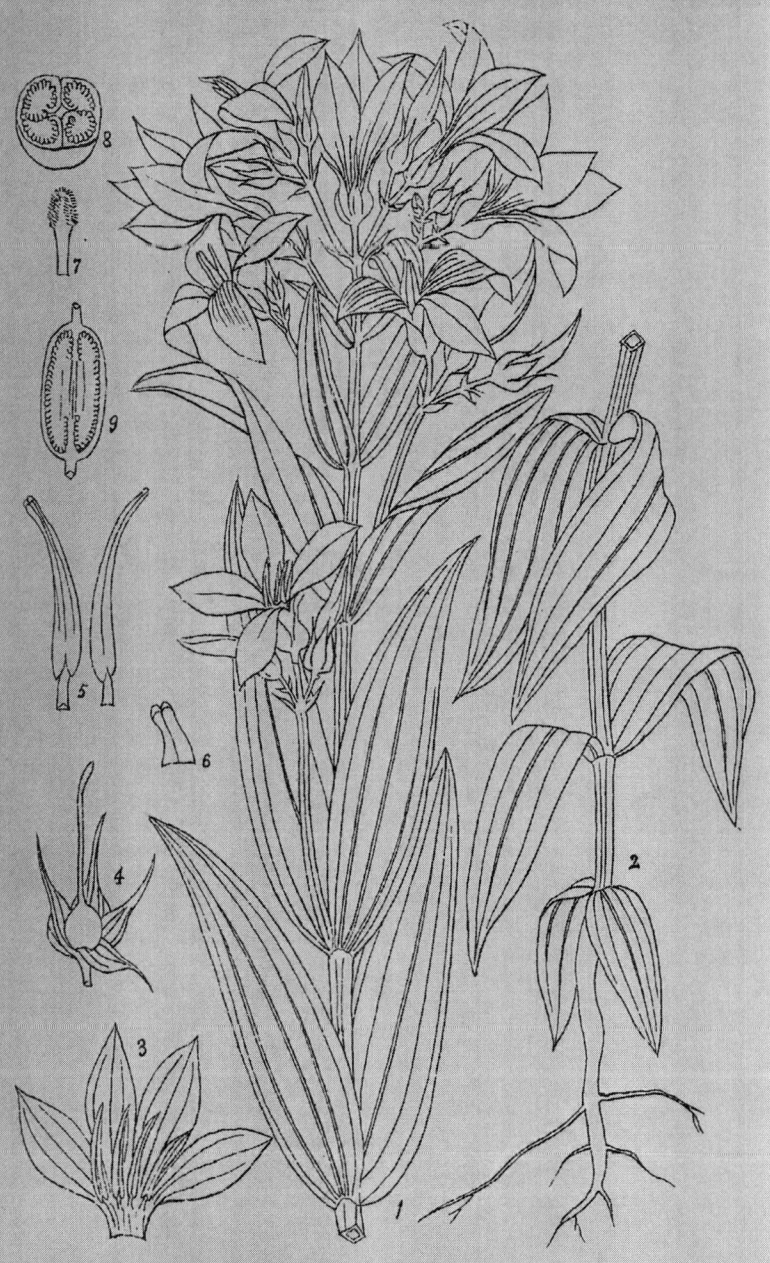

EXACUM BICOLOR, *ROXB.*

PLATE No. 636.

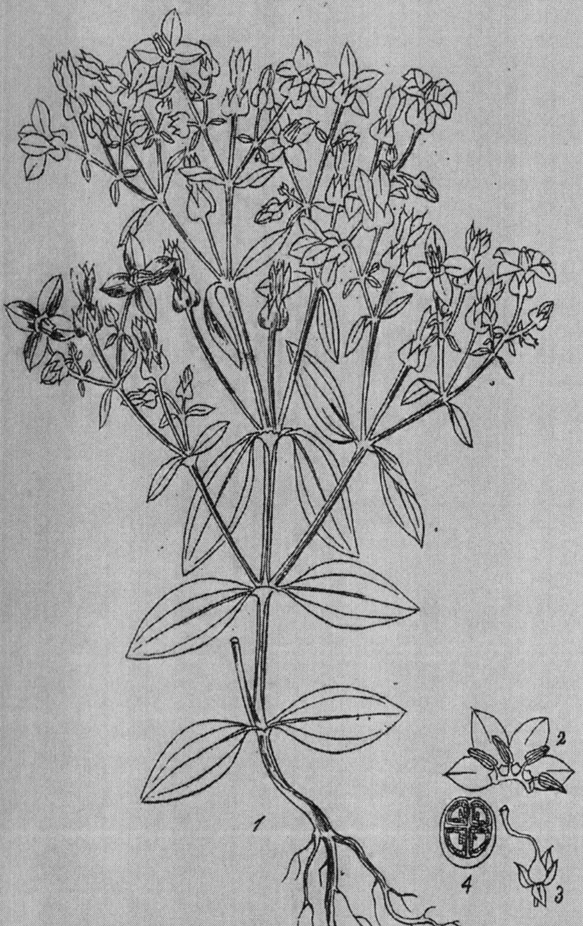

EXACUM PEDUNCULATUM, LINN.

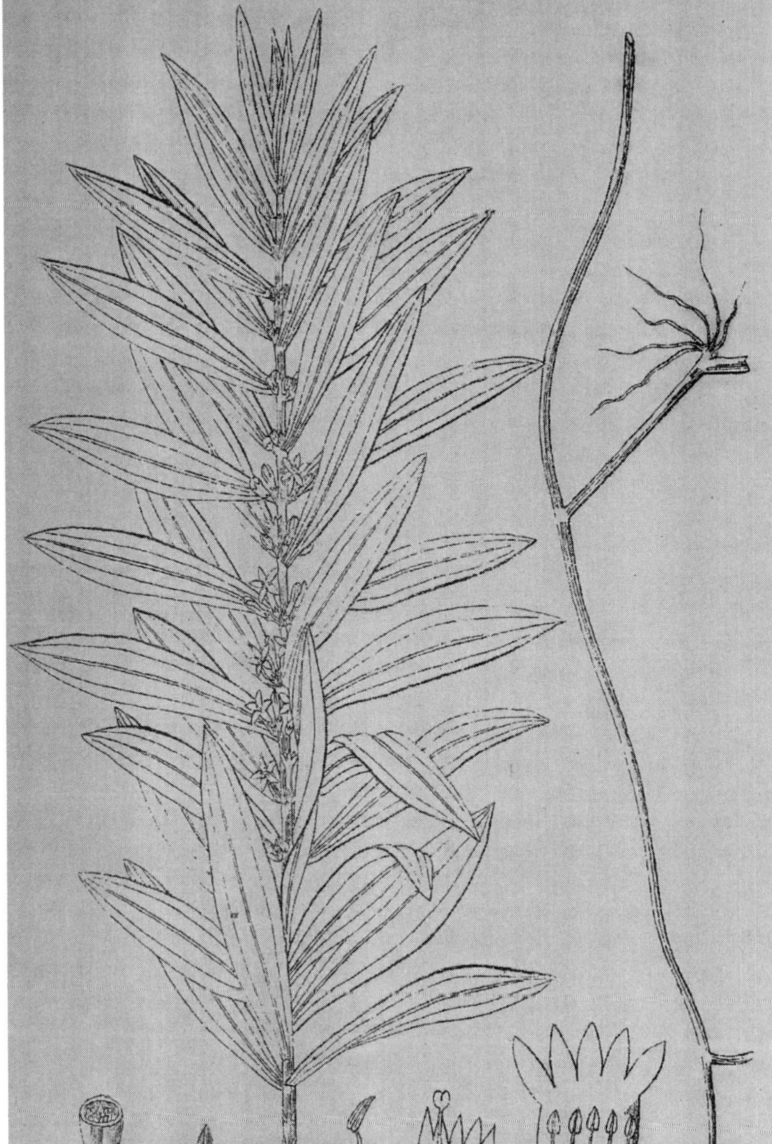

ENICOSTEMA LITTORALE, *BLUME.*

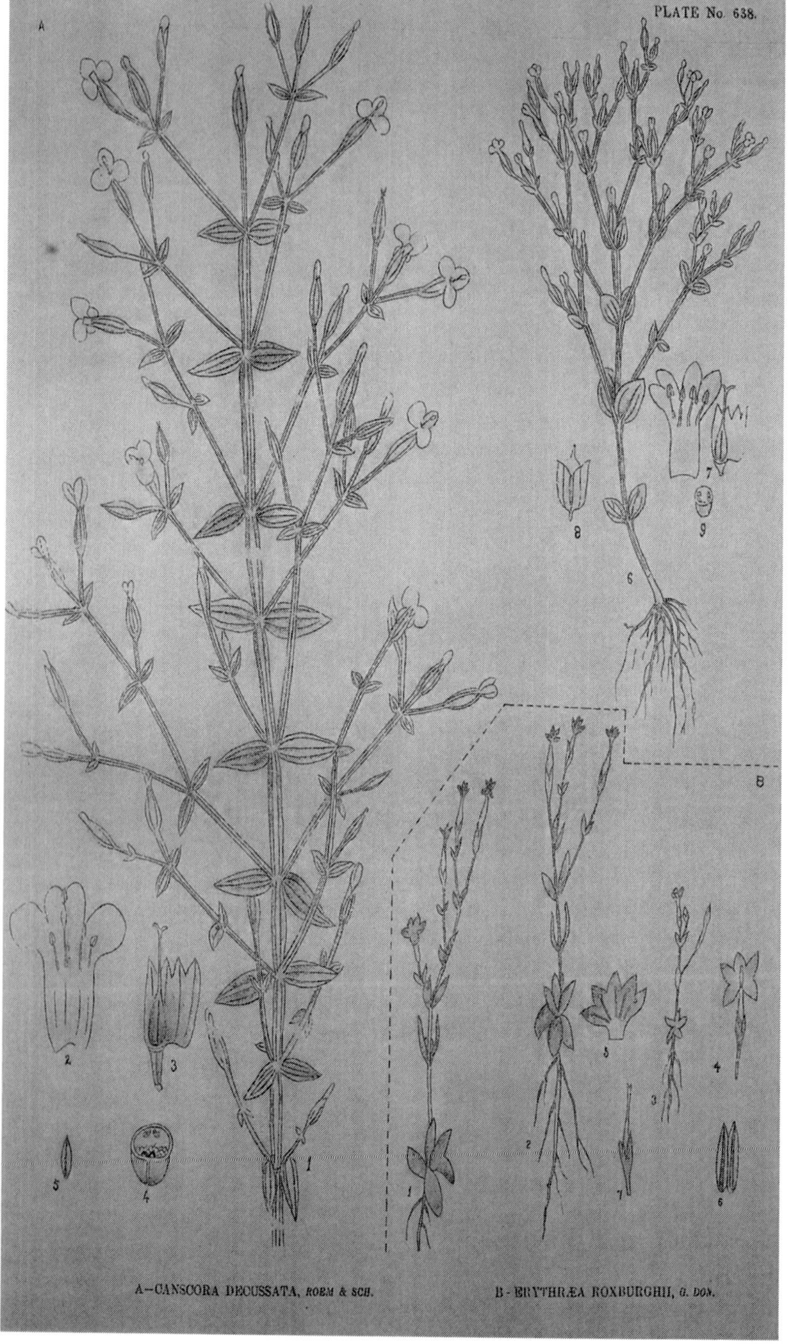

A—CANSCORA DECUSSATA, ROEM & SCH.   B—ERYTHRÆA ROXBURGHII, G. DON.

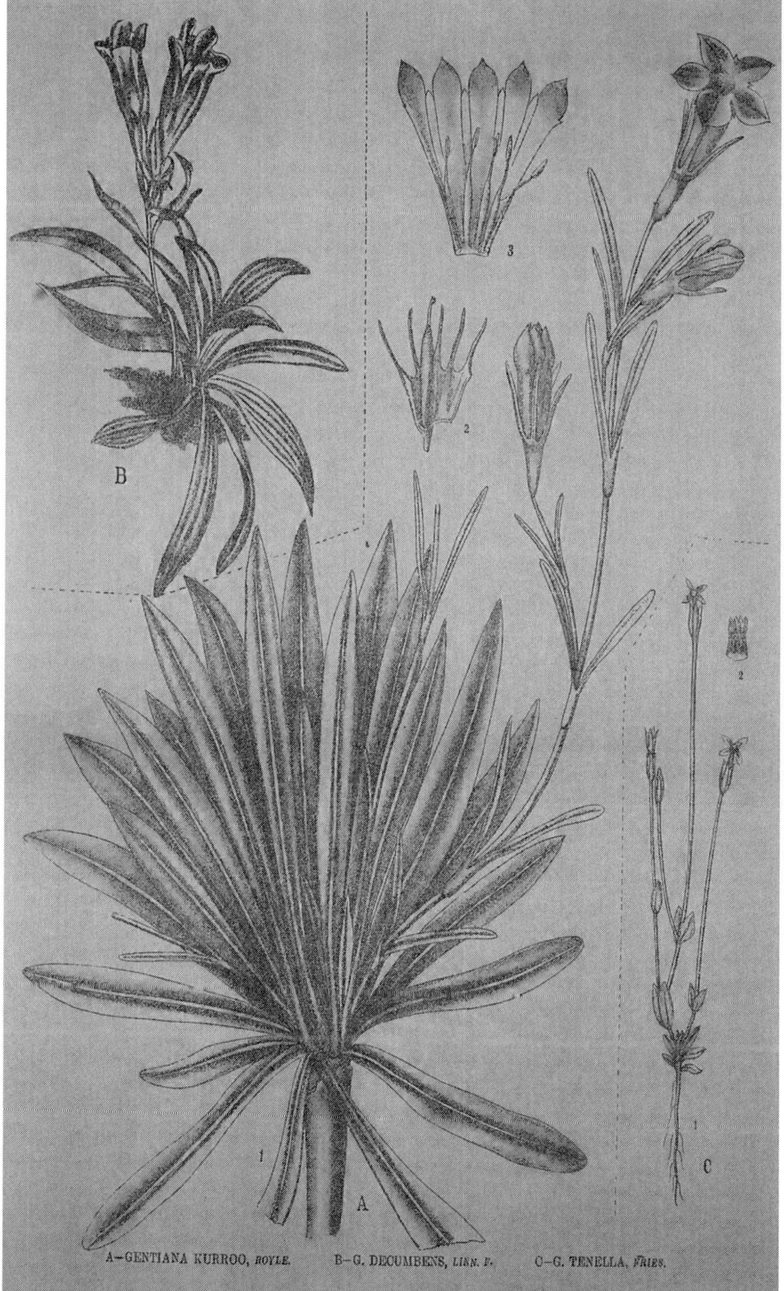

A—GENTIANA KURROO, *Royle*. B—G. DECUMBENS, *Linn. f.* C—G. TENELLA, *Fries*.

PLATE No. 640

A—SWERTIA PANICULATA, *Wall.* B—S. PURPURASCENS, *Wall.*

PLATE No. 641

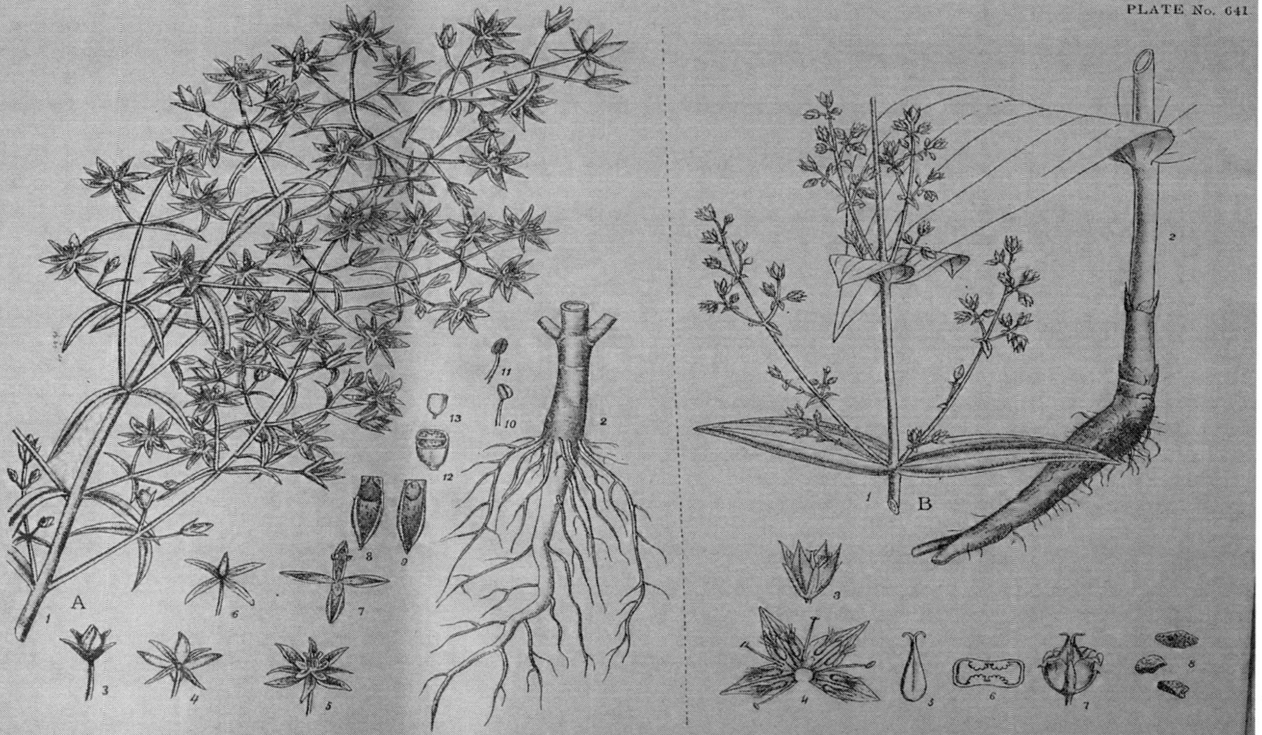

A–SWERTIA ANGUSTIFOLIA, HAM.

B—S. CHIRATA, HAM.

PLATE No. 642.

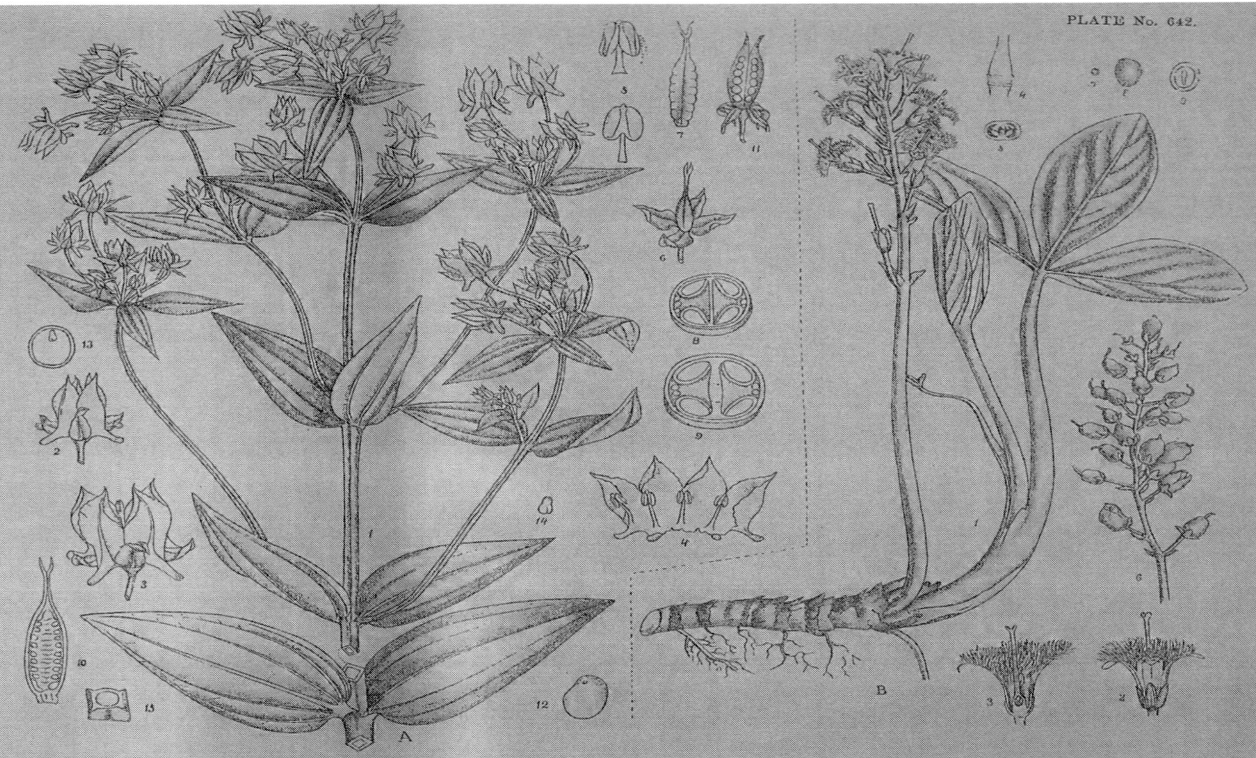

A–SWERTIA AFFINIS, *CLARKE.* B–MENYANTHES TRIFOLIATA, *LINN.*

PLATE No. 643.

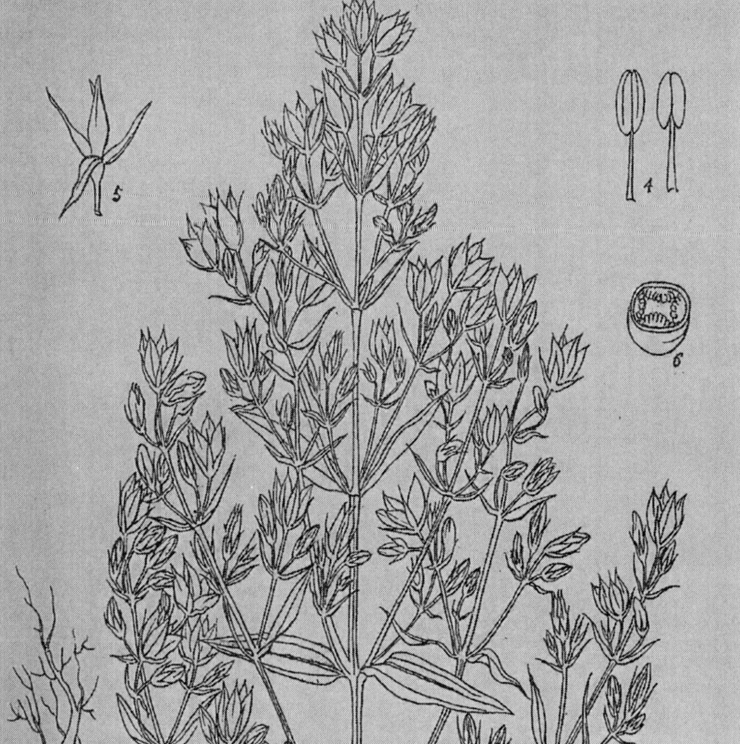

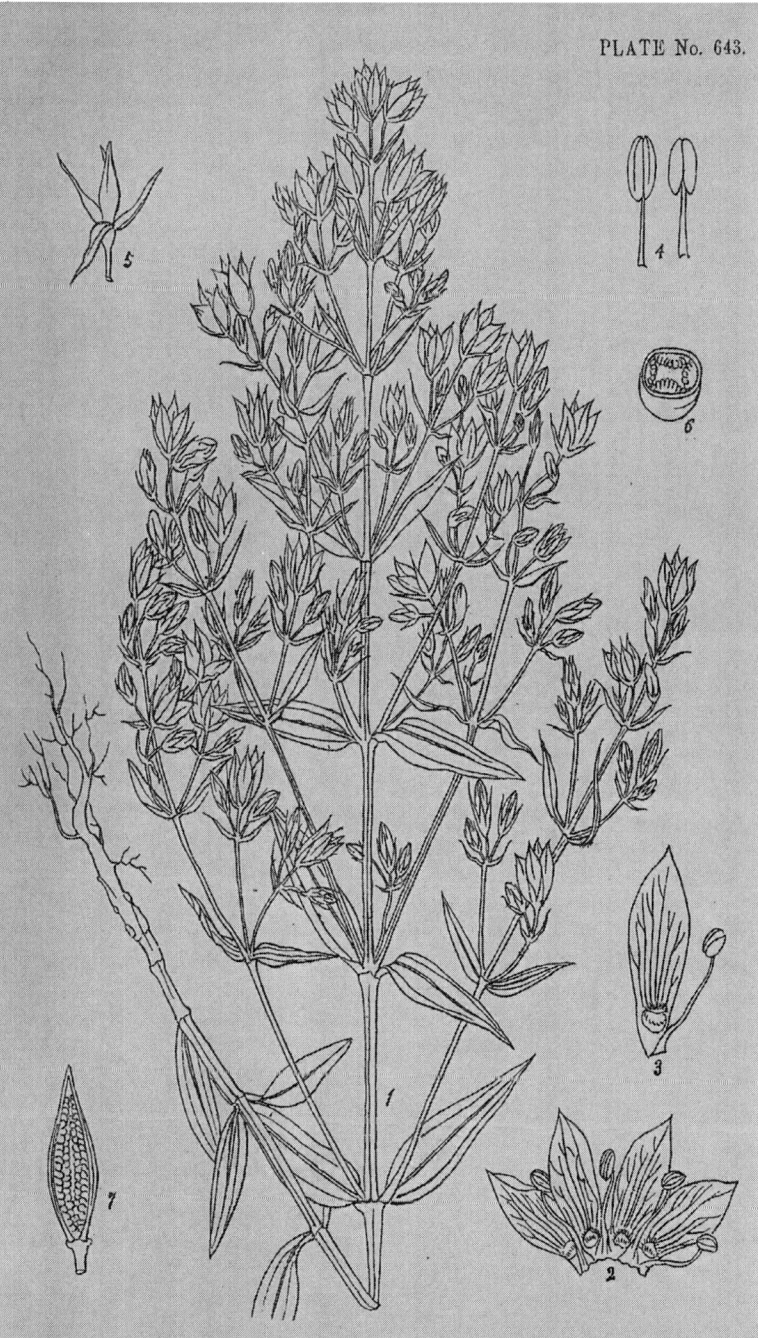

SWERTIA DECUSSATA, *NIMMO.*

PLATE No. 644.

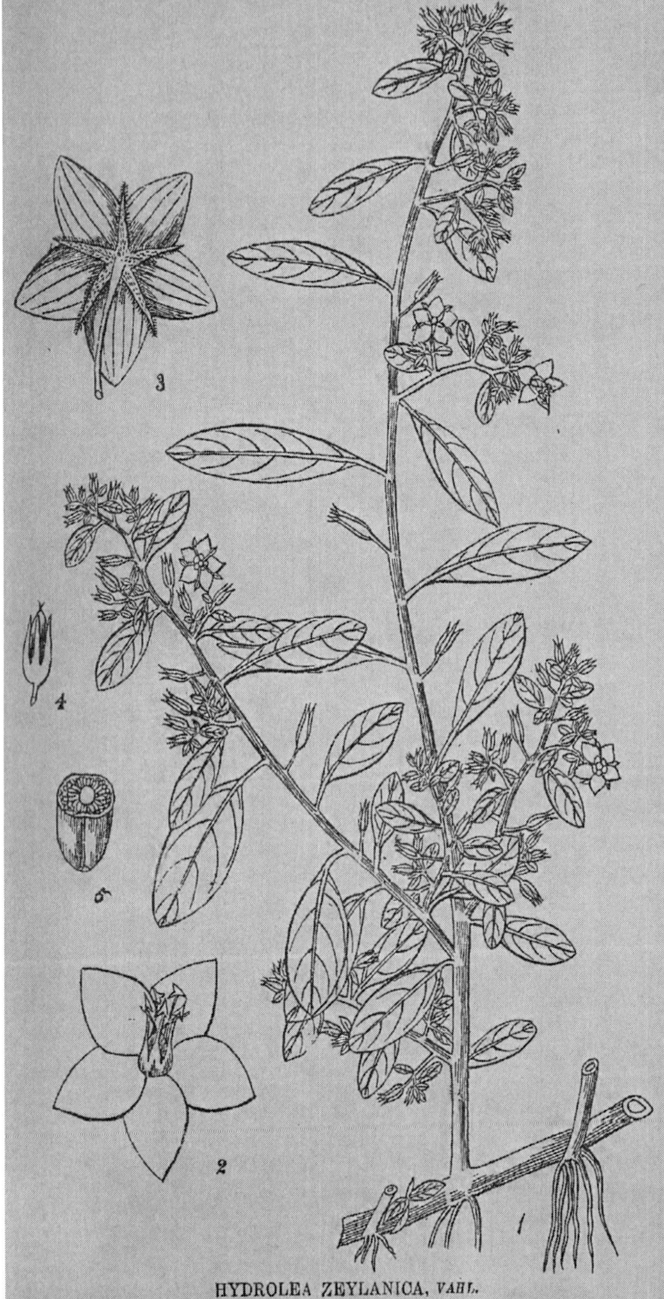

HYDROLEA ZEYLANICA, VAHL.

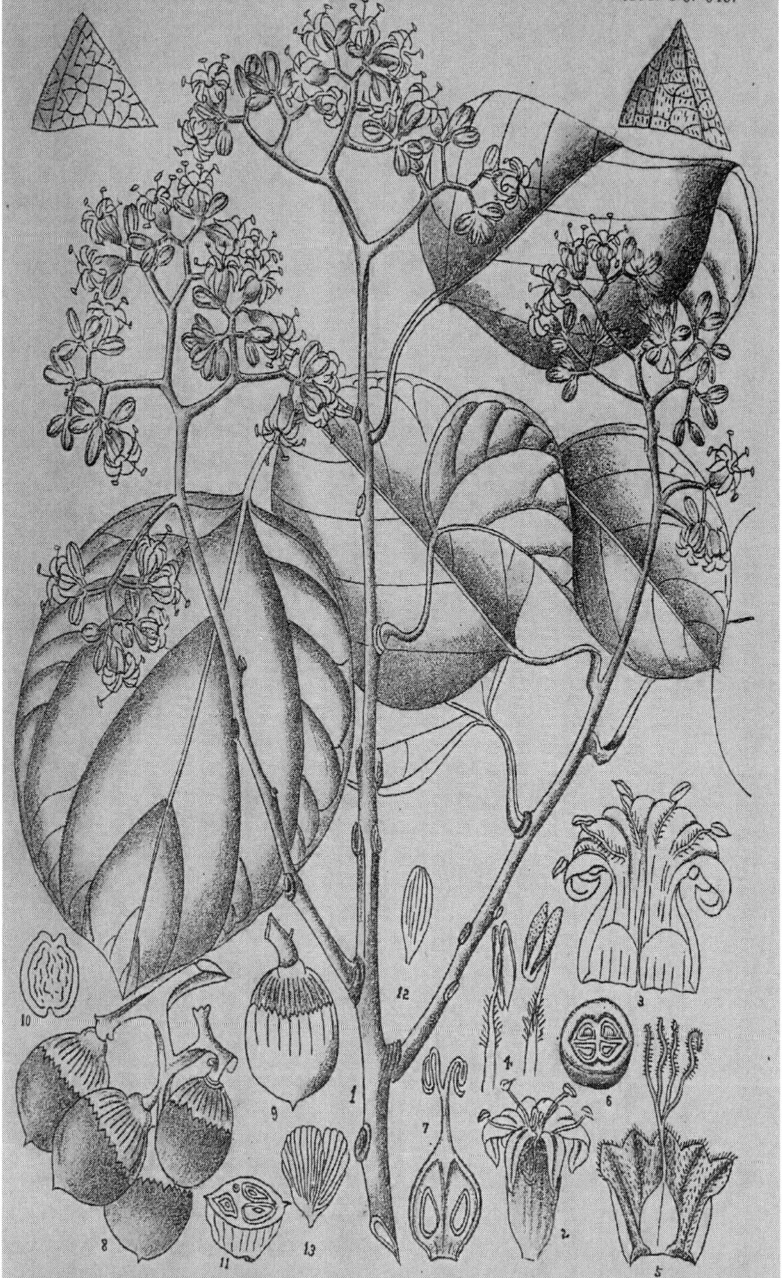

CORDIA MYXA, *LINN.*

PLATE No. 646.

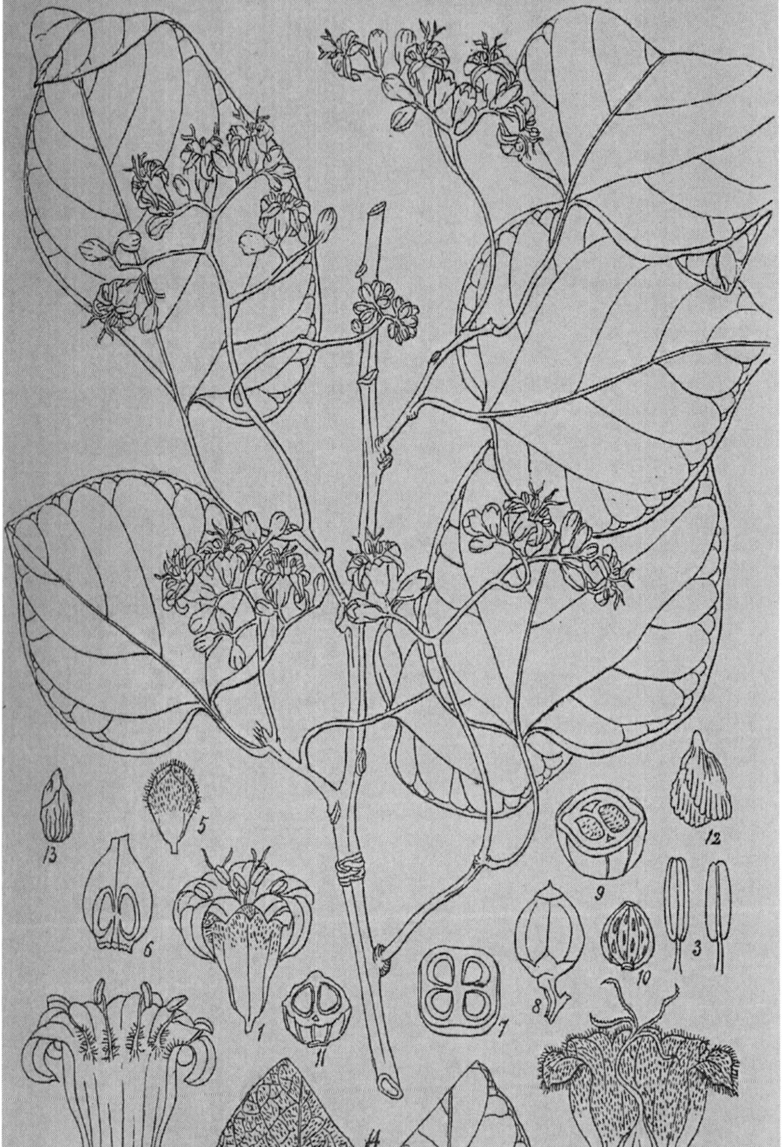

CORDIA OBLIQUA, *WILLD.*

PLATE No. 647.

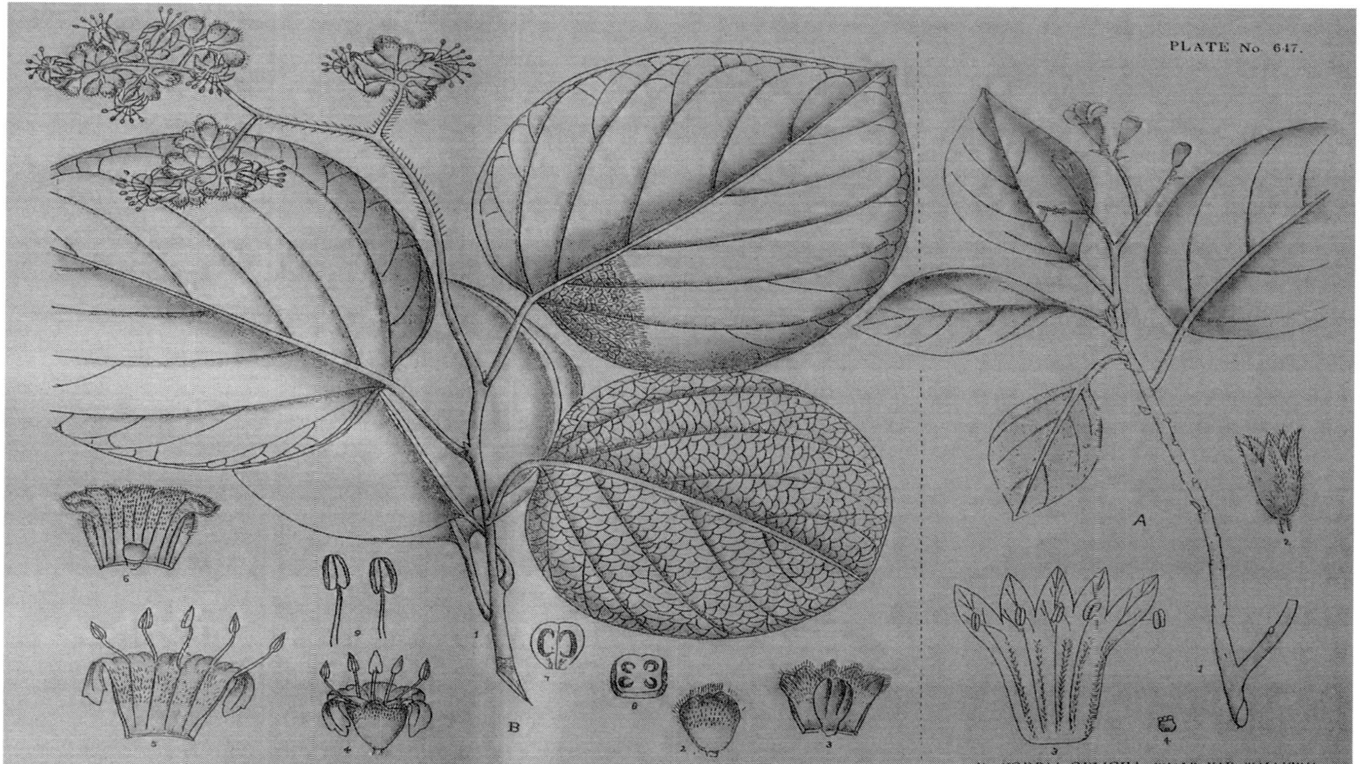

A—CORDIA VESTITA, *Hk. F. & T.* B—CORDIA OBLIQUA, *Willd. var. Wallichii*

PLATE No. 648.

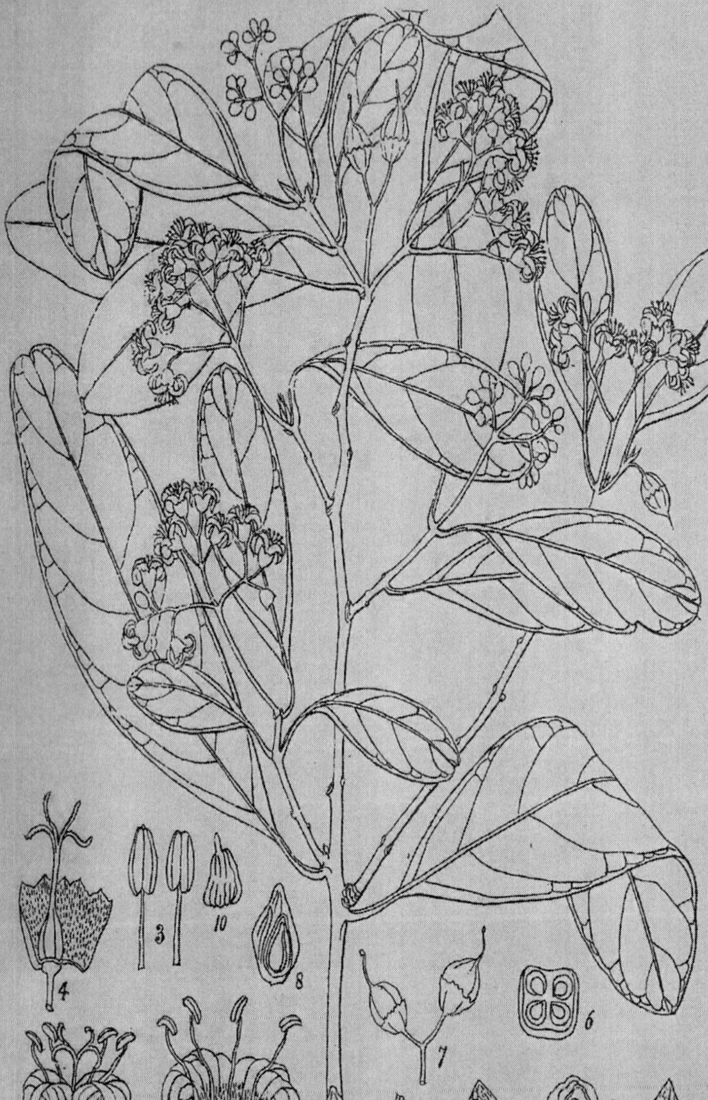

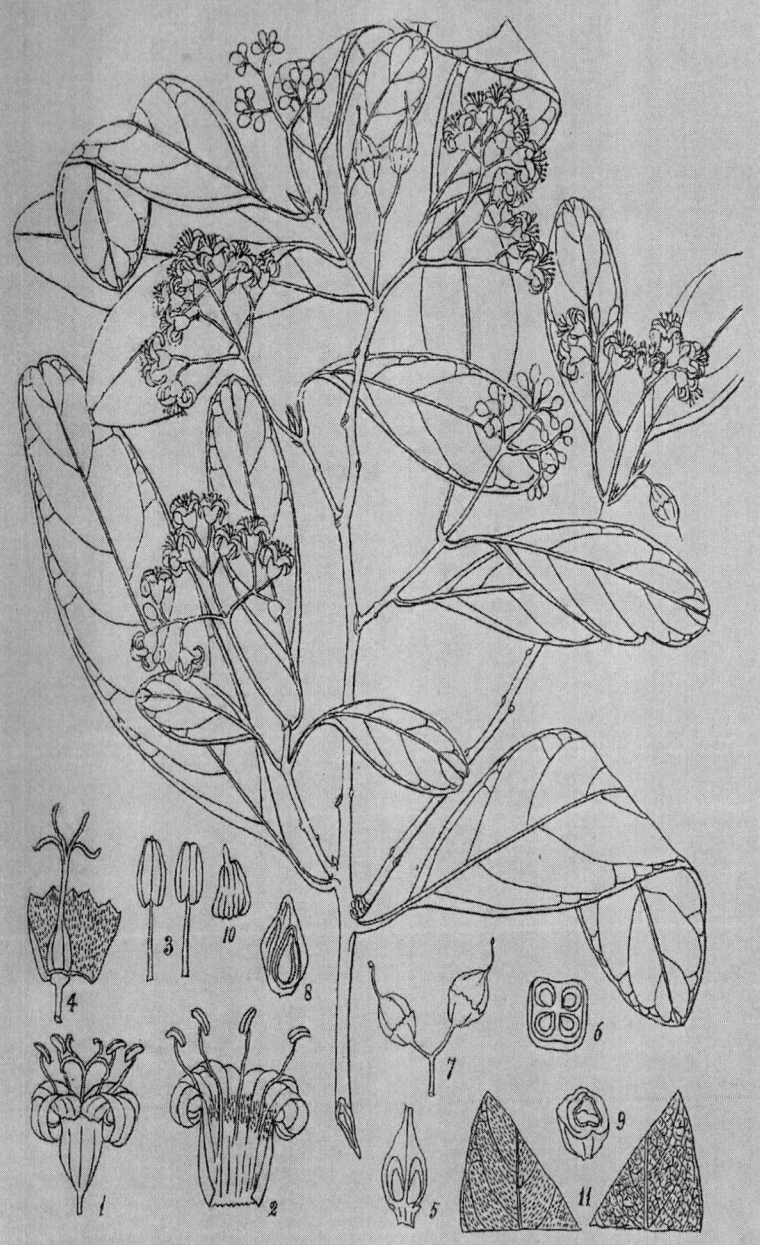

CORDIA ROTHII, *RŒM. & SCH.*

PLATE No. 649.

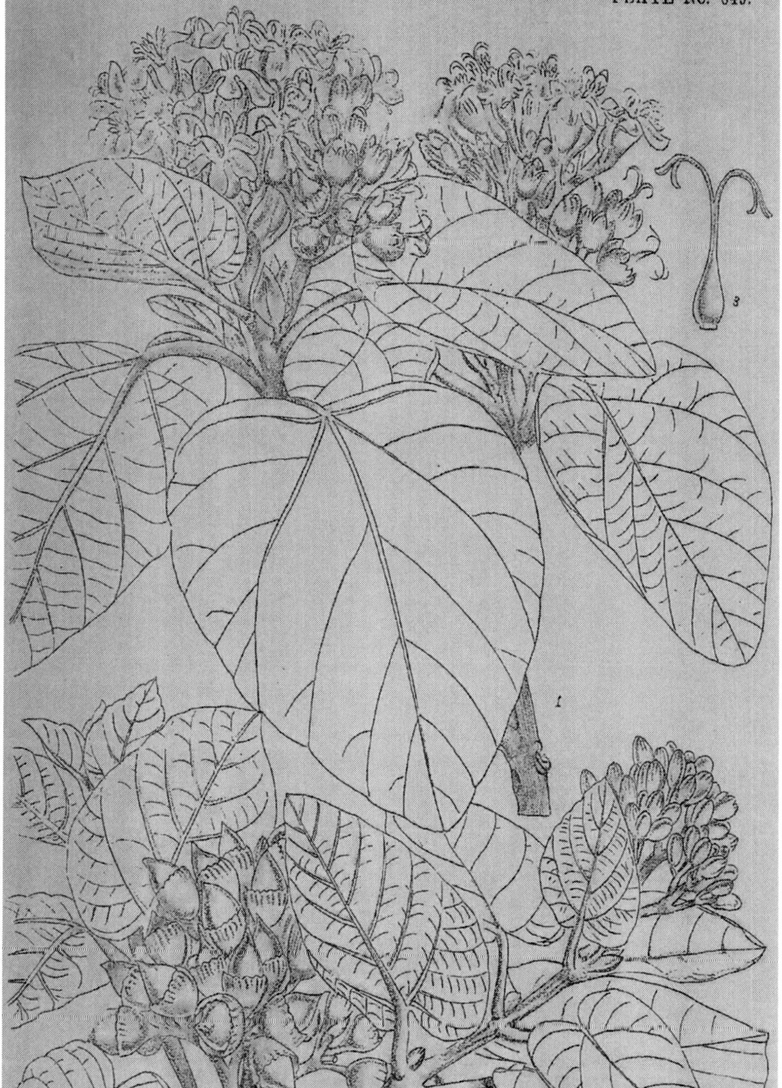

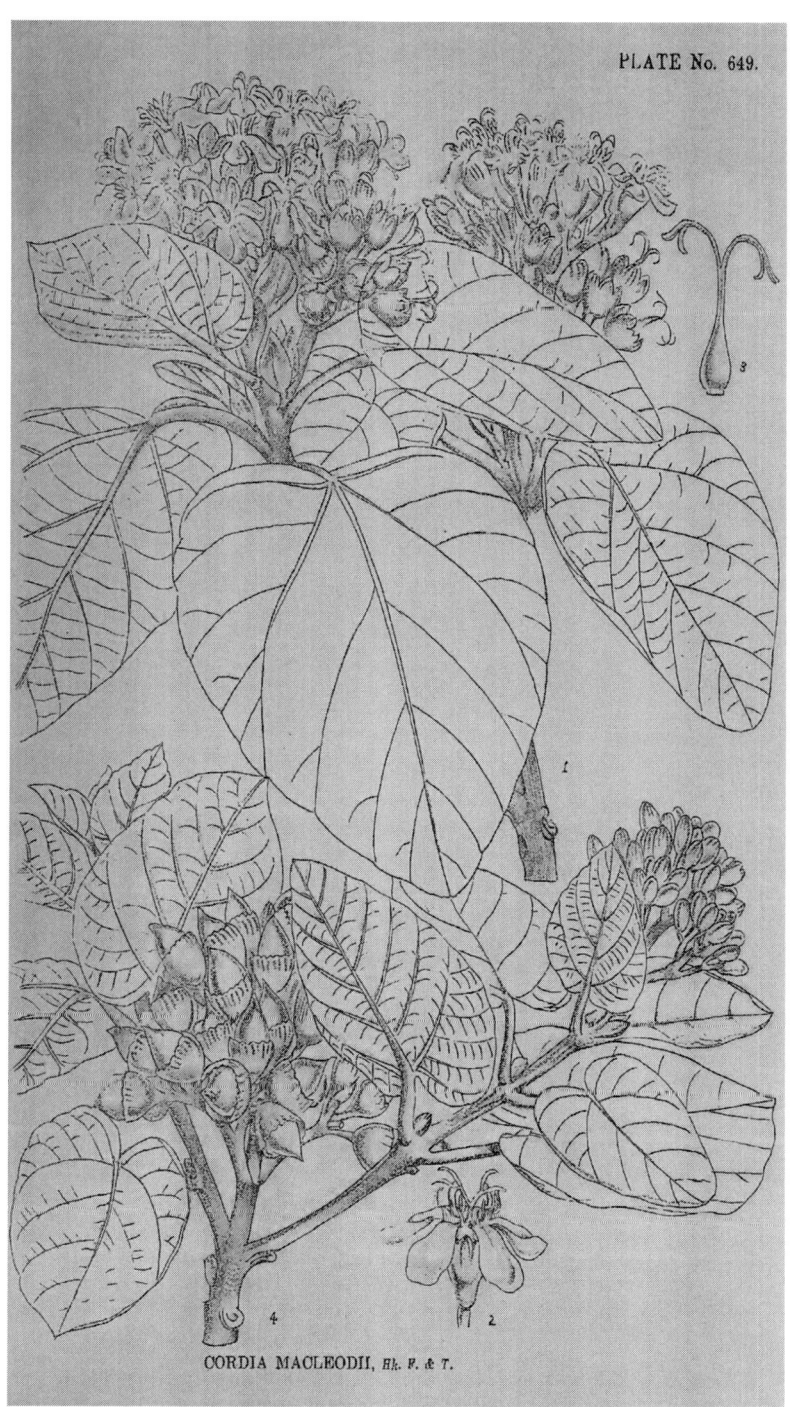

CORDIA MACLEODII, *Hk. F. & T.*

PLATE No. 650.

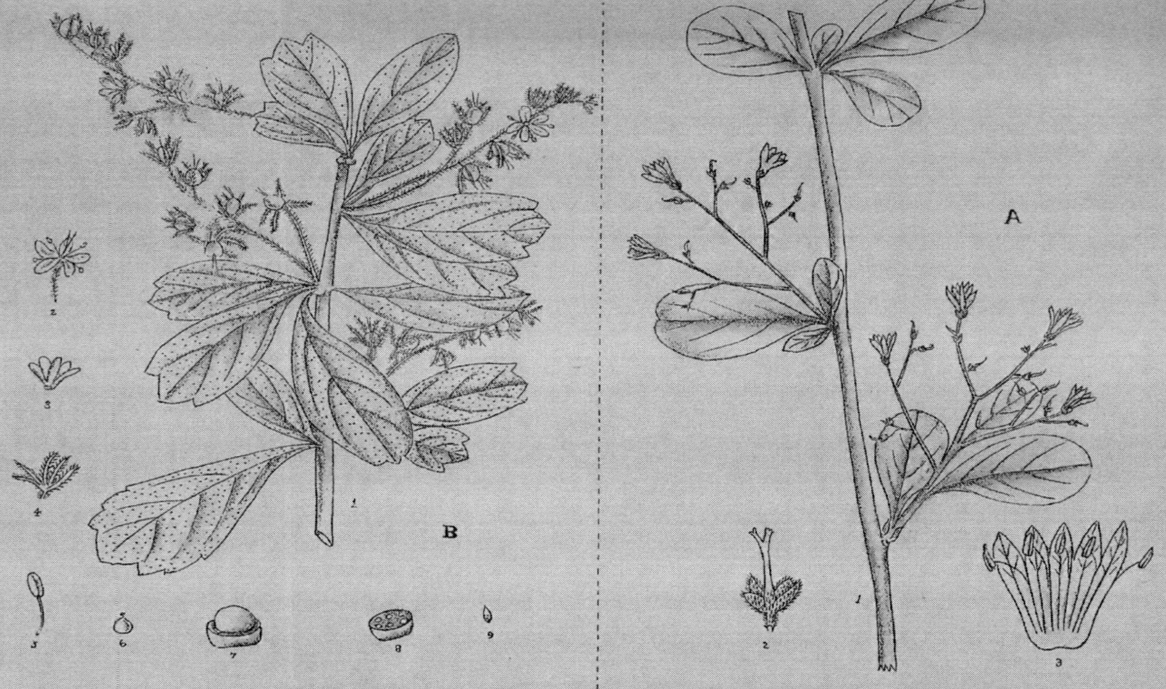

A—EHRETIA OBTUSIFOLIA, HOCHST.

B—EHRETIA BUXIFOLIA, ROXB.

PLATE No. 651.

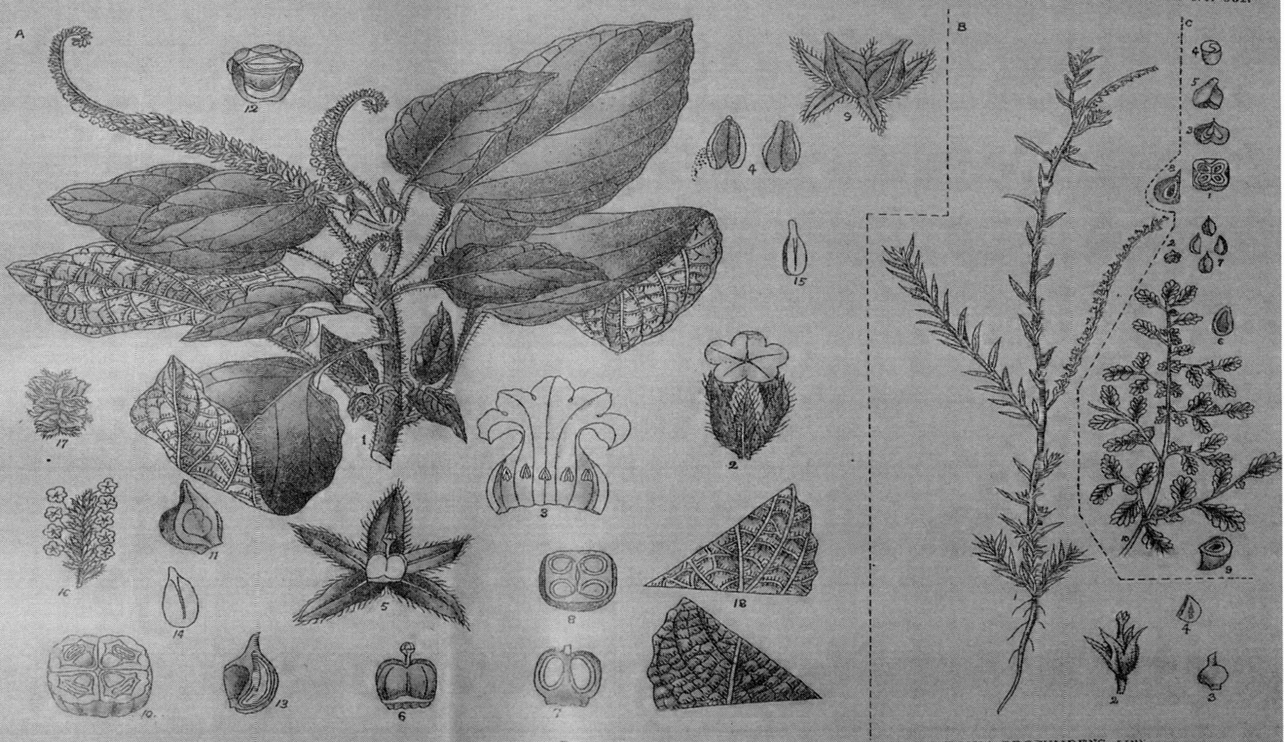

A—HELIOTROPIUM INDICUM, LINN.   B H. STRIGOSUM, WILLD.   C -COLDENIA PROCUMBENS, LINN.

PLATE No. 652

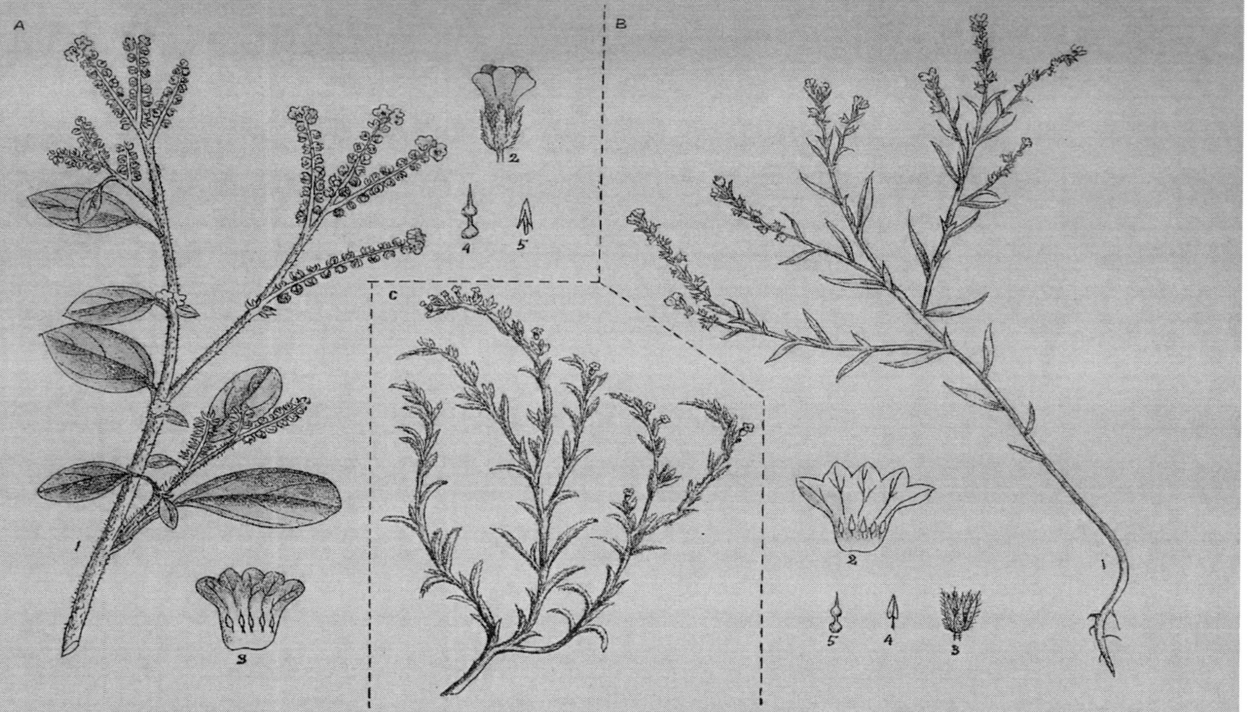

A—HELIOTROPIUM EICHWALDI, *STEUD.* C—H. UNDULATUM, *VAHL.* B—H. STRIGOSUM, *WILLD, VAR. BREVFOLIA.*

PLATE No. 653.

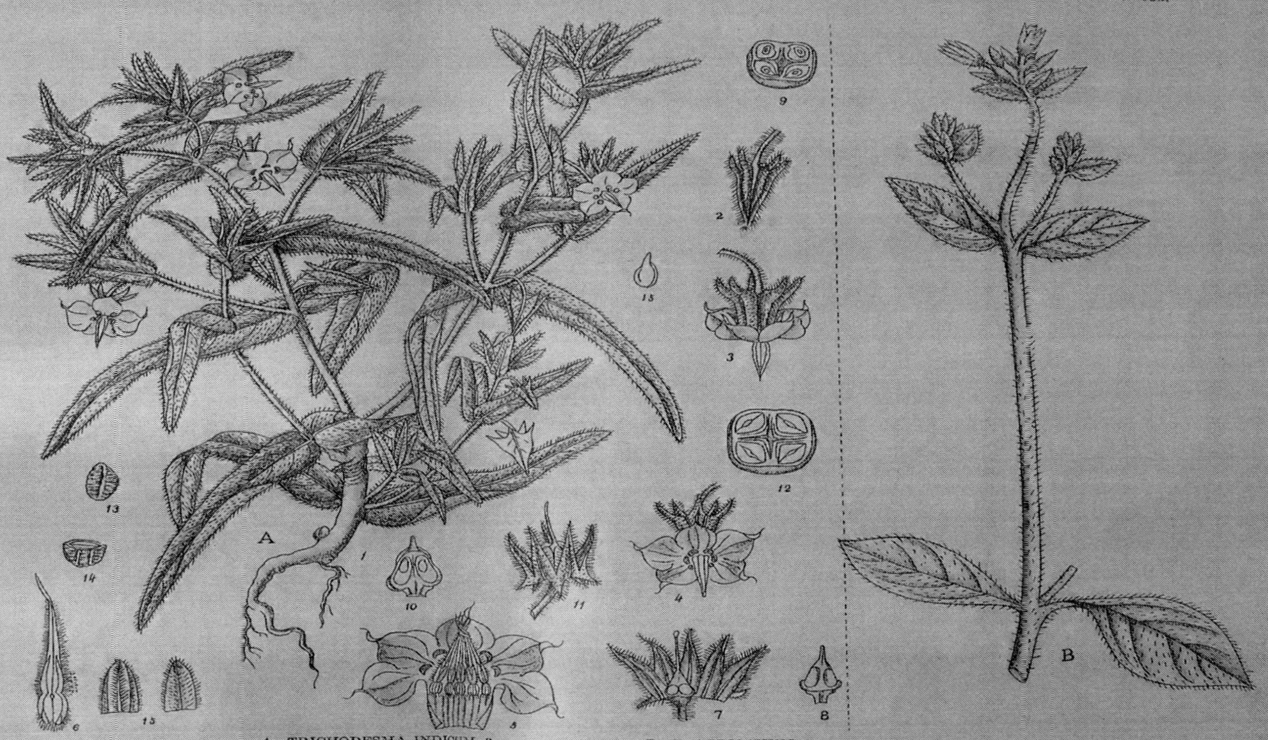

A—TRICHODESMA INDICUM, Br.

B—T. AFRICANUM, Br.

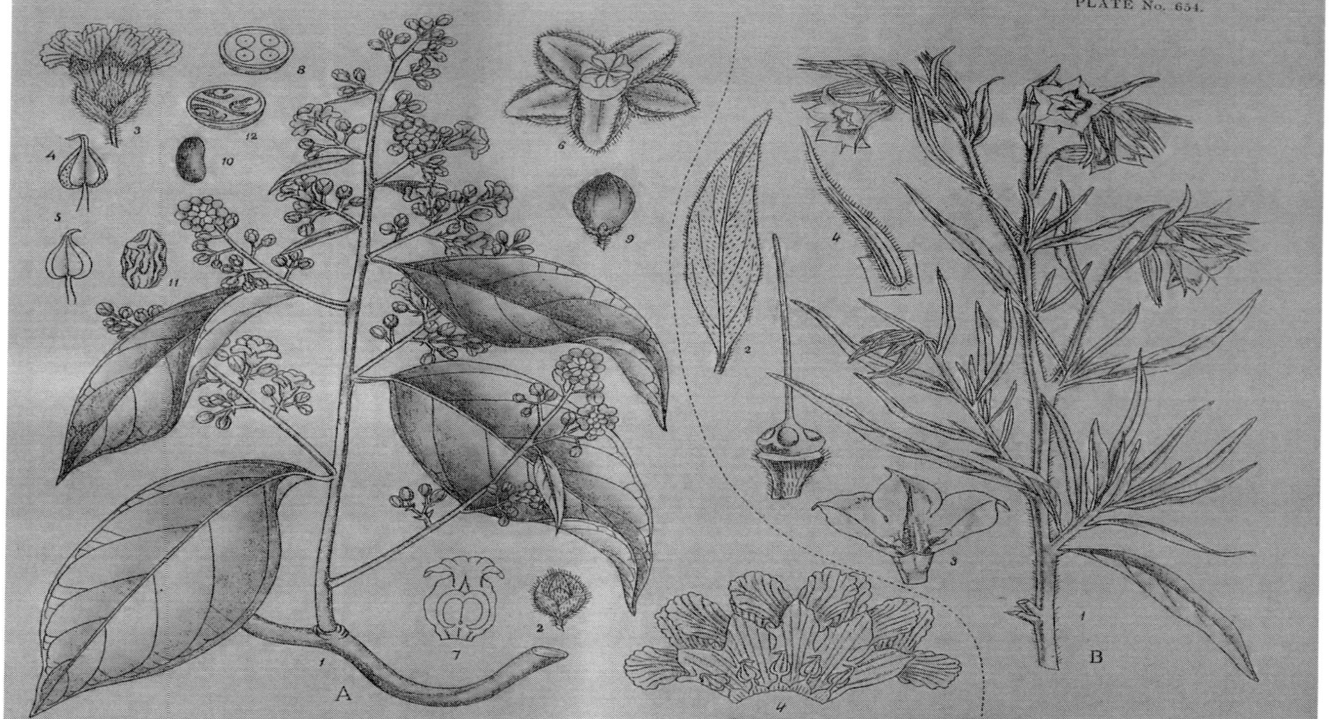

A—ERYCIBE PANICULATA, ROXB.

B—TRICHODESMA ZEYLANICUM, BR.

PLATE No. 655.

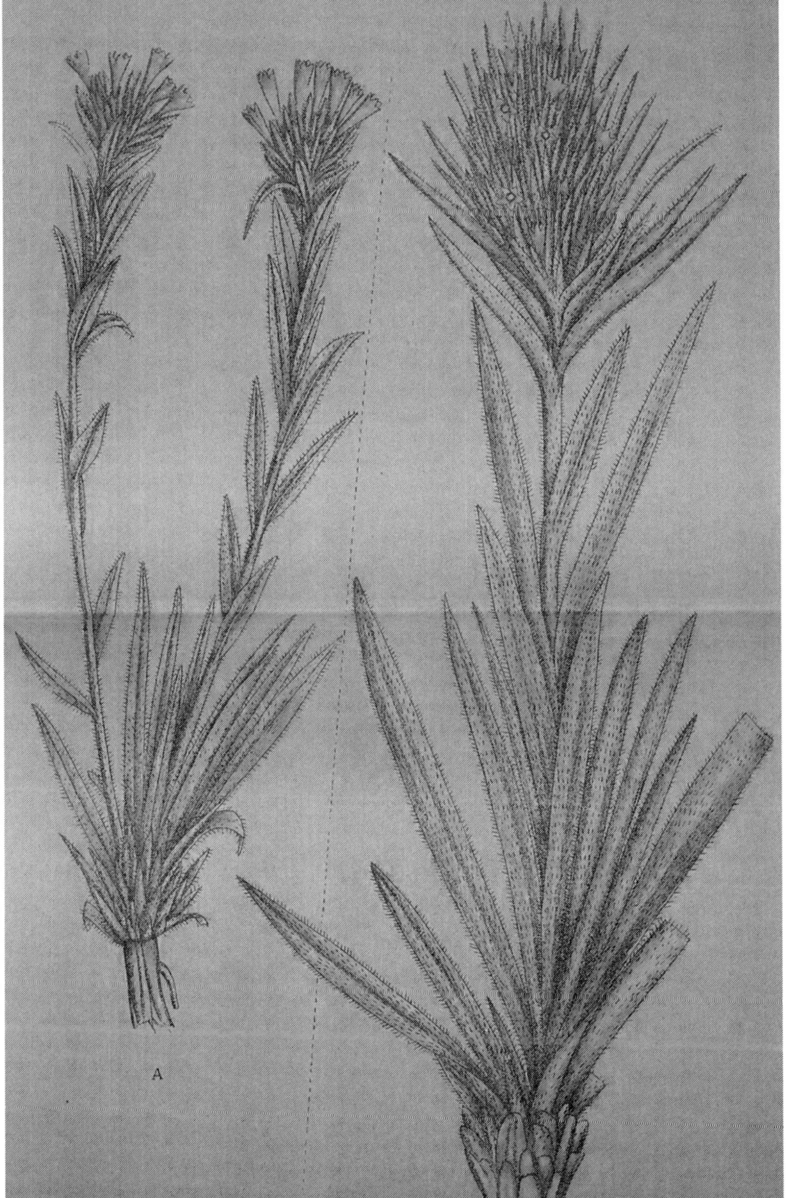

A—MACROTOMIA PERENNIS, BOISS.   B—MACROTOMIA BENTHAMI, DC

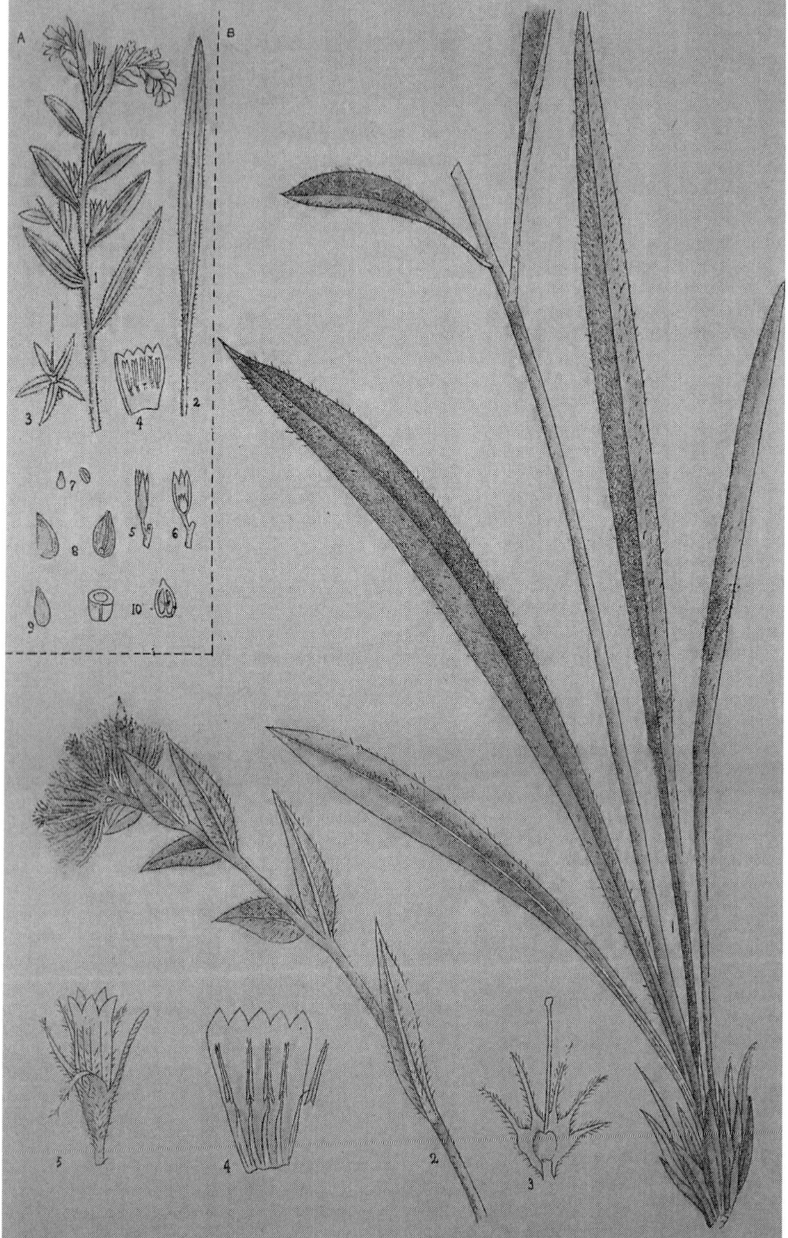

A—ONOSMA ECHIOIDES, *LINN.*

B—ONOSMA BRACTEATUM, *WALL.*

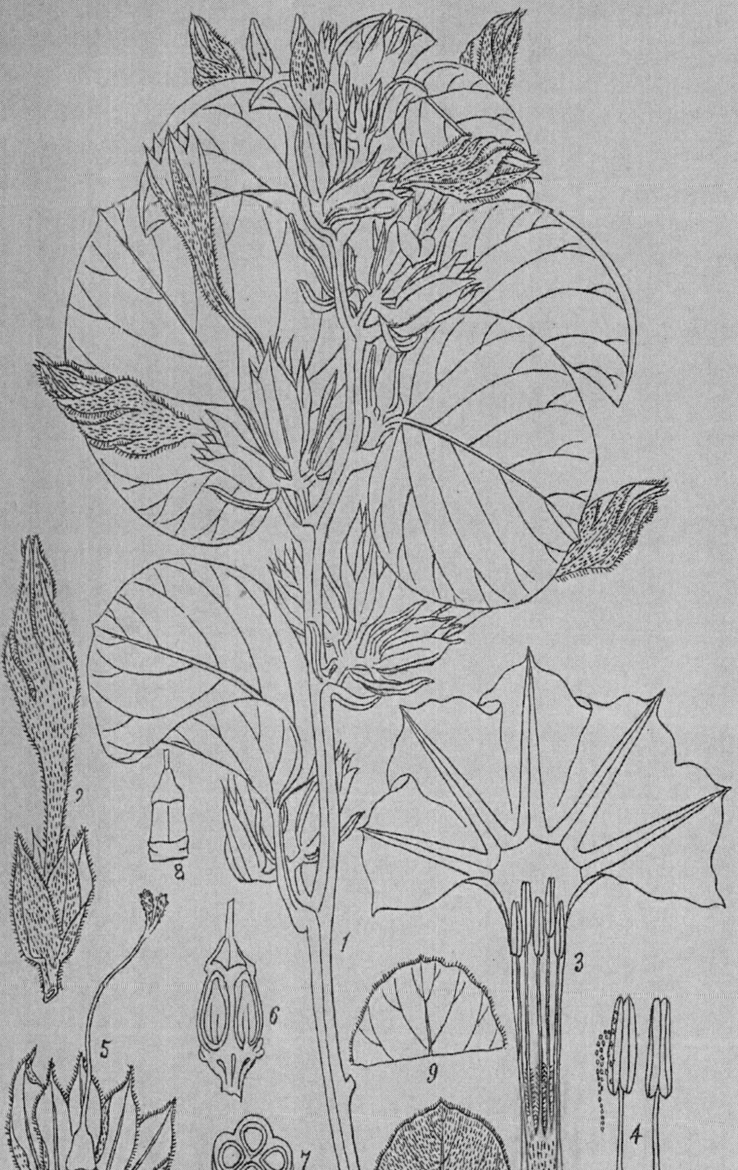

RIVEA ORNATA, CHOIS.

PLATE No. 658

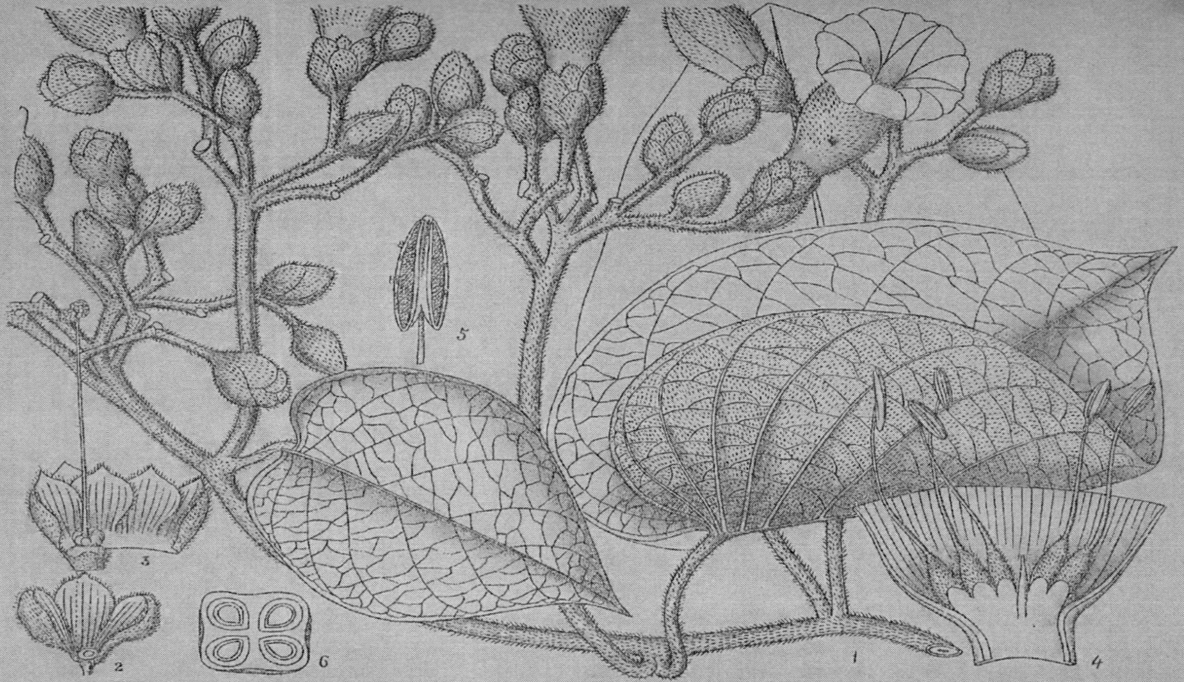

ARGYREIA SPECIOSA, *SWEET.*

PLATE No. 659.

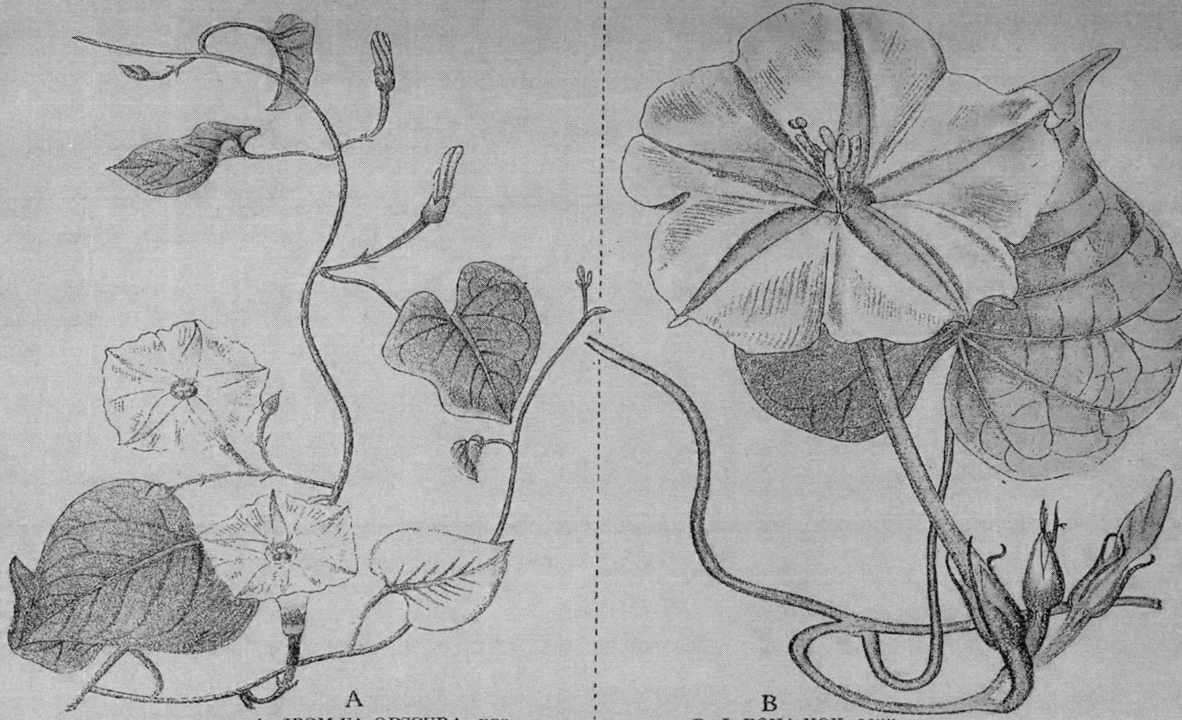

A—IPOMÆA OBSCURA, *Ker.* B—I. BONA-NOX, *Linn.*

PLATE No. 660

IPOMÆA MURICATA, JACQ.

PLATE No. 661.

IPOMÆA HEDERACEA, *JACQ.*

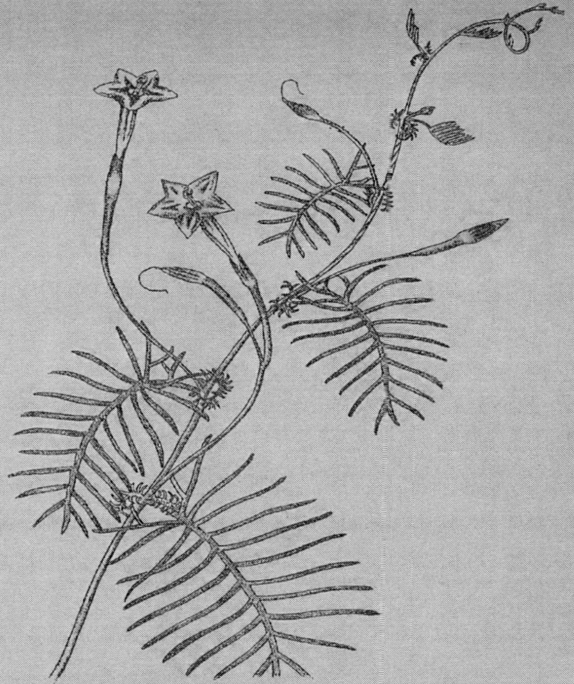

IPOMÆA QUAMOCLIT, *LINN.*

IPOMÆA DIGITATA, LINN.

PLATE No. 663.

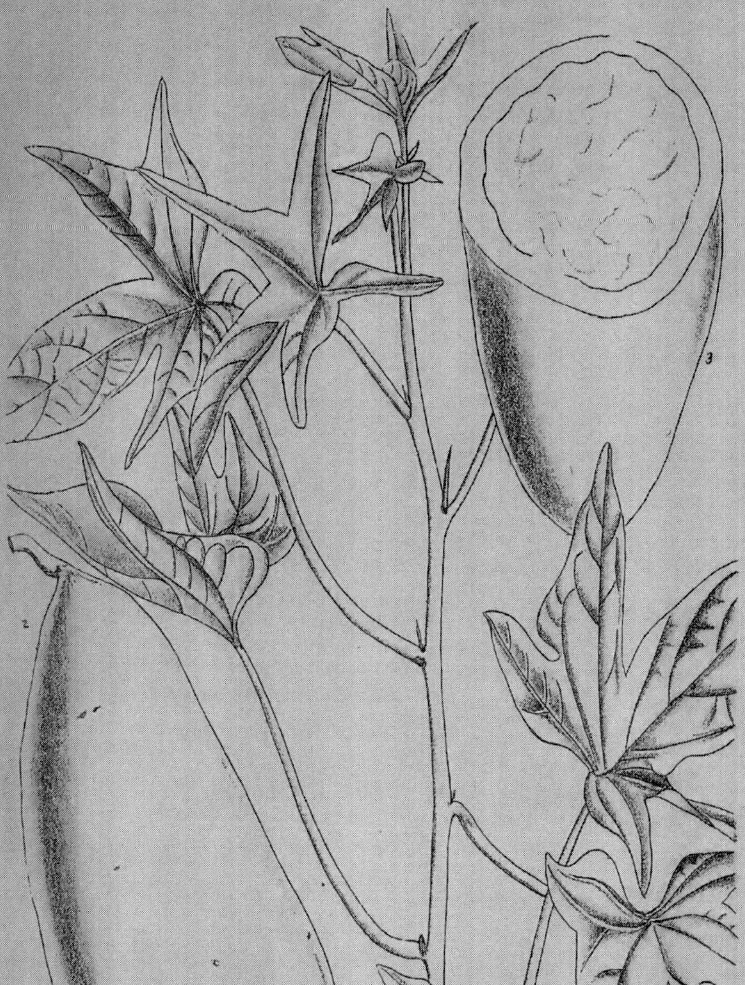

IPOMÆA BATATAS, *LAMK.*

PLATE No. 664.

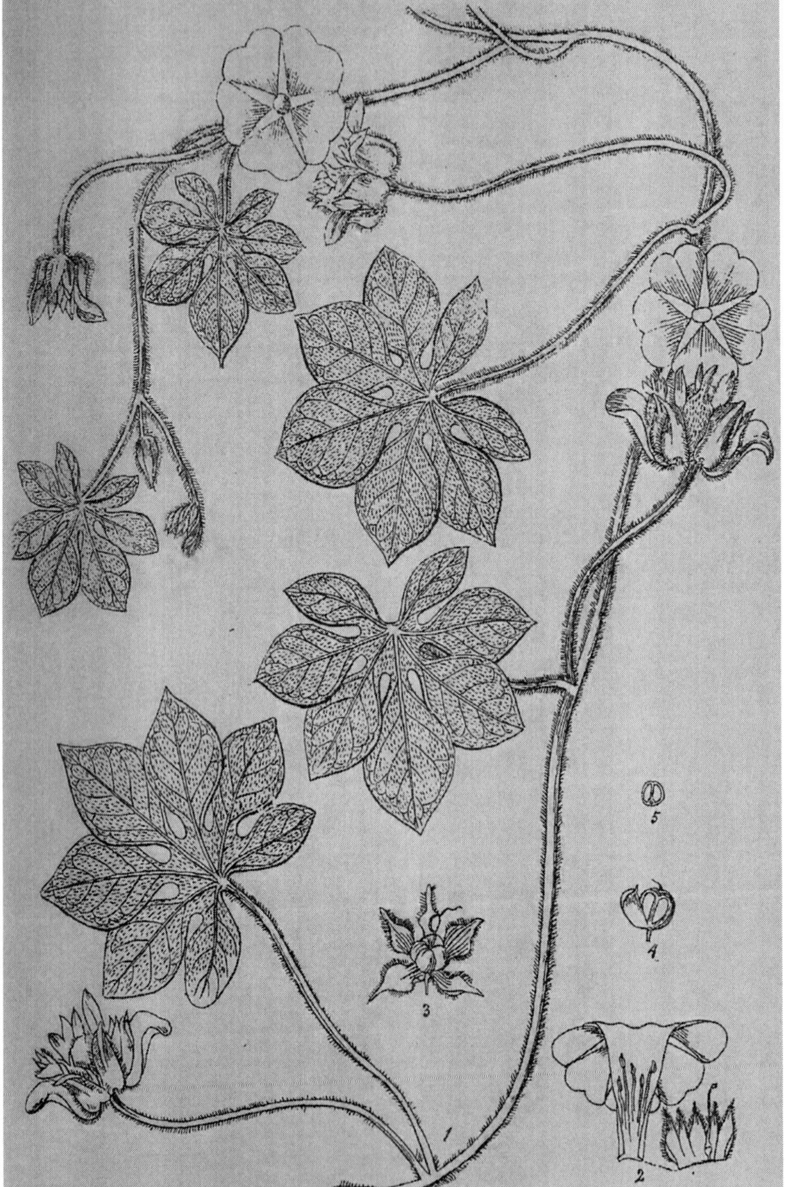

IPOMÆA PES-TIGRIDIS, *LINN.*

PLATE No. 663.

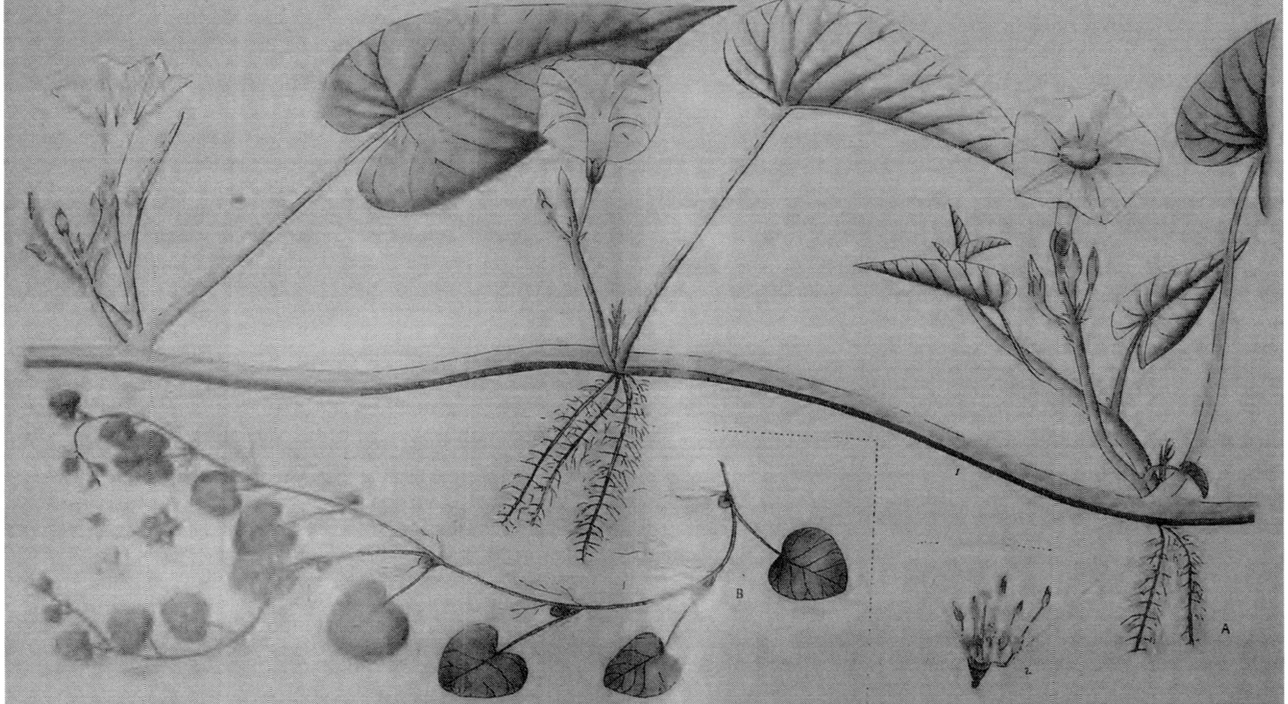

A IPOMÆA AQUATICA, FORSK.　　B I. RENIFORMIS, CHOIS.

PLATE No. 666.

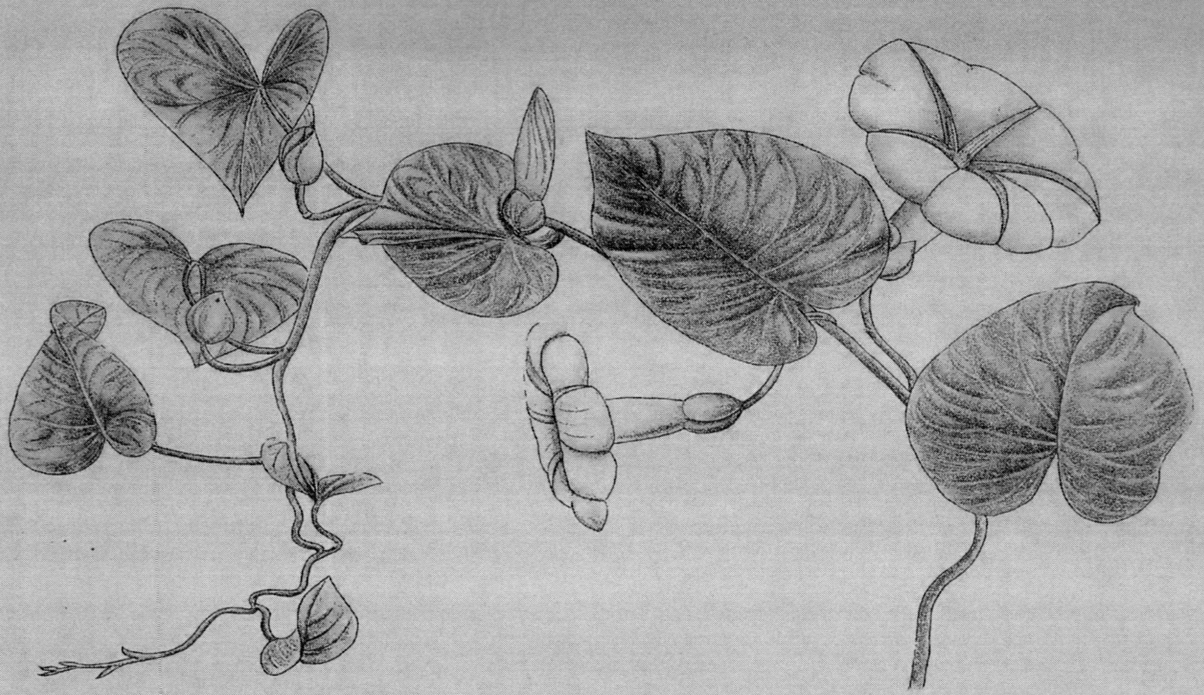

IPOMÆA TURPETHUM, *Br.*

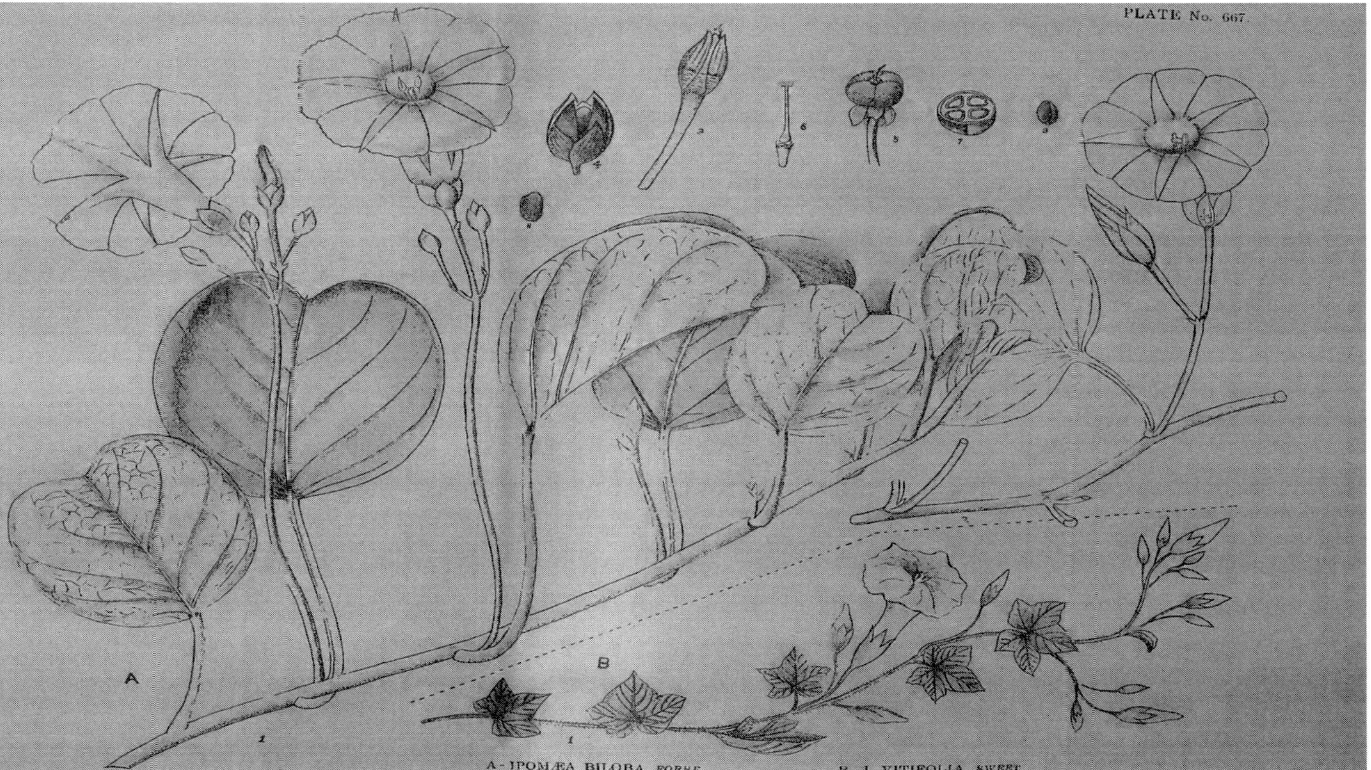

A-IPOMÆA BILOBA, *FORSK*　　B-I. VITIFOLIA, *SWEET*

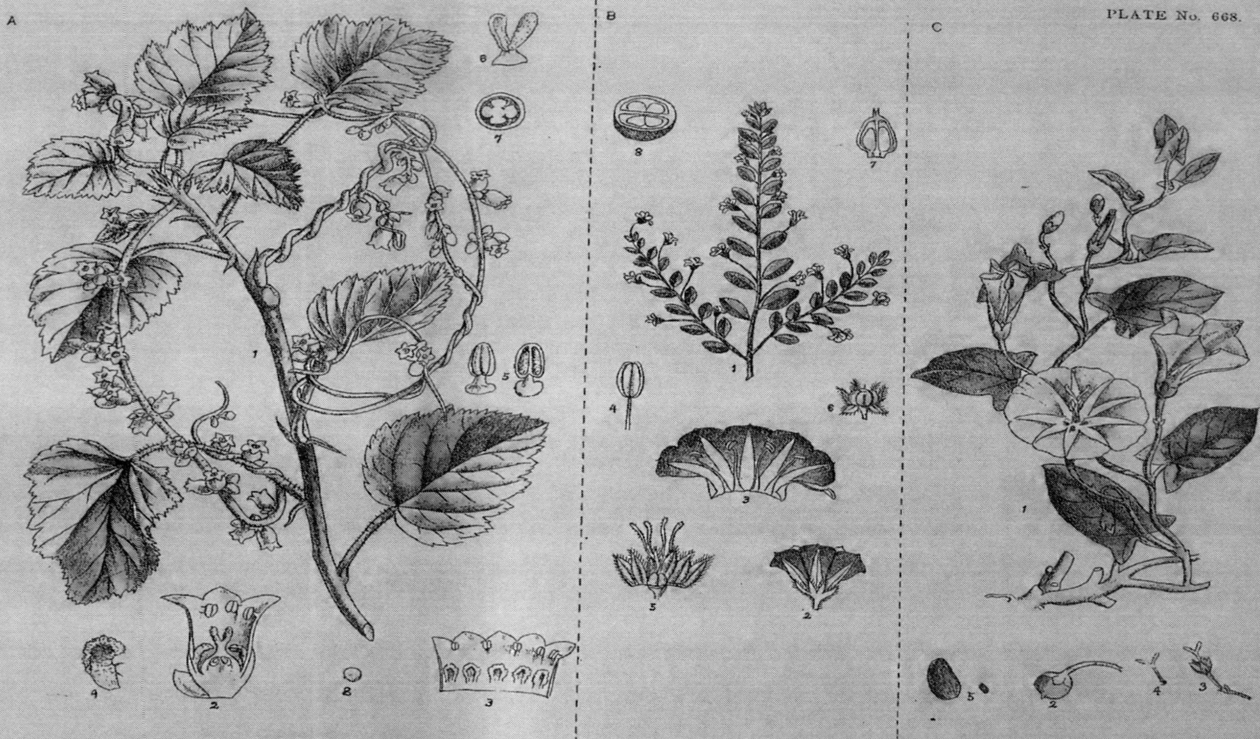

A– CUSCUTA REFLEXA, *ROXB.*

B—EVOLVULUS ALSINOIDES, *WALL.*

C—CONVOLVULUS ARVENSIS, *LINN.*

PLATE No. 669.

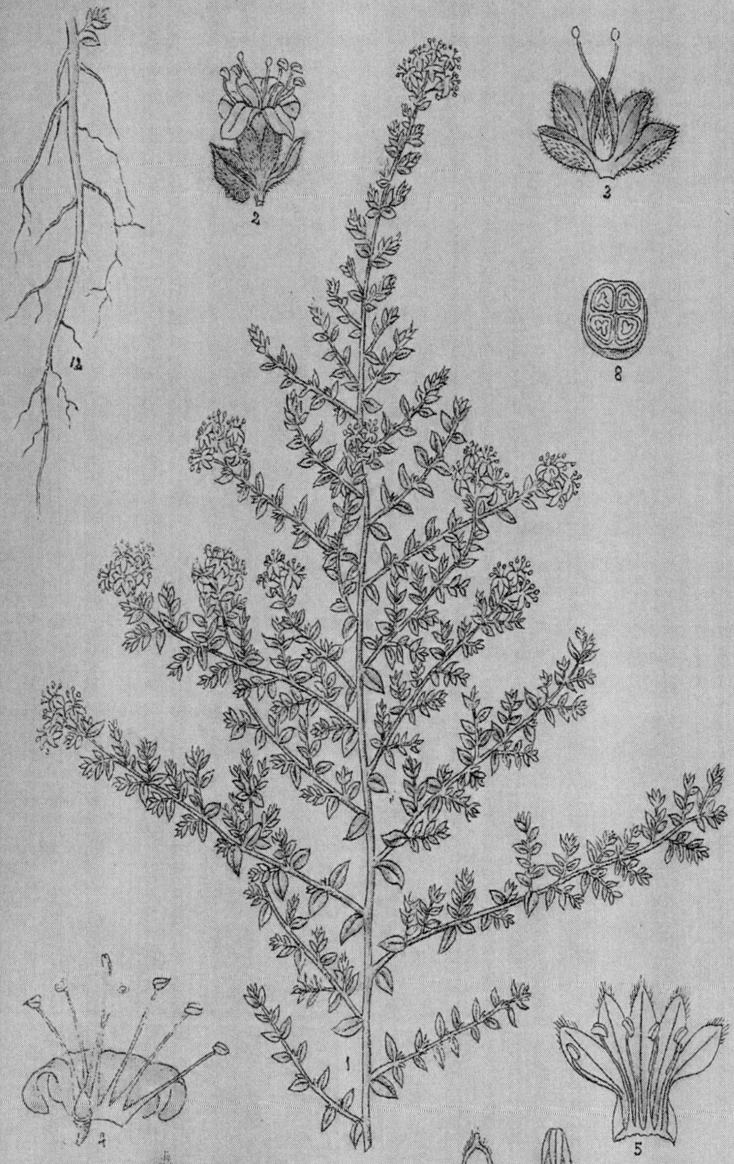

CRESSA CRETICA, *LINN.*

SOLANUM NIGRUM, *LINN.*

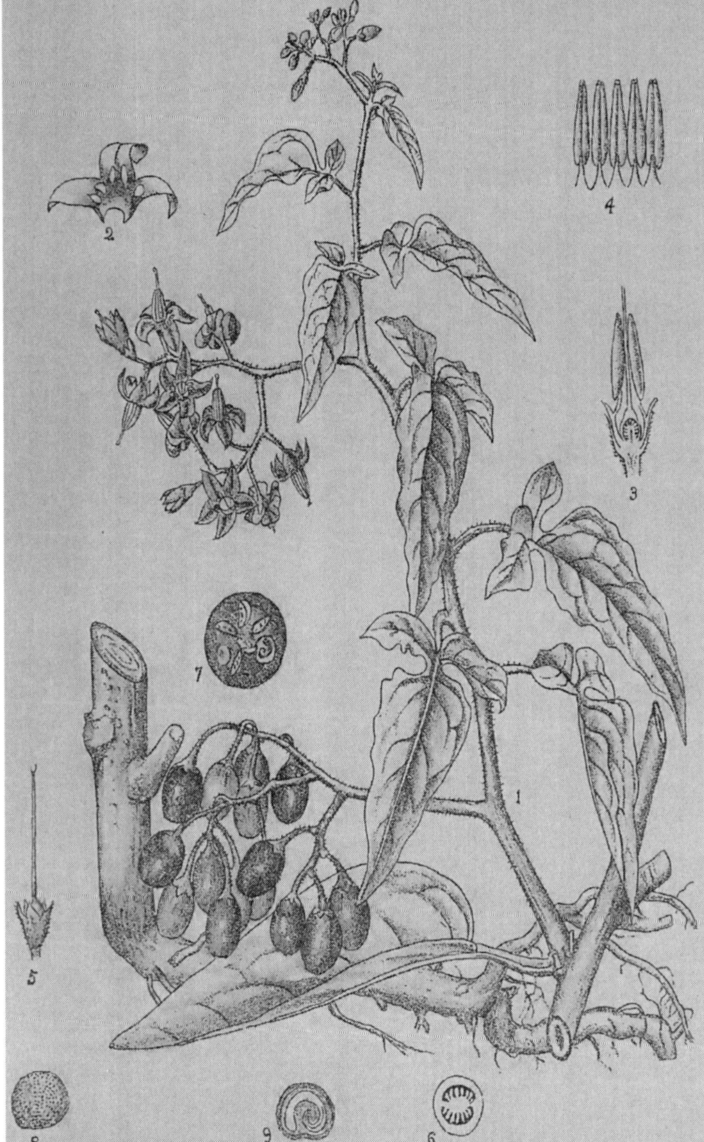

SOLANUM DULCAMARA, *Linn.*

PLATE No. 672.

SOLANUM SPIRALE, *ROXB.*

PLATE No. 673.

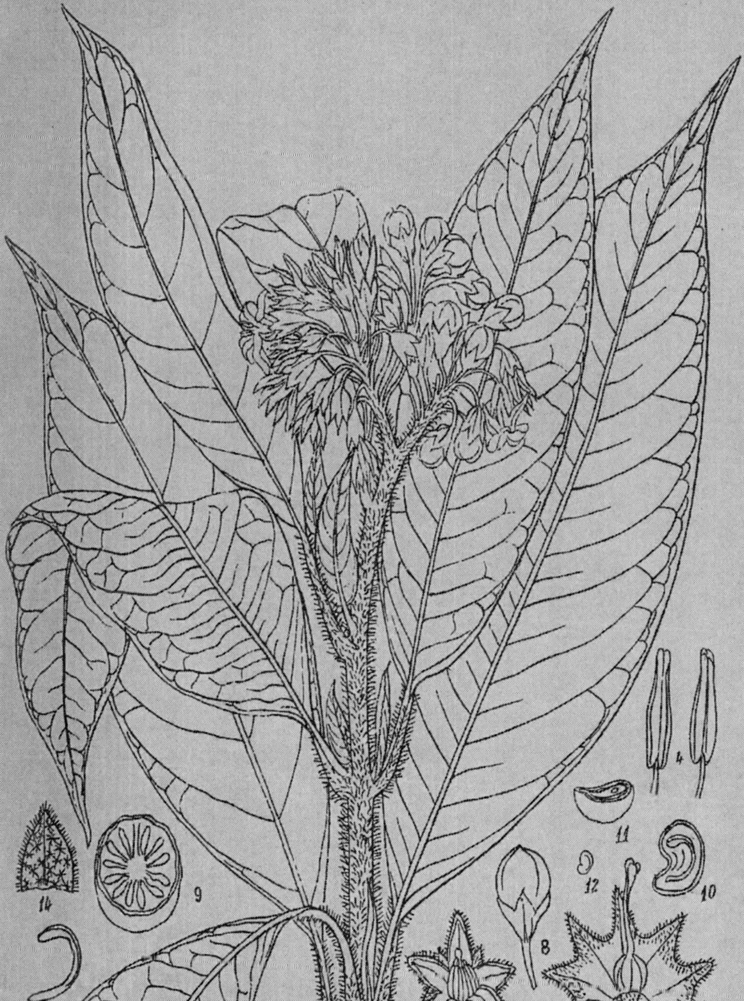

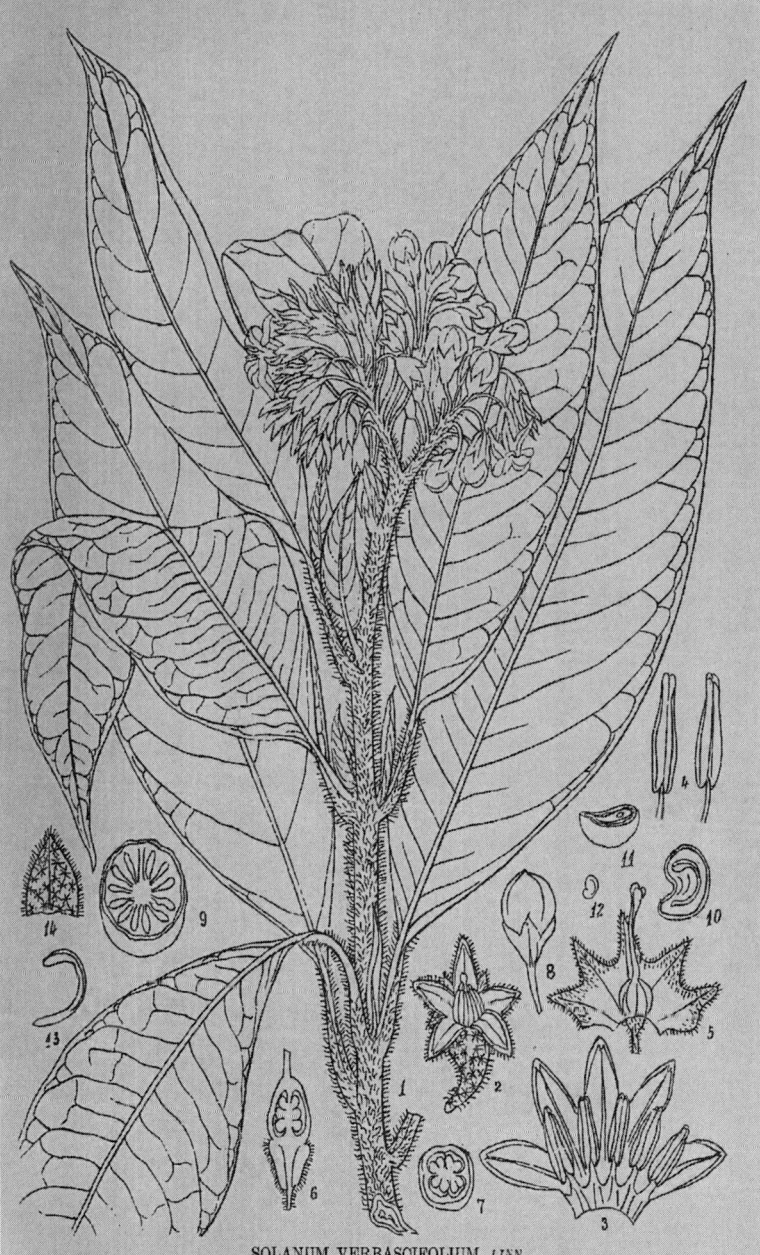

SOLANUM VERBASOIFOLIUM, *LINN.*

PLATE No. 674.

SOLANUM FEROX, Linn.

PLATE No. 675.

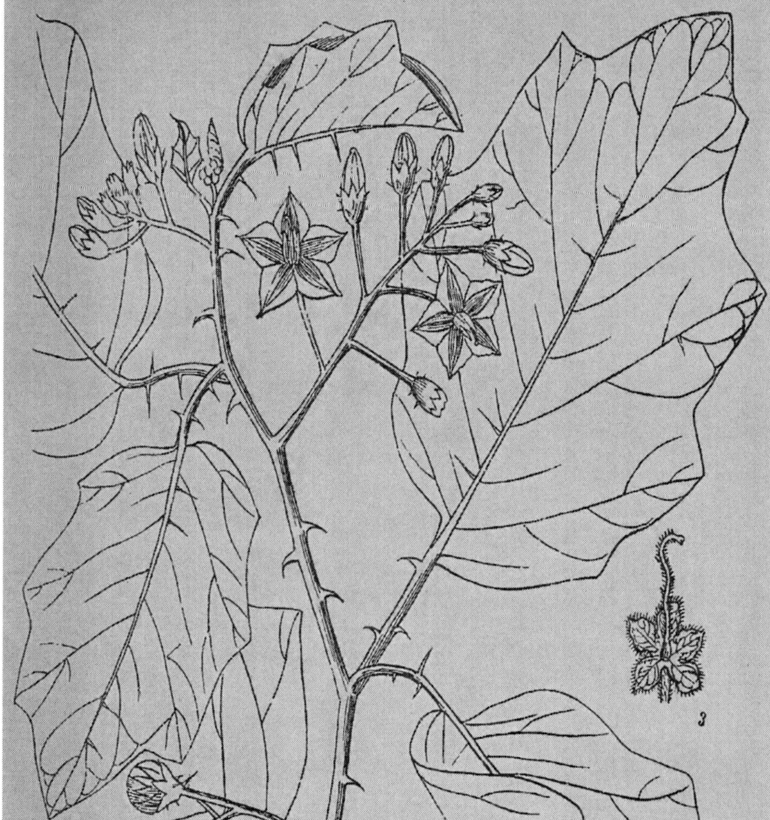

SOLANUM INDICUM, *LINN.*

PLATE No. 676.

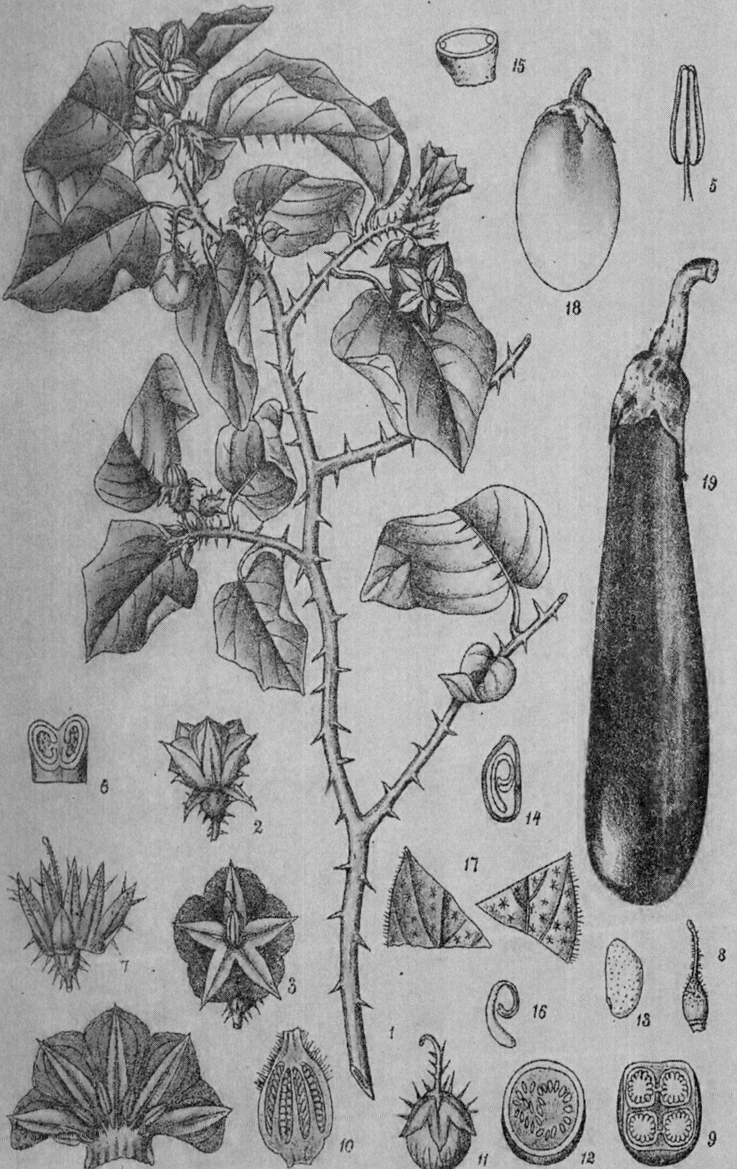

SOLANUM MELONGENA, *LINN.*

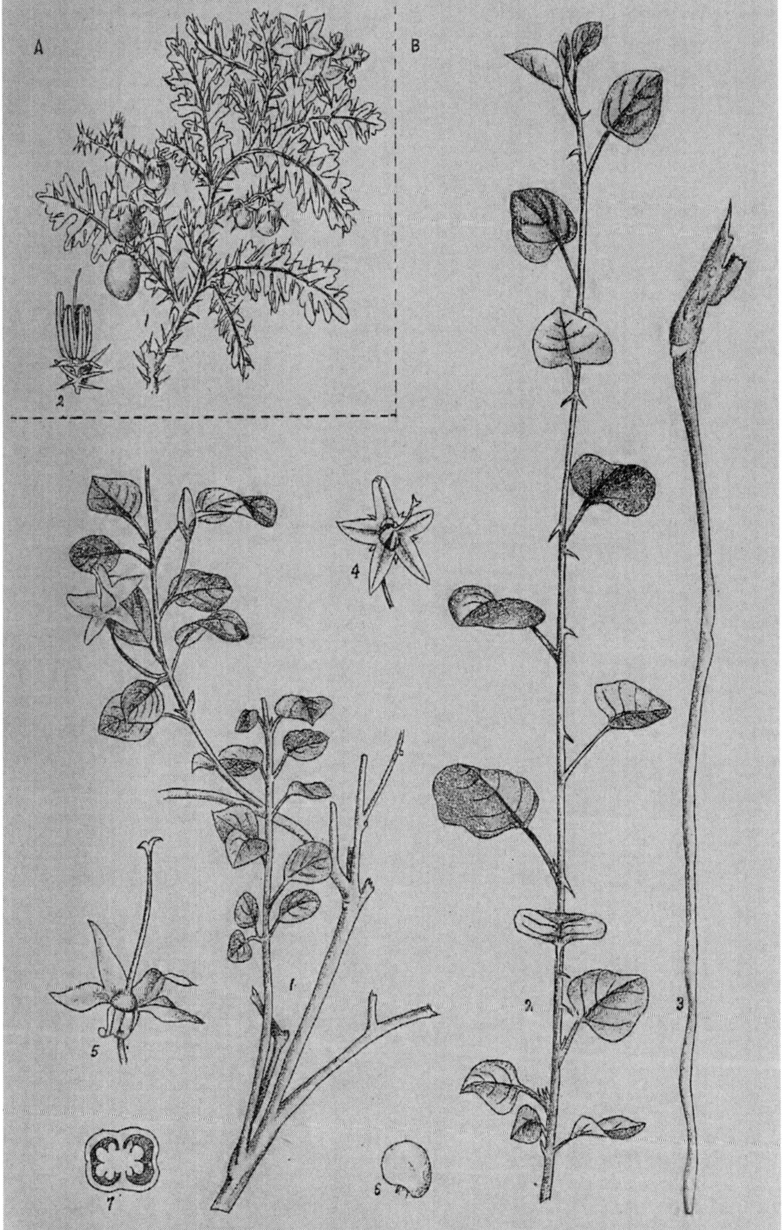

A—SOLANUM XANTHOCARPUM, *SCHRAD. & WENDL.*

B—SOLANUM GRACILIPES, *DCNE.*

PLATE No 678.

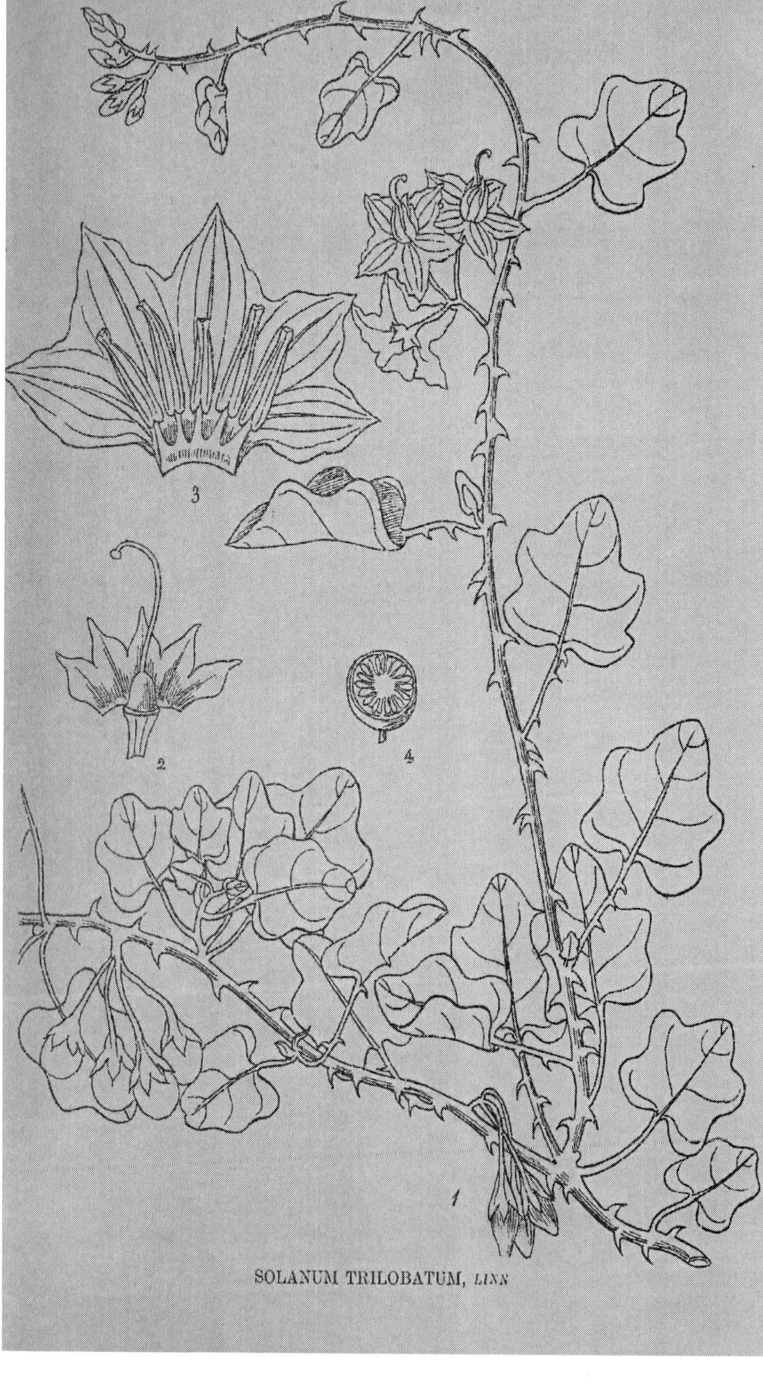

SOLANUM TRILOBATUM, *LINN*

PLATE No. 679.

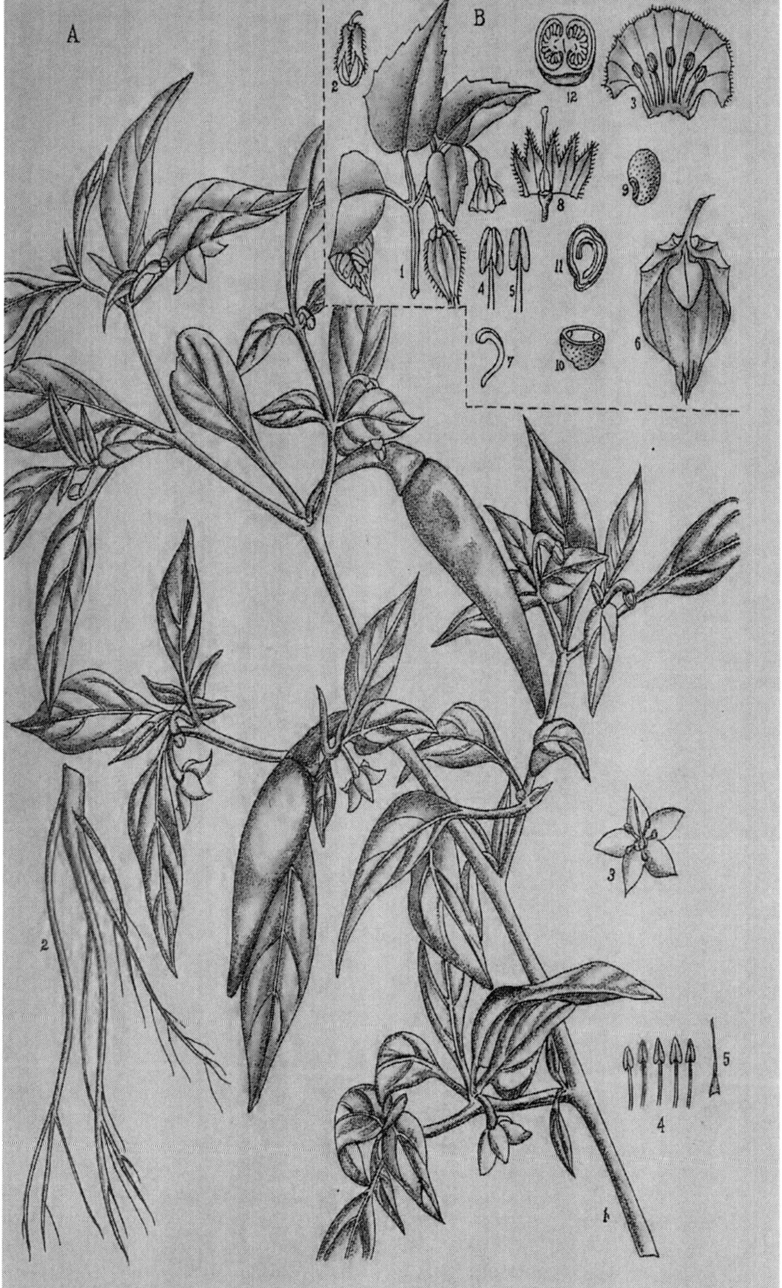

A—CAPSICUM FRUTESCENS, *LINN.* B—PHYSALIS MINIMA, *LINN.*

PLATE No. 680.

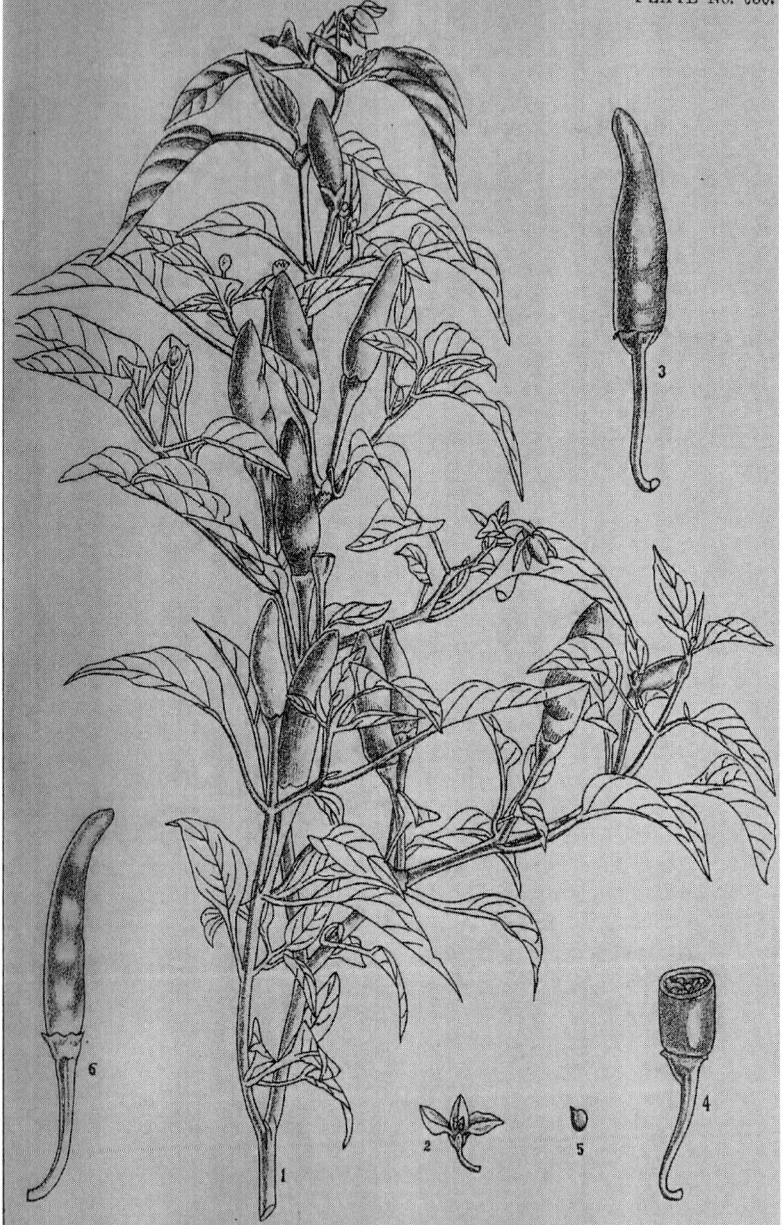

CAPSICUM MINIMUM, *ROXB.*

PLATE No. 681.

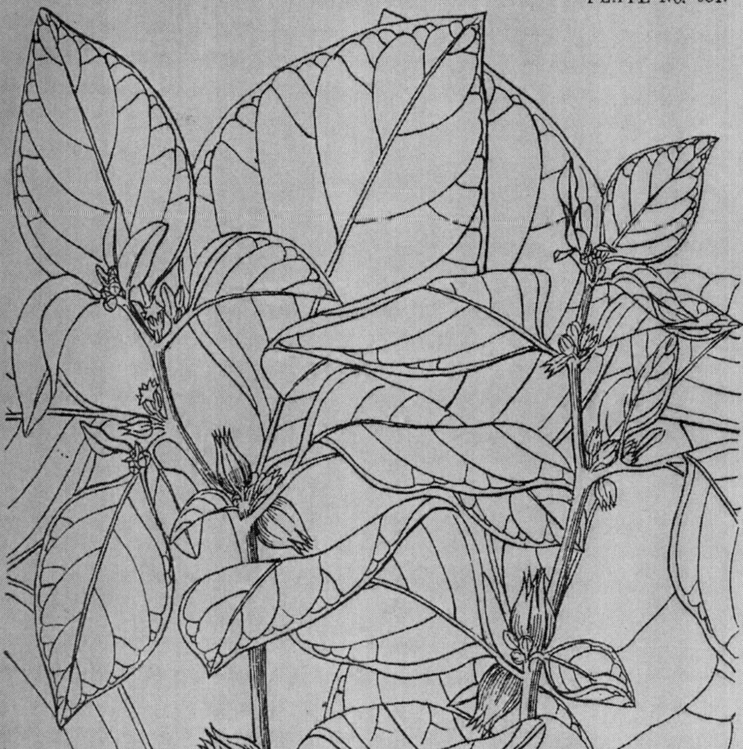

WITHANIA SOMNIFERA, *Dunal.*

PLATE No. 682.

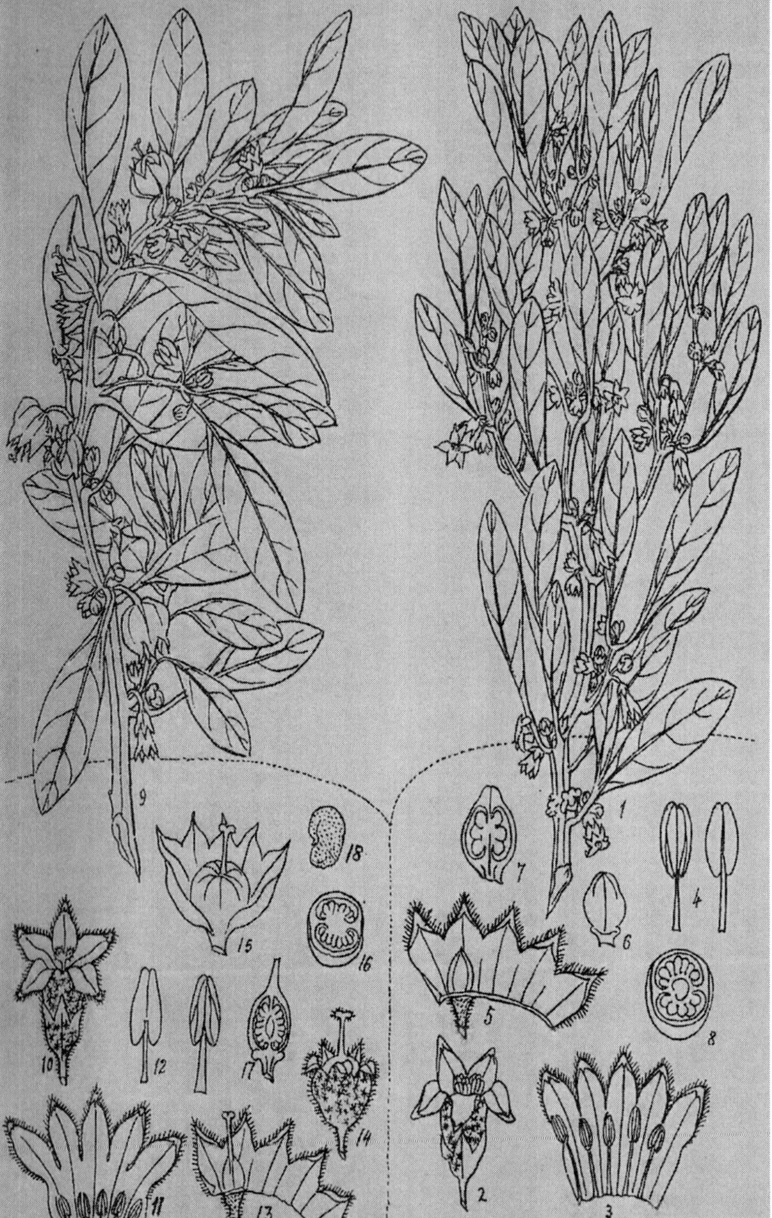

WITHANIA COAGULANS, *DUNAL.*

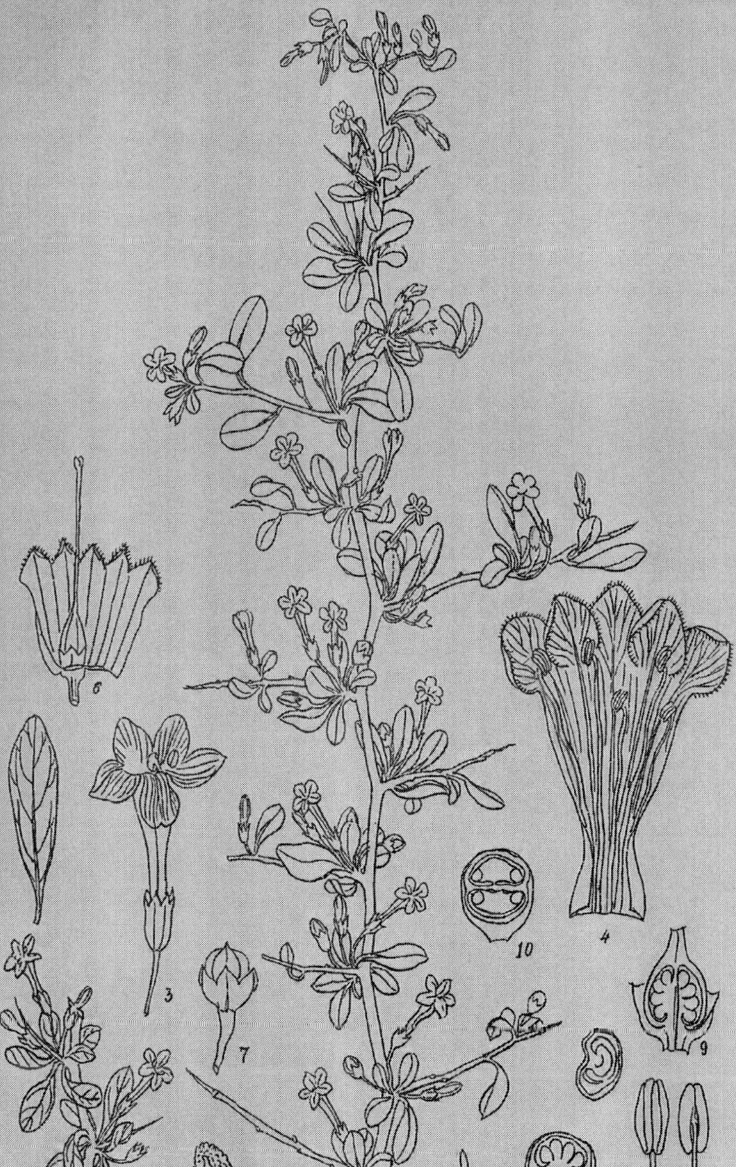

LYCIUM EUROPÆUM, *LINN.*

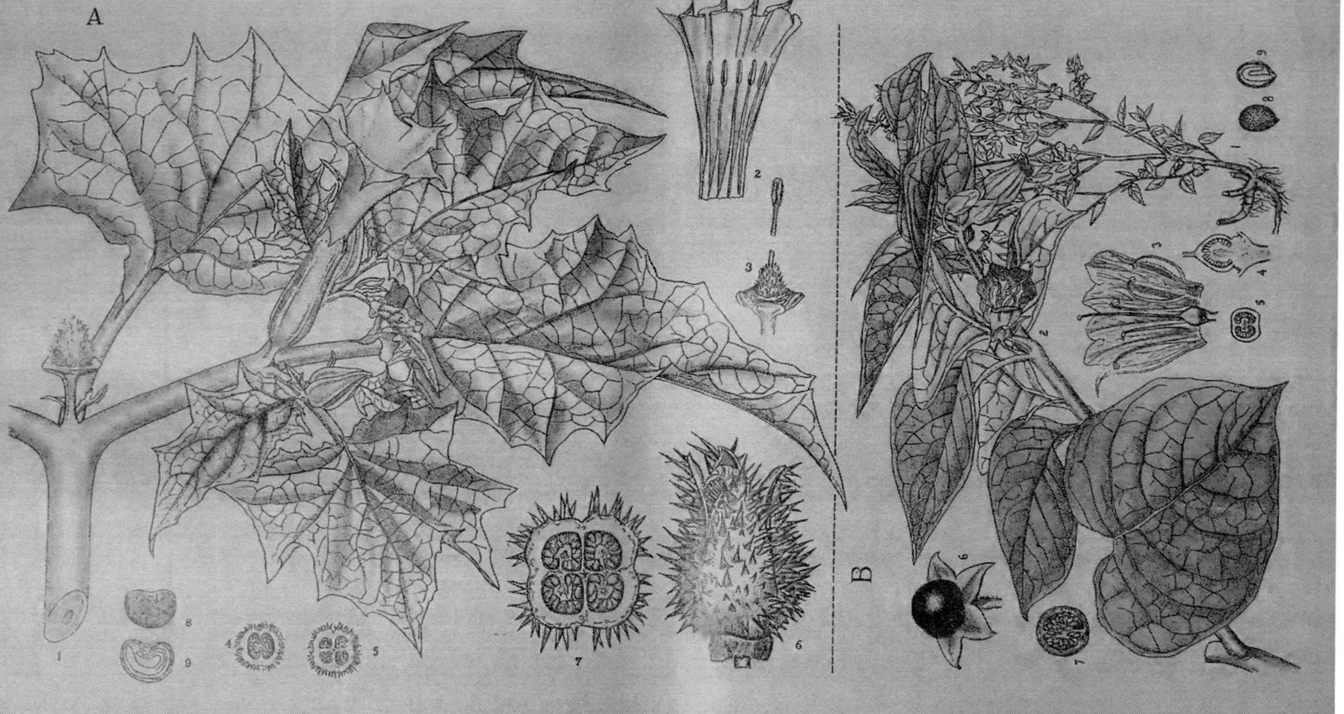

A—DATURA STRAMONIUM, *Linn.*   B—ATROPA BELLADONNA, *Linn.*

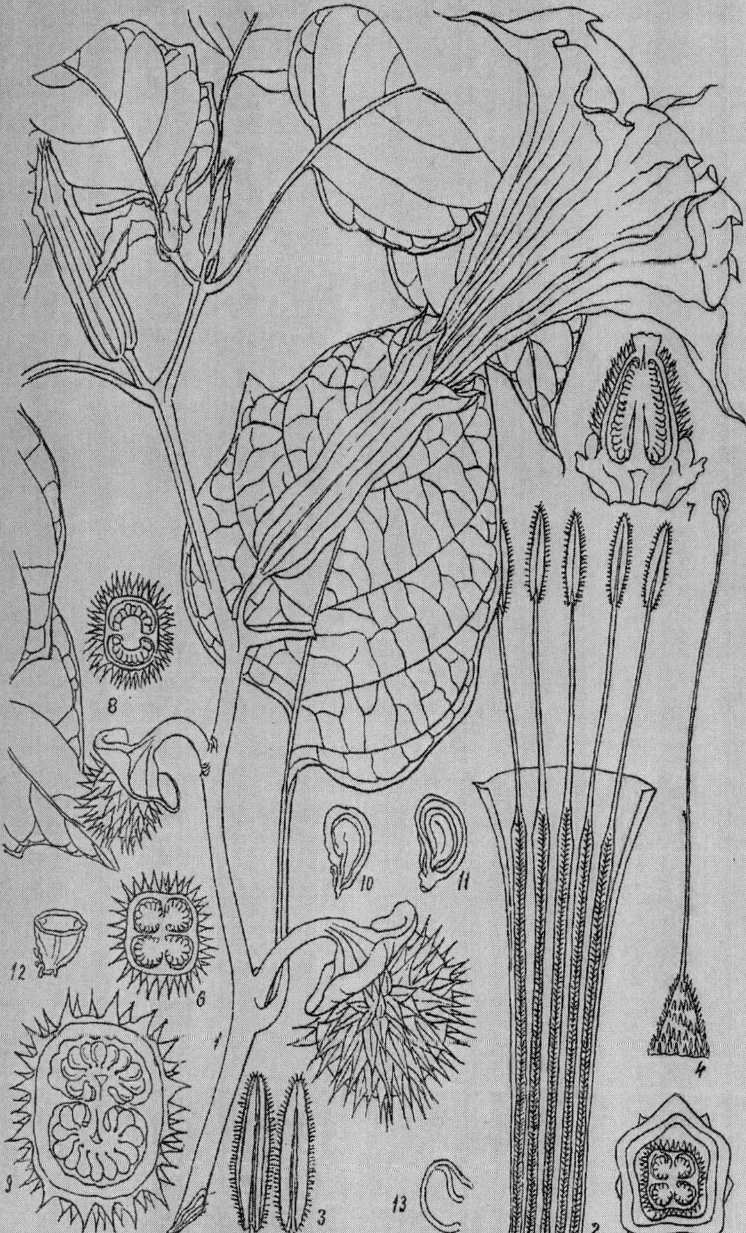

DATURA FASTUOSA, *Linn.*

PLATE No. 686.

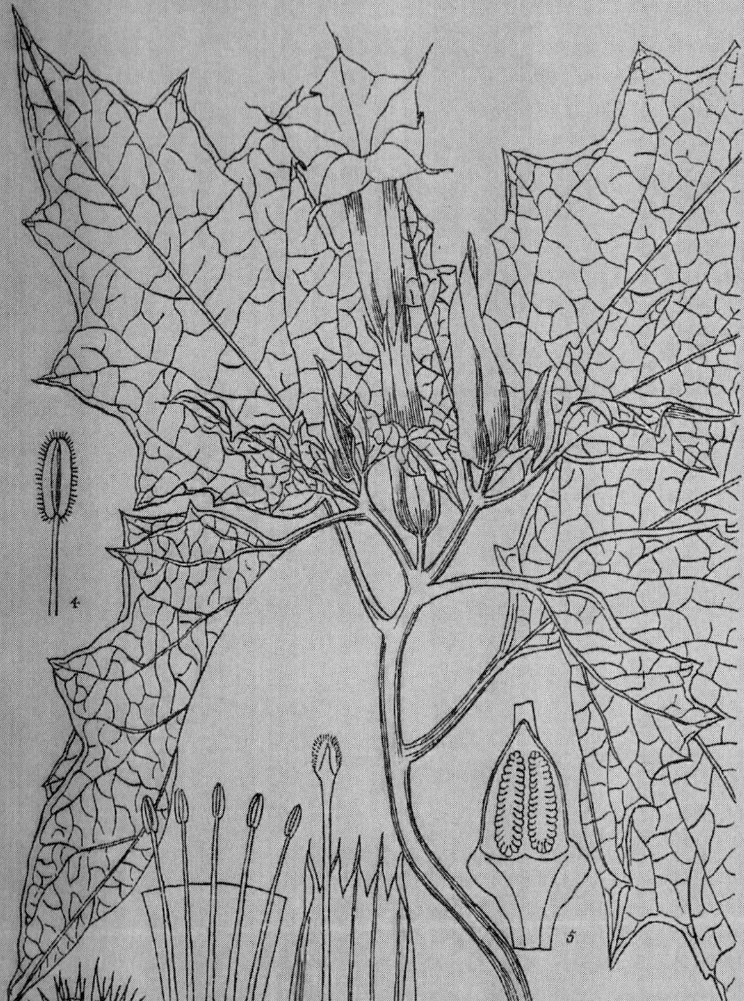

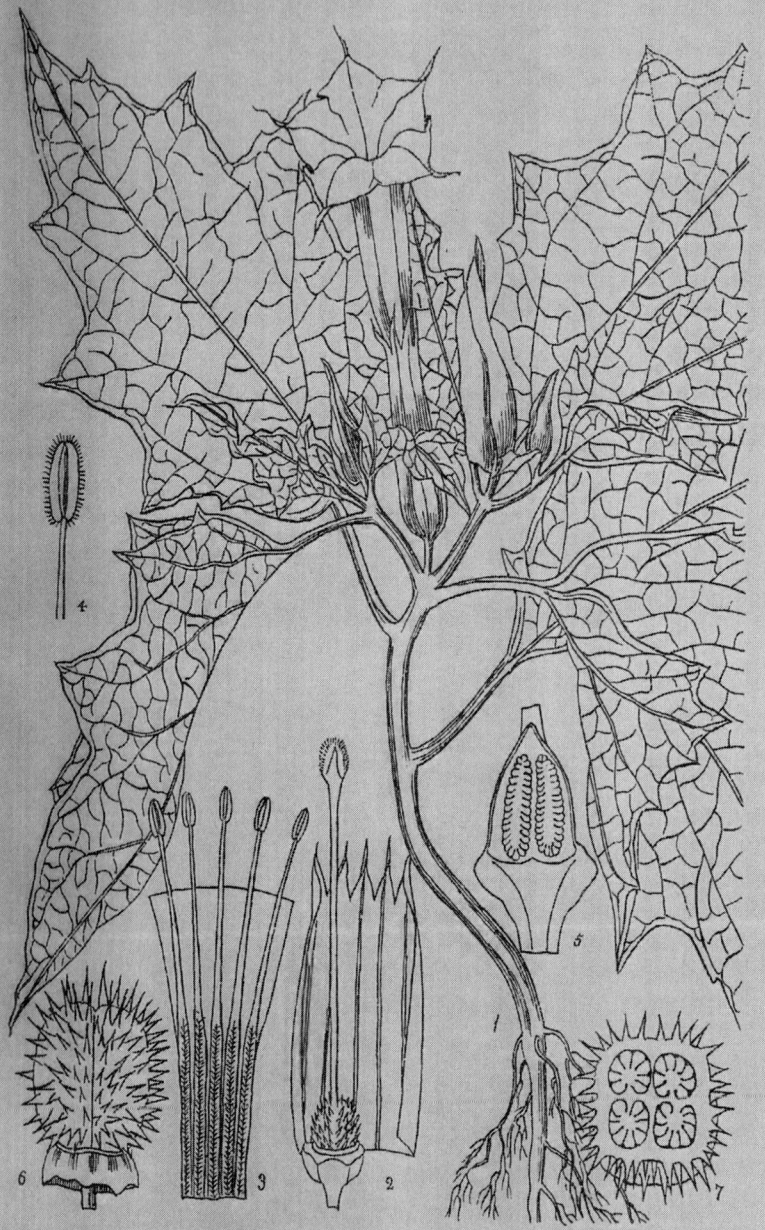

DATURA FASTUOSA, *LINN. VAR. ALBA.*

PLATE No. 687.

A—SCOPOLIA LURIDA, *DUNAL.*

B—HYOSCYAMUS NIGER, *LINN.*

C—PHYSOCHLAINA PRÆALTA, *HOOK. F.*

PLATE No. 688.

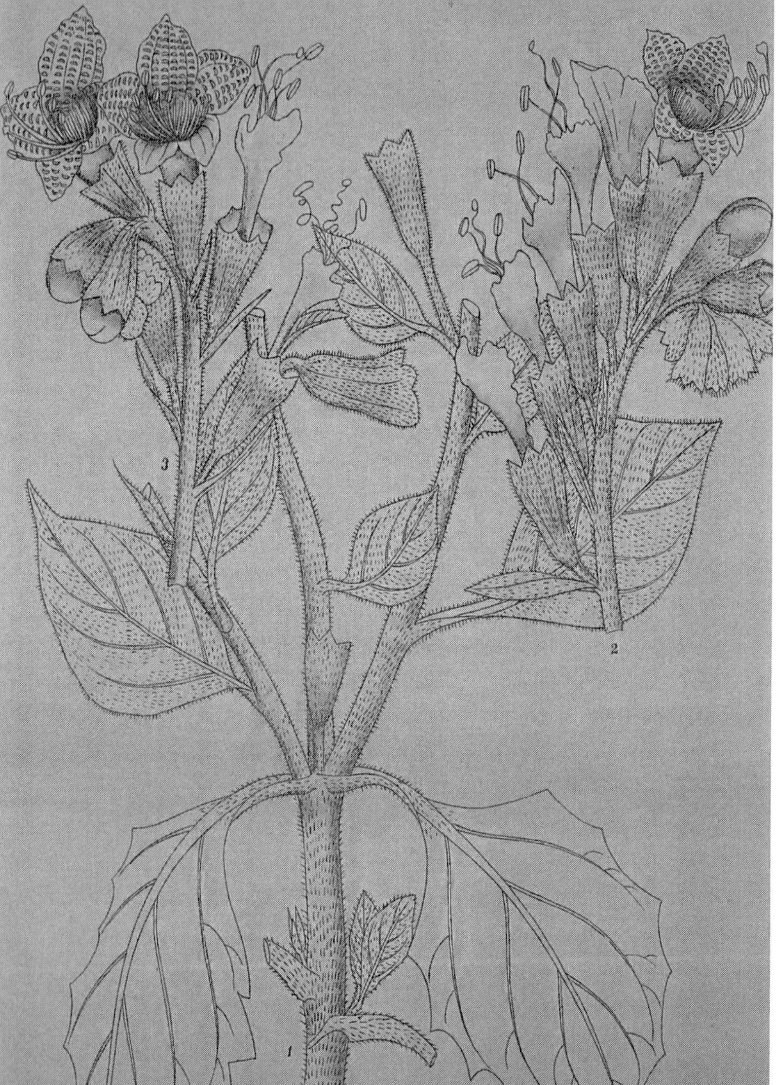

HYOSCYAMUS MUTICUS, *LINN.*

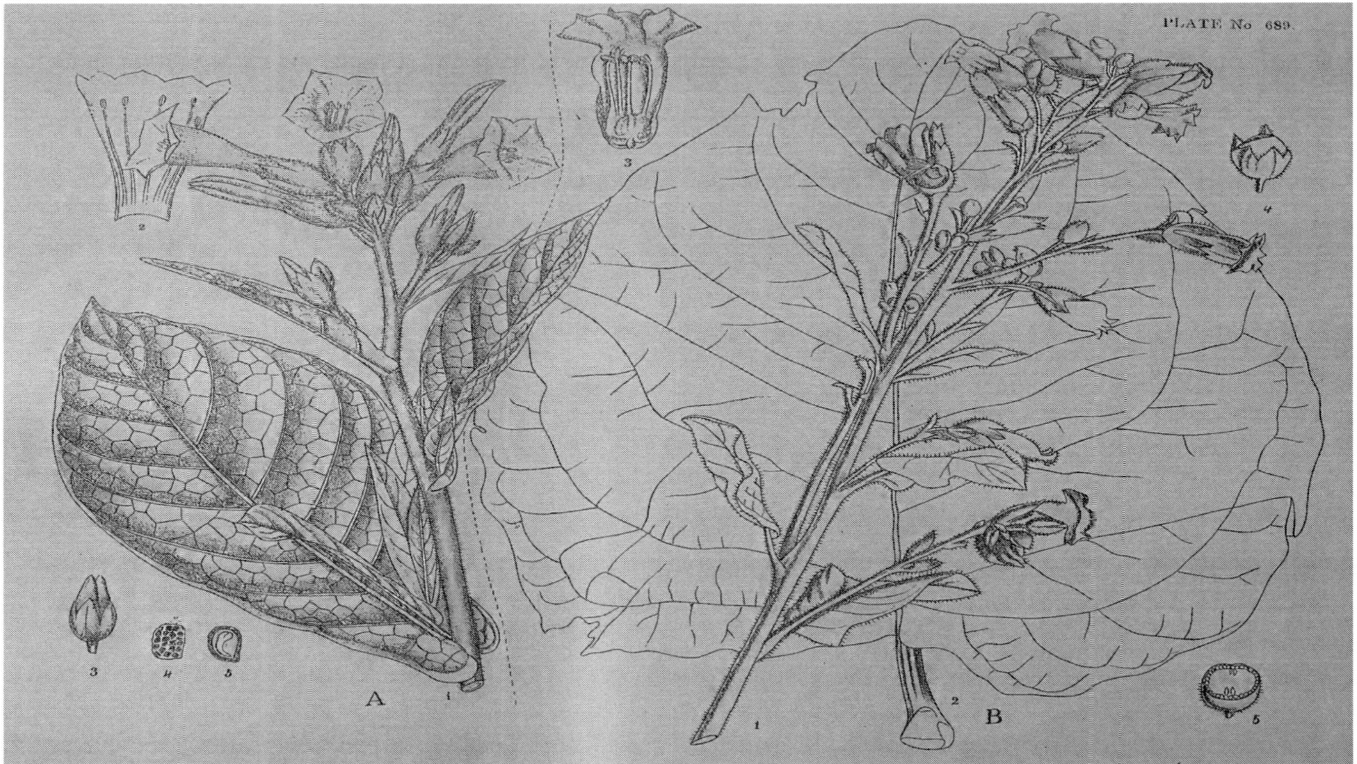

A–NICOTIANA TABACUM, *Linn.* B–NICOTIANA RUSTICA, *Linn.*

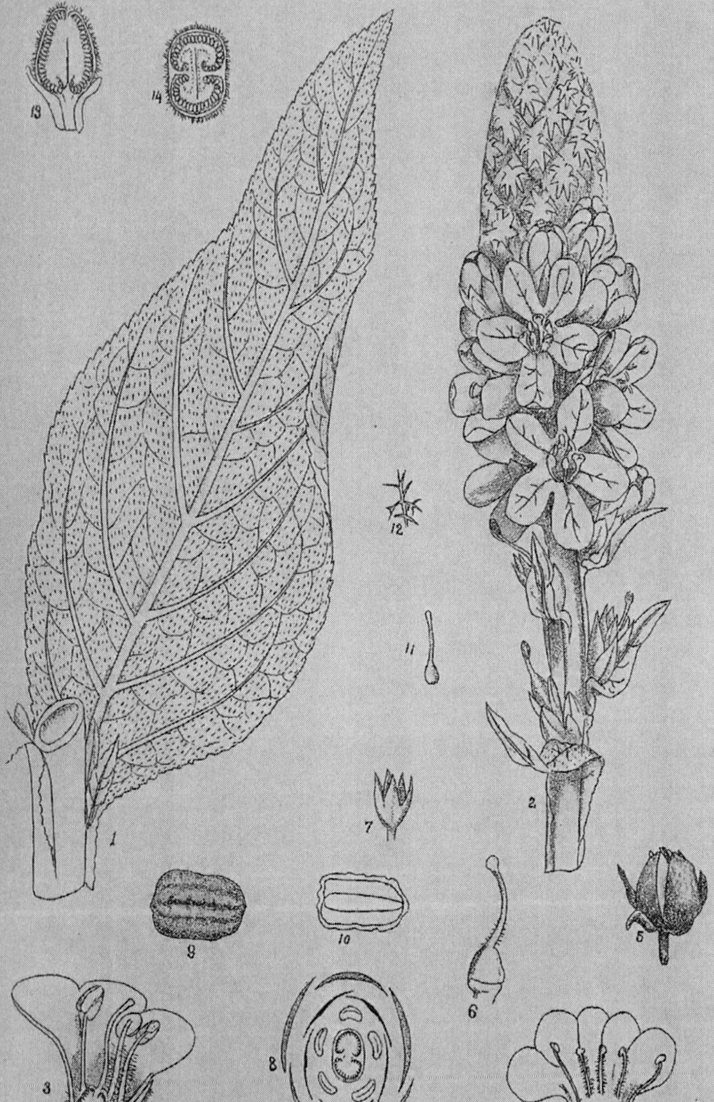

VERBASOUM THAPSUS, *LINN.*

PLATE No. 691.

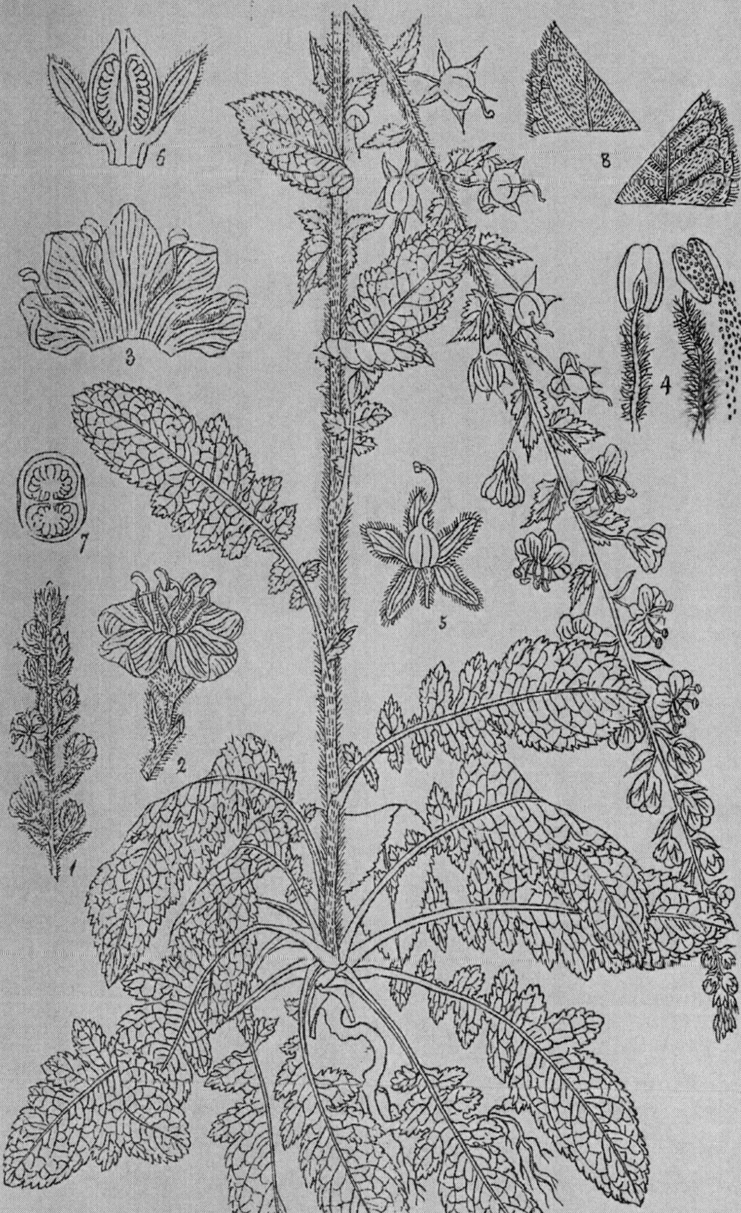

CELSIA COROMANDELIANA, *VAHL.*

PLATE No. 692.

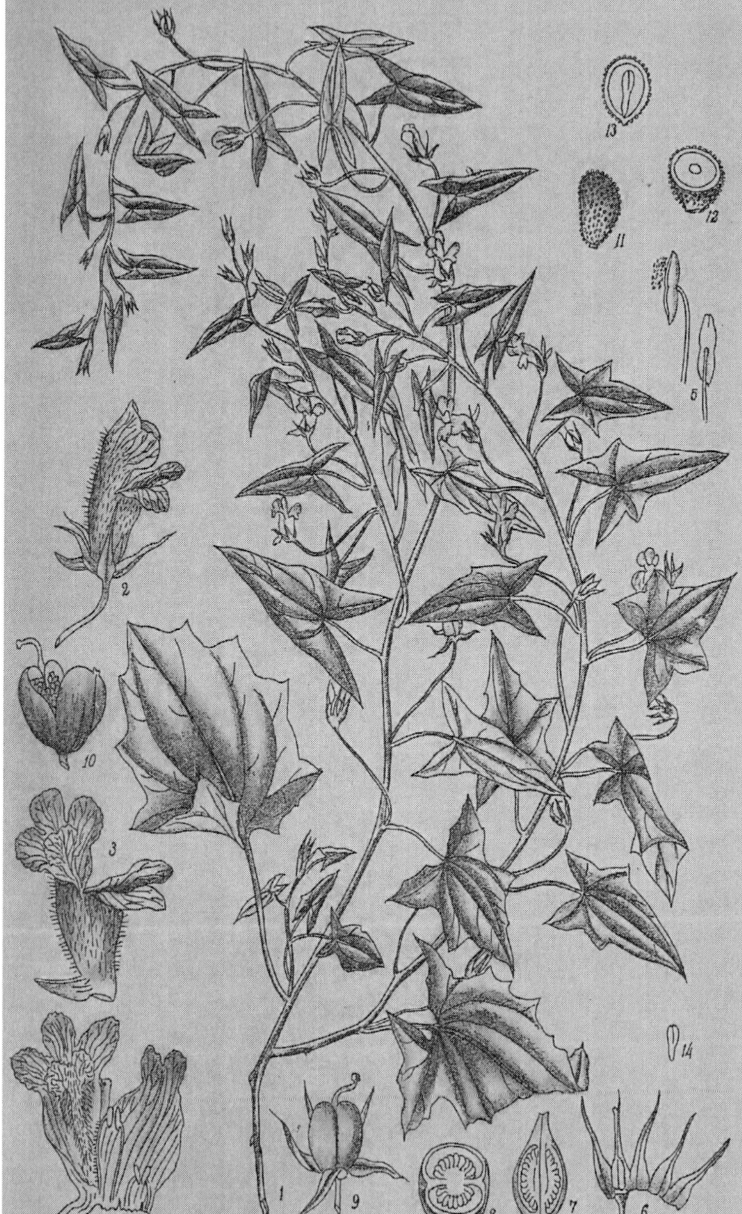

LINARIA RAMOSISSIMA, *WALL.*

PLATE No. 693.

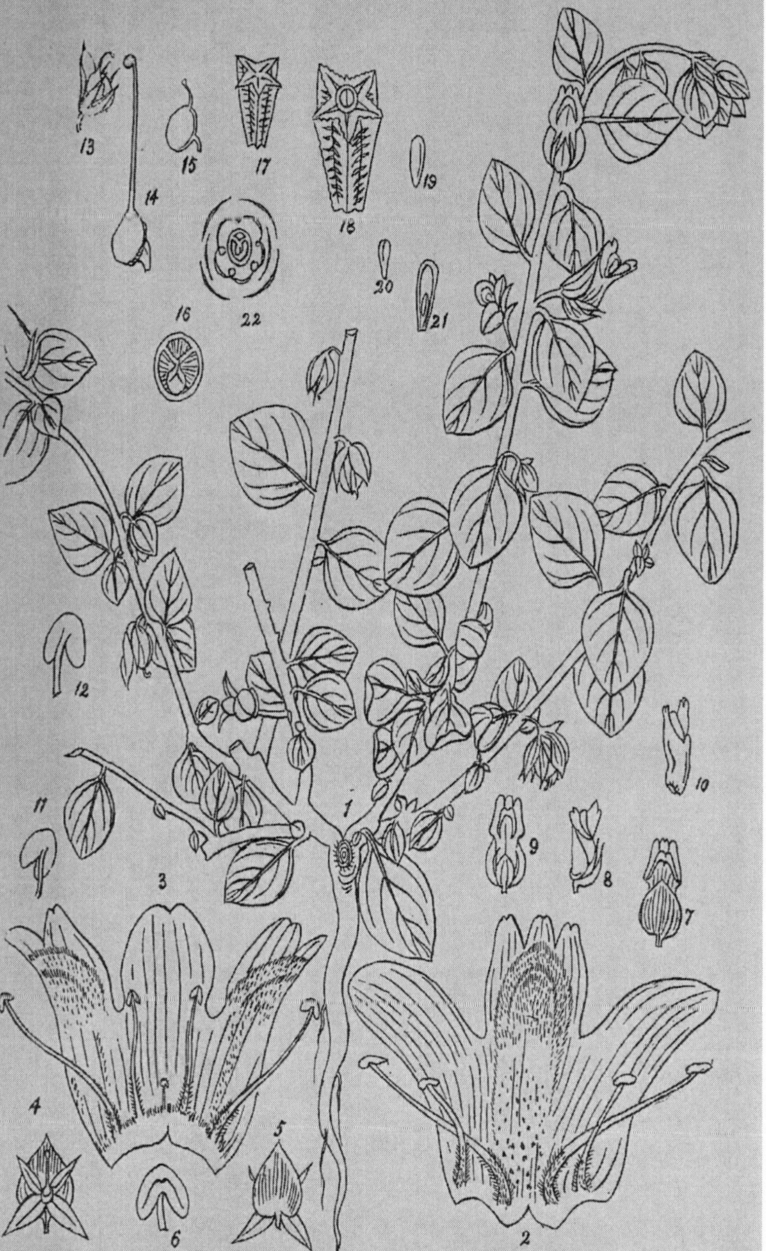

SCHWEINFURTHIA SPHÆROCARPA, *A. BRAUN.*

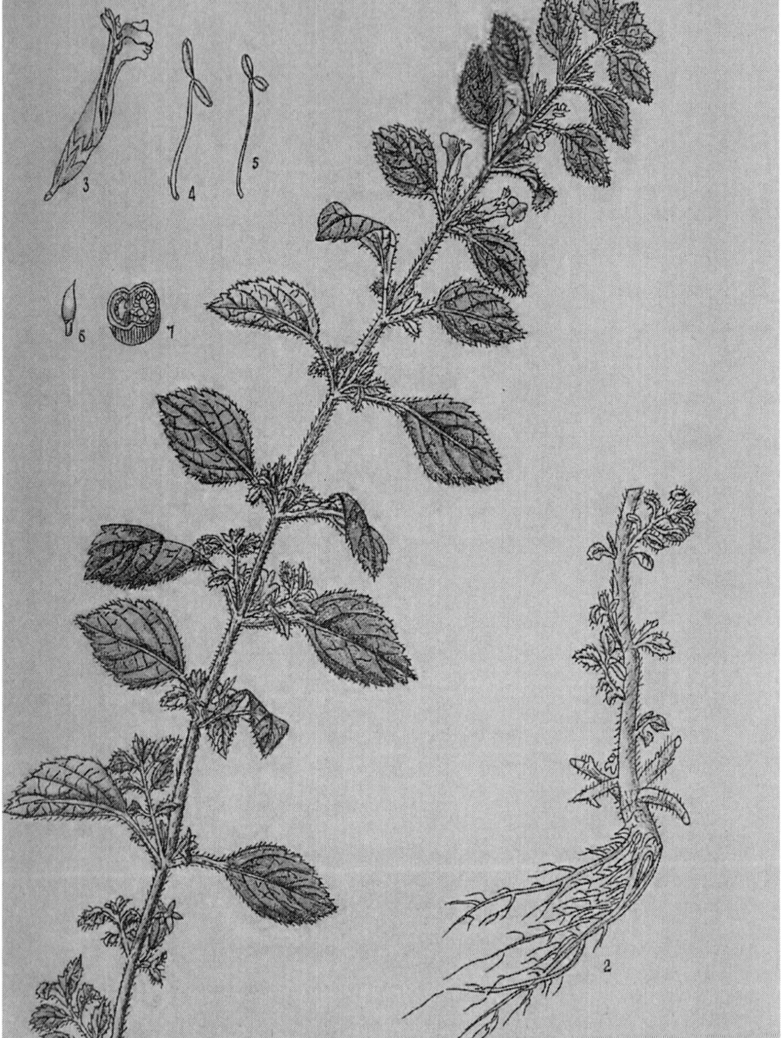

LINDENBERGIA URTICÆFOLIA, *LEHM.*

PLATE No. 695.

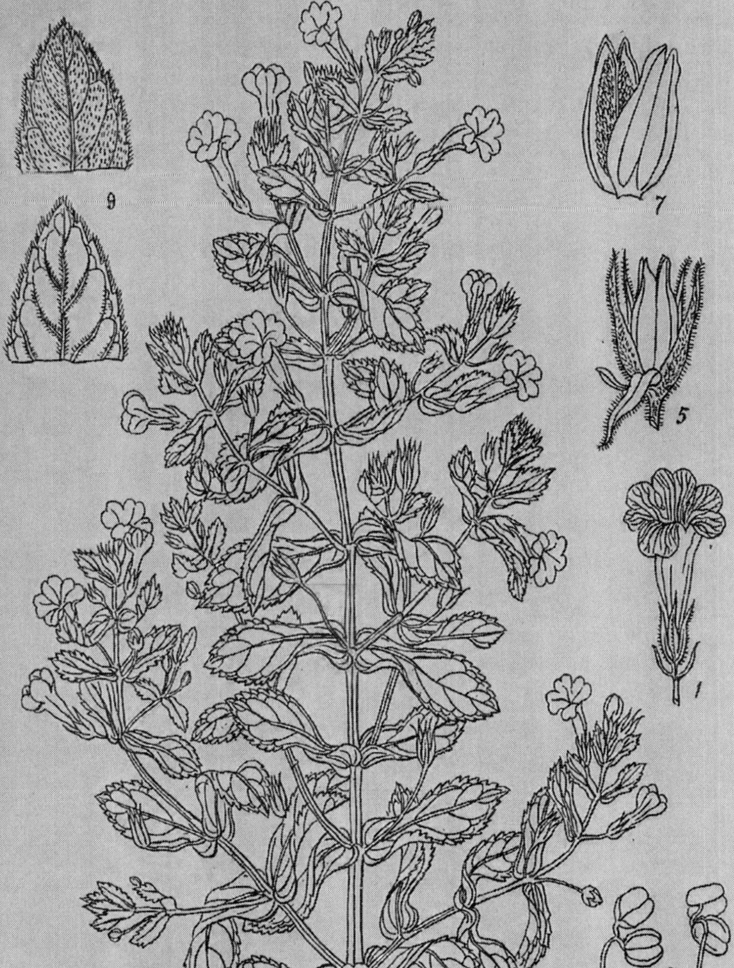

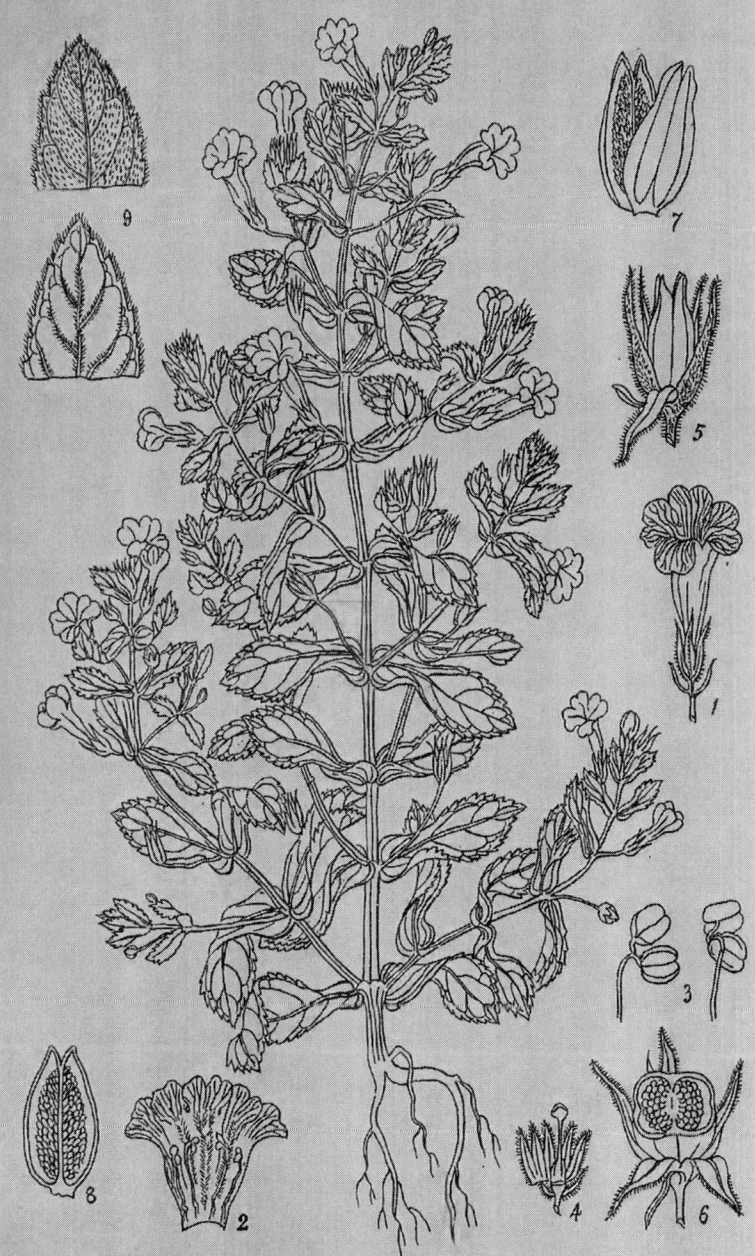

STEMODIA VISCOSA, *ROXB.*

PLATE No. 696.

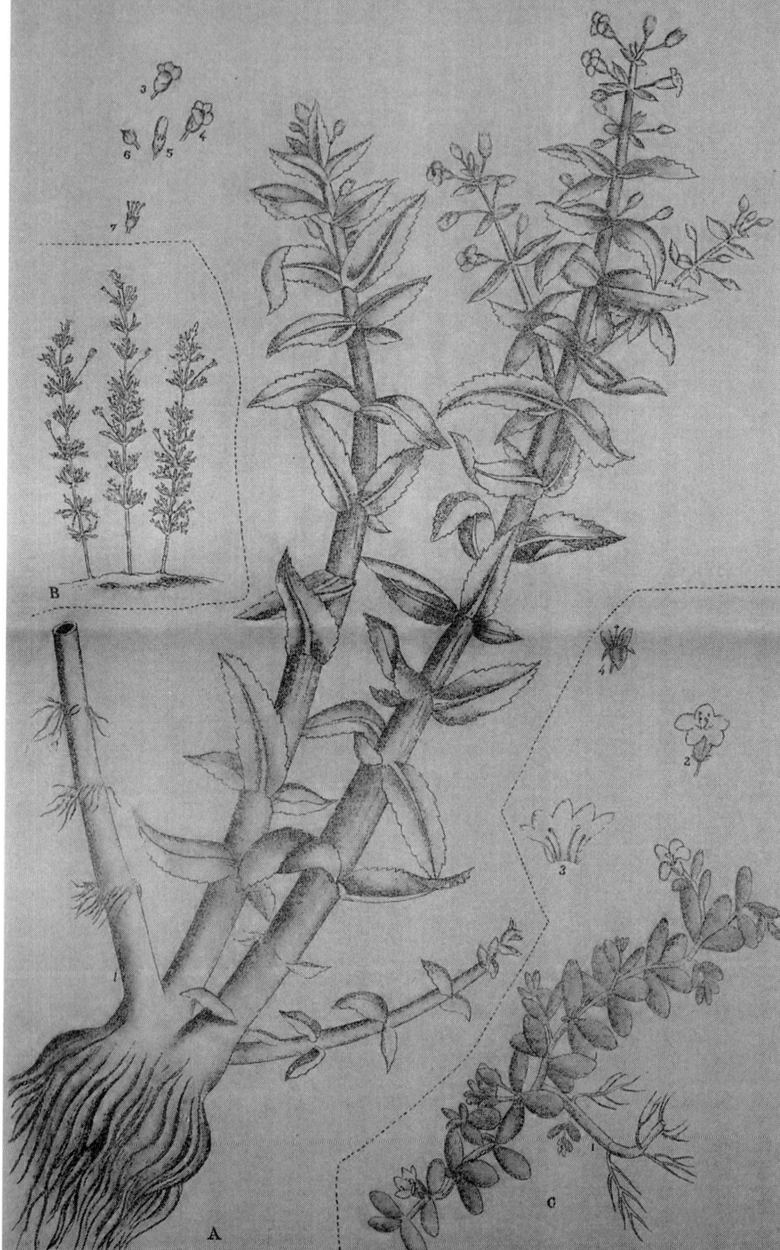

A—LIMNOPHILA GRATISSIMA, *Blume.* B—L. GRATIOLOIDES, *Br.* C—HERPESTIS MONNIERIA, *H. B. K.*

PLATE No. 697.

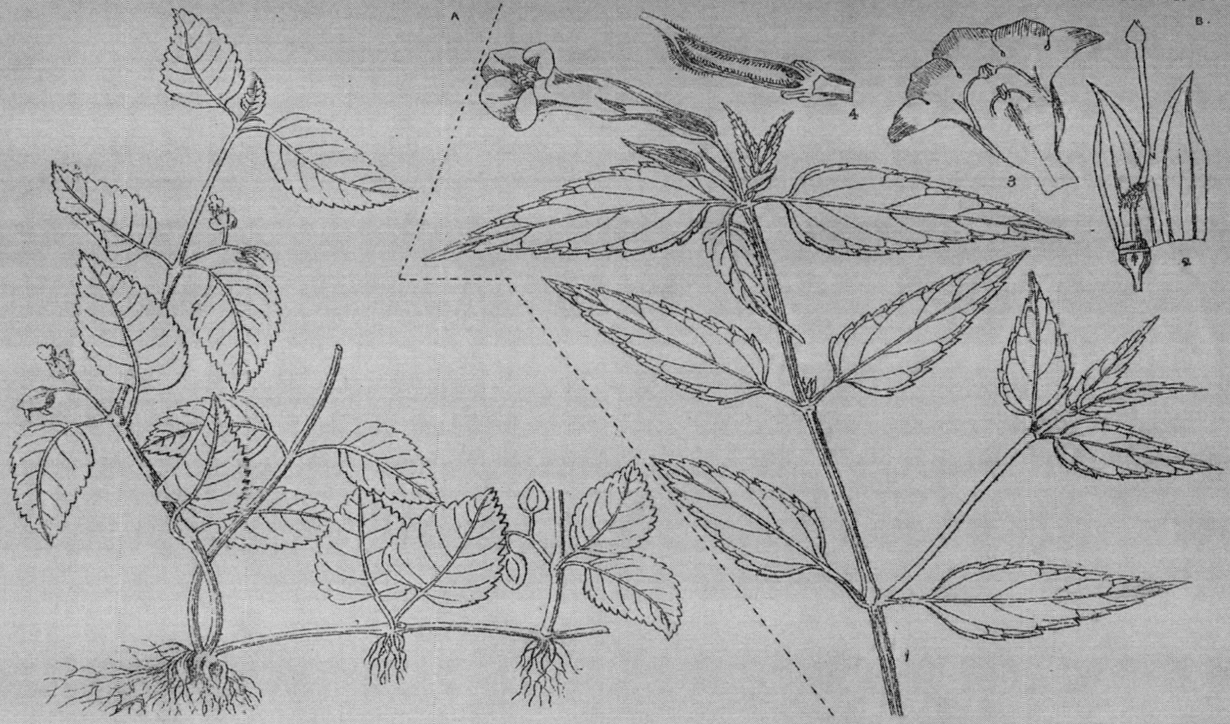

A--CURANGA AMARA, *JUSS.*

B—TORENIA ASIATICA, *LINN.*

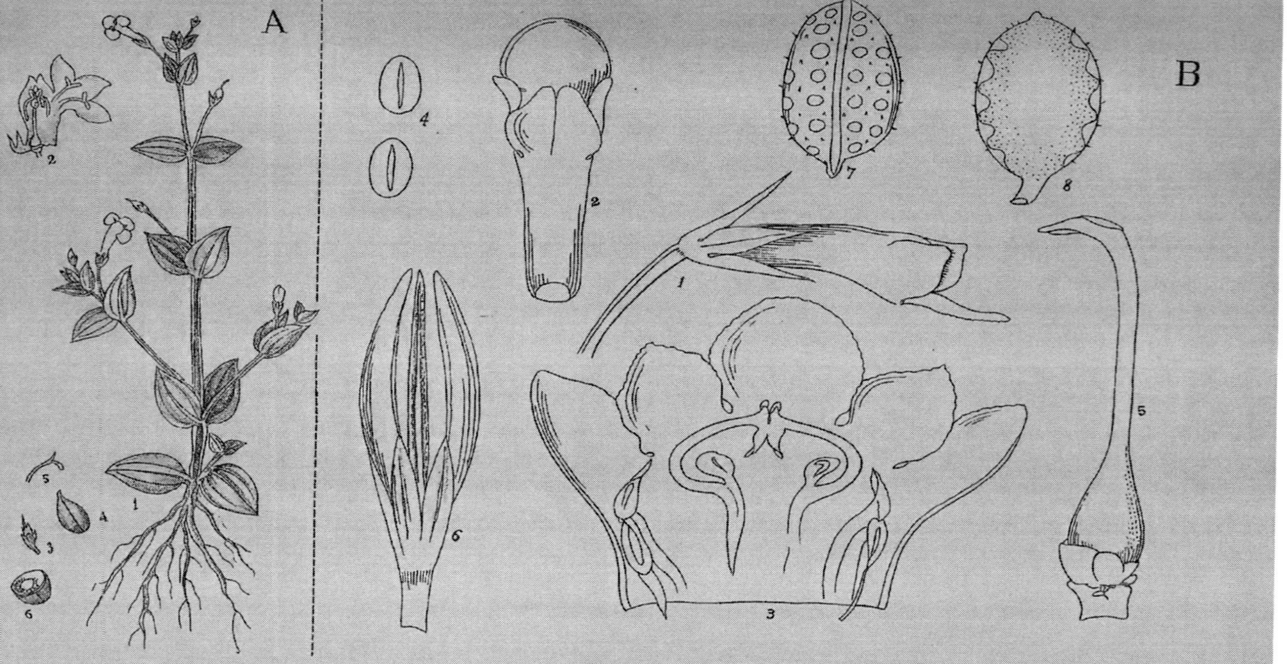

A—VANDELLIA ERECTA, *Benth.*

B—VANDELLIA PEDUNCULATA, *Benth.*

PLATE No. 699.

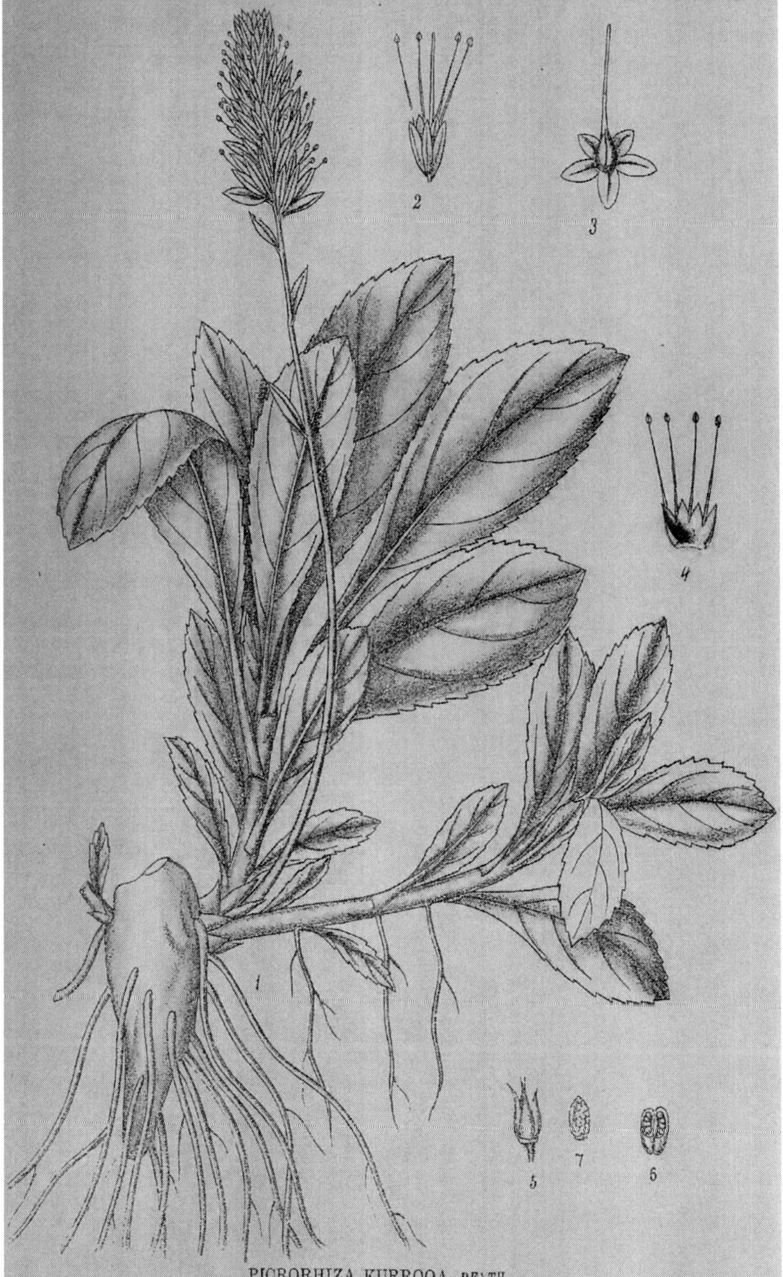

PICRORHIZA KURROOA, BENTH.

PLATE No. 700.

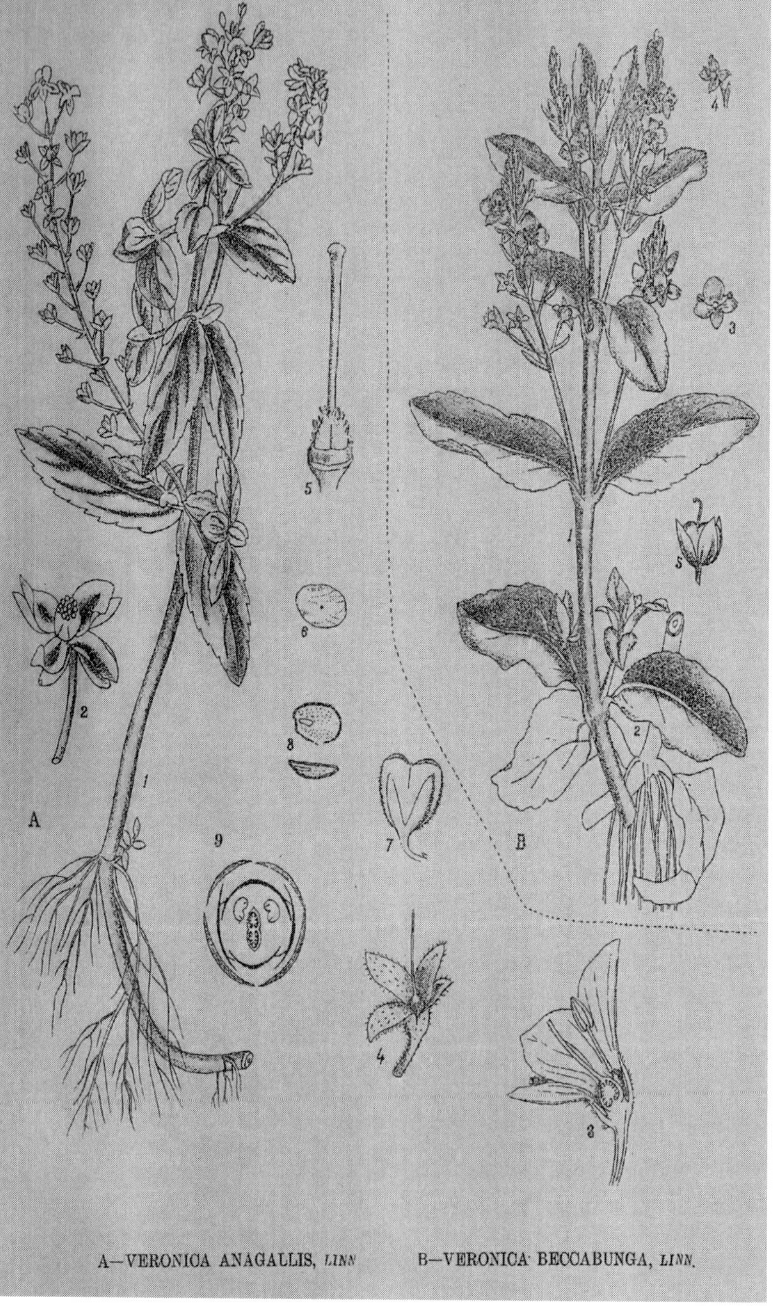

A—VERONICA ANAGALLIS, *LINN*   B—VERONICA BECCABUNGA, *LINN.*

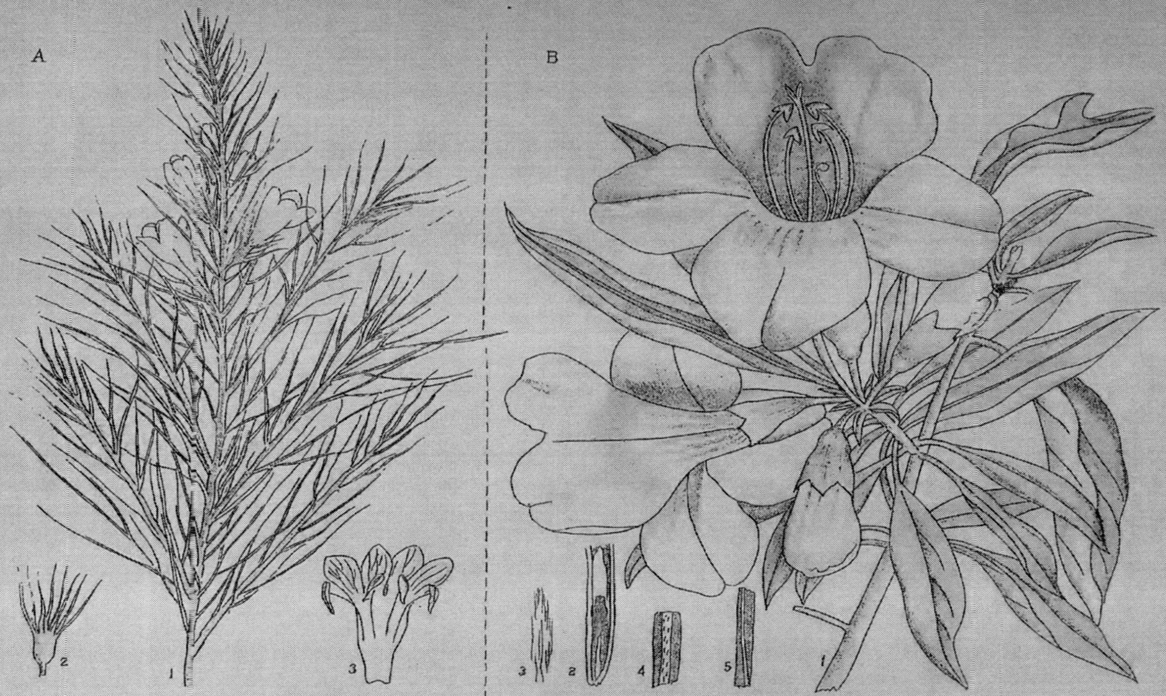

A—SOPUBIA DELPHINIFOLIA, *G. Don* B—TECOMA UNDULATA, *G. Don*

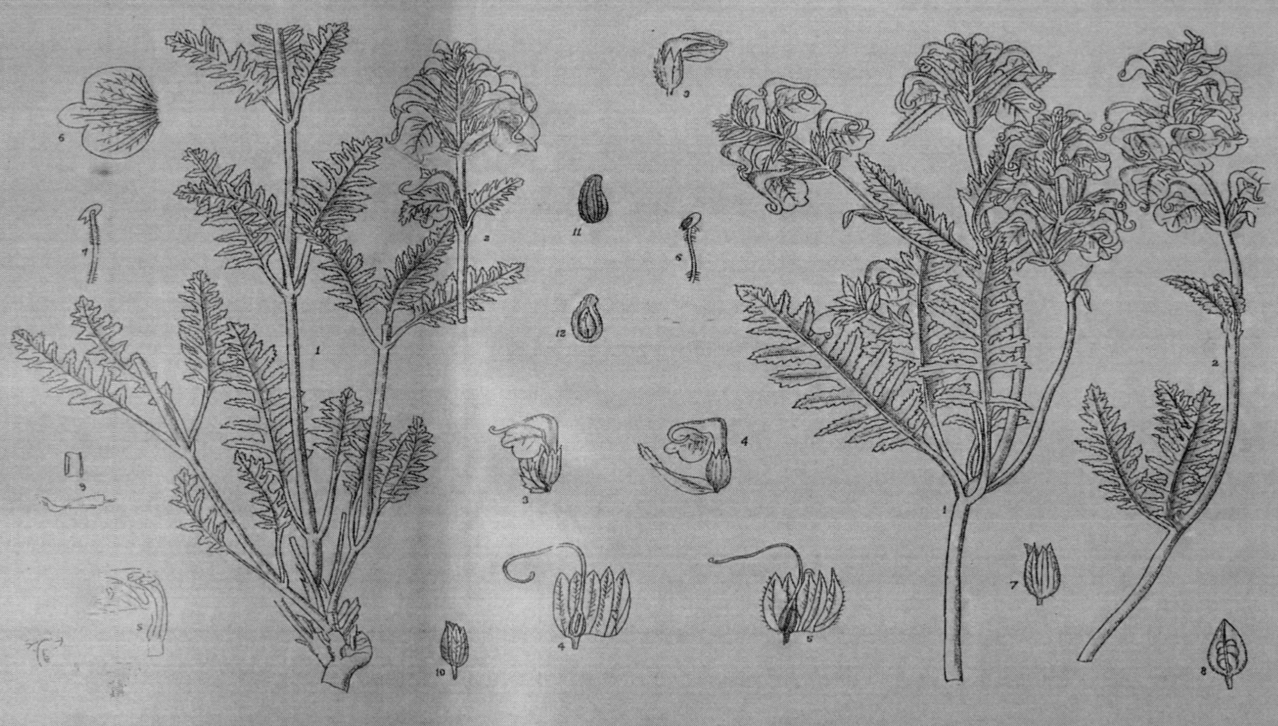

PEDICULARIS, PECTINATA, *Wall.*

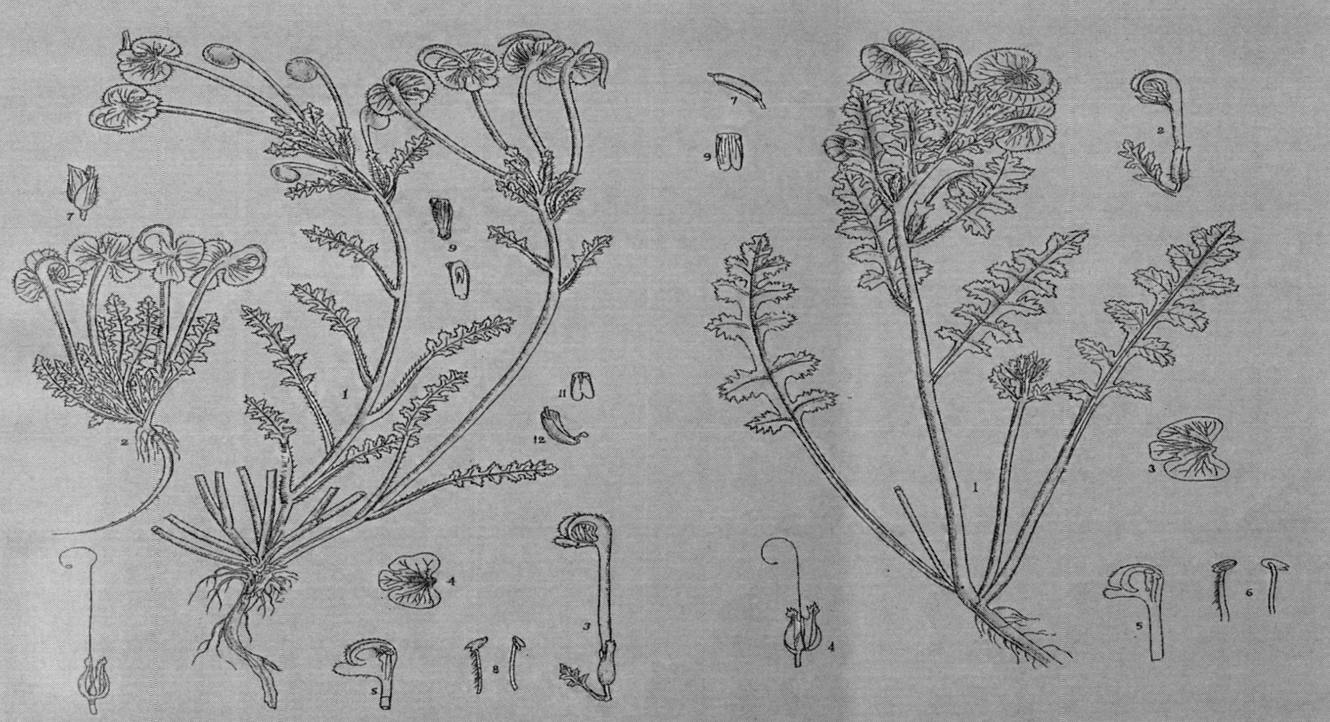

PEDICULARIS SIPHONANTHA, *D. DON.*

OROXYLUM INDICUM, Vent.

PLATE No. 705.

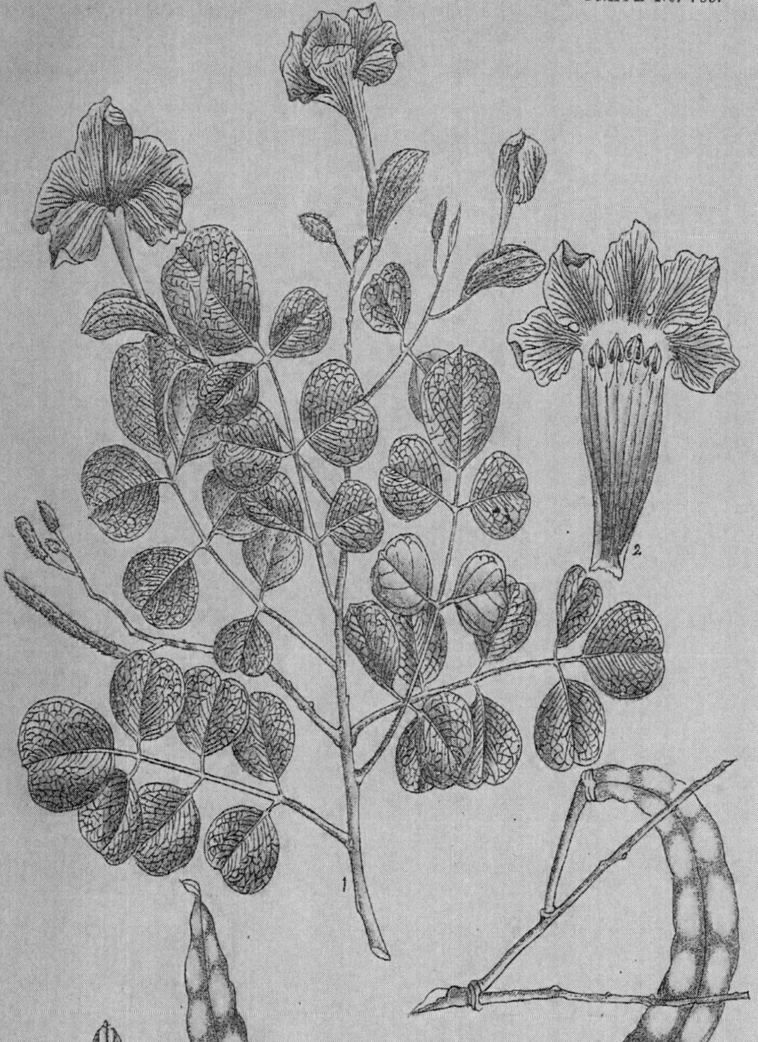

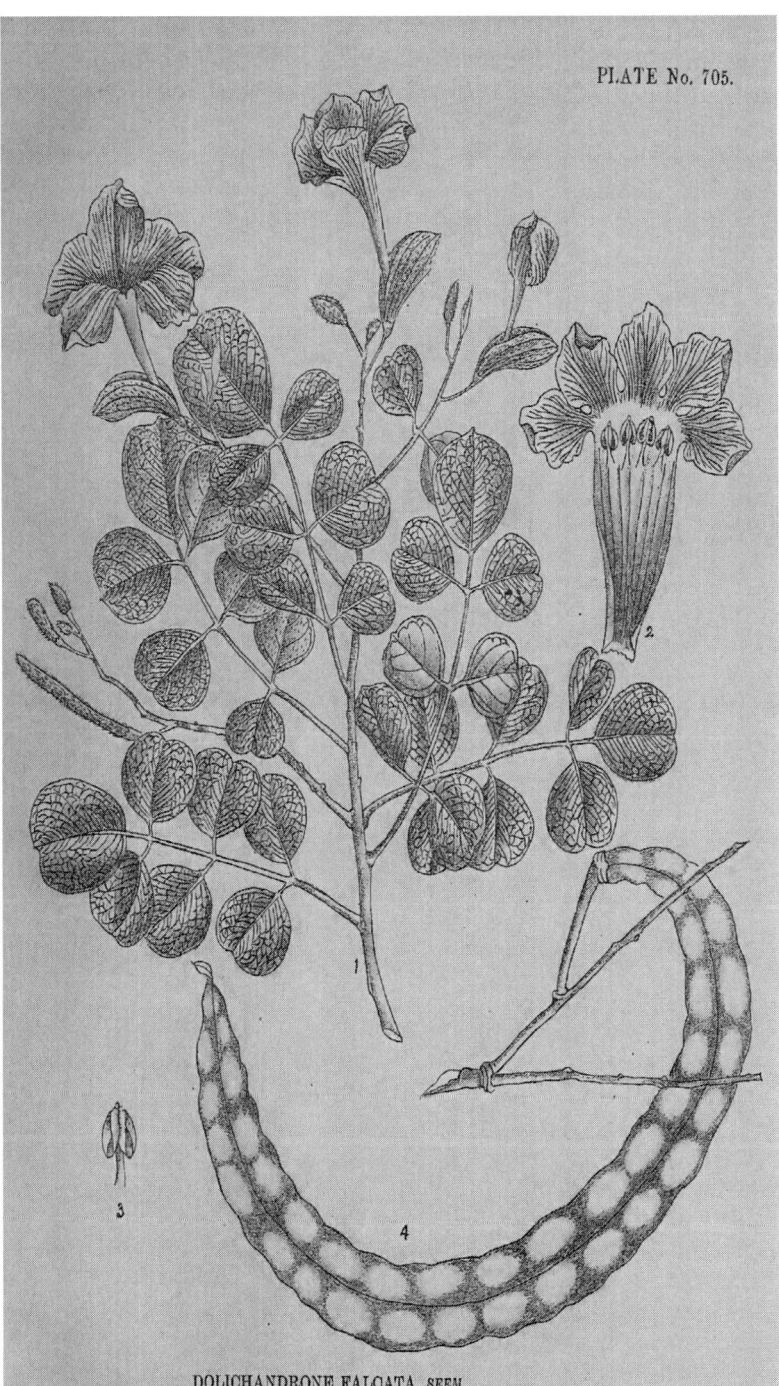

DOLICHANDRONE FALOATA, SEEM.

PLATE No. 706.

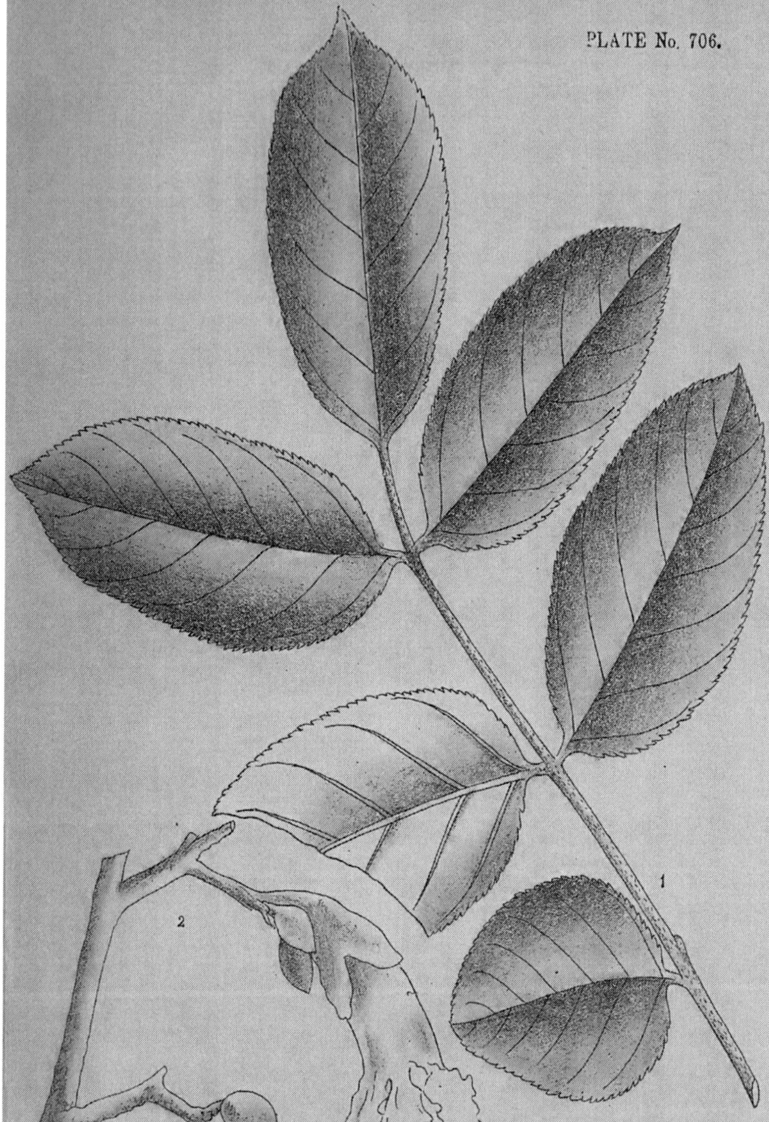

HETEROPHRAGMA ROXBURGHII, DC.

PLATE No. 707

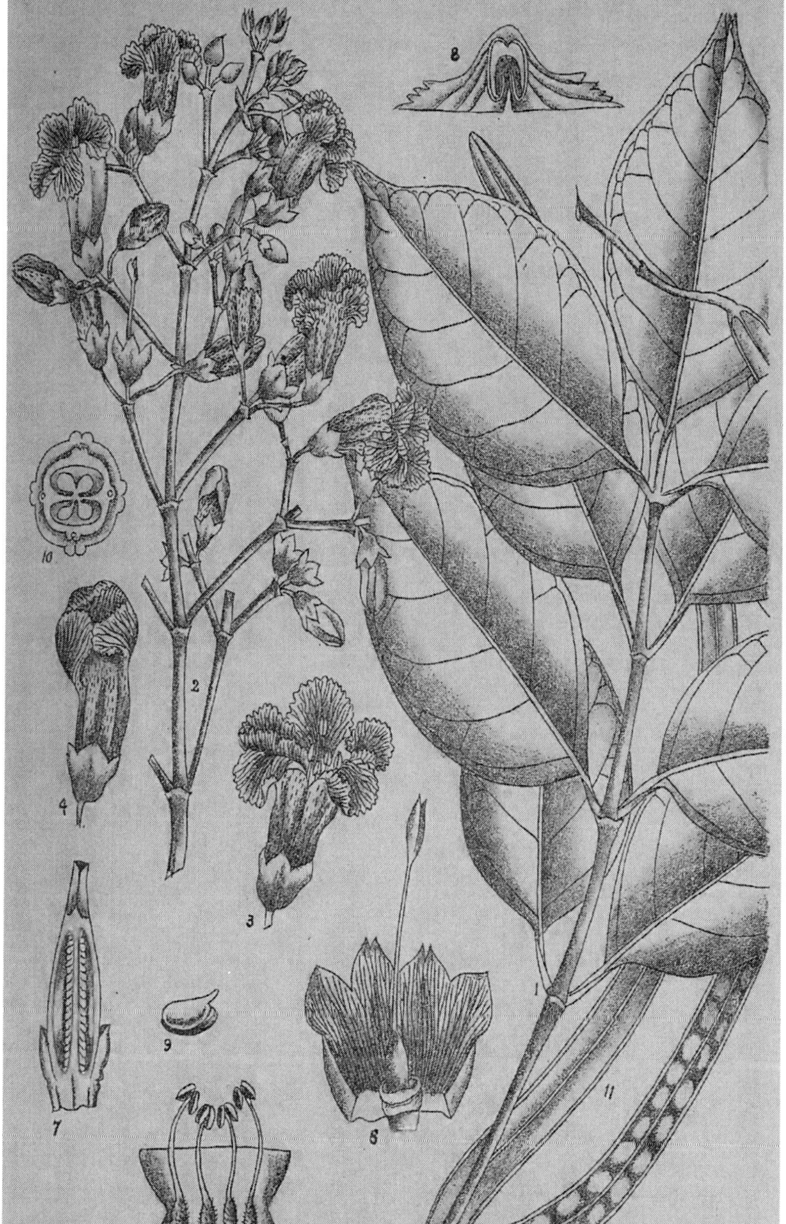

STEREOSPERMUM CHELONODIES, DC.

STEREOSPERMUM SUAVEOLENS, *DC.*

PLATE No. 709.

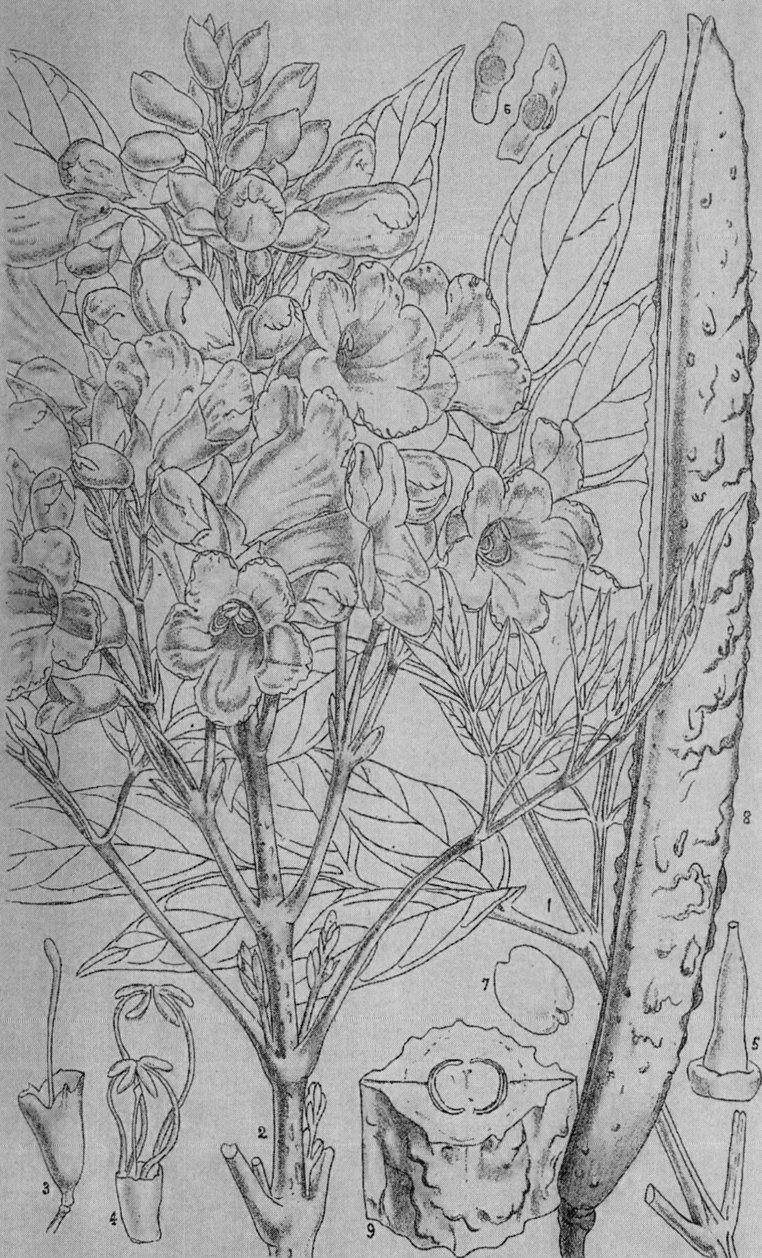

STEREOSPERMUM XYLOCARPUM, *WIGHT.*

PLATE No 710.

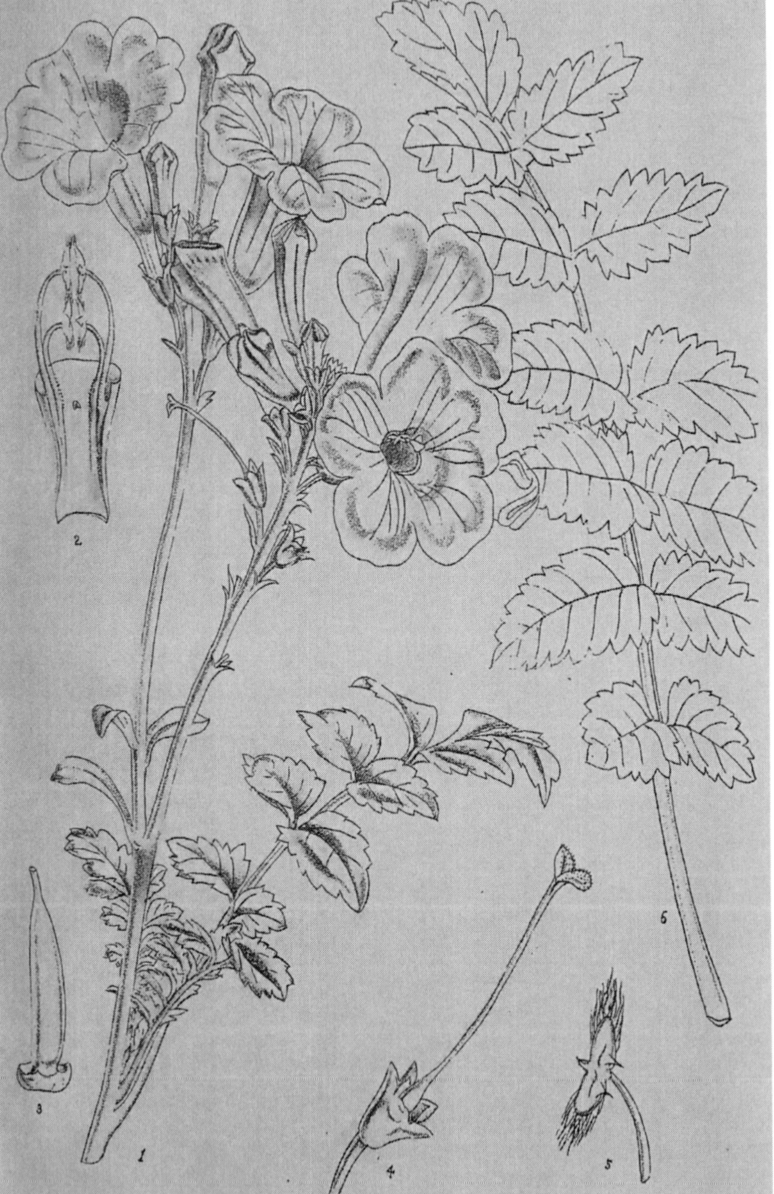

AMPHICOME EMODI, Lindl.

PLATE No. 711.

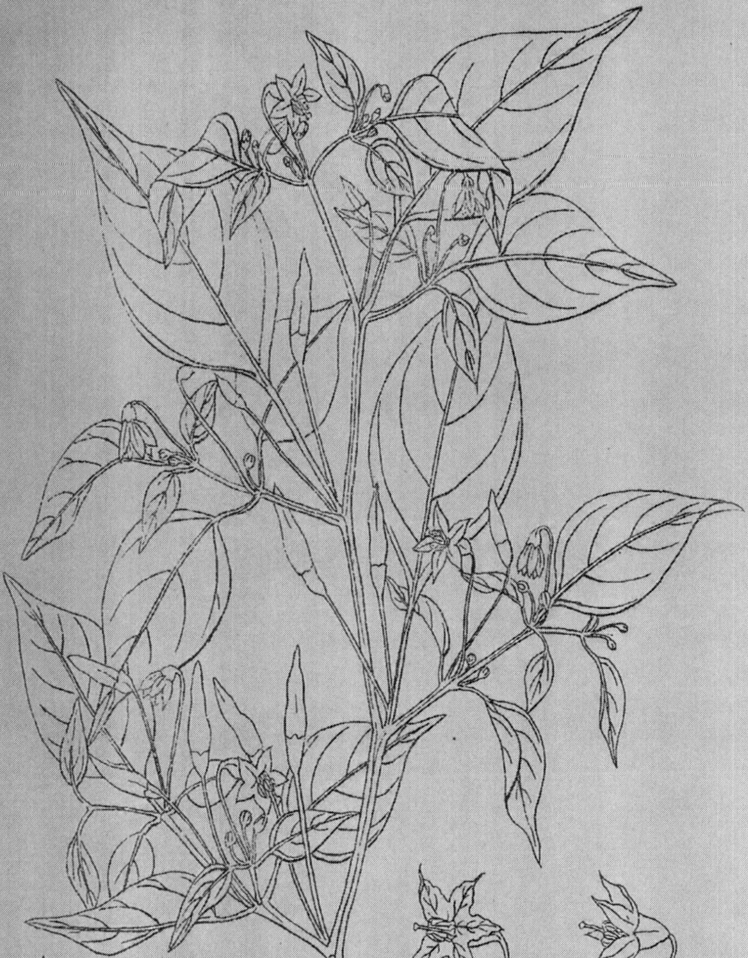

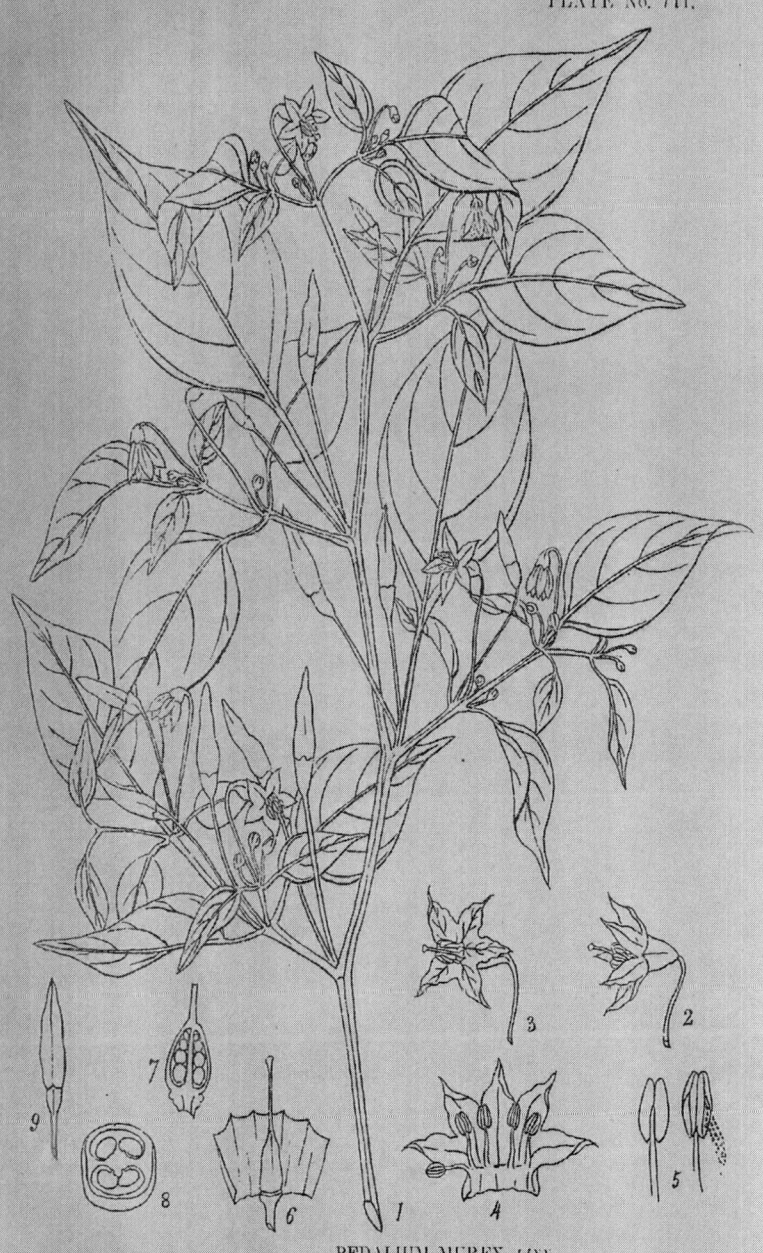

PEDALIUM MUREX, *LINN.*

PLATE No. 712.

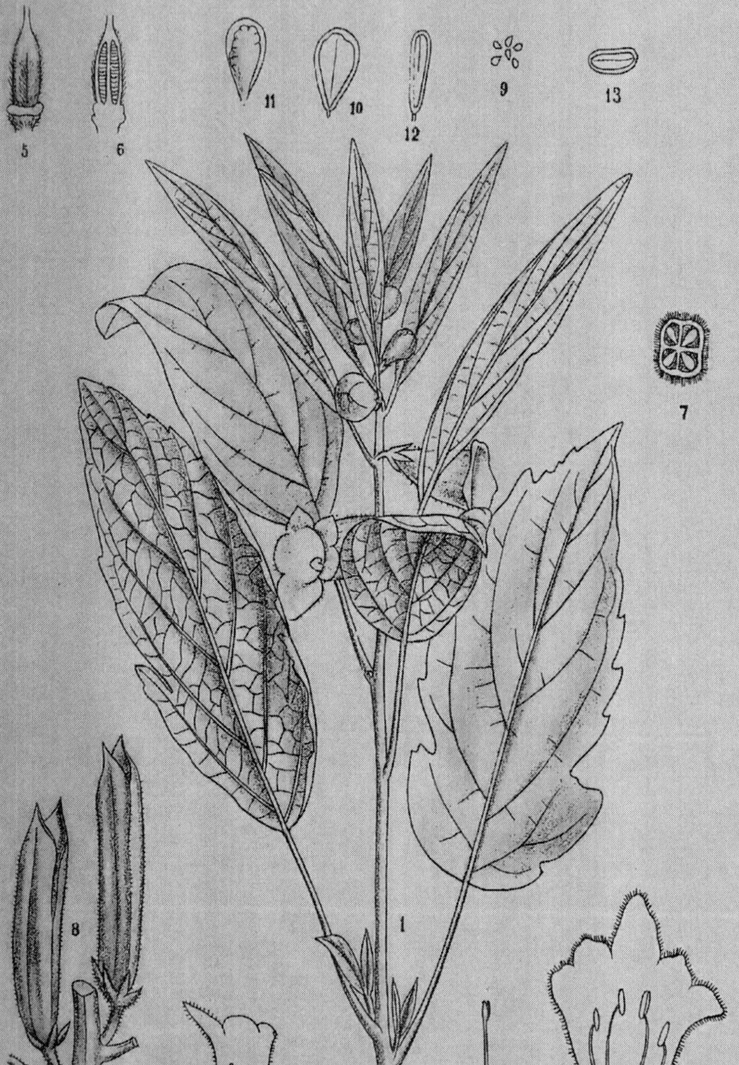

SESAMUM INDICUM, DC.

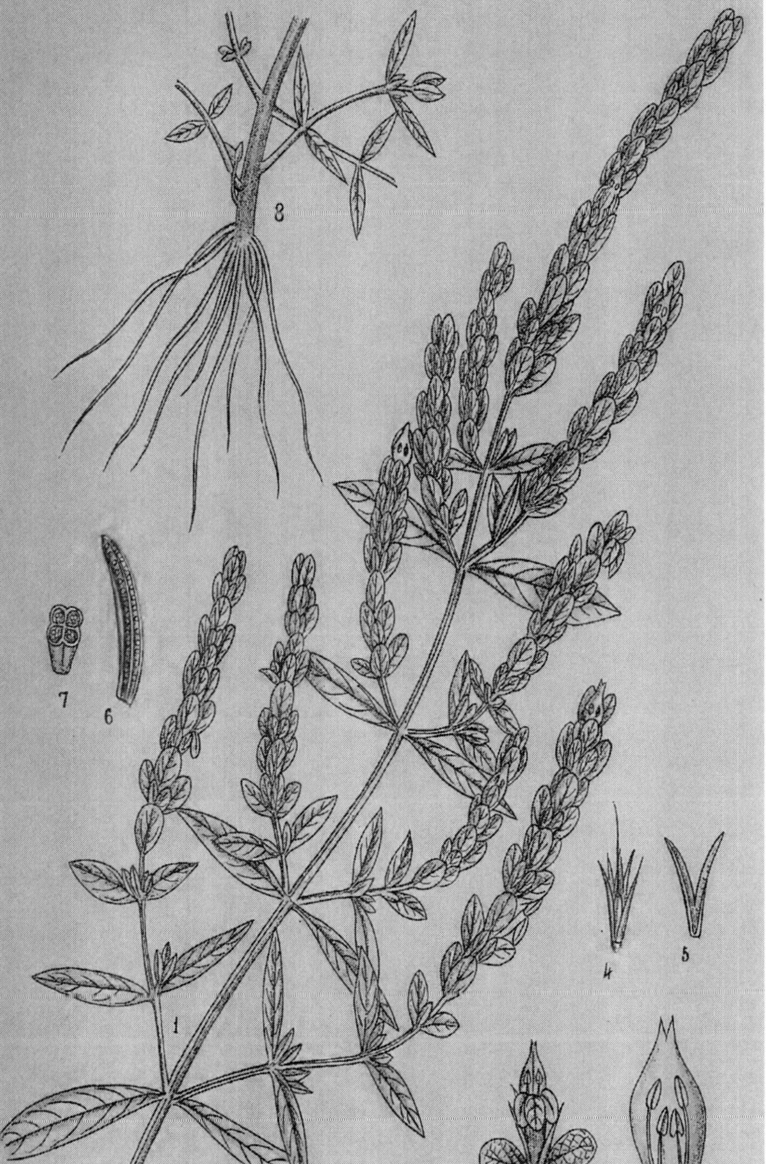

CARDANTHERA ULIGINOSA, HAM.

PLATE No. 714.

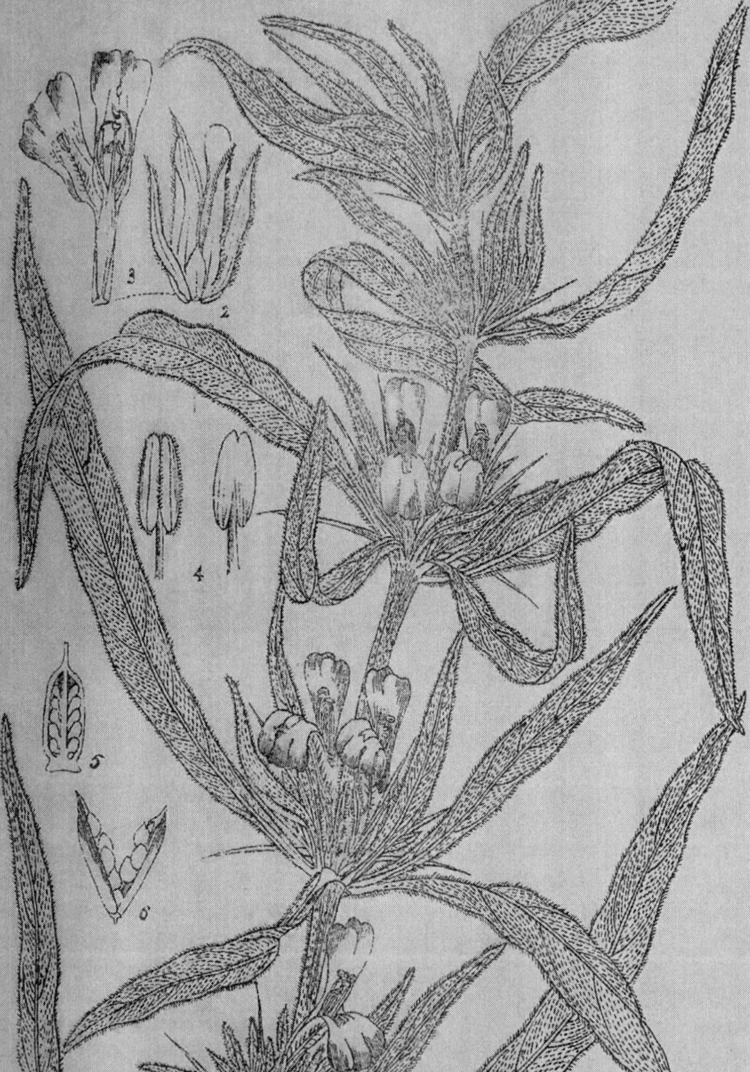

HYGROPHILA SPINOSA, T. ANDERS.

PLATE No. 715.

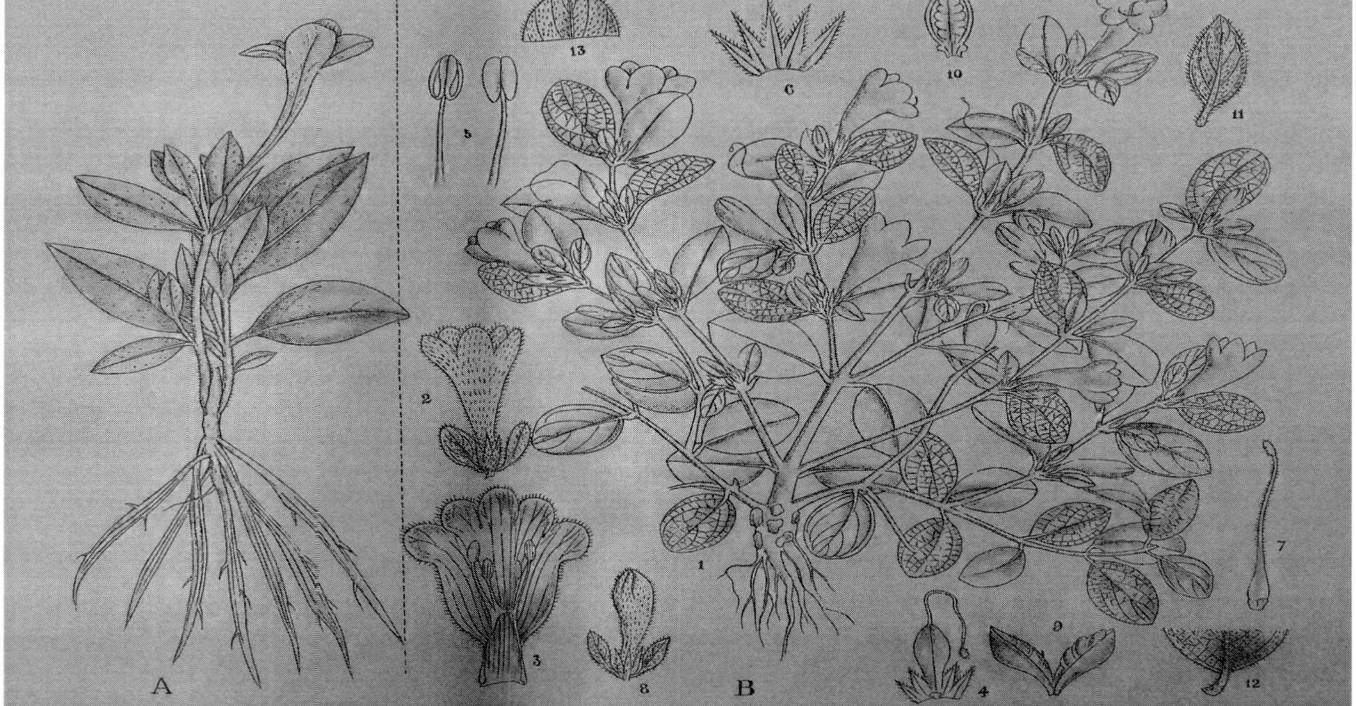

A—RUELLIA SUFFRUTICOSA, *Roxb.*　　B—RUELLIA PROSTRATA, *Lamk.*

DÆDALACANTHUS ROSEUS, *T. Anders.*

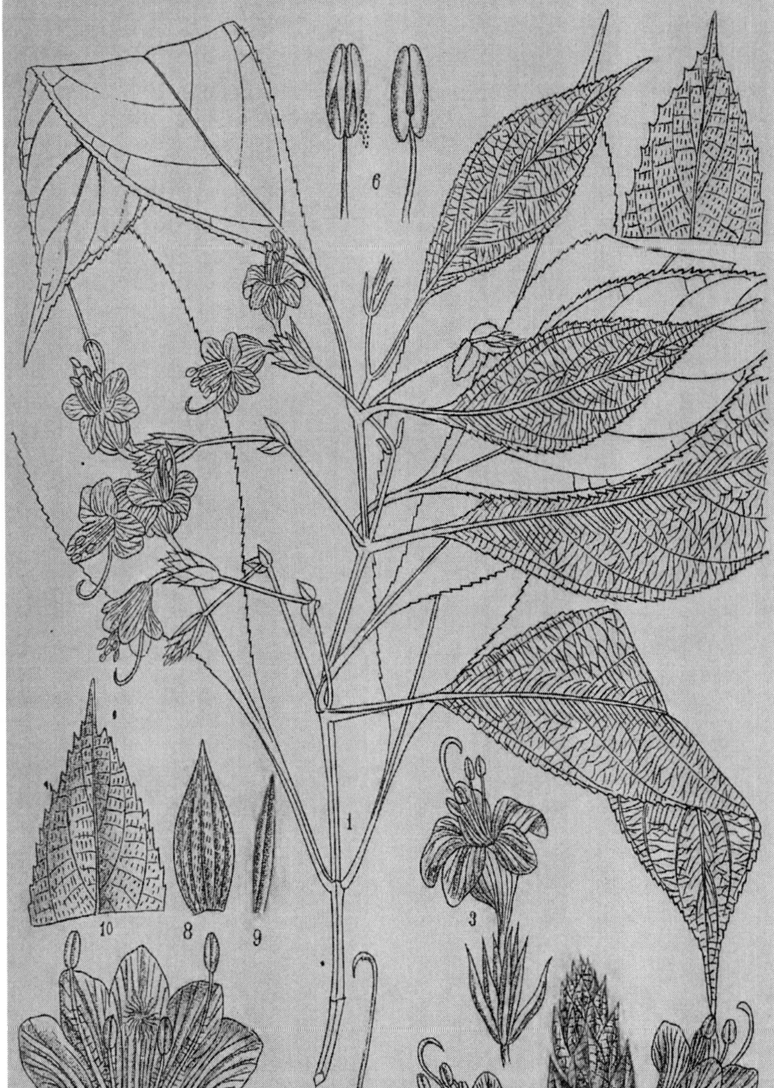

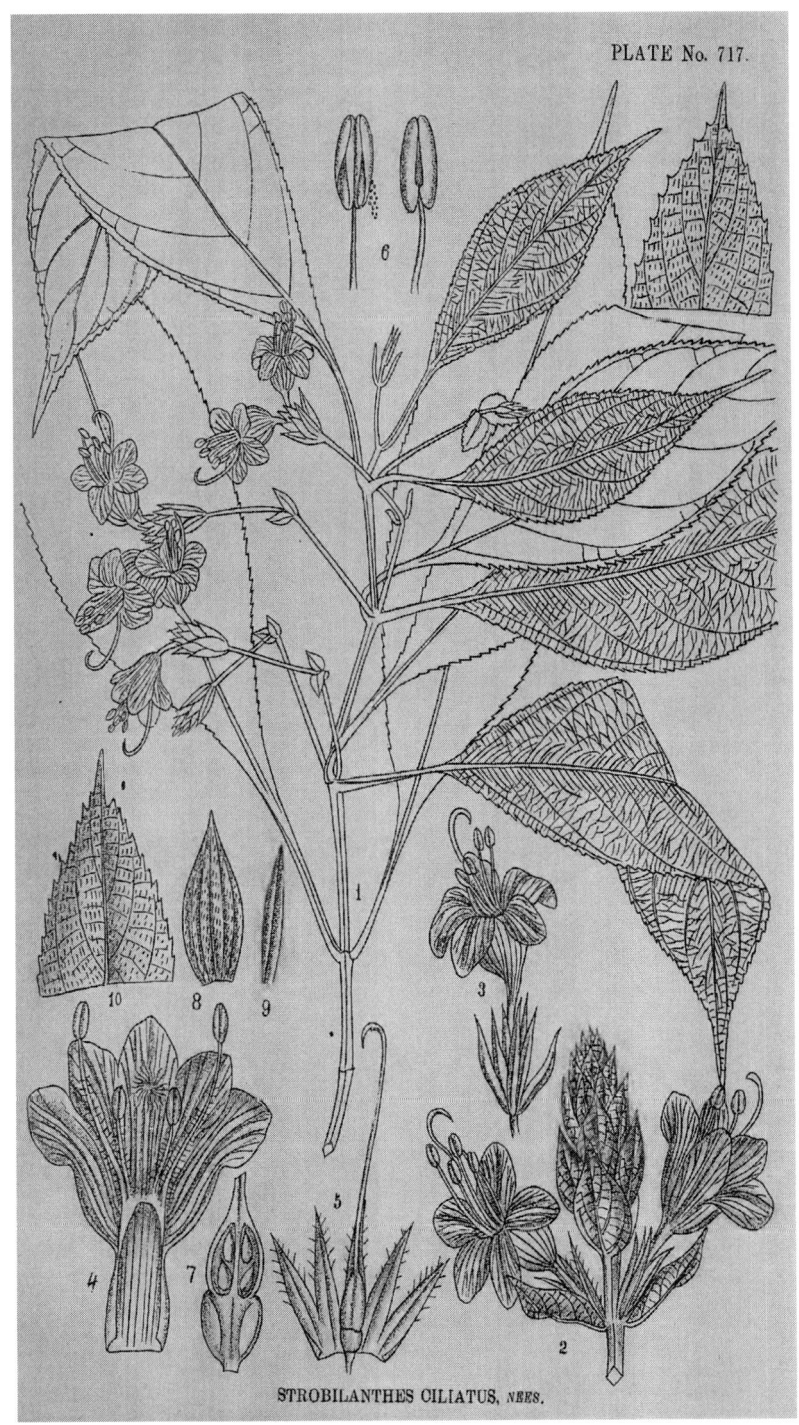

STROBILANTHES CILIATUS, *NEES.*

PLATE No. 718.

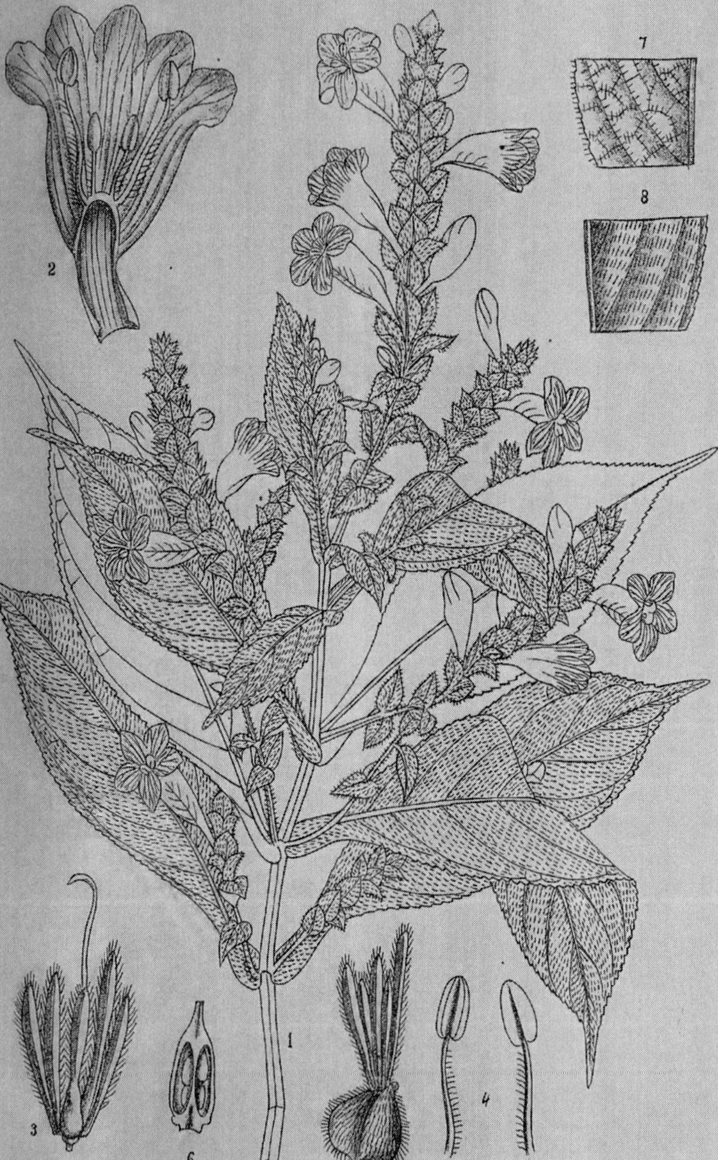

STROBILANTHES AURICULATUS, NEES.

A—ACANTHUS ILICIFOLIUS, *LINN.* B—BLEPHARIS EDULIS, *PERS.*

PLATE No. 720.

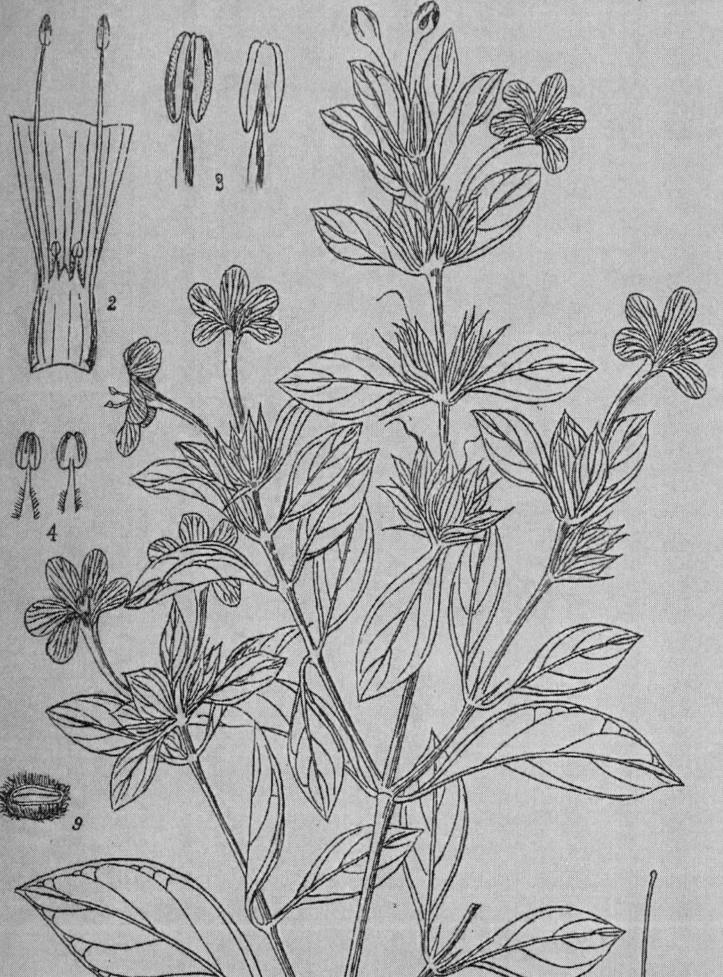

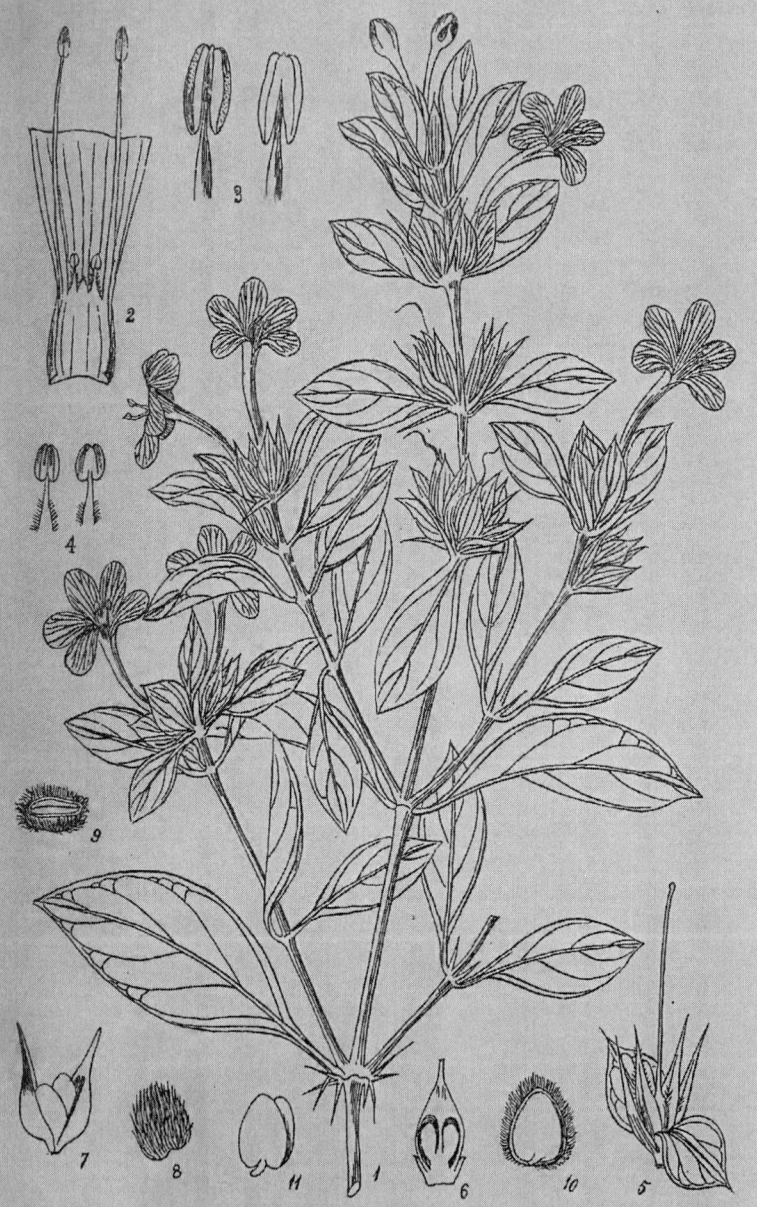

BARLERIA PRIONITIS, *LINN.*

PLATE No. 721.

BARLERIA CRISTATA, *LINN.*

PLATE No. 722.

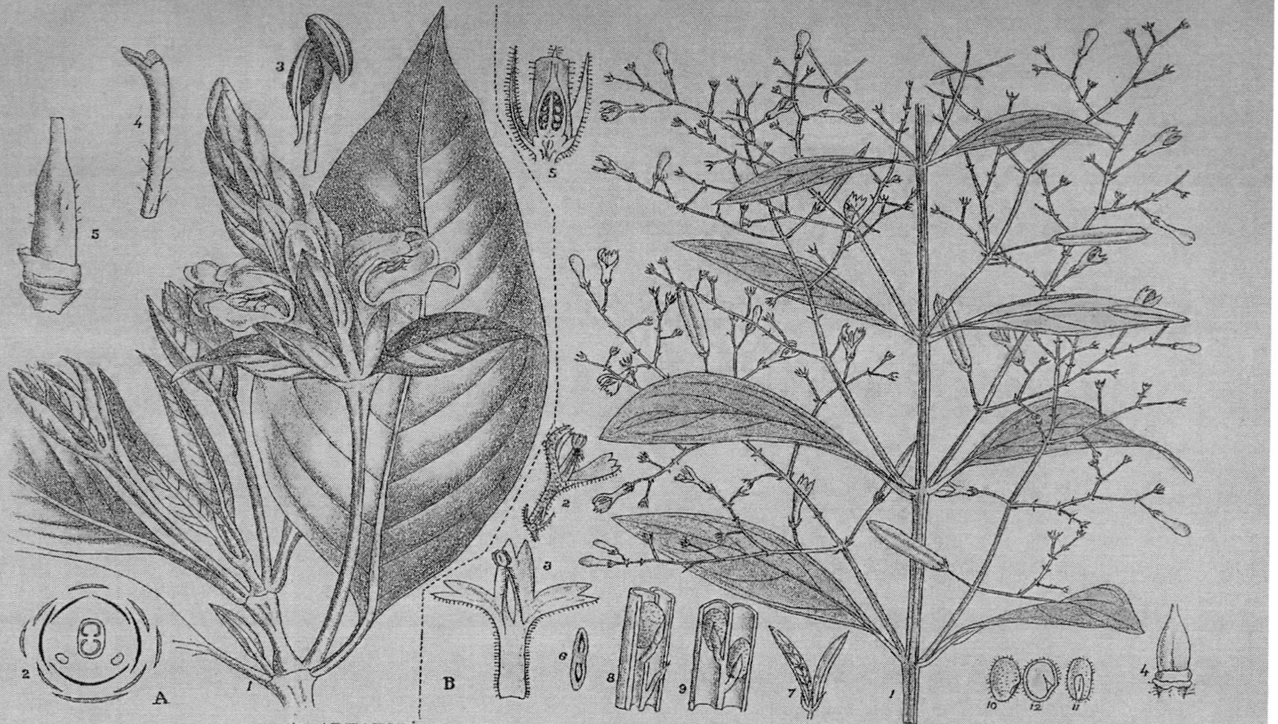

A—ADHATODA VASICA, *NEES*. B—ANDROGRAPHIS PANICULATA, *NEES*.

PLATE No. 723.

LEPIDAGATHIS CRISTATA, *WILLD.*

PLATE No. 724.

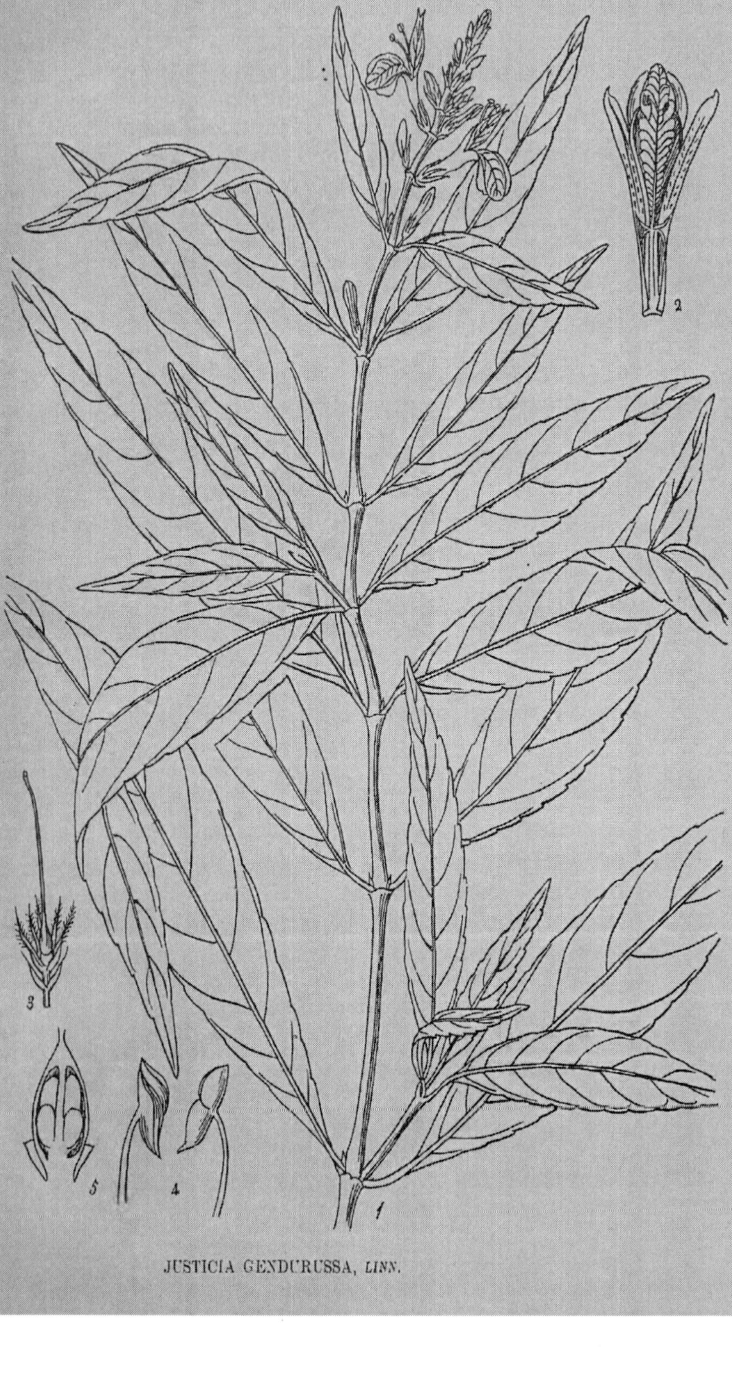

JUSTICIA GENDURUSSA, *LINN.*

PLATE No. 725.

JUSTICIA PROCUMBENS, *Linn.*

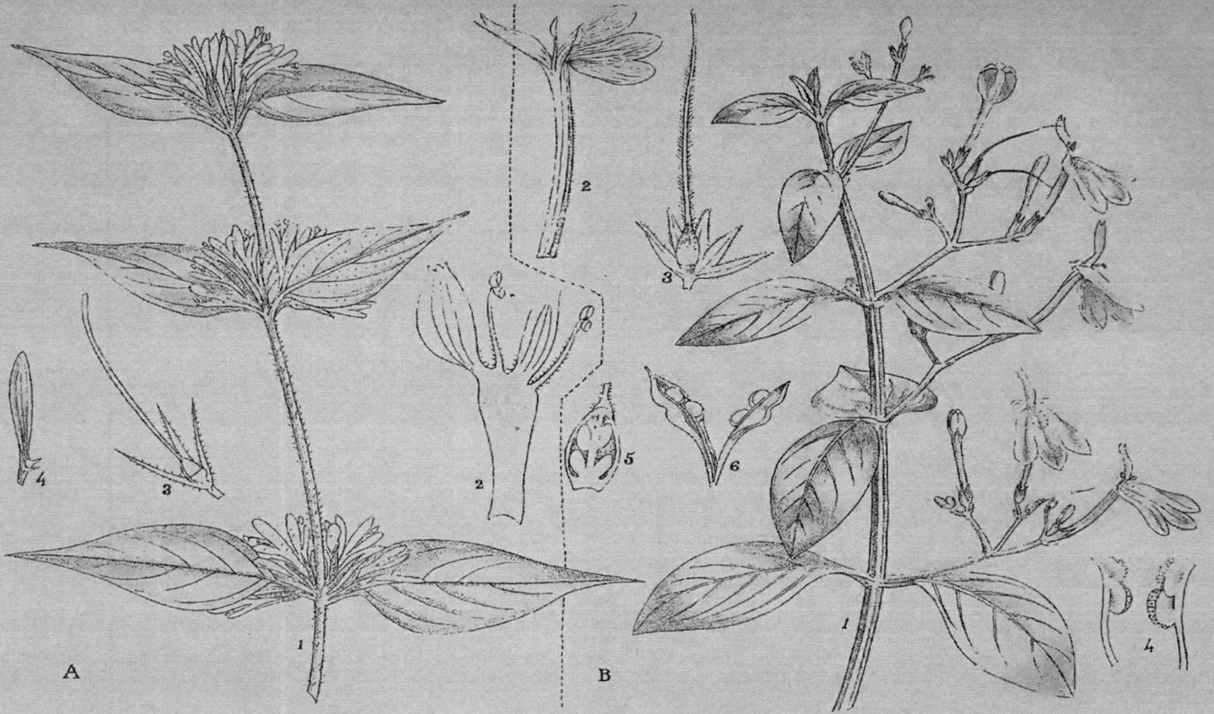

A—DICLIPTERA ROXBURGHIANA, *NEES.* B—RHINACANTHUS COMMUNIS, *NEES.*

PLATE No. 727.

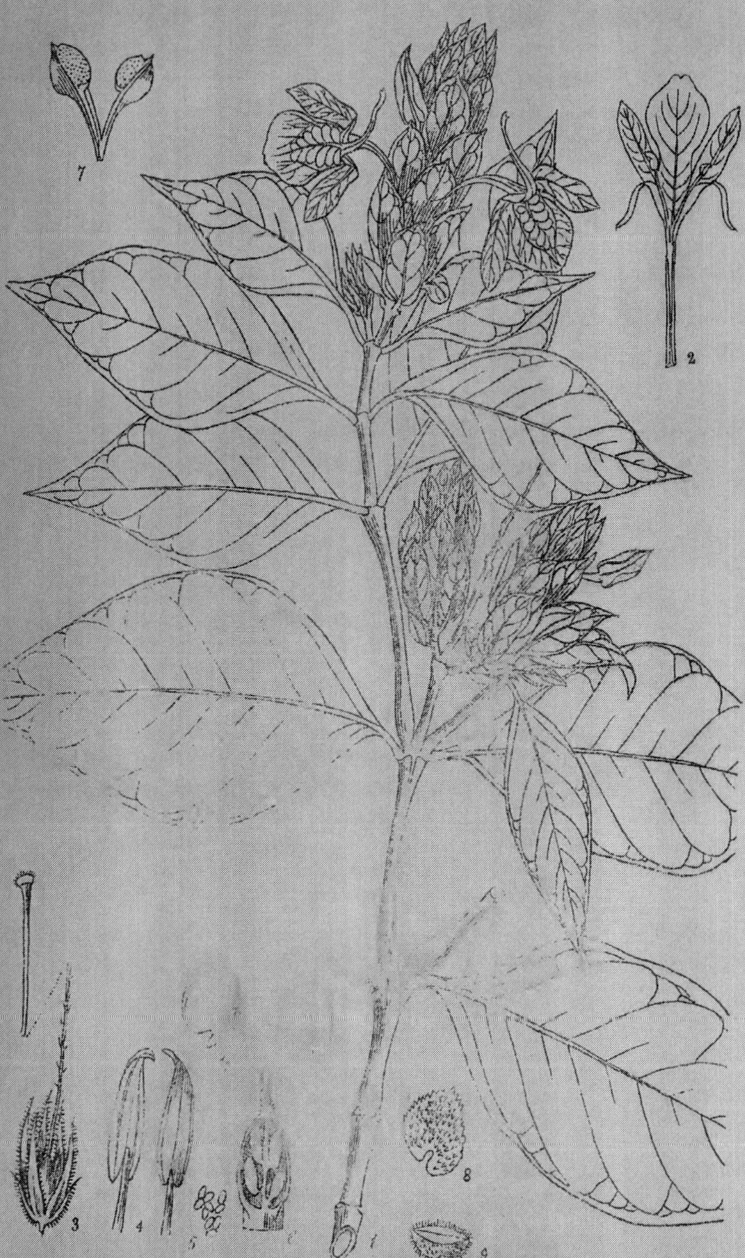

ECBOLIUM LINNEANUM, *KURZ.*

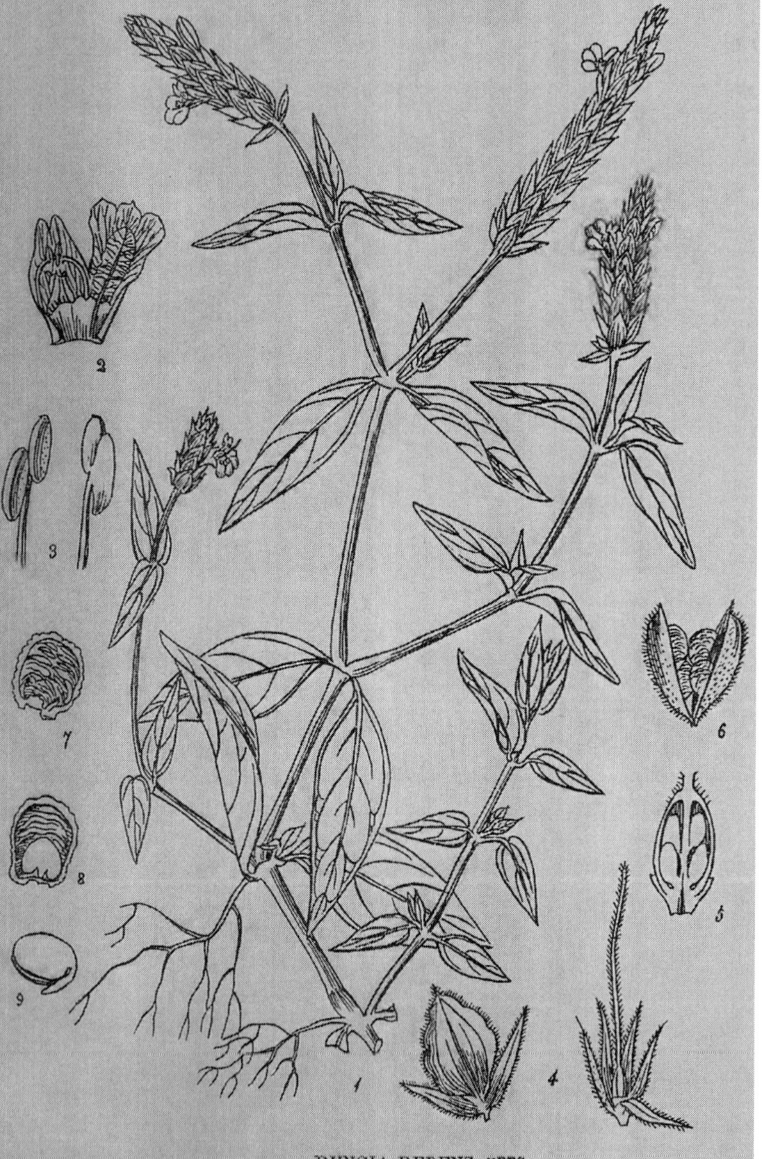

RUNGIA REPENS, *NEES.*

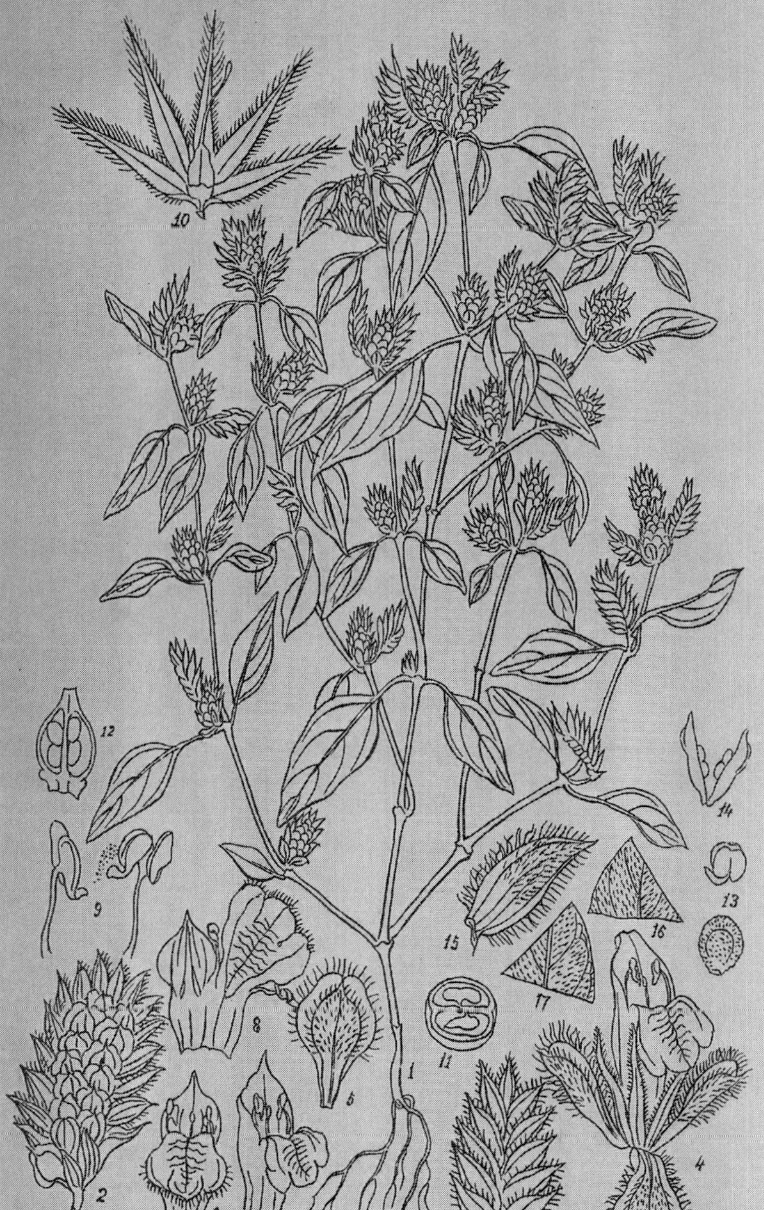

RUNGIA PARVIFLORA, NEES.

PLATE No. 730.

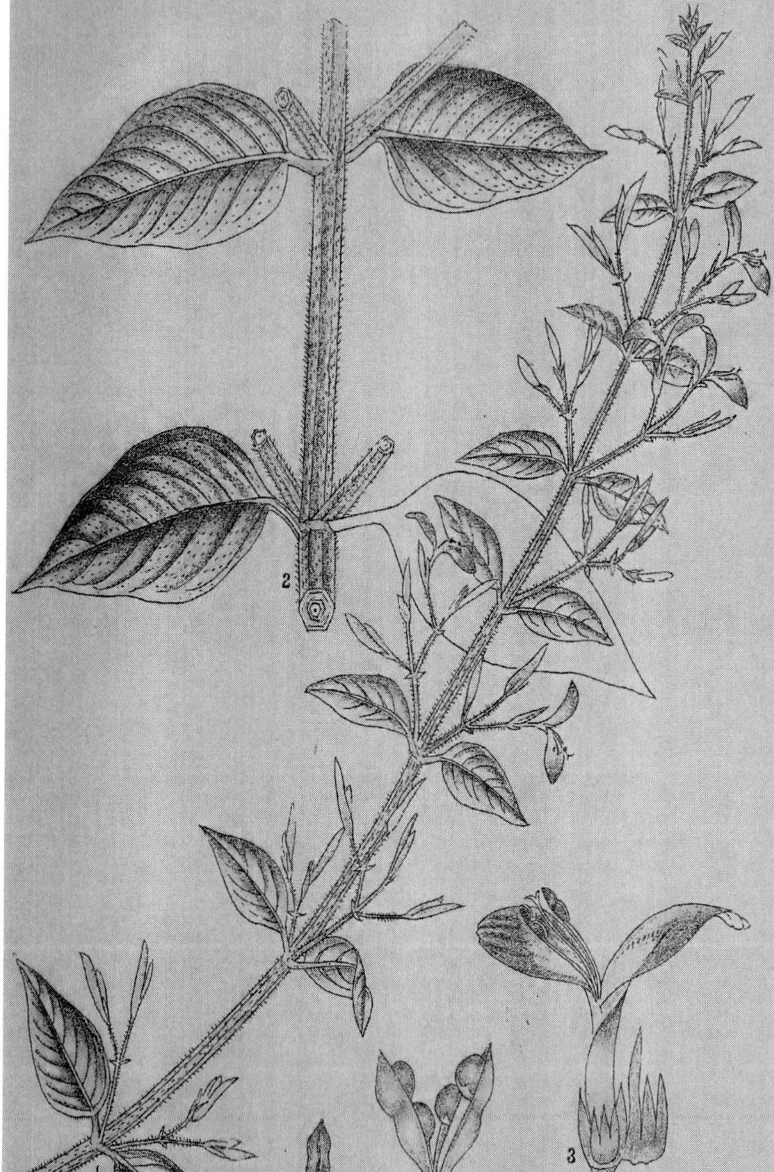

PERISTROPHE BICALYCULATA, NEES.

PLATE No. 731.

LIPPIA NODIFLORA, Rich.

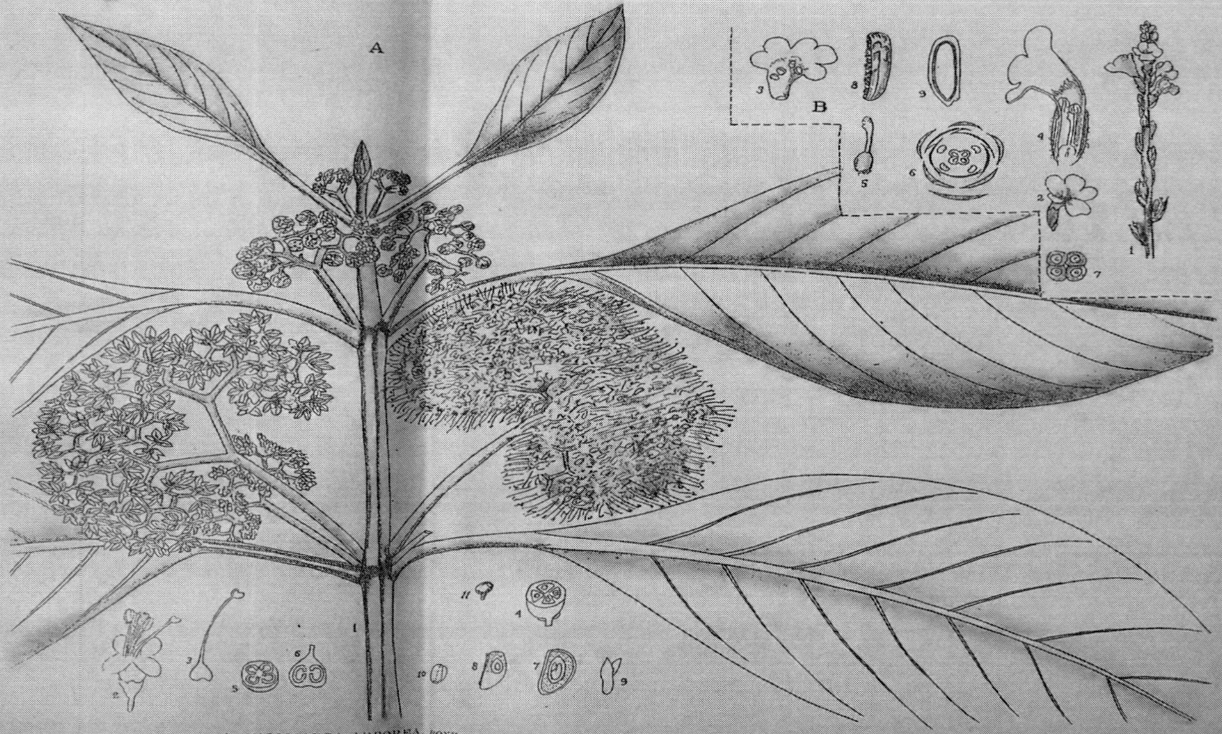

A—CALLICARPA ARBOREA, ROXB.　　B—VERBENA OFFICINALIS, LINN

CALLICARPA LANATA, LINN.

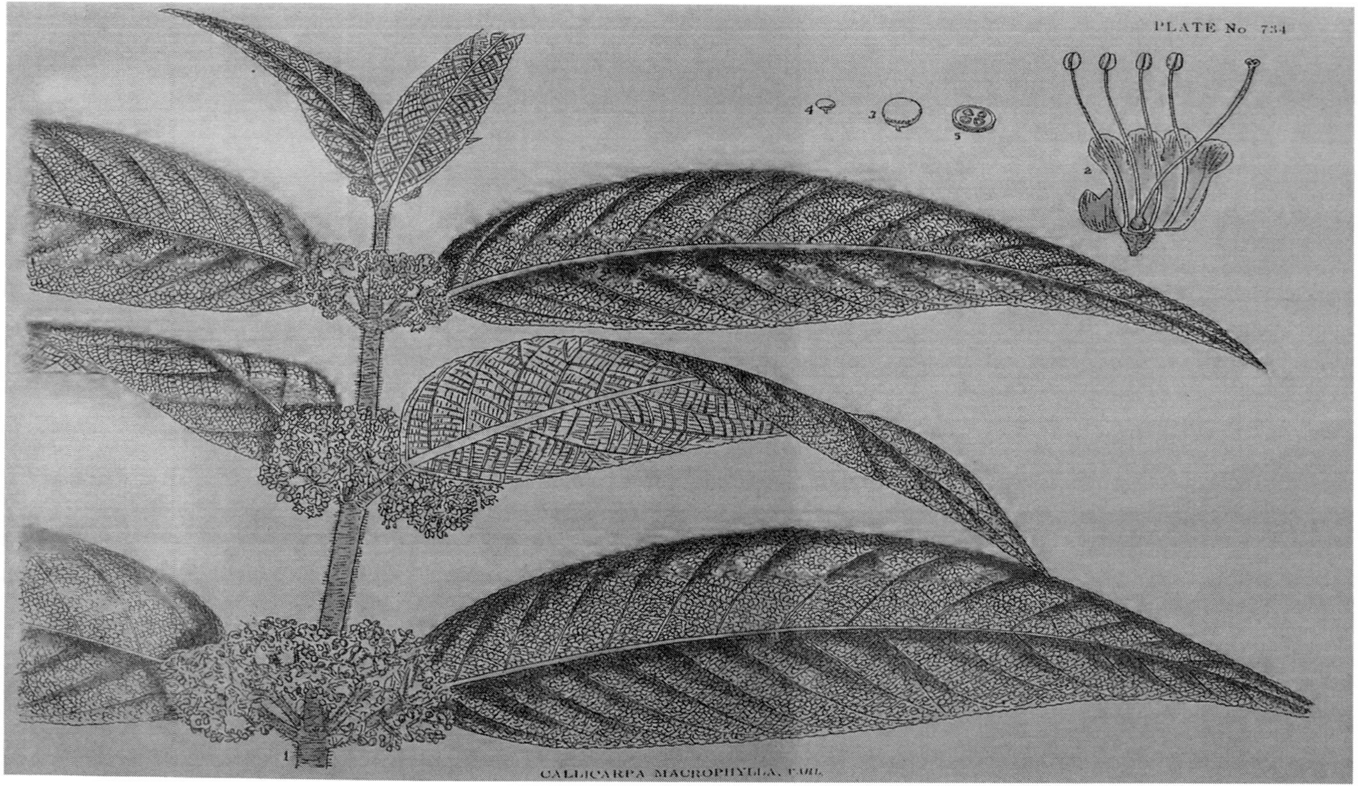

CALLICARPA MACROPHYLLA, Vahl.

TECTONA GRANDIS, *LINN. F.*

PLATE No. 736.

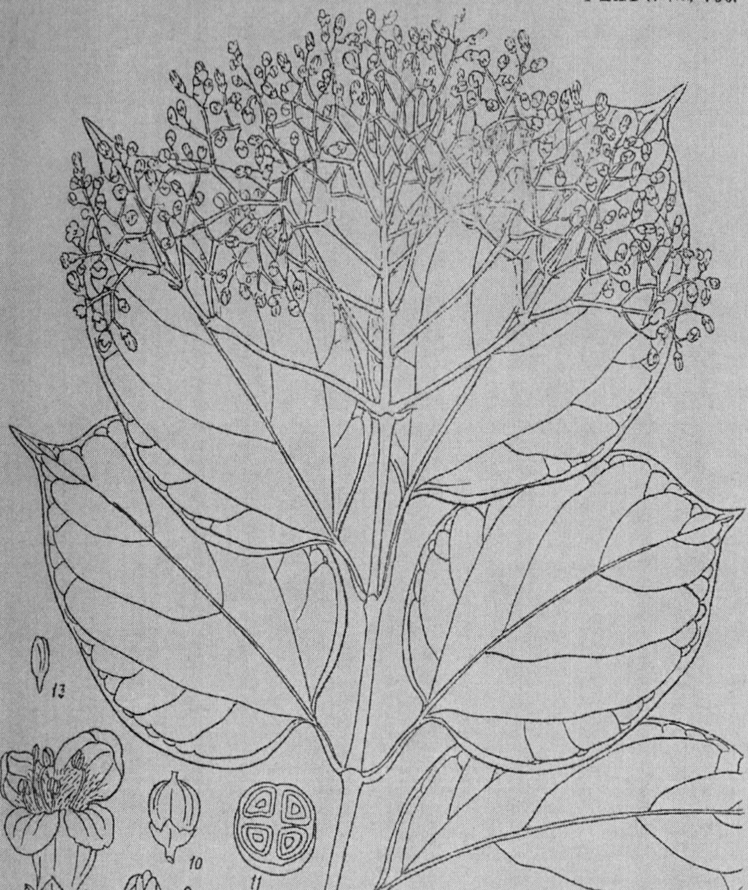

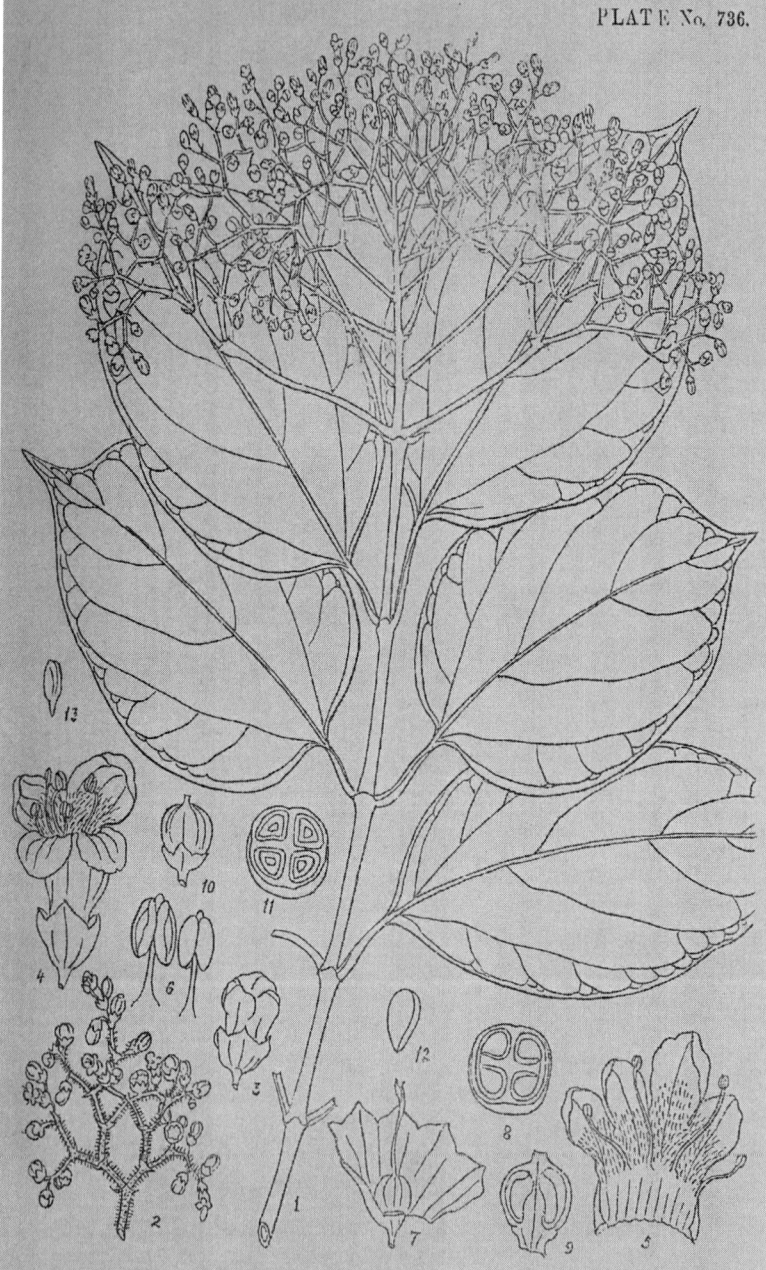

PREMNA INTEGRIFOLIA, *LINN.*

PLATE No. 737.

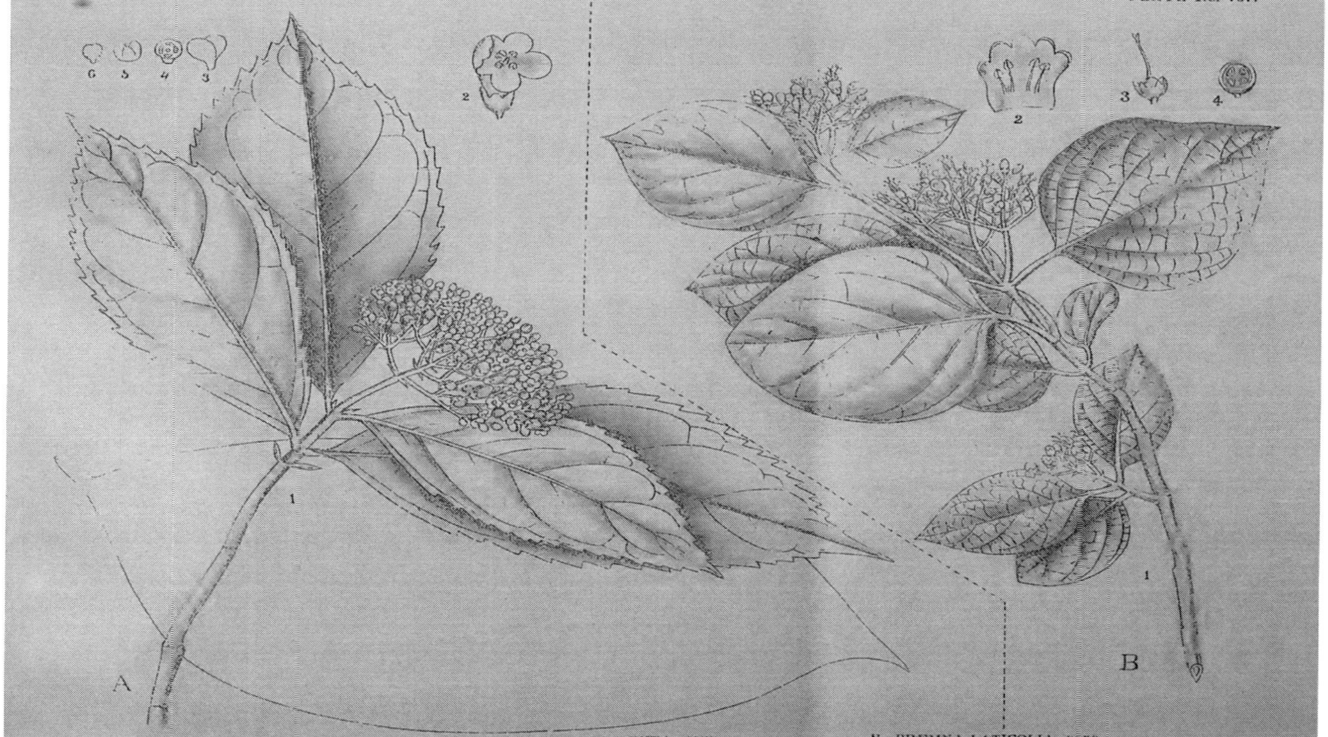

A—PREMNA ESCULENTA, Roxb.   B PREMNA LATIFOLIA, Roxb.

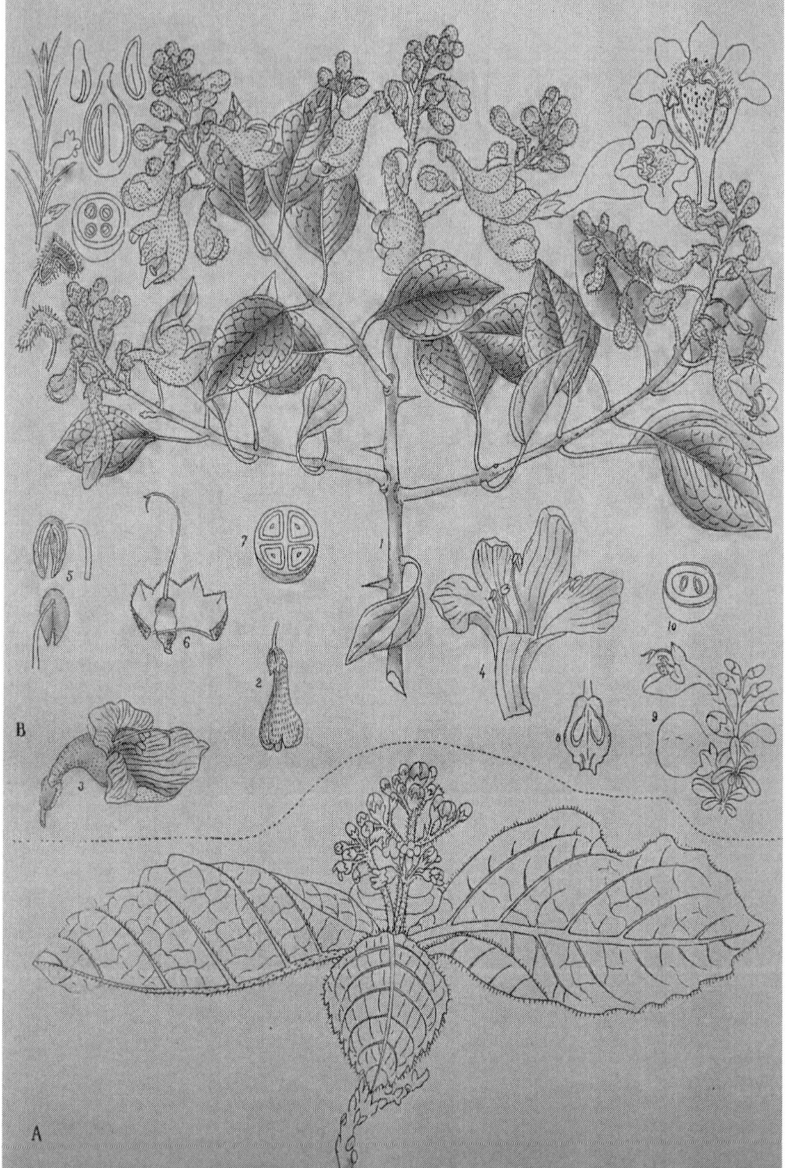

A—PREMNA HERBACEA, *ROXB.* B—GMELINA ASIATICA, *LINN.*

PLATE No. 739.

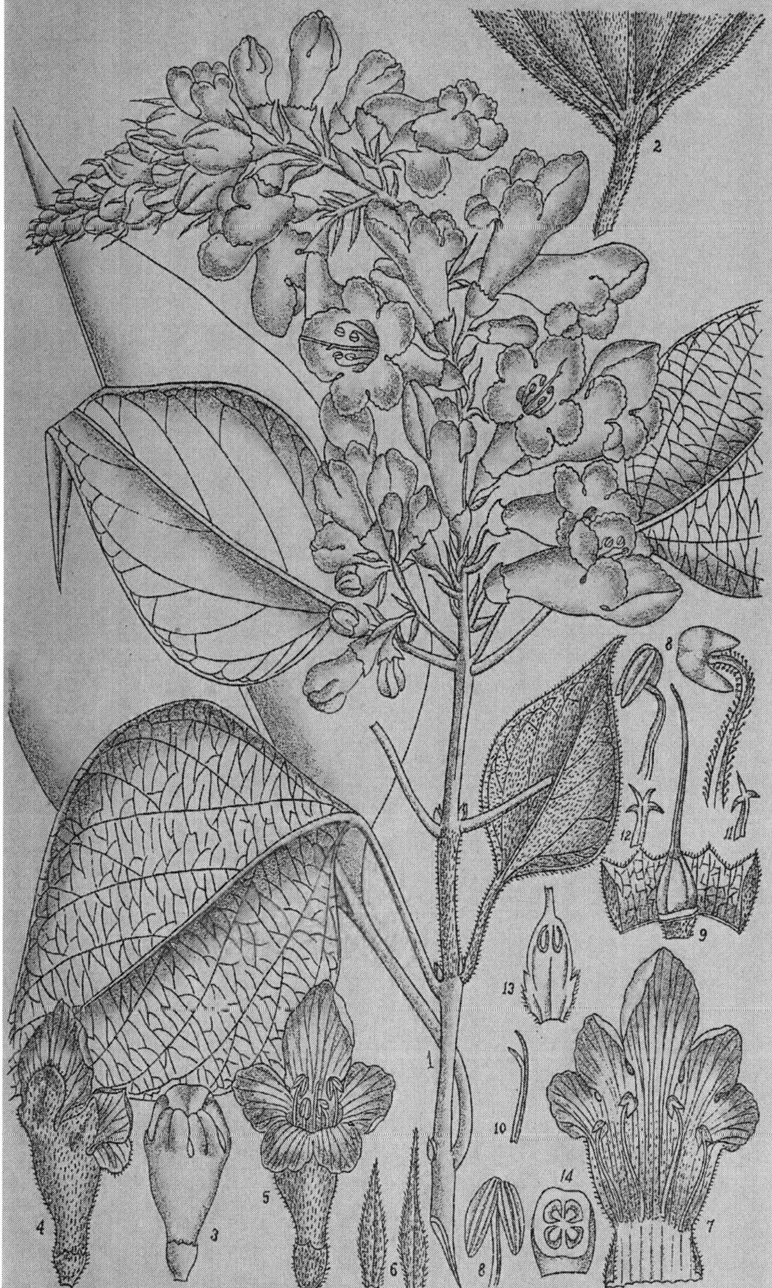

GMELINA ARBOREA, *ROXB.*

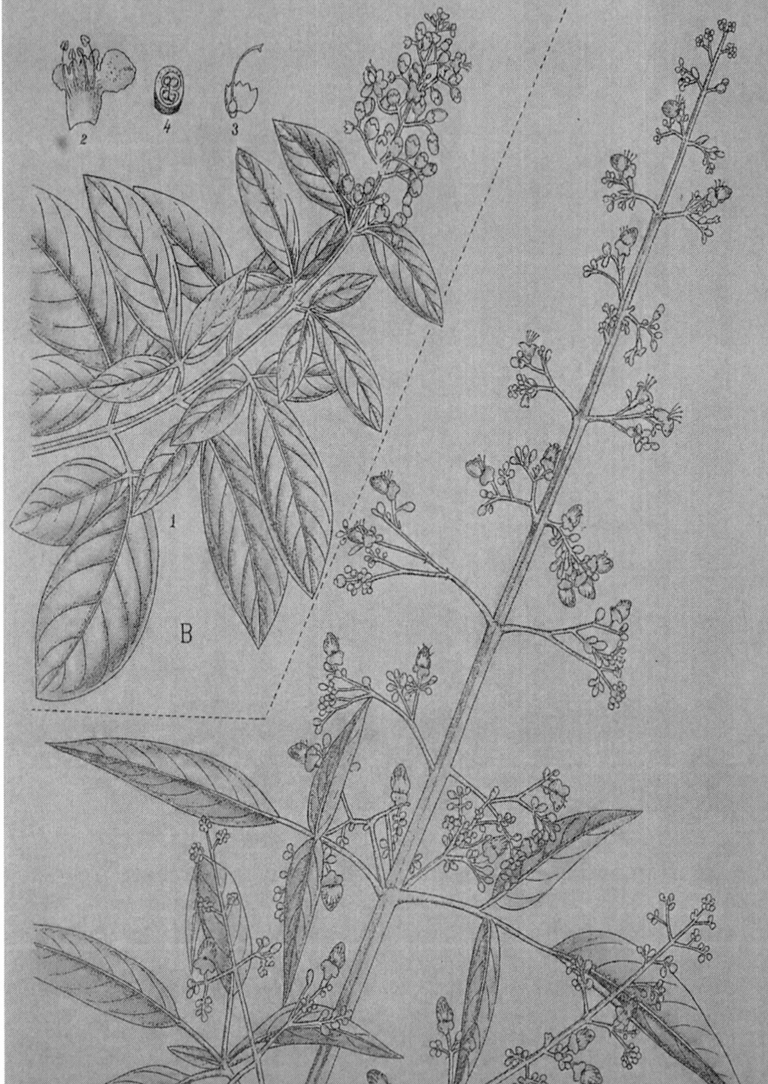

A—VITEX NEGUNDO, *LINN.*　　　B—V. TRIFOLIA, *LINN. F.*

PLATE No. 741.

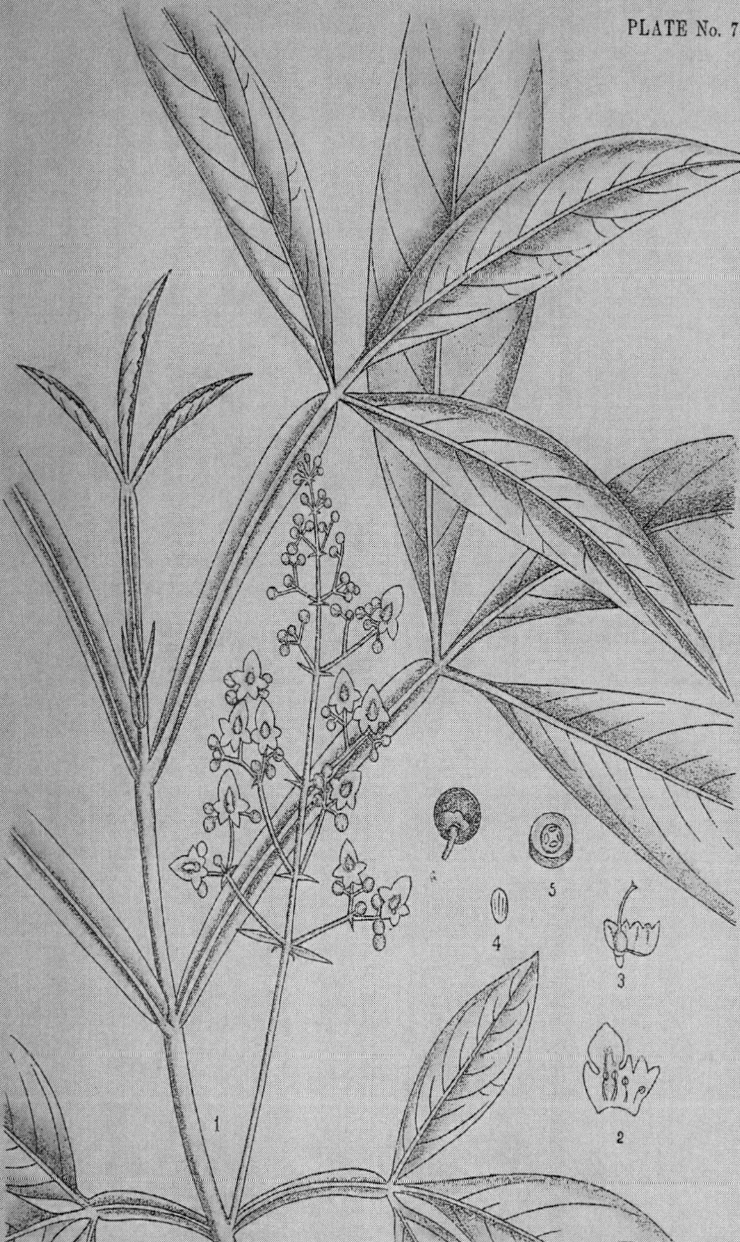

VITEX PEDUNCULARIS, WALL.

PLATE No 742.

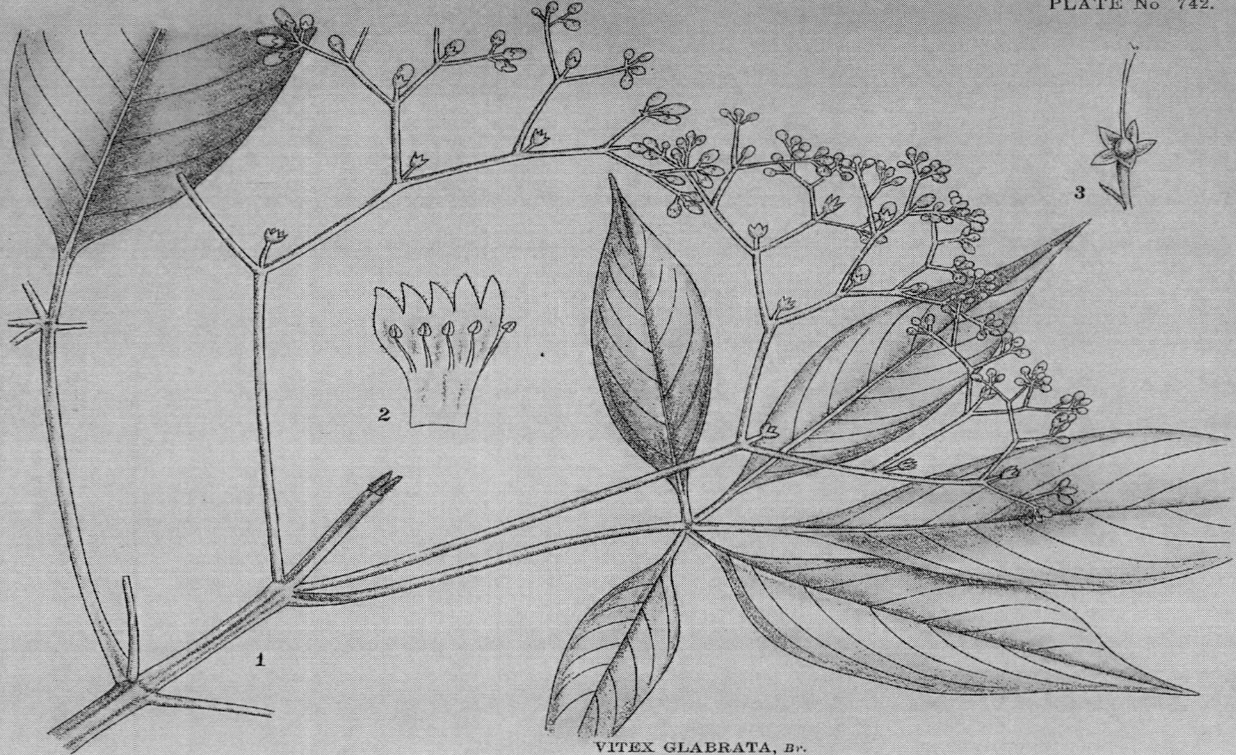

VITEX GLABRATA, *Br.*

PLATE No 743.

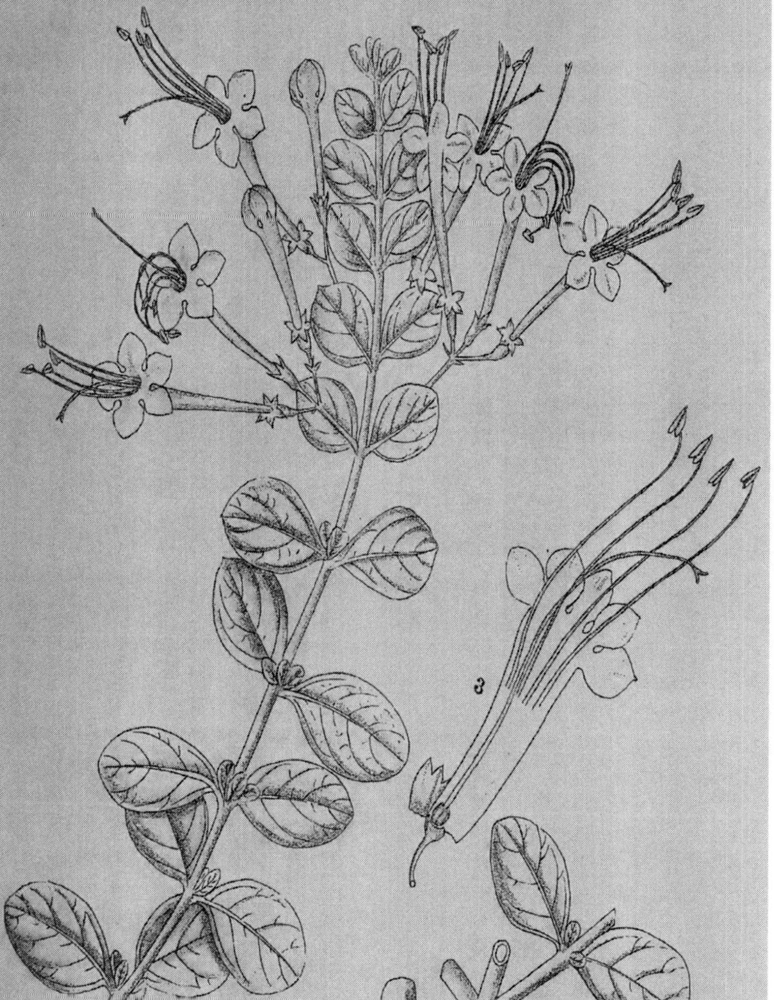

CLERODENDRON INERME, GÆRTN.

PLATE No. 744.

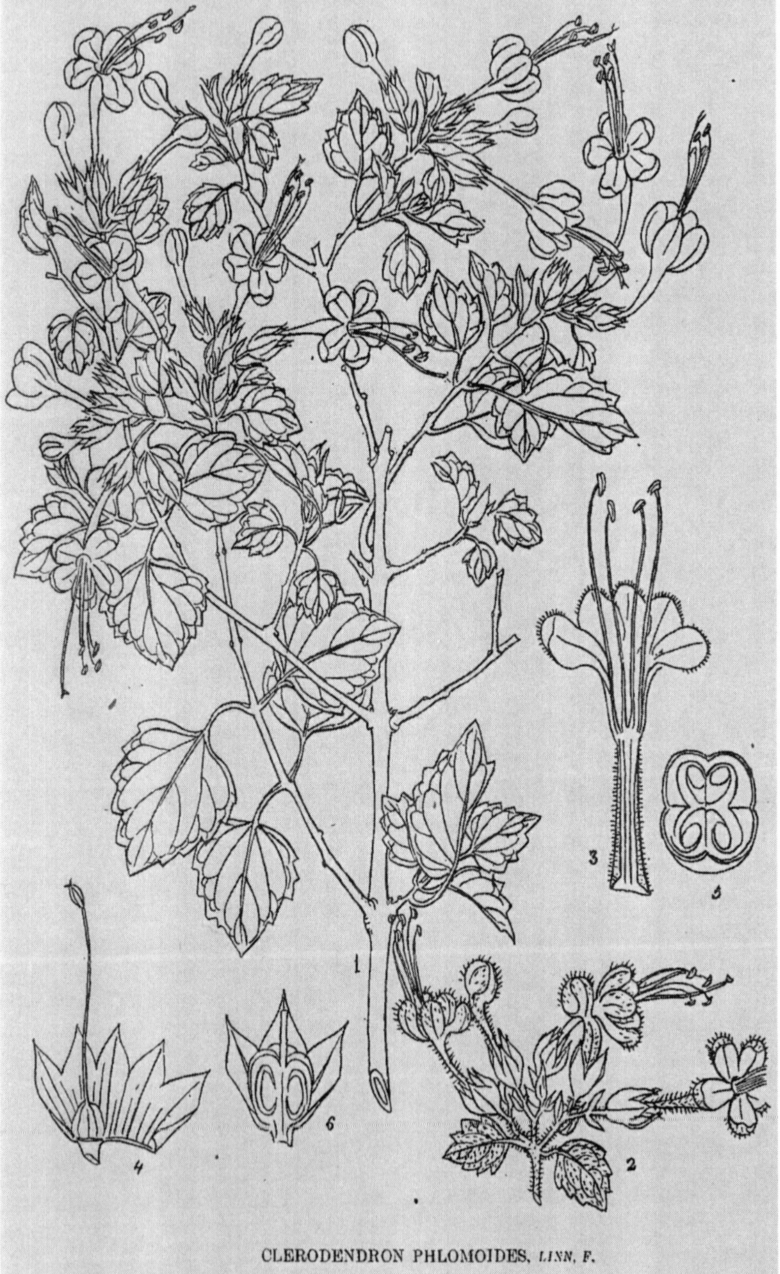

CLERODENDRON PHLOMOIDES, *LINN, F.*

PLATE No. 745.

CLERODENDRON SERRATUM, *SPRENG.*

PLATE No. 746.

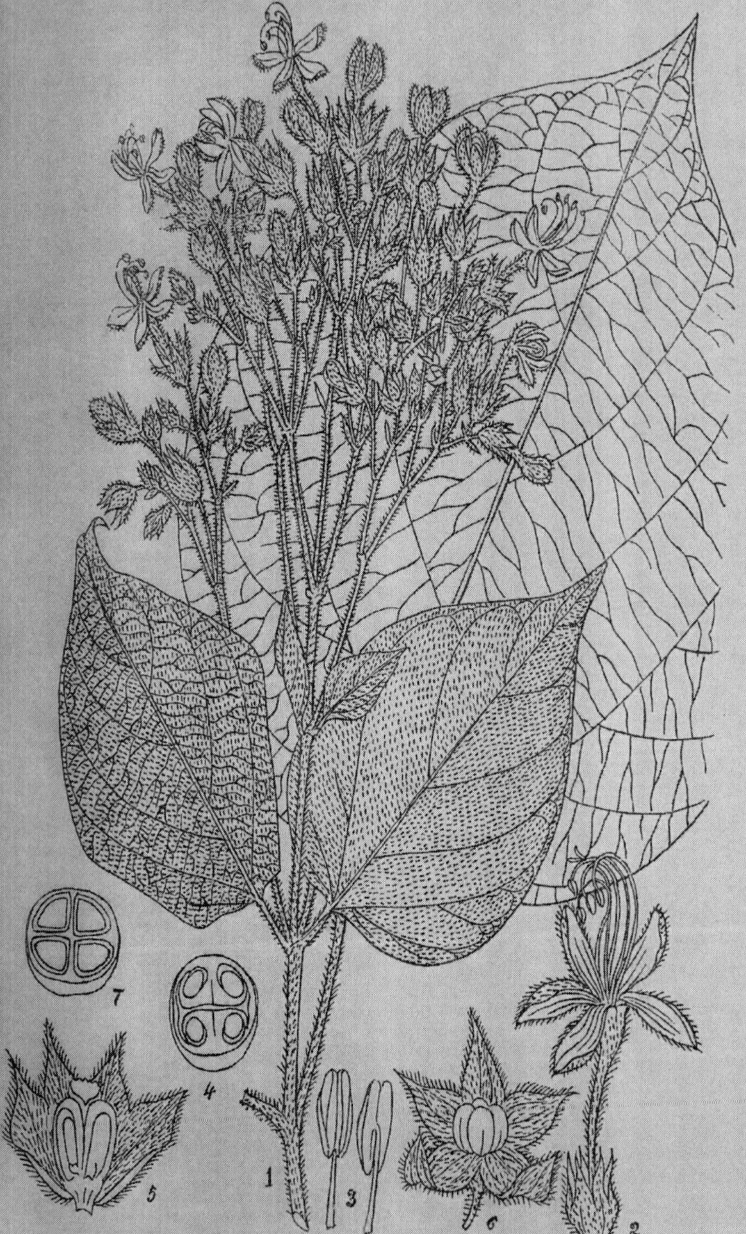

CLERODENDRON INFORTUNATUM, *GÆRTN.*

PLATE No. 747.

CLERODENDRON SIPHONANTHUS, Br.

PLATE No. 748.

AVICENNIA OFFICINALIS, LINN.

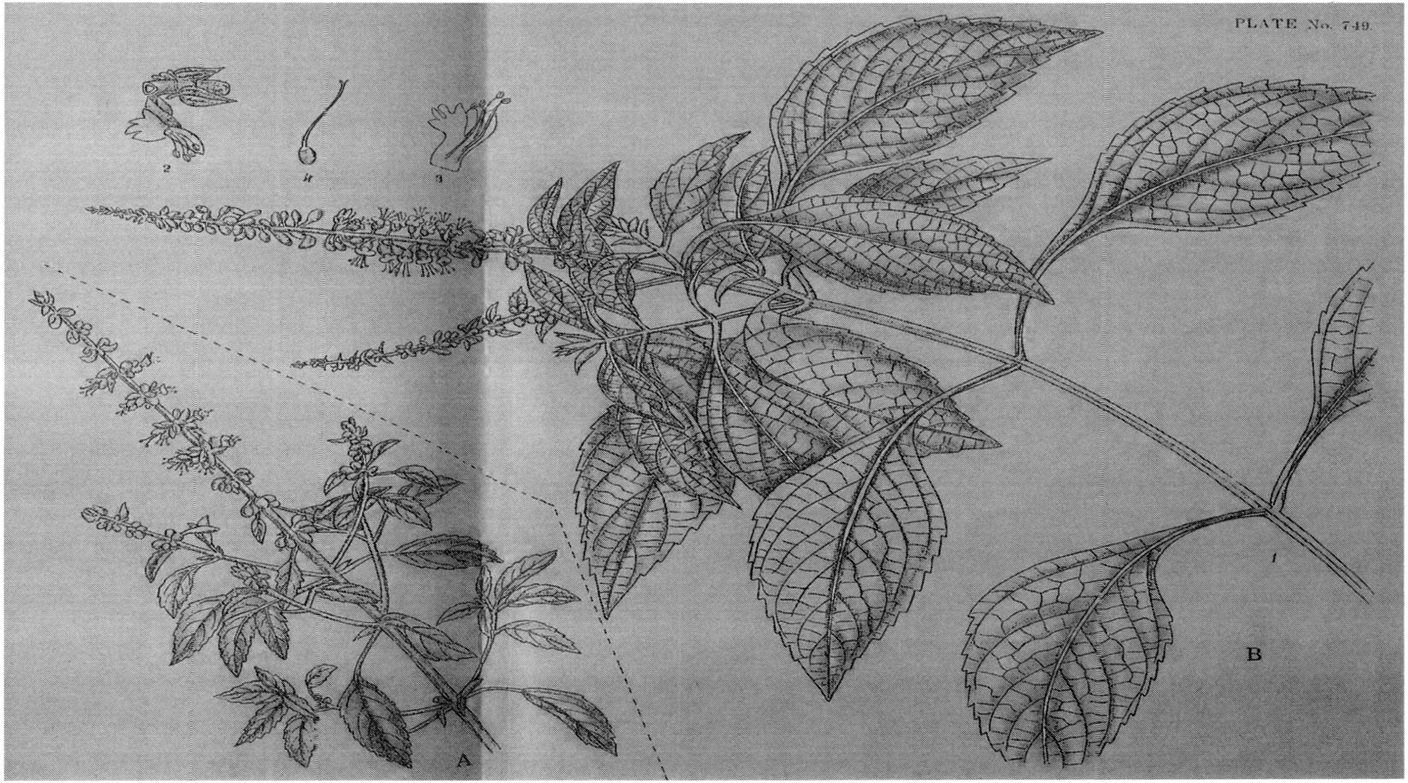
2
4
3
1
A
B

PLATE No. 750.

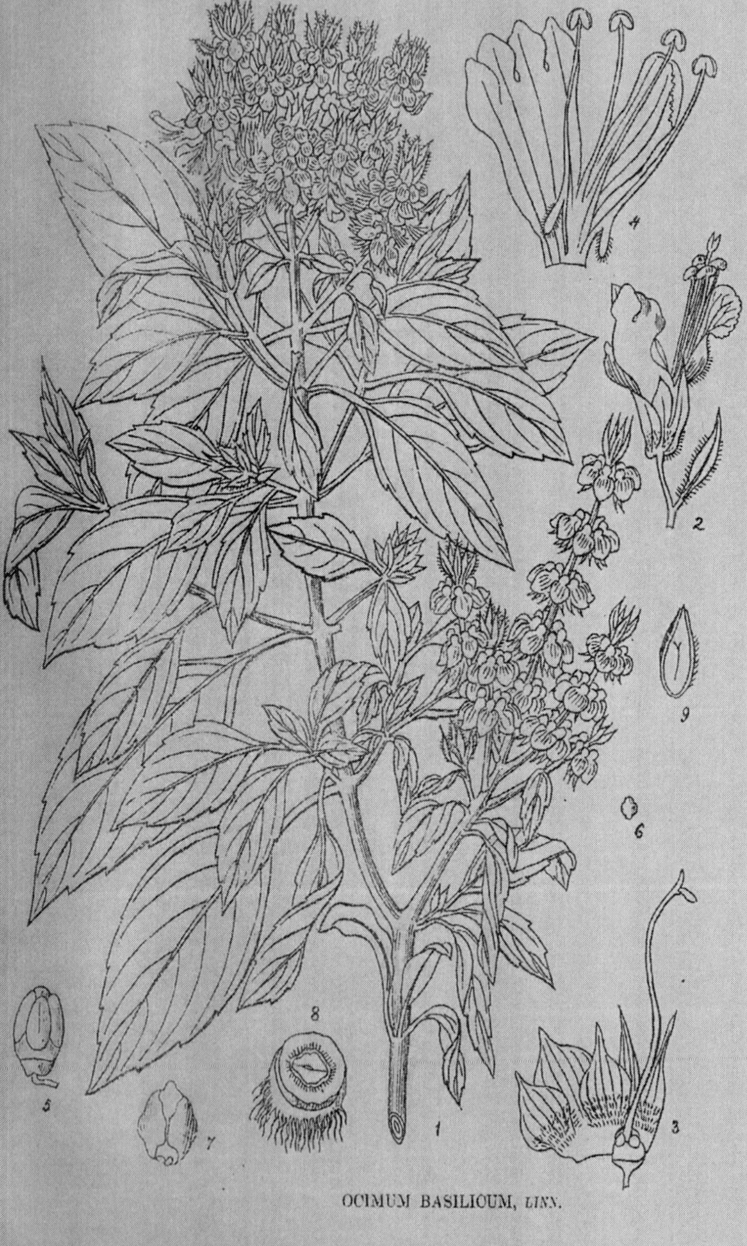

OCIMUM BASILIOUM, *LINN.*

PLATE No. 751.

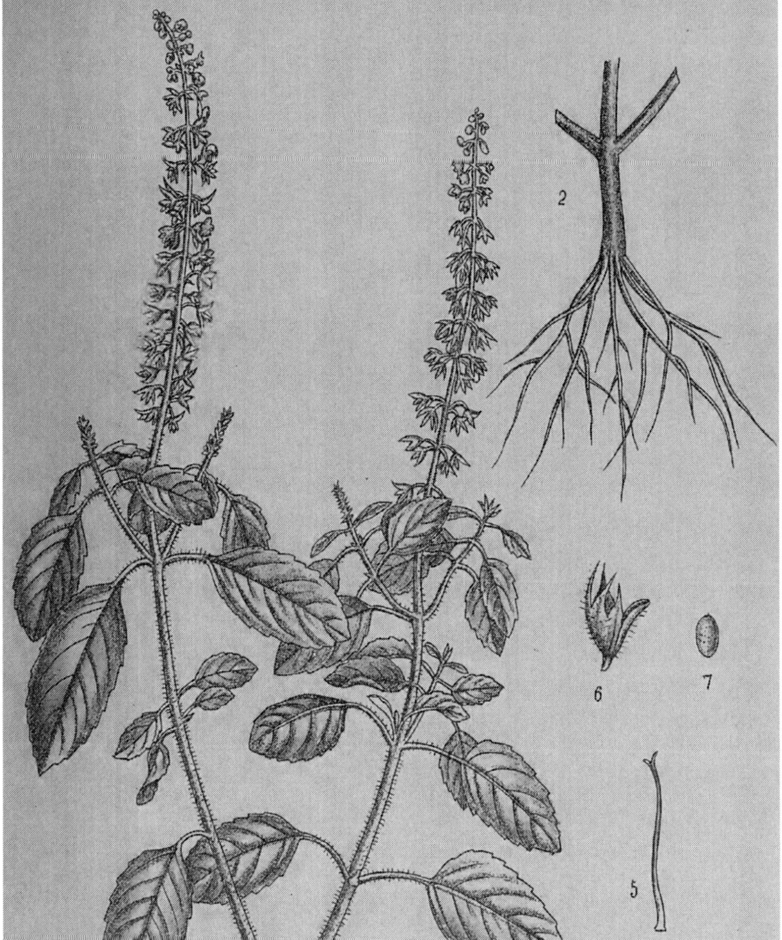

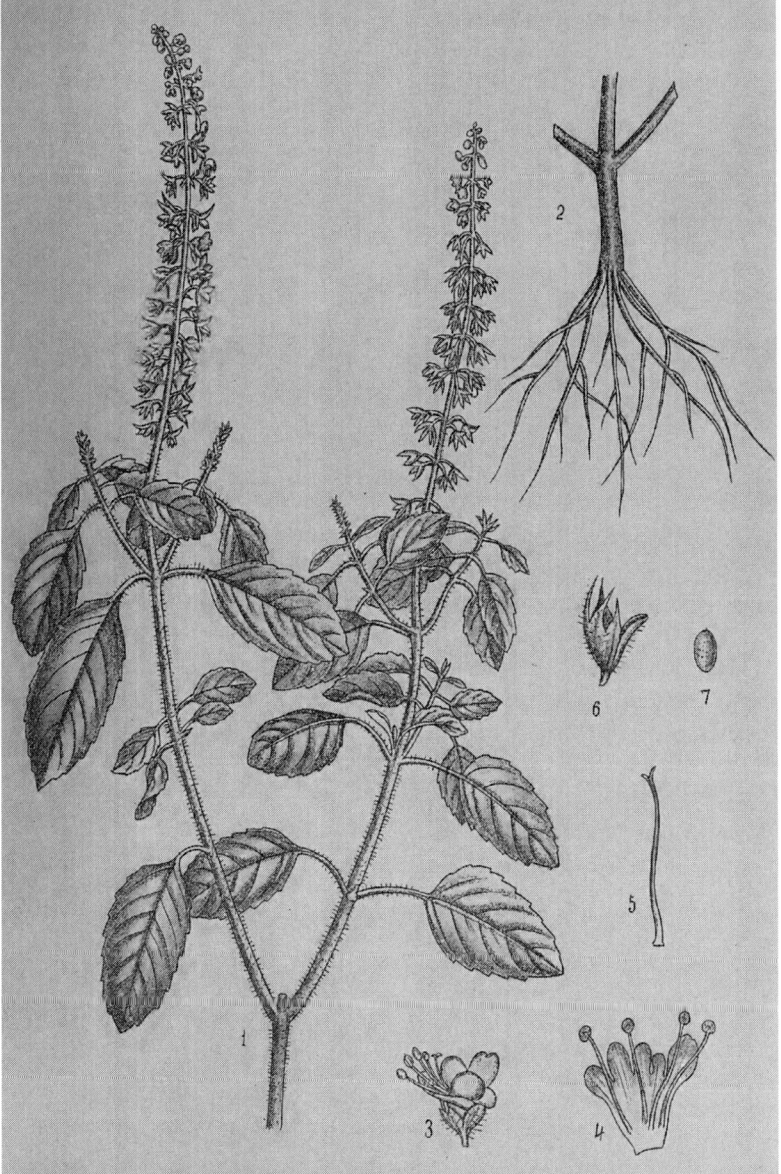

OCIMUM SANCTUM, *LINN.*

PLATE No. 752.

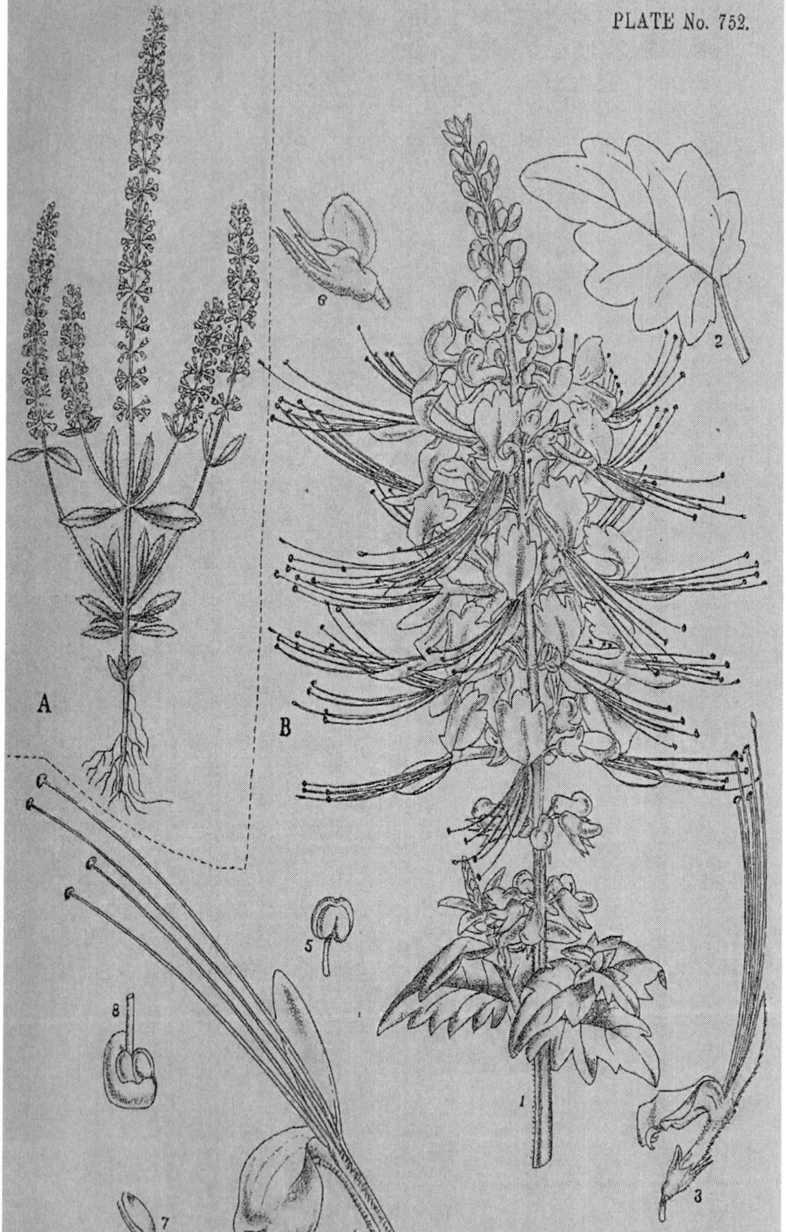

A—GENIOSPORUM PROSTRATUM, *BENTH.* B—ORTHOSIPHON STAMINEUS, *BENTH.*

PLATE No. 753.

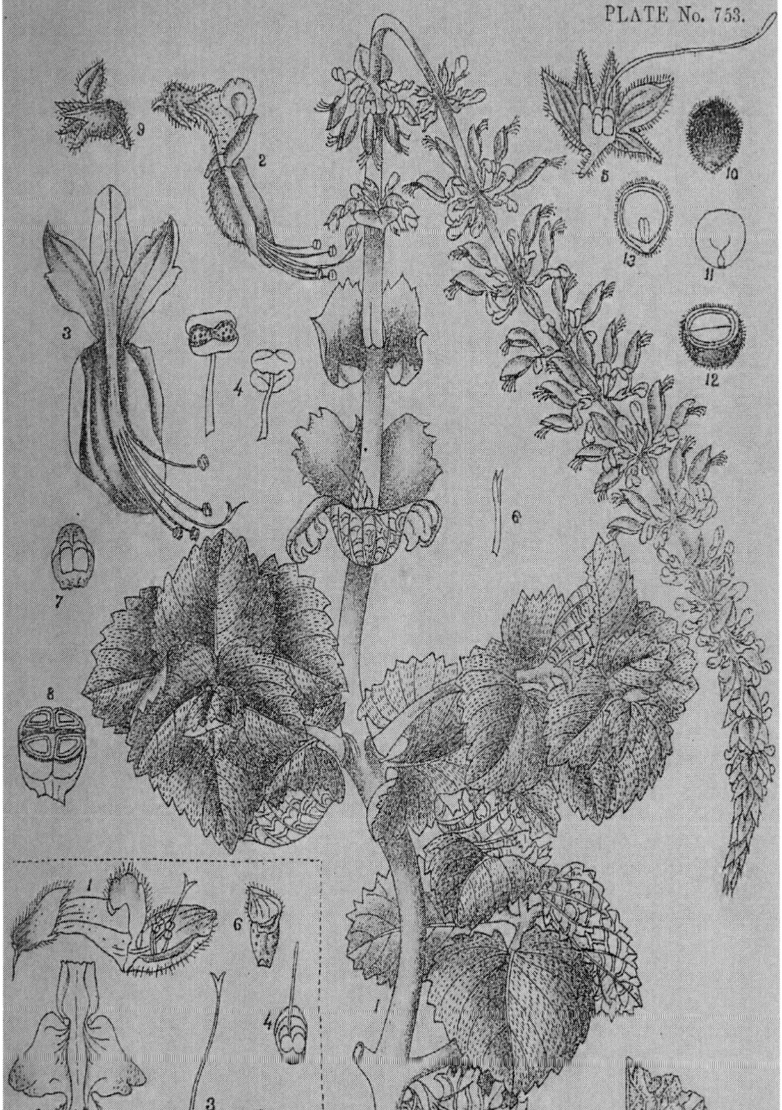

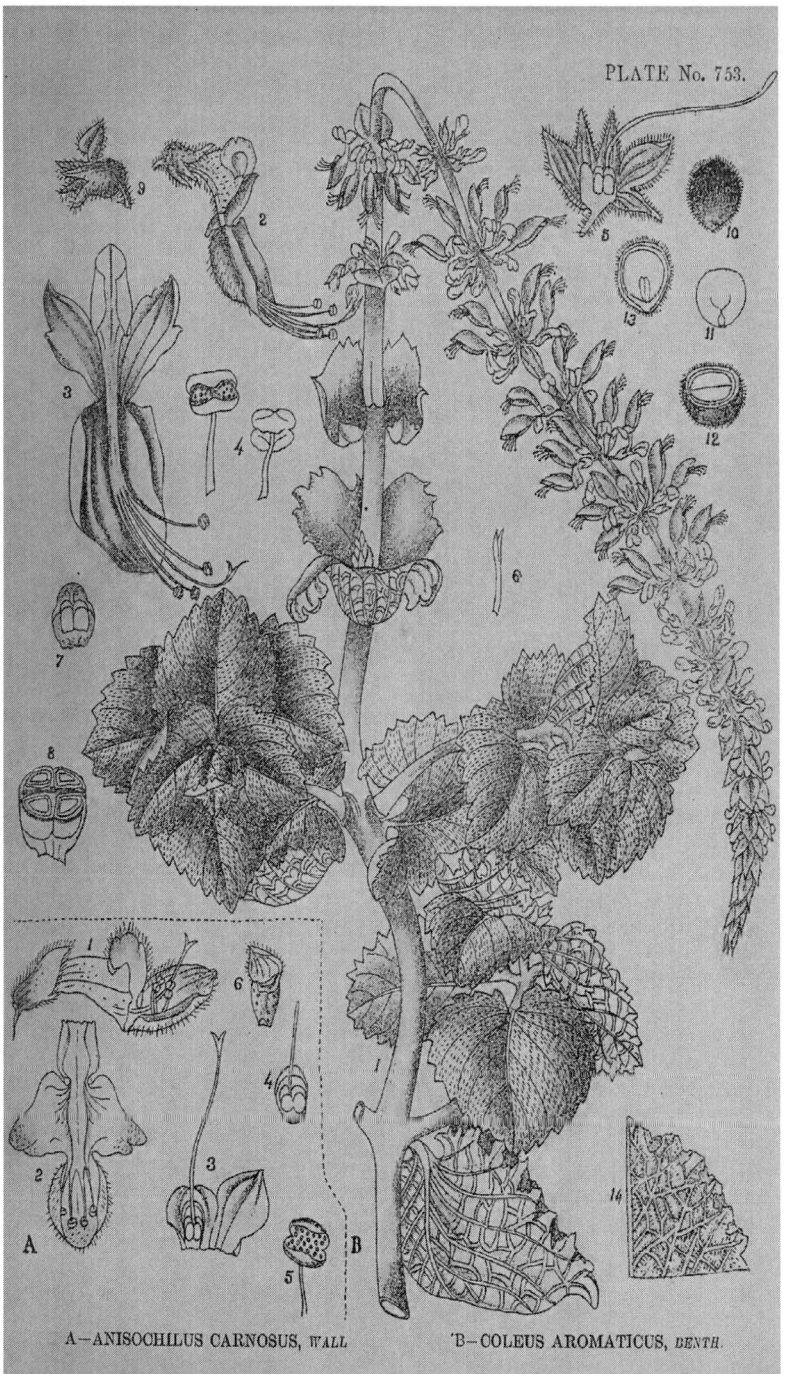

A—ANISOCHILUS CARNOSUS, *WALL* B—COLEUS AROMATICUS, *BENTH.*

PLATE No. 754.

POGOSTEMON PLECTRANTHOIDES, *DESF.*

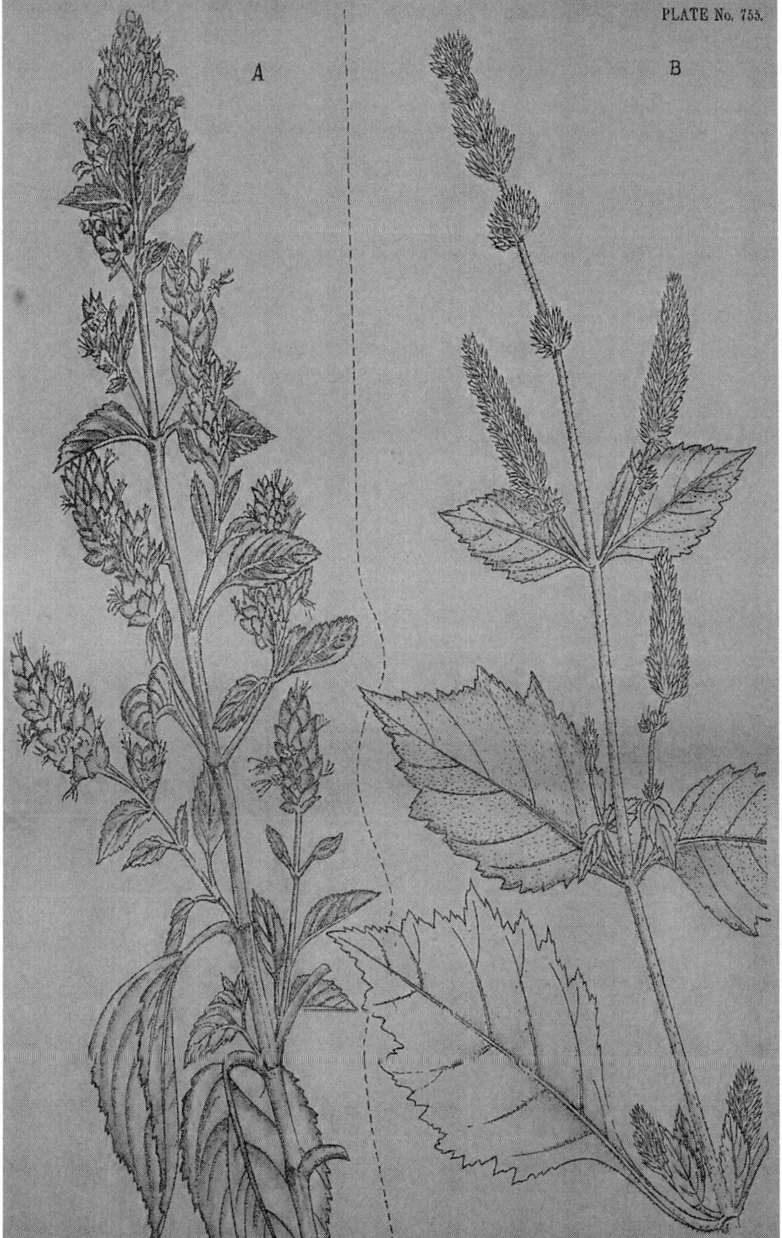

A—POGOSTEMON PARVIFLORUS, BENTH.

B—POGOSTEMON PURPURASCENS, DALZ.

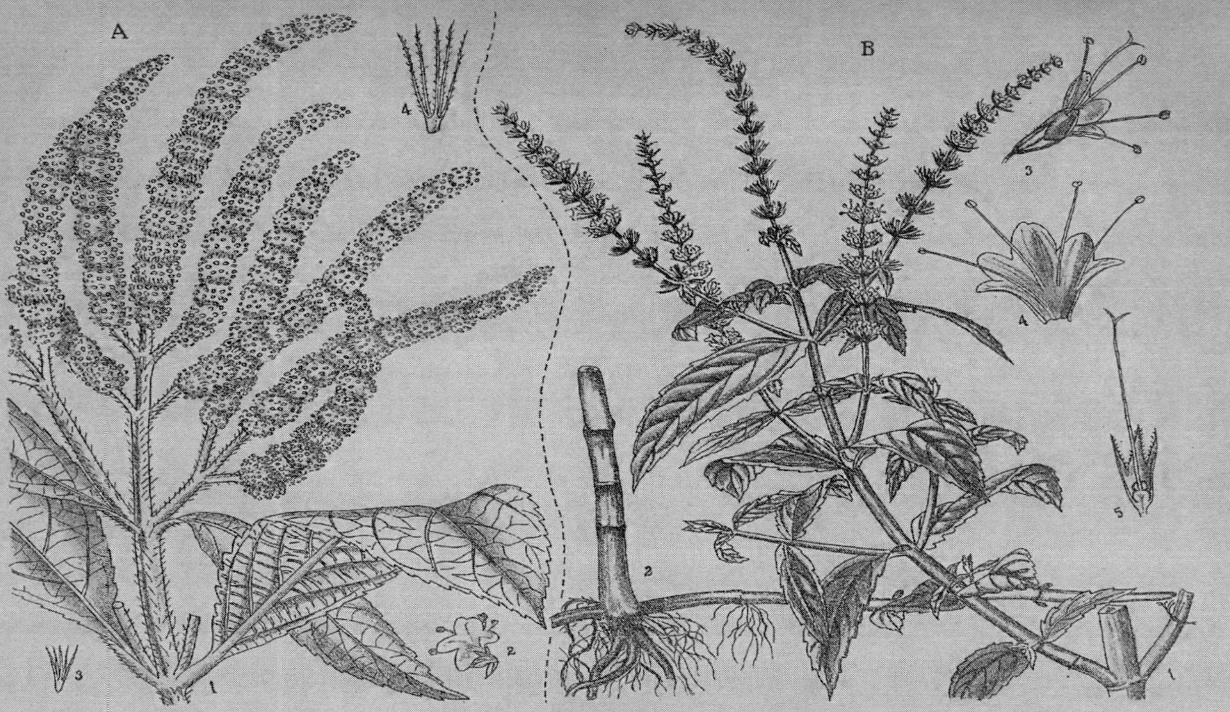

A—COLEBROOKEA OPPOSITIFOLIA, *Smith.* B—MENTHA VIRIDIS, *Linn.*

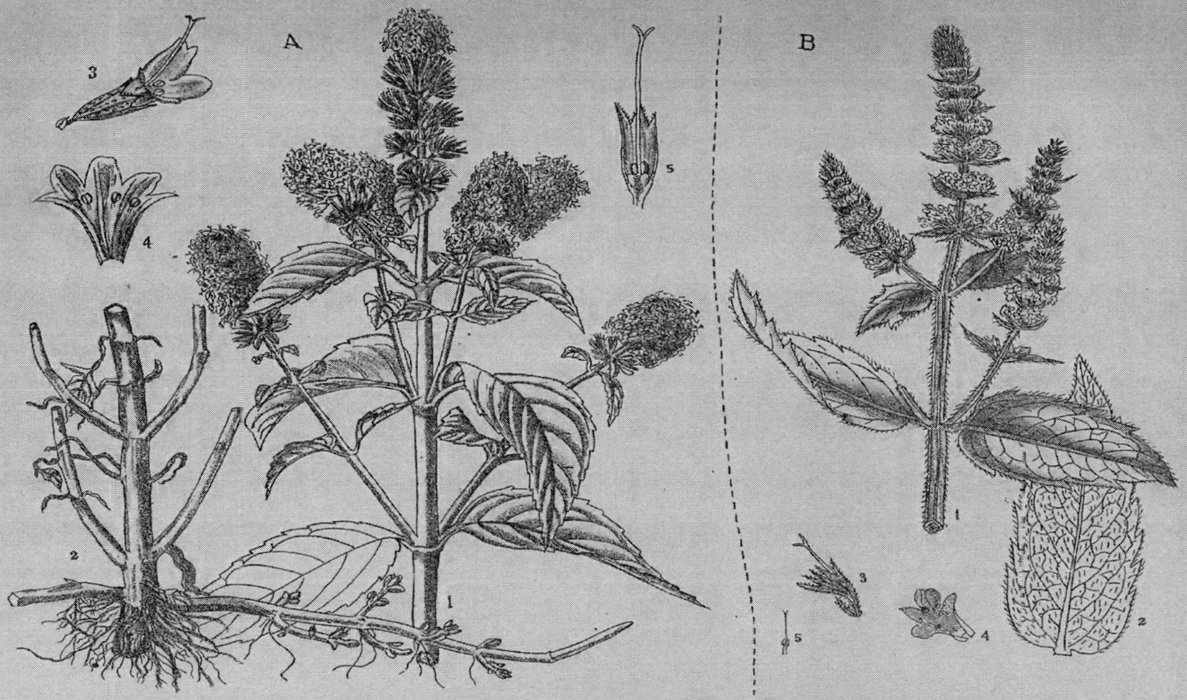

A.—MENTHA PIPERITA, LINN. MENTHA SYLVESTRIS, LINN.

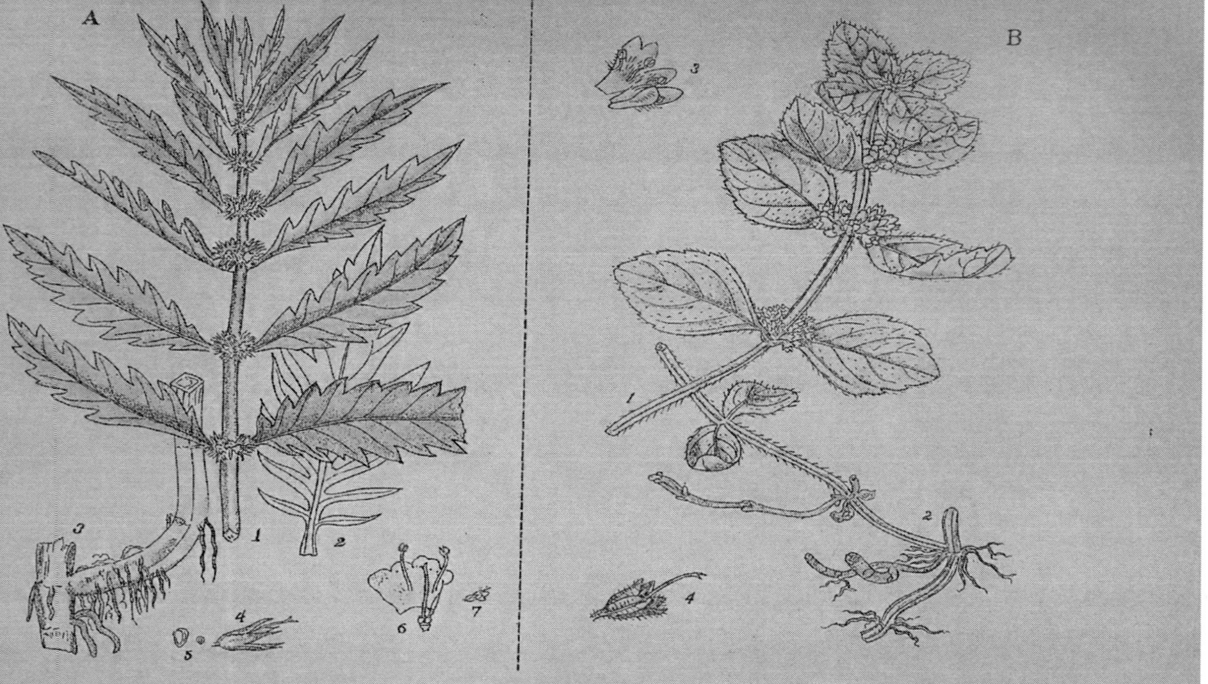

A—LYCOPUS EUROPÆUS, *LINN.*　　B—MENTHA ARVENSIS, *LINN.*

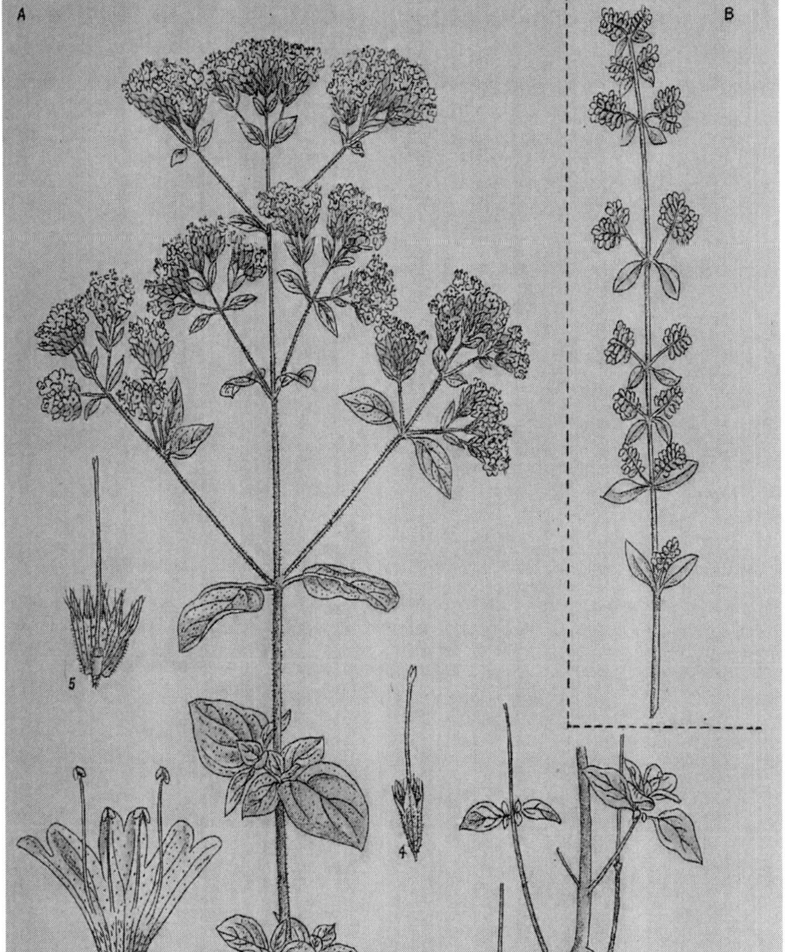

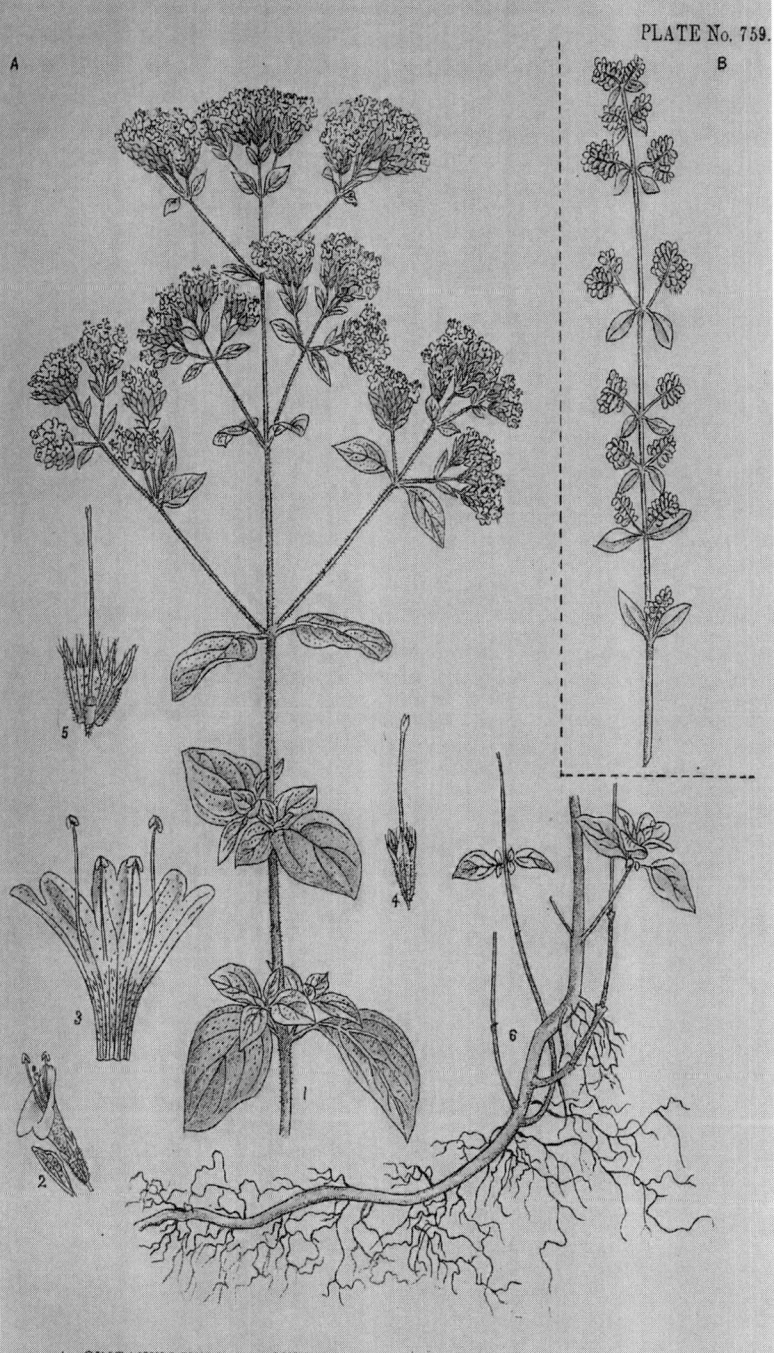

A – ORIGANUM VULGARE, *LINN.* B–ORIGANUM MAJORANA, *LINN.*

PLATE No. 760.

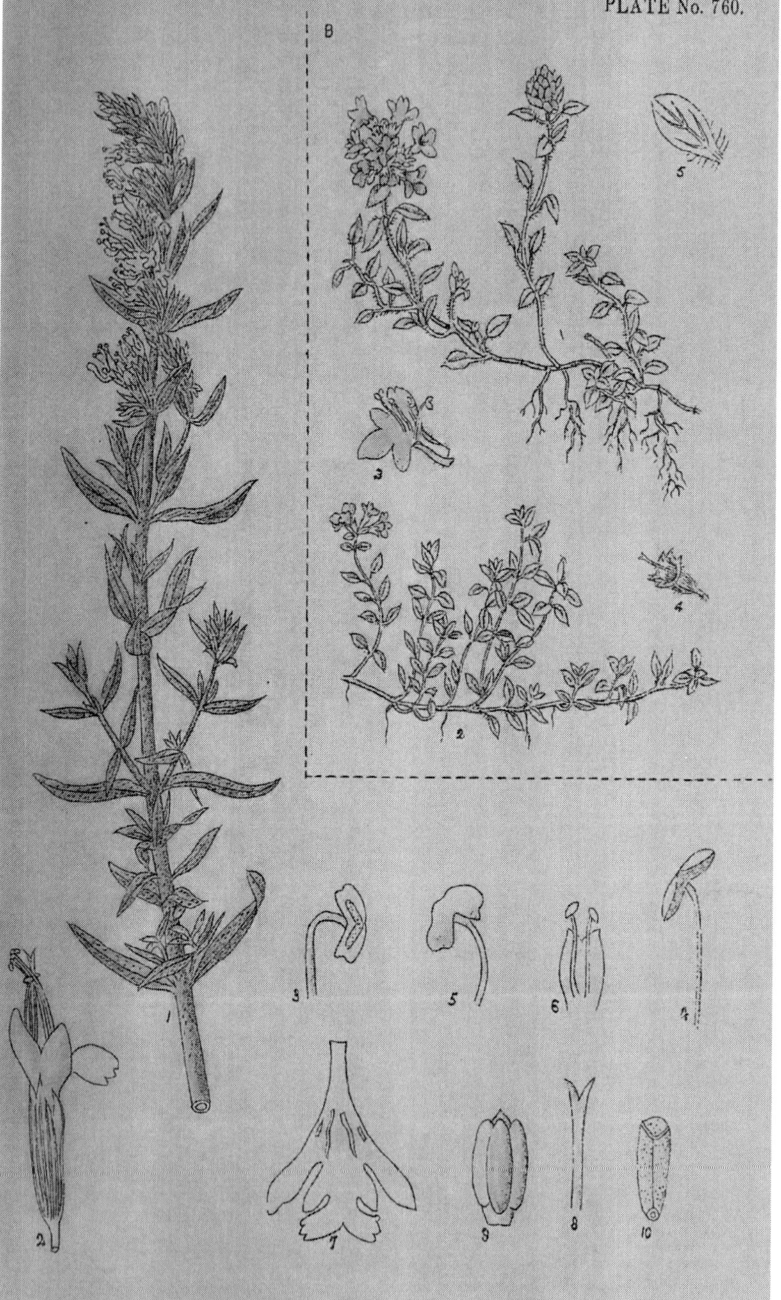

A—HYSSOPUS OFFICINALIS, *LINN.* B—THYMUS SERPYLLUM, *LINN.*

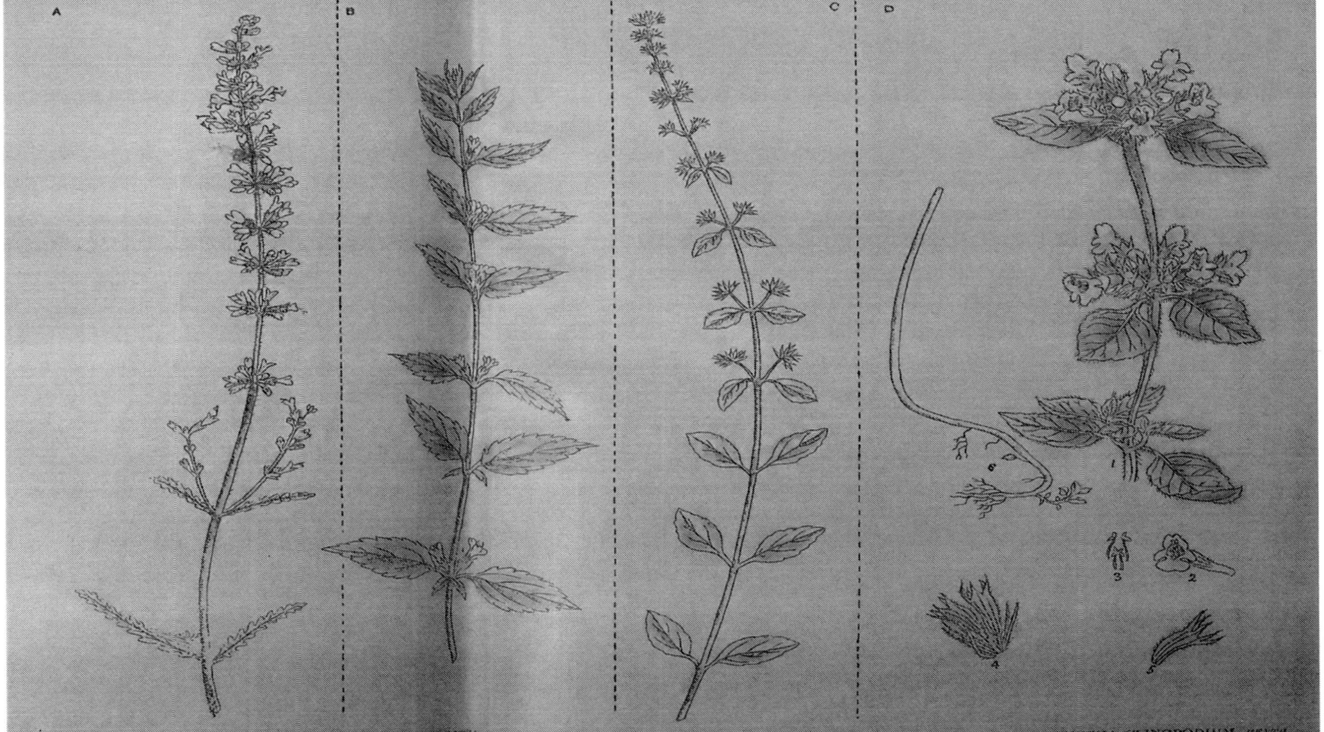

A—PEROWSKIA ABROTANOIDES, *Karel.* B—MELISSA PARVIFLORA, *Benth.* C—MICROMERIA CAPITELLATA, *Benth.* D CALAMINTHA CLINOPODIUM, *Benth.*

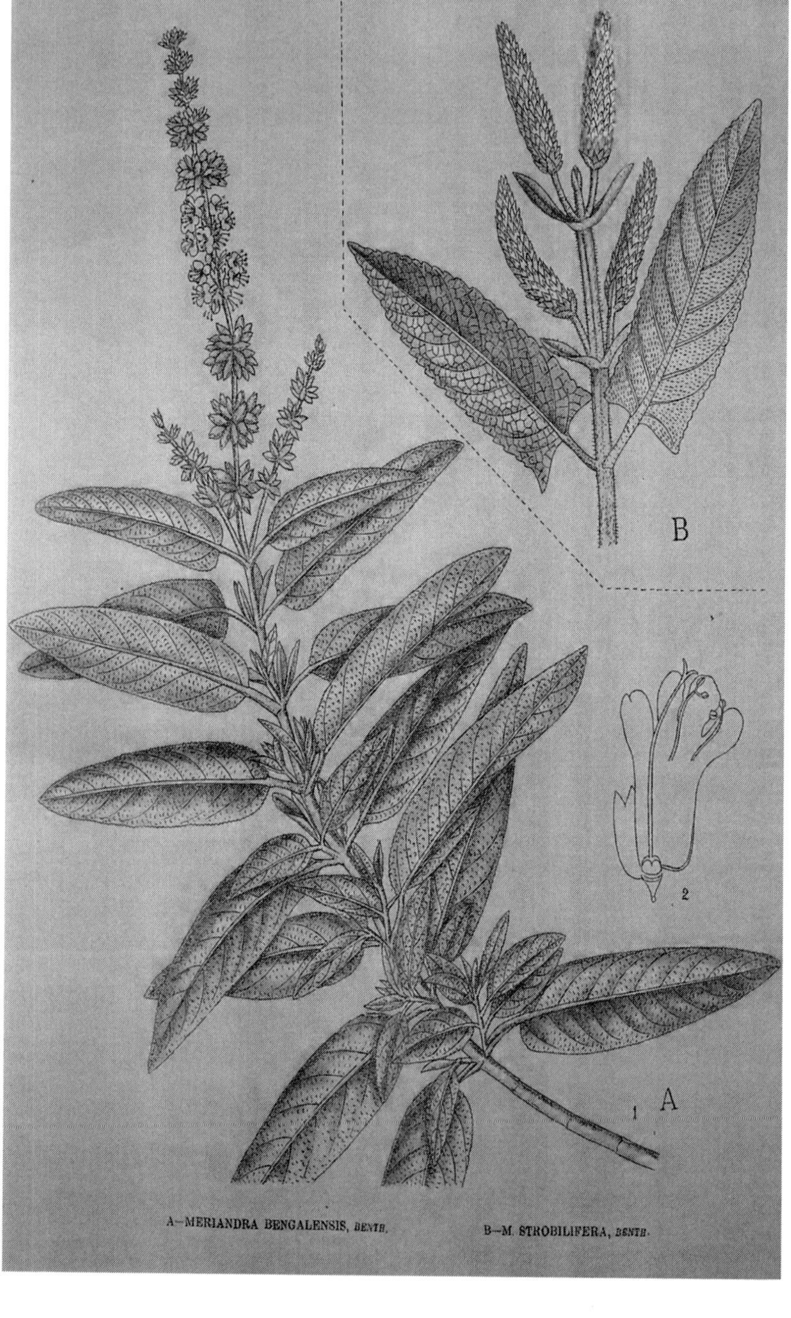

A—MERIANDRA BENGALENSIS, BENTH.

B—M. STROBILIFERA, BENTH.

PLATE No 763.

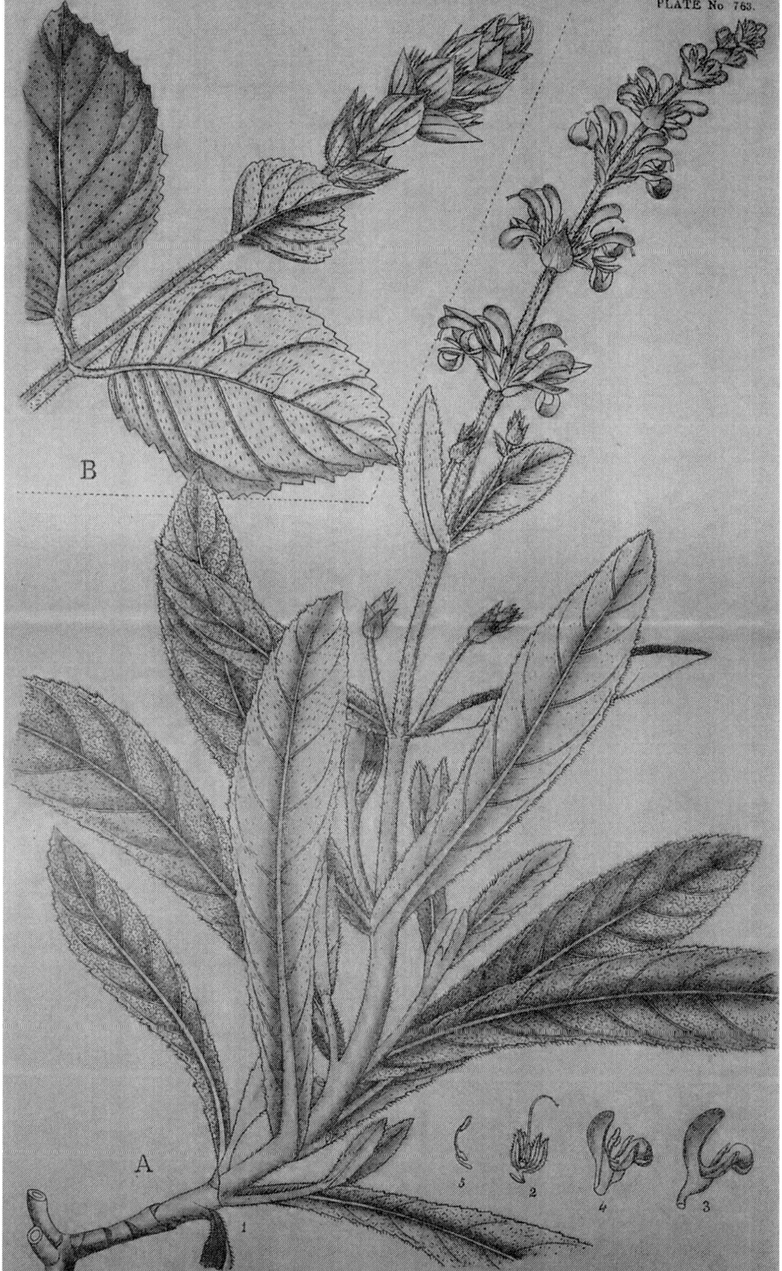

A—SALVIA LANATA, ROXB. B—SALVIA MOORCROFTIANA, WALL

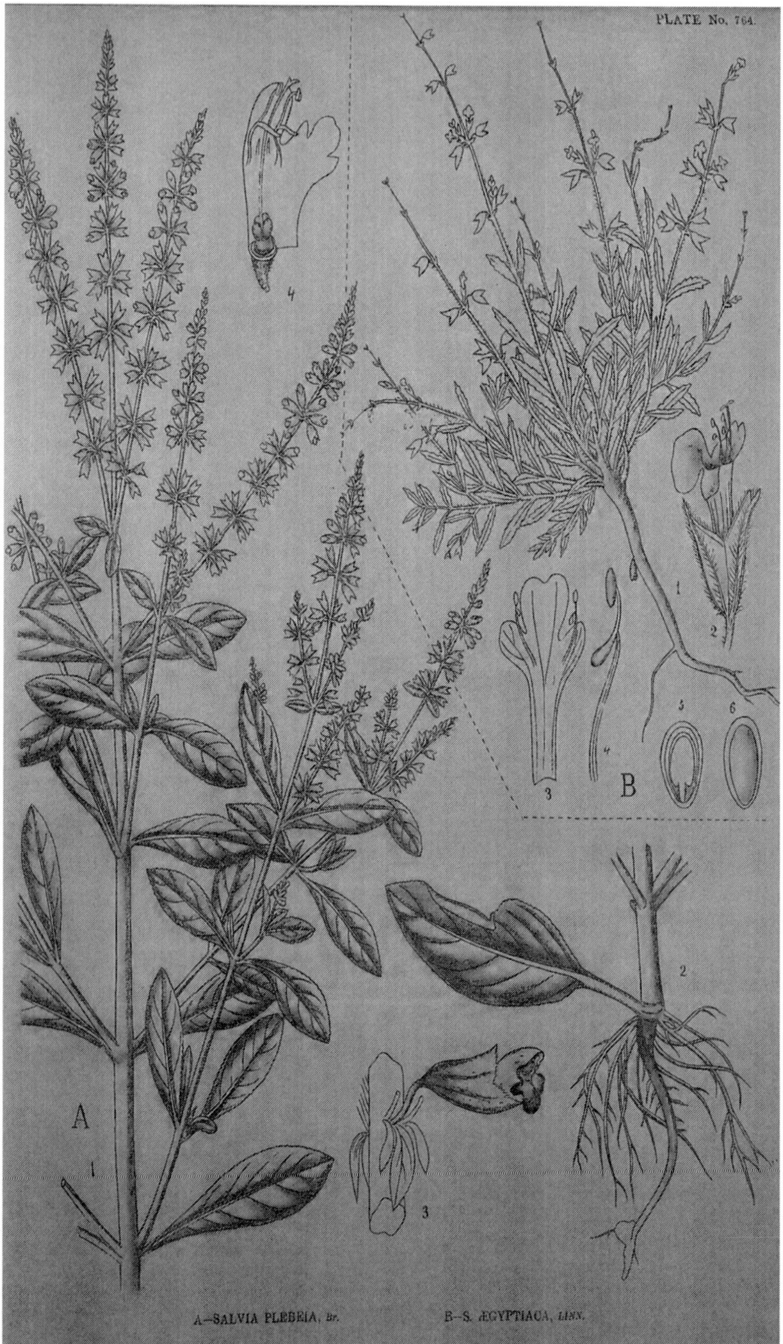

A—SALVIA PLEBEIA, *Br.* B—S. ÆGYPTIACA, *LINN.*

PLATE No. 765.

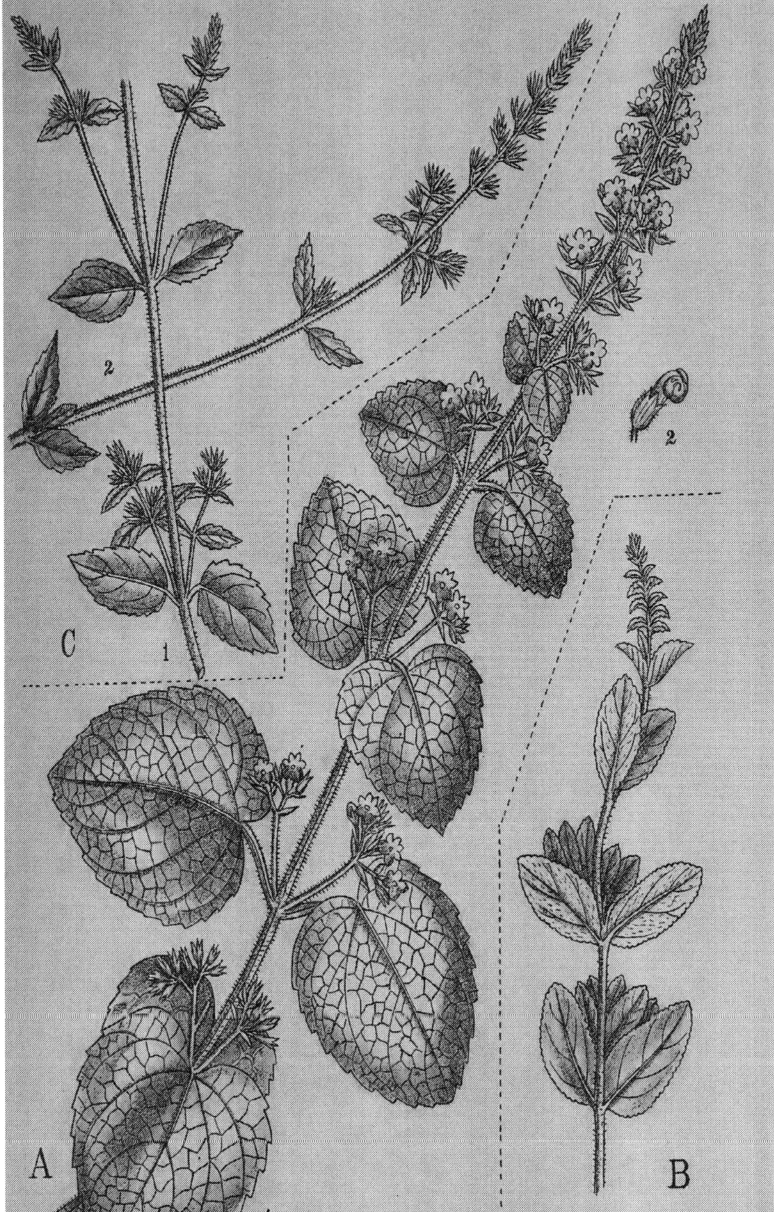

A—NEPETA RUDERALIS, *HAMILT.* B—NEPETA ELLIPTICA, *ROYLE.* C—N. CILIARIS, *BENTH.*

PLATE No. 766.

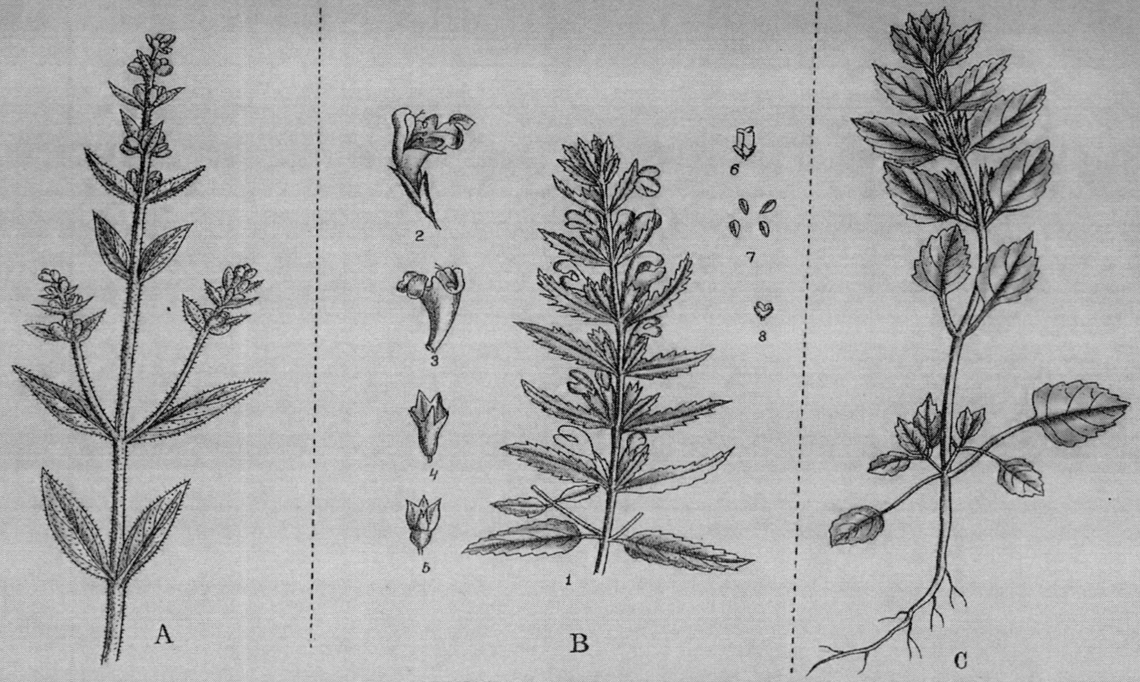

A—STACHYS PARVIFLORA, *Benth.* B—DRACOCEPHALUM MOLDAVICUM, *Linn.* C—LALLEMANTIA ROYLEANA, *Benth.*

PLATE No. 767.

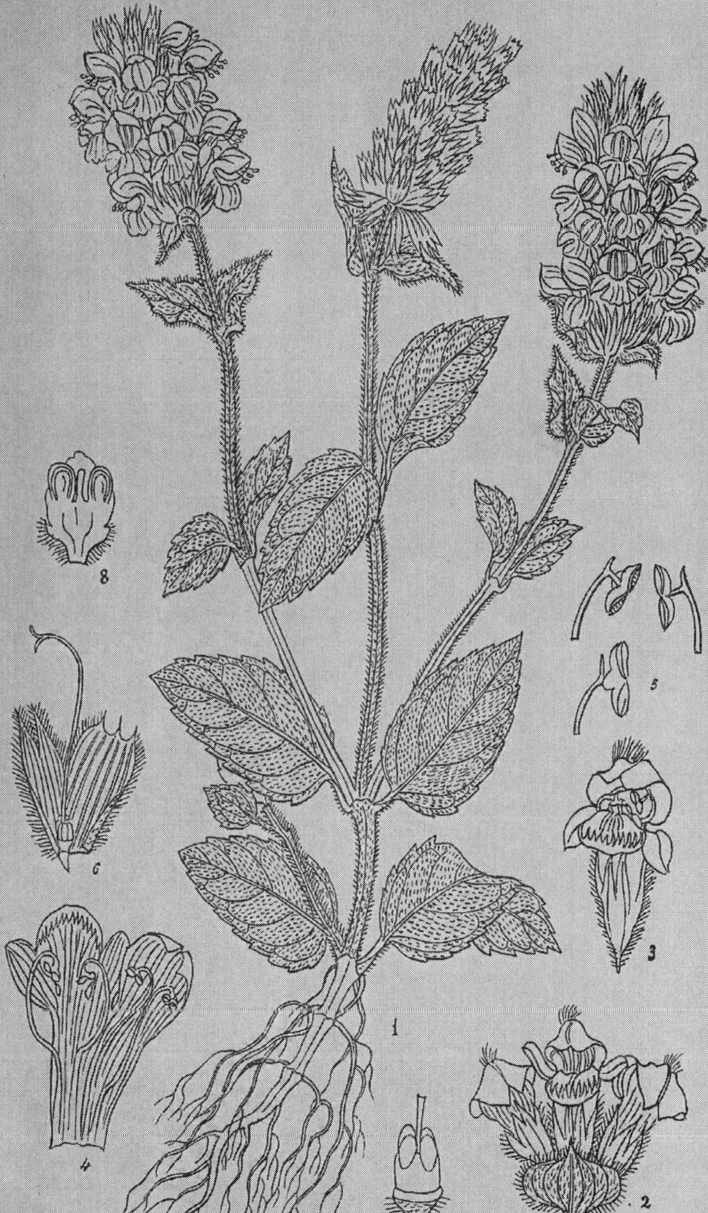

BRUNELLA VULGARIS, *LINN.*

PLATE No. 768.

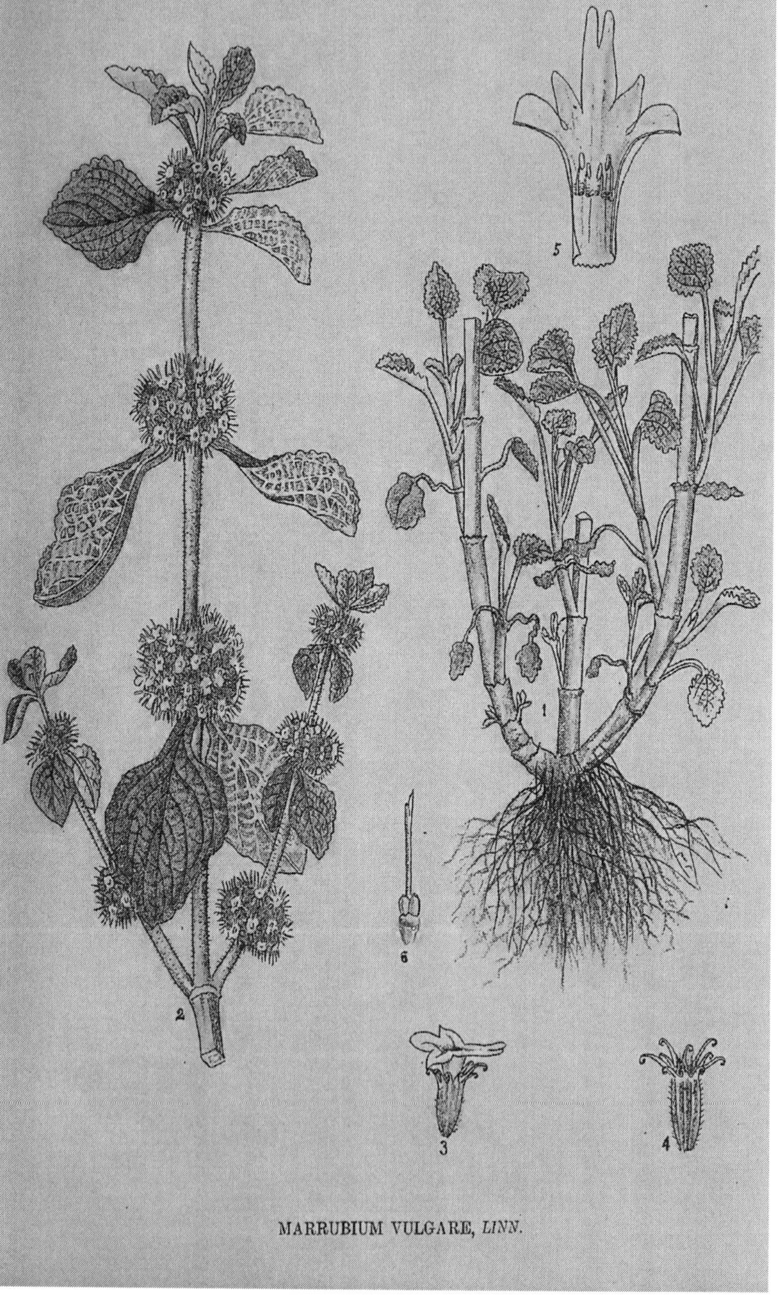

MARRUBIUM VULGARE, *LINN.*

PLATE No. 769.

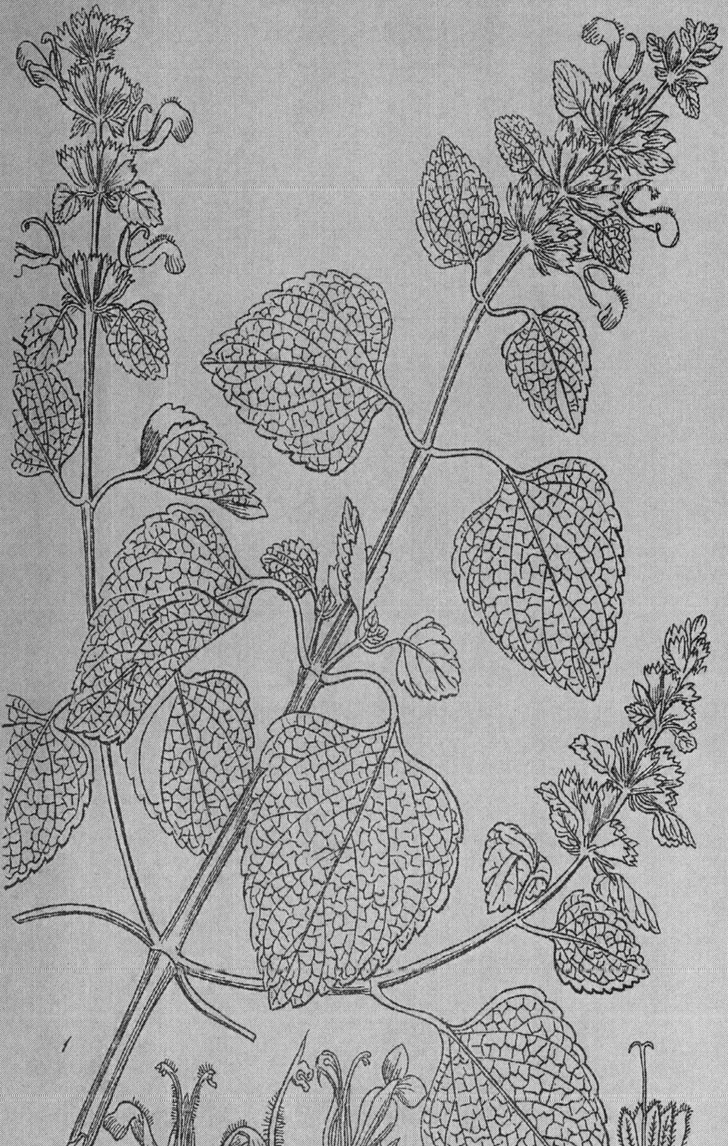

ANISOMELES OVATA, BR.

PLATE No. 770.

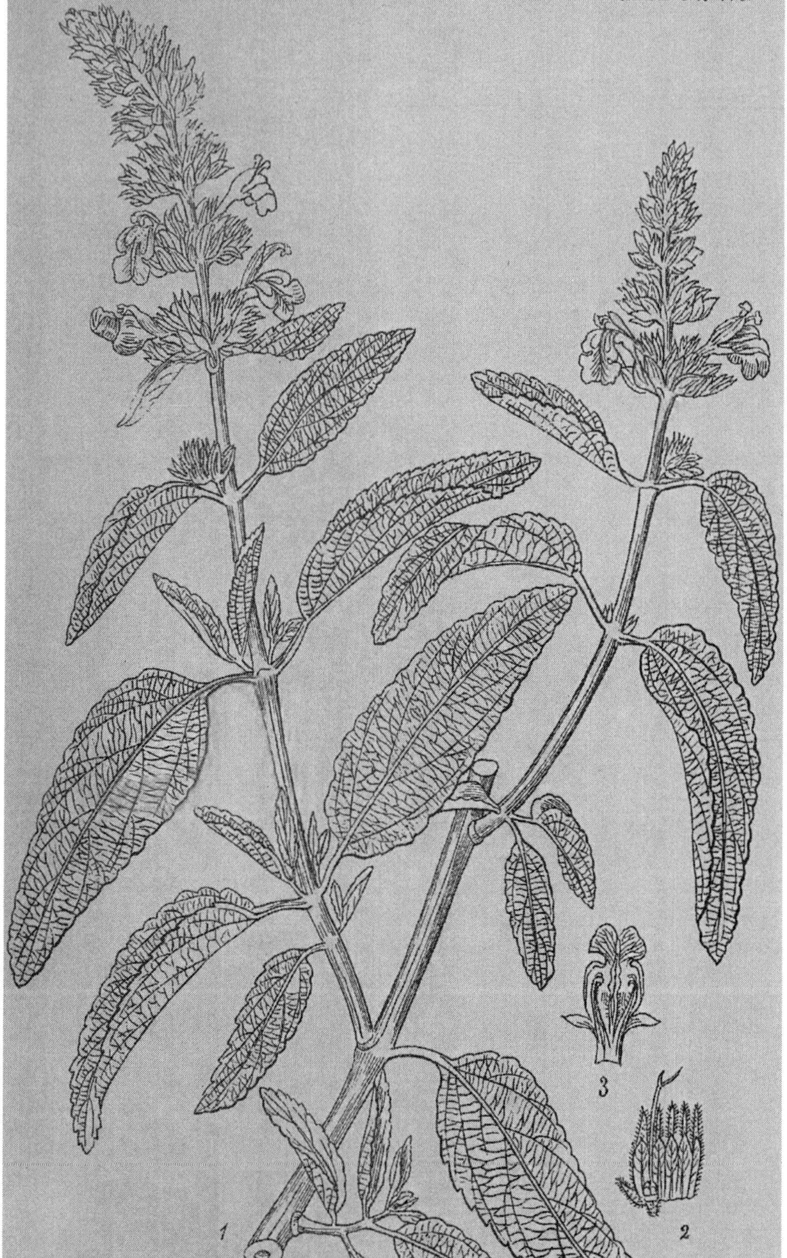

ANISOMELES MALABARICA, BR.

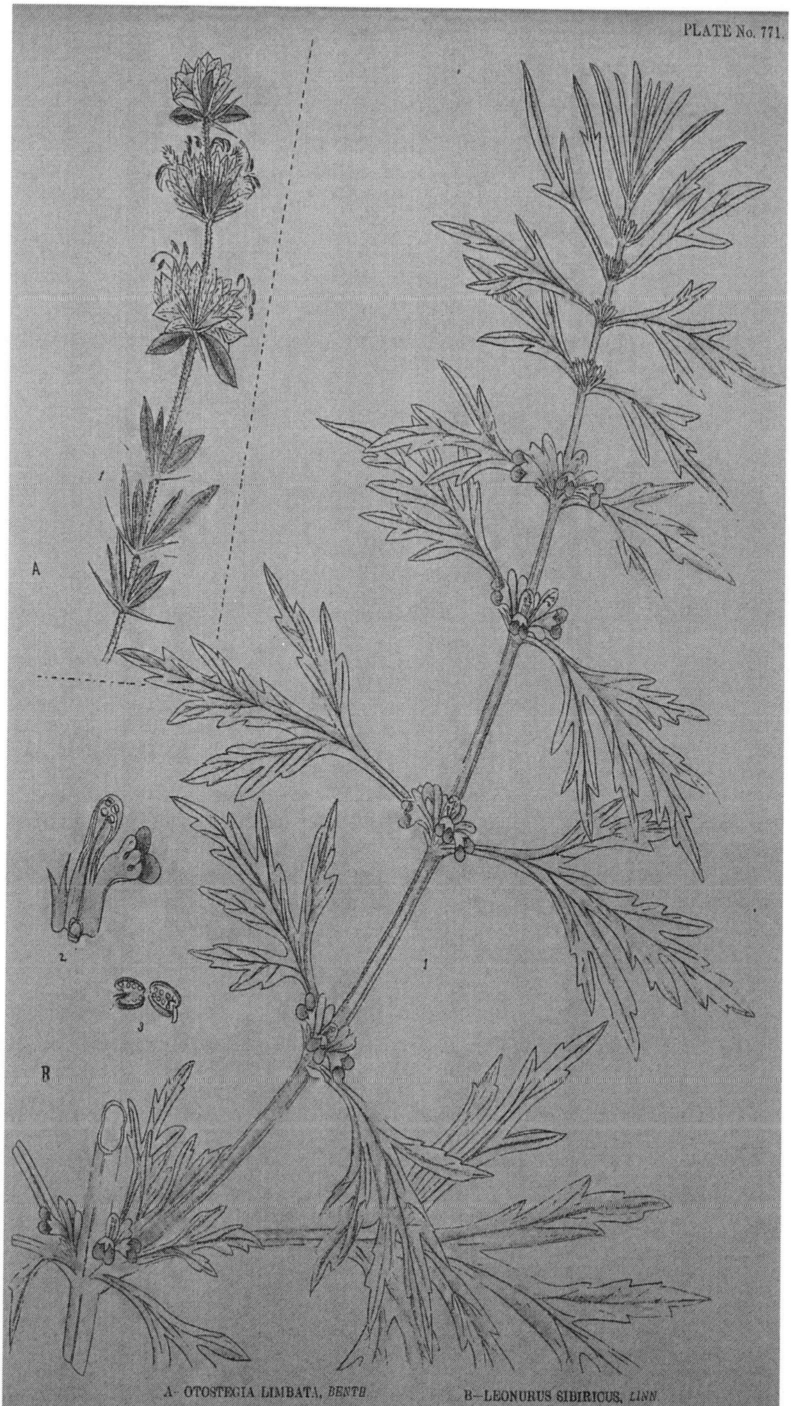

A- OTOSTEGIA LIMBATA, *BENTH*

B—LEONURUS SIBIRICUS, *LINN*

PLATE No. 772.

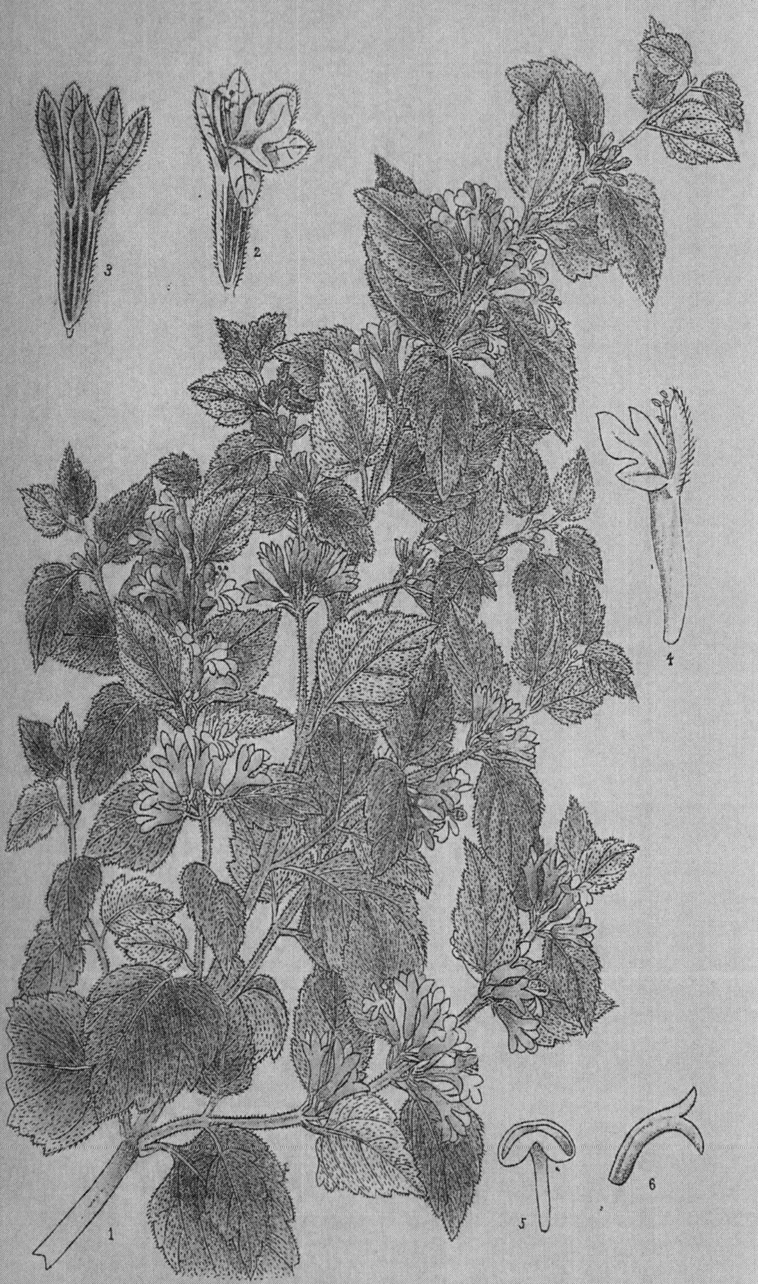

ROYLEA ELEGANS, *WALL.*

PLATE No 773.

LEUCAS CEPHALOTES, *SPRENG.*

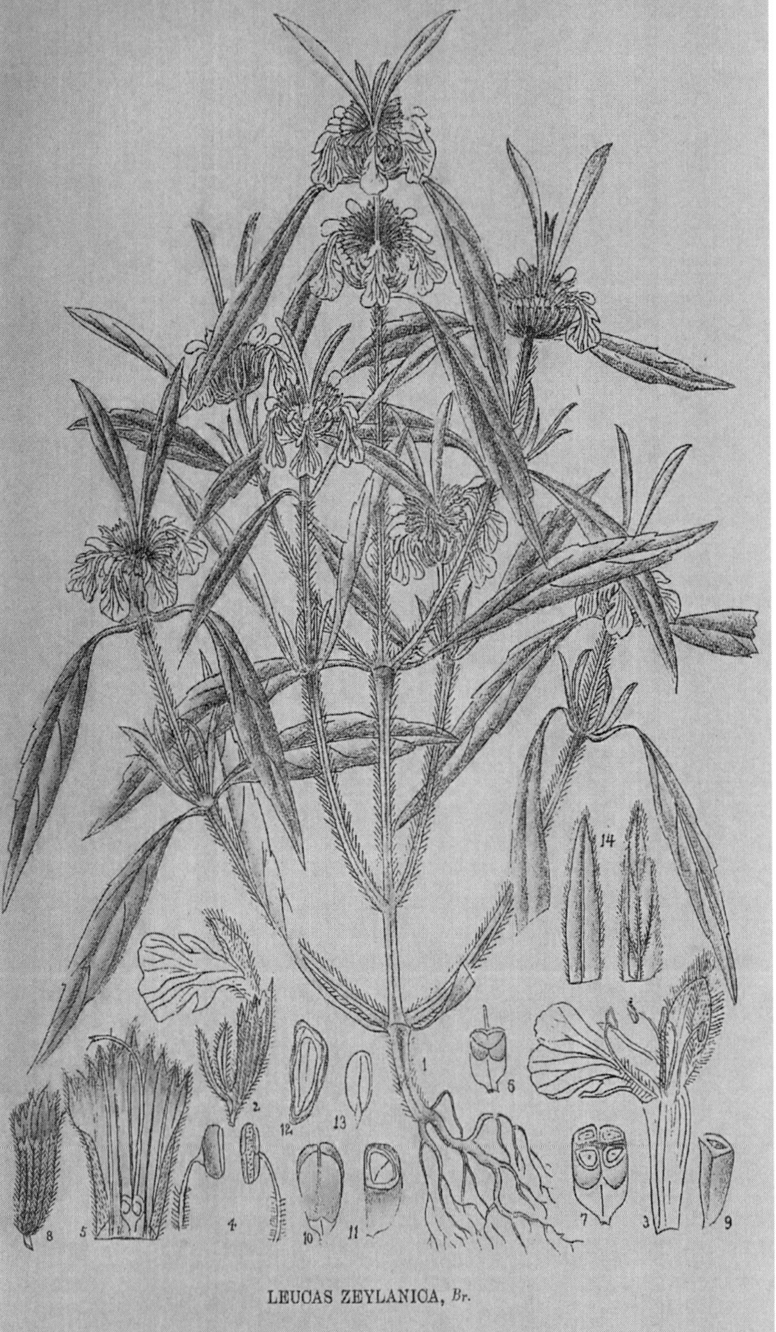

LEUCAS ZEYLANICA, *Br.*

PLATE No. 775

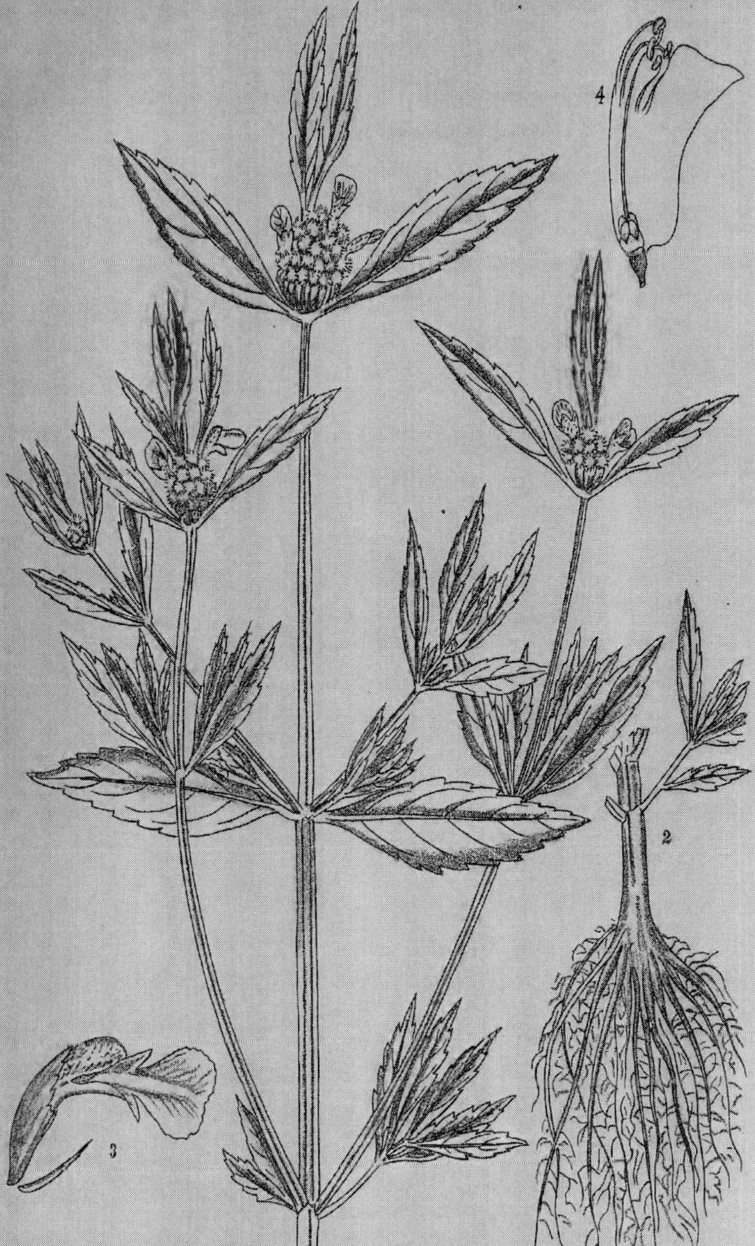

LEUCAS ASPERA, SPRENG.

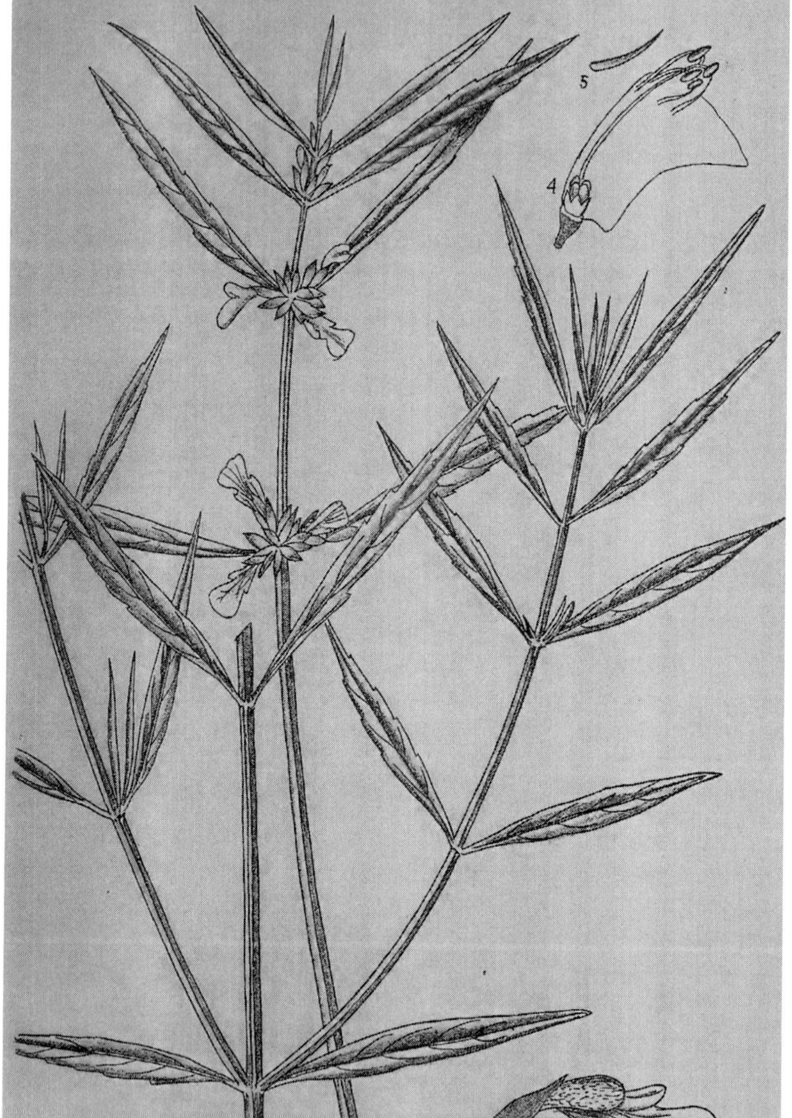

LEUCAS LINIFOLIA, *SPRENG.*

PLATE No. 777.

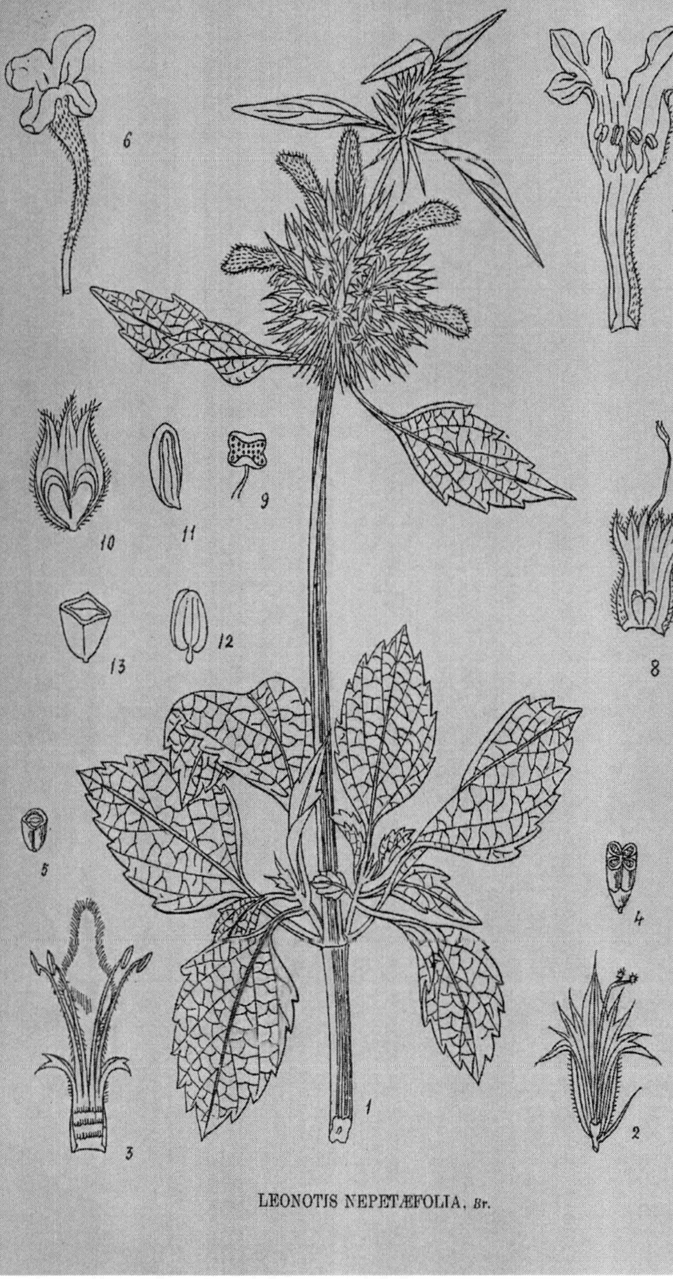

LEONOTIS NEPETÆFOLIA, *Br.*

PLATE No. 778.

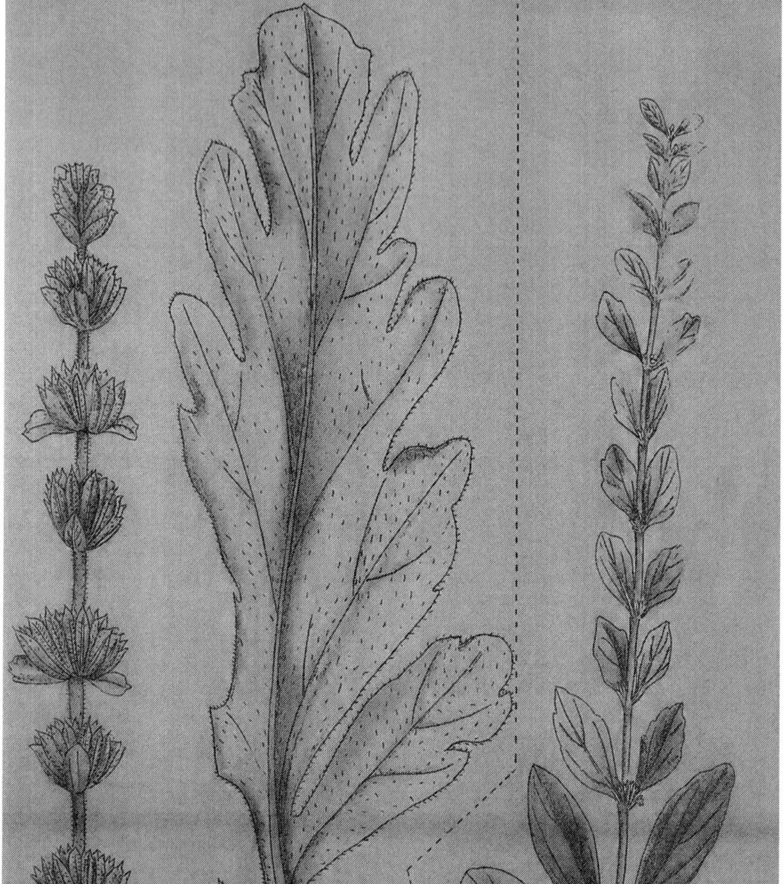

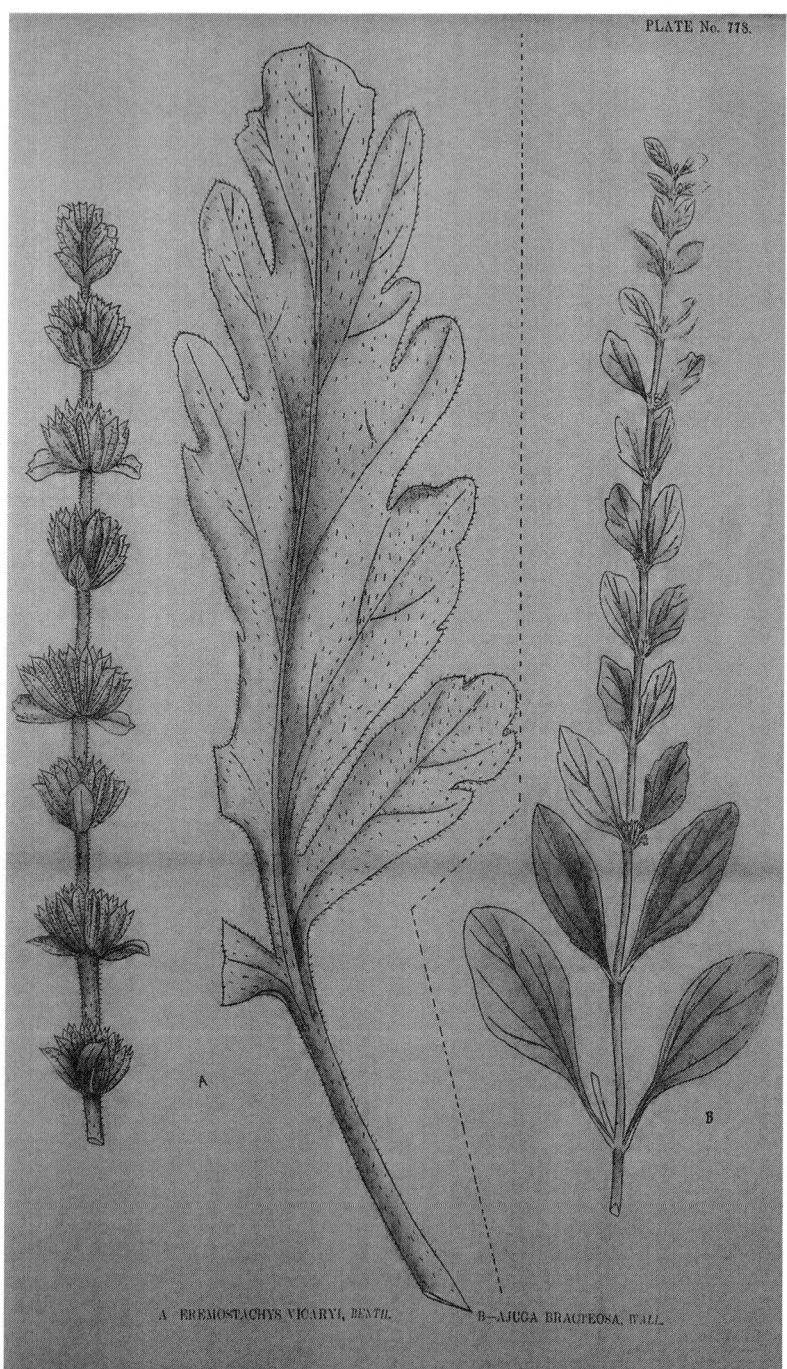

A—EREMOSTACHYS VICARYI, *Benth.* B—AJUGA BRACTEOSA, *Wall.*

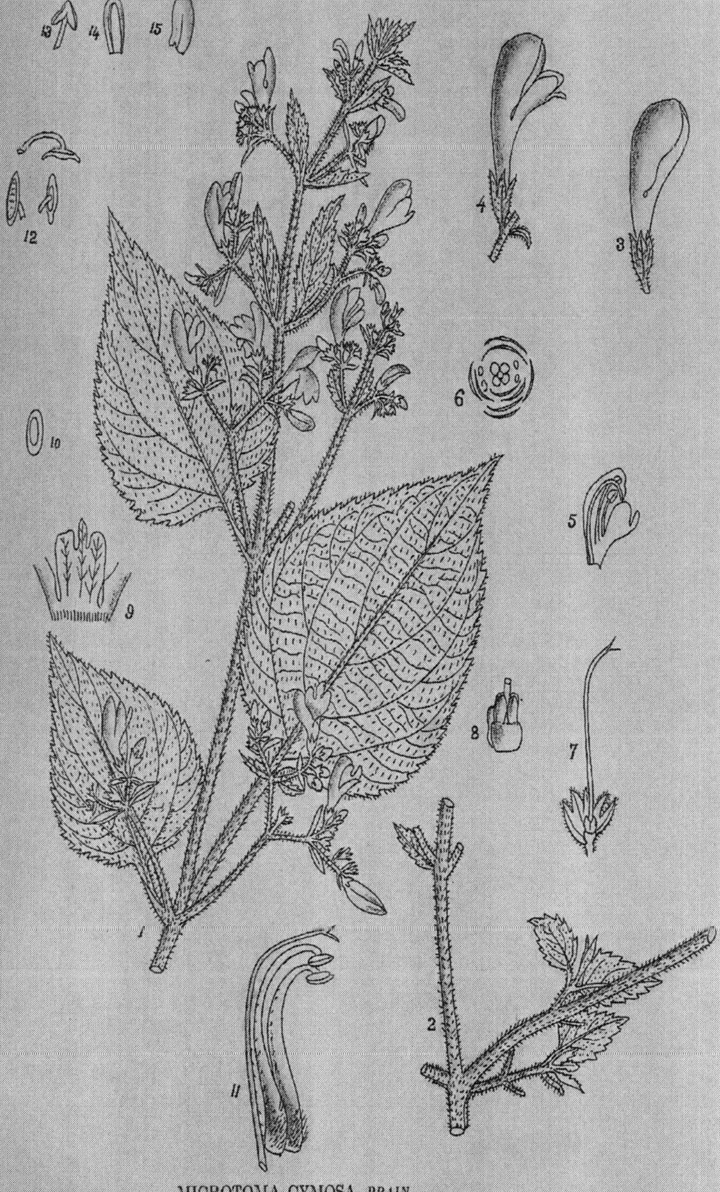

MICROTOMA CYMOSA, *PRAIN.*

PLATE No. 780

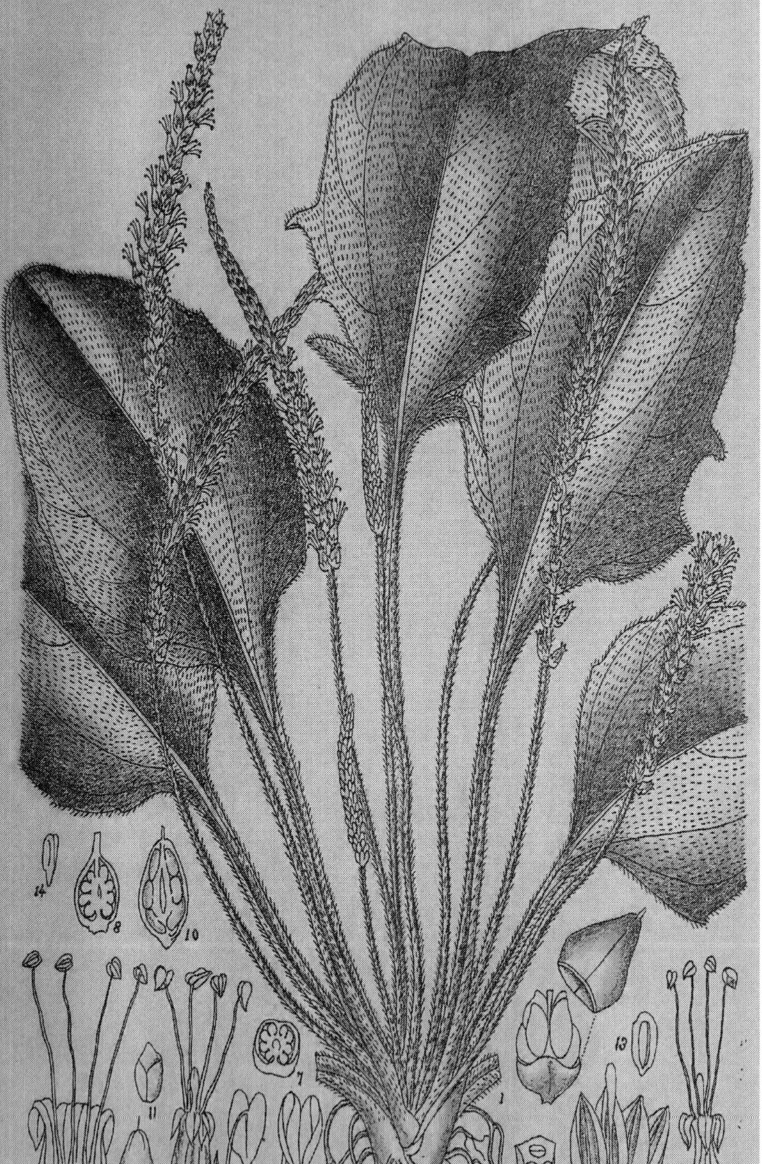

PLANTAGO MAJOR, *LINN.*

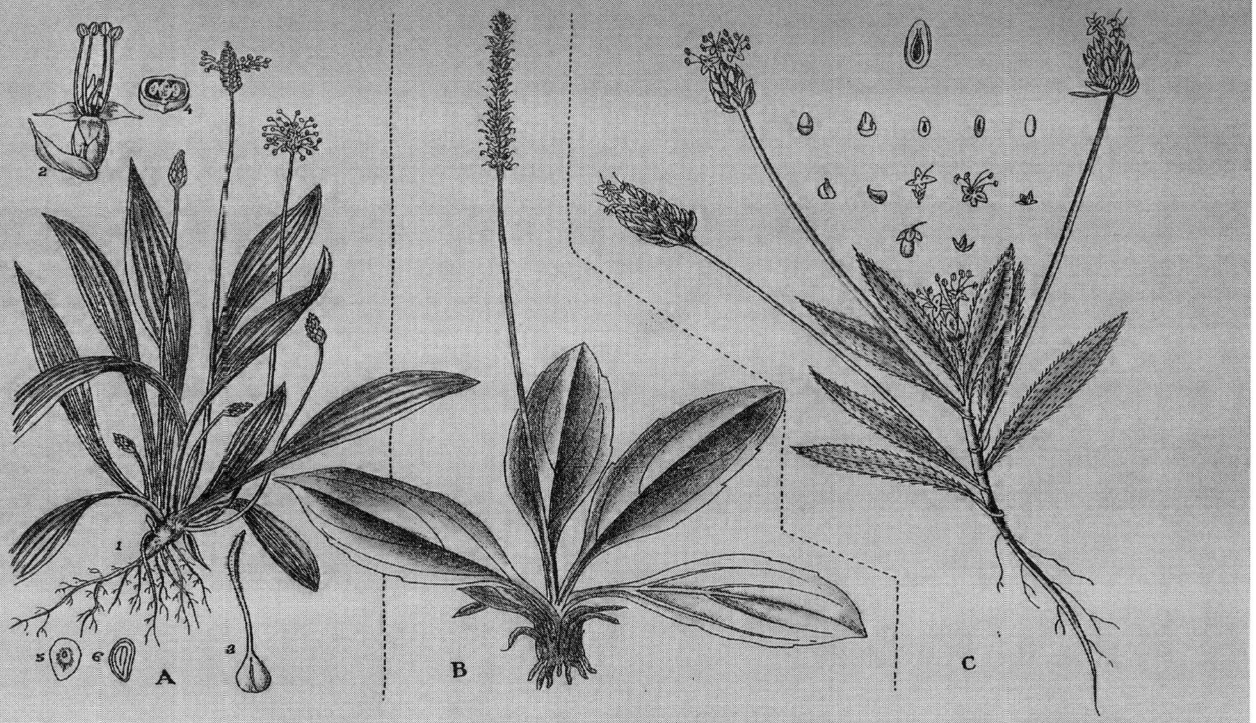

A—PLANTAGO LANCEOLATA, *LINN.* B—P. BRACHYPHYLLA, *EDGEW.* C—P. AMPLEXICAULIS, *CAV.*

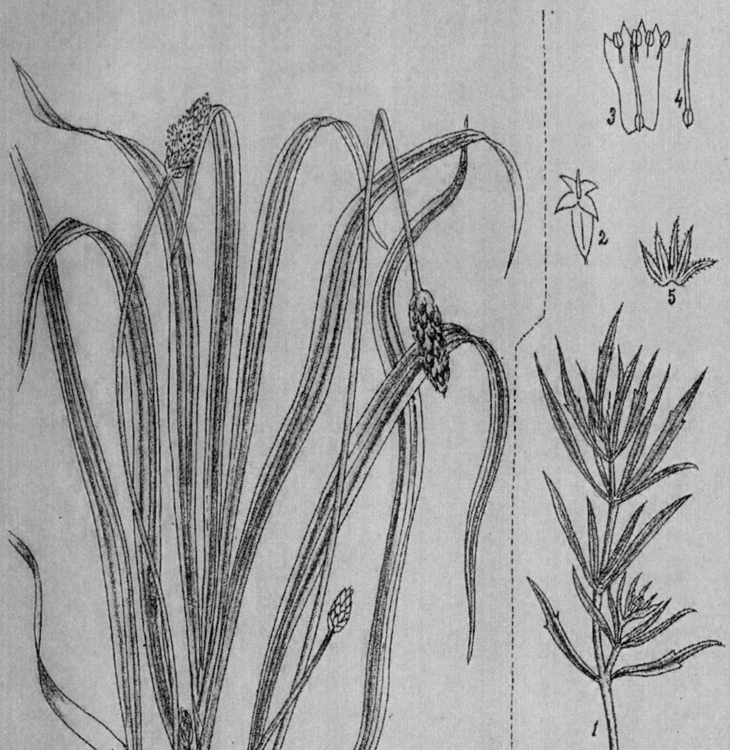

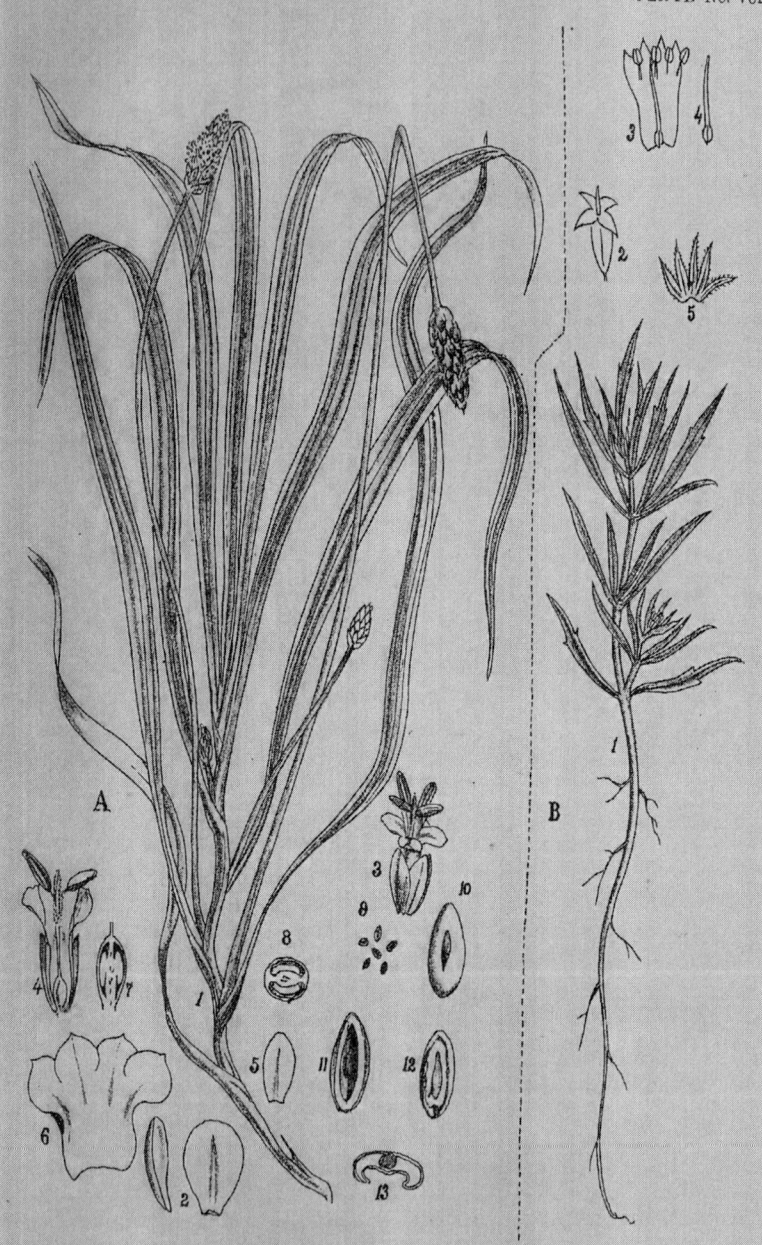

A—PLANTAGO OVATA, *Forsk.*   B—P. PSYLLIUM, *Linn.*

PLATE No. 783.

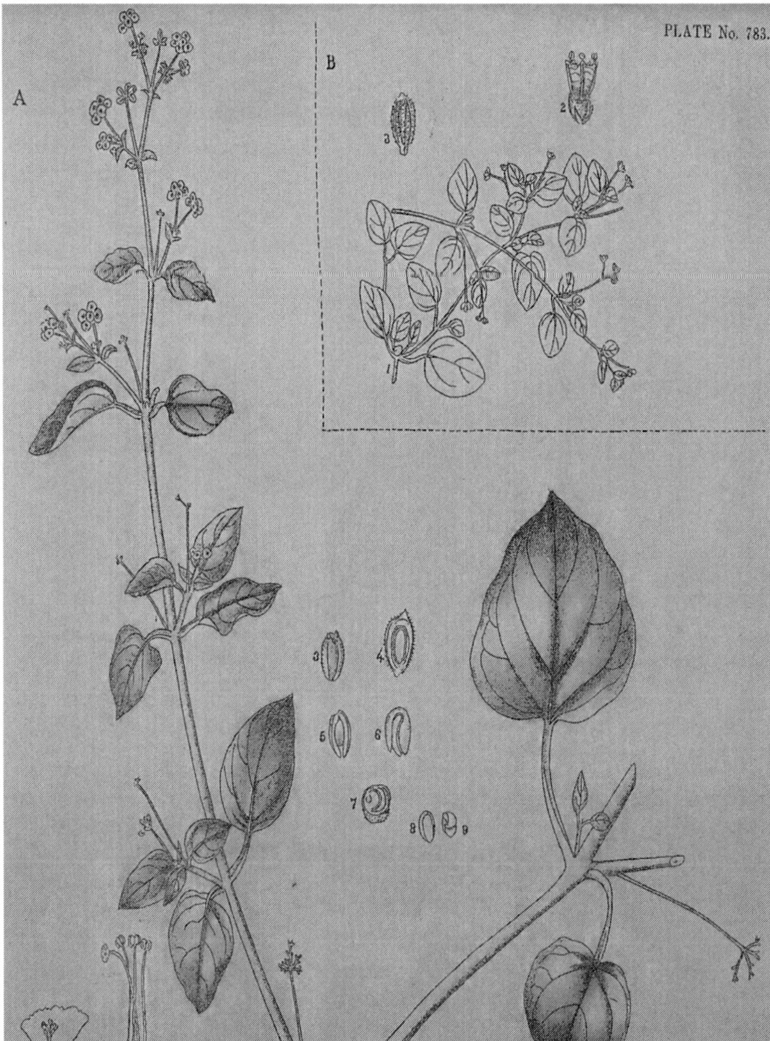

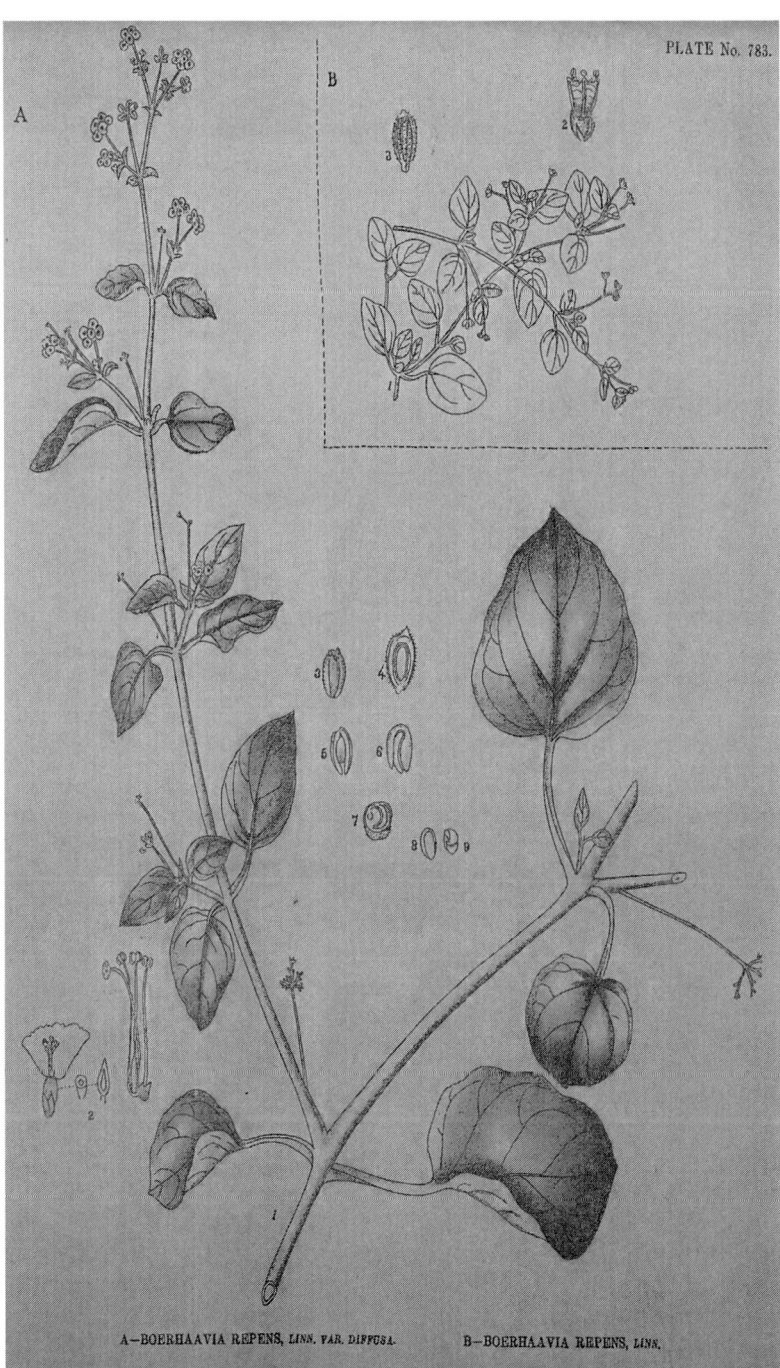

A—BOERHAAVIA REPENS, *LINN. VAR. DIFFUSA.* B—BOERHAAVIA REPENS, *LINN.*

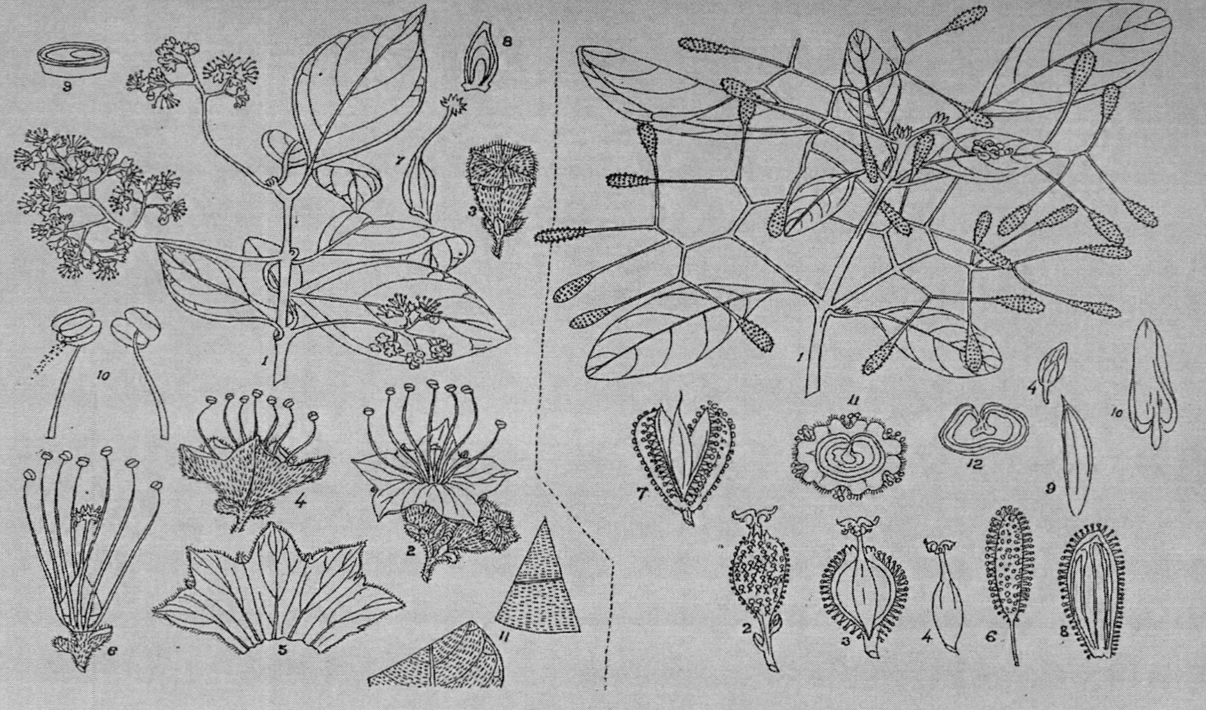

PISONIA ACULEATA, *LINN.*

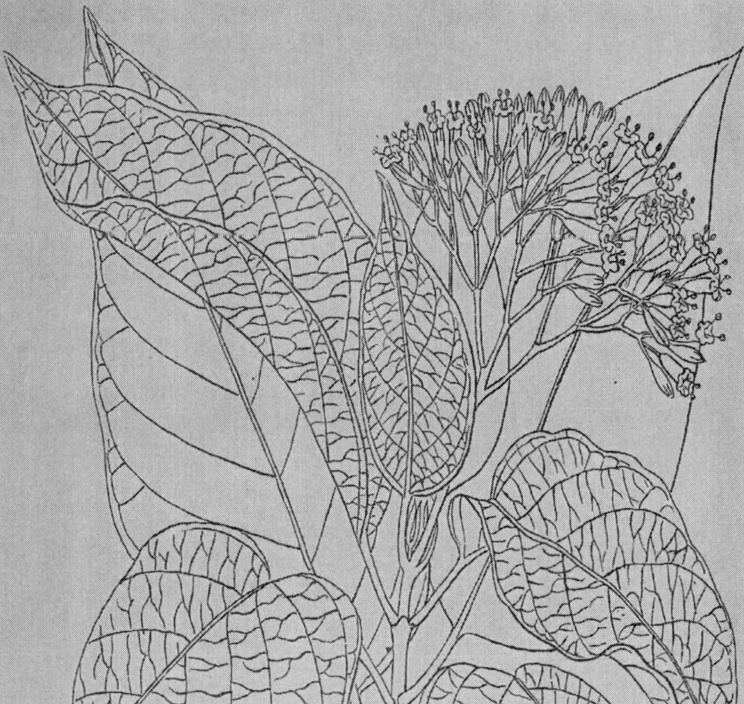

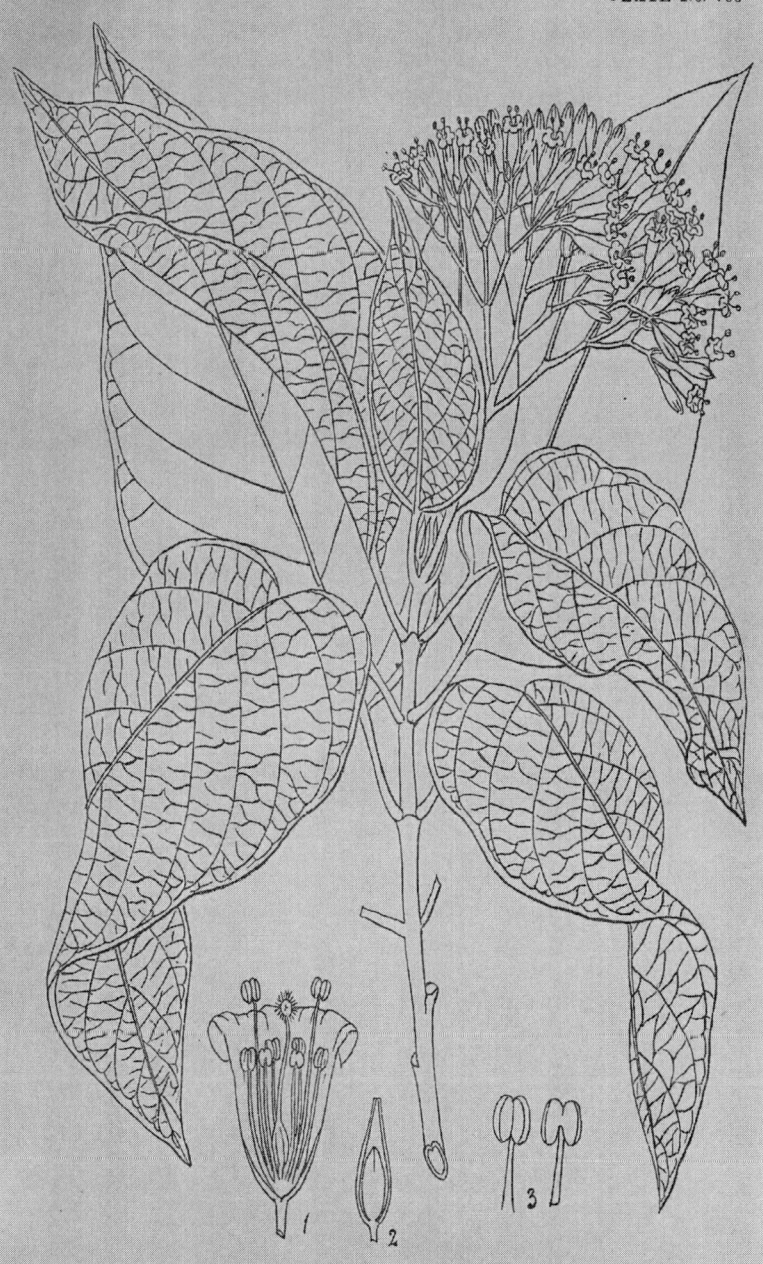

PISONIA ALBA, *SPANOGHE*

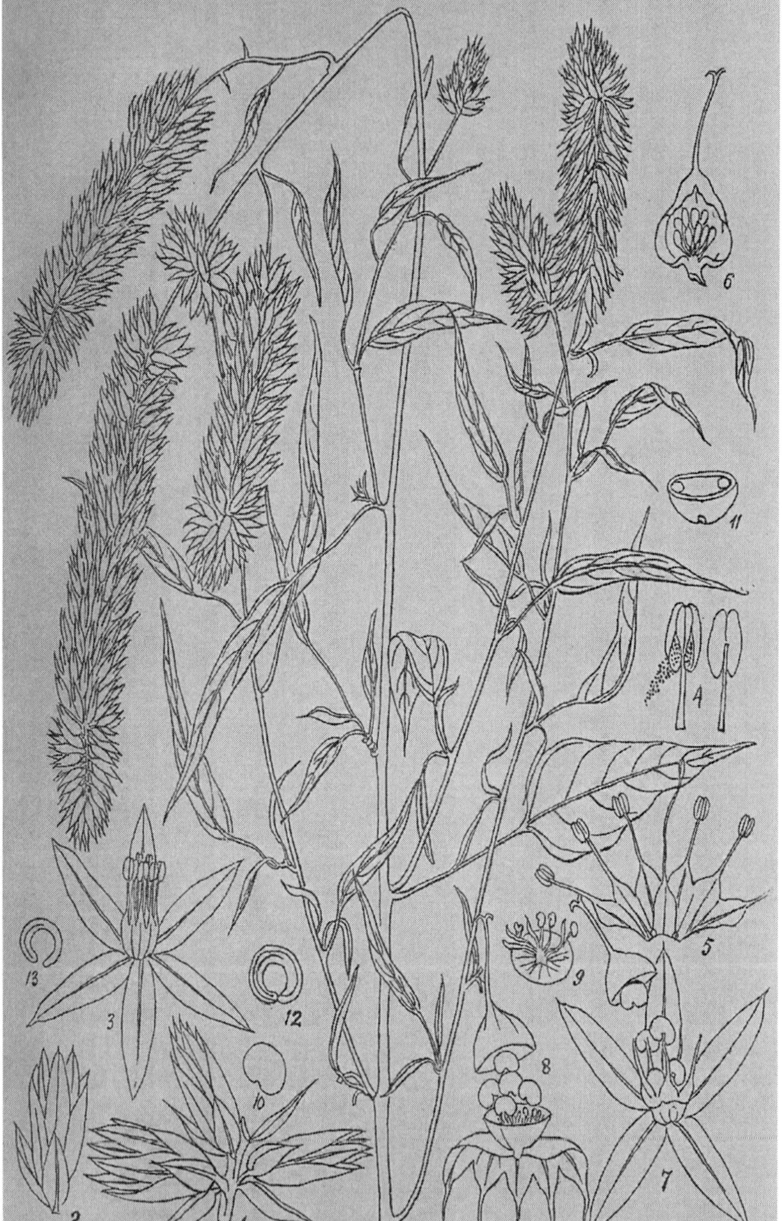

CELOSIA ARGENTEA, *LINN.*

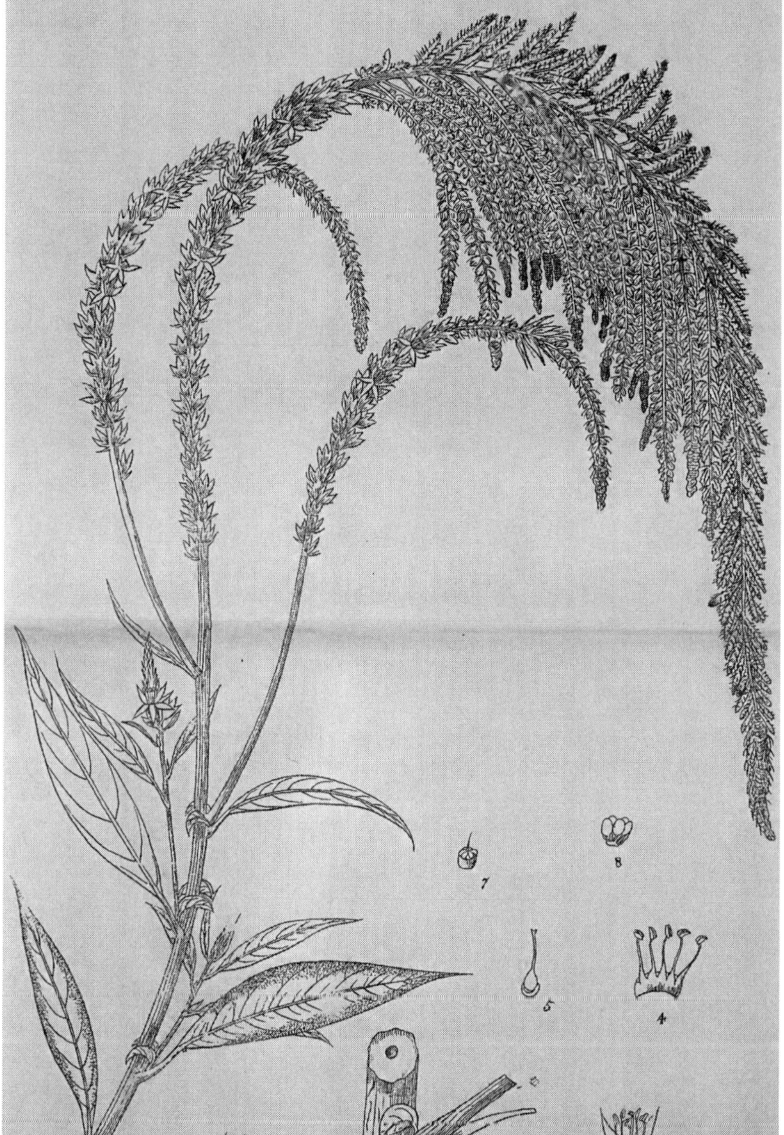

CELOSIA CRISTATA, *LINN.*

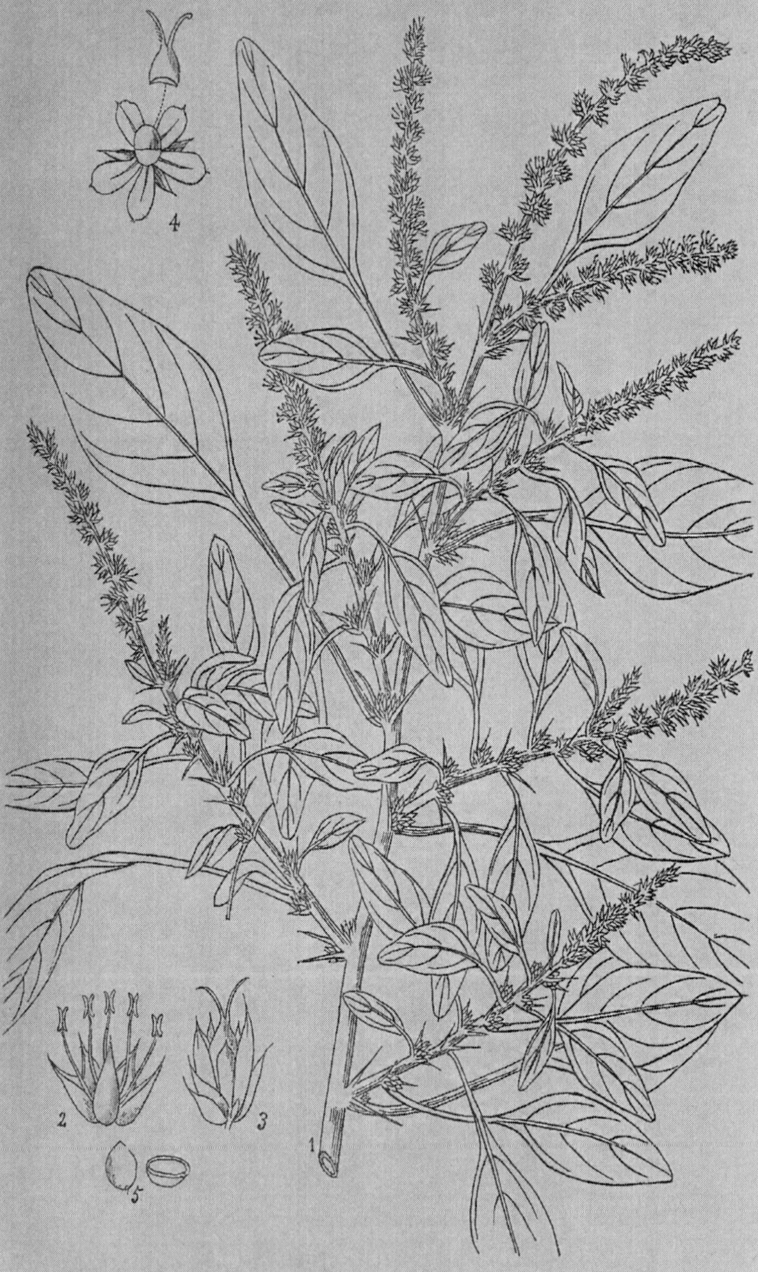

AMARANTHUS SPINOSUS, LINN.

PLATE No. 789.

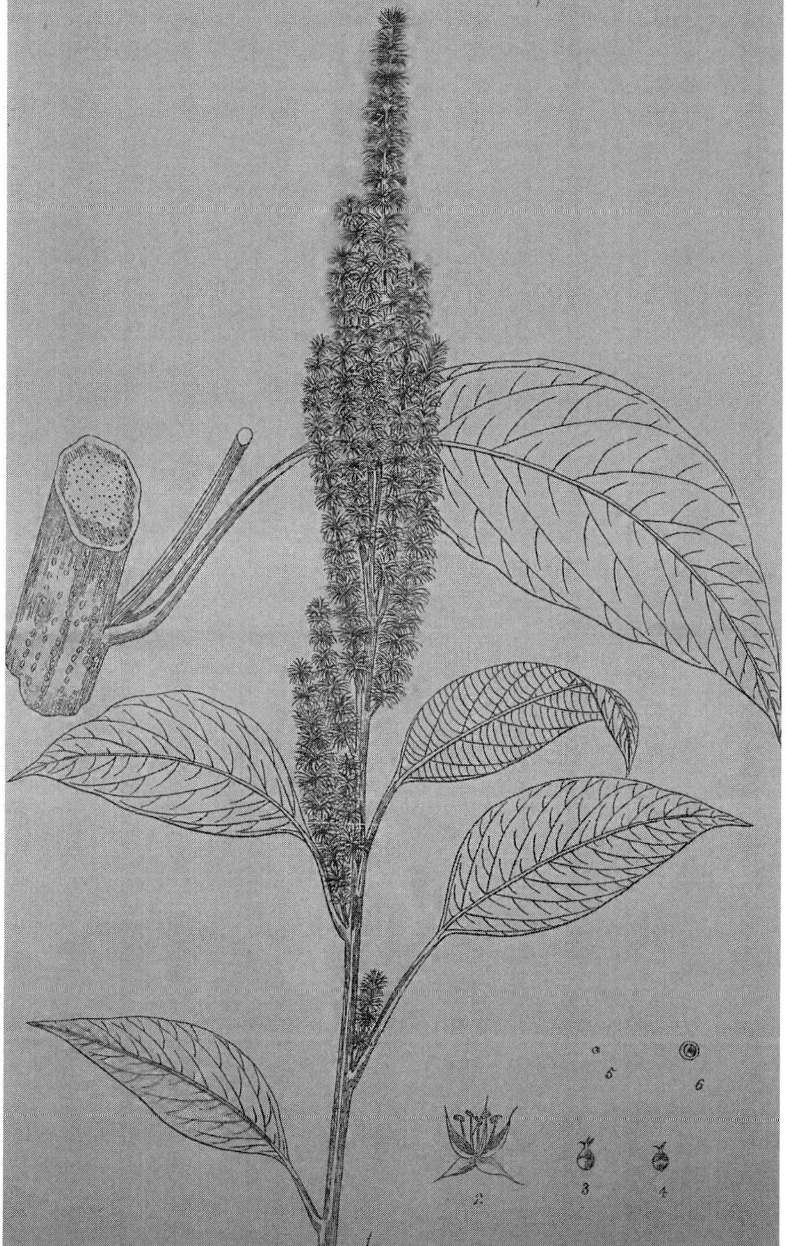

AMARANTHUS PANICULATUS, *LINN.*

PLATE No. 790.

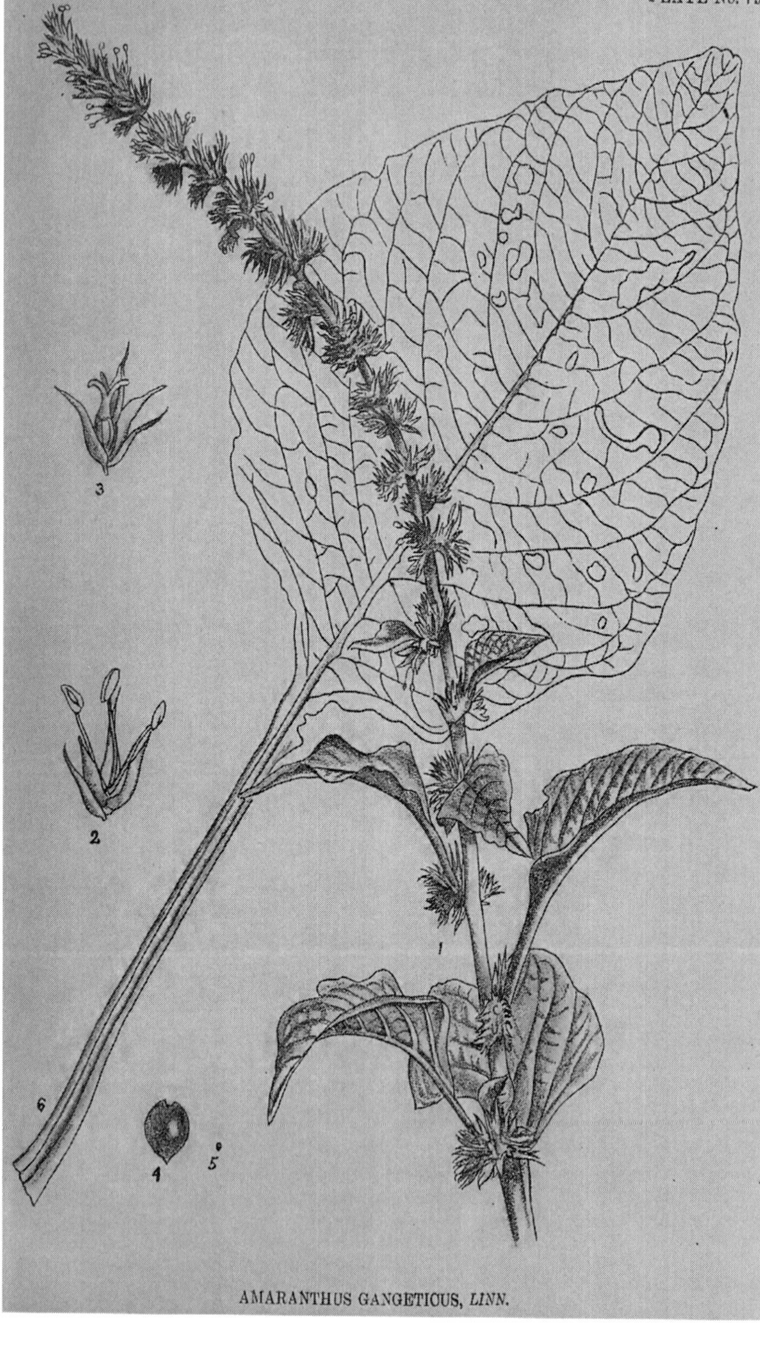

AMARANTHUS GANGETICUS, *LINN.*

PLATE No. 791.

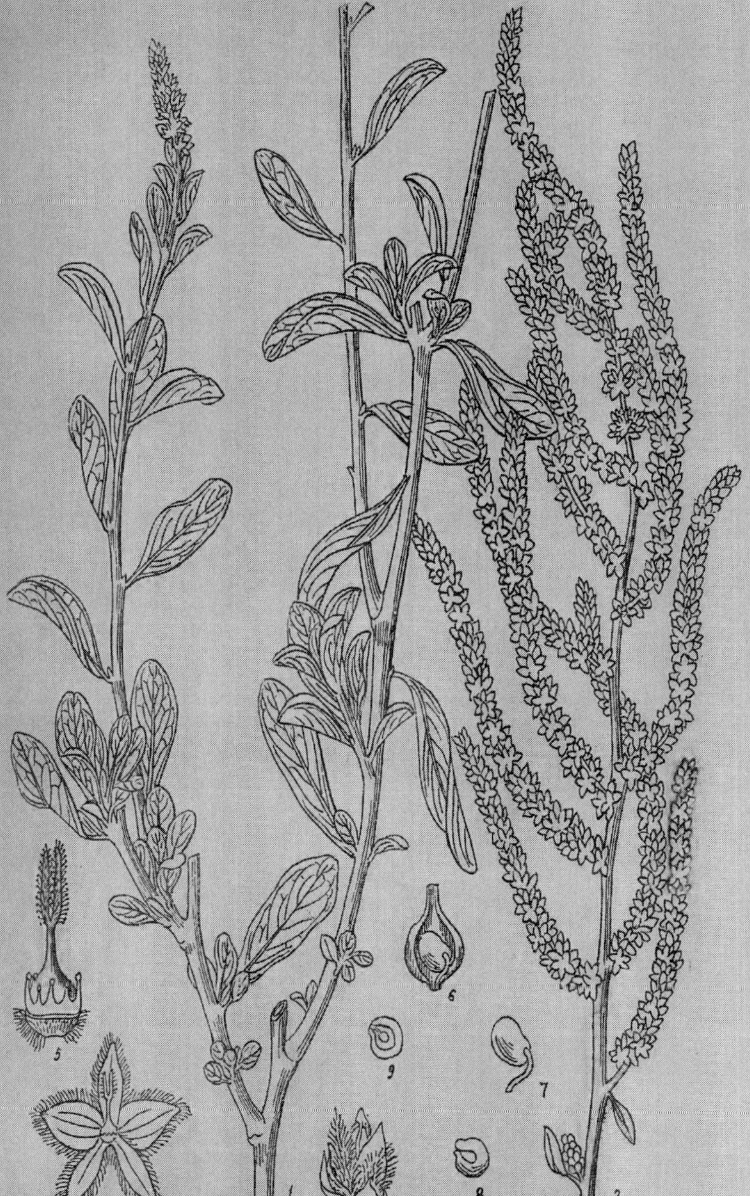

ÆRUA JAVANICA, JUSS.

PLATE No. 792.

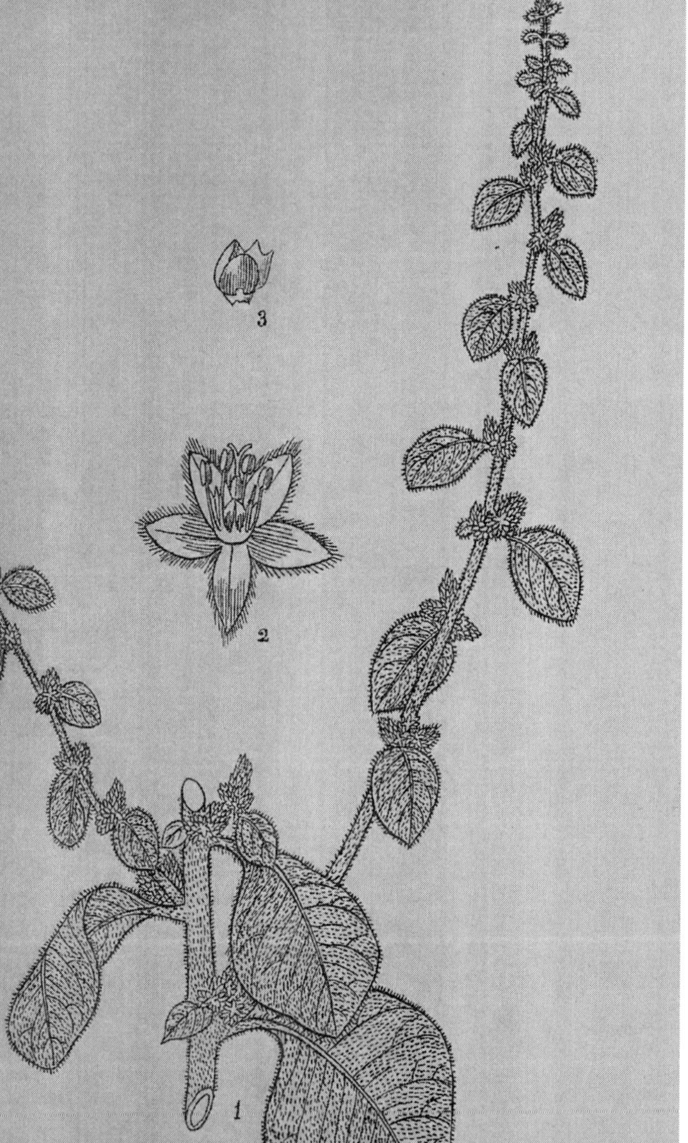

ÆRUA LANATA, *JUSS.*

PLATE No. 793.

ACHYRANTHES ASPERA. *LINN.*

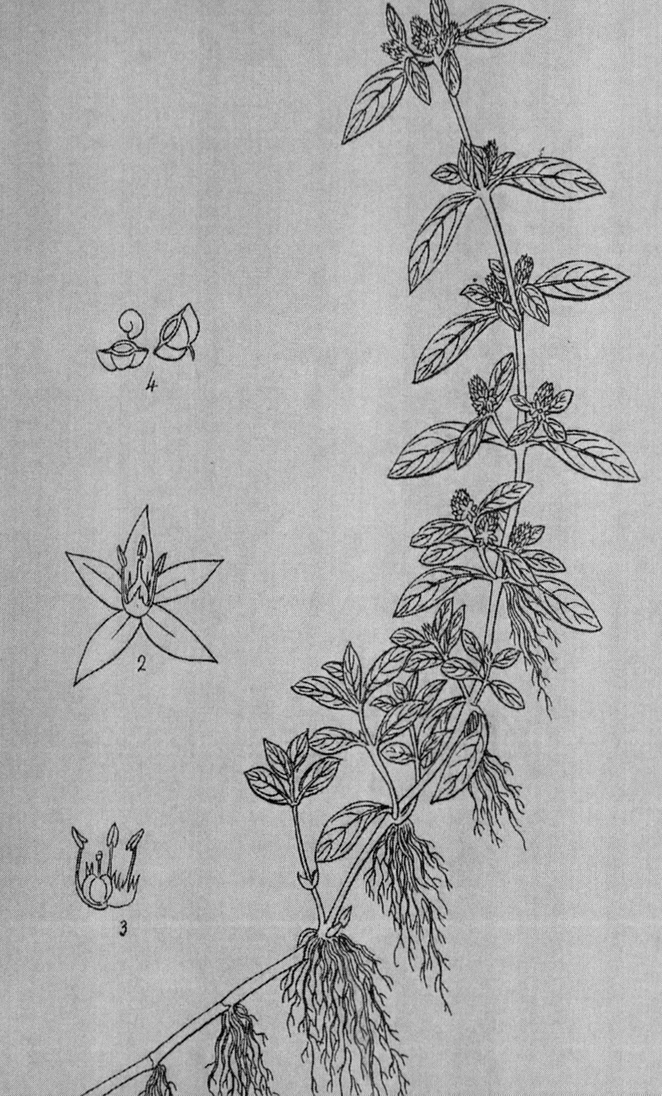

ALTERNANTHERA SESSILIS, *Br.*

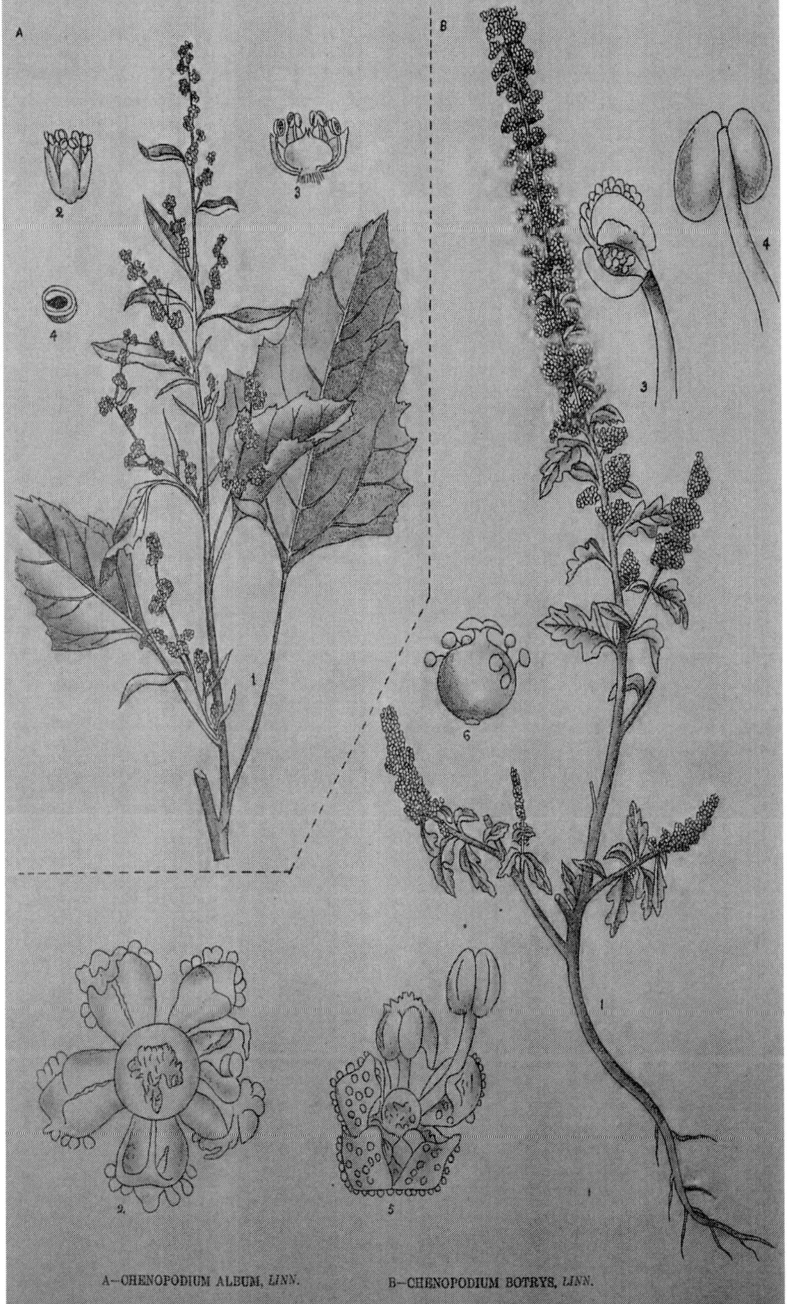

A—CHENOPODIUM ALBUM, *LINN.* B—CHENOPODIUM BOTRYS, *LINN.*

PLATE No. 796.

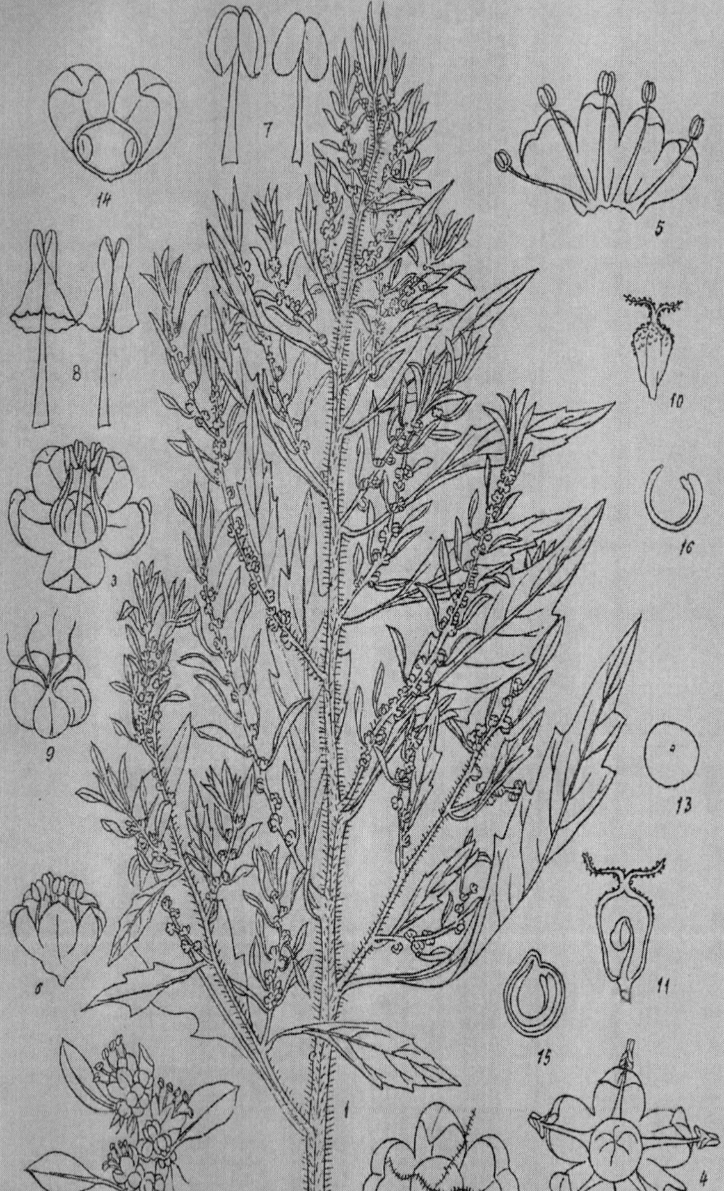

CHENOPODUM AMBROSIODES, LINN

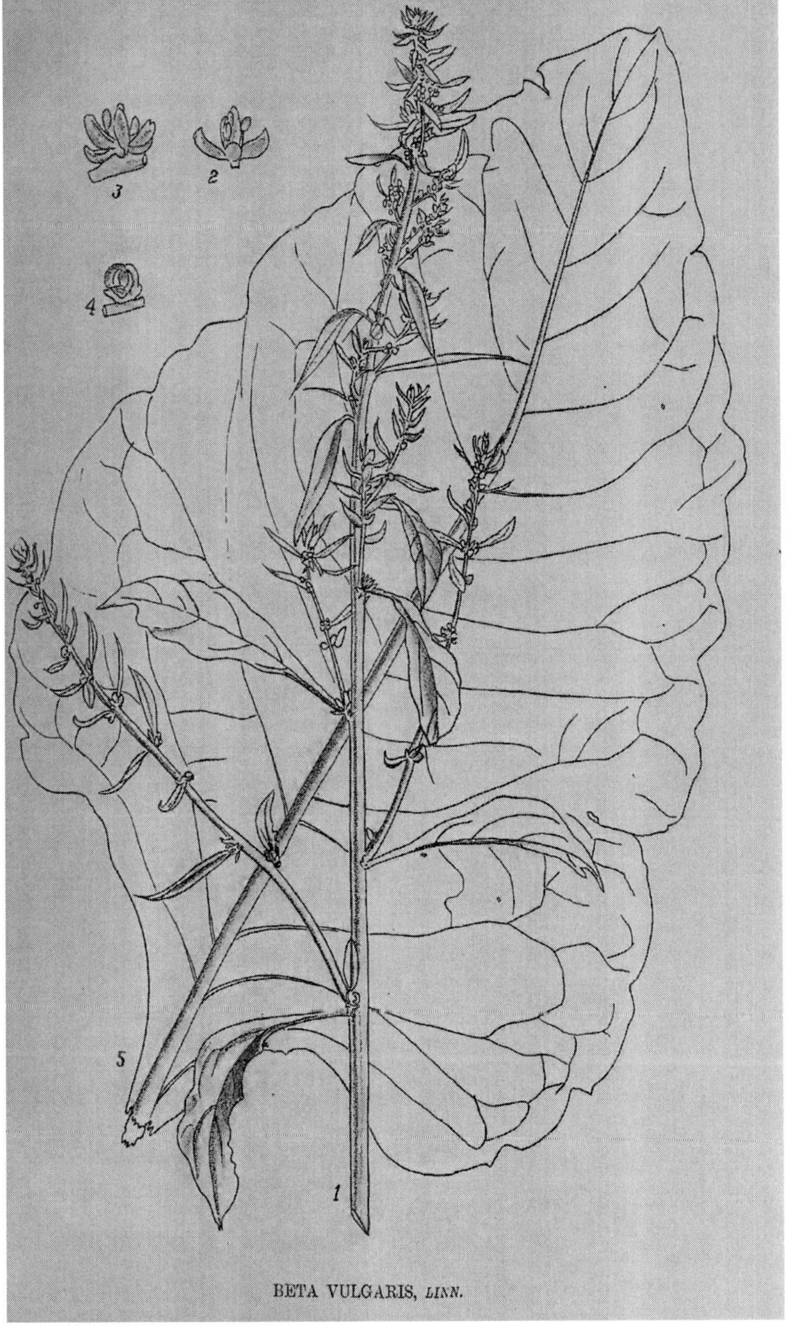

BETA VULGARIS, *LINN.*

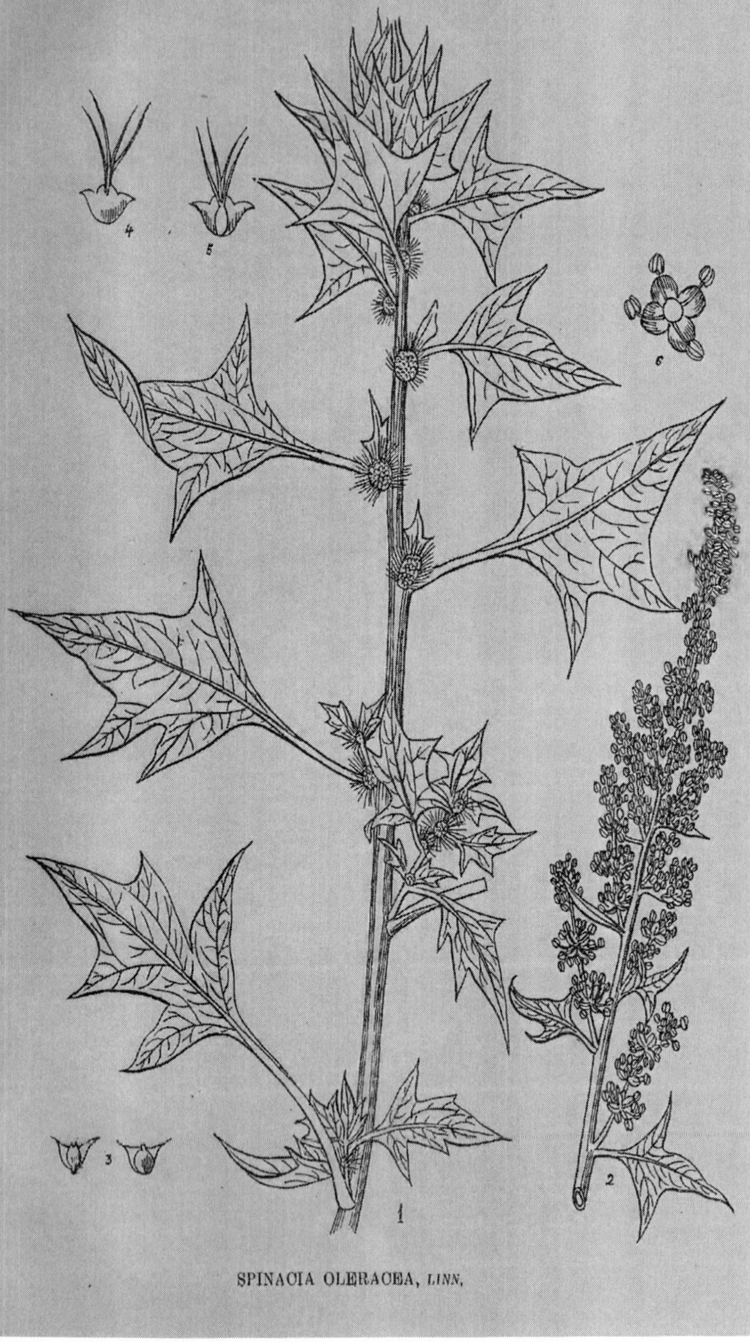

SPINACIA OLERACEA, *LINN*,

PLATE No. 799.

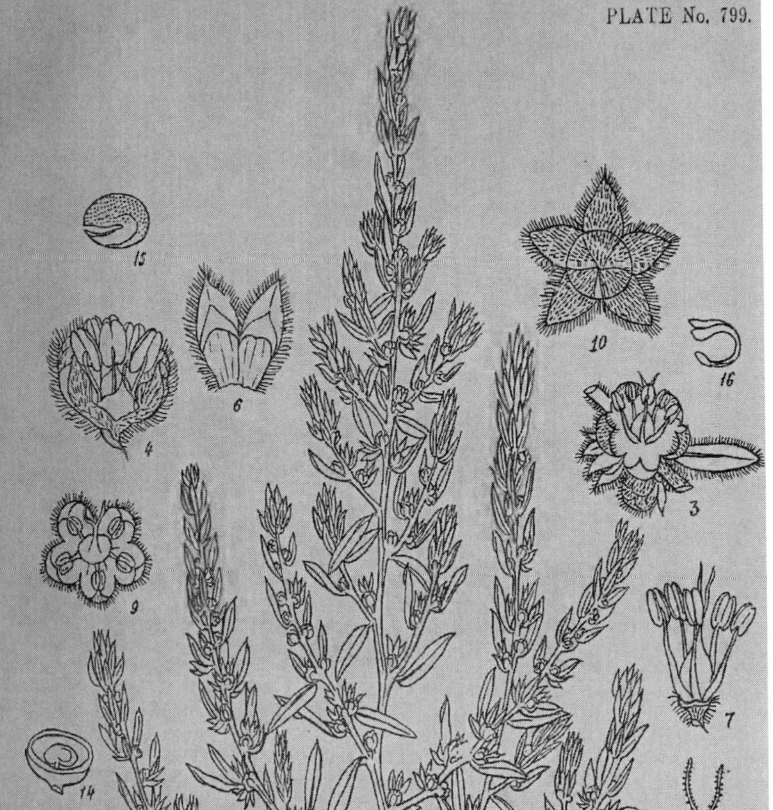

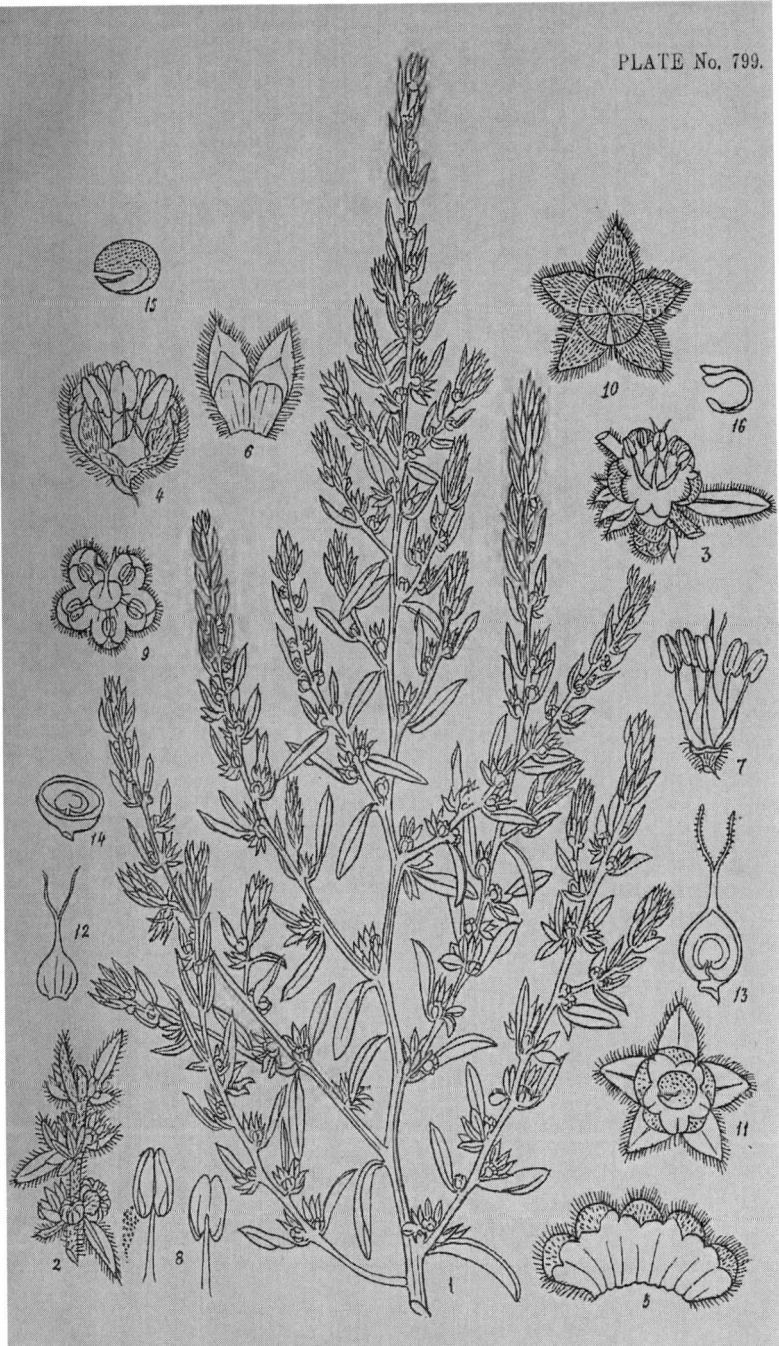

KOCHIA INDICA, *WIGHT.*

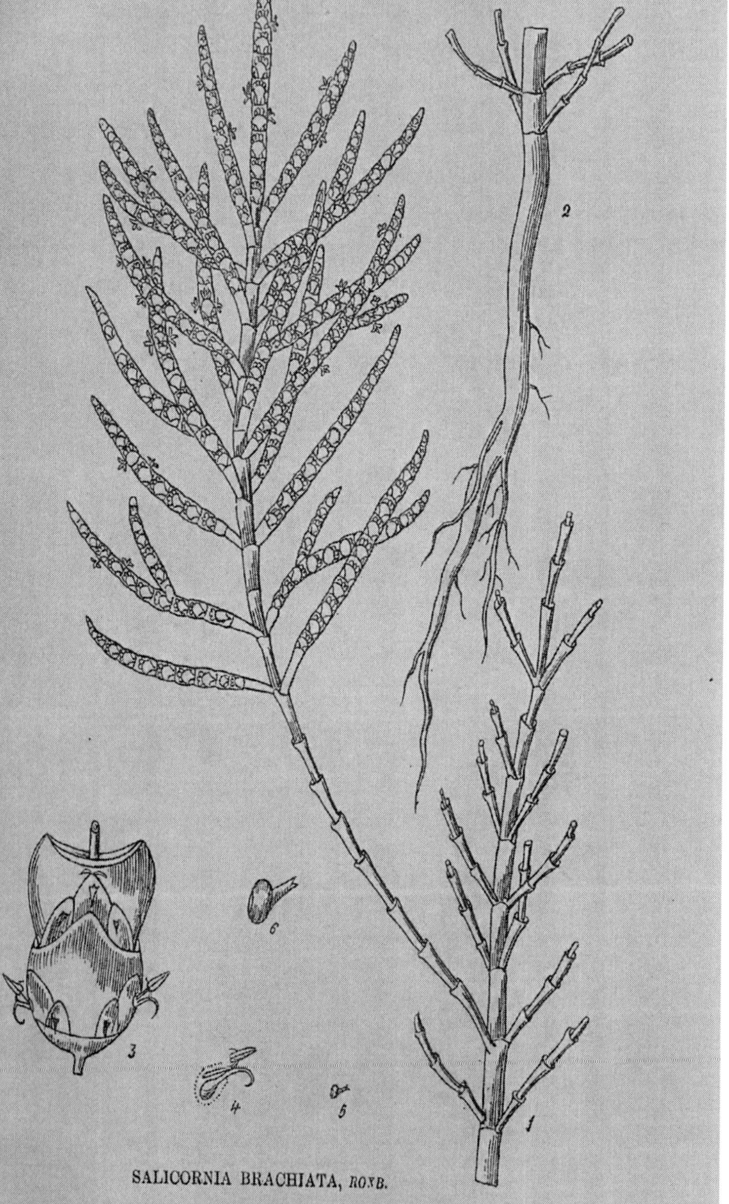

SALICORNIA BRACHIATA, *ROXB.*

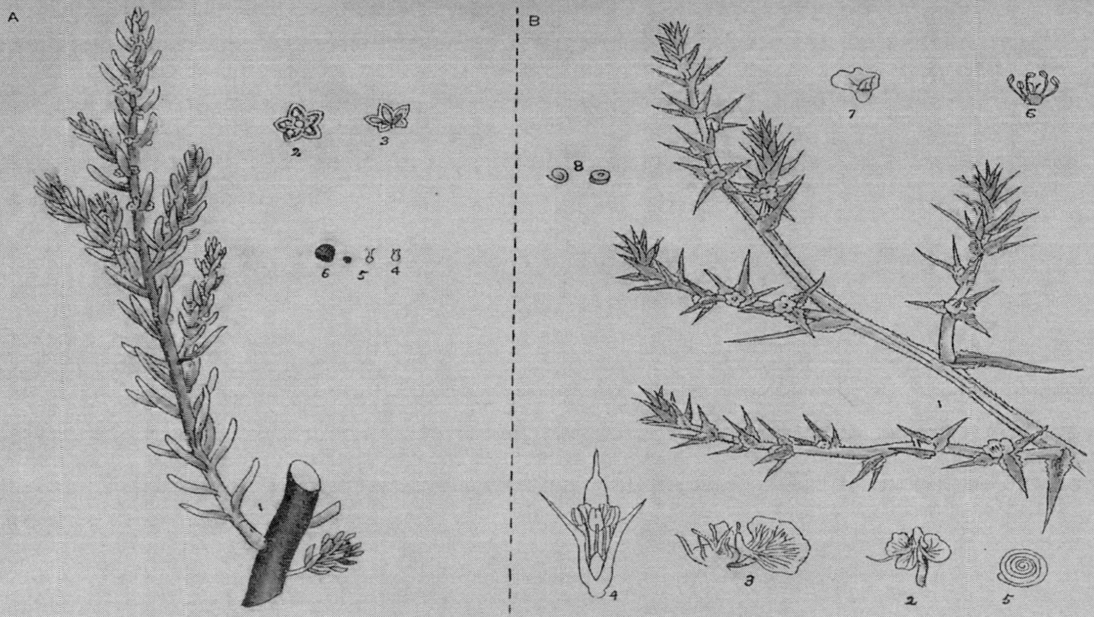

A—SUÆDA FRUTICOSA, *Forsk.*

B—SALSOLA KALI, *Linn.*

PLATE No. 802.

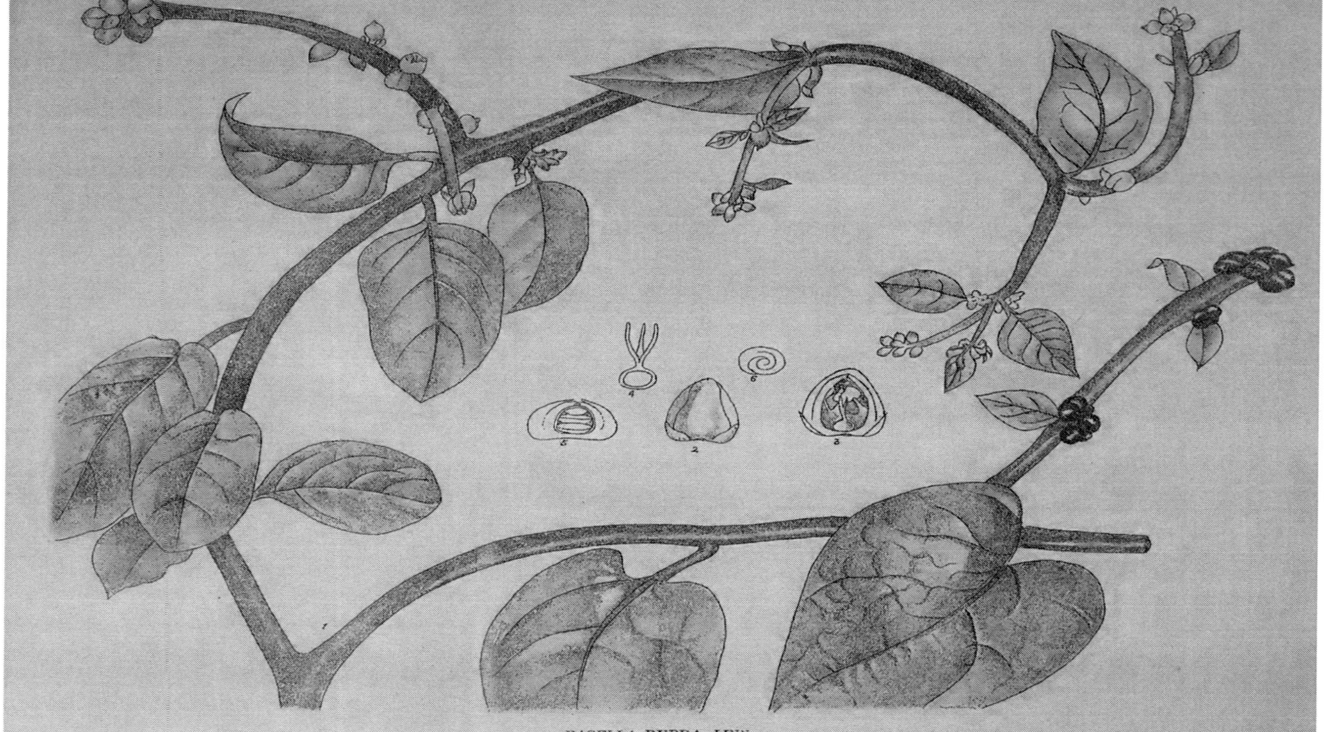

BASELLA RUBRA, *LINN.*

PLATE No. 803.

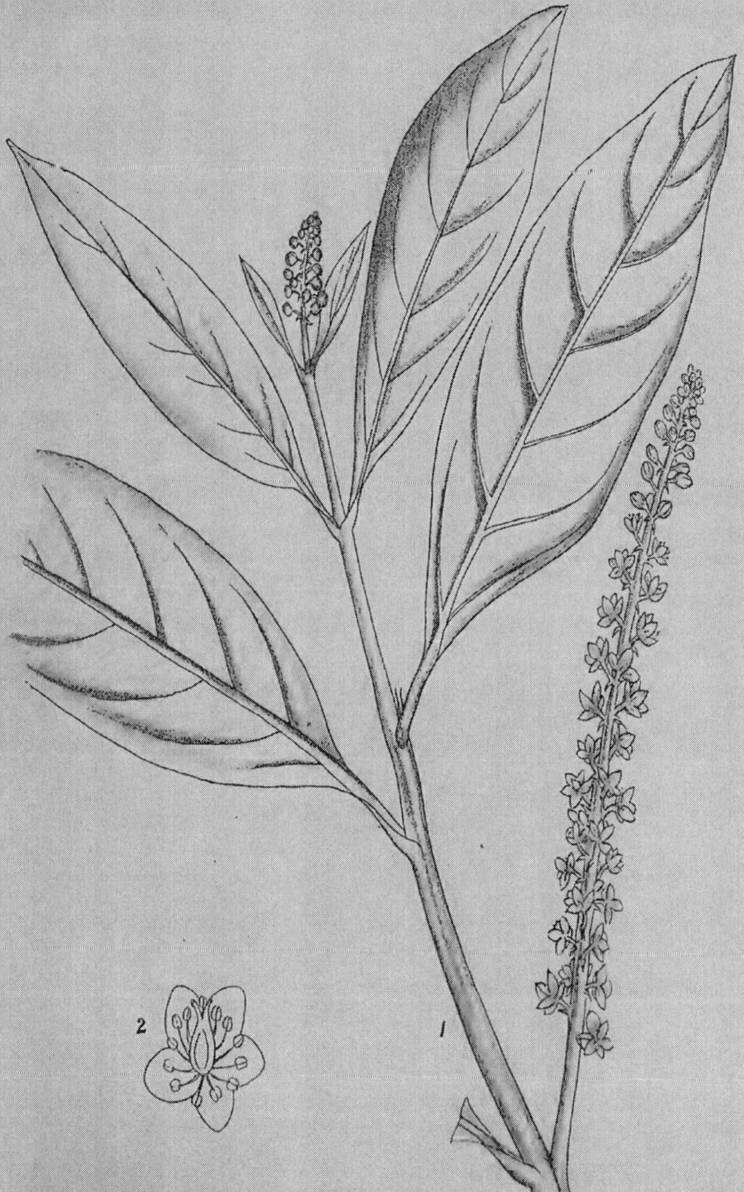

PHYTOLACCA ACINOSA, *ROXB.*

PLATE No 804

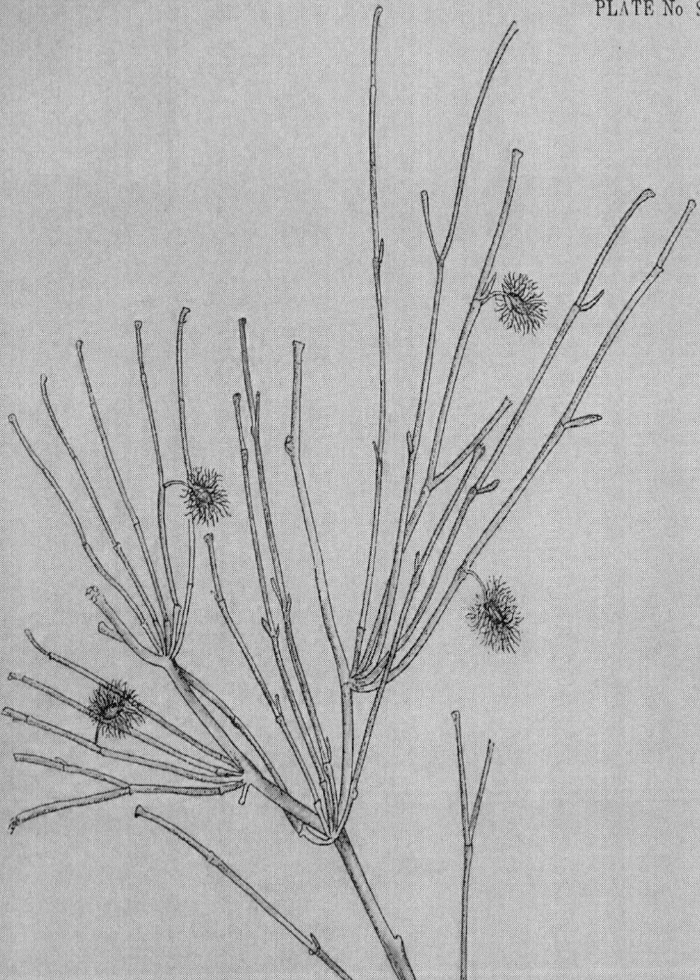

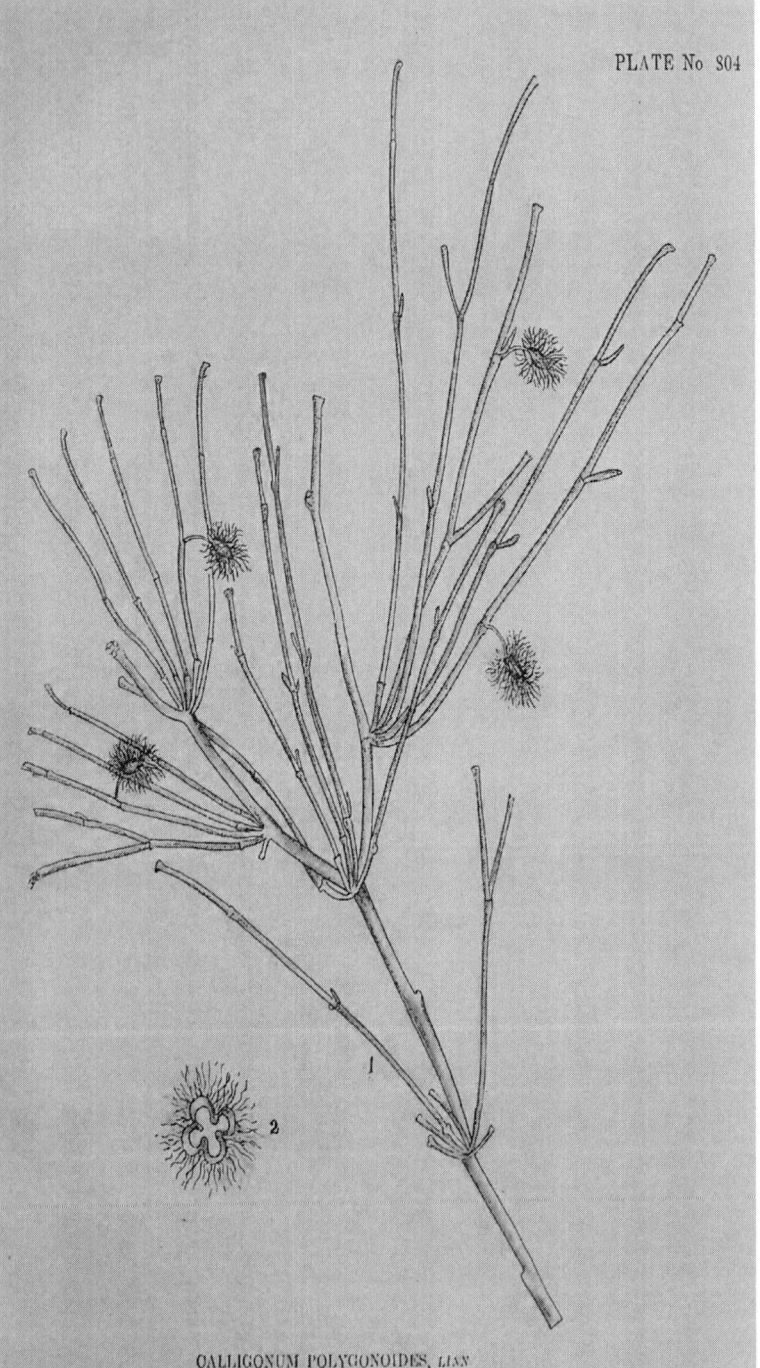

CALLIGONUM POLYGONOIDES, *Linn.*

PLATE No. 805.

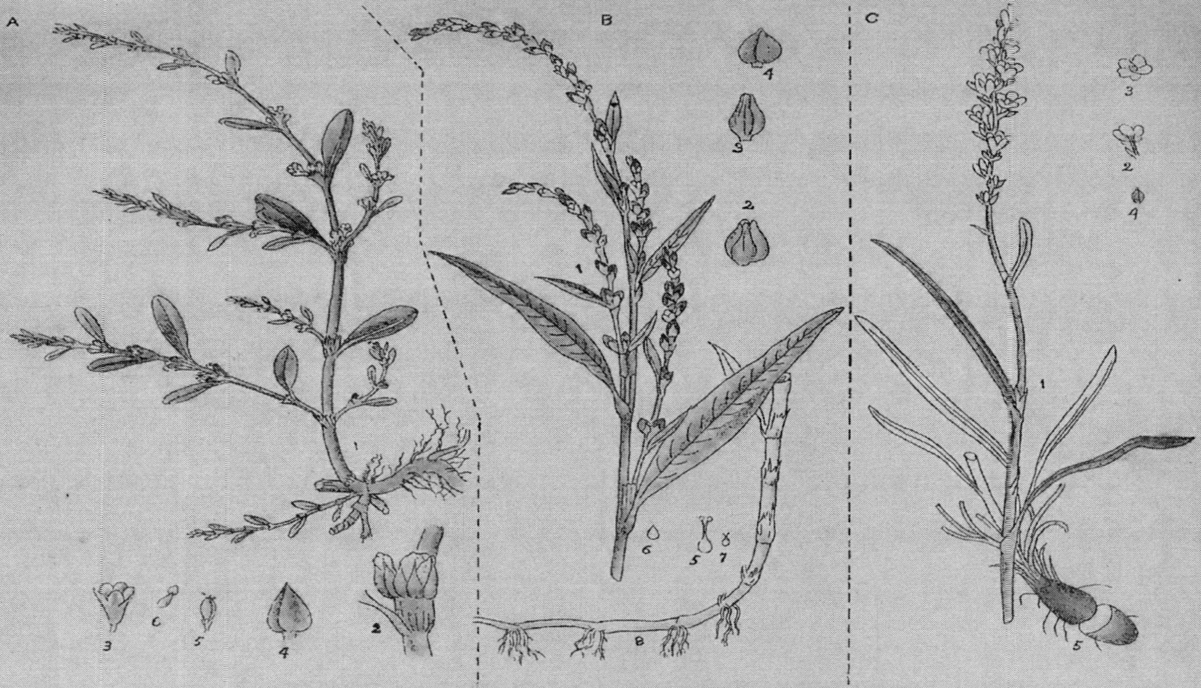

A—POLYGONUM AVICULARE, *LINN.* B—POLYGONUM HYDROPIPER, *LINN.* C—POLYGONUM VIVIPARUM, *LINN.*

PLATE No. 806

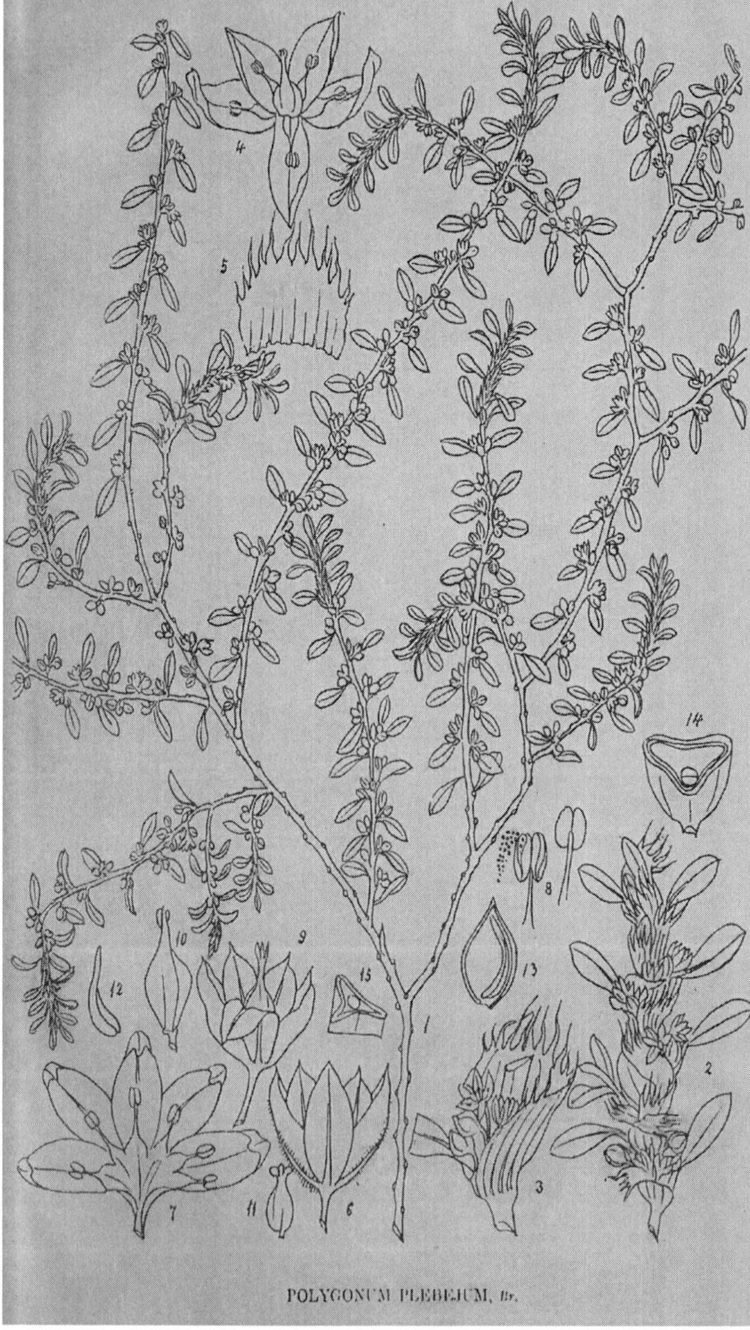

POLYGONUM PLEBEJUM, Br.

PLATE No. 807.

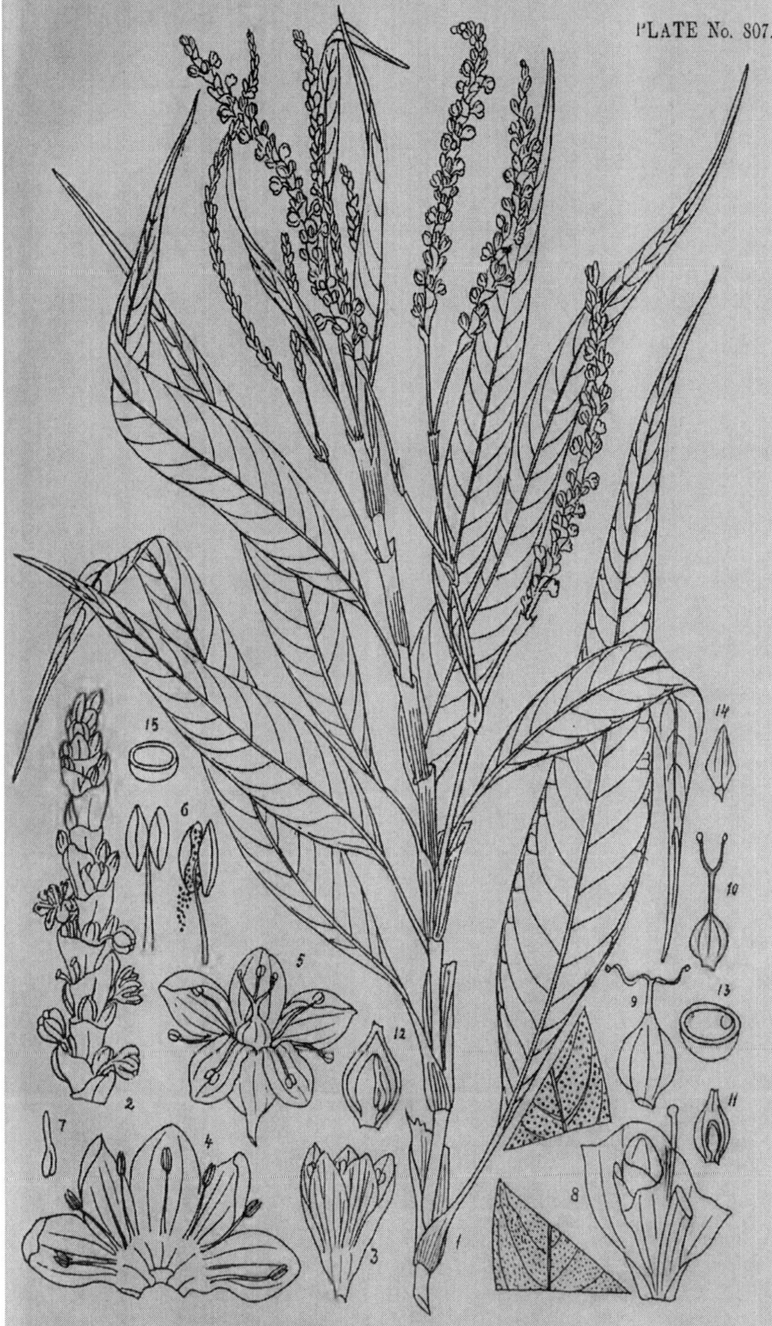

POLYGONUM GLABRUM, *WILLD*

PLATE No 808.

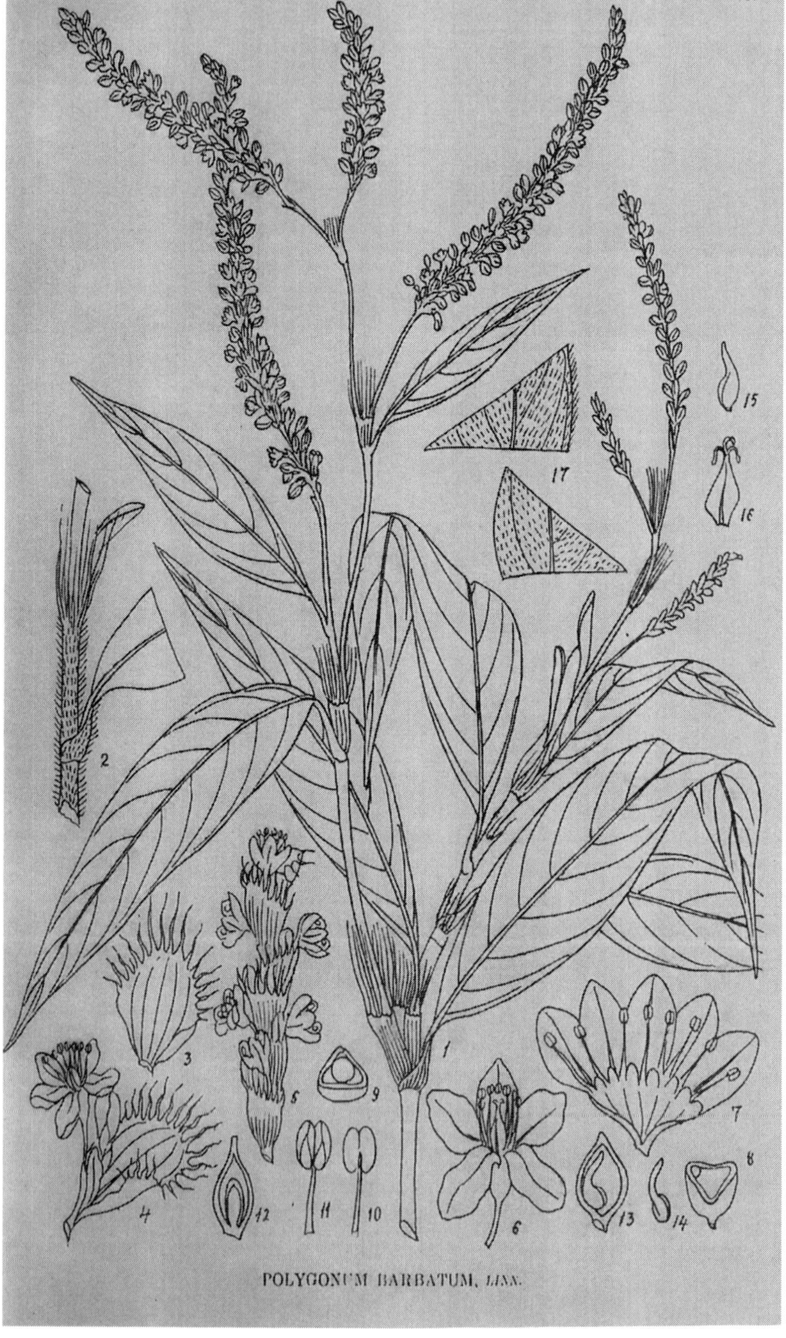

POLYGONUM BARBATUM, LINN.

POLYGONUM ALATUM, HAM.

PLATE No. 810.

POLYGONUM MOLLE, D. DON.

PLATE No. 811.

A—RHEUM SPICIFORME, *Royle.* B—RHEUM WEBBIANUM, *Royle.*

PLATE No. 812.

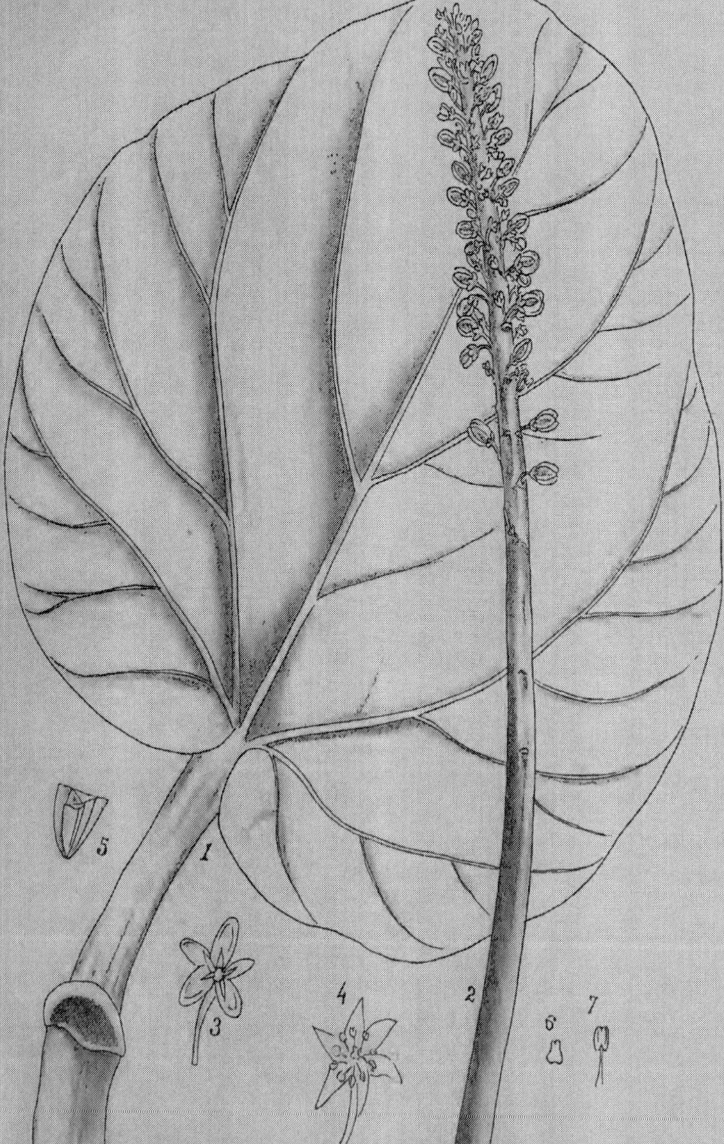

RHEUM MOORCROFTIANUM, ROYLE

PLATE No. 813.

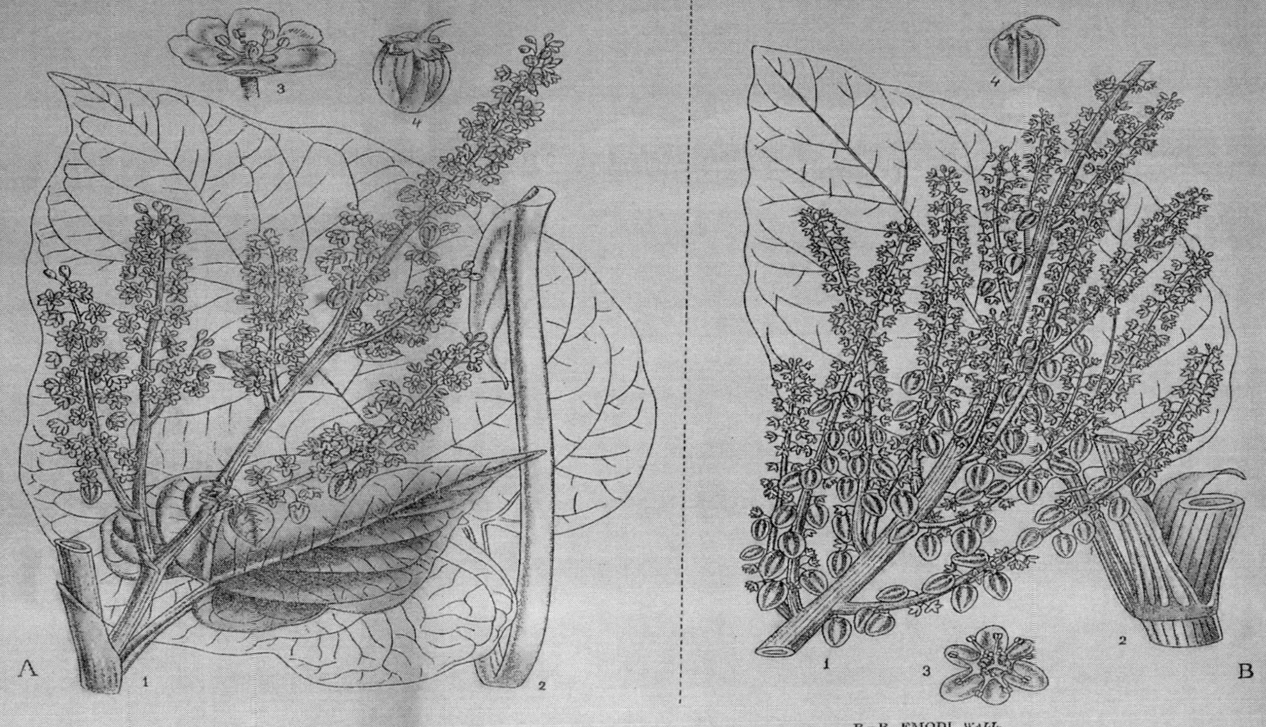

A—RHEUM ACUMINATUM, *Hook, f. & T.*

B—R. EMODI, *Wall.*

PLATE No. 814.

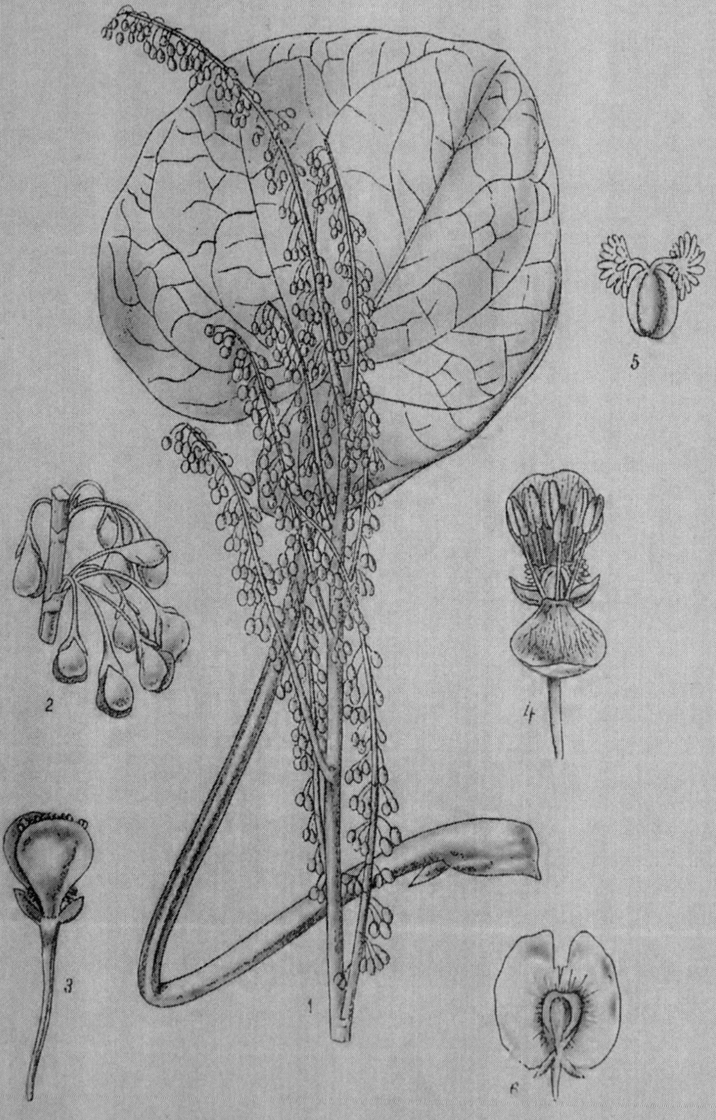

OXYRIA DIGYNA, *Hill.*

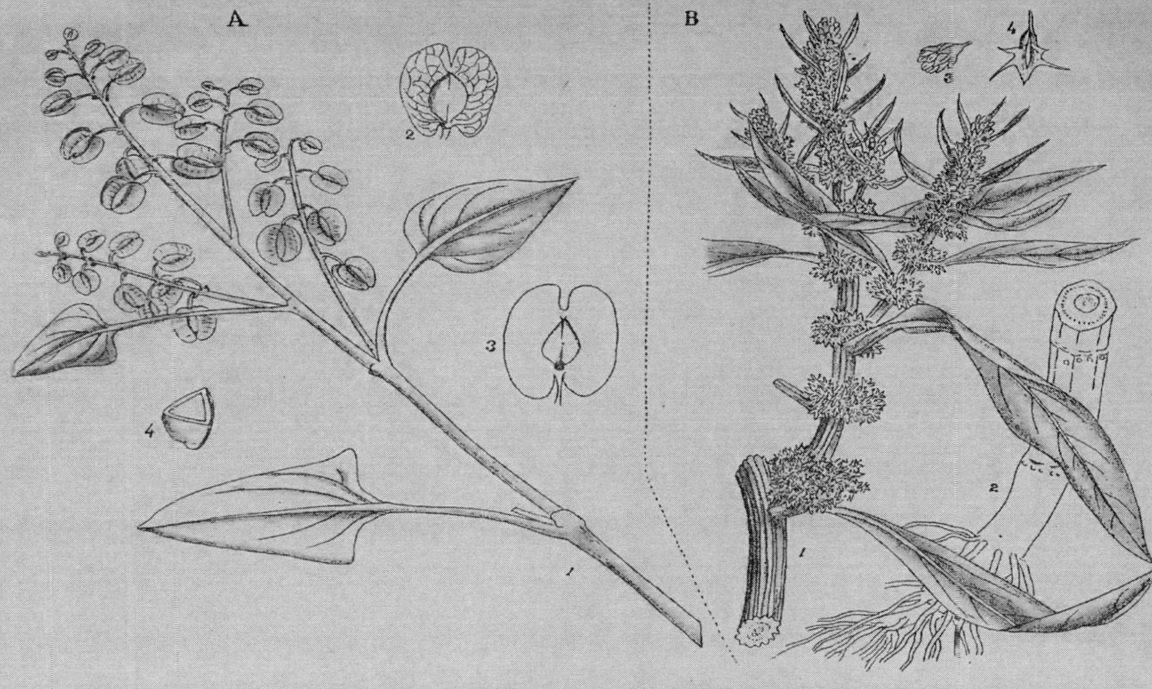

A—RUMEX VESICARIUS, *Linn.*

B—RUMEX MARITIMUS, *Linn.*

PLATE No. 816.

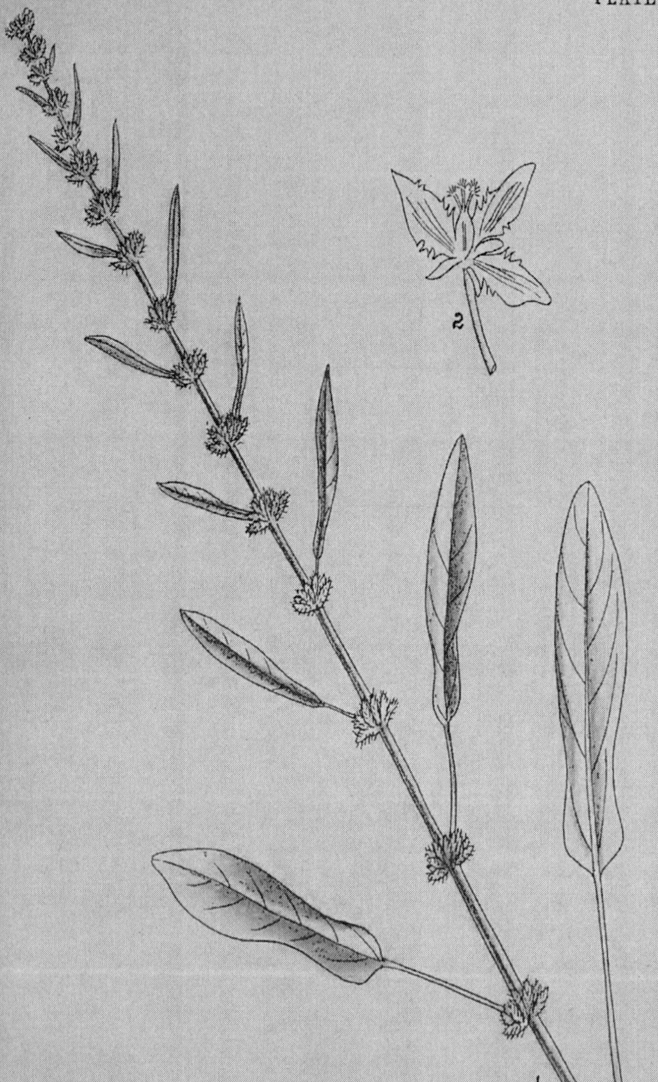

RUMEX DENTATUS, LINN.

PLATE No. 817.

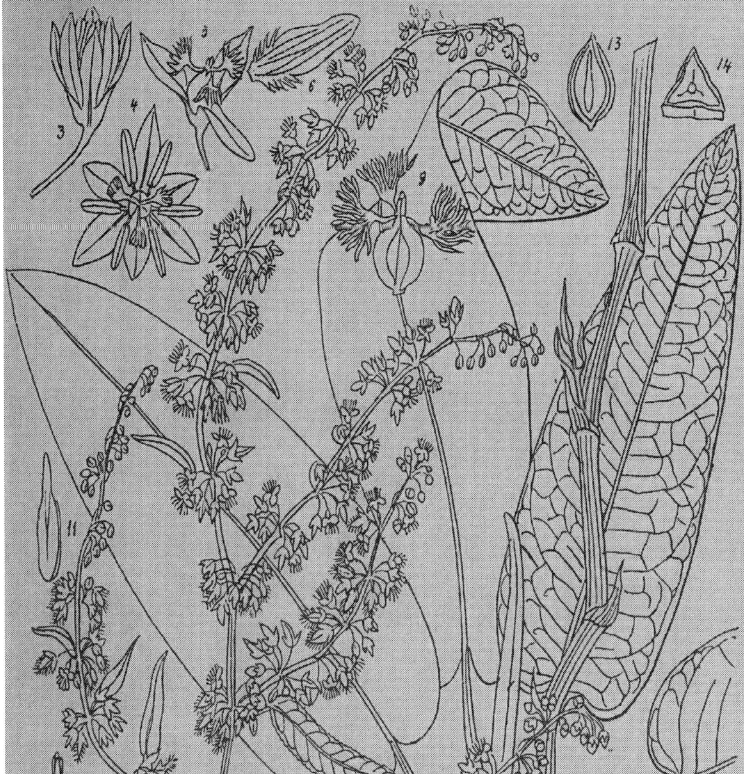

RUMEX NEPALENSIS, SPRENG.

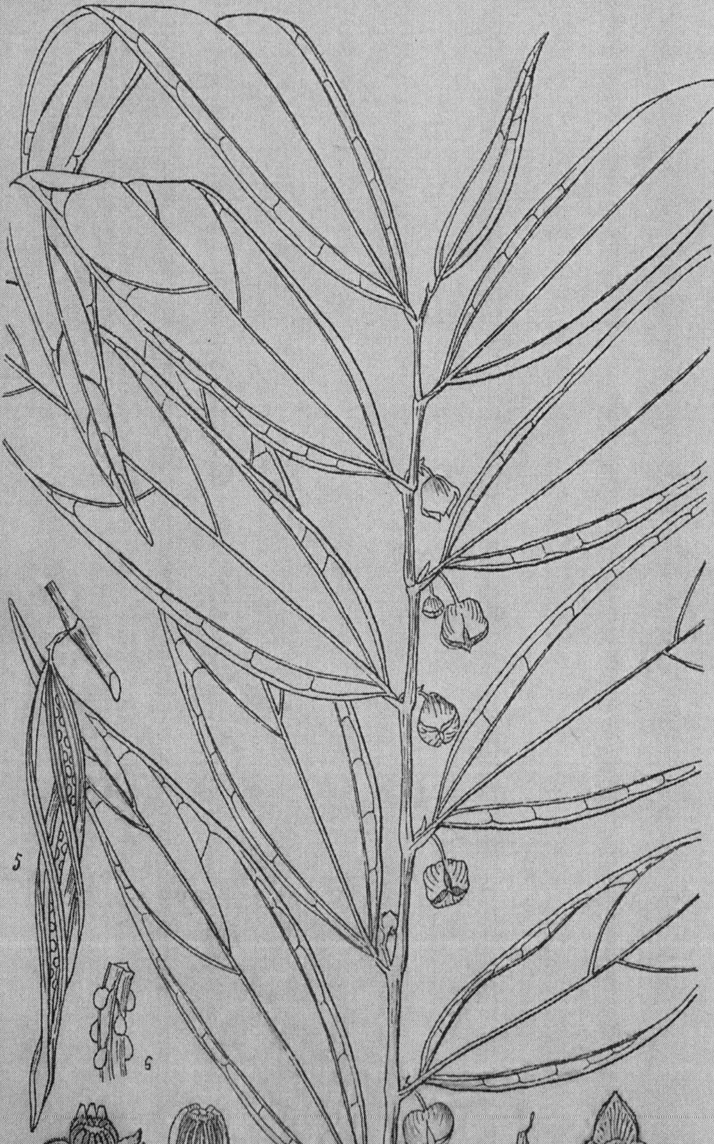

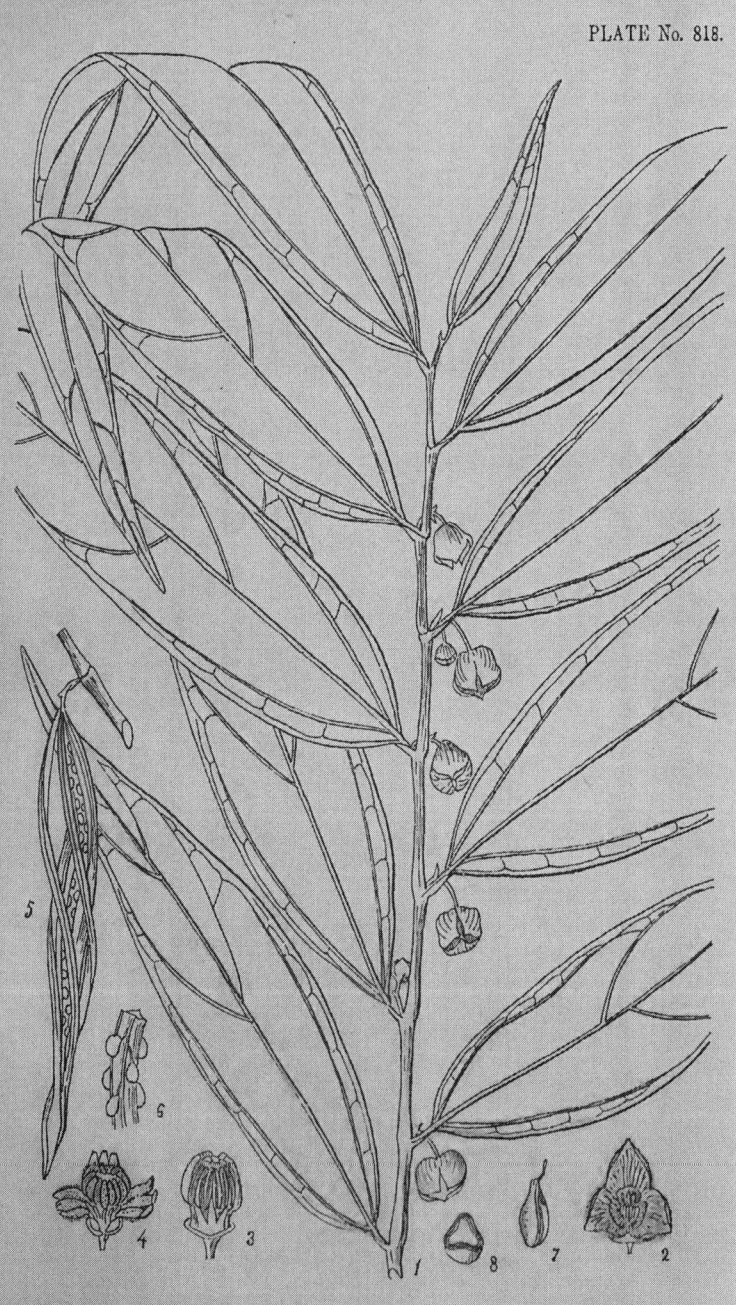

BRAGANTIA WALLICHII, Br.

PLATE No. 819.

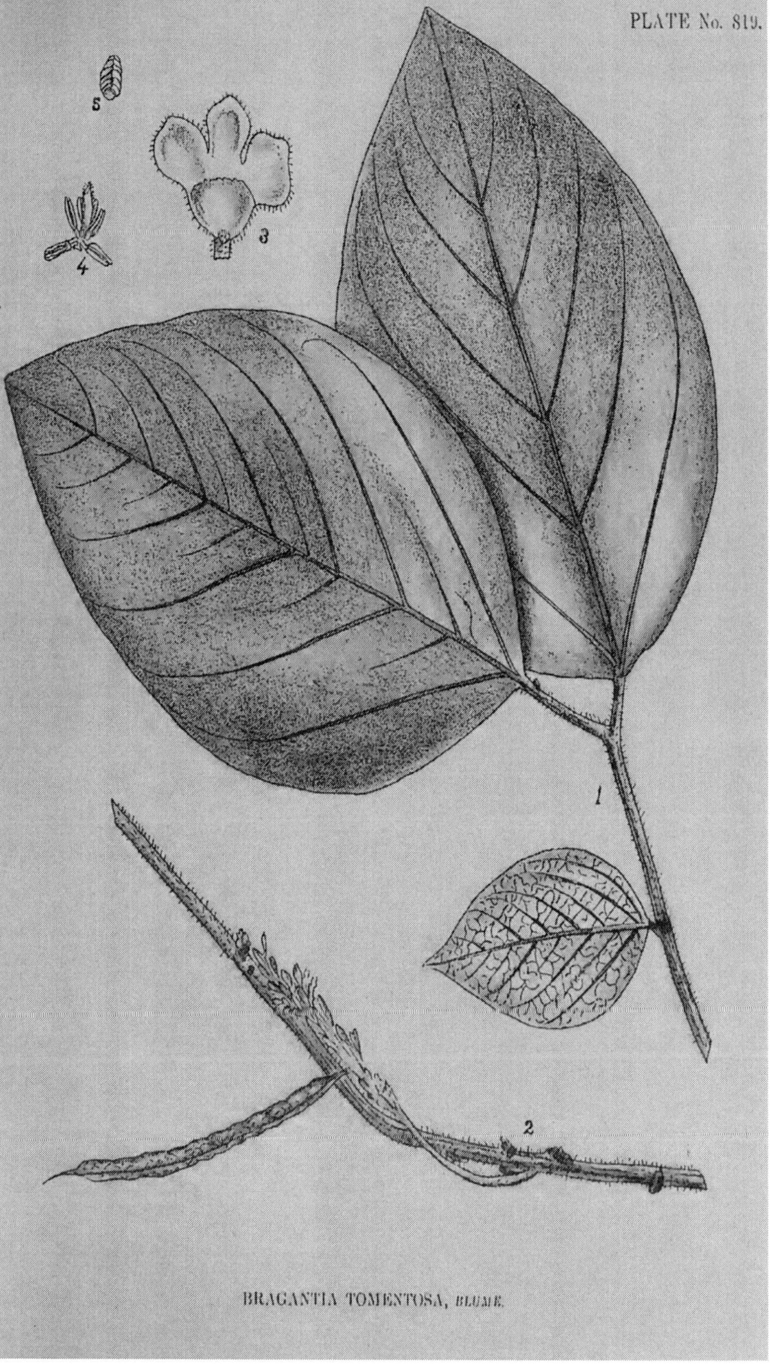

BRAGANTIA TOMENTOSA, *BLUME.*

A—ARISTOLOCHIA BRACTEATA, *Retz.* B—ARISTOLOCHIA INDICA, *Linn.*

PLATE No. 821.

A—PIPER LONGUM, *Linn.* B—PIPER NIGRUM, *Linn.*

PLATE No. 822.

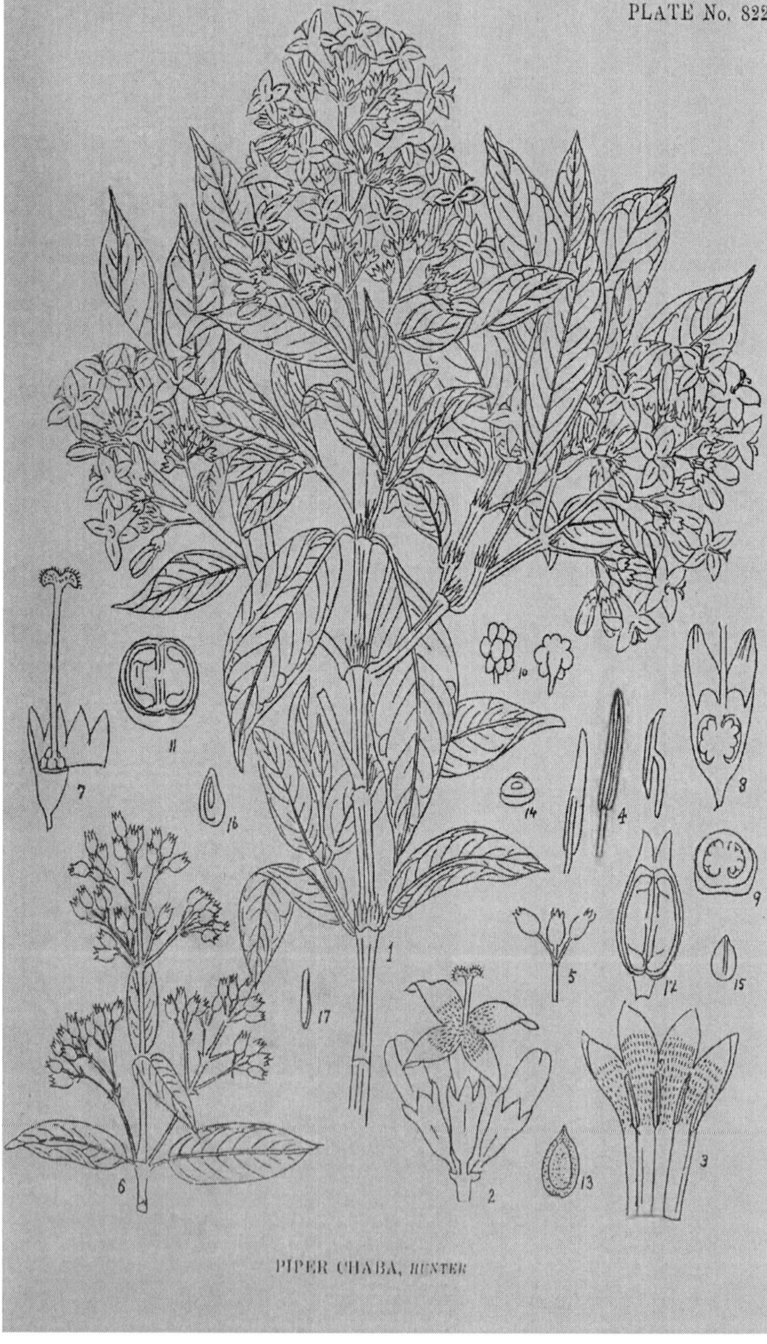

PIPER CHABA, *Hunter*

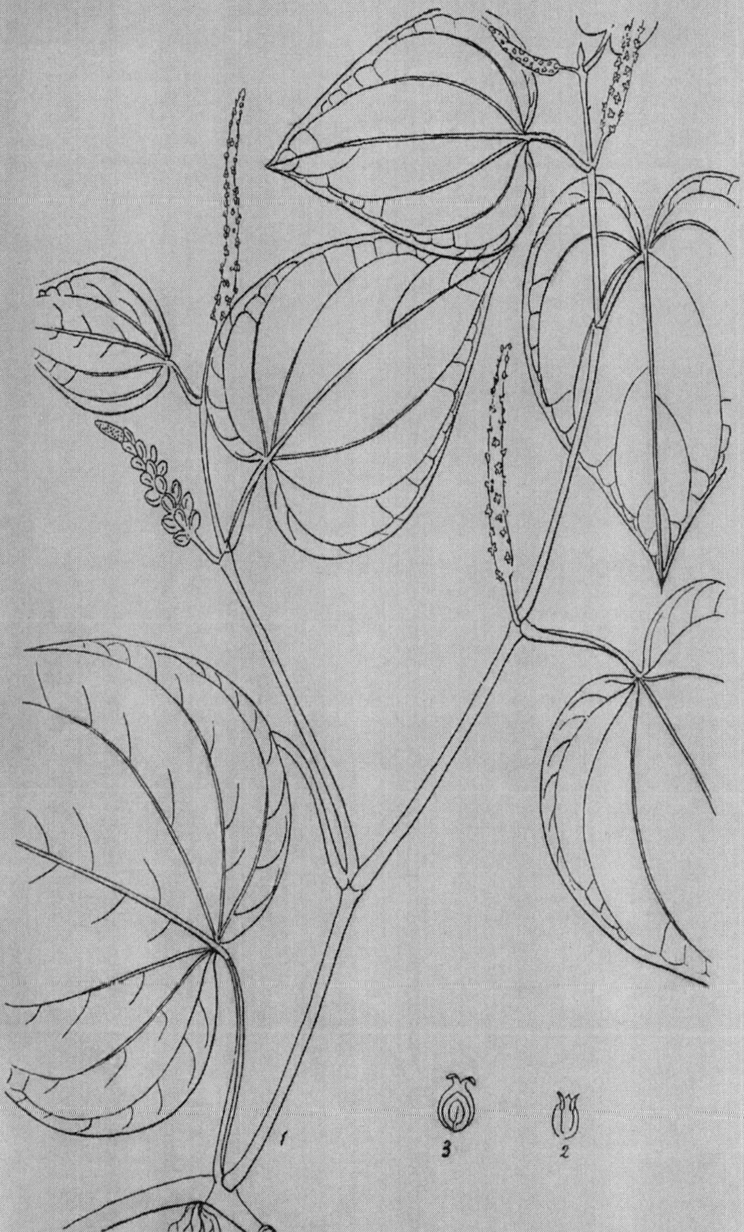

PIPER SYLVATICUM, ROXB.

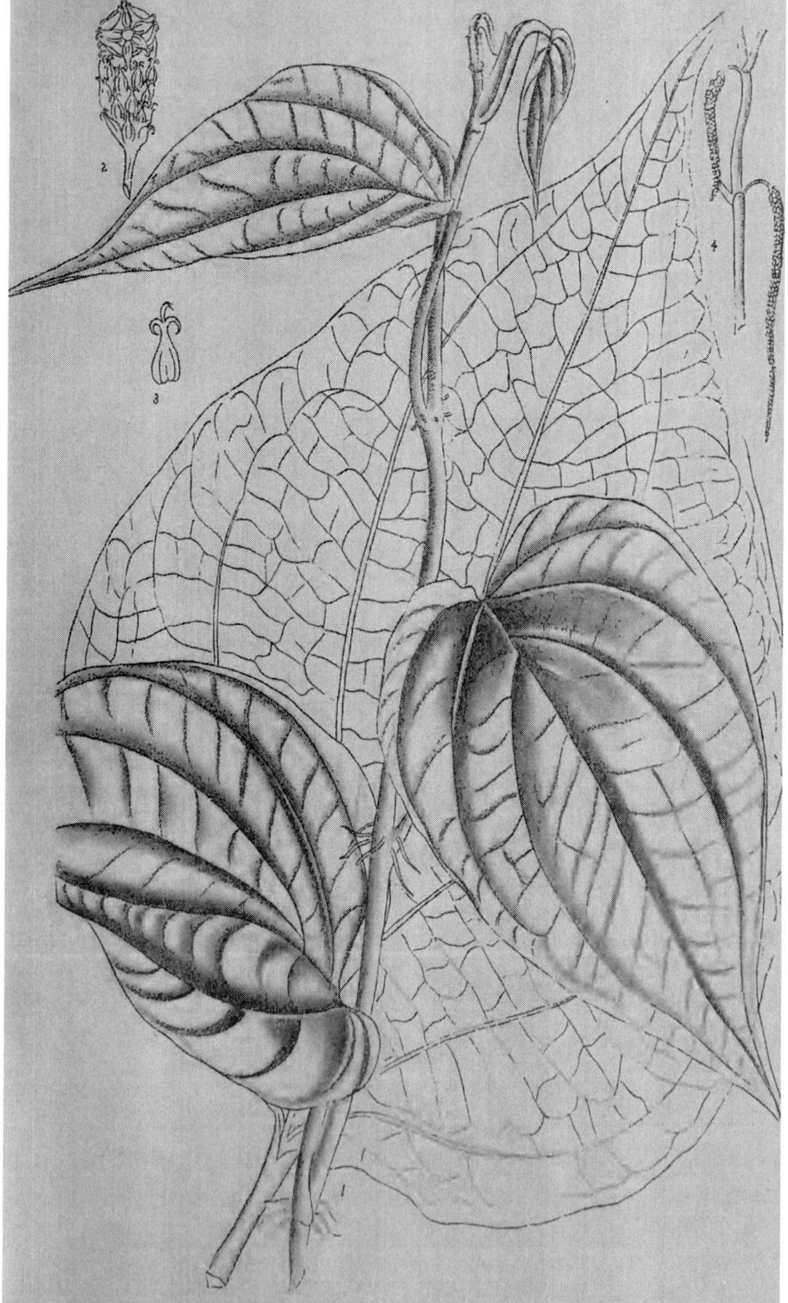

PIPER BETLE, *Linn.*

MYRISTICA MALABARICA, LAMK.

PLATE No. 826.

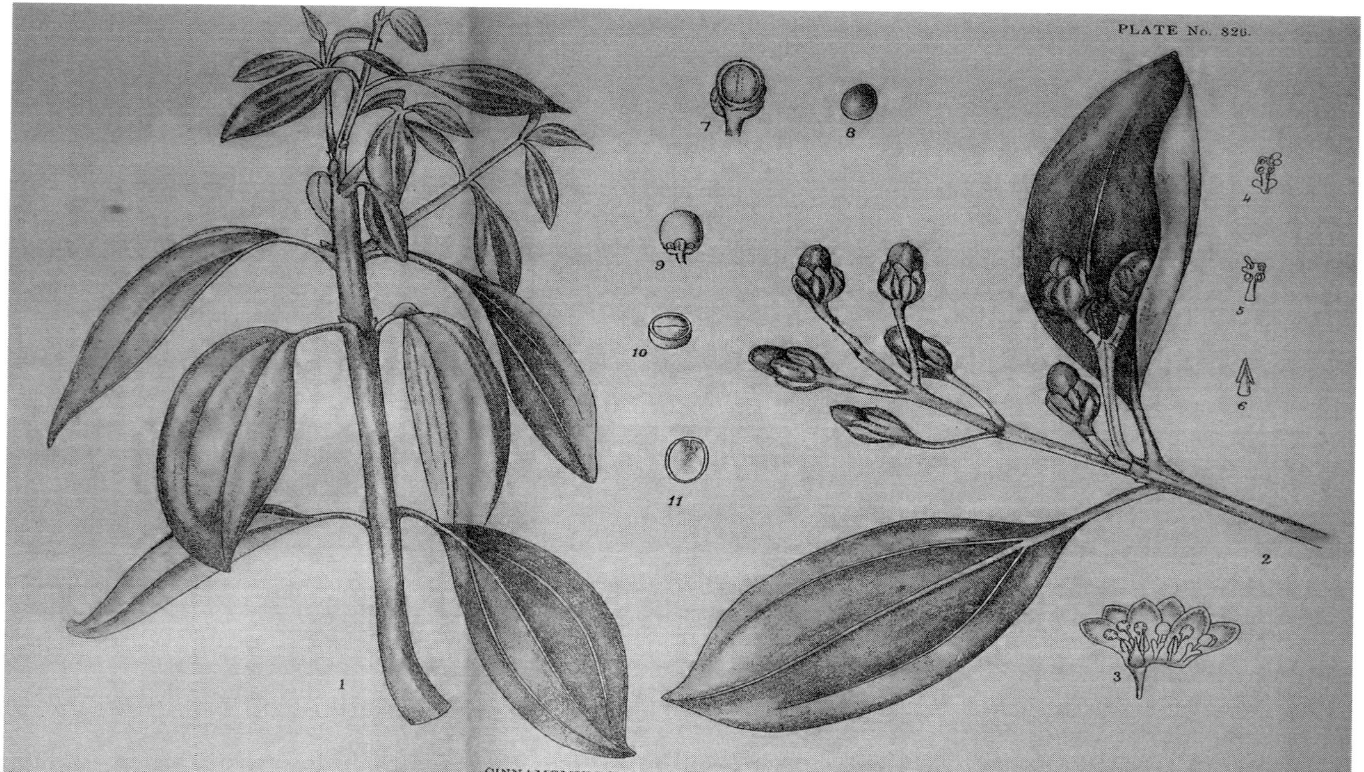

CINNAMOMUM TAMALA, *FR. NEES.*

PLTAE No. 827.

CINNAMOMUM OBTUSIFOLIUM, NEES

PLATE No. 828.

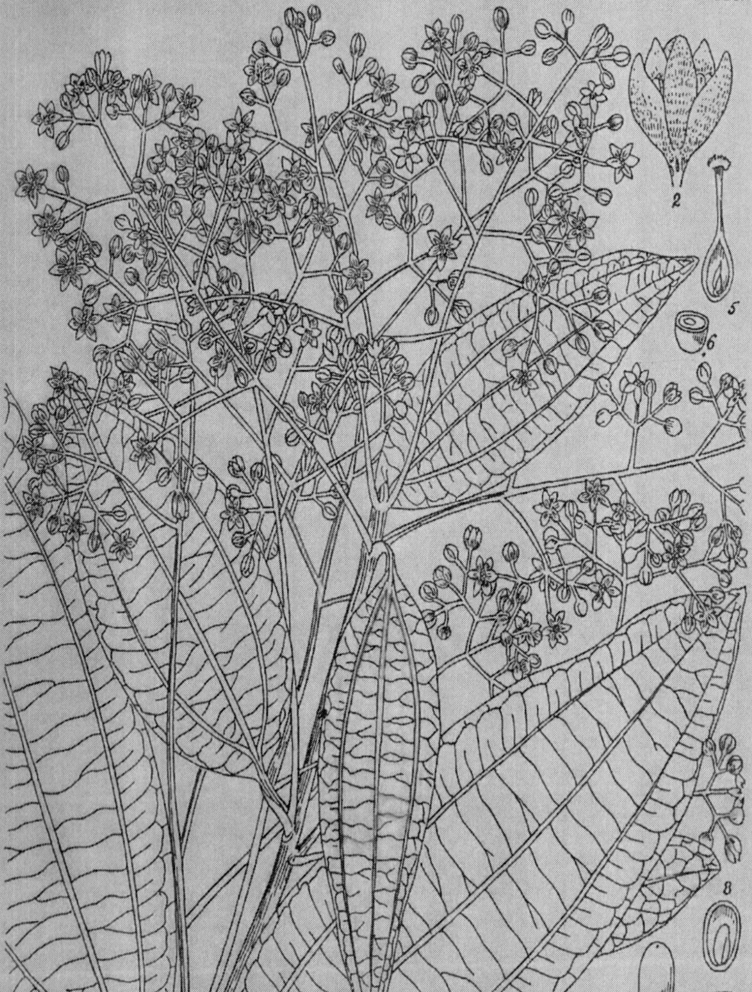

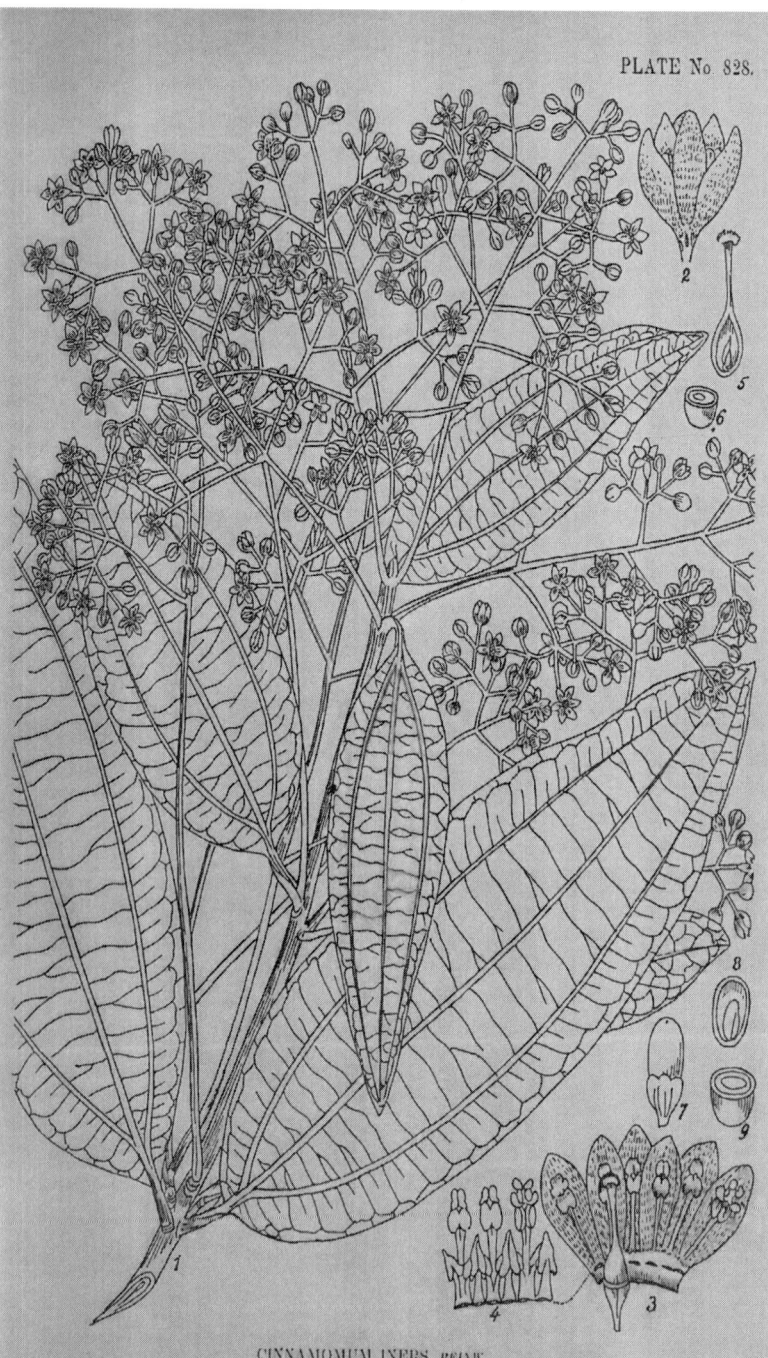

CINNAMOMUM INERS, REINW.

PLATE No. 829

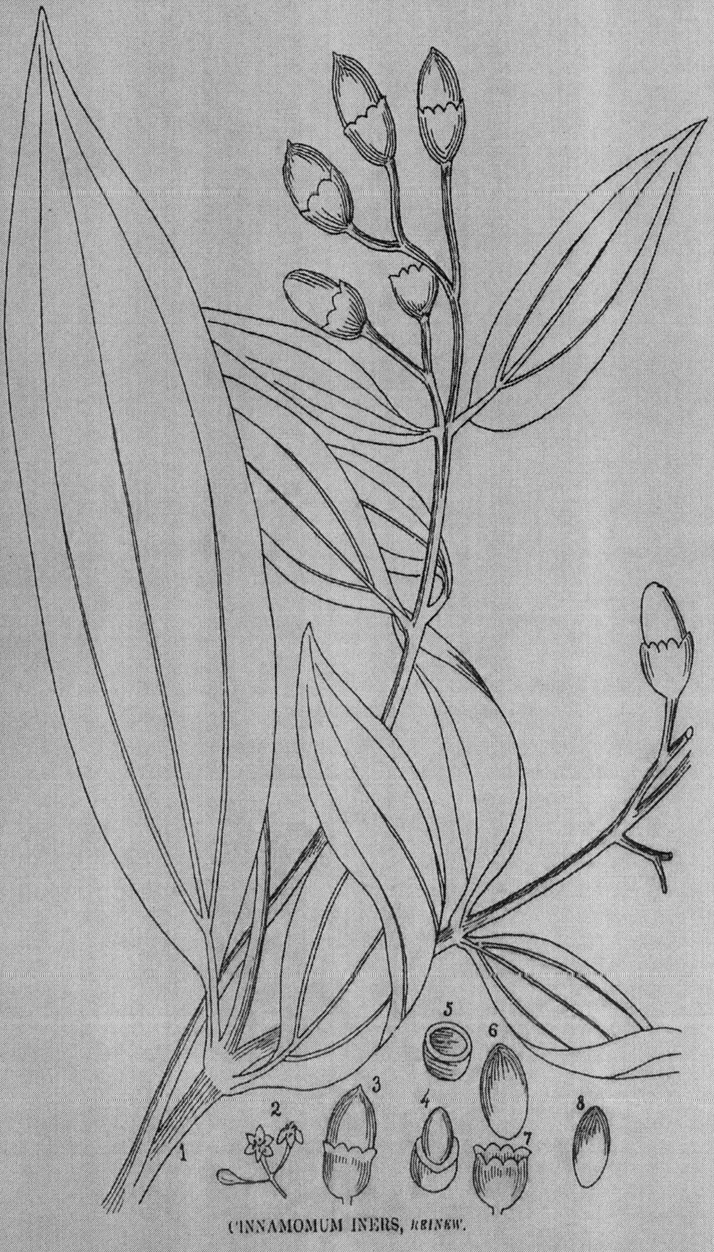

CINNAMOMUM INERS, REINW.

PLATE No. 830

A—CINNAMOMUM ZEYLANICUM, *Breyn.*　　B—C. GLANDULIFERUM, *Meissn.*

PLATE No. 831

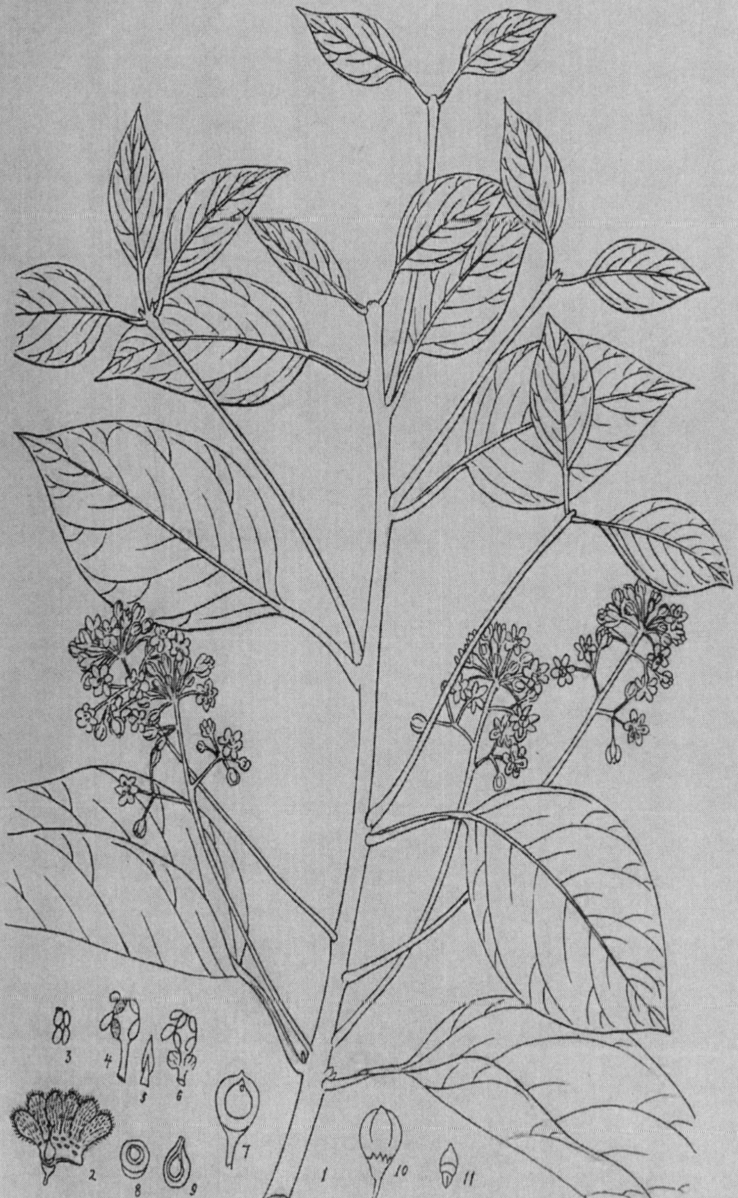

CINNAMOMUM PARTHENOXYLON *MEISSN.*

PLATE No. 832.

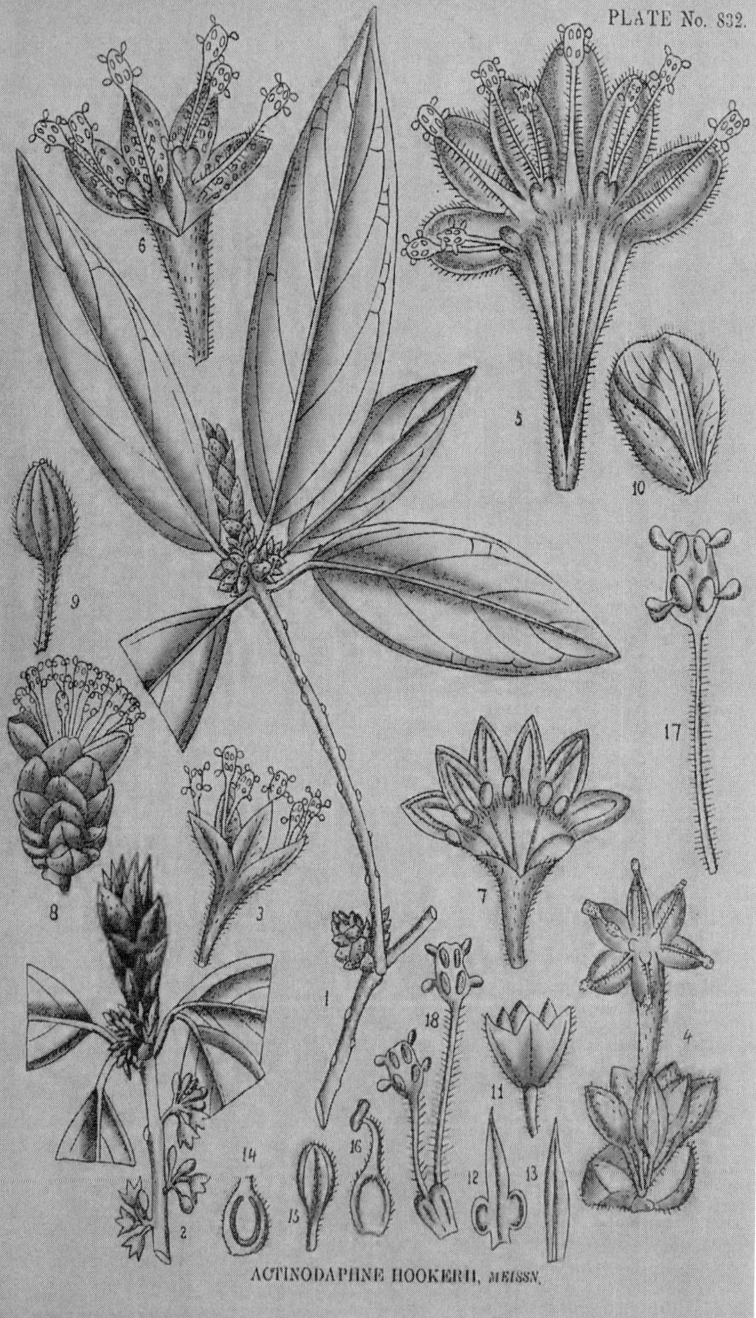

ACTINODAPHNE HOOKERII, MEISSN.

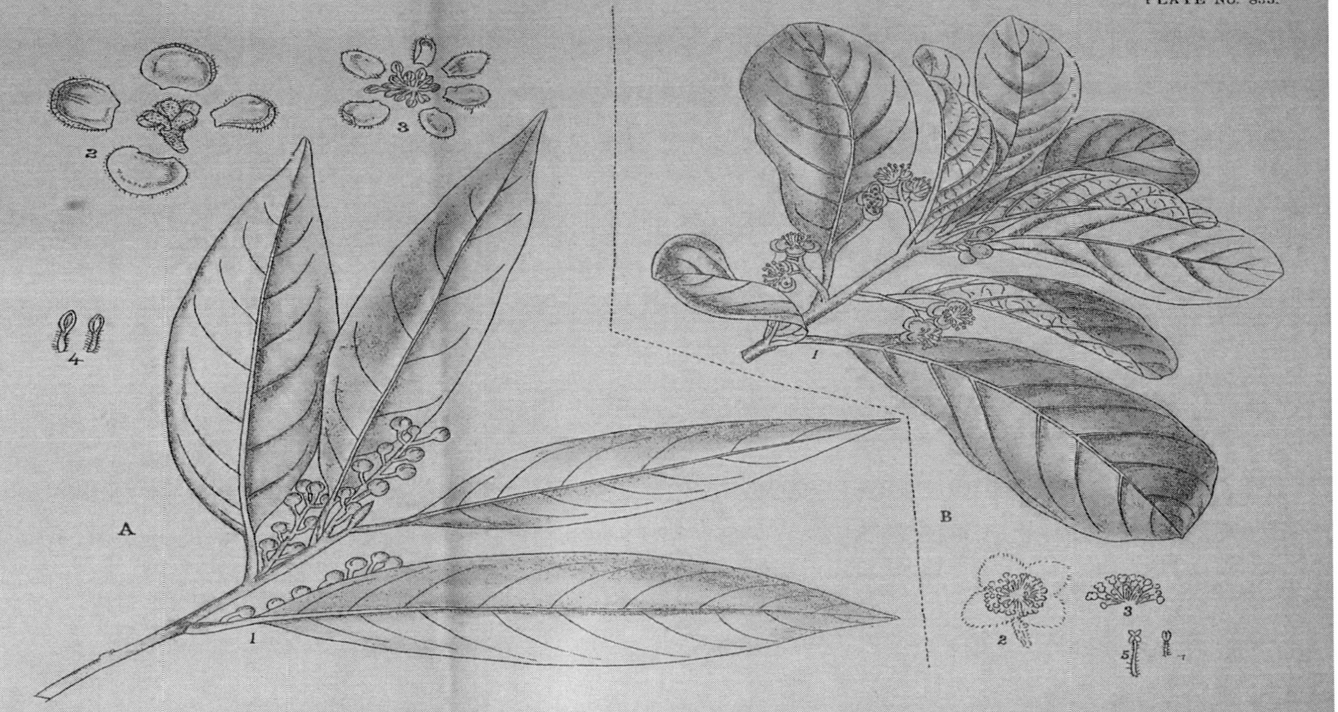

A—LITSÆA STOCKSII, *HOOK. F.*   B—LITSÆA SEBIFERA, *PERS.*

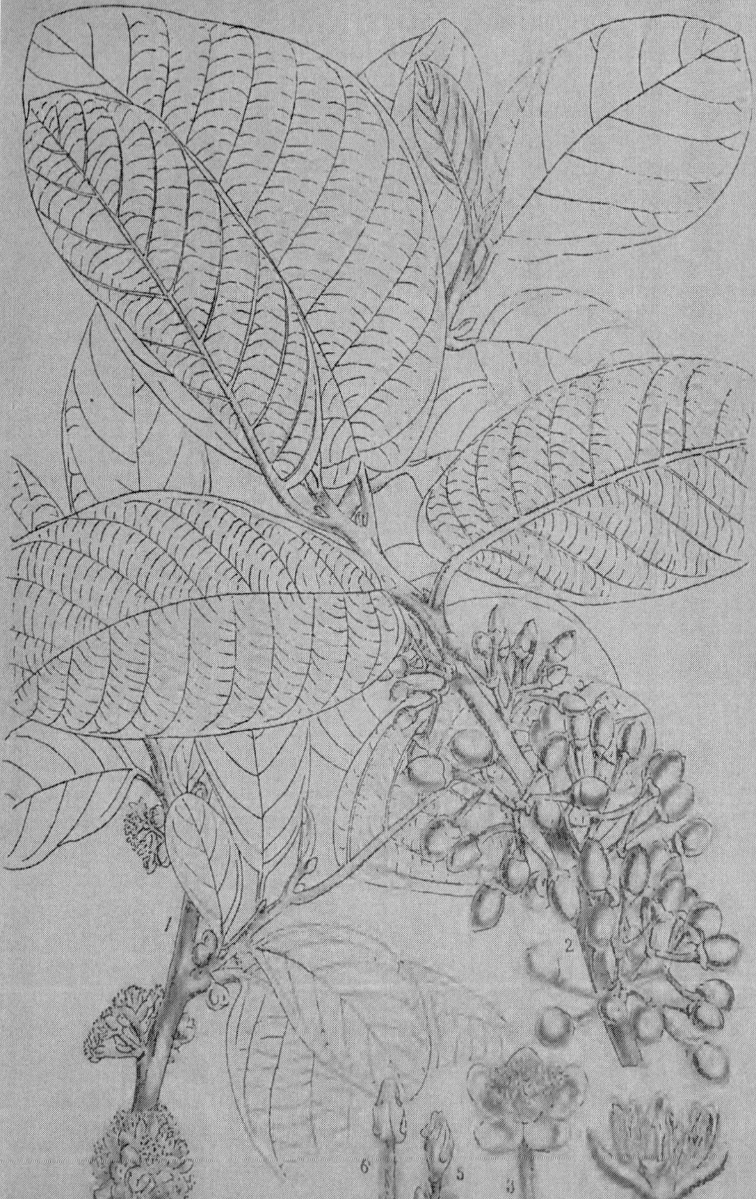

LITSEA POLYANTHA, JUSS.

PLATE No. 835.

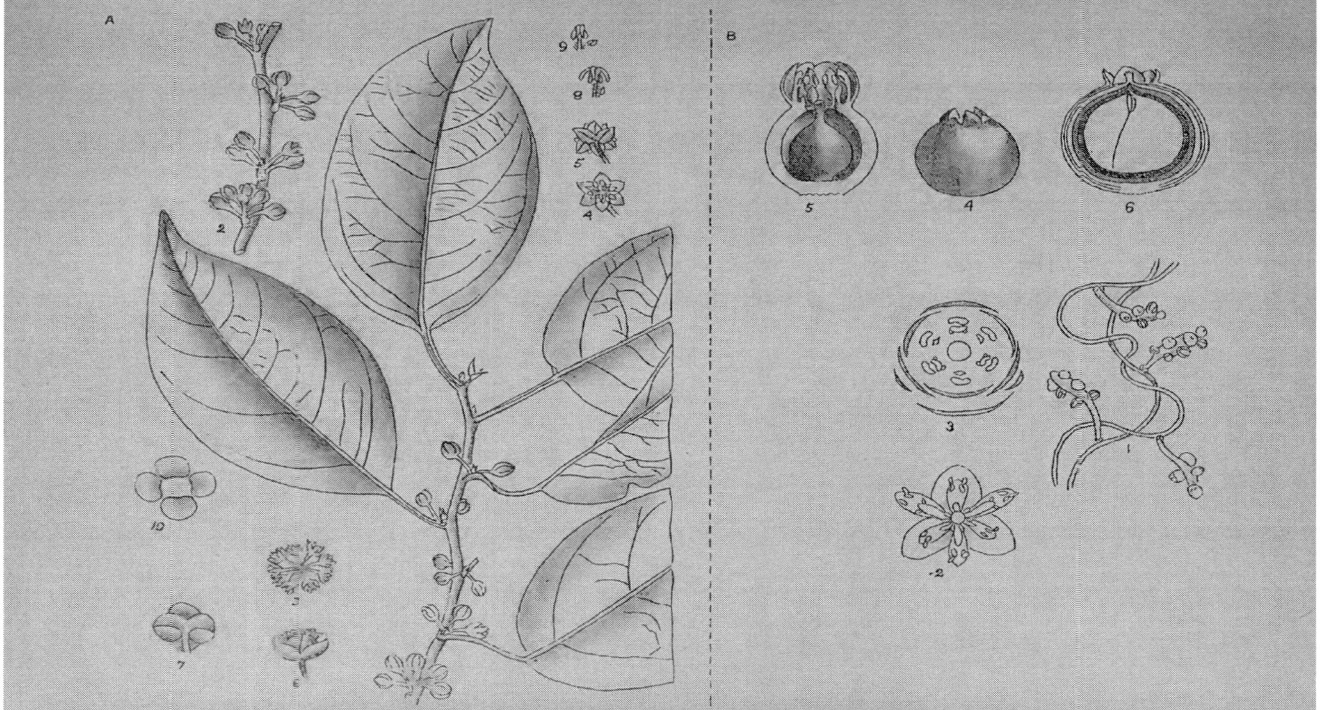

A—LINDERA NEESIANA, *BENTH.* B—CASSYTHA FILIFORMIS, *LINN.*

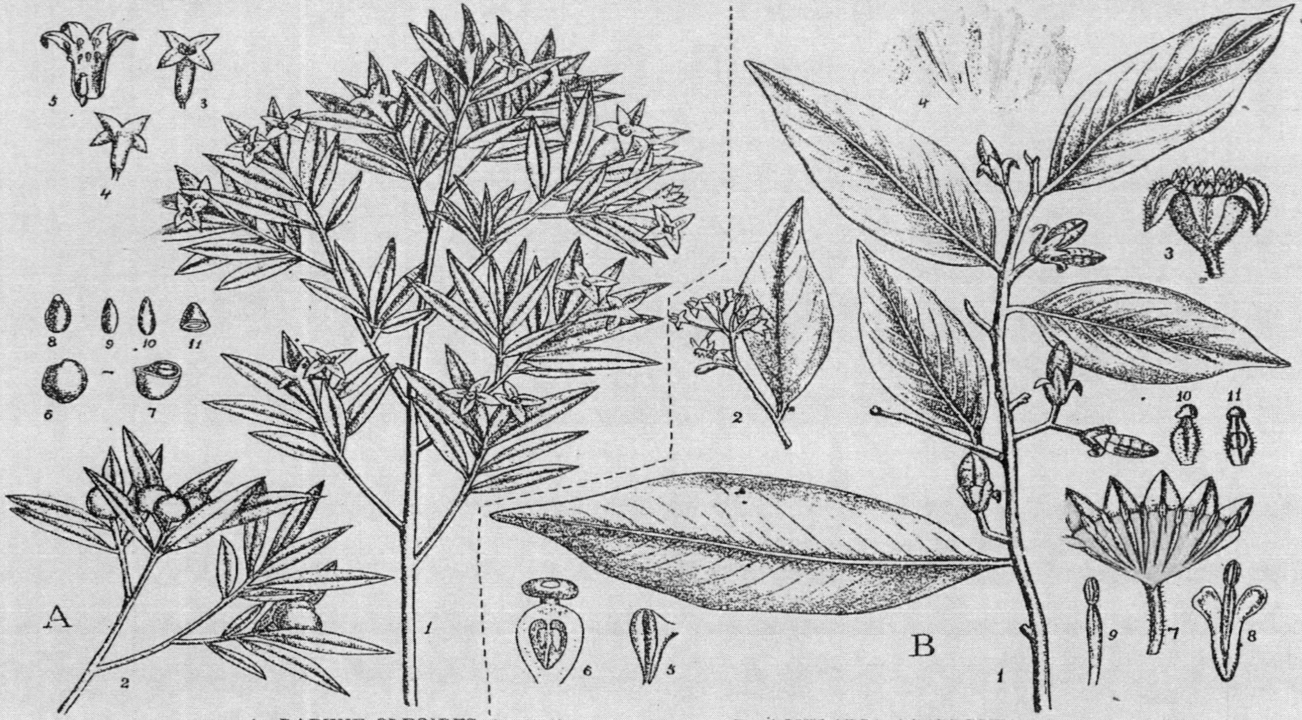

A—DAPHNE OLEOIDES, *SCHREIE.* B—AQUILARIA AGALLCOHA, *ROXB.*

PLATE No. 837.

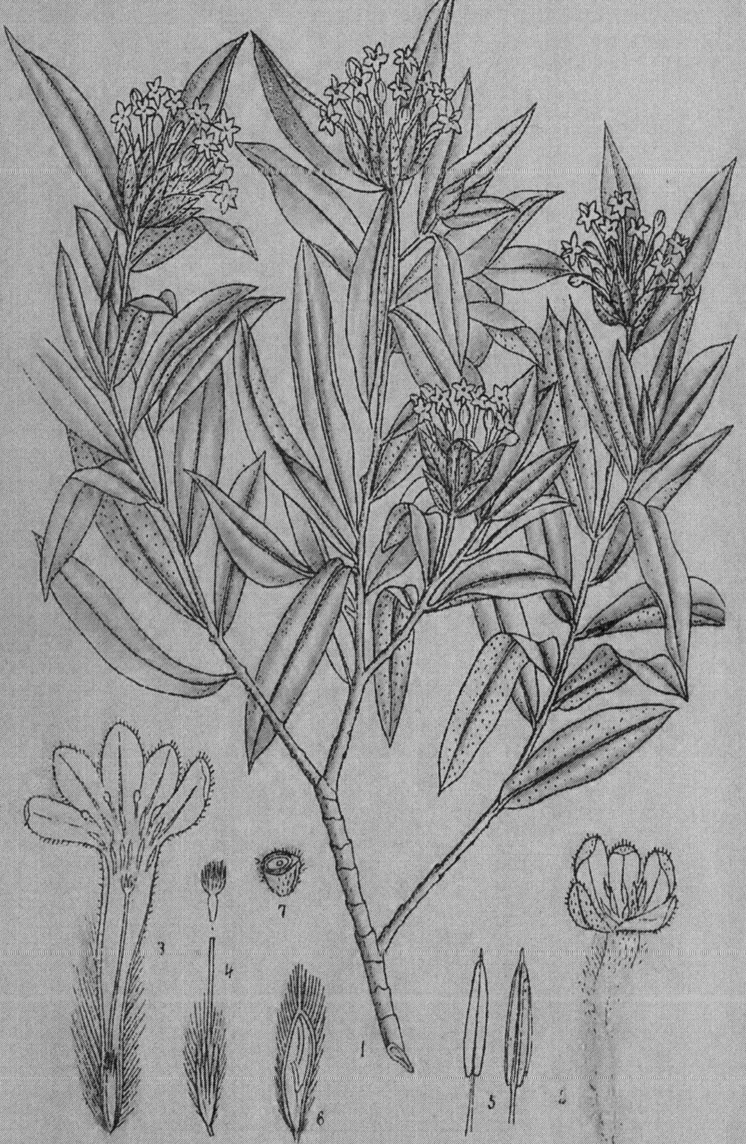

LASIOSIPHON ERIOCEPHALUS, *DCNE.*

PLATE No. 838.

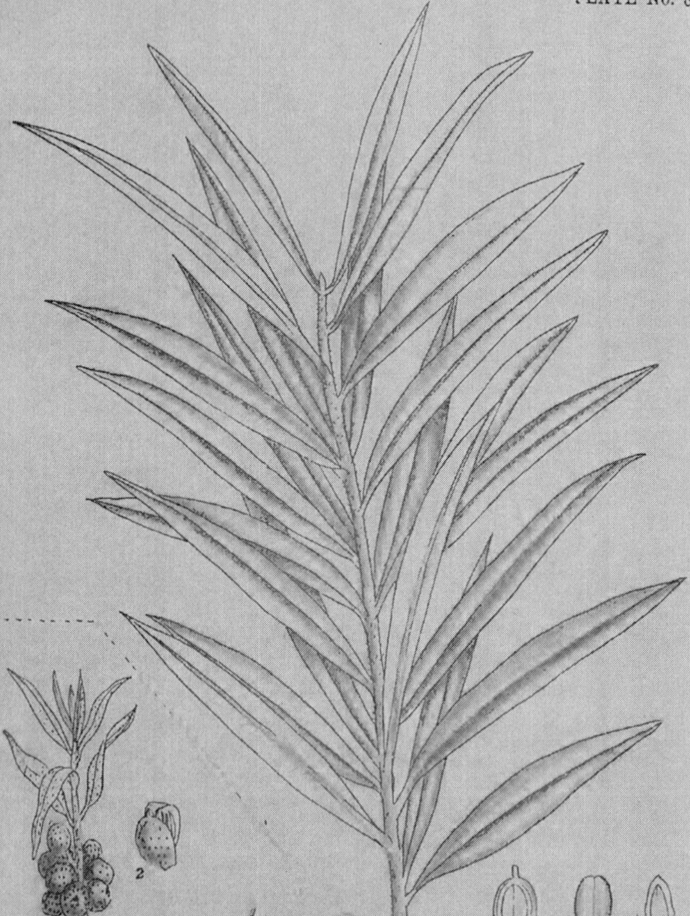

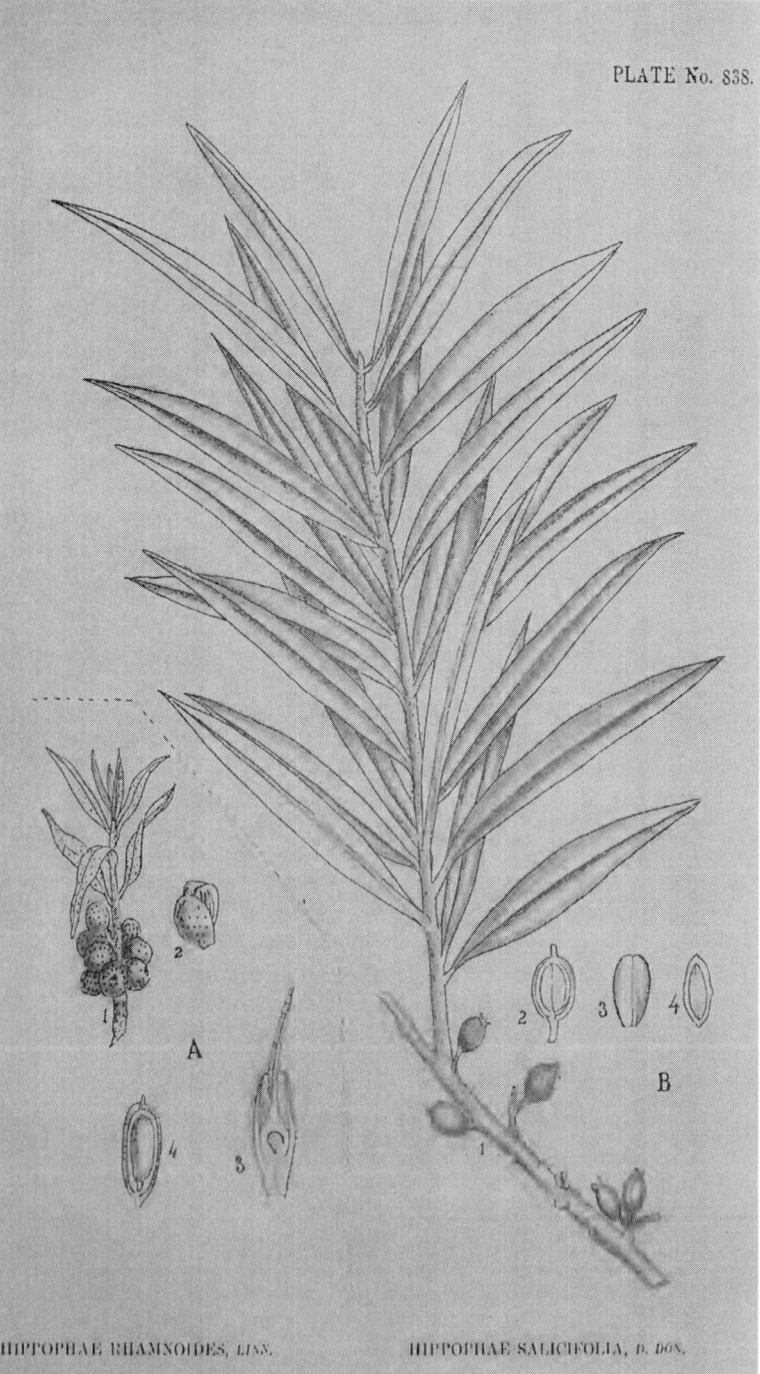

HIPPOPHAE RHAMNOIDES, *LINN.* HIPPOPHAE SALICIFOLIA, *D. DON.*

PLATE No. 839.

A—ELÆAGNUS HORTENSIS, *M. BIEB.* B—ELÆAGNUS UMBELLATA, *THUNB.*

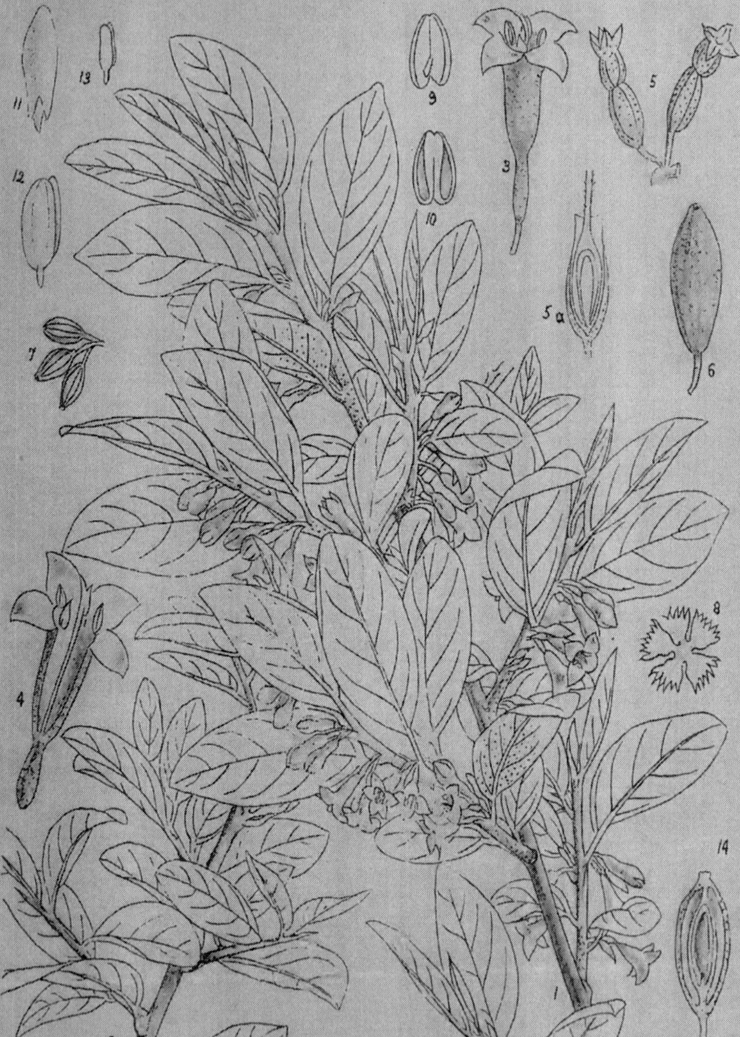

ELÆAGNUS LATIFOLIA, LINN

PLATE No. 841.

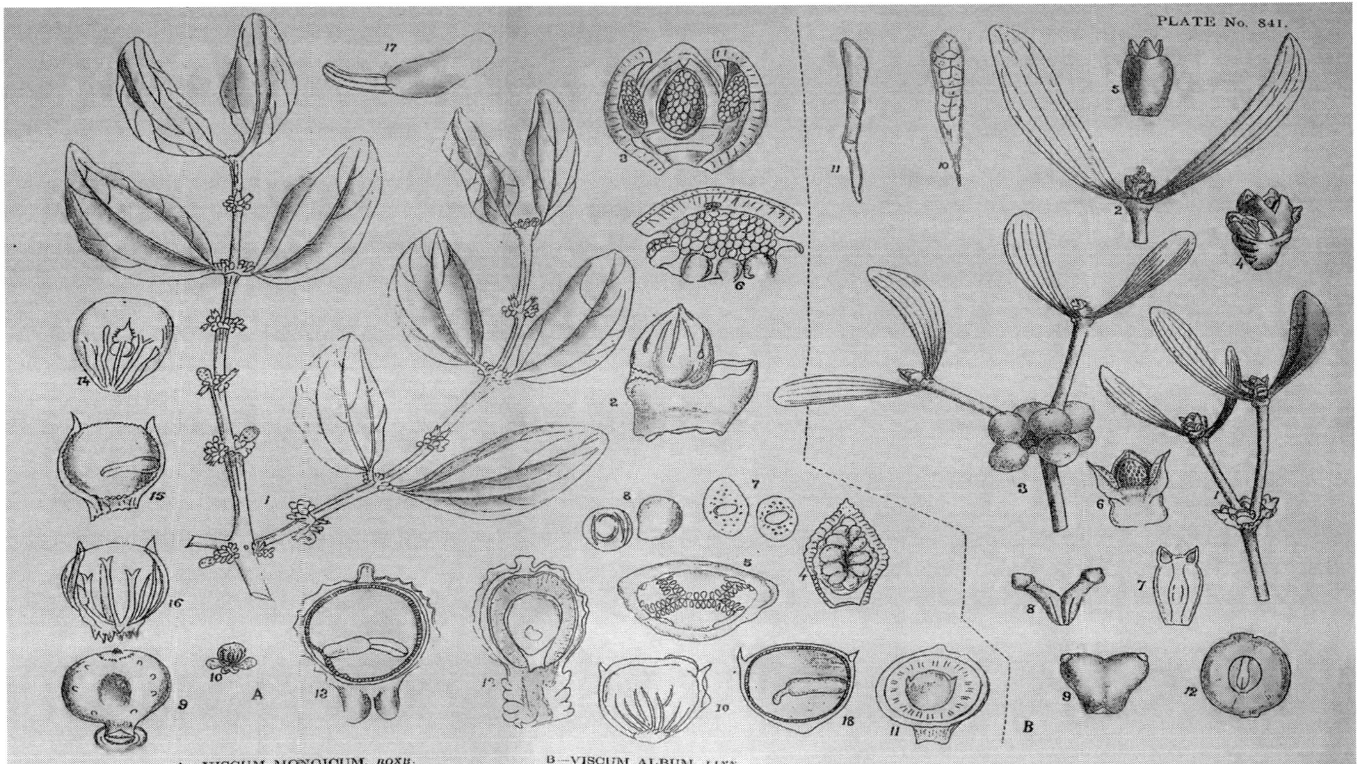

A.—VISCUM MONOICUM, *Roxb.* B.—VISCUM ALBUM, *Linn.*

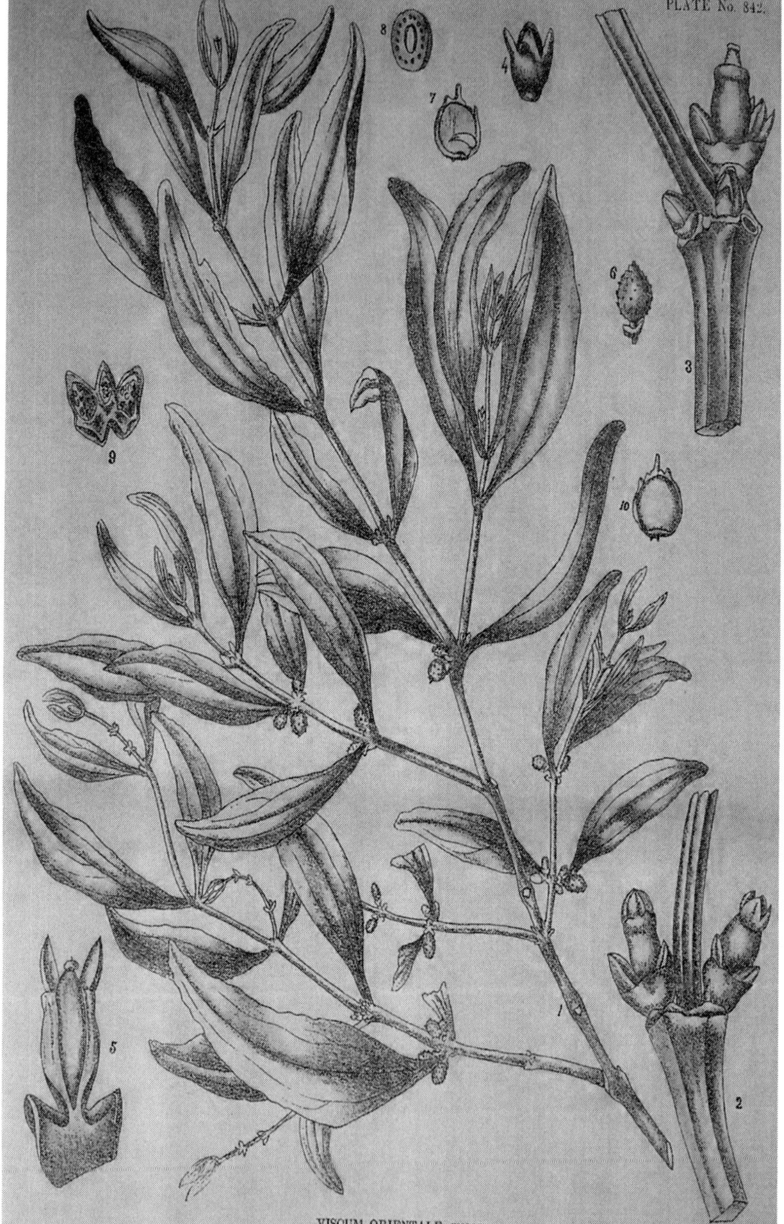

VISCUM ORIENTALE, WILLD

PLATE No 843

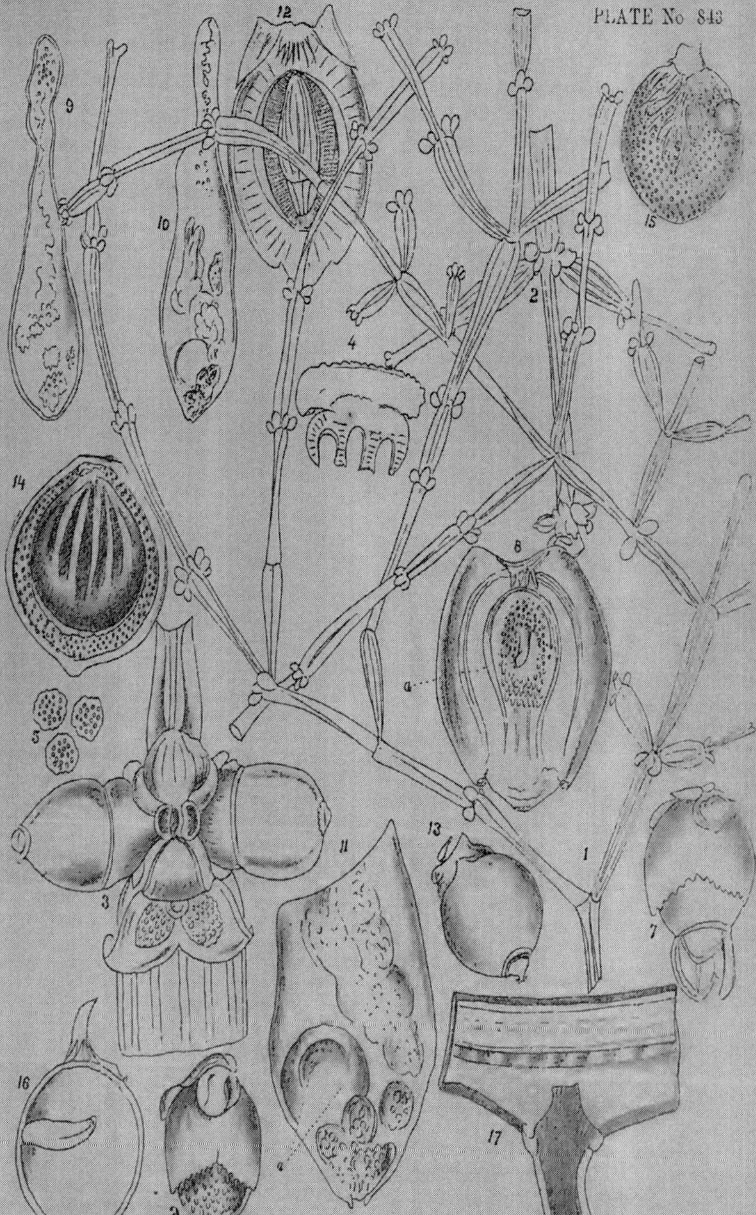

VISCUM ARTICULATUM, *Burm.*

PLATE No. 844.

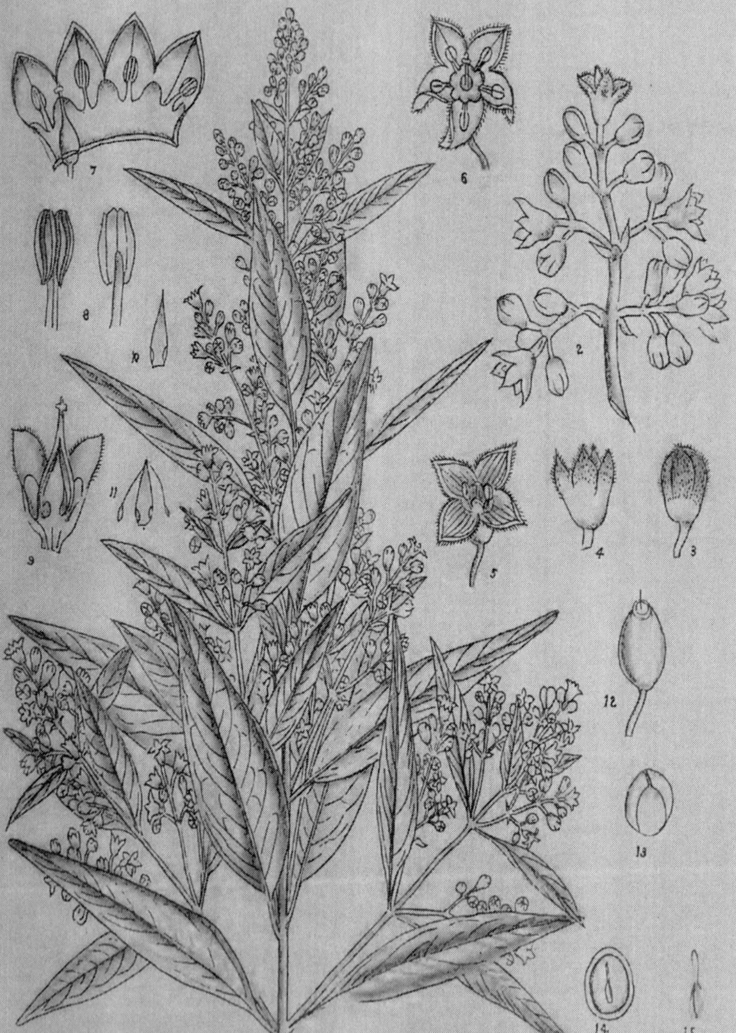

SANTALUM ALBUM, LINN

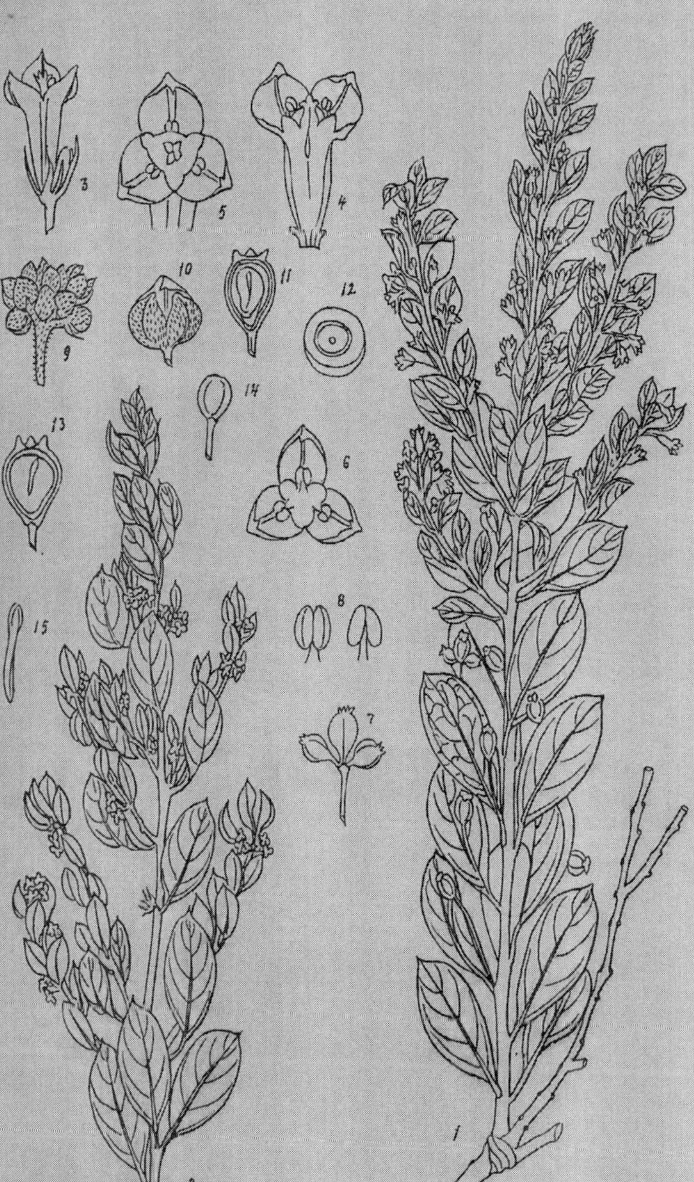

OSYRIS ARBOREA, WALL.

PLATE No. 846.

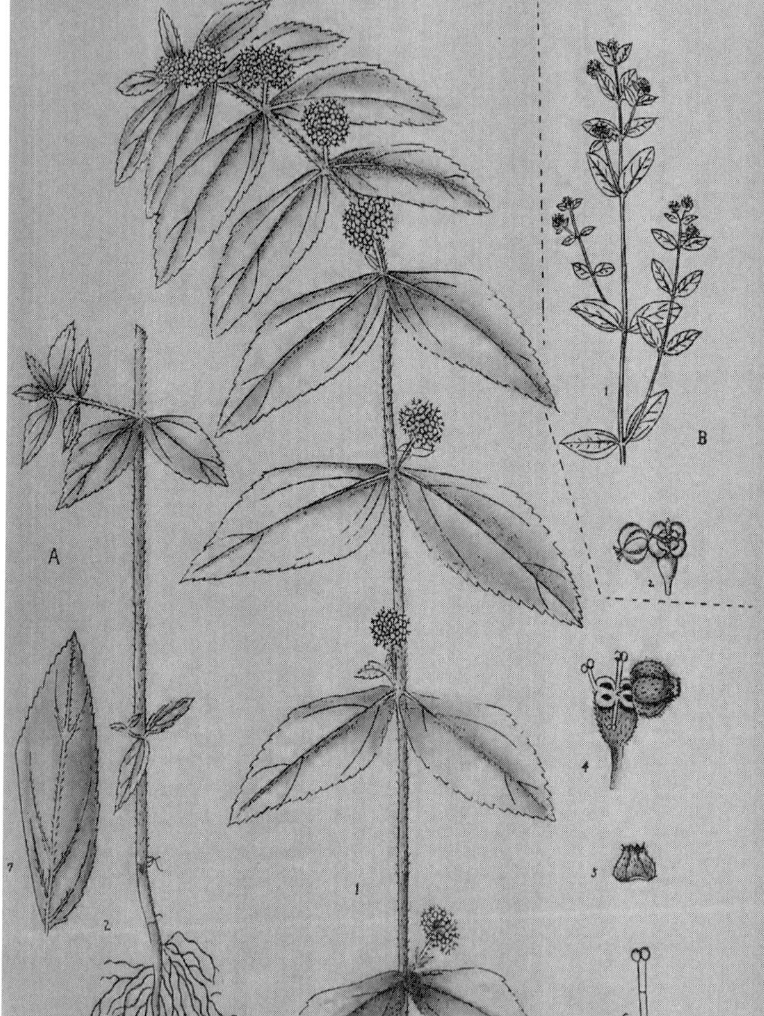

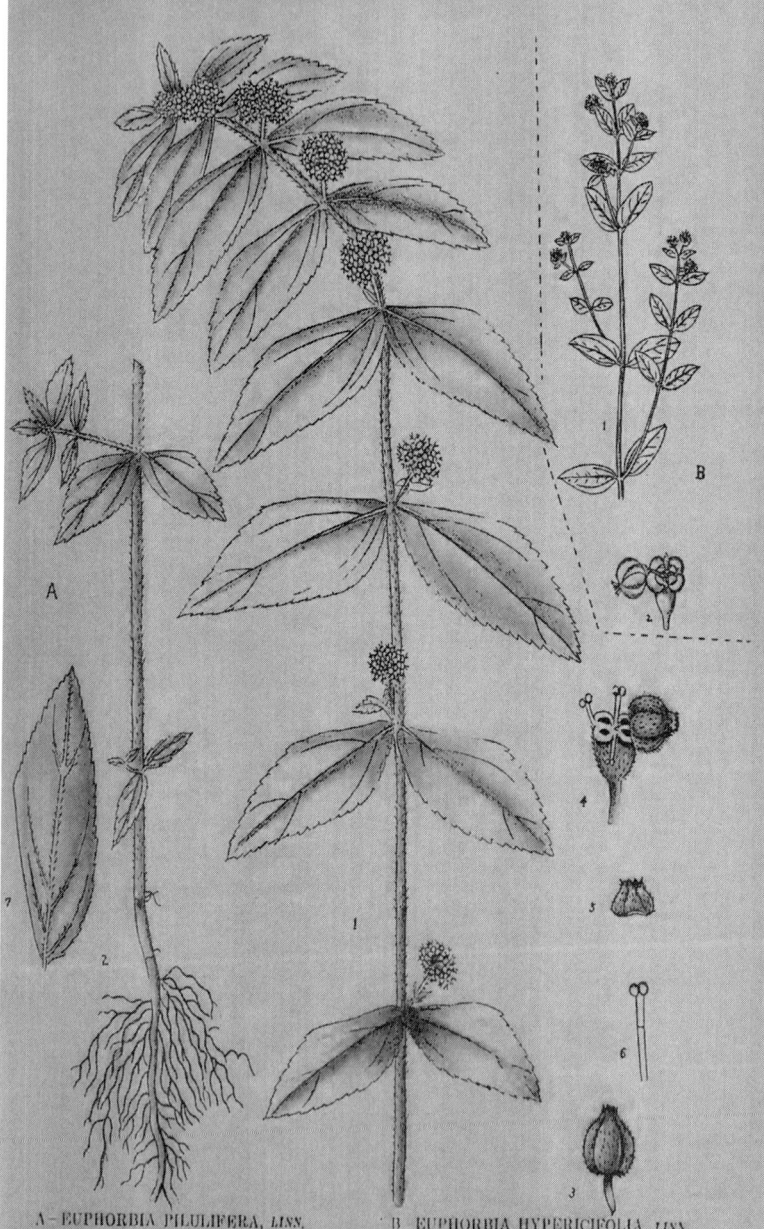

A—EUPHORBIA PILULIFERA, *LINN.*   B EUPHORBIA HYPERICIFOLIA, *LINN.*

PLATE No. 847.

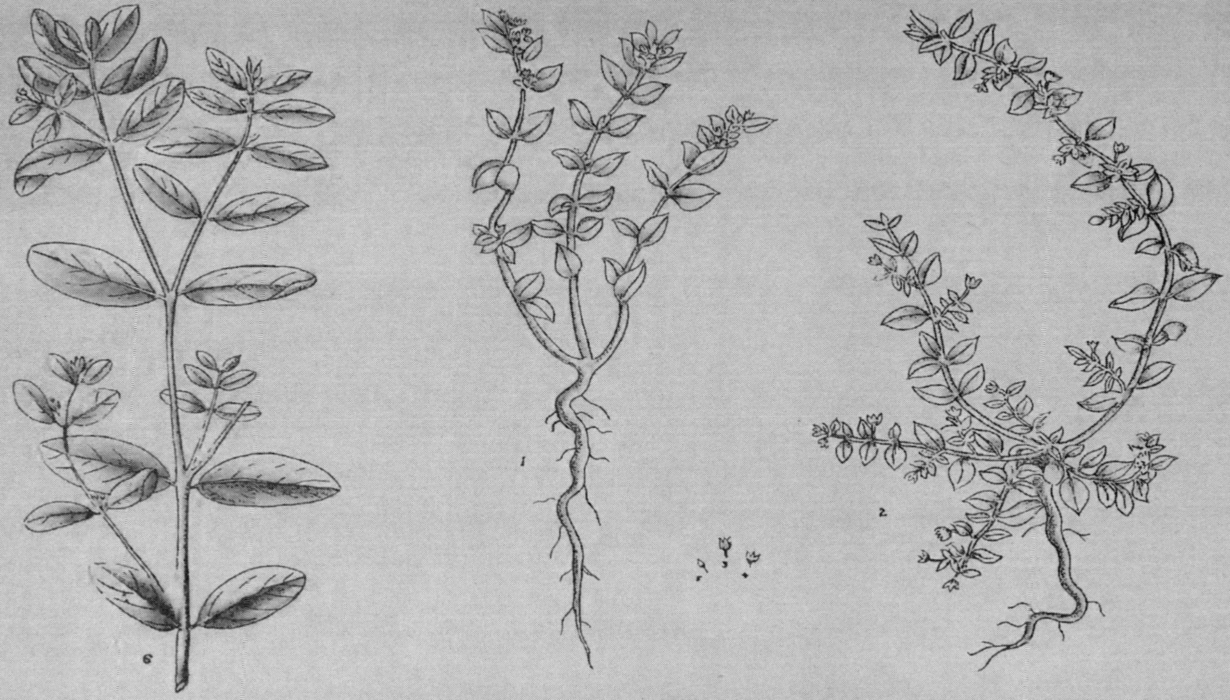

EUPHORBIA THYMIFOLIA, *Burm.*

PLATE No. 848.

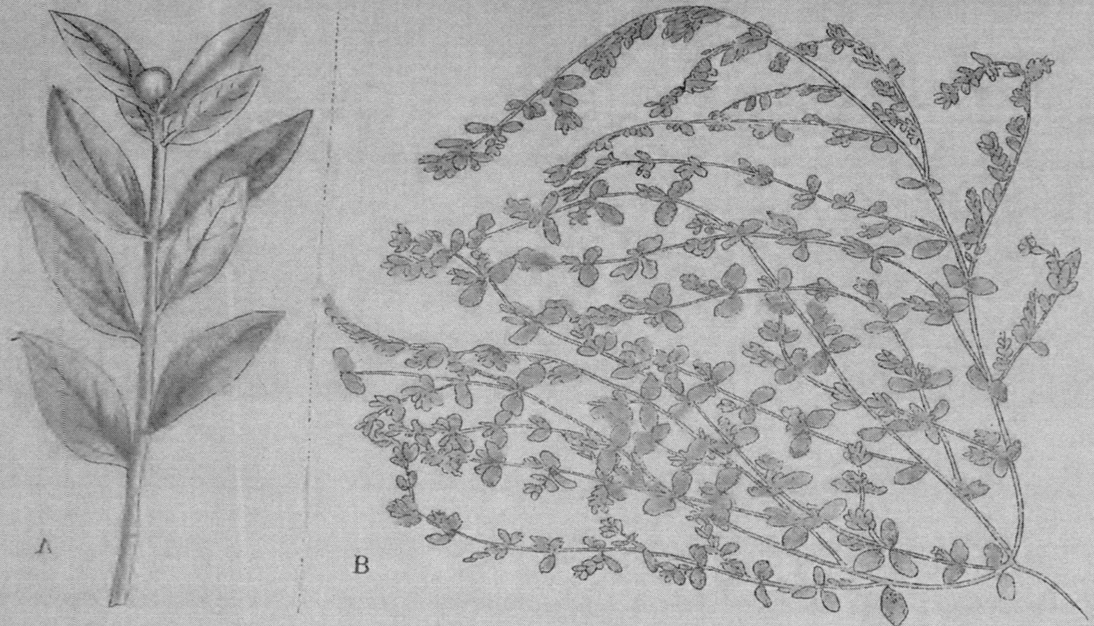

A—EUPHORBIA THOMSONIANA, *BOISS.* B—EUPHORBIA MICROPHYLLA, *HEYNE.*

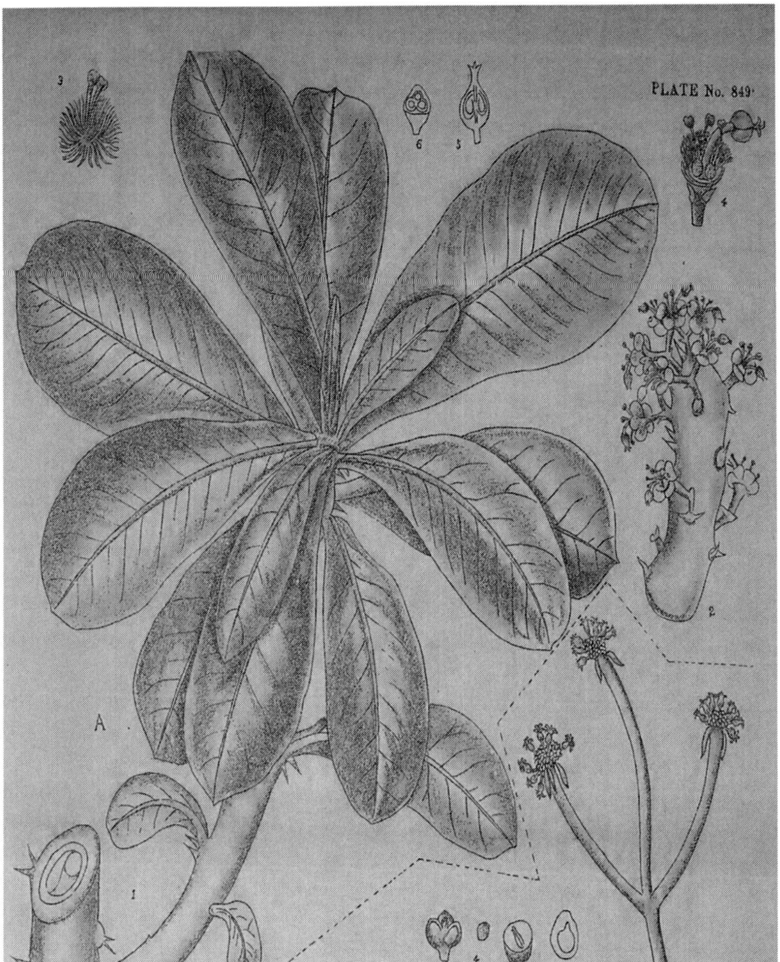

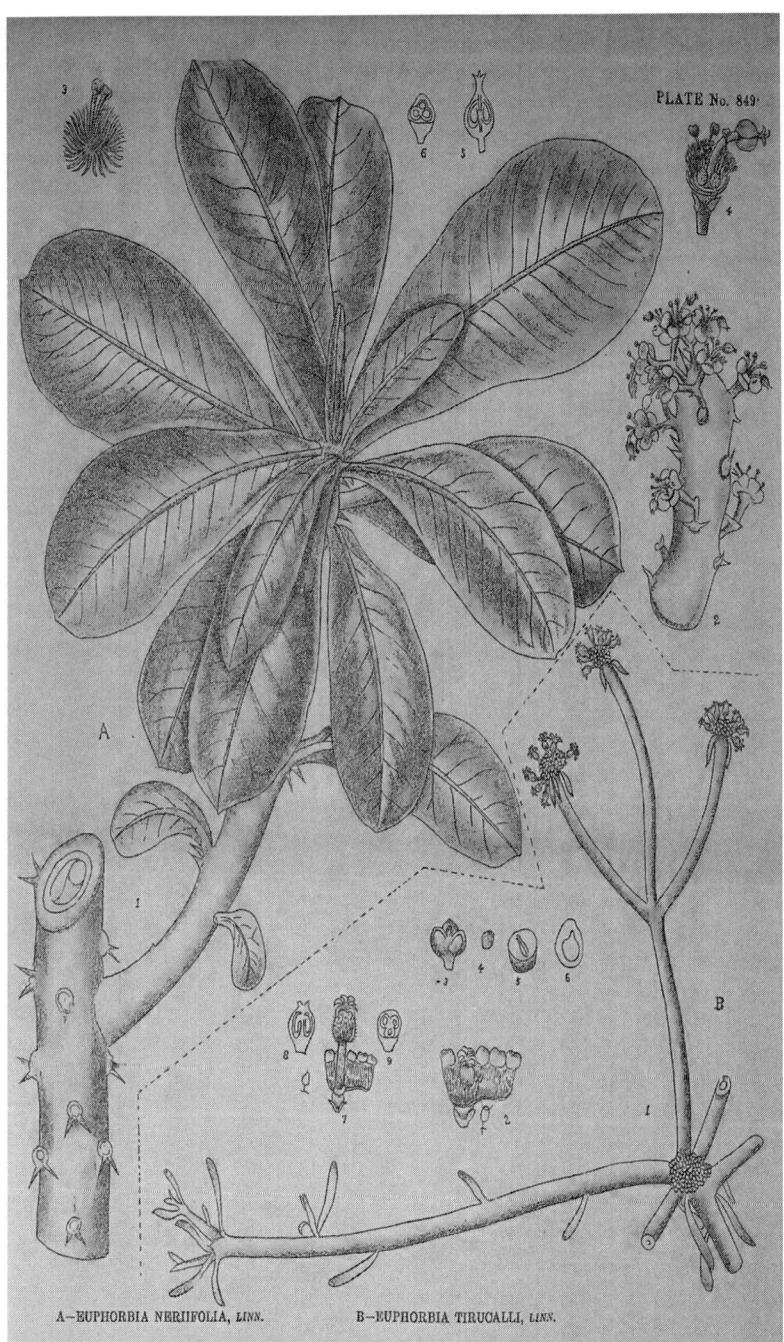

A—EUPHORBIA NERIIFOLIA, *LINN.* B—EUPHORBIA TIRUCALLI, *LINN.*

PLATE No. 850.

EUPHORBIA NIVULIA, *HAM.*

PLATE No. 851.

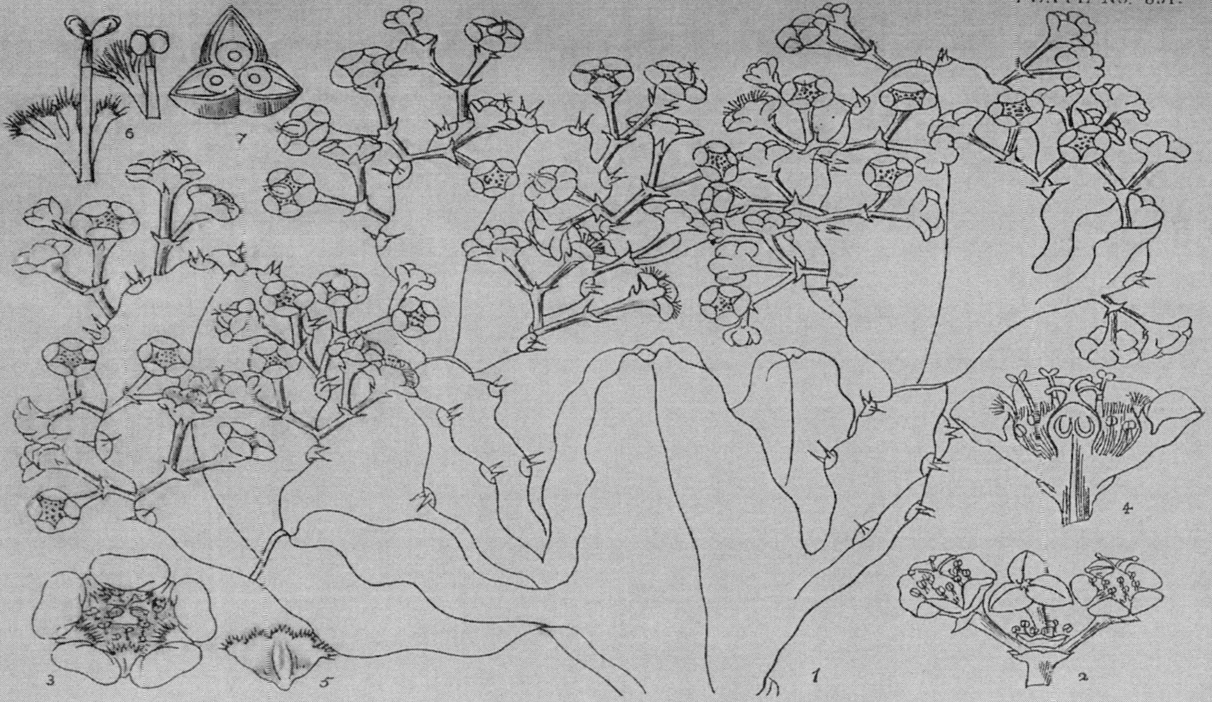

EUPHORBIA ANTIQUORUM, *LINN.*

PLATE No. 852.

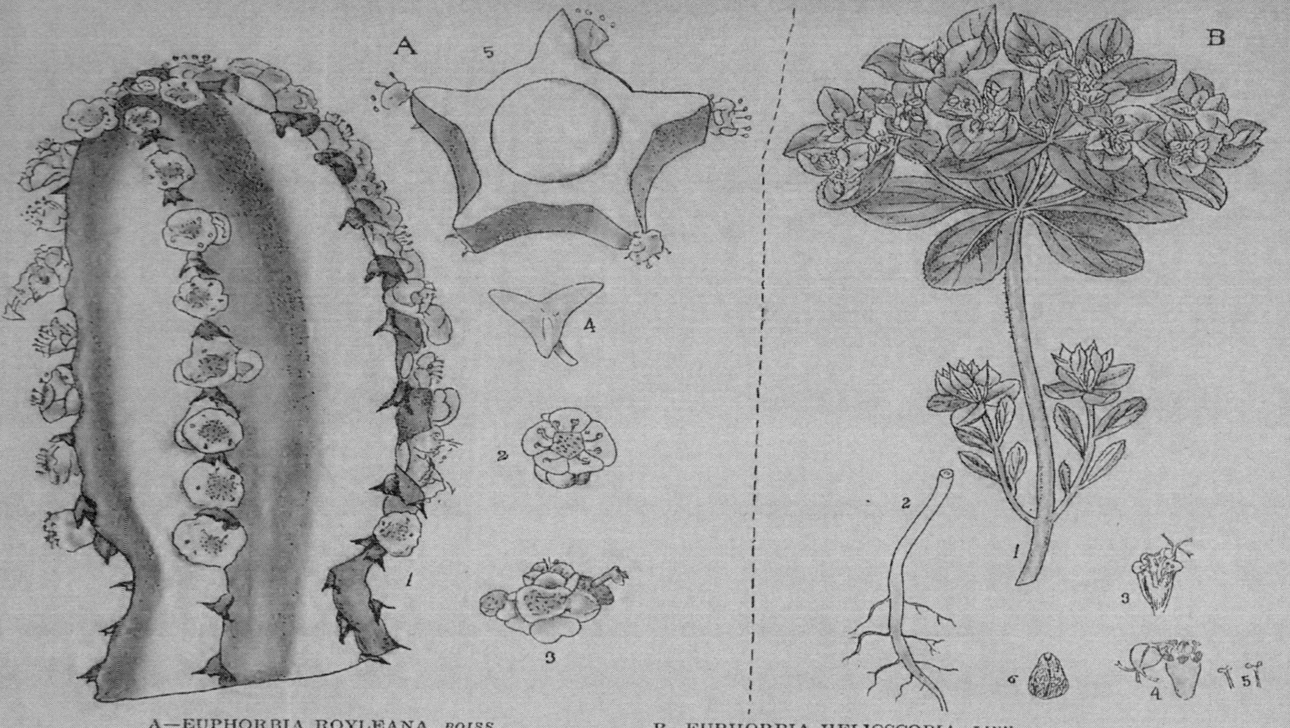

A—EUPHORBIA ROYLEANA, *Boiss.*

B—EUPHORBIA HELIOSCOPIA, *Linn.*

PLATE No 853.

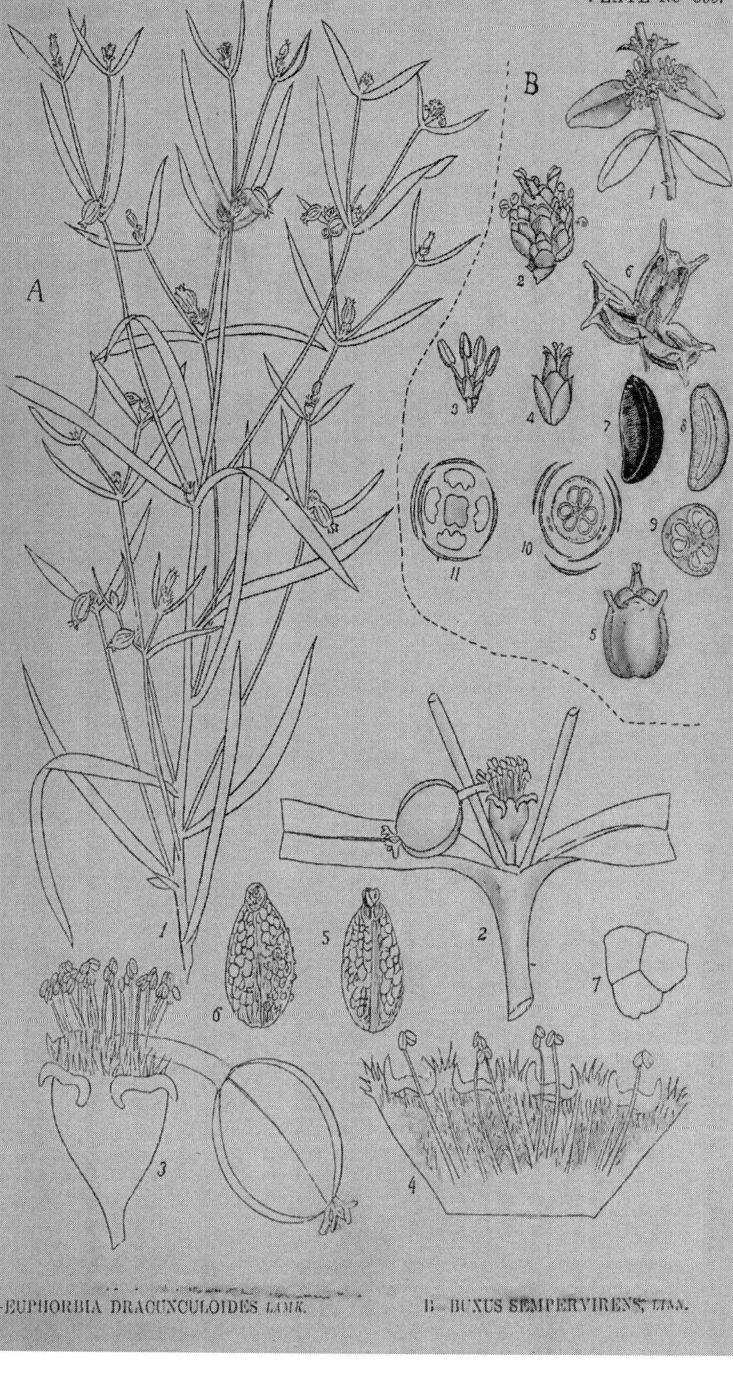

A—EUPHORBIA DRACUNCULOIDES *Lamk.* B—BUXUS SEMPERVIRENS, *Linn.*

PLATE No. 854.

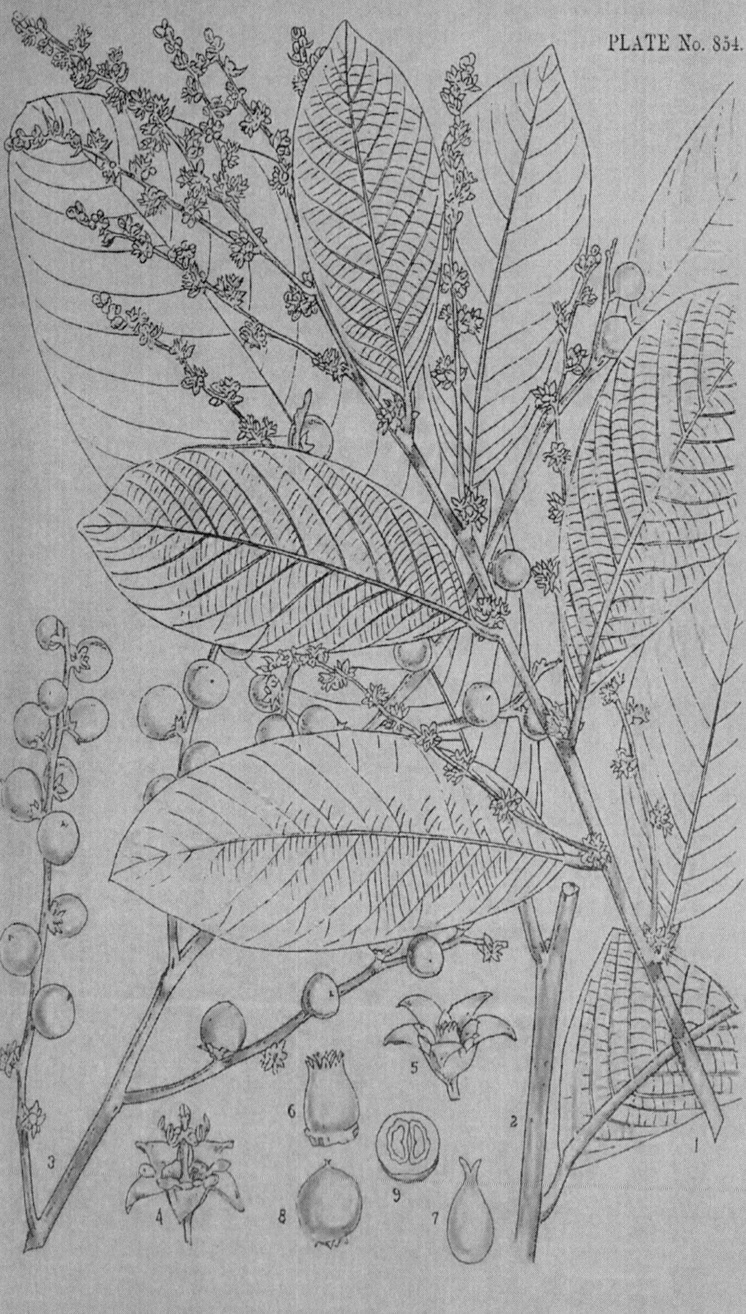

BRIDELIA RETUSA, SPRENG.

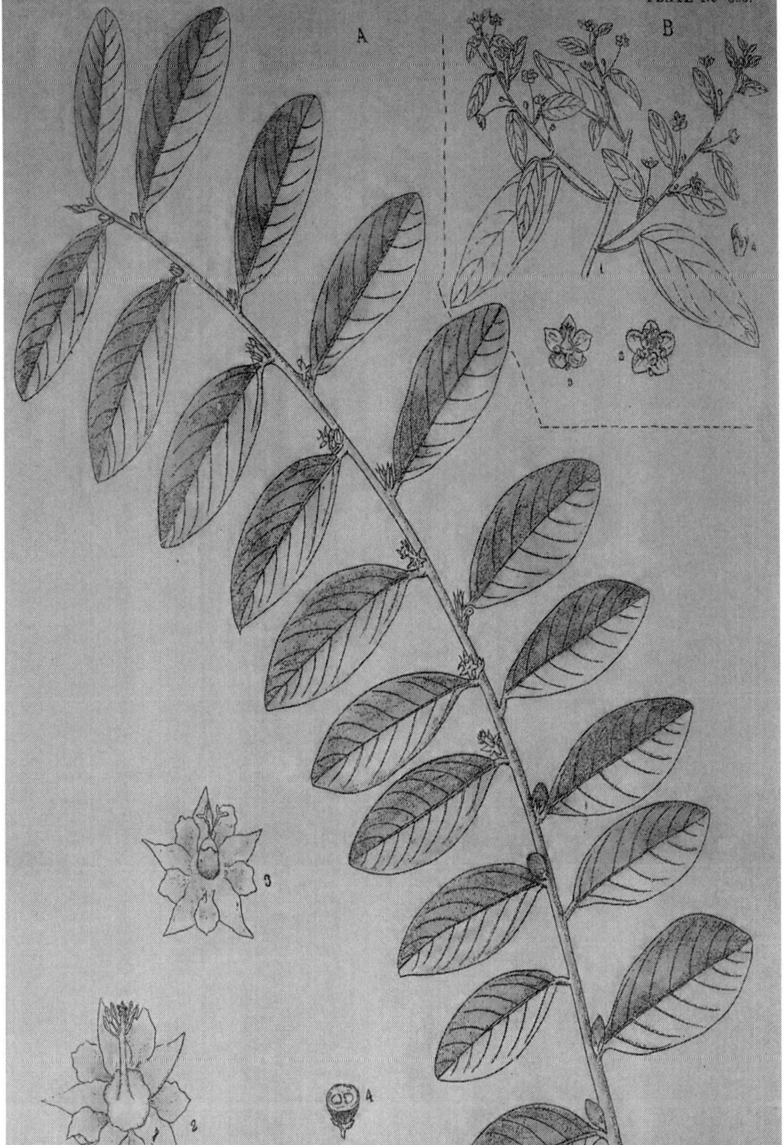

A—BRIDELIA MONTANA, *WILLD.* B—ANDRACHNE CORDIFOLIA, *MUELL.*

PLATE No. 856.

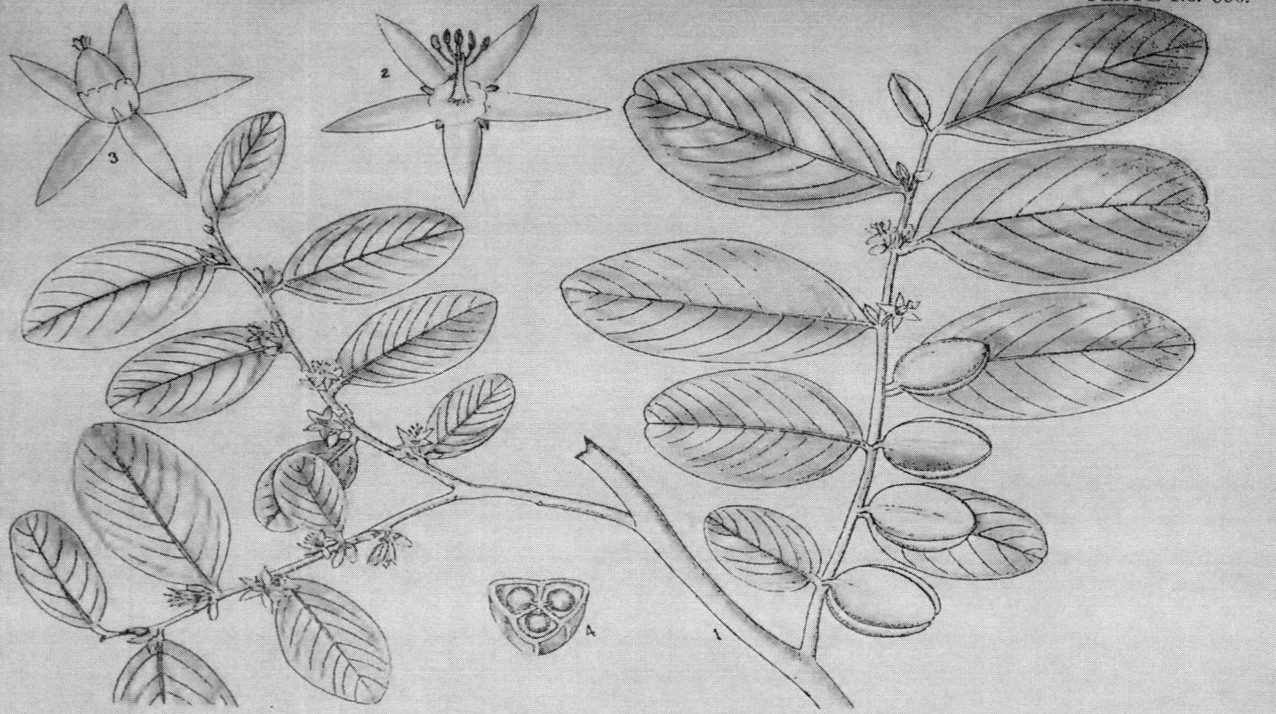

CLEISTANTHUS COLLINUS, *Benth.*

PLATE No. 859.

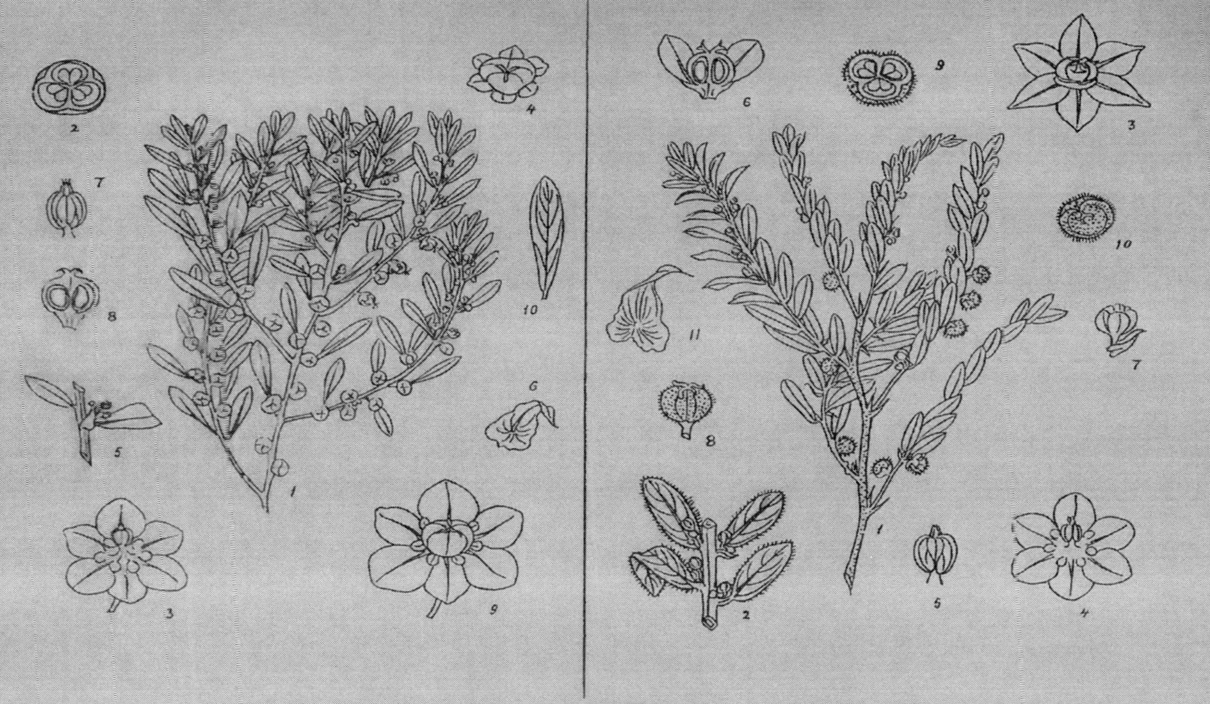

A—PHYLLANTHUS MADERASPATENSIS, *Linn.*   B—PHYLLANTHUS URINARIA, *Linn.*

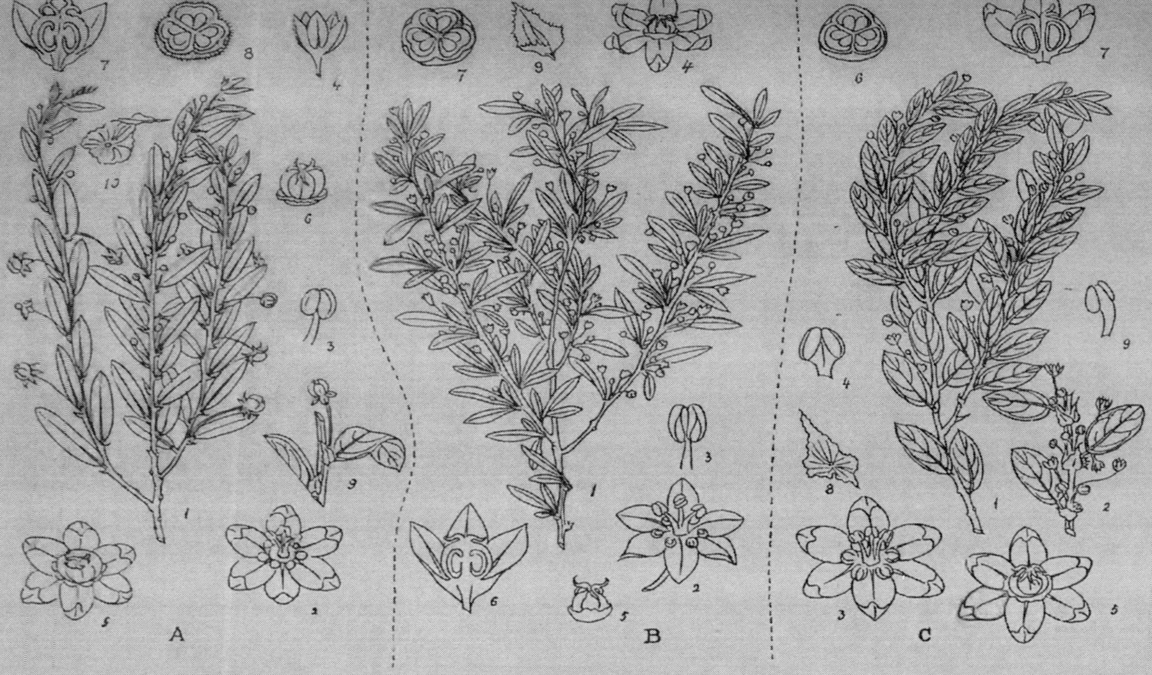

PHYLLANTHUS SIMPLEX, *RETZ.*

PLATE No. 861.

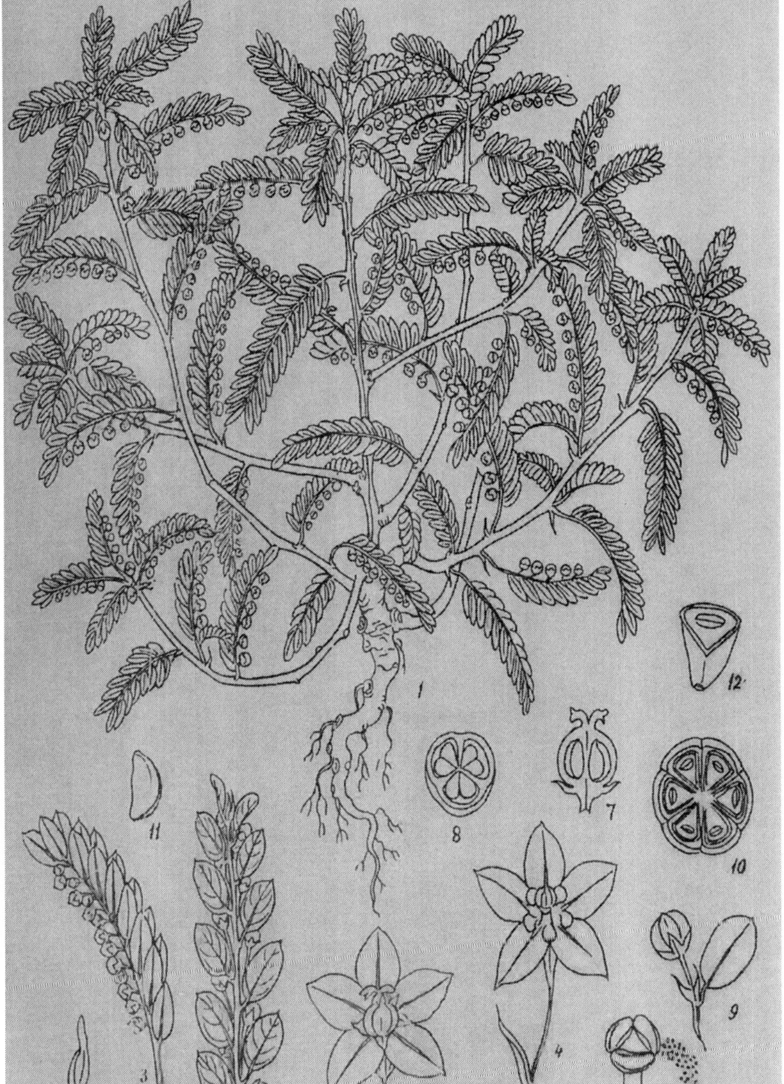

PHYLLANTHUS NIRURI, LINN.

A—PHYLLANTHUS DISTICHUS, *MUELL.* B—FLUEGGEA MICROCARPA, *BLUME.*

PLATE No 863.

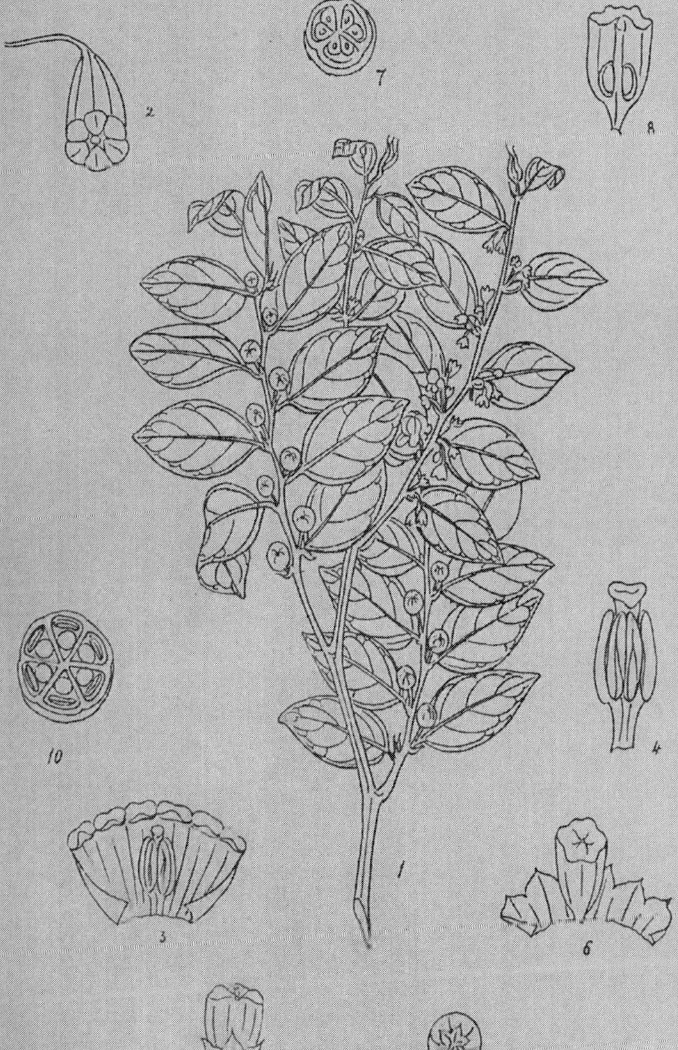

BREYNIA RHAMNOIDES, MUELL

PLATE No. 864.

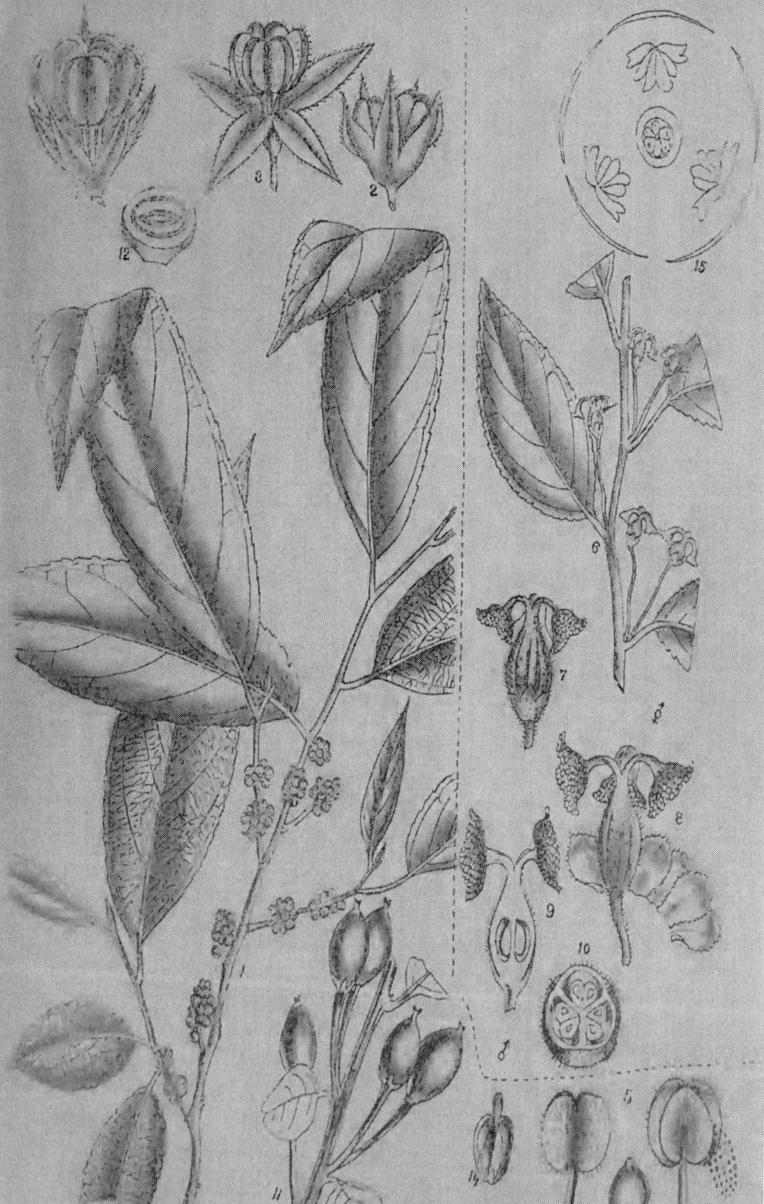

PUTRANJIVA ROXBURGHII, WALL.

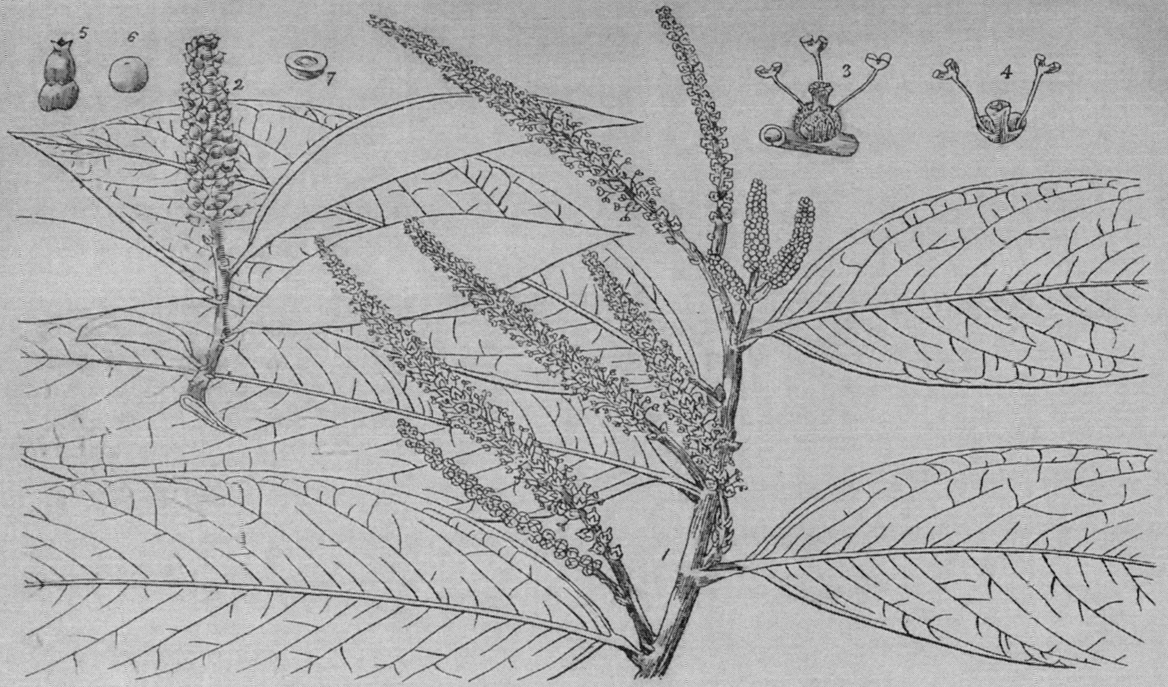

ANTIDESMA BUNIUS, *SPRENG.*

PLATE No. 866.

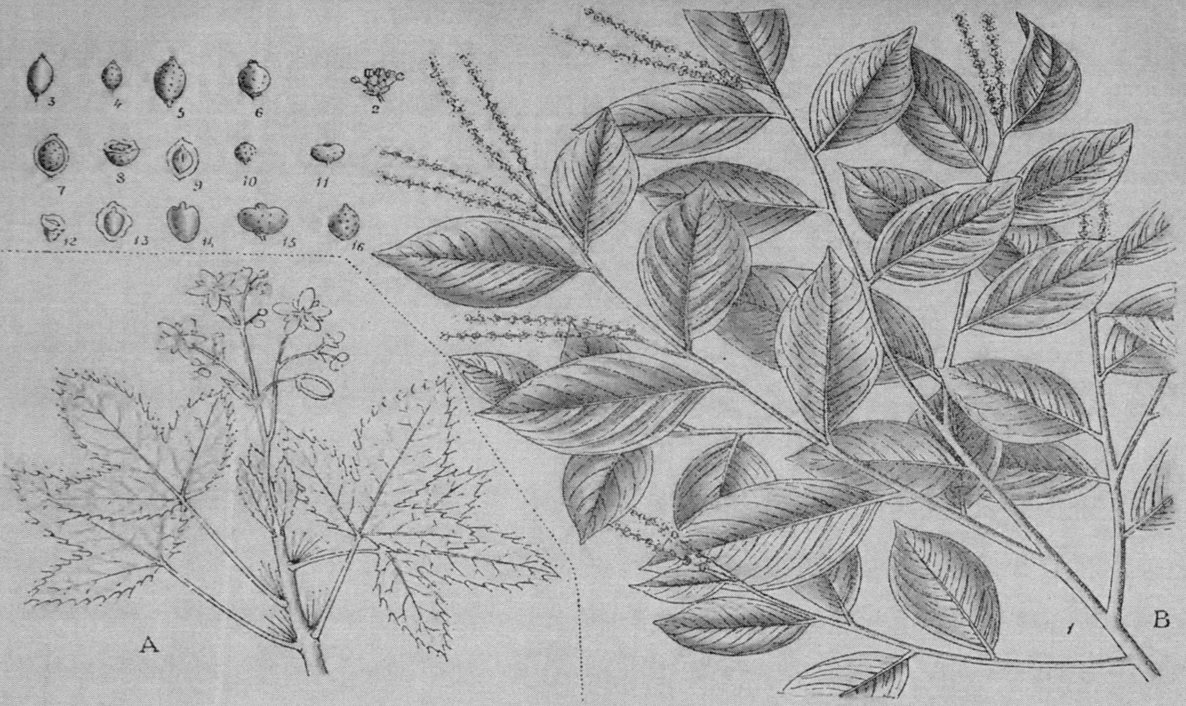

A—JATROPHA GLANDULIFERA, *ROXB.*　　B—ANTIDESMA ALEXITERIA, *LINN.*

PLATE No. 867.

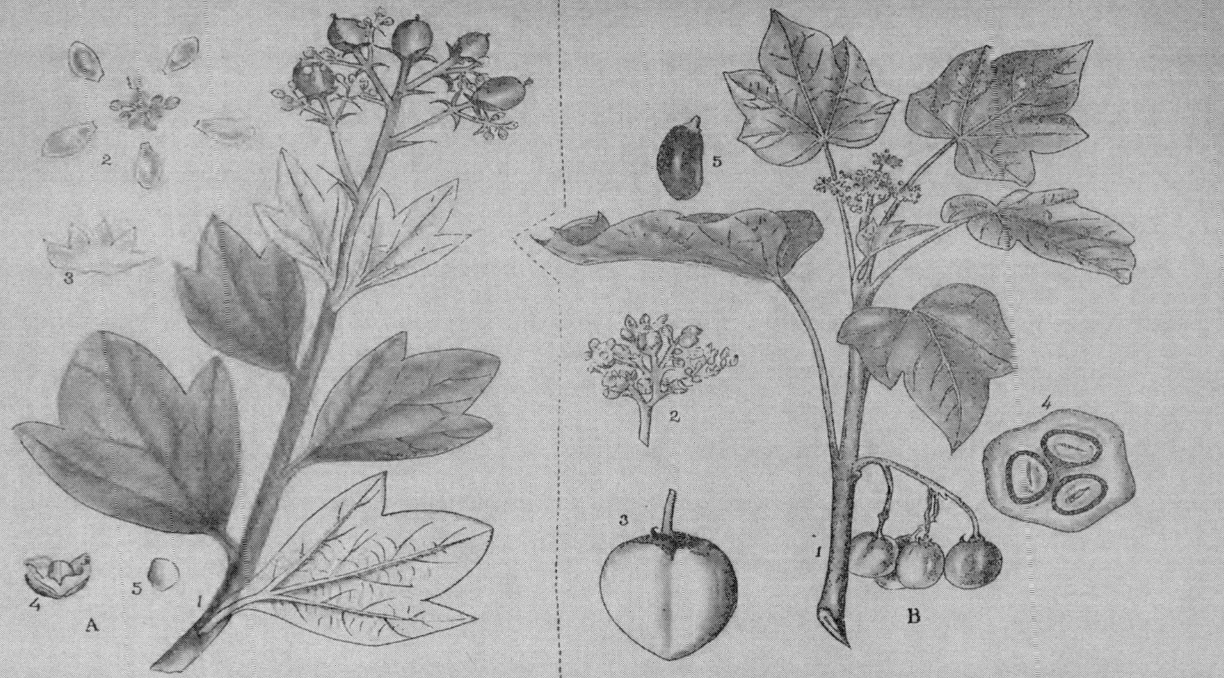

A. JATROPHA NANA, DALZ. & GIBS.   B.–JATROPHA CURCAS, LINN.

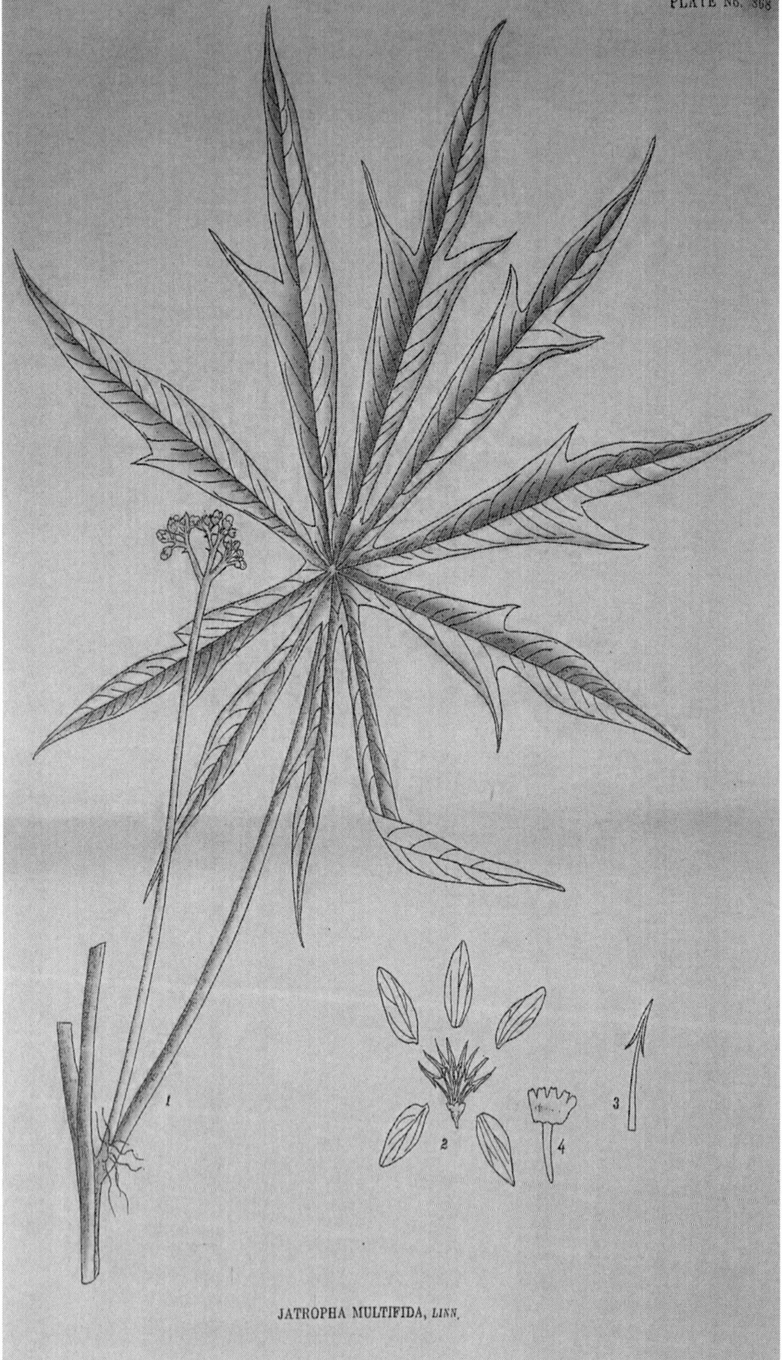

JATROPHA MULTIFIDA, *LINN.*

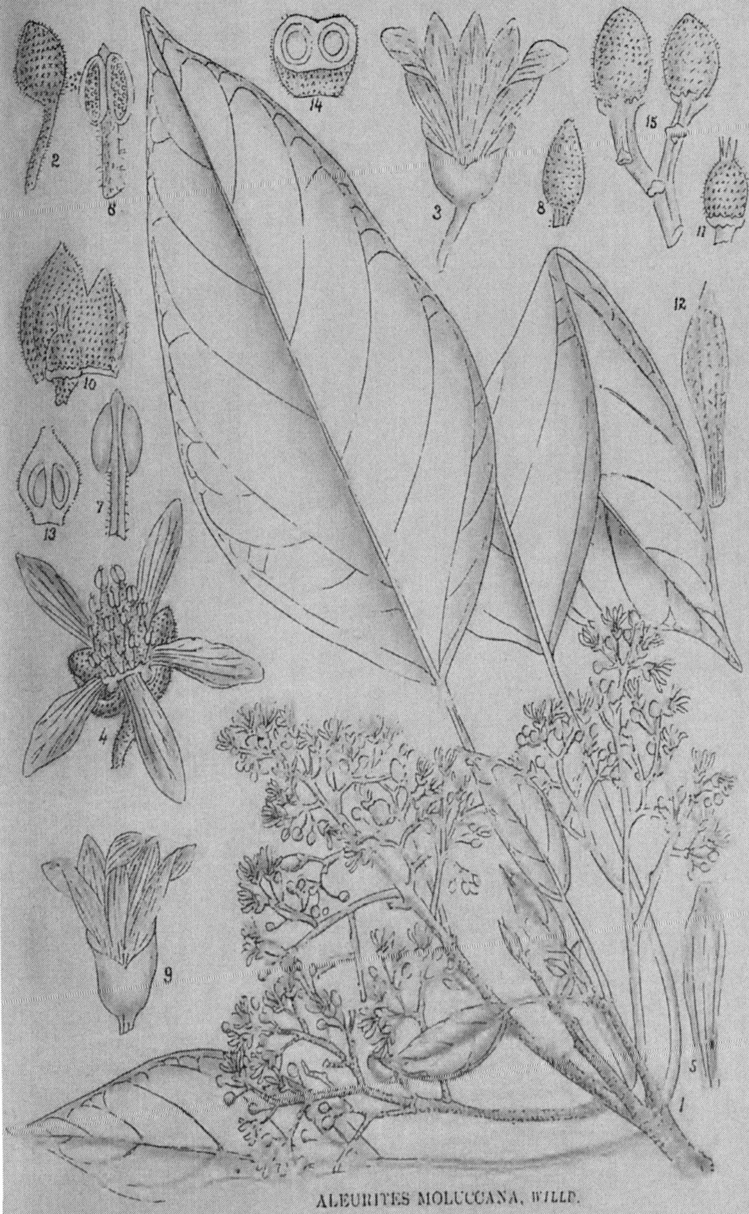

ALEURITES MOLUCCANA, WILLD.

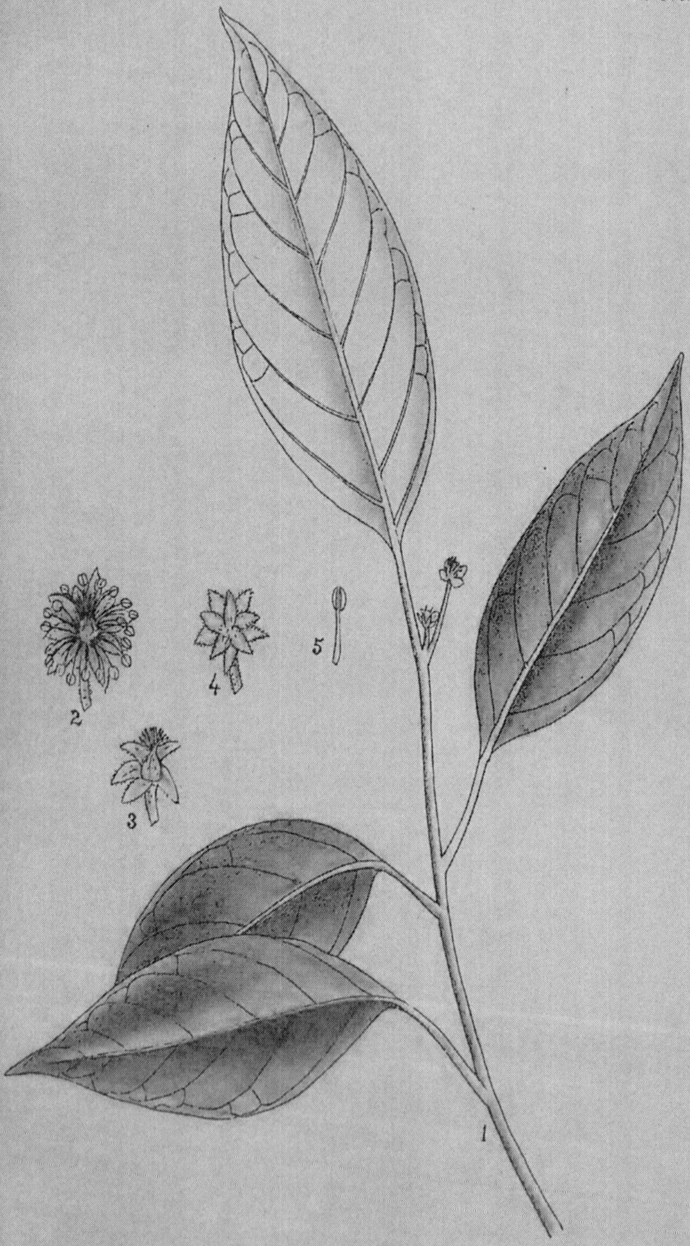

CROTON RETICULATUS, HEYNE.

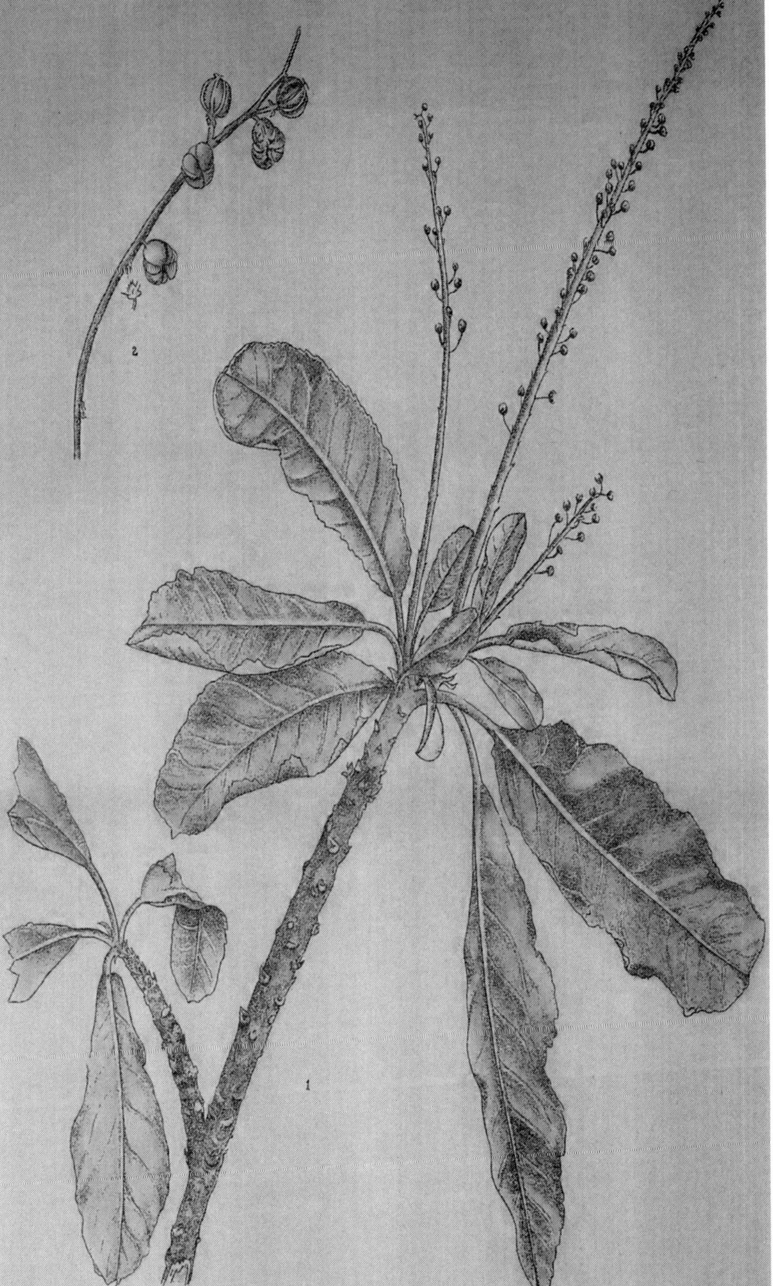

CROTON OBLONGIFOLIUS, ROXB.

A–CROTON CAUDATUS, *GEISEL.* B–CROTON TIGLIUM, *LINN.*

PLATE No. 873.

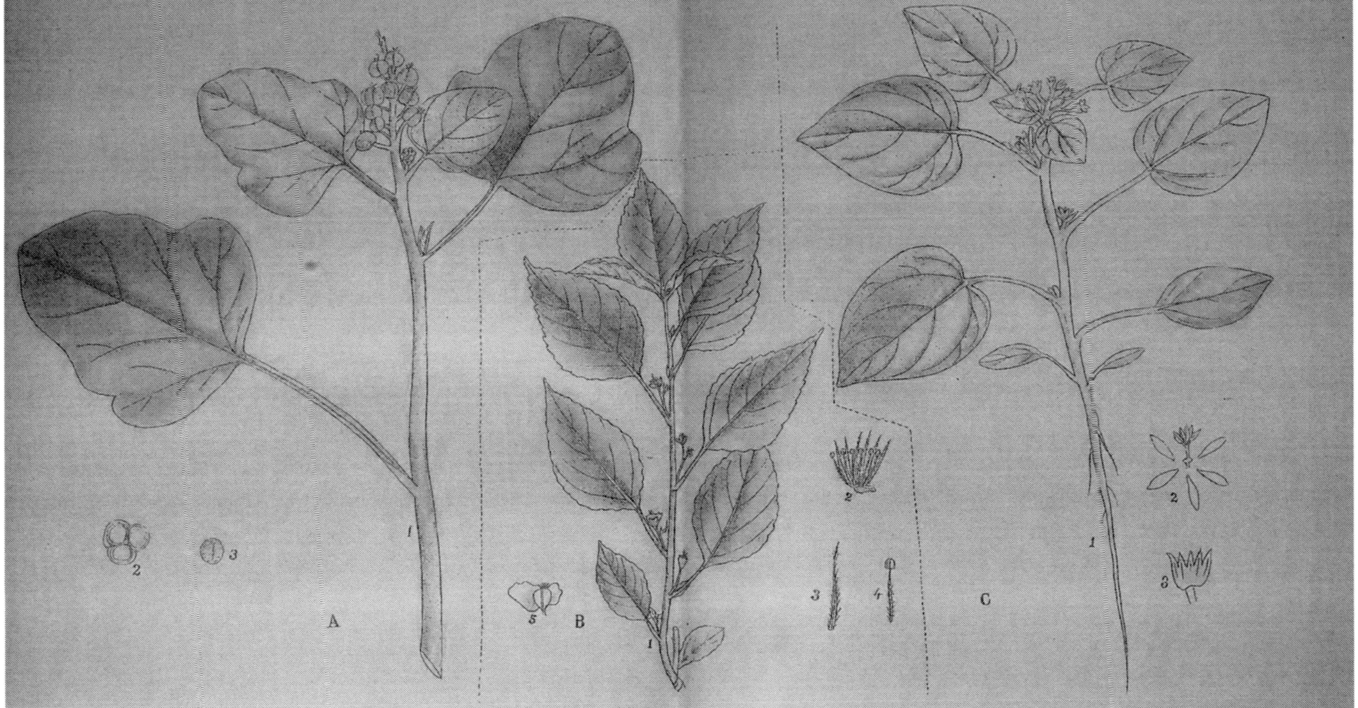

A—CHROZOPHORA PLICATA, *A. JUSS.* B—ACALYPHA FRUTICOSA, *FORSK.* C—CHROZOPHORA TINCTORIA, *A. JUSS.*

PLATE No 874.

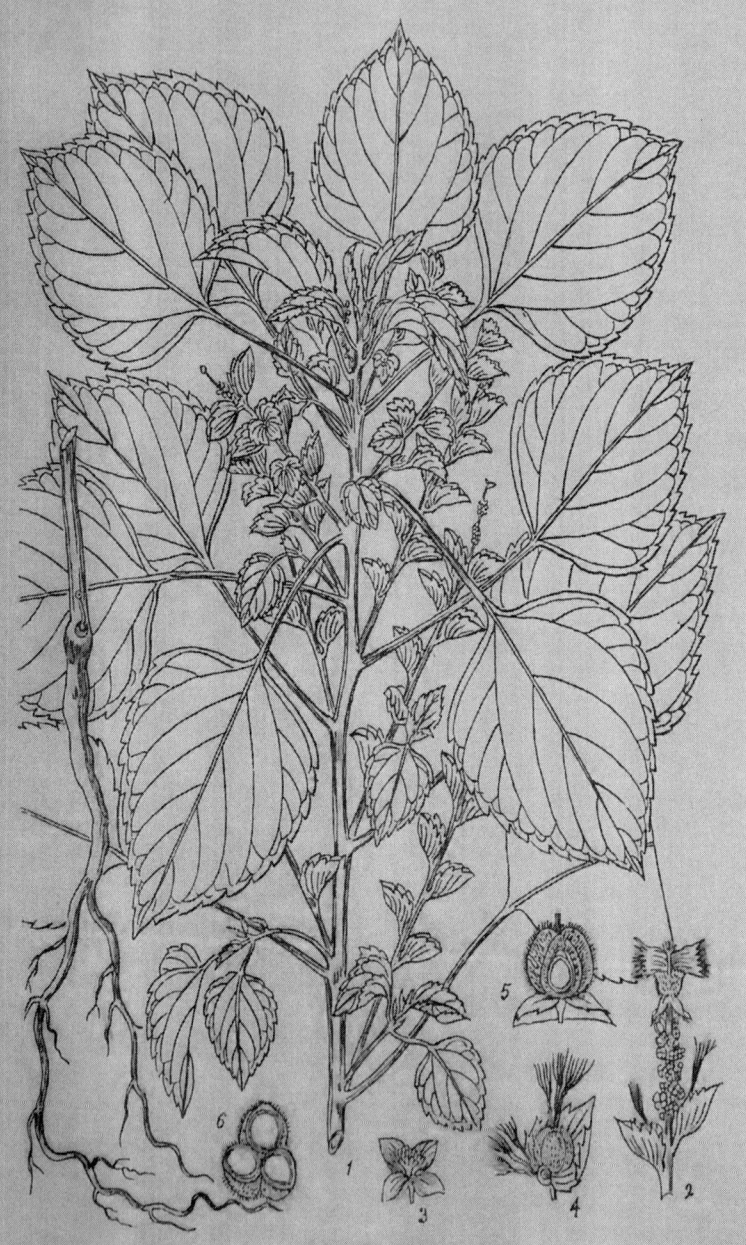

ACALYPHA INDICA, LINN

PLATE No. 875.

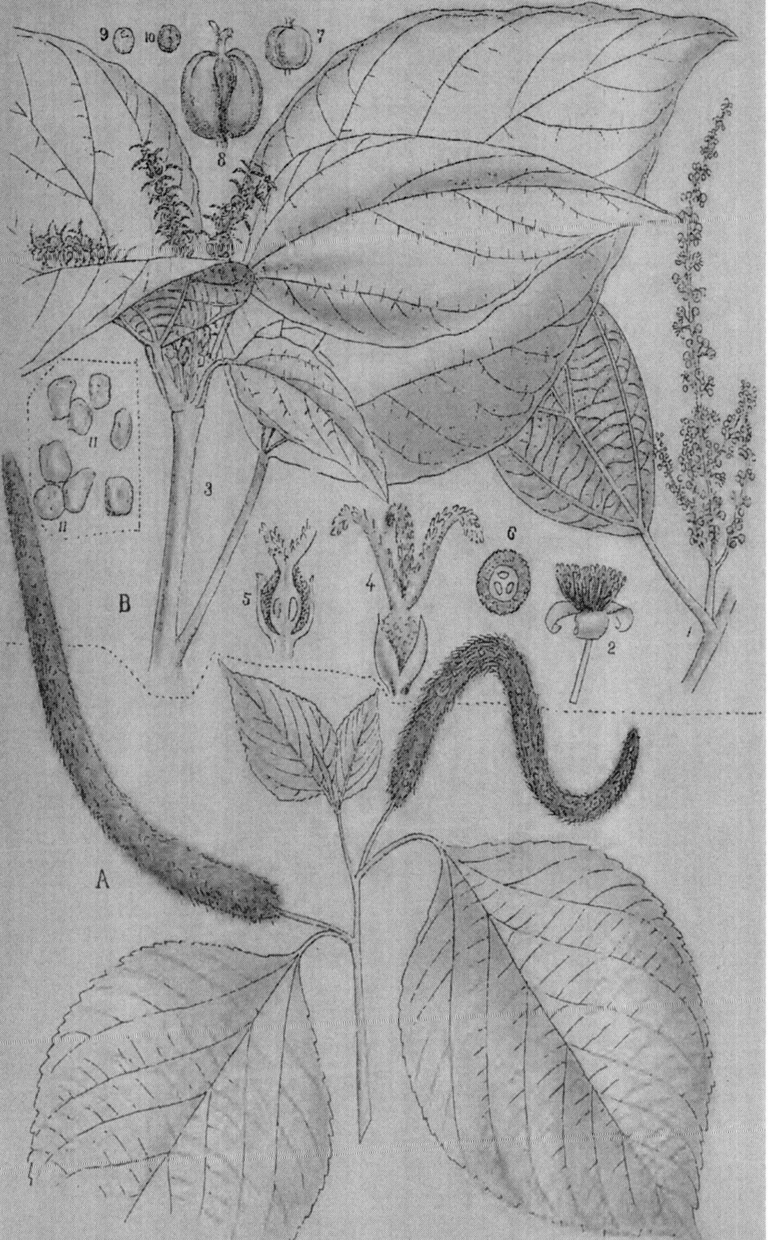

A—ACALYPHA HISPIDA, *Burm*

B—MALLOTUS PHILIPPINENSIS, *Muell.*

PLATE No. 876.

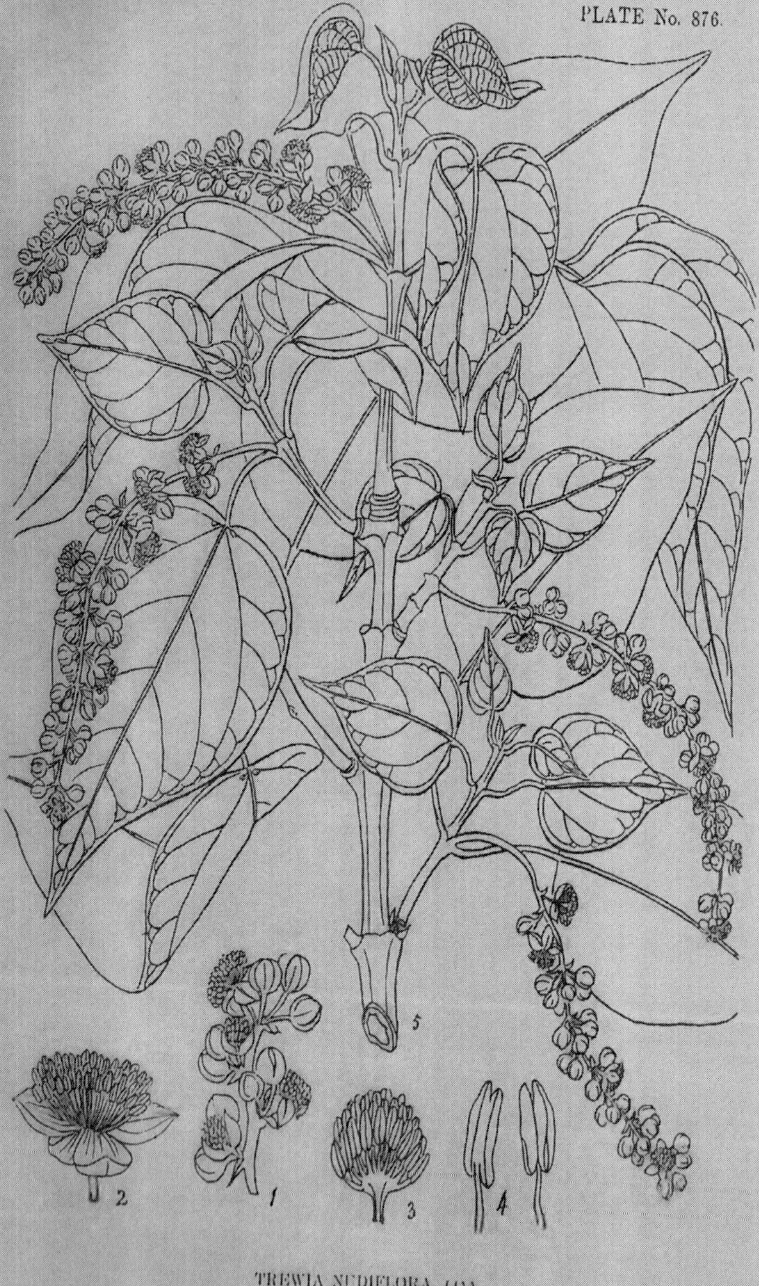

TREWIA NUDIFLORA, Linn.

PLATE No. 877.

MACARANGA ROXBURGHII, WIGHT.

PLATE No. 878.

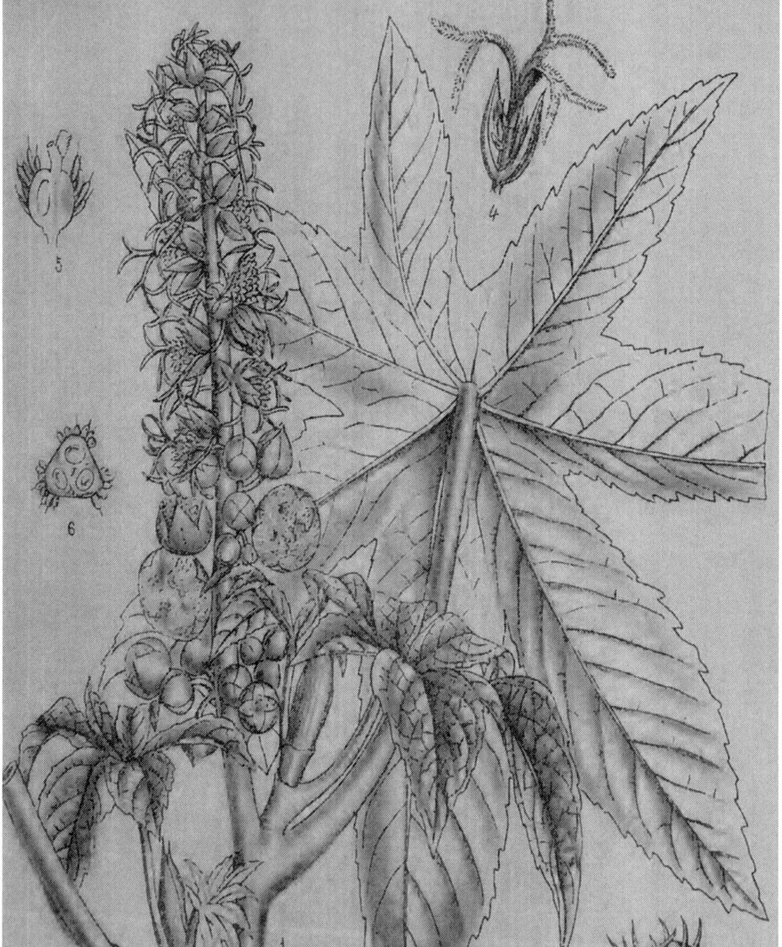

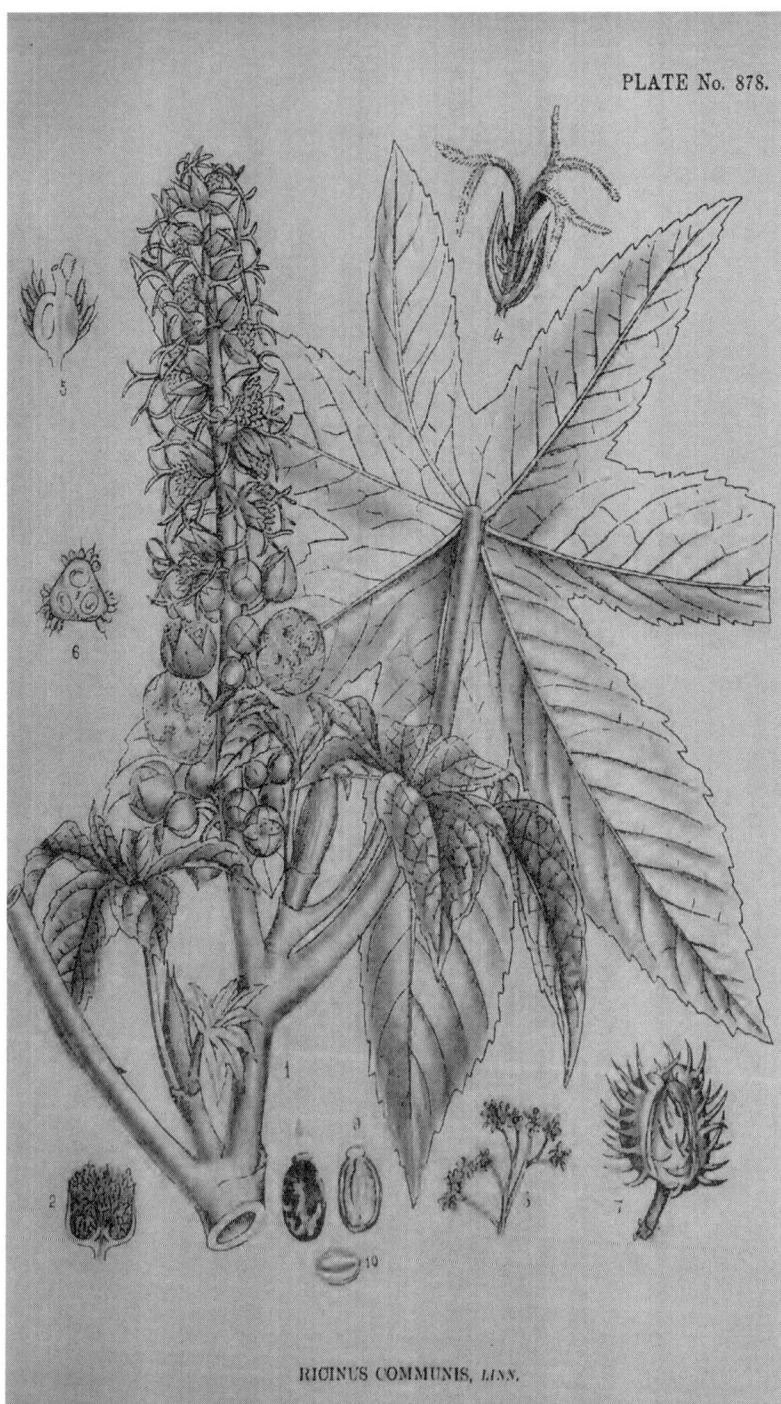

RICINUS COMMUNIS, *LINN.*

BALIOSPERMUM AXILLARE, BLUME.

PLATE No. 880.

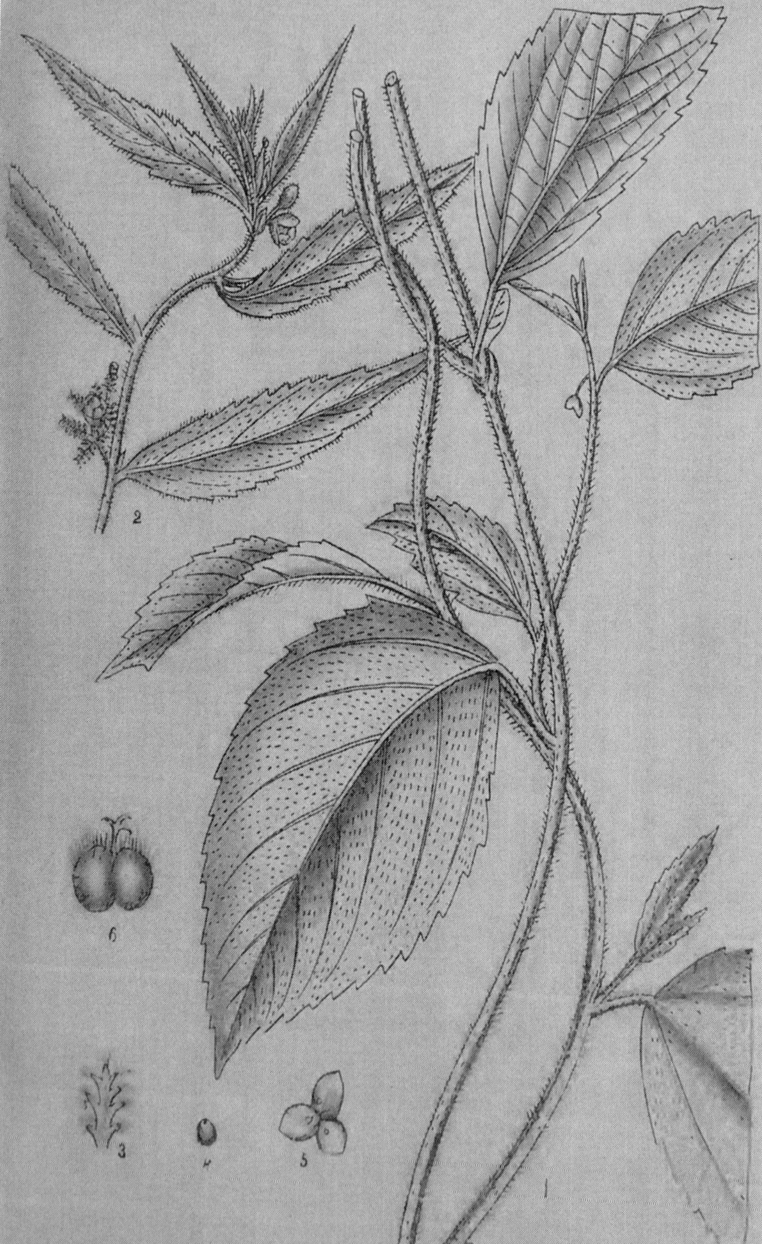

TRAGIA INVOLUCRATA, *Linn.*

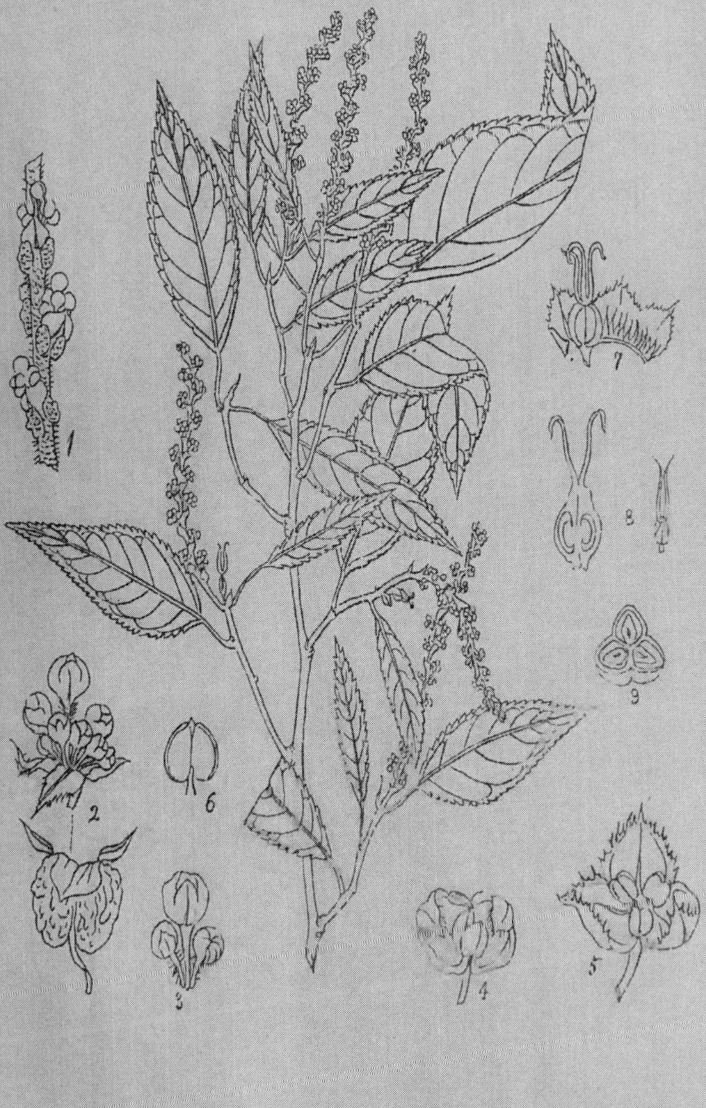

SAPIUM INDICUM, WILLD.

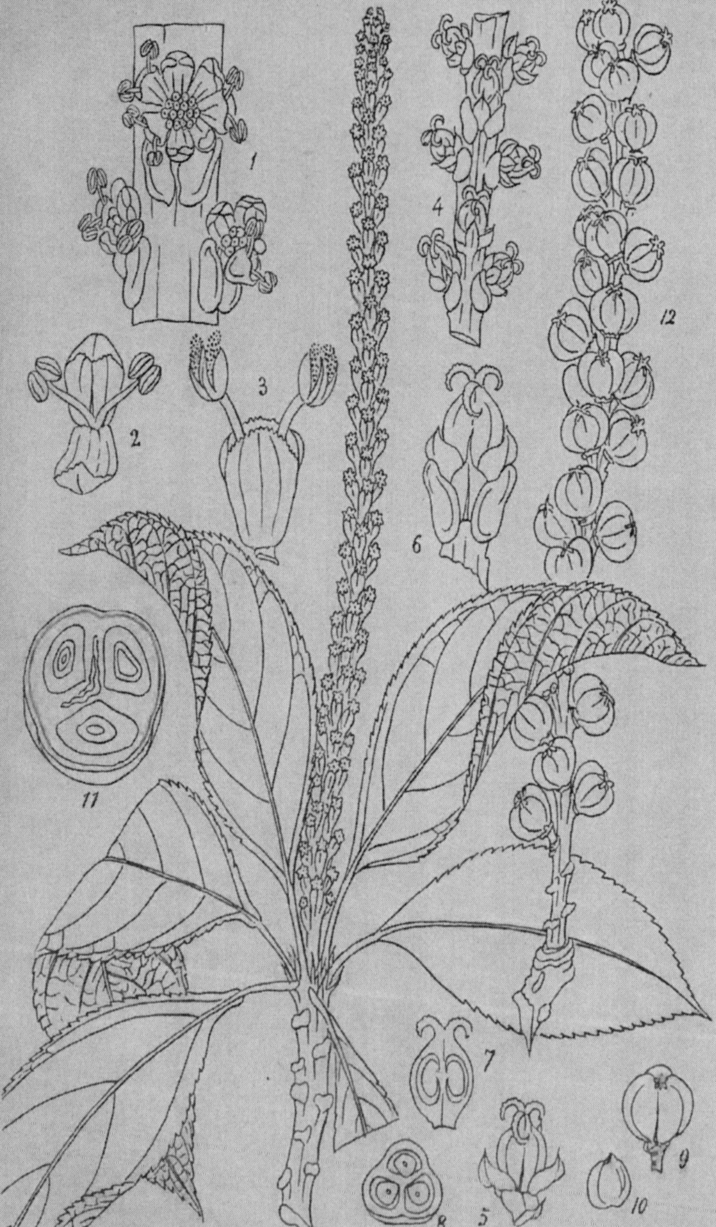

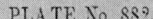

SAPIUM INSIGNE, BENTH.

PLATE No. 883

EXCŒCARIA AGALLOCHA, LINN.

PLATE No. 884.

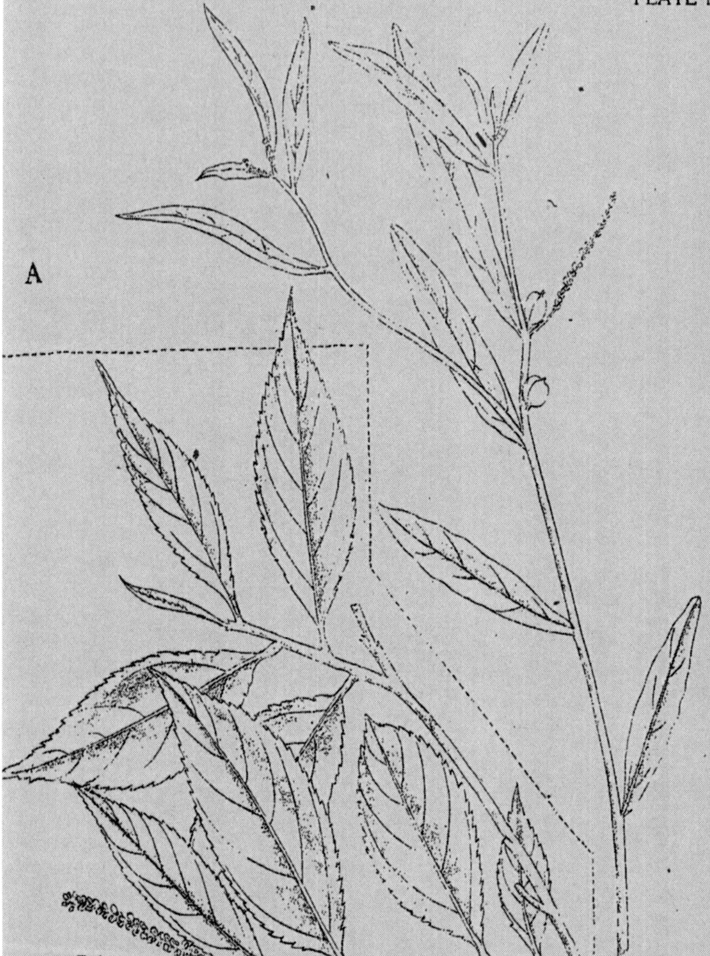

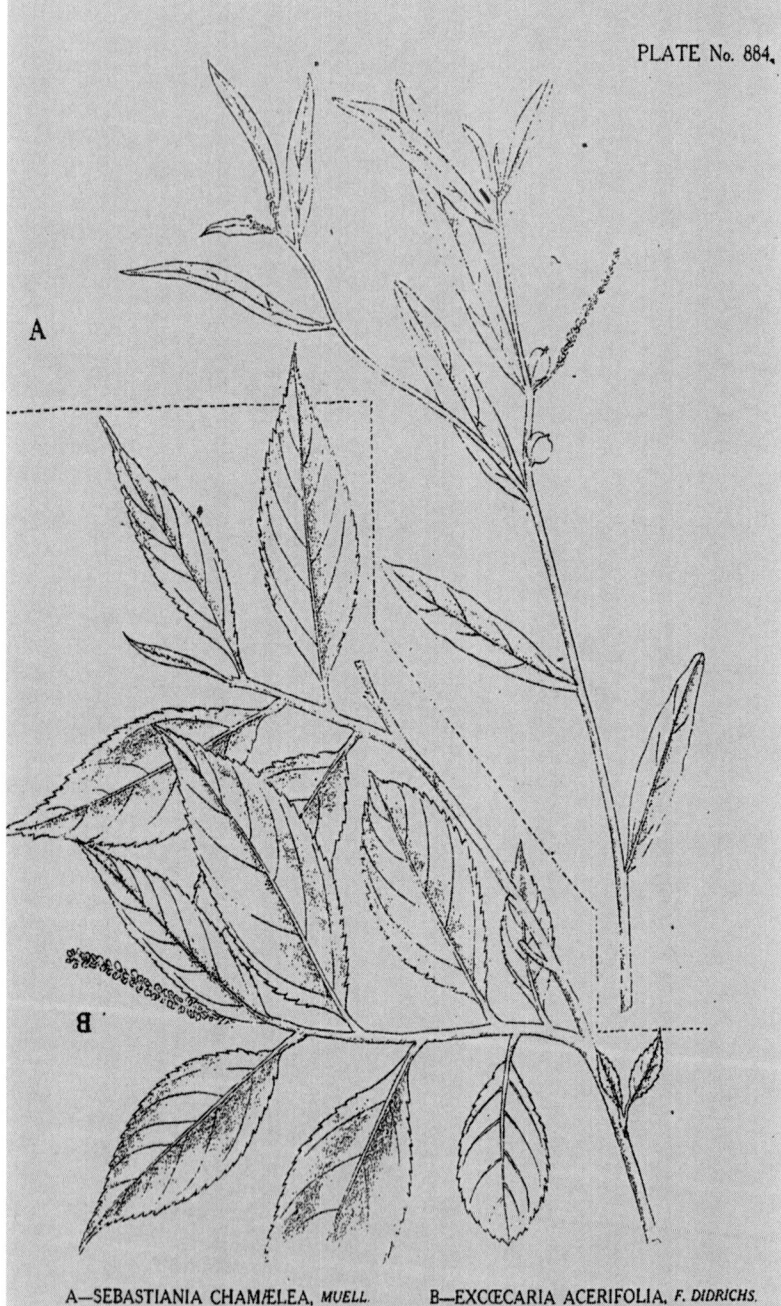

A—SEBASTIANIA CHAMÆLEA, *MUELL.* B—EXCŒCARIA ACERIFOLIA, *F. DIDRICHS.*

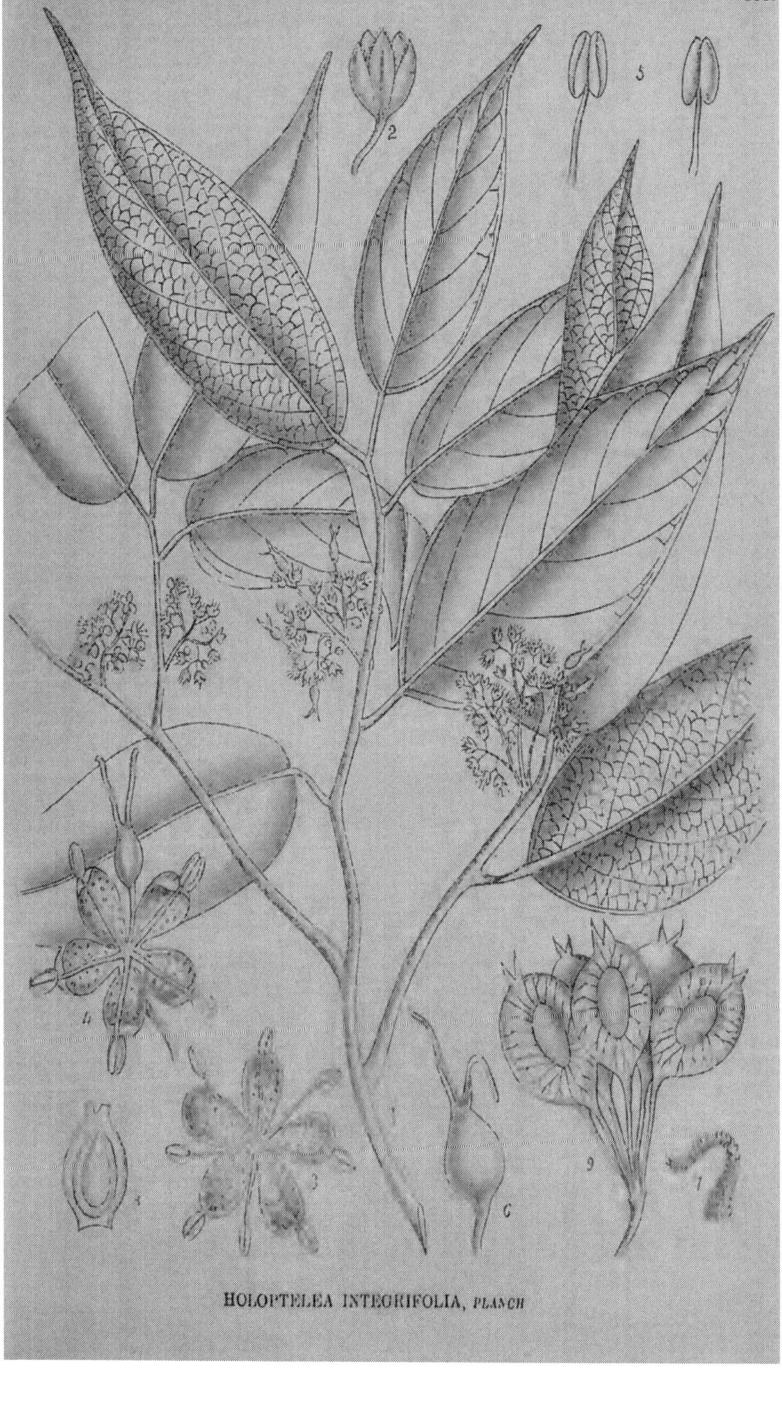

HOLOPTELEA INTEGRIFOLIA, PLANCH

CELTIS AUSTRALIS LINN.

PLATE No. 887

A—HUMULUS LUPULUS, *LINN.*

B—GIRONNEIRA RETICULATA, *THWAITES.*

PLATE No. 888.

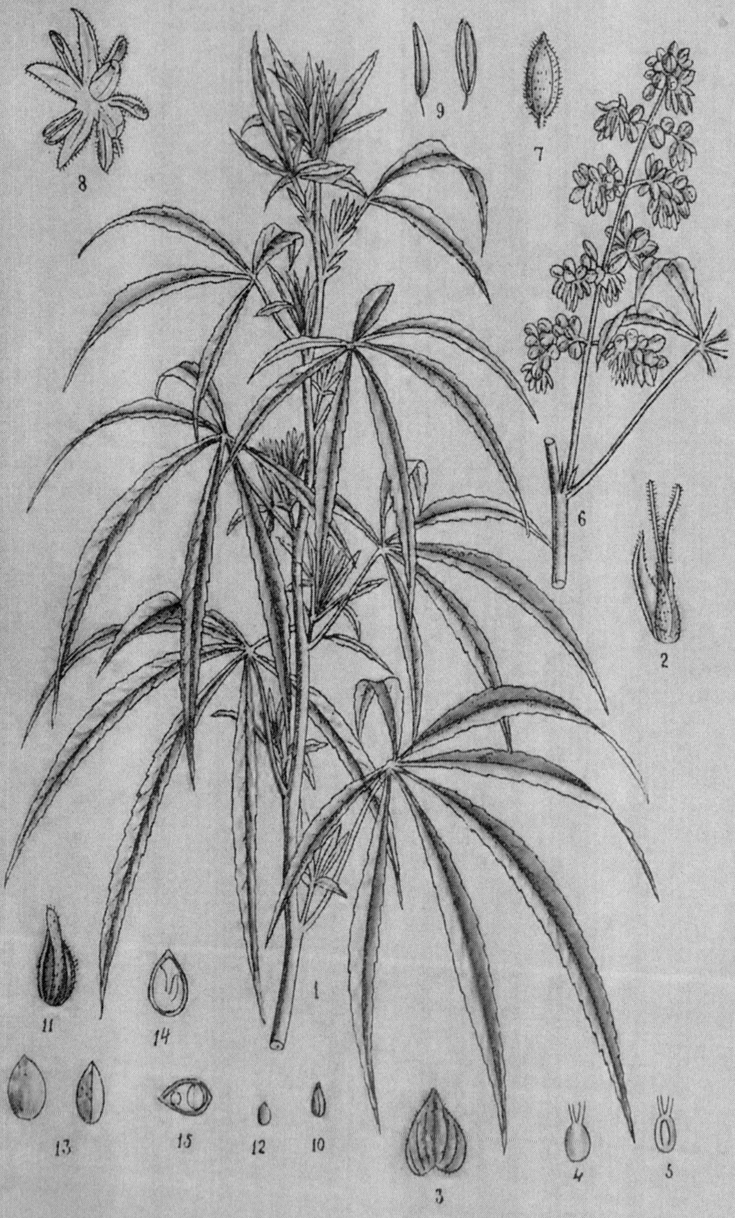

CANNABIS SATIVA, *LINN.*

STREBLUS ASPER, Lour.

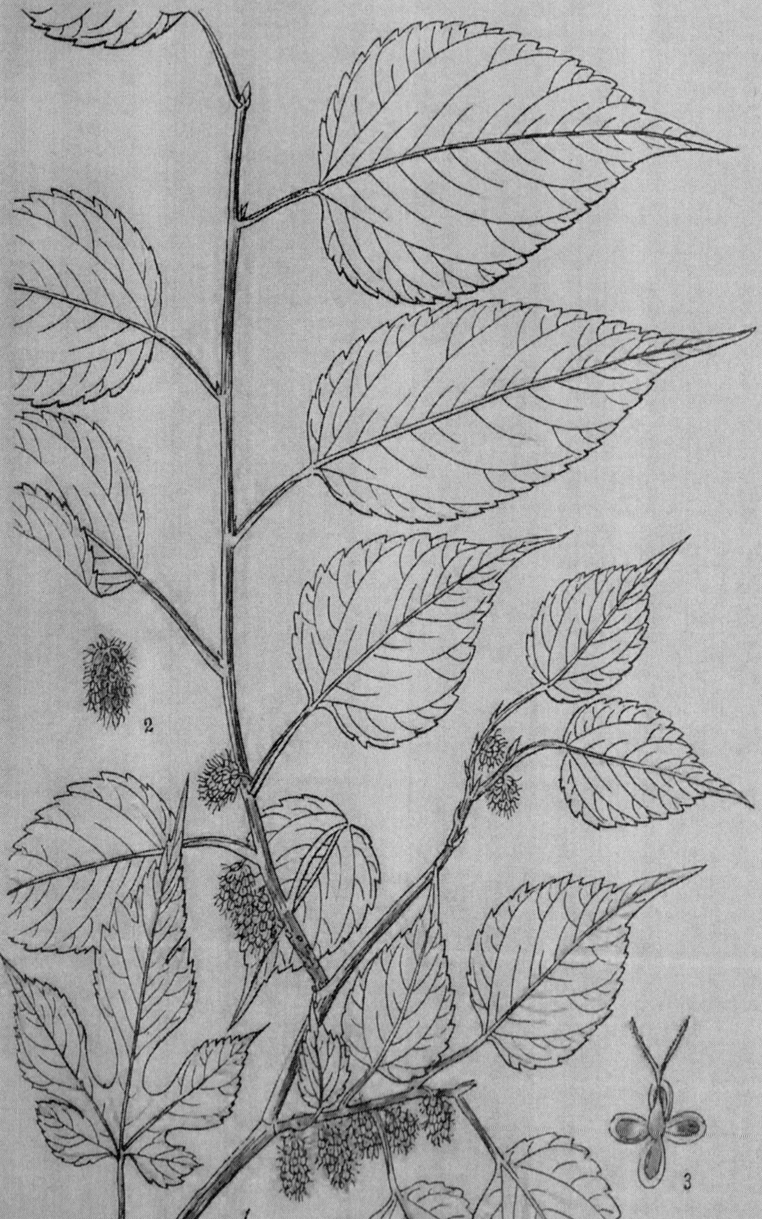

MORUS INDICA, *Linn.*

PLATE No. 891.

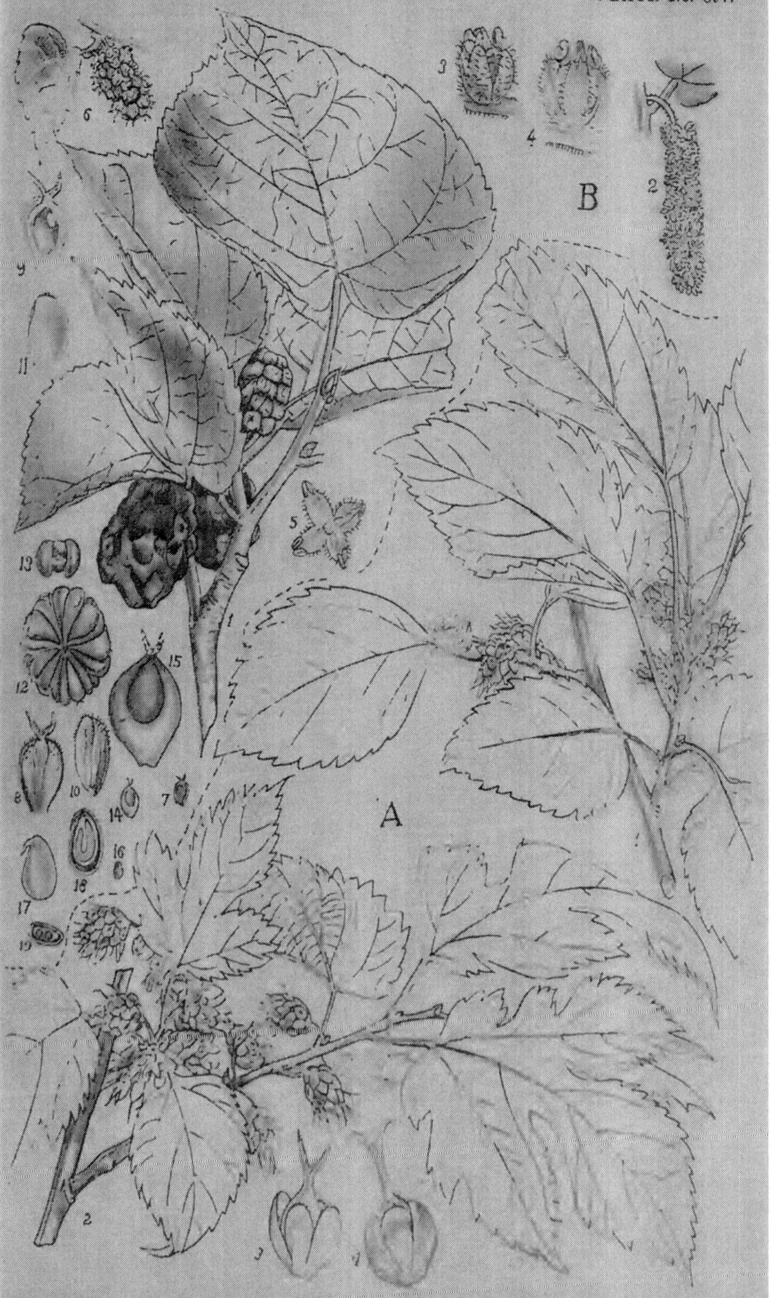

A—MORUS ALBA, LINN. B—MORUS NIGRA, LINN.

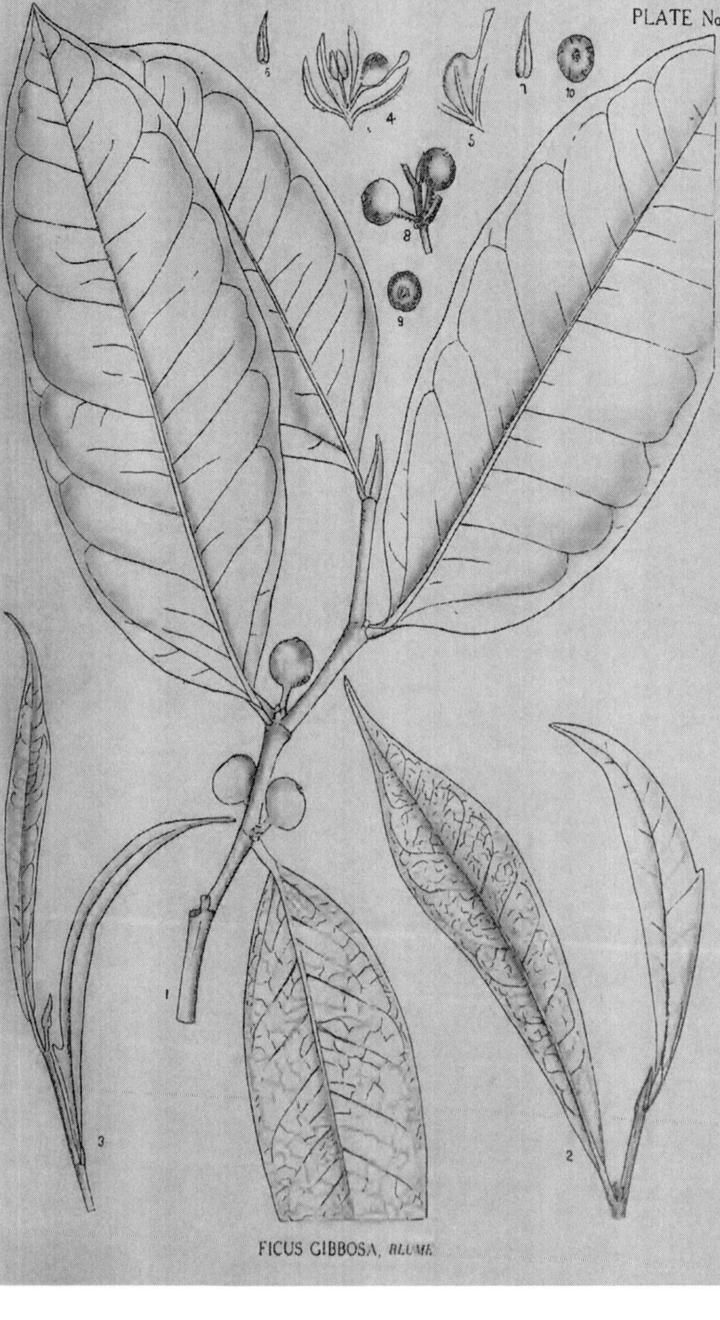

FICUS GIBBOSA, *BLUME*

PLATE No. 893.

FICUS BENGALENSIS, *Linn.*

PLATE No. 894.

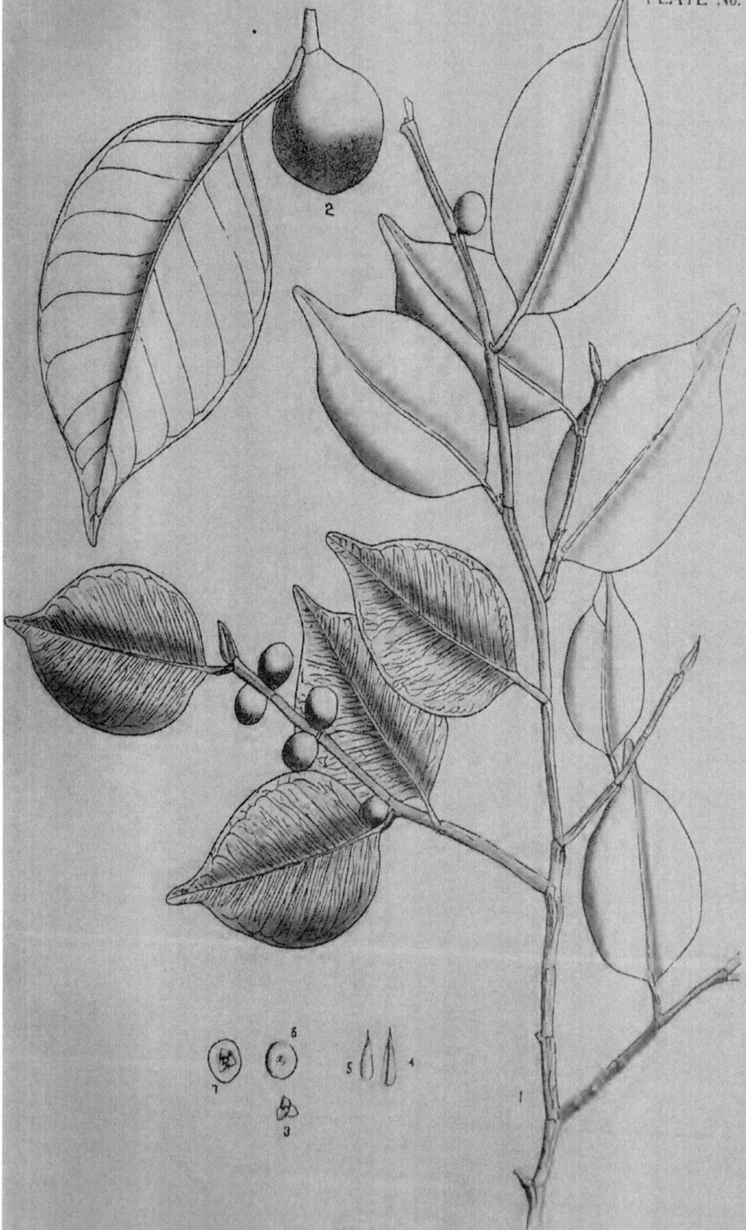

FICUS BENJAMINA, *Linn.*

PLATE No. 895.

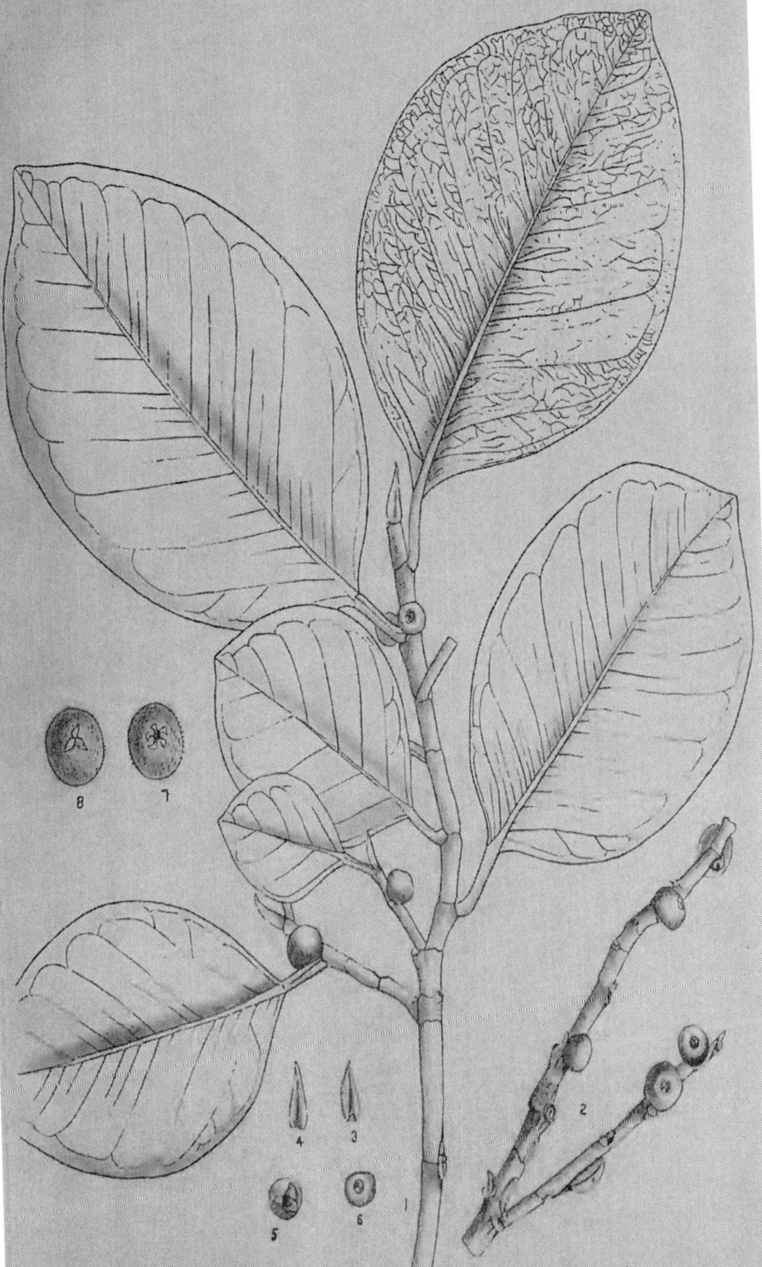

FICUS RETUSA, LINN.

PLATE No. 896.

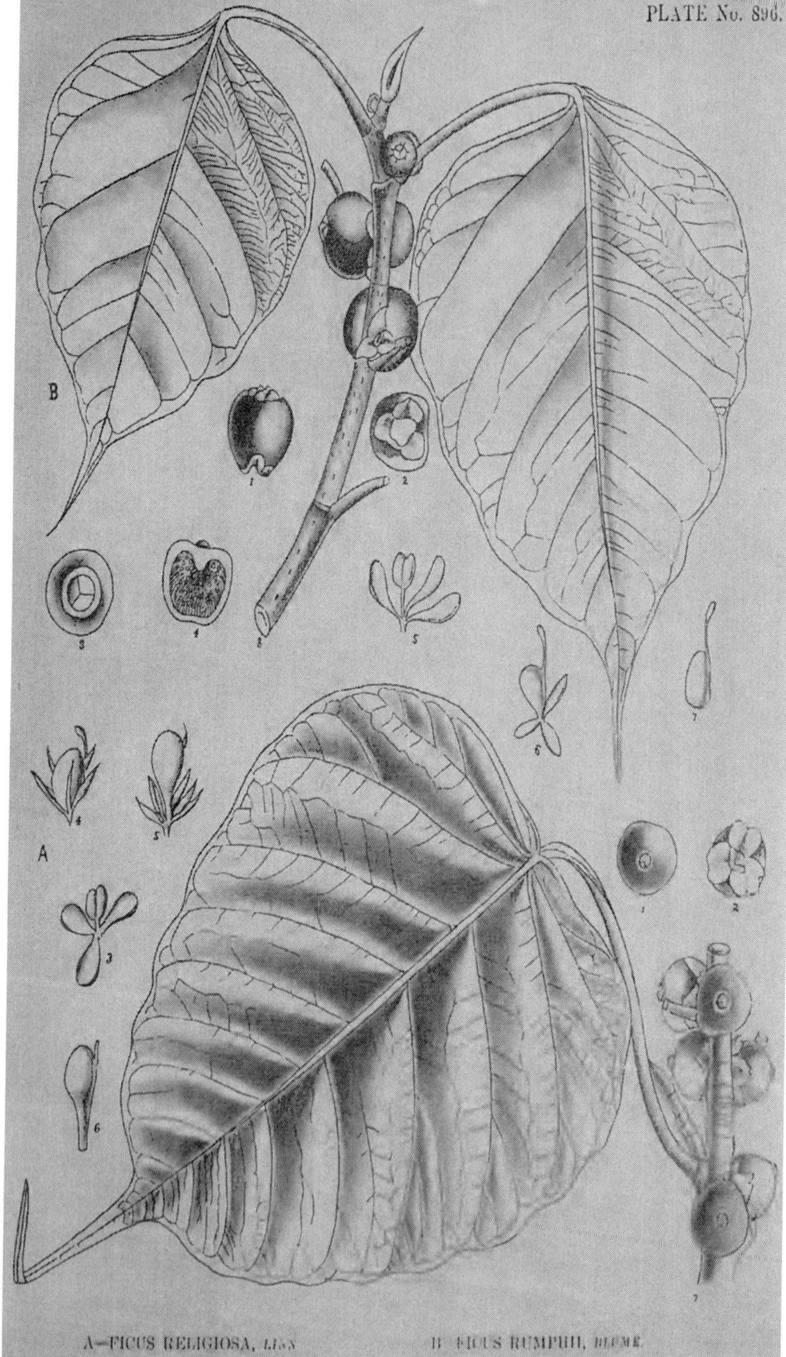

A—FICUS RELIGIOSA, *Linn.* B—FICUS RUMPHII, *Blume.*

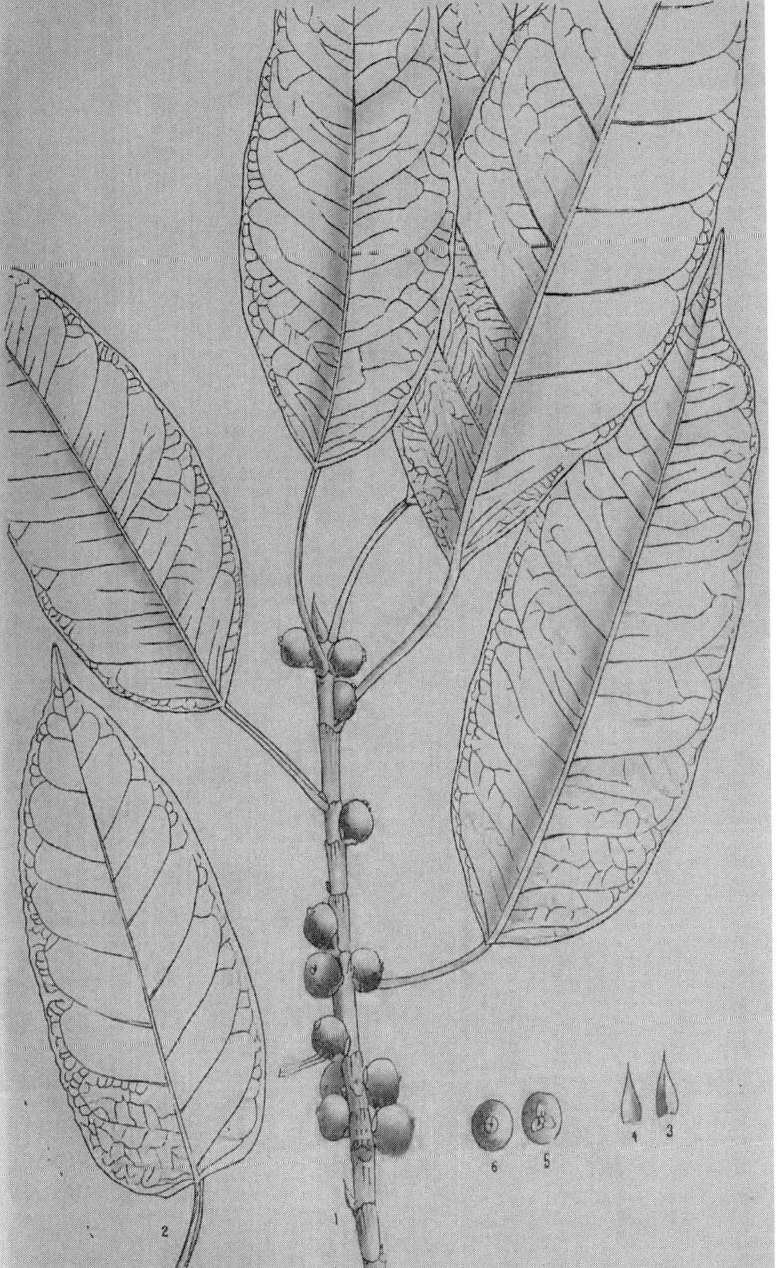

FICUS INFECTORIA, ROXB.

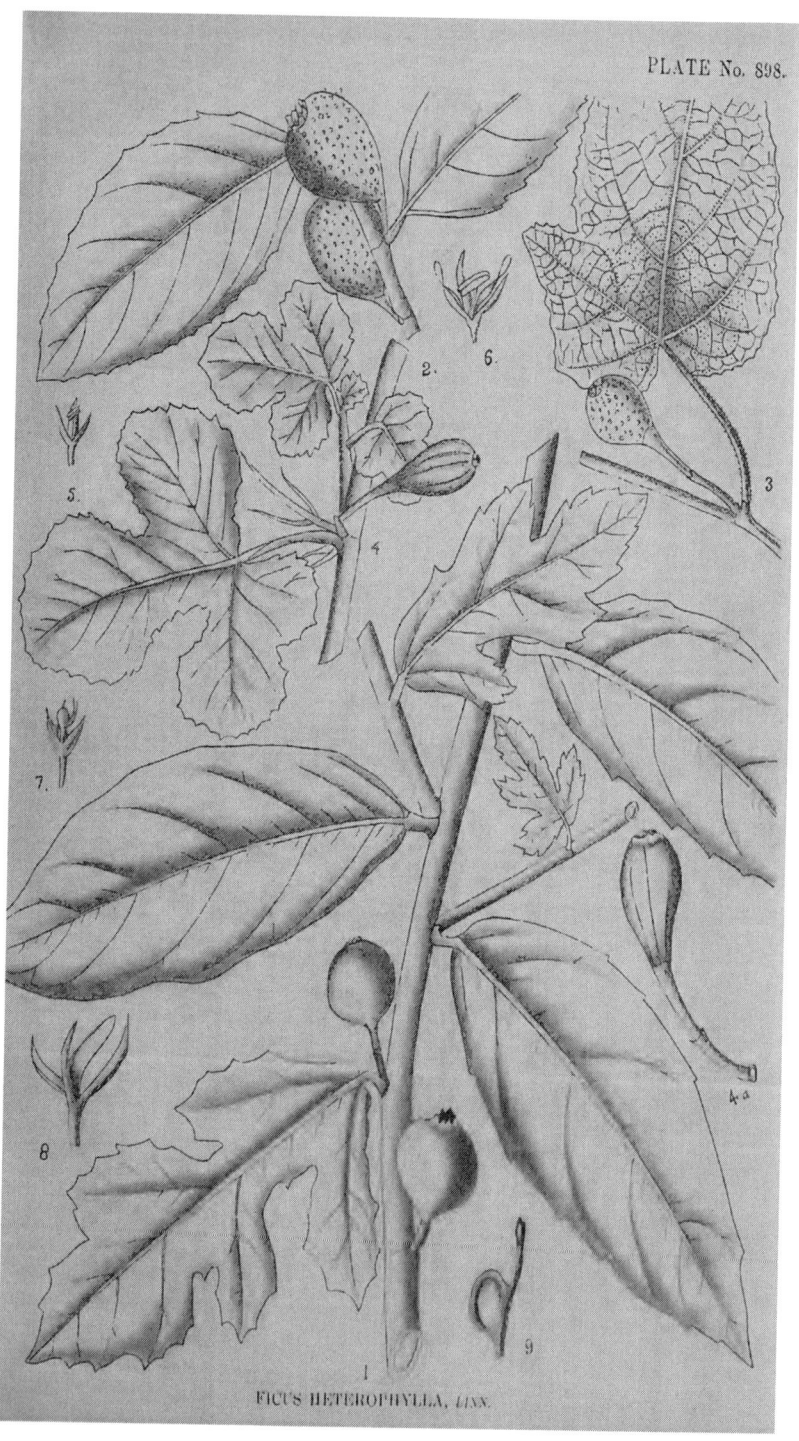

FICUS HETEROPHYLLA, LINN.

PLATE No. 899.

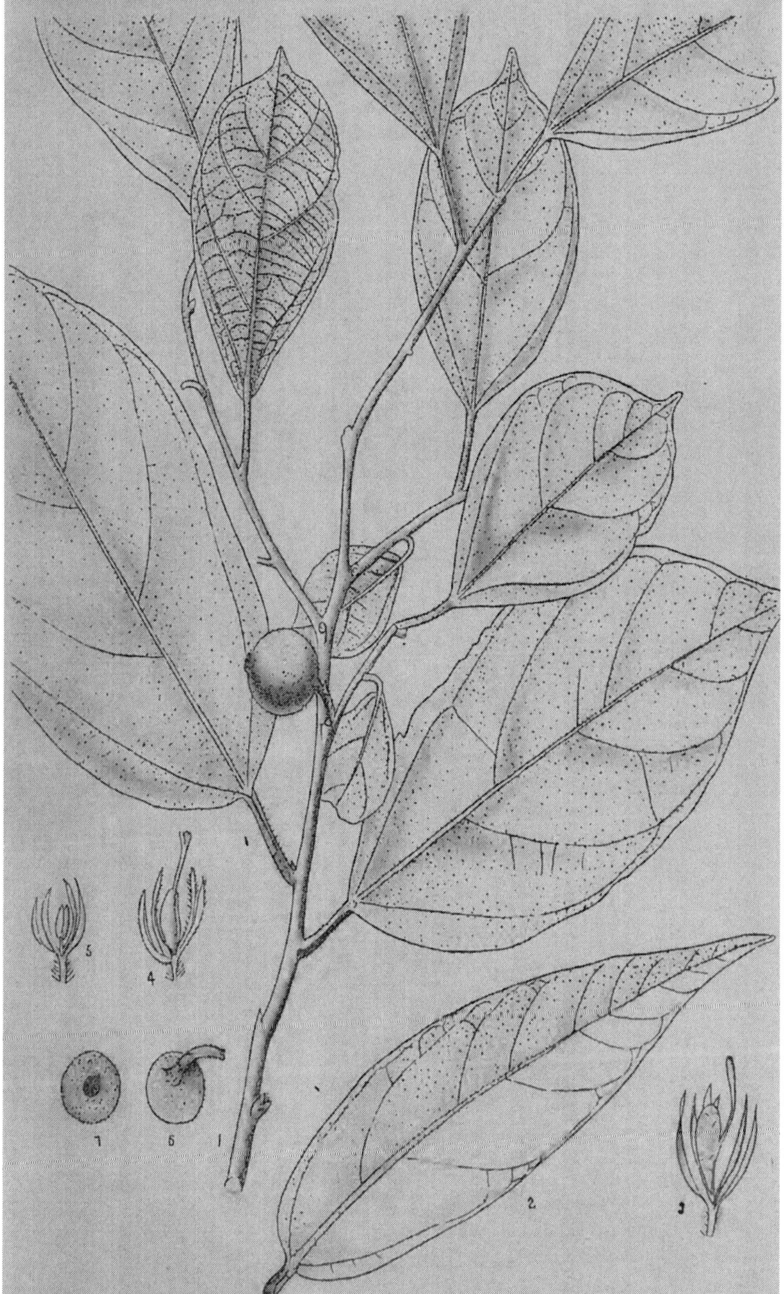

FICUS ASPERRIMA, ROXB

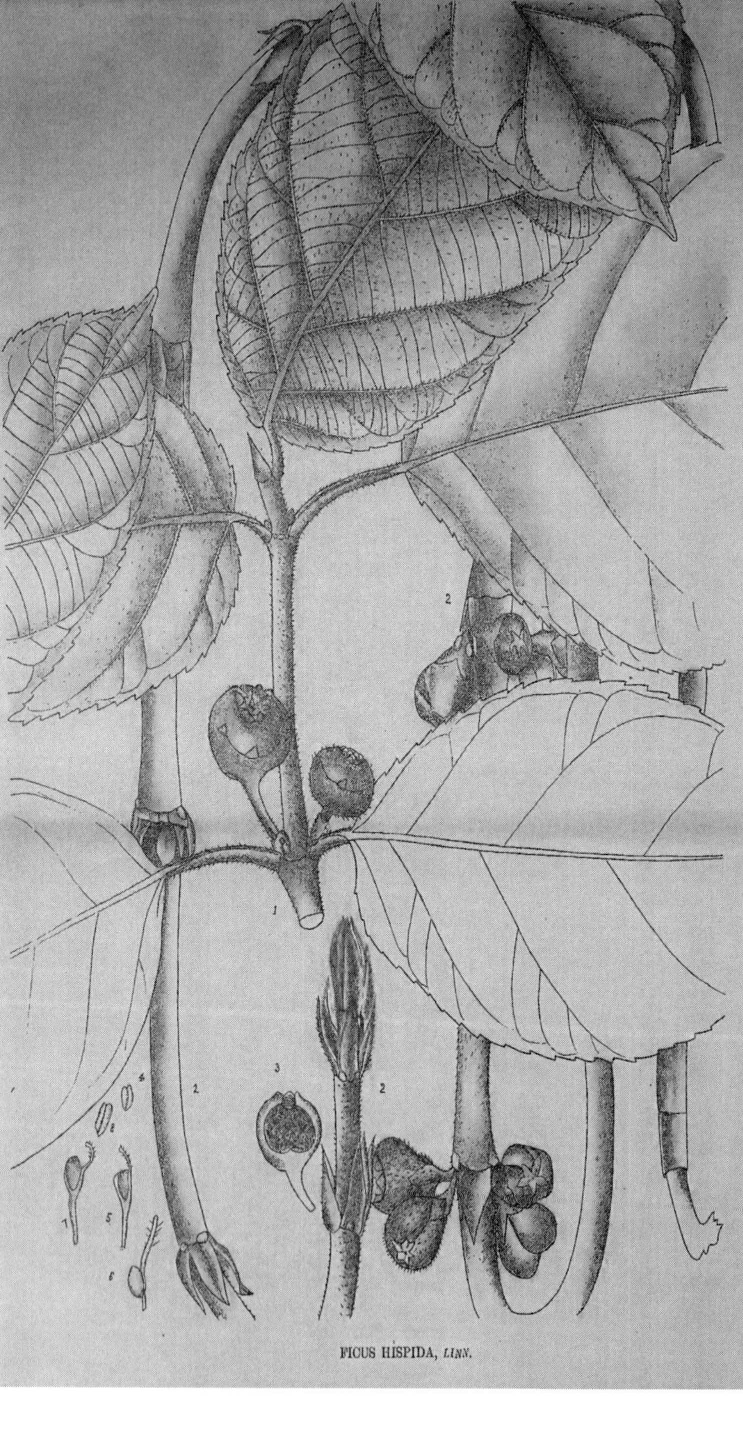

FICUS HISPIDA, *LINN.*

FICUS HISPIDA, *Linn.*

PLATE No 901.

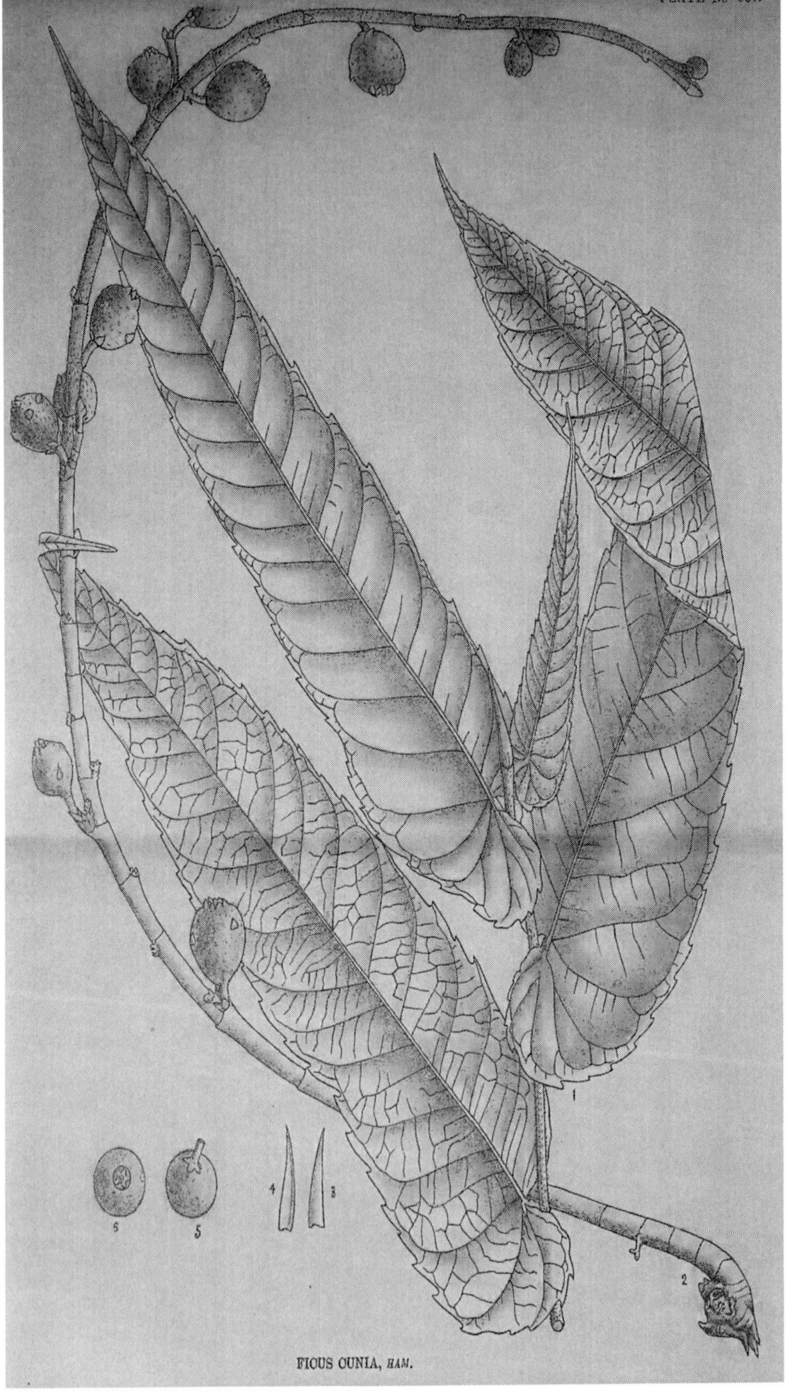

FICUS CUNIA, HAM.

PLATE No. 902.

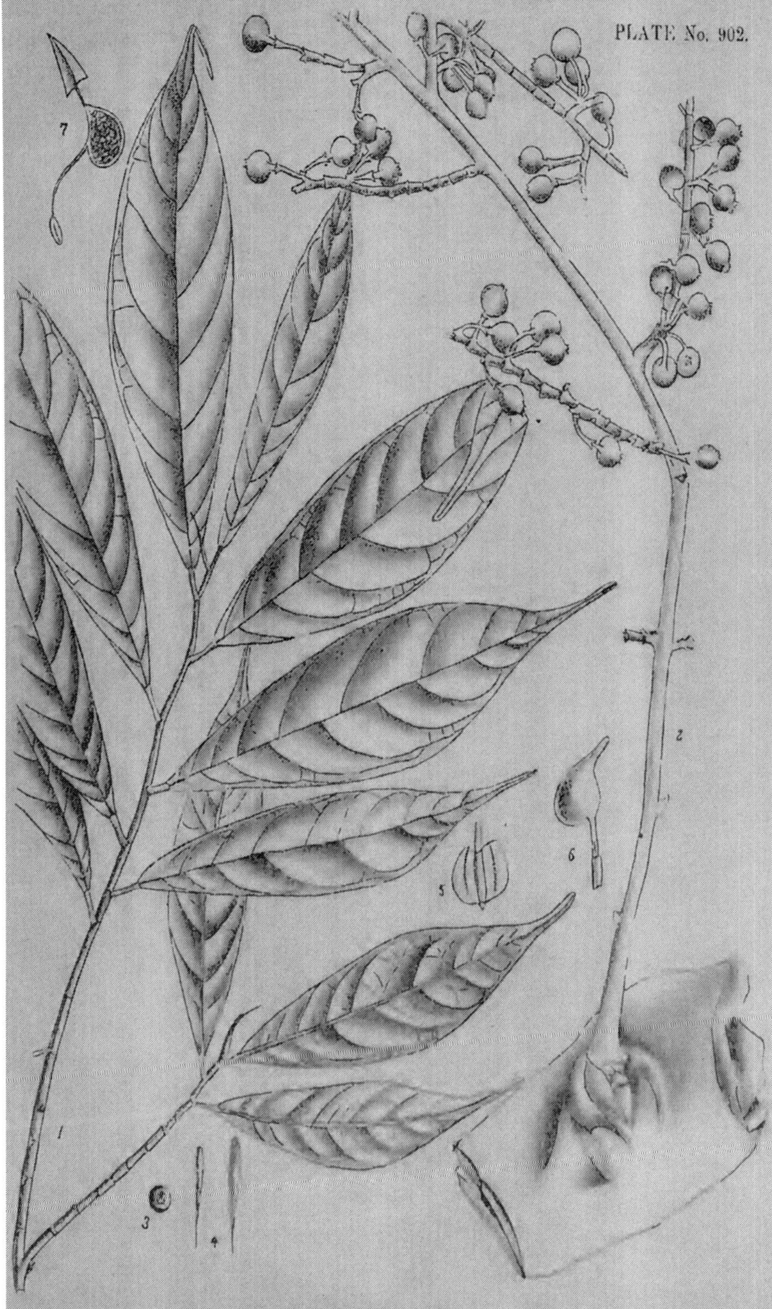

FICUS RIBES, REINW.

PLATE No. 903.

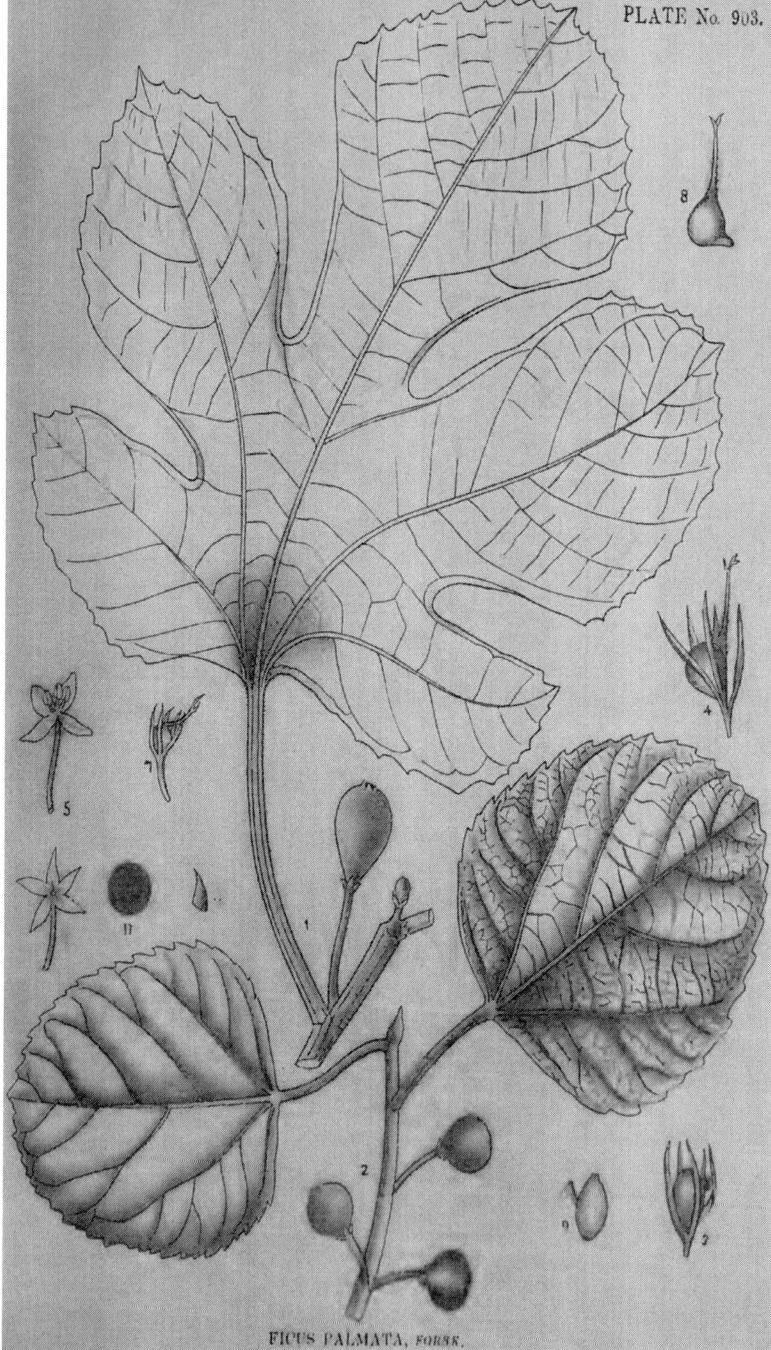

FICUS PALMATA, FORSK.

PLATE No. 904.

A—FICUS GLOMERATA, *ROXB.*

PLATE No. 905.

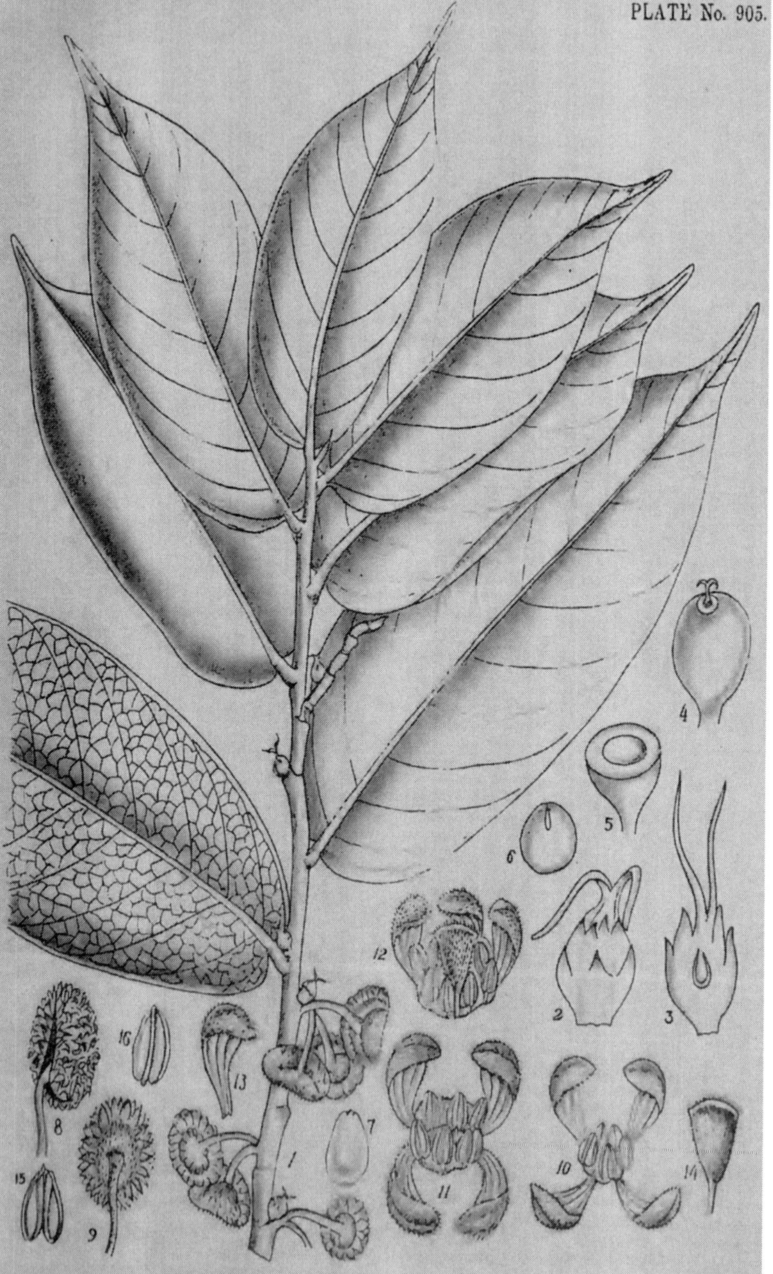

ANTIARIS TOXICARIA, LESCHEN.

PLATE No. 906.

ARTOCARPUS INTEGRIFOLIA, LINN. F.

PLATE No. 906A

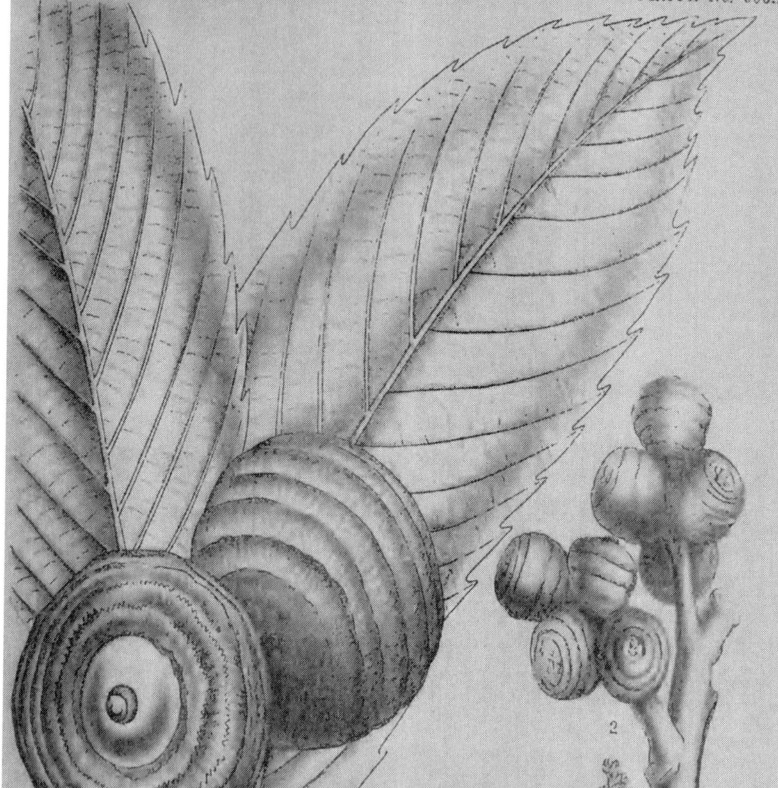

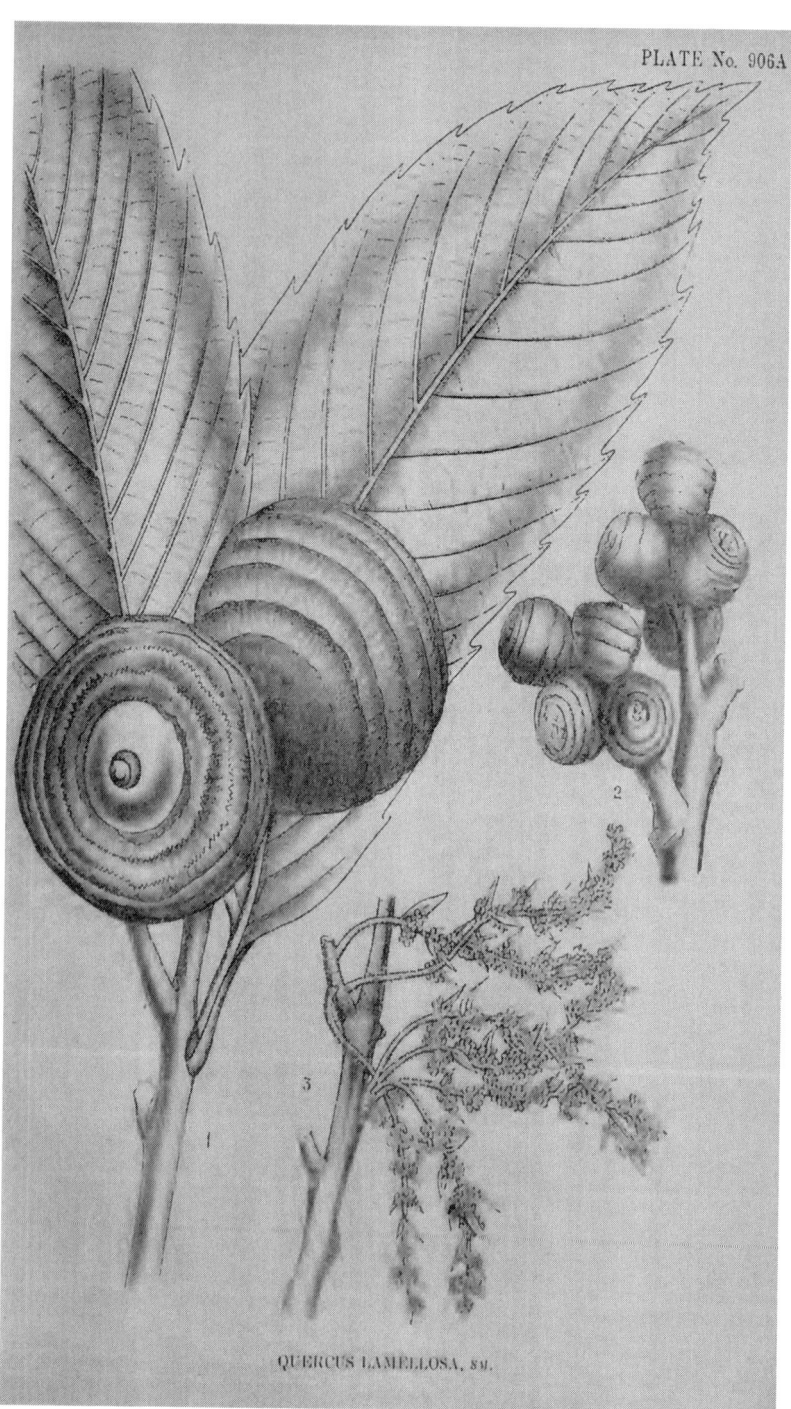

QUERCUS LAMELLOSA, Sm.

PLATE No. 907.

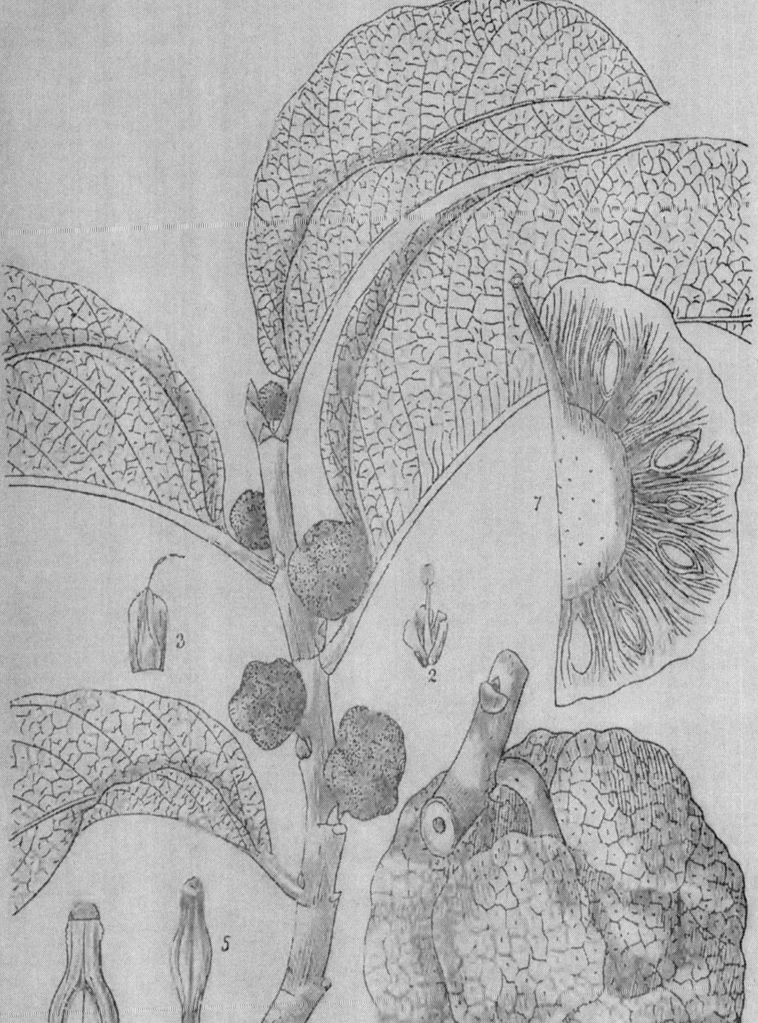

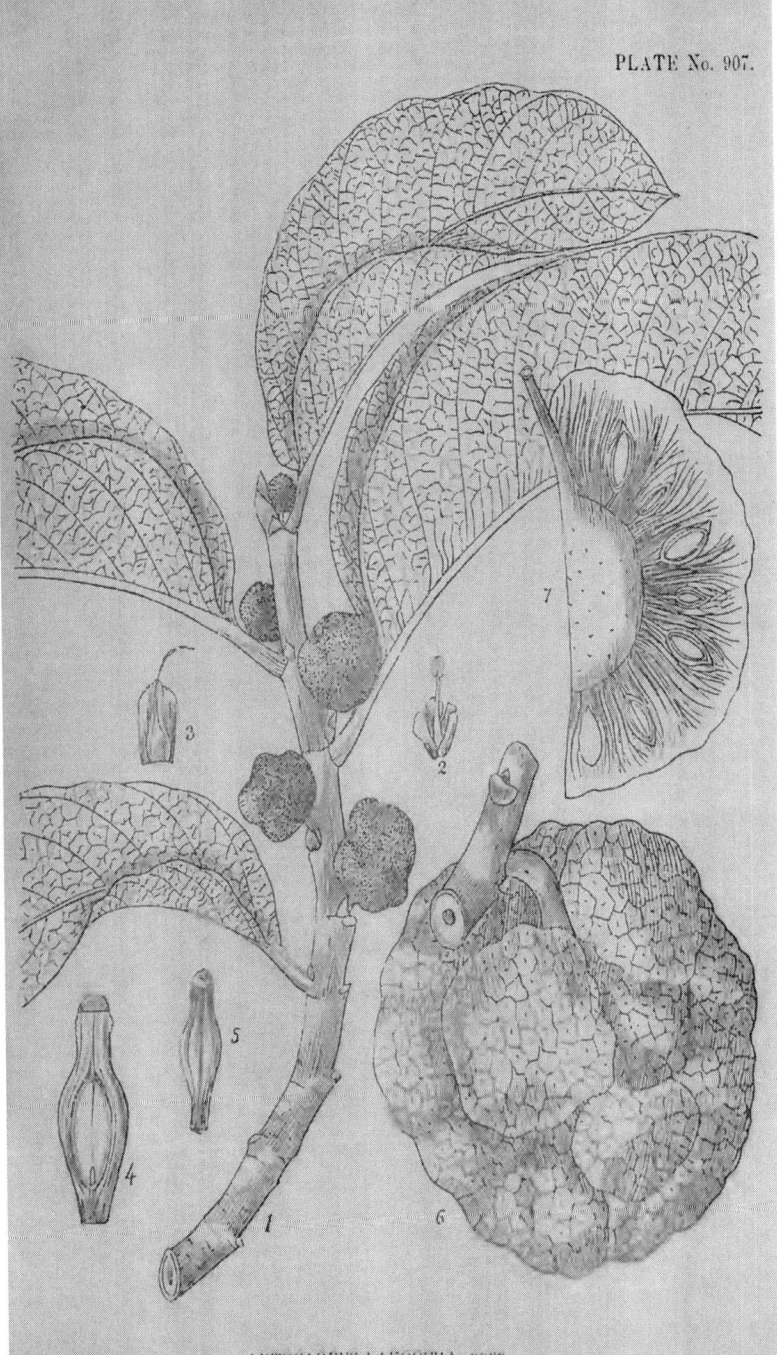

ARTOCARPUS LAKOOCHA, ROXB.

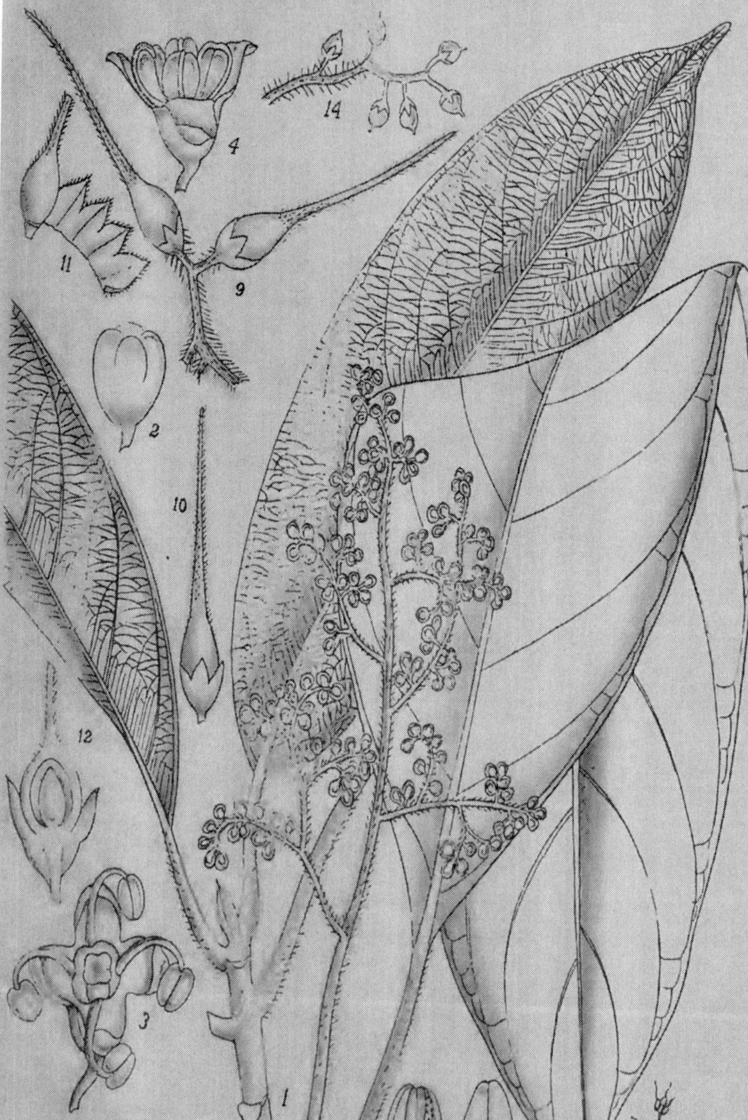

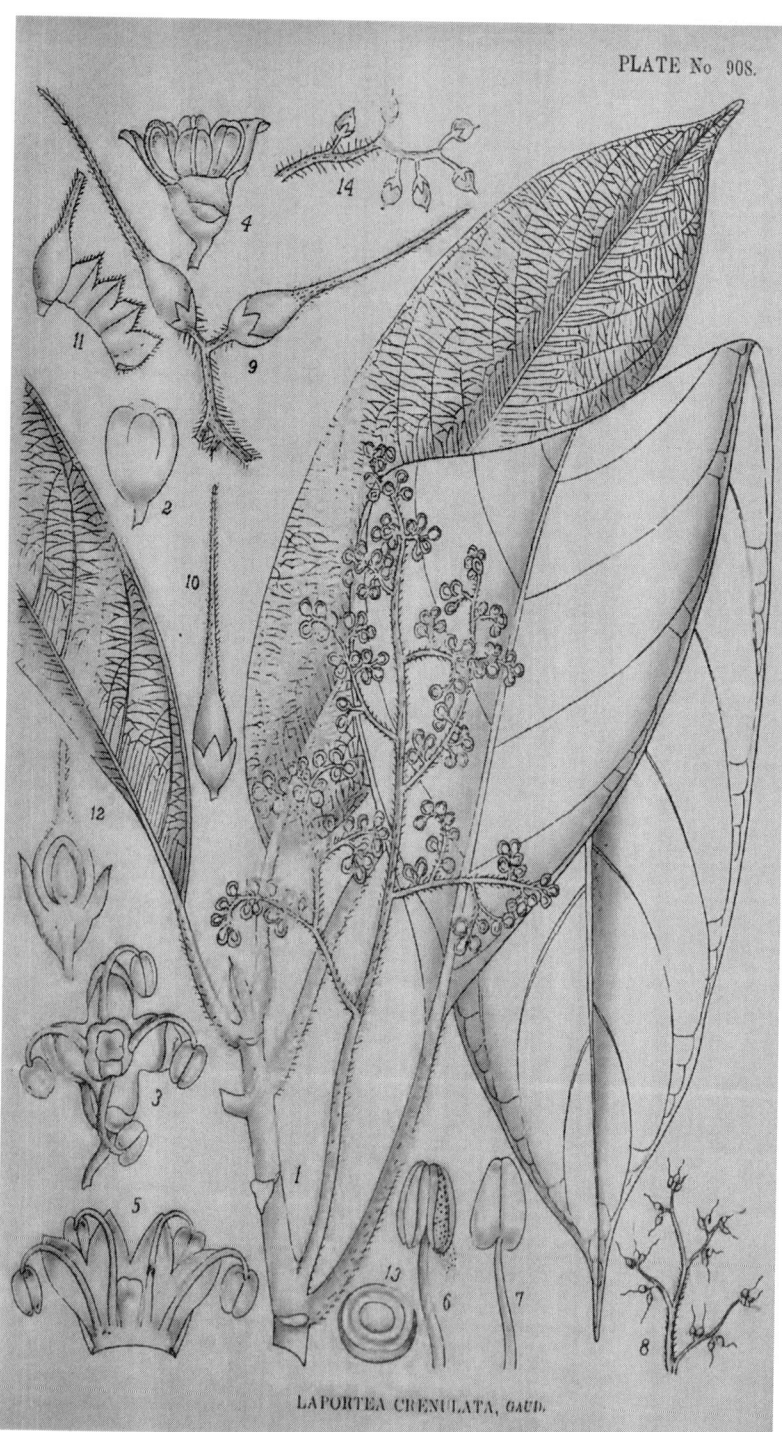

LAPORTEA CRENULATA, GAUD.

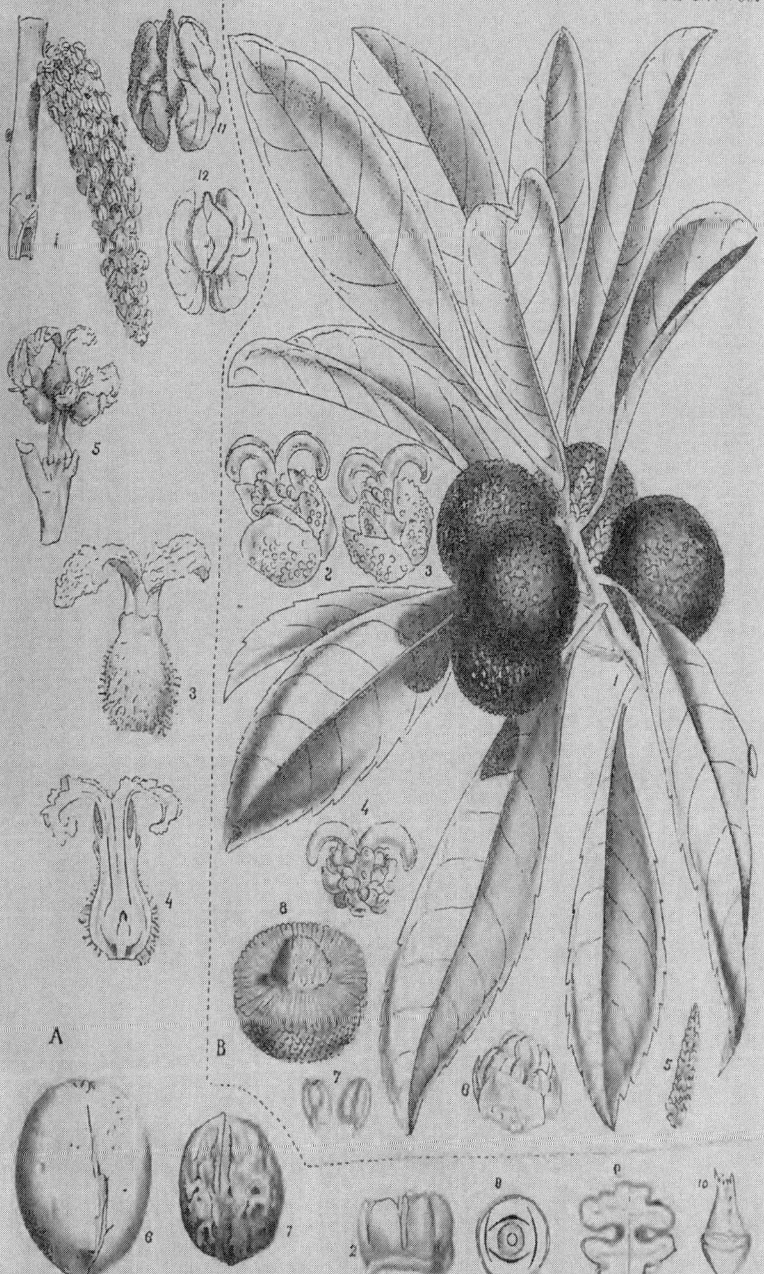

A JUGLANS REGIA, *LINN.* B—MYRICA NAGI, *THUNB.*

PLATE No. 910.

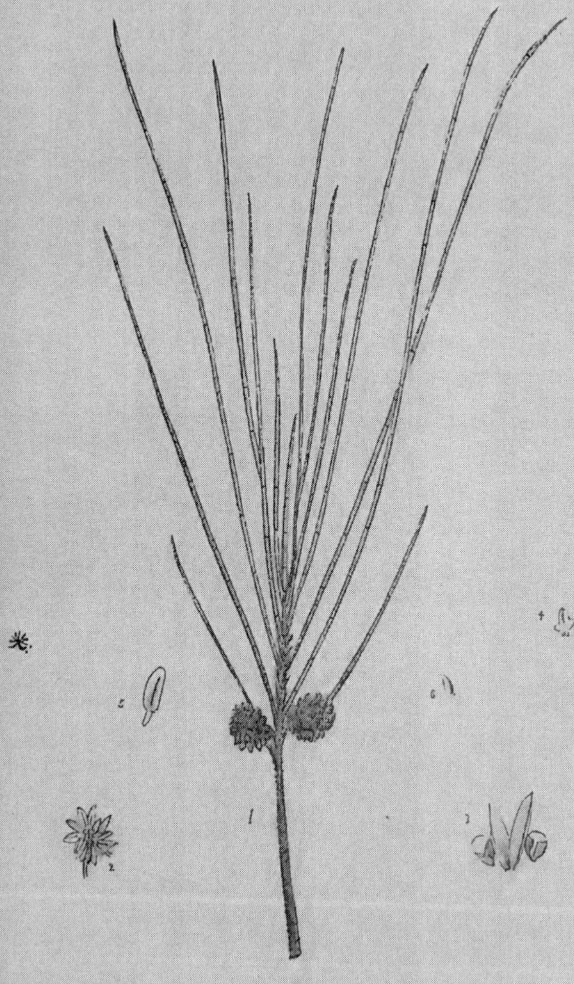

CASUARINA EQUISETIFOLIA, Forst.

PLATE No. 911.

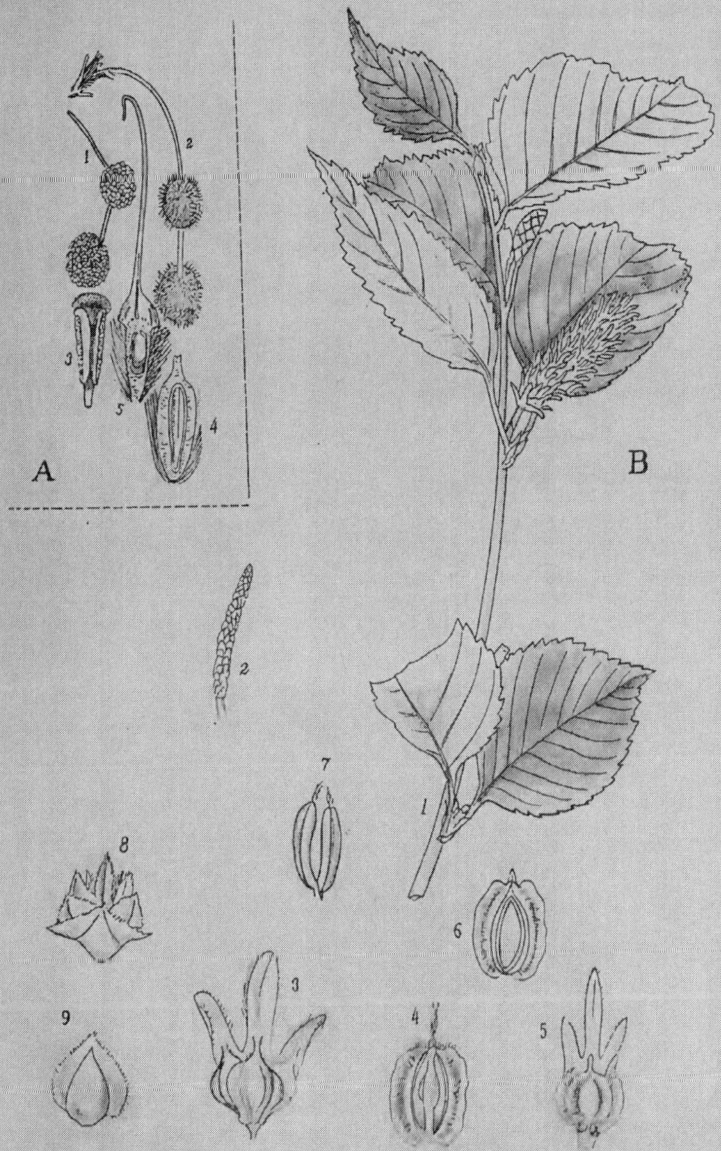

A—PLATANUS ORIENTALIS, *Linn.* B—BETULA UTILIS, *D. Don.*

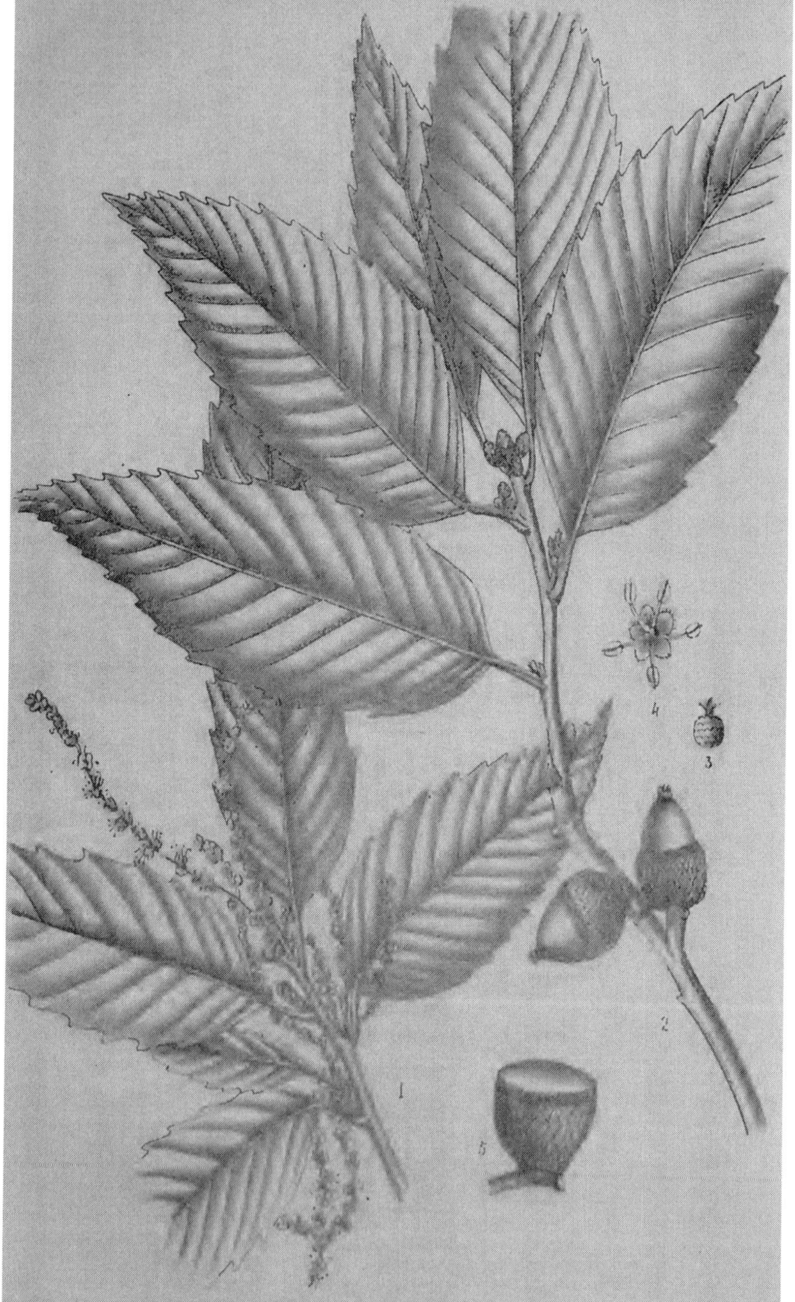

QUERCUS INCANA, *Roxb.*

PLATE No. 913.

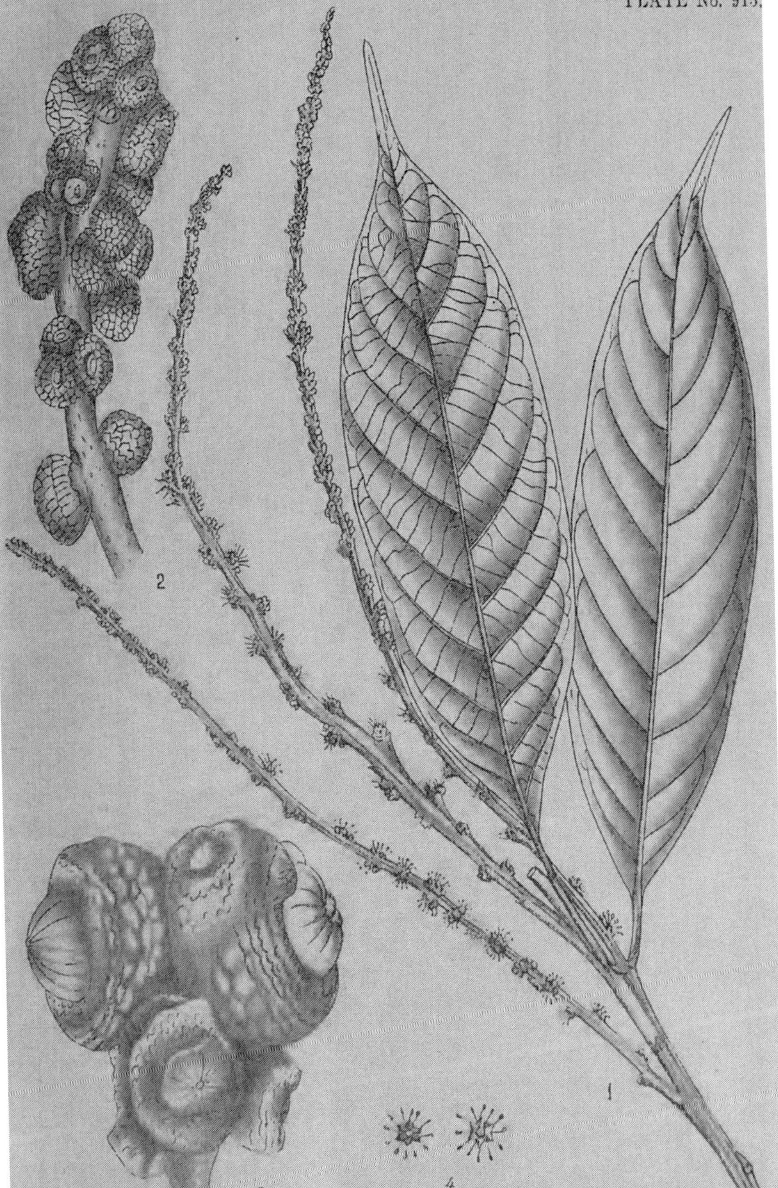

QUERCUS PACHYPHYLLA, *KURZ*

CORYLUS COLURNA, LINN.

PLATE No. 915.

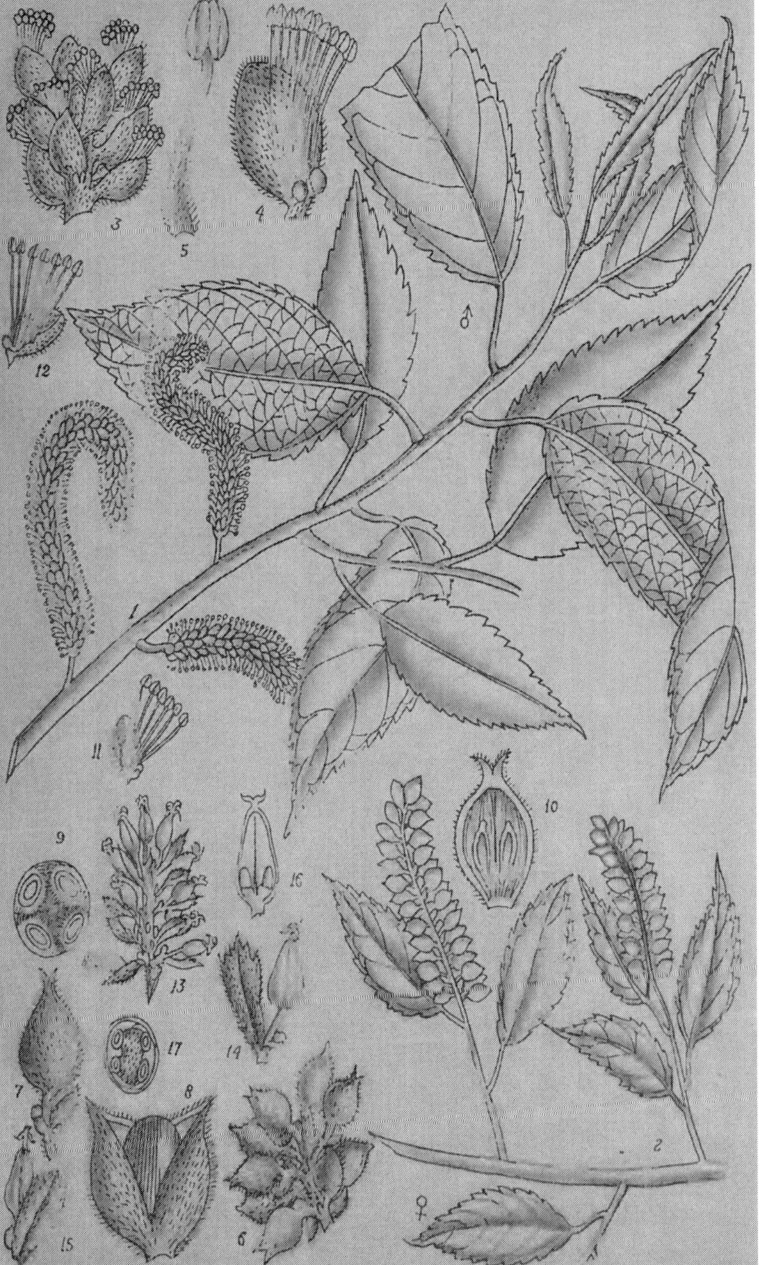

SALIX TETRASPERMA, ROXB.

PLATE No. 916.

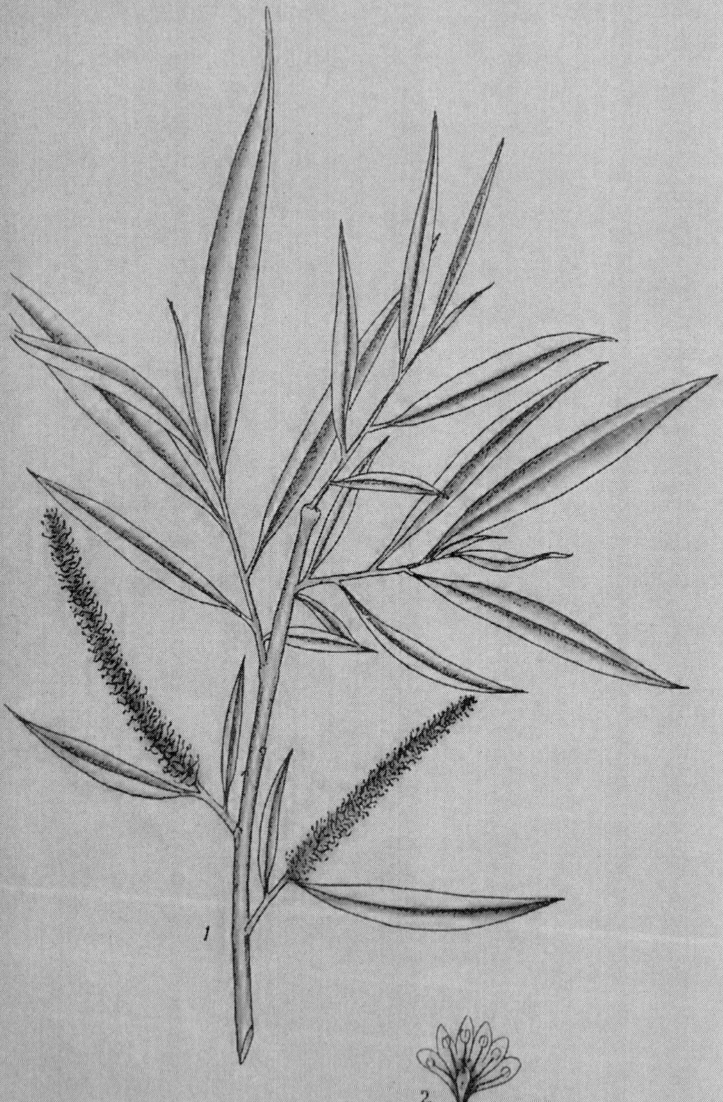

SALIX ACOMPHYLLA, BOISS.

PLATE No. 917.

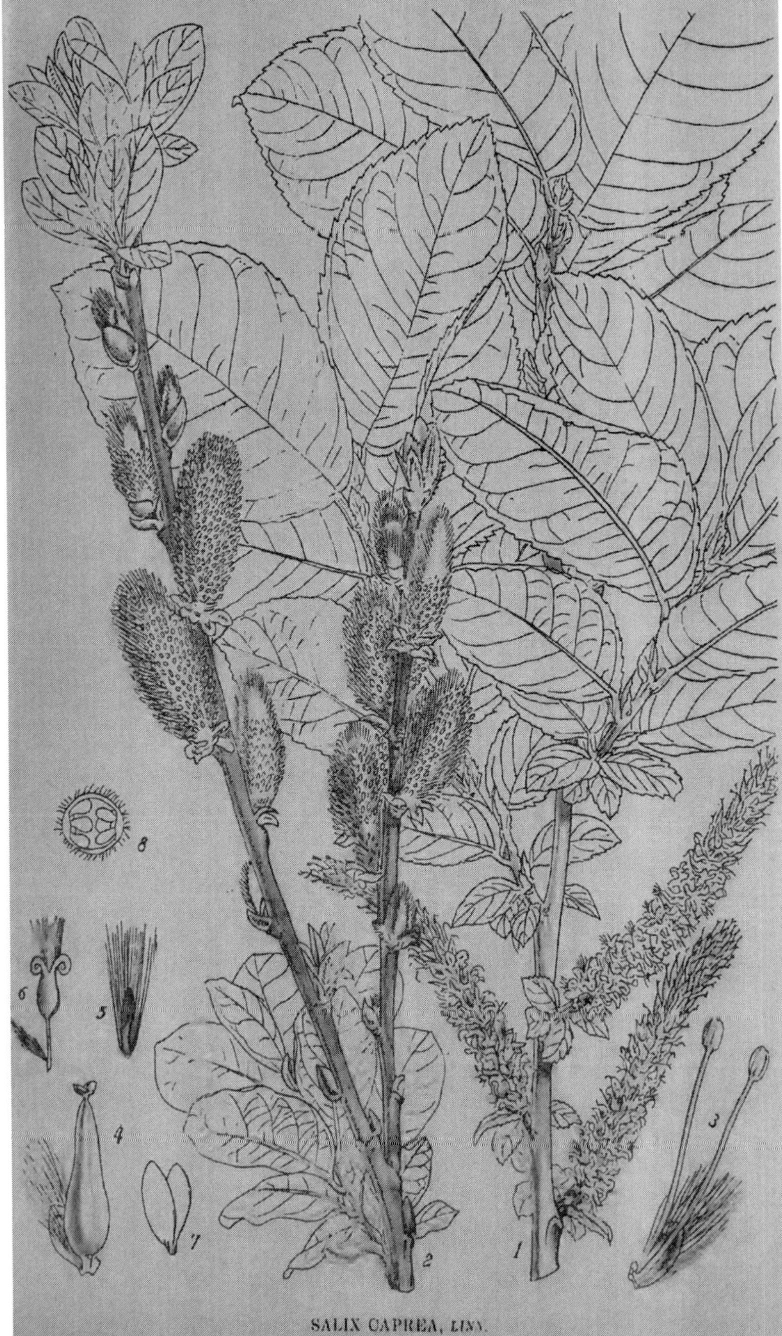

SALIX CAPREA, *Linn.*

PLATE No. 918.

A—SALIX ALBA, *Linn.* B—S. BABYLONICA, *Linn.*

PLATE No. 919.

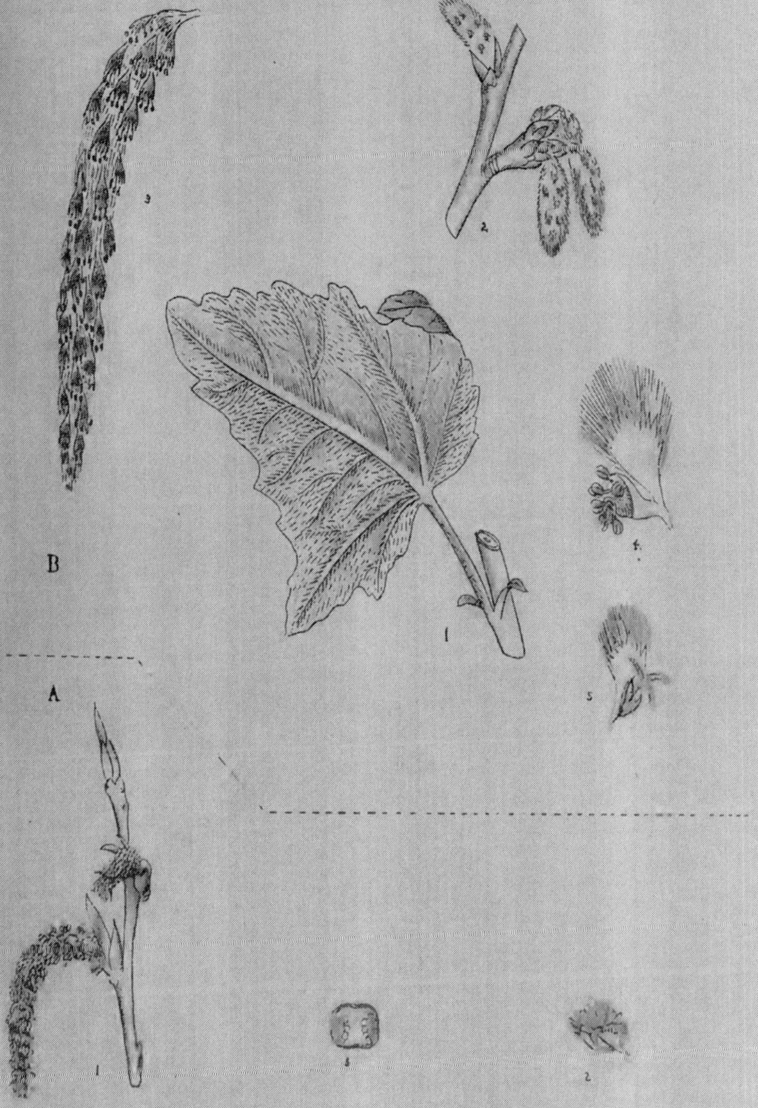

A—POPULUS NIGRA, LINN. B—POPULUS ALBA, LINN.

PLATE No. 920

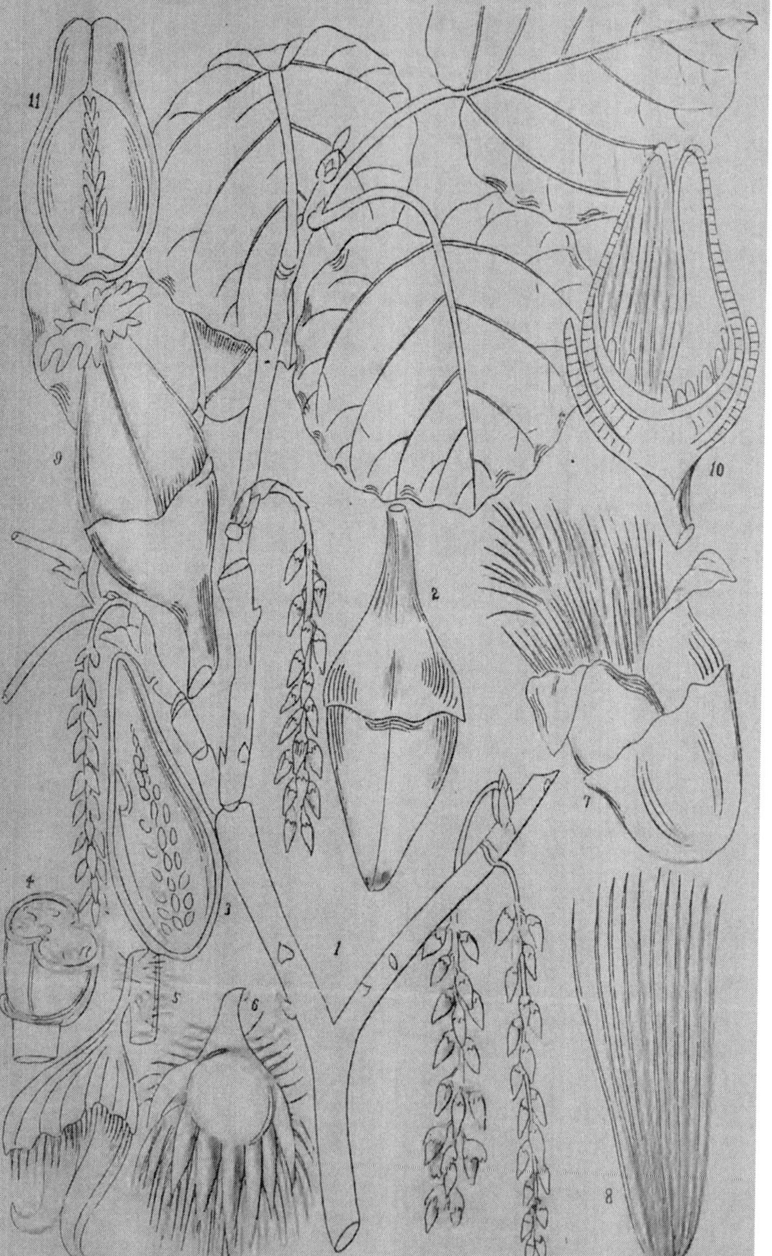

POPULUS CILIATA, WALL.

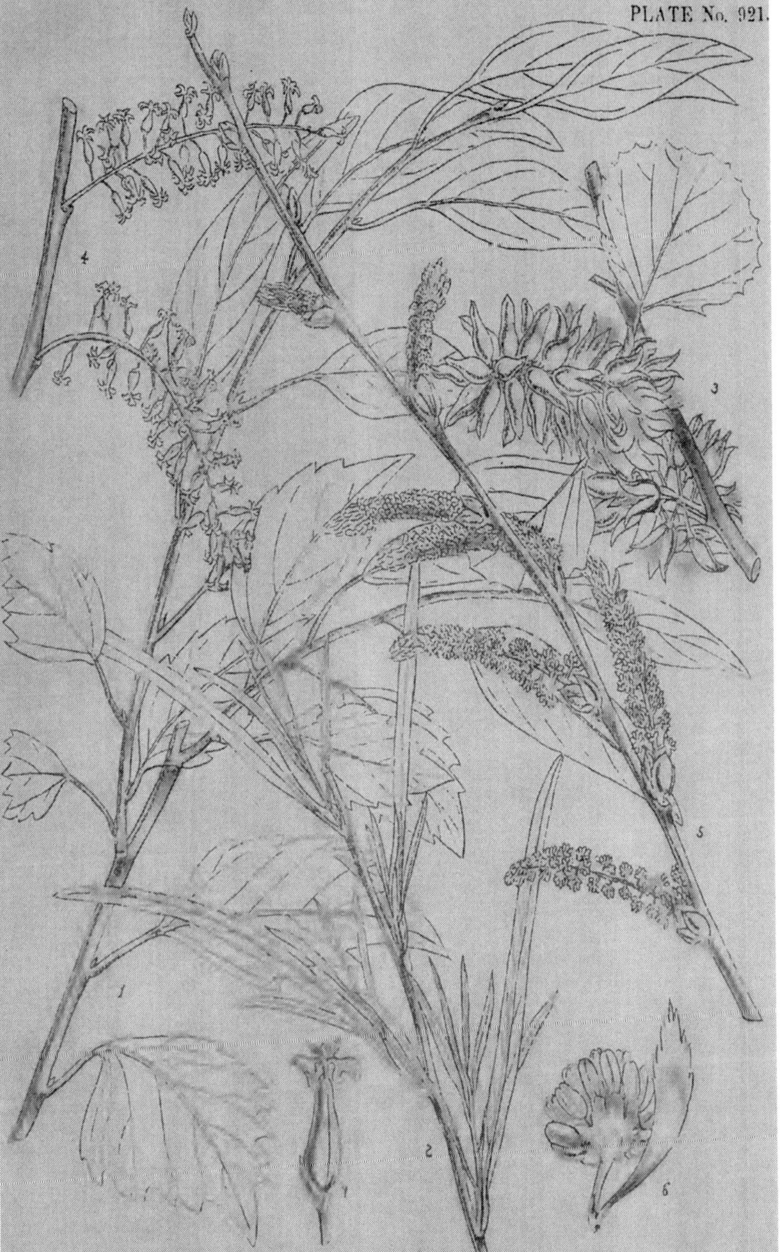

POPULUS EUPHRATICA, Oliv.

PLATE No. 922.

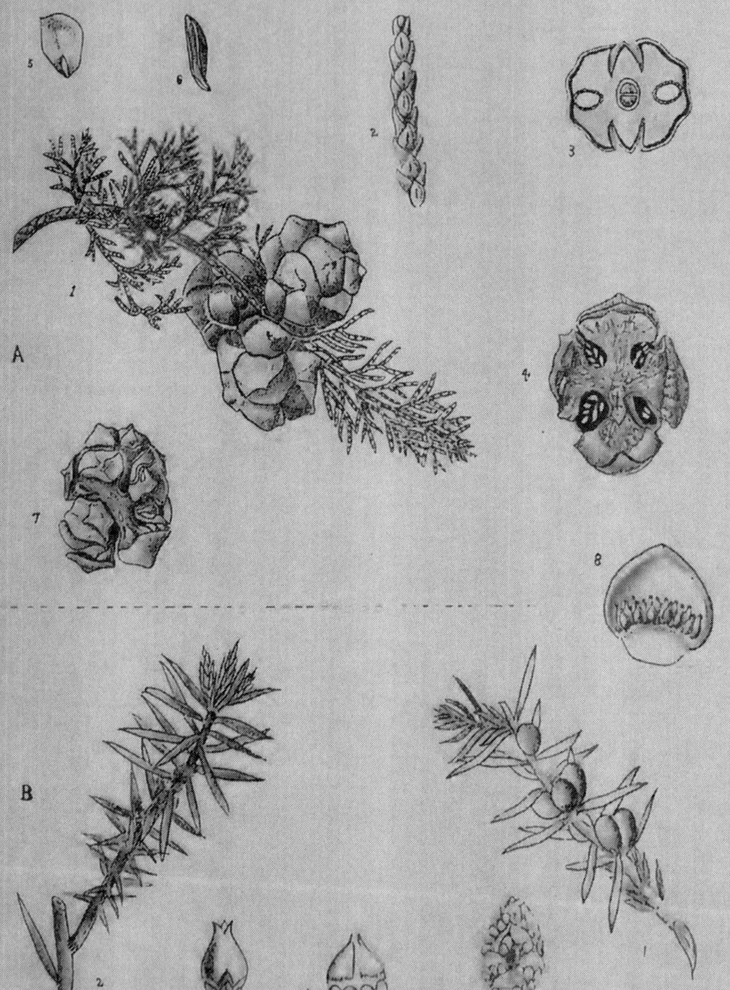

A—CUPRESSUS SEMPERVIRENS, *Linn.*　　B-JUNIPERUS COMMUNIS, *Linn.*

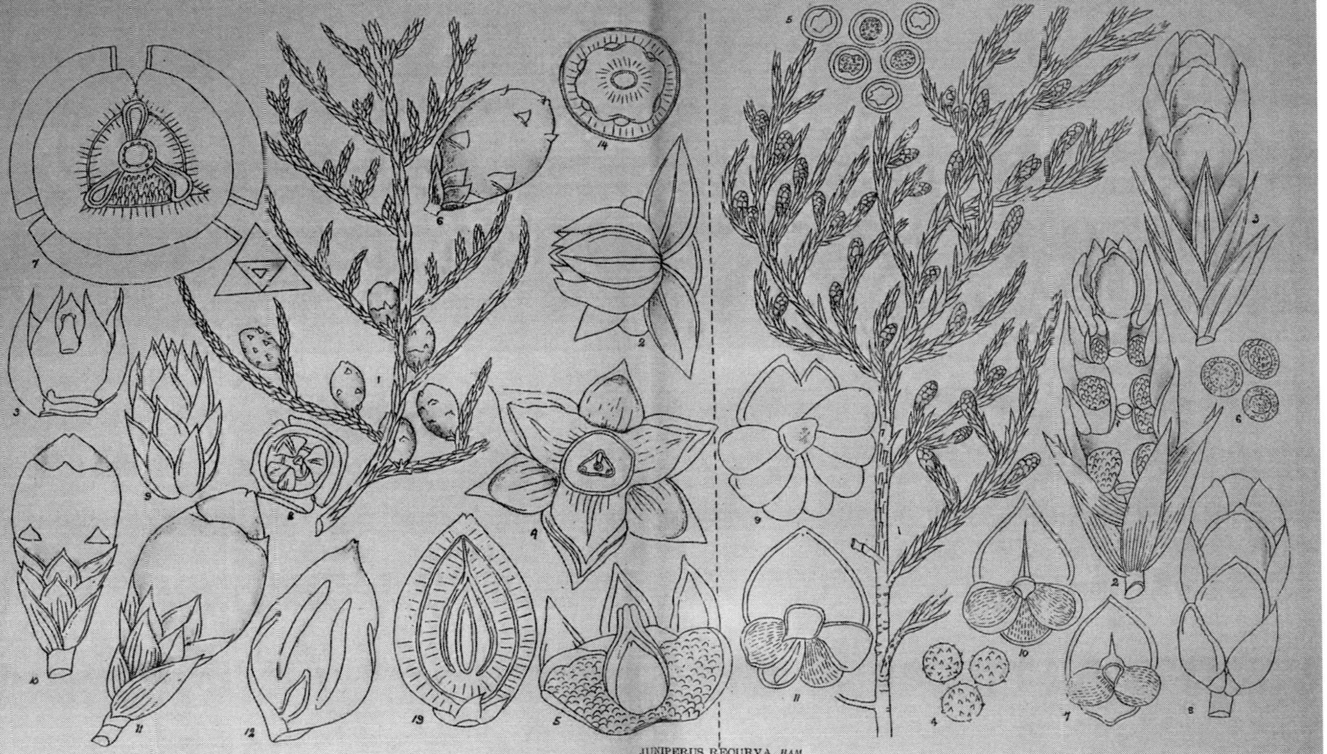

JUNIPERUS RECURVA, HAM

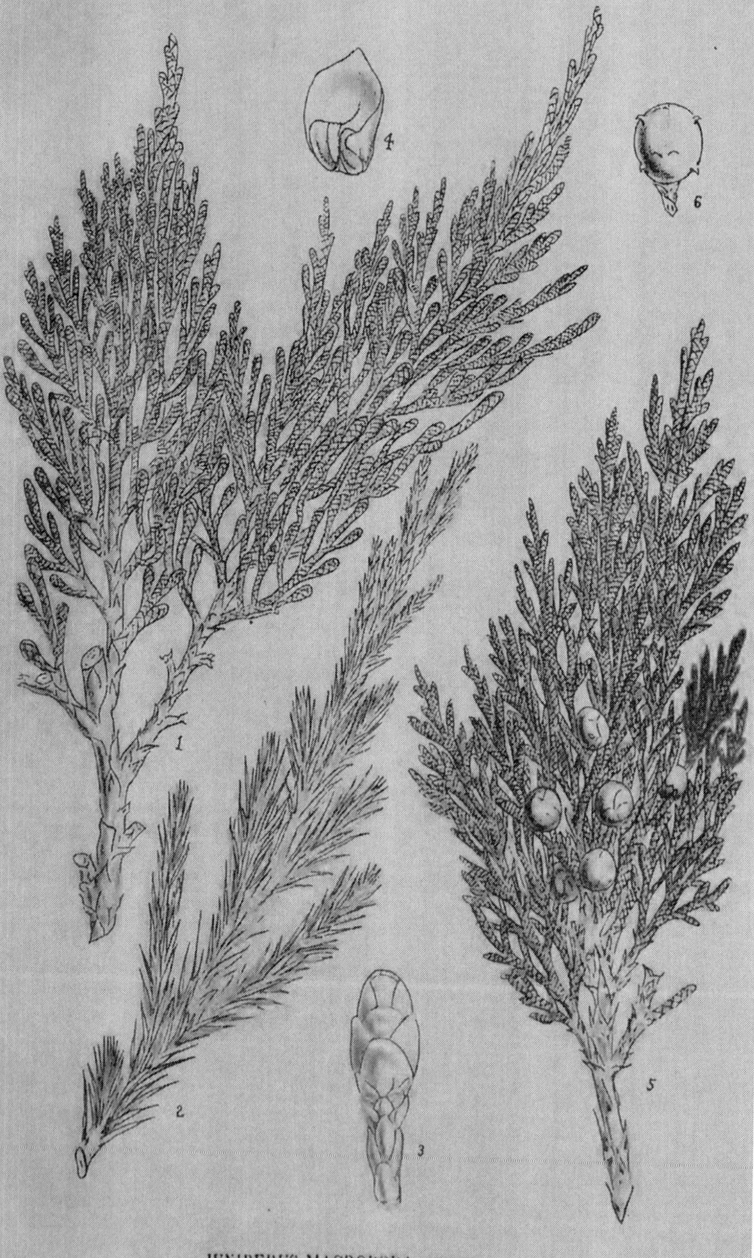

JUNIPERUS MACROPODA, BOISS.

PLATE No. 925.

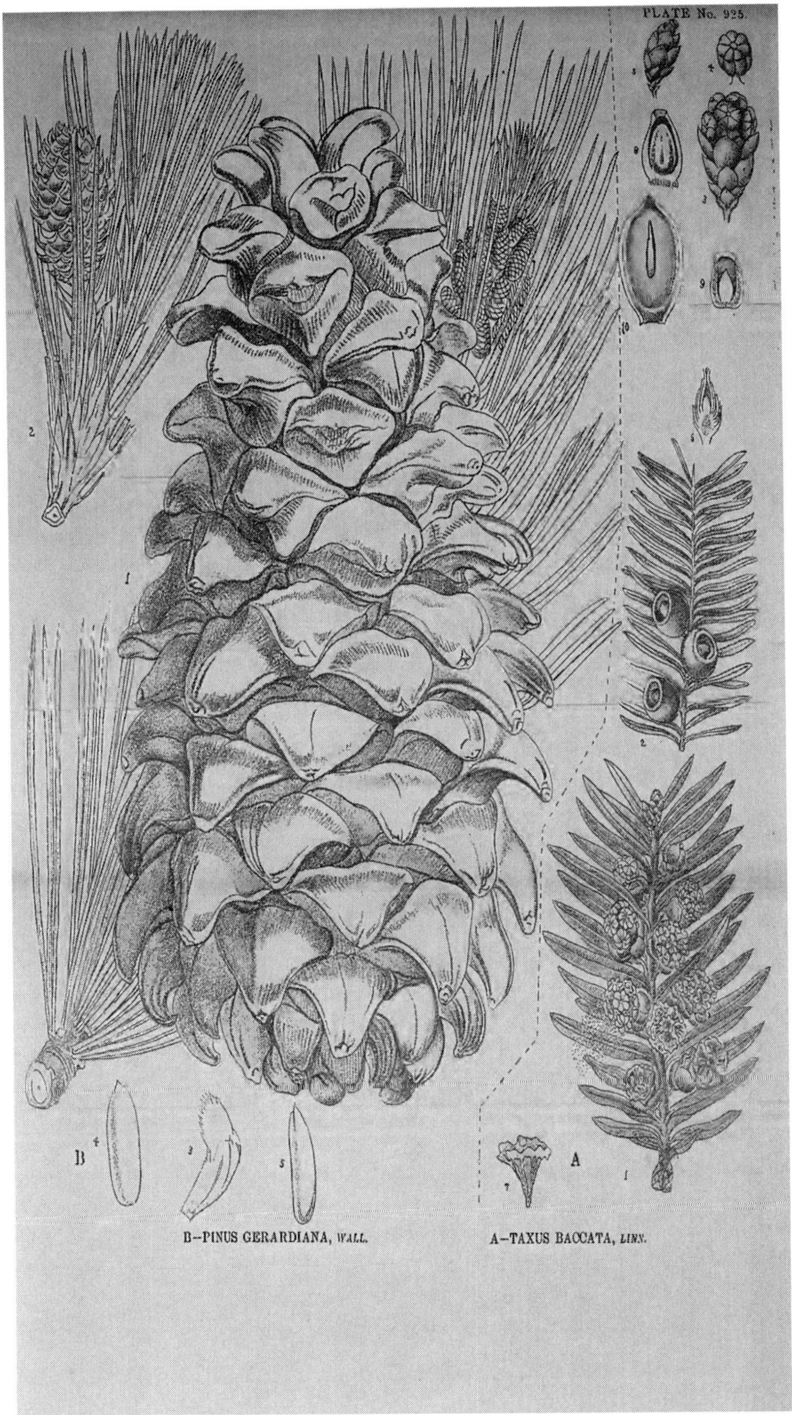

B—PINUS GERARDIANA, *WALL.*

A—TAXUS BACCATA, *LINN.*

A. PINUS LONGIFOLIA, ROXB.   B. PINUS LONGIFOLIA, ROXB.

PLATE No. 927.

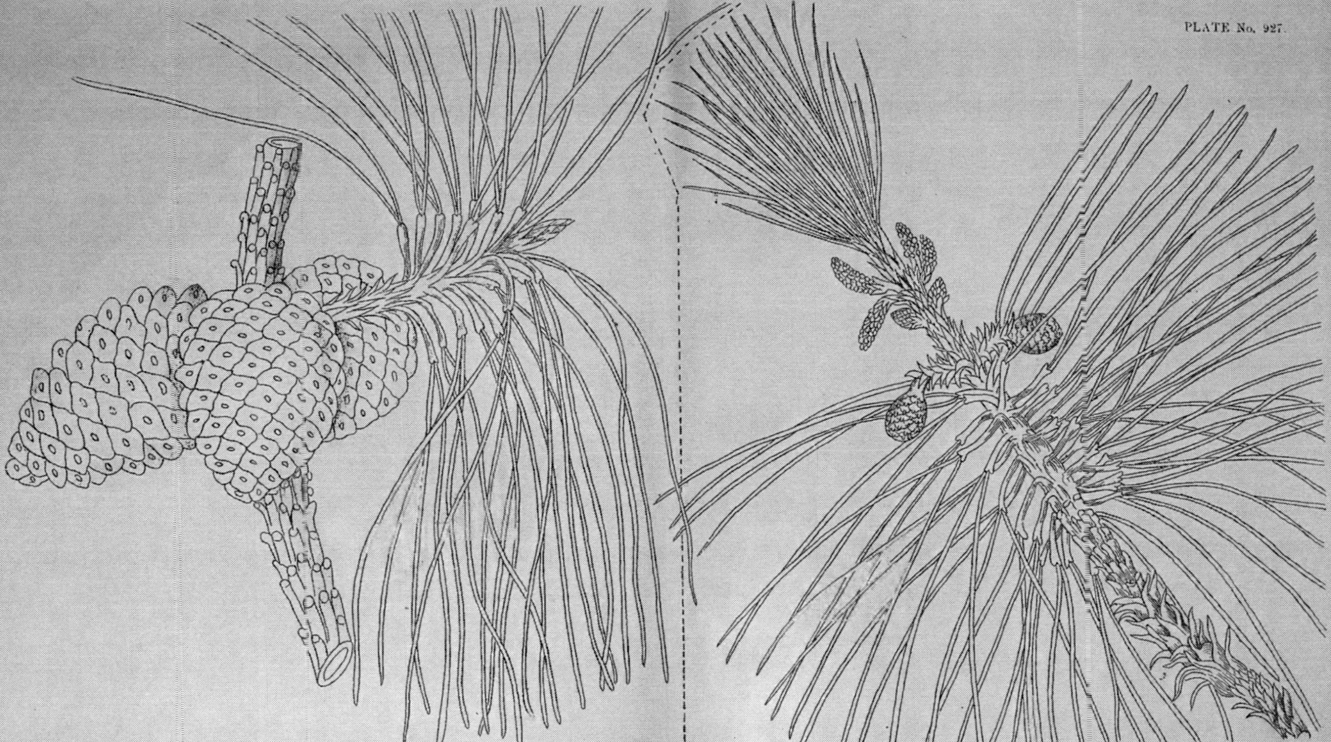

PINUS KHASYA, *ROYLE.*

PLATE No. 928.

A—CEDRUS LIBANI, *BARREL.* B—CEDRUS DEODARA, *LOUD.* C—ABIES WEBBIANA, *LINDL.*

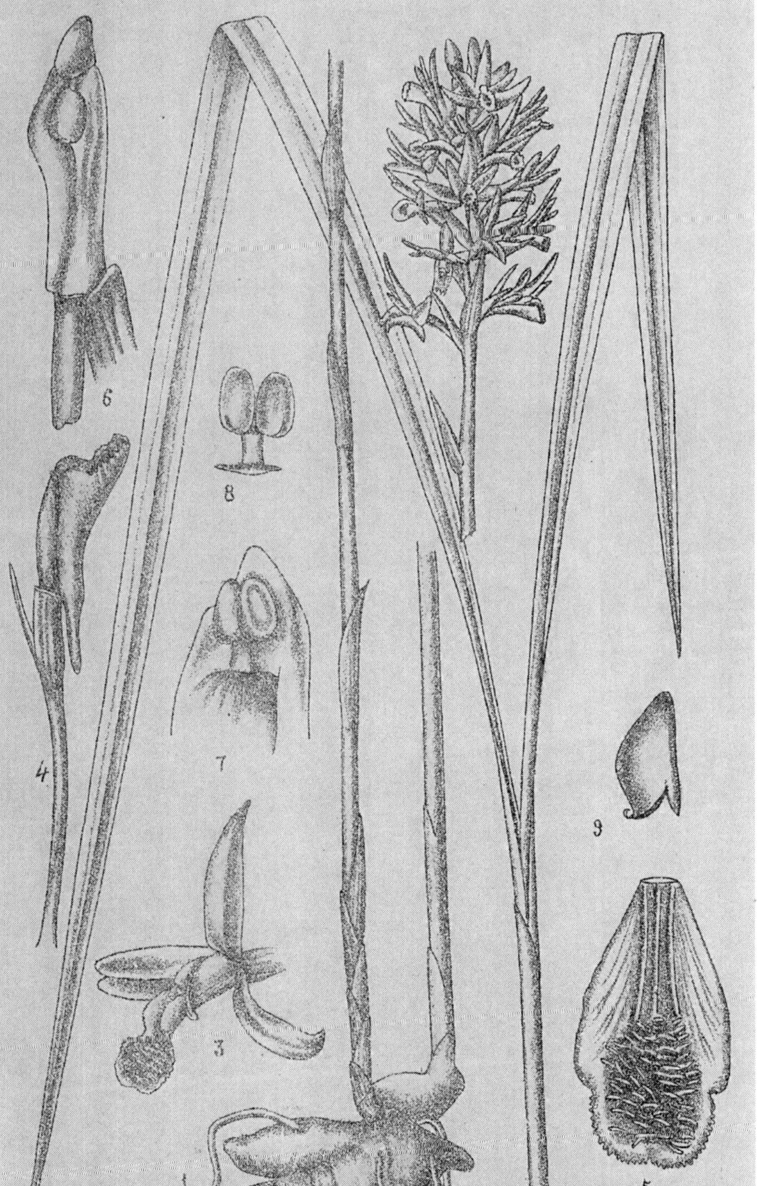

EULOPHIA CAMPESTRIS, *WALL.*

PLATE No. 930.

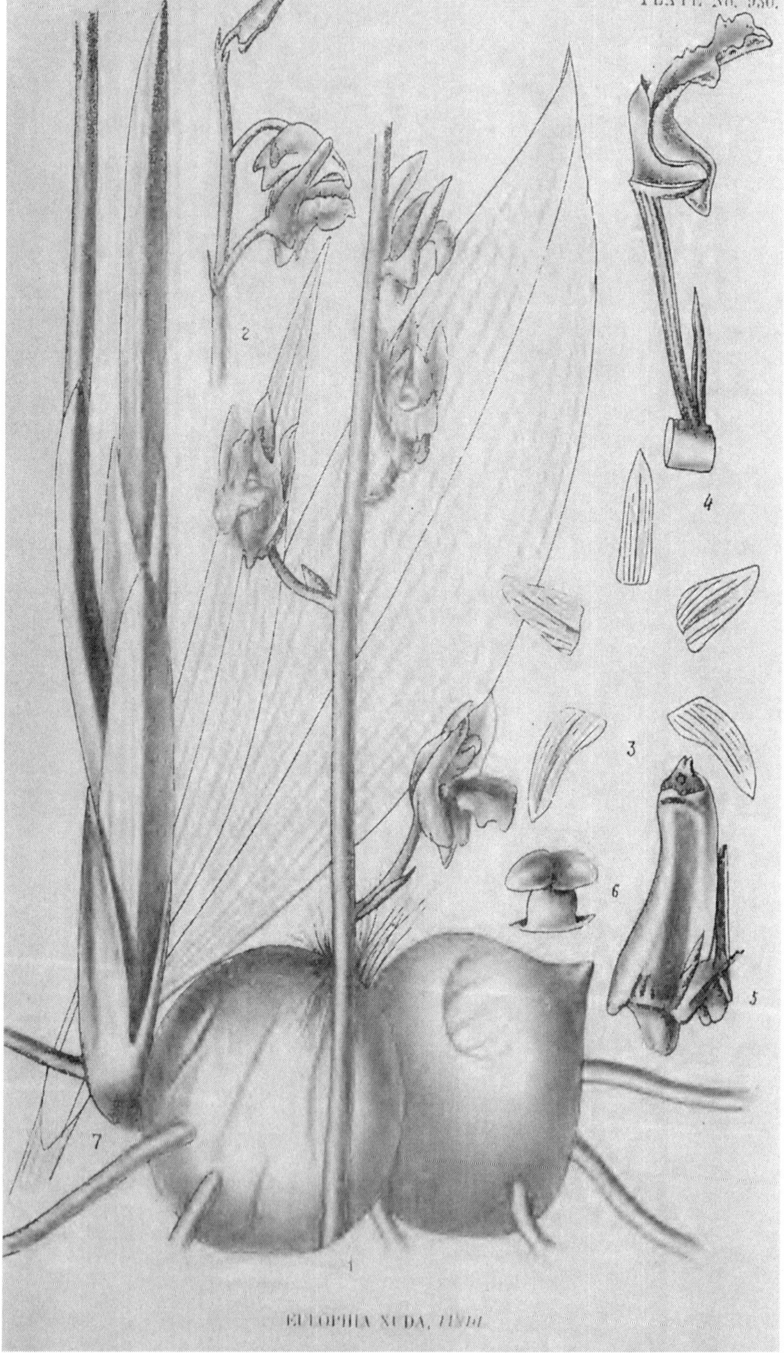

EULOPHIA NUDA, *Lindl.*

PLATE No. 931

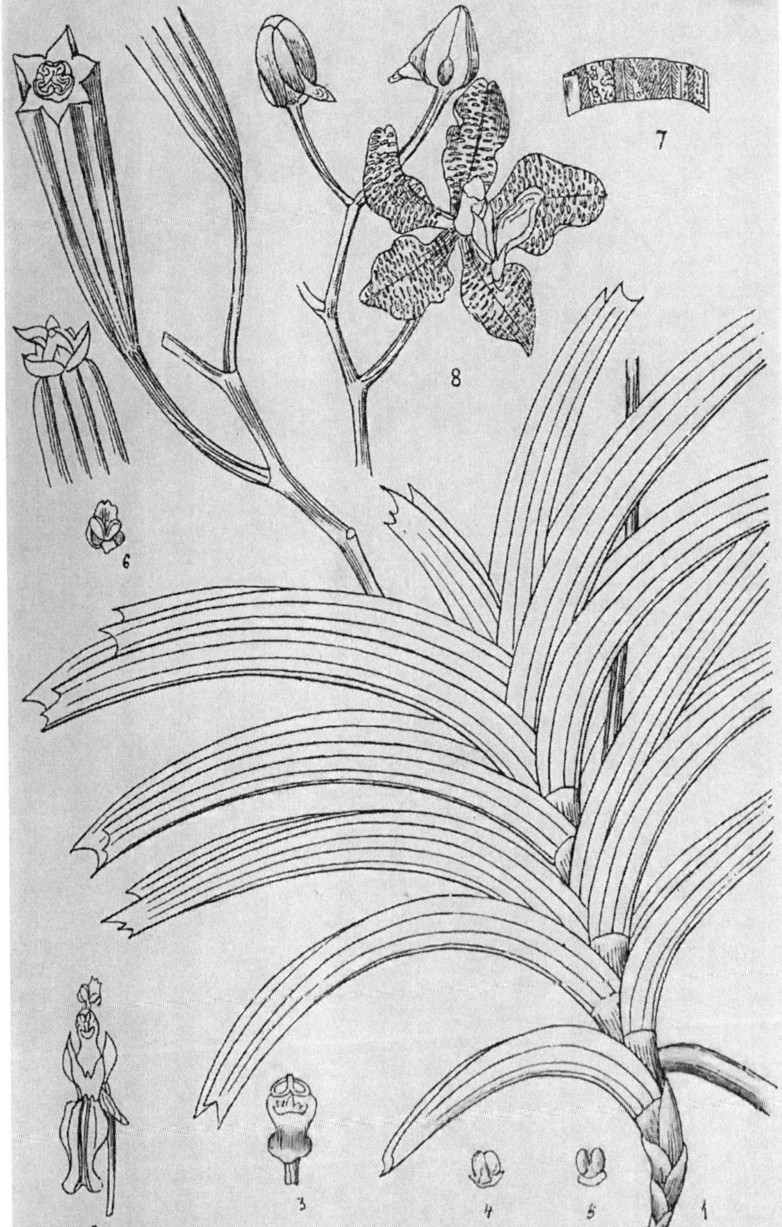

VANDA ROXBURGHII, Br.

PLATE No. 932

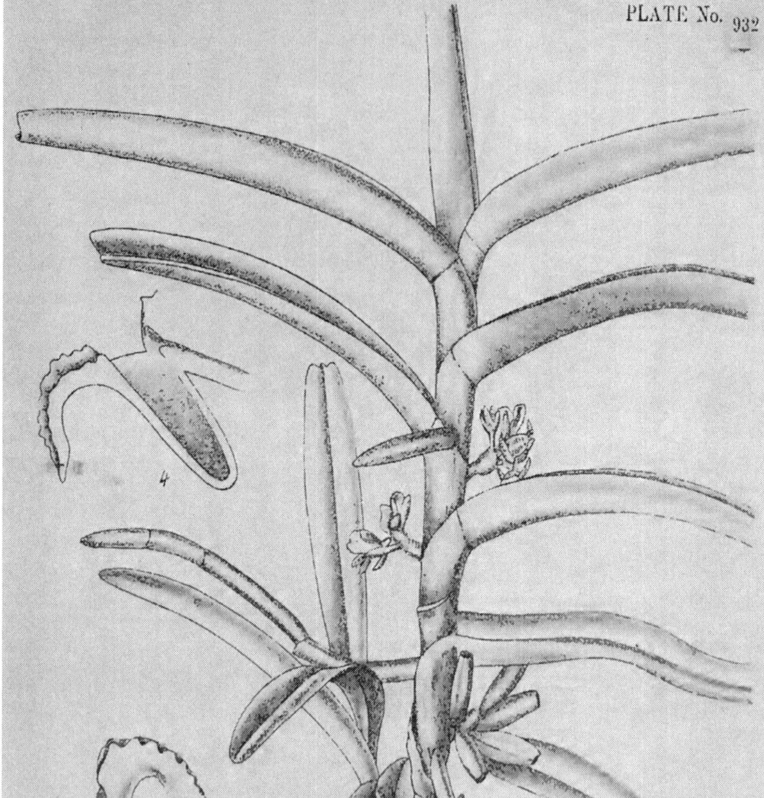

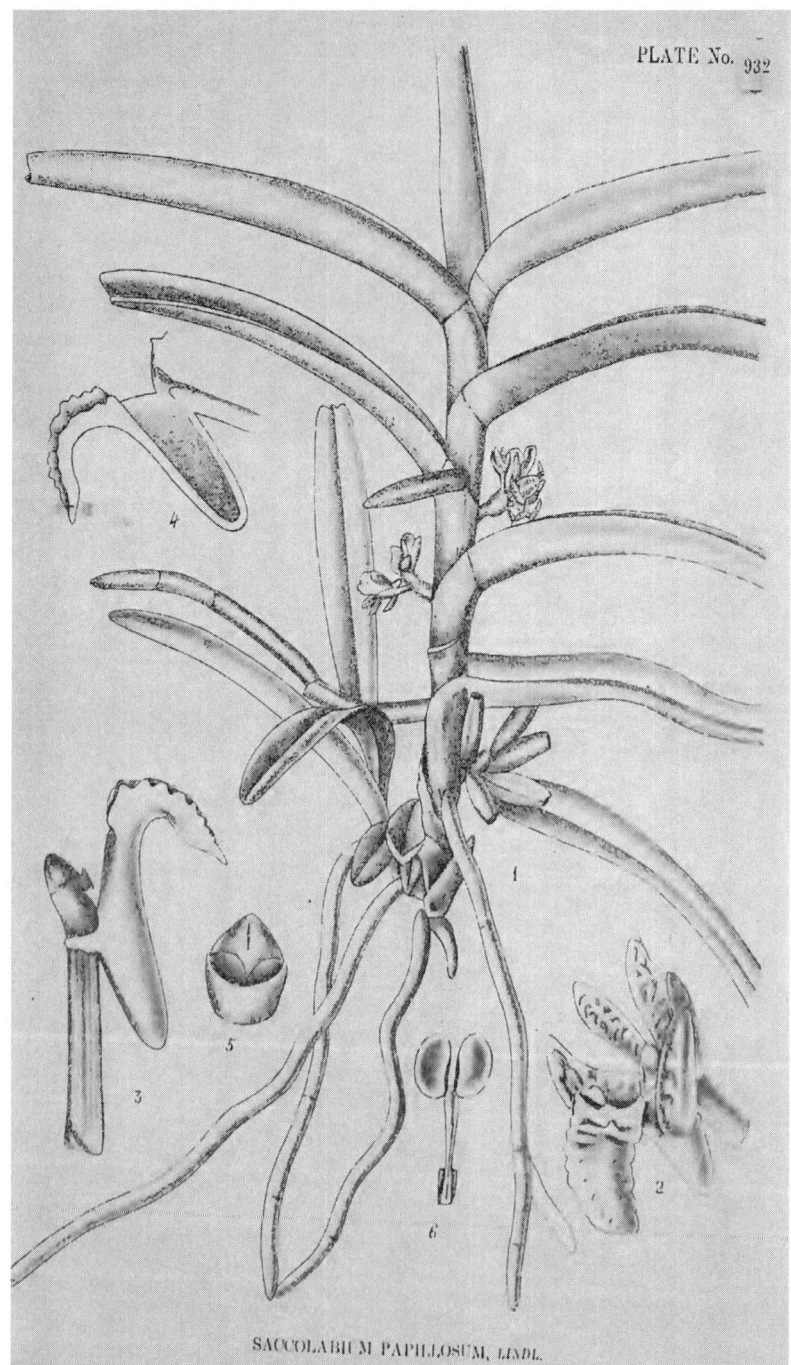

SACCOLABIUM PAPILLOSUM, *LINDL.*

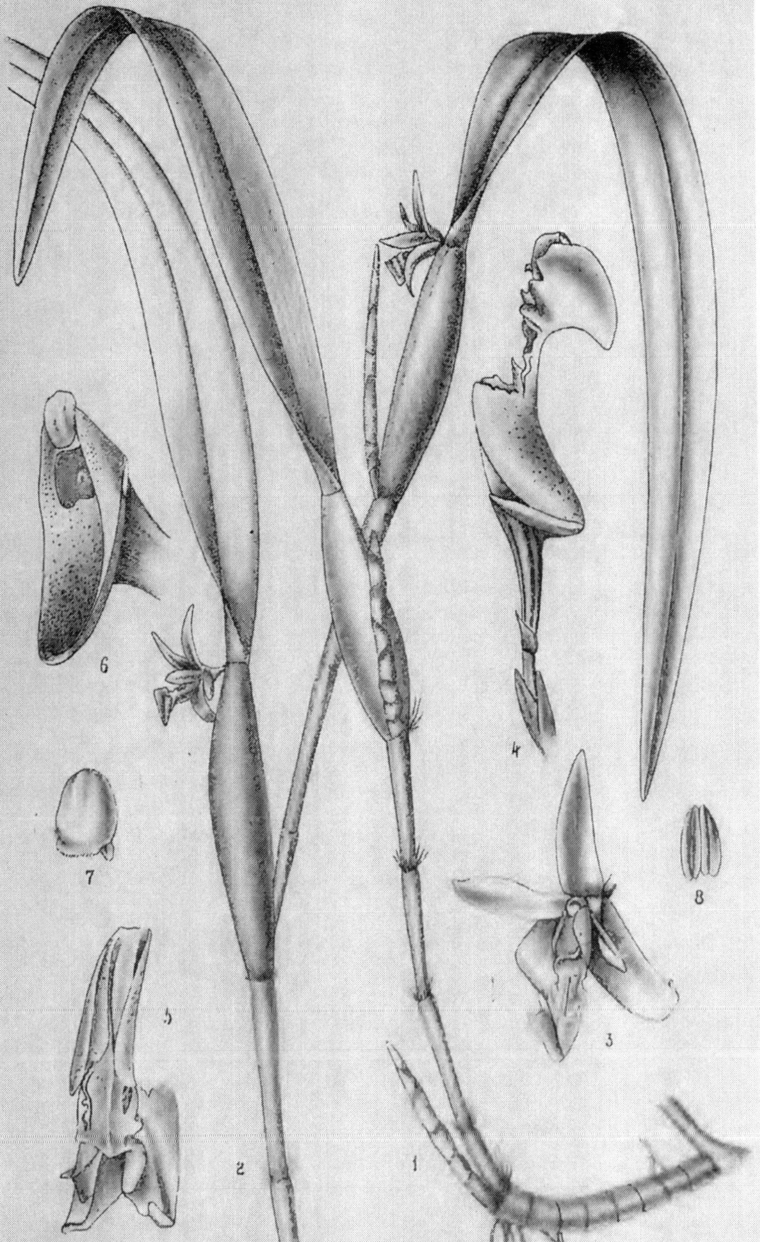

DENDROBIUM MACRAEI, LINDL.

PLATE No. 934.

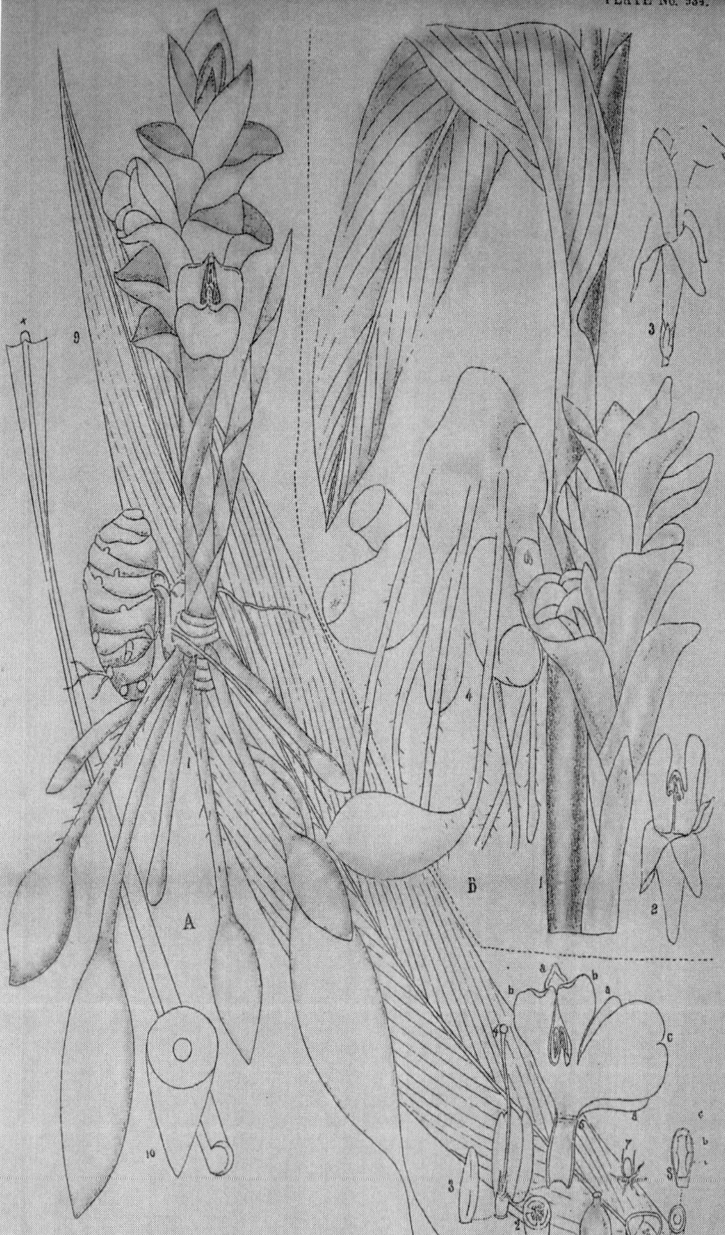

A—CURCUMA ANGUSTIFOLIA, *ROXB.*

B—CURCUMA ZEDOARIA, *ROSC.*

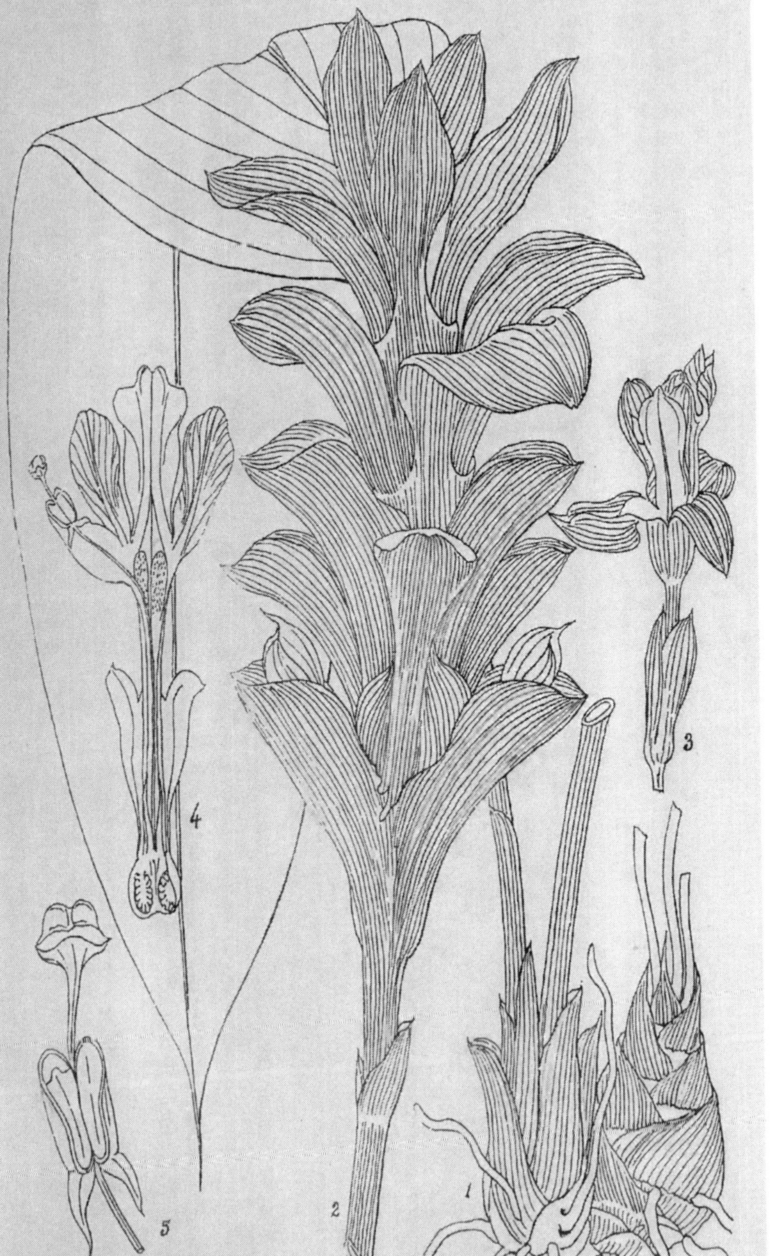

CURCUMA AROMATICA, *SALISB.*

PLATE No. 936.

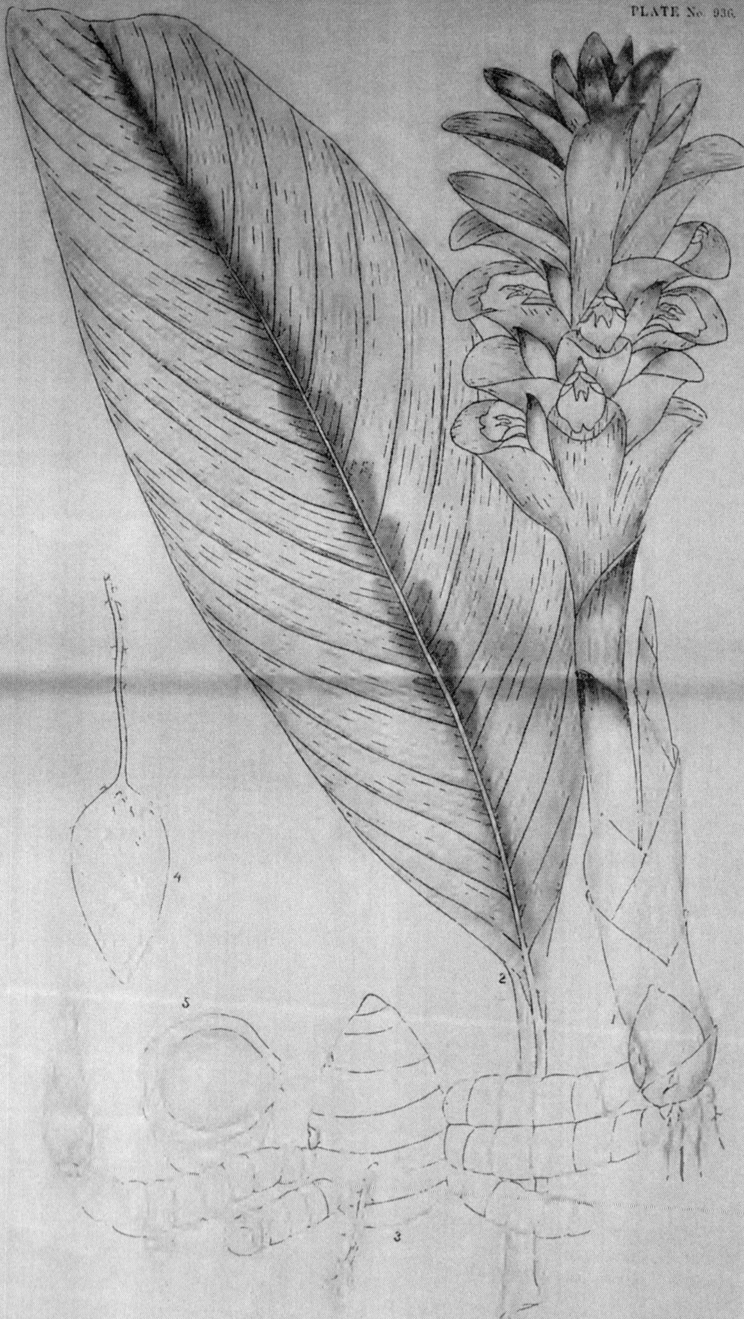

CURCUMA CÆSIA, ROXB.

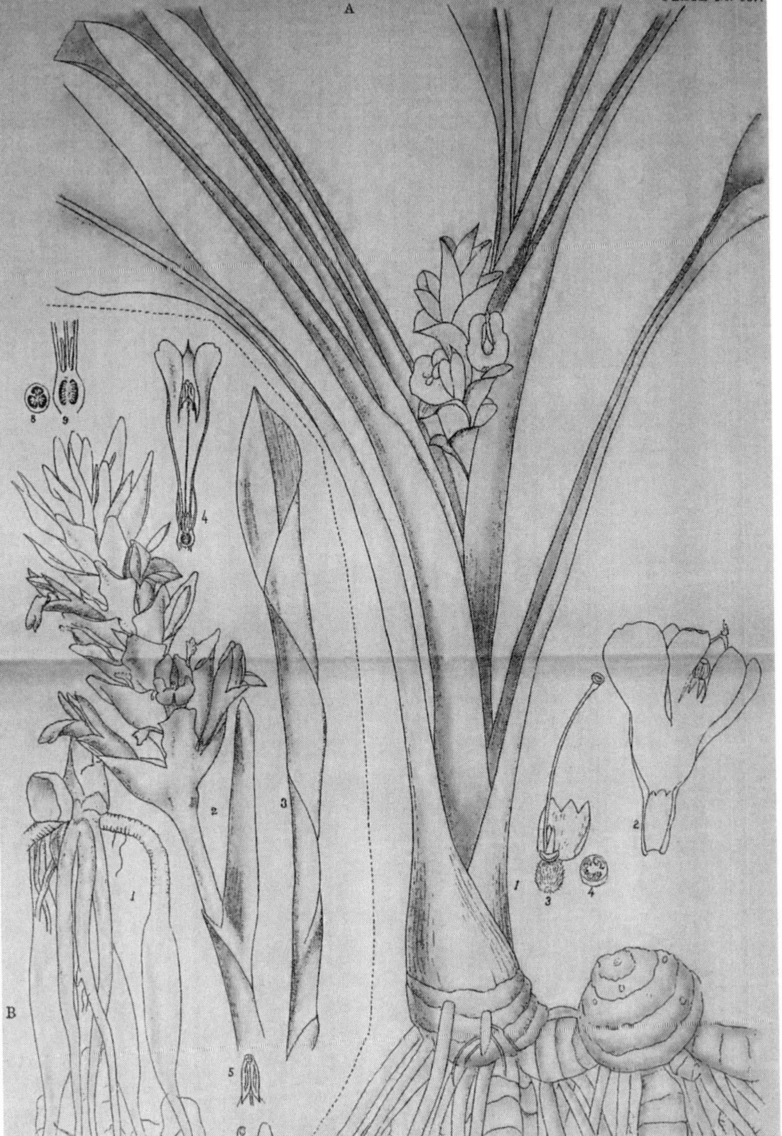

B—CURCUMA LONGA, *Linn.*   A—CURCUMA AMADA, *Roxb.*

PLATE No. 938.

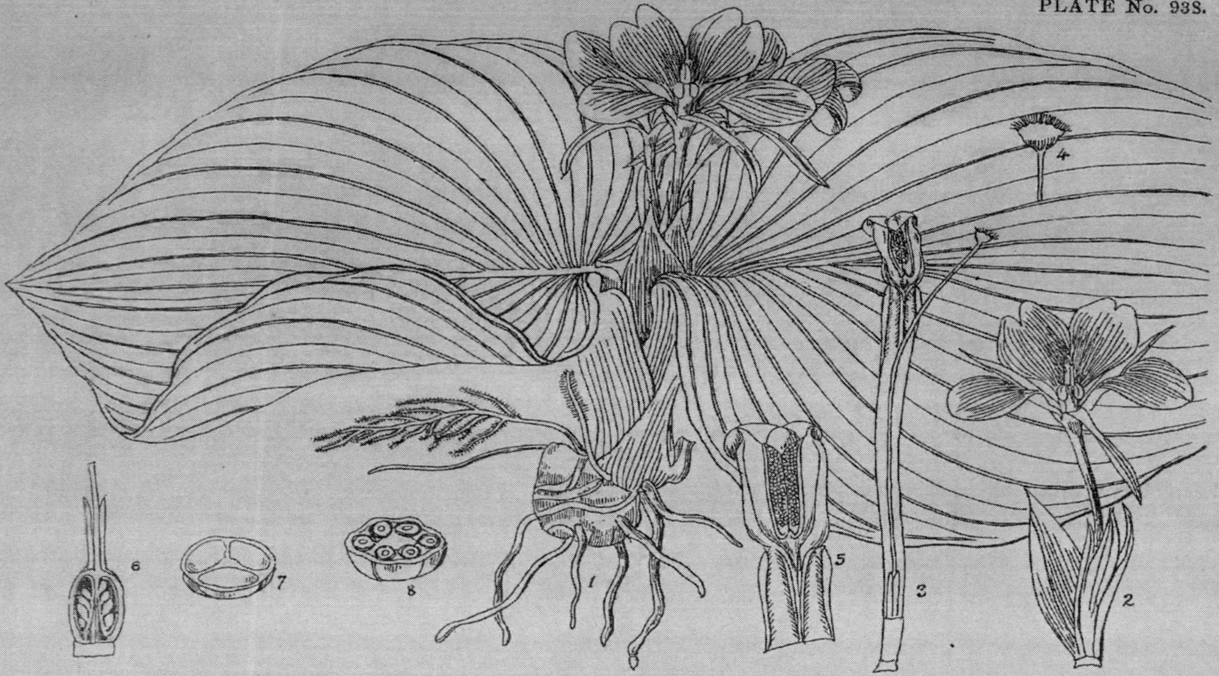

KÆMPFERIA GALANGA, *Linn.*

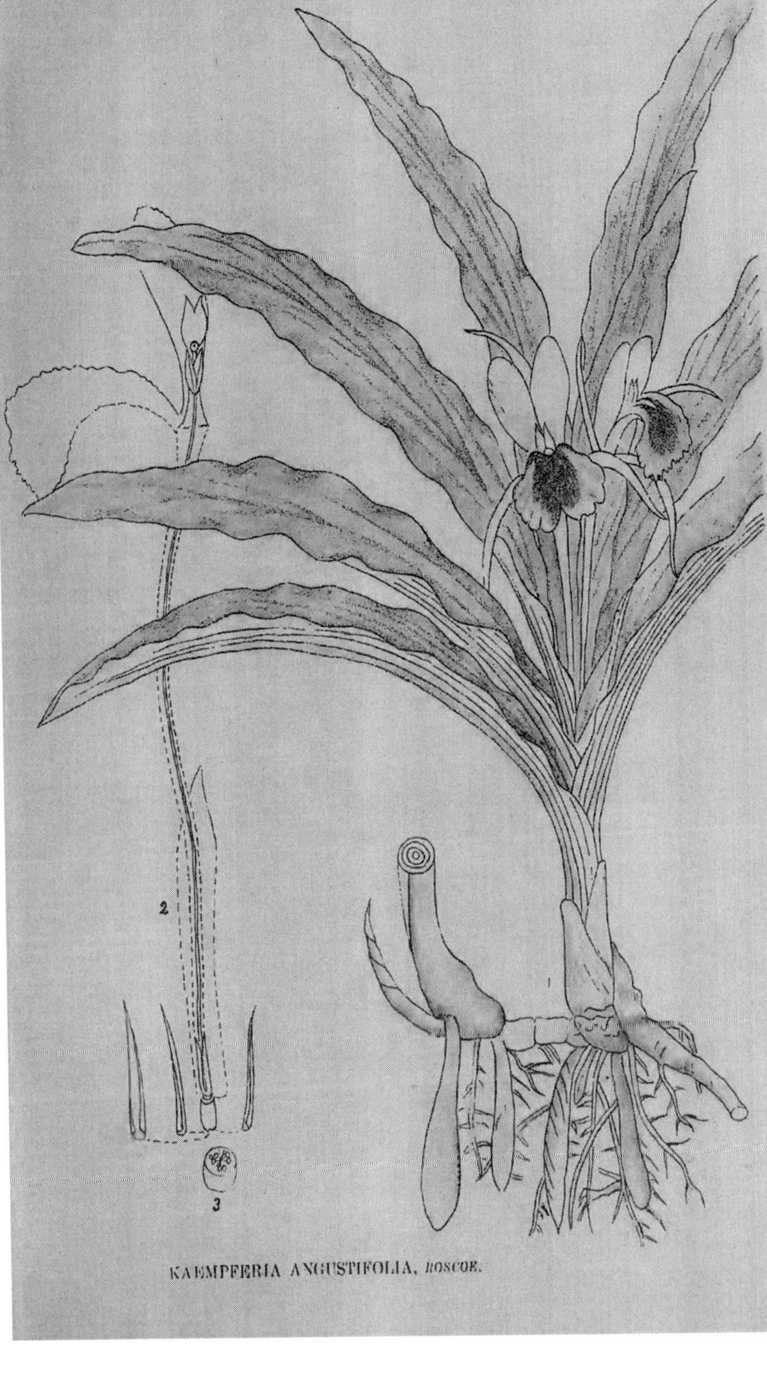

KAEMPFERIA ANGUSTIFOLIA, *ROSCOE.*

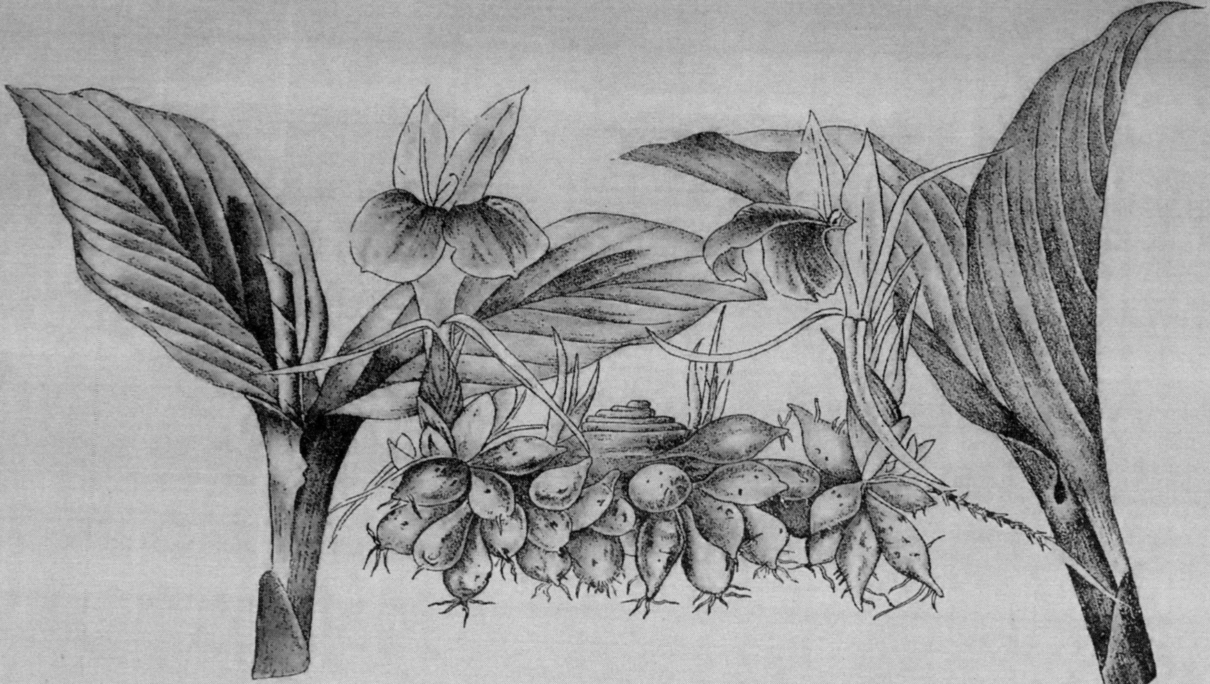

KAEMPFERIA ROTUNDA, *LINN.*

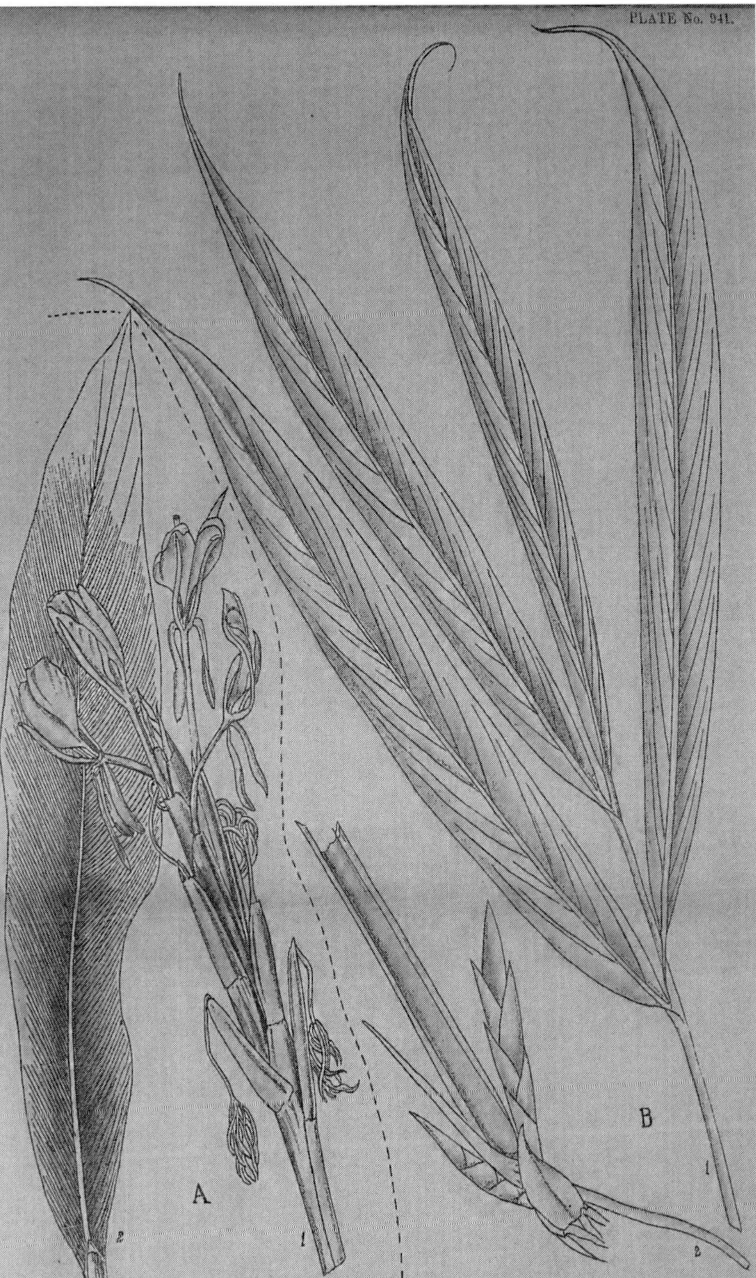

A—HEDYCHIUM SPICATUM, *Hamilt.* B—AMOMUM XANTHIOIDES, *Wall.*

PLATE No. 942.

AMOMUM SUBULATUM, ROXB

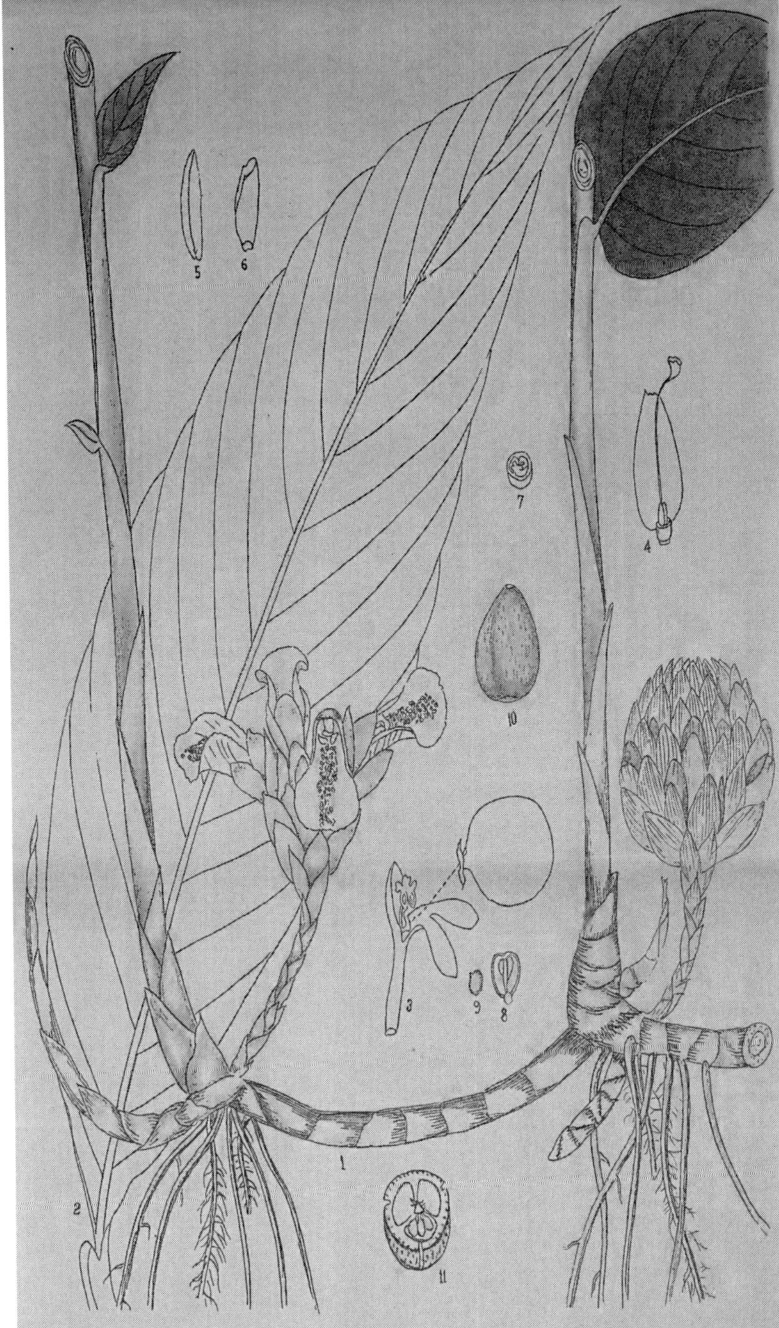

AMOMUM AROMATICUM, ROXB.

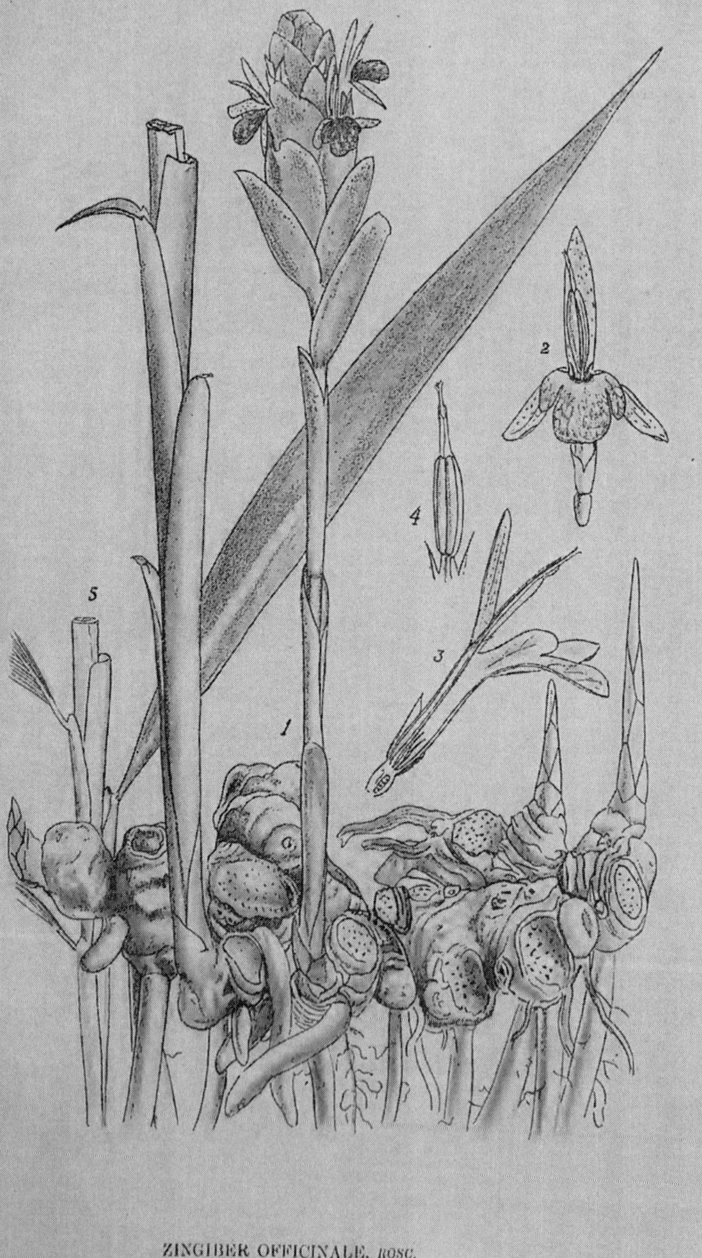

ZINGIBER OFFICINALE, *Rosc.*

PLATE No. 945.

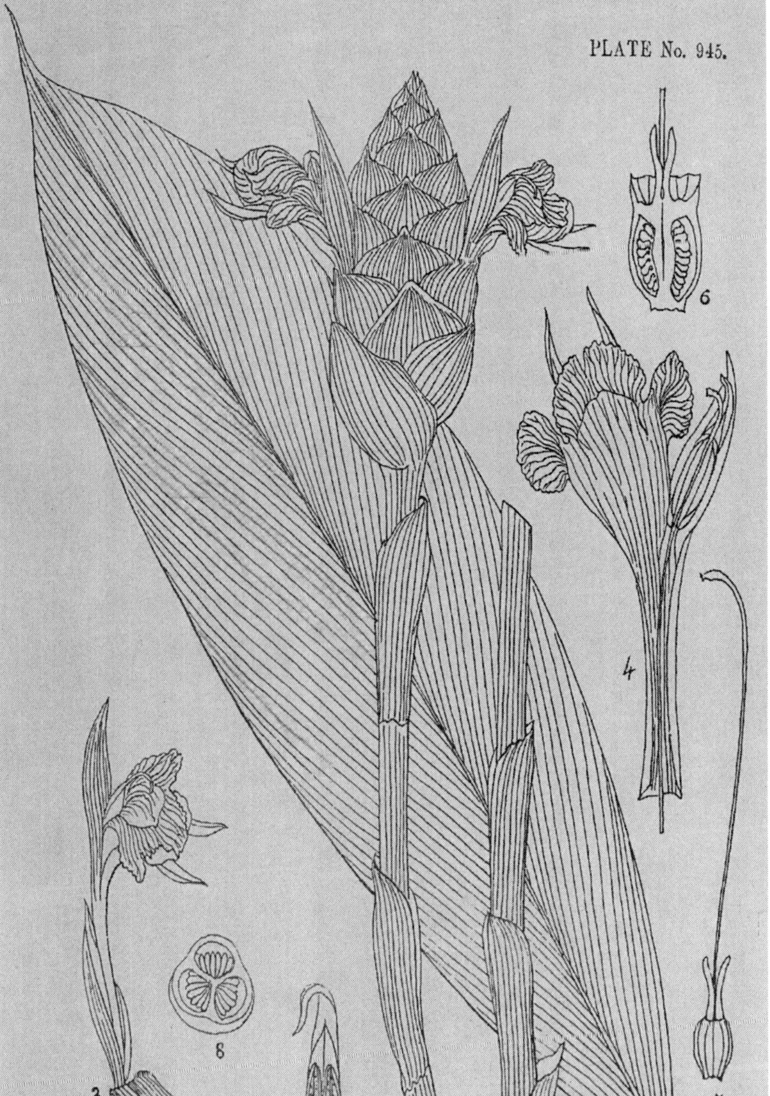

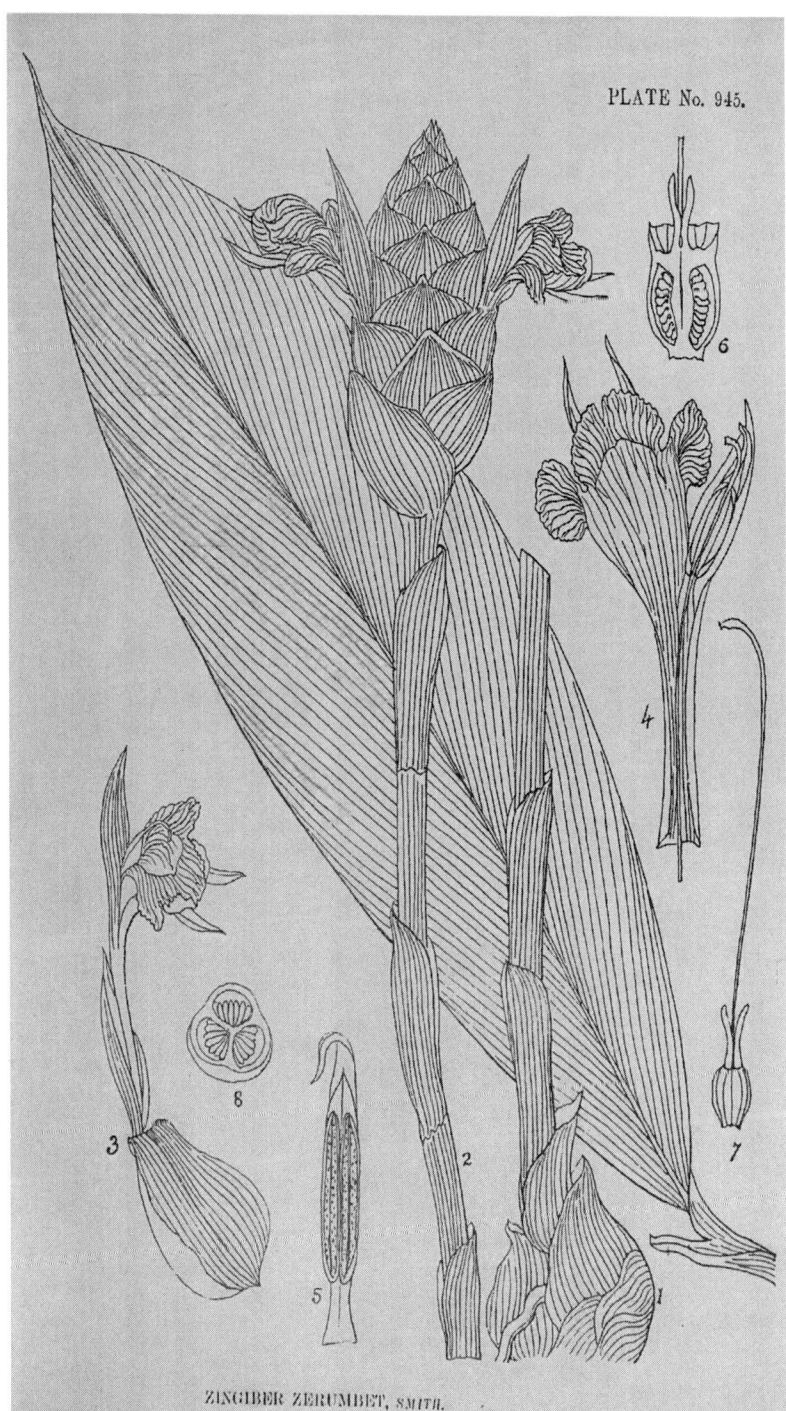

ZINGIBER ZERUMBET, SMITH.

ZINGIBER CASUMUNAR, ROXB.

PLATE No. 947.

COSTUS SPECIOSUS, SMITH.

PLATE No. 948.

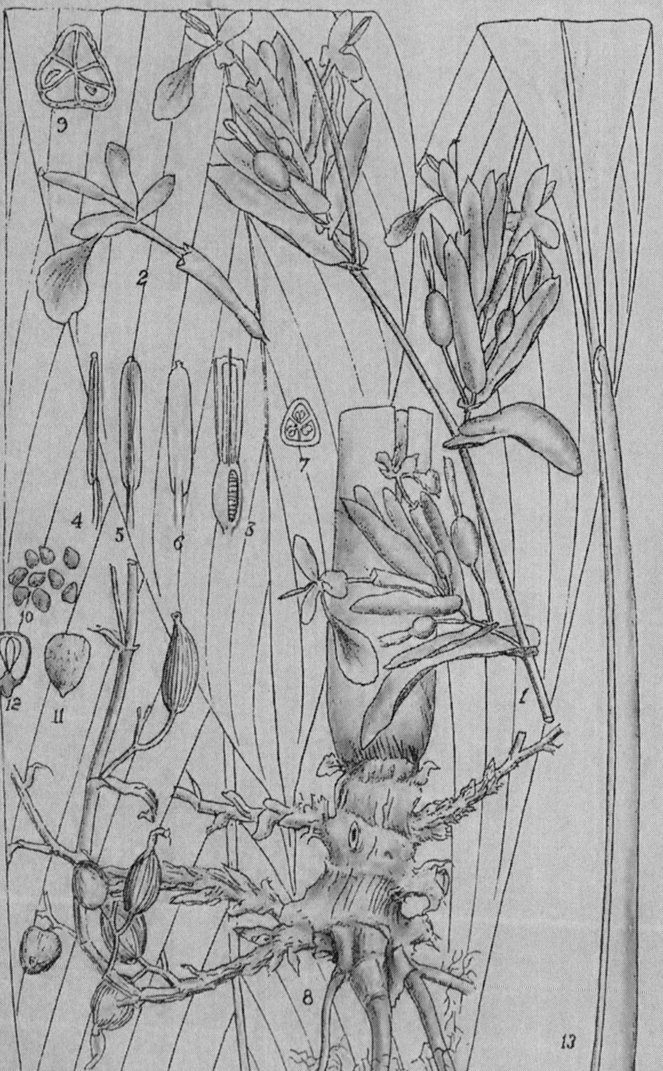

ELETTARIA CARDAMOMUM, MATON

PLATE No. 949

ALPINIA GALANGA, Sw.

PLATE No 950

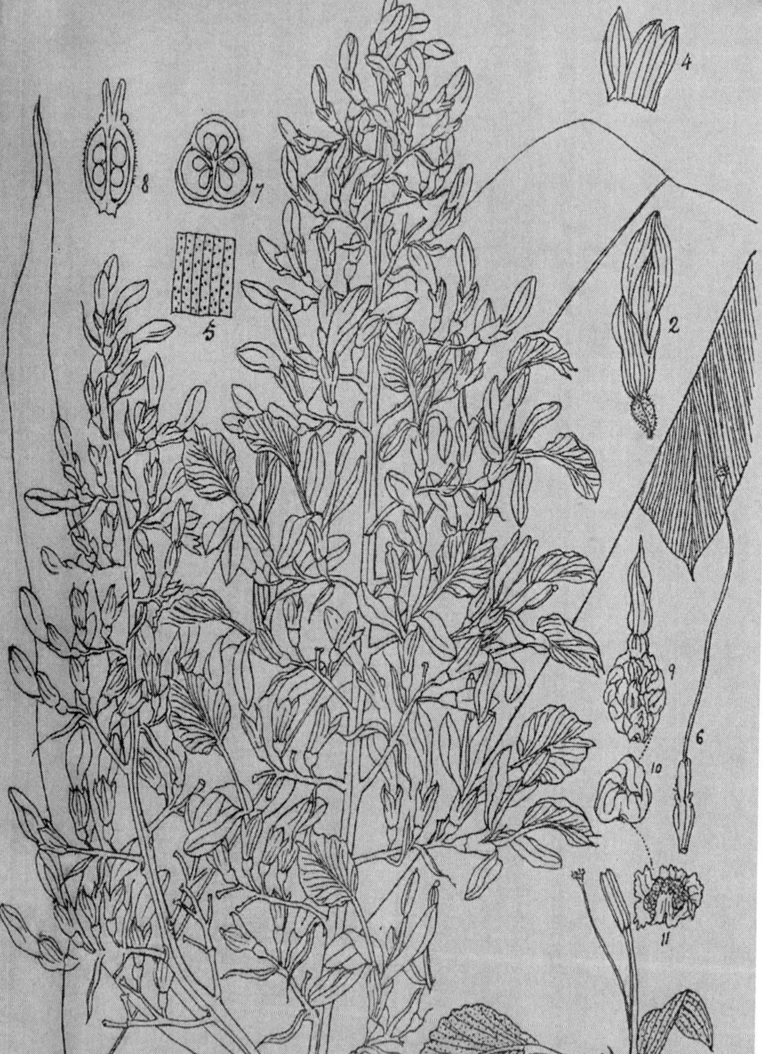

ALPINIA ALLUGHAS, ROSC.

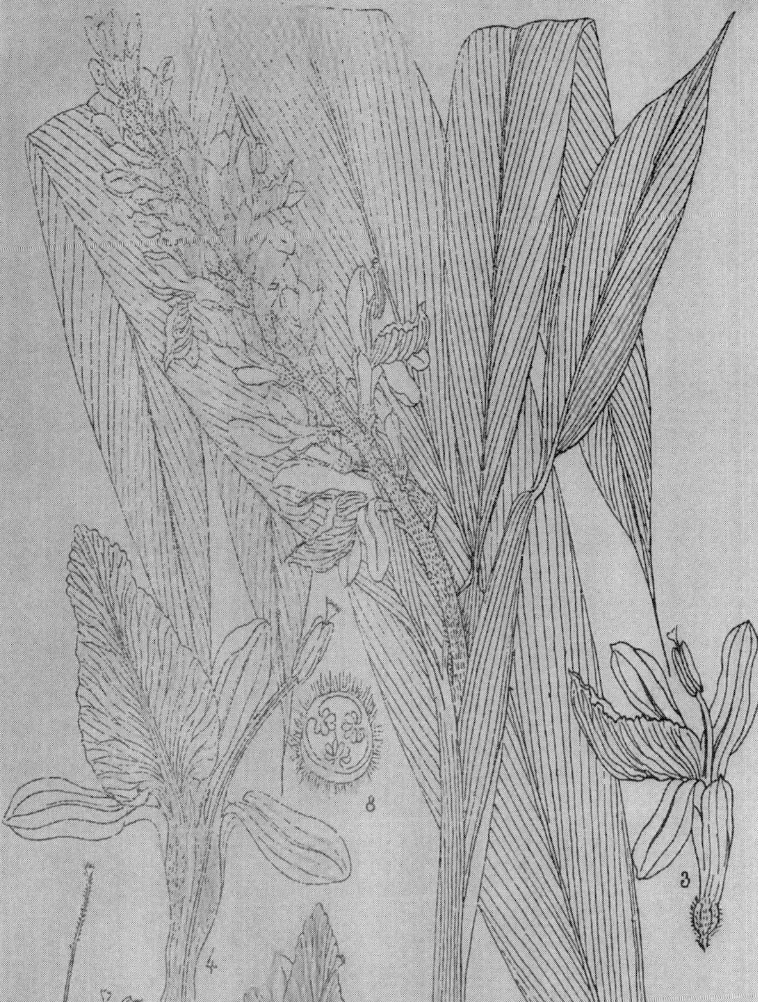

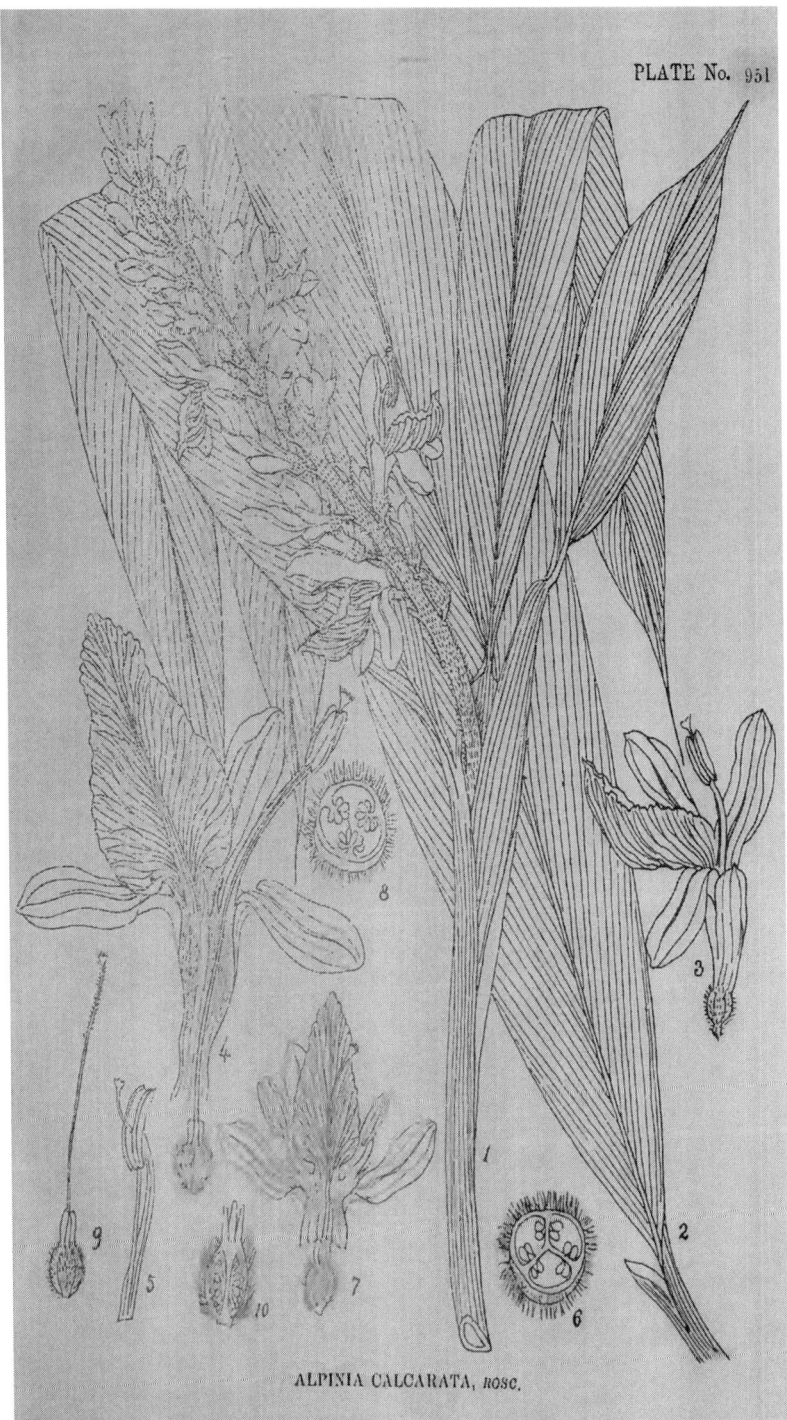

ALPINIA CALCARATA, *Rosc.*

PLATE No. 952.

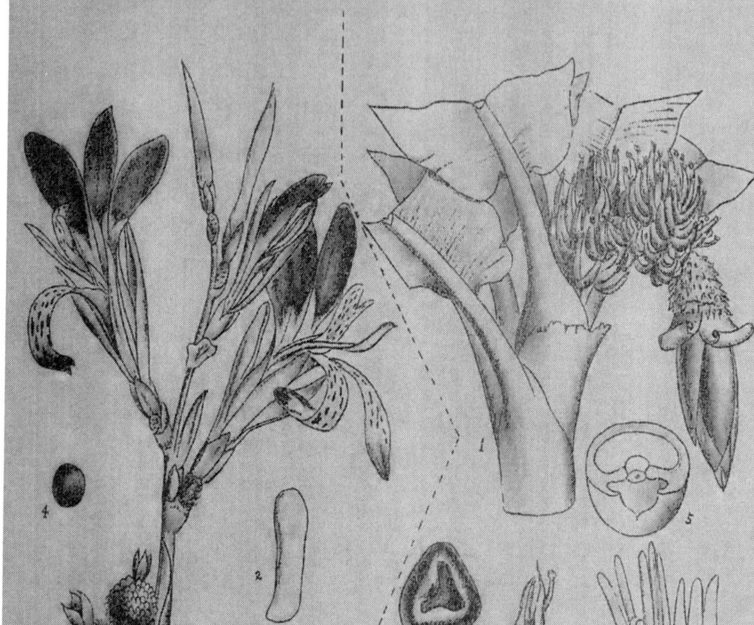

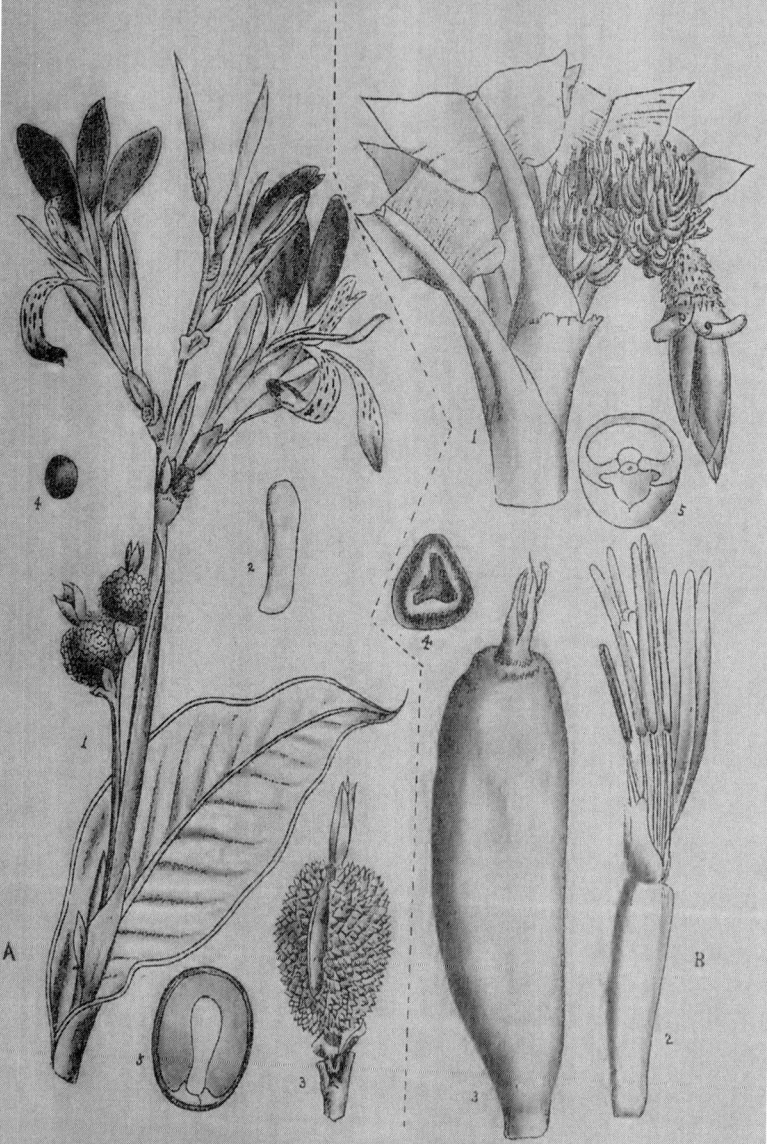

A—CANNA INDICA, *Linn.*

B—MUSA SAPIENTUM, *Linn.*

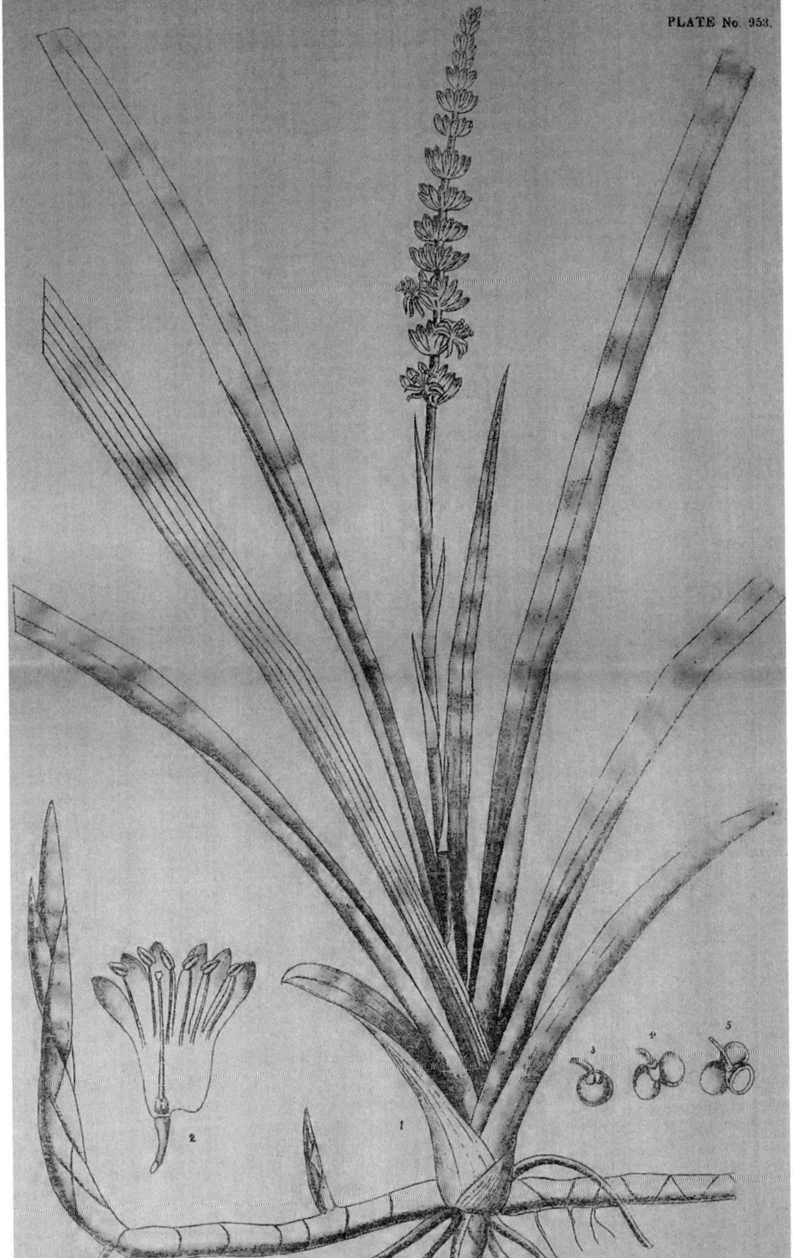

SANSEVIERIA ROXBURGHIANA, *Schult.*

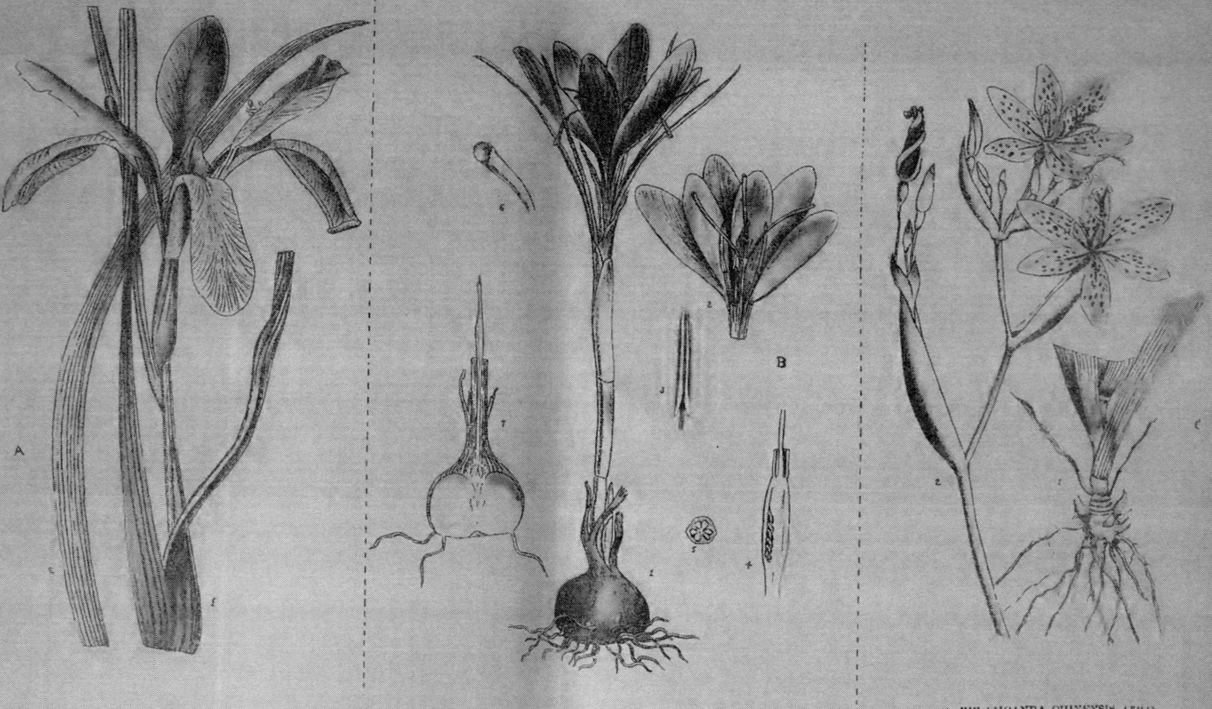

A–IRIS ENSATA, *THUNB* B–CROCUS SATIVUS *LINN.* C–BELAMCANDA CHINENSIS, *LEMAN.*

A—IRIS NEPALENSIS, *D. Don.*

B—IRIS KUMAONENSIS, *Wall.*

PLATE No. 956.

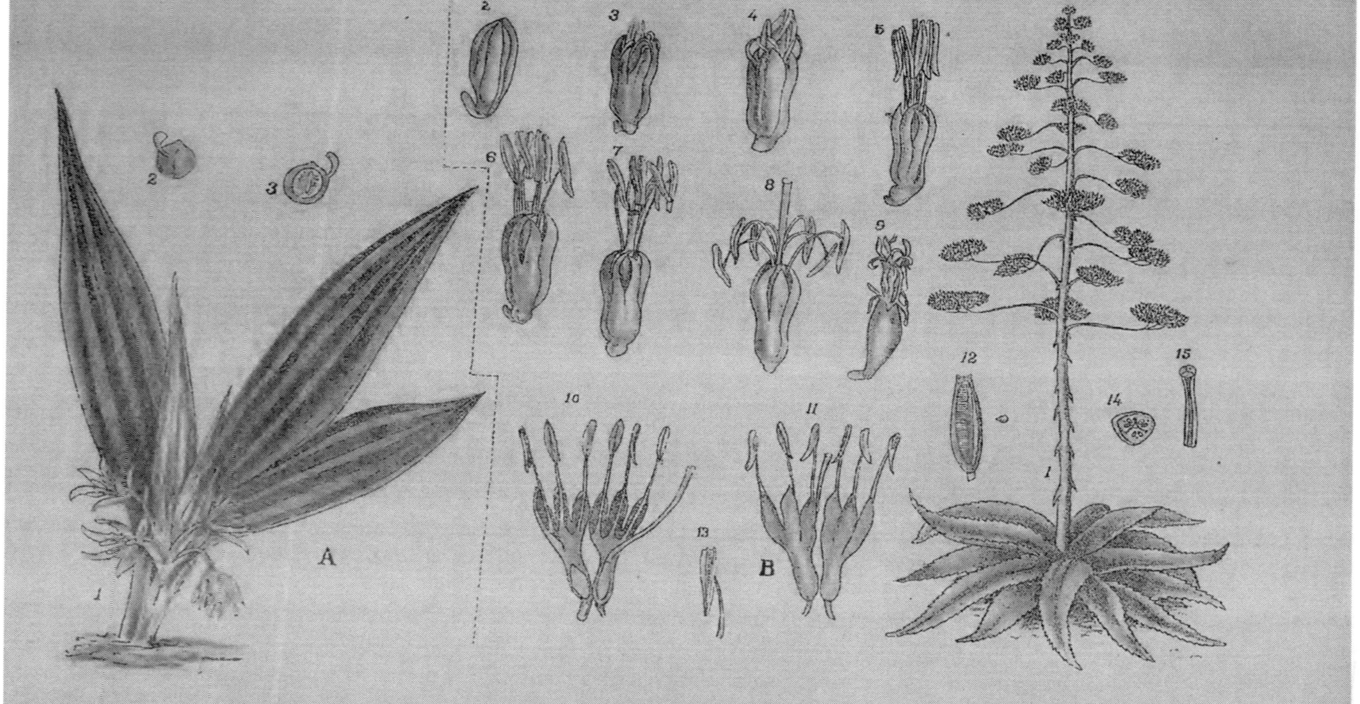

A—CURCULAGO ORCHIOIDES, *GAERTN.*   B—AGAVE AMERICANA, *LINN.*

CRINUM ASIATICUM, *Linn.*

PLATE No. 958.

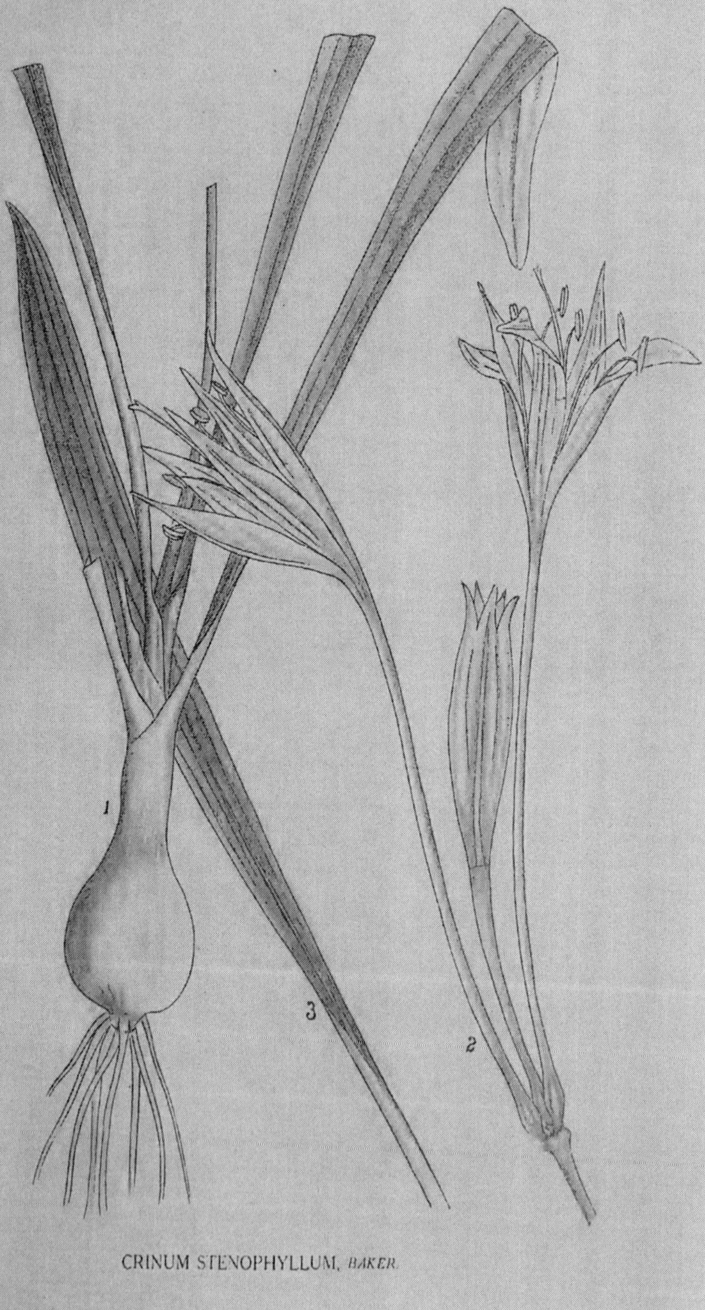

CRINUM STENOPHYLLUM, *BAKER.*

PLATE No 959.

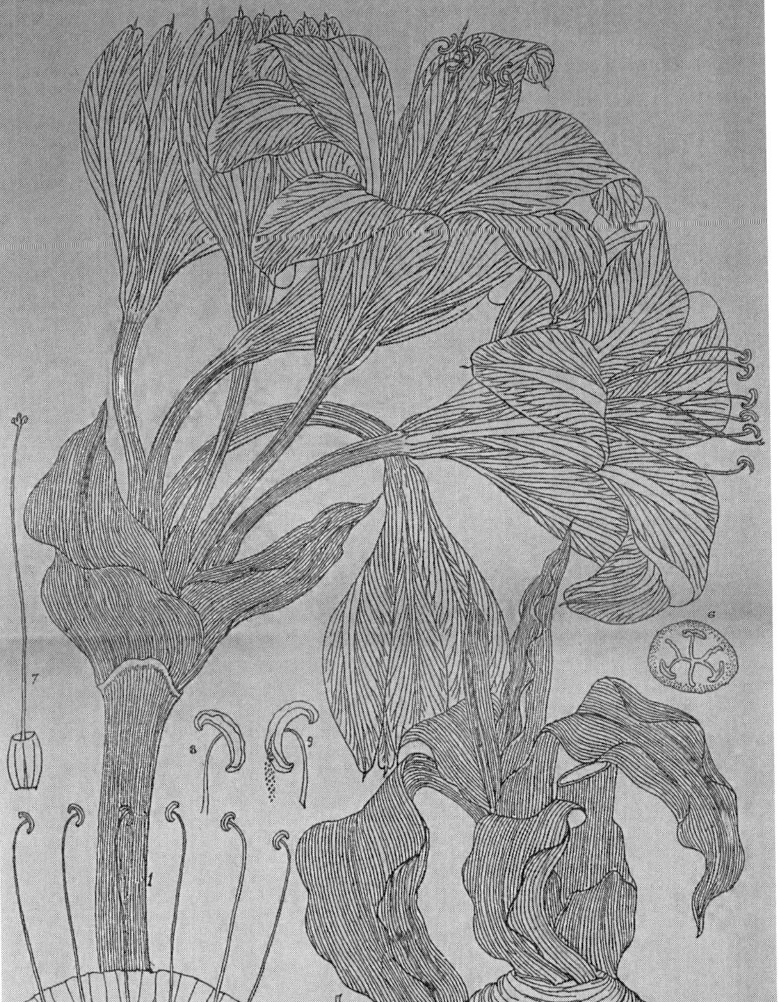

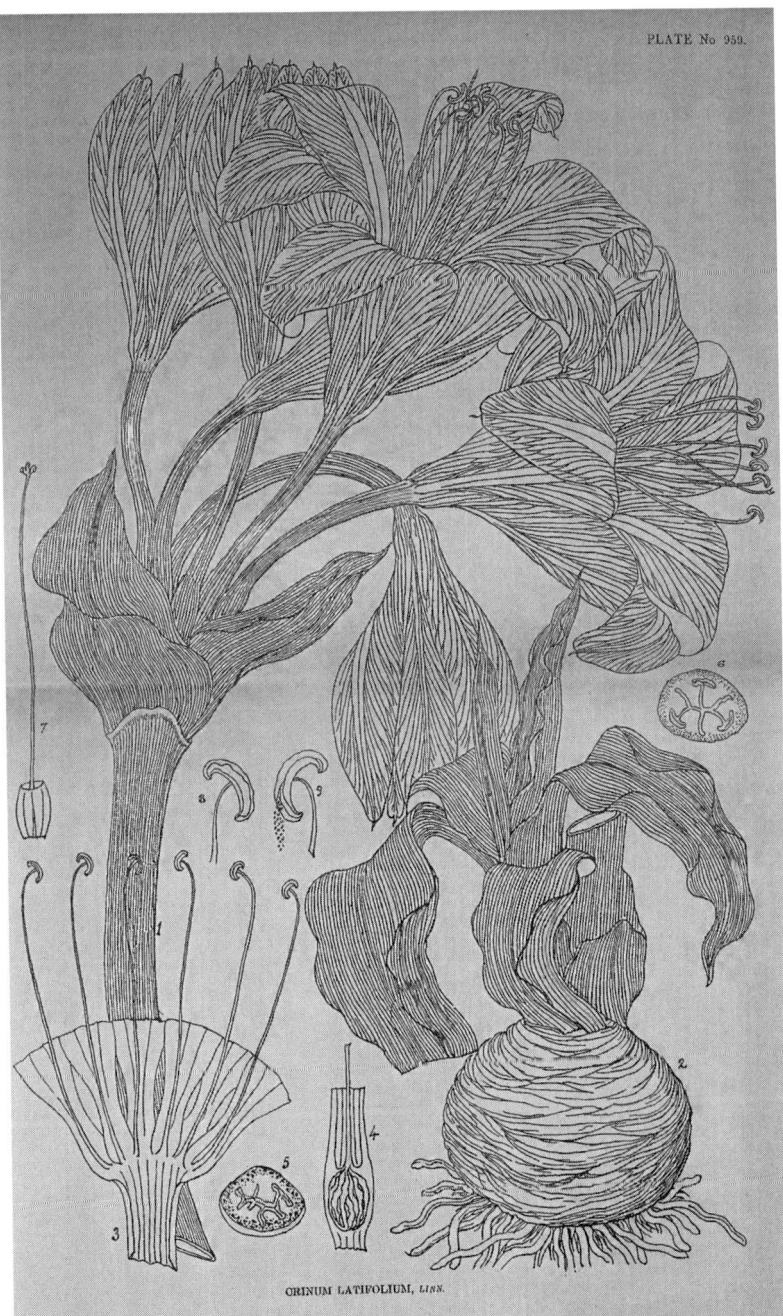

CRINUM LATIFOLIUM, *Linn.*

PLATE No. 960.

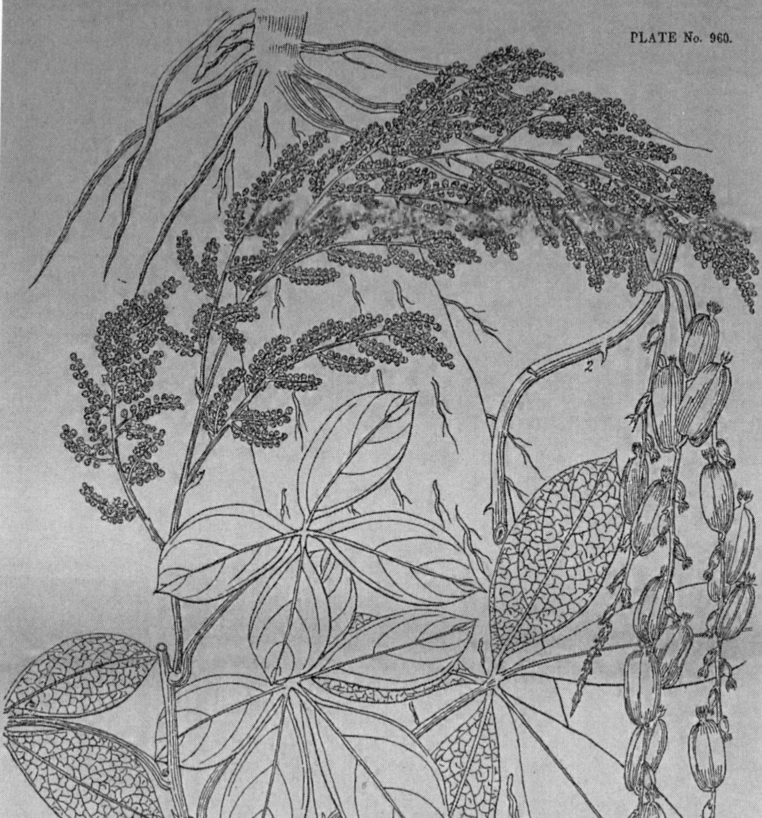

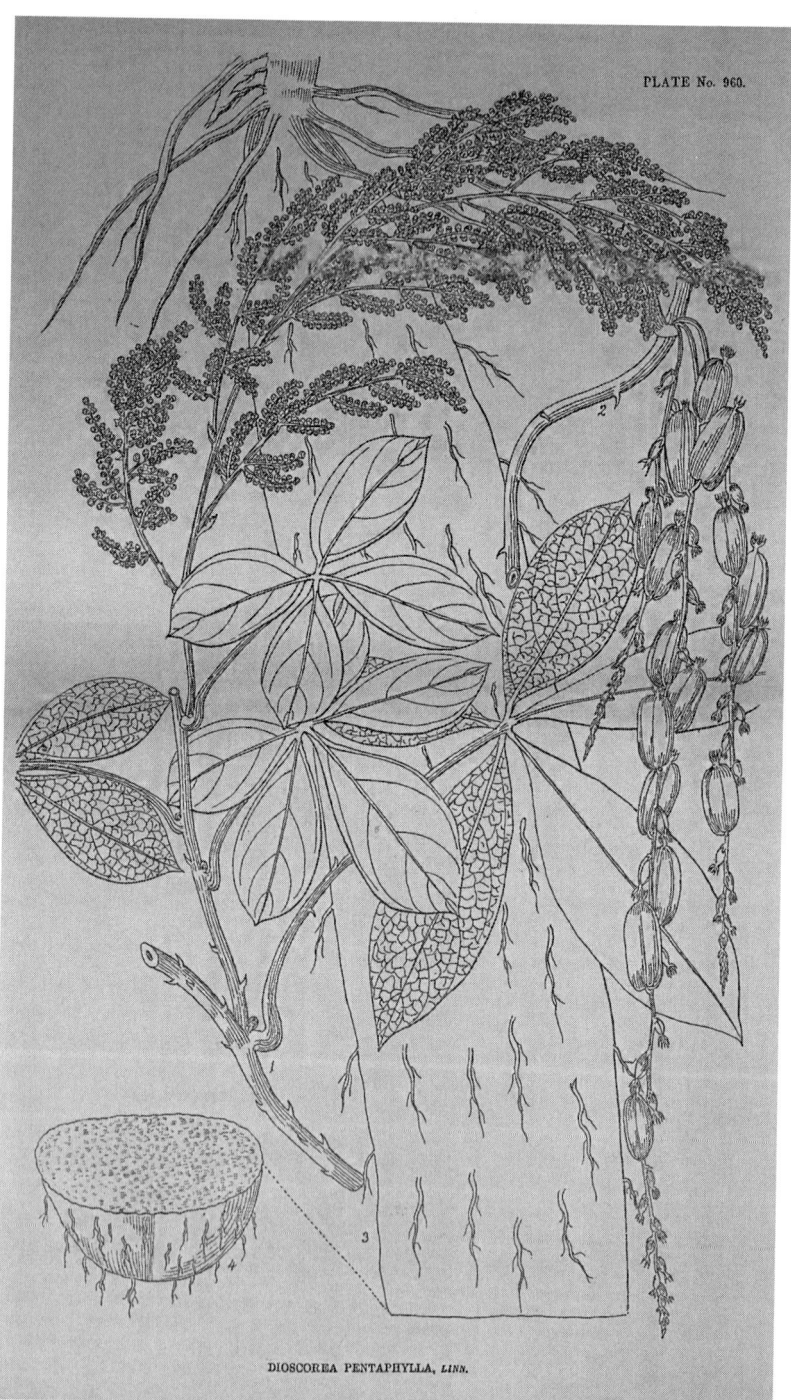

DIOSCOREA PENTAPHYLLA, *LINN.*

PLATE No. 961.

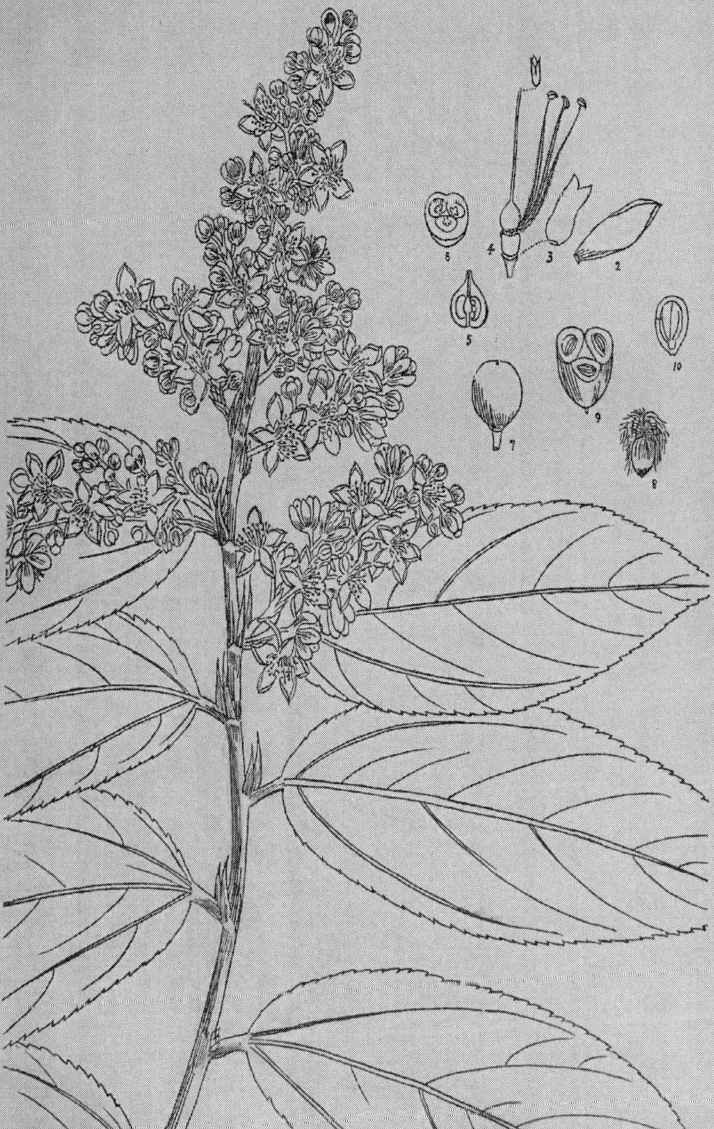

DIOSCOREA OPPOSITIFOLIA, LINN.

PLATE No. 962.

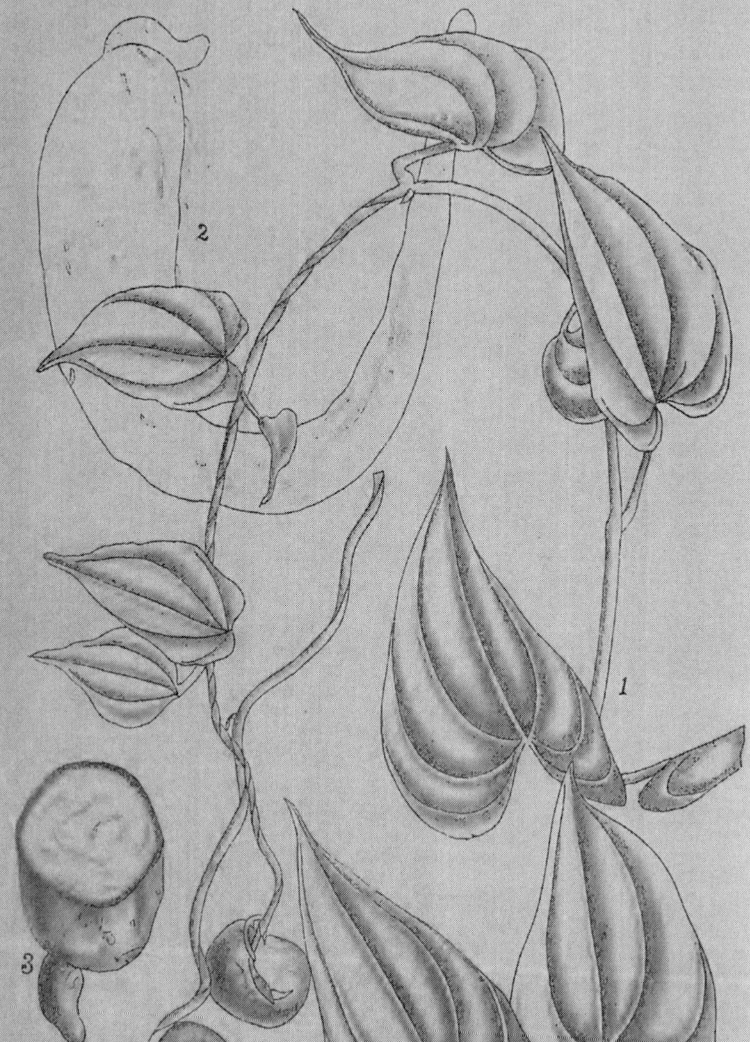

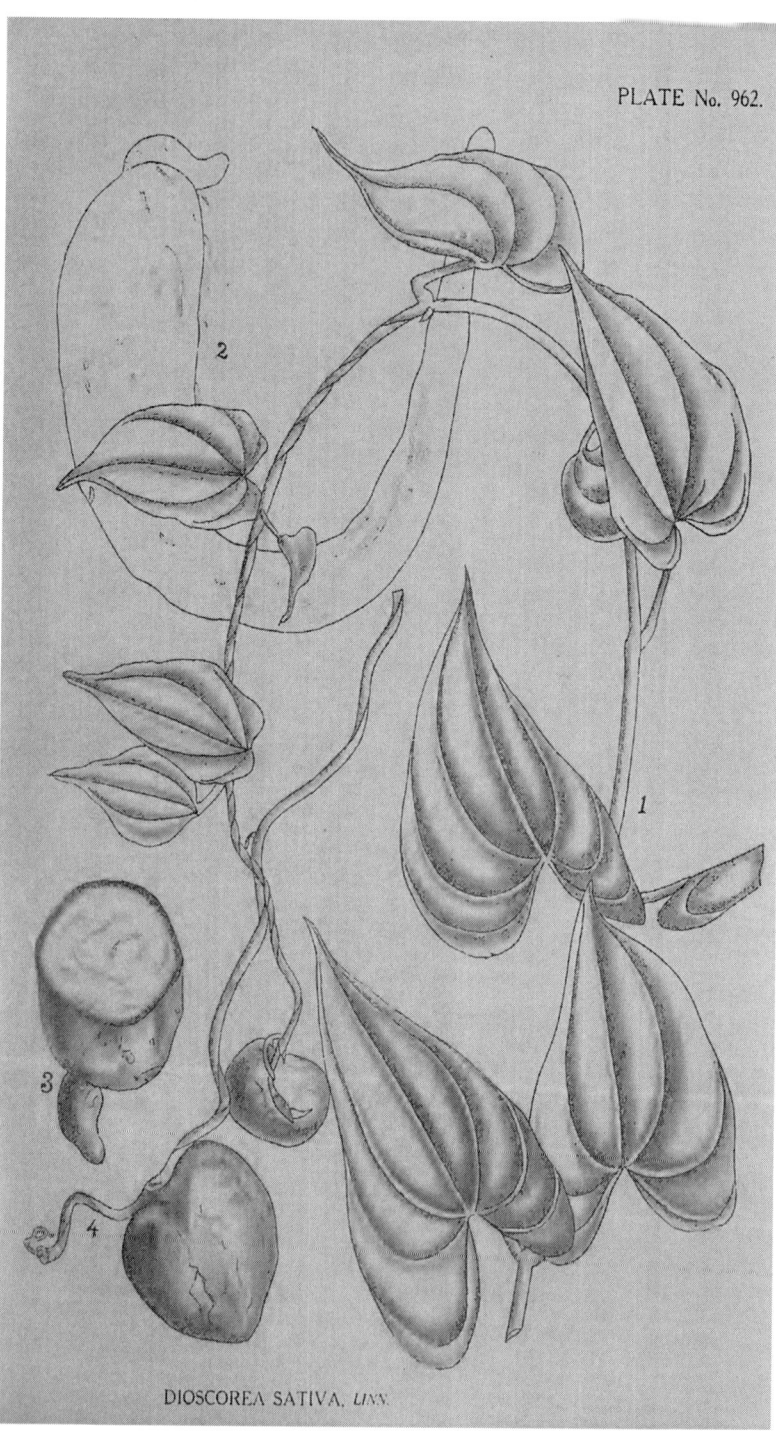

DIOSCOREA SATIVA, *LINN.*

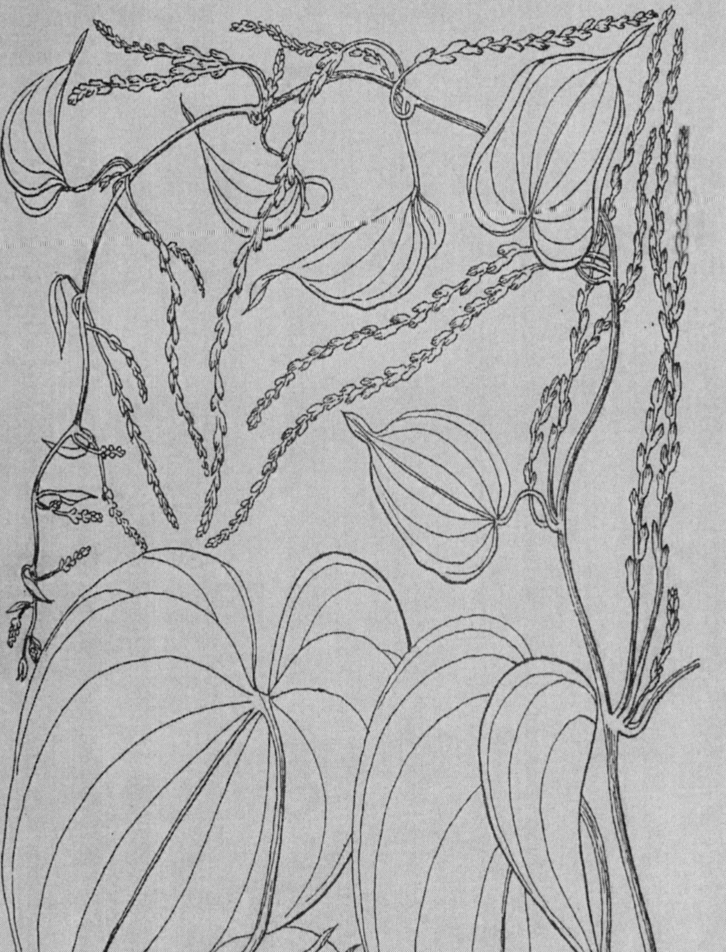

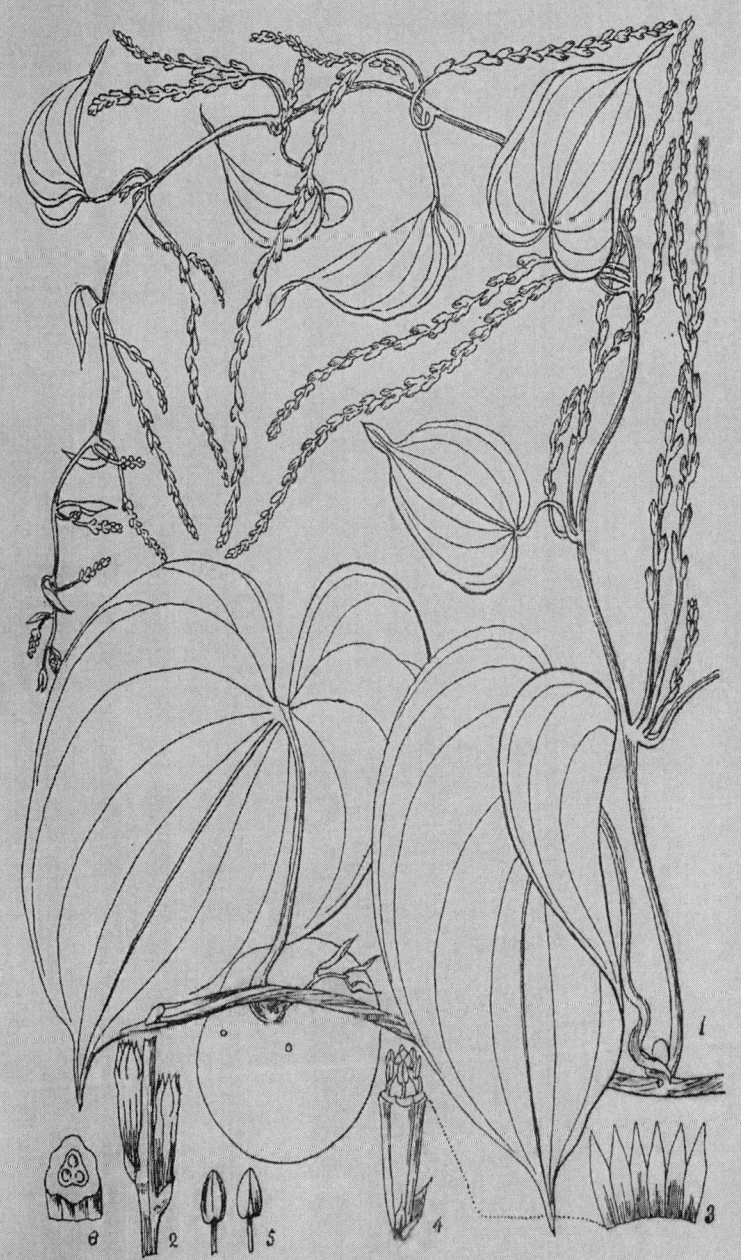

DIOSCOREA BULBIFERA, *Linn.*

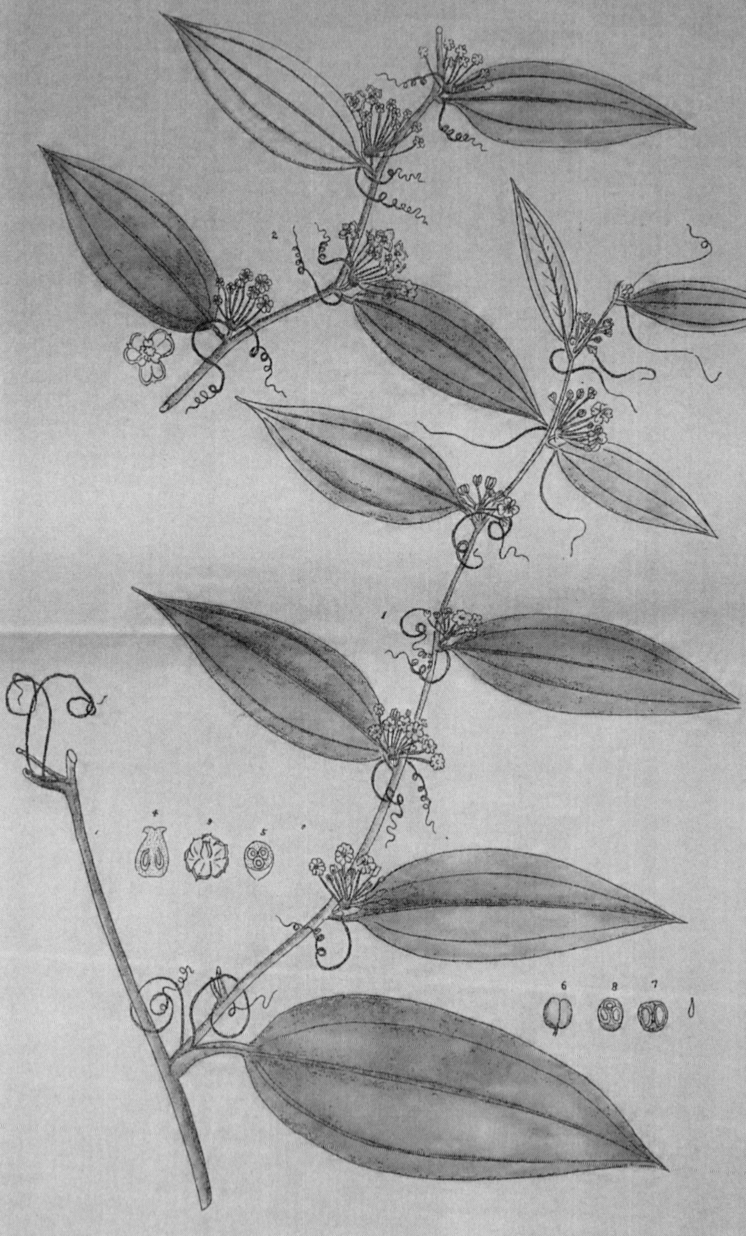

SMILAX GLABRA, ROXB.

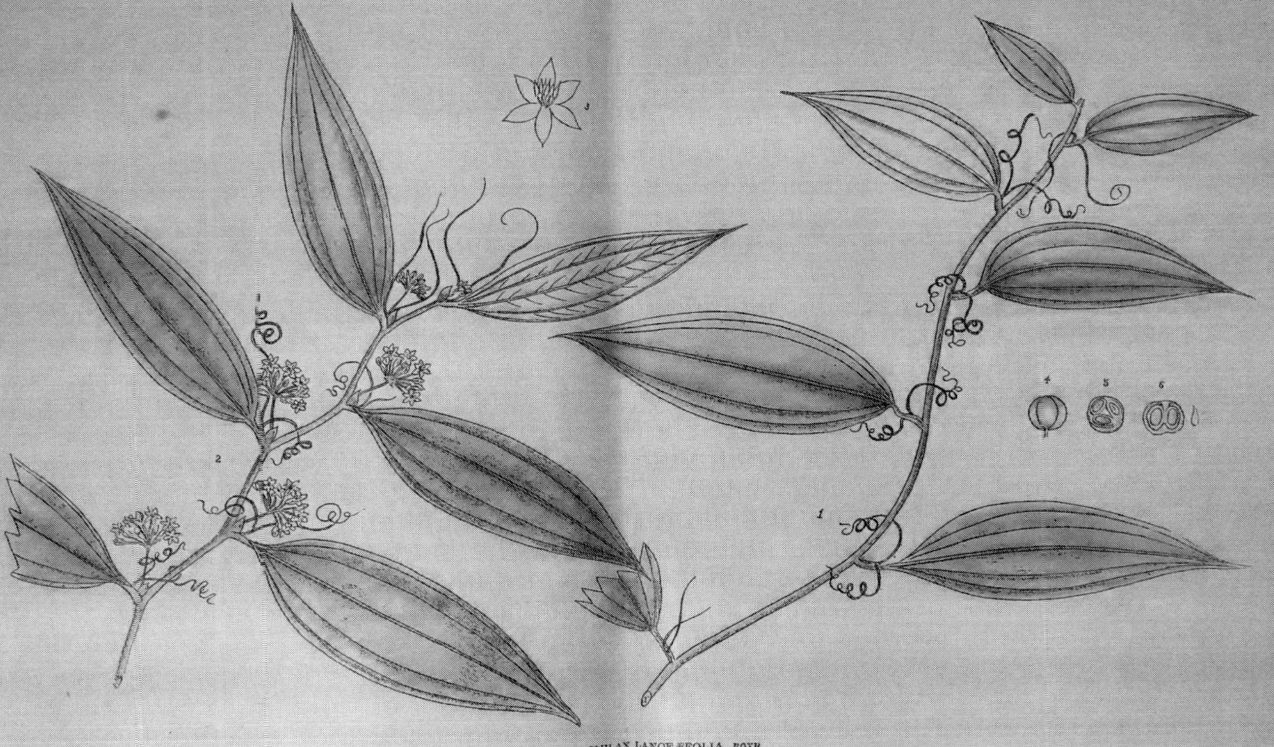

SMILAX LANCEÆFOLIA, *ROXB.*

PLATE No. 966.

SMILAX MACROPHYLLA, ROXB.

PLATE No. 967.

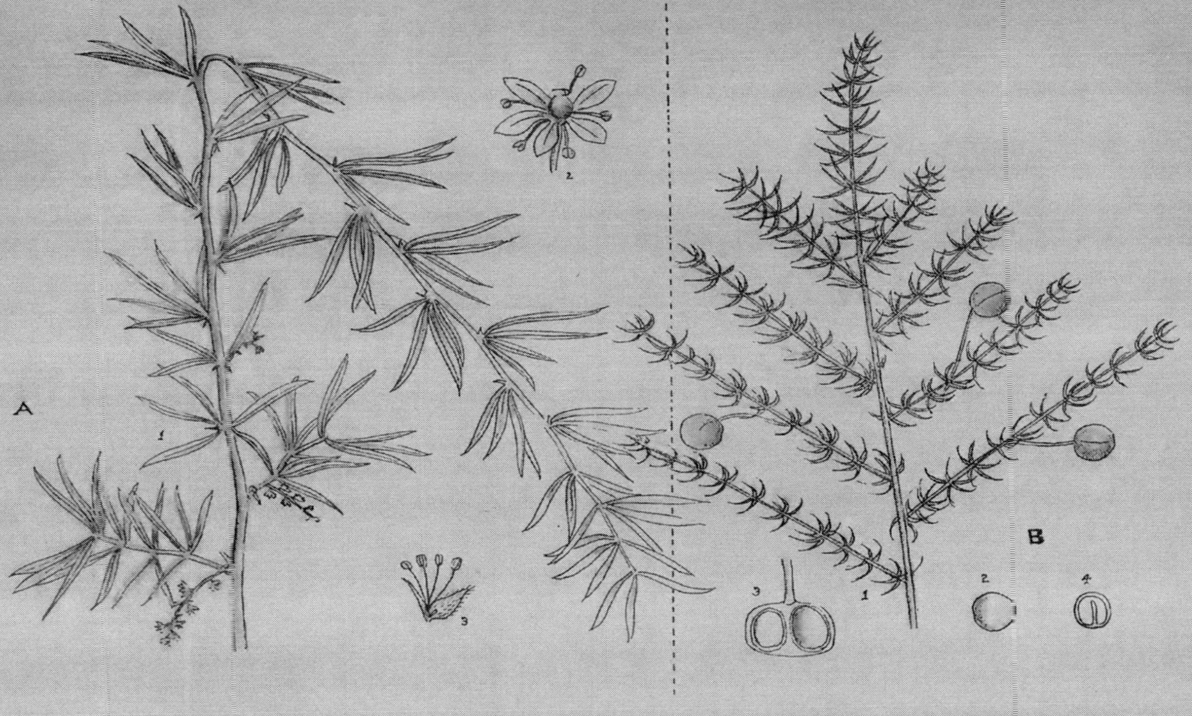

A- ASPARAGUS GONOCLADOS, *BAKER*　　　B—A. FILICINUS, *HAM.*

ASPARAGUS RACEMOSUS, WILLD.

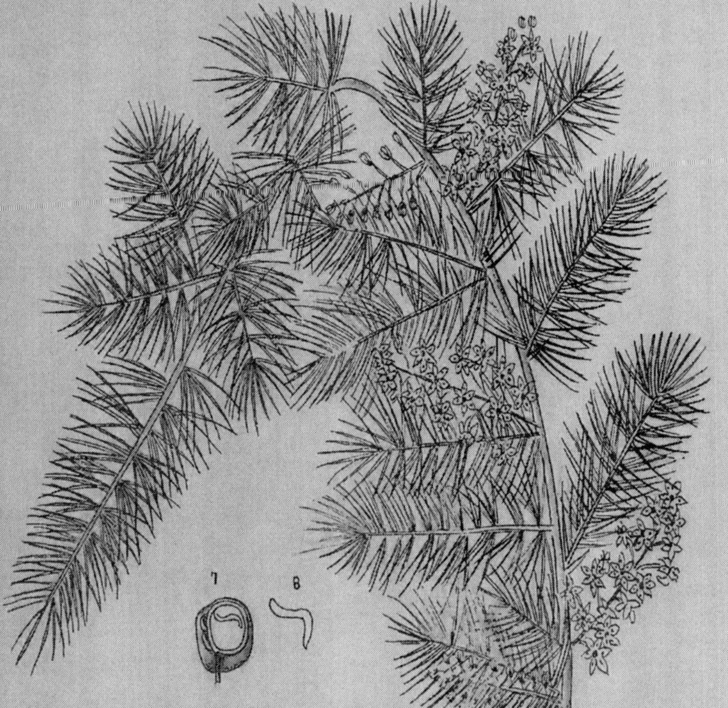

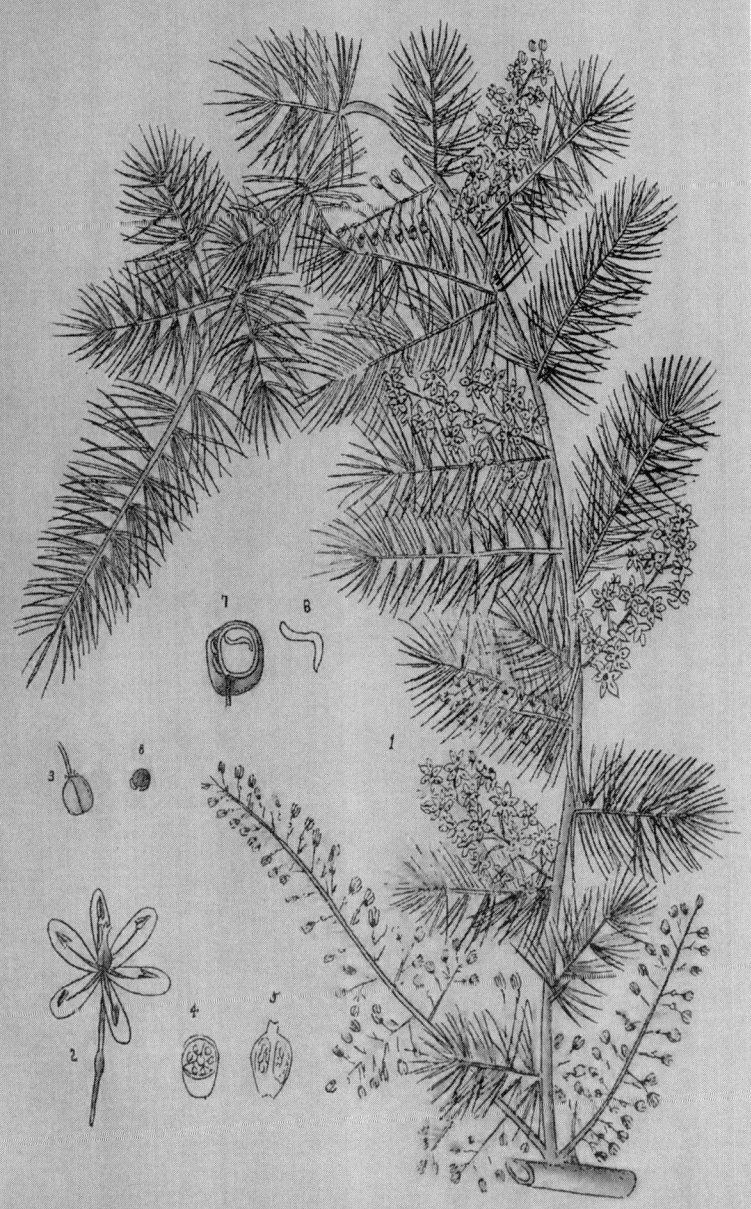

ASPARAGUS ADSCENDENS, *ROXB*

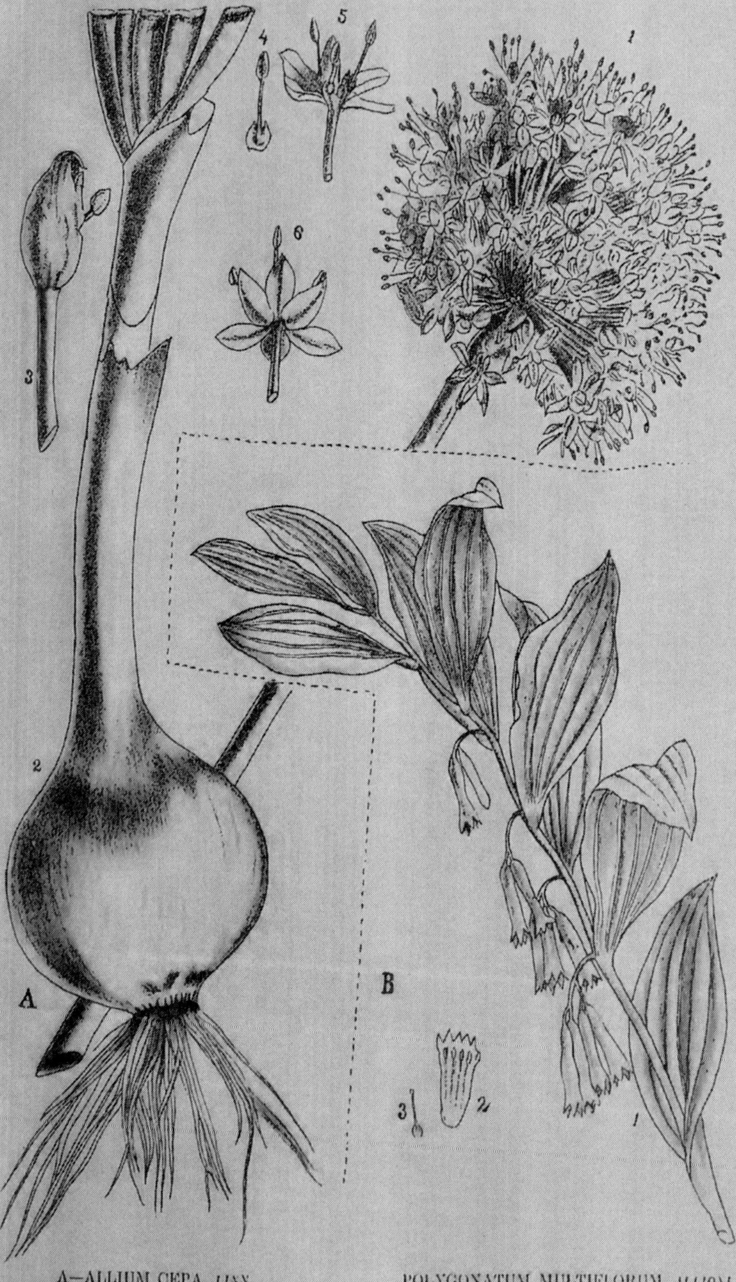

A—ALLIUM CEPA, *LINN.* POLYGONATUM MULTIFLORUM, *ALLIONI.*

PLATE No. 971.

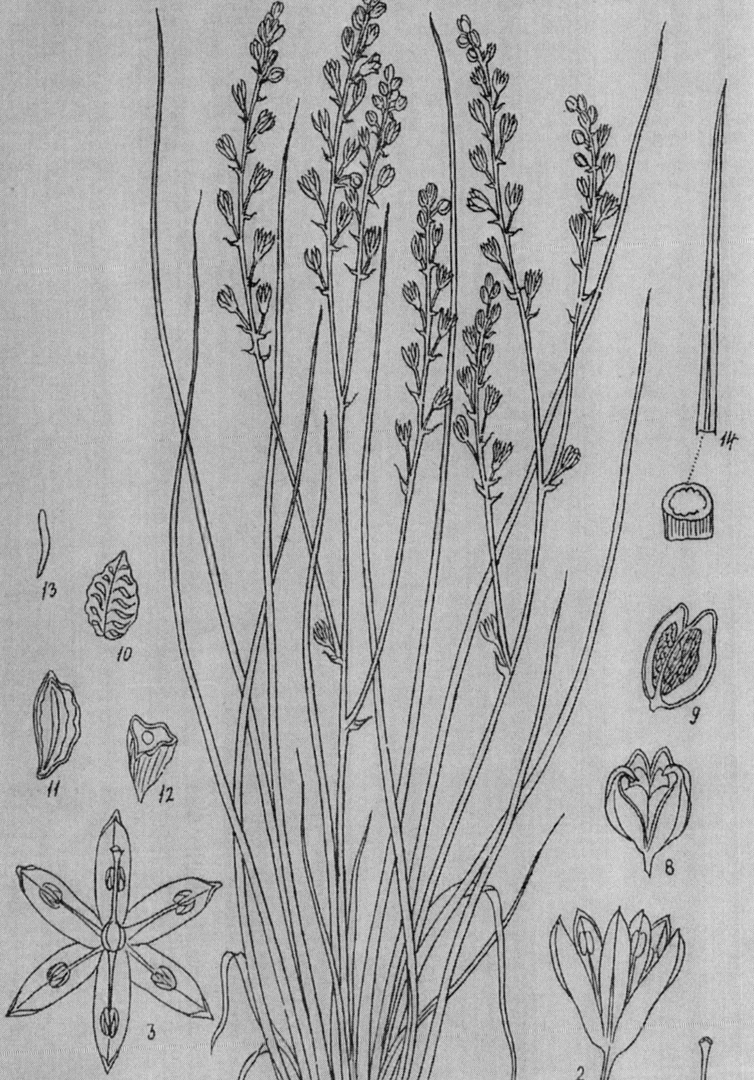

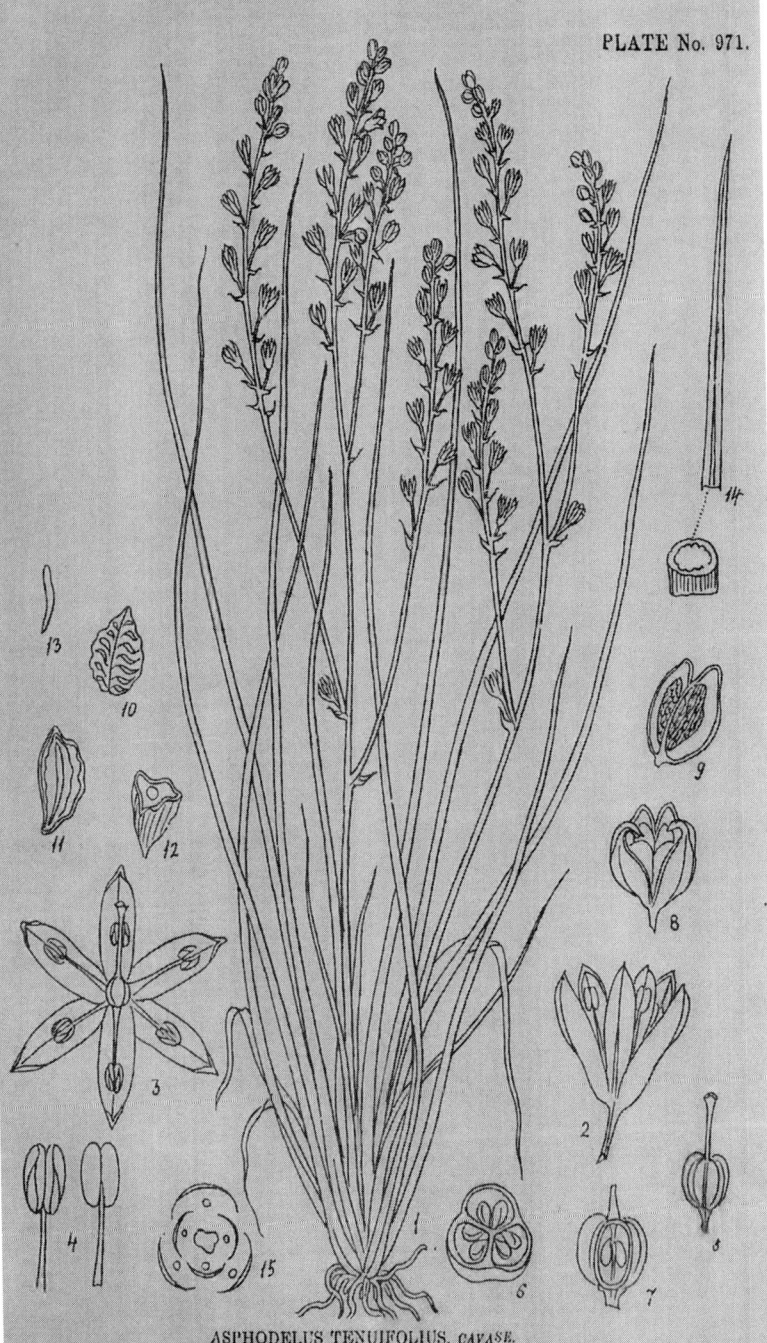

ASPHODELUS TENUIFOLIUS, *CAVASE.*

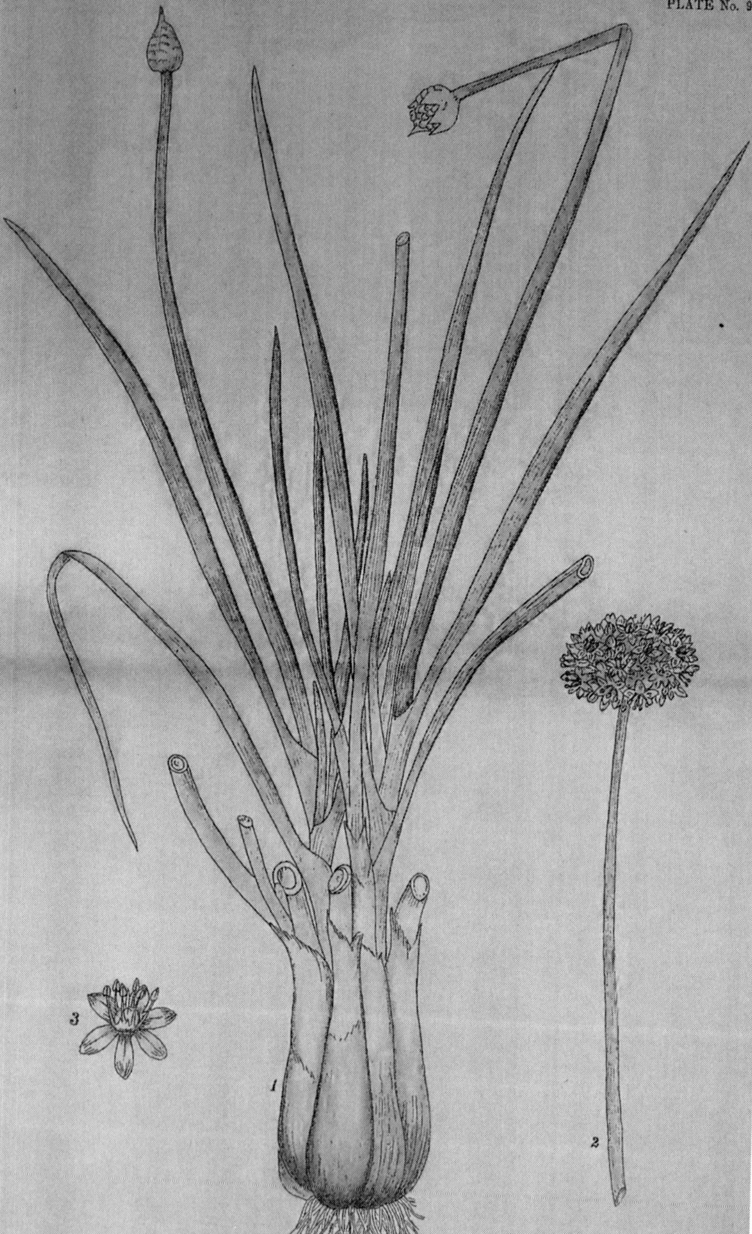

ALLIUM ASCALONICUM, *LINN.*

PLATE No. 973.

ALLIUM SATIVUM, *LINN.*

PLATE No. 974.

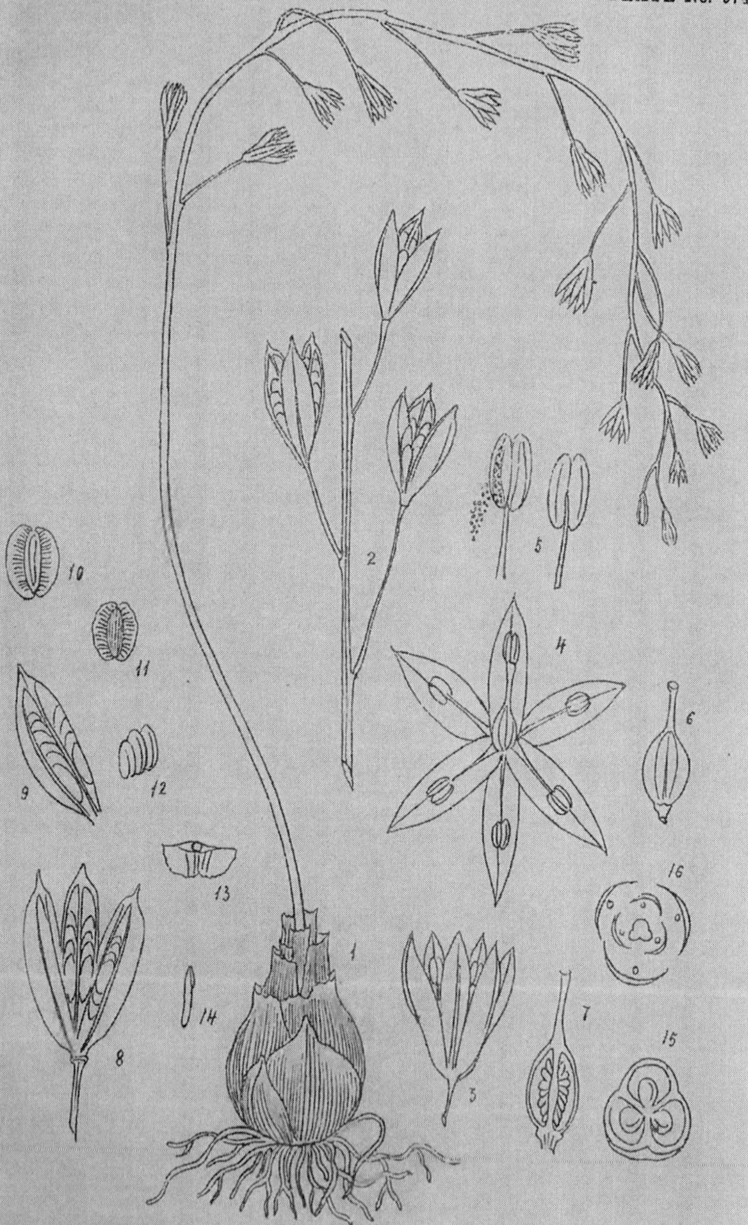

URGINEA INDICA, KUNTH

PLATE No. 975.

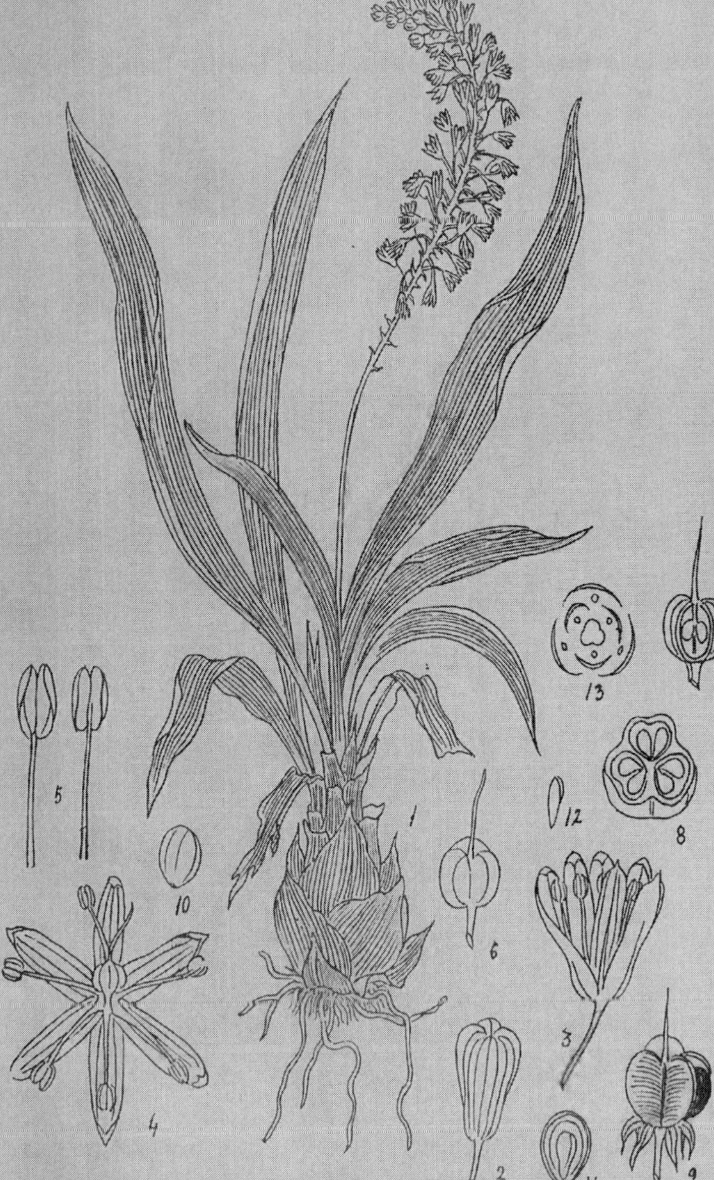

SCILLA INDICA, BAKER

PLATE No. 976.

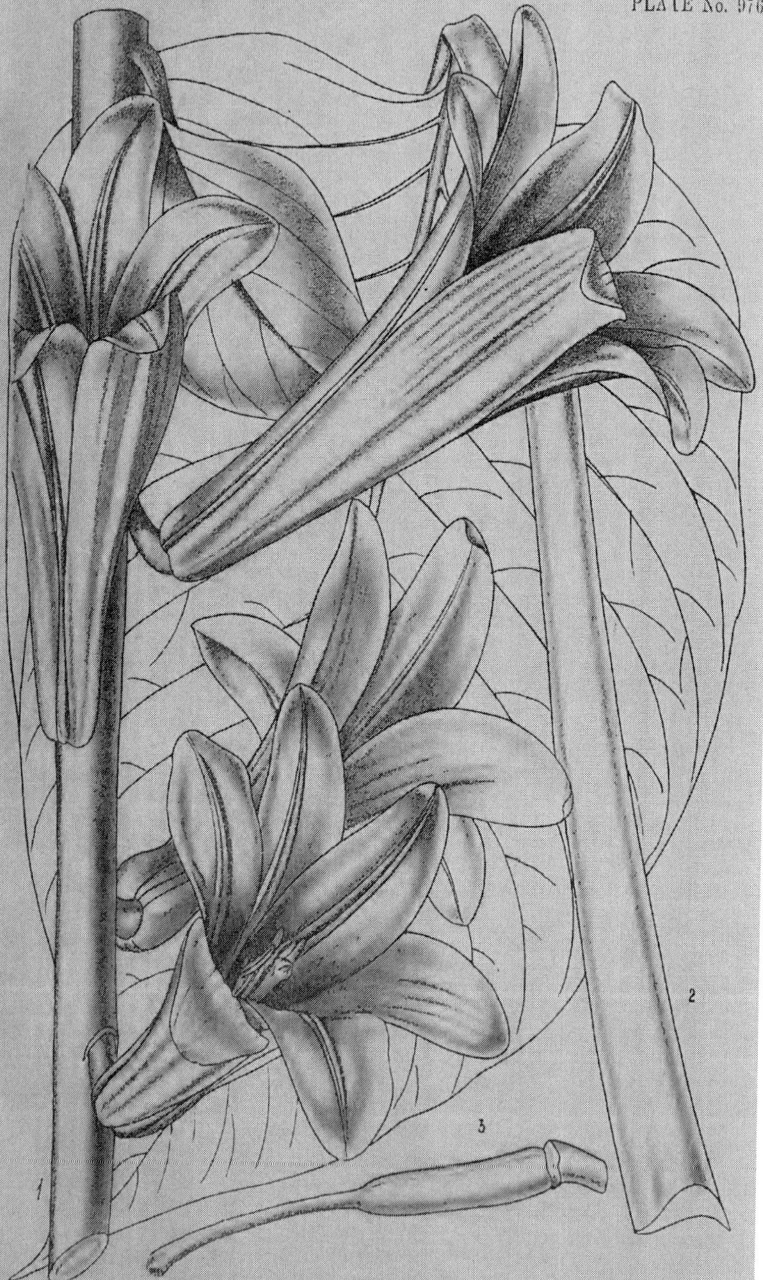

LILIUM GIGANTEUM, *WALL.*

LILIUM WALLICHIANUM, *SCHULTES F.*

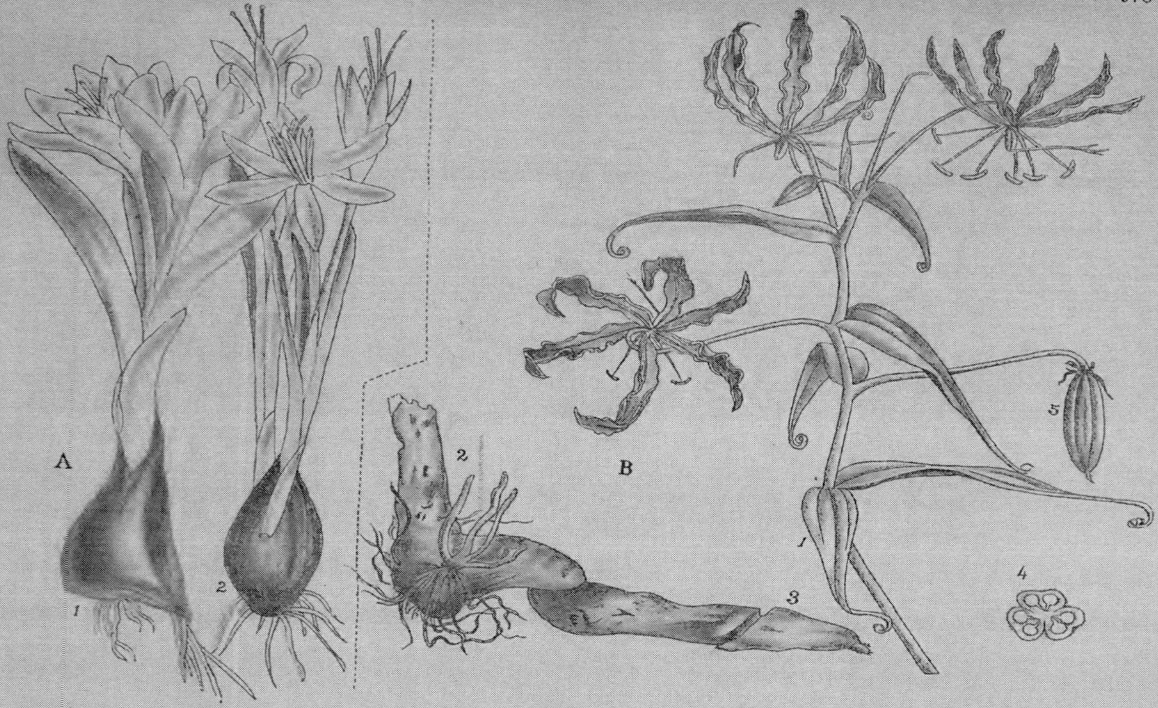

A—COLCHICUM LUTEUM, *BAKER.*   B—GLORIOSA SUPERBA, *LINN.*

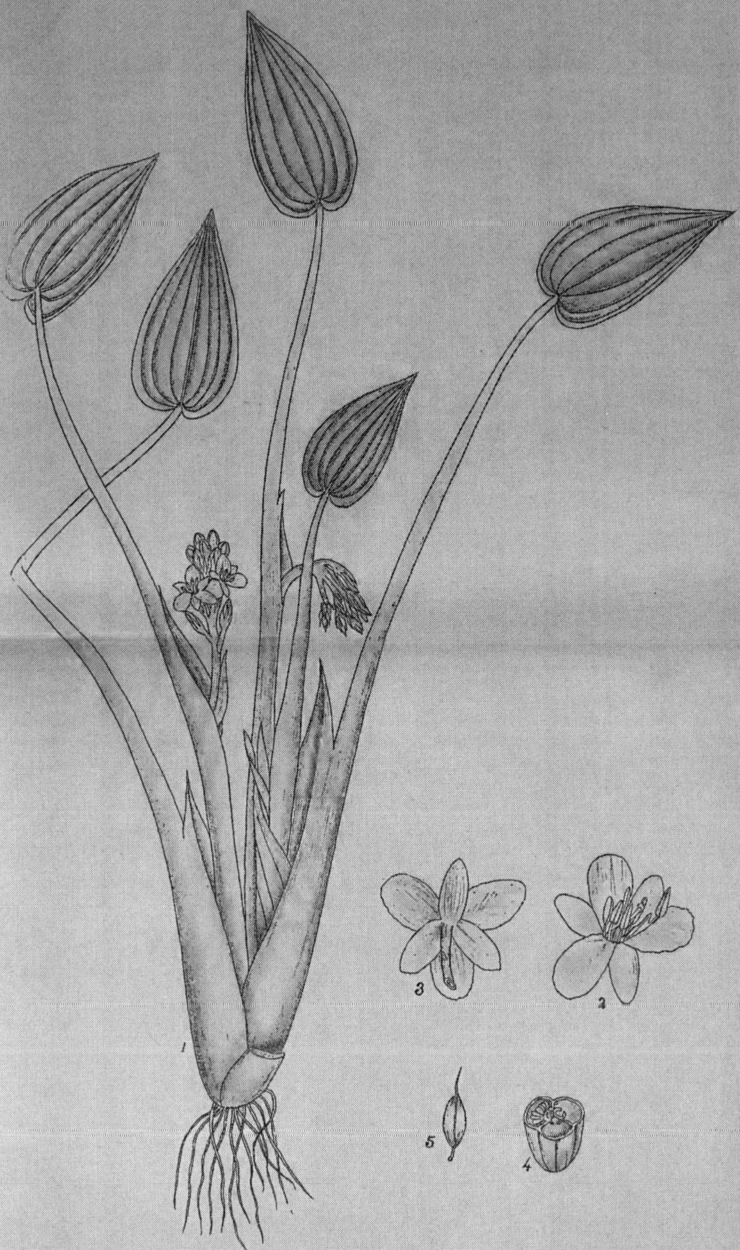

MONOCHORIA VAGINALIS, *PRESL.*

PLATE No. 980.

XYRIS INDICA, *Linn.*

PLATE No. 981.

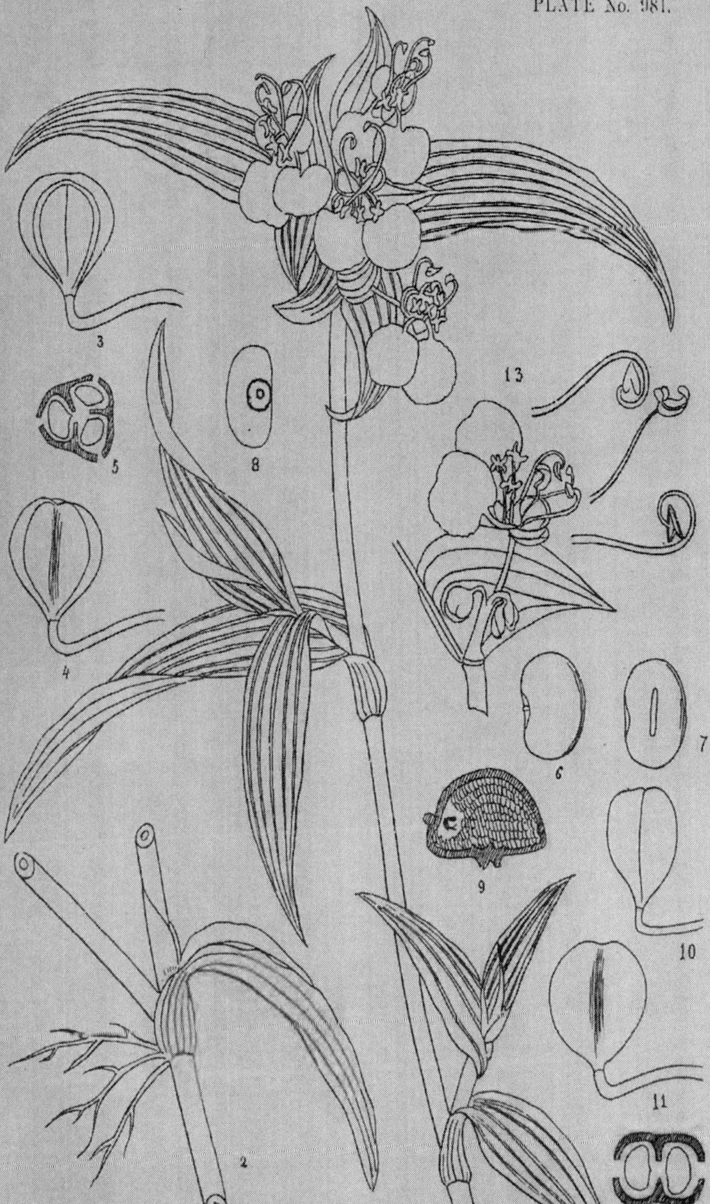

COMMELINA OBLIQUA, *HAM.*

PLATE No. 982.

COMMELINA SUFFRUTICOSA, BLUME.

PLATE No. 983.

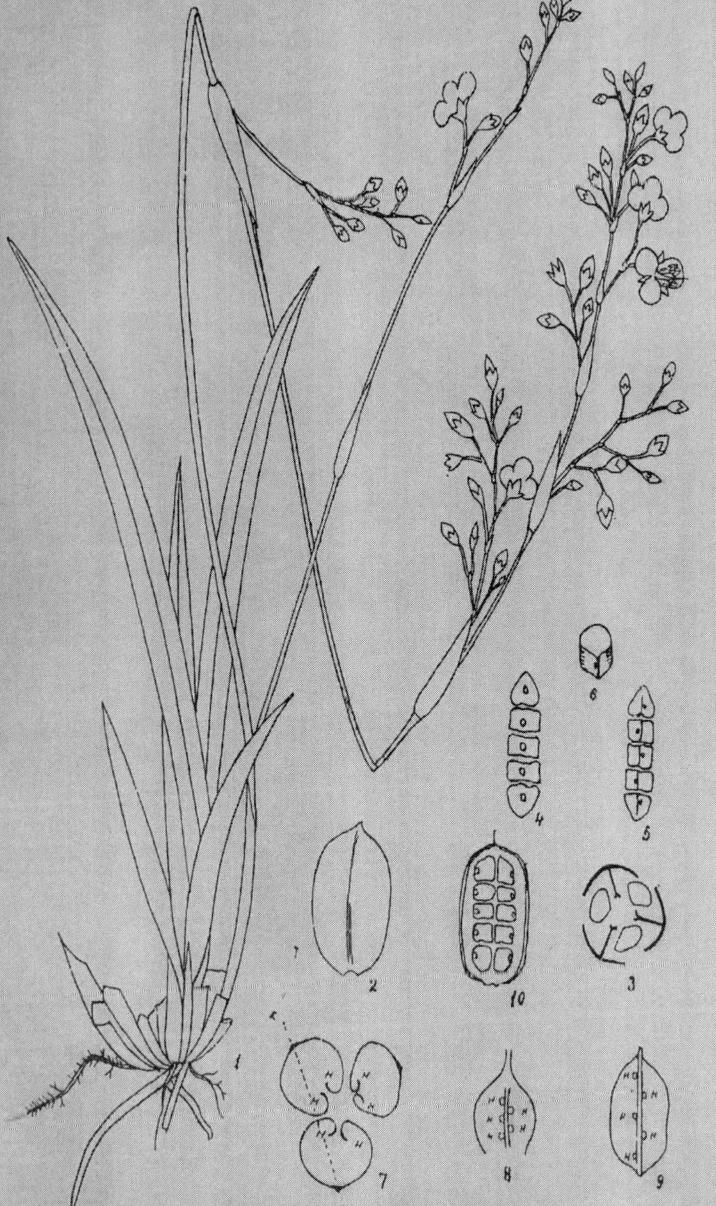

ANEILEMA SCAPIFLORUM, *Wight*.

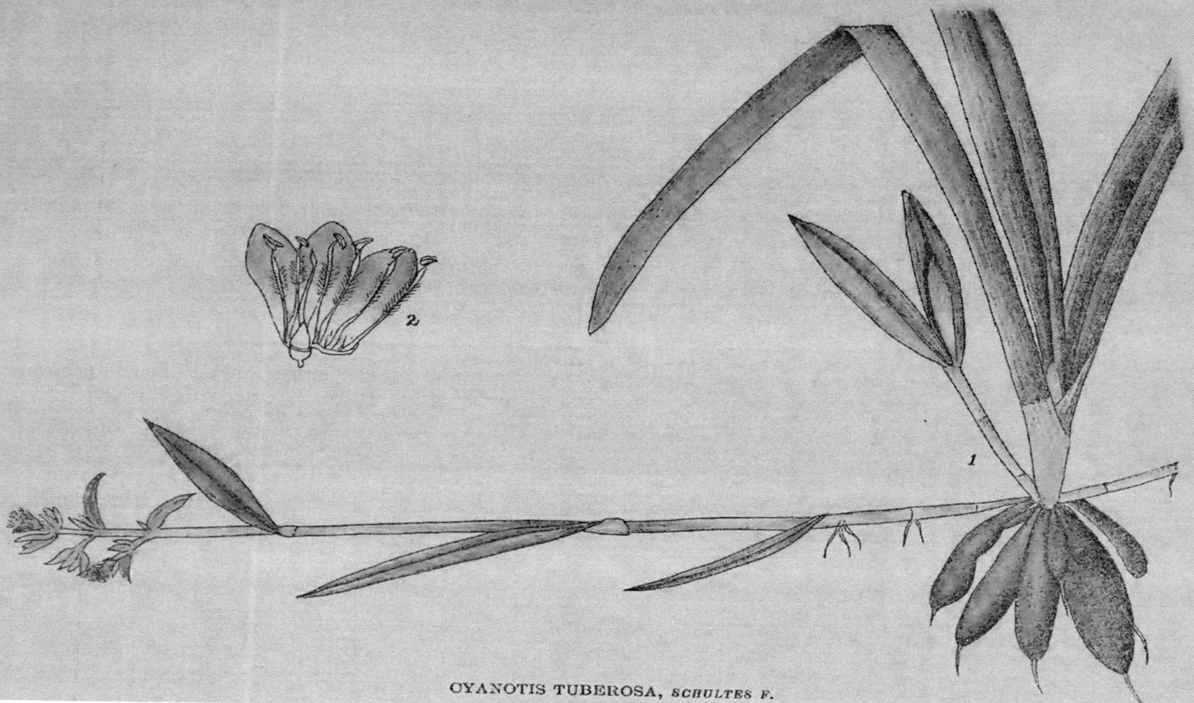

CYANOTIS TUBEROSA, *SCHULTES F.*

PLATE No. 985

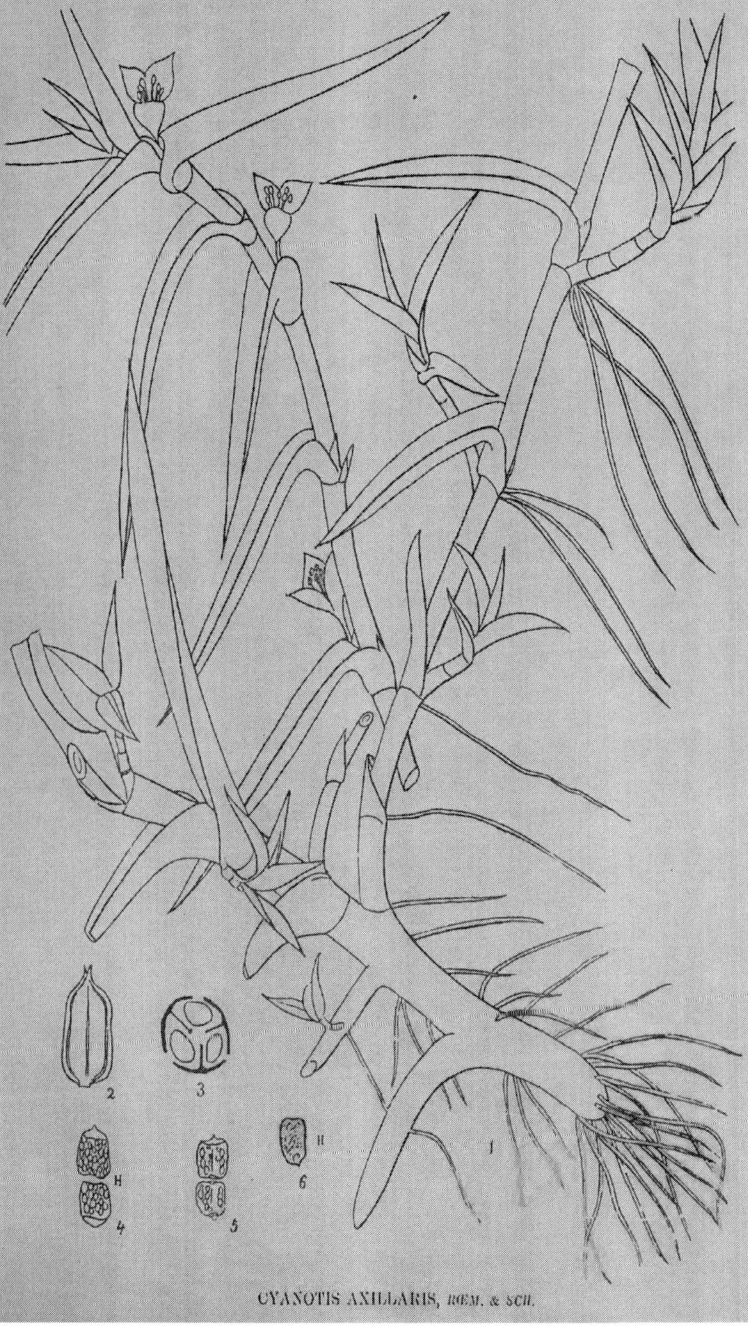

CYANOTIS AXILLARIS, ROEM. & SCH.

PLATE No 980

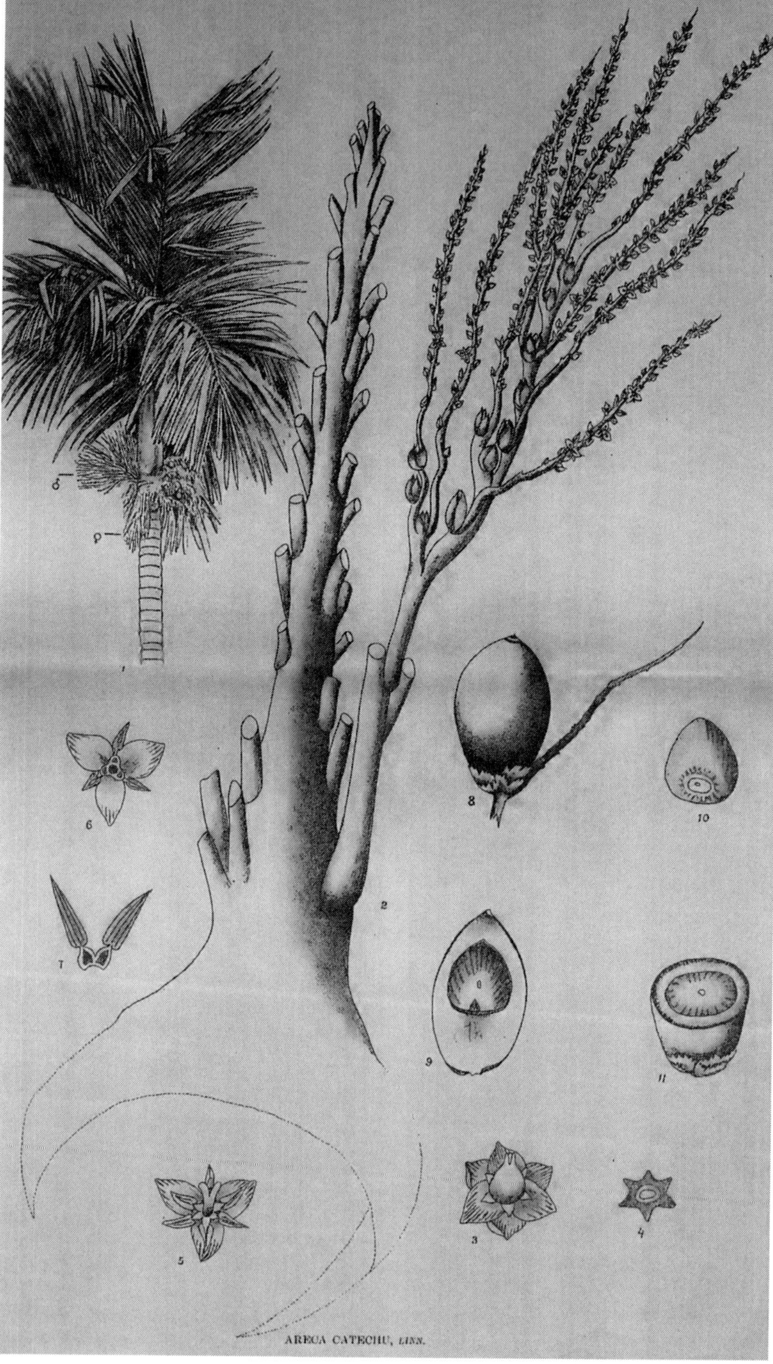

AREGA CATECHU, *LINN.*

PLATE No. 986A.

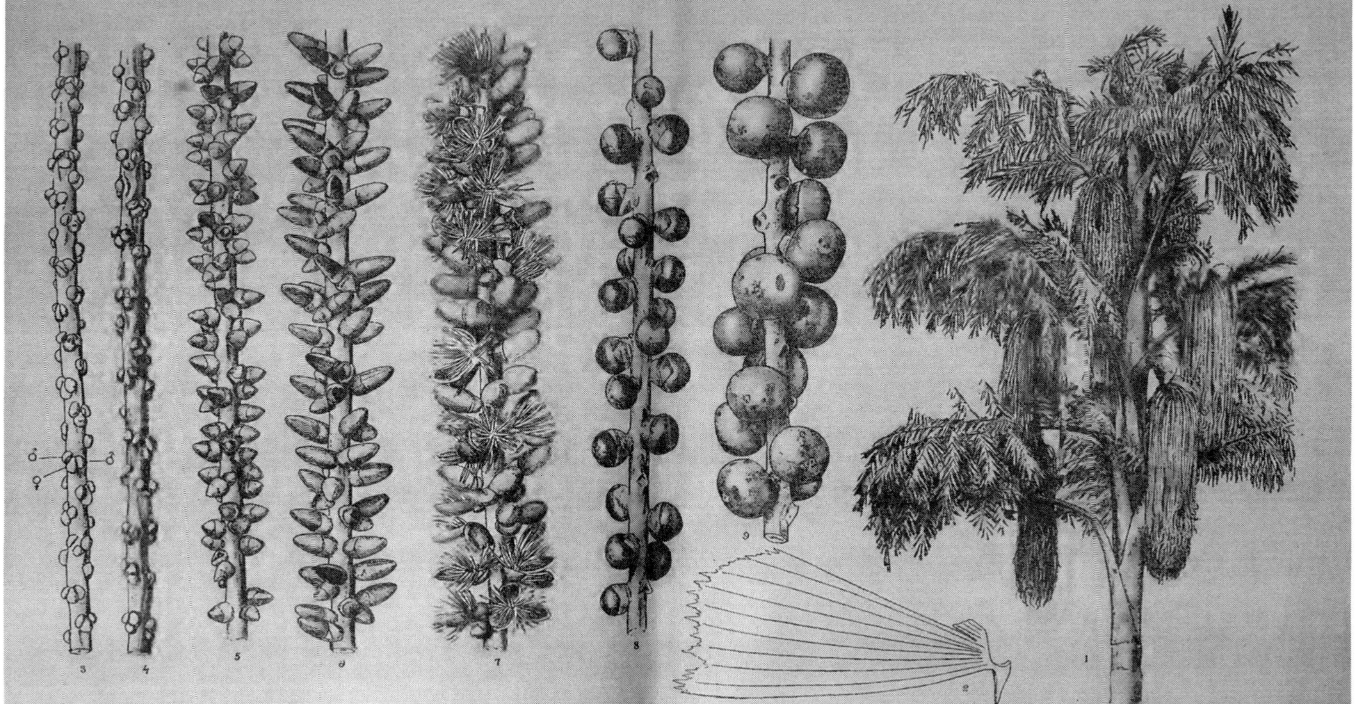

CARYOTA URENS, LINN.

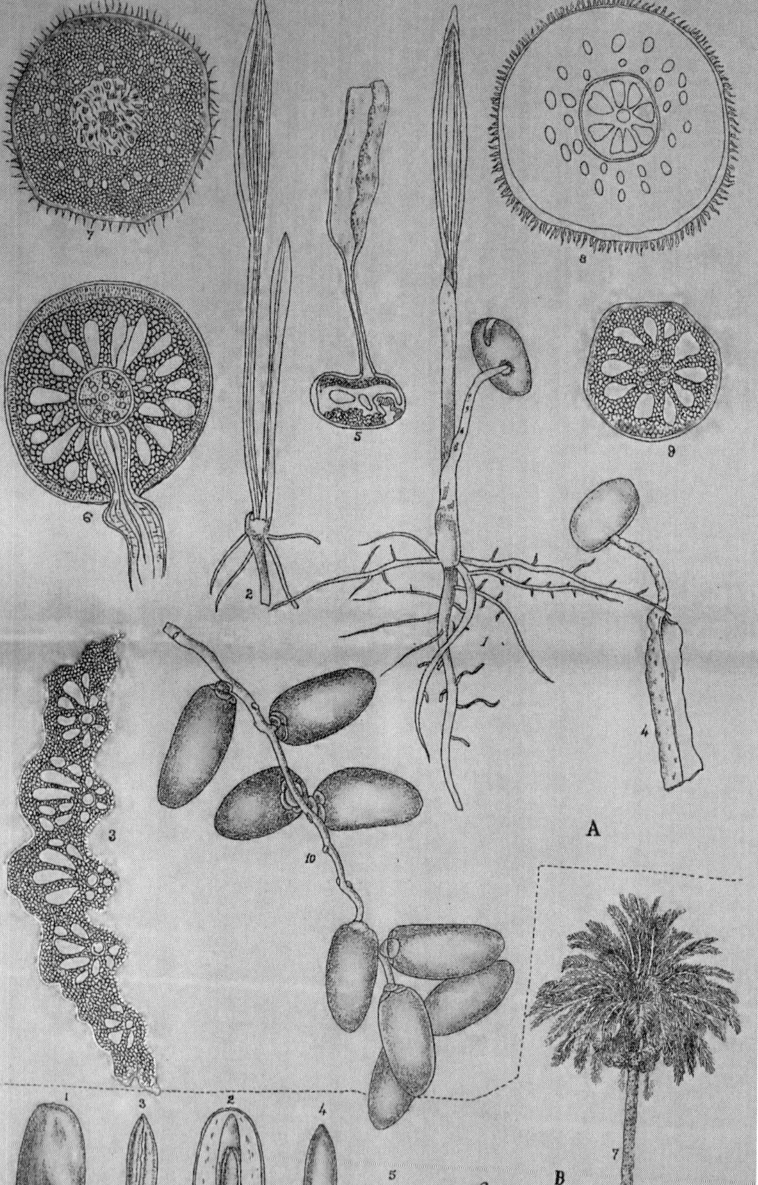

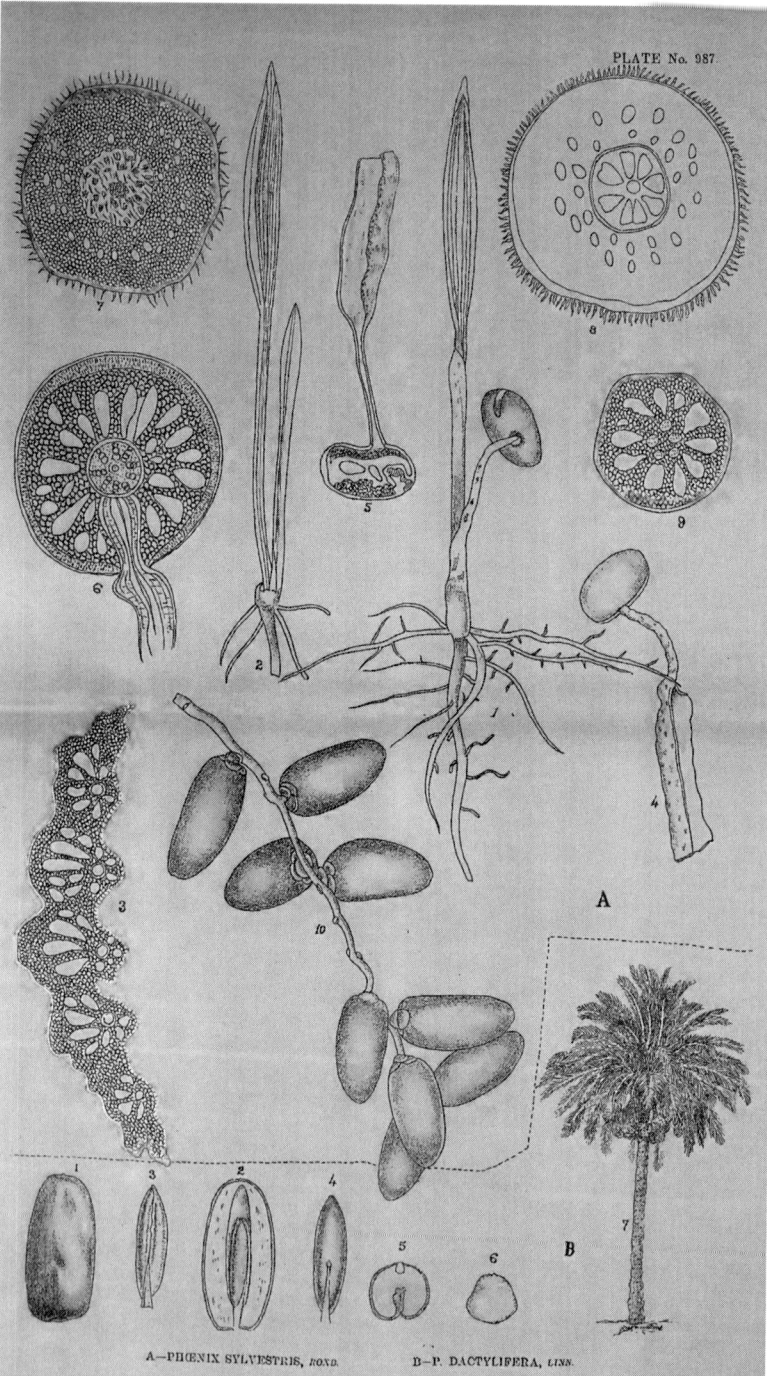

A—PHŒNIX SYLVESTRIS, *ROXB.*   B—P. DACTYLIFERA, *LINN.*

PLATE No. 988.

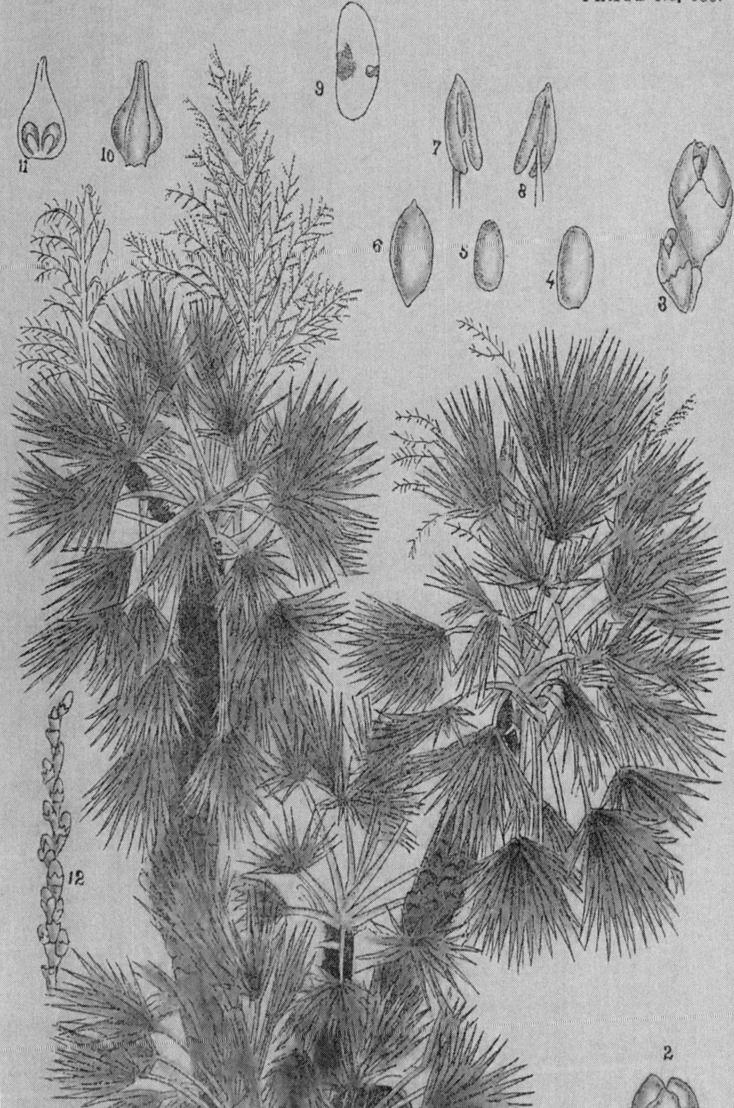

NANNORHOPS RITCHCINA, *H. Wdl.*

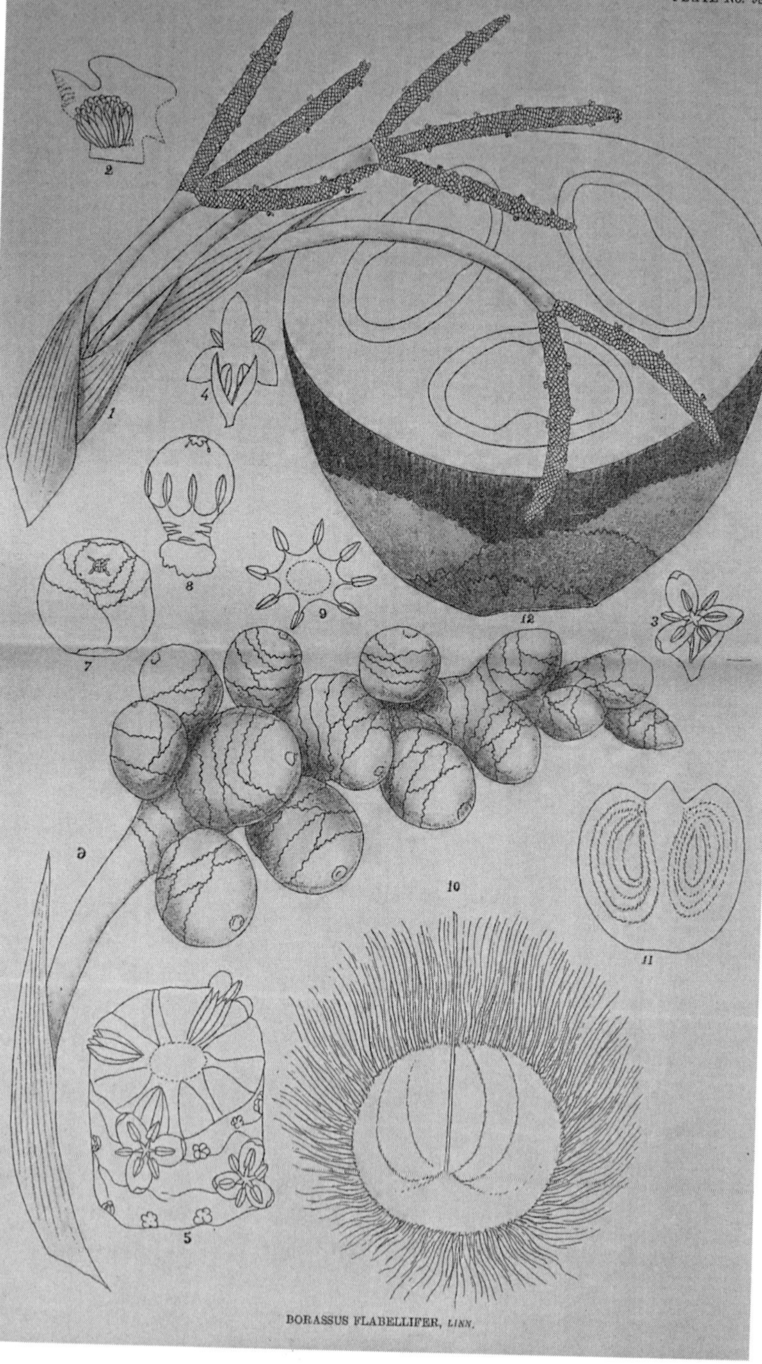

BORASSUS FLABELLIFER, *LINN.*

PLATE No. 990.

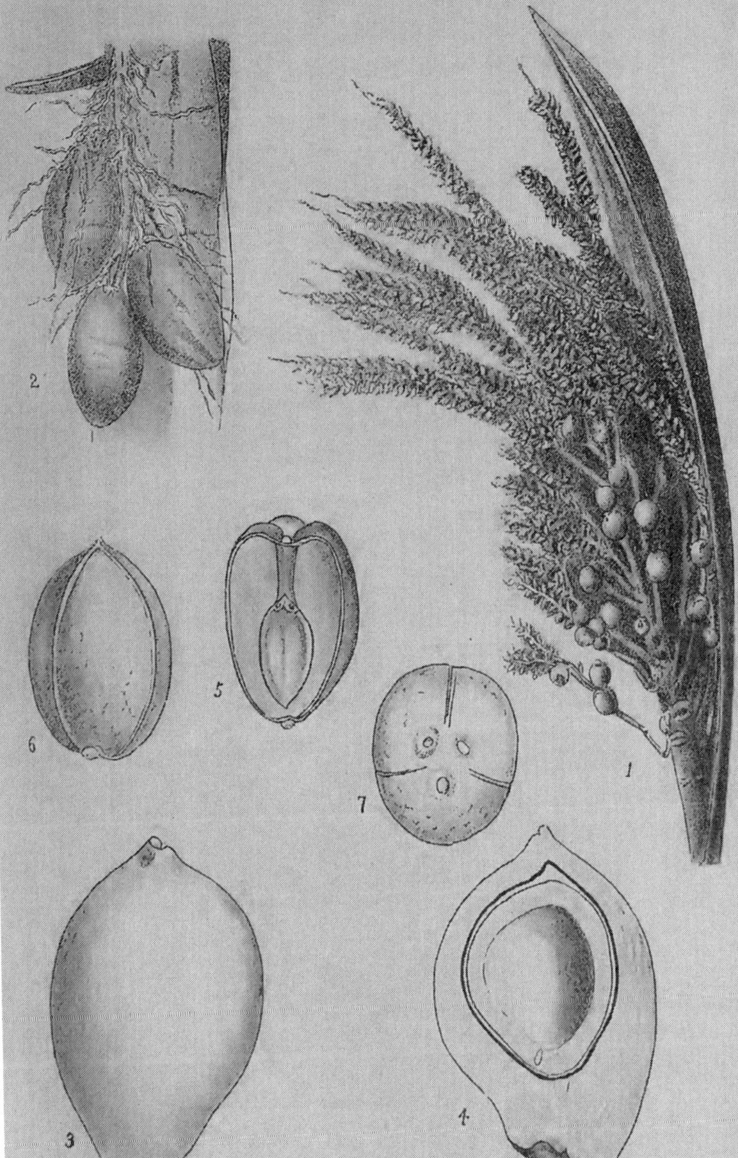

COCOS NUCIFERA, *LINN.*

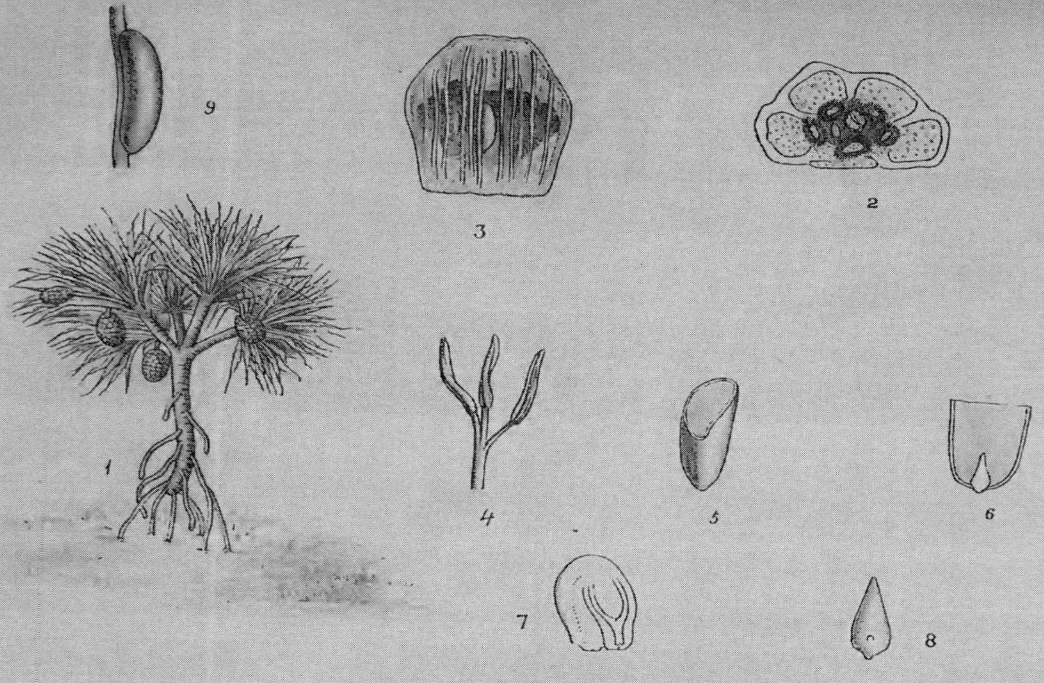

PANDANUS FASCICULARIS, LAM.

PLATE No. 992.

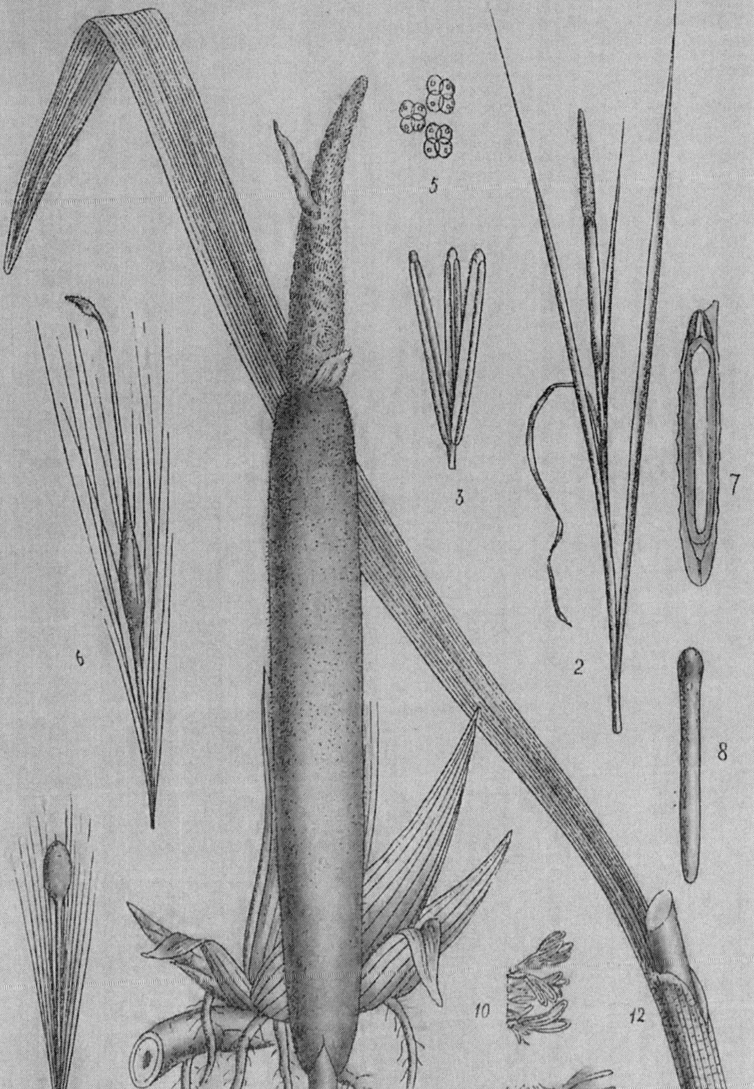

TYPHA ELEPHANTINA, ROXB

PLATE No. 993.

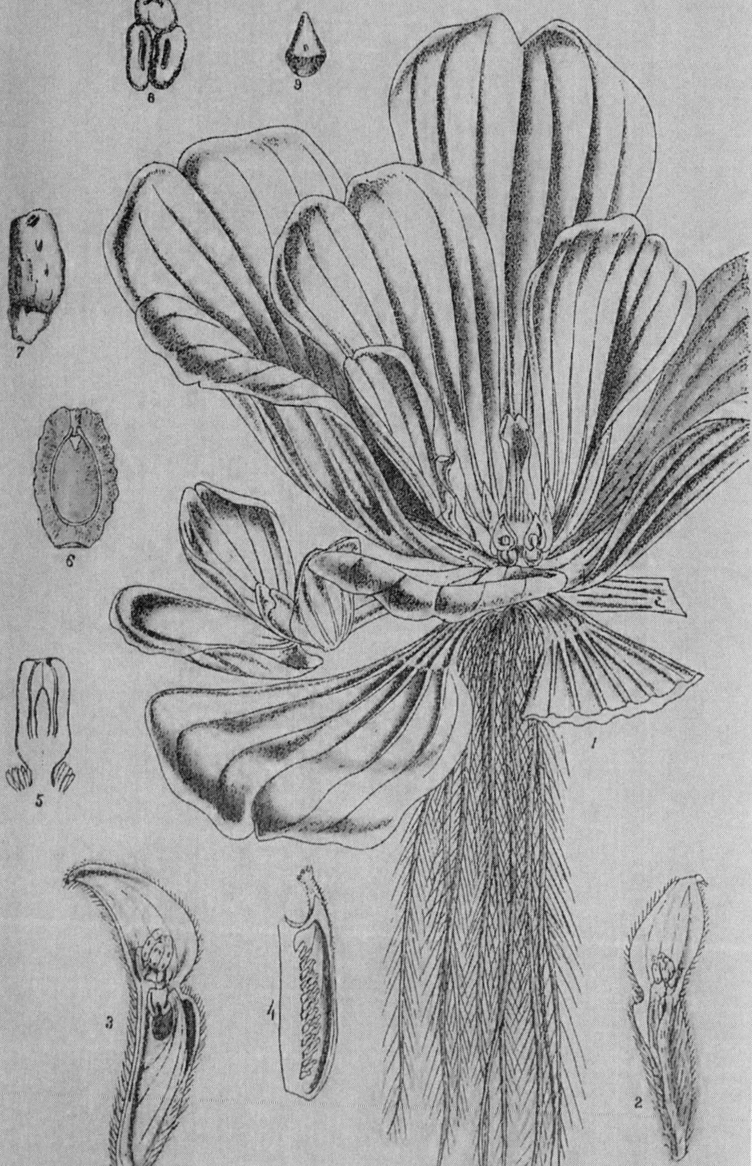

PISTIA STRATIOTES, LINN.

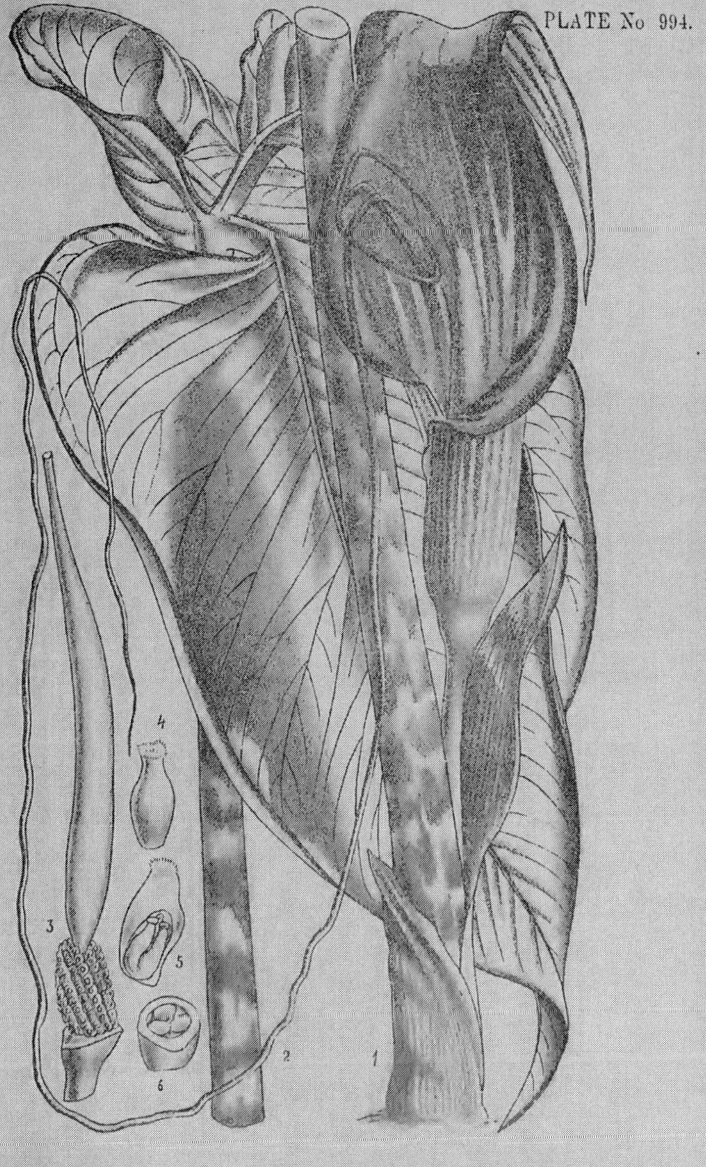

ARISÆMA SPECIOSUM, *MART.*

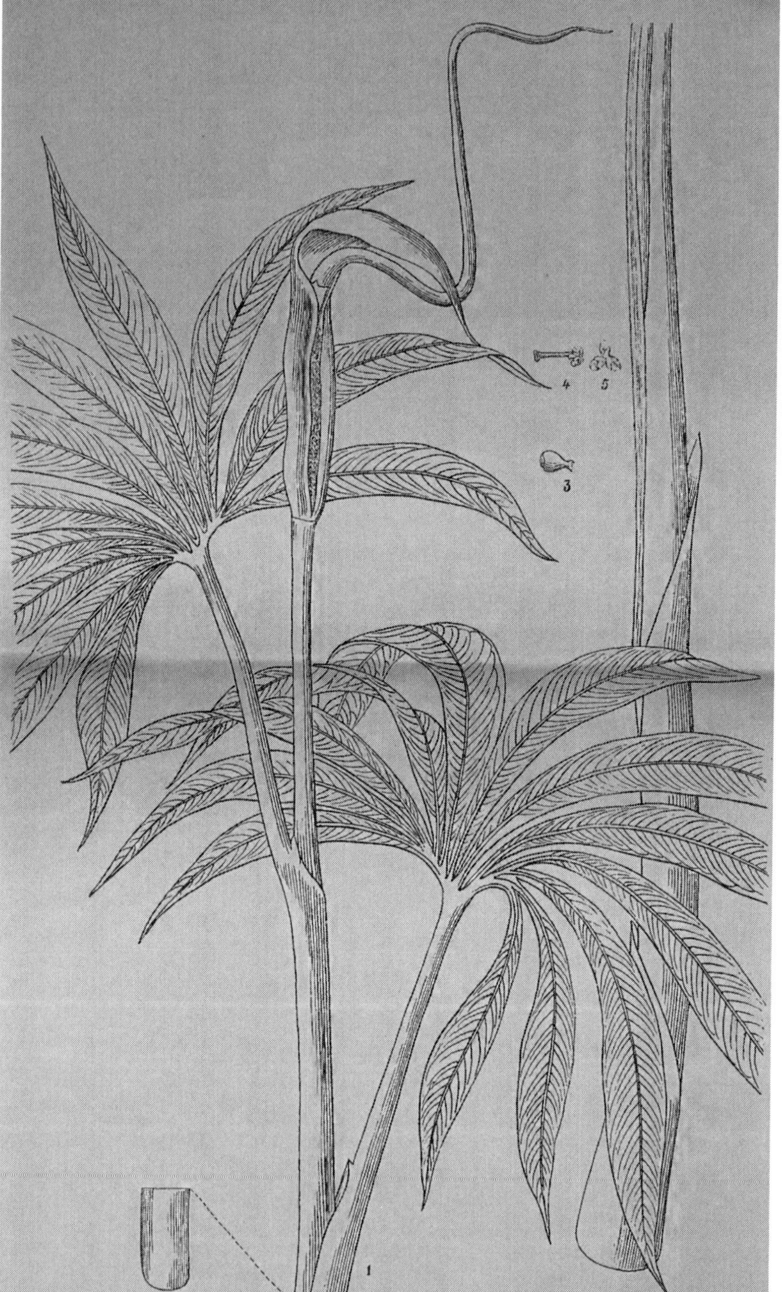

ARISÆMA TORTUOSUM, *SCHOTT.*

PLATE No 996.

ARISÆMA LESCHENAULTII, *BLUME.*

SAUROMATUM GUTTATUM, *SCHOTT.*

PLATE No. 998.

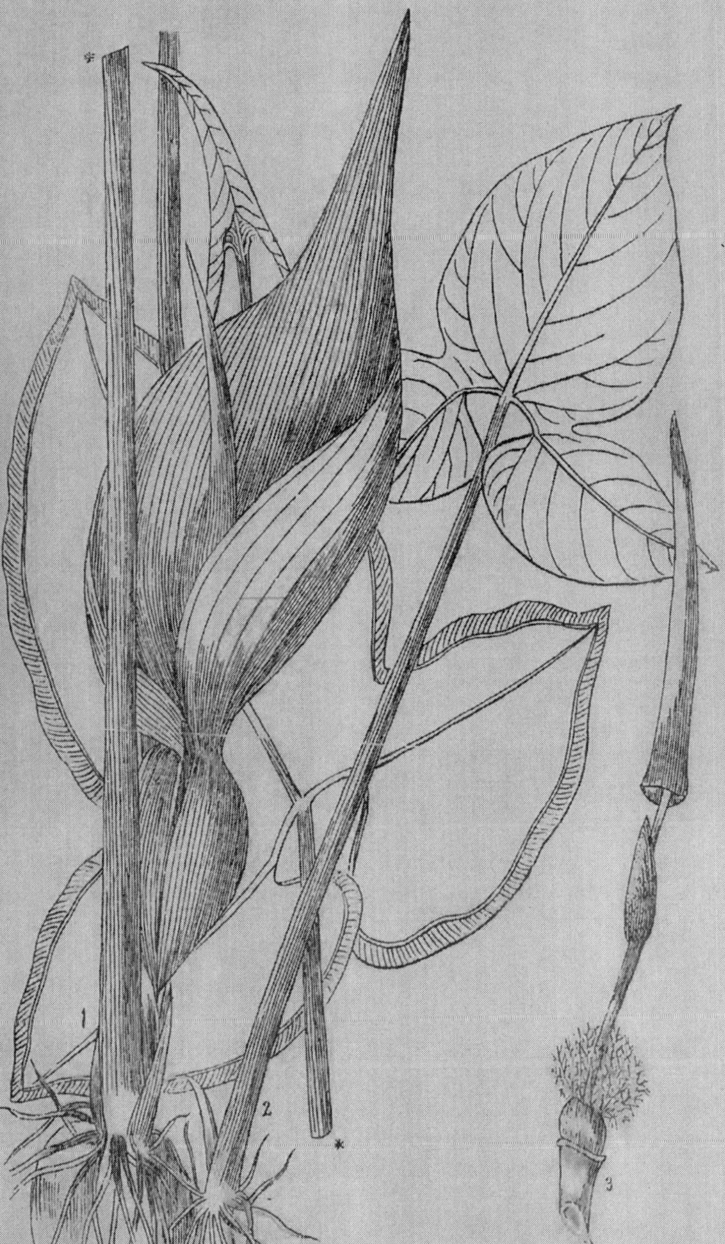

TYPHONIUM TRILOBATUM, *SCHOTT.*

PLATE No. 999.

AMORPHOPHALLUS CAMPANULATUS, *Blume.*

PLATE No. 1000

SYNANTHERIAS SYLVATICA, SCHOTT.

PLESMONIUM MARGARITIFERUM, SCHOTT.

PLATE No. 1002

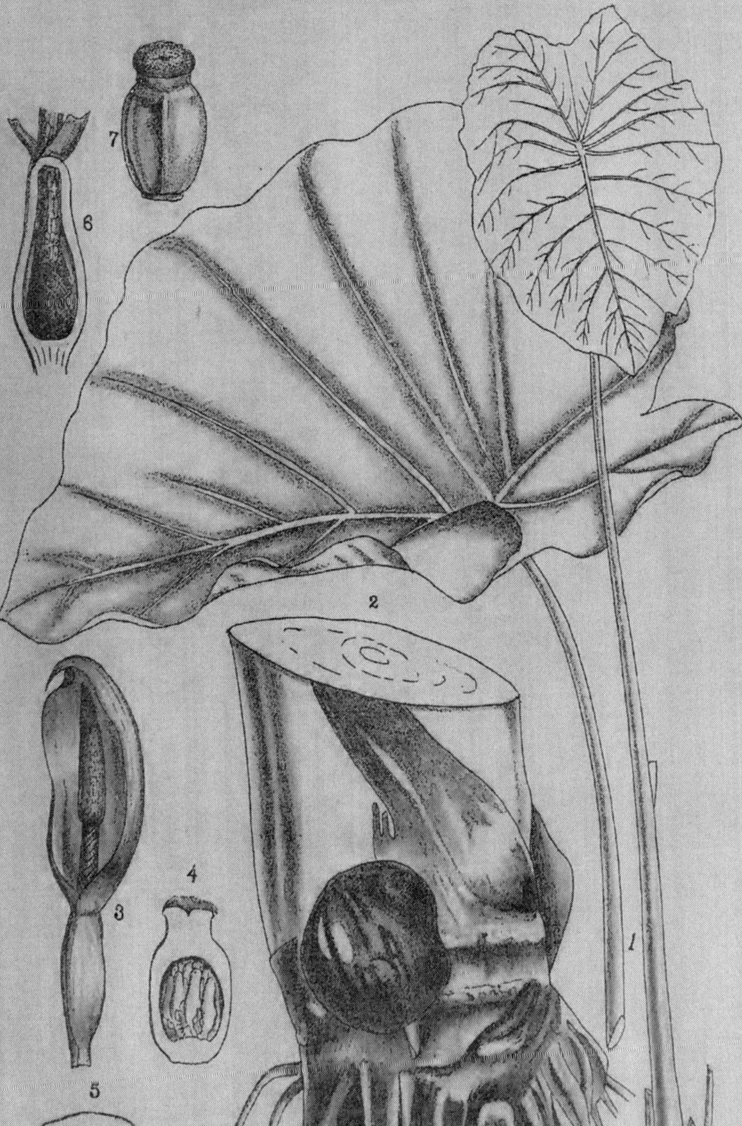

COLOCASIA ANTIQUORUM, SCHOTT

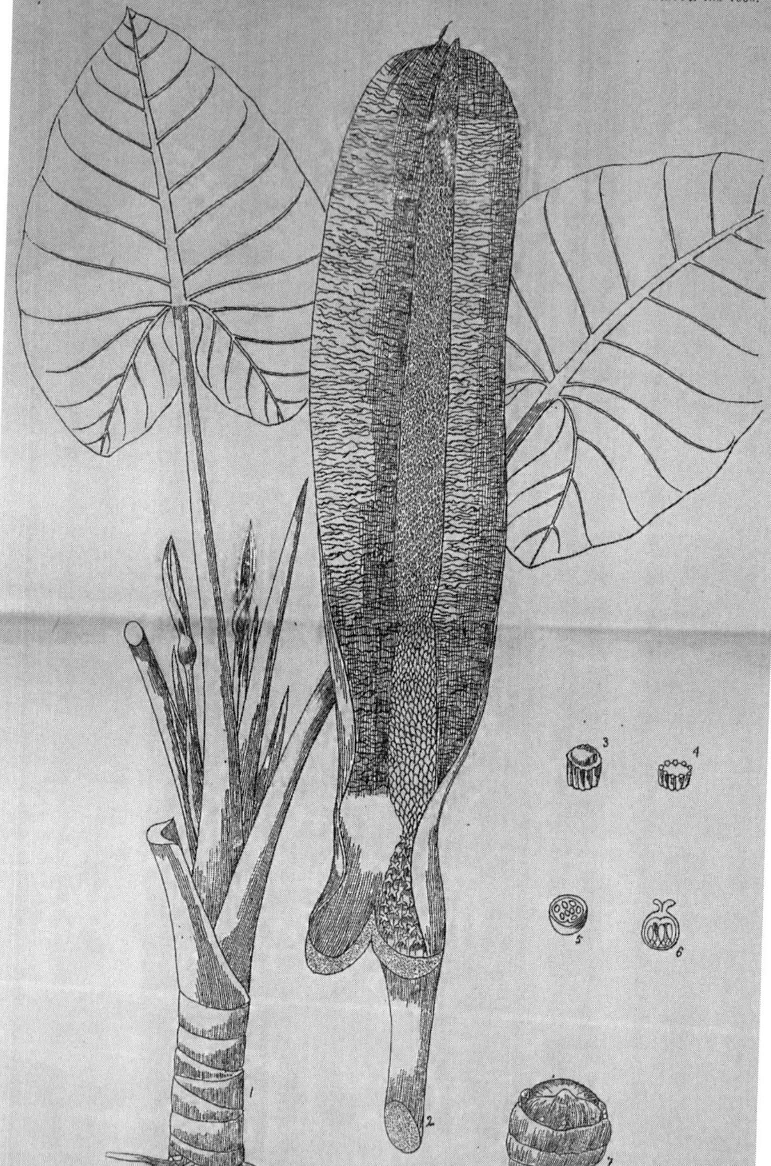

ALOCASIA INDICA, SCHOTT.

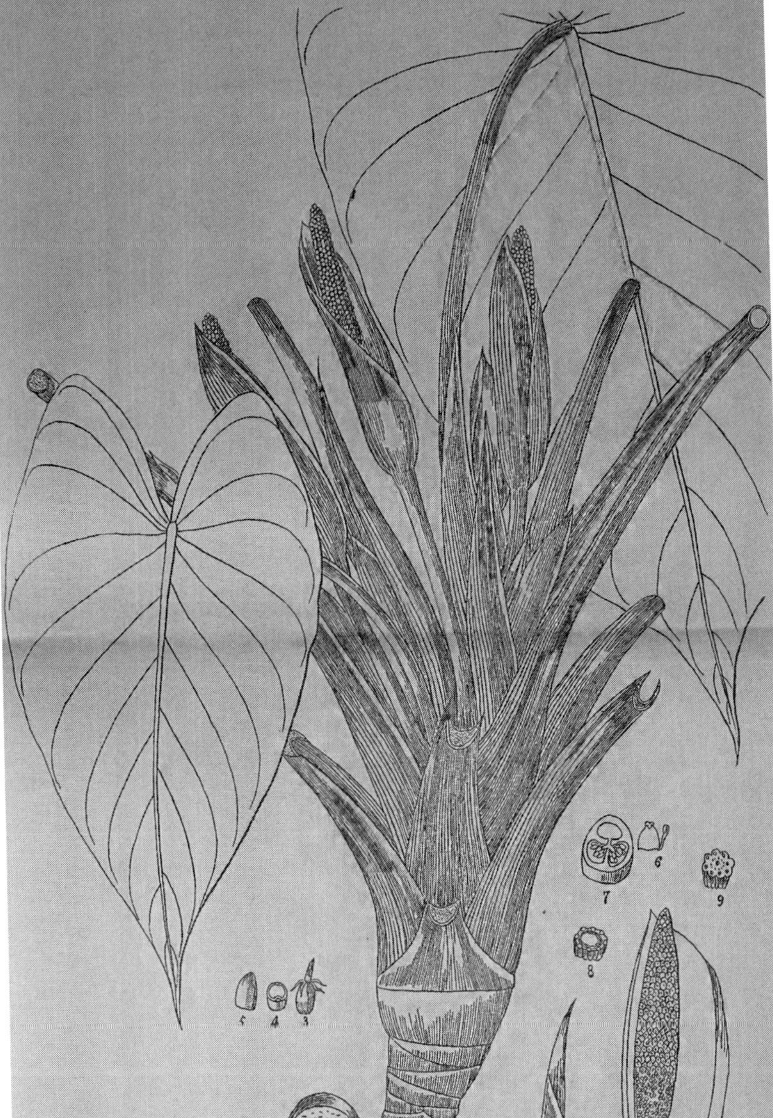

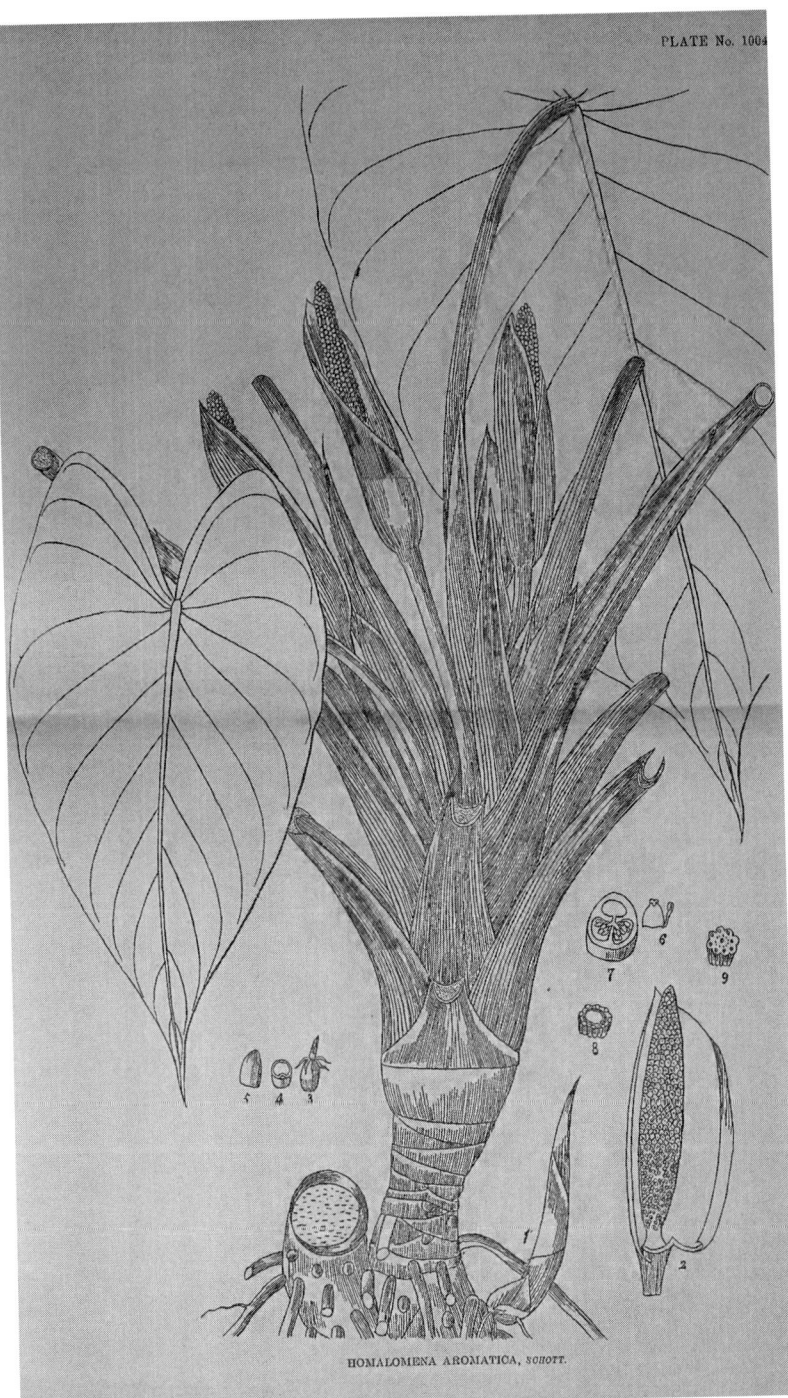

HOMALOMENA AROMATICA, SCHOTT.

PLATE No. 1005.

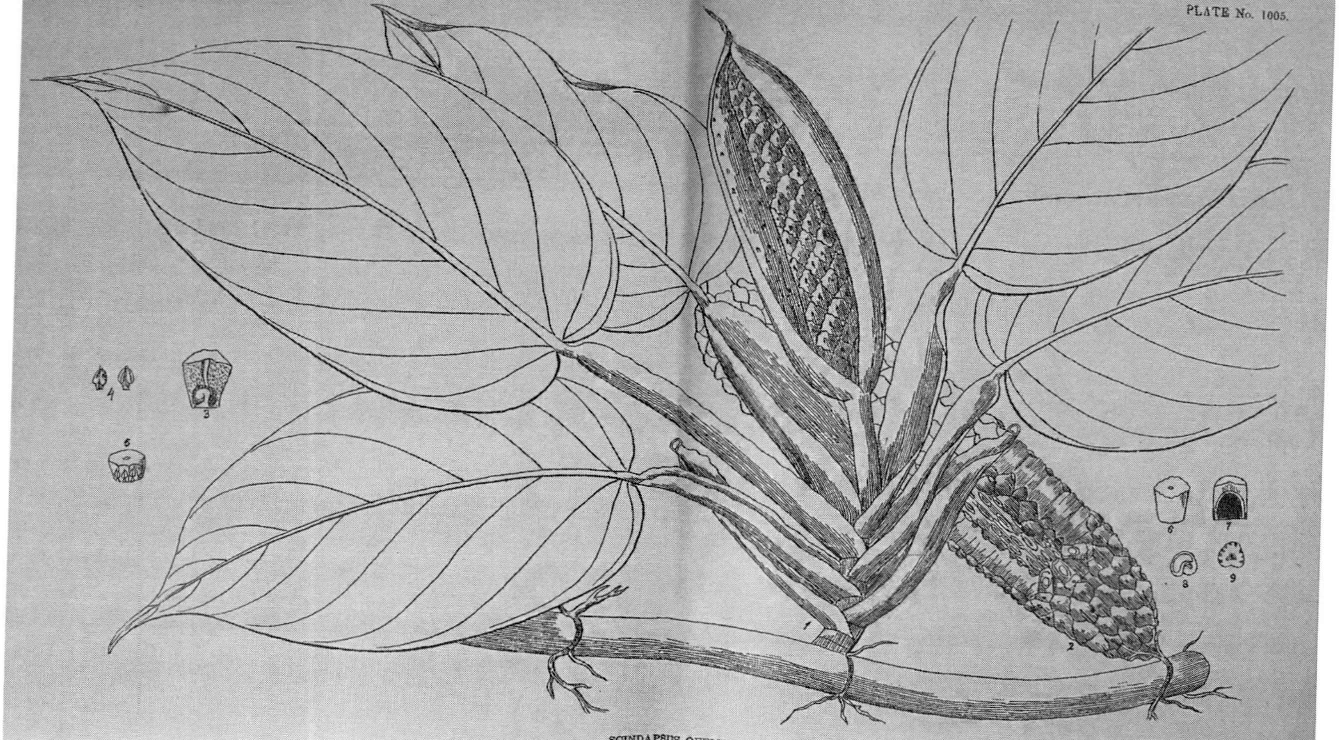

SCINDAPSUS OFFICINALIS, *SCHOTT.*

PLATE No. 1006.

RHAPHIDOPHORA PERTUSA, SCHOTT.

PLATE No. 1007.

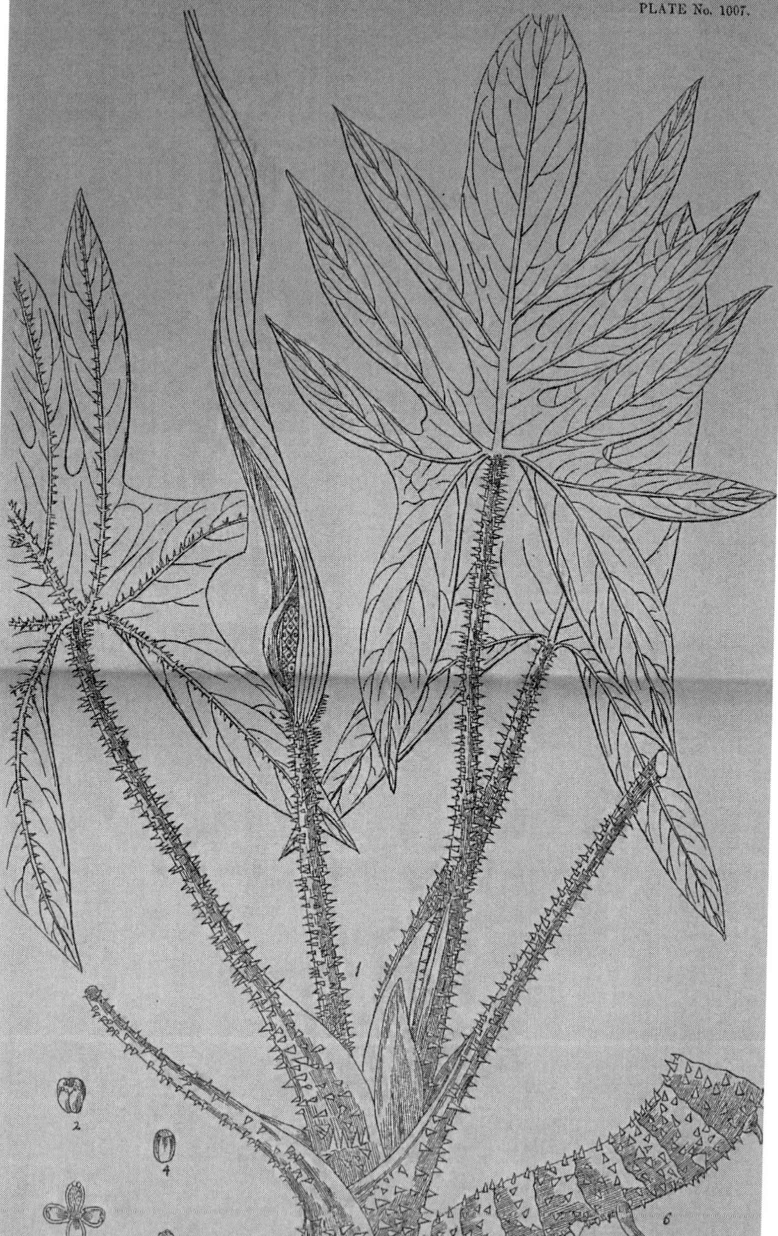

LASIA HETEROPHYLLA, *SCHOTT.*

PLATE No. 1008.

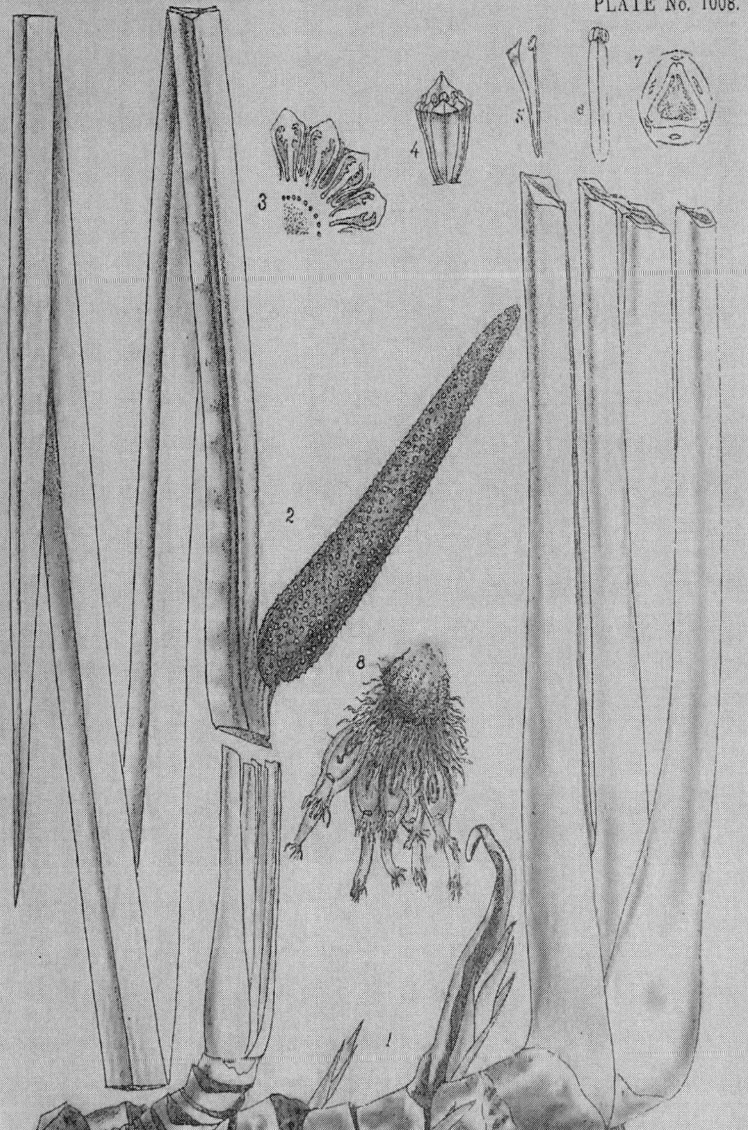

ACORUS CALAMUS, *Linn*

PLATE No. 1009.

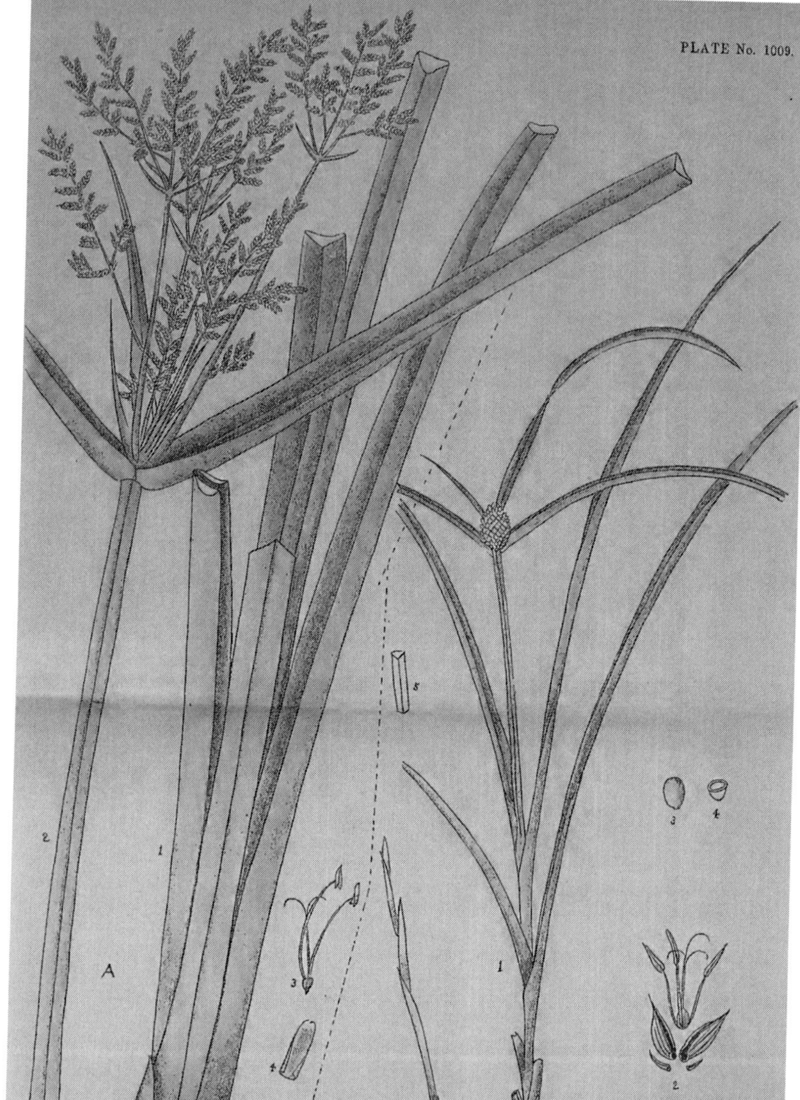

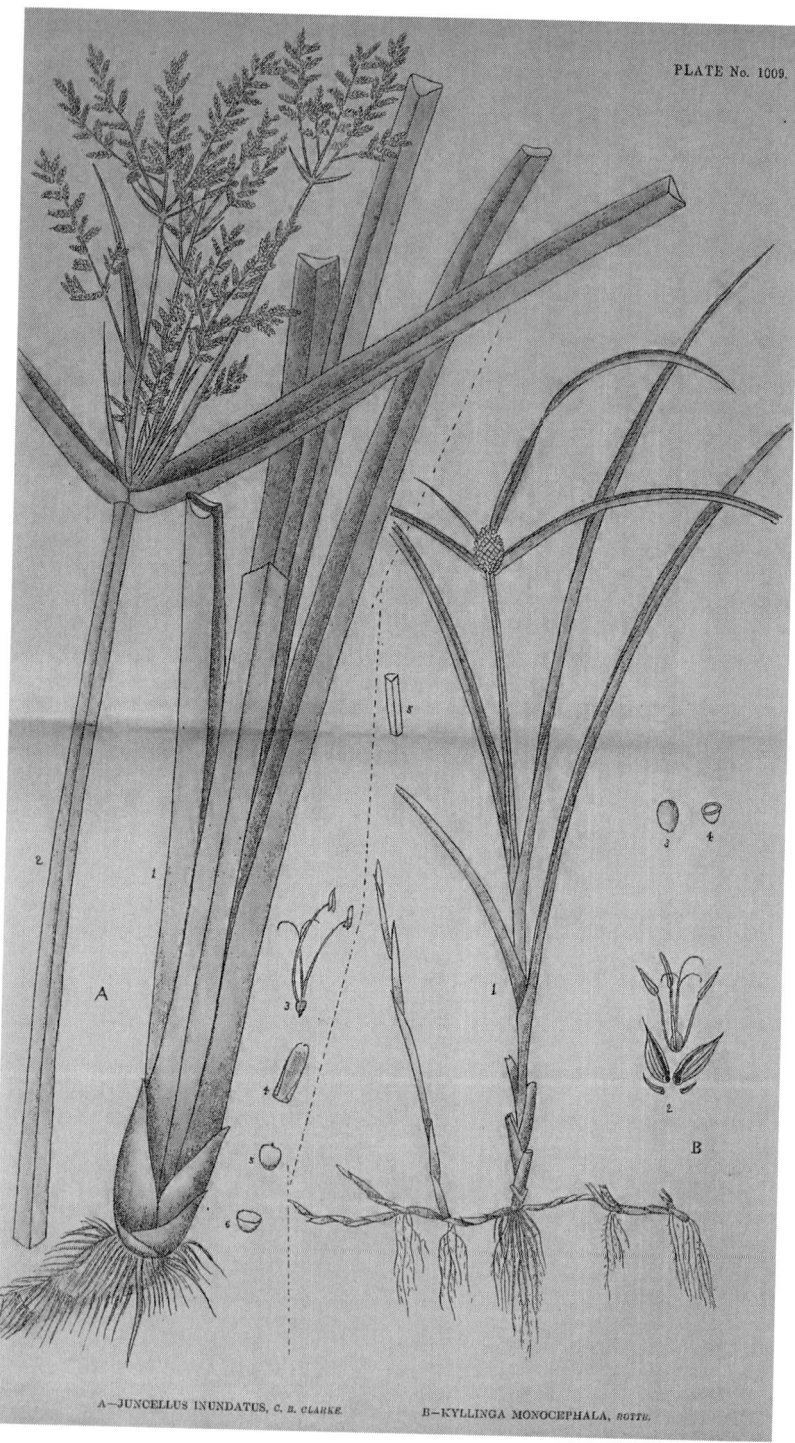

A—JUNCELLUS INUNDATUS, *C. B. CLARKE.* B—KYLLINGA MONOCEPHALA, *ROTTB.*

PLATE No. 1010.

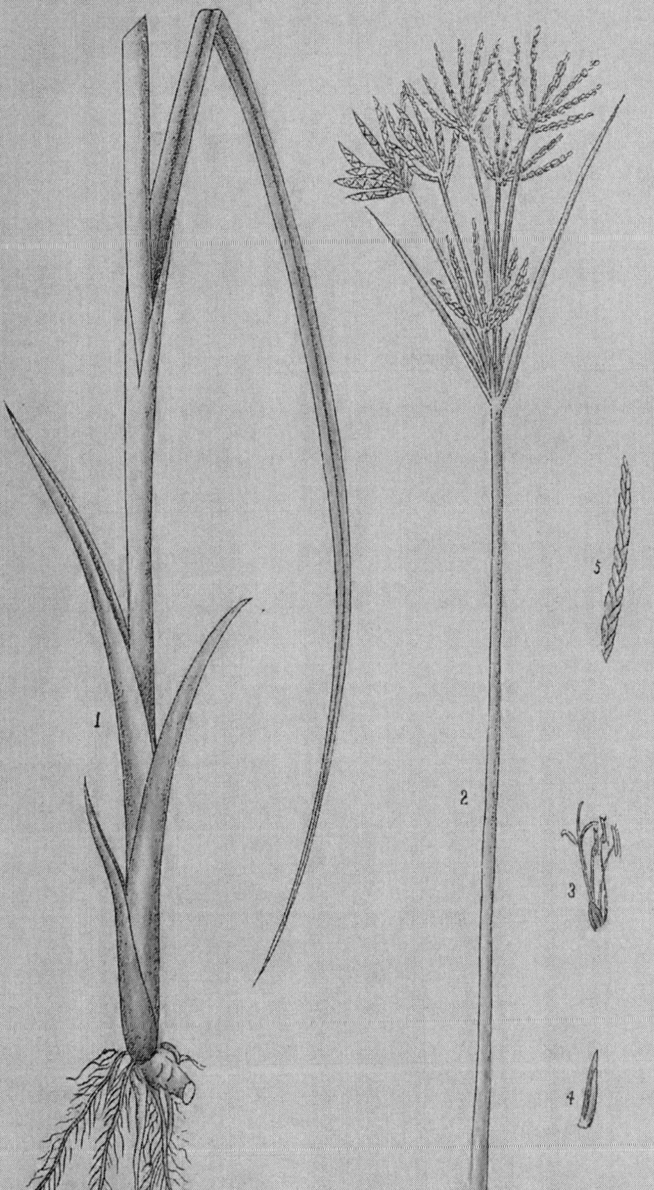

CYPERUS SCARIOSUS, Br.

PLATE No. 1011.

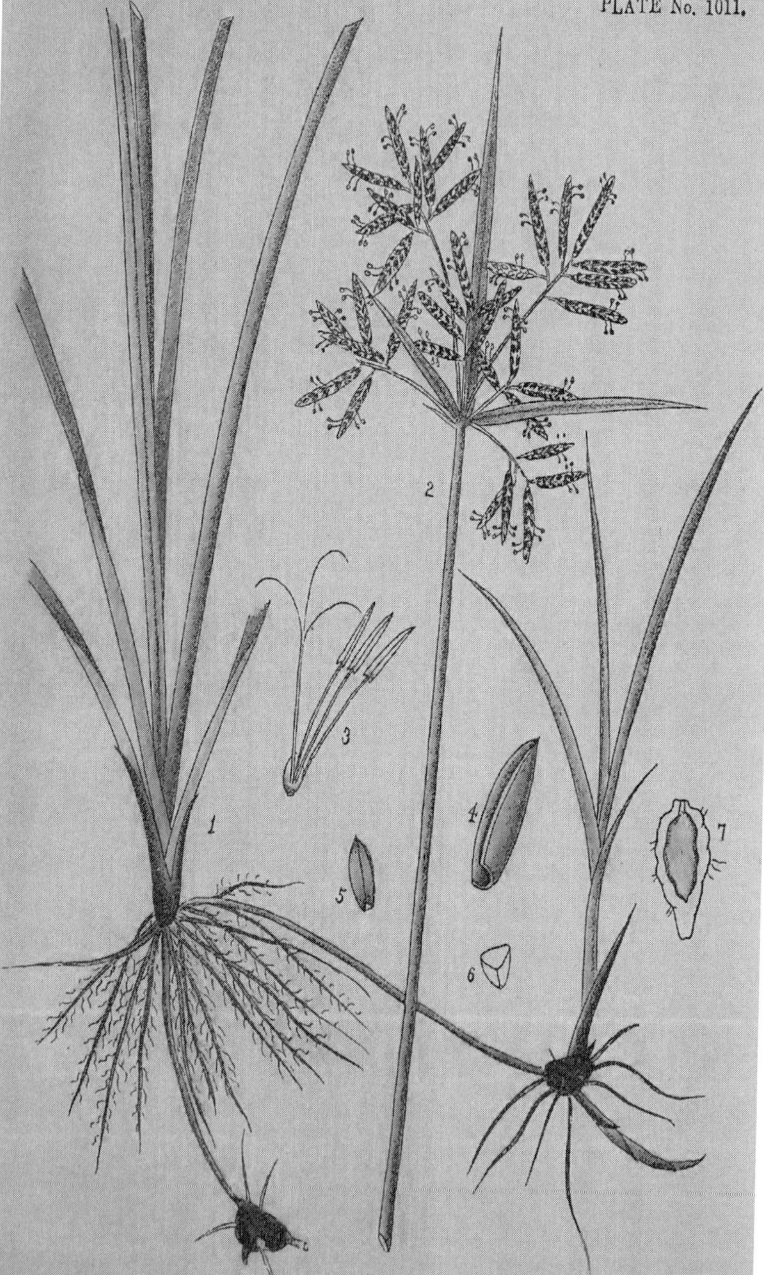

CYPERUS ROTUNDUS, LINN.

PLATE No. 1012.

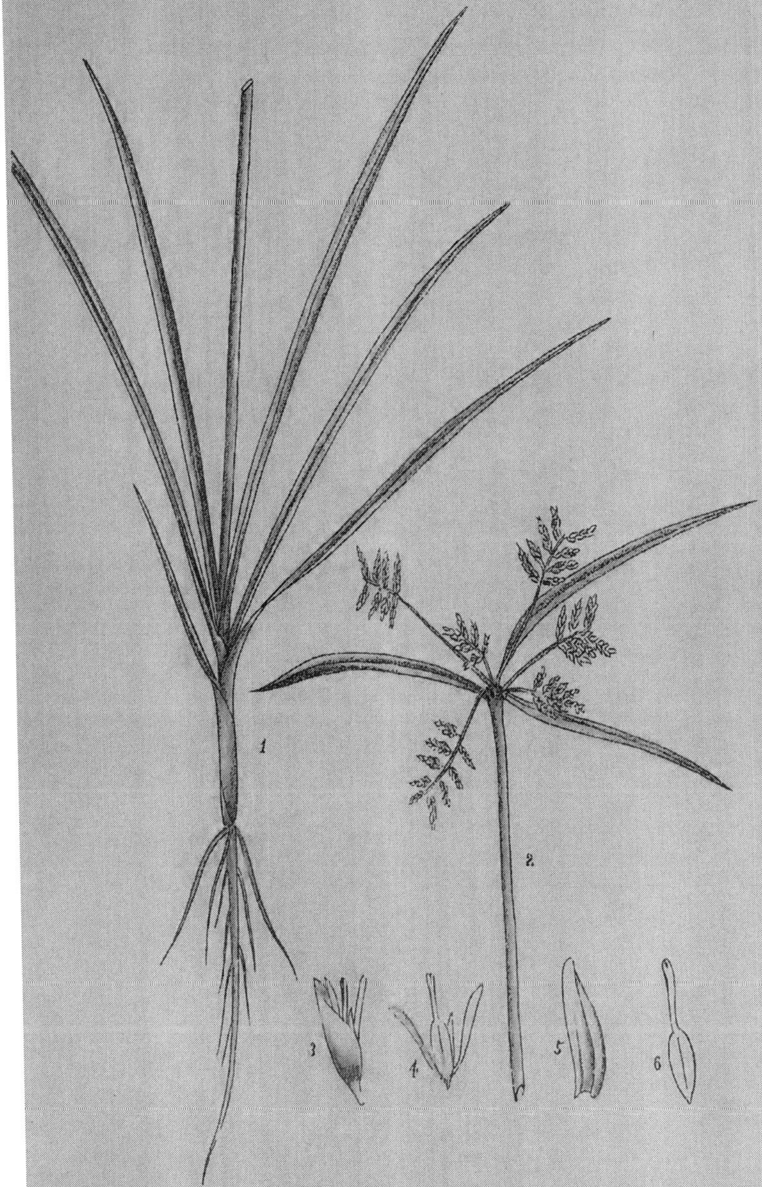

CYPERUS ESCULENTUS, LINN.

PLATE No. 1013

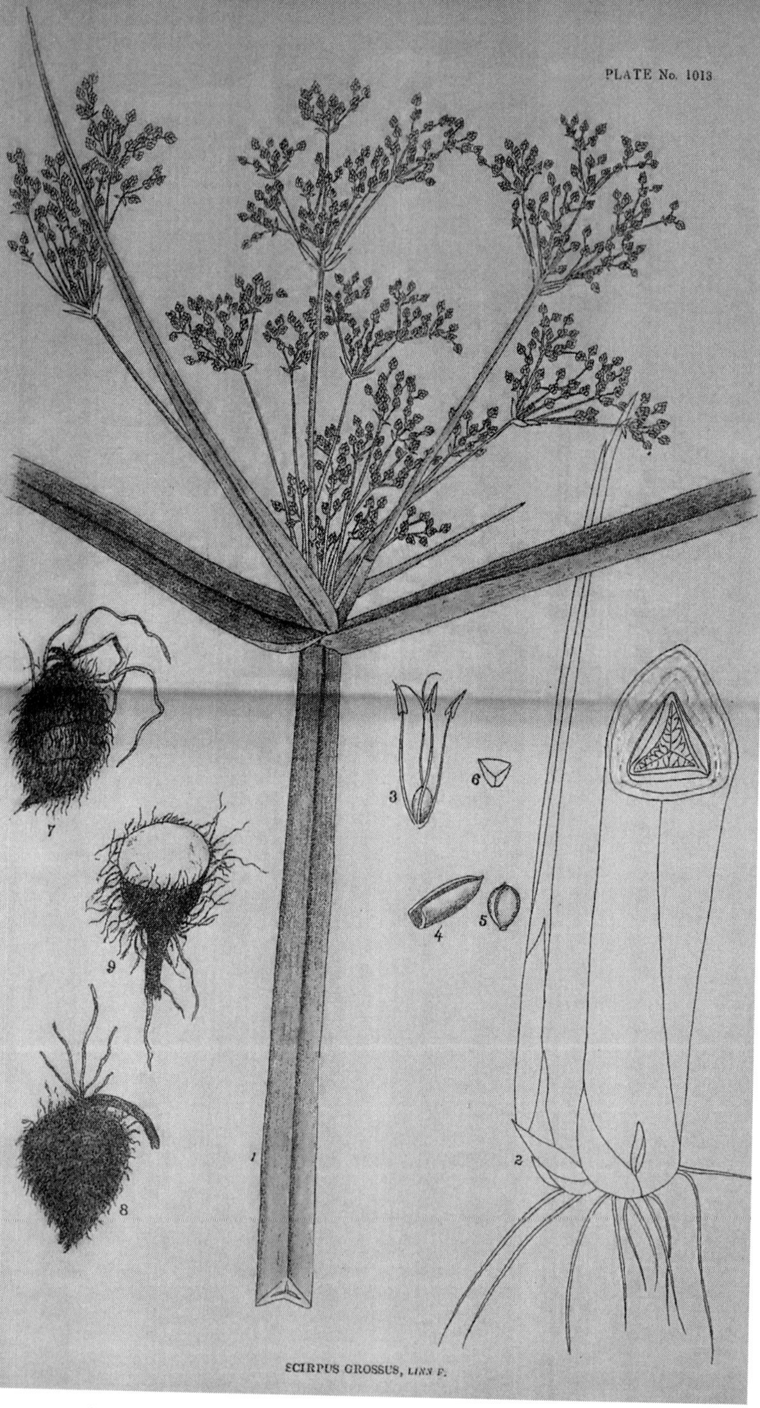

SCIRPUS GROSSUS, LINN F.

PLATE No. 1014.

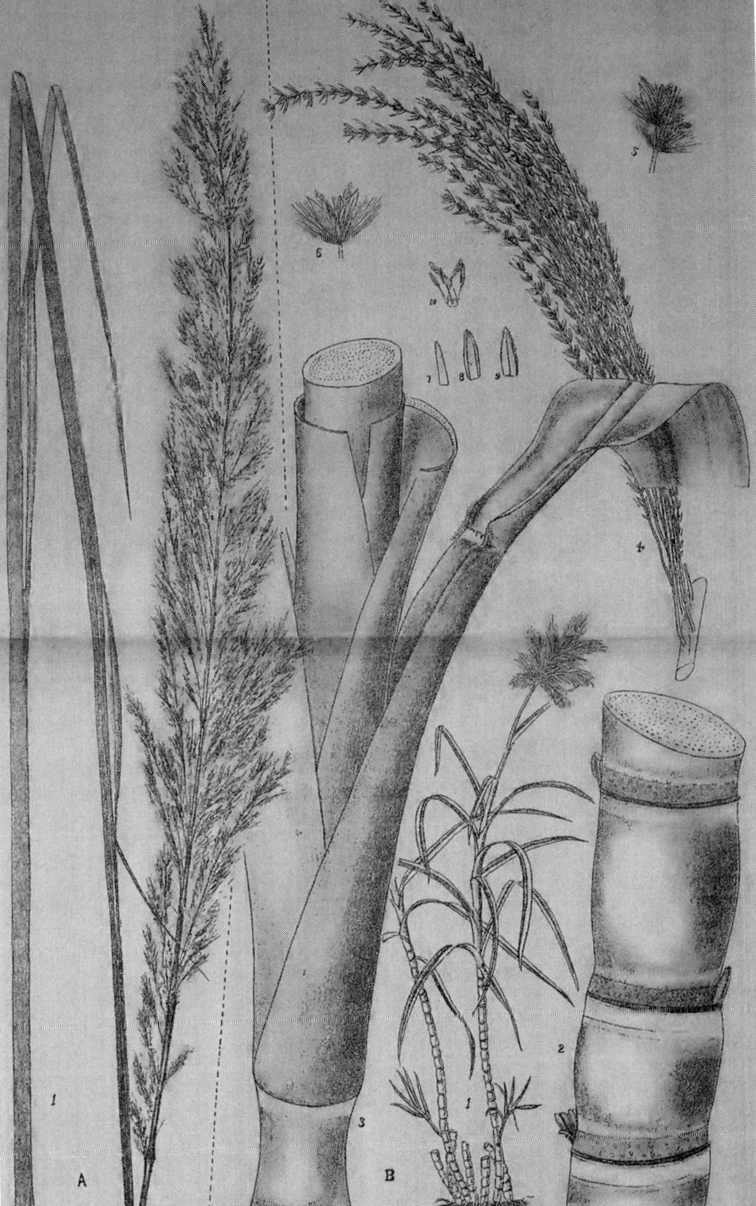

A—SACCHARUM ARUNDINACEUM, *Retz.* B—SACCHARUM OFFICINARUM, *Linn.*

PLATE No. 1015.

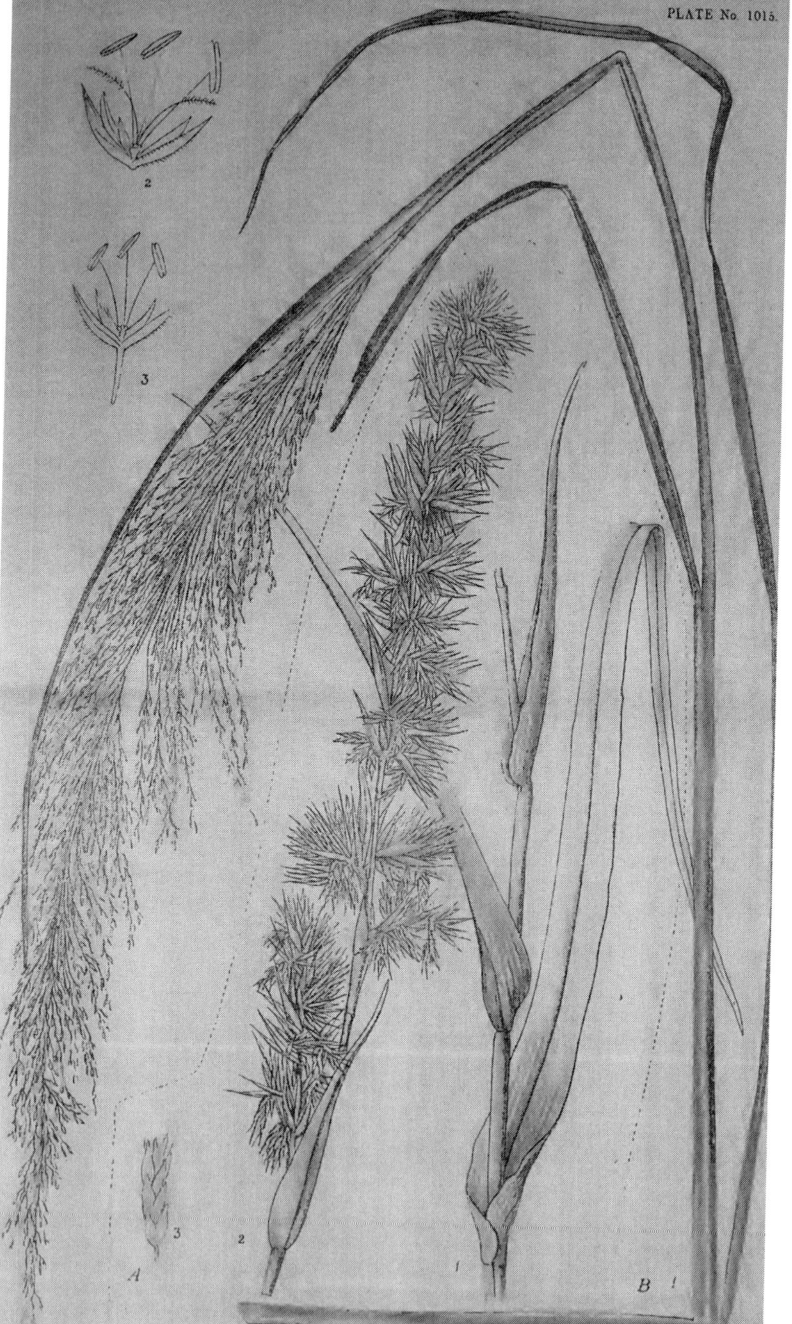

A—ANDROPOGON SCHŒNANTHUS, *Linn.* B—ANDROPOGON SQUARROSUS, *Linn. f.*

PLATE No. 1016.

ANDROPOGON LANIGER, *DESF.*

PLATE No. 1017.

ANDROPOGON NARDUS, LINN.

PLATE No. 1018.

ANDROPOGON CITRATUS, D.C.

AVENA FATUA, LINN.

CYNODON DACTYLON, PERS.

PLATE No. 1021

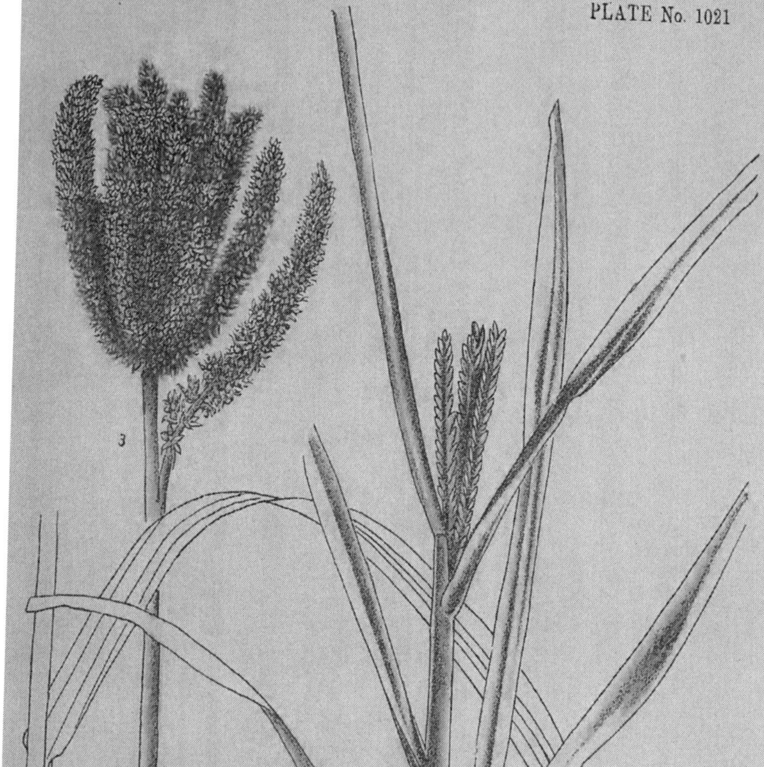

ELEUSINE CORACANA, GÆRTN.

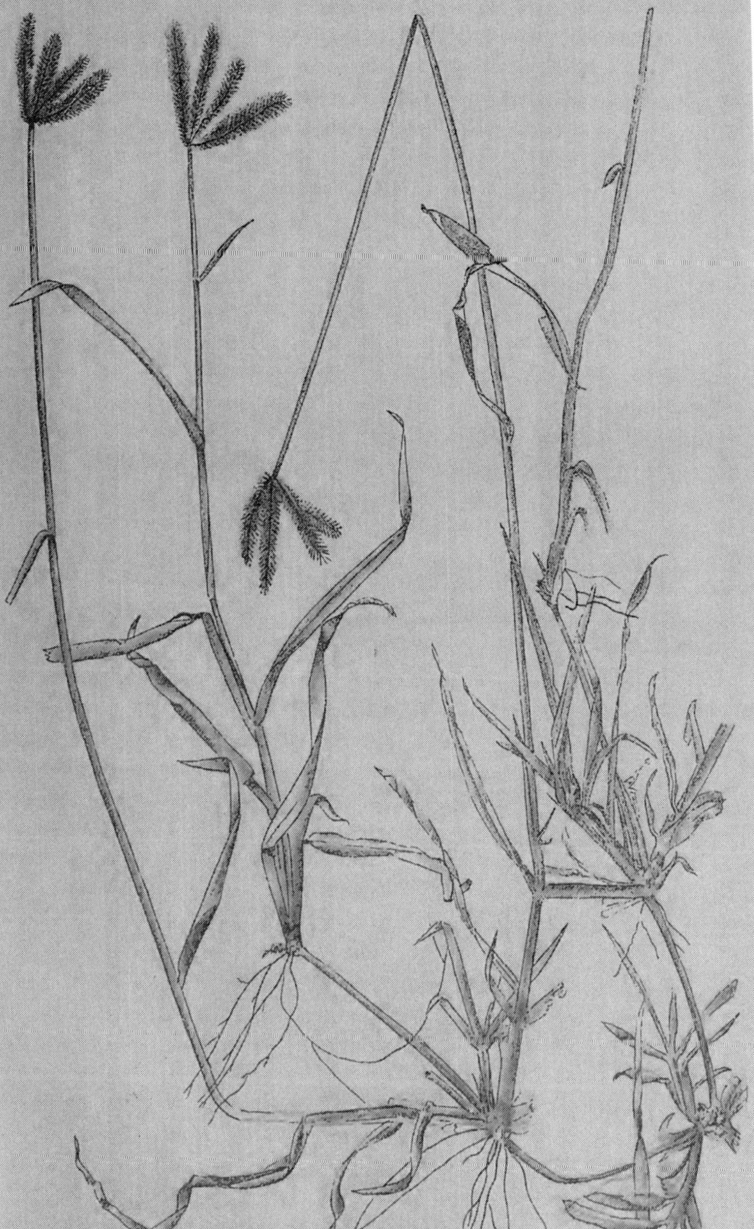

ELEUSINE ÆGYPTIACA, DESF

PLATE No. 1023.

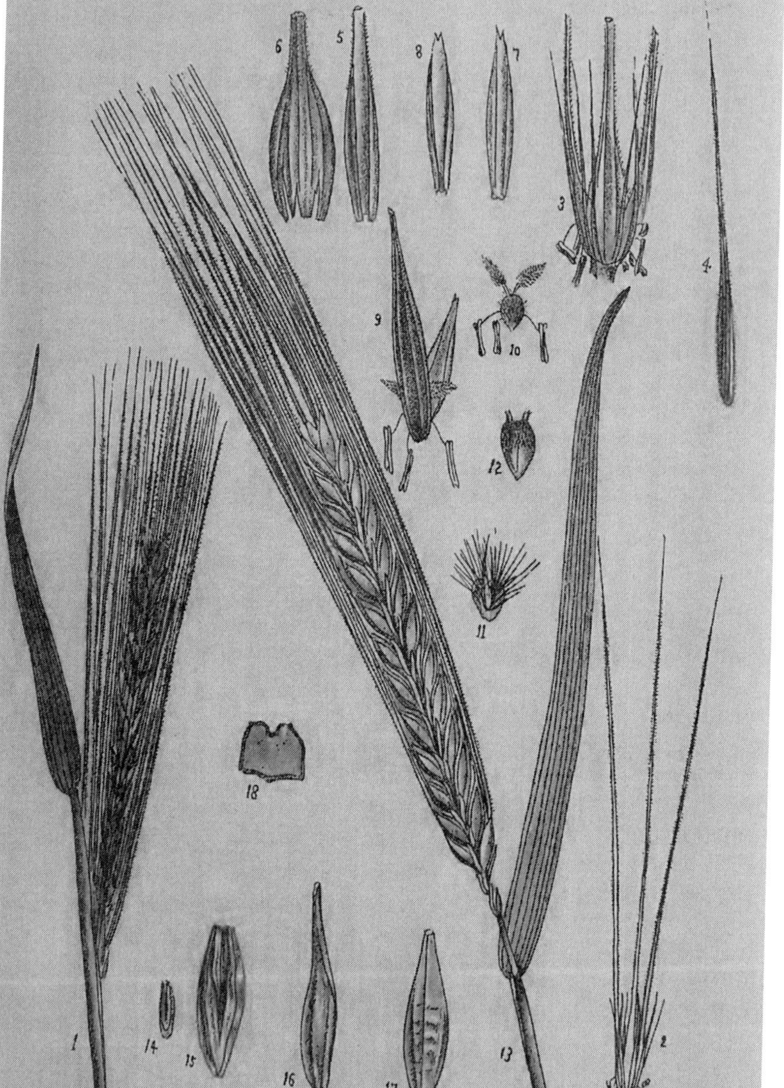

HORDEUM VULGARE, LINN

PLATE No. 1024.

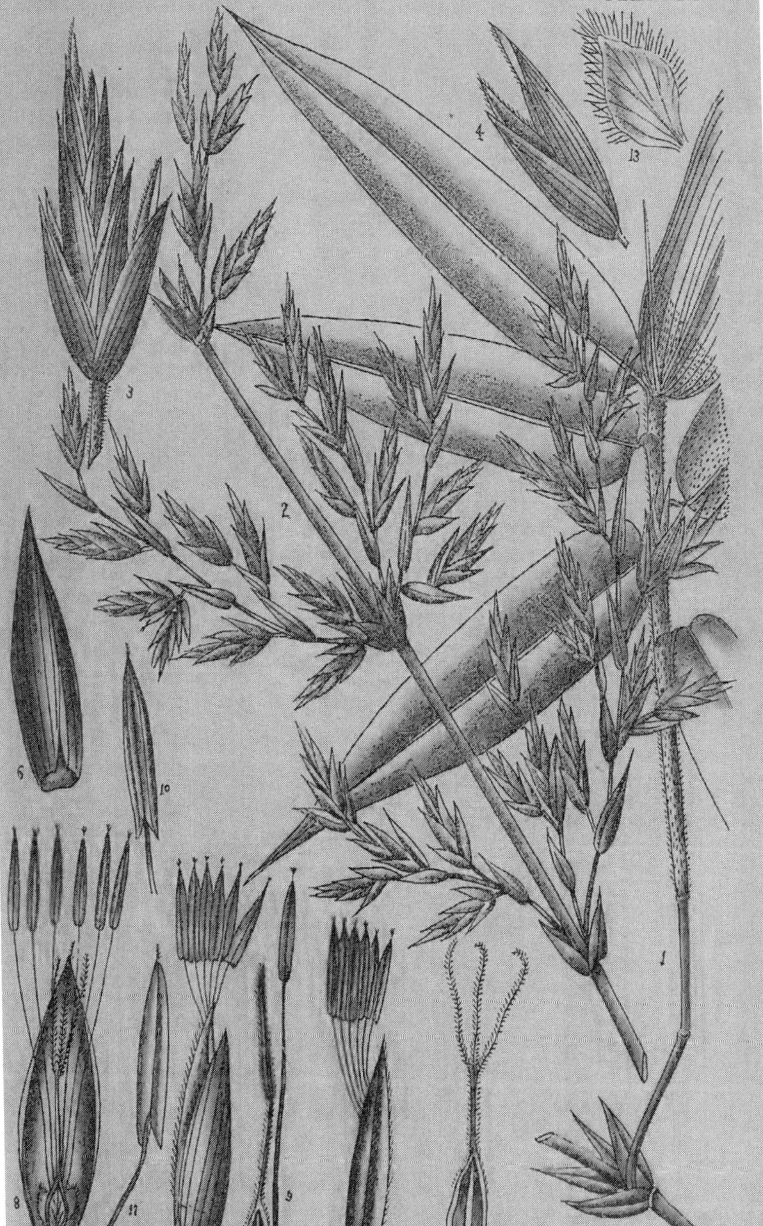

BAMBUSA ARUNDINACEA, *WILLD.*

PLATE No. 1025.

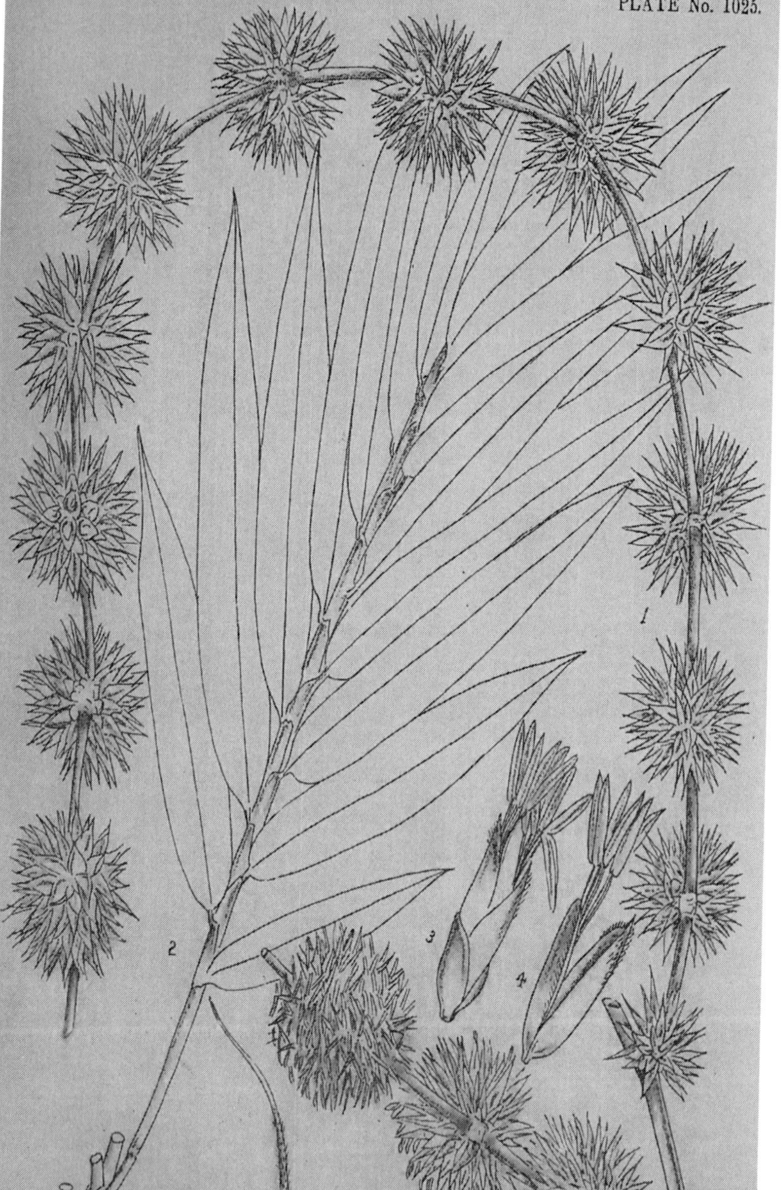

DENDROCALAMUS STRICTUS, NEES.

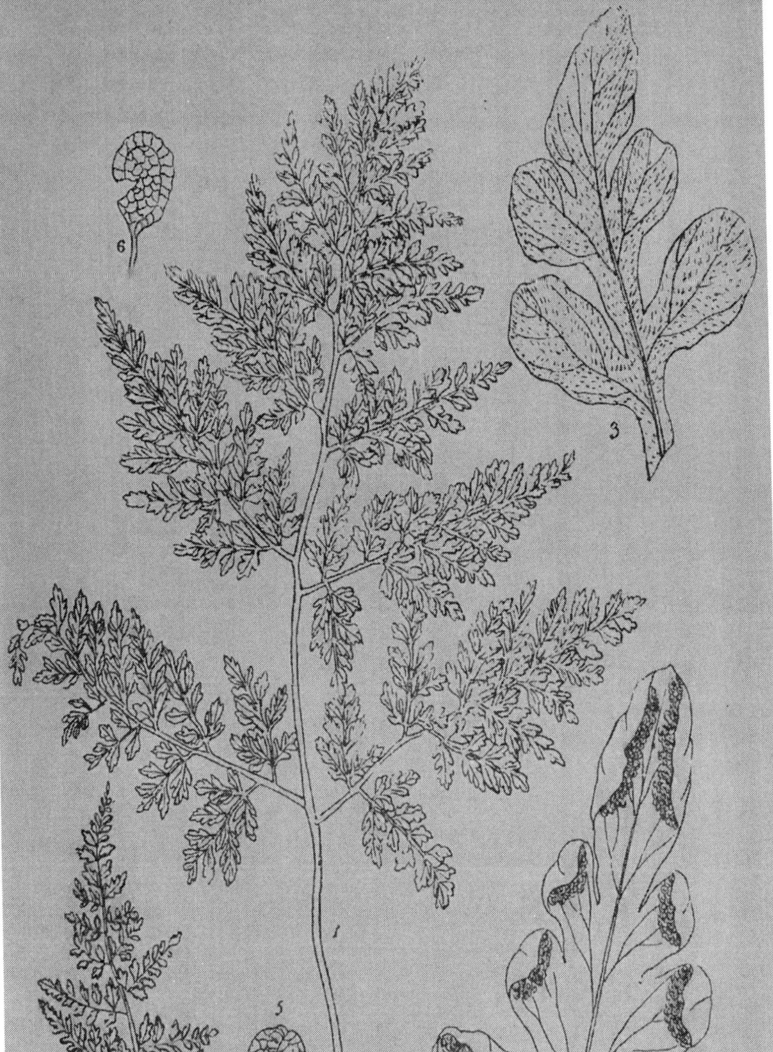

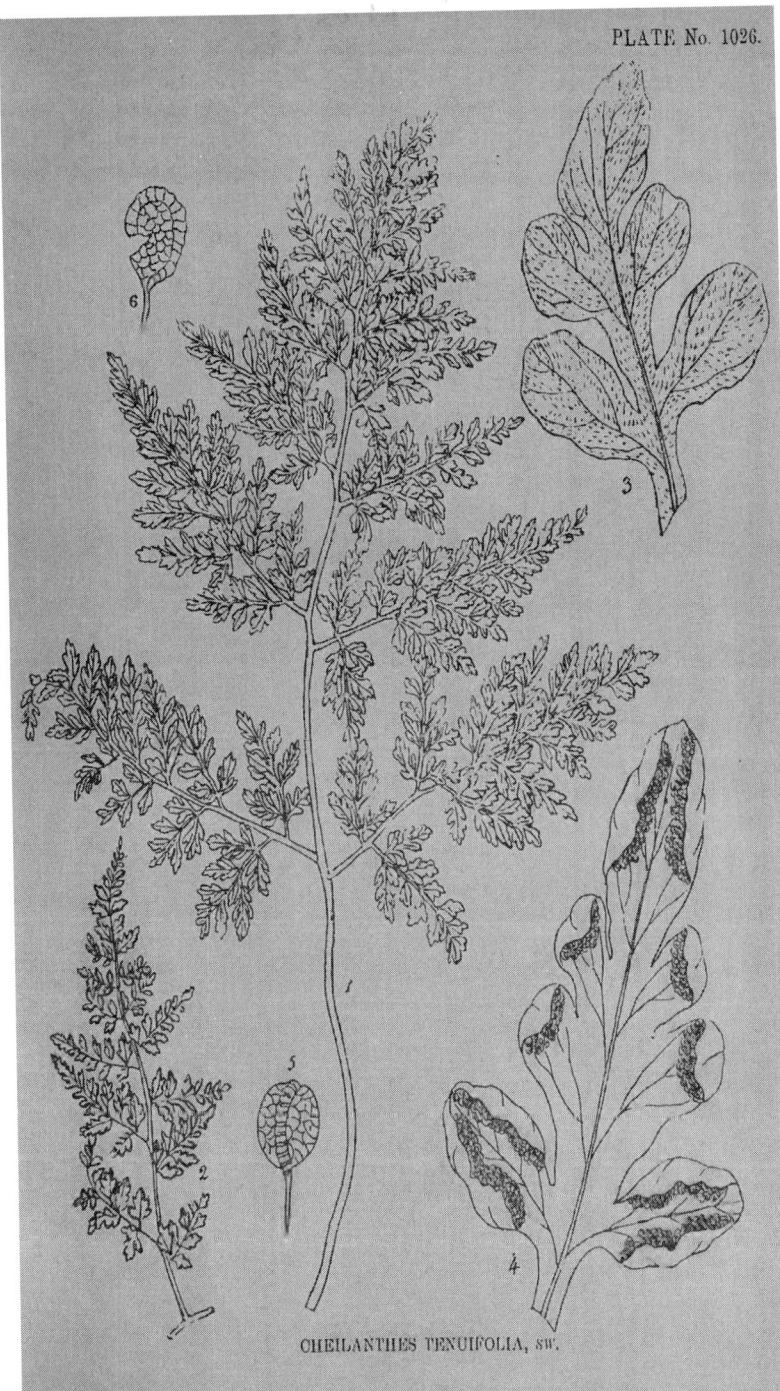

CHEILANTHES TENUIFOLIA, SW.

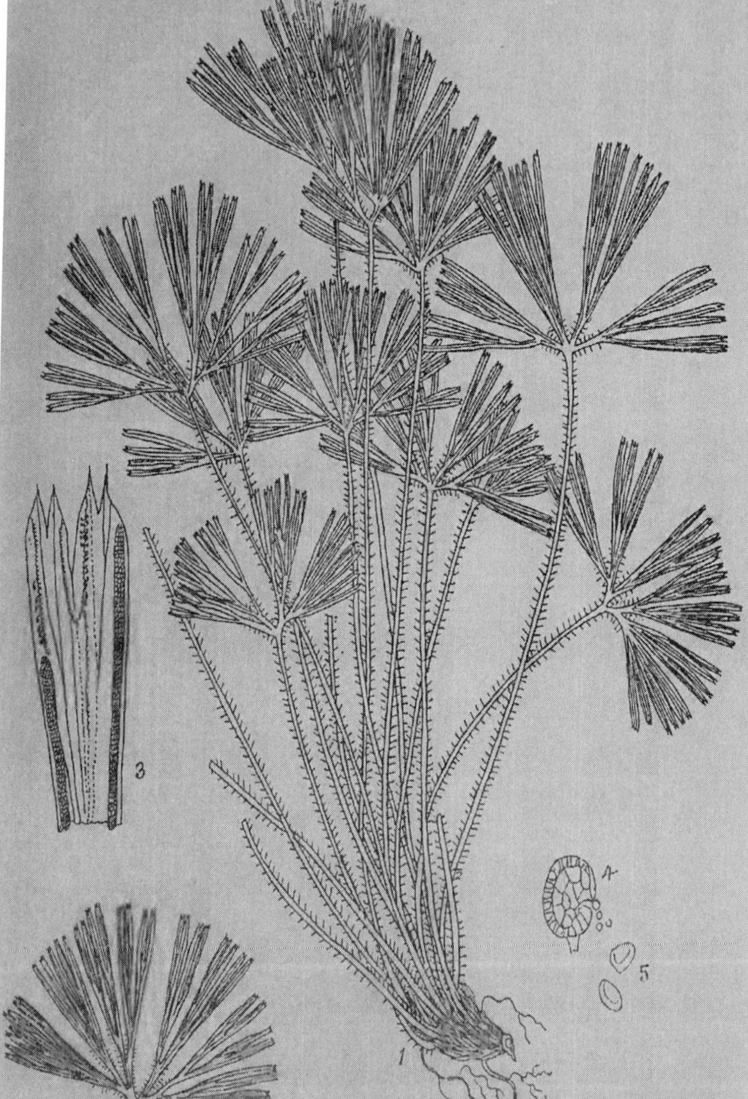

ACTINIOPTERIS DICHOTOMA, FORSK.

PLATE No. 1028.

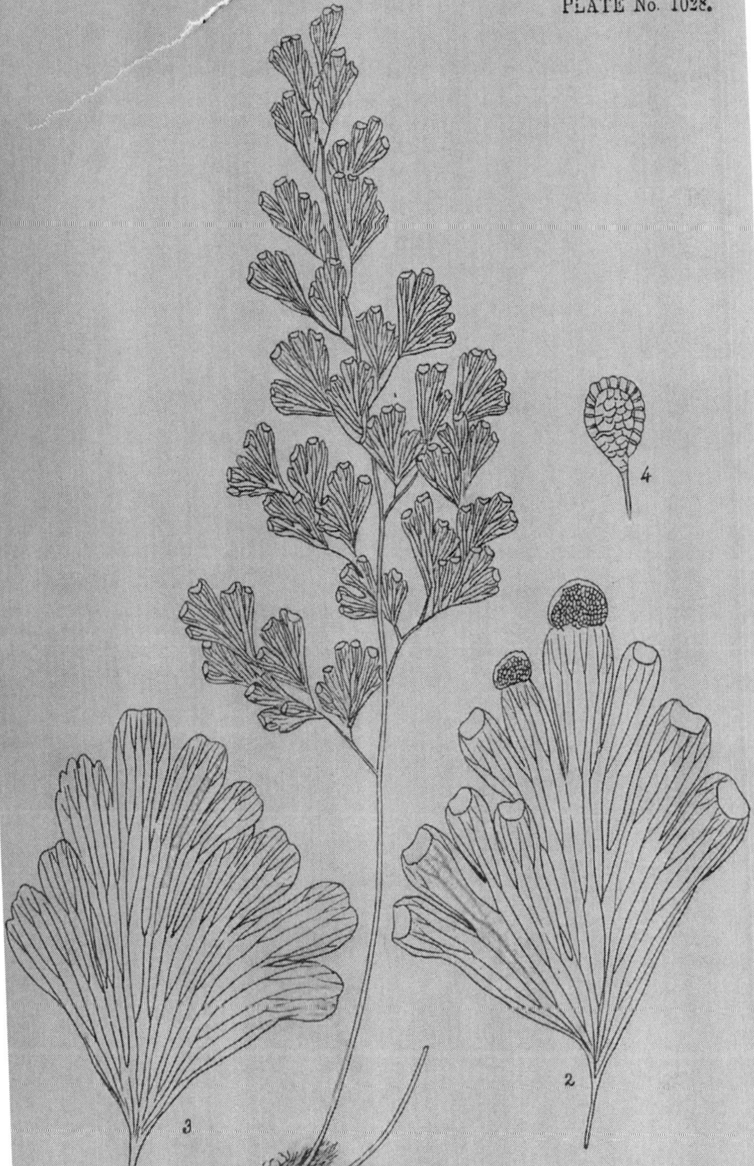

ADIANTUM CAPILLUS-VENERIS, *LINN.*

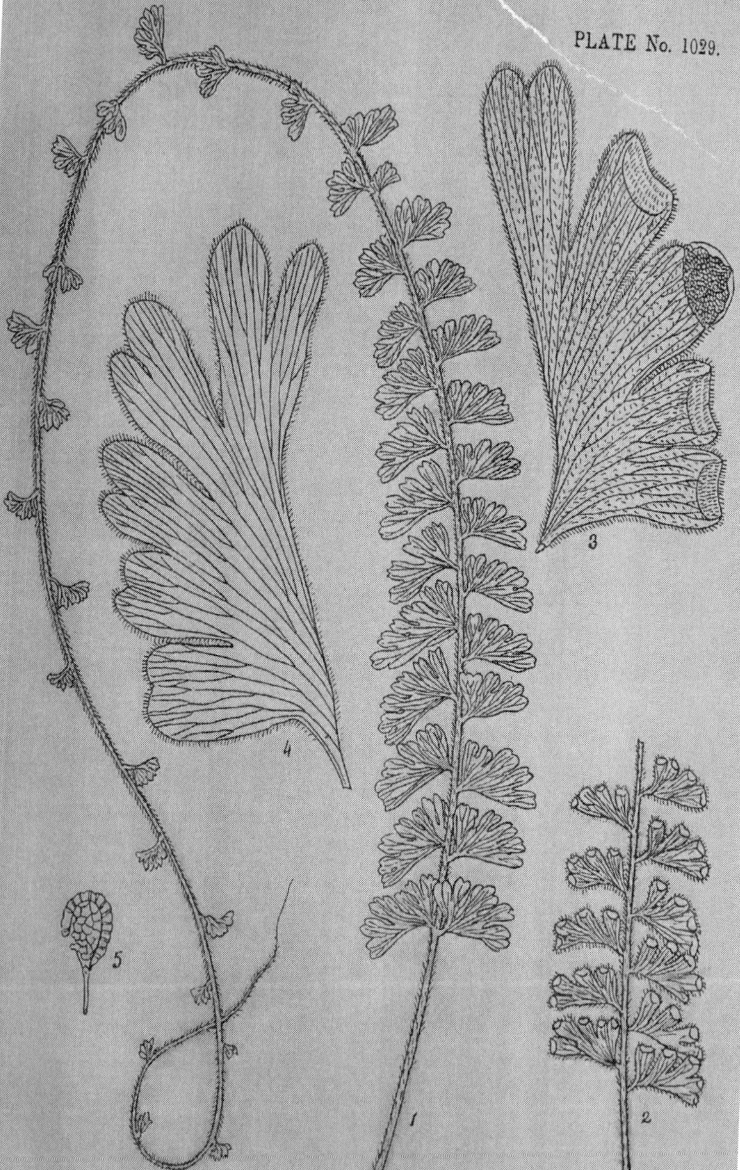

ADIANTUM CAUDATUM, *LINN.*

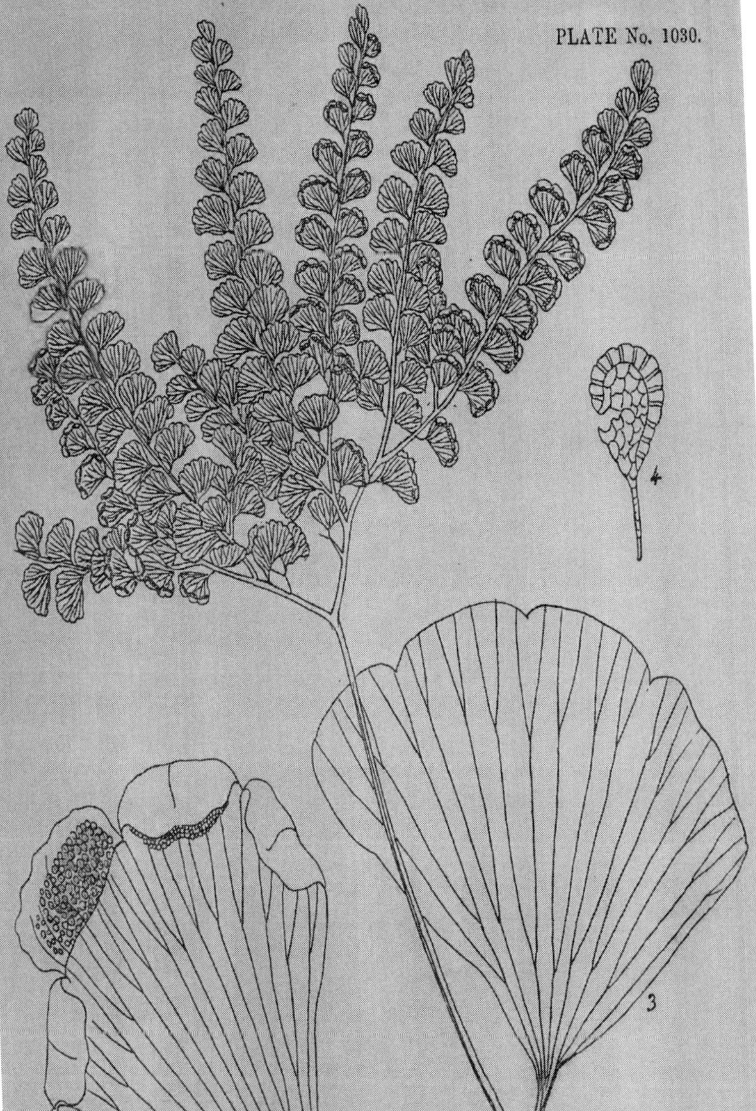

PLATE No. 1030.

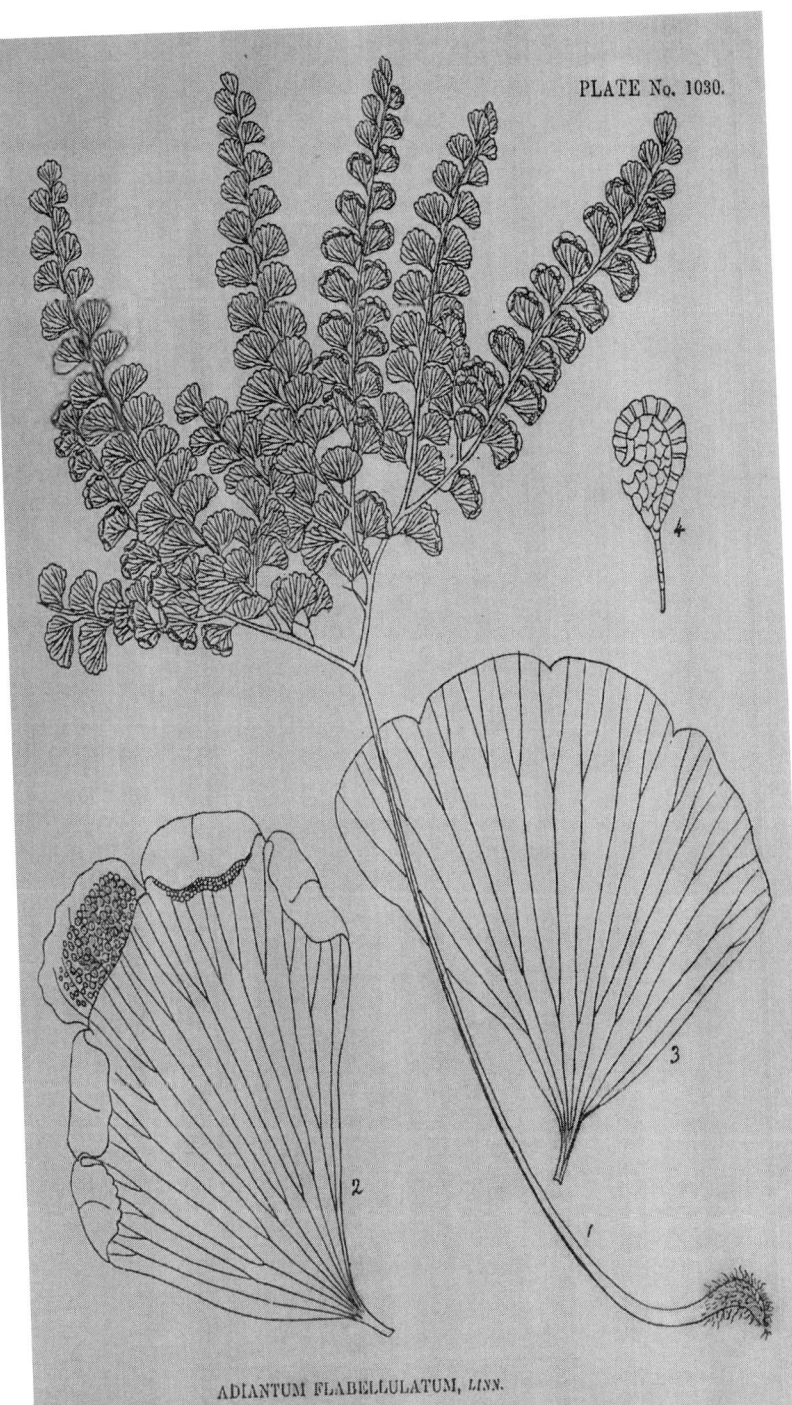

ADIANTUM FLABELLULATUM, LINN.

PLATE No. 1031.

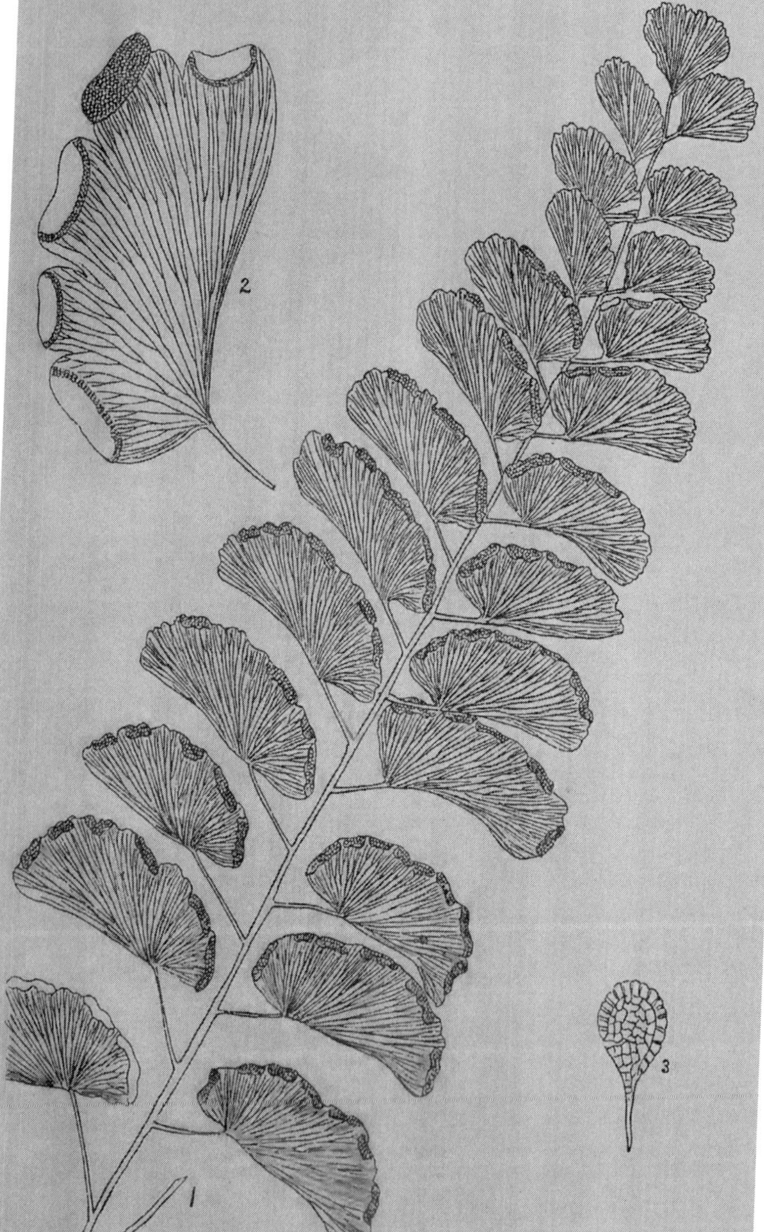

ADIANTUM LUNULATUM, *BURM.*

PLATE No. 1032.

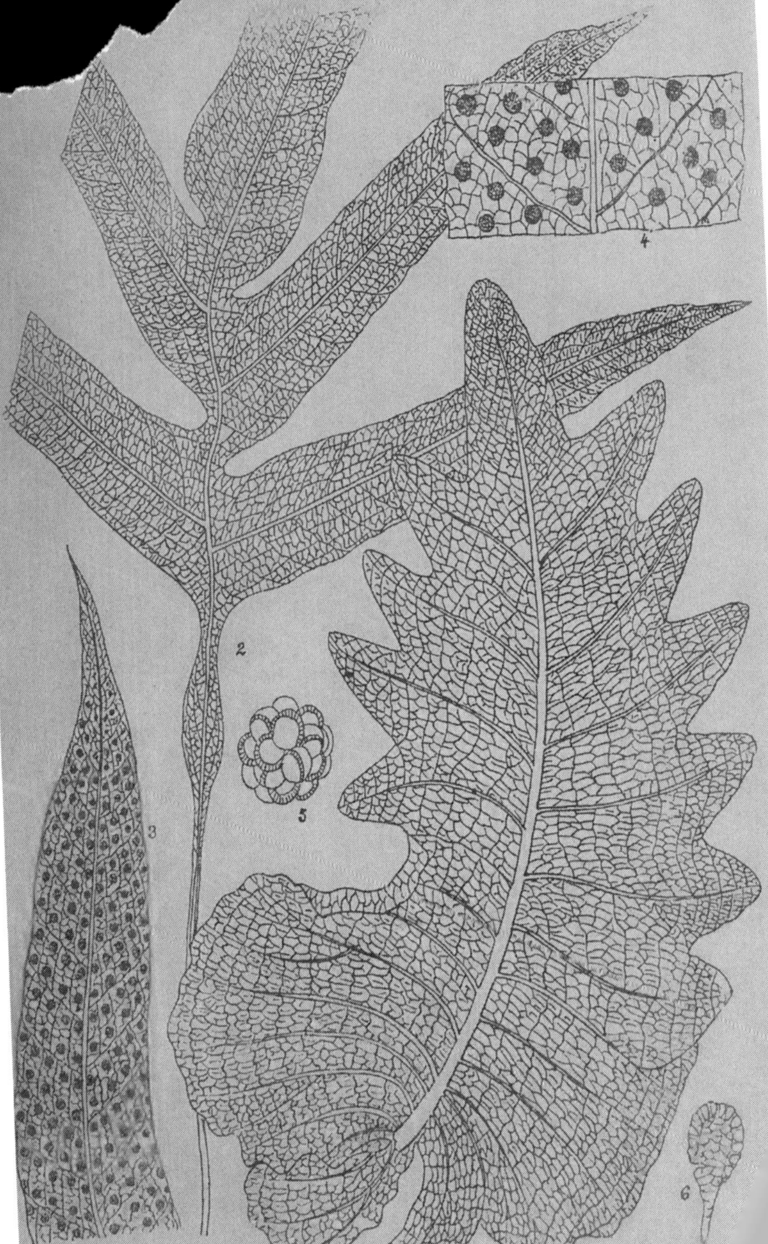

DRYNARIA QUERCIFOLIA, LINN.

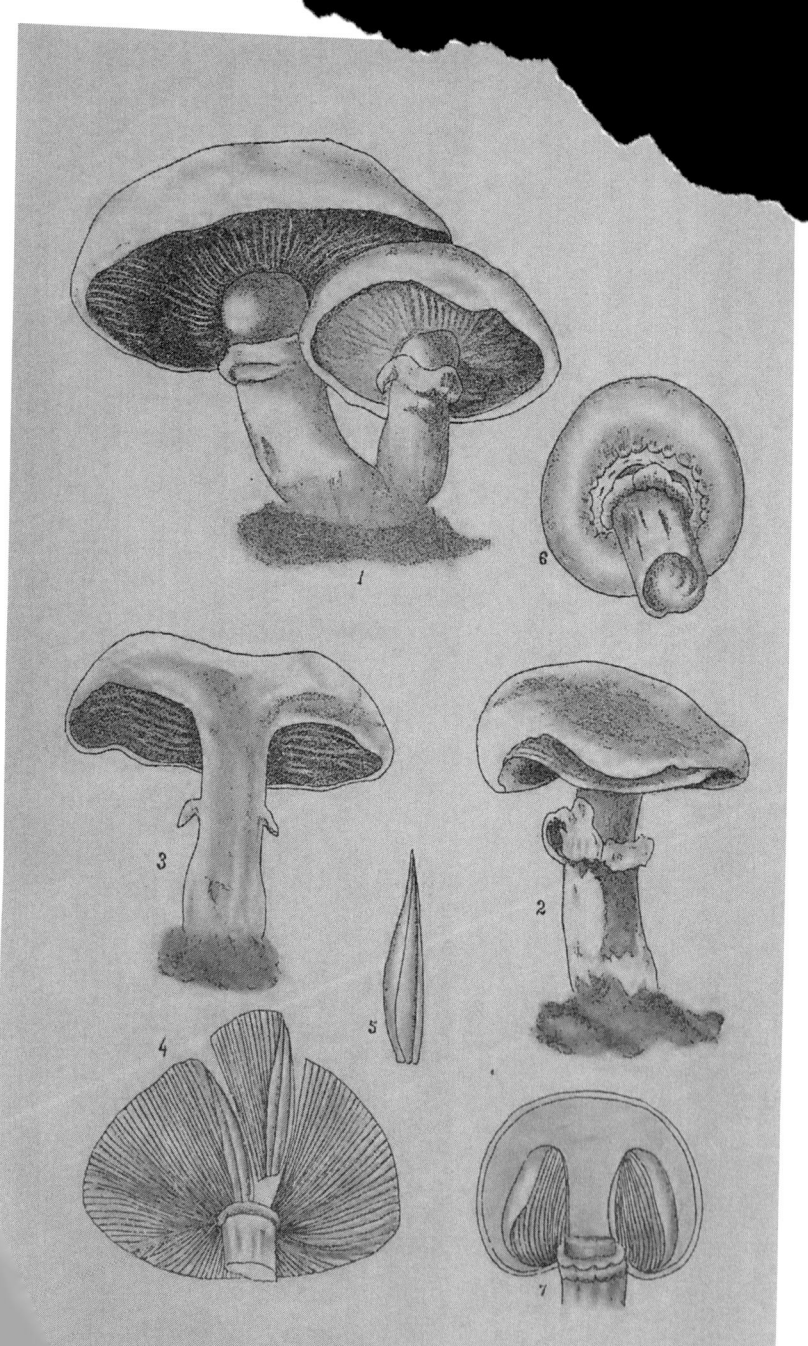

AGARICUS CAMPESTRIS, *LINN.*